D1616154

Biographical Directory of Negro Ministers

Second Edition

by

Ethel L. Williams

The Scarecrow Press, Inc.
Metuchen, N. J. 1970

ISBN 0-8108-0328-3

Foreword

The role of Negro ministers in the revolution now gripping the nation is a crucial one. They are demonstrating religion in action in the true Christian sense. The author of this book provides a readily available resource for biographical data concerning them. Included are familiar names but also can be found many ministers whose names and roles will be unknown generally. All, however, are active and influential in local or national affairs.

James M. Nabrit Jr.
President
Howard University
Washington, D. C.

Contents

Preface

The idea of compiling a biographical directory of living Negro ministers came to me as a result of my frequent inability as a librarian to answer requests for this type of material. These requests have doubled in volume during the last few years because of the social revolution in America and the responsible leadership role that the Negro minister has assumed. Existing publications containing biographical materials are either out-of-date or limited in their inclusion of Negro ministers. Also, those sources that are current are often inaccessible and scattered in denominational reports and yearbooks.

Four years have now elapsed since the publication of the first edition of the Biographical Directory. The apparent usefulness of the directory and the ever-increasing demand for current information on Negro ministers has prompted me to revise and enlarge the old edition.

It is hoped that, in addition to serving as a much needed reference book on the American Negro Clergy, this new directory will serve as a source-book for governmental and community organizations. National, state, city and county officials may use it in selecting ministers to serve on community organizations and projects. To facilitate this type of use, a geographical index has been added to the present edition.

The editor wishes to emphasize that this compilation is not a "Who's Who" in the strict sense. An effort is not made to evaluate or endorse the ministers included or to list all the ministers who are rendering valuable service to their parishes, denominations and community.

Many of the ministers contacted did not return their questionnaires. Limitations in finances, staff and time did not permit second requests or verification by the biographee before printing. Biographies that are included from the first edition have been revised to include new positions and addresses, to the extent that we were able to secure the information. Biographical accounts of deceased ministers have been deleted and approximately eight hundred new biographies have been added.

In the appendix is a list of sources to help the user secure information about ministers that did not return the questionnaire and information regarding the traditional Negro churches in America.

I am grateful to all who have assisted in making this revised and enlarged edition possible, particularly Dean Samuel L. Gandy and the officials of Howard University for the various forms of assistance provided me while engaged in this compilation. Grateful acknowledgment is made to Mr. Clifton Brown, Assistant Librarian, School of Religon, who has been most helpful in all phases of the project. Also, I wish to express my gratitude to the Rev. Daniel McLellan, Mrs. Judith Dobbins, Mrs. Delores Carpenter, Mrs. Evelyn Dwimoh and Miss Brenda Johnson who helped in the research and the typing of the manuscript.

Ethel L. Williams

Abbreviations

The following list includes the most frequent abbreviations used in the biographies and those with which some laymen might not be familiar. An asterisk (*) used to begin an entry in the main text indicates that the biographee is an alumnus of the Howard University School of Religion, Washington, D. C.

A.A.	Associate in Arts
A.B.	Bachelor of Arts
Amer.	America, American
Amer. Bapt. Conv.	American Baptist Convention
A.M.	Master of Arts
A. M. E.	African Methodist Episcopal
A. M. E. Z.	African Methodist Episcopal Zion
Assn.	Association
Asst.	Assistant
b.	born
B.A.	Bachelor of Arts
B.D.	Bachelor of Divinity
B.S.	Bachelor of Science
B.T.U.	Baptist Teachers Union
B.Th.	Bachelor of Theology
Bapt.	Baptist
Bd.	Board
Bn.	Battalion
Br.	Branch
B.W.I.	British West Indies
B.Y.P.U.	Baptist Young Peoples Union
CAAP	Community Action Against Poverty
Cath.	Catholic
Ch.	Church
Chap.	Chaplain
Chmn.	Chairman
Christn. Chs.	Christian Churches (Disciples of Christ)
C. M. E.	Christian Methodist Episcopal
Coll.	College
Com.	Committee

Conf.	Conference
Congr'l	Congregational
Contbr.	Contribution
Conv.	Convention
CORE	Congress of Racial Equality
D.D.	Doctor of Divinity
dau.	daughter
del.	delegate
D.E.L.	Doctor of Ecclestical Law
D.Litt. or L.H.D.	Doctor of Literature
Denom.	Denomination
Dept.	Department
D.H.L.	Doctor of Human Letters
D.S.T.	Doctor of Sacred Theology
D.S.Litt.	Doctor of Sacred Literature
Dir.	Directors
Div.	Division
D.R.E.	Director of Religious Education
Ed.	Editor
Edn.	Education
Ed.D.	Doctor of Education
Ed.M.	Master of Education
Elks	Protective Order of Elks
EOA	Economic Opportunities Act
E.T.O.	European Theatre of Operations
Evang.	Evangelical
Exec.	Executive
Fgn.	Foreign
FOR	Fellowship for Reconciliation
Foun.	Foundation
Hdqtrs.	Headquarters
Hon.	Honorary
Hosp.	Hospital
Inf.	Infantry
Inst.	Institute
Instr.	Instructor
Interch.	Interchurch
I.O.O.F.	Independent Order of Odd Fellows
Interdenominat.	Interdenominational
K. of P.	Knights of Pythias
L.H.D.	Doctor of Humane Letters

Litt. D.	Doctor of Letters
Luth.	Lutheran
LL.B.	Bachelor of Laws
LL.D.	Doctor of Laws
LL.M.	Master of Laws
m.	married
M.A.	Master of Arts
Mason	Free and Accepted Masons or Prince Hall Masons
M.D.	Doctor of Medicine
M.D.S.	Master of Dental Surgery
M.S.	Master of Science
M.S.T.	Master of Sacred Theology
Meth. ch.	Methodist Church
M.R.E.	Master of Religious Education
NAACP	National Association for the Advancement of Colored People
Nat. Bapt. Conv. Amer.	National Baptist Convention of America
Nat. Bapt. Conv. U.S.A.	National Baptist Convention, U.S.A.
NSS and BTUC	National Sunday School and Baptist Training Union Congress
Nat., Nat'l	National
Odd Fellows	Grand United Order of Odd Fellows
OIC	Opportunities Industrialization Centers
Ph.D.	Doctor of Philosophy
pres.	President
Presbyn.	Presbyterian
Presbyn. Ch. U.S.A.	Presbyterian Church in the U.S.A.
Prot. Epis. Ch.	Protestant Episcopal Church
rep.	representative
s.	son
sch.	school
S.C.L.C.	Southern Christian Leadership Conference
S.D.A.	Seventh-Day Adventist
sec.	secretary
sem.	seminary
soc.	society
S.T.B.	Bachelor of Sacred Theology

theol.	theology
treas.	treasurer
U. C. C.	United Church of Christ--formerly the Methodist Church
United Presbyn. Ch. U. S. A.	United Presbyterian Church in the United States of America
Univ.	University
vice pres. or v. p.	vice president

Biographical Directory

ABNEY, Albert, b. Marshall, Texas, Dec. 18, 1914; s. Hayes and Annis (Devers) A.; B.Th., providence Bapt. Theol. Sem., Los Angeles, Calif., 1961; m. Elvie Richardson; 1 dau. Albert Deloris (Robinson): pastor, Mt. Carmel Holy Assembly Bapt. Ch., 1947--; mem. progressive National Bapt. Conv., Inc. Home: 1342 W. 103st., Los Angeles, Calif. 44 Church: 254 E. 94 St., L.A. 3 Calif.

ACKERMAN, Amos Abraham, b. Walterboro, S. C., May 12, 1917; s. Asbury and Alice (Gones) A.; Th.B., Malone Coll., 1949; m. M. Ruth Glover; children--Patricia A., Ruth Yvonne; asst. pastor, St. Paul's African Methodist Episcopal Zion Church, Cleveland, Ohio, 1936-50; church school teacher, 25 years; current pastor, Bethel African Methodist Episcopal Zion Ch., Cleveland, Ohio; Mem., Ohio Annual Conference, 1937--; Mayor's Committee; Operation City of Cleveland; A.M.E. Zion Ministers Union; National Council of Churches; Cleveland Church Federation; NAACP; Urban League; Interdenominational Ministers Ass'n; YMCA Board; Glenville Community Council of Cleveland; Mason; Home: 10915 Lee Ave., Cleveland 6, Ohio; Office: 1428 East 110th St., Cleveland 6, Ohio.

ADAIR, Joseph H., b. Chester, S. C., Dec. 30, 1924; s. Aton A. and Margaret (Jones) A.; A.B., Johnson C. Smith University, 1941-43; B.D., 1948-51; m. Justine Godley; children--Daisy Ellen, Godley Maurice; pastor, Mattoon Presbyterian Ch., Greenville, S.C., 1951-58; Walker's Chapel U. Presbyn. Ch., Reidsville, S. C.; Bower's Chapel U. Presbyn. Ch., Wellford, S.C., 1958-63; pub. sch. tchr. Greenville Co.,'1953-63; US Navy, 1943-46; Home: Rte 4, Box 577, Greenville, S. C.

ADAMS, Clyde, b. Cherry Valley, Ark.; attended Univ. of Cincinnati; Univ. of Toledo; Fort Wayne Bible Coll.; D.D. (Hon.) Mich. State Bapt. Sem.; Ministers Instit. & Coll., West Pt., Miss.; baptist chs., Addyston,

Toledo, Ohio, pastor, Union Bapt. Ch., Ft. Wayne, Ind., present; Chmn. Bd. of dir. Nat. Bapt. Youth Camp, Constintine, Mich.; bd. of dir. Nat. Bapt. Conv. (5 yrs.); present, mem. ex. bd., Frontiers Club; NAACP (Fort Wayne); Associated Chs. of Fort Wayne & Allen Co.; United Community Services; Y.M.C.A.; Equal Opportunity Coun. of Ft. Wayne; Chmn. Civic Com. of Ministerial Alliance; mem., Police Community Relations Commn.; Inter-faith commn.; Home: 907 Colerick St., Ft. Wayne, Ind. 46806.

ADAMS, James A., b. Holly Springs, Miss., April 12, 1898; A.B., Lane Coll.; B.D., Gammon Theol. Sem., 1951-53; Graduate Courses, Fisk Univ. and Garrett Biblical Institute; m. Augusta Person; pastor, Christian Methodist Episcopal Churches, McKensie, Jackson, Brownsville, Tenn.; current pastor, FarmerChapel C.M.E., Ch., Brownsville, Tenn.; Prof., Phillips Sch. of Theol., 1944-58; Mem., Judiciary Count, C.M.E. Ch.; Home: 351 Berry St., Jackson, Tenn.

ADAMS, John Hurst, b. Columbia, S. C., Nov. 27, 1929; s. Eugene A. and Charity A.; A.B., Johnson C. Smith, 1948; S.T.B., S.T.M., Boston Univ.; further Study, Harvard Univ., Union Theol. Sem., N.Y.; D.D. (Hon.), Wilberforce Univ., 1956, Campbell Coll. (Miss.), 1959; Urban Training Center, Chgo.; m. Dolly Jacqueline Desselle; Children--Gaye Desselle, Jann Hurst, Madelyn Rose; asst. pastor, Charles St. African Meth. Epis. Ch., Boston, Mass., 1949-50; pastor, Bethel A.M.E. Ch., Lynn, Mass., 1950-52; Prof. Payne Theol. Sem., Wilberforce, Ohio, 1952-56; pres. Paul Quinn Coll., Waco, Texas; 1956-62; pastor, First A.M.E. ch., Seattle, Wash., 1963-68; Grant A.M.E. Ch., Los Angeles, 1968-present; A.M.E. Ch. Gen. Bd. Ed., Repres. Consultation on Ch.; Comm. on Restructuring A.M.E. Ch.; A.M.E. Stewardship Commn.; Cons., Jt. Strategy & Action Com., Chm. & Organizer, Central Area Citizens' Com. (Seattle); Chmn. of Bd., Central Area Motivation Program; vi.-Chmn., Seattle-King Co. Eco. Opp. Bd. Vi - Chmn. Seattle, O.I.C.; Bd. mem. NAACP; Coun. of Chs., Seattle; World without War coun. (Seattle); Y.M.C.A. (Seattle); Organizer & Chmn., Freedom Patrol Movement, 1965; Co-sponsor & Chmn., Seattle Sch. Boycott Co., 1966; Co-founder, Seattle Eco. Growth Organization; Bd. mem Urban League (Seattle); awards, "Man of Yr.," B'nai B'rith (Seattle

Lodge); Community Leadership award, Seattle League, 1966; mem. Alpha Phi Alpha; Sigma Pi Phi; Home: 3766 Crestway Pl.; Office: 1157 E. 105th St., L. A., Calif.

ADAMS, L. Bryant, b. Henderson, Tex., Jan. 7, 1907; s. Gus and Amy (Montgomery) A.; B. A., Bishop Coll., 1934; B. D., Southern Theol. Sem., Fort Worth, 1940; m. Fern Kurkendall Crutchfield; Children--Maxine Marle (Mrs. Williams Walker); pastor, Mt. Olive Bapt. Ch., Albuquerque, N. Mexico; Mt. Zion Bapt. Ch., Sweetwater, Tex.; Mt. Zion Bapt. Ch., Brownwood, Tex.; current pastor, Second Bapt. Ch., El Paso, Texas, 1953--; former civilian chaplain, Camp Bowie, 6 years; teacher, Sweetwater, Texas, 1949-51; Mem., Community Develop. Assn., Sweetwater; dean, Original West Texas Dist. S. S. & B. T. U. Congress; Mem., NAACP; Bd. Mem. of the McCall Day Nursery; Public Relations Chairman, Interdenominational Ministerial Alliance; former pres., El Paso Ministerial Alliance; editorial staff, Bishop Bears; Brownwood Community News Letter; contributing editor, Southwest Trade Guide (The Interpreter) El Paso, Texas; Home: 311 South Tornillo St., El Paso, Texas 79901; Office: Second Baptist Church, 401 South Virginia St., El Paso, Texas.

ADAMSON, Norman R., b. Center Point, Ark., March 21, 1937; s. Morris & Nobie L.; A. A., Southwestern Christian Coll., Terrell, Texas, 1957; courses, North Park Coll. & Theol. Sem.; m. Helen J. Bond; Children--Norman Jr., Darryl, Noel, Tracy; Assoc. pastor, Michigan Ave. Church of Christ, Chicago, 1961-66; Stony Island Christian Ch., 1967-present; Chgo. U. S. Post Office Dep.; Customer Relations Representative Officer, 1958-present; Home: 8110 S. Dante St., Chgo., Ill. 60619; Office: 1600 E. 84th St., Chgo., Ill. 60617.

ADJAHOE, Alfred Amedjorgbenu, b. Keta, Ghana, W. Africa, June 8, 1900; s. Kofi and Aloeke (Badonu); S. T. B., Johnson C. Smith Univ., Charlotte, N. C., 1925; B. A., Livingstone Coll., Salisbury, N. C., 1927; D. D. (hon.), Livingstone Coll., 1948; m. Juanita Graham; Children--Jane Ablewah (Mrs. Willie Tsitsiwu), Marie, Alfred, Agnes Ablewavi (Mrs. Thomas F. Ribeiro), Stanley, Edgar; pastor, AMEZ Chs., 8 yrs.; Bishop Deputy, missionary, AMEZ E. Ghana, W. Africa, 15 yrs.; returned to Am., pastored AMEZ Chs.; present presiding elder, AMEZ Mass. Area; tchr., Davie Co., Mocksville, N. C.,

8 yrs.; mem., NAACP; vi-pres. Human Rights Club, Attleboro, Mass., 1968-; mem., Alpha Tau Omega; Christn. Coun.; Min. Assoc., Attleboro, Mass.; Home: 32 Leroy St., Attleboro, Mass. 02703.

ALBERT, Xavier Robert, b. Houston, Texas, Sept. 10, 1931; s. Robert and Cora (Tillman) A.; B. S. Pharmacy, Texas Southern Univ.; Loyola Univ.; Bellarmine College; Wayne State U., Passionist Seminary; Ordained priest, Roman Cath. Ch., May 26, 1963; Home: 23300 Davison Ave., W., Detroit, Mich. 48223.

ALEXANDER, George W. II, b. Dec. 21, 1936, Louisville, Ky.; s. Jesse W. and Reella D.; A. B. Central State Coll., Wilberforce, Ohio, 1958; B. D. Southern Bapt. Theol. Sem., Louisville, Ky., 1962; Clinical Pastoral Tng., Louisville Gen. Hosp., 1960; m. Norma Jean Moody; Children--Joy Renee, Hope Reinette; Juvenile Court Chaplain, Hamilton Co., Cincinnati, Ohio, 1961-62; U. S. Army Chaplain, 1962-present; Youth Activities Sup., Ft. Campbell, Ky., 1964-65; mem. Fort Campbell's Sch. Bd., 1964-65; mem. Equal Employment Opportunities sub. com., Ft. Sill, Okla.; Decorations, Bronze Star Medal, Parachutist Medal; mem. Alpha Phi Alpha; Alpha Kappa Mu Honor Soc.; Toastmaster's Inc., Military Chaplain's Assoc.; Assn. of U. S. Army; 101 Airborne Asso. Home: 1222 Bob Perrel Rd., Ft. Sill, Okla. 73503; Office: Office of the Chaplain, HQ 2d AIT BDE, USATC, FA, Ft. Sill, Okla. 73503

ALEXANDER, Lloyd Matthew, coll. prof.; b. Meredithville, Va., June 3, 1903; s. William Alexander and Millie (Brown) A.; St. Paul's Jr. College (Now St. Paul's College), Lawrenceville, Va., 1929-31; St. Augustine's College, Raleigh, N. C., 1931-33, B. A.; B. D., Bishop Payne Divinity School, Petersburg, Va., 1933-36; Union Theo. Sem. and Teachers Coll., Columbia Univ., NYC, M. A., 1938, 1946; m. Helen Eugenia Arrant; Children--Juanita Lucille, Lloyd Matthew, Jr., Leonard Arrant; Chaplain Ft. Valley School, Ft. Valley, Georgia, 1937-40; Priest-in-charge, St. Mark's Episcopal Church, Bracey, Va., 1940-43; chaplain, Armed Forces (Capt. in 5th Air Force), 1943-46; chaplain, St. Augustine's College, Raleigh, N. C., 1947-49; Priest-in-charge, St. Cyprian's, Hampton & St. Augustine's, Newport News, 1950-60; vicar, St. Augustine's Newport News, 1960--; teacher, Ft. Valley School; teacher of philosophy at St. Augustine's College, Raleigh;

award: Man of the Year in Hampton, Va. (Omega Psi Phi); Home: 1207 Aberdden Rd., Hampton Va.; Office: 2515 Marshall Ave., Newport News, Va.

ALEXANDER, Robert Henry, Sr., b. Camilla, Ga., Feb. 14, 1914; s. Moses Taylor and Mariah Androna (Melver) A.; A.B., Morris Brown Coll., 1940; B.D. Turner Theol. Sem., 1942; S.T.M., Boston Univ., 1948; m. Ruby Artelia Johnson; Children--Sheila Ann (Mrs. Lavonne), Robert Henry, James Avery; Ordained to ministry, African Methodist Episcopal Church, 1935; pastor, Rock Temple, Conyers, Ga., 7 yrs.; pres., Shorter Coll., North Little Rock, Arkansas, 1948-52; pastor, Avery Church, Oklahoma City, 1952--; Mem., General Bd., Publication Bd., Com. on Education, 12th Episcopal Dist., A.M.E. Ch., 1952--; U.S. Army, Chapalin Corps, Maj., 1942-46; Mem., Oklahoma City Counc. of Churches (pres. 1957-59; v.p. 1953-57); Oklahoma City Interdenominational Ministerial Alliance (pres. 1954-59); dir., Urban League, 1952-58; Mason; Home: 1109 NE 17th St., Oklahoma City, Okla.; Office: 1425 N. Kelham Ave., Oklahoma City, Okla.

ALEXANDER, William Alphonso, Sr., b. Newport News, Va., Dec. 20, 1921; s. Samuel Roscoe and Carrie (Allen) A.; A.B., Fisk Univ., 1949; M.A., 1957; B.D., McCormick Theol. Sem., Chic., Ill., 1951; m. Fay Janet Hampton; Children--William, Jr., Paul Garvin, Peter Hadley; assoc. pastor, St. Augustine Presbyterian Church, Bronx, N.Y.; pastor, St. Andrew Presbyterian Ch., U.S.A.; pastor, Nashville, Tenn., Dec. 1951--; Moderator of Nashville Presbytery, 1961; Visit monthly since 1956, to State Prison (Nashville); chaplain, Fisk Gen. Alumni Assn.; chaplain, Davidson County Independent Political Counc. (Nashville, Tenn.); chaplain, Frontier's International, Nashville Chapter, 1956--; Home: 901 37th Ave. N., Nashville, Tenn.; Office: 949 37th Ave. N., Nashville, Tenn.

ALEXANDER, William Peter, b. Columbus, Miss., Aug. 5, 1897; Douglas Univ., Coll. of Rel., 1927-28; McKendree Coll., 1932; Univ. of Ill., 1941; Midwest Bible Coll., 1959-60; D.D. (hon.) Central Miss. Coll., 1957; Ark. Bapt. Coll., 1963; 6 children; pastor, Mt. Olive Bapt. Ch., East St. Louis, Mo., 1927-39; Mt. Nebo Bapt. Ch., 1939-44; current, New Hope Bapt. Ch., 1944--; dean, East St. Louis Extension, Amer. Bapt. Sem.; moderator,

New Salem Bapt. District Assn., 1953-63; pres., Ill. Bapt. Gen. State Congress of Christn. Ed.; instructor Adult Div. Nat. Sunday Sch. and B. T. U. Congress; mem. East St. Louis Chamber of Commerce; former pres., NAACP; Bd. of Governors and Bd. of Directors, United Fund of Greater East St. Louis; mem., All America City Steering Com.; East St. Louis Centennial Com.; vice chairman, East St. Louis Human Relations Com.; Appointed by Mayor, Ill. Emancipation Centennial; Mason; Home: 4247 Piggott Ave., East St. Louis, Ill.; Office: 2122 Missouri Ave., East St. Louis, Ill.

ALLEN, Frank Murphy, b. Ansley, Ala., Apr. 17, 1908; s. John Wesley; B. Th., Hood Theol. Sem., Livingstone Coll., Salisbury, N. C.; m. Flora Stringer; Children--George, Marcia, John, Sheila; pastor, Jeff Chapel AMEZ Ch., Goshen, Ala., 1938-39; New Hope AMEZ Circuit, Lapine, Ala., 1939-40; Troy Chapel, Montgomery, Ala., 1940-42; St. Paul AMEZ Ch., Tuskegee, Ala., 1942-44; St. Matthew AMEZ Ch., Miami, Fla., 1944-48; Payne Chapel, Little Rock, Ark., 1948-51; St. John AMEZ Ch., Mocksville, N. C., 1951-53; Gethsemane AMEZ Ch., Charlotte, N. C., 1953-present; mem., N. C. Coun. of Chs., Com. on Christn. Social Morals; Clergyman's Christn. and Civic Action Assn.; mem., Charlotte chapt., NAACP; YMCA; Office: 326 Cemetery St., Charlotte, N. C.

ALLEN, John Claude, bishop, b. Talladega, Ala., April 5, 1899; A. B., Talladega Coll.; 1 dau. Claudia Mae (Shannon); licensed to preach, Detroit, Mich., 1926; admitted into S. E. Missouri and Ill. Conf.; pastor, Christian Methodist Episcopal Ch., Mich.; pastor, Israel C. M. E. Ch., Gary, Indiana; presiding elder, Chicago District, C. M. E. Ch.; Treas., S. E. Missouri & Ill. Conf.; sec., Kingdom Extension C. M. E. Ch., 1946-58; established and pastored C. M. E. Churches in Pacific Coast area; Bd. mem., Bd. of Education, Public Schools, Gary, Ind.; Elected 28th bishop C. M. E. Ch., Memphis, Tenn., May 1954; Home: 755 W. 26th Ave., Gary, Ind.

ALLEYNE, Lawrence Edward D., teacher, b. Brooklyn, N. Y., June 14, 1928; s. Edward C. and Wilhelmina (King) A.; Jordan Sem., Menominee, Mich.; Mother of the Savior Sem., Blackwood, N. J.; Catholic Univ. of America, Washington, D. C., 1954-57, B. A. 1956; Ordained priest, Roman Cath. Ch., 1960; Instructor, Greek,

Latin, Religion, Mother of the Savior Sem., Blackwood, N. J., 1960--; Treas. of Seminary, 1961--; Home and Office: Mother of the Savior Seminary, Blackwood, N. J.

ALLISON, Jonathan Wm., b. Leavenworth, Kansas, April 23, 1913; s. John W. & Lona V. (Oden); Oakwood Coll., Huntsville, Ala., 1935-36; A. B., Andrews Univ., Berrien Springs, Mich., 1939; Grad. courses, U. C. L. A., Los Angeles; m. Bessie Lou Cort; Children--Frederick Dan, Carole Anne, John Wm., Camille Yvonne; pastor, Beacon Light Seventh-Day Adventist Ch., Phoenix, Ariz., 1940-43; Inkster S. A. D. Ch., Inkster, Mich., 1943-45; Capitol Ave. S. A. D., Ch. Indianapolis, Ind., 1945-48; City Temple, Detroit, 1948-54; Univ. S. A. D. Ch., Los Angeles, 1954-present; mem. Senior Citizens Committeeman, Los Angeles; Democrat; Chmn., Sch. Bd., Los Angeles Parochial Union Sch.; Co.-Chmn., Lynwood Academy Bd.; mem. Pacific Union Conf. Com. of S. A. D. Ch.; Home: 1147 W. 39th Pl., Los Angeles, Calif., 90037; Office: 1135 W. Santa Barbara, Los Angeles, Calif., 90037

*Alston, Charlie, b. Warren County, N. C., Oct. 17, 1921; s. Wayman and Elizabeth (Jordan) A.; A. B., Va. Union Univ., Richmond, Va., 1951; Graduate work, Univ. of Alaska, 1956; B. D., Howard Univ. Sch. of Rel., Wash., D. C., 1963; specialized training: Clinical Pastoral Training; Children's Center; Dept. of Pub. Welfare, D. C.; Laurel, Md.; Personnel Supervision; Air Training Command; Scott Air Force Base, Ill.; pastor, St. John's Bapt. Ch., Fairbanks, Alaska, 3 years; minister of education, Pilgrims Baptist Ch., Wash., D. C., 2 years; juvenile counselor, Children's Center, Dept. of Pub. Welfare, D. C.; Laurel, Md.; instructor, Systematic Theol., The Wash. Bapt. Sem., Wash., D. C., 3 years; institutional chaplain, Council of Churches of Greater Washington, Wash., D. C.; senior clinical chaplain, Milledgeville State Hospital, 1963--; pres., NAACP, Alaska; 1st Amer. Negro to pastor a Southern Bapt. Convention Church; mem., Fairbanks Ministers Assn., Alaska; The Executive Comm. of the Alaska Bapt. Convention; U. S. Air Force, three years active duty as Air Transportation Technician; four years active duty as Personnel Supervisor; mem., Urban League; NAACP; Georgia Public Health Assn.; Campaign medal with three bronze stars; Home: P. O. Box 725, Milledgeville, Ga. 31061; Office: Milledgeville State Hospital, Milledgeville, Ga.

ALSTON, Edward Deedom, b. Norfolk, Va., Sept. 29, 1911; s. Deedom and Berderlee (Redden) A.; 1935 B.S. North Carolina Coll., Durham; 1942, B.D. Bishop Payne Divinity Sch., Petersburg, Va.; m. Elouise Williams A.; Children--Edward Deedom, Jr., Virnal Jeffery; St. James Episcopal Ch., Emporia, Va.; St. James Episcopal Ch., Portsmouth, Va.; Our Merciful Saviour Episcopal Ch., Louisville, Ky.; Activities: Home visitor, Staff, Louisville Municipal Housing Commission; Ky. Committee on Illegitimacy; Mayor's Comm. on Human Relations; Bd., Chestnut St. Branch YMCA; Ky. Civil Liberties Union; mem. Frontiers of America; Kappa Alpha Psi; Home: 1016 S. 43rd St., Louisville, Ky.; Church: 473 S. 11th St., Louisville, Ky.

ALSTON, Justus M., b. Oxford, N.C., April 15, 1905; s. L. L. and Mary A.; A.B., Johnson C. Smith University, 1928; B.D., Johnson C. Smith Univ., 1931; D.D. (hon.), Johnson C. Smith Univ., 1940; m. Nannie McClure; Children--Jeffery Myron; Former moderator Catawba Presbytery; pres. pastor, New Hampton United Presbyterian Ch.; mem. Mason, Phi Beta Sigma; former Master, Myersville Lodge, F. & A.M.; Pres., Johnson C. Smith Alumni; Home: 2012 Oaklawn Ave., Charlotte, N.C.

ALSTON, Percel Odel, Sr., church official; b. Norfolk, Va., Jan. 27, 1926; s. Robert James Sr. and Louise (Harrison) A.; A.B., Va. Union Univ., 1950; B.D., Andover Newton Theol. Sem., 1954; S.T.M., Andover Newton Theol. Sem., 1954; m. Maybelle Helene Kelly; Children--Taitu Zawdu, Karen Louise, Percel Odel, Jr.; pastor, Midway Congregational Ch. (United Church of Christ), McIntosh, Ga.; dir., Dorchester Coop. Center, McIntosh, Ga., 1954-56; minister, Chrstn. Education, Convention of the South; United Church of Christ, Greensboro, N.C. 1956-64; sec., Leadership Development, Div. of Christian Education, Bd. of Homeland Ministries, United Church of Christ, 1964--; mem., Com. on Administration and Leadership, Div. of Christian Ed., National Counc. of Churches; consultant, The Church and Urbanization, United Church of Christ; consultant, Education for Vocational Decision for Ministry Group Youth Work Party, Technological Revolution; Office: 1505 Race St., Philadelphia, Pa.

AMOS, Walter Hansel, bishop, b. Milan, Tenn., March 16, 1908; s. E.F.B. and Alice E.; Lane Coll.; A.B., Univ.

of Wisconsin; B. D., Garrett Biblical Institute; M. A. Univ. of Chicago Sch. of Divinity; Wayne Univ.; Ph. D., Univ. of Michigan; Admitted on trial Christian Methodist Episcopal Ch., 1935; Ordained deacon, 1936; Full Connection, 1936; Ordained Elder, 1938; Elected 32nd bishop, Christian Methodist Episcopal Ch., St. Louis, Mo., May 1962; Home: 2111 La Salle Gardens, So., Detroit, Mich.

ANDERSON, Benjamin J., b. B'ham, Ala.; s. Charles and Gertrude (Fisher) A.; A. B., Morehouse Coll., 1939; B. D., Andover Newton Theol. Sem., 1942; m. Louise Gaillard; Children--Marjorie; Gertrude; pastor, Gloucester Meml. Presbyn. Ch., 1941-47; Witherspoon Presbyn. Ch., Princeton, N. J., 1948-64; currently, chap., Smith Coll., 1964--; past, missionary to China by Presbyn. Bd. of Foreign Miss.; mem., Bd. of Pensions; moderator, Presbytery, New Brunswick; pres., Princeton Pastors' Assn.; Exec. Dir., Commn. on Rel. and Race, Synod of N. J., United Presbyn. Ch., 1963; chmn. Standing Com. Nat. Miss., 175th Gen. Assembly, U. P. Ch., nominated candidate moderator, 176th Gen. Assembly, Presbytery, New Brunswick; present mem., Bd. of Managers, Central Dept. of Evangelism; Nat. Counc. of Chs. of Christ; trustee, Westminster Foun., Princeton Univ., dir., trustee, TriCo. Mental Health Assn.; Holyoke, Mass.; frequent lectr. coll. and univ.; Office: Chaplains Office, Smith Coll., Northampton, Mass.

ANDERSON, Felix Sylvester, bishop, b. Wilmington, N. C., Oct. 3, 1893; Charles and Bettie (Foye) A.; A. B., Livingstone Coll., 1920; courses, Hood Theol. Sem.; B. D., Western Theol. Sem., 1922-24; m. Bessie B. Bizzel; Children--Felix S. Jr., Herman L., Mrs. Wright, Paul Robinson, Joseph D., Theodore M., Mrs. Alfred Haney; pastor, AMEZ Chs., Rocky Creek Circuit, 1915; Mainville Circuit, 1916; Mt. Lebanon AME Zion Ch., Elizabeth City, N. C.; Kadesh Edenton, N. C.; Hunters Chapel, Tuscaloosa, Augusta, Ga., Southern Pines, N. C., Big Zion, Mobile, Ala; Broadway Temple, Louisville, Ky., 1948-60; present bishop, Eighth Epis. Dist. A. M. E. Z. Ch.; instr., P. W. Moore High Sch., Elizabeth City, N. C., 1929-32; mem., Gen. Assem. Repre. 42nd Dist., 1954-60; trustee, Livingstone Coll., Pres., Bd. of Statistics, A. M. E. Z. Ch.; citation, A. M. E. Z. Ministers Alliance, 1958; Ky. Teachers Assoc., 1955; NAACP; Urban League; mem., Fraternal Order of Police; Home: 741 S. 44th St., Louisville, Ky. 40211.

ANDERSON, Herbert Forgys, b. Jamaica, B. W. I., May 31, 1884; s. Henry Dorman and Frances Augusts; A. B. S. T. B., Lincoln Univ., 1916, 1931; m. Luevinia Burell Sullivan; pastor, Timothy Darling Presby. Ch., USA, Oxford, N. C., 1919-20; Cumberland Presby. Ch., Va., 1920-21; Holbrook St. Presby Ch., 1921-23; Chestnut St. Presby. Ch., 1923-24; 9th St. Bristol, Tenn. St. Mark Rogerville, 1924-31; Christ Presby. Ch., Augusta, Ga., 1931-64; teacher, Oxford, N. C.; Danville, Va.; Bristol, Tenn.; Rogerville, Tenn.; mem., Omega Psi Phi; former treas., Hodge Presby. Ch., 1945-60; moderator, commissioner, General Assembly, 1939, 1948, 1945; mem. Interdenominational Alliance, Augusta, Ga.; Advisory Bd., U. S. A., Augusta, Ga.; Home: 1136 Cecilia St., Augusta, Ga., 30901; Office: 1316 Gwinnette, Augusta, Ga., 30901.

ANDERSON, Herman Leroy, b. Wilmington, N. C., Feb. 23, 1923; Felix S. and Bessie (Bizzell) A.; B. S., Tuskegee Inst., 1943; B. D., Hood Theol. Sem., 1959; m. Ruth Rogers; Children--Deborah Ruth; Herman Leroy; Derrick Rushion; pastor, Hood Meml. A. M. E. Z. Ch., Belmont, N. C., 1956-59; St. James A. M. E. Z. Ch., Ithaca, N. Y., 1959-62; Soldiers Meml., A. M. E. Z. Ch., Salisbury, N. C., 1962--; Self-employed Fuel Business operator, Wilmington, N. C., 1946-48; tchr., City School System, Wilmington, N. C., 1947-53; mail carrier, Wilmington, N. C., 1953-56; mem., Rowan County Bd. of Pub. Welfare; Alpha Phi Alpha; NAACP; Democrat; N. C. Coun. of Chs.; Home: 212 W. Liberty St., Salisbury, N. C., 28144.

ANDERSON, Jesse Fosset, b. Plainfield, N. J., April 3, 1910; s. Jefferson Charles and Mary (Fosset) A.; A. B., Lincoln Univ., 1932; S. T. B., Genl. Theol. Sem., 1935; m. Elizabeth Reynolds Jackson; children--Jesse, Jr., John, Louis; curate, St. Philips Ch., New York City, 1935-38; priest-in-charge, St. Philips Ch., Grand Rapids, Mich., 1938-42; priest-in-charge, St. Matthews Ch., Wilmington, Del., 1942-44; rector, St. Thomas Ch., Philadelphia, Pa., 1944--; Mayor's Commn. on Higher Education (Phila., Pa.); mem.: Diocesan and National Offices; Standing Committee (Bishop's Counc. of Advice); Executive Committee of Diocese; Dept. of Christian Social Relations; Dept. of Missions; Committee on Racial Understanding; Bd. of Episcopal Community Services; Twice delegate, Dioceses to National Gen. Convention; teacher, Provincial and Diocesan Adult and Youth Conferences;

Home: 1427 No. 56th St., Philadelphia, Pa.; Office: 52nd & Ponish Sts., Philadelphia, Pa.

ANDERSON, Leslie Otto, b. Steelton, Pa., Nov. 5, 1933; s. John Richard and Mamie Cordella (Caldwell) A.; B.A., Oakwood Coll., 1959; M.A., Andrews Univ., 1960; m. Mary Alyce Branche. Present: District pastor, Muskegon-Grand Rapids-Idlewild, Michigan, 1960--; U.S. Air Force, 1952-56; National Defense Award; Good Conduct (military); Home: 715 Paris Ave., S.E., Grand Rapids, Mich. 49503; Office: 111 Graham St., S.W., Grand Rapids, Mich.

ANDERSON, Louis Lloyd, b. Steubenville, Ohio, Jan. 1, 1922; s. Cecil H. L. and Maggie Beachum A.; A.B., Univ. of Pittsburgh, 1948; B.S., M.A., Religious Education; Courses Ph.D., Univ. of Chicago; m. Pauline Dinkins; pastor, Metropolitan Bapt. Ch., Pittsburgh, Pa., 1940-43; Calvary Bapt. Ch., Duluth, Minn., 1950-52; North Montgomery Bapt. Ch., Montgomery, Ala., 1954-55; current pastor, Tabernacle Bapt. Ch., Selma, Ala., 1955--; mem., Dallas County Voters League, Southern Christian Leadership Conference; Home: 817 First Ave., Selma, Ala.; Office: 1431 Broad St., Selma, Ala.

ANDERSON, Vinton Randolph, b. Somerset, Bermuda, July 11, 1927; s. C. L. Rabberway (foster parents) and Francis; B.A., Wilberforce Univ., 1952; B.D. Payne Theo. Sem., 1952; M.A. Kansas Univ., 1962; D.D. (hon.), Paul Quinn Coll., 1964; m. Vivienne Louise Cholmondeley; Children--Vinton R. Jr., Jeffrey Charles, Carlton Lawson; pastor, St. Mark African Methodist Episcopal Ch., Topeka, Kan., 1952-53; Brown Chapel A.M.E. Ch., Parsons, Kan., 1953-55; St. Luke A.M.E. Ch., Lawrence, Kan., 1955-59; St. Paul A.M.E. Ch., Wichita, Kan., 1959-64; St. Paul A.M.E. Ch., St. Louis, Mo., 1964--; mem., Gen. Bd. of Education of the A.M.E. Ch.; First v-p., Wichita Branch of the NAACP; church work chairman NAACP, Kansas; pres., Bd. of Trustees, Wichita Counc. of Churches; mem., Bd. of Dir. Christian Stewardship for the Kansas-Nebraska Conference of the A.M.E. Ch.; Zeta Sigma Pi National Honorary Social Science Fraternity; Alpha Phi Alpha; delegate, World Methodist Conference, Oslo, Norway, 1961; mem., President's Comm. on Equal Employment Opportunities, 1963; representative, A.M.E. Ch. to the Commission of Higher Education of the Nat. Counc. of Churches in the USA;

Mayor's Committee; Episcopal Committee of the A. M. E. Ch.; attended Yale Univ. Conf. for the Ministry; Home: 5357 Batmear St., St. Louis, Mo.; Office: 1260 Hamilton St., St. Louis, Mo.

ANDERSON, William H., b. March 11, 1919, South Carolina; s. Jackson, Jr., and Isabella (Bibbs) A; Morehouse Coll., 1941-44; Univ. of Pa., 1954; A. B. Miller Univ., 1945; Courses, Rutgers Univ.; D. D. (Hon.) Morris Coll., 1956; pastor, First Bapt. Ch., Bound Brook, N. J., 1946-49; Belmont Bapt. Ch., Phila., Pa., 1949-51; Second Bapt. Ch. of Frankfort, Pa., 1951-58; Northeast Bapt. Ch., Phila., Pa., 1958-present; pres. Bapt. Minister's Conf., Phila., 1955; ex. sec. Coun. of Bapt. Organizations, 1956-present; ex. dir. Coun. of United Negro Charities, 1960-present; pres. Pa. Bapt. Conv., 1968-72; Dir.-Gen., Progressive Nat. Congress of Christian Ed., 1967-present; Dir. Excelsior Housing Corp.; Dir. Gen. Bd. Nat. Coun. of Chs. awards, The Phila. Tribune Service Award, 1959; mem. Mason; Knights of Phythians; I. B. O. P. E.; author Saved from the Sea, Sermons, 1955. Home: 1635 W. Grange, Philadelphia, Pa., 19141; Office: Foulkrod and Tackawanna Sts., Phila., Pa. 19124.

*ANDREWS, Richard Taylor, Jr., b. Houston, Texas, Sept. 8, 1912; s. Richard Taylor and Julia (Sommerville) A.; A. B., Fisk Univ., 1932; B. D., Sch. of Rel., Howard Univ., 1953; m. Marjory Jackson; Children--Stephen B., Richard Taylor III; Pastor, Mt. Zion Congregational (United Church of Christ), Cleveland, Ohio, 1953-present; Consultant, Social Action Comm. of United Ch. of Christ; vice-moderator, Ohio Synod of United Ch. of Christ; board mem., NAACP (Cleveland Branch), 1956-60; board mem., YMCA, 1959-present; Honorable discharge, World War II; Omega Psi Phi; Citizen's League; Consumer's League; all in Cleveland, Ohio; Article pub. in Social Action, 1962; Home: 9703 Parmelee Ave., Cleveland, O.; Office: 10723 Magnolia Dr., Cleveland, O.

*ANONYE, Albert, Chinedozi, college professor, b. Alaenyi Ogwa, Nigeria, W. Africa, June 9, 1925; s. Aaron M. and Isabella Eleonu (Nwachukugwobi) A.; B. A., Central State Coll., Wilberforce, O., 1953; M. A., Boston Univ., Boston, Mass., 1954; B. D., Sch. of Rel., Howard Univ., 1961; m. Archiong Ewa Ewa Eke; Children--Anita Chinwe, Stella Ulunma, Betty Ngozi, Columbus K., Theodosia, Rose; Prof., Aggrey Mem. Coll., Arochuku, Nigeria,

1955-56; principal, Emmanuel Coll., Owerri, E. Nigeria, 1957-59; missionary pastor, Twelfth St. Christian Ch., Wash., D.C., 1960-63; Present: assoc. prof., and chrmn., History Dept., Talladega Coll., 1963-68; Prof., Morgan State Coll., 1968-present; former Sec.-Gen., N'Dian Estate br. of Calabar Mercantile Workers' Union; founder, Ndi-Uhu Village Family Union, Nigeria, 1956; pres., Intl. Relations Club, Inc. of N. Amer., 1952-53; Office: Morgan State Coll., Balto., Md.

ANTHONY, Irving, b. Trinidad, West Indies; s. Alexander A. and Martha (Jemmott) A.; A.B., M.S., Coll. of the City of New York, 1927, 1938; m. Cicely Olivia. Curate: St. Ambrose Ch., N.Y.C., 1945; St. Andrew's Church, N.Y.C., 1946-49; St. Phillip's Ch., N.Y.C., 1949-60; rector, St. Andrew's Ch., N.Y.C., 1960-present; teacher, N.Y.C Public Schools; advisory board, Harlem Hospital Sch. of Nursing; mason; Master's thesis: "Factors Influencing Truancy Among Boys of Junior High School Age." Home: 2588 Seventh Ave., New York, N.Y.; Office: 2067 5th Ave., New York, N.Y.

*ARMSTRONG, Ernest W., b. Bluff Route, Soper, Okla., May 1, 1915; s. Giles H. and Vinnie (Jones) A.; A.B., Dillard Univ., 1942; B.D., M.A., Howard Univ., 1946, 1947; m. Luella Whitaker; Children--Ernest W., Jr., Earl M., Everett W.; Chaplain to Bapt. students at Howard Univ. and asst. pastor, Shiloh Bapt. Ch., Wash., D.C., 1946-48; coll. minister and assoc. prof., social sci., Savannah State Coll., Savannah, Ga., 1948-49; U.S. Army chaplain, 1949-69; Prof., Triton Com. & Tech. Coll., River Grove, Ill.; Bronze Star (V) medal; Amer. Defense medal; German Occupation medal; 10 years U.S. Army Reserve medal; U.N. Campaign medal; Korean War medal; mem. Omega Psi Phi; Mason, cited "Mason of the Year" by the Oklahoma Grand Lodge, 1962; rec'd. "Scroll of Honor," Omega Psi Phi, 1964 for "outstanding achievement in the field of Int'l. Brotherhood;" Deputy Sovereign Grand Comm., Scottish Rite Masonry in Europe, Southern Jurisdiction; Office: Triton Com. & Tech. Coll., River Grove, Ill.

ARNOLD, James Alridge; s. Roy and Pauline; A.B., Butler Univ., Indianapolis, Ind., 1943; M. Div., Hood Theol. Sem., Salisbury, N.C., 1967; m. Irene Miller; Pastor, Jones Tabernacle A.M.E.Z. Ch., Indianapolis, Ind., 1937; Penick Chapel A.M.E.Z. Ch., 1940-45; A.M.E.Z.

Ch., White Plains, N.Y., 1945-52; Hood Mem. A.M.E. Z. Ch., Bristol, Tenn., 1952-58; Fair Promise A.M.E. Z. Ch., Sanford, N.C., 1958-present; mem., Urban League; YMCA; NAACP; State Coun.of Chs., N.C.; Sanford Housing Commn.; Good Neighbor Counc.; mem., A.M.E.Z. Ch., Finance Com.; Examing Com., in-coming ministers; Budget and Apportionment Com., Gen. Conf.; Home: 508 Ramseur St., Sanford, N.C.

ARNOLD, Lionel A., b. Aug. 30, 1921, Greenville, Pa.; s. J.P. and Gertrude (Dowe); A.B., Thiel Coll., Greenville, Pa., 1943; B. Th. Anderson Coll. and Theol. Sem., 1944; M.A., B.D., Oberlin Coll. Sch. of Theol., 1946-47; S.Th.M. Harvard Div. Sch., 1955; L.H.D. (Hon.) Thiel Coll., 1964; Coll. Minister, LeMoyne Coll., Memphis, Tenn., 1947-60; Dean and Prof. Philosophy and Rel., LeMoyne Coll., 1963-68; Ed. leave, 1968-69; mem. Am. Acad. of Rel., Faculty Christn. Fellowship; Tchr. Adult Ed. Program; Crosscut Club; Home: 384 Gaston Ave., Memphis, Tenn. 38126; Office: LeMoyne Coll., Memphis, Tenn. 38126.

ARTERBERRY, Rufus, Sr., b. Fairfield, Ala., May 9, 1937; A.B., Wilberforce Univ., Wilberforce, Ohio, 1959; B.D., Payne Theol. Sem., 1963; m. Juanita Houston; Children--Rufus, Jr.; Asst. pastor, Univ. Chapel, Wilberforce, Ohio, 1959-60; pastor, St. Paul A.M.E. Ch., Cedarville, Ohio, 1960; pastor, St. James A.M.E. Ch., Bellefontaine, Ohio, 1962-64; present pastor, St. James A.M.E. Ch., Erie, Pa.; presently chaplain, Pa. State Senate; mem. Exec. Bd. NAACP; mem. Bd. of Booker T. Washington Center; pres., Erie Minority Anti-Poverty Com., mem. Opportunity Industrial Center Bd.; sec. Erie Interdenominational Minister's Union; chaplain, Migrant workers, summer, 1966; sub.-tchr. Jr. and High Sch., Erie City Sch. Sys.; mem., Rel. and Labor Coun. of Amer.; Nat. Coun. of Chs.; Citizen's Action Com.; Erie Human Rel. Commn.; Alpha Phi Alpha; Home: 517 W. Third St., Erie, Pa., 16507.

ARTIS, George Henry, b. Wilmington, N.C., July 2, 1931; s. George H. and Hazel (Smith) A.; B.A., St. Mary's Sem., Techny, Ill., 1952-58; Divine Word Sem., Bay St. Louis, Miss., 1948-52, 1958-62; Springhill Coll., Mobile, Ala.; Catholic U. of Amer., Wash., D.C.; Ordained March 17, 1962, priest, Roman Cath. Ch.; Asst. Pastor, The Immaculate Heart of Mary Church, Lafayette, La.;

Office: Immaculate Heart of Mary Church, P. O. Box 2398 Surrey & 12th St., Lafayette, La.

ASBURY, Howard DeGrasse, coll. prof., b. Boston, Mass., Aug. 28, 1907; s. Jasper DeGrasse and Adelaide (Hart) A.; A. B., Clark Univ., Atlanta, Ga., 1936; M. A., S. T. B., Boston Univ., 1936-39; m. Doris Wade; Children--Shirley Evone (Mrs. Robert H. Downs); pastor, Main St. Meth. Ch., Ronceverte, W. Va., 1939-41; Trinity Meth. Ch., Fairmont, W. Va., 1941-43; coll. minister, prof., Samuel Huston Coll. (later Huston-Tillotson Coll.), Austin, Tex., 1943-54; current pastor, St. Paul Meth. Ch., Jamaica, L. I., 1954--; mem., Alpha Phi Alpha; Phi Kappa Theta; Sons of Union Veterans of the Civil War; chaplain, New York Dept., Camp No. 20; Home: 104-20 189 St., Hollis, L. I.; Office: 173-01 108 Ave., Jamaica, L. I.

ASHBY, John Lynwood, Sr., b. Virginia Beach, Fa., Feb. 19, 1934; s. John and Ella; Va. State Coll., 1967; m. Louise Taylor; Children--John, Darlene; present pastor, 1st Bapt. Ch., Chesapeake, Va.; mem. Norfolk, Portsmouth, Va. Beach Bapt. Min. Conf.; v.-pres., Chesapeake Br., SCLC; dir., Boy Scout Troop, 1st Bapt.-Westmunden, Chesapeake, Va.; chmn., Newlight Rec. Com.; (former) pres., Newlight Civic Leage; advisor, Westmunden Civic League, Chesapeake, Va.; award, Korean Citation Medal, Good conduct medal, U. N. Medal; mem. Grand Lodge Loc. 39; Home: 200 Stauffer Way, Portsmouth, Va., 23701; Office: 1900 Lyons Ave., Chesapeake, Va.

ASHFORD, George, b. Winnsboro, S. C., June 23, 1929; June 23, 1929; s. Richard and Pearl Leitner A.; student, Allen Univ., Columbia, S. C., 1950-51, 1953-55; m. Rhudene Reeves; Children--Valerie G.; pastored African Meth. Epis. Chs., S. C.; pastor, Pine Grove A. M. E. Ch., S. C., 1964-present; tchr., S. C., 1955-57; Exec., N. C. Mutual Ins. Co., Durham, N. C., 1962-present; Exec. Bd., W. H. Burton Ele. Sch.; pres., John Merrick Club, Columbia Dist., N. C. Mutual Ins. Co.; served in Armed Forces; rec'd. Korean Service Medal; U. S. Service Medal; Democrat; Home: 1835 Columbia Coll. Dr., Columbia, S. C. 29203.

ASHURST, Harold Teen, b. Houston, Tex., June 23, 1929; s. Charlie and Beatrice W.; B. A., Huston Tillotson Coll.,

Austin, Tex.; Pres. B.D., Perkins Sch. of Theol., Dallas, Tex.; pastor, C.M.E. Ch., 1937-57; Meth. Ch., 1957-present; tchr., High Sch., Austin, Tex., 1959; mem. Omega Psi Phi; Ecum. Com. of Perkins Sch. of Theol., Dallas, Tex.; Home: 1118 E. Tucker St., Ft. Worth, Tex.; Office: 308 Martin Hall, (S.M.U.), Dallas, Tex. 75222.

ATCHISON, Wallace William, presiding elder; b. Edgefield, S.C., Mar. 31, 1876; s. Jarrett and Charity A.; Paine College, Augusta, Ga., 1908; m. Mahala Field; Pastored Christian Meth. Episcopal Chs. in Ga., Ky., Tenn., Okla., Ark., Ala., and New Jersey, 1907-35; presiding elder, Jersey City District and Camden, N.J. District, 1935-64. Retired April 1964. Home: 1588 W. Front St., Red Bank, N.J.

AUSTIN, Junius Caesar, b. Buckingham, Va., Aug. 1, 1887; s. Carey and Mary (Harvey) A.; A.B., Lynchburg Theol. Sem. & Coll., Lynchburg, Va.; B.S., Temple Univ., Philadelphia, Pa.; LL.D. (Hon.), Wilberforce Univ.; m. Inez Klosking Pollard; Children--Dorothea (Mrs. Jerome Brown); Rev. J.C. Austin Jr.; pastor, First Bapt. Ch., Appomattox Court House, 1903; Liberty Bapt. Ch., Belmar, N.J.; Main St. Bapt. Ch., Clifton Forge, Va., 1910-12; Mt. Zion Bapt. Ch., Staunton, Va., 1912-15; Ebenezer Bapt. Ch., Pittsburgh, Pa., 1915-25; Pilgrim Bapt. Ch., Chicago, Ill., 1926--; chrmn., Foreign Missn. Bd., 1917-25; regional chrmn., Foreign Missn. for the Progressive Nat. Bapt. Convention; served as food conservator during World War I; agricultural collaborator; pres., Square Deal Civic League; pres., Bapt. State Convention of Ill.; served as volun. camp pastor, World War I; author, So You Want to be Happy and Seven Deadly Sins; Home: 3932 S. Parkway, Chicago, Ill. 60616.

*AUSTIN, Miles Jonathan, b. Sanford, Fla., July 10, 1933; s. Simeon L. and Charity A.; B.S., Fla. A.&M. Univ., 1959; B.D., Howard Univ., Sch. of Rel., 1964; m. Jeanne M. (Sistrunk); Children--Miles Jr., Maria; graduate courses, Springfield Coll.; YMCA Certificate Secretary, 1966; D.C. government Youth Coun., 1961-62, Children's ctr.; Social Worker, Junior Citizens Corps, Wash., D.C., 1962-64; Asst. youth dir. YMCA, Newark, N.J.; Youth dir. YMCA, Princeton, N.J., 1966-67; Project dir., Essex Co. Neighborhood Youth Corps, 1967-68;

currently, dir. of Disaster Relief and Service to Military families, Essex, N. J. Chap. Amer. Red Cross; former asst. pastor Bethany Bapt. Ch., Newark, N. J.; mem. East Orange, N. J. Community Action Com. (Anti-poverty program); Democratic 4th Ward Assn., Newark, N. J.; Home: 134 Steuben St., East Orange, N. J. 07018; Office: 710 High St., Newark, N. J. 07102.

AUSTIN, Samuel Quincy, b. Alabama, May 4, 1935; s. Ira and Katherine, A.; B. S., Univ. of Buffalo, 1958; B. Th. Buffalo Bible Coll., 1960; State Univ. of N. Y., Buffalo, courses towards Masters degree; m. Naomi Brown; Children--Samuel Q., Jr., Cynthia Lorraine; pastor, Pilgrim Bapt. Ch., Buffalo, N. Y.; Grace Bapt. Ch., Mt. Vernon, N. Y.; currently tchr. & principal Buffalo City schs. (4 yrs.); pres. Sunday Sch. & Bapt. Tr. Union Congress, instructor Bapt. Empire State Sunday Sch. & Bapt. Training Union; pres. Buffalo Improvement Assn.; tchr Harlem Training School (Abyssinian Bapt. Ch. -NYC.); Head, SCLC, Operation Breadbasket (Westchester, N. Y.); Bd. dir. NAACP, (N. Y.); Counc. of Chs.; Negro Voters' Registrations (Mt. Vernon); Civic Unity League; vice-moderator, United Missionary Bapt. Assn.; Chmn. Martin Luther King Meml. Scholarship Fund (Mt. Vernon); Chmn. Human Rights Commn (Mt. Vernon); vice-pres. Westchester Crime Commn.; candidate "New Voice Party" for Mayor Mt. Vernon; Home: 152 The Explanade, Mt. Vernon, N. Y., 10553; Office: 52 So. 6th Ave., Mt. Vernon, N. Y. 10550.

BABER, George W., bishop, b. Cleveland, Ohio, Aug. 29, 1898; s. William and Emma Effie (Griffin) B.; A. B., Payne Theol. Sem.; B. D., Chicago Theol. Sem.; D. D. (hon.), Wilberforce Univ.; Morris Brown Coll.; Shorter Coll.; Payne and Campbell Coll.; m. Alma Marie Wims (deceased); Children--June (Mrs. Woodson), Flora A. (Mrs. J. S. Benn, III), George W., Benjamin S., Barbara (Mrs. Crawford); pastor, African Meth. Epis. Chs., Indiana, Mich., 1924-27; Elected bishop, 1944; current, presiding bishop of the First Episcopal District; founder, Camp Baber, Cassopolis, Mich.; organizer, The Pastors Seminar; Young People's Congress; Trustee of Bd. and chairman of Finance Bd., Payne Sem.; mem. Detroit Interracial Com.; Welfare Bd., Flint, Mich.; Home Federal Savings & Loan Assn.; NAACP; sec., General Bd., Bishops' Council, 1959-60; pres., Bishops' Council, 1960-

61; chmn., General Bd., Bishops' Council, 1961-62; delegate, World Meth. Conf., Oxford, England, 1951; delegate, World Meth. Conf., Oslo, Norway, 1961; World Council of Chs., New Delhi, India, 1961; mem., Advisory Bd., Amer. Bible Society, 1952--; Home: 800 4th St., S.W. Apt. S-120, Washington, D.C.

BAGWELL, Clarence W., b. Onancock, Va., Oct. 12, 1907; s. Clarence P. and Hazel Rose (Bushrod) B.; A.B. Clark Coll., B.D. Gammon Theol. Sem., D.D. Miller Univ.; m. Cora Collins; Children--Clarence H., Carroll Stephen; Ministry, Ferry Ave. U. Meth. Ch., 1961--present, Camden; mem., Mason; Chaplain, N.J. Civil Defense Corp.; Home: 768 Ferry Ave., Camden, N.J.; Office: 8th & Ferry Ave., Camden, N.J.

BAILEY, A. Leon, b. Washington, Ga., May 20, 1902; s. A.S. and Hattie Nora (B); A.B., Morris Brown Coll., Atlanta, Ga., 1924-28; B.D., Garrett Inst., Northwestern Univ., Evanston, Ill., 1928-31; M.A., Northwestern Univ., 1936-67; D.D. (hon.) Morris Brown, Atlanta, Ga.; m. Portia H. Thomas; Children--P. Andrea, Nora Cornelia; Asst. pastor, Woodlawn A.M.E. Ch., Chicago, Ill., 1933-41; pastor, Parks Meml. A.M.E. Ch., Chicago, 1941-42; Institutional A.M.E. Ch., Chicago, 1942-53; Carey, A.M.E. Ch., Chicago, 1953-67; Quinn Chapel A.M.E., Chicago, 1967-present; Case worker and Supervisor of Case workers, Cook Co. Bureau of Pub. Welfare, Chicago, Ill., 1933-43; Exec. dir. Illinois Commn. on Human Relations, 1943-52; dir., Christian Education, Chicago Annual Conf. of A.M.E., Chicago, 1945-67; Chmn., Minister's Welfare Com., Chicago, 1957-60; Citation, Commn. on Human Relations, State of Illinois, 1952; Minister of the year, Chicago Annual Conf., A.M.E. Ch., 1962; Citation, Minister of the Year, Wilberforce Univ., Payne Theol. Sem., 1964; vi-p., Ch. Fed. of Greater Chicago 2 yrs.; pres. Chicago A.M.E. Ministerial Alliance 2 yrs.; mem. Phi Beta Sigma; Home: 7359 S. Oglesby, Chicago, Ill., 60649; Office: 2401 S. Wabash Ave., Chicago, Ill. 60616

BAILEY, Charles Buford, b. Kansas City, Kans., Mar. 29, 1923; s. Benjamin and Esther; A.B., Kan. State Coll., 1952; B.Th. Western Bapt. Sem., 1955; m. Geneva Stephens; Children--Charles, Nozella, Wilson, Gelain; pastor, Salem Bapt. Ch., Kansas City, Kansas; exec. bd., Ec. Opportunity Found., K.C., Kans.; U.S. Army, 3 yrs.;

mem. Min. Alliance; Kans. State Bapt. Conv.; Nat. Bapt. Conv.; NAACP; Home: 1136 Routand Ave., K. C., Kans.; Office: 1824 N. 11th St., K. C., Kans.

BAILEY, Howard Andrew, b. Denton, Md., April 10, 1901; s. Doro D. and Sara (B); A. B. Howard Univ., Wash., D. C. 1928; Howard Univ., Sch. of Rel., B. D., 1933; courses, Temple Univ. Sch. of Theol., Phila., Pa.; m. Nora Jefferson; Children--Wayne H.; pastor, United Meth. Chs., Haddonfield, N. J., 1933-35; Atlantic City, N. J., 1935-38; Newport, Del., 1938-42; Salem, N. J., 1942-43; Exec. Sec. Bd. of Ed., Delaware Conf., United Meth. Ch. (Phila., Pa.), 1943-65; Assoc. Dir. Education of the Peninsula Conf. of the United Meth. Ch. (Dover, Del.), 1965-present; Trustee, Morgan State Coll. Christ Ctr., Baltimore, Md.; Trustee, Morristown Coll. (Tenn.); former dean of the Baltimore Area Leadership Sch. - Bennett Coll., Greensboro, N. C.; Chmn. Comm. on Continuing Ed. Annual Conf. Bd. of Ministry (United Meth. Ch.); mem. Gen. bd. of ed., com. of curriculum resources; Home: 622 No. West St., Dover, Del., 19901; Office: 217 N. Bradford St., Dover, Del. 19901.

BAILEY, Jack Simpson, b. Brunswick, Ga., June 2, 1937; s. Henry D. and Sylvia Williamson, B.; A. B., Johnson C. Smith Univ., 1960; B. D., 1963; Graduate work at Chicago Theol. Sem. 1963--; m. Mary Roberts; student pastor Cedar Grove and Bethpage Presby. Chs., Kannapolis and Concord, N. C.; 1962-63; student pastor Sec. Presby. Ch., Cheraw, S. C., 1962-63; asst. pastor, Lawndale Presby. Ch., Chicago, Ill. (post. grad. intern); mem. Chicago Urban League, Alpha Kappa Mu and Sigma Rho Sigma Nat. Honor Societies, Phi Beta Sigma Fraternity; Home: 5751 S. Woodlawn Ave., Chicago, Ill.; Office: 1908 S. Millard Ave., Chicago, Ill.

BAILEY, John Henry, b. Lancaster, S. C., May 22, 1910; s. Nathaniel and Carry (Spring) B.; A. B., B. D. Johnson C. Smith Univ., Charlotte, N. C., 1950-56; m. Mary Stinson; Children--John Henry, Nathaniel; Mary Lee B. Herron, Alice B. Smith, Mamie B. Crawford, Flossie B. Woodards, Carrie B. Wiley, Sallie Ann, Virginia, Betty Ann and Patricia Ann; Pastor, Nazareth Bapt. Ch. and The Cross Road Bapt. Ch., Rock Hill, S. C.; Dean Christian Ed., York County, S. C.; vice-pres., State Sunday School Convention, York County, S. C.; mem. Trustee Bd., Friendship Jr. Coll., Rock Hill, S. C.; Democrat; Home:

929 N. Davidson St., Charlotte, N.C. 28202; Church: RFD 1, 5 Rock Hill, S.C.

BAILEY, John Seth, bishop; b. Mobile, Ala., June 9, 1896; s. Edmond and Caroline (B); Trinity Hall Coll. and Sem., Springfield, Ill., 1959; m. Anne Lee Garrett; pastor, founder Bailey Temple Ch. of God in Christ, Inc., 1926, founder, Seth Temple Church of God in Christ, Inc., 1953, Detroit, Mich.; ordained Bishop of Mich. Diocese, 1951--present; currently, Chmn. Internat. Bishop's Bd., Dir. Bailey Gen. Hospital, Detroit; mem. NAACP; YMCA; Interdenominational Min. Alliance; Citation, Common Counc. of the City of Detroit 1966; Veteran World War I; Home: 3230 Cambridge Rd., Detroit, Mich. 48221; Office: 3230 Cambridge Rd., Detroit, Mich. 48221.

BALL, William Franklin, bishop, b. Mt. Pleasant, S.C., Aug. 3, 1906; s. Charles F. and Delia (Blake) B.; A.B., Bd., Edward Waters Coll., Walker Business Coll., Wilberforce Univ.; m. Agnes Marie Moton; Children--Frankie (Mrs. Harold), William F., Jr.; pastor, African Meth. Episcopal Chs., Mission Chs. in Fla., Ky., Tenn.; presiding elder, W. Jacksonville Dist.; Elected bishop, 1956; current, bishop 11th District; chairman, Bishops' Committee on Evangelism; Committee on Compilation of the Discipline; delegate, World Council of Methodism; Mem., Mason; Phi Beta Sigma; former evangelistic preacher and held many revivals; Home: 7530 NW 10th Ave., Miami, Fla.

*BANKS, Allen A., Jr., b. Bryan, Tex.; s. Allen A. and Idell (Turner) B.; A.B., Bishop Coll., 1937; B.D., M.A., Howard Univ., Sch. of Rel., 1939; 1943; D.D., Arkansas Bapt. Coll., 1955; m. Victoria Allen; Children --Allen Arthur, III, Teta Victoria; current pastor, Second Bapt. Ch., Detroit, Mich., 1947--; pres., Wolverine State Missionary Bapt. Conv., 1960-64; Corresponding sec., Metropolitan Missionary Bapt. Assn.; former mem. General Board, Nat. Counc. of Chs.; vice-pres., Mich. Counc. of Chs.; vice-pres., Detroit Counc. of Chs.; mem. Mich. State Civil Rights Comm.; Detroit Comm. on Children and Youth; Detroit Urban League; YMCA; Higher Education Opportunities; Kappa Alpha Psi; Pioneer Club; Home: 2340 Chicago Blvd., Detroit, Mich., 48206; Office: 441 Monroe Ave., Detroit, Mich. 48226.

BANKS, William Love, b. Philadelphia, Pa., Feb. 19, 1928;

B. A., Univ. of Pa., 1953; B. D., Lincoln Sem., Oxford, Pa., 1957; Th. M., Eastern Bapt. Sem., Phila., 1959; m. Thelma Congleton; pastor, Nazarene Bapt. Ch., Phila., Pa., 1956-present; faculty, Manna Bible Inst., Phila.; faculty (evening sch.) Phila. Coll. of Bible; Bible tchr., Hol-Reba Bible Conf., Cullen, Va.; Bible tchr., Pa. State Bapt. Congress of Christian Ed.; conducts radio Bible Class; Armed Forces, 1946-49; author: Jonah: The Reluctant Prophet, Moody Press, 1966; Home: 1327 E. Cliveden, Phila., Pa. 19119.

BARBER, Jesse Belmont, b. Charlotte, N. C., Nov. 2, 1893; s. Henry and Cecelia (Lyles) B.; A. B., Lincoln Univ., 1915; S. T. B., 1918; M. Th., Auburn Theol. Sem., 1936; D. D., Lincoln Univ., 1940; m. Mae Valeria Fortune; Children--Jesse Belmont, Jr.; pastor, Grace Presby. Ch., Seattle, 1918-22; supervisor, S. S. Missions, Presby. U. S. A., 1922-26; pastor, Leonard St. Presby. Ch., Chattanooga, Tenn., 1926-43; dean, Theol. Sem., Lincoln Univ., Pa., 1943-50; sec. Presby. Work in the South-Div. of Evangelism until retirement, 1960; minister of visitation, 1961--; co-chairman, Presby. Inst. on Racial and Cultural Relations, 1946-48; leader, preaching missions in Mexico, Cuba, Puerto Rico, and Dominican Republic, 1954-59; mem. Bd. of Dirs. of Red Cross, Advisor to Housing Authority, YMCA; mem. Mason; Alpha Phi Alpha; Alumni Assn. of Lincoln, Auburn and Union; Editor, The New Advance; author: Climbing Jacob's Ladder; Home: 24-50 Gilmore St., E. Elmhurst, N. Y.

BARBER, William Joseph, teacher, social worker, b. Free Union Community, Jamesville, N. C., Mar. 21, 1927; A. B., St. Augustine's Coll., Raleigh, N. C.; B. D. and M. S., Butler Univ., Indianapolis; Courses: Elementary ed., Radio-technology; also courses--College of the Bible; m. Eleanor Lucille Patterson; Children--William Joseph, II; pastor, Market St. Christn Ch., Carthays, Ind., supply pastor, Indiana Missouri and No. Carolina; current pastor-dir., Hillside Christian Center, Indianapolis, Ind.; tchr. Warrenton High School, Ga.; Social case worker, Martion Co., Dept. of Pub. Welfare; Counselor, Eastside Christian Center; Staff asst., Flanner House; Field worker, Wash., N. C., Norfolk, Va., Disciples of Christ; mem. Alpha Phi Alpha; United College Fund; Disciples of Christ, Historical Society; Indianapolis Social Workers Club; Indiana Registry of Social Workers; author: A History of the Origin and Development of a Rural Negro Church Group in Eastern N. C.,

The Disciple Assemblies of Eastern North Carolina, A Partial History of the Free Union Community; Home: Hillside Christian Ch. Center Parsonage, 1731 Ingram St., Indianapolis, Ind. 46218; Office: Hillside Christian Ch. Center, 1731-37 Ingram St., Indianapolis, Ind. 46218.

BARBOUR, Josephus Pius, b. Galveston, Tex., June 8, 1894; s. Alfred and Ellen; A.B., Morehouse Coll., Atlanta, Ga., 1917; B.D., Th.M., Crozier Theol. Sem.; m. Lee Littlejohn; Children-- Pius, Almanina; tchr. Tuskegee Inst.; pastor Calvary Bapt. Ch.; ed., Natl. Bapt. Voice; mem. Chester Water Authority; Soc. of Bible Lit., Alpha Phi Delpha; Hist. Soc.; Amer. Bapt. Conv.; Home: 1614 W. 2nd, Chester, Pa., 19012; Office: 1616 W. 2nd, Chester, Pa. 19012.

*BARNES, Frederick William, b. Washington, D.C., Jan. 2, 1920; s. William Richard and Annie (Quander) B.; A.B., Howard Univ., 1949; B.D., Sch. of Rel., 1958; m. Vivian Elizabeth Thomas; Children--Cynthia, Michael, Ivan, Candas; Asst. pastor, John Wesley African Meth. Episc. Zion Ch., 1952-56; pastor, Contee A.M.E.Z. Ch., 1956-present; Pres., Adams Elem. School PTA, 1960-62; Army Air Force, 1943-46. Kappa Alpha Psi; treas., Far Northeast Min. Alliance; vice-pres., Meth. Ministers Assn., Wash., D.C.; Home: 36 53rd Place, S.E., Wash., D.C.; Office: 903 Division Ave., N.E., Wash., D.C.

*BARNES, Kenneth Pearle, b. Wayside, P.O. Charles County, Md., Sept. 6, 1904; s. William Humphrey and Mary Jane (Thomas) B.; B.S. Howard U. 1926, D.D. Howard U. Sch. of Rel. 1934; m. Mildred Lois North; Children--Kenneth William, Barrington Benton, Barbara Lois V. Smith; tchr., Douglas High School, Staunton, Va. 1926-27; Ministry: Upper Marlboro, Md. 1935; Brookville, Md. 1947, Mt. Vernon, Washington, D.C., 1939, Upper Marlboro, Md., 1941, Jones Meth., Wash., D.C., 1943, Alexandria, Va. 1953; Present: Supt. of W. Baltimore Dist., Washington Annual Conf. of the Meth. Ch. (since 1959); Pres. of Brown Junior High PTA, Wash., D.C. 1951-52; mem. Elks, Odd Fellows, Masons, Eureka Lodge, Wash., D.C. and Omega Psi Phi Fraternity; Post-grad. work in psychiatry and education; Home: 3702 Dennlyn Rd., Baltimore, Md.; Office: 828 N. Carrollton Ave., Baltimre, Md.

*BARNES, William Heard, Sr., b. Grenada, Miss., June 15,

1918; s. Wm. Edward and Mary (Allen) B.; B. S., Campbell Coll.; B. D., Wilberforce Univ. Payne Theol. Sem., Wilberforce, O.; grad. study: Union Theol. Sem., N. Y.; D. D. (hon.), Campbell Coll., Jackson, Miss.; m. Louise Trigg; Children--Sylvia Louise, Wm. H., Jr., Valarie V. Frederick Van Douglas; pastor, African Meth. Episcopal Chs., Miss., Pa., S. C., 1937-63; current pastor, Bethel A. M. E. Ch., Kingston, S. C., 1963--; Trustee mem., Allen Univ., Columbia, S. C.; mem. The Interdenominational and Inter-Faith Minis. Alliance; vice-pres., The Connectional Dept. of A. M. E. Ch.; mem. Alpha Phi Alpha; Mason; Democrat; Editorial Bd. mem. The Christian Recorder of A. M. E. Ch.; Home: 300 W. Main St., Kingston, S. C.; Office: same.

BARNETTE, James William, b. Pineville, N. C., April 25, 1913; s. William W. and Tetsie (Thompson) B.; B. A., Johnson C. Smith Univ., Charlotte, N. C., 1937; B. D., 1940; m. Etta P. Lee; pastor, Miranda Presby. Ch., Charlotte, N. C.; pastor, Central Presby. Ch., Lynchburg, Va., 1940-43; Rocky Mount, N. C., Mt. Pisgah Presby. Ch. (1943-54); Bethesda Ch., Nottoway, Va. (1954-60); Goodwill Presby. Ch., 1960-62 and Presby. Ch. of our Saviour, Wilmington, Del. 1962--; present - Delaware-Inner City Project; Legal Redress Chairman of the local chap. in NAACP, Rocky Mount, N. C.; mem. Mason; the Order of Eastern Star; Home: 1013 E. 27th St., Wilmington, Del.; Church: 1017 E. 27th St., Wilmington, Del.

BARNETTE, Paul B., b. York, S. C., June 23, 1909; s. Cleve and Ida (Tolbut) B.; Friendship Coll., 1931; B. A., B. D., Benedict Coll., 1958, 1961; D. D. (hon.) Friendship Coll.; m. Addie Mae Garvin; Children--Marvin; Mamie E., Roosevelt, Mrs. Charlotte P. Walker, Robert C., Thomas N., Mrs. Ida Mae Graham, Mrs. Geneva Hall; pastor, Flat Rock Bapt. Ch., Clover, S. C., 1931-41; Weeping Mary, Bowling Green, S. C., 1932-44; Nazareth, Rock Hill, S. C., 1942-54; Tabernacle Bapt. Ch., Gastonia, N. C., 1941--present; tchr & principal, Cedar Grove Sch., York, S. C.; Crowford Sch., Ogdom, S. C., 1942-43; principal, Mt. Zion Sch., McConnels, S. C., 1944-57; chmn. Exec. Bd., Friendship Coll., 1950-60; mem. Clergymen's Christn. & Civic Action Assn., Charlotte, N. C.; NAACP; Citizens Voters League, Gastonia, N. C.; Home: 3219 Sutton Dr., Charlotte, N. C. 28208.

BARON, Herman Alexander, b. New York, N. Y., Jan. 22,

1920; s. Linus and Agnes; B.A., N.Y. Univ.; M.S.W., N.Y. Univ. Sch. of Social Work, 1944; B.D., Union Theol. Sem., New York City, 1949; m. Valerie Thompson; Children--Linda, Herman; asst. pastor, Williams Inst. C.M.E. Ch., N.Y.C.; pastor, Mt. Pisgah C.M.E. Ch., Baltimore, Md., 1953; Russel Tabernacle C.M.E. Ch., Philadelphia, Pa., 1955; Russel Inst. Ch., Bronx, N.Y., 1957; Nazarene Congl. Ch., Brooklyn, N.Y., 1960-pres.; chaplain, Brooklyn House of Detention, N.Y., 1962; pres., Greater Harlem Youth Coun., 1951; dir., Harlem Fund Center, St. Philips Epis. Ch., N.Y.C.; regional dir., Christn. Ed., E. Episc. Dist. C.M.E. Ch., 1954-59; co-founder, McDonough St. Community Center and Half-way House Pilot Project, Brooklyn, N.Y.; assoc. instr., asst. chaplain, Md. State Coll., Princess Ann, Md.; assoc. instr., Coppen State Coll., Baltimore, Md.; cons., O.E.O., N.Y.C.; social worker, Rockaway Project Head-Start Opportunity Center, McDonough St. Comm. Center Proj. Head-Start, Brooklyn, N.Y.; exec. dir., Registrar and Vote Campaign, Baltimore, Md.; chmn., Md. State Chapt. of Com. on Racial Equality; sec. Mayor's Com. of Rel. Leaders, N.Y.C., 1962; chmn., Christn. Soc. Action Com., United Ch. of Christ; pub. relations dir., Brooklyn Interdenominational Min. Alliance; mem. Amer. Sociological Soc.; NAIUC; (formerly) NBC staff composer, Manhattan Rhapsody, Echoes of Broadway, Harlem Moods, Safari, The Rainbow Symphony; Home: 144-20 Village Road, Jamaica, N.Y., 11435; Office: 506 McDonough St., Brooklyn, N.Y. 11233.

BARRETT, William Emanuel, Sr., b. Quinque, Va., Sept. 16, 1925; s. Stephen Emanuel and Ethel Clisten (Moten) W.; A.B., Virginia Union Univ., 1950; B.D., 1953; Lutheran Theol. Sem., Phila., 1960-61; m. Loretta Katherine Williams; Children--William E., Katherine Denise; pastor, Antioch Bapt. Ch., Culpeper, 1949-53; pastor, Mt. Zion Bapt. Ch., Staunton, Va., 1953-57; pastor, Mt. Calvary Bapt., New Kensington, Pa., 1957-60; pastor, Tabernacle Lutheran Ch., Phila., 1961--; consultant and lecturer, Phila. Psychiatric Inst., 1963--; pres., 18th Dist. Youth Referral Committee, Phila., 1962-63; chrmn., Education Committee, Cobbs Creek Civic Assoc., 1963; Bd. of Directors, 1964; mem. NAACP; mem. Philadelphia 400 Ministers; mem. Philadelphia Fellowship Commn; State Repr. of the Luth. Ch. to the Counc. of Chs.; Service in the U.S. Army, 1943-46; award: American Theater; Good Conduct; Home: 5933 Pine St., Philadelphia,

Pa., Church: 59th and Spruce Sts., Phila., Pa.

BARRON, Richard Edward, b. Newark, N. J., Nov. 29, 1931; s. Edward and Cora (Crowell) B.; B. A., Oakwood Coll., 1962; Andrews Univ., 1963; D. D. Coll. Div. Metaphysics, 1963; m. Vivian Virginia Steele; Children --Teresa Ann, Shelley Renee, Carol Marie; Present: New Hope Seventh-Day Adventist Ch., Pueblo, Colo., 1963--; U. S. Army, 1952-54; Good Conduct medal; NAACP award, Newark, N. J., Branch for religious activities, 1958; Home: 1448 Stone Ave., Pueblo, Colo., Office: 714 Arroya St., Pueblo, Colo.

BASKIN, Lee Roy, presiding elder, tchr., b. Bullock County, Ala., Sept. 29, 1897; s. Lee Roy and Ibbie (Curry) B.; B. S. Ed., Ala. State Coll., 1917; B. S., Tuskegee Inst., 1918; M. A. Ed., Univ. of Cincinnati, 1934-35; m. Johnnie Mae Pickett; Children--Lee M. Myrtle, Bennie E., Warren E.; pastor, A. M. E. Zion Ch., 1921-47; tchr., the School System, 23 yrs.; Presiding elder, 17 yrs.; U. S. Forces, 1918-20 (1st Lt.); mem., Democrat; Chmn. Adult Committee; Sec. Budget Commn, A. M. E. Zion Ch., Ala.; delegate, General Conf. A. M. E. Zion Ch. for 48 yrs.; Home: Rte 2, Box 125, Tuskegee, Ala.

BASS, Richard Oliver, b. Nashville, Tenn., June 24, 1923; s. D. W. and Ethel M. (McCorkle) B.; A. B., Lane Coll.; Wichita Univ.; B. D. Garrett Bible Inst., Evanston, Ill.; m. Edith V. Thomas; Children--Richard O., Jr., Claude Anderson; pastor, Christian Meth. Episc. Chs., Fla., Kansas, S. C., Ind.; current pastor, Lewis Metropolitan C. M. E. Ch., Los Angeles, Calif.; tchr., Leadership Training Schs., Ohio, N. C., S. C., Ga., Kansas, Miss., Calif.; has served as pres. of various ministerial assoc.; pres., Natl. Youth Conf. - C. M. E. Ch., 1944-48 (Greenville County); participated actively in interracial activities in all communities; operating commissioner, U. S. O.; mem. Bd. of Urban League, Gary, Ind.; YMCA, Wichita, Kansas & Evanston, Ill.; awards: Michigan-Indiana Conf. -C. M. E. Ch. for Fellowship & Cooperation among chs.; Los Angeles County Bd. of Supervision; mem. Alpha Phi Alpha; Mason; Democrat; Frontiers of Amer.; Home: 1632 49th St., Los Angeles, Calif. 90062; Office: Lewis Metropolitan C. M. E. Ch., 4900 So. Western Ave., Los Angeles, Calif. 90062.

BATEMAN, Melvin, b. Indianapolis, Ind., June 17, 1924; s. George Hall and Julia Mae; Th. B., The Bethel Sch. of Theol., Detroit, Mich., 1953; m. Beatrice Laverne Anderson; Children--Jack, Melanie, Gregory, Donielle, Marcia; pastor, Bethlehem Temple, Terre Haute, Ind., 3 yrs.; St. Paul A. M. E. Z. Ch., Covington, Ky., 1 yr.; Findlay St. Ch., 1960-64; Sec. the Ministerial Fellowship (Scioto County), Portsmouth, O.; handwriting expert-grapho-analyst (the science of reading the personality through the handwriting); work with Ministers and business organizations; professional ventriloquist - 2 dummies, Ike and Mike, Radio and TV programs, WCPO-TV, Cincinnati, WHTN-TV Huntington, W. Va., Channel 10, Columbus, O., WCIN - radio, Cincinnati. "Let Youth be Heard" originated and moderated program in Portsmouth; organized the Commnity Rec. Soc.; Have natl. award for outstanding work with the Red Cross and from the city for a Race Relation Program titled "An Approach to Understanding;" served in the Medical Corps 2 yr. and 4 mos. of the Air Force; Good Conduct medal; Home: 1009 13th St., Portsmouth, O.

BATTLES, Richard Arthur, Jr., b. Little Rock, Ark., Jan. 15, 1928; s. Richard A., Sr. and Amelia Z. (B); courses, Arkansas Bapt. Coll; Union Theol. Sem.; m. Betty Everett; Children-- Richard Ian, Robin Amelia; pastor, Mt. Olive Bapt., Hartford, Conn., 1960--present; Regional Dir., S. C. L. C., 1960--present; Human Relations Commn., Hartford, Conn., 1965-67; mem. Bd. Ed., Hartford, Conn.; mem. Rockefeller Foundation, 1967--present; U. S. Navy, 1946-48; Republican; Alpha Phi Alpha; Home: 241 Colebrook St., Hartford, Conn.; Office: 12 Suffield St., Hartford, Conn.

BEANE, John Solomon, asst. presiding bishop, Bible Way Church of our Lord Jesus Christ World-Wide, Inc.; b. Boons Mill, Va., May 23, 1888; s. Joe and Elzina (Napper) B.; A. B., Bluefield Coll., 1905; D. D. (hon.), Amer. Bible Coll., 1957; asst. presiding bishop, Bible Way Ch.; m. Miranda Jannie Carter, June 13, 1906; 1 daughter (deceased); mem. Odd Fellows, NAACP, Petersburg Virginia Civic and Political groups; Home: 614 Harding St., Petersburg, Va.; Office: 459 Harding St., Petersburg, Va.

BEARDEN, Harold Irvin, bishop, b. Atlanta, Ga., Mar. 8, 1910; A. B., Morris Brown Coll.; B. D. Turner Theol.

Sem., D. D. (hon.), Morris Brown Coll.; Campbell Coll.; Kittrell Coll.; LL. D. (hon.), Daniel Payne Coll.; Monrovia Coll.; Wilberforce Univ.; m. Lois M. Mathis; Children--Mrs. Jo Ann B. Vickers, Harold Irvin, Jr., Mrs. Gloria B. Pearson, Lloyd Colbert, Sharon Delores, Richard Louis; pastor, Foundation Chapel African Meth. Episc. Ch., Atlanta, Ga.; St. John A. M. E. Ch., Atlanta, Ga.; Austell Circuit, Austell, Ga.; Greater Bethel A. M. E. Ch., Blandtown, Ga.; Turner Chapel A. M. E. Ch., Marietta, Ga.; First A. M. E. Ch., Athens, Ga.; St. James A. M. E. Church, Columbus, Ga.; St. Paul A. M. E. Ch., Atlanta, Ga.; Big Bethel A. M. E. Ch., Atlanta, Ga.; trustee, Morris Brown Coll., 1933-64; pres., Atlanta Branch, NAACP, 1958-59; Civic Leagues: Marietta, Athens, Columbus, Atlanta, all in Georgia; elected bishop May 17, 1964, A. M. E. Ch., 17th Episc. Dist.; Home: 644 Skipper Drive, N. W., Atlanta, Ga., 30318.

BEASLEY, Louis James, b. Florence, Ala., April 18, 1907; s. Rufus and Mary (Sneed) B.; A. B., Clark Coll., Atlanta, Ga., 1935; B. D., Gammon Theol. Sem., Atlanta, Ga., 1936; m. Lauvenia C. Minor; Children--George F., Louis J., Jr., Sadye M., Winnie C., 1944; pastor, Rush Mem. Congregational Ch., Atlanta, Ga., 1934-39; First Congregational Ch., Marietta, Ga., 1936-39; current chaplain, U. S. Army: 24th U. S. Infantry Regiment; 9th U. S. Calvary; 92nd Inf. Div., Post chaplain, Camp Kilmer, N. J.; Staff chaplain 1st Corps; Post chaplain Hq. USAG, Ft. Devens, Mass.; Deputy chaplain USA COMZEUR (France); Bronze star, Purple Heart, Army commendation with one oak leaf cluster; Office: Chaplain Div., HQ. USACOMZEUR, APO 58, New York, N. Y.

*BEASLEY, Moses W., church official, b. Memphis, Tenn., April 16, 1906; s. Moses P. and Irene (Potts) B.; A. B.; Lane Coll., Jackson, Tenn., 1938; B. D., Howard Univ. Sch. of Rel., 1941; M. A., New York Univ., Sch. of Ed.; m. Hattie Mae Walton; Children--Moses, Muriel L. (Mrs. Julian Bertran), Louise (Mrs. Wm. Steward), Jacquelyn (Mrs. John Henry), William Nathaniel; asst. pastor, Mt. Carmel Bapt. Ch., 1939-46; current pastor, Shiloh Bapt. Ch., Alexandria, Va., 1948--; pres., Va. State Bapt. Educa. Congress; organizer Natl. State Bapt. Educa. Congress; vice pres., Natl. Bapt. B. T. U. and S. S. Congress, U. S. A., Inc.; Bd. mem., Mental Health Assn., 15 yrs.; Alexandria Branch, 10 yrs.; Third Vice Moderator, Northern Va. Bapt. Assn.; tchr, D.C. public schs, 1950--; Natl. Bapt. S.S. and B.T.U. Congress, U.S.A., Inc.; Exec. Bd., NAACP, Alexandria; pres., Lane Coll. Alumni, Wash., D.C.; mem. N.E.A.; D.C.E.A.; Mason; Republican; tour leader, Europe and Holy Land; five years with the National Negro Opera Company; Home: 647 Franklin St. N.E., Wash., D.C. 20017; Office: 1401 Duke St., Alexandria, Va.

BEATTY, Joseph Henry, b. Mar. 31, 1914, Bryan Co., Ga.; s. Noah and Emma (B); A.B., Va. Sem., Lynchburg, Va., 1939; S.T.B. Lincoln Univ., Lincoln Univ., Pa., 1943; m. Clara Elizabeth Meade; Children--Emma Henrietta, Charles H., Joseph H. II, Alicia Leona; pastor, First Bapt. Ch., Appomatox, Va., 1938-39; Friendship Bapt. Ch., Corning, N.Y., 1944; First Bapt. Ch., Glassboro, N.J., 1947-50; Holy Cross Bapt. Ch., Philadelphia, Pa. 1950-present; spec. asst. to exec. sec. Bapt. For. Mission Bur. of Prog. Natl. Bapt. Conv.; mem. Bd. Dirs. of the Phila. Housing Developt. Corp.; former Pres. Bapt. Minister's Conf. of Phila.; U.S. Army Signal Corps, 1943-45; awards, S.W. Pacific decoration; OIC award; mem. Omega Psi Phi; ed. Mission Outlook, official organ, Bapt. For. Mission Bureau, Prog. Bapt. Conv.; Home: 6146 Callowhill St., Phila., Pa. 19151; Office: 236-40 N. 60th St., Philadelphia, Pa., 19139.

BEDENBAUGH, David Roosevelt, b. Newberry, S.C., May 17, 1917; s. R.O. and Mary B.; A.B., B.D., D.D. (hon.) Allen Univ., Columbia, S.C., 1937, 1950, 1952; m. Fannie Parris; Children--Mary McLeod; David; pastor, African Meth. Episc. Ch., S.C., Clinton, Iowa; St. Luke A.M.E. Ch., E. Chicago, Ind., 1961-present; tchr. and principal S.C.; partner, Robinson Bedenbaugh Funeral Estab., Clinton and Prosperity, S.C.; del. Gen. Conf. A.M.E. Ch.; chmn., Com. of Evangelism (7th Episc. Dist.); ch. chmn., NAACP (S.C.); treas., Ind. Annual Conf., A.M.E. Ch.; sec.-treas., E. Chicago Ministerial Assn.; mem., Econ. Opportunity Coun. of E. Chicago; chmn., Div. of Planning Ser., United Community Services; trustee, Allen Univ. (16 yrs.); former sec., Piedmont & Columbia Annual Conf., A.M.E. Ch. (7th Episc. Dist.); del. Palmetto Tchrs. Assn. (4 yrs.); v. pres., Palmetto State Parent-Tchrs. Assn. (4 yrs.); charter mem. and stockholder Palmetto Leader, weekly newspaper;

mem., Bd. of dir., Bethlehem Center, Spartanburg, S.C.; Office: 3889 Penn. Ave., E. Chicago, Ind.

BELL, Asa Lee, b. Martin County, N.C., Sept. 13, 1930; s. Frank and Lula (Moore) B.; A.B., B.D., Shaw Univ., Raleigh, N.C.; courses, A. & T. Coll., Greensboro, N.C., Va. Union Univ., Richmond, Va.; m. Melvine Richards; Children--Florita Lenise, Asa Lee, Jr.; pastor, Salem Miss. Bapt. Ch., Columbia, N.C.; currently First Bapt. Ch., Ballard St., Wadesboro, N.C.; mem. Bi-Racial Com., Wadesboro; pres., Anson Recreation Corp.; auditor, Zion Miss. Bapt. Assn.; mem. Exec. bd. of the Anson County Sunday Sch. Conv.; vice-pres., Anson County Inter-racial Min. Alliance; mem., Ad. Com. of Anson County Credit Union; vice pres., Anson Shaw Club; dir., Anson Development Counc.; Home: 622 Ballard St., Wadesboro, N.C. 28170

*BELL, Harold Lloyd; b. Evanston, Ill.; s. Roy C. & Carrie Louise (B); A.B., Howard Univ., 1956; B.D., Howard Univ. Sch. of Rel., 1966; pastor, Baltimore Conf. United Meth. Ch., 1965-present; Dir. Wesley Found., Howard Univ., Wash., D.C.-present; Consult., Vista 1965; Soc. service head, Head Start Program, Howard Co., Md., 1966-67; Home and Office: 100 Bryant St., N.W., Washington, D.C. 20001.

BELL, Howard William, b. Troy, Ala., July 31, 1905; s. William and Emma (Early) B.; B.Th., Payne Sem., Wilberforce Univ., 1945; A.B., Allen Univ., 1953; D.D. (hon.) Kittrell Coll., 1963; m. Mary Copeland; pastor, John G. Mitchell A.M.E. Ch., Galapolice, Ohio, 1940; A.M.E. Ch., Jamestown, Ohio; Bethel A.M.E. Ch., Lebanon, Ohio, 1943-45; Mitchell Chapel A.M.E., Mansfield, Ohio, 1945-47; A.M.E. Ch., Glendell, Ohio, 1948-49; A.M.E. Ch., Martins Ferry, Ohio, 1949; Jenkinsville, Whitehall A.M.E. Ch., 1950-52; Prosperity Circuit, 1952-56; Bethel A.M.E. Ch., Glassboro, N.J., 1956; New Mt. Olive A.M.E. Ch., S. Norfolk, Va., 1957-59; Macedonia A.M.E. Ch., 1959-present; instruc., Ga. Tyler Elementary & High Schs., Windsor, Va.; Oaklawn Elem. Sch., Suffolk, Va.; pres. of Suffolk-Nansemond Branch, NAACP, 1961, 1963-65; active in civil rights activities in Suffolk, Va.; honored as "write-in" candidate for membership in the House of Delegates, Commonwealth of Va.; mem. State Independent Voters League; pres., Suffolk-Nansemond and Vicinity Min. Alliance; pres., A. M. E. Ministerial All. of Tidewater, Va.; chrmn., co-ordinating comm. NAACP Suffolk; Home: 132 Pine St., Suffolk, Va. 23434; Office: 135 Pine St., Suffolk, Va. 23434.

BELL, Virgil L., Sr., b. Dallas, Tex., Feb. 25, 1930; s. George W. and Virginia B.; B. A., Bishop Coll., 1953; B. Th., Hall St. Sem., Dallas, Tex.; m. Queenah Ruth; Children--Sonja Michel, Virgil Jr., Jonathan Lemuel, Gregory Allen; pastor, Tyree Chapel A. M. E. Ch., Ballinger, Tex., 1954-55; Smith Chapel A. M. E. Ch., Eastland, Tex., 1955-56; Mt. Olive A. M. E. Ch., Wallis, Tex., 1959-60; Emmanuel A. M. E. Ch., San Antonio, Tex., 1960-63; Tyree Chapel A. M. E. Ch., Bay City, Tex., 1963-65; Grant Chapel A. M. E. Ch., Palestine, Tex., 1965-present; dean, Inst. Work of Greater NE Tex. Conf.; Bible instr. Palestine Ministers Assn.; tchr. Pub. sch. system, Tex.; chmn. Ministerial Efficiency Commn., Greater NE Conf.; sec., Anderson Ct. Civic League of Palestine; chaplain, Bus. & Prof. Womens Club, Palestine; U. S. Army, 1946-49; award: Airborne Jump Wings; Glider Flight Wings; Home: 708 South St., Palestine, Tex. 75801.

BENNETT, Robert Avon, Jr., b. Baltimore, Md., Jan. 11, 1933; s. Robert Avon (deceased) and Irene (Harris) B.; 1954; B. A. (Phi Beta Kappa), Kenyon Coll.; 1954-55, Fulbright Fellowship, Univ. Copenhagen, Denmark; 1958, S. T. B., Gen. Theol. Sem. (NYC); m. Patricia Ann Grieg B.; Children--Mark Robert, Ann Elizabeth; graduated, Gen. Sem., 1958; ordained deacon, Epsic. Ch., 1958; priest, 1959; asst. priest, St. James' Episc. Ch. Baltimore, Md., 1958-63; Episc. chaplain, Morgan State Coll. 1959-63; at present tutor (faculty asst.) Gen. Theol. Sem., 1963 Episc. chaplain, Provident Hospital; Baltimore, Md., 1959-63; mem. Christian Social Relations Commn., Episc. Diocese of Md., 1959-63; Phi Beta Kappa, Kenyon Coll.; NAACP; Episc. Soc. for Cultural & Racial Unity; Home: 175 Ninth Ave., New York, N. Y. 10011.

BENTON, Elijah, b. Mayersville, Miss., Nov. 4, 1896; s. Lewis and Lubertha (Pitts) B.; B. T. H., Amer. Bapt. Theol. Sem. & Sch. of Rel., Detroit, Mich., 1947; D. D. (hon.) Greenville Ind. Coll., Greenville, Miss., 1959; m. Fannie Howard; ordained Bapt. min., 1924; pastor, Mt. Zion Bapt. Ch., Toledo, O., 1928--; mem. Bd. Dirs.,

Nat. Bapt. Conv., USA, Inc.; mem. Coop. Bd., Nat. Sunday Schs. and BTU Pub. House, Nashville, Tenn.; pres., Ohio State Bapt. Conv., Inc.; Marr. Counselor; Instr., Ohio Bapt. State Inst.; mem. Bd. of Community Relations; Sel. Serv. Bd. No. 8, Toledo, O.; Vet. WW I (10 mos., France); Mason; Home: 706 O'Brien, Toledo, Ohio, 43602; Church: 701 Vance, Toledo, O.

BERRY, Benjamin Donaldson; b. Wash., D.C., Dec. 22, 1939; s. Benjamin and Otis; B.A., Morehouse Coll., Atlanta, Ga., 1962; S.T.B., Harvard Div. Sch., Cambridge, Mass., 1966; m. Linda Baker; Children--Richard, Kathleen, Thena; assoc. dean, Chapel, Fisk Univ., 1964-65; pastor, Plymouth UCC, Louisville, Ky., 1966-pres.; soc. worker, Cambridge, Mass., 1963-66; mem. adv. comm. on Sex and Family Living, Pub. Sch.; chmn., W. Louisville Coop. Ministry, 1968; mem. IMAGE, Inc., Louisville Jaycees; Alpha Phi Alpha; Rockefeller Fellow, 1962-66; Merrill Scholar, 1960; Home: 3033 Grand Ave., Louisville, Ky. 40211; Office: 1630 W. Chestnut St., Louisville, Ky., 40203.

BETTIS, Joshua, b. Jackson, Ala., Nov. 27, 1912; s. Johnnie and Emma; courses, Ala. State Coll., Montgomery, Ala., m. Maggie Law; pastor, Oakgrove, Mt. Nebo A.M.E.Z. Chs., Greenvile, Ala., 1949-52; Simpson Chapel, 1953-55; Mt. Zion Jerusalem, Rainbow A.M.E.Z. Chs., 1956-66; Pettys Mem. Ch., Demopolis, Ala., 1967-68; Clinton Chapel, Montgomery, Ala.; trustee, Lomax-Hannon Jr. Coll., Greenville, Ala.; treas. Cahaba Annual Conf., A.M.E.Z. Ch., military duty, 1943-46; award, European African Middle-Eastern Campaign ribbon, 3 bronze starts, Victory ribbon, Good conduct medal; mem. Mason; A.M.E.Z. Min. Alliance, Montgomery, Ala.; Home: 1517 Weaver, Selma, Ala. 36701

BIBBONS, Jeffery Clarence, b. New Orleans, La., Dec. 12, 1907; s. Simon and Albertine Pardo; B; Straight U., 1926-28, Tuskegee, 1929-30, A.B. Dillard U., 1945-49, Certificate in Rel. Educa., Garrett Theol. Sem.; m. Evelyn Skillings; Children--Jeffreda Antoinette; Social worker, 1949-58, pastor, 1941-present; Pres. of Dunbar Community Civic League, 1959--present; 33d degree Mason; mem. Democratic Party, Sec. of Meth. Min. Alliance; Home: 9014 Palm Street, New Orleans, La.; Office: 2001 Simon Bolivar Ave., New Orleans, La. 70113

BILLOUPS, Edward Doyle, church official, b. West Baton Rouge, Dec. 16, 1896; s. Luke and Julia (Prince) B.; B. Th., Baton Rouge Coll., 1912; Leland Coll., 1931-34; D. D. (hon.), Leland Coll., 1947; LL. D. (hon.), Natchez Coll., 1952; m. Helen Rucker; Children-- L. E., Mildred, Ceola, Norma; pastor, Second Bapt. Ch.; New St. John Bapt. Ch., Baton Rouge, La., 1922--; pres., 4th Dist. Bapt. Assn., 1946-64; pres., La. Bapt. State Conv., 1949--; pres., Interdenominational Alliance, Baton Rouge, La., 1948--; pres., Leland Coll. Trustee Bd., 1951--; mem., Bi-racial Com. Baton Rouge, La.; vice pres. at-large, Natl. Bapt. Conv. USA Inc.; Adv. Bd., Union Theol. Sem., New Orleans, La., 1953; Adv. Bd., United Theol. Sem., Monroe, La., 1955; Certificate of Appreciation from Pres. F. D. Roosevelt, 1942; mem. NAACP; Mason; Democrat; Home: 1678 79th Ave., Baton Rouge, La.; Office: 908 No. 33rd St., Baton Rouge, La.

*BIRCH, Adolphus Augustus, b. British Honduras, Feb. 28, 1898; s. Joshua and Ella (Franklin) B.; Hampton Coll., 1919 Bishop Payne Div. Sch. B. Th., Howard Univ.; Va. Theol. Sem.; m. Mary Jefferson; Children--Adolpho, Kennard. Entered ministry in 1926; pastored Prot. Episc. Chs. in Va., Tex., and Wash., D. C.; retired: rector, St. George's Prot. Episc. Ch., Wash., D. C.; pres., Clericus, 1948; chaplain, Freedmen's Hosp., Wash., D. C.; former chaplain, Episc. students, Howard Univ. Alumni award, Sch. of Rel., Howard Univ.; Republican; Home: 701 Joseph Ave., Nashville, Tenn.

BIRCHETTE, John Fletcher, Jr., b. Asheville, N. C., June 4, 1915; s. John Fletcher and Carolyn (Goodrum) B.; A. B., Morehouse Coll., 1937; Atlanta U., 1938-39; Eckels Coll. of Mortuary Sci., 1946-47; m. Bessie Allen Hurt; 1 son, John Fletcher, III; pastored, St. John A. Bapt. Church, Asheville, N. C., 1949-51; Thankful Bapt. Ch., Johnson City, Tenn., 1951--; tchr., Franklin City, Fla. Pub. Sch., 1939-42; Allen-Birchette Funeral Home, Asheville, N. C., 1949-63; Birchette Mortuary, Johnson City, Tenn., 1959--; mem. Mayor's Adv. Comm., Mayor's Comm. on Human Relations; trustee, Owen Coll.; S/Sgt., U. S. Army, 1942-44; mem. Omega Psi Phi; Home: 807 No. Boone St., Johnson City, Tenn.; Church: 219 E. Millard St., Johnson City, Tenn.

BIRD, Van Samuel, b. Waycross, Ga., Sept. 6, 1924; A. B.,

Fort Valley St. Coll., 1948; B.D., Seabury-Western Sem., 1951; Diploma, St. Augustine's Coll., Canterbury, England, 1958; courses: Johns Hopkins Univ., summer 1963; m. Eva Ruth Brown; Children--Amanda D., Van S., Lesley S.; curate, St. Thomas Episc. Ch., Phila., Pa., 1951-53; founder and vicar, Holy Trin. Episc. Ch., Baltimore, Md., 1953--present; Omega Psi Phi; Home: 909 N. Bentalou St., Baltimore, Md.; Office: Lafayette & Wheeler Ave., Baltimore, Md.

*BISHOP, Cecil, b. Pittsburgh, Pa., May 12, 1930; s. Ross Mance and Diana Briggs (Wilson) B.; A.B., Knoxville Coll., Knoxville, Tenn., 1954; Hood Theol. Sem., 1954-56; B.D., Sch. of Rel., Howard Univ., 1958; S.T.M., Wesley Theol. Sem., 1960; m. Wilhelma Jones; pastor, Center Grove African Method. Episc. Zion Ch., Tobaccoville, N.C., 1954-56; asst. pastor, John Wesley A.M.E.Z. Ch., Wash., D.C., 1956-58; pastor, Clinton A.M.E.Z. Ch., Rockville, Md., 1958-60; present: pastor, Trinity A.M.E.Z. Ch., Greensboro, N.C., 1960--; lecturer, Bd. of Dirs. United Southern Chrtn. Fellowship Found., A & T Coll.; mem. Bd. of Management, Hayes-Taylor YMCA, Greensboro, N.C., mem., former pres., Greensboro Ministers' Fellowship; Home: 2011 Asheboro St., Greensboro, N.C.; Office: 445 E. Washington St., Greensboro, N.C.

BLACK, Garland, b. Endora, Ark., Jan. 17, 1903; b. Richard and Cora (Jones) B.; m. Maria James; Children --Calvin, Mrs. Ivory L. Burts, Carneal, Jessie Bea, Arthur, James Edward, Nathan, Marjorie, George Earl; pastor, James Chapel A.M.E.Z. Ch., Eudora, Ark, 1920-present; Home: Rt. 1, Box 307, Eudora, Ark., 71640.

BLACK, Jakie Bernard, Jr., b. Clarksville, Tex., Jan. 6, 1925; s. Jakie B. and Velma (Simington) B.; Tex. Coll., 1949; Wiley Coll. intermittently, 1958-62; compl. Conf. course of study required by the Meth. Ch., 1962; ordained elder in 1964; m. Eloise Mathis; Children--Jacquelyn Sue Jones (married); Cheryl Annette, Margaret Ann; pastor, Bagwell Circuit, 1953-57, Clarksville, Tex., Daingerfield Circuit, 1957-61, Daingerfield, Tex.; Liberty Sta., 1961-62, Hughes Springs, Tex.; St. Paul, 1962-65, Clarksville, Tex.; St. Paul, 1965-present; Texarkana, Tex.; Exec. bd. mem. of Bowie Co. Econ. Advancement Corp., 1966, treas. Texarkana Min. Alliance, 1966; dir.,

Christn. Soc. Concerns of the Marshall Dist., 1964-66; mem. Texas Conf., Meth. Ch.; mem. NAACP; Home: 2417 West 9th St., Texarkana, Tex. 75501.

BLACKMAN, Herman Elliott-Constantine, b. Bridgetown, Barbados, T.W.I., Dec. 25, 1912; s. Joseph Constantine and Amanda (Barrow) B.; Barbados & St. Vincent (W.I.) London and Oxford Univ., Bishop Payne Div. Sch., Union Theol. Sem., B.A., M.A.; Post grad. lectures from the Union Theol. Sem. & Va. Theol. Sem.; m. Henrietta Vinton Henry; since ordination worked only in the Diocese of Long Island; tchr., Lay reader, Deacon, 1949; Priest, 1949; curate, St. Augustine's, Brooklyn, N.Y.; vicar, St. Martin's, Diocesan Missioner; rector, St. Stephen's & St. Martin's; Past sec. and vice pres., Long Island Clericus; tchr., Dept. of Rel. & Psychological Therapy; The Anglican Soc.; Dept. of Chrstn. Soc. Relations in the city of New York; mem., scholarship examining bd. of Gil Hodges Found., Inc.; Academy of Rel. and Mental Health; The Fellowship of the Inst. for Rel. and Soc. Studies; served for the British forces, 1940-46; mem. Brooklyn Democratic Club, Masonic Lodge & Mechanics Lodge, Bermuda Benevolent Society, West Indian League, Dept. for the Racial and Cultural improvement of Minority Races, Church Hist. Soc.; Natl. Geographical Soc.; author, The Being of God, 1954 research work on Existentialism by Jean P. Sartre; Editor of the Church Steeple magazine; Home: 541 Franklin Ave., Brooklyn, N.Y.; Office: 809 Jefferson Ave., Brooklyn, N.Y.

*BLACKMON, Thomas O'Dell Vinci, b. Americus, Ga., Oct. 1, 1932; s. Sam Pratt Benjamin and Mattie Wilson; B.S. Fort Valley St. Coll., 1955; Howard Univ., Sch. of Rel., 1964; ordained, The Primitive Bapt. Ch., 1956; Inst. Counselor Children's Center, Maple Glen Sch., Laurel, Md., 1966-present; tchr. Macon Co. Training Sch., Montezuma, Ga., 1955-57; Discussion leader Amer. Foreign Policy Great Decisions Program, UN Assn. Capital Area; Dir., The Inst. of Chrstn. Ed. (Wash. area Coun. of Chs.) 1966; mem. Democrat; "For Love of Children" (Wash., D.C.); UN Assn. Capital Area; founder and pres. The Soc. for Ecumenical Dialogue (Howard Univ.); mem. United World Federalist; The Fellowship of Religious Humanists; contrib. Luth. Theol. Sem., Phila., Pa. Pamphlet, "The Nature & Place of Theol. in the Ch., a Bapt. Understanding," 1963; Home: 4228 Benning Rd.,

N. E. No. 305, Washington, D. C., 20019.

BLAIR, James Lowell, b. Cleveland, O., Sept. 4, 1931; s. Joseph and Clara; B. A. Univ. of Kan., 1954; B. D., Christn. Theol. Sem., 1958; m. Vida Shirley; Children --James II, Darren, Monica; student pastor, Dunham Christn. Ch., Cleveland, O., 1954-63; Central Christn. Ch.; present; mgr. Lawson Milk Co., 1963-; pres. Inter-denom. Min. Alliance; vi-pres. Coun. of Rel. and Race; pres. Christn. Min. Assn.; Bd. Human Resources Corp.; Bd., Exec. Com. Christn. Ch. in Mo.; v.-pres. Clergy for Coun. for United Action; mem. Exec. Com., Metro Christn. Ch. Commn.; Pres. Midtown Min. Assn., 1966-67; sec. Inner-city Dept. Coun. of Chs.; v.-pres., Coun. of Chs.; NAACP; mem. Alpha Phi Alpha; Home: 3200 Mersington, Kansas City, Mo.; Office: 3801 Linwood Blvd., Kansas City, Mo. 64128

BLAKE, Charles Carlos, b. Pierce Co., Ga., June 9, 1918; s. Samuel and Emma Bell; B.; A. B., Morris Brown Coll., Atlanta, Ga., 1941; B. D.; Turner Theol. Sem., Atlanta, Ga., 1943; M. A. Boston Univ., Sch. of Theol., Boston, Mass., 1948; D. D. (hon.) Jackson Theol. Sem., No. Little Rock, Ark.; ordained elder, Rome, Ga., 1942; m. Christine R.; Children--six; pastored in Ga., Ark., Mass., Conn., N. Y.; present pastor, Macedonia A. M. E. Ch., Camden, N. J.; founder and present dir., Southern N. J., Opportunities Industrialization Center; served two yrs., Prot. chaplain for adolescent drug addicts, Riverside Hosp., North Brother Is., N. Y.; Civil Rights Commissioner for 8 yrs.; presently, Commissioner, Mental Hosp., Camden Co., N. J.; Dir., Christn. Ed., First Episc. Dist. of A. M. E. Ch., Del., Pa., N. J., N. Y., New England states, Bermuda; chmn., Bd. of Dir., Southern N. J. O. I. C.; Dir., Macedonia Community Action Program, Manpower Title II on Job Training, Camden, N. J.; chaplain, WW II and Korean Police Action, retired 1964; Mason; NAACP; Kappa Alpha Psi; The Kiwanis; author, Handbook for Members of the A. M. E. Church (3rd ed.); Home: 1450 Wildwood Ave., Camden, N. J. 08103; Office: 301 Market St., Camden, N. J.

BLAKE, David A., Sr., b. Wake County, N. C., Aug. 7, 1887; s. John Addison and Mintia (Hooker) B.; Howard Univ., Sch. of Rel., B. D. 1915; D. D. (hon.) Wilberforce Univ., m. Grace Rogers (deceased) Ruby Ray; Children--David Jr., George, Richard, Mrs. Grace Johnson;

pastored, Campbell Chapel African Meth. Episc. Ch., Carrollton, Va.; presiding elder, So. Detroit Michigan Dist., A. M. E. Ch.; pastor, St. Stephens A. M. E. Ch., Chicago; St. Paul A. M. E. Ch., Des Moines; St. Paul A. M. E. Ch., Springfield, Ill, 1961--to date; tchr. 4 years; former mem., County Bd. of Supervisors, Wash. Co., Mich.; Home: 1116 S. 16th St. Springfield, Ill. 62703

BLAKELY, George Wayman, bishop, b. Ashley County, Ark., Aug. 30, 1905; s. Richard and Alice B.; A. B., Western Univ., Quindaro, Kansas, 1924; B. D., Iliff Sch. of Theol., Denver, Colo., 1928; D. D. (hon.), Payne Theol. Sem., Wilberforce, Ohio, 1948; Daniel Payne Coll., Birmingham, Ala., 1948; Monrovia Coll., Monrovia, Liberia, 1953; Kittrell Coll., Kittrell, N. C., 1963; m. Annie Marion King (deceased), Vera Corrine Doyle; Children-- George Wayman, Jr., Alyce Vera; pastor, Turner Mission African Methodist Episc. Ch., Kansas City, Mo., 1923-24; Mt. Olive A. M. E. Ch., Sheridan, Wyo., 1924-25; Ward Mission A. M. E. Ch., Denver, Colo., 1925-28; Ward Chapel A. M. E. Ch., Junction City, Kans., 1928-29; Bethel A. M. E. Ch., Leavenworth, Kans., 1929-30; St. John A. M. E. Ch., Pine Bluff, Ark., 1930-31; Visitors Chapel A. M. E. Ch., Hot Springs, Ark., 1931-35; Carter Chapel, Helena, Ark., 1936-37; Big Bethel A. M. E. Ch., Little Rock, Ark., 1939-53; St. Paul A. M. E. Ch., St. Louis, Mo., 1953-64; presiding elder, Monticello Dist., 1935-36; Pine Bluff Dist., 1937-38; Little Rock Dist., 1938-39; elected and consecrated bishop, A. M. E. Ch., Cincinnati, O., May 17, 1964; 16th Episc. Dist. (Carribean-So. American Area; delegate, World Counc. of Chs., Amsterdam, Holland, 1948; Evanston, Ill., 1954; fraternal delegate, Gen. Conf. of Meth. Ch., Boston, Mass., 1948; delegate and mem. World Meth. Counc., Oslo, Norway, 1962; mem. Bd. of Trustees, Wilberforce Univ., Wilberforce, Ohio; Bd. of Dirs., Douglas Hospital, Kansas City, Kans.; Exec. com., Senior Citizens Home, Kansas City, Kans.; pres., Interdenominational Min. Alliance, two terms, Little Rock, Ark.; Exec. Comm., Fraternal Counc. of Chs.; Exec. Com., Urban League; YMCA; NAACP; Exec. Com., Metropolitan Ch. Fed., St. Louis, Mo.; Grand Jury, Pulaski Co., Ark.; Being one of the first Negro members since reconstruction days; chrmn. Citizens Com. for Equalization of Salaries of Negro tchrs., Pulaski Co., Ark.; chrmn., Comm. that organized USO, YMCA, Little Rock,

Ark.; One of the first Negro mem. of State Central Com. Republican Party, Ark.; pres., Interde. Alliance; vice pres., Metropolitan Ch. Fed. Minis. Alliance, St. Louis, Mo.; representative, Interde. Alliance, March, Washington; mem., Mason; Kappa Alpha Psi; Home: 4940 Northland Place, St. Louis, Mo.

BLAKEY, Durocher Lon, publisher, b. Macon City, Ala., June 14, 1909; s. Frank Robert Blakey and Watty Ann (Walker) B.; A.B., Livingstone College, Salisbury, N.C., 1947; Johnson C. Smith Univ. (Summers) 1945, 1946; further study at Miles Coll., Birmingham, Ala., 1955; Hood Theol. Sem., 1947-50; 1952-53; B.D., Southeastern Bapt. Theol. Sem., Forest, N.C., 1961-63; m. Etta Florine Carter; pastor, North Ala., Western No. Carolina, Georga, Arkansas, and North Carolina Conf. of A.M.E. Zion Ch.; current, Gen. mgr. African Meth. Episc. Zion Ch., Publishing House, Charlotte, N.C., 1963--; Pastoral counseling, St. John A.M.E. Zion Ch.; tchr., Walter Southland Inst., Lexa, Ark., 1950-51; and pub. sch. systems in Fayette, Ala., 1958-60; Nash and Edgecombe counties, N.C., 1963-64; mem.: Elks, Masons, Knights of Pythians; Rocky Mt. Voter and Improvement League, Rocky Mt. Ministers' Fellowship, N.C. Counc. on Human Relations, N.C. Jt. Counc. on Health and Citizenship, Souther Chrstn. Leadership Conf., NAACP, YMCA, YWCA, pres. Livingstone College Alumni Assn. of Rocky Mt., N.C.; Citizenship award by the Alpha Omicron Chapter, Fraternity, 1963; Home: 908 Leggett Rd., Rocky Mt., N.C.; Office: St. John A.M.E. Zion Ch., Rocky Mt., N.C.

BLAND, Frank Leon, B. Newellton, La., Jan. 9, 1908; s. Louis and Catherine (Monroe) B.; Oakwood Academy and Oakwood Coll., 1926-31; Dillard Univ., La., 1932-33; m. Alga Lois Bailey; bible worker, Ark.-La. Conf. of Seventh-Day Adventists, New Orleans, 1932-34; singing evangelist, South. Union Conf., Decatur, Ga., 1943-45; pastor, Carolina Conf., Charlotte, N.C., 1935-38; Ala.-Miss. Conf., Meridian, Miss., 1938-42; Sec-Treas. Allegheny Conf., Pine Forge, Pa., 1945-48; pres., Central States Conf., Kansas City, Mo., 1948-59; So. Central Conf., Nashville, Tenn., 1959-62; Assn. sec., Regional Dept. Gen. Conf., 1962-66; gen. v.p., Gen. Conf. of Seventh-Day Adventists, June, 1966; chrmn., Oakwood Coll. Bd., Huntsville, Ala.; chrmn., Riverside Hospital Bd., Nashville, Tenn.; mem. Oakwood Coll. Alumni Assn.; mem., editorial bd., The Message magazine and Review & Herald, the paper of Seventh-Day Adventists pub. at Review & Herald Pub. Assn., Takoma Park, Wash., D. C.; Home: 5209 New Hampshire Ave., N. W., Washington, D. C.

BLASSINGAME, James Matthew, b. Anderson County, S. C., Jan. 13, 1913; s. Moses and Maggie B.; Paine Coll., 1935-36; Benedict Theol. Sem., Columbia, S. C., 1941-43; B. D., Virginia Theol. Sem., 1945; m. Hester Lee Thompson; pastor, Chrstn. Meth. Episc. Chs., South Carolina, Virginia, N. Carolina; present: pastor, Beebe Chrstn. Meml. Episc. Ch., Wash., N. C.; former instr. Christian Inst., Winston-Salem, N. C.; chrmn, Comm. on Admissions, C. M. E. Ch., pres., NAACP (Polk Co., N. C.) 3 yrs.; Interdenominational Min. Alliance; councilman, scoutmaster; ex. bd., Wash. United Fund, N. C.; Office: P. O. Box 300, Washington, N. C.

BOBBITT, Matthew Douglas, b. N. C., Sept. 6, 1911; s. Henry and Mamie; Shaw Univ., 1937-38; Pa. Sch. of Bible; New Aery Theol. Sem.; m. Annie (Smith); missionary, Bapt. Chrstn. Union, 1940-45; pastor, Second Bapt. Ch., Mt. Holly, N. J., 1943-present; pres., New Light Missionary Bapt. Union, So. Jersey, 1955-60; mem., Ch. and Community Group Scholarship Fund, Mt. Holly, N. J.; Mason; Bethany Bapt. Assn.; Gen. Bapt. Conv.; Bapt. Min. Conf., Phila. and vicinity; Home: Kings Hwy., Moorestown, N. J., 08057.

BODLEY, Simon, Jr., b. Camden, Ala., June 5, 1932; s. Simon and Bella (Ethridge); Concordia Lutheran College, Ft. Wayne; Immanuel Lutheran Sem.; m. Jemima Sessons; Children--Chenita Maria, Simon Lemoyre, Kelvin Derell; missionary at large, 1957-60; pastor, Ala. Victory Lutheran Ch., Youngstown, O., 1960--; Home: 350 Falls Ave., Youngstown, O.; Church: Victory Lutheran Ch., 336 Blender, Youngstown, O.

BOLDEN, Vernie L., b. Seebert, W. Va., Aug. 30, 1938; s. Robert and Dabota; A. B., Marshall Univ., Huntington, W. Va., 1960; B. D., Crozer Theol. Sem., Chester, Pa., 1963; spec. studies, Colgate-Rochester Div. Sch., 1965; m. Margie Cobbs; Children--Beth, Tara, Vernie, Jr.; chaplain, W. Va. Home for Aged & Infirm; 1959-60; Interim pastor, First Bapt. Ch., Huntington, W. Va., 1959-60; ministerial asst. Shiloh Bapt. Ch., Phila., Pa.

1961; student pastor, St. Andrews U. Ch. of Christ, Phila., Pa., 1961-63; dir., Pastoral guidance, Milton Project, N.Y. State Coun. of Chs., 1963-67; pastor, St. Johns' Congregational Ch., Springfield, Mass., 1967-present; founder, The Family Sharing Program; lecturer, Urban issues and race relations; specialist, conditions and problems of migrant agri. workers; former pres., Highland Progressive Club, 1966; vi-chmn. S.U.M.A.C. Corp., Inc., 1966-67; present, v-p., Greater Springfield Clergy Assn.; v-p., Hampden Ministers Assn.; mem. Ex. Bd. Northern Ed. Service; Bd. of Dirs., Springfield YMCA; Bd. of managers, Crozer Sem. Alumni Soc.; Ex. Com. Hill Neighborhood Coun.; Screening Com. Springfield Big Brothers, Inc.; mem. Personnel & Urban Ministry Com., Springfield Coun. of Chs.; mem. Ch. & Mission Com. Mass. Conf. United Ch. of Christ; Springfield pastor's Coun.; Springfield Ad Hoc Urban Crisis Com.; Home: 239 Cortland St., Springfield, Mass. 01109; Office: 643 Union St., Springfield, Mass. 01109.

BOHLER, Lewis Penrose, Jr., b. Augusta, Ga., Nov. 28, 19 ; s. Lewis P., Sr. and Margie A. (Fisher) B.; Hampton Inst., 1944-46; W. Va. State Coll., 1949-51, A.B.; B.D., Oberlin School of Theol.; Kenyon Coll.; m. Gloria Elizabeth Jackson; Children-- Carmen LeJeune, Stephen Craig; pastor, St. Augustine's Episc. Ch., Youngstown, O., 1955-61; current rector, Episc. Ch. of the Advent, Los Angeles, Calif., 1961--; consultant, Psychology of Race Relations, Episc. Diocese of L.A.; v-p., Wilshire Community Coordinating Coun.; mem. NAACP; Urban League; USO; Com. on Human Relations; US Air Force, 1946-49; Good Conduct Medal; Marksman; Soldier of Year; mem., PTA; Ex-disc jockey; ex-boxer, Republican; appears frequently on TV and radio; Home: 1739 Buckingham Pl., Los Angeles, Calif.; Office: 4976 W. Adam's Blvd., Los Angeles, Calif. 90016.

BOLINGS, Blaine Arlington, b. Esmont, Va., June 13, 1919; s. Joseph F. and Mamie (Wagner) B.; Wiley Coll., 1950-55; m. Edith Joseph; 5 sons, Blaine Jr., Lemie, Beryl, Joseph, David; 3 daus., Mamie, Sheryl, Maude; pastored Anahuae Circuit, Anahuae, Tex., 9 yrs.; Marshall Circuit, Marshall, Tex., 3 yrs.; mem. PTA; Boy Scouts; military service, 1941-45; P.O. Box 483, Anahuae, Texas.

BONNER, Isaiah Hamilton, bishop, b. Camden, Ala., July

27, 1890; s. Richard and Prescilla B.; A. B., Knoxville Coll., 1912; B. D., 1914; D. D. (hon.), Payne Coll., 1942; m. Nannie Jones; Children--Isaiah Hamilton, Jr., Helen Marie, Samuel; pastor, African Meth. Episc. Chs. in Uniontown, Mobile, Dothan, Montgomery, Selma, Ala.; presiding elder, Montgomery Dist., 1937; elected bishop, 1948; current, presiding bishop 9th Dist.; trustee, Daniel Payne Coll., 1929--; chrmn., Missionary Bd., A. M. E. Ch., 1952-56; mem. Civil League, Montgomery, Ala.; pres., State Interdenominational Alliance, 3 yrs.; sec., Bishops' Coun. A. M. E. Ch., 1960; pres., Bishops' Coun., 1961; Home: 1721 Sylvan St., Selma, Ala.

BOOKEE, Austin A., b. King & Queen Co., Va., May 29; s. Robert and Julia (Berry); Storer Coll., 1946-48; Va. Sem. & Coll., 1948-52; courses, Va. Union Univ. and Princeton Univ.; m. Cordelia Bookee (deceased); Children--William, Theadore, Cordelia; pastor, Ebenezer Bapt. Ch.; chrmn. Exec. Northern Va. Assn.; mem., Exec. Bd., NAACP, Alexandria, Va.; mem. Bd. of Corp., Alexandria Hospital; tchr. pub. sch. sys.; worked with N. S. P. Project; Order of King David; mem. Ed. Scholarship Fund; Exec. Bd. Lott Carey Foreign Conv.; published pamphlets on the meaning of tithing in the Bapt. Ch.; Home: 117 N. Peyton St., Alexandria, Va., 22314.

*BOOKER, Merrel Daniel, b. July 9, 1908; A. B., Howard Univ.; B. D., Howard Univ. Sch. of Rel.; Union Theol. Sem., New York; N. Y. Sch. of Soc. Work; Wash. Sch. of Psychiatry; Boston Univ., S. T. M.; Inst. of Pastoral Care, Mass. Gen. Hospital, Boston, Mass.; Pastoral Clinical Training: Mass. Mem'l. Hosp.; Charlestown State Hosp. for the Mentally Ill, Norristown, Pa.; Bellevue Hosp., N. Y.; Gallinger Mun. Hosp., Wash., D. C.; m. Erma E.; Children--Merrel, Sue; pastor, Fountain Bapt. Ch., Summit, N. J., 6-1/2 yrs.; dean of men, Talladega Coll., Talladega, Ala.; staff mem., Wash. Fed. of Chs., Wash., D. C.; resident chaplain, Freedmen's Hosp., Wash., D. C.; Fed. Corr. Institution, Chillicothe, O.; chrmn., Div. of Rel., Bishop Coll., Marshall, Tex.; pastor, New Hope Bapt. Ch., Dallas, Tex., 1952-56; pastor, St. Timothy's Community Ch., Gary, Ind., 1956--; feature writer, Informer Chain of Newspapers, Minister Speaks His Mind; mission magazine, Int'l. Pulpit and Parsonage Exchange; Home: 7007 So. Creiger St., Chicago, Ill.

BOONE, Theodore Sylvester, educator, author, b. Winchester, Tex., Dec. 28, 1896; s. Alexander Lorenzo and Ida (Chaney) B.; A. B., Des Moines Coll., 1918; B. A., Sioux Falls Coll., 1918; LL. B., Chicago Law Sch., 1922; A. M., Ark. Bapt. Coll., 1924; other schools and colleges, Prairie View, 1915; Bishop Coll., 1915-17; U. of Iowa, 1918-20; U. of Chgo., 1920-21; Perfect Voice Inst., Chgo, Ill., 1929; Houston Coll., 1930 LL. D. (hon.); Moody Bible Inst., Chgo., 1930; U. of Mich., 1949-50; m. Ruby Beatrice Alexander; pastor, 8th St. Bapt. Ch., Temple, Texas, 1924-31; Mt. Gilead Bapt. Ch., Ft. Worth, Tex., 1931-36; Greater Mt. Gilead Bapt. Ch., 1936-44; King Solomon Miss. Bapt. Ch., Det., Mich., 1944--; lecturer, Bishop Coll., 1938-45; spec. instr., Southwestern Bapt. Theol. Sem., 1941-43; lec., instr., Natl. Sunday Sch. & B. T. U. Cong., 1921-62; Progressive Natl. Sunday Sch. & B. T. U. Cong. instr., 1963--; dean, Okla. Sch. of Rel., 1943-44; instr. Negro hist. Lexington U., 1943-44; dir., Historical Commn. & Historiographer, Natl. Bapt. Conv., USA, Inc., 1939-53; pres., Ft. Worth Sch. of Rel., 1933-36; Bible instr., I. M. Terrell High Sch., 1937-38; editor, Western Star, Bapt. Miss. & Edu. Conv., Texas; Fort Worth Light; Open Door, Women's Aux., B. M. & E. Conv., Texas; Flaming Sword; practiced law, Indianapolis, Ind., 1922-24; 1st pres., Corpus Juris Club; recipient, Most Famous Negro Citizen Award, Ft. Worth, 1933; Distinguished Service Plaque, Citizen's Comm., Detroit, Mich.; Alumni Plaque, Bishop Coll., 1963; mem. Knights of Pythian, Odd Fellows, United Bros. of Friendship, Elks, Masons, Kappa Alpha Psi; author: The Philosophy of Booker T. Washington, Racial Development, Baptists, Know Yourselves and Others, What Baptists Should Know and Do, and many other books; Home: 590 E. Boston Blvd., Detroit, Mich.; Church: 6125 Fourteenth St., Detroit, Mich.

*BOOTH, Lavaughn Venchael, b. Collins, Miss., Jan. 7, 1919; s. Frederick D. and Mamie (Powell) B.; A. B., Alcorn A & M Coll., Miss., 1940; B. D., Howard Univ., Sch. of Rel., 1943; L. H. D., (hon.), Wilberforce Univ., 1963; m. Georgia Ann Morris; Children--Lavaughn V., Jr., William D., Anna M., Paul M., Georgia A.; pastored: First Bapt. Ch., Warrenton, Va., 1942-43; First Bapt. Ch., Gary, Ind., 1944-52; present: Zion Bapt. Ch., Cincinnati, 1952--; lecturer, Nat'l. Bapt. Conv. Inc., Women's Aux., 1946-62; founder, Nat'l. Prayer League,

Inc.; founder, Progressive Nat'l. Bapt. Conv. Inc.; author: Showers of Blessing (book of sermons), and several songs, inc. Brothers Joined in Heart (1960) and You Need Not Walk Alone (1963); Prot. Scout Comm.; Citizens' Comm. on Youth; Comm. of Management, YMCA; Republican; master's thesis - Christian Philanthropy and the Uplift of the Negro in the South, 1865-1900. Home: 3415 Dury Ave., Cincinnati, O., Office: 630 Glenwood Ave., Cincinnati, O.

BORDERS, William Holmes, educator, b. Bibb Co., Ga., Feb. 24, 1905; s. James B. and Leila (Birdsong) B.; A. B., Morehouse Coll., 1929; B. D., Garrett Theol. Sem., 1932; M. A., Chgo. Univ., 1936; honorary degrees: D. D., Morris Brown Coll., 1940; Shaw U., 1942; Gammon Theol. Sem., 1947; L. H. D., Wilberforce Univ., 1962; m. Julia Pate; Children--William Holmes, Jr., Mrs. Juel Borders Benson; pastor, 2nd Bapt. Ch., Evanston, Ill., 1937; Wheat St. Bapt. Ch., Atlanta, Ga., 1937--; Prof., Psych., Morehouse Coll., 1937-39; active YMCA worker; recipient, Omega Psi Phi Frat., Man of the Year award, 1950; Phi Beta Sigma Frat., Social Action Achievement Award, 1949; Natl. Sunday Sch. and B. T. U. Award, 1955; mem. Masons; Prog. Natl. Bapt. Conv., Bapt. World Alliance, NAACP (life), Kappa Alpha Psi Frat.; author: Follow Me, 7 Minutes at the Mike in the Deep South, Thunderbolts; (religious poems) "I'm Somebody!" "Men Must Live as Brothers," and others; Home: 1426 Mozley Drive, S. W., Atlanta, Ga., 30314; Church: 18 Yonge St., N. E., Atlanta, Ga., 30312.

BOSWELL, Hamilton Theodore, b. Dallas, Texas, Aug. 11, 1914; s. Warren A. & Grace Louise (B); A. B., Wiley Coll., Marshall, Tex., 1938; M. Th., Univ. of S. Carolina, 1943; m. Eleanor Bernice Gragg; Children--Jeri Lynn, Ronald Fuqua, Eleanor Louise, Michael; pastored United Meth. Chs., Shaw Chapel, Los Angeles, 1939-43; Bowen Meml. Ch., Los Angeles, 1943-47; Jones Meml. United Meth. Ch., San Francisco, 1947--; promoter-builder, Jones Meml. Homes (Senior Citizens), San Francisco; organizer, Jones Meth. Credit Unon; mem. San Francisco Housing Authority, 1964--; San Francisco Juvenile Justice Commn., 1960-64; dir. Jones Meml. Homes; awards, The Silver Spur award; San Francisco Planning & Urban Renewal Commn., Bd. dirs., Western Region, Natl. Assn. Housing Redevelopment Officials; San Francisco Conf. Rel. & Race, 1964-67; author, newspaper column, "The Race Problem and the Social Gospel," "The Pulpit Voice"; Home: 45 Cleary Ct., San Francisco, Calif. 94109; Office: 1975 Post St., San Francisco, Calif. 94115.

BOTTOMS, Lawrence Wendell, church official, b. Selma, Ala., Apr. 9, 1908; s. Wilbur McDonald and Gussie Adolphus (Shivers) B.; A. B., Geneva Coll., Beaver Falls, Pa.; B. D., The Ref. Presby. Sem., Pittsburgh, Pa.; further study: Atlanta Univ.; m. Elizabeth Letisha Stallworth; Children--Lawrence Wendell, Jr., Jean (Mrs. Julian Perry), Letisha (Mrs. DeWitt Alfred), Janice; ordained by Presby. of Ill., Ref. Presby. Ch., Nov. 18, 1936; pastor, Ref. Presby. Ch., Selma; rec'd into Presby. U. S. Church, 1938; pastor, Grace Presby. Ch., Louisville, Ky., 1938-49; while serving Grace Ch., served as part-time Reg. Dir., Chrstn. Educ. Snedecor Meml. Synod, Presby. U. S., 1938-49; served as full-time dir., 1949-51; asst. sec., Div. of Negro Work, Presby., U. S., Bd. of Ch. Extension, 1951-52; sec. in full-time 1953--; asst. sec., Div. of Home Missions, Bd. of Ch. Extension Presby. Ch., U. S.; mem. The Coun. of Chs., Louisville, Ky.; mem. Bd. of Chrstn. Edu. and Bd. of World Missions; mem. The Commn. on Missionary Edu. of the National Coun. of Chs.; moderator, Synod of Ky., 1962-63; assoc. ed., Presbyterian Outlook; 1960 Distinguished Service award from Geneva Coll., Beaver Falls, Pa.; author: The Policies and Rationale Underlining the Support of Negro Colleges and Schools Maintained by the Presbyterian Church in the United States." Home: 182 Chicamauga Pl., S. W. Atlanta, Georgia; Office: 341 Ponce de Leon Ave., N. Atlanta, Georgia.

BOUIE, Simon Pinckney,, b. Columbia, S. C., Oct. 3, 1939; B. A., Allen Univ., 1961; B. D., Interdenominational Theol. Center, 1966; courses, Sch. of Soc. Work, Atlanta Univ., 1961-62; courses, Pastoral Clinical Trng., So. Carolina Mental Hosp., 1967; m. Willie Omia Jamison; Children--Harold Simone; Soc. Studies & Music tchr., Rosemary Sch., Andrews, S. C., 1961-62; asst. pastor, Big Bethel A. M. E. Ch., Atlanta, Ga., 1963-65; college minister, Allen Univ., 1966-67; pastor, Bishops' Meml. A. M. E. Ch., present; chaplain, Crafts-Farrow State Hosp., Columbia, S. C., 1967; chaplain, Coun. of Chs., Coun. Migrant Commn., N. Y.; mem. chrmn., Richland & Lexington Co. NAACP Drive; mem. YMCA; Columbia Min. Alliance; Hosp. Chaplains; mem. Urban League; Alpha Phi Alpha; Home: 1833 McFadden St., Columbia, S. C., 29204; Office: Bishops' Meml. A. M. E. Ch., 2221 Washington St., Columbia, S. C.

BOURNE, Charles Nathaniel, b. Cambridge, Mass., Dec. 7, 1918; s. Joseph T. and Beatrice (Wilson) B.; Eastern Nazarene Coll., 1948-52, A. B., Wollaston, Mass.; S. T. B., Boston Univ. Sch. of Theol., Boston, Mass., 1952-55; D. D. (hon.), Kittrell Coll., N. C., 1957; m. Marjorie Earmine Burke; Children--Charlene, Carmella, Charles, Jr.; asst. pastor, St. Paul A. M. E. Ch., Cambridge, Mass., 1946-48; pastor, St. James A. M. E. Ch., Jamestown, R. I., 1948-50; pastor, Bethel African Meth. Episc. Ch., Plymouth, Mass., 1950-52; pastor, Bethel A. M. E. Ch., Lynn, Mass., 1952-55; pastor, Bethel A. M. E. Ch., Cambridge, Md., 1955--; U. S. Army and European Theater, 1942-46; mem. Bi-Racial Commn., City of Cambridge, 1960-62; v-p., Dorchester Co. Inter-Racial Minister's Assn., 1960-62; Ex. Bd. Dorchester Co. NAACP, 1960--; sub. tchr., Cambridge, Md. Ele. schs.; mem. Mason; spec. articles to A. M. E. Ch. Review; Home: 621 Pine St., Cambridge, Dorchester Co., Md.; Office: Bethel A. M. E. Ch., 623 Pine St., Cambridge, Dorchester Co., Md.

BOWEN, Kenneth Athelston, b. Boston, Mass., Jan. 2, 1922; s. Rufus W. and Martha E. B.; A. B., Gordon Coll., Mass., 1949; B. D., Andover Newton Theol. Sem., Mass., 1952; m. Sylvia G. Clark; Children--Kenneth A. Jr., Yvonne A., Elaine L.; pastor, First Bapt. Saugus, Mass., 1945-47; Messiah Bapt., Brockton, Mass., 1953-58; exec. dir., Hickory St. Chrstn. Edu. Ctr, Buffalo, N. Y., 1958--; pres., Buffalo Br. NAACP, 1954-56; mem Econ. Opp. Bd., Milwaukee; pres., Wis. State Sun. Sch. & B. T. U. Trng. Union Cong.; v. p., Natl. Sun. Sch. & B. T. U. Cong.; Faculty Club; faculty mem., Natl. Laymen's Conv.; mem. Bd. Human Relations; rec'd Good Neighbor Award, Buffalo, N. Y., 1955; Phi Beta Sigma, Frontiers Internat.; Masons; Rel. editor, Milwaukee Star; Home: 418 W. Christine Lane, Milwaukee, Wis. 53212; Office: Mt. Moriah Bapt. Ch., 6th & Galena, Milwaukee, Wis.

BOWENS, Charles Haywood, Jr., b. July 26, 1922, Norfolk, Va.; s. Charles H. and Clara J. A. B., Va. State Coll., Petersburg, Va., 1953; m. Beatrice Andrew; Children--

Charles H. III, Cynthia, Curtis; pastor, New Hope Bapt. Ch. and Little Zion Bapt. Ch., Portsmouth, Va.; tchr. pub. schs., present; pres. Minister's Fellowship Alliance; Minister's Interdenominational Forum; Minister's Conf. Pres.; Portsmouth NAACP; mem. Natl. Bapt. and Amer. Bapt. Assn.; pres. Portsmouth Norfolk Citizen's Com. (Pol.); painter of murals; awards, pub. ser.; mem. 100 Women's Organization, 1968; NAACP pub. service award, 1967; WW II Pacific; Home: 408 Beechdale Rd., Portsmouth, Va. 23707

BOWIE, Harry John, b. Long Branch, N.J., Nov. 12, 1935; s. Walter William and Esther (Lester) B.; B.A., Hobart Coll., 1954-58; S.T.B., The Gen. Theol. Sem., 1958-61; present rector, Chapel of the Annunciation, Lawnside, N.J., 1961--; St. John's Episc. Ch., Camden, N.J., 1961--; Episc. Chaplain-Camden Hosps., 1961-62; N.J. State Sch. for the Mentally Retarded, 1962--; mem. Planning Bd. Boro of Lawnside, 1962; Phi Beta Kappa; Lawnside Jaycees; Home: 16 Warwick Rd., Lawnside, N.J.

BOWMAN, John, b. Wash., D.C., Mar. 16, 1908; s. Francis; 2 yrs. novitiate, prof. of first vows, E. Troy, Wis., ordained to priesthood, 1939; asst. pastor, St. Benedict's, Duson, La., 1939-41; Immaculate Heart of Mary Parish, Lafayette, La.; U.S. Army chaplain, 1941-42; pastor, Immaculate Heart of Mary Parish, present; appt. provincial superior, Divine Word Missionaries' Southern Province, U.S., 1965--; Office: Immaculate Heart of Mary Parish, Lafayette, La.

BOYD, Braxton Julian, teacher; b. Princeton, Kentucky, Jan. 21, 1921; s. Hugh Lee and Margaret (Duke) B.; A.B., Garrett Biblical Inst., 1942; B.D., St. Paul Meth. Sem., 1947; further study, Northwestern Univ., 1962-63; m. Dorothy Harrison; children--Karen, Braxton II, Thurston, James; pastor, Chrstn. Meth. Episc. Chs. in Ark., Tex., Mich., Ill., Mo., and D.C., 1948-64; present: pastor, Israel Metro. C.M.E. Ch., Wash., D.C.; tchr. Walker High School, Magnolia, Ark.; Flint, Mich.; Decatur, Ill.; U.S. Navy, WW II; mem. Omega Psi Phi; Mason; State's chrmn., Columbia Democratic Voters League, 1948-50; sec. Voters Registration 1948-50; youth coun. advisor, K.C., Mo.; NAACP Adv. Coun., K.C., Mo.; mem. Amer. Civil Lib. Union, K.C., Mo. and POAU; Home: 632 Randolph St., N.W., Wash., D.C.;

Office: 557 Randolph St., N.W., Wash., D.C.

BOYD, Cauthion T., chaplain, (Col.); b. Spencer, N. Carolina; A.B., Hampton Inst., Hampton, Va.; B.D., Anderson Sem., Indiana; m. Mary; Children-- Carl, Barbara Ann, Gerald; enlisted Ft. Harrison, USA, 1945; chaplain, Guam, 1945-48; Ft. Lewis, Wash., 1949-50; Ft. Meade, Md., 1951-52; Frankfurt, Germany, 1953-56; Korea; Selfridge, AFB, Detroit, Mich., 1956-61; Germany, 1962-63; Asst. Post Chaplain, Ft. George Meade, Md.; Asst. 1st Army Chaplain, June 1965; Vietnam, 1966; Post Chaplain, Ft. Harrison, 1967--; decorations, Silver Star; Bronze Star (Korea); Bronze Star, Oak Leaf Cluster (Vietnam); Army Commendation Medal Oak Leaf Clusters; Office: Post Chaplain, Ft. Benjamin Harrison, Ind.

BOYKIN, Isaac, b. Wilmington, N.C., July 9, 1895; s. Thomas and Ida (B).; Gregory Inst., N.C., 1909-16; courses, Livingston Coll., Ministers' & Laymen's Inst., Cape Fear Conf. A.M.E.Z. Ch. (Summers); pastored African Meth. Episc. Z. Chs., Cape Fear Conf., N.C., 1938-59; presiding elder, A.M.E.Z. Ch., Wilson, N.C. District, 1959--; U.S. Railway clerk (ret.); former mem. Cham. of Comm.; Elks; Pythians; Democrat; Home: 713 S. 7th St., Wilmington, N.C. 28401

BRADFORD, Charles Edward, church official, b. Washington, D.C., July 12, 1925; s. Robert Lee and Etta Elizabeth (Littlejohn) B.; Oakwood Coll, Huntsville, Ala., 1946; spec. course, S.D.A. Theol. Sem.; m. Ethel Lee McKenzie; Children--Sharon, Charles, Jr., Dwight; pastor, New Orleans, La., 1946; Berean S.D.A. Ch., Baton Rouge, La., 1946-51; Oakland Ave. S.D.A. Ch., Dallas, Tex., 1951-52; Berean S.D.A. Ch., St. Louis, Mo., 1953-57; sec. Home Missionary Dept. for Central States Conf. of S.D.A. Kansas City, Mo., 1952-53; sec., Home Missionary Dept. Northeastern Conf. and pastor of the City Tabernacle S.D.A. Ch., New York City, 1957-61; pres., Lake Region Conf., Chicago, Ill, 1961--; mem. Lake Union Conf. ex. comm.; Andrews Univ. Bd.; Oakwood Coll. Bd., Review and Herald Publishing Assn. Bd., Wash., D.C.; Hinsdale Hosp. Bd., Hinsdale, Ill.; Riverside Hosp. Bd., Nashville, Tenn.; contributing ed., The Message Magazine, Nashville, Tenn.; contributed article to the S.D.A. Encyclopedia on History of the Lake Region Conf. of S.D.A.; Home 8560 S. Kenwood St., Chicago,

Ill.; Office: 8517 S. State St., Chicago, Ill.

BRADFORD, Ernest Marvin, b. East St. Louis, Ill., April 21, 1927; s. Shelby and Leora (Barnes) B.; B.A., Morehouse Coll., 1952; B.D., Morehouse Coll. Sch. of Rel., 1958; m. Adnee Marie Byrom; Children--Althea Bettye, Aleta Marie (twins); pastor, Mt. Pisgah Presby. Ch., U.S.A., Hartsville, S.C., 1960-62; current pastor, Northern Heights Presby. Ch., Selma, Ala., 1962--; mem. County Improvement Assn.; US Army Chaplain asst., 1946-47; Home: 1571 Range St., Selma, Ala.; Office: 1575 Range St., Selma, Ala.

BRADLEY, David H., editor, college prof., b. Franklin, Pa., Sept. 20, 1905; s. Daniel F. and Cora A. (Brewer) B.; A.B., Livinstone College, 1929; A.M., University of Pittsburgh, 1932; grad. course: N.Y. Univ., 1940-42; m. Harriette Marie Jackson; Children--Laverne Findlay (Mrs. George), David, Jr.; pastor, Mercer, Pa. W. Bridgewater, Pa., Bellevue, Pa., Altoona, Pa.; Prof. of History, Livingstone Coll., 1933-35; pastor, Ridgewood, N.J., 1935-49; current ed., A.M.E.Z. Quarterly; conf. dir., Chrstn. Edu., N.J., 1936-48; Denominational dir. Ministers Inst., 1938-55; asst. sec., Chrstn and Leadership Edu. Schs., 1949-55; Bergen Co. T.B. Soc.; Natl. Coun. of Chs. Comm. on Ed. Evangelism, Home Missions; Ad. and Leadership; mem.: Meth. His. Soc.; Phi Beta Sigma; Mason, Republican; author: The Federal Elections Bill of 1890 (1932); History of the A.M.E.Z. Ch., (1956); contributor, Dictionary of Christn. Ed. by Cully, 1964; Home: P.O. Box 146, Bedford, Pa.

*BRADLEY, Fulton Obadiah, coll. prof., b. Bishopville, S.C., Dec. 23, 1926; s. Henry Herbert and Florence (Ruth) B.; m. Lettie Myrtle Powell; Children--Fulton Adrian, Raymond Arnold; B.A., Morehouse Coll., Atlanta, Ga., 1947; B.D., Howard Univ. Sch. of Rel., Wash., D.C., 1950; M.A., Howard Univ. Sch. of Rel., 1957; further study: American Univ., Wash., D.C.; Student Interm Pastor, Friendship Bapt. Ch., N.Y.C., 1950; pastor, First Inst. Bapt. Ch., Winston-Salem, 1951-54; First Bapt. Ch., W. Wash., D.C., 1954-62; dean, Dept. of Theol., Va. Union Theol. Sem. and Coll., Lynchburg, Va., 1950-51; dean, Baptist Ed. Congress, D.C.; faculty mem., Natl. Bapt. Sunday Sch. and Bapt. Trng. Union Cong., Natl. Bapt. Convention, USA, Inc., 1956; instr., Howard Univ., Sch. of Rel., Wash., D.C., 1958-62;

former mem., Bd. of Rel. Ed., Natl. Bapt. Conv., USA, Inc.; Bd. of Trustees, Stoddard Home, Wash., D.C.; current mem., Rel. Ed. Assn. of US and Canada; mem., Min. Adv. Comm., Planned Parenthood Assn. of Detroit; Metropolitan Dist. Assn.; Wolverine State Bapt. Conv.; Booker T. Washington Bus. Assn.; Baptist Min. Conf. of Detroit and Vicinity; Metropolitan YMCA, Fisher Br.; Detroit Coun. of Chs.; Pastors' Union; Evangelism Comm., Detroit Coun. of Chs.; Interde. Min. Alliance, Detroit; Comm. of Management, Fisher YMCA; co-chrmn. Membership Campaign, Fisher Branch, YMCA. contributing ed., Bapt. Teacher, Sunday Sch. Pub. Bd., Natl. Bapt. Conv., USA, Inc., Nashville, Tenn.; Inst. of Rel., Howard Univ. Sch. of Rel., Wash., D.C.; Frontiers Intl.; Home: 3814 Leslie St., Detroit, Mich; Office: 6125 Beechwood St., Detroit, Mich.

*BRADY, Crawford Wm., b. Milwaukee, Wis., Feb. 15, 1924; s. William and Sedalia Lovings (Trent) B.; Rel. Trng. Inst., Columbus, O., 1947; B.S., Marquette Univ., Milwaukee, 1954; B.D., Howard Univ. Sch. of Rel., 1955-58; m. Well Harper; Children--Clifford, William; pastor, Walls Meml. A.M.E. Zion Ch., Toledo, 1961-62; St. Paul's African Meth. Episc. Zion Ch., Blairsville, Pa., 1962-64; Aide to Congressman, 84th Cong.; ed., Milwaukee Defender, 1951-55; US Air Forces, 1943-45; Writer's award, 1954 (Defender); mem. Alpha; Home: 5423 13th St., N.W., Washington, D.C.

BRANCH, Emanuel Sylvestre, b. Phila., Pa., July 1, 1921; s. Emanuel Sylvestre, and Miley Anderson (Dean); B.A., Yale Univ., 1950; B.D., Yale Div. Sch., 1955; m. Gloria Cleopatra Connolly; Children--Crystal Alice, Colleen Ann; pastor, First Bapt. Ch., Milford, Conn., 1947-50; Union Bapt. Ch., Hartford, Conn., 1953-60; Asst. Ex. Dir. Coun. of Chs., Cleveland, O., 1961-64; pastor, Antioch Bapt. Ch., Cleveland, O., 1961-pres.; lectr., Intergroup Rel., Western Res. Univ., 1962-4; former mem. Bd. of Dir., Conn. Bapt. Conv.; Fam. Serv. Soc.; Hartford Sem. Found.; Hartford Soc. Adj. Commn.; Hartley-Salmon Child Guidance Clinic; Interdenom. Min. Alliance; present Cleveland Coun. of Chs., Dir. of Radio and TV; Dir. Comm. Rel. Dept., Dir. Spiritual Life Dept., 1961-64; mem. Public Affairs Com. of Ohio Coun. Chs.; Amer. Assembly on Arms Control, Western Res. Univ., 1962; Delegate Assembly, Natl. Urban Leage; Pres. Bd. Dirs., Urban League of Cleveland; Min. Assn.

Greater Cleveland, 1966-67; Home: 16633 Lomond Blvd., Shaker Heights, O. 44120; Office: 8869 Cedar Ave., Cleveland, O. 44106.

BRANCH, George Murray, sem. prof. and dir., b. Prince Edward Co., Va., Apr. 18, 1914; s. George McGuffie and Annie Pearl (Clark) B.; B.S., Va. Union Univ., 1938; B.D., Andover Newton Theol. Sch., 1944; M.A., Drew Univ., 1946; courses: Hebrew Union Coll., 1952; Drew Univ., 1952-53, 1962-63; m. Jamima Wall; Children-- Dianne Everett; pastor, Peoples Bapt. Ch., Portsmouth, N.H., 1940-41; First Bapt. Ch., Madison, N.J., 1941-44; field sec., Natl. Student Coun. of YMCA, Southern Area, 1944-47; asst. prof., Morehouse Coll., Atlanta, Ga., 1947-56; assoc. prof., 1956-59; current assoc. prof., Interdenom. Theol. Center, Atlanta, Ga., 1959--; dir., Morehouse Sch. of Rel. in I.T.C., 1963--; mem., Campus Work Com., Southern Area Coun. of YMCA, 1947-60; Adv. Com., West Side Br., Butler St. YMCA, 1963--; Adv. Com., Area I, Atlanta Pub. Sch., 1955-56; Bd. of Dir., Atlanta Br., Amer. Civil Liber. Union, 1964--; mem. Amer. Acad. of Rel., Soc. of Biblical Lit. and Exegesis, Amer. Sch. of Oriental Res., Soc. for the Scientific Study of Rel., Howard Univ. Inst. of Rel., Amer. Assn. of Univ. Prof., Soc. for Rel. in Higher Edu., Kappa Alpha Psi; Home: 841 Fair St., SW, Atlanta, Ga. 30314; Office: 645 Beckwith St., SW, Atlanta, Ga. 30314.

BRANNON, Thomas Edward, b. Martinsburg, W. Va., Oct. 14, 1919; s. Betnie and Vally B.; attended Carnegie Inst. of Tech., 1950-54; Univ. Pitts., 1956-58; m. Virginia Kirk; Children-- Thomas E., Jr., Nanette K., Jeffrey N.; pastor, Van Port Community A.M.E.Z. Ch., Pa., 1954-56; Avery Meml. A.M.E.Z. Ch., Pa., 1957-65, presently assoc. pastor, St. Matthew's A.M.E.Z. Ch., Pa.; mem., Sewickley Human Rel. Com.; served in Armed Forces; rec'd Good Conduct Medal and Battle Stars; Home: 440 Duff Rd., Sewickley, Pa. 15143.

*BRANTFORD, Gerald Henry, b. Lorain, Ohio, Dec. 28, 1919; s. Ernest and Mary (Perkins) B.; A.B., Western Res. Univ., Cleveland, O., 1949; B.D., Howard Univ. Sch. of Rel., 1953; m. Georgene Sweatt; Children-- David Alan; assoc. pastor, Asbury Meth. Ch., 1953-55; dir., Wesley Found., Howard Univ., 1955-57; pastor, St. James Meth. Ch., Milwaukee, 1957-62; Exec. sec.,

Lexington Conf., Bd. of Ed., The Meth. Ch., 1962-64; pastor, Ingleside-Whitfield Meth. Ch., Chicago, Ill., 1964--; former mem., Ex. Bd., NAACP, Milwaukee; Milwaukee Commn. on Human Rights; Home: 924 East 76th St., Chicago, Ill. 60619; Office: 929 E. 76th St., Chicago, Ill. 60619.

BRAZILL, Ernest Stonewall, b. Albany, Ga., Apr. 23, 1910; s. George Henry and Sallie (Jackson) B.; B.Th., Conroe Normal & Indus. Coll., Conroe, Tex.; m. Lily McDavid; Children--Nathaniel E., Mrs. Robert Miller; pastor, Wright Grove Bapt. Ch., Altair, Tex., 1946-49; Sinclair Bapt. Ch., Bremerton, Wash., 1950-55; Shiloh Bapt. Ch., Tacoma, Wash., 1955-present; pres., Sun. Sch. and B.T.U. of the No. Pacific Bapt. Conv.; pres. of the Puget Sound Minister's Conf.; mem. of the Tacoma Min. Alliance; Mason; mem., Mayor's Comm. on Housing and Soc. Welfare; Bd. mem., NAACP; mem., Natl. Bapt. Conv. of Amer.; Home: 1723 S. Kay St., Tacoma, Wash.; Office: 1211 S. Eye St., Tacoma, Wash., 98405.

BREEDEN, James Pleasant, b. Minneapolis, Minn., Oct. 14, 1934; s. Pleasant and Florence; B.A., Dartmouth Coll., 1956; B.D., Union Theol. Sem., N.Y., 1960; m. Jeanne Marie Savoye; Children--Margaret, Johanna, Frederick; curate, St. James Episc. Ch., Roxbury, Mass., 1960-63; canon, adv. to Bishop, St. Pauls Cath., Boston, Mass., 1963-65; asst. dir., Commn. on Rel. and Race, NCC of N.Y., 1965-67; dir., commn. on Ch. and Race, Mass. Coun. of Chs., Boston, Mass.; mem., Mass. State Adv. Com.; US Civil Rights Commn.; chmn., Gov. Task Force on Human Rights and Urban Tensions; NCNC; awards, Outstanding Young Men, Boston Jaycees, 1965; Natl. Assn. of Soc. Workers, 1964; mem., Bd. and exec. com., ACLU, Mass.; Home: 15 Montrose St., Roxbury, Mass., 02119; Office: 14 Beacon St., Boston, Mass. 02108.

*BREEDING, M. L., Miles Coll., Ala.; Paine Coll., Ga.; Howard Univ. Sch. of Rel.; pastor, Chrstn. Meth. Episc. Chs., Wash., D.C., Chicago, Pittsburgh, Asheville, N.C., Dayton and Cleveland, Ohio and Indiana; currently Gen. Sec., Bd. of Missions of the Chrstn. Meth. Episc. Chs. (Home and Intl. Missions); mem., Com. on Cooperation and Coun. between the Meth. Ch. and the C.M.E. Ch.; mem. Gen. Com. on Chaplains and Armed Forces

Personnel; mem., Mason; Office: 307 Berkeley Rd., Indianapolis, Ind.

BREWER, Harold Cole, b. Kansas City, Mo., s. John Cole and Evelyn B. (Wright) B.; B.A., Oakwood Coll., Union Coll., 1957; M.A., Andrews Univ., 1958; m. Gaynell Tyler B.; daughter, Deanne M.; pastor-evangelist, Central States Conf. of Seventh-Day Adventist; pastored: Pueblo, Colo., 1958; St. Joseph, Mo. and Leavenworth, Kansas, 1959; St. Joseph, Mo., 1959-62; Atchinson, Kansas, 1959-63; present: pastor, Topeka, Kansas Seventh-Day Adventist Church, 1962-; mem. Amer. Temp. Soc., NAACP, Min. Assn.; Home: 3304 Colfax St., Topeka, Kans.; Office: 954 College St., Topeka, Kansas.

BRIDDELL, David Wesley, b. Berlin, Md., Nov. 28, 1931; s. Wm. T. and Elsie C.; A.B., Morgan State Coll., 1952; S.T.B. Boston Univ., Sch. of Theol., 1955; m. Jocelyn LaVerne Weston; Children--Jocelyn, Mark; pastor, St. Andrew's United Meth. Ch., Worcester, Mass., 1954-55; Shiloh Meth. Ch., Crisfield, Md., 1955-57; Emmanuel Meth. Ch., Phila., Pa., 1957-64; Assoc. Dir. Audio-Visual Dept., Bd. of Missions United Meth. Ch., New York City, 1964-67; Dir. Audio-visual Resources, Bd. of Missions, New York, 1967--; Bd. mem. Planned Parenthood Assoc., Phila., Pa., 1960-64; Wharton Neighborhood Association, 1960-64; N.E. Community Organization, Teaneck, N.J., 1968-; awards, Community Serv.; Crime Prevention Assn., 1964, Phila., Pa.; mem. Democrat; Rel. Pub. Rela. Coun.; New York Film Coun.; writer, Film utilization guides; Home: 1146 Anna St., Teaneck, N.J. 07666; Office: 475 Riverside Dr., New York, N.Y. 10027.

*BRIDGES, Ramsey May,' b. Darbun, Miss., Aug. 25, 1912; s. Simon P. and Dora (May) B.; B.A., Dillard Univ., New Orleans, La., 1938; B.D., Howard Univ. Sch. of Rel., Wash., D.C., 1942; Th.M., Pittsburgh-Xenia, 1958; m. Helen U. Deas; Children--Sarah Lee; dir., Wesley Found., 1942-43; pastor, McKendree Meth. Ch., Cumberland, Ind., 1943-46; Hartford Meml. Meth. Ch., Hickory, N.C., 1946-49; Simpson Meth., Charlotte, N.C. 1949-52; Brooklyn, N.Y., 1952-54; Warren Pittsburgh, 1954-61; Dist. Supt., Meth. Ch., Charleston Dist., 1961-65; Dist. Supt. Meth. Ch., Parkersburg Dist., The Meth. Ch., 1965--; mem., Kappa Alpha Psi; Mason; Republican;

Home: 1716 Market St., Parkersburg, W. Va., 26102.

BRIGHT, John Douglas, bishop, Americus, Ga., Oct. 11, 1917; s. Turner and Estella (Williams) B.; A. B., Wilberforce Univ., Th. B., Payne Sem., 1942; hon. degrees, Daniel Payne, Allen Univ., and Wilberforce Univ.; m. Vida M.; Children--John, Jr., and Gwendolyn; pastor A. M. E. Ch., So. Charlston, O., 1937-38, Wayman Ch., Hillsboro, O., 1938-40, Wayman Ch., Bainbridge, O., 1938-40, Shorter Chapel, Greenfield, O., 1940, Lee Chapel, Cincinnati, O., 1940-42, St. Paul Ch., Lima, O., 1942-43, Bethel Ch., Pittsburgh, 1943; elected bishop May 1960, Los Angeles, Calif.; first assignment as bishop was to Central Africa, 1960-62; 12th Episc. Dist., comprising Arkansas and Okla., 1962-64; 1st Espisc. Dist. May 1964-; mem. of the World Coun. of Chs., the World Conf. of Meth., Natl. Coun. of Churches; Masons; Elks; NAACP; pub. articles: Christian Recorder, Southern Chrstn. Recorder, Pittsburgh Courier; Home and Office: 6608 Lincoln Drive, Phila., Pa.

BRIGHTMAN, Edward Scipio, b. Charleston, S. C., Jan. 26, 1914; s. Peter Jackson and Katie (Johnson) B.; B. A., Coll. of the City of New York, 1949; B. D., Va. Episc. Theol. Sem., Alexandria, Va., 1957; m. Lucy Frasier; Children--Laura, Edwina, Edward, Jr., John, Samuel, James; Asst. in charge, St. Philip's Episc. Ch., Brooklyn, N. Y., 1952-53; priest in charge, St. Simon's Episc. Ch., Springfield, Mass., 1953-55; Christ. Episc. Ch., Halifax, Va., 1955-57; St. Thomas Episc. Ch., Tulsa, Okla., 1957-61; curate, All Saints Episc. Ch., St. Louis, Mo., 1961-63; rector, St. Philip Episc. Ch., 1963--; Home: 2009 Locust St., Omaha, Nebr.; Office: 2532 Binney St., Omaha, Nebr.

BRITTON, John Henry, b. LaGuardo, Tenn., Sept. 16; s. John and Amanda B.; Fisk Univ., Sch. of Rel., Nashville, Tenn., 1930-33; Tenn. A. & I. Univ. summer Rel. Inst.; m. Martha M. Parrish; Children--Naomi Louise, John Henry, Jr.; pastored the foll. Chrstn. Meth. Episc. Chs. in Laguardo, Tenn.: St. Andrews, 1913, 1915-16; Odom's Bend & Powell's Grove, 1913-15; Cherry Valley, 1961-21; Payne Chapel, Avondale, Tenn., 1921-24; Lane Tabernacle, Nashville, Tenn., 1924-26, 1933-36; St. Luke C. M. E. Ch., Nashville, Tenn., 1926-27; presiding elder, Clarksville Dist., Tenn. Conf., 1927-33; ret. from pastorate, 1961; statistician, Tenn. Annual Conf., C. M. E.

Ch., 1930-54; mem., NAACP; Nashville Chrstn. Leadership Conf.; Sigma Rho Sigma; Mason; Home: 1510 South St., Nashville, Tenn. 37212.

BROCKMAN, Nathaniel J., b. Greenville, S. C., June 20, 1933; s. Isaac A. and Addie M. (Smith) B.; B. Th., Am. Bapt. Theol. Sem., Nashville, Tenn., 1957; m. Mattie Elizabeth Todd; Children--Elaine Patricia, Joel Malcolm, Elizabeth Regene, Anita; chapel minister, Natl. Sch. of Business; pastor, New Liberty Bapt. Ch., Fountain Inn, S. C.; Griffin Ebenezer Bapt. Ch., Dickens, S. C., Mt. Calvary Bapt. Ch.; present Dir. Bapt. Center, Greenville, S. C.; mem. NAACP; dir. Voter Educ. Project, Greenville City, S. C.; Mason; Young Democrat; S. C. Human Rela. Coun.; Home: 407 Green Ave., Greenville, S. C. 29601.

BRONSON, Oswald Perry, sem. prof., b. Sanford, Fla., July 19, 1927; s. Uriah Perry and Flora (Hollinshed) B.; B. S., Bethune Cookman Coll., 1950; B. D., Gammon Theol. Sem., 1959; Ph. D. courses: Northwestern Univ.; m. Helen Carolyn Williams; Children--Josephine Suzette, Flora Helen, Oswald Perry, Jr.; pastor, The Meth. Chs., St. Joseph, Deland, Fla., 1948-50; St. John, Ft. Pierce, Fla., 1948-50; Kenney Chapel, Tampa, Fla., 1952-53; Rocky Ford Circuit, Ga., 1959-60; Ch. of the Redeemer, and Ingleside-Whitfield Meth., 1960-64; Dir. of Field Edu. & Assoc. Prof. of Chrstn. Edu. at Interdenom. Theol. Center, Atlanta, Ga., 1964-64; Pres. Interdenom. Theol. Center, Atlanta, Ga., 1968--; Rehabilitation Cent., Marianna Fla.; chaplain, Southwest State TB Hosp., Tampa, Fla., 1952-53; mem., Alpha Kappa Mu Honor Soc.; Home: 9 McDonough Blvd., Atlanta, Ga. 30315; Office: 671 Beckwith St., Atlanta, Ga. 30314.

BROOKINS, H. Hartford, b. Miss., June 8, 1925; B. A., Wilberforce Univ.; B. D., Payne Theol. Sem.; D. D. (hon.) Payne Theol. Sem.; grad. work, Univ. of Kan.; m. Helene Winona Howard; pastored, A. M. E. Chs., 1950-to date; pastor, First A. M. E. Ch., Los Angeles, 1959-present; former pres., Wichita Inter-Racial Min. Alliance; v. p., Wichita Coun. of Chs.; present chrmn., 10th Dist. Recall Commn. (amassed more than 13,000 votes in protest to a City Coun.; chrmn., Campaign Com., Los Angeles' first elected Negro Councilman; apptd. to Bd. of Institutional Management by Gov. Geo. Docking; mem., NAACP; Urban League; Business & Prof. Men of L. A.;

Mason; Alpha Phi Alpha; Bd. mem., Los Angeles Fed. of Chs.; Home: 1809 Wellington Rd., Los Angeles, Calif. 90019.

BROOKINS, Houston Daniel, b. Yazoo County, Miss., July 24, 1910; s. J. A. and Georgia Ann B.; A. B., Alcorn Coll., Miss., 1932; M. R. E., Tuskegee Inst., Ala., 1934; m. Maggie Wade; ordained Deacon African Meth. Episc. Ch., 1934; ordained Elder, A. M. E. Ch., 1936; pastored in Okla. and Ark., the following chs.: St. Paul A. M. E. Ch., Dover, Okla., 1935-36; Allen Temple A. M. E. Ch., 1936-41; St. Paul A. M. E. Ch., Arkadelphia, Ark., 1941-46; St. Luke Forest City, 1946-48; Carter Chapel, Helena, Ark., 1948-52; Bethel A. M. E., Stuttgart, Ark., 1952-56; Gates Chapel, 1964--; Most valuable citizens award, Crosset Ala., 1960; pres., Negro group for civil rights, Crossett; mem., PTA; Democrat; Trustee mem., Shorter Coll., No. Little Rock, Ark.; Hon. mem., City Coun., Crossett, Ala.; mem., NAACP; Home: 400 N. Alabama St., Crossett, Ark. 71635; Office: 305 W. Third Ave., Crossett, Ark., 71635

BROOKS, Charles DeCatur, church official, b. Greensboro, N. C., July 24, 1930; s. Marvin B. and Mattie (Reaves) B.; B. A., Oakwood Coll., 1951; m. Walterene L. Wagner; Children-- Diedra Yvonne, Charles DeCatur, Jr.; pastored Seventh-Day Adventist Chs.: Wilmington, Del., 1951-52; Chester, Pa., 1951-53; Camden, N. J., 1953-56; Columbus, O., 1956-60; Cleveland, O., 1960-63; present: sec. and revivalist, Columbia Union Conf. of Seventh-Day Adventists, 1963--; mem., Pine Forge Inst. Bd., 1960-63 and Exec. Comm., Columbia Union Conf., 1963--; Home: 1728 Varnum St., N. W., Wash., D. C. Office: 7710 Carroll Ave., N. W., Takoma Park, D. C.

BROOKS, David Henry, chaplain, b. Decatur, Ga., Dec. 6, 1908; s. Joseph Wood and Ft. Sumter (Smith) B.; Morehouse Coll., 1927-30; Va. State Coll., 1945-47; Bishop Payne Div. Sch., 1944-47; B. D., 1949; A. B., Fla. Agr. and Mech. Univ., 1948; m. Vivian Lucia Stallsworth; ordained deacon, 1947; ordained priest, 1948 (The Episc. Ch. Diocese of Fla.); priest-in-chge., St. Michael and All Angels Episc. Ch.; Episc. chaplain, Fla. A & M Univ. Tallahassee, Fla., 1947--; mem., The Coll. Commn.; Dept. of Mission; Church Extension of the Diocese of Fla; local and state officer, NAACP; mem. Phi Beta Sigma Frat.; tchr., Sociology, Florida A & M Univ., 1948-51;

Omega Phi Psi; Citizen of the Year Award; mem., Democrat; B.D. Thesis: Community Determinations for Church Action--In the City of Hampton, Va., 1947; Home: 2109 Owens St., Tallahassee, Fla.; Office: 1405 Melvin St., Tallahassee, Fla.

BROOKS, Elemit Anthony, b. Norfolk, Va.; A.B., Lincoln Univ., 1950; B.D., Drew Univ. Theol. Sem., 1953; courses: John Carroll Univ., Human Relations, 1956; m. Doris Kearsley; daughter--Bethella Annette; pastor, Chrstn. Ed. and youth pastor, First Presby. Ch., Oxford, Pa.; Trin. & Metro. Meth. Ch., NYC; youth advisor, Meth. students, Cleveland Ch. Fellowship, 1956-58; pastor, Werner Meth. Ch., Cleveland, O. 1953-58; pastor (assoc.), Bushwick Ave. Meth. Ch., Brooklyn, N.Y., 1960-63; pastor, First Meth. Ch., Bronx, N.Y., 1963--; Bd. mem., Min. Trng. & Qualification; Bd. of Hosps. and Homes; Bd. of Dirs., NY East. Conf., Health Care Agency; Bd. of Dirs., Brooklyn-Long Is. Ch. Soc.; mem., Bd. of Prot. Coun., Bronx Div.; mem. local sch. bd.; chrmn, the So. Bronx Housing Com.; the Mayors Commn. on Rel. Leaders of NYC.; Bd. of Managers of the Neighborhood Adv. Serv.; chrmn., the Mott Haven Citizen Com.; mem., The Adv. Comm. of the Natl. Coun. Negro Women, Bronx Div., Community Educ. Comm., Mem., NAACP; Urban League; Home: 401 E. 141 St., Bronx, N.Y.

BROOKS, Henry Curtis, sem. prof., b. Alexandria, Va., May 7, 1929; s. Houston George, Sr. and Evelyn (Lemon) B.; B.A., Storer Coll., 1950; B.D., S.T.M., Andover Newton Theol. Sch., 1954; Ph.D., Boston Univ., 1964; m. Aeolus Jones; Children--Steven Jeffrey; ordained, Amer. Bapt. minister, 1953; asst. min., Shiloh Bapt. Ch., W. Medford, Mass., 1953-54; pastor, St. John's Bapt. Ch., Waburn, Mass., 1954-58; visiting lecturer, Andover Newton Theo. Sch., Newton, Mass., 1958-64; asst. prof., Andover Newton Theol. Sch., 1964--; Prot. chaplain, Boston City Hosp., Boston, Mass., 1955--; chaplain supervisor, The Andover Theol. Sch. Summer Sch. of Clinical Training at the Boston City Hosp., 1955-61; asst. dir., The Summer Sch., 1961--; sec., Bd. of Governors, Inst. of Pastoral Care; v.p., Bd. of Dirs., Prot. Youth Center, Baldwinville, Mass.; Adult Program Comm. of New England Area Coun. of YMCA; Comm. on Juvenile Delinquency of the Dept. of Soc. Relations of the Mass. Coun. of Chs.; Soc. Concerns Com. of the Newton

Coun. of Chs.; Assn. of Sem. Profs. in the Practical Field; Accredited Hosp. Chaplain by the Amer. Prot. Hosp. Assn.; Accredited Chaplain Supervisor by the Inst. of Pastoral Care; Home: 31 Paul St., Newton Centre, Mass. 02159; Office: 210 Herrick Rd., Newton Centre, Mass. 02159

BROOKS, Jerome Bernard, educator, b. Houston, Tex., Mar. 20, 1932; s. Osburn B. and Agnes (Harrison) B.; M.A. Eng., Notre Dame Univ.; Columbia U.; Loyola, Los Angeles; Coll. teaching, 1962--; Week-end parish worker; author, "The Negro Priest in White Parishes," Religious Education (Jan-Feb. 1964); Home and Office: 5700 N. Harlem Ave., Chicago, Ill., 60631.

*BROOKS, Thomas Howard, b. Annapolis, Md., Nov. 22, 1919; s. Thomas and Ethel (Osborne) B.; B.S., Morgan State Coll., 1944; B.D., Sch. of Rel., Howard Univ., 1947; candidate for Master's degree in Rel. Ed.; m. Myrtle Holloway. Pastored: Ridgely-Huntsville Meth. Ch., Seat Pleasant, Md., 1945-48; Upper Marlboro, Md. Union Meth. Ch., 1948-50; St. James Meth. Ch., White Sulphur Springs, W. Va., 1950-53; Sharp St., Meth. Ch., Sandy Spring, Md., 1953-61; present: Jerusalem Meth. Ch., Rockville, Md., 1961-66; Hughes Meml. United Meth. Ch., 1966-present; pres., Bd. of Ed. of Wash. Conf., Meth. Ch.; v.p., Montgomery Coun. NAACP; v.p., Rockville Min. Alliance; mem., Bd. of Dirs., Wesley Found., Howard Univ.; Mason; Office: 18 54th St., SE, Wash., D.C.

BROOMFIELD, Oree, Sr., b. Mississippi, May 19, 1927; s. F.M. and Hettie (Thomas) B.; Lane Coll., 1950-52; A.B., Miss. Indust. Coll., 1954; B.D., Gammon Theol. Sem., 1957; m. Wylene A. Parham; Children--Oree, Jr., Leonard Bernard; ordained minister in Chrstn. Meth. Episc. Ch., 1952; pastor, Rock of Ages, Augusta, Ga., 1954-56; Emanuel Chapel, West Point, Ga., 1956-58; Anderson Chapel, 1958-64; St. John, Wash., D.C., 1964-present; Dept. of Rel., M.I. Coll., Holly Springs, Miss., 1959-64; pres., Marshall County Voter's League, 1959-62; sec. to two Bishops of the C.M.E. Ch.,; mem., Bd. of Dir. ofJ.H. Meridith Edu. Found., Jackson, Miss.; Mason; Oddfellow; part-time Dir. of Chrstn. Educ. of the N.Y.-Wash. Annual Conf. of the C.M.E. Ch.; Home: 2301-36th St., S.E., Wash., D.C. 20020; Office: 2801 Stanton Rd., S.E., Washington, D.C.

BROWN, Benjamin Harrison, tchr., b. Roberson Co., N.C., May 28, 1888; s. Angus and Mary Jane B.; B.S., Johnson C. Smith, 1915-19; B.D., 1920-22; m. Mamie Phar; Children--Mary Harriet, Chasten, Atmos Chasten, Benjamin A., Jr., Barbet Chasten; pastor, Faison Meml. United Presby. Ch., Clinton, N.C.; tchr. Hayswood Sch., 1923-24; pastor, The Second Presby. Ch., 1926-40; tchr. the County & Bladen C.H.S. for eight years; commissioner from Cape Fear Presbytery, Catawba Synod to the Gen. Assembly of the United Presby. Ch., Cincinnati, O.; Home: P.O. Box 393 W&D Elizabethtown, N.C.; Church: Faison Mt. United Presbyterian Ch., Clinton, N.C.

BROWN, Clifton H., b. Oct. 3, 1918, Danville, Ky.; s. Rufus H. and Lucinda; A.B., Wilberforce Univ., 1939-43; Ohio State, 1954-56; Paine Sem., 1956-57; m. Betty K. Fleming; Children--Clifton, Deborah; pastor, Bethel A.M.E. Ch., Lebanon, O.; St. Paul A.M.E. Ch., So. Charleston, O.; Quinn A.M.E. Ch., Marion, O.; St. Paul A.M.E. Ch., London, O.; present: Dir. Pub. Safety and Park Rec., Marysville, O.; Consult. Dir. Personnel, Ray, Lewis & Sons, Marysville, O.; Dir. of Lib. and Trng., O.M. Scott & Sons, Co., Marysville, O., present; Adv., Dist. Boy Scouts of Amer. Explorers, 1956-64; City Councilman, Marysville, O., 1968-72; v. chrmn. Central Ohio Water and Pollution Bd., 1958-60; mem. Am. Legion Post 79, 1946-68; v. chrmn. Co. Bd. of Mental Health, 1968; mem. Co. Bd. of Retarded Children, 1964-68; Pres. Union Co. Coun. of Chs. (2 yrs.); WW II, European Theatre, 1943-45; Awards, 6 Bronze stars, Citation Combat; mem. Minister's Ohio Annual Conf. A.M.E., mem. Masons; Omega Psi Phi; Republican; articles on: Pollution abatement; Home: 240 N. Maple St., Marysville, Ohio 43040; Office: 505 W. Third St., Marysville, Ohio 43040

BROWN, Edward Lynn, b. Tenn., Apr. 2, 1936; s. Willie T. and Ocie (Royal) B.; A.B., Lane Coll, 1960; B.D., Interdenom. Theol. Center, 1963; m. Gladys Stephens; Children--Alonzo Victor; pastor, Salem C.M.E. Ch., Jackson, Tenn., 1936--; New Hope C.M.E. Ch., Gibpson Co., 1957-58; St. Paul C.M.E. Ch., 1958-60; Bolivar, Tenn.; St. Mary C.M.E. Ch., Chattanooga, Tenn., 1961-; Greenwood C.M.E. Ch., 1963--; Memphis, Tenn.; Assoc. Dir., Youthwork, First Episc. Dist., C.M.E. Ch.; lesson writer, Intermediate's Sun. Sch. Quarters, C.M.E. Ch.; chrmn., Church work, Memphis Branch, NAACP;

v.p., C.M.E., Memphis Min. Alliance; sec.; Interdenom. Min. Alliance, Memphis; Alpha Phi Alpha; Intl. Soc. of Theta Phi; staff mem. (writer), Gen. Bd. of Chrstn. Educ., C.M.E. Ch.; co-author, Reconciliation: A Mission of the Christian Church, Bible Study Booklet; Home: 1066 S. Bellevue, Memphis, Tenn.

BROWN, Ertemus Temmie, b. Memphis, Tenn. 1909; s. Chesterfield and Eliza B.; Howe Inst., Jackson, Tenn.; Lane Coll., Jackson, Tenn.; B.Th., B.D., Phillips Sch. of Theol., 1951, 1954; m. Katie Mae Tipton; Children--Mrs. Albertine Bell, Sheila; pastor, Tenson C.M.E. Ch., Rossville, Tenn.; Henning C.M.E. Ch., Henning, Tenn.; John Chapel C.M.E. Ch., Whitehaven, Tenn.; Phillips Chapel C.M.E. Ch., Miland, Tenn.; St. Paul C.M.E. Ch., Jackson, Tenn.; Featherstone Temple C.M.E. Ch., Memphis, Tenn.; Cater Tabernacle Ch., Orlando, Fla.; Trinity C.M.E. Ch., Miami, Fla.; Bowel Meml., Kan. City, Mo.; present pastor, Lewis Temple C.M.E. Ch., Grambling, La.; mem., Judicial Counc., C.M.E. Ch.; NAACP; mem., Bd. of Trustees, Miles Coll., Birmingham, Ala.; Home: J.F. Kennedy Ave., PO Box 514, Grambling, La. 71245.

BROWN, Frank Reginald, b. June 24, 1902, New York, N.Y.; s. Frank B. and Mary Virginia (Warren); A.B., Lincoln Univ., Oxford, Pa., 1932; M.A., Columbia Univ., N.Y., 1936; Diploma Adult Ed., 1953; Ed.D., Union Theol. Sem., N.Y., 1952; courses, Ohio State Univ. Sch. of Div., Univ. of Chicago, Hartford Sem. Found.; m. Fletcher Beatrice; Children--Reginald Willis; ordained Bapt. Chaplain, 1937; ordained A.M.E. Zion Ch., 1943; pastored New England, New York, Allegheny, West Central and Western, North Carolina Conf., A.M.E.Z. Ch., Commn. 1st Lt. Chaplains Corps, USA, Mar. 7, 1943; chaplain, 1943-46; Dean Hood Sem., Salisbury, N.C.--present; Hd., Sci. Dept. Va. Sem. and Coll., 1936-39; Prof. Hood Sem., 1946-53; del. A.M.E.Z. to 3rd World Coun. of Chs., Canada, 1964; 2nd Conf. Theol. Ed., Bristol, England, 1966; 11th World Meth. Conf., London, 1966; mem. Adult Ed. Assn. of Amer.; Natl. Coun. of N.C., Comm. on Fam. Life; Rel. Ed. Assn.; Amer. Acad. of Rel.; N.C. Tchrs. of Rel. Assn.; Rel. Research Assn.; Alpha Phi Alpha; Natl. Coun. of Chs. of Christ, N.C.; Home: 815 W. Thomas St., Salisbury, N.C. 28144; Office: Hood Sem., 800 Thomas St., Salisbury, N.C. 28144

BROWN, Henry, Junior bishop, b. Orangeburg, S. C., Jan. 5, 1914; s. John and Henrietta (Muller) B.; Pub. Sch., Orangeburg, S. C., Bible Way Trng. Sch.; m. Minnie Lee Onabitt; Children--Valarie, LaVonne, Henry Lewis, Joe Nathan, Maxine; pastor, Bible Way Church World Wide, Prince Frederick, Md., Organizer and Builder; Junior Bishop, Diocese in Eastern N. C.; mem. The Apostolic Inter-organizational Fellowship Conf.; Organized Recreation Area, Prince Frederick, Md.; Home: Route 1, Box 66-A, Prince Frederick, Md.

BROWN, James Walter, b. Edisto Island, S. C., Aug. 14, 1932; s. Benjamin J., Sr. and Viola (Searbrook) B.; A. B., Johnson C. Smith Univ., 1952-56; B. C., 1956-59; m. Katherine Hope; Children--Veronica Oveta, Alton Tyrone, Jacqueline Nina; pastor, Hopewell and Aimwell United Presby. Chs., of Walterboro, S. C., 1958-59; Sun. Sch. Missionary at Headquarters at Spartanburg, S. C.; current pastor, the Ladson United Presby. Ch., Columbia, S. C.; Home: 1401 Gregg, Columbia, S. C.; Church: 1720 Sumter, Columbia, S. C.

BROWN, Johnny Mack, b. Selma, Ala., Aug. 23, 1928; s. Ruben and Buela (Steel) B.; Ala. Luth. Coll., 1946; Immanuel Luth. Coll., Greensboro, N. C., 1951; m. Janet Odessa Colemon; Children--Mattie, Johnnie, Debra; current pastor, Holy Cross Luth. Ch. (Mo. Synod), Camden, Ala.; Home: P. O. Box N, Camden, Ala.

BROWN, Joseph Bernard, b. Canton, Miss., Oct. 1, 1912; s. Joseph and Easea L. (Davis); A. B. Rust. Coll., 1944; courses Garrett Theol. Sem., 1950; Northwestern Univ., 1955; M. A. Chrstn. Ed., McCormick Theol. Sem., 1963; m. Ida Eiland; ordained, Meth. Ch., pastored chs. Northern Miss., 1949-51; Smith Meml. Meth. Ch., Chgo.; assoc. pastor, St. Mark Ch., St. James, Woodlawn Meth. Chs., Chgo. area; present pastor, Clair Meth. Ch., Chgo.; tchr. public schs., Miss., 1944-46; Home 7254 S. Champlain Ave., Chgo., Ill. 60619; Office: 3540 W. 15th St., Chgo., Ill.

BROWN, Philip Rayfield, III, educator, b. New Orleans, La., Oct. 7, 1917; s. Philip R., Jr. and Eleanora B.; A. B., Xavier Univ., 1939; B. Th., Union Theol. Sem., 1943; D. D. (hon.), United Theol. Sem., 1964; m. Bertha Duckett, 1938; 2 sons, Lt. Philip R., IV, James Elliot; 2 daus., Eleanor Brown Miller, Norma Brown West;

pastor, Pleasant Grove Bapt., Ch., N. O., La., 1947-59; Calvary Miss. Bapt. Ch., W. Monroe, La., 1959--; Instr., Natl. Sun. Sch. & B. T. U. Cong., 1942--; Instr., United Theol. Sem., Monroe, La.; pastor, Travelers Rest Miss. Bapt. Ch., Tallulah, La., 1962--; pres., Ideal Bapt. Sun. Sch. & B. T. U. Cong., N. O. La., 1942-59; Dean, La. State Bapt. Conv., Dept. Chrstn.
E Edu., 1945--; Dir. Pub. Rel., La. Bapt. Conv., 1950--; Dean, Chrstn. Edu., 10th Dist. Bapt. Assn., Northeast, La.; Dean, Twin City Leadership Trang Inst., Monroe-West Monroe, La.; Pres., Monroe Chap. NAACP, 1959-62; Spec. Investigator, City of N. O. Utilities Dept., 1950-59; Sec. Bd. Trustee, United Theol. Sem., Monroe, La.; v. chrmn., Negro Chamber of Comm., Monroe, La.; Recipient Highest Merit Award, City of N. O., La.; Office: Calvary Miss. Bapt. Ch., Ninth & Linderman Sts., W. Monroe, La.

BROWN, Revl Amos, b. Macon, Ga., Sept. 6, 1919; s. Eugene & Julia Wynn (B); Univ. of Alaska Bible Sch., 1956-58; Manhattan Bible Inst., currently; ordained, 1965; Assoc. pastor, Little Widows Might Bapt. Ch., NYC, (2-1/2 yrs.); Upper Room Bapt. Ch., Brooklyn, N. Y.; pastor Greater Friendship Bapt. Ch., Brooklyn, currently; refrig. & air condition instr.; U. S. Army, 1941-62; awards, Good Conduct Medal; mem., Mason; Home: 952 Lafayette Ave., Brooklyn, N. Y. 11221

BROWN, Robert Leslie, soc. worker, b. Little Rock, Ark., May 26, 1927; s. William R. and Verlie (Acklin) B.; 1944, B. A. Jarvis Chrstn. Coll., Hawkins, Tex.; m. Vera Mae (Bowser) B.; Children-- Robert Jr., Carol, William Arthur; pastor, 1948-59, 12th St. Chrstn. Ch., Austin, Tex.; 1951-present, Maple St. Christian Ch., Lockland, O.; Soc. worker, 1959-present; Hamilton Coun. Welfare Dept., Cincinnati, O.; mem. Pride of the Valley Prince Hall Masonic Lodge (Master); Interdenom. Min. Alliance of Greater Cincinnati; Soc. Serv. Assn. of Greater Cincinnati; NAACP; Home: 608 Maple St., Lockland, Ohio 45215

BROWN, Theophile Waldorf, tchr., b. Richmond, Va., Aug. 24, 1925; s. Thomas Harvey and Sarah Etta (Taylor) B.; B. A. Ed., Classics, Phil., St. John's Univ., Collegeville, Minn., 1952; M. A., Latin, Univ. of Ottawa, Can., 1961; ordained priest, Roman Cath. Ch., 1956; Chrmn. of

Classics, St. Augustine's Coll., Nassau, 1957--; Monastery organist and choir dir.; Home: St. John's Abbey, Collegeville, Minn.

BROWN, Thomas Emerson, b. Crystal Springs, Miss., Dec. 7, 1888; s. Augustus G. and Lula (Scott) B.; Moody Bible Inst., Chgo., Ill.; m. Clarinda Bridges; Olivet Bapt. Ch., Chgo., Ill., 1916; Lily Dale Bapt. Ch., 1918; Progressive Bapt. Ch., Chgo., Ill., 1919; mem. Bd. Dir., Providence Hosp., Chgo., Ill., 1945-55; Bd. Dirs., Chgo. Bapt. Inst., 1958; Bd. Dirs., M. I. & E. Min. Coll., West Point, Miss.; recipient, Citation for Human Brotherhood, Citizen's Salute, Station WBEE; mem. NAACP; Home: 3616 Wentworth Ave., Chgo., Ill. Church: 3658 Wentworth Ave., Chgo., Ill.

BROWN, Warren M., b. Knoxville, Tenn., Aug. 14, 1941; s. Wm. M. & Edith M. (B); A. B., Knoxville, Coll., Tenn., 1964; Interdenom. Theol. Center, Atlanta, courses, 1964; m. Aurelia Elizabeth Sanders; Children--Angelyne, Anita Elise; pastor, Oak Grove Afr. Meth. Episc. Zion Ch., 1958-61; Youngs Temple, Morristown, Tenn., 1961-62; Jones Temple, Waynesville, N. C., 1962-65; Walls Temple, Albany, N. Y., 1965-present; former dir., Postal Services, Knoxville, Coll., 1964-65; Asst. dir., Trinity Inst., Albany, N. Y., Jan. 1966-67; dir. Survey & Service, Troy, N. Y., O. E. O., Mar., 1968; mem. Bd. & Treas. Albany Urban League, 1967; Bd. Coun. of Chs., Albany, N. Y.; Chrmn. Auditor, Western N. Y. Conf. A. M. E. Z. Ch.; mem. Kappa Alpha Psi; Adv. Bd. NY State Com. on Adult Ed., 1966; Home: 39 Delaware St., Albany, N. Y. 12202; Office: 27 Delaware St., Albany, N. Y. 12202.

BROWN, Willard Gardner, b. Chester, Pa., April 11, 1915; s. Willard Albert and Alberta (Gardner) B.; B. A., Wilberforce Univ., 1944; B. D., Payne Theol. Sem., Wilberforce Univ., 1946; courses, Jersey City Coll. of Educ.; m. Evelyn Morgan; Children--Willard, Mrs. John C. Brown, Mrs. Alvin Chisolm, Paul; pastor, Zion Meth. Ch., Sharptown, Md., 1947-49; St. Paul's Meth. Ch., Berlin, Md., 1949-57; Clair Meml. Meth. Ch., Jersey City, N. J., 1957-62; St. Marks Meth. Ch., Montclair, N. J., 1962--; tchr., Pub. sch. sys., Jersey City, N. J., 1960-62; mem., NAACP; Bd. of Rel. Ed.; Northern N. J. Conf.; Div. of Radio & TV of N. J. Coun. of Chs.; Clergy Club of Montclair; Min. Assn. Montclair; Alpha Phi Alpha;

Masons; articles to Montclair Times; Home: 36 Fulton St., Montclair, N.J. 07042; Office: 51 Elm St., Montclair, N.J. 07042.

BROWN, William Henry, tchr.; b. Rockford, Ill., Apr. 2, 1915; s. Harry Leslie and Mary Magdaline (Crosswright) B.; 1948, A.B. Washburn Univ.; 1960, No. Carolina Univ.; m. Ruth Margaret Bynes B.; Children--Jessie Curtis, Gerald Andrew, Rosemary, William, Jr., Willa Ruth; pastor, 1935-39 Second Chrstn. Ch., Atchison, Kan., 1939-48, Second Chrstn. Ch., Topeka, Kans.; 1942, Third Chrstn. Ch., Kansas City, Kans.; 1948-49, Ninth St. Chrstn. Ch., Des Moines, Iowa; 1949-53, Cleveland Ave. Chrstn. Ch., Winston-Salem, N.C.; 1953-56, Jones St. Christian Ch., Bluefield, West. Va.; 1956 (present), Min. Gen. Program, Piedmont Tri-State Dist. tchr: Dir. of Night Sch. for Adults, Reidsville, N.C. (typing, shorthand, business English); Kappa Alpha Psi; Home: 703 Melrose St., Reidsville, N.C.; Church: 1103 Ware St., Reidsville, N.C.

*BROWNE, Hosea Harold, b. Ark., June 29, 1918; s. E.B. and Sarah; B.A., Philander Smith Coll., Little Rock, Ark., 1941; B.D., Howard Univ., Sch. of Rel., 1948; Children--Sallie, Barbara, Hosea, Marshal; pastor, Good Will Bapt. Ch., Wash., D.C., 1954-66; Good Shepherd Bapt. Ch., Wash., D.C., 1966-67; Good Shepherd Bapt. Ch. 1967-present; tech. librarian, Navy Dept., 1956--; mem., former bd. of trustees, Holiday House, Wash., D.C.; former Kalorama Rd. Coun.; Adams Morgan Better Neighborhood Conf.; Coun. for Neighborhood Projects Community; Civic Midway Assn.; Bapt. Min. Conf.; Mason; hon. mem., IDU; U.S. Army, 4 yrs.; award, Soldiers Medal for bravery; ed., Crack Your Sides Laughing; Home: 610 Rittenhouse St. N.W., Wash., D.C.; Office: 6300 E. St. S.E., Capital Hghts, D.C.

*BRUCE, John Carlyle, b. British Guiana, Feb. 20, 1923; s. Samuel Alexander and Susan (Adams) B.; A.B., Livingstone Coll., 1958; B.D., Howard Univ. Sch. of Rel., 1962; summer courses, Amer. Univ. Wesley Sem., Wash. D.C., 1961; m. Jossie C. Wilson; Children--Denise Christine; Carlyle Alexander; Lynda Verleigh; tchr., British Guiana; ordained a min. Afr. Meth. Episc. Zion Ch., 1955; pastor, Calvary & Salem A.M.E.Z. Chs., Lancaster, S.C., 1955-56; St. John's A.M.E.Z. Ch., Mocksville, N.C., 1956; asst. pastor, John Wesley

A. M. E. Z. Ch., Wash., D. C., 1956-58; pastor, Green Meml. A. M. E. Z. Ch., Portland, Me., 1958-62; St. Paul A. M. E. Z. Ch., Johnson City, Tenn., 1958-62; Petersburg A. M. E. Z. Ch., Circuit, Rogersville, Tenn., 1964-65; mem., NAACP Central Maine; Portland Coun. of Human Relations; Ministerial Assn.; Coun. Community Concerns; Civil Rights Commn.; Home: Fairground Rd., Greenville, Tenn. 37743.

BRYANT, Harrison James, bishop, b. Georgetown, S. C., Nov. 20, 1899; s. Richard and Annie B.; A. B., Allen Univ., 1932; B. D., Payne Theol. Sem., 1935; D. D. (hon.) Payne Theol. Sem.; Wilberforce Univ., Ohio; Kittrell Coll., N. C.; LL. D. (hon.), Campbell Coll., Jackson, Miss.; Monrovia Coll., Liberia, W. Africa; m. Edith Drusesella Holland; Children--Cynthia Ann, Hazel Joan, Harrison, J., Jr., John Richard, Eleanor Louise; pastor, Jones Chapel African Meth. Episc. Ch., Lexington Co., S. C., 1926-27; Chappell Sta. A. M. E. Ch., Columbia, S. C., 1927-32; First A. M. E. Ch., Xenia, O., 1932-35; dean, Jackson Theol. Sem. and pastor of River View A. M. E. Ch., 1935-36; St. Paul A. M. E. Ch., Zanesville, O., 1936-39; St. Paul A. M. E. Ch., Lexington, Ky., 1939-42; St. John's A. M. E. Ch., Baltimore, Md., 1942-49; Bethel A. M. E. Ch., Baltimore, Md., 1949-64; elected bishop, A. M. E. Ch., May 1964; vice-pres., Md. Coun. of Chs., 1960-62; mem. Exec. Bd., Baltimore Branch NAACP, 1964--; chaplain, Mason; Home: 3513 Dennlyn Rd., Baltimore, Md.

*BRYANT, Lawrence Chesterfield, college prof., b. Battleboro, N. C., Feb. 16, 1916; s. Emmitt and Gattie Bland (Cooper) B.; B. S., Shaw Univ., 1940; B. D., Sch. of Rel., Howard Univ., 1950; M. A., New York Univ., 1950; Ed. D., Univ. of Va., 1959; m. Ila Thomas; Children--Lawrence Michael, Cynthia Ann; pastored: First Bapt. Ch., Mt. Hope, W. Va., 1950-51; First Bapt. Ch., Harrisonburg, Va., 1953-56; Fla. Meml. Coll., 1956-60; New Mount Zion Bapt. Ch., Orangeburg, S. C., 1960-61; Prof. of Educ., Jackson Coll., Jackson, Miss., 1956; Fla. Meml. Coll., St. Augustine, Fla; present, prof. ed., So. Carolina State Coll., Orangeburg, S. C., 1960-64; Alpha Phi Alpha, Palmetto Edu. Assn., Nat. Ed. Assn., Amer. Tchrs. Assn., Amer. Personnel and Guidance Assn.; Chairman, Research Comm.; managing ed., Exploration in Education (Research journal at So. Carolina State Coll.) Home: Box 1615, College Station,

Orangeburg, S. C.

BUDFORD, Kenneth Leroy, b. Pulaski, Va., Aug. 17, 1917; s. C. Jordan and Marie (Jenkins) B.; A. B., City College, New York, 1939; B. Th., Bloomfield Sch. of Rel., Newark, N. J., 1942; D. D., Miller Univ., Phila., Pa., 1960; m. Lillian M. Glanton; Children--Selma L. (Mrs. D. Ross Turpeau); Kenneth Leroy, Jr., Lawrence J. Thompson (step-son); Myron H. Thompson (step-son); pastor, Brighton Rock A. M. E. Z. Ch., Portsmouth, Va., 1939-41; St. James A. M. E. Z. Ch., Matawan, N. J., 1941-45; St. Luke A. M. E. Z. Ch., New Castle, Pa. 1945-47; Martin Chapel A. M. E. Z. Ch., Los Angeles, Calif., 1947-56; Butler Chapel A. M. E. Z. Ch., Tuskegee, Ala., 1956--; v. p., Tuskegee Civic Assn., and Chrmn. of its Community Welfare Comm.; mem. Tuskegee, Ala., Bi-Racial Comm.; mem., Macon County (Ala.) Progressive Democratic Comm.; A. M. E. Z. chaplain to students, Tuskegee Inst.; Chrmn, Comm. on counseling - Rel. life Council, Tuskegee Inst.; mem. and past-pres., Tuskegee Min. Coun.; mem. Bd. of Trustees, Chrstn. Educ. Dept.; mem., Home and Ch. Div. Chrstn. Educ. Dept.; mem. Connectional Budget Bd.; mem. Episc. Comm.; Trustee, Lomas Hannon Jr. Coll., Greenville, Ala.; Chrmn. Bd. of Examiners, Ala. Conf.; Chrmn. Budge Comm., Ala. Conf.; Office: Butler Chapel, A. M. E. Zion Church, Tuskegee, Ala.

BUIE, George Charles, Jr., b. Detroit, Mich., Mar. 21, 1929; s. George and Rosie Anna Buie; A. B., Livingstone Coll., 1960; B. D., Hood Theol. Sem., 1960; advanced studies, Pacific Sch. of Rel.; m. Helen Abner; Children --Catrina L.; Michael V.; pres., Minis. Assn., Vallejo, Calif., 1961; Vallejo Federated Leadership Coun., 1962; pastor, Greater Cooper Zion Ch., Oakland, Calif.; YMCA; instruc., Jr. & Sr. High Sch., 1961-65; Army, 1961-63; Korea Medical Corps; Syngman Rhee medal; four battle stars; Mason; Home: 1626 65th Ave., Oakland, Calif.; Office: 1420 Myrtle St., Oakland, Calif.

BULLOCK, Richard David, Jr., educator, b. Drewry, N. C., May 6, 1908; s. Richard D. and Mary (Burwell) B.; Shaw Univ., Raleigh, N. C., 1929-34; No. Carolina Coll., Durham, N. C., 1948; m. Verlena Rowland (dec.) 1 dau., Ernestine V. Boon; Malnaye Bullock; pastored: Children's Chapel Cong. Ch., Graham, N. C., 1946-52; Corinth Cong. Ch., Youngsville, N. C., 1959-64; present pastor: Mt.

Zion Cong. Ch., Henderson, N. C., 1960-64; principal, Sandy Grove Elem. Sch., 1934-38; principal, Nutbush Sch., Manson, N. C., 1938-52; mem. N. C. Teacher's Assn.; Steering Comm. on By-laws and Constitution, United Ch. of Christ; Home: Box 25, Manson, N. C.; Office: Route 1, Drewry, N. C.

BUNTON, Henry Clay, bishop, b. Tuscaloosa Co., Ala., Oct. 19, 1904; s. Isaac and Sarah L. B.; B. D., Fla. A & M Coll., Tallahassee, Fla., 1941; Th. M., Iliff Sch. of Theol., Denver, Colo., 1952; D. D. (hon.) Texas Coll., Tyler, Tex., 1955; m. Estelle McKinney, Alfreda Gibbs; Children--Mattye Lou, Marjorie, Henry C., Jr., Joseph Ronald; pastor, C. M. E. Ch., Ala., Fla., Ark., Tex., Denver, Colo., and Memphis, Tenn.; elected Bishop, C. M. E. Ch., May 1962; now serving Seventh Episc. Dist., C. M. E. Ch., 1962--; mem., C. M. E. Bd. of Chrstn. Edu.; dir., Adult and Youth Work for the Gen. Bd.; dean, Fla. Sch. of Chrstn. Workers; dir., Chrstn. Edu. for Jackson-Memphis Tenn. Annual Conf.; Bd. of Dir., Henderson Coll.; mem. Southern Christian Leadership Conf.; trustee of Miles Coll.; Bd. of Trustees, Paine Coll. Frat. organizations; Mason; Phi Beta Sigma; Chaplain, US Army, 1943-46, 1948-50; Major; 3 Battle Stars; Awards from: The Citizens Non-Partisan Registration Comm., Memphis, Tenn.; The Interdenom. Min. Alliance, Memphis, Tenn.; NAACP, Memphis, Tenn.; Award of Merit, Radio Sta. WDIA, Memphis, Tenn.; Democrat; asst. ed., Chrstn. Index and Sun. Sch. Lesson writer for the C. M. E. Ch. (formerly), now chrmn. of the Publishing Bd. of the C. M. E. ch.; Home: 6524 16th St. NW, Wash., D. C.

BURGESS, John Melville, bishop, b. Grand Rapids, Mich., Mar. 11, 1909; s. Theodore Thomas and Ethel Inez (Beverly) B.; B. A., M. A., Univ. of Mich.; B. D., Episc. Theol. Sem., 1934; LHD (hon.), Univ. of Mich., 1963; LL. D., Augustine's Coll, 1963; m. Esther Taylor; Children--Julia, Margaret; priest-in-charge: St. Phillip's Grand Rapids, Mich., 1934-39; St. Simon of Cyrene, Woodlaw, Cincinnati, O., 1938-46; Epsc. chaplain, Howard Univ., Wash., D. C., 1946-56; Canon, Wash. Cathedral, 1951-56; Arch-deacon of Boston, Supt. Episc. City Mission, 1956-62; Suffragan Bishop of Mass., 62-69; Bishop of Mass. 1969--present; Del. Central Com. World Coun. Chs., India, 1952; Del. World Coun. Chs., New Delhi, 1961; Del. Gen. Conv. Episc. Ch., 1951-61;

Spec. lecturer, Episc. Theol. Sch. ; trustee, St. Paul's Coll. , Lawrenceville, Va. ; chrmn. , Boston Comm. on Race and Rel. ; Home: 46 Berwick Rd. , Newton Centre, Mass. ; Office: One Joy St. , Boston, Mass.

BURGESS, Monroe Abel, church official, b. Baltimore, Md. , June 19, 1910; s. Monroe Abel and Gertrude (Anderson) B. ; Oakwood Coll. , Huntsville, Ala. ; Union Coll. , Lincoln Nebr. ; m. Willie Mae Herbin; Children-- Monroe A. , III, James Edward; pastored: Calvary Seventh-Day Adventist Ch. , Norfolk, Va. , 1933; Gill St. , S. D. A. Ch. , Petersburg, Va. , 1936; Ethan Temple S. D. A. Ch. , Pittsburgh, Pa. , 1941; Ebenezer S. D. A. Ch. , Phila. , Pa. , 1948-52; tchr. , Wash. Union Acad. , 1932; Departmental sec. , Allegheney Conf. of S. D. A. , 1945-47 and 1952-56; present: Depart. sec. , Central States Conf. of S. D. A. , 1956--; Pres. Interdenom. Min. Alliance, 1961-63; Ch. sec. , NAACP-Region IV, 1961-63; comm. mem. K. C. Coun. on Rel. and Race, Citizens Co-ordinating Comm. , Operation Alphabet; Democrat; Independent Voters Assn. ; Kansas City, Mo. ; Home: 3028 Agnes St. , Kansas City, Mo. 64128; Office: 2528 Benton Blvd. , Kansas City, Mo. 64127.

BURKE, DeGrandval, teacher, b. Matthews, N. C. , Dec. 25, 1909; s. Crawford A. and Florence (McCauley) B. ; 1934-38, B. S. , 1944, B. D. (Sem.), Johnson C. Smith Univ. ; 1946-47, M. A. , McCormick Theol. Sem. ; m. Mattie Cannon; Child--DeGrandval, Jr. ; tchr. , 1944-61, Boggs Academy, Keysville, Ga. ; pastor, Emmanuel United Presbyterian Ch. , Charlotte, N. C. ; co-pastor, 1961-63, Biddleville-Emmanuel United Presby. Ch. ; instr. Religious Edu. , J. C. Smith Univ. , 1946-50, 1962; awards: "Minister of the Year" of Catawba Synod, 1956; mem. Alpha Kappa Mu Nat. Soc. ; Phi Beta Sigma; Republican; initiated two spec. projects in Chrstn. Edu. , which were pub. in our church's nat. magazine, and were adopted by the Synod of Catawba as part of its adult work program. They were known as Project 20 and the Alpha Chi Omega Chrstn. Fellowship; Home: 1414 Onyx St. , Charlotte, N. C. ; Office: Box 314, Johnson C. Smith Univ. , Charlotte, N. C.

BURKS, Olliw Allen, presiding elder, b. Montgomery, Miss. , Sept. 3, 1883; s. Sylas and Mary Ann (Johnson) B. ; Campbell Coll. , Jackson, Miss. , 1919-21; D. D. (hon.), Payne Theol. Sem. , 1925; m. Madora Harris; Children--

Morjorie May Tutus Sims; pastor, Afr. Meth. Episc. Chs., Miss., Ohio, W. Va., N. C.; current presiding elder, A. M. E. Ch.; mem. Democratic Party; Mason; Oddfellow; Pythian; Home: P. O. Box 1265, Logan, W. Va.

BURNETT, Marshall H., b. Trenton, Tenn., Aug. 18, 1907; s. Wilson H. and Lizzie (Witson) B.; A. B., Lane Coll., 1933; S. T. B., Lane Coll., 1934; courses, A. I. State Univ.; m. Estella Sykes; daughter--Brenda Neal; pastor and supr., C. M. E. Chs., Jones & New Hope, 1933-34; Beach Grove; Milan Ct., Brownsville Ct., 1935-44; Lane Chapel C. M. E. Ch., Humboldt, Tenn., 1950-56; Dist. supr., Brownsville Dist., 1960--present; prin., Jr. High Sch., 4 yrs.; tchr., High Sch., Humboldt City Schs., 26 yrs.; state dir., Young People's Jubilee, 16 yrs.; trustee, Lane Coll., 12 yrs.; sec. of Bd. of Trustee, Lane Coll.; pres., Humboldt Civic Club; pres. Humboldt Min. Alliance; Mason; Democrat; Home: 502 W. Main St., Humboldt, Tenn. 38343

BURNS, Charles Dixon, b. Greenville, Miss., June 23, 1932; s. Washington and Charlie (Dixon) B.; Catholic Univ., Wash., D. C., 1963; Divine Word Sem., Bay St. Louis, Miss. (4 yrs. theol.); ordained priest, Roman Cath. Ch., Mar. 17, 1962; Vocation. Dir., Divine Word Missionaries South. Province; Ex. Sec. Natl. Urban Task Force, US Cath. Conf., 1969--; second v. p. of Interreligious Found. Comm. Organization (IFCO); mem. Com. of Black Churchmen; Home: 4001 14th NE., Wash., D. C.; Office: 1313 Mass. Ave., N. W., Wash., D. C.

*BURRELL, Emma Pinkney, tchr., b. Prince Geo. Co., Md., Aug. 9, 1912; d. Arthur Phillip and Florence Butler P.; A. B., Howard Univ.;, Miner Teachers Coll., B. D., Howard Univ., 1959; m. George W. Burrell; prin., Fanguire High Sch., Irvin, Va., 1932-34; tchr., D. C. Eve. Sch. and sub. tchr., 1934-40; government employee, 1940-58; pastor, St. Mary's Larger Parish, 3 yrs.; St. Luke Meth. Ch., Jackson, 1956-63; asst. pastor, Asbury Meth. Ch., Wash., D. C., 1954-55; pastor, Mt. Vernon Meth. Ch., 1963--; First woman in Central Jurisdiction to rec. full clerigical status; Home: Rt. 1 Box 306A, Jessup, Md., 20794; Office: Mt. Vernon Meth. Ch., 1910 W. Va. Ave. N. E., Wash., D. C. 20002.

BURRELL, Louis Stephen, S. V. D., Franklin, Pa., May 28,

1936; s. Luther and Vera (Jackson) B.; A.A., Divine Word Sem., Conesus, N.Y., 1959; B.A., Div. Word Sem., Techny, Ill., 1965; asst. curate, St. Anselm's Cath. Ch., S. Mich. Ave., Chicago, Ill., 1965--; mem. Soc. of Divine Word; Home: 1003 Elm St., Franklin, Pa. 16323; Office: S. Michigan Ave., Chicago, Ill. 60637.

BURRUS, Lloyd Andros, b. Fairfield, N.C., June 29, 1920; s. George B. and Mallissia (Johnson) B.; B.A., Shaw Univ., 1945; B.D., Crozer Theol. Sem., Chester, Pa., 1949; further study: McGill Univ., Canada; widower; Children--Cecilia Elizabeth; asst. pastor, Queen St. Bapt. Ch., Norfolk, Va., 1942-45; pastor, Zion Bapt. Ch., Camden, N.J., 1949-54; Ebenezer Bapt. Ch., Newburgh, N.Y., 1954-58; founder and pastor, Zion Temple Bapt. Ch., Jamaica, N.Y., 1958--; chrmn., Home Missions Bd., Progressive Natl. Bapt. Conv., Ind.; tchr., Bordentown Sch., N.J., 1950-51; guest lecturer, O.T. History, Camden, N.J., YMCA, 1953; consultant, So. Jersey Bd. of Probation & Parole, 1950-53; pres., Newburgh, N.Y. Branch NAACP, 1955-57; organizer, Newburgh, N.Y. Citizens' Comm., 1956; one of 12 honorees for 1952 Afro-Amer. Newspapers, Camden, N.J., and Pa. area; Democrat; mem., Phi Beta Sigma; Home: 1147 Noble Ave., Bronx, N.Y.; Office: Zion Temple Bapt., Van Wyer Expressway, 105th Ave., Richmond Hill, Jamaica, N.Y.

BURTON, H.L., editor; A.B., Lane Coll.; North Western Coll.; Th.M., Sch. of Rel. - Butler Univ.; D.D. (hon.), Lane Coll.; further studies at Cath. Univ. of America; pastor, 6 yrs. Mt. Olive, So. Carolina, St. Mathew (N. Carolina - 6 mos.); Israel Metropolitan, Wash., D.C., 9-1/2 yrs; present: pastor, Phillips Temple Chrstn. Meth. Episc. Ch., Indianapolis, Ind. Annual Conf. sec.-treas., C.M.E. Ch.; Dean, dir., tchr., Leadership Trng. Schs., C.M.E. Ch.; mem. ex. bd., Church Federation, Indianapolis, Ind. and vicinity; pres., Interdenom. Min. Alliance; plaque award, Lane Coll.; Branch pres., NAACP; Basileus chapter Omiga Psi Phi; Mason; Elks; Editor, C.M.E. Official magazine, The Eastern Index, 1954-62; Office: 1226 North West St., Indianapolis, Ind.; Home: 135 W. 21st St., Indianapolis, Ind.

BURTON, Horace Edward, b. Wilmington, Del., Oct. 23, 1923; s. Frederick D. and Bessie (Stewart) B.; Del.

State Coll., 1941-42; B.S., Wilberforce Univ., 1946-49; B.D., Payne Theol. Sem., 1949-50; Rutgers Univ., 1958-present; courses, Andover Newton Sem., 1961-62; m. Margaret Sammons; Children--Cynthia, Horace, Jr., Tracee Kim, Zina Ruthann; pastor, Clayton Circuit, A.M.E. Ch., 1951-53; Richard Allen A.M.E. Ch., Bermuda, 1953-57; Bethel A.M.E. Ch., Woodbury, N.J., 1957-60; St. Paul A.M.E. Ch., Cambridge, Mass., 1960-62; Bethel A.M.E. Ch., Springfield, Mass., 1962--; tchr., Pub. Sch. Sys., Woodbury, N.J.; staff, Boston Weekday Rel. Ed. Mass. Coun. of Chs.; sec., New England Annual Conf.; mem., Bd. of Trustees, New England Conf.; mem., Mayor's Citizens Adv. Comm., Cambridge, Mass., 1961; pres., Central Square Interdenom. Min. Alliance, 1962; mem., NAACP; Steering Com of Conf. on Rel. and Race, 1965; Human Relations Commn., Springfield, Mass., 1966; US Army, 1943-46; mem., Alpha Kappa Mu; Senmer-Rekh; Alpha Phi Alpha; Home: 146 Thompson St., Springfield, Mass.

BUSSEY, Talmage D., b. Camden, Ala., Nov. 22, 1897; s. Annie E. Williams; A.B., Miles Coll., Birmingham, Ala., 1946; courses, Iowa State; B.D.; D.D. (hon.), Birmingham Bapt. Coll., 1942; Selma Univ., Selma, Ala., 1948; m. Viola L. Long; Children--Mrs. Timothy Bottoms; pastor, Rising Star Bapt. Ch., 1921-31; Triadstone Bapt. Ch., 1931-37; sec., Ala. Bapt. Sun. Sch. & B.T.U. Congress, 1932-67; sec.-treas., Birmingham Bapt. Coll., 1927-47; pres., Birmingham Bapt. Coll., 1947-67; instr., Birmingham Bapt. Coll., 1927-60; trustee, Selma Univ., Selma, Ala.; author pamphlets, Some Biblical and Historical Facts on the Jewish Sabbath and the Lord's Day; Christian Education; Tithing; Home: 1300 2nd Ave., W., Birmingham, Ala.

BUTLER, Charles William, educator, b. Dermott, Ark., May 4, 1922; B.A. Philander Smith Coll., Little Rock, Ark.; B.D., Union Theol. Sem., NYC.; res. Ph.D.; Columbia Univ.; further study, U. of Nancy, Nancy, France, Wayne State Univ., Clinical Trng., Harper Hosp., Detroit, Mich., Merrill Palmer Inst., Detroit, Mich.; m. Helen Odean Scoggins; Children--Charles, Jr., Keith, Kevin, Beverly; military service, WW II, 4 campaign stars; asst. pastor, St. James Presby. Ch., N.Y.; Released Time Instr., NYC Mission Soc.; instr., Bapt. Center N.Y.; instr., Biblical Lit. & Rel., Morehouse Coll., Atlanta, Ga., 1951-54; pastor, Metropolitan Bapt. Ch.,

Detroit, Mich, 1954-63; pastor, New Calvary Bapt. Ch., Detroit, Mich., 1963--; Supervisor, Gen. Div., Natl. Bapt. Sun. Sch. & B. T. U. Cong., Chrmn., Christian Educ. Commn., Wolverine Bapt. State Conv., Mich.; mem. Theol. Study Commn., Priorities Evaluation Commn. Bd., Met. Det. Council of Chs., Mayor's Comm., Commission on Children & Youth (Det.) Mich. Coun. of Chs., Interdenom. Min. Council, Ministerial Counc., Home Fed. Savings & Loan Assn., Detroit; Boy Scouts; YMCA; Natl. Negro Bus. League; Booker T. Washington Bus. Assn., the Pioneers, Alpha Phi Alpha; Office: 3975 Concord Ave., Det., Mich., 48207.

BUTLER, Ernest Daniel, b. Connersville, Ind., Oct. 11, 1913; s. Daniel Taniel and Margaret Lucile B.; Franklin Coll., 1933; Moody Bible Sch., 1935; Payne Theol. Sem., 1936; m. Mary Louise Jones; Children-- Ernest E., Robert J., William D., Albert R., James L., Grayce L. Florence (Mrs.), Mary Ann; pastored, Mt. Zion Bapt. Ch., Connersville, Ind.; First Bapt. Ch., Noblesville, Ind., 1949-59; Second Bapt. Ch., Bloomington, Ind., 1959--; Dir. Southeastern Dist. Youth Camp, 1946-49; 1960-64; Dir. Youth Work, Ind. Bapt. State Conv., 1964; Chrmn., Southeastern Dist. Benevolent Bd., 1962--; Dir., YMCA, Indiana U., 1962-65; mem. Bd. Dir., Blomington Family Counciling Agency, 1963--; Chrmn., Bloomington Fair Housing Comm., 1960-64; vice-chrmn., Bloomington, Mayor's Human Relations Com.; vice-chrmn. Indiana Citizens Fair Housing Comm., 1963--; Rec., Service Award, Boy Scout Activities, 1962-63; mem. Campus Ministers, Ind. U., Inter-Faith Council, Ind. U.; Author, The Church Looks at Sex, 1963; Home: 509 W. 8th, Bloomington, Ind.; Church: 321 N. Roger St., Bloomington, Ind.

BUTLER, Grady, b. Greenville, S. C., June 29, 1935; s. Clarence E. and Nina (Westfield) B.; B. S., Tuskegee Inst., 1955-59; B. D., Interdenom. Theol. Center and Morehouse Sch. of Rel., 1959-62; m. Berthea LaConyea; Children-- Danielle LaClaire, Louise LaConyea; asst. minister, Emmanuel Bapt. Ch., Atlanta, 1959-60; chaplain, Migrant Ministry, Va. Coun. of Chs., Summer 1960; asst. minister, W. Hunter St. Bapt. Ch., 1961-62, 1965--present; pastor, Jubilee Bapt. Ch., Taylors, S. C., 1962-65; camp counselor, Bethlehem Center Camp, summer, 1962-66; program worker, Bethlehem Community Center, Atlanta, Ga., 1962--present; mem., Mason; Big Brothers of Atlanta; Atlanta Soc. Workers Club; Home: 803 Duffield Dr., N.W. Atlanta, Ga. 30318

BUTLER, J. Ray, educator, b. Roseboro, N.C., Aug. 5, 1923; s. Amos D., Sr. and Mary F. B.; A.B., Shaw Univ., 1951; B.D., Shaw Div. Sch., 1953; D.D. (hon.) Friendship Coll., Rock Hill, S.C., 1964; m. Marion Geola Lucas; 4 sons; pastorates: Mt. Olive Bapt. Ch., Fayetteville,. N.C. (2 yrs.) ; First Bapt. Ch., Creedmoor, N.C. (6 yrs.); New Chrstn. Bapt. Ch., Rose Hill, N.C. (3 yrs.); Ebenezer Bapt. Ch., Wilmington, N.C., 1954--; Pres., Interdenom. Min. Alliance, Wilmington & vicinity, 1956-58; Sec., 1960--; Pres., Wilmington Civic League, 1960--; mem. Adv. Bd., Phyllis Wheatley YWCA, Exec. Bd. mem., Wilmington Adult Chap. NAACP; mem. Alpha Phi Alpha; Vice chrmn., Gen. Bd., Gen. Bapt. State Conv., N.C., Inc., 1960--; mem. Extension teaching staff, Shaw Univ., In-service Ministers, 1957--; Moderator, Western Union Association, 1956--; mem. Exec. Bd., Theol. Alumni Assn., Shaw Univ., Raleigh, N.C.; mem. Exec. Bd., Lott Carey Bapt. For. Miss. Conv., Inc.; Exec. Bd., Hampton Min. Conf.; Natl. Bapt. Conv. USA, Inc; Home: 211 S. Seventh St., Wilmington, N.C.; Church: 209 S. Seventh St., Wilmington, N.C.

BUTLER, Joseph LeCount, b. Washington, D.C.; s. Xavier and Edith (Davis) B., B.A., Union College; m. Noetta Melvene Keller; Children--Joseph, Jr., Davis Meredith, Joel Kenneth; pastored Seventh Day Adventist Chs. in Lincoln, Nebr., 1 yr., Topeka, Kans., 6 yrs., Wichita, Kansas, 5 yrs.; present: Omaha, Nebr. Home: 2114 Sprague St., Omaha, Nebr. 68110; Office: 3028 Bedford St., Omaha, Nebr.

BUTTS, E. Wellington II, b. April 17, 1937, Newport News, Va.; s. Wm. Davis Sr. and Leona Elanor (B); A.B. Fisk Univ., Nashville, Tenn.; B.D. McCormick Sem., Chgo., Ill.; courses, Princeton Sem.; m. Bennie E. Booker; Children--E. Wellington III, Kelem Briam Amakari; asst. pastor, W. Presbyn. Ch., St. Louis, Mo., 1962-64; pastor, Bethany Presbyn. Ch., Englewood, N.J., 1964--; mem. Natl. Com. of Inquiry; chrmn. Ecum. Relations Com. of Palisades Presbytery; mem. Gen. Coun. Presby.; v.p. Englewood Min. Assn.; Teaching Assn., N.Y. Theol. Sem.; treas., Com. on Ch. and Race, N.J.; Bd. of Dirs., Nat. Com. Negro Churchmen; Asst. State Clerk, Gen.

Clerk, Gen. Assembly United Presbyn. Ch.; mem. Com. for Dept. of Min. Relations; mem. Concerned Presbyn.; Presby. Interracial Counc.; treas., Churchmen's Coalition; Leader Ecum. Encounter to Greece and Ethiopia; mem. Com. of Preparations for World Coun. of Chs. Assembly of Missions; awards, Man of the Year, 1967, Englewood, N. J.; Home and Office: 309 Englewood Ave., Englewood, N. J. 07631.

*BYRD, Cameron Wells, b. Ithaca, N. Y., Nov. 10, 1935; B. A., Univ. of Buffalo, N. Y., 1953-57; B. D., Howard Univ. Sch. of Rel., 1957-60; Certificate Clinical Pastoral Care, Andover Newton Theol. Sch.; m. Maxine; Children--two; research aide, Bd. of Redevelop., Buffalo, N. Y., 1954; chaplain of Migrant Agr. Workers, New York State Coun. of Churches, 1958; pastor, Bradley Meml. Bapt. Ch., Oak Bluffs, Mass., 1959; advisor, Student Chrstn. Assn., Howard Univ., 1958-59; student asst., Peoples Cong. Ch., Wash., D. C., 1960-62; asst. pastor, Peoples Cong. Ch., Wash., D. C., 1960-62; dir. of Halfway House, Plymouth Cong. Ch., Detroit, Mich., 1962-63; pastor, Christ Ch., United Ch. of Christ, Detroit, Mich., 1962-69; dir. Ecu. Center, Roxbury, Mass., 1969-present; award, Fellow of The Amer. Assn. of Theol. Schs. in the US and Canada, 1959; mem. Camp Management Com., Detroit Metro. Assn., Unit Ch. of Christ; Comm. on Soc. Concerns, Mich. Conf., UCCC; Chrstn. Ed. Com., Detroit Assn., UCC; Chrstn. Ed. Fellowship, UCC; Audio-Visual Review, Detroit Coun. of Chs.; Greater Detroit Ministerium Detroit Coun. of Chs.; Interdenom. Min. Alliance of Greater Detroit; S. W. Detroit Inter-Faith Redevelop. Project; Legislative Principles Com., Mich. Coun. of Chs.; Div. of Chrstn Ed., Natl. Council of Chs.; World Serv. Com., Downtown YMCA; Youth Com., Downtown YMCA; Ministerial-Advisory Com., Planned Parenthood League, Inc.; chrmn. Grass Roots Organization Workers (GROW) of S. W. Detroit; Bd. of Dir., Prot. Comm. Services, Detroit, Mich.; Office: The Ecumenical Center, 75 Crawford St., Rox-Bury, Mass. 02121.

BYRD, Vernon Randolph, b. Enoree, S. C., July 1, 1931; s. Syfellas and Josephine; A. B., Allen Univ. 1949-51; Boston Univ., 1951-63; D. D. (hon.), Kittrell Jr. Coll.; m. Theora Lindsey; Children--Michele, Vanesa Dawn, Vernon, Jr., Christopher Paul; asst. pastor, Charles St. African Meth. Episc. Ch., Roxbury, Mass., 1951-53;

pastor, Macedonia A. M. E. Ch., Seaford, Del., 1954-59; pastor, St. Paul's African Meth. Episc. Ch., Hamilton, Bermuda, 1959--; pres., Min. Assn., Bermuda; arbitrator bet. gov't and local Bermuda Industrial Union; mem., Phi Beta Sigma; Mason; Home: 196 Sharpnack, Phila., Pa.; Office: St. Paul A. M. E. Ch., Box 361, N. Shore, Pembroke West, Hamilton, Bermuda.

BYRD, William Theodore, Jr., b. Mocksville, N. C., Dec. 22, 1921; s. Wm. Theodore and Mattie (Wilson); A. B., Lincoln University 1941; S. T. B. 1944; m. Perzealia (Holmes); Children--Cecelia Alice; Wm. Theodore III (deceased), Paul Anthony; Dir. of Friendship House, Lackawanna, N. Y., 1944-49; Minister of Grace Presby. Ch., U. S. Louisville, Ky., 1949-60; Minister of Lawrence Chapel United Presby. Ch. and Bethel Presby., 1960, Dandridge, Tenn.; mem. NAACP, Min. Alliances, Morristown Assn. (Interracial and Interdenom.); pres., Louisville Branch NAACP 1957; pres., Min. Alliance - Morristown, 1964; mem. Omega Psi Frat.; Elks; Knight of Pythian Lodge; sermons pub. (newspaper) and radio broadcasts; Home: 414 Harrison St., Morristown, Tenn.; Office: Lawrence Chapel United Presby. Ch., 414 Harrison St., Morristown, Tenn.

CABEY, Edwin Herbert, b. Montserrat, West Indies, Aug. 17, 1930; s. John Matthew and Alfredine (Donoghue) C.; A. B. Phil., Divine Word Sem., Techny, Ill., 1958; S. T. B., S. T. L., Pontifical Gregorian Univ., Rome, Italy, 1959-63; Pontifical Biblical Inst., Rome, Italy, 1963--; ordained priest, Roman Cath. Ch., Mar. 17, 1962; Home: Divine Word Sem., Bay St. Louis, Miss.; Office: Collegio del Verbo Divino, Roma-Ostiense 5080, Italy.

CADDELL, Gerwood Lincoln, b. Woodbrook, Trinidad, W. I., Jan. 10, 1906; s. Benjamin and Margaret; B. A., Wilberforce Univ., 1934; B. D., Payne Theol. Sem., 1936; D. D. (hon.); Shorter Coll., Little Rock, Arkl., 1941; Campbell Coll., Jackson, Miss., 1941; Payne Theol. Sem., 1946; Edward Waters Coll., Jacksonville, Fla., 1948; LL. D. (hon.); Campbell Coll., Jackson, Miss., 1943; Monrovia Coll., Liberia, W. Africa, 1955; m. Virginia Jackson; Children--Karen (Mrs. Blair); pastor, Bethel A. M. E. Ch., N. Y. C., 1931; ordained Deacon, 1932; ordained Elder, Allen Chapel, Dayton, O., 1934; pastor,

Bethel Franklin, Payne Chapel, Huntingdon, Pa., 1937; Dean of Theol., Campbell Coll., Jackson, Miss., 1937-38; pastor, Asbury Chapel, Waynesburg, O.; Quinn Chapel, Cleveland, O., 1938; St. Paul, Westside, Cleveland, O., 1939; lectr., Men's Study Club of Blessed Sacrament Guild; sec., N. O. Annual Conf., 1943-51; mem., Trustee, Coll of Ed. and Indust. Arts, Wilberforce, O.; trustee, O. Annual Conf., 1952; mem., O. Annual Conf. Finance Com.; chaplain, Civil Defense Corps, Steubenville, O.; inst. officer, Boy Scouts of Amer., Ft. Steuben, 1952; exec. bd., Prot. Coun. of Chs., Steubenville, 1953-57; pres., Negro Community Coun., Steubenville, 1953-54; pres., O. Valley Min. Alliance, 1953-57; mem., Steubenville Boxing and Wrestling Commn., 1954-58; pres., Phyllis Wheatley Fellowship Assn., Steubenville, 1954-55; tchr., Steubenville Pub. Sch. System, O., 1956; mem., Adv. Com., Jefferson Planning Commn., 1956; Notary Public, Jefferson Co., Steubenville, 1957-60; mem., Akron Min. Assn., 1959; trustee, Summit Co. Mental Health Assn., 1962-67; chmn., trustee bd., Coun. of Chs. of Greater Akron, 1964; Bd. of dir., Payne Theol. Sem.; mem., Adv. Housing Commn., 1965; treas., N. O. Conf., 1966; chrmn., Bd. of Exam., N. O. Conf., 1966; awards--Citation of Merit, 3rd Episc. Dist., AME Ch., 1954; Cert. of Merit, Quinn Meml. AME Ch., Steubenville, O.; Alumni Citation of Honor, Wilberforce Univ., 1956; Cert. of Appreciation, Heart Fund Assn., 1956; Citation, Mental Health Assn., Summit Co., 1964; mem., Phi Beta Sigma; in preparation--book, History of Abraham; author, Barbara Heck: Pioneer Methodist; Home: 746 Kolb St., Akron, O. 44307; Office: 739 St. Clair St., Akron, O. 44307.

CALBERT, William Edward, Chaplain, Lt. Col., b. Lemoore, Calif., June 11, 1918; s. Wm. R. and Sadie (Hackett) C.; A. B., San Francisco St. Coll., 1949; B. D. Berkeley Bapt. Div. Sch., 1952; M. A. Teachers Coll., Columbia Univ., N. Y., 1963; U. S. Army chaplain's sch., courses, 1952, 60, 62; m. Madlyn Williams; Children--Rose, Muriel, Katherine, Yvonne, Wm. E., Jr.; pres. Berkeley Bapt. Div. Sch., 1951-52; Commissioned Chaplain, 1952--present; Camp Roberts, Calif., 1952-53; Korea, 1953-54; Ft. Knox, Ky., 1954-56; Germany, 1956-57; Group Chaplain, Travis AFB, Calif., 1958-63; Military Scholarship Student, Columbia Univ., NYC., 1962-63; Staff & Faculty, US Army Chaplains Sch., Ft. Hamilton,

N. Y., 1963-67; Vietnam, 1967-68; instr., Ft. Hamilton, N. Y., 1963-65; Dep. Chrmn. of Non-resident Instruction Dept., & Chief of Reserve Components Br., Asst. dir. Army-wide extension course program; dir. Professional Studies of Army Reserve Component Chaplains; Monitor, Army-wide character guidance program; part-time dir., Rel. Ed., Concord Bapt. Ch., Bklyn, N. Y., 1964-67; Bapt. Leadership schs.; mem. Prot. Chapel Com.; v. p., Fairfield, Travis-Vacaville Min. Assn., 1961-62; awards--Bronze Star Medal (Oak Leaf Cluster); Army Commendation Medal; European Campaign Medal; WW II Victory Medal & Army Occupation Medal; Korean Service & U. S. Service Medals; Vietnam Campaign Medal; Army Reserve; Amer. Campaign; Army Certificates of Achievement; author: "Army Subjects Schedule 21-42, Character Guidance Instruction During Basic Training"; pub. by Dept. Army, Oct. 1964; contributor, Army Field Manual, 16-5, The Chaplain, 1967; author, Character Guidance Program Course (for Army Service Schs.); ed. of many correspondence courses, U. S. Army Chaplains Sch.; Home: 1226 Jackson St., N. E., Wash., D. C. 20017; Office: Hdqs., 1st U. S. Army, Office of the Army Chaplain, Ft. George C. Meade, Md., 20755.

CALDWELL, John Martin, b. Henry County, Ky., Sept. 15, 1902; s. John Martin and Anna (Hobbs) C.; A. B., Evansville Coll., 1949; B. Th., Simmons Univ., 1930; D. D. (hon.), Simmons Univ., 1945; m. Maude Alice Johnson; Children--James, Naomi, John R., Evelyn Ruth, Gloria D., James Martin, Ann Mary; pastor, Riverview Bapt. Ch., Louisville, Ky., 1 yr.; Pleasant Point Bapt. Ch., 2-1/2 yrs.; Zion Bapt. Ch., Evansville, Ind., 1932--; moderator, Southern Dist. Assn.; State Dean of Rel. Ed. of Ind., 14 yrs.; tchr., Natl. Bapt. Cong., 15 yrs; v. p., Bi-racial Minister's Assn.; Citation by Pres. Roosevelt for service on the draft bd. in WW II; pres., NAACP, Evansville Branch, 15 yrs.; mem., Mason; author: Zion Pulpit (annual pamphlet of sermons); Home: 830 E. Gum, Evansville, Ind.; Office: 1800 So. Governor, Evansville, Ind.

CALHOUN, Clyde Livingston, b. Marlboro Co., South Carolina, Feb. 20, 1926; s. Hugh Livingston and Isadora (Stubbs) C.; A. B., Claflin Coll., 1951, B. D., Gammon Theol. Sem., 1955; m. Birdadean Jamison; ministry, Walhalla, S. C., 1854. 56, Barberg Co., 1957-59; Jefferson Charge, Jefferson, S. C., 1960-63--; Old Bethel Meth.

Ch., Charleston, S.C.; mem., Mason; Home: 20 Felix St., Charleston, S.C.; Office: 222 Calhoun St., Charleston, S.C. 29403.

*CALHOUN, Raymond L., b. Ennis, Tex., Mar. 27, s. Carl C. and Sallie (Warner) C.; B.S., Lane Coll., 1942; B.D., Howard Univ. Sch. of Rel., 1945; MTW Catholic Univ., Wash., D.C., 1959; m. Mary U. Jackson; Children-- Carl, Raymond, Marilyn; pastor, Williams Temple Chrstn. Meth. Episc. Ch., Phila., Pa., 1945; instr., Texas Coll., Tyler, Tex., 1947; pastor, Hopps Meml. C.M.E. Ch., Syracuse, N.Y., 1948-55; Miles Meml. Ch., Wash., D.C., 1956-59; Williams Inst. C.M.E. Ch., NYC, 1959-63; Dir. Program & Service, Congreg. Ch., Broadway, NYC, 1963--; mem., Alpha Phi Alpha; Bd. mem., NAACP; former pres., NAACP; Thesis: Action Research in Community Planning; Office: 211 W. 56th St., New York, N.Y. (Broadway Congregational Church).

CALHOUN, William Edward, b. Carrollton, La., Dec. 26, 1932; s. Fred D. and Henrietta (Hill) C.; Morehouse Coll., 1949-53; The Sch. of St. Philip Neri for Delayed Vocations, Latin Cert., 1957; Catholic Univ., Wash., D.C., Grad. studies, 1963--; ordained priest, Roman Cath. Ch., May 25, 1963; served U.S.A.F., 1952-56; mem. Alpha Phi Alpha; Home: 135 Griffin, N.W., Atlanta, Ga.; Office: Caldwell Hall, Box 74, Cath. Univ. of Amer., Wash., D.C. 20017.

CALLENDER, Eugene St. Clair, b. Boston, Mass., Jan. 21, 1926; s. Arthur St. Clair and Eva Valeria (Graham); A.B., Boston Univ., 1947; B.D., Westminster Theol. Sem., 1950; grad. studies: Union Theol. Sem., 1953-55; m. Lemoine DeLeaver; Children--Renee, William, Leslie; assoc. pastor, Second Chrstn. Ref. Ch., Paterson, N.J., 1950-53; founder of The Mid-Harlem Community Parish, 1955-59; assoc. pastor, Ch. of Master, 1959-61; current pastor, Ch. of the Master, 1961--; consultant to the Taconic Found., N.Y., chrmn., Harlem Neighborhoods Assn.; moderator, The Presbytery of NYC United Presby. Ch.; mem., Bd. of Dir., Sheltering Arms Children Service; v.p., NY Branch, NAACP; Bd. of Harlem Youth Opportunities Unlimited; Omega Psi Phi; Mason; Home: 2160 Madison Ave., New York, N.Y.; Office: 360 Morningside Ave., New York, N.Y.

CALVIN, Willie James, b. Dallas, Tex., Mar. 31, 1913; s. Will and Lula (Page) C.; B.D., Bishop Coll.; m. Bernice Fields; Children--Sylvia, Willette; pastor Galilee Bapt. Ch., Marshall, Tex., 10 yrs.; Mt. Zion Bapt. Ch., 1961--; mem., Bapt. Missionary & Educational Conv.; contributing ed., Natl. Voice, Nat. Bapt. Conv., Inc.; mem., Bd. of Urban League, Milwaukee; dean, Wisconsin State Congress, Natl. Bapt. Conv.; mem., Mason; Home: 4346 N. 16th St., Milwaukee, Wisc. 53209; Office: 210 Garfield, Milwaukee, Wisc.

CAMERON, Johnnie Earl, b. Hattiesburg, Miss., June 11, 1932; s. A.C. and Courtney; B.S., Rust Coll., 1957; B.D., Amer. Bapt. Sem., 1956; m. Mrs. Johnnie Earl Cameron; Children--Jonetta, John Earl, Jr.; pres., Natl. Bapt. Student Union, 1954; Ambassador to Republic of Panama for 10 wks., 1954; pastor, Second Bapt. Ch., Oxford, Miss., 1955-56; New Hope Bapt. Ch., Meridian, Miss., 1958-59; Calvary Bapt. Ch., Laurel, Miss., 1960-63; current pastor, Faith Tabernacle Bapt. Ch., Hattiesburg, Miss.; candidate, U.S. Fifth Cong. Dist., 1964; dir., Hattiesburg Ministers' Project for the Natl. Coun. of Chs.; mem., Assn. for Civic Improvement; chrmn., Hattiesburg Assn. for Civic Improvement; mem., Southern Leadership Conf.; Home: 401 Ashford St., Hattiesburg, Miss.

CAMPBELL, Abraham Alexander, b. Jackson, Tenn., Apr. 16, 1909; s. Alfred J. and Melvinnie (Ellison) C.; courses, Am. Bapt. Theol. Sem., 1944; m. Nancy Alberta Grandberry; Children--Abraham Alexander, Jr., pastor, Lower Salem & New Hope Bapt. Chs., 1935-40; Columbus M.B. Ch., 1945; moderator, Hickory Grove Dist. Ann., 1940; pres., Tenn. Regular State B.M. & E. Conv., 1951; mem., Bd. of Dirs., Amer. Bapt. Theol. Sem., Nashville, Tenn., 1956; v.p., Natl. Bapt. Conv., USA, Inc., 1957; mem., Bi-Racial Com., 1959; sec., Terrell Meml. Hosp., 1956; Republican; Home: 2500 Carnes Ave., Memphis, Tenn.; Office: 324 N. Decatur, Memphis, Tenn., 38105

CAMPBELL, Amos B., b. Jan. 31, 1927, Montego Bay, Jamaica; s. Amos B. and Drucilla (Chennis) C.; A.B. Va. Union Univ., 1952; B.D. Va. Union Theol. Sem., 1955; M.A. Hartford Theol. Sem. Found., 1957; m. June 9, 1956; children--Alexis Maria, Paula Lynn, Edwin Alexander, Susan Winifred; supply pastor, Mt. Zion Bapt.

Ch., Staunton, Va., 1955; migrant chaplain, N.J. Coun. of Chs., Trenton, N.J., summer 1956; Dir. Rel. Ed., Middlefield Fed. Ch., Conn., 1956-57; Minister of Ed. and Assoc. Pastor Horace Bushnell Congl. Ch., 1960-62; Minister Chrstn. Ed., R.I. United Ch. of Christ, 1962--; 1958 Age Group Consult.; Ch. Sch. Leaders Club of Hartford; former tchr. British West Indies, 1945-47; lecturer Negro History; Chrstn. Ed. Com. Hartford Assn. Congl. Chs. and Ministers, 1959-61; v.p. Greater Hartford Coun. of Chs., 1962; mem., Housing Com. Hartford Coun. of Chs.; treas., Alumni Coun. Hartford Sem. Found., 1960-62; mem., Bd. of dirs. New England United Ministries in Higher Ed.; bd. mem. R.I. People Against Poverty; R.I. Asson. for Retarded Children; mem., Alpha Phi Alpha; NAACP; R.I. Coun. of Chs.; R.I. Congl. Chrstn. Min.; author: The Total Church Plans for Christmas (Booklet) Home: 32 Winsor Dr., Barrington, R.I. 02806.

CAMPBELL, Egbert Alexander, b. Jan. 31, 1927, Montego Bay, Jamaica; s. Amos and Drucilla; A.B., Va. Union Univ., 1952; B.D., Va. Union Theol. Sem., 1955; M.A., Hartford Sem. Found., 1957; m. Estelle Marie Jones; Children--Alexis, Paula, Edwin, Susan; ordained to ministry United Ch. of Christ, 1959; Dir. Rel. Ed., Middlefield Federated Ch., Middlefield, Conn., 1956-57; asst. pastor, Horace Bushnell Congl. Ch., Conn., 1957-61; Minister Chrstn. Ed., R.I. Congl. Chrstn. Conf. --present; Hist. tchr., high school, Jamaica, 1947-49; dorm. dir., Va. Union Univ., 1954-55; migrant chaplain, N.J. Coun. of Chs., 1956; Age Group Consult.; Ch. Sch. Leaders Club of Hartford, 1958-61; lecturer, R.I.; Bd. mem. R.I. People Against Poverty, 1966; Barrington Action Com., 1968; Bd. mem. R.I. Assn. for Retarded Children, Inc., 1967; awards - honorary Citizen of Rehoboth, Mass., 1968; mem. Bd. of Trustees, New England United Ministers in Higher Ed. Assn. (R.I.); mem., Alpha Phi Alpha; Home: 32 Winsor Dr., Barrington, R.I. Office; 2 Stimson Ave., Providence, R.I.

CAMPBELL, Jeffrey, tchr., A.B., B.D., St. Laurence Univ., 1933, 1935; ordained minister Unitarian Universalist Ch. 1935; present: tchr., Putney School, Putney, Vt., Office: Putney School, Putney, Vt.

CAMPBELL, Jesse, bishop, b. Dec. 24, 1910, Little Rock, Ark.; s. James C.; m. Agnes Goodwin; Children--Jessie, Clarola, J. Lorraine, Lillie, Eunice, Willie, J. Maurice,

Frezell, Wardell, Kenneth; ordained 1942; served as Deacon, asst. pastor; pastor, St. James Ch. of God in Christ, Chgo., Ill. (founder-present); Campbell Temple Ch. of God in Christ (founder), Robbins, Ill.; present, Bishop of sixth Diocese of Ill. and Africa of Ch. of God in Christ; Home: 1529 S. Central Park, Chgo., Ill. 60623; Office: St. James Ch. of God in Christ, 4147 W. Roosevelt Rd., Chicago, Ill.

CAMPBELL, Stephen Calhoun (Dynamo), educator, administrator, b. Newberry, S.C., June 6, 1895; s. Major and Melinda C.; Morris College, A.B., B.Th., 1920; D.D. (hon.) 1959; Benedict Coll., A.B., 1931; B.D., 1933; Wayne State, Ed. M., 1947; A.M., 1956; m. Beulah Clinkscales (1st); Pauline Finley; Children--Stephen, Jr., Finley C., Major C., Anthony C., Russell C., Ansonia; minister, 1911; tchr, 1920; pastor, St. Paul Bapt., 1924-42; pastor, Russell St. Bapt. Ch., Det., Mich., 1942--; Pres. Edu. Conv., Abbeville-Greenwood, 1922-42; Sec. Bapt. State Conv., S.C. 1931-36; moderator, Rocky River Bapt. Assn., 1927-43; Dean, State Sun. Sch. & BTU Cong., S.C., 1931-43; Dean, Wolverine State Cong., Mich., 1944-60; Sec., Met. Dist. Assn., Mich., 1944-60; Dir., Chrstn. Edu., Bapt. State Conv., Mich., 1963--; Pres., State Cong. of Chrstn. Edu., 1962--; Recipient, Ch. Leadership Award, 1954; Educational Leadership, 1962; Pub. Sch. Leadership, 1963; mem. Phi Delta Kappa, Alpha Kappa Delta, The Acad. of Rel. and Mental Health, Soc. for Scientific Study of Rel.; Author, <u>A Baptist Church Organized for Action;</u> and several other publications; editor, <u>Sr. B.T.U. Manual</u>; Home: 301 Boston Blvd., Detroit, Mich; Church: 8700 Russell St., Detroit, Mich.

CANNON, James Alexander, Sr., b. Gastonia, N.C., Mar. 13, 1920; s. U.S. and Emma (Grant) C.; Johnson C. Smith Univ., A.B. 1942; M.A. 1960; B.D. McCormick Theol. Sem., 1945; m. Edna Mae (Jones) C.; sons: James, Charles, Joseph; dau., Merrie Sue; 1945-52, pastor, Covenant Presby. Ch., Durham, N.C.; 1945-52 Coll. minister, N.C. at Durham, N.C.; 1955, asst. minister, Presby. Ch. of the Covenant, Det., Mich.; 1954-60, pastor, Lawndale Presby. Ch., Chgo., Ill.; 1960-62, Calvary Presby. Ch., Asheville, N.C.; current: Dir. of the Westminster Found. of the Synod of Catawba of the United Presby. Ch., USA; State of No. Carolina of the United Campus Chrstn. Ministry; mem. Asheville and Buncombe County Citizens Organization 1961-62; NAACP award, Psi Phi Frat. Man of the Year in Community Service; mem. Omega Psi Phi; N. C. Human Relation Council; Home: 1102 Gorrell St., Greensboro, N. C.; Church: 1102 Gorrell St., Greensboro, N. C.

CANNON, James Romeo, b. Marion, S. C., Nov. 2, 1911; s. Christopher Columbus and Rose (Green) C.; B. T. H., Howard Univ., Wash., D. C., 1932; S. T. B., Boston Univ., 1936; S. T. M., Boston Univ., 1946; courses, Amer. Univ., Wash., D. C., 1957; m. Mary Elizabeth Roberts; Children--James Forrester; David Wesley; pastor, John Wesley Ch., Salem, Va., 1935-40; E. Calvary Meth. Ch., Wash. D. C., 1941-44; asst. pastor, Asbury Ch., part-time dir. of Wesley Found., Howard Univ., 1947-48; Simms Meml. Ch., Wash. D. C., 1948-52; prof., Rel. and Phil., Wiley Coll., 1945-46; dir., Rel. activities and instruc. in Ethics and the Humanities, Morristown Coll., 1952-58; instr., Youth Inst., and WSCS Schs. of Miss., Md. Univ. and Morgan State Coll., 1947-64; del., Natl. Sem. on Human Rights, United Nations Plaza, N. Y., 1966; del., Meth. World Conf., London, Eng., 1966; pastor, Buena Vista Meth. Ch., Pittsburgh, Pa., 1959-64; mem., Citizens Coun. of Pa.; Outpost Mayor's Com. on Human Relations; mem. of the Neighborhood Coun. on Human Resources, organizer and sponsor of the Child Care Service Center in North Side, Pittsburgh; served civilian duty on Dist. of Columbia Ration Bds. and as Air Raid Warden Organizer; Omega Psi Phi; Mason; NAACP; mem., Boston Philosophical Club; has rec'd. cash awards for the following pub. articles: "Educating Youth for Value Ends," "The Family in God's Plan," "Three Links in God's Purpose," "The Profile in John Brown's Struggle for Freedom;" a newspaper series, Pittsburgh Courier, "The Negro Renaissance in America," "A New Revival," "Negro in the Methodist Church;" Home: 616 Taylor Ave., Pittsburgh, Pa. 15212.

CAREY, Archibald J., Jr., lawyer, b. Chicago, Ill., Feb. 29, 1908; s. Bishop Archibald J. and Elizabeth (Davis) C.; A. B., Lewis Inst., Chgo., Ill., 1928; B. D. Northwestern Univ., 1932; LL. B. Chgo., Kent Coll. Law, 1935; D. D. (hon.) Wilberforce Univ., Ohio, 1943; LL. D., Campbell Coll., Jackson, Miss., 1950; LL. D. (hon.) John Marshall Law School, 1954; m. Hazel Harper, Jan. 31, 1931; Children-- Carolyn Eloise; ordained to ministry, A. M. E. Ch., 1930; pastor, Woodlawn A. M. E. Ch., Chgo., 1930-49; Quinn Chapel A. M. E. Ch., Chgo., 1940--;

admitted to Ill. bar, 1936--; mem. Prescott, Taylor, Carey & Cooper; dir., counselor, Unity Mutual Life Ins. Co.; dir.-pres., Ill. Fed. Sav. & Loan Assn.; elected alderman, 3d Ward, Chgo., 1947, 51; Rep. nominee 1st Ill. Dist. U. S. Congress, 1950; Chrmn. Pres.'s Comm. on Govt. Employment Policy, 1957-61; v. chrmn., 1955-57; mem. U. S. del. 8th Gen. Assembly, UN, 1953; recd. 1st prize, Daily News Oratorical Contest, 1924; Edmund W. Burke law scholarship, 1935; mem. Chgo. Coun. Against Racial and Rel. Discrimination; Amer. Brotherhood (Chgo. br. Natl. Conf. of Christians and Jews); Alpha Phi Alpha Award of Honor, 1953; Abraham Schwartz Award for Human Relations, 1954; "Useful Citizen" award, 1954; Northwest Sertoma Club of Chgo. "Service to Mankind" award, 1956; Order of Eastern Star Natl. Citation, 1960; Home: 4934 S. Mich. Ave., Chgo., Ill. Office: 188 W. Randolph St., Chgo., Ill.

CARLEN, Gray L., b. Prentiss, Miss., Dec. 15, 1919; s. Sandy and Estella S.; Prentiss Inst., 1934; Children--Dorothy Nell McLendon, Joe McLendon; pastor, Brown Chapel Chrstn. Meth. Episc. Ch., Mt. Olive, Miss., 1949-50; Little Bethel, Terry, Miss., 1951; Warm Springs C. M. E. Ch., Terry, Miss., 1952; Garden C. M. E. Ch., Chgo., Ill., 1959-61; St. Paul C. M. E. Ch., Charleston, Miss., 1965; Center C. M. E., Indianola, Miss., 1967--; v. p., NAACP, Charleston, Miss.; Home: 501 Chandler St., Indianpola, Miss. 38751.

CARPENTER, Charles William, b. Stanford, Ky., May 1, 1886; s. James and Amanda C.; Tuskegee Normal and Indus. Inst., 1909; Garrett Biblical Inst., Evanston, Ill., 1917; Payne Theol. Sem., Wilberforce, Ohio; m. Linnia H. Hopkins; pastor, Afr. Meth. Episc. Ch., 18 yrs., New Duluth, Minn., Joliet, Ill., Crawfordville, Ind., French Lick, Ind., Marion, Ind., Muncie, Ind., Toronto, Ontario, Canada; presiding elder, Ontario Conf.; pastor, Second Baptist Ch., 1929--; v. p., Ann Arbor Ministerial Assn., 3 yrs.; Community Fund, YMCA Bd., Ann Arbor; Home: 216 Beakes, Ann Arbor, Mich. 48104.

CARRINGTON, Charles L., b. Austin, Tex., Oct. 27, 1909; s. Essex and Palice (Langham) C.; A. B., Samuel Huston Coll., Austin, Tex., 1930; B. D., Gammon Theol. Sem., Atlanta, Ga., 1933; M. A., Drew Univ., Madison, N. J., 1934; Columbia Univ.; New York Univ.; m. Muriel Jervis; Children--Charles Langham C. Jr.; asst. pastor, dir. of Rel. Edu., St. Mark's Meth. Ch., NYC, 1934-36; ordained Elder, The Meth. Ch., West Texas Conf., 1936; dir., Adult Guidance Bureau, NYC Bd. of Edu., 1936-38; pastor, Butler Meml. Meth. Ch., Bronx, N.Y., 1938-48; pastor, Brooks Meml. Meth. Ch., Jamaica, N.Y., 1941-64; Exec. sec., Bd. of Missions, The New York Conf., The Meth. Ch., 1964; mem., Del. Conf., 1937-64; dean, Conf. of Meth. Youth Fellowship Assembly, 6 yrs.; Dean of Area Pastor's Sch., 13 yrs.; chrmn, Conf. of Bd. of Chrstn. Soc. Concerns; Organizer and chrmn., Citizens' Com. on Juvenile Problems; Exec. mem., pres. (former), Jamaica Br., NAACP; Charter and bd. mem., Comm. Coun. of S. Jamaica; v.p., Queens Fed. of Chs.; mem., NY Metropolitan Area Planning Com., The Meth. Ch.; Home: 223-43 111th Ave., Queens Village, N.Y.; Office: 1228 North Ave., New Rochelle, N.Y.

CARRINGTON, John Elmer, b. New Rochelle, N.Y., Nov. 28, 1925; s. William O. and Pearl M. (Robinson) C.; B.S., New York Univ., 1950; B.D., Drew Univ., 1952; Union Sem., NYC, 1956; New York Univ., 1958-59; m. Virginia T. De Pass; Children--Marlene Diane, Jeanette Elaine; pastor, St. Luke Afr. Meth. Episc. Zion Ch., Westfield, N.J., 1949-50; Wallace Chapel A.M.E.Z. Ch., Summit, N.J., 1950-59; Willis Ave. Meth. Ch., Bronx, N.Y., 1959-63; Springfield Gardens Meth. Ch., NYC, 1963--; chaplain, Harlem Hosp., NYC Dept. of Hospitals, 1960--; dir., Chrstn. Edu., N.J. Annual Conf., A.M.E. Zion Ch., 1951-57; mem., NYC local sch. for Districts 15, 16, 1962-63; US Army Air Corps, 1944-46; Home: 131-29 Farmers Blvd., Jamaica, N.Y. 11434.

CARRINGTON, William Orlando, b. Georgetown, British Guiana, Oct. 30, 1879; m. Pearl Robinson; began pastorate 1906 in So. Tenn. Conf. Afr. Meth. Episc. Zion Ch.; pastor, First A.M.E. Zion Ch., Brooklyn, N.Y., 1936--; retired 1964; former prof., Hood Theol. Sem.; Howard Univ. Sch. of Rel.; author: Carry A Little Honey (book of sermons); Home: 480 Tompkins Ave., Brooklyn, N.Y.

CARROLL, Edward Gonzalez, chaplain, ch. official, b. Wheeling, W.Va., Jan. 7, 1910; A.B., Morgan Coll., 1930; B.D., Yale Univ., 1933; M.A., Columbia Univ., 1941; m. Phenola Valentine; children--Edward, Jr., Nansi Ethelene; pastor, St. Andrews Meth. Ch., Mt. Wash., Md

1933-34; pastor, John Wesley Meth. Ch., Salem, Va., 1934-35; pastor Meth. Ch., Grafton, W. Va., 1936-37; instr. in Bible and Philosophy at Morgan Coll., 1937-41; US Army Chaplain, 1941-45; assoc. sec. student YMCA, 1945-49, in NYC; assoc. pastor, St. Marks Meth. Church, NYC, 1949-53; pastor, Epworth Meth. Ch., NYC, 1953-55; pastor, Sharp St., Meml. Meth. Ch., Baltimore, Md., 1955-62; Dist. supt. Wash. Dist. Meth. Ch., Wash. D. C., 1962-68; pastor, Marvin Meml. U. Meth. Ch., Silver Spring, Md., 1968-present; mem., Gov. Comm. for the Employment of the Handicapped; Bd. of Balto. Urban League and NAACP, 1955-62; citation by the Gov. Safety Comm., 1961; Mason; author: "The Military Chaplaincy," in book We Have This Ministry. Home: 1710 Varnum, Wash. D. C.; Church: 1010 Dale Drive, Silver Spring, Md.

CARROLL, Richard Allen, b. Beachville, Md., May 14, 1928; s. Allen and Gladys; Va. Sem. & Coll., Lynchburg, Va., 1951-61; Howard Univ., Wash., D. C., 1961-63; Amer. Univ., Wash., D. C., 1964-; assoc. pastor, Rock Creek Bapt. Ch., Wash., D. C., 1962-68; founder, Mt. Zion Bapt. Ch., Wash., D. C., 1968--; pres. Mt. Bethel Leadership Training Sch.; asst. chaplain, D. C. Receiving Home; U. S. Army, 1946-49; mem. Omega Psi Phi; Mason; Urban League; Home: 5610 New Hampshire Ave., Wash., D. C. (N. E.) 20012; Office: 1300 Ingraham St. N. W., Wash., D. C. 20011.

CARTER, Churchill, b. Louisville, Ky., July 30, 1922; s. Churchill and Ethel (B.) C.; B. S., Wilberforce Univ., 1945; B. D., Payne Theol. Sem., 1945; M. Litt., Univ. of Pittsburgh, 1947; m. Alice Edwina Roston; Children--Toinette Ernestine, Kimberly Ann, Stephen Earl; pastor, St. James Afr. Meth. Episc. Ch., 1945-47; pastor, Mallory Chapel A. M. E. Ch., Edenborn and Masontown, 1947-48; St. Mark A. M. E. Ch., Wilkinsburg, 1948-50; pastor, Bethel A. M. E. Ch., Canonsburg, Pa., 1950; St. James A. M. E. Ch., Erie, 1950-57; current pastor, Park Pl. A. M. E. Ch., Homestead, Pa., 1957--; parole advisor, Penn. State Parole Bd.; former probation officer, Juvenile Court, City of Pittsburgh; part-time phys. ed. instr.; Salvation Army (former); ex. sec. Tawawa Sch. of Rel., Wilberforce Univ.; mem. Gov. Lawrence's State Juvenile Commn.; chrmn. Republican Party, Borough of Homestead, Pa., 1963-64; Bd. of Dir., Homestead Comm. Center, 1959-64; Bd. of Dirs., Payne Theol. Sem., 1960-

64; mem., Ex. Bd. Penn. Coun. of Chs., 1958-62; former Dean, Tawawa Sch. of Rel., Wilberforce Univ.; mem., Phi Beta Sigma, Mason, Frontiers Intl., Republican; Home: 215 E. Tenth Ave., Homestead, Pa.; Office: Park Pl. A. M. E. Ch., Homestead, Pa.

CARTER, George Washington, Jr., b. Houma, La., Oct. 1, 1901; s. George W. and Grace (Butler) C.; Columbia Univ.; Nebr. Wesleyan Univ.; B. D., Dillard Univ.; B. D., Gammon Theol. Sem.; M. S. T., Boston Univ.; D. D. (hon.), New Orleans Univ. & Gammon Theol. Sem.; m. W. Ruth Grissette; Children-- Carol Elaine, (Mrs. Manassas McGowan); superintendent, Peoples Community Center; supt., Mather Acad. and Browning Home, Woman's Div.; pastor, Omaha Neb., Lincoln, Neb., Manhattan, Kans.; Taylor Meml. Meth. Ch., Oakland, Calif.; Camphor Meml. Meth. Ch., Scotlandville, La.; supt., New Orleans Dist.; present pastor, First St. Meth. Ch., New Orleans; tchr., area pastor Sch. Meth. Ch.; sec. La. Conf., Meth. Ch., 12 yrs.; sec., Central Jurisdiction, US Forces, WW I; award, Plaque, Outstanding Work in Ministry to Youth; mem., Mason, Omega Psi Phi, Ch. Fed. (Interracial), New Orleans; Home: 4703 Annette St., New Orleans, La.

CARTER, Grover Hester, editor, b. Lishon, La., Jan. 14, 1889; s. William J. and Cora E. C.; A. B., Walden Univ.; B. D., Paine Coll., 1919; D. D. (hon.), Paine Coll.; principal, Minden High Sch., 1915-16; pastor, Mt. View Ch. of the Chrstn. Meth. Episc. Ch., Iva, S. C.; Holsey Temple C. M. E. Ch., Atlanta, Ga.; Holsey Temple, Macon, Ga.; Mitchell St., Atlanta, Ga.; editor, Eastern Index, C. M. E. Ch.; pastor of Trinity C. M. E. Ch., Augusta, Ga.; publishing agent of C. M. E. Ch., Jackson, Tenn.; pres., NAACP, Augusta, Ga.; mem., YMCA Bd. of Dirs., Atlanta, Ga; Trustee Bd., Paine Coll., Augusta, Ga.; Republican; instrumental in defeating the Speaker of the House as representative, 1947; also as pres. of NAACP, revived the Negro vote in Augusta; Home: 109 Shannon, Jackson, Tenn.; Office: 109 Shannon, Jackson, Tenn.

CARTER, Harold A., b. Selma, Ala., Dec. 24, 1936; s. Nathan M. and Liccie Beul; B. S., Ala. State Tchrs. Coll., Montgomery, Ala., 1956; B. D., Crozier Theol. Sem., Chester, Pa., 1959; D. D. (hon.) Lynchburg Sem., 1965; courses, Hebrew Univ., Jerusalem, Israel, 1963; Children--Weptanomah Washington; pastor, Court St. Bapt. Ch.

Lynchburg, Va., 1959-64; New Shiloh Bapt. Ch., Balto., Md., 1964-pres.; Instr. Va. Union Sem., Lynchburg, Va., 1959-64; pres. Lynchburg Bapt. Min., 1961-63; Bd. v.p., Balto. O.I.C.; Bd., NAACP; Convener Min. of Balto. for SCLC; Home: 3501 Sequoia St., Balto., Md. 21215; Office: New Shiloh Bapt. Ch., Balto., Md.

CARTER, James E., B.A., Lincoln Univ., Jefferson City, Mo., 1960; B.D., Garrett Theol. Sem. at Northwestern Univ., Evanston, Ill., 1964; grad. work, Lincoln Univ.; m. Mossie Blanton; dir., Chapel, Morristown Coll., Morristown, Tenn.; soc. worker, Cook Co. Dept. of Public Aid, Chgo., Ill.; pastor, Fowler-Clifton Meth. Ch., Chgo., Ill.; Arnold Meml. Meth. Ch., Chgo., Ill.; Home: 2243 S. Millard Ave., Chgo, Ill.; Office: 1330 S. Fairfield Ave., Chgo., Ill.

CARTER, John F., Jr., b. Yazoo City, Miss., Oct. 3, 1924; s. John F. and Mary C.; B.S., Alcorn A & M Coll., 1950; courses, Chicago Tchrs. Coll., 1953-55; Garrett Biblical Inst., 1955-57; Minister's Trng. Inst., 1959-61; m. Annie Ruth Evans; Children--Valerie Ann; Business tchr., Miss., 1950-51; soc. worker, Chgo., Ill., 1951-55; tchr., Chgo. pub. sch., 1955-66; pastor, Bethel A.M.E. Ch., Michigan City, 1965--; mem., Bd. of the Pre-Readiness Sch., Mich. City, 1965-67; chrmn. Bd. of Pre-Readiness Sch., Mich. City, 1967--; mem., Human Rel. Commn., 1965--; chrmn. Ministers' Union, 1967--; Michigan City, Ind.; Army, 1943-46; rec'd. four Battle Stars for service; Home: 317 E. Fourth St., Michigan City, Ind. 46360

CARTER, Lymell, b. Rusk, Tex., May 19, 1932; s. Lee and Annie; A.B., Tex. Coll., 1954; B.D., Lincoln Univ., 1957; m. Betty Jean; Children--Lymell, Annie, Nestor; Natl. Coun. of Chs., 1959-61; pastor, St. James C.M.E. Ch., Lynchburg, Va., 1961; Freeman Chapel C.M.E. Ch., Hopkinsville, Ky., 1962; Wesley Chapel, Clarksville, Tenn., 1963; Trinity C.M.E. Ch., Magnolia, Ark., 1963-65; St. Vestal C.M.E. Ch., El Dorado, Ark., 1965--; tchr.; mem., bd. of dir., Coun. on Human Rel., Ark.; pres., Min. Alliance, Magnolia, Ark.; Coun. on Human Rel., El Dorado, Ark.; v.p., Min. Alliance and program chrmn., mem., SCLC; NAACP; Home: 901 N.W. Ave., El Dorado, Ark. 71730

CARTER, Lynell Hampton, b. Burkeville, Va., Apr. 6, 1938;

s. Wm. & Eda Elizabeth; A. B., Boston Univ.; B. D., Lutheran Sch. of Theol., Chgo.; pastor, Christ Luth. Ch., Saskatchewan; St. Peters, Meacham, Saskatchewan, Canada, currently; Student chaplain, Grand Canyon; Mass. Gen. Hosp.; mem. TKE Fraternity; Home: Box 59, Young, Saskatchewan, Canada.

CARTER, Matthew Gamaliel, b. Danville, Va., Oct. 16, 1913, Clarence and Henrietta (Curley) C.; B. A., Va. Union Univ., 1939; B. D., 1942; courses, Columbia Univ. and Union Sem.; D. D. (hon.), Va. Union Univ., 1960; m. Frances Hill; Children--Bettye Frances, Nanette Carolyn C.; pastor, Zion Bapt. Ch., Petersburg, Va., 1940-41; ex. sec., Leigh St. YMCA, Richmond, Va., 1941-48; assoc. sec., SW Area Coun. YMCA, 1948-51; exec. sec., Spring St. YMCA, 1951-58; asst. dir., Assn. Press, Publication Dept., Natl. Coun. YMCA, 1958--; deputy mayor and dir. of public works, Montclair, N. J.; "Man of the Year" award, Phila., YMCA, 1962; Dis. Service award, United Negro Coll. Fund (No. Jersey Inter-Alumni) 1963; award for leadership in local govt. (Montclair Council Natl. Negro Women), 1964; mem., Kappa Alpha Psi; Sigma Pi Phi; Office: 215 Orange Rd., Montclair, N. J.; Office: 291 Broadway, New York, N. Y. 10007.

*CATCHINGS, Lincoln Maynard, YMCA sec., b. Houston, Tex., Oct. 30, 1914; s. Robert M., Sr., and Bessie G. (Maynard) C.; B. S., Prairie View Coll., Tex., 1935; B. D., Hoard Univ., 1941; M. A., Howard Univ., 1942; Univ. of Chicago, summer sessions; m. Rose M. Withers; Children--Lincoln M., Jr.; tchr., Jackson High Sch., Rosenberg, Tex., 1936-38; Southern Reg. Sec., Natl. Student YMCA, 1942-44; "Common Ground" worker, spec. consultant for chs. and rel. organizations, Dept. of Race Relations, Amer. Miss. Assn.; pastor, Plymouth Congr. Ch., Wash., D. C., 1947-53; asst., Dept. of Soc. Sci., Fisk Univ., 1945-47; chaplain, Congre. Chrstn. students, Howard Univ.; Natl. Assn. Sec., Commn. on Interracial and Intercultural Relations, Natl. Student Coun. YMCA, 1953-65; Dir. Develp. Coun. for Chrstn. Soc. Action, U. C. Christ Office of Intl. Develp. Coun. of Ch., Wash. D. C., present; mem., Bd. of Pub. Welfare for the Dist. of Columbia, 1952--; Bd. of Dirs., Wash. Urban League chrmn., Commn. on Community Life of the Wash. Fed. of Chs.; Dir. of Edu., Eastern Region of Alpha Phi Alpha Bd. of Trustees, United Comm. Serv. of the D. C.; Bd.

of Dirs., Wash. Fed. of Chs.; The Jesse Mitchell Club; nominating committee of Family and Child Welfare, Sec. of United Community Services; commentator: "Religion in the News" - Newscast over WCPM; awarded plaque for outstanding community service by Wash. Afro-Amer. Newspaper; mem., Bd. of Trustees, Planned Parenthood Assn., Wash. D.C.; ex. comm., Family and Child Welfare Sec., U.C.S.; Philosophy Club, Howard Univ.; Inst. of Religion, sponsored by Sch. of Rel., Howard Univ.; Bd. of Freedom Rally, Inc.; Fact Finding Committee of Interdenom. Min. Alliance (chrmn.); chrmn. committee to draft statement to Pres. Eisenhower on elimination of segregation for Frat. Coun. of Chs.; mem., nominating committee of the Gen. Coun. of Congre. Chrstn. Chs.; Chrstn. Citizenship Comm. of the Coun. for Social Action of the Congre. Chrstn. Chs.; Natl. Adv. Comm. on Race Relations, Amer. Missionary Assn.; assoc. dir., International Work Camp in La Chambon, France, 1950; Exec. Coun. of Chrstn. Action; Exec. Com. of the Fellowship of Southern Chs.; Alpha Kappa Delta; citation by Bd. of Commissioners of Wash., D.C. for distinguished public service; Office: 110 Maryland Ave., N.E., Washington, D.C.

CARY, William Sterling, b. Plainfield, N.J., 1929; A.B., Morehouse Coll.; B.D., Union Theol. Sem.; m. Marie Belle Phillips, 1952; Children--Yvonne Eileen, Denise Marie, William, Jr.; pastor, Grace Congre. Ch., Harlem; mem., UCC Comm. on Racial Justice Now; UCC Bd. of Homeland Ministries; former v.p., Prot. Coun. of N.Y. (Manhattan div.); Home: 11-29 196th St., Hollis, N.Y.; Office: 310 W. 139th St., New York, N.Y.

CAUTION, Tollie LeRoy, Sr., church official, b. Baltimore, Md., Aug. 20, 1902; s. Gustave Orville and Blanche (Johnson) C.; A.B., Cum Laude, Lincoln Univ., Pa., 1926; S.T.B., Magna Cum Laude, Phila. Div. Sch., 1929; M.A. Univ. of Penn., 1929; D.D. (hon.), Lincoln Univ., 1947; D.D., Phila. Div. School, 1954; m. Cora Marie Gosnell; Children--Tollie LeRoy, Jr.; ordained 1930; vicar and rector, parishes in Md., Pa., and N.Y.; asst. sec., Home Dept., Natl. Coun. of the Prot. Episc. Ch., working with Negroes, Orientals, Puerto Ricans and Mexican Americans, 1945--; trustee, St. Augustine's Coll., Raleigh, N.C.; trustee, Voorhees Coll., Denmark, S.C.; Bd. of Trustees, Okolona Coll., Okolona, Miss.; Bishop Payne Div. Sch.; Phila. Div. Sch.; Fort Valley Coll. Center, Fort Valley, Ga.; sec., Amer. Ch. Inst., dir., summer schs. of Rel. Edu. for St. Augustine's, Voorhees and Okolona Coll.; Comm., Episc. Natl. Coun.; Committee, Natl. Coun. of Chs. of Christ, USA; mem., Mason, Kappa Alpha Psi, Rural Workers Fellowship; life mem., NAACP; mem., Southern Chrstn. Leadership Conf.; Southern Conf. Edu. Fund; author: A Decade of Progress in Negro Work; The Prot. Espiscopal Church: Policies and Rationale Upon Which Support of its Negro Colleges is Predicated; Home: 549 W. 123rd St., New York, N.Y. 10027; Office: 815 Second Ave., New York, N.Y. 10017.

CHAMBERS, David Ernest, Jr., b. Dallas, Tex., May 18, 1934; s. David and Mattie C. (Nayles) C.; A.B., Bishop Coll., Dallas, Tex., 1959; B.D., Oberlin Sch. of Theol., Oberlin, Ohio, 1960; Grad. study, Wayne State Univ., Detroit, toward M.A.; m. Nelva LaVaughn Haynes; pastor, Ebenezer Bapt. Ch., Idabel, Okla., 1953-56; Family counselor, Dept. of Probation, Cleveland, O., Juvenile Court, 1960-65; Assoc. pastor, Mt. Zion Congre. Ch., Cleveland, O., currently; mem., Glenville Ex. Bd., Cleveland, 1966--; mem., Adv. Bd., Cleveland Bd. of Edu., 1967-68; Chrmn. Operation Equality, Cleveland, 1967-68; pres. Cleveland United Ch. of Christ. Min. Assn. 1968-69; sec. Operation Breadbasket, 1966--; mem. Mayor's Com. of 100, Cleveland, O.; politically Independent; Home: 10723 Magnolia Dr., Cleveland, O. 44106.

CHAMBERS, James Coolidge, s. John and Mary Elizabeth (Cunningham) C.; A.B., Va. Union Univ.; B.D., Yale Div. Sch., Recipient Jessey Hayes Fellow at Yale; m. Yolande Hargraves; Children--Esther, James and Timothy; pastor, organizaing minister Covenant Presby. Ch.; Norfolk Presby., Norfolk, Va.; organized Community United Presby. Ch., Presby. of Va., United Presby. Ch., Portsmouth, Va.; current: St. John's Presby. Ch., Detroit, Mich.; mem., Chrmn. United Negro Coll. Fund Financial Drive in Va.; Detroit Fellowship of Urban Ch.; chrmn. Steering Committee for Central City Redevelop't. Corp. Housing Commnr., City of Detroit, Mich.; Home: 2326 Atkinson, Detroit, Mich.; Church: 1410Jos Campau, Detroit, Mich.

CHAMBERS, Timothy Moses, b. Mt. Pleasant, Texas, June 19, 1899; s. C.C. and Jeraldine C.; Bishop Coll., Marshall, Tex.; Princeton Theol. Sem., 1921; S.T.D. (hon.), Princeton Univ.; D.D. (hon.), Coleman Coll.; m. Hazel

Thomas; Children-- Timothy, Jr., Jonnie Madlock, Eunice M.; Dir. Extension Work, Ark. Bapt. Coll., Pine Bluff, Ark.; pres., Bapt. Miss. & Ed. Conv., Texas, 1946-50; pastor, Zion Hill Bapt. Ch., Los Angeles, Calif., 1950--; pres., Progressive Natl. Bapt. Conv. of Amer., Inc., 1962--; instruc., Min. Inst., Ark. Bapt. Coll.; mem., Seminar & Preacher's Staff, Natl. L. K. Williams Inst., Bishop Coll.; instr. Sch. of Leadership Trng, W. Bapt. Conv., Calif. and Bapt. Minister's Union, S. Calif.; pres., Interdenom. Min. Alliance, L. A. & vicinity; trustee, Bishop College; "Minister of the Year," 1960; recd. Distinguished Service Award, Bishop Coll.; Ch. Administration Award, Southern Bapt. Conv.; Democrat; speaker, Bapt. World Alliance, Copenhagen, Denmark, 1947; author: Chambers at the Blackboard, The Revival Pattern, The Petical Mouthpiece; Home: 3890 6th Ave., Los Angeles, Calif; Church: 5025 S. McKinley Ave., Los Angeles, Calif.

CHAMBLISS, Carroll Randolph, chaplain, b. Jackson, Miss., May 29, 1925; s. Jesse R., Sr. & Nora V. (Robinson) C. (deceased); A. B., Wilberforce Univ., Wilberforce, Ohio, 1951; B. D., Payne Theol. Sem., Wilberforce, O., 1951; Th. M., Princeton Theol. Sem., 1968; m. Christene Helen Knew; Children--Randolph, Francis, Christopher, Phillip; pastor, St. Mathew Afr. Meth. Episc. Ch., St. Louis, Mo., 1951-56; The Ch. of the Master, St. Louis, Mo., 1953-56; Chaplain, U. S. Navy, 1956--; awards, Amer. Theater; Asiatic-Pacific; WW II Victory Medal; Home: 903 Hangford St., Oceanside, Calif., 92054; Office: Comsubron 15 REP, FPO San Francisco 96610.

CHANDLER, James Cleveland, b. State-line, Miss., June 20, 1911; s. Bose and Lucy (Lang) C.; A. B., Dillard Univ.; Th. M., Union Bapt. Sem.; m. Hallowene Inez Reed; Children--Charles E., James C., Jr.; pastor, St. Elmo Bapt. Ch., Laurel, Miss.; pres., East Sun. Sch. & Bapt. Training Union Congress; State vice pres., Natl. Sun. Sch. and B. T. U.; instr., E. Miss. Dist. Sun. Sch. & B. T. U. Congress; leader, Voter Registration Movement, Hattiesburg, Miss., 1961; mem., Natl. Bapt. Conv., USA, Inc.; NAACP; Phi Beta Sigma; Mason; Home: Laurel, 512 S. 6th Laurel, Miss. 39440; Office: 512 S. 6th Ave., Laurel, Miss. 39440

*CHAPPELLE, Ezekiel Emerson, Jr., sem. prof., b. Greenwood, S. C., May 31, 1915; s. E. E. and Susie A. C.; A. B., Benedict Coll., 1937; B. D., Howard Univ., 1940; S. T. M., Oberlin Grad. Sch. of Theol., 1941; D. R. E., Central Bapt. Sem., 1958; m. Thelma Dunston; Children--Charles Wesley, Bernice Virginia; Second Bapt. Ch., Elyria, O., 1 yr. while in sch. at Oberlin; pastor, First Bapt. Ch., Suffolk, Va., 4 yrs.; Second Bapt. Ch., Kansas City, Mo., 1946--; tchr., Western Bapt. Coll., 12 yrs.; mem., Adv. Bd., Queen of World Hosp.; Rehabilitation Inst.; Coun. of Chs.; vice moderator, Fellowship Dist. Assn.; author: The Voice of God, by the Carlton Press, NYC; Home: 3224 E. 29th Kansas City, Mo.; Office: Second Baptist Church, 39th Monroe, Kansas City, Mo.

CHAPPELLE, Thomas Oscar, dean; b. Sapulpa, Okla., Oct. 15, 1915; s. Peter A. and Sacannah B.; A. B., Bishop Coll., 1934; B. Th., Amer. Bapt. Theol. Sem., Nashville, Tenn., 1936; m. Elizabeth Louise; Children--Flora, Thomas, Carlos; dir., Chrstn. Edu. Third Bapt. Toledo, O., 1937-40; dean, Okla. Sch. of Rel., 1940-42; pastor, Morning Star Bapt. Ch., Tulsa, 1942--; owner, Rest Haven Nursing Home, Tulsa, Okla.; pres., Moton Meml. Hosp. Bd.; pres., Okla. Bapt. Congress of Christian Edu.; assoc. dir., Gen. of the National Sun. Sch. and B. T. U. Congrèss; D. D. (hon.), Wright Sch. of Rel., Morris Booker Bapt. Coll., Birmingham Bapt. Coll.; Distinguished Service Award, Tulsa Coun. of Chs.; mem., NAACP, Tulsa Urban League, The Prince Hall Masonic Lodge; Democrat; author: How We Do It, 1960; Home: 1136 E. 26th Pl., N., Tulsa, Okla.; Office: 1014 E. Pine St., Tulsa, Okla.

*CHASE, Lendall Warren, b. Wash., D. C., s. Berry Raymond and Carrie (Jackson) C.; A. B., Lincoln Univ., Pa., 1937-42; B. D., Howard Univ. Sch. of Rel., Wash., D. C., 1950; m. Elnora Elizabeth Ellis; Children--Lendall W. Jr., Patricia G., Larry W., Percy R., Elaine E.; asst. pastor, Tabernacle Bapt. Ch., Wash., 1949-53; pastor, High St. Bapt. Ch., Danville, Va., 1953--; Bd. of Managers, Brodnax Branch YMCA, 1954-56; v. p., Danvile Ministerial Assn., 1953-60; pres., Min. Alliance of Danville & vicinity; sec., Chr. of Civic Affairs Comm.; sub. tchr., Pittsylvania County Sch. System; mem. Bd., of Danville Branch NAACP; pres., Danville Chrstn. Progressive Assn. (affiliate of So. Christian Leadership Conf.) US Army, 1942-45; Home: 632 High St., Danville, Va.;

Office: 630 High St., Danville, Va.

CHEATHAM, William Lee, church official, b. Belzonia, Miss., Aug. 25, 1899; s. William and Lydia (Dixon) C.; Oakwood Coll., Huntsville, Ala., 1921; m. Laura Elizabeth Muir; Children--6 sons and 2 daughters; pastor, Dover and Wilmington, Del., 1937-44; Berea Temple, Balto., Md., 1944-53; pres., Allegheny Conf. of Seventh-Day Adventists; chrmn. Bd. of Pine Forge, Pa. Acad., 1953-63; vice-chrmn., Bd. of the Hadley Hosp., Wash., D. C.; trustee, Riverside Hosp. Board, Nashville, Tenn.; mem., Trustee Bd. of Oakwood College, Huntsville, Ala., Columbia Union Coll., Wash., D. C., Chas. F. Kettering Meml. Hosp., Dayton, O.; Mem., Human Relations Committee, Gen. Conf. of S. D. A., Wash., D. C.; Ex. Committee, Columbia Union Conf., Takoma Park, Md.; Home: Manatawny Rd., Pine Forge, Pa.; Office: P. O. Box 21, Pine Forge, Pa.

CHEEK, James Edward, b. Dec. 4, 1932, Roanoke Rapids, N. C.; A. B., Shaw Univ., Raleigh, N. C., 1955; B. D., Colgate Rochester Div. Sch., Rochester, N. Y., 1958; Ph. D., Drew Univ., Madison, N. J., 1962; m. Celestine Juanita Williams; Children--James Edward, Jr., Janet Elizabeth; tchr. asst., Drew Theol. Sch., Madison, N. J., 1959-60; instr., Union Jr. Coll., Cranford, N. J., 1960 (summer); visiting instr., Upsala Coll., E. Orange, N. J., 1960 (summer); asst. prof. The Sch. of Rel., Va. Union Univ., Richmond, Va., 1961-63; pres., Shaw Univ., Raleigh, N. C., 1963-69; pres., Howard Univ., Wash., D. C., July 1969--; Alpha Kappa Delta Natl. Hon. Sociological Soc., 1954; Colgate-Rochester Graduate Fellow, 1958; Lily Found. Fellow, 1958 and 1959; Rockefeller Doctoral Fellow, 1960; mem., Soc. of Biblical Lit. and Exegesis; Amer. Soc. of Ch. History; Nat. Assn. of Biblical Instrs.; Amer. Assn. of Univ. Professors; Rel. Research Assn.; past civic activities, Sec. of the Edu. Sub-committee of the Va. Adv. Comm. to the U. S. Commission on Civil Rights; Research consultant to Mich. State Univ. Study of Prince Edward County sponsored by the U. S. Office of Edu.; Bibliographer and consultant on lit. and publications for the Va. Coun. on Human Relations; mem., of Special Comm. on Edu. Opportunity for Negro Youth under the auspices of the Va. Coun. on Human Relations; present civic activities, N. C. Good Neighbor Coun.; Mayor's Community Relations Coun.; Bd. of Dir., the United Fund of Wake County; Bd. of Dir., Family Serv. of Raleigh; Bd. of Dir., Fund for the Advancement of Theol. Edu.; Bd. of Trustees, Urban America, Inc.; Bd. of Trustees, Colgate Rochester Div. Sch.; Bd. of Dir. and Exec. Committee, the United Negro Coll. Fund, Inc.; Comm. on Intl. Edu. of the Coll. Entrance Examination Board; Comm. on Planning and Policy of the Amer. Coun. on Edu.; mem., Alpha Phi Alpha; U.S. Air Force, 1951-52; listed in Who's Who in American Education; listed in the 1968 ed. of Outstanding Young Men in America; Office: Office of the President, Howard Univ., Wash., D.C. 20001

CHERRY, Charles Alexander, b. Anderson, S.C.; s. Charles E. and Florence C. C.; A.B., Benedict Coll., 1935; B.D., Oberlin Grad. Sch. of Theol., Ohio, 1949; m. Verna Mungin; Children-- Ruth Deborah, Charles A., Jr.; pastor, Dunn's Creek Bapt. Ch., Ware Shoals, S.C., 1940-44; chaplain, US Army, 1944-46, served at Camp Ellis, Ill., Camp Howrah, Calcutta, India; coll. pastor, Benedict Coll., 1949-58; pastor, Central Bapt., Ch., Charleston, S.C., 1951-53; current, field representative, Benedict Coll. and pastor, Liberty Hill Bapt. Ch., Catawba, S.C., tchr, pub. sch. of S.C., 1935-44; decorations: Asiatic-Pacific Campaign Medal; Amer. Campaign Medal; World War II Victory Medal; mem., Omega Psi Phi; Home: Benedict Coll., Columbia, S.C.

CHERRY, Henry C., b. Benoit, Miss., Mar. 20, 1905; s. Nealy Cherry; Eng. Bible Diploma, Miss. Bapt. Sem., Inc.; D.D. (hon.) Natchez Coll., Natchez, Miss.; m. Rachel Simmons; 1 son, Archie L. Adams; pastored, Strangers Home Bapt., Shaw, Miss.; First Bapt., Memphis, Tenn.; Macedonia Bapt. Ch., Benoit, Miss.; Mod. Bolivar Co. Gen. Bapt. Assn.; v.p. at large, Progressive Bapt. State Conv., Miss.; Trustee, Miss. Bapt. Sem., Inc.; mem. Bd. Management, Taborian Hosp., Mound Bayou, Miss.; trustee, Natchez Coll., Natchez, Miss.; Church: Box 123, Benoit, Miss.

*CHERRY, Maurice Stallworth, b. Cordele, Ga., Dec. 2, 1932; s. Jeffery Lee and Olivia (Dean) C.; B.A., Paine Coll., 1952; B.D., Howard Univ. Sch. of Rel., 1955; m. Joyce Lundy; dir. of Youth Work, Chrstn. Meth. Episc. Chs. of Ga., 1955-59; pastor, Davisboro Circuit C.M.E. Ch., 1955; pastor, Montezuma Circuit C.M.E. Ch., 1955-59; chaplain, Paine Coll., 1959-61; chaplain and dean of men, Paine Coll., 1961--; grad. study in

O. T., Emory Univ., 1963--; counselor, Paine Coll. Student Movement, 1960-63; mem., Amer. Acad. of Rel.; Bd. of Chrstn. Edu., C. M. E. Ch., 1956-60; pres., Natl. Chrstn. Youth Fellowship, C. M. E. Ch., 1956-60; Home: 851 Clifton Court Circuit, Apt. 7, Atlanta, Ga. 30329.

*CHRISTIAN, George Benjamin, b. Winston-Salem, N. C., Dec. 8, 1908; s. Joseph Benjamin and Hattie (Patterson) C.; B. S., Shaw Univ., Raleigh, N. C.; B. D., Howard Univ. Sch. of Rel., Wash., D. C., 1949; m. Margaret Delores Odom; Children--Randolph Harrison; tchr. pub. sch. W-Salem, N. C., 1930-38; US Employment Serv., interviewer, 1938-41; Youth Counselor, Natl. Youth Adm., 1941-42; War Manpower Recruiting Officer, US Employment Serv., Eastern, N. C., 1942-44; Program dir., USO, Norfolk, Va., 1944-46; chaplain and organizer, Westminster Found., Howard Univ., 1949-51; dir., Knox Community Center, Baltimore, 1951-53; pastor, Bethel Presby. Ch., Plainfield, N. J., 1953--; Bd. of Dirs., Red Cross, Plainfield Chapt., 1955-60; Bd. of Dirs., Community Serv. Coun., 1956--; Bd. of Dirs., Neighborhood House, 1957-58; Mayor's Civil Rights Commn., 1958-63; current mem., Mayor's Commn. on Human Rights; Staff of chaplains, Vet. Hosp., Lyons, N. J.; Trustee, Presby. of Elizabeth; moderator, Presby. of Elizabeth (former); Certificate of Appreciation, Red Cross, Plainfield Chap., for 5 yrs. serv., 1960; mem., Phi Beta Sigma; Frontiers; Intl. Serv. Club; Mason; Fellow-Inst. of Rel. Studies, Jewish Theol. Sem., NYC.; alumnus, Rutgers Human Relations Workshop; Home: 751 Webster Pl., Plainfield, N. J.; Office: 300 E. 5th St., Plainfield, N. J.

CHRISTIAN, Gerald Chilton, b. Antigua, B. W. I., Feb. 28, 1916; s. Joseph Martin and Maria (Frances) C.; A. B., City Coll., New York, 1939; B. D., Chgo. Theol. Sem., 1943; M. A., Drew Univ., 1947; pastor, St. Luke Congregational Ch., Little Rock, Ark., 1939-43; St. Luke's Congre. Ch., 1947-52; Oak Park United Ch. of Christ, Sacramento, Calif., 1952--; sec., Urban League, Little Rock, Ark.; pres., Boys Work, YMCA, Ark.; pres., Neighborhood Council; moderator, Sacramento Valley Assn., United Ch. of Christ; Oral Panel Bd. member, State of Calif.; mem., Mason; Phi Beta Sigma; Ministerial Assn.; licensed Rel. Edu. tchr., Natl. Counc. of Chs.; Home: 2761 Santa Clara Way, Sacramento, Calif; Office: 3308 4th Ave., Sacaramento, Calif.

CHRISTOPHER, Claude, b. Jacksonville, Tex., Oct. 26, 1929; s. W. V. and Ora (C).; A. B., Prairie View A & M Coll., Prairie View, Tex., 1951; M. A., De Paul Univ., Chgo., Ill., 1958; m. M. Olivia Walker; Children--Gery James, Sharon Denise; ordained Afr. Meth. Episc. Zion Ch. after 4 yr. Ministers course; pastor, Gordon Meml. Afr. Meth. Episc. Ch., 1960-63; merged with St. Mathew A. M. E. Z. Ch., 1963--; tchr. Chgo. pub. sch., 1957-68; pres. Prairie-Halsted Fed. Ch. Assn., 1965-68; chrmn. Supervisory Com. Bd. of Dirs. Prairie-Halsted Ch. Credit Union; US Army, 1951-54; statistician, Mich. Conf. A. M. E. Z. Ch.; Home: 16560 Honore St., Markham, Ill. 60426; Office: 9448 S. Eggleston St., Chgo., Ill. 60620.

CHRISTOPHER, Olden Walter, b. Napoleonville, La., Jan. 5, 1911; s. Alix and Ellen; Gilbert Academy, 1928; Natchitoches Trng, 1932; Dillard Univ., 1946-48; So. Univ., 1949; m. Onesophorus Lunnon; Children--Olden, Barbara Jean; pastor, Shaw Temple Ch., New Orleans, La.; Cane River Circuit Natchitoches, La., 1939; Valena Jones, St. Louis, Miss., 1944; Jeanerette Cir. 1941-2; Peoples Meth., 1946; St. Mathew, New Orleans, 1948; Thirkield, Bogalusa, 1952; Wesley, New Orleans, 1958; Philip Mem., New Orleans, 1961; Grace Meth., New Orleans, 1964--; tchr., Jefferson Parish sch., Boy Scouts; YMCA; citation, Outstanding Leadership, Bogalusa, New Orleans; mem., La. tchrs. Assn.; NAACP; Meth. Min. of New Orleans; Intl. Min. Alliance; Boy Scouts of Amer.; Home: 400 Thayer St., New Orleans, La. 70114; Office: 2001 Iberville St., New Orleans, La.

*CHURN, Serenus T., b. June 19, 1939; s. Charles and Violet; A. B., Morgan State Coll., Balto., Md., 1962; B. D., Howard Univ., Sch. of Rel., Wash. D. C., 1965; m. Shirley Brown; Children--Serenus T.; pastor, Messiah Bapt. Ch., Yonkers, N. Y., 1965--; Union Bapt. Ch., Easton, Md., 1961-65; asst. pastor, Union Temple Bapt. Ch., Balto., Md., 1955-61; chrmn., Housing Code Enforcement Commn., Yonkers, N. Y., 1965--; chrmn., voter registration, Easton, Md., 1961-65; Bates Investigating Com., Yonkers; v. p., Min. Fellowship Coun., Yonkers; mem., Phi Sigma Tau; Home: 281 Warburton Ave., Yonkers, N. Y. 10701; Office: 76 Warburton Ave., Yonkers, N. Y.

CLAIR, Matthew Walker, Jr., bishop; b. Harpers Ferry,

W. Va., Aug. 12, 1890; s. Matthew Wesley and Fannie Meade (Walker) C.; Syracuse Univ., 1909; B. A. Howard Univ., 1915; S. T. B., Boston, Univ., 1918; S. T. M., Iliff Sch. of Theol., 1927; D. D. (hon.) Morgan Univ., 1934; Gammon Theol. Sem., 1936; m. Ethel C. Smith, Nov. 25, 1920; Children--Phyllis Ann, Ethel Maxine (Mrs. Jasper Wilson); ordained to ministry, Meth. Ch., 1917; prof. practical theol., Gammon Theol. Sem., 1936-40; pastor, St. Mark Meth. Ch., Chgo.; bishop, Meth. Ch.; Coun. Bishops, NYC.; mem. Bd. of Dirs., E. Stanley Jones Union; chaplain, 380 Labor Bn., US Army, WW I; mem., Ch. Fed. of Greater Chgo., Gen. Conf. Com. Min. Trng. of Meth. Ch.; Pi Gamma Mu; Alpha Phi Alpha; Home: Box 234 Main Post Office, St. Louis, Mo.

CLANCY, Bryant Edward, b. Catherine, Ala., Jan. 23, 1937; s. Bryant and Ida (Clark) C.; Immanuel Luth. Coll. & Sem., Greensboro, N. C., 1956-61; 1958, A. B. (Magna Cum Laude) 1961 Diploma of Graduation from Sem. (Cum Laude); m. Elma Pearl Neely; vicar, St. Andrew Luth. Ch., Charlotte, N. C. and Grace Luth. Ch., Concord, N. C., 1953-62; pastor, St. Andrew's Luth. Ch., Charlotte, N. C.; mem. Luth. Human Relation Assn. of Amer.; mem. NAACP; mem. Democratic Party; sec., Tri-Circuit Conf. sec. Charlotte Luth. Min. Assn.; Home: 2607 Abelwood Rd., Charlotte, N. C.; Church: 213 N. McDowell, Charlotte, N. C.

CLARK, Harold, Chaplain (Capt.), b. Ashburn, Ga., Oct. 20, 1930; s. Oliver and Ophelia (Buckles) C.; A. B., Benedict Coll., Columbia, S. C., 1955; B. Th., Amer. Bapt. Theol. Sem., Nashville, Tenn., 1952; courses, Fisk Univ., Nashville, 1952-53; Southern Bapt. Theol. Sem., Louisville, Ky., 1962-66; m. Clara Milligan; Children--Harold, Jr.; pastor, First Bapt. Ch., Estill Spring, Tenn., 1951-53; asst. pastor, Second Nazareth Bapt. Ch., Columbia, S. C.; 1953-55; Oakland Bapt. Ch., Louisville, Ky., 1962-66; US Army, 1955-62; Chaplain, 1967--; founder, the Christian Life Commn., Detroit and NYC; mem. Natl. Bapt. Conv.; Medals, Joint Service; Good Conduct; Occupation Armed Forces Res.; Natl. Defense; Armed Forces Exp.; author, The Negro and the Southern Bapt. Conv.; The Negro and His Relations with Whites; Home: 1715 W. Grand Ave., Detroit, Mich. 48238; Office: First Bde, 2nd Inf. Div., APO San Francisco 96224.

CLARK, Isaac Rufus, sem. prof., b. New Castle, Pa., Feb. 15, 1925; s. James H. and Lillian (Alexander) C.; B.A., Wilberforce Univ., 1951; B.D., Payne Theol. Sem., 1952; Th.D., Boston Univ. Sch. of Theol., 1958; post-doctoral studies, summers of 1959, 1962, 1963, Union Theol. Sem., N.Y.; m. Betty Jane Clark; Children--Isaac R., Jr., Karen E.; pastor, Bethel Afr. Meth. Episc. Ch., Lynn, Mass., 1952-53; Bethel A.M.E. Ch., New Bedord, Mass., 1953-55; asst. & assoc. prof., Systematic Theol., Payne Theol. Sem., Wilberforce, Ohio, 1955-60; dean & assoc. prof., Paul Quinn Coll., Waco, Tex., 1960-62; current prof., Interdenom. Theol. Center, Atlanta, Ga., 1962--; dir., Field Edu., Interdenom. Theol. Center; Rel. News Broadcasting each Sun. over WAOK, Atlanta; dir., Kitty Haven Nursery Sch., 1960; US Navy, 1943-46; Conduct & Asiatic-Pacific Medals from Navy; mem. (former), Natl. Assn. Collegiate Deans & Registrars; mem., Alpha Kappa Mu Honor Soc.; Assn. of Texas Coll. and Univs.; Assn. of Field Work Dirs. of Theol. Sems.; AAUP; NAACP; Democrat; YMCA; Collaborating with profs. in Homiletics at Candler and Columbia Sems. on Value of TV media in the teaching of Homiletics, work done at Prot. Radio and TV Center; Home: 157 Kevin Ct., Atlanta, Ga.; Office: 671 Beckwith SW, Atlanta, Ga.

CLARK, James I., bishop, b. Trinidad B.W.I., Sept. 6, 1906; s. William and Alberta (James) C.; Governor Sch., Elen. 1921, W.I. Shelton Coll., Natl. Bible Inst. 1946-63; Certificate and Th.B., Coll. of Paterson, 1945-47; Bloomfield Coll, 1949, Amer. Bible Coll. Chgo., Th.D., D.D., 1952; Further study: Genl. Jewish Theol. Sem.; m. Rachel Johnson; Children--James I., Jr., Wm. S., Mrs. Albertha Thomas, Alvin Thomas, Benjamin W., Joseph Alan, Mary, Hubert, Henrietta, Lois, Frances; ordained 1932 in the Bible Way Ch. of Our Lord Jesus Christ World-wide Inc., 1932 after 2 yrs. of evangelistic work; pastor, Bible Way Ch., Paterson, N.J., 1941-55; dean, The Bible Inst., 1955-58; pastor, Straight Gate Ch., Mamaro, N.Y., Overseer, states of N.C. and Conn.; organized, Christ Temple Ch.; Consecrated Bishop of Diocese of NY and West Indies, 1962--; conducts: Bible Sch. for Training of Christian Workers, in Westchester County, N.Y.; mem. Mason; Interdenom. Min. Conf., N.Y.; YMCA; chrmn. Bd. of Edu., Prot. Coun., N.Y.; Home: 25-63 98 St. E. Elmhurst, L.I., N.Y.; Office: 507-09 W. 125th St., New York, N.Y.

CLARK, Moses Julius, b. Catherine, Ala., July 4, 1925; s. Madison and Lola (Funish) C.; Ala. Luth. Acad.; Immanuel Luth. Coll., Greensboro, N. C., 1950-55; m. Lucille E. Dale; m. Miriam Marie; children-- Moses J. Jr., Lydia L., Cynthia D.; pastor, St. Matthew Luth. Ch., Arlington, Ala., St. Luke Luth. Ch., Laminson, Ala., 1955-57; St. Paul Luth. Ch., Oak Hill, Ala., 1957-63; Christ Luth. Ch., Rosebud, Ala.; Gethesamane Luth. Ch., Hamburg, Ala.; St. Mark Luth. Ch., Ackerville, Ala.; Augustana Luth. Ch., Alexandria, La.; St. Paul Luth. Ch., Mansura, La.; Service: US Air Force, 1943-46; awards: America Service, Good Conduct, WW II Victory Medal; Church: Augustana Luth. Ch., Alexandria, La.

CLARKE, Aloysius Roland, tchr., b. Washington, D. C., Oct. 17, 1928; s. Wm. Lownes and Lottie (Johnson) C.; St. Augustine Sem., Bay St. Louis, Miss., 1945-49; B. A., S. T. B., Benedictine Mission Sem., Newton, N. J., 1950-59; Univ. of Wurzburg, 1960-61; Fordham Univ., NYC, 1961-63, M. A., Prefect and Instr., Benedictine Mission Sem., 1959-60; Asst. pastor, St. Charles Borromeo Ch., NYC, 1962+ instr. Benedictine Miss. Sem., 1962--; v. p. Sussex County Comm. Rela. Coun., 1963--; Home: St. Paul's Abbey, Newton, N. J.

CLARKE, Elisha Salathiel, b. Miami, Fla., July 30, 1921; s. Elisha Salathiel and Theodora (Johnson) C.; A. B., St. Augustine Coll., Raleigh, N. C., 1945; B. D., Bishop Payne Div. Sch., Petersburg, Va., 1948; m. Julia Rebecca Smith; Children--Sheila Coleen, Elisha Salathiel III, Alison Trinette; rector, St. Matthew's Episc. Ch., Delray Beach, Fla.; St. James Episc. Ch., Tampa, Fla.; The Ch. of the Incarnation, Miami, Fla.; The Ch. of the Transfiguration, Opa Locka, Fla.; mem., Bd. of Dirs., James E. Scott Comm. Assn.; Alpha Psi Alpha; Home: 1984 N. W. 153rd St., Opa Locka, Fla.

CLARKE, Jimmy Ed., librarian, b. Tyler, Tex., Feb. 20, 1934; s. Junius and Lillie (M.) C.; B. S., Tex. Coll., Tyler, Tex., 1954; Perkins Sch. of Theol. S. M. U., 1954-55; B. D., No. Tex. State Univ., Denton, Summer 1959; M. S., Ill., 1962; m. Norma Jean Tilley; 1 son, Chandran Edward; pub. sch. tchr., Kerens, Tex., 1955-57; pastor, Powell Chapel C. M. E. Ch., Kerens, Tex.; Brookins C. M. E. Ch., Malakoff, Tex., 1953-57; circulation librarian, Bridwell Library, Perkins Sch. of Theol., So.

Meth. Univ., 1959-62; pastor, Magnolia C.M.E. Ch., Dallas, 1962-64; present librarian, Interdenom. Theol. Center, Atlanta, Ga., 1964-; instr. in the Tex. Pastor's sch. each summer at Tex. Coll., Tyler, Tex.; mem., Bd. of Chrstn. Edu. of the Dallas-Ft. Worth Conf. of the C.M.E. Ch., and the Adv. Coun. of the Dallas Youth Coun. of the C.M.E. Ch.; chrmn., Leadership Edu. Sec. of the Natl. Chrstn. Edu. Coun. of the C.M.E. Ch.; asst. sec., Dallas C.M.E. Min. Alliance; sec.-treas., Bd. of Dirs., Youth Opportunities Inc.; awarded a Lilly Fellowship to study at Illinois; Kappa Alpha Psi; Beta Kappa Chi in undergrad. sc.; Office: Interdenominational Theol. Sem., Atlanta, Ga.

*CLATER, Bobbie Daniel, coll. dean, b. Dallas, Tex., April 3, 1927; s. Marshall and Pauline Lillian W.; A.B., Bishop Coll., 1948; M. Ed., Bishop Coll., 1951; B.D., Howard Univ. Sch. of Rel., 1954; m. Virginia Alice Douglas; Children-- Brian Daniel, Robert Douglas; pastor, New Hope Bapt. Ch., Como, Tex.; Liberty Bapt. Ch. and St. Mark Bapt. Ch., Marshall, Tex., 1945-51; asst. pastor, Lane Chrstn. Meth. Ch., Wash. D.C.; dean of men and tchr. in Rel., Bishop Coll., 1949-51; dean of students and chrmn. of Dept. of Practical Theol., Oklahoma Sch. of Rel., Langston, Okla., 1954-56; dir., Bapt. Student Work and Chair of Bible, Lincoln Univ., Jefferson County, Missouri, 1956-63; pastor, Mt. Zion Bapt. Ch., Bunceton, Mo., 1963-68; pastor, Second Bapt. Ch., 1968--; mem., Mo. Coun. of Soc. Welfare; Coun. on Rel. and Race, NAACP; Natl. Coun. on Family Life; pres., Min. Alliance, 1965--; dean, Sun. Sch. and B.T.U. Cong., Mt. Carmel Dist., Mo.; mem. Coun. of Rel. and Race; Omega Psi Phi; Democrat; Home: 413 N. 5th St., Columbia, Mo.; Office: Second Bapt. Ch., 4th and Broadway, Columbia, Mo.

CLAY, W. Benjamin, b. Yazoo City, Miss., Feb. 16, 1927; s. Rev. Henry C. Sr. and Clara C.; A.B. Rust College, B.D. Gammon Theol. Sem., D.D. Natl. Bible Sch.; m. Ruth D. Clay; Children--W. Benjamin, Jr., Jonothan, Margo; present: pastor of Gammon Meth. Ch., Chgo., Ill; pres. of Interracial Meth. Group, YMCA; Home: 229 S. Central Park, Chicago, Ill; Office: 1959 W. Maypole Ave., Chicago, Ill.

CLAYTON, Robert Louis, Jr., b. Pensacola, Fla., Feb. 25, 1934; s. Robert L. Sr. and Louise Clayton (Hardy); A.B.,

Talladega Coll., 1955; Gammon Sem., 1955-56; B. D., Hood Sem., Livingstone Coll., 1959; Emory Univ., 1964; S. T. M. candidate, Interdenom. Theol. Center, 1963-64; m. Minnie Harris; Children--Robert Joel, Myrna Audiness; ordained pastor, The A. M. E. Ch.; pastor, Union Temple A. M. E. Ch., Athens, Ga., 1955-56; Pleasant Grove, Cheraw, S. C., 1958-59; Tenn. Valley Community Ch., Florence, Ala., 1961-63; asst. dean of Chapel, Dillard Univ., New Orleans, La., 1957-58; acting chaplain and instr., Ala. A & M Coll., Normal, Ala.; current instr. and dir. of pub. and placement, Interdenom. Theol. Center, Atlanta, Ga.; youth consultant, Chrstn. Edu. Conv.; Advancement chrmn., Monto Sano Dist., Boy Scouts of Amer.; Football and basketball official for high schs.; pres., Grad. Chapter of Fraternity initiating Adult Literacy programs for Voter Registration, 1962-63; worked in Harris Home for Children Program; mem., Ala. Interscholastic Athletic Assn.; Ala. Sociologist and Anthropologist Assn.; Ala. State Teachers Assn.; Alpha Phi Alpha; Amer. Tchrs. Assn.; Assn. for the Coordination of Univ. Rel. Affairs; Boy Scouts of America; Natl. Assn. of Coll. and Univ. Chaplains; Natl. Edu. Assn.; Rel. Edu. Assn.; Southern Intercollegiate Athletic Assn.; NAACP; The Passive Revolution of Jesus, The Many Faces of God, and The Person of Christ in the New Testament are lectures now being used Nkawkaw Training Coll., Ghana, W. Africa; The Danforth Found. Sem. Internship Award, 1957; Home: 653 Beckwith St., Atlanta, Ga. 30314.

CLEAGE, Albert Buford, Jr., b. Indianapolis, Ind., June 13, 1911; s. Albert Buford and Pearl (Reed) C.; A. B., Wayne State Univ., Detroit, Mich., 1937; B. D., Oberlin Grad, Sch. of Theol., Oberlin, Ohio; Univ. of Southern Calif., Los Angeles, Calif; Wayne State Univ. Grad. Sch.; m. Doris Graham; Children--Kristin, Pearl; case worker, Detroit Dept. of Pub. Welfare, 1937-38; pastor, Chandler Meml. Congre. Ch., Lexington, Ky., 1942-43; Fellowship Ch. of All Peoples, San Francisco, Calif., 1943-44; St. John's Congre. Ch., Springfield, Mass., 1946-51; St. Mark's Community Ch., Detroit, Mich., 1951-52; Shrine of the Black Madonna, 1952--; chrmn., Housing Com., Ex. Bd. NAACP, 1948-51; mem., Round Table Conf. of Christians and Jews, Springfield, Mass., 1950-51; NAACP Ex. Bd., Detroit, Mich., 1951, 1963--; Group on Advanced Leadership Exec. Bd., Detroit, Mich., 1962--; The Freedom Now Political Party, Mich. State Chrmn,

1963--; The United Ch. of Christ Ministerium, Detroit, Mich., 1964; The Congre. Min. Assn., Detroit, Mich., 1959-60; contributing ed., The Illustrated News, Detroit, Mich., 1962--; author, The Black Messiah, Sheed & Ward, 1968; Home: 2042 Clavert, Detroit, Mich; Office: 7625 Linwood, Detroit, Mich.

CLEMENT, Harold, A. L., s. Gustavius and Florence (Smith) C.; A. B., Livingstone Coll., Salisbury, N. C., 1937-41; Hartford Sem. Found., Hartford, Conn., 1941-42; Yale Div. Sch., 1942; S. T. B., Boston Univ., 1943-45; m. Olivia B. Tucker; Children--Ricardo Tucker; pastor, First A. M. E. Z. Ch., San Francisco, Calif.; Mt. Zion A. M. E. Z. Ch., Montgomery, Ala.; John Wesley, Pittsburgh, Pa., 1958-61; Varick Meml. A. M. E. Z. Ch., New Haven, Conn., 1961--; tchr., Livingstone Coll., 1945-46; case worker, Pa., 1960-63; counsellor, Domestic. Rel. Ct., Allegheny Co., Pittsburgh, Pa., 1963-64; mem., Ex. Bd., NAACP, San Francisco Br.; Bd. dirs., San Francisco Coun. Chs., 1952-53; sec.-treas., Home Mission Dept., Calif. Conf., A. M. E. Z. Ch., 1952-56; chrmn. budget finance com., New England Annual Conf., A. M. E. Z. Ch., 1966--; Trustee Bd., Lomax-Hannon Coll., Greenville, Ala., 1956-57; Commn. mem., Dept. Home Missions, Natl. Coun. Chs., 1960--; award, Silver Shield, Inc.; contributor, Rel. mag.; Bd. mem., Urban League, New Haven, Conn., 1966--; mem. Chrstn. Ed. Com., Urban League; Home: 11 Charles St., New Haven, Conn. 06511

CLEMENTS, George Harold, b. Chicago, Ill., Jan. 26, 1932; s. Samuel G. and Aldonia (Peters) C.; Quizly Prep. Sem., 1945-50; B. A., M. A., S. T. B., St. Mary of the Lake; asst. priest, St. Ambrose, 1957-62; St. Dorothy, 1962--; mem. Cath. Interracial Council, NAACP, Urban League, H. O. M. E., Cath. Black Caucas; Home: 450 E. 78th St., Chicago, Ill.

CLEVELAND, Edward Earl, b. Huntsville, Ala., Mar. 11, 1921; s. William Clifford and Eunice (Clifford) C.; courses, Oakwood Coll., Huntsville, Ala.; m. Celia Marie Adney; Children--Earl Clifford; pastored for 5 yrs., 1942-47; served as Conf. Evangelist, 1948-50; evangelist, So. Union of Seventh-Day Adventists, 1950-54; assoc. sec., Min. Assn. of the Gen. Conf. of Seventh-Day Adventists, 1954--; tchr. for two sessions, Andrews Univ.; visiting lecturer, Oakwood Coll., 15 yrs.; assoc. ed., The Ministry Magazine; Home 915 Lawrence St. NE, Wash., D.C.; Office: 6840 Eastern Ave. NW, Wash., D.C. 20012

CLEVELAND, Frank C., b. Dallas, Tex., Mar. 10, 1913; s. George Frank and Elizabeth C.; Simmons Univ., Louisville, Ky. 1946; Capitol Univ., Columbus, O., 1956-58; m. Minnie Wyms; Children--Frank C., Jr., Allan S.; pastor, New Salem Bapt. Ch., Columbus, O.; v.p., No. Central Coun. of Chs.; 1967--present, moderator, Eastern Union Dist. Bapt. Assn.; Dir. gen. Ohio State Sun. Sch. & B.T.U., Congress, 1960--; pres., Columbus Bapt. Min. Alliance, 1962-64; Chrmn. Civil Betterment Com.; mem. Mayor's Advisory Bd. on Police Brutality, Columbus, O.; Home: 2985 South Field Dr., Columbus, O., 43207; Office: 487 N. Champion Ave., Columbus, O. 43203.

*CLIFFORD, Richard Lorenzo, b. Romney, W. Va., April 23, 1916; s. Earl Overton and Ruth (Fisher) R.; A.B., Clark Coll., 1940; A.M., W. Va. Univ., 1952; B.D., Howard Univ. Sch. of Rel., 1963; m. Robertine Lewis; Children--Sharon Louise, Linda Marie, Nancy Kay; pastor, The Meth. Ch., Johnstown, Pa., 1940; Frostburg, Md., 1941; Crafton, Morgantown, W. Va., 1946-47; Wheeling, W. Va., 1946-53; Washington, D.C., Simpson, 1953-55; Centenial, Baltimore, Md., 1955-59; supt., The Va.-Wash. Dist. of the Wash. Annual Conf. of the Meth. Ch.; exec. sec., Bd. of Chrstn. Edu., N.C., Va. Conf. of Meth. Ch.; present pastor, Van Buren United Meth. Ch., Wash. D.C.; visiting clergy service, Johns Hopkins Hosp. Baltimore, Md., 1955-59; Bd. of Dirs., Wesley Found., Howard Univ., 1960--; mem., Amer. Sociological Soc.; Soc. for the study of Soc. Problems; Home: 35 Van Buren St., N.W., Wash., D.C.

CLINKSCALES, John William, b. Chgo., Ill., Mar. 5, 1925; s. John W. and Nannie Lucille (G.); A.B., Va. Union Univ., Richmond, Va., 1946; B.D., McCormick Theol. Sem., Chgo., Ill., 1950; Asst. pastor, Beth. Eden Bapt. Ch., 1942-55; Lebanon Bapt. Ch., Chgo., Ill., 1955--; mem. Chgo. Bapt. Assn. (Amer. Bapt. Conv.); Chgo. Bapt. Min. Dept. of Chrstn. Edu.; Bd. of Dir., Englewood Sen. Citizens Center; Bd. of Dir., Southtown YMCA; Adv. Bd. Englewood Urban Prog. Center; mem. Military Chap. Assn.; Chap. 4th Bde, 85th Div., USAR; Kappa Alpha Psi; Home: 9545 So. Prairie Ave., Chgo., Ill.

60628; Office: Lebanon Bapt. Ch., 1501 W. Marquette Rd., Chgo., Ill.

COAN, Josephus Roosevelt, sem. prof., b. Spartanburg, S. C.; Nov. 26, 1902; s. Andrew Johnson and Mary Ann (Foster) C.; A. B., Howard Univ., 1930; B. D., Yale Div. Sch., 1933; M. A., Yale Univ. Grad. Sch., 1934; D. D. (hon.), Morris Brown Coll., 1938; Ph. D., Hartford Sem. Found., 1961; m. Sammye Elizabeth Fuller; pastor, Rhode Island, 1933-34; Adairsville Ga., 1935; Dallas, Ga., 1936; Morris Brown Coll., Atlanta, 1934-38; 1948--; missionary, So. and Central Africa, 1938-47; assoc. ed., A. M. E. Journal of Rel. Edu.; writer of Adult Sunday Sch. Quarterly; Hd. of the Div. of Philosophy and Rel., Morris Brown Coll.; current prof., Christian Edu. & Missions, Interdenom. Theol. Center, Atlanta, Ga.; dir. of Rel. Edu., A. M. E. Ch. in Ga.; mem., Exec. Comm. of the Ga. Coun. Chs.; NAACP; AAUP, AHA, AMSAC, Theta Phi, Phi Beta Sigma, MABI, NACUC, REA; author: Daniel Alexander Payne: Christian Education, 1935; Ph. D. Dissertation, "The Expansion of Missions of the A. M. E. Ch. in So. Africa, 1896-1908; "Education Among the Bantu People of So. Africa;" 1949; Home: 244 W. Lake Ave., Atlanta, Ga.; Office: 671 Beckwith St., SW, Atlanta, Ga.

*COATES, James Elliott, b. Dec. 30, 1929; s. George and Louise; B. A., B. D., Howard Univ., 1953, 1956; m. Sandra M. Parker; Children--James Jr., Donna, Keith, Kevin; chaplain, Migrant Workers, 1956; Dir. Rel. Ed., Mt. Carmel Bapt. Ch., 1956-58; pastor, Bethlehem Bapt. Ch., 1958--; Dir. Anti-Poverty Program, 1964-67; chaplain, D. C. Dept. of Corrections, 1960-61; instr., Wash. Bapt. Sem.; Ed. Congress, Progressive Bapt. Conv., consult., Dist. of Columbia, Mental Health Assn.; Off. of Ed.-Health, Ed., Welfare; Ed. Chrmn. S. E. Unit Amer. Cancer Assn.; pres., Bd. of Ed., D. C. pub. schs mem. Urban Coalition, SCLC, Chrmn., Anacostia Com. Planning Coun.; author: Community Participation Proposal; Home: 1210 Howard Rd. S. E., Wash. D. C.; Office: 2458 Nichols Ave. S. E., Wash., D. C. 20020.

*COBB, Charles Earl, b. Durham, N. C., Sept. 28, 1916; s. James Samuel and Mary (Cox) C.; A. B., N. C. Coll., 1940; B. D., Howard Univ. Sch. of Rel.; S. T. M., Boston Univ.; residential requirements for Th. D., Boston Univ.; m. Martha Bea Kendrick; Children--Charles E., Jr.,

Ann C., M. Adrienne, Janet E.; pastor, St. John's Afr. Meth. Episc. Ch., Frankfort, Ky., 1947-51; St. Mark Congre. Ch. and Soc. Center, Boston, Mass., 1944-47; chaplain and dean of min., Ky. State Coll., 1947-51; pastor, St. John's Congre. Ch., 1951-68; Ex. Coord. Com. for Racial Justice, U. C. C., 1968--; organizer, Sch. of Civic Responsibility, Springfield, Mass.; dir., Dramatics, St. John's Players, St. John's Congre. Ch., Springfield, Mass.; chrmn., Legal Redress Committee, Publicity Comm., Springfield Br., NAACP; organizer and first pres., Springfield Civic Assn.; Exec. Com., Citizen's Action Commn. (by Major) Springfield, Mass.; commissioner, Pub. Welfare Commn., Springfield, Mass.; pres., Eisenhower's Comm. on Govt. Contracts, Rel. Leaders Conf., Wash. D. C.; award: New England Reg. Conf., NAACP award 1958, Maine, New Hampshire, Vermont, Conn., Mass., Rhode Island; Pastor's Council (Spearhead and Fought - rec'd plaque) "For distinguished service in attacking the barriers of discrimination and in uniting the spirits of men in understanding and brotherhood, done according to the highest democratic ideals and motivated with the living spirit of true Christianity;" annual award Brotherhood Club, Greenfield, Mass., "Distinguished Award for Outstanding Community Service and High Standards in your profession;" Man of the Year, Omega Psi Phi Fraternity, New England Region, 1954; Bd. of Dirs., Hampden County Mass. Assn. for Retarded Children; Bd. of Dirs., Child and Family Service, Springfield, Mass.; Exec. Bd., Mass. Coun. of Chs., Boston, Mass.; Exec. Bd., McKnight Civic Assn., Springfield, Mass.; Exec. Committee, Springfield Br., NAACP, Springfield, Mass.; chrmn., Comm. on Ministry, Hampden Assn. of Congre. Chrstn. Chs.; Committee on Urban Church, Mass. Congre. Chrstn. Conf.; Inter-racial Action Committee, Greater Springfield Coun. of Chs.; Steering Committee, Scholarship Clearing House; Comm. for Students of Prince Edward County, Va.; mem., Greater Springfield Min. Assn.; Springfield, Mass.; Congregational Min. Club.; Pastors Coun., Springfield; NAACP, Springfield Branch; Urban League, Springfield; Omega Psi Phi Frat.; Delta Chi Chapt., Springfield; Meridan Sun Ludge, No. 26 Free and Accepted Masons; Hampden Assn. Congre. Chrstn. Chs.; Office: 297 Park Ave. S., New York 10010

COBHAM, Dudley DeCosta, b. New York City, New York, April 5, 1922; s. Clement Leroy and Ruth Naomi (Waithe) C.; B. A., Lincoln Univ., 1945; B. D., Gen. Theol. Sem.,

1949; ordained deacon, 1949; ordained priest, 1950; curate, St. Philips, 1949-52; vicar, St. Clement's, 1952-54; rector, St. Clement's, 1954--; chaplain, Mt. Vernon NY Police Dept., 1959--; Bd. of Dirs. Mental Hygiene Assn., Mt. Vernon, NY; Bd. of Dirs. of the Boys Club of Mt. Vernon; Bd. of Dir. of the Community Chest, Mt. Vernon; Bd. of Dirs. of the Community Center, Mt. Vernon; Chrmn., Ed. Comm., NAACP, Mt. Vernon Chap.; Mt. Vernon, Min. Assn.; mem., Phi Beta Sigma Frat.; Progressive Lodge No. 64 F. & A. M.; Men of St. Clement's Ch.; Priest Assn. S. S. J. E.; NY Confirmation Commn. appt. by the Bishop; Research on the His. of Confirmation for the Confirmation Commn. with particular emphasis on Youth; Home: 42 No. High St., Mt. Vernon, N. Y.; Office: 126 So. Ninth Ave., Mt. Vernon, N. Y.

COCHRAN, Morris Bartlett, tchr., b. Charlotte, N. C., June 19, 1910; s. Arthur Myron and Sarah J. (Bly) C.; B. A., Fisk Univ., 1932; B. D., Bishop Payne Div. Sch., 1937; m. Carrie Watson; Children--Janeice Farrar, Brenda Louise, Morrisena Bartlett, Carol Ann; chaplain, Gaudet Normal & Indus. Sch., New Orleans, La., 1937-38; chaplain & tchr., the Gailor Indus. Sch., Mason, Tenn., 1938-40; priest-in-chge., W. Tennessee Missions, 1938-44; priest-in-charge, St. Timothy's, Daytona Beach, Fla., and St. John's, Orlando, Fla., 1945-49; instr., Business Dept. of Bethune Cookman Coll., Daytona Beach Fla., 1947-49; rector of St. Margaret's Prot. Episc. Ch. Dayton, O., 1949--; sec., the Memphis Chamber of Commerce, 1942-44; mem., The Dayton Urban League Bd., 1950-61; mem., Soc. Health Bd., 1954-59; present mem. The Human Relations Commn. of Dayton, O.; campaign coordinator, Dayton United Negro Coll. Fund Campaign, 5 yrs.; former sec. and pres., the Dayton Min. Assn.; award from the Natl. United Negro Coll. Fund - citation for services to the Dayton & Montgomery County Soc. Hygiene Assn.; award from the Eta Phi Beta Sorority, for services in Religion, Education, etc.; Home: 6380 Germantown Pike, Dayton, O.; Office: 3010 McCall St., Dayton, O.

COLE, Wilbert C., b. Miss.; attended, Amer. Bapt. Theol. Sem., Nashville, Tenn.; Storer Coll.; United Theol. Sem. N. Y.; current pastor, St. Philips Bapt. Ch., Wash., D. C., 1945--; organizer, Natl. Capital Bapt. Conv.; men Walter H. Brooks Bd. of Dirs.; vice moderator, Mt. Betl el Bapt. Assn.; active in politics, Wash., D.C.; Office: St. Philips Bapt. Church, 10 K St. NE, Wash., D.C.

COLEMAN, David Cyrus, b. Thomasville, Ga., Jan. 24, 1901; s. James Emmanual and Crecy C.; attended Fla. Meml. Coll.; Albany State; Lane Coll.; D.D. (hon.) Monrovia Coll., Monrovia, Liberia (Africa); m. Tennie Mildred Anderson; Children--David Cyrus, Jr., W. Coleman, E.H. Coleman, Mildred L.; pastor, Campbell Chapel A.M.E. Ch., Denver, Colo.; former princ., Douglass High Sch., Live Oak, Fla.; mem., Gen. Bd., A.M.E. Ch., E. Denver Min. Alliance, Exec. Com. Denver Area Coun. of Chs.; treas., Colo. Annual Conf., A.M.E. Ch.; mem. NAACP; Home: 2815 Dahlia St., Denver, Colo. 80207; Office: 1500 E. 22nd Ave., Denver, Colo.

COLEMAN, Frederick Douglas, Jr., physician, b. Louisville, Ky., Jan. 25, 1921; s. Frederick Douglas, Sr. and Jamye (H.) C.; Fisk Univ.; Meharry Med. Coll., M.D., 1944; D.D., Monrovia Coll., Liberia, 1955; m. Ann Gleaves; Children--Frieda Ann, Frederick Douglas III; pastor, Afr. Meth. Episc. Ch., Hartsville Circuit, 1940-42; Trinity, Nashville, 1942-45; presiding elder, Clarksville Dist., 1945-49; pres. elder, North Nashville Clarksville Dist., 1956-64; practicing physician, Clarksville, Tenn., 1945--; staff physician, Meml. Hosp., Clarksville, Tenn., 1956--; examiner, Metropolitan Life Ins. Co., 1958--; mem., Montgomery County Med. Soc. (integrated); Tenn. Med. Assn.; Amer. Med. Assn.; Natl. Med. Assn.; US Army, Med. Corps, Capt., 1953-55; Commanding Officer, 765th Med. Detachment; Chief Physical Examiner US Army Hosp., Ft. Campbell; Battalion Surgeon 47th Armored Med. Bn. 1st Armored Div.; repr., A.M.E. Ch. Med. Missions Bd. Natl. Coun. Chs.; mem. Mason; American Legion; Home: 847 Woodwart Dr., Clarksville, Tenn.; Office: 224 8th St., Clarksville, Tenn.

COLEMAN, Harry Alexander, b. Piedmont, W. Va., Aug. 3, s. Paul Abraham and Marguerite (Howard) C.; Johnstown Cent., Univ. of Pittsburgh, 1953-55, A.B. Univ. of W. Va., 1955-57, S.T.B., Boston Univ. Sch. of Theol.; m. Helen Threasa Price; ministry: asst. pastor, Trinity Meth. Ch., Johnstown, Pa. 1953-55; asst. to pastor, Jones Meth. Ch., Morgantown, W. Va., 1957; asst. to pastor, Warren Meth. Ch., Pittsburgh, Pa. summers of

1957 and '58, Minister to Youth of First Meth. Ch., Everett, Mass., 1958-60; pastor, Logan Meml. Meth. Ch., Parkersburg, W. Va., 1960-62; pastor, Ebenezer Meth. Ch., Huntington, W. Va., 1962-64; Charleston Dist. Dir. of Youth Work, 1960-64; mem. NAACP; chrmn., Legal Defense Fund of NAACP 1963-64; sec. Brotherhood of Chrstns. & Jews, 1961-62; US Army, 1951-53; mem. W. Va. Univ. Philosophical Soc.; Sigma Theta Epsilon Fraternity; Home: 1647 Eighth Ave., Huntington, W. Va. 25703

COLEMAN, Nelson Garfield, b. Union Springs, Ala., Nov. 15, 1909; s. Nelson and Mittie; B. S., Ala. State Coll., Montgomery, Ala.; Ala. Lutheran Bible Inst., Montgomery, Ala.; m. Vesta Emily; Children--Bettye, Patricia, Nelson, Thelma, Bessie, Presley, Vesta; pastor, Grace Luth. Ch., Anniston, Ala., 1956--; mem., Miami Valley Conf. and O. Dist.; tchr., prin., sch. in Ala., 1932-35, 1935-43; cons., Univ. of Ala., Cap. Univ., Columbus, O.; Univ. of Chgo.; Augsburg Coll., Mpls., Minn.; pres., Mutual Co-op. Grocery Store, 1957-60; Anniston Br. NAACP, 1946-49; sec., Emancipation League, 1962-68; Amer. Fed. of Govt. Employees; US Army, 1944-45; award, Medal of Honor; mem. AFGE Lodge; Voters League; Civic League; Min. Alliance; Anniston Min. Conf.; coordinating com., Black Luth. Clergymen; Home: 1100 W. 14th St., Anniston, Ala.; Office: 1301 W. 15th St., Anniston, Ala. 36201.

COLEMAN, Rudolph Wesley, b. Liveoak, Fla., Aug. 19, 1929; s. David Cyrus and Tennie Mildred; B. S., Wilberforce Univ., 1954; B. D., Payne Sem. 1956; Th. M., Princeton Sem.; m. Cecile M. Bryant; Children--Princess Cheryl; pastor, Bethel Afr. Meth. Episc. Ch., Schenectady, N. Y., 1956; Vernon Temple A. M. E. Ch., Southampton, Bermuda, 1956-61; Union Chapel A. M. E. Ch., Newark, N. J., 1961-66; Mt. Zion A. M. E., Dover, Del., 1966--; dir. Chrstn. Ed., New Jersey Conf., 1961-66; mem. Coun. of Chs., Redevelopment Bd., 1962-66; Trustee, Bapt. El. Conf., 1967--; First v. p., NAACP (Dover Br.); 1945-48; Air Force; mem., Phi Beta Sigma; Home: 28 Queen St., Dover, Del. 19901.

COLEMAN, William Hannan, Jr., tchr., b. Detroit, Mich., Jan. 5, 1926; s. Wm. J., Sr. and Willie C.; Livingstone Coll., 1943-45; Detroit Inst. of Tech., 1945-46; Univ. of Calif., 1947-48; A. B., San Francisco State, 1949; Grad.

study, Univ. So. Calif., Los Angeles State; Stephanie Cornelius, David William (deceased), Paul Frederick; pastor, Shiloh A. M. E. Z. Ch., Monrovia, 1950-52; First A. M. E. Z. Ch., Pasadena, Calif., 1952-57; Martin Chapel A. M. E. Z. Ch., Los Angeles, 1957-58; Second A. M. E. Z., Los Angeles, 1958--; tchr., John Muir Jr. Coll., Pasadena, 1953-54; Wilson High Sch., Pasadena, 1955-57; Los Angeles Sch. Sys., 1957-58; office mgr., Commercial Express Trust of Arcadia, Calif., 1951-52; Fourth v. p., Ministers & Laymen's Assn. (A. M. E. Z. Ch.); faculty mem., San Fran. Coun. of Chs. Dept. of Chrstn. Edu.; faculty mem., West Coast Conferences, A. M. E. Z. Ch. Leadership Training Inst.; area dir., Chrstn. of Conf. Bd., dir. of youth (presently) sec., Dist. Conf.; sec., the Budget Committee of the S. W. Rocky Mountain Conf.; chrmn., Committee on Admissions, and Conf. field sec. of the Committee on Soc. Action (A. M. E. Z. Ch.); award for outstanding community service by the Consolidated Realty Bd. of Los Angeles, 1964; Recommended for Edu. Award for Los Angeles Ministers Awards Annual Event, 1961; mem, Democrat, Alpha Phi Alpha, Civil Rights Non-Violence Workers Committee, Inc., NAACP, Urban League, UCRC Edu. Committee, Friends of Student Non-Violent Coordinating Committee; research area: Howard Becker's Sacred Secular Theory, 1963 (unpub.); Soc. Teachings of John Wesley and Black Muslims in the USA; Home: 2117-1/2 Palm Grove Ave., Los Angeles, Calif.; Office: 1201 East 43rd St., Los Angeles, Calif.

COLERIDGE, Clarence Nicholas, b. Georgetown, British Guiana, S. Africa, Nov. 27, 1930; s. Charles and Ina (De Weever) C.; Lincoln Univ., 1950-51; B. S., Howard Univ., 1951-54; B. D., Drew Univ. Sch. of Theol., 1960; Gen. Theol. Sem., 1960-61; curate, St. Philip's Ch., NYC, 1961; curate, St. George's Episc. Ch., Brooklyn, N. Y., 1962--; Home: 845 Putnam Ave., Brooklyn, N. Y.; Office: 800 March Ave., Brooklyn, N. Y.

*COLES, Joseph Carlyle, Jr., b. Wash., D. C., Feb. 15, 1926; s. Joseph Carlyle and Rubie (Banks) C.; A. B., B. D., Howard Univ., Wash., D. C., 1947, 1950; m. Geneva Rose Hamilton; Children--Rubie, Jocelyn; pastor, St. Paul Chrstn. Meth. Episc. Ch., Halifax, Va., 1949-50; Ebenezer C. M. E. Ch., So. Boston, Va., 1950-53; Lane Metro C. M. E. Ch., Cleveland, O., 1953-63; Williams Institutional C. M. E. Ch., NYC, N. Y., 1963--;

dean, The Ohio Leadership Training School (C. M. E.), 1955-59; mem., Cleveland Bd. of Edu., 1962-63; pres., Meth. Min. Alliance, Cleveland, O., 1959-61; Exec. Comm., NAACP, Cleveland, O.; picture appeared in Ebony Magazine in 1955 under caption "Bright Young Men of God;" mem., 11th Ward Democratic Club, Cleveland, O., 1961-63; Alpha Phi Alpha; former contributing ed., The Christian Index (official organ of the C. M. E. Ch.); Home: 1270 E. 222nd, Bronx, N. Y.; Office: 2225 7th Ave., New York, N. Y.

*COLLIER, Arthur James, Jr., b. June 8, 1930, Macon, Ga.; s. Arthur James, Sr. and Bessie Rozier (C.); B. S., Florida N. & I. Coll., St. Augustine, Fla., 1957; B. D., Howard Univ. Sch. of Rel., Wash., D. C., 1960; grad. courses, Barry Coll., Miami, Fla.; Fla. State Univ., Tallahassee, Fla.; m. Jacquelyn Lightsey; Children--Arthur III, Joel Emerson, Jacquelyn J., Avis; Minister to migrants, Milton, N. Y., 1958-59; Pompano Farm Labor, Fla., 1960-63; pastor, St. Matthews Bapt. Ch., Wabasso, Fla., 1963-66; Project. dir., Adult Migrant Ed., Fla. State Dept. of Ed., 1966--; tchr. to migrant children, Broward Co.; Opportunity Coun. Adult Ed. Program, 1963-66; Consult. Adult Basic Ed., State Dept. of Ed. (Fla.); paratrooper, US Army, 3 yrs.; mem. Phi Beta Sigma; Fla. Adult Ed. Assn.; Adult Ed. Assn. of the USA; Natl. Assn. for Pub. Sch. Adult Ed.; Ed., Handbook of Contemporary Ed. Concepts for Reaching and Enriching Adult Migrant and Seasonal Farm Workers; Bulletin 71H-6, 1968, State Dept. of Ed., Tallahassee, Fla.; Home: 1328 Victoria St., Tallahassee, Fla. 32304; Office: 319 Pepper Bldg., State Dept. of Ed., Tallahassee, Fla.

COLLINS, George Napoleon, bishop, b. Quincy, Fla., June 8, 1899; s. Charles C. and Fannie (Armstead) C.; A. B., Edward Waters Coll., 1926; B. D., B. F. Lee Sem., 1926; D. D. (hon.), Shorter Coll., 1944; Moody Bible Inst. Chicago, 1943-45; m. Lottie Phyllis Miller (deceased), Oneida B. Mickens; Children--George N., Jr., Charles C., William L.; pastor, Sunbeam Afr. Meth. Episc. Ch., Mirroui, 1919; St. Paul A. M. E. Ch., May Port, Fla., 1919-24; St. James A. M. E. Ch., Commers Mill, Jacksonville, Fla., 1925-26; St. James A. M. E. Ch., Miami, Fla., 1926-28; Mt. Moriah A. M. E. Ch., Cocoa, Fla., 1928-29; St. Mark A. M. E. Ch., Orlando, Fla., 1929-31; Mt. Zion A. M. E. Ch., Daytona Beach, Fla., 1931-33;

Mt. Hermon A. M. E. Ch., Ft. Lauderdale, Fla. 1933-40; St. Paul A. M. E. Ch., Tampa, 1940-41; Visitors Chapel A. M. E. Ch., Hot Springs, Ark., 1945; elected bishop, 1964, 18th Dist.; pres., Interdenom. Coun.; mem., Race Relation Coun. of Hot Springs; Mason; NAACP; Elk; Alpha Phi Alpha; author: Practical Jr. Ch. Work; Home: 4426 So. Liberty St., New Orelans, La. 70115.

COLLINS, Leon C., b. Locust Grove, Ga., 1910; graduate, Wilberforce Univ., Ohio; m. Eva Mae Brown; Children --seven; pastor, Zion Ch., Deanwood, Md., 1948--; coun., Receiving Home for Children, Wash., D. C., 1956--; Office: 1234 Kenilworth Ave. NE, Washington, D. C.

COLLINS, Noel Virginia, b. Uniontown, Ky., Nov. 2; d. Joseph and Margaret (Wagner) Churchill; Indiana State Tchrs. Coll., 1919-21, 1939-40; B. S., Ill. Inst. of Tech., 1948; grad. work at DePaul and Roosevelt Universities, Chgo., Ill.; m. Edward J. Collins (deceased); asst. pastor, Cosmopolitan Community, 1935-65, Chicago; Christ Temple Chrstn. Ch., 1965--; Chcgo; tchr., Chicago, Ill., 1921-62; mem. Natl. Writers Club, Christian Writers Press Club, Retired Teachers Assn., Amer. Assn. of Women Ministers; pub., Crossword puzzles, stories, anecdotes; Home: 5768 S. LaSalle, Chicago, Ill. 60621.

COLLINS, William, b. St. Louis, Mo., July 3, 1924; s. William and Rosetta Elizabeth; B. S., St. Louis Univ., 1956; B. D., Colgate Rochester Div. Sch., 1960; Ed. M., Univ. Rochester, 1960; m. Margaret Elizabeth Brown; Children--Sylvia Annett, Deirdre Lynn, William III; caseworker, Mo.; migrant min., N. Y. Coun. of Chs.; Min. of Ed., Antioch Bapt. Ch., 1960-61; Dir. Field Rel. and Asst. Registrar, Bluefield State Coll., Bluefield, W. Va.; pastor, Antioch Bapt. Ch., 1961--; mem., Landmark and Urban Design Commn. Adult Welfare Serv. Com., 1965--; parole bd., St. Louis; Nurses Adv. Bd., St. Louis, Bd. Annie Malone Children's Home; Bd. Interfaith Clergy Coun., St. Louis; US Army, 1943-46; Alpha Phi Alpha; Home: 5770 Waterman, St. Louis, Mo. 63112; Office: Antioch Bapt. Ch., 4213 W. No. Market St., St. Louis, Mo. 63113.

COMPTON, John Robert, b. Oct. 13, 1925, Canton, O.;

s. S. John and Lillie Pearl (C.); B.S.L., Jarvis Chrstn. Coll., Hawkins, Tex., 1947; B.D., Chrstn. Theol. Sem., Indianapolis, Ind., 1963; D.D. (hon.) Chrstn. Theol. Sem., 1968; courses, Yale summer sch. of Alcohol Studies, New Haven, Conn., 1956; m. Lucile A. Wheaton; Children--John, Jr., Lenita Jacqueline; pastor, Fulton St. Chrstn. Ch., Palestine, Tex., 1944-48; United Chrstn. Ch., Cincinnati, O., 1948-66; Dir., Cleveland Met. Comm., Ohio Soc. of Chrstn. Chs., Cleveland, O., 1966-68; asst. to Gen. Minister and Pres. of Chrstn. Ch. (Disciples of Christ), and dir. "Reconciliation-Urban Crisis Program," 1968--; Bible lecturer, 84th Conv. Disciples of Christ, Jamaica, 1964; mem. Spec. Comm. to Congo to study Disciples of Christ Mission Program, 1963; Faculty lecturer, Chrstn. Theol. Sem., Indianapolis, Ind., 1969--; Trustee, Victory Neighborhood Services Agency, 1965-66; Steering Com., O.I.C., Cincinnati, 1966; v.p., NAACP (Cincinnati Br.) 1964-66; mem. Bd. of Mgrs., Intl. Conv. of Christ. Chs.; Mayor's Friendly Relations Com., (Cincinnati); Seminar on Integration in Ohio; author: sermon in Vital Pulpit, ed., by Hunter Beckelhymer; Home: 25530 Westwood Rd., Westlake, Ohio, 44145; Office: 221 Ohmer Ave., Indianapolis, Ind. 46219.

CONE, James Hal, b. Fordyce, Ark., Aug. 8, 1938; s. Charlie M. and Lucille; Shorter Coll., Rome, Ga., 1954-56; A.B., Philander Smith Coll., Little Rock, Ark., 1958; B.D., Garrett Theol. Sem., Evanston, Ill., 1961; M.A., Ph.D., Northwestern Univ., Evanston, Ill., 1961, 1965; m. Rose Hampton; Children--Michael Lawrence, Charles Pierson; asst. pastor, Woodlawn, Afr. Meth. Episc. Ch.; Prof. Philander Smith Coll., 1964-66; Adrian Coll., Adrian, Mich., 1966-67; Asst. prof. Theol. Union Theol. Sem., NYC, 1967-present; mem., Amer. Acad. Rel. Amer. Theol. Soc.; contrib. author to Is Anybody Listening to Black America by E. Lincoln; author, Black Theology and Black Power, N.Y. Seabury Press, 1969; Home: 1368 Spencer Pl., Adrian, Mich.; Office: Adrian Coll.

COOK, James E., b. Lancaster, S.C., Mar. 25, 1925; s. Neely and Grebilue; B.A., Livingstone Coll., 1949; B.D., Hood Theol. Sem., 1951; m. Mildred Washington; Children--Diaon, Gloria, Roslyn; pastor, Warner Temple, Lancaster, S.C., 1950-51; Baum Temple, Summerville, S.C., 1951-61; Butler Chapel A.M.E.Z. Ch., Greenville, Ala., 1961--; Dean of Rel., Lomax-Hannon Jr. Coll.,

1962--; chrmn. Bd. of Dir., City Reaction; mem., Adv. Com., Bd. of Dir., Community Action Program, 1966--; Trustee, Bd. of Lomax-Hannon Jr. Coll.; mem., Omega Psi Phi; Eaton Lodge, Knights of Pythias; Masons; Min. and Laymen Coun. of A. M. E. Z. Ch.; NAACP; Civic Democratic League; author, articles, Star of Zion; Home: 407 Oglesby St., Greenville, Ala.; Office: 407 Oglesby St., Greenville, Ala. 36037.

*COOK, Payton Brailsford, b. Griffin, Ga., Mar. 10, 1931; s. Marcus E., Sr. and Mary (Daniel) C.; A. B., Paine Coll., Augusta, Ga., 1953; B. D., Howard Univ., Sch. of Rel., Wash., D. C., 1959; Grad. study in Sociology, Grad. Sch., Howard Univ., Wash., D. C., 1960; certificate: Univ. of Ga., Southeastern Sch. for Alcohol Studies, 1964; m. Mary Prudence Murray; Children--Pamela Yvonne, Lisa De Nell; asst. pastor, First Bapt. Ch., Wash., D. C., 1959-62; migrant chaplain, NY State, Coun. of Chs., Camden, New York, 1958-60; counselor Children's Center, Laurel, Md., 1960-63; Senior Clinical Chaplain, Milledgeville State Hosp., 1963--; mem., Natl. Assn. for the Advancement of Colored People & Natl. Urban League; US Army, 1953-55; Good Conduct Medal; Defense Medal; mem., Ga. Pub. Health Assn.; The Amer. Correctional Chaplain's Assn.; Amer. Prot. Correctional Chaplains Assn.; Home: 548 Boundary St., Milledgeville, Ga.; Office: Milledgeville State Hosp., Milledgeville, Ga.

COOK, Wallace Jeffery, b. El Reno, Okla., July 14, 1932; s. Walter and Della Mae; B. A., Ariz. State Coll., 1953; B. D., Crozer Sem., 1964; D. D. S., Howard Univ., 1957; m. Martha Charles; Children--Cheryle Louise; pastor, First Bapt. Ch., Yardley, Pa., 1963-64; Ebenezer Bapt. Ch., Providence, R. I., 1964--; Dr. of Dental Surgery, US Air Force, 1957-61; mem., Bd. John Hope Settlement House; Urban Leage, Providence, R. I.; v. p., Greater Providence Min. Alliance, 1965-67; sec., Greater Providence Min. Alliance, 1967--; Capt., USAF, 1957-61; mem., R. I. Bapt. State Conv., bd. mem., United Bapt. Conv. of Mass. and R. I.; Steering Com. of Sun. Sch., B. Y. F. Cong. of United Bapt. Conv.; 1st. v. p., United Bapt. Conv. of Mass. and R. I.; Home: 54 Adelaide Ave., Providence, R. I. 02907; Office: 135 Dodge St., Providence, R. I. 02907.

COOLEY, James Franklin, tchr., b. Rowland, N. C., Jan.

11, 1926; s. James F. and Martha (Buie) C.; A.B., Johnson C. Smith Univ., 1953; B.D., Johnson C. Smith Univ. Thol. Sem., 1956; m. Lourenia McCallum; Children--Virginia Mae, James Francis, Gladys, Franklin D.; pastor, Grant Chapel Presby. Ch., Darien, Ga., 1956-57; current pastor, St. Andrews Presby. Ch., Forrest City, Ark., 1956--; tchr., Lincoln Jr. High Sch., Forrest City, Ark., 1957--; advisor to Youth Group (conf.), Stillman Coll., Tuscaloosa, Ala., 1956--; mem., Civic League; del., state-side meetings on Community Service Programs, Juvenile Problems; US Forces, 1944-46; award and decorations: E.T.O. Ribbon; P.T.O. Ribbon, Ribbon for Liberation of France & Philippines; Good Conduct Medal; two battle stars; mem., Omega Psi Phi, Mason, Ark. Teachers Assn., Forrest City Prof. Tchrs. Assn.; Min. Alliance, Juvenile Probation Officer, Juvenile Bd. & Forrest City voters league; Spec. recognition in newspaper for Juvenile Work; Ex-official mem. of public welfare dept.; Lion Club consultant with juvenile, municipal, and circuit courts on all Negro violators; Home: 222 S. Beach St., Forrest City, Ark.; Office: 715 S. Center St., Forrest City, Ark.

COOPER, Austin Rellins, b. Miami, Fla., Aug. 8, 1933; s. Benjamin Leon, Jr. and Louise (Bethel) C.; 1953-57, B.A., St. Augustine's Coll., Raleigh, N.C.; 1957-60, B.D., Evanston, Ill.; m. Patricia Ann Hopkins; son--Austin, Jr.; ordained deacon, 1960; ordained priest, 1961; vicar, ch., Transfiguration & St. Andrew's Episc. Ch., Hollywood, Fla., July-Sept., 1960; vicar, St. Matthews Episc. Ch., Delray Bch., Fla., & St. Marys Ch., Deerfield Bch., Fla., Oct. 1960-Feb. 1962; curate, St. Simons Rochester, N.Y., Mar.-Oct. 1962; vicar and headmaster, St. Augustine Espisc. Ch., Dallas, Tex.; activities: pres. Delray Bch. (Fla.) br. NAACP, July '61-Feb. '62; mem., Dallas (Tex.) br. NAACP; Dallas Committee for Full Citizenship, Edu. Comm.; Amer. Civ. Liberties Union; Alpha Phi Alpha; Home: 3940 N. Hampton Rd., Dallas, Tex.; Church: 3930 N. Hampton Rd., Dallas, Tex.

*COOPER, John, Jr., b. Jonesville, Tex., Feb. 28, 1928; s. John and Sue Milla Owen; A.B., B.D., Howard Univ.; m. Eleanor J. James; asst. pastor, Shiloh Bapt. Ch., Wash., D.C., 1942-55; First Bapt. Ch., Lexington, Va., 1955-58; current pastor, New Monumental Bapt. Ch., Chattanooga, Tenn., 1958--; tchr., Bible Center, Chattanooga, Tenn.; sec., Chattanooga Min. Alliance; pres.,

Interdenom. Min. Alliance; Democrat; mem., NAACP; Home: 1112 E. Fifth St., Chattanooga, Tex.

*COOPER, Marcus Lanstern, Jr., b. Austin, Tex., June 23, 1917; s. M. L., Sr. and Celestine (Black) C.; Sam Huston Coll., 1936-37; B. A., Tillotson Coll., 1940; B. D., Howard Univ., Sch. of Rel., 1949; m. Minnie Patterson; Children--Esther Lynette, Marcus L., III; pastor, Gay Hill Bapt. Ch., Georgetown, Tex., 1950-58; Second Bapt. Ch., Waco, Tex., 1958--; pres., Austin br. NAACP, 1950-58; pres., Waco br. NAACP, 1959--; pres., Bapt. Min. Union, Austin, Tex., 1956-57; pres., Round Rock Sub-Dist. Bd.; recording sec., Doris Miller YMCA Bd. of Management, Waco, Tex., 1960--; recording sec., Waco Min. Alliance, 1966; Home: 1215 S. 2nd St., Waco, Tex. 76706; Office: Second Bapt. Ch., 1205 S. 2nd St., Waco, Tex.

COOPER, Quincy Darnell, b. Republic, Pa., Feb. 14, 1938; s. Lafayette S. and Jannie C.; A. B., Maryland State Coll., 1956-60; S. T. B., Wesley Theol. Sem., 1960-63; m. Deborah Lynn; pastor, Lewes Charge, Lewes, Del., 1958-63; assoc. pastor, Salem Meth. Ch., NYC, 1963-64; pastor, John Wesley Meth. Ch., Brooklyn, NY, 1964--; research dir., Morningside Teen Council, 1963-64; Community Voters Assn. Inc., Bklyn, NYC; mem., Harlem br. YMCA, Bedford br. YMCA; Prot. Coun. of Bklyn; Rockefeller Found. award for Theol. Students; mem., Kappa Alpha Psi, Mason, Kappa Alpha Mu Honor Soc.; Home: 378 Nostrand Ave., Brooklyn, N. Y.; Office: 260 Quincy St., Brooklyn, N. Y.

COOPER, Theodore Walter, b. New Orleans, La., April 28, 1929; s. Walter and Irene C.; m. Margie Luvada Thompson; Children--Monica; pastor, St. Andrews Luth. Ch.; pastor, Bethlehem Luth. Ch., New Orleans, La.; pastor, St. John Luth. Ch., Kansas City, Mo.; pastor, New Hope Luth. Ch., Detroit, Mich.; mem. Bd. Dirs., Luth. Human Relations Council; Home: 4055 Seebaldt, Detroit, Mich; Church: 1658 Holden, Detroit, Mich.

COSTEN, James Hutten, b. Omaha, Nebr., Oct. 5, 1931; s. Wm. Theodore and Mary (Brookings) C.; A. B., Johnson C. Smith Univ., 1953; B. D., Johnson C. Smith Univ., 1956; Th. M., Southern Bapt. Theol. Sem., 1963; m. Melva Wilson Costen; Children--James Hutten, Jr., Craig Lamont, Cheryl Leatrice; pastor, Mt. Pisgah United

Presby. Ch., Rocky Mount, N. C., 1956--; mem. Mayor's Good Neighbor Comm., Rocky Mount, N. C.; pres. NAACP; sec. Voters League; Dir. T. B. Assn.; awards: United Fund Award 1961 for Outstanding Citizenship, Rocky Mount, N. C.; Citizen of theYear award 1962 by Alpha Omicron Chapter Omega Psi Phi Frat.; mem., Alpha Phi Alpha Frat.; Home: 312 Park Ave., Rocky Mount, N. C.; Church: 614 Goldleaf St., Rocky Mount, N. C.

COSTNER, Dwight Augustus, b. Gaston Co., N. C., Apr. 9, 1897; s. Alonzo Lee and Sarah Perlina; A. B., Johnson C. Smith Univ., 1927; B. D., Va. Union Univ., 1931; courses, Howard Univ., 1939-41; 1944; m. Jessie Mae Gidney; pastor, Pine Grove Ch., Blacksburg, S. C., 1928-32; Fairview Ch., Cherryville, N. C., 1939-40; New Zion Ch., Spindale, N. C., 1940-42; Ebenezer Ch., Kings Mt., N. C., 1945-49; St. James Bapt. Ch., Bessemer City, 1945-52; sec., Ebenezer Sun. Sch. Conv., 1922-27; Gold Hill Assn., 1931-32; asst. sec., Mt. Peace Assn.; 1936; Ebenezer Bapt. Assn., 1942-present; retired 1963; tchr., N. C. pub. schs.; dir., Cleveland Co. Tchrs. Civic League; v. p., Cleveland Co., N. C., NAACP; chrmn. Head Start, Shelby, N. C.; mem. Trustee's Bd., Cleveland Meml. Hosp.; Mason; Democrat; Omega Psi Phi; chrmn. Retired Tchrs., S. W. Dist. of N. C.; rec'd Cert. of appreciation and plaque for service as tchr., May, 1963; Home: Rt. 3, Box 412A, Shelby, N. C. 28150.

*COUNCILL, Richard Alvin, b. Suffolk, Va., Apr. 19, 1917; s. Richard C. and Rosa E. (Williams) C.; certificate, Elizabeth City State Tchr. Coll., 1934-36; Drew Univ. & Howard Univ. Sch. of Rel., 1944-46; B. S., M. A., Columbia Univ., 1948-51; D. D., Livingstone Coll., 1957; m. Dorothy L. Coston; Children--Faith Maria, Sheila Marie; pastor, St. James A. M. E. Z. Ch., Eliz. City, N. C., 1941-43; Good Hope and Center Chapel A. M. E. Z. Chs., Curritucks Co., N. C., 1943-44; Shrewsbury Ave. A. M. E. Z. Ch., Red Bank, N. J., 1945-52; Logan Temple A. M. E. Z. Ch., Knoxville, Tenn., 1952-56; Metropolitan A. M. E. Z. Ch., Norfolk, Va., 1956-present; instr., Knoxville Coll., 1953-56; instr., Evening Coll., Norfolk Div. of Va. State Coll., 1956-present; mem., Bd. Management, Hunton YMCA; treas., Norfolk Min. Assn.; 1959; pres., A. M. E. Z. Min. Alliance, 1964-present; mem., NAACP; Mason; Exec. Com. Va. Coun. Chs., 1963-present; treas., Va. Annual Conf., 1956-present;

Home: 1305 Merrimac Ave., Norfolk, Va. 23504.

*COURSEY, John Henry, b. Marshall, Tex., Sept. 22, 1931; s. Wm. and Mackie (Ford) C.; B.A., B.D., Howard Univ., Sch. of Rel., 1955, 1963; pastor, Liberty Town Meth. Charge, Liberty Town, Md., 1960-61; Atholton Meth. Chge., Simpsonville, Md., 1961-67; instr., Cortez Peters Business Sch., Wash., D.C., 1962-63; mem., Bd. of Dirs., Tsuga Day Camp, Guilford, Md., 1964; Political Action Comm., NAACP Howard Co. br., 1963--; 5th Dist. Democratic Club, Howard Co., Md.; Kappa Alpha Psi; chaplain, Howard Univ. Business Alumni; Glenwood Country Club; author: "A Second Look;" Home: 5549 So. Dakota Ave., Wash. D.C., 20011; Office: 1100 Vermont Ave. NW, Wash., D.C.

COUSIN, Lee Andrew, chaplain, b. Roxboro, N.C., Mar. 17, 1915; s. Nathaniel Theodore and Sadie Fisher (Duncan) C.; B.D., Payne Theol. Sem., 1936; m. Mary Evelyn Lunsden; Children--Myrna Lee (Choates), Evelyn Elayne, Jesse Andrew, Joan Elizabeth; pastor, A.M.E. Chs., Huntington, Pa., W. Bridgewater, Pa., Greenburg, Pa., Tampa, Fla., 1936-40; pastor, Monessen and Wilkenburg, Pa., 1945; US Army Chaplain 1943-45, 50; Service in the European and Pacific Theatres of operation during WW II; Office: Chaplain, Headquarters, USA, Material Command, Wash., D.C. 20315.

*COX, Benjamin Elton, b. Whiteville, Tenn., June 19, 1931; s. Charlie and Ada C.; A.B., Livingstone Coll., Salisbury, N.C., 1954; Hood Sem., Salisbury, N.C., 1954-55; B.D., Howard Univ. Sch. of Rel., Wash., D.C., 1957; courses: Episc. Theol. Sch., Cambridge, Mass., 1957; youth minister, Caldwell Chapel Afr. Meth. Episc. Zion Ch., Kankakee, Ill., 1948-51; pastor, Jonesville A.M.E.Z. Ch., Matthews, N.C., 1953-55; youth min., John Wesley, A.M.E.Z. Ch., Wash., D.C., 1955-56; lay reader, St. Luke's Episc. Ch., Wash., D.C., 1956-57; student minister, All Saints' Episc. Ch., Lynn, Mass., 1957; current pastor, Pilgrim United Ch. of Christ, High Pt., N.C., 1958--; asst. chaplain, Boys' Village of Md., Chetleham, Md., 1956-57; tchr., Wm. Penn High Sch., High Pt., N.C., 1958-59; Bd. mem., Carl Chavis YMCA, High Pt., 1962; active in non-violent protests; Natl. Youth Sec. for NAACP, 3 mos.; field sec., CORE, 1961; one of the first 13 Freedom Riders; jailed 17 times; face sentence of 10 years if ever convicted by highest court; spent more than 4-1/2 mos. in jails in N. C., Ark. and La.; Home 619 No. Elwood Dr., High Pt., N. C.; Office: 600 Fairview St., High Pt., N. C.

COX, James Alexander, educator, b. Pittsburgh, Pa., Aug. 17, 1913; s. Samuel R. and Mary Francis Mayo C.; Va. Sem. & Coll., 1932-35; A. B., Va. Union Univ., 1937; M. A., Univ. of Pittsburgh, 1957; Adv. studies, Harvard & Yale; pastored, Mt. Zion Bapt. Ch., Bridgeport, O., 1938-42; Act. pastor, 2nd Bapt., Steubenville, O., 1943; pastor, Macedonia Bapt., Wheeling, W. Va., 1947-53; pastor, Calvary Bapt., Pittsburgh, Pa., 1953--; princ., Westmoreland Co., Va., 1937-38; tchr., Lincoln High Sch., Wheeling, W. Va., 1938-43; US Army Chaplain (Maj.), WW II, 1943-46; recipient, Bronze Star (action beyond call of duty); achievement award, Courier WAMO, 1960; Salute award, Sta. WZUM, Outstanding contribution to Community, 1964; Mr. Pastor Plaque Award, Elks of World, 1957; Meritorious Serv. Placque, Soc. Worker at Morals Court, Bapt. Min. Conf., Pittsburgh & Vicinity, 1961; soc. worker, Moral Court, Pittsburgh, Pa., 1954-60; pres., Bapt. Min. Conf., Pittsburgh & Vicinity, 1963--; mem., Bd. Dirs., NAACP; asst. dean, fac. mem., Pittsburgh Extension, Amer. Bapt. Theol. Sem.; mem., United Negro Protest Committee, Pittsburgh; Mason; Home: 512 Junilla St., Pittsburgh, Pa., 15219; Church: 2629 Wylie Ave., Pittsburgh, Pa. 15319.

COX, Milton Edward, tchr., b. Sanford, N. C., Nov. 10, 1921; s. Wm. Francis and Rose (Smith) C.; A. B., Johnson C. Smith Univ., Charlotte, N. C., 1932-36; B. D., Johnson C. Smith Univ., 1936-39; M. A., McCormick Theol. Sem., Chgo., Ill, 1947-48; m. Margaret Elizabeth Robinson; pastor, Logan-New Center Chs., RFD, Statesville, N. C., 1937-41; Antioch Presby. Ch., Eliz. City, N. C., 1941-43; Ladson Presby. Ch., Columbia, S. C., 1943-60; Cheraw Second Presby. Ch., Cheraw, S. C., 1960-62, Trinity Presby. Ch., Tallahassee, Fla., 1962--; instr. Benedict Coll., Columbia, S. C., 1953-61; chaplain, Police Dept., Columbia, S. C.; mem. Bd. of Dir., Boys Club, Columbia, S. C., mem., Adv. Bd.; mem. Nat. Found. of Infantile Paralysis, Richland; mem. USA Committee, pres., Interdenom. Min. Alliance, all of Columbia, S. C.; mem., Min. Alliance of Tallahassee, Boy Scouts of Amer., Inter-Civic Council, NAACP, and Kappa Alpha Psi Fraternity; Home: 1901 S. Boulevard, Tallahassee, Fla; Office: Corner of Gore and Pasco,

Tallahassee, Fla.

COX, Sherman Haywood, b. Baltimore, Md., Aug. 10, 1934; s. Squire Masco and Kathleen William (Hall) C.; Morgan State Coll., 1957; B.A., Oakwood Coll., 1960; Andrews Univ., M.A., 1961; DD., Coll. of Div. Metaphysics, 1962; pastor, Seventh-Day Adventist Ch., in Paducah, Ky., 1961; Seventh-Day Adventist Ch., Lexington, Covington, Berea and Richmond; present, pastor, Hattiesburg, McComb, Laurel, Brookhaven, Soso and Gulfport Seventh-Day Adventist Chs., Mississippi; mem., Ky. Bd. for Mental Health; Lexington, Ky. interracial Min. Assn.; Bd. mem. of one of the two mentally retarded schs. for Negroes in the state of Miss.; assoc. dir., 1964 March of Dimes for the Regional work in Hattiesburg, Miss.; Lexington, Ky. and Hattiesburg, Miss. PTA; editorial, Lexington Herald Leader in 1962; two articles in The Message magazine, 1961-63; Home: 209 Rose Ave., Hattiesburg, Miss.

CRAGG, Christopher Morton, b. N.Y.C., June 26, 1923; s. Christopher M., Sr. and Mary E. C.; diploma, God's Bible Coll., Cincinnati, O., 1948; B.Th., Roosevelt Coll., Chg., Ill., 1951; diploma, Yale Hebrew Theol. Sem., Bklyn, N.Y., 1954; B.D., St. Basil's Sem., N.Y.C., 1964; D.S. Litt. (hon.) Free Episc. Sem., London, Eng., 1964; D.D. (hon.), Daniel Payne Coll., Birmingham, Ala., 1951; L.H.D. (hon.) Imperial Philo-Byzantine Univ., Madrid, Spain, 1966; m. Frances Elaine Laurel; Children--Helena Gwedit; convert from Jewish Rel. to Christianity; served as pres., Union of Ethiopian-Hebrew Congregations & Rabbis; ed., "The African Israelite;" rector, St. Moses, The Black Orthodox Ch.; Cathedral Ch. of the Holy Resurrection, N.Y.; Archbishop, The Amer. Orthodox Ch. and Patriarchal Exarch. and Primate, N.Y.; served as adjunct prof., St. Francis Sem., Bklyn, N.Y.; mem., Holy Synod of Bishops, Turkish Orthodox Patriarchate, Istanbul, Turkey; Bd. of Trustees, Holy Inst., London, England; Bd. of Dirs., St. Basil's Youth Hosp., Auburn, N.H.; Bd. of Dirs., Anti-poverty program, upper Harlem, N.Y.; US Army, 1942-43; rec'd Knight Grand Cross of Justice, Knights of Malta, Order of St. John of Jerusalem; mem., Order of St. Constantine The Great; Mason; mem., Assn. for Study of Negro Life; NAACP; Amer. Liberal Party; mem., N.Y. Coun. of Chs.; mem., Interdenom. Min. Meeting, N.Y.; Amer. Min. Assn.; ed., American Orthodoxy; Falasha Mazgaba Hayimanit

(Ethiopian-Hebrew Treasury of Faith); co-editor, The Divine Liturgy for English-Speaking Orthodox (official liturgy of Amer. Orthodox Ch.); Home: 461 W. 153rd St., N.Y.C. 10031; Office: Holy Theotokos Cathedral, P.O. Box 1294, Woodhaven, L.I., N.Y. 11421.

*CRAIG, Benjamin Howard, b. Clanton, Ala., Oct. 1, 1907; s. Abraham and Mamie C.; A.B., Miles Coll.; B.D., Howard Univ. Sch. of Rel.; courses for M.A., Amer. Univ.; m. Lillie Hendrieth; 1 dau., Annette; sec., YMCA, Birmingham, Ala., 8 yrs.; supply minister, Calvary Presby. Ch., Anniston, Ala., 1948; stated supply minister, Bethel Presby. Ch., Alexandria, Va., 6 yrs; present: pastor, Faith United Presby. Ch., Wash., D.C., 6 yrs.; Counselor and soc. worker, Dept. of Pub. Welfare, D.C. Gov't., 9 yrs.; mem., S.E. Civic Assn. and treas., S.E. Ministerial Assn., Wash. D.C.; former chrmn., precinct 80, Democrat, Washington, D.C.; mem., Comm. Inter-racial Committee; Home: 1629 Fort Davis Pl., S.E., Wash., D.C.; Office: 3129 20th St., SE, Washington, D.C.

CRAIG, Lawrence Lauman, Sr., b. E. St. Louis, Ill., Feb. 4, 1938; s. Charles A., Sr., and Martha F. C.; A.B., Lane Coll., Jackson, Tenn., 1960; B.D., Iliff Sch. of Theol., Denver, Colo., 1963; m. Zenobia Yvonne Barge; Children--Kennethia LaTrace, Conchita DeElla, Lawrence L., Jr., Charles John Presley; pastor, Spring Creek Circuit Chrstn. Meth. Episc. Ch., Tenn., 1958-60; St. Luke C.M.E. Ch., Denver, Colo., 1960-63; Miles Meml. C.M.E. Ch., Wash., D.C., 1963-65; St. Paul C.M.E. Ch., Norfolk, Va., 1965-present; tchr., Chester Co. Training Sch., Chester, Tenn.; Norfolk Sch. Va., shoe salesman, 1952-60 (part-time), St. Louis, Mo.; vocalist, St. Louis, Mo.; St. Louis dir., Youth Christian Endeavor, St. Louis, 1954-56; Choir dir., 1954-56; Dist. dean, Wash.-Va. Dist., Conf. C.M.E.; Bd. mem. S.C.L. Conf., Norfolk Assn.; Dir. of Youth, Norfolk Min. Assn.; Leader, Young Park Civic League, Norfolk; YMCA; Amer. Coll. & Univ. 1960; mem., Alpha Phi Alpha; politics, Independent; Home: 525 W. 27th St., Norfolk, Va. 23517; Office: 310 E. Virginia Beach Blvd., Norfolk, Va. 23510.

CRAWFORD, Evans Edgar, Jr., dean, professor, b. Templ Tex., July 2, 1923; s. Evans Edgar, Sr. and Mary (Inge C.; A.B. Samuel Huston Coll. (now Huston-Tillotson),

Austin, Tex., 1943; S. T. B., Boston Univ. Sch. of Theol., 1946, Ph. D., Boston Univ., Grad. Sch. 1957; m. Elizabeth Pinder Bailey; Ministry: Student minister at Morgan Meml. Ch. of All Nations, Boston, 1943-46; staff pastor, Ch. of All Nations, 1946-49; Interim min., Pond St. Bapt. Ch., Providence, R. I., 1949-54; coordinator, Student Activities, Boston Univ. Sch. of Theol., 1956-58; asst. prof. of practical theol., Howard Univ., Sch. of Rel., 1958; Dean of chapel, Howard Univ., 1959-64; Bd. of Dirs., Providence Urban League, 1953; Bd. of Dirs., John Hope Comm. Center, 1952; mem., Alpha Phi Alpha; NAACP; Exec. Comm., Natl. Assn. of Coll. and Univ. Chaplains, 1963; Home: 4130 Arkansas Ave., NW, Wash., D. C.; Office: Howard Univ., Chapel Office, Wash., D. C.

CRAWFORD, Peter Griffin, b. Aberdeen, Miss., Apr. 6, 1910; s. George and Mary Frances C.; A. B., Rust Coll., 1934; B. D., Payne Theol. Sem., 1941; D. D. (hon.), Mercer Univ., 1951; m. Fannie DeZon; Children--Peter Marlin; Ronald G.; Mark; Mary; pastor, Jr. Ch., St. Stephen's, Detroit, 1933; pastor St. Luke A. M. E. Ch., E. Detroit, 1934; pastor, Wabash, Ind., 1934-37; Kalamazoo, Mich., 1937-38; pastor, Asbury Chapel, Louisville, Ky.; Bethel Ch., Chattanooga, Tenn., 1943-51; pres , Ga. Bapt. Coll., Macon, Ga.; pastor, Charlotte, N. C., 1951-65; present pastor, St. John's A. M. E. Ch., Nashville; former pres. State conf. brs. NAACP, 1947; chrmn., Ch. Com. NAACP, Charlotte, N. C.; Memphis; present v. p., Nashville br. NAACP; chrmn. Skills Bank, Natl. Urban League, 1961-65; mem., Training Program, Natl. Coun. of Chs., USA; ed. and reporter, The Anvil, pub. for 13th Episc. Dist., A. M. E. Chs. of Tenn. and Ky.; Home: 1402 South St., Nashville, Tenn. 37212; Office: 1822 Formosa St., Nashville, Tenn.

CRAWFORD, William Richard, b. Winston-Salem, N. C., June 18, 1910; s. Walter and Henrietta (Evans) C.; A. B., W. Va. State Coll., 1937; B. D., Gammon Theol. Sem., 1947; m. Givendolyn Scales; Children--Gloria Yvette; ordained elder, 1947; pastor, Mt. Pleasant Meth. Ch., Winston-Salem, N. C., 1947--; mem., The Mayor's Civic Betterment Comm., 1950-51; Bd. of Aldermen, Winston-Salem, N. C., 1951-61; Bd. of Dirs., United Fund; Div. chrmn., United Fund, 1951-53; Pub. Safety Comm. Bd., Bd. of Alderman; Winston-Salem Sch. Bd.; Comm. of Management YMCA, chrmn., Urban League-Welfare Com.;

Recreation Comm.; Sec., N.C. Annual Conf. of the Meth. Ch.; Bd. of Dirs., The Eye Bak for Restoring Sight, Inc.; Chief Warden, Civil Defense, So. Third Ward; PTA Council; N.C. Sch. Bd. Assn.; Alcoholic Rehabilitation Comm.; Interdenom. Min. Alliance; The Forsyth Min. Fellowship; Alpha Phi Alpha; NAACP; Mason; Hon. mem., Soc. Promoters Club; Les Bonne Filles; v.p. and dir., Safe Bus Inc.; v. chrmn., Exec. Comm. Democratic Party of Forsyth Co.; Trustee, Winston-Salem Tchrs. Coll.; Bd. of Dirs., Meml. Indust. Sch.; awards: "Man of the Year," 1953 Winston-Salem Jaycees; Service and Civic Award, 1954; Omega Psi Phi, Citation for Service Award; Patterson Ave. YMCA, 1954; The Nathan W. Collier Meritorious Serv. Award, Fla. N & I Coll.; article "Where Does the Church Stand?" Central Chrstn. Advocate; "The Church and Community Outreach" Central Chrstn. Advocate; Home: 1701 Shadymount Ave., Winston-Salem, N.C.; Office: 1003 E. 14th St., Winston-Salem, N.C. 27105.

CREWS, Clarence Leo, b. Newark, N.J., Aug. 10, 1929; s. Lundy and Cynthia Hester; A.B., Bloomfield Coll., Bloomfield, N.J.; B.D., Va. Union Univ., Richmond, Va.; courses: Psychiatry for ministers, Wayne State Univ., Med. Sch., Detroit, Mich.; m. Felecia Juanita Martin; dau. Cynthia Bethania (deceased); pastor, Union Grove Bapt. Ch., Petersburg, Va.; assoc. pastor, Tabernacle Bapt. Ch., Detroit, Mich.; Dir. Rel. Ed. & Prof., Texas Coll., Tyler, Tex.; social worker, Prot. Comm. Services, Detroit, Mich.; Asst. youth dir., YMCA, Detroit; pastor, Hopewell Missionary Bapt. ch. and probation officer, Recorder's Court, Detroit, Mich.-present; sec. Interdenom. Min. Alliance, Detroit, 1959-61; ex. com., Hampton Min. Conf., 1959-61; Exec. com. Southwest Faculty Conf., 1963-65; Biracial Com., Tyler, Tex., 1964-65; mem. Amer. Acad. of Rel., 1961-65; Natl. Chaplains' Assn. for Univ. & Coll.; mem. Menninger Found., 1965-present; Amer. Bapt. Conv.; Progressive Bapt. Conv.; Fellowship of Chrstn. Athletes, Kansas City, Mo.; Home: 17206 Woodingham, Detroit, Mich. 48221; Office: 2911 Kendall, Detroit, Mich. 48238

CREWS, William Hunter, b. Winston-Salem, N.C., Mar. 18, 1932; s. Bynum Curlee and Ruth (Penn) C.; B.A., Va. Union Univ., 1955; M.A., New York Univ., 1964; courses: Union Theol. Sem., NYC; m. June Day; Children--William H., Jr.; dir. of Chrstn. Edu., Bethel

Afr. Meth. Episc. Ch., Detroit, Mich., 1955-57; current pastor, The Mount Pleasant Bapt. Ch., Norfolk, Va., 1957--; chrmn., Budget Com., Norfolk Com. for the Improvement of Edu.; v.p., Bapt. Min. Conf. of Norfolk; mem., Omega Psi Phi; Interracial Fellowship, Norfolk Com. for Improvement of Edu.; Home: 118 Mt. Pleasant Ave., Norfolk, Va.; Office: 934 W. Little Creel Rd., Norfolk, Va.

CRIGLAR, Edmond, b. Sunflour, Miss., Sept. 2, 1889; s. Grant and Eliza C.; minister's course, Amer. Bapt. Bible Sem.; D.D. (hon.) Coleman Coll.; m. Inez Martha Mc Coulough; pastor, Hickory Grove Bapt. Ch., Castalian Springs, Tenn., chrmn., Commn. Student Fund, Bapt. Min. Conf.; chaplain, Amer. Legion, Nashville, Tenn.; dean, East Folk Sun. Sch. and B.T.U. Cong., E. Folk Assn.; tchr., Min. Ethics, Min. Conf., Nashville; tchr., Meaning of Ch. Membership, Stones River Assn.; pres., Progressive Com. Civic League, Nashville, Tenn.; recd. certificate of Progress, Natl. Coun. of Chs.; Democrat; author pamphlets: Fronts for Boys; Acrostic Church Covenant; Dispensation in Genesis; Union or Unity; Which Are We; Home: 2137 Burns Ave., Nashville, Tenn. 27206.

CRISS, George Washington, b. Jacksonville, Tex., Oct. 17, 1919; s. Lum C. and Jessie (Cary) C.; B.D., Western Sem., Kansas City, Mo.; D.D., Friendship Coll., 1963; m. Doris Williams; Children--George, Jr.; asst. pastor, Highland Bapt. Ch., Kansas City, Mo., 1945; organized Friendship Bapt. Ch., Kansas City, Mo., 1949; Metropolitan Bapt. Ch., NYC, 1951-52; pastor, Providence Bapt. Ch., Marlin, Tex., 1952-53; Marvella Park Bapt. Ch., Calif., 1954-56; Sharon Bapt. Ch., L.A., Calif., 1956-61; current, Sharon Bapt. Ch., Bronx, N.Y.; Trustee, Interfaith Health Assn., NYC; Home: 947 Grant Ave., Bronx, N.Y.;' Office: 827 Forest Ave., Bronx, N.Y.

CROSBY, Isaac, b. Bayspring, Miss., Feb. 21, 1936; s. Obadiah and Flossie (Moncrief) C.; B.A., Stillman Coll., 1958; B.D., Union Theol. Sem. (Presby.), 1962; m. Willirean Jackson; Dir., Recreation Rel. Activities, Summer '58; asst. pastor of All Souls Presby. Ch., 1958-59; current pastor, Faith Presby. Ch., 1962--; Dir. of United Chrstn. Fellowship, 1962--; awards: Highest scholastic average, State NFA Quiz Contest, 1953;

Outstanding Achievements Award upon grad. from coll.; Pres. of Stillman Coll. Alumni Assn. 1960-61; Home: 913 N. Cedar St., Pine Bluff, Ark.; Office: 24 Watson Blvd., Pine Bluff, Ark.

*CROSSON, Calvin Perry, b. Clinton, S. C., May 25, 1921; s. Calvin Luther and Eula S. (Murles) C.; A. B. Howard Univ., 1956; B. D., Sch. of Rel., Howard Univ. 1961; m. Ronetta Collyne Swann; 1 dau., Delores C. (Mrs. Philip Jones); pastor, Eastern Meth. Ch., Balto., Md., 1956-65; WW II - Asiatic Pacific Theater, 1942-45; Asiatic Pac. Theater ribbon; Philippine Liberation ribbon; Good Conduct Medal; mem., Interdenom. Min. Alliance; Meth. Ministers Wed. Morning Fellowship; Meth. Min. Fellowship; E. Balto. Clergymen's Assn.; Republican; pastor, Jones United Meth. Ch., Wash., D. C., 1968-present; Home: 4325 New Hampshire Ave., Wash., D. C.

CUMMINGS, James L., b. Allensville, Todd Co., Ky., Dec. 2, 1926; s. Andrew and Fannie Robbie C.; A. B., Lane Coll., Jackson, Tenn., 1948; Butler Univ. Sch. of Rel., Ind., B. D., 1959; m. Norma J. Cravens; Children--Denise Marie; pastor, Trinity Chrstn. Meth. Episc. Ch., Indianapolis, Ind., 1956--; mem. Bd. of Dirs. for Ch. Fed.; pres., Indianadpolis Min. Assn.; Interdenom. Min. Alliance; sec., The Ohio Annual Conf. Chrstn. Meth. Episc. Ch.; mem., Bd. of Indianapolis Zoning Appeals; City Coun., Indianapolis, Ind., 1963--; Fall Creek Parkway YMCA; Bd. mem. NAACP; Fed. Associated Club; Scout Award, Region Seven; Democrat; Alpha "Man of the Year," 1960; Citation from Crispus Attucks High Sch. from "Hall of Fame" for service to community, nation and profession, 1962; mem., Mason, Alpha Phi Alpha; Office: 2253 Martindale Ave., Indianapolis, Ind.

CUNNINGHAM, Frank, coll. pres., b. Okolona, Miss., Oct. 10, 1912; s. Frank and I. B. C.; B. A., Mt. Union Coll., Alliance, O., 1937; M. A., Boston Univ., 1939; S. T. B., Boston Univ. Sch. of Theol., 1940; Ohio State Univ.; Ph. D., Boston Univ., 1951; LL. D. (hon.), Paul Quinn Coll., 1952 m. Elizabeth Holmes; asst. prof., Wilberforce Univ., 1942-45; dean, Turner Theol. Sem., 1945-58; visiting prof., Atlanta Univ. Summer Sch., 1948-58; assoc. pastor, Ch. of All Nations, Boston Univ., 1939-42; pastor, Comm. Afr. Methodist Episc. Ch., Cleveland, O., 1942; current pres., Morris Brown Coll., Atlanta, Ga., 1958--; pres., The Ga. Philosophical Soc.

and Psych.; mem., Amer. Philo. Assn.; Inst. of Rel., Howard Univ.; Phi Beta Sigma; Kappa Boule of Sigma Pi Phi; Danforth Fellow in Philosophy, Univ. of Minn., 1958; Fullbright Scholar in India, 1962; Office: Morris Brown Coll., Atlanta, Ga.

CUNNINGHAM, Richard Theodore, b. Princeton, La., May 30, 1914; Edd and Ida (Henry) C.; A.B., Paul Quinn Coll., Waco, Tex., 1936-39; B.D., Dallas Coll. of the Bible, 1944; Children--Richard Theodore Jr.; current pastor, Bebee Tabernacle C.M.E. Ch., Houston, Tex.; faculty mem., Pastor's Sch., Tex. Coll., Tyler, Tex.; civilian chap., Riverside Hosp., Houston, Tex.; mem., Minister's and Laymen Coun., C.M.E. Ch.; Democrat; Mason; NAACP; Bd. of Chrstn. Soc. Concerns, C.M.E. Ch.; contributing ed., <u>Christian Index</u>; mem., Com. that wrote social creed for C.M.E. Ch.; Home: 917 Saulwer St., Houston, Tex. 77019

CUNNINGHAM, Theodore Francis, b. Omaha, Neb., May 22, 1928; s. Theodore, Sr. and Lilly Mae (Addie) C.; B.S., phil., Creighton Univ., 1951; M.A. Eur. Hist. St. Louis Univ., 1960; Conv. to Catholicism, Aug. 1948; ordained priest, Roman Cath. Ch., June 11, 1964; tchr., history, Eng. speech, dramatics, Creighton Prep, Omaha, 1957-59; mem. Alpha Phi Alpha; Home: St. Mary's College, St. Mary's, Kansas.

CURRY, John Wesley, b. Ashville, Ala., Jan. 10, 1908; s. James Arthur and Zilla (Arnold) C.; A.B., Claflin Coll., Orangeburg, S.C., 1927-30; B.D., Gammon Theol. Sem., Atlanta, Ga., 1930-33; further study, Garrett Sem. 1955, D.D., Claflin College; D.D. Gammon Theol. Sem.; m. Willa Mae Ogletree; Children--John Wesley, Jr., James Adam; ministry, St. Marks Meth. Ch., Mayesville, S.C., 1933-38; Centenary Meth. Ch., Charleston, S.C., 1939-45; supt., Charleston Dist. of the S.C. Conf., 1945-46; Florence Dist., 1946-51; pastor, Cumberland Meth. Ch., Florence, S.C., 1951-57; supt., Florence Dist. 1957-62; pastor, Trinity Meth. Ch. Orangeburg, S.C., 1962 to present; mem., The Meth. Ecumenical Conf., Oxford, England, 1951; World Meth. Conf., Norway, 1961; del. to the Meth. Genl. and Jurisdictional Confs., 1948, '52, '56, '60, '64; mem., Co-ordinating Coun. of The Meth. Ch., 1956-64; Genl. Coun. on World Service and Finance, 1964; treas. of the S.C. Annual Conf.; trustee, Claflin Coll.; mem., Phi Beta

Sigma, Mason, Exec. Com. NAACP; author of column, "Know Your Church" in the Central Chrstn. Advocate of The Meth. Ch.; Home: 191 Boulevard, N. E. Orangeburg, S. C.

CURRY, Lacey Kirk, b. Wichita Falls, Tex., Oct. 8, 1926; s. Milton and Lena (Easter); A. B., Univ. of Denver, 1959; courses, Colo. Univ., Berkeley Bapt. Div. Sch., Weber State Coll.; m. Dorothy Davis; Children--L. K. Seneca, Donald Eugene, Theresa Lynne, Augustus; pastor, St. John Bapt. Ch., Tulare, Calif., 1962-65; New Zion Bapt. Ch., Ogden, Utah, 1965-present; mem., Bd., Comm. Action, Ogden, Utah; military duty, 1945-46; Home: 2929 Lincoln, Ogden, Utah 84401; Office: 2935 Lincoln Ave., Ogden Utah 84401.

CURRY, Morris Alexander, b. Magnolia, Ark., Apr. 17, 1913; s. Luther and Mattie E. C.; B. A., Ark. Bapt. Ch., 1945; M. A., Phillips Univ., Enid, Okla., 1962; m. Zarah Mae Gholston; Children--Morris Alexander, Jr.; pastor, First Bapt. Ch., Idabel, Okla., 1937-51; Shiloh Bapt. Ch., Camden, Ark., 1951-54; Calvary Bapt. Ch., Oklahoma City, Okla., 1955--; dean, Southeastern Dist. Sun. Sch. & B. T. U. Cong., 1941-46; moderator, Southeastern Dist. Bapt. Assn., 1949-51; vice moderator, E. Zion Dist. Assn., 1962--; v. p., NAACP, Okla. City br., 1959-61; mem., House Comm. YMCA East Side br. 1961--; pres., Okla. City Interdenom. Min. Alliance, 1960-62; mem., Pythian; Mason; Democrat; Home: 1918 NE Grand Blvd., Okla. City, Okla.; Office: 300 No. Walnut, Okla. City, Okla.

CURRY, Norris Samuel, bishop, b. Naples, Tex., Aug. 16, 1910; s. Lonnie and Fannie (Hervey) C.; A. B., Texas Coll., 1942; B. D., Drew Univ., 1947; LL. D., Texas Coll., 1957; m. Mary Cleopatra Reynolds; Children--Betsy Gail, Norris Duane; pastoral ministry began in 1928, E. Texas Conf., Central Tex. Conf. to 1944; to N. J. through 1949 in Drew Univ. on leave via pastoral duties; to Los Angeles, Calif. as pastor, Phillips Temple C. M. E. Ch., 9 yrs.; ed., Christian Index, official organ of C. M. E. Ch., 1958; elected 31st Bishop of C. M. E. Ch. in 1962 Genl. Conf., St. Louis, Mo.; presently presiding bishop of the Fourth Episc. Dist., La. and Miss., C. M. E. Ch., residing in New Orleans, La.; tchr. Texas Coll., 1947; del. World and Natl. religious bodies: World Meth. Conf., Natl. Coun. of Chs. Gen. Assemblies;

Faith and Order Conf., in Europe and the U. S.; chrmn. Miss. Indus. Coll. Trustee Bd., Holly Springs, Miss.; mem., Home Mission Div., Natl. Coun. of Chs.; Trustee Bd., Phillips Sch. of Theol., ITC, Atlanta, Ga.; chrmn., governing bd. of Gen. Bd. of Lay Activities, C. M. E. Ch.; Mason; Democrat; Home: 9141 S. Claiborne Ave., New Orleans, La. 70118

DADE, Malcolm Gray, canon, b. New Bedford, Mass., Feb. 27, 1903; s. I. C. and Margaret (Warfield); B. A., Lincoln Univ.; Episc. Theol. Sem., Cambridge, Mass.; D. D. (hon.), Wilberforce Univ.; m. Bonnie Jean Denham; Children--Malcolm, Jr., Duwain, Margaret, Julia; rector, St. Cyprian Prot. Episc. Ch., 1936--; appt. Honorary Canon of the Cathedral Ch. of St. Paul, Mich.; mem., Mayor's Civic Commn. (Mich.); Bd. of Wayne Co. Training Sch., 1960-62; chaplain, Det. House of Correction, 1961-62; del., Prot. Episc. Genl. Convention; chaplain Mich. State Troops during WW II; cited for distinguished comm. service by District-Historic Soc. and Omega Psi Phi; Mayor of Detroit proclaimed a "Canon Dade Day;" hon. mem., WAW-CIO (Local 600); author: "Inside Michigan;" Home: 18834 Charest, Detroit, Mich.; Office: 6114 28th St., Detroit, Mich.

DALY, Samuel Franklin; A. B., Livingstone Coll., Salisbury, N. C.; B. D., Gammon Theol. Sem., Atlanta, Ga.; A. M. Drew Univ., Madison, N. J.; courses, Union Theol. Sem., N. Y.; pastor, First Bapt. Ch., Rocky Mount, N. C. and other chs.; pastor, First Bapt. Ch., Franklin, Va.; tchr., elementary sch., N. C.; princ., High Sch., N. C.; sec., Bapt. State Sun. Sch. Conv., N. C.; dir., Central Div., Bapt. Gen. Conv., N. C.; asst. prof., Shaw Univ. Sch. of Rel., Raleigh, N. C.; sec., Sharon Bapt. Conv., Tidewater area; pres., Southampton Interracial, Interdenom. Min. Union; pres., NAACP, Franklin, Va.; pres., Franklin-Southampton Chap., Va. Human Relation Coun.; mem., State Bd. Va. Human Coun.; mem., Ex. Bd., Bapt. Gen. Conv., Va.; booklet: How to Register and Vote in N. C.; editor, The Living Stone (coll. paper); Home: Box 622, Franklin, Va. 23851

DAMES, Jonathan Alexander, b. Key West, Fla., Feb. 9, 1883; s. R. H. and Malvina J. D.; Edward Waters Coll., A. B. & B. D., Howard Univ., 1920-24; grad. wk. Butler

Univ., Indianapolis, and Union Theol. Sem., NYC; D.D. & LL.D. (hon.), Douglas Univ., St. Louis and Monrovia Coll., Monrovia, Liberia, W. Africa; m. Annie L.; pastor, Lakeland, Md., 1920-24; Cambridge, Md., 1924-27; St. Paul Afr. Meth. Episc. Ch., 1928; pastor, Campbell A.M.E. Ch., Wash., D.C., 1928-29; pastor, St. James A.M.E. Ch., St. Louis, Mo., 1929-40; Pasadena, Calif., 1940-44; Bethel, Detroit, 1944-49; Bethel, Indianapolis, Ind., 1949-57; Woodlawn A.M.E. Ch., Chgo., 1957--; Trustee chrmn., Indiana Conf., 1956-7; Trustee, Wilberforce Univ., 1934-39; princ., Sch. at Thompsontown, Md., 1924-25; organized Clerk Circle in St. Louis seeking jobs integration; Interracial pastoral activities in each city pastored, with emphasis on better race relations; mem., Phi Beta Sigma; Mason; Democrat; author, The A.M.E. General Budget Catechism, Copyright 1957 (pamphlet); The Probationer's Guide, published 1956 (pamphlet); Home: 7842 S. Maryland Ave., Chicago, Ill.; Office: 6456 S. Evans Ave., Chicago, Ill.

DANIEL, Wilbur Nathan, b. Louisville, Ky., Jan. 2, 1918; s. Nathan Daniel and Fannie B.D.; Ft. Wayne Bible Inst.; B.Th., Amer. Bapt. Theol. Sem., Nashville, Tenn., 1948; B.S., Tenn. State Univ., 1949; M.A., Austin Peay State Coll., 1957; m. Marguerite Richards; 2 sons, Wilbur Nathan and Richard Eugene; pastored, Macedonia Bapt. Ch., Garrett, Ind., 1944-47; Pilgrim Emmanuel Bapt., 1947-49, Nashville, Tenn.; St. John Bapt., Clarksville, Tenn., 1949-57; Antioch Miss. Bapt., Chgo., NAACP; v. chrmn., Chgo. Bapt. Inst., vice moderator, North Woodriver Bapt. Dist. Assn.; pres., Chgo. br. NAACP, 1962; Cand. for Cong., 1st Cong. Dist., Ill., 1964; Rec. "Minister of the Year" award, 1960; D.D., Va. Theol. Sem. and Coll., 1960; D.D., Ark. Bapt. State Coll., 1961; "Good American" award, Chgo. Com. of 100 organizations, 1964; Home: 8445 S. Calumet, Chicago, Ill.; Church: 415 W. Englewood Ave., Chicago, Ill.

DANIELS, Reginald James, b. Orangeburg, S.C., Aug. 2, 1916; s. Malachi Samuel and Sallie Garret (Adams) D.; B.S., S.C. State A & M Coll., 1937; S.T.B., Lincoln Univ. Sem., 1943; m. Marguerite Wade Younger; Children--Reginald II, Judith M., Freda A.; served City and Indus. Unit, Bd. of Natl. Missions, Presby. Ch., USA, Phila., 1943; Dayton, O.; current pastor, Madison

Ave. Presby. Ch., Balto., Md., 1944--; tchr., Chester Co., S. C., 1937-40; sec., Bd. of Chrstn. Managers, Druid Hill br. YMCA, 1958; chrmn., Adv. Com., Family and Children's Soc., 1954--; Bd. mem., Family & Children's Soc., 1963--; Office: Madison Ave. Presby. Ch., Baltimore, Md.

DARBY, Walter A., Jr., b. Oct. 22, 1922; s. Walter A. and Iris (Newman) D.; B. A., Oakwood Coll., 1949; m. Florence Burton; Childre--Walter A. III, Edythe Vanessa; pastor, St. Petersburg and Palmetto, Fla., 1949-50; dir. of 20th Century Bible Sch. for the So. Atlantic Conf. of Seventh-Day Adventists, Atlanta, Ga., 1950-51; mgr. of the So. Atlantic Book and Bible House, 1951-57; organized church, Mt. Olives, Athens, Ga., 1957; Winston-Salem, 1957-59; Wilmington, N. C., 1959-61; Macon, Ga., 1961-63; present: pastor, S. D. A. Ch., Wichita, Tex., 1963--; night sch. tchr., Reid Business Coll., Atlanta, Ga., 1955-56; US Army, 3 yrs., former mem., Interdenom. Min. Alliance; Home: 1639 No. Volutsia, Wichita, Kan.; Office: 1121 Wabash Ave., Wichita, Kan.

DAVID, Lawrence T., b. Cherau, S. C., Jan. 14, 1930; s. Marion; A. B., Morris Coll., Sumpter, S. C., 1954; B. D., Gammon Theol. Sem., 1958; course, Columbia Bible Coll. Grad. Sch. of Missions, 1964-65; m. Hilda L. Black; Children--Lawrence Kenneth, LaDonna, Chappelle, Marc Charleton; pastor, St. John Bapt. Ch., Gainesville, Ga., 1957-59; US Army 1959; Chaplain, Ft. Knox, Ky., 1959-61; Wurzburg, W. Germany, 1961-64; Ft. Jackson, Reception Sta., 1964-66; Vietnam, Aug. 1966-Aug. 1967; study, US Army Chaplain Sch., 1967-68; Ft. Jackson, July 1968-present; mem. Mason; So. Side Chamber of Commerce; awards: Army Commendation Medal; Airborne Wings; Air Medal; Vietnamese Combat and Service award; Natl. Ser. Defense Medal; Home: 2300 Adams St., Columbia, S. C., 29203; Office: Post Chaplain Office, Ft. Jackson, S. C. 29207

DAVIES, Everett Frederick Samuel, b. Freetown, Sierra Leone, Africa, July 21, 1902; s. Frederick and Elizabeth; B. A., Tallageda Coll., 1927; B. D., 1928; M. A., Yale Univ., 1930; Ed. D., Columbia Univ., 1946; m. Marguerite Marion Buckner; prof., Bishop Coll., 1932-35; assoc. dir., Detroit, Mich. Survey, 1935-36; prof. and dir. of Religious Activities, Va. State Coll., Petersburg, Va., 1936-46; prof., 1946--; mem., 5-Man Town Comm., Ettrick, Va.; 1st v.p., Va. Coun. on Human Relations; mem., Ed. Bd. of Psych. (publication); Alpha Phi Alpha; sec., Va. Philosophical Assn.; Amer. Philosophical Assn.; Fellow, Amer. Sociological Assn.; sec., Va. Philosophical Assn.; Ed. Bd. of Psychology; Home: 54 Third Ave., Ettrick, Va.; Office: 202 Va. Hall, Va. State Coll., Petersburg, Va.

*DAVIES, Lawrence Anderson, b. July 7, 1930, Houston, Tex.; s. Lawrence Anderson and Autrey (Thomas) D.; B.S., Prairie View A & M Coll., 1949; B.D., Howard Univ. Sch. of Rel., 1957; S.T.M., Wesley Theol. Sem., 1961; m. Janice J. Pryde; Children--Lauren Andrea, Karen Michelle, Sharron Lynie; pastor, Good Samaritan Bapt. Ch., Wash., D.C., 1956-61; asst. pastor and dir. of Rel. Edu., Shiloh Bapt. Ch., Wash., D.C., 1961-62; current pastor, Shiloh (Old Site) Bapt. Ch., Fredericksburg Area Min. Assn., 1962--; pres., Fredericksburg Area Min. Assn.; Bd. of Dir., Fredericksburg Area Counseling Service; 2nd v.p., Pratt Chapt.; mem., Va. Assn. for Mental Health; Exec. Bd., Lott Carey Foreign Missions Conv.; Fredericksburg Area Personal Counseling Service; Chrstn. Edu. Div., Va. Coun. of Chs.; pres., Walker Grant PTA, Fredericksburg bi-racial Commission; Progressive Natl. Bapt. Conv.; US Army, 1952-54; Certificate of Commendation for service and counselor by Pratt Chapter, Va. Mental Health Assn.; mem., Alpha Phi Alpha; Home: 1205 Cardwell St., Fredericksburg, Va. 22401; Office: 801 Sophia St., Fredericksburg, Va.

DAVIS, Abraham Eric, tchr.; b. New Orleans, La., Nov. 16, 1934; A.B., Southern Univ., 1954-58; Gammon Theol. Sem. (Interdenom. Theol. Center) 1958-60; m. Muriel McCall; Children--four daus.; Ministry: Student asst. pastor, Bowen Meth. Ch., Atlanta, Ga., 1958-59, Trinity Meth. Ch., 1960-63, St. Paul Meth. Ch., Shreveport, La. 1963-present; instr. and counselor, Godman Elem. Sch., Baldwin, La., Sagen Brown Home for Underprivileged Children, Baldwin, La.; mem., La. Conf. Bd. of Chrstn. Soc. Concerns of the Meth. Ch., NAACP, Citizens Com. of Shreveport; rec'd the Frank W. Clelland Award; mem., Interdenom. Min. Alliance, Institutional repr. Boy Scouts of America; YMCA, Democratic Party; Home: 1852 Abbie St., Shreveport, La.; Office: 1001 Pierre Ave., Shreveport, La.

*DAVIS, Arnor S., rel. educator, b. Ga., Dec. 30, 1919; s. Alex and Bessie D.; B. S., Ga. State Coll., 1948; B. D., Howard Univ. Sch. of Rel., 1953; M. A., 1958; m. Virginia; Children--Arnetta, Timothy, Alex; dir., Rel. Edu., Galbraith Afr. Meth. Episc. Zion Ch., Wash. D. C., 1958-60; current dir., Rel. Ed. New Bethel Bapt. Ch., Wash., D. C., 1960--; staff asst., Howard Univ. Community Serv. Project, 1963; mem., Bd. of Dirs., Iona Whipper Home, Wash., D. C.; Clergymen's Adv. Comm., Planned Parenthood, Wash., D. C.; US Army, 1942-46; Home: 631 Jefferson St. NE, Wash., D. C.; Office: New Bethel Ch., 812 S St. NW, Wash., D. C.

DAVIS, Corneal A., b. 1902, Tougaloo Coll., Tougaloo, Miss.; Moody Bible Institute, Chgo., Ill.; John Marshall Sch. of Law, Chgo., Ill.; m. Elma Howell; Children--Yvonne (Mrs. Maule); asst. pastor, Quinn Chapel A. M. E. Ch., Chgo.; present State Repr., State of Ill.; mem. Bd. of Local Improvements, Chgo.; present mem. Mayor's Cabinet; mem. Ill. Gen. Assembly, (26 yrs.); Democratic State Central Comm.; pres., Second Ward Regular Democratic Organization; Chrmn., Comm. Am. Negro Emancipation Centennial Comm.; Bd. mem., Wabash YMCA; Ada S. McKinley Comm. Services; Grand Chaplain, Masons, Ill.; chaplain, Geo. L. Giles Post, Amer. Legion; Past Imperial Potentate, Shriners; Grand Traveling Deputy Elks; Omega Psi Phi; awards: Shriner of the Year, 1954; Chgo. Urban League Award, 1961; Amer. Friendship Award, 1961; Sigma Omega Excellence Award, 1963; Prince Hall Mason of Year, Ill. Grand Lodge, 1964; Civil War Centennial Award of Merit (Ill.), 1965; Amer. Legion Meritorious Serv. Award, Ill., 1965; Home: 3223 S. Calumet Ave., Chgo., Ill.; Office: 3435 S. Indiana Ave., Chgo, Ill.

DAVIS, Cyprian, tchr., b. Wash., D. C., Sept. 9, 1930; s. Clarence Wm. and Evelyn (Jackson) D.; A. B., St. Meinrad Coll., 1953; S. T. L. Cath. Univ. of Amer, 1957; Licencie en sciences historiques, Universite Catholique, Louvain, Belgium, 1963; solemn vows as Benedictine monk, St. Meinrad, 1954; ordained priest, Roman Cath. Ch., 1956; instr., Church Hist., Sch. of Theol., Instr., French & Eur. Hist., St. Meinrad Coll., 1963-64; mem., Medieval Acad., The Cath. Historical Assn.; Home: St. Meinrad Archabbey, St. Meinrad, Ind. 47577

DAVIS, Edsel M., b. Monroeville, Ala., Jan. 2, 1935; s.

N. A. and Clevia (D.); A. B., Selma Univ., Ala. 1956; B. D., Interdenom. Theol. Center, Atlanta, Ga., 1960; m. Ida Louise Tolbert; Children--Edsel M. Jr., Kerry Lance; pastor, Tabernacle Bapt. Ch., Beatrice, Ala., 1956-58; Shiloh Bapt. Ch., Montevallo, Ala., 1958-63; New Hope, Hobson City, Ala., 1963-65; New Pleasant Grove Bapt. Ch., Macon, Ga., Nov. 1965-present; tchr., Amer. Bapt. Theol. Training Extension Sch., Macon, 1966-present; pastor's div., Gen. Missionary Bapt. State Conv. (Ga.) 1967-68; sec., Operation Breadbasket (Macon, Ga.); mem., NAACP; Mayor's Citizen's Com. on Patriotism; Citizens Hosp. Adv. Com. (Macon); Mason; pres., Bapt. Min. Brotherhood (Macon); contrib., "Our Daily Bread," Nat. Bapt. Conv. Series, vol. 9, no. 3, Townsend Press, 1968, p. 36-66; Home: 1745 Kitchen Rd., Macon, Ga. 31201; Office: 833 Cowan St., Macon, Ga. 31201

DAVIS, Enoch Douglas, b. June 13, 1908, Waynesboro; s. Abraham and Mozell D.; A. A., Fla. Meml. Coll., St. Augustine, Fla.; B. A., Fla. A & M Univ., Tallahassee, Fla.; M. R. E., Interdenom. Theol. Center, Atlanta, Ga.; m. Trigpen Hazel; Children--Leroy Douglas; pastor, Second Bethel Bapt. Ch., 33 yrs.; chaplain, Gibbs Jr. Coll.; mem., Trustee Bd. Fla. Meml. Coll., 1951--; Citizens Cooperative Com.; Exec. Com. Gen. Bapt. State Conv. of Fla.; Boy Scouts of America, Pinellas Div.; award: Citation for distinguished service by Ambassador Club, Inc.; citation for service from United Negro Coll. Fund; Oscar, United Giver's Fund; Mason; Democrat; Home: 550 16th St. S., St. Petersburg, Fla. 33705; Office: 506 16th St., St. Petersburg, Fla. 33705

DAVIS, Grady Demus, sem. dean, b. Pleasant Hill, N. C., Dec. 23, 1919; s. Willie E. and Elenora D.; A. B., Shaw Univ., 1942; B. D., Andover-Newton (Mass.), 1949 Ph. D., Boston Univ. 1953; m. Dorothy Mae Hicks; 2 sons--Grady D., Jr., Mahatma Gandhi; 3 daus., Deryl Gradette, Psyche Darzette, Crystal Tara; student pastor, Ebenezer Bapt. Ch., Boston; Zion Bapt., Everett, Mass.; pastor, Oberlin Bapt., Raleigh, N. C., 1953-67; Union Bapt., Durham, N. C., 1963--; Dean, Shaw Univ. Div. Sch., 1953--; Prof. of Psych., Univ. of N. C., 1967-pres.; pres., Raleigh Citizens Assn., 1961; cand., House of Rep. Wake Co., N. C., 1960; apptd. Gov. Comm. on Juvenile Delinquency & Youth Crime, 1962; US Army, 1942-46;

recipient Raleigh's Negro Family of the Year, 1959; mem., Amer. Psychol. Assn., N.C. Psych. Assn., Amer. Assn. Univ. Profs.; Soc. for Scientific Study of Rel., NAACP, Phi Beta Sigma; lectr., Coll. & Univ. Rel. Emphases Weeks and Retreats; Office: Univ. of North Carolina, Fayetteville, N. C.

DAVIS, Guildford Kenneth, b. Long Branch, N. J., Nov. 24, 1924; s. Isaiah and Betty D.; Bible Trng. Inst., Goldsboro, N. C.; m. Ida Mae Hicks; Children--Hattie, Betty Jean, Vivian, Iris, Vernon; pastor, St. Stephen AMEZ Ch., Warsaw, N. C., 1952; St. James AMEZ Ch., Southport, N. C., 1954; Clinton Ct., Clinton, N. C., 1955; St. Thomas, New Shrewsbury, N. J., 1957; St. James, Perth Amboy, N. J., 1959; Price Meml., Atlantic City, N. J., 1965; Metropolitan, Ridgewood, N. J., 1967-present; US Air Force 1943-46; pres., Perth Amboy (N. J.) Prot. Min. Assn., sec., Salvation Army Adv. Bd., mem. Middlesex Co. TB and Health League; Raritan Soc. Plan. Coun., P. B. A. Chap., Worship Comm., Atlantic Co. Coun. of Chrs., YMCA; NAACP; Edu. Comm., Atlantic City Chapter; Home: 261 S. Broad St., Ridgewood, N. J. 07450; Office: 259 S. Broad St., Ridgewood, N. J. 07450

DAVIS, John Candler, b. Webster, N. C., Sept. 12, 1907; s. John Harden and Carrie (Love) D.; B. A., St. Augustine Coll., 1932; B. D., Bishop Payne Div. Sch., 1936; M. A., Western Reserve Univ., 1959; D. D. (hon.), Wilberforce Univ., 1956; m. Ethel Norris; rector, St. Matthias Ch., Asheville, N. C., 1936-39; curate, St. Philips Ch., NYC, 1939-42; prof., Bishop Payne Div. Sch., 1942-43; rector, St. Andrew's Ch., Cleveland, O., 1942-58; chaplain, Cleve. State Hosp., 1945-58; vicar, Meade Meml. Episc. Ch., Alexandria, Va., 1959; certificate in Clinical Trng., Boston State Hosp., 1950; certificate in Group Life Laboratory, Bethel, Maine, 1958; mem., Acad. of Rel. and Mental Health; Bd. of Trustees, Alexandria Welfare Coun. Com. on Day Care, Greater Wash. Area; Durant Civic Assn., Alexandria, Va.; Mason; Shriner; Knight Templar; Omega Psi Phi; Assn. of Mental Hosp. Chaplains; Amer. Prot. Hosp. Chaplains Assn.; (Life) NAACP; Home: 382 Beacon Hill Rd., Groveton, Va. 22306; Office: 322 N. Alfred St., Alexandria, Va. 22314

DAVIS, Leon Houston, ch. official, b. East St. Louis, Ill.,

May 8, 1920; s. James Roy and Viola (Reid) D.; Oakwood Jr. Coll., 1943; Emmanuel Missionary Coll., 1945; m. Althea Lightner; 1 son--Leon Houston, Jr.; pastored, Marion and Muncie, Ind. Seventh-Day Adventist Ch., 1945-46; Springfield and E. St. Louis, Ill. S. D. A. Ch., 1946-49; youth dir., and edu. supt., Lake Reg. Conf. of S. D. A., Chgo., Ill., 1949-54; present: youth dir. and edu. supt., Northeastern Conf. of S. D. A., NYC, 1955--; Amer. Temp. sec. and Civil Defence sec. of Northeastern Conf., NYC; Natl. Selective Servicement repr.; press sec.; committee mem., Northeastern Conf. Academy Bd. of S. D. A., 1955--; Northeastern Conf. of S. D. A., Ex. Com.; Atlantic Union Bd. Edu., Comm., So. Lancaster, Mass.; testimonial luncheon, Americana Hotel, Feb. 10, 1962, NYC, for outstanding achievement as Youth Dir. of Northeastern Conf. of S. D. A.; Pathfinder Dir.; Victory Lake Camp; Youth Camp Dir., Hyde Park, N. Y.; Home: 1257 Carroll St., Brooklyn, N. Y.; Office: 560 W. 150th St., NYC.

DAVIS, Samuel Matthew, b. Shortersville, Ala., Sept. 7, 1908; s. Alexander A. and Mahala D.; B. D., Daniel Payne Coll., 1927; D. D. (hon.), Payne Coll., 1945; LL. D., Monrovia Coll., W. Africa, 1955; LL. D., Daniel Payne Coll., 1961; m. Alma D.; Children--Rebecca (Mrs. Ullessee Fletcher), Dorothy (Mrs. C. E. Murphy), Coleman, Robert, Joseph, James, Solomon, Bester J., Walter; pastor, since 1928, Afr. Meth. Episc. Chs.; Cole Bluff, Miss., St. Stephen, Crighton, 1929; Fairhope, 1930, Pinegrove Mobile, 1931, Thomaston, 1932-33, Pleasant Hill, Magnolia, 1934, St. John, Swicha, 1935-36, Prattsville, 1937; presiding elder, The Camden Dist., 1938; presiding elder, the Prattsville Dist., 1939; pastor, St. James A. M. E. Ch., Pratt City, 1940; Jones Chapel, Clayton; St. Mark A. M. E. Ch., Toscaloosa, 1947; St. James Anniston, 1948; presiding elder, Florence Huntsville Dist., 1949; current pastor, St. Paul Afr. Meth. Episc. Ch., Birmingham, Ala.; pres., Brotherhood of A. M. E. Ch.; Trustee, Daniel Payne Coll.; pres., Smithfield Civic League, 4 yrs.; mem., Episc. Comm. A. M. E. Ch., 1952-56; pres., United Order of Brotherhood of State of Ala.; Republican; Mason; Citation from Payne Theol. Sem.; Award of Merit, Pi Lambda Sigma Honor Soc., 1962; Award, WENN (radio) in field of human relations, 1963, Birmingham, Ala.; Home: 320 Ninth Court, W. Birmingham, Ala.; Office: 300 Fourth Court, Birmingham, Al.

DAW, Matthew Leonard, b. Youngstown, O., Jan. 28, 1921; s. Lane and Myrtle (White) D.; A. B., Univ. of Pittsburgh, 1947; B. D., Ref. Preby. Sem., 1959; m. Lenore Estella Owens; Children--Andrea, Matthew L., Alan Lane; licensed to ministry, 1941; interim pastor, Mt. Olivet Bapt. Ch., Newport, R. I., 1943; New Hope Bapt. Ch., Braddock, Pa., 1947-49; South Hills Bapt. Ch., Pittsburgh, Pa., 1950-51; pastor, St. John Bapt. Ch., Pittsburgh, Pa., 1951-52; Second Bapt. Ch., Ford City, Pa., 1952-56; Triumph Bapt. Ch., Sweickley, Pa., 1956-62; Calvary Bapt. Ch., 1962--; former soc. worker, Morals Court, Pittsburgh, Pa.; area moderator, Kiski Valley Area (Auba), Pittsburgh, Pa.; chrmn., Bi-racial Comm., Spokane; mem., Bd. of Dirs., Coun. of Chs., Spokane; Alpha Phi Alpha; Home: E. 207 Third Ave., Spokane, Wash. 99202

DAWKINS, Maurice Anderson, b. Chicago, Ill., Jan. 29, 1921; s. Anderson Maurice and Marie Von (Dickerson) D.; A. B., Columbia Univ., NYC, 1943; M. A., Union Theol. Sem. & Columbia Univ., 1950; further study: Columbia Univ.; D. D. (hon.), 1964; m. Doris Myrtle Scott; Children--Kimball Maurice, Susan Scott; min. of edu. and assoc. pastor, The Community Ch. of New York, 1948-54; min. & dir., People's Independent Ch. of Christ, Natl. Coun. of Community Chs.; former pres., Intl. Coun. of Comm. Chs.; mem., Natl. Urban League, Western Regional Bd.; Amer. Leadership Conf. on Afr. Amer. Assn.; UN World Affairs Council; former pres., NAACP (Los Angeles); founder and former pres., Western Chrstn. Conf.; West coast coordinator, Natl. Day of Prayer, 1956; Prayer Pilgrimage to Wash., 1957; Youth March on Wash., 1958, 1963; Gov.'s Commn. on Metro. Area Problems, 1959-63; Atty. Gen's Adv. Com. on Constitutional Rights, 1959-63; Mayor's Com. on Human Rights, 1960-61; Calif. State Com. on Urban Policy; League Award for Promoting Interracial Understanding; George Washington's Carver Award for Human Rights; Natl. Coun. of Negro Women Award for Rel. Leadership; Weekly Radio broadcast Los Angeles, Column "The Christian Answer" in Calif. Eagle; Weekly guest columnist, L. A. Sentinel; Office: Peoples' Independent Ch. of Christ, 1025 E. 18th St., Los Angeles, Calif.

DAY, Roland Frederick, Chaplain (Maj.), b. Mecklenburg, Va., Nov. 18, 1933; s. Walter A. and Minnie S. (D.); A. B., B. D., Va. Union Univ., Richmond, Va., 1954,

1957; Ed. M., Indiana Univ., Bloomington, Ind., 1968; m. Delores Johnson; Children--Roland F. II, DeLanda Denese; Dean of boys, Va. State Sch. for Blind & Deaf, Hampton, Va., 1957-59; US Army, Chaplain, 1959-present; awards: Natl. Defense Ser. Medal; Army Commendation Medal; Home: 4526 Kinmount Ave., Lanham, Md. 20801; Office: Dept. of the Army, Office of the Chaplains (Chief), Wash., D. C. 20315

DAYE, Linwood Thomas, b. Hillsboro, N. C., Dec. 16, 1931; s. Allen and Maude (Lee) D.; A. B., N. C. Coll., 1960; B. D., Shaw Univ., Raleigh, N. C., 1963; D. D. (hon.), Guadolupe Coll., 1966; m. Daisy Virginia Rudd; Children--Sherron, Gwenivere, Linwood, Alvis; Orange Cross Rds. Bapt. Ch., Hillsboro, N. C.; Mt. Olive Bapt. Ch., Efland, N. C.; First Bapt. Ch., Mebone, N. C.; Shiloh Bapt. Ch., Henderson, N. C.; Zion Bapt. Ch., Newport News, Va., 1966-present; instr., Central High Sch., Hillsboro, N. C. mortician, N. C.; notary pub., N. C.; mem., bi-racial coun., Burlington, N. C.; US Army, 5 yrs.; mem. NAACP; New Hope Assn.; Tidewater Peninsula Assn.; Mason; Home: 1018 Wickham Ave., Newport News, Va.; Office: 633 20th St., Newport News, Va.

DAYS, Morgan M., b. Pine Level, Ala., May 30, 1891; s. William and Louvenia; Crozier Theol. Sem., Chester, Pa.; D. D. (hon.), Va. Sem. and Coll., Lynchburg, 1957; Courses, Cornell Univ., 1935-37; m. Fannie Bell; pastor, Bethel Bapt. Ch., Troy, Ala., 1917-18; asst. chaplain, 366th Inf., 1918-19; Friendshp Bapt. Ch., Corning, N. Y., 1919-25; Friendship Bapt. Ch., Schenectady, N. Y., 1925-37; Shiloh Bapt. Ch., Rockville Centre, N. Y., 1937-present; moderator, Capital Dist. Bapt. Assn., 1930-37; pres., West End Civic Assn., Rockville Centre, N. Y., 1938-41; v. p., Coun. Chs. Nassau City, N. Y., 1941-43; pres., Interracial Prot. Min. Assn.; mem., L. I. Human Rights Coun.; Mayor's Com. of Rockville Center Urban Renewal; Grievance Com. of Rockville Centre; Chrmn., Human Rights Com., Rockville Centre, N. Y., Awards: Bapt. Min. Fellowship, Queens, Nassau and Suffolk Cos., N. Y.; Empire St. Bapt. Conv., Lions Club, Rockville Centre; citation, Pres. Harry Truman, Race Rel. in Nassau Co.; Cert. of Public Vol. Service; low-housing park re-named the "Rev. Morgan Days Park;" sponsored these prog. in ch., organized child day center; adult ed. program; Rec. and Youth Center; Home: 15 Wilson Lane,

Rockville Centre, N. Y. 11570; Office: 96 N. Centre Ave., Rockville Centre, N. Y.

*DeBERRY, David, b. Mainline, Pa., May 22, 1932; s. Jonathan Robert and Mary Ellen (Thomas) D.; A. B., Va. Union Univ., 1952; courses, Sorbonne, Paris, France; M. S., Colo. Univ., 1962, B. D., Howard Univ., Sch. of Rel.; m. Clara Jayne Terry; migrant minister, Delaware Natl. Coun. of Chs.; assoc. pastor, St. Paul Meth. Ch., Laurel, Md.; pastor, Winchester, Va. Meth. Ch.; pastor, John Mann Meth. Ch.; pres., Recruit. Coordin., United Meth. Ch.; counselor, Boy Scouts of Amer.; mem., Civic Voters League, Roanoke, Va.; Roanoke Min. Alliance; former pres., Winchester NAACP; mem., Omega Psi Phi; served with US Force (Korean War); Home: 809 Madison Ave. NW, Roanoke, Va.; Office: 4016 W. Broad St., Richmond, Va. 23230

DEBRO, W. L., b. Springhill Co., N. C., Jan. 26, 1884; s. Melchia and Mary D.; D. D. (hon.), Campbell Coll., 1945; m. Mary Eliza Bishop; Children--Beatrice; pastored Afr. Meth. Episc. Chs. in Miss., La.; present pastor, Rankin Chapel, Rayville, La.; former presiding elder, A. M. E. Ch., trustee, Campbell Coll.; Democrat; Home: 606 Second St., Lake Providence, La.

DeGRAFFENREIDT, Kermit Jesse, b. Durham, N. C., Oct. 3, 1937; s. Jesse Roscoe and Minnie (Ellis) D.; A. B., North Carolina Coll., Durham; B. D., Hood Theol. Sem., 1963; course: Wesley Theol. Sem., 1963--; m. Guytanna Maria Horton; asst. pastor, St. Mark A. M. E. Z. Ch., Durham, N. C., 1958-60; Mt. Moriah A. M. E. Z. Ch., Henderson, N. C., 1960-63; current pastor, Clinton A. M. E. Z. Ch., Rockville, Md., 1963--; NAACP participant in N. C. demo., 1960-63; v. p., Comm. Youth Improvement Assn. of Rockville, 1964; mem., Omega Psi Phi; Min. Alliance of Rockville & Wash. Dist. A. M. E. Z. Chs.; Home: 223 Elizabeth Ave., Rockville, Md. 20850; Office: 814 Westmore Ave., Rockville, Md.

DeLAINE, Joseph A.; b. Manning, S. C., July 2, 1906; s. H. C. and Tisbia (D.); A. B., Allen Univ., Columbia, S. C., 1931; B. D., Dickerson Sem., Columbia, S. C., 1945; D. D. (hon.), 1954; summer sch., State Agr. Coll., S. C.; Morris Coll., Sumter, S. C.; m. Mattie Lee Belton; Children--Joseph A., Jr., Ophelia E., Brumit B.; pastored, Afr. Meth. Episc. Chs., Fairfax, S. C., Pine

Grove Ct.; Spring Hill Ct.; Rimini, S.C., 1926-50; pastor, St. James Ch., 1950-55; founded DeLaine-Waring A.M.E. Ch., Buffalo, N.Y., 1955-60; Calvary A.M.E. Ch., 1956-present; leader in Clarendon Co. sch. segregation case, 1954; trustee, Allen Univ., Columbia, S.C., 13 yrs.; mem., Palmetto Tchrs. House of Delegates, 3 yrs.; del., A.M.E. Gen. Conf., 1936, 1940, 1943, 1948; organizer, Clarendon Co., NAACP, 1943; pres., Summerton Parents Group, Summerton, S.C.; monthly article, A.M.E. Christian Recorder, "Our Part in a Revolution;" Office: Calvary A.M.E. Ch., 790 Herkimer St., Brooklyn, N.Y.

DENNIS, Walter Decoster, b. Wash., D.C., Aug. 23, 1932; s. Walter Decoster, Sr. and Helen (Maddux); asst. pastor, S. Philip's Ch., Bklyn, N.Y., 1956; asst. pastor, The Cathedral of St. John The Divine, 1956-60; adjunct asst. prof., Amer. history, Hampton Inst. consultant, Natl. Coun. of the Episc. Ch., mem., Bd. of Dirs. of Episc. Soc. of Racial Cultural Unity; author: "Puerto Rican Neighbors," "Mexican-American Neighbors;" Home: 551 E. Murcury Blvd., Hampton, Va.; Office: 55 E. Tyler St., Kecoughtan Sq., Hampton, Va.

DeVEAUX, William Phillips, chaplain, b. Ft. Huachuca, Ariz., Aug. 3, 1941; s. John Allen and Della (Phillips) D.; A.B., Howard Univ., Wash., D.C., 1962; S.T.B., Boston Univ., 1968; m. Patricia Ann Morris; Children--Dawn Della, Dana Golder, Wm., Jr., Paul John; asst. pastor, Metro. A.M.E. Ch., Wash., D.C., 1960-62; Charles St. A.M.E. Ch., Boston, Mass., 1963-66; Bethel A.M.E. Ch., Lynn, Mass., 1966-68; chaplain, May 1968-present, 82d Airborne Div., Ft. Bragg, N.C.; awards, Expert Infantryman Badge; Military parachutist; mem. Omega Psi Phi; Home: 121 Luzon Dr., Ft. Bragg, N.C.; Office: Brigade Chaplains' Office, HHC 2d Bde 82 Airborne Div., Ft. Bragg, N.C.

DIAL, James Samuel, b. Darlington, S.C., Aug. 17, 1912; s. Sammie S. and Mary (Burch) D.; Claflin Coll., 1930-31; A.B., Clark Coll., 1950; B.D., Gammon Theol. Sem. 1952; m. Gertrude Alma Brevard; Children--Michael Sylvester; pastor, Meth. Chs., Landrum, S.C., 1932-33, Cowpens, S.C., 1934-35, Blacksburg, S.C., 1936-37, So. Greenville, S.C., 1958-63; Dist. Supt., Beaufort Dist., 1963-64; Dist. Supt., Orangeburg, S.C., 1964--; pastor (current), Mt. Zion Meth. Ch., Kingstree, S.C.;

tchr., 11 yrs. (ele. sch., 7 yrs., high sch., 4 yrs.); mem., Claflin Coll. Trustee Bd.; chrmn., S. C. Conf. Com. on World Service & Finance, The Meth. Ch.; mem., Mason; Home: 319 W. Main St., Kingstree, S. C.

DICKERSON, Adolphus Summer, sem. prof., b. Greenville, Ga., May 25, 1914; s. Dixie and Mary Bessie (Ogletree) D.; A. B., 1943, Clark Coll., Atlanta, Ga.; B. D., Gammon Theol. Sem., 1945; M. A., Atlanta Univ., S. T. M., Boston Univ. Sch. of Theol., 1960; m. Virginia Griffin; pastor, Barnesville Meth. Ch., Ga., 1937-38; St. Mark Meth. Ch., Augusta, 1938-40; Palen Meth. Ch., Savannah, Ga., 1940-41; Centenary Meth. Ch., Atlanta, Ga., 1941-42; So. Atlanta Meth. Ch., Atlanta, Ga., 1942-48; Ariel Bowen Meth. Ch., 1948-54; Dist. Supt., Atlanta South, 1954-60, 1960--; prof., Gammon Theol. Sem. and Interdenom. Theol. Center; "Minister of Year" 1958; first Negro chaplain to serve in a Fed. prison, 1945--; columnist, Atlanta Daily World; contributor, Central Christian Advocate; Home: 1507 Mozley Pl. S. W., Atlanta, Ga.; Office: 583 Mitabell St. S. W., Atlanta, Ga.

DICKERSON, Noy Jasper, tchr., b. Elkhorn, W. Va., Sept. 17, 1892; s. Charles Marion and Maria (Higginbotham) D.; 1932, B. S., Bluefield State College; 1942, M. A. Mich. Univ.; m. Frances Louise Anderson D.; tchr., 1923-24 Mercer Co. Schools (W. Va.); 1925-37, McDowell Co. Schs. (W. Va.); 1937-44, Mercer Co. Schs. (W. Va.) 1944-50, interviewer: W. Va. State Employment Service; pastor, Community Chrstn. Ch., 1946-present; US Army, 1918-19; Home: 309 Allen St., Bluefield, W. Va.; Office: 315 Marshall St., Bluefield, W. Va.

DICKINSON, Richard Charles, b. Kimbrough, Ala., Mar. 20, 1925; s. Armstead and Alice; B. S., Barber Scotia Coll., Concord, N. C., 1959; B. D., Immanuel Luth. Coll. and Sem., Greensboro, N. C., 1952; m. Blanchie Watson; Children--Richard, Bernard, Deborah, Dwight; dir., Luth. Worship Hr., 1952-55; chrmn., Com. on Youth Work for Ala. and No. Fla. Conf. Chs., 1952-55; pastor, Mt. Calvary Luth. Ch., Kannapolis, N. C., 1956-60; sec., Bd. of Control Immanuel Luth. Coll. and Sem., 1956-60; pastor, Good Shepherd Luth. Ch., Gary, Ind., 1960-66; Chatham Fields Luth. Ch., Chg., Ill., 1966-present; mem., Bd. Luth. Human Rel. Assn., Chg., Ill., rep. Bd. of Soc. Welfare; Home: 8100 S. St. Lawrence,

Chgo., Ill. 60619; Office: 8050 S. St. Lawrence, Chgo., Ill. 60619

DICKS, Abel Joseph, b. Beaumont, Tex., Apr. 5, 1933; s. Abel and Winnie (Premeau) D.; B.A., Divine Word Sem., Techny, Ill., 1959; ordained priest of Roman Cath. Ch., Mar. 19, 1962; mem. Soc. of the Divine Word; Home: 1025 Michigan Ave., NE, Wash., D.C. 20017

DICKSON, Melvin Curtis, b. Texas, Oct. 25, 1912; s. David M. and Lizzie (De Laney) D.; A.B., Southern Chrstn. Inst., 1935; Butler Univ., 1935-39; m. Eunice S. King; Children--Melvin, Joseph, Larry, Brenda; pastor, Louden Ave. Chrstn. Ch., Roanoke, Va., 1939-43; Forest Ave. Chrstn. Ch., Tex., 1943-53; Louden Ave. Chrstn. Ch., Roanoke, Va., 1953-56; current pastor, Forest Ave. Chrstn. Ch., Dallas, Tex., 1956--; pres., Tex. Chrstn. Missionary Committee, present: consultant, Youth Conf., Chrstn. Ch.; mem., Civic Com. Housing Com.; Democrat; Home: 1814 Peabody, Dallas, Tex. 75215; Office: 1802 Forest Ave., Dallas, Tex. 75215

*DIXON, Edward Parker, chaplain, b. Madison, N.J., Oct. 11, 1922; s. Edward P. and Nora (Ghee) D.; B.A., Lincoln Univ., Pa., 1945; B.D., Howard Univ. Sch. of Rel., 1949; m. Patricia Ann Foster; Children--Leslie Dawn; chap., Peoria State Hosp., Peoria, Ill.; chap., Burgen Pines Hosp., Paramus, N.J.; visiting lecturer, Garrett Theol. Sem., Evanston, Ill.; instr., Chgo. Bapt. Inst., field work supervisor, McCormick Theol. Sem., Chgo., Ill.; mem., Clergy for Quality & Equality in Chgo.: Urban League Rel. Leaders of Chgo.; NAACP; Omega Psi Phi; Home: Teaneck, N.J.; Office: Burgen Pines Hospital, Paramus, N.J.

DIXON, James Inman, b. Nashville, Tenn., Oct. 10, 1910; s. William Henry and Mary (Pitt) D.; M.S., A & I State Tchrs. Coll., Nashville, Tenn., 1935; M.A., Dept. Psych. Rel., 1946; M.S. Butler Univ., Indianapolis, Ind.; m. Tommie Hinton; B.D., Gammon Theol. Sem., 1938; served as a minister-in-the pastorate 30 yrs.; Dist. Supt., 5 yrs., founder, 5 Meth. Ch. bodies, and have developed much interest in working with alcoholism patients, after rec'g. much information in regards to working with Sch. of Alcoholic Studies, Yale Univ., 1946, and at other times; pastor, So. Atlanta Meth. Ch., 1939; Anderson Indiana-Second Meth. Ch., 1942-47; Dayton, O., McKinley Meth. Ch., 1947-52; founder Dixon Meth. during this period, 1950; Indianapolis, Ind., Simpson Meth. Ch.; established Christ Meth. Ch. while pastoring here; Cincinnati, O. Dist. Supt., 1959--; current pastor, Grace Meth. Ch., Cincinnati, O.; given much time to pastoral counseling, in family life, etc.; mem., Bd. of Wesley Foundations in Colleges; pres., NAACP; YMCA; Mason; writer of many articles to papers and poems of a rel. nature; Home: 830 Lexington Ave., Cincinnati, Ohio.

*DOBSON, Vernon Nathaniel, b. Baltimore, Md., Oct. 29, 1923; s. Spencer and Estelle; A. B., Howard Univ., 1949; B. D., Howard Univ., Sch. of Rel., 1953; m. Napoleon Pleasants; Children--Rosalind, Sandra, Michael, Keith, Kevin, Kim, Donna; probation officer, Criminal Court of Baltimore, 1953-66; pastor, Emmanuel Bapt. Ch., Over-lea, Md., 1953-58; asst. dir., Knox Presby. Com. Center, 1956-58; dir., asst. minister, Harvey Johnson Center, Union Bapt. Ch., 1958-66; pastor, Union Bapt. Ch., 1967-present; tchr., Md. Bapt. Ch.-Wide Inst.; chrmn. Bd. Activists for Fair Housing; Trustee Bd., Sch. of Rel. Md. Bapt. Conv.; chrmn. Foster Care, Md. Coun. Chs.; Com. on Coop. Southern Bapt., Md. Bapt. Conv.; mem., NAACP; chrmn., Min. Div. United Negro Coll. Fund.; Navy, 1943-46; mem., Interdenom. Min. Alliance; Home: 3104 Cedardale Rd., Baltimore, Md. 21215; Office: Union Bapt. Ch., Druid Hill Ave., Dolphin St., Baltimore, Md. 21217

DOGGETTE, Jackson Michael, b. Virginia, Dec. 11, 1930; s. Herbert Richard and Sally (Robertson) D.; studied architecture, 1944-48; B. A., Oakwood Coll., 1954; doing grad. work at Andrews Univ.; m. Edythe Marie Young; Children--Linda, Jackson, Jr., James; pastored Seventh-Day Adventist Chs. in--Lubbock, Tex., Roswell, N. M., El Paso, Tex., 1954-55, Wichita Falls, Tex., Ardmore, Okla., 1956-57; present, pastor, S. D. A. Ch., Santa Monica, Calif., 1958--; mem., Sch. Bd. of Santa Monica Jr. Acad. & Glendale Acad.; Home: 1904 19th St. Santa Monica, Calif.; Office: 1845 20th St., Santa Monica, Calif.

DOGGETT, John Nelson, Jr., b. Phila., Pa., Apr. 3, 1918; s. John and Winola (Ballard) D.; A. B., Lincoln Univ.,

Pa., 1942; B.D., Union Theol. Sem., N.Y., 1945; m. Frances Brown; Children--Lorraine, William Ballard, John Nelson; youth pastor, Ch. of the Master, NYC, 1942-43; youth pastor, Salem Meth. Ch., NYC, 1943-45; pastor, South Gate Community Ch., San Francisco, Calif., 1945-46; pastor-organizer, Downs Meml. Meth. Ch., Oakland, Calif., 1947-49; pastor, Scott Meth. Ch., Pasadena, Calif., 1950-53; pastor, Hamilton Meth. Ch., Los Angeles, Calif., 1953-64; transferred from So. Calif.-Ariz. Conf. to Central West Conf., 1964; pastor, Union Meml. Meth. Ch., St. Louis, Mo., 1964; chrmn.-coordinator, Martin Luther King Western Chrstn. Leadership Rallies, 1961-63; treas., Univ. of So. Calif.; Los Angeles Co. Bd. of Supervisor's Human Rel. Bd., 1963-64; consultant to So. Central Area Welfare Planning Coun., So. Central Coordinating Coun., Ch. Welfare & Soc. Service Bds.; chrmn., Inter-Jurisdictional Rel. Com. for merger of Central West Conf.; Area Adv. Com., Central Jurisdiction; Area repre., So. Central Jurisdiction Adv. Com.; Del., World Meth. Conf., London, England, 1966; Conf. minister to Mexico City, D.F., 1965; initiator, Head Start Pre-School "Kinder-Cottage," St. Louis, Mo., 1965; Democrat; mem., Urban League; Fair Housing Com.; Job Equality Coun.; Jewish War Veteran's Star of David award for outstanding community service; Human Relations Plaque for outstanding service in Human Relation, Los Angeles Consolidated Realty Bd.; Certificate of Merit, So. Calif. Conf. of Chrstns. and Jews; meritorious award for services to Los Angeles Ch. Welfare Bd.; Phi Kappa Epsilon Honorary Scholarship Soc.; Delta Rho Forensic Soc.; Alpha Phi Alpha; Home: 6949 Julian Ave., St. Louis, Mo. 63130; Office: 1141 Belt Ave., St. Louis, Mo. 63112

DONALD, Grady H., b. Belton, S.C., June 19, 1929; s. Alonza C. and Ella (Calhoun) D.; A.B., Benedict Coll., Columbia, S.C., 1951; B.D., Amer. Bapt. Theol. Sem., Nashville, Tenn., 1954; m. Clara G. Phillips; Children--Grady H., Jr., Michael Thomas, Angelyn Yvonne; pastor, Hopewell Bapt. Ch., Glasgow, Ky., 1953-55; First Bapt. Ch., Murfreeshers, Tenn., 1955-58; current, Kayne Ave. Bapt. Ch., 1958--; faculty mem., Amer. Bapt. Theol. Sem. Extension Sch., 1963--; Missionary to Jamaica, 1951; tchr., Natl. Sun. Sch. & B.T.U. Congress; assoc. dean-at-large, Leadership Edu. Cong. of Tenn. B.M. & E. Conv.; 1st v.p., The Nashville Chrstn. Leadership

Coun.; mem., Bd. of Dirs., So. St. Community Center; charter mem., The Nashville Coordinating Coun. for Civil Rights; mem., The NAACP and The Davidson Co. Independent Political Council; Alumni Award, 1960, for Outstanding Service to Race, Country and Ch.; mem., Alpha Phi Alpha; Mason; Home: 1423 Edgehill Ave., Nashville, Tenn. 37212; Office: 1109 12th Ave., So. Nashville, Tenn. 37212

DONALDSON, Spurgeon Booker, b. Orangeburg, S.C., Apr. 11, 1900; s. James S. and Maria (Thomas) D.; courses, Crozer Theol. Sem., Pa., 1935; D.D. (hon.), Indianapolis, Ind.; m. Vieillian M. Drewitt; Children-- Ellen, Edward; pastor, Emmanual Bapt. Ch., Jamestown, N.Y., 1937-54; Shiloh Bapt. Ch., Port Norris, N.J., 1955-present; mem., NAACP, Port Norris, N.J.; Republican; Home: Fortescue Rd., Newport, N.J.; Office: Memorial St., Port Norris, N.J.

DOUGLAS, Jesse L., b. New Orleans, La., Aug. 19, 1930; s. William and Isabella D.; Dillard Univ., 1952-56; A.B., Lane Coll., Jackson, Tenn., 1957-59; B.D., Interdenom. Theol. Center, Atlanta, Ga., 1959-64; S.T.M. candidate; m. Blanche Y. Gordon; Children--Jesse L., Jr.; asst. to the Gen. Sec. of Evangelism of the Chrstn. Meth. Episc. Ch.; Conf. soloist for the Georgia Conf., 1959-62; current pastor, The First C.M.E. Ch., Montgomery, Ala.; mem., Bd. of Dirs., Montgomery Improvement Assn.; v.p., Interdenom. Min. Alliance, Montgomery, Ala.; A Commissioner's Com. on Community Affairs; Home: 716 Glass St., Montgomery, Ala.; Office: First C.M.E. Ch., 776 So. Holt St., Montgomery, Ala.

DOUGLASS, Robert Lewis, b. Dec. 12, 1927, Memphis, Tenn.; s. John A. and Maggie Brown (D.); A.B., Lane Coll., Jackson, Tenn., 1964; M. Div., Howard Univ. Sch. of Rel., 1968; D.D. (hon.), Baltimore Coll. of the Bible and Sem., 1968; pastor, Chrstn. Meth. Episc. Ch., Jackson, Tenn.; Youngstown, O.; Wash., D.C.; Alexandria, Va.; St. John C.M.E. Ch., Gadsden, Ala., 1968-present; program chrmn. NAACP, Youngstown, O., 1960-61; pres., NAACP, Gadsden, Ala., pres., Etowah Co. Ala. Hous. Dev. Corp.; US Navy 1950-64; awards, Korean Service Decoration; Omega Psi Phi; Home: 823 Avenue G, Gadsden, Ala. 35901

DOYLE, Bertram Wilbur, bishop, b. Lowndesboro, Ala., July 3, 1897; s. Henry Sebastian and Anna Magnolia (Walker) D.; A. B., Ohio Wesleyan Univ., 1921; A. M., Univ. Chicago, 1924, Ph. D., 1934; D. D., Lane Coll., 1934; Dr. of Laws (hon.), Miles Coll., 1958; m. Pansy Ray Stewart, Aug. 12, 1918; Children--Vera Corinne, Annie Glenn, Grace Margaret, Pansy Henrieta, Bertram Wilbur; tchr., Samuel Houston Coll., 1921-22, Claflin Coll., 1922-24, Clark Coll., 1924-26; dean, Paine Coll., 1925-27; tchr. Fisk Univ., 1927-37, personnel dean, 1928-30; ordained to ministry of Chrstn. M. E. Ch., 1925; pastor, Orangeburg, Allendale, S. C., Nashville, Good-lettsville, Tenn.; faculty summer schs. Atlanta Univ., 1939, Hampton Inst., 1940-41; dean, Louisville Municipal Coll., 1942-50; sec. edn. Chrstn. M. E. Ch., 1937-50; elected bishop 7th dist., 1950, 6th dist., 1954, 8th dist., 1958; exec. com. Meth. World Conf., 1951, mem. 1956, mem. Ecumenical Conf., 1951; mem., exec. com. World Meth. Council, 1951--; chrmn. Chrstn. M. E delegation to World Meth. Conf., Oslow, Norway, 1961; Chrmn. bd. trustees Tex. Coll. Meml. Natl. Coun. Chrstn. Chs. (gen. bd. 1950--; mem. constituting conv. 1950), Natl. Prot. Coun. Higher Edu. (sec. exec. com. 1948-50), New Deal Progressive League, Phi Beta Kappa, Kappa Alpha Psi, Sigma Pi Phi; author: Etiquette of Race Relation in the South, 1937; editor, A Study of Negro Business and Employment in Louisville, 1944; contributor articles mags; Home: 1702 Heiman St., Nashville, Tenn.

*DRAYTON, Jerry, b. Savannah, Ga., June 15, 1918; s. Solomon and Marie D.; certificate clinical psychiatry, Bowman Gray Sch.; A. B., Morehouse Coll., 1943; B. D., Howard Univ., Sch. of Rel., 1946; D. D. (hon.), Va. Theol. Sem., Lynchburg, Va.; m. Susie E. Jones; Children--Jerry Alphonso, Jr.; pastor, New Bethel Baptist Ch., Winston-Salem, N. C.; pres., Forsyth Min. Fellowship, Winston-Salem, N. C.; v. p., Interracial N. C. Bapt. Fellowship; chrmn., Exec. Bd. of Interracial Urban League, Winston-Salem, N. C.; chrmn., Comm. on Pub. Accommodations; Bd. mem., Forsyth Co. Alcoholic Program; chrmn, Edu. Comm.; Exec. Bd. of Interracial N. C. Coun. of Chs.; Counseling staff of the Domestic Relations Court; chrmn., Interracial Comm. studying complete desegregation of all recreational facilities in Winston-Salem, N. C.; historian, Bapt. State Conv., N. C.; v. p., Exec. Bd., NAACP; Edu. Bd., Natl. Bapt.

Conv., Inc.; mem., Exec. Bd. Lott Carey Foreign Mission Conv.; Home: 2025 K Court Ave., Winston-Salem, N. C.; Office: 1016 No. Trade St., Winston-Salem, N. C., 27101

DUCKETT, Zelma E., (Mrs.), b. Chattanooga, Tenn., Dec. 25, 1909; dau. Wm. Hayden Ferguson and Gallie (Baker); tchr. certificate, Tenn. State Coll., 1930; B. S., Brockport, N. Y., 1954; m. Gilbert C. Duckett; founder and pastor, Ferguson Afr. Meth. Episc. Zion Mission, Albion, N. Y., 1956-present; Counselor to migrants; licensed missionary, 1959; Holds worship services at migrant camp sites; assists migrants with housing health problems and child welfare; tchr., Athens, Tenn., Clewiston, Fla., Athens, Zanesville, Ohio; (Peace Corps), Niagara Falls, N. Y., Ex. sec., NAACP (Orleans Co.); sec. & bd. mem. Economic Opportunity Community Action Group, 1965; Voter registration bd.; certificate of appreciation, Orleans Co., Migrant ministry; NAACP; Home: 129 Clarendon St., Albion, N. Y.; Office: P. O. Box 92, Albion, N. Y. 14411

DUDLEY, Charles Edward, church official, b. South Bend, Ind., Feb. 1, 1927; s. Joseph and Julia (Talley) D.; Emanuel Missionary Coll.; B. A., Oakwood Coll., 1947; m. Etta Mae Maycock; Children--Bonita Andrea, Charles E. II, Albert Leroy; pastored, Jackson and Memphis, Tenn., Seventh-Day Adventist Chs., 1949-54; Montgomery, Ala. S. D. A. Ch., 1954-55; Baton Rouge S. D. A. Ch., 1955-58; Dallas, Tex., City Temple, 1958-62; Sec.-treas., Southwest Region Conf., summer of 1962 (Dallas); present: pres., So. Central Conf. of S. D. A., Nashville, Tenn.; mem., Riverside Hosp. Board, Nashville, Tenn., Madison Hosp. Bd., Madison, Tenn.; Exec. Comm., So. Union Conf., Decatur, Ga.; Oakwood Coll. Bd., Huntsville, Ala.; Southern Publishing Assn., Nashville, Tenn.; Home: 1604 White's Creek Pike, Nashville, Tenn.; Office: 715 Young's Lane, Nashville, Tenn.

DUKES, Billie Edward, b. Roe, Arkansas, Feb. 3, 1913; s. Edward & Cora (D.); City Coll., NYC, A. B., Va. Union Univ., 1960; Biblical Sem., N. Y.; B. D., M. A., Hartford Sem. Found., 1964, 1965; widower; Children--LaRee (Mrs. Bell, Jr.), Florence (Mrs. Miller); pastor, St. John Bapt. Ch., W. Hempstead, L. I., 1948-52; Antioch Bapt. Ch., Bedford Hills, N. Y., 1960-64; Minister of Youth & Christn. Ed., S. Congregational Ed.

Dir. (5 chs.) 1967-68; pastor, Lemuel Haynes Congre. United Ch. of Christ, Jamaica, N.Y., 1968-present; former mem., Crisis Com., Western Assn., Buffalo, N.Y., 1967; mem. Amer. Acad. of Rel.; Steering Com., Crisis Com. (White Racism in Christian Chs.); Ex. bd. Ch. Extension Comm., N.Y. Conf. United Ch. of Christ; Home: 160-35 119th Drive, Jamaica, N.Y. 11434; Office: 146-09 116th Ave., Jamaica, N.Y. 11434

DUMAS, Floyd Earl, b. Muskogee, Okla., Jan. 27, 1926; s. William and Ada (Tate) D.; Langston Univ., 1953; Okla. Sch. of Rel., 1951; m. Grace Lorine Provo; Children--Floyd E., Milton Vance; pastor, New Hope Bapt. Ch., Okla. City, Okla., 1955-56; Mt. Zion Bapt. Ch., Guthrie, Okla., 1954-55; Bethel Bapt. Ch., So. Bend, Ind., 1956-57; Galilee Bapt. Ch., Gary, Ind., 1958-63; Metro. Bapt. Ch., Gary, Ind., 1963-present; worked as employment counselor; tchr., social worker; pres., local co., Office Economic Opportunity, Lake Co., Ind., Democrat; mem., NAACP; US Navy Reserve; mem., Mason; Natl. Bapt. Conv., USA; Progressive Natl. Bapt. Conv.; Urban League; Bapt. Ministerial Conf. Coun. of Chs.; Home: 459 W. 20th Pl., Gary, Ind., 46401

DUNGEE, John Riley, Jr., chaplain, b. Roanoke, Va., Mar 6, 1900; s. John Riley, Sr. and Flossie Belle (Wingfield) D.; A.B., Johnson C. Smith Univ., 1923; B.D., 1926; D.D. (hon.), 1957; courses, Union Theol. Sem., NY Summer, 1946; pastor, Green St. Presby. Ch., Morganton, N.C.; Trinity Presby. Ch., Marion, N.C., 1923-26; Lebanon Presby. Ch., Ridgeway, S.C., 1926-36; tchr., Henderson Inst., Henderson, N.C.; pastor, Townsville United Presby. Ch., Townsville, N.C., 1936-42; chaplain, US Army, 1942-46; pastor, Cotton Meml. United Presby. Ch., 1946--; Stated clerk Presby. of Tenn. (U.P.) 1950-58; Gen. Assembly Commissioner-1931, 1940, 1947, 1950, 1953, 1957, 1961; Permanent Clerk Synod of Catawba, United Presby. Ch., USA; pres. Vance Co. br. NAACP, 1948-49; v.p., 1959; pres. Vance Co. Min. Alliance, 1952-58; pres., Vance Co. Voters' League, 1953-60; chaplain, US Army, 1942-46; awards: Amer. Theater Ribbon, Asiatic-Pacific Theater Ribbon; certificate of commendation, Army Service Forces Hq., Camp Shelby, Miss.; Certificate of Award for Meritorious Service, Gen. Commission on Army and Navy Chaplains; mem., Charter pres., Alpha-Omicron Chapter, Alpha Phi Alpha; Johnson C. Smith Univ., 1923;

Jr. Grand Warden, S.C. Grand Lodge, A. F. & A. M., Asst. Rabban, Cairo Temple, A. E. A. O. Nobles of the Mystic Shrine, 1932-36; Home: 439 W. Rock Spring St., Henderson, N. C.; Office: 511 N. Chestnut St., Henderson, N. C.

DUNLAP, Theodore Roosevelt, b. Wewoka, Okla., April 21, 1903; s. Robert Green and Sylvia (Trotter) D.; B. D., Union Theol. Sem., 1949; San Diego State Coll., San Diego, Cal., A. B., 1946; m. Sadie Altin Fields; pastor, Oak Park Community Ch., Sacramento, Calif., 1948-51; Chandler Meml. Congre. Ch., Lexington, Ky., 1951-54; Meth. Chs., Ky., Tenn., Ark., Kan., and Ill., 1954--; An interim term on the Bd. of Hosps. and Homes, The Meth. Ch., 1958-60; mem., Mason; Home: 611 South 15th St., Springfield, Ill. 62703; Office: 15th and Edward Sts., Springfield, Ill. 62703

DUNNAVILLE, Marshall Edward, b. Roanoke, Va., April 12, 1921; s. Marshall E. and Effie D.; A. B., B. A., Va. Sem. & Coll., Lynchburg, Va., 1940-46; m. Mildred Morgan; Children--Romell; chaplain, Carter Nursing Home, 1940-46; pastor, First A. M. E. Z. Ch., Marion, Va., 1946-48; pastor, Gum Spring, Va., 1948-55; Big Hill, Va., 1955-61; pastor, White Meml. A. M. E. Z. Ch., Middleboro, Ky.; Neal Chapel, Tazwell, Tenn., 1965-present; tchr., Marion High Sch., Marion, Va., 1946-47; chap., The Applaican Hosp., Middlesboro, Ky., 1962-65; trustee, Old Folks Home, Bristol, Va.; mem., Middlesboro Min. Assn.; Bd. mem., O. E. O., Bell Co.; mem., Bd. of Dir., Human Rights Coun.; Mason; Research Bd., A. M. E. Z. Ch.; Home: 107 W. Rochester St., Middlesboro, Ky.; Office: White Meml., A. M. E. Z. Ch., Iron Wood Rd., Middlesboro, Ky.

DUNSTON, Alfred G., Jr., bishop, b. Coinjock, N. C., June 25, 1915; s. Alfred G. and Cora (McNair); A. B., Livingstone Coll. & Hood Sem.; M. A., Drew Univ., 1939-41; D. D. (hon.), Allen Univ.; D. C. L. Monrovia Coll., Liberia; Children--Carol, Aingred, Armayne; elected bishop, Indianapolis, Ind., May 20, 1964, 12th Episc. Dist.; Mt. Sinai A. M. E. Z. Advance, N. C., 1936-67; St. John A. M. E. Z. Thomasville, N. C.; Wallace Temple, A. M. E. Z. Ch., Bayonne, N. J., 1939-41; Price Meml. A. M. E. Z. Ch., Atlantic City, 1941-43; Wallace Chapel, Summit, N. J., 1946-48; Logan Temple, Knoxville, Tenn., 1948-52; Big Wesley, Phila., Pa., 1952-63; Mother Zion, NYC, 1964;

mem., Commission on Human Relations, Phila., Pa., 1963; mem., Selective Patronage Program, Phila., 1960-63; mem., Bd. Dirs. Mercy-Douglas Hosp., Phila.; co-founder, Opportunities Industrialization Center, Phila., 1963; trustee, Berean College, Phila., Pa., 1956-64; trustee, Shapp Scholarship Fund, 1960-63; mem., Bd. Dirs., Western Community House, 1954-64; Member, Bd. Dir., Phila. Coun. of Chs., 1960-63; chaplain, WW II, 92nd Infantry Div. Artillery; 92nd Inf. Div. Citation for meritorious service in support of combat troops; mem., Alpha Phi Alpha; Mason; Narrator of film "The Rising New Africa" produced by Trans-Continental featured in television documentary film "The Run From Race" 1963; Home: 5901 Cobbs Creek Parkway, Philadelphia, Pa.

*DURDEN, Lewis Minyon, b. Diboll, Tex., Sept. 16, 1911: s. Lewis Minyon and Devilla Emma (D.); A. B., Clark Coll., 1938; Gammon Theol. Sem., Atlanta, Ga. 1935-40; B. D., Howard Univ., Sch. of Rel., 1942; M. A., Rel. Ed., S. T. M., Yale Div. Sch., 1951-52; m. Erma Ruth Clark; Children--Tempie Anita (Mrs. Frank Jones); Denise L., Ricardo L.; pastor, Newlight Bapt. Ch., Minden La., 1935-36; Chaplain, US Army, 1942-64 (Col.); assoc. pastor, Zion Bapt. Ch., 1966-present; Administr., Zion Bapt. Nursing Home, 1967-present; founder and pres., Durwilma Finance Co., 1968-present; High sch. principal, prof., Cincinnati Bible Coll.; awards, Army Commendation Medal with two Oak Leaf Clusters, Purple Heart, Legion of Merit; served as chap. in Europe, Asia, Africa, Guam, Hawaii, Korea, 1942-64; mem., Phi Beta Sigma; Retired Persons Assn.; NAACP; Mason; Retired Officers Assn.; Cincinnati Bapt. Min. Conf.; Democrat; exec. v. p., Lighthouse Life Ins. Co.; editor, Nations Prayer Call (newspaper); author The Army Character Guidance Program; Home: 3707 Washington Ave., Cincinnati, O. 45229; Office: Nursing Home, 3610 Washington Ave., Cincinnati, O. 45229

DYKES, DeWitt Sanford, church official, b. Gadsden, Ala., Aug. 16, 1904; s. Henry Sanford R. and Mollie Wade D.; A. B., Clark Coll., 1930; B. D., Gammon Theol. Sem., 1931; S. T. M., Boston Univ. Sch. of Theol.; m. Viola G. Logan; Children--Reida Belle (Mrs. George L. Gardiner), DeWitt S., Jr.; pastor, Mt. Pleasant Meth. Ch., Marion, Va., 1932-36; Wiley Meml. Meth. Ch., 1936-46; E. Vine Ave. Meth. Ch., Knoxville, Tenn.,

1946-53; dist. supt., Chattanooga Dist., The East Tenn. Conf., 1953-54; present, staff mem. of the Div. of Natl. Missions of the Bd. of Missions of the Meth. Ch., Section of Ch. Extension, Dept. of Finance and Field Service, 1955--; pres., Clark Coll. Alumni, 1942-44; mem., Alpha Phi Alpha; Home: 2139 Dandridge Ave., SE, Knoxville, Tenn. 37915.

DYSON, William Andrew, radio announcer, b. Norfolk, Va., May 20, 1935; s. Eddie E. and Leola (Jackson) D.; Virginia State Coll.; Univ. of Bordeoue, France; Virginia Theol. Sem.; now engaged in historical research; m. Mildred Marianne Saunders; Children--Michael, William Andrew II, San Deo Paul; business exec., Bar-Charis, Recreational Facilities; asst. pastor, St. Paul's Chrstn. Meth. Episc. Ch., Norfolk, Va.; pastor, Walker Meml. C. M. E. Ch., Spartanburg, S. C., 1963; current pastor, Metro. C. M. E. Ch., Phila., Pa.; radio announcer (before entering clergy), WRAP, Norfolk, Va.; WLOW, Portsmouth; WBRG, Lynchburg, Va.; mem., Va. Coun. Human Relations; US Air Force (European area), 4 yrs.; Amer. Legion, Merit award, while in High Sch.; chap., Civil Air Patrol Unit, Wash., D. C.; mem., The Natl. Collegiate Panel of America; contrib. ed. to Mail-Mat, official organ of Interdenom. ministers coun. of Amer. and the British West Indies; Home: 3432 No. 17th St., Philadelphia, Pa.

EASLEY, Paul Howard, chap., b. Charleston, W. Va., Sept. 7, 1930; s. Alexander P. and Estella A.; B. S., W. Va. State Coll., Inst., W. Va.; B. D., Gammon Theol. Sem., Atlanta, Ga.; courses, Scarritt Christ. Coll., Nashville, Tenn.; m. Sarita Elvira Payne; Children--Paul H., Jr., Verita Jean, David Allen; pastored chs., Lewisburg, W. Va., 1954-55; Brownsburg, W. Va., 1955-56; Fairmont, W. Va., 1959-61; Roceverte-White Sulphur Charge, 1961; US Army chap., 1960-present; former, youth worker, Bethlehem Community Center, Atlanta, Ga.; YMCA, Charleston, W. Va. & Atlanta, Ga.; chap., migrant ministry, Va. Coun. of Chs., 1958; mem., Omega Psi Phi; Military Chaplains Assn.; Mason; Military awards, Army Commendation Medal (Clusters); Certificate of Appreciation, Chief of Chaplains of Korea; Home: 321-1 Pelham St., Fort Riley, Kan. 66442; Office: Correctional Training Facility, Ft. Riley, Kan. 66442

*EATON, Herbert Hoover, b. Creedmoor, N. C., Dec. 8, 1928; s. Hugh Dee and Flossie (Moss) E.; Hampton Inst., 1956; B. S., No. Carolina Coll., Durham, 1956; B. D., Howard Univ., Sch. of Rel., 1956; S. T. M., Boston Univ. 1957; m. Delores Costella Sankey; Children--Eric Renard; US Army, 1951-53; asst. pastor, Zion Bapt. Ch., Wash., D. C.; student asst. to Dean of Andrew Rankin Meml. Chapel, Howard Univ., 1954-56; dir. of student Chrstn. Assn., Howard Univ., 1957-60; pastor, Dexter Ave. Bapt. Ch., Montgomery, Ala., 1960-65; pastor, Kenwood United Ch. of Christ, 1965-69; present, chaplain, N. C. Coll., Durham; chrmn, Bd. of Dirs. Montgomery Improvement Assn., 1963--; mem., City Commissioners Comm. on Community Affairs; v. p., Tuskegee-Montgomery; Howard Univ. Alumni Club, present; Inst. of Rel.; Mason; Alpha Phi Alpha; circulation mgr., Journal of Religious Thought, 1957-60; editor, Sch. of Rel. "NEWS;" Home: 1001 Plum St., Durham, N. C., 27701

*EATON, James Alonza, coll. chaplain, b. Portsmouth, Va., Dec. 26, 1921; s. Lloyd R. and Mary (Massenburg) E.; A. B., Virginia State Coll., 1943; B. D., Howard Univ., Sch. of Rel., 1946; M. A. Boston Univ., 1952; Ed. D., Columbia Univ., 1959; pastor, Wentz Meml. Congre. Ch., Winston-Salem, N. C., 1946-48; chaplain, US Army, 1950-54; acting chaplain, Tuskegee Inst., 1954-55; assoc. pastor, Friendship Bapt. Ch., NYC, 1955-58; dir., Rel. Activities, Elizabeth City State Coll., Elizabeth City, N. C., 1959-63; counselor to students, City Coll. of New York, 1958-59; dir. of Testing and Guidance Savannah State Coll., 1963--; mem., Amer. Assn. of Univ. Professors; Southern Student Personnel Assn.; Amer. Personnel and Guidance Assn.; Amer. Psychological Assn.; Kappa Delta Pi Honor Soc.; Home: Box 188, Savannah State Coll., Savannah, Ga. 31404

EDDLEMAN, William Thomas, b. Rockwell, N. C., Jan. 1, 1900; s. William and Emma (Carrie); B. D., Emmanuel Luth. Coll. and Sem., Greensboro, N. C., 1924; courses, Temple Univ.; m. Lela Mae (Young); Children--Loretta Winfred (Mrs. Hollis Gordon); Myrtress Goretha; pastor, Pilgrim Luth. Ch., Birmingham, Ala., 1925-present; prin. Pilgrim Luth. Day Sch. and Kindergarten, Birmingham., Ala.; Birmingham Min. Assn.; award, citation for long-standing and distinguished service Payne Coll., Birmingham, Ala., 1960; Home: 6304 3rd Crt. S., Birmingham, Ala. 35212; Office: 447 N. 1st St., Birmingham, Ala.

EDINGTON, Charles Arthur, b. Loudon, Tenn., April 10, 1889; s. Joseph and Sarah E.; A. B., Swift Meml. Coll., 1906-10; S. T. B., M. A., Lincoln Univ., 1912-15; D. D. (hon.), Johnson C. Smith Univ.; m. Della Mae Reid; Children--Marie Alease (Mrs. Charles F. Chisolm), Arthur Reid, H. Clifford, Sarah Elizabeth (Mrs. James H. Houston); asst. pastor, Grace Presby. Ch., Pittsburgh, Pa., 1915-17; pastor, St. Mark's Presby. Ch., Rogersville, Tenn., 1917-35; Calvary Presby. Ch., Asheville, N. C., 1935-59; retired, Dec. 31, 1959; tchr., Swift Meml. Coll.; dean, Swift Meml. Coll.; concurrent with duties as pastor, St. Mark's Presby. Ch.; stated clerk, Rogersville Presbytery; chrmn., Natl. Missions of Presbytery and Synod; Bd. of Management, Market Street YMCA (Asheville, N. C.); Bd. of Dirs., Amer. Red Cross; served as civilian chap. at Camp Croft, S. C. (WW II); Home: Rt. 5, Box 182, Asheville, N. C.

EDMONDS, Edwin Richardson, tchr., b. Austin, Tex., June 19, 1917; A. B., Morehouse Coll., 1938; S. T. B., Boston Univ. Sch. of Theol., 1946; Ph. D., Boston Univ. Grad. Sch., 1949; m. Maye Frances Bailey; 4 daus., Lynette Edmonds Johnson, Karen, Cheryl, Toni; pastor, Dixwell Ave. Congre. Ch., New Haven, Conn., 1959-64; prof. Soc., Bennett Coll., 1956-59; Inst. Soc. and Dean of Students, Del. State Coll., 1948-50; asst. prof. Soc. and Dir. of Inst. Research, Langston Univ., 1950-56; instr. Soc. (part-time), Quinnipiac Coll., New Haven, Conn.; Bd. of Dir., Community Progress, Inc., United Appeal, New Haven Coun. of Chs.; mem., Conn. Adv. Comm. to the U. S. Civil Rights Commission; author: "Demographic Study of the Negro of Oklahoma, 1910-1950," Annals, Oklahoma Academy of Science, 1954; "A Program of Student Discipline," Negro Educational Review, Oct. 1953; "The Myrdalian Hypothesis of Rank Order Discrimination," Phylon, 2nd Quarter, 1955.; Home: 40 Bellevue Rd., New Haven, Conn.; Office: 100 Dixwell Ave., New Haven, Conn.

EDWARDS, Chancy Rudolph, b. Nash County, N. C., Feb. 28, s. Buck Hilliard and Lucy Kearney E.; A. B., Shaw Univ., Raleigh, N. C., B. D., Shaw Div. Sch., 1949; D. D. (hon.), Shaw Univ., 1963; m. Luella Dickens; Children--Jewyl Anita; pastor, Spring Garden Bapt. Ch., Wash., N. C., 1948-53; First Bapt. Ch., Fayetteville, N. C., 1953--; dir., Roanoke Inst., Elizabeth City, N. C., 1950-53; current visiting pastor, McCaine Sanitorium,

McCaine, N. C., 1963--; tchr., Dept. of Rel. Promotion, Shaw Univ.; trustee, Shaw Univ., Raleigh, N. C., 1960--; Democrat; Mason; Home: 312 Moore St., Fayetteville, N. C.; Office: 302 Moore St., Fayetteville, N. C.

EDWARDS, Isadore, Jr., b. Jacksonville, Fla., Oct. 15, 1926; s. Isadore and Rebecca; B. S., Fla. Meml. Coll., St. Augustine, Fla., 1963; B. S. (Rel.) Fla. Meml. Coll., St. Augustine, Fla.; m. Elizabeth Hardy; Children-- Jerome, Brenda; pres., Aristocrat Club, Jacksonville, Fla., 1953-55; Scout master, Troop 73, St. Johns Bapt. Ch., Jacksonville, Fla., 1956-58; asst. pastor, Bethel Inst. Ch., Jacksonville, Fla., 1958-60; pastor, Friendship Bapt. Ch., Ft. Myers, Fla., pres; mem. Adv. Comm. U.S. Civil Rights Commn., 1965--pres.; Del. Natl. Bapt. Conv. of Amer. Foreign Mission Bd., 1966-present; Coord. Comm. for Farm Workers, 1966-pres.; chrmn., NAACP State Migrant Prot. Com., 1965-present; Natl. Bd. of Dir., NAACP; Dean of Instr., First So. Fla. Dist. Sun. Sch. and B. T. U. Conv., 1966-pres.; instr. Prog. Bapt. State Conv.; US Army Air Force, 1945-46; awards, Plaque for Comm. Ser., Hghts. Elem. Sch., 1965; Cert. of Appreciation for Spec. Ser., Ft. Myers Beach Rotary Club, 1967; Spec. award Meritorious Serv., Fla. NAACP, 1967; Plaque, Delta Sigma Theta Sor. Inc., Outstanding contrib. to Human Rel., 1968; Home: 2965 Lafayette St., Ft. Myers, Fla., 33901; Office: 2976 Anderson Ave., Ft. Myers, Fla. 33901

EDWARDS, Joseph DuMaine, Sr., church official, b. St. Louis, Mo., Mar. 27, 1907; s. Lewis James and Belle (Berry) E.; A. B., B. Th., Douglas Univ., 1934-41; m. Bessie Mae Johnson; Children-- Mrs. Lois M. Henry, Joseph DuMaine, Jr.; prof. baseball player, 1929-30 (St. Louis Stars); prof. musician, 10 yrs.; insurance salesman, waiter, cook, butler, laborer construction work, etc., 1930-39; began ministry as local preacher, 1939; pastor, St. Charles Ch., Mo., 1939-42; Colo. People's Meth. Ch., 1942-43; St. Joseph Meth. Ch., Mo., 1943-45; Key Meth. Ch., 1945-47; Dist. supt. So. Nashville Dist., 1947-53; pastor, Pitts Meth. Ch., Springfield, 1953-60; dist. supt. The Meth. Ch. (Kansas City Dist.), 1960--; Office: Kansas City Dist. Central West Conf., The Meth. Ch., 3219 Lockridge, Kansas City, Mo.

EDWARDS, Kenneth Pennington (chaplain), b. Kingston,

W. Va., Aug. 31, 1931; s. Cornelius E. and Pearl (E.); B. A., Barrington Coll., Barrington, R. I., 1958; M. Th., S. C. Sch. of Theol., Claremont, Calif., 1966; m. Rosalie E. Hart; Children--Peta Gay, Kerry Kay, Joseph K., Jonathan K.; Dir. of Rel. Ed., Mass. Ave. Bapt. Ch., Cambridge, Mass., 1957-58; Union Bapt. Ch., 1958-59, Cambridge; Dir. of Youth, Second Bapt. Ch., Los Angeles, Calif., 1959-61; Dir. of Rel. Ed., Immanuel Bapt. Ch., 1961-63, Los Angeles, Calif.; supply pastor, Immanuel Bapt. Ch., 1964-65; chaplain, Air Force, 1951-53; chaplain, Army, 1967-present; pastor, Immanuel Bapt. Ch., Los Angeles, Calif., 1965-67; chrmn., Community Improvement Organization, Los Angeles, Calif., 1966-67; Good Conduct Medal; Korean Conflict Medal; Natl. Defense Medal; Home: 1991 Miramar St., Pomona, Calif. 91767; Office: CH (CPT) Kenneth P. Edwards-02332989, 116th Engr. Bn. (Cbt), APO San Francisco, Calif. 96314

EDWARDS, Vinson Allen, educator, administrator, b. Crawfordville, Ga., July 12, 1897; s. Alexander and Fannie B. E.; A. B., Morehouse Coll., 1927; B. D., Drew Theol. Sem., 1930; M. A., Cornell Univ., 1940; m. Lillian Dixon; instr., Morehouse Coll., 1930-35; Sup. Adult Edu., Ga., 1935-36; Dean of Instruction, Forsyth Teach. Coll., 1937-39; Dir. Rel. Ext., Home Missions Div., Natl. Coun. of Chs., 1940-46; Dir. Rural Ch. Div., Nat. Bapt. Conv., USA, Inc., 1946-52; Dir., Leadership Edu. Div., Home Missions, Natl. Coun. of Chs., 1952-64; pastor, County Church, 1932-33; 1953-54; instr., Amer. Bapt. Sem.; Collaborator U. S. D. A. in Rural Areas Development; mem., Tuskegee Civic Assn., 1952-64; nominated, Bd. of Revenue, Macon Co., Ala., 1964; mem., Rural Sociological Soc., Masons, Democratic party; ala. Coun. of Human Relations, Ala. Coun. of Chs.; Research: Study of Negro Leadership in Rural Ga., Negro Ch. in 5 Ala. Counties; Author: The Church at Work in Rural Communities, and others; traveled abroad (1956 sum.), Seminar on Study of Rural Life in Europe; Home: P.O. Box 58, Tuskegee Inst., Ala.

*EGGLESTON, George Watkins, b. Martinsville, Va., Oct. 21, 1924; s. Raymond James and America (Payton) E.; A. B., Va. State Univ., Petersburg, Va., 1951; M. A., Va. State, 1952; B. D., Howard Univ. Sch. of Rel., 1960; journalist, Norfolk Journal and Guide, 1953-55; mem., European Seminar for Chrstn. Edu. (United Ch. of Christ),

1956; asst. chaplain, United Chrstn. Fellowship; supply min., Bethel Presby. Ch., Alexandria, Va., summers; current, asst. pastor, 15th St., Presby. Ch.; instr., Inst. of Modern Language, 1960-62; Va. State Citizenship Award; Howard Shields Award for Poetry, Va. State; recipient, Amer. Found. Scholarship for the Blind; Home: 1308 Clifton St. NW, Wash., D.C.; Office: 15th St. Presby. Ch., 15th & R Sts., NW, Wash., D.C.

ELLIGAN, Irvin, b. Chattanooga, Tenn., Nov. 24, 1915; s. Irvin and Annie; B.S., Knoxville Coll., Knoxville, Tenn., 1938; Th.B. Pittsburgh-Xenia Sem., 1944; D.D. (hon.), Stillman Coll., 1965; courses, Union Theol. Sem., 1966-67; m. Florence Coston; Children--Rachel, Irvin; tchr., Camden Acad., Camden, Ala., 1939-41; pastor, 1st U.P. Ch., Norfolk, Va., 1944-48; 1st U.P. Ch., Knoxville, Tenn., 1948-52; All Souls Presby. Ch., Richmond, Va., 1952-57; Eastminster Presby. Ch., Richmond, Va., 1952-63; chaplain, Knoxville Coll., 1941-52; assoc. sec., Div. Ch. and Soc., U.S. Presby., 1963-67; assoc. pastor, Lakeview Presby. Ch., St. Petersburg, Fla., 1967-present; mem. Bd. Friends Assn. for Children, Richmond, Va., 1962-66; chrmn., dist., R.E. Lee Boy Scout Coun., Va., 1961-67; Va. Gov. Com. on Youth; Bd., Leigh St. YMCA; awards, Silver Beaver, Boy Scouts of Amer.; citizenship, Delver Woman's Club; Richmond, Red Cross Service pin; outstanding citizenship, Astoria Club, Richmond, Va.; mem., Crusade for Voters; Democrat; NAACP; Natl. Com. of Negro Churchmen; former pres., Frontiers Internatl., Richmond, Va.; author, articles; mem., ed. com., Covenant Life Curr. Bks. and Studies; Home: 2127 14th St. S., St. Petersburg, Fla. 33705; Office: 1310 Lakeview Ave. S., St. Petersburg, Fla. 33705

ELLIS, Thomas H., b. Farmville, Va., Sept. 2, 1918; s. William E. and Clara (Anderson) E.; B.A., Morgan State Coll., 1950; Colgate Rochester Div. Sch., 1955-58; m. Frances Anderson; 4 daus., Sylvania, Yvonne, Geneva, Frances, 1 son, Thomas; asst. min., First Pentecostal Ch., Chester, Pa., 1946-52; minister, Bethel Tabernacle Ch., Buffalo, N.Y., 1952-57; dir., Inner city Parish, Asbury Delaware Meth. Ch., 1957-58; chaplain, migrant ministry, N.Y. State Coun. of Chs., Niagara Co., 1958; minister, Lincoln Meml. Congre. Ch., Chgo., Ill., 1959--; v.p., Woodlawn Organization, 1962; pres., Greater Woodlawn Pastors Alliance, 1963; US Navy, 1945-

46 (R.); Home: 6329 St. Lawrence, Chicago, Ill.; Office: 6454 Champlain Ave., Chicago, Ill.

ENGLAND, Frank, b. July 30, 1932; s. Peter and Anna (Verse); Passac Voc. Sch., 1951; No. Bapt. Sch. of Rel., 1942; founder, Pastor Timothy Bapt. Ch., Passaic, N. J., 1965--present; carpenter and cabinet maker; mem., and chap. U. S. Jr. Chamber of Commerce, Passaic Chapter; Bd. of Dir., Pasaaic Co. Mental Health Assn.; Home: 52 Morris St., Paterson, N. J.

ENWRIGHT, John Thomas, b. Birmingham, Ala., Sept. 20, 1904; s. Thomas Jefferson and Emma Laws (Strothers) E.; B. S., Clark Coll., 1929; B. D., Gammon Theol. Sem., Atlanta, Ga.; m. Eula Clyde; Children--Florence Marjorie (Mrs. Miller); pastor, Midway Congre. Ch., McIntosh, Ga., 1936-67; First Congre. Ch., Greensboro, N. C., 1937-39; Beecher Meml. Congre. Ch., New Orleans, La., 1939-50; Plymouth Congre. Ch., Charleston, S. C., 1950-present; mem., Bd. of Dirs., of the World Ministries of the UCC, 1964-present; Bd. of Dirs., Cannon St. YMCA, 1957-present; mem., Interdenom. Min. Assn., Charleston Co.; Min. Assn. of Charleston; Omega Psi Phi; Home: 32 Bull St., Charleston, S. C. 29401

EPPS, Saint Paul Langley, b. Norfolk, Va., Feb. 18, 1916; s. William and Azarina; B. A., Knoxville Coll., Knoxville, Tenn., 1939; B. Th., Pittsburgh-Xenia Theol. Sem., Pittsburgh, Pa., 1942; D. D., Sterling Coll., Sterling, Kansas, 1957; m. Kathryn Gilliam; Children--Frances, Braxton, Sheldon; pastor, United Presby. Chs., Henderson, Townsville, N. C., 1942-46; Bel-Vue Ch., L. A., Calif., 1946-64; sec., Synods, Presbyteries, Dept. of Interpretation and Stewardship, 1964-66; assoc. for Racial Ministries, Div. of Evangelism, Bd. of Natl. Missions, 1966-present; moderator, Tenn. Presbytery, 1944-45; L. A. Presbytery, 1952; mem., Bd. Ch. Ext., 1958-64; Spec. Com'. of Consolidation, Commn. on Rel. and Race, Gen. Assembly; Bergen Co. Urban League; NAACP; Northeast Citizen's Coun.; pres., Watts Health Coun., L. A., Calif., 1954-present; Bd. of Dirs., So. Area Boys Club, 1956-present; Bd. of Dir., Health, Edu., V. D., 1955-present; v. p., S. L. A. Com. for Better Edu.; author, The Cry of the Black Ghetto; Home: 165 Van Buskirk Rd., Teaneck, N. J. 07666; Office: 475 Riverside Dr., New York, N. Y. 10027

*EUBANKS, John Bunyon, coll. pres., b. Clinton, La., Feb. 28, 1913; s. Frank and Ella (Collins) E.; Th. B., Howard Univ., Sch. of Rel., 1935, A. B., 1936; A. M., 1938, Ph. D., 1947, Univ. of Chgo.; additional study: Harvard Univ.; Syracuse Univ.; Children--Judith Anne, John B., Jr., David; edu. sec., Senate Ave. YMCA, Indianapolis, Ind., 1937-41; area sec., Natl. Council YMCA, 1941-43; prof. and chrmn., Soc. Science, Morris Brown Coll., Atlanta, Ga., 1946-49; pres., Jarvis Chrstn. Coll., Hawkins, Tex., 1949-53; community development officer, Intl. Cooperation Administration, Baghdad, Iraq, 1953-55; chrmn. and prof., Soc. Science, Jackson State Coll., Miss.; prof. of philosophy and foundations of education, Tuskegee Inst., 1960--; mem., Advisory Bd. of Boggs Acad., Keyesville, Ga., 1963--; mem., Gen. Edu. Bd. Fellow in Comparative Religions, 1943-44; Alpha Kappa Delta Natl. Honorary Sociological Soc.; African Studies Assn.; Acad. of Rel. and Mental Health; Ala. Philosophical Soc.; Soc. for Applied Anthropology; Soc. for Internatl. Development; Home: 624 So. 15th St., Baton Rouge, La.

EVANS, Benjamin Bonaparte, tchr., b. Gloucester, Va., May 26, 1892; s. Ransom and Alice (Holmes) E.; B. A., Knoxville Coll., 1920; B. D., Pittsburgh Theol. Sem., 1925; Ed. M., Univ. of Pittsburgh, 1943; D. D. (hon.), Knoxville Coll., 1950; m. Theresa Hamlet; pastor, United Presby. Ch., Norfolk, Va., 1926-37; Dir. of Rel., Knoxville Coll., 1937-44; current pastor, United Presby. Ch., Cincinnati, 1944--; mem., Knoxville Coll., Bd. of Ministers, 1955; YMCA; NAACP, 1946; Cincinnati Mayors Friendly Relations Comm.; Home: 3549 Reading Rd., Cincinnati, Ohio

EVANS, Charles Lawrence, administrator, b. Pleasantville, N. J., May 2, 1908; s. Charles Lawrence and Florence (Gray) E.; A. B., Lincoln Univ. (Pa.), 1933; S. T. B., Lincolun Univ. Sch. of Rel., 1936; A. M., Lincoln Univ.; D. D. (hon.), Va. Union Univ., 1958; minister, First Bapt., Suffolk, Va., 1937-42; Zion Bapt., Petersburg, Va., 1942-45; Exec. Sec., Bapt. Allied Bodies of Va., 1945--; m. Alice Priscilla Rasin; 1 dau., Sandra Elizabeth; mem., Exec. Bd., Va. Ch. Temperance Council, Va. Coun. of Chs.; Va. Negro Bapt. Children's Home, Inc.; Lott Carey Foreign Mission Conv.; Publishing Bd., Natl. Bapt. Conv. of Amer., Inc.; Interdenom. Rel. Work Foundation; pres., West End Civic & Improvement

League, Richmond, Va. ; author: S. S. Lessons, Norfolk Journal & Guide, 1939--; Tour leader, Europe and Holy Land, 1955 & 1963; So. America, 1960; Office: Virginia Union Univ., Richmond, Va.

EVANS, Clay, b. Brownsville, Tenn., June 23, 1925; s. Henry and Estanauly (E.); Chgo. Bapt. Inst., 4 yrs.; Univ. of Chgo. Sch. of Divinity; m. Lutha Mae Hollingshed; Children--Diane, Michael, Ralph, Claudette, Faith Renee; pastor, Woodlawn Bapt. Ch., Brownsville, Tenn., 1935; asst. pastor, Taberncale Bapt. Ch., Chgo., Ill., 1945; founder and pastor, Fellowship Missionary Bapt. Ch., 1950--; pres., Bapt. Ministers Conf. of Chgo., 1965, 1966; co-chrmn., Chamber of Commerce, NAACP, Chgo.; Home: 9657 S. Indiana Ave., Chicago, Ill. 60628

EVANS, John Marvin, chaplain, b. Cincinnati, O., Sept. 3, 1925; s. John Thomas and Addie G. (Smith) E.; B. S., Howard Univ., 1950; Amer. Univ., 1952-54; Episc. Theol. Sch., 1955-58; m. Lillian M. Swann; 1 son--John Edward; pastor, All Saint Prot. Episc. Ch., Toledo, O., 1958-62; army chap., 4th Inf. Div. Support Command, Ft. Lewis, Wash., 1963-present; federal employee, Bur. of Census, H. E. W., Dept. of Welfare, D. C., 1950-55; Bd. mem., Planned Parenthood League; businessman mem., YMCA, Toledo, O.; Bd. mem., Group work div. of Toledo Coun. of Soc. Agencies and Toledo Chapter of Boy Scouts; pres., Neighborhood Areas Council; membership chrmn. and housing chrmn. and selective buying chrmn., Toledo Chapter of NAACP; official del., Ohio Coun. of Chs. for Diocese of Ohio, 1961-62; mem., Housing Comm. (State level) of NAACP, Ohio; served in Europe and Pacific theaters of operations, WW II, 1944-46; enlisted man, 1/Lt. Chap. of 4th Inf. Div., Support Command, 1962-present; battle star - European campaign; Citizen's cert. for community work, Toledo, O., given by Frederick Douglas Community Center; Omega Psi Phi; Episc. Soc. for Cultural and Racial Unity; one of the Episc. clergymen jailed in Jackson, Miss. during prayer pilgrimage, Sept. 1961; Home: Quarters 2546-E, Ft. Lewis, Wash; Office: Chapel No. 2, Bldg. 1645, Ft. Lewis, Wash.

EVERETT, Ezra, chaplain (Major), b. Cairo, Ga., April 8, 1929; s. Horace and Annie (Lee) E.; A. B., Clark Coll., Atlanta, Ga., 1951; B. D., Gammon Theol. Sem., Atlanta, Ga., 1954; m. Marvalinia Ruth Bell; Children--

Conycee Marvele, Lynette Ruth; ordained Elder United Meth. Ch., 1953; pastor, Ga. Oliver Meth. Ch., Atlanta, Ga.; Warren Temple Meth. Ch., La Grange, Ga.; chaplain, US Army, 1954-present; served Ft. Jackson, S.C., 1954-55; Korea, 1955-56; Japan, 1956-58; Ft. Campbell, Ky., 1958-61; Germany, 1961-64; Aberdeen Proving Grounds, Md., 1964-66; Vietnam, 1966-67; Ft. Gordon, Ga., 1967-68; Ft. Benning, Ga., 1968-present; Office: US Army, Inf. Center, Ft. Benning, Ga. 31905

EWING, Isaiah, b. Nashville, Tenn., Dec. 25, 1928; s. Isaiah and Valine; A.B., Fisk Univ., 1949; B.D., Chgo., Theol. Sem., 1954; M.A., Fisk Univ., 1960; m. Polly Ann Eslick; Children--James Waller, Benita Cordellia, Waller; ordained elder, Afr. Meth. Episc. Ch., 13th Episc. Dist.; pastor, McGavock Chapel, Charlotte, Tenn.; Salters Chapel, Waverly, Tenn.; St. John, A.M.E. Ch., McEwen, Tenn.; current pastor, St. Paul A.M.E. Ch., Fayetteville, Tenn.; tchr., pub. schs., Nashville, Tenn., Waverly, Tenn., and Fayetteville, Tenn.; mem., Natl. Adv. Comm.; CORE; Natl. Adv. Comm., So. Chrstn. Leadership Coun.; US Army Chaplain, 1954-58; mem., Mason; Alpha Phi Alpha; Sigma Pi Phi; Home: 326 West College, Fayetteville, Tenn.; Office: 328 West College, Fayetteville, Tenn.

EXUM, John M., editor, b. Memphis, Tenn., Jan. 3, 1909; s. John W. and Lena (Turner) E.; B.A., Univ. of Denver, 1947; M.Th., Iliff Sch. of Theol., 1950; m. Lola Thelma Gibbs; 1 dau., Yvonne Lois; pastored: Rock of Ages Chrstn. Meth. Episc. Ch., Memphis, Tenn., 1942-44; Cleaves Meml. C.M.E. Ch., Denver, 1944-50; Jamison Mem. Temple, Kansas City, Mo., 1950-59; Grace C.M.E. Ch., Detroit, Mich., 1959-61; Carter Metro. C.M.E. Ch., Detroit, 1961-present; dir., Chrstn. Edu. Kansas, Mo. Conf. C.M.E. Ch., 1950-59 and Chrstn. Edu., Michigan-Indiana Conf., 1960--; Achievement award, Omega Psi Phi fraternity, Kansas City, Mo., 1952; Omicron Delta Sigma; Masons; Knights of Phythians; editor, Eastern Index, C.M.E. Ch.; Home: 1804 W. Grand Blvd., Detroit, Mich.; Office: 1512 W. Grand Blvd., Detroit, Mich.

FAIR, Frank Thomas, b. Clinton, S.C., Oct. 19, 1929; s. Leo and Verda Drucilla; A.B., Benedict Coll., Columbia, S.C., 1950; B.D., Crozier Sem., 1955; S.T.M. Gammon

Sem., 1959; m. Thelma Barbara Belton; Children--Frank Thomas, Iamera L., Donna Machelle, Selwyn Tyrelle; tchr., S. C. area trade sch., Denmark, S. C., 1950-52; Min., Bright Hope Bapt. Ch., Philadelphia, Pa., 1952-53; Mt. Olivet Bapt. Ch., Phila., Pa., 1954-55; pastor, Royal Bapt. Ch., Anderson, S. C., 1955-61; New Hope Bapt. Ch., Norristown, Pa., 1961-pres.; tchr., Benedict Ext. Ser., Benedict Coll., Columbia, S. C., 1956-61; J. J. Starks Sch. of Theol., Benedict Coll., 1959-61; New Life Boys Ranch, Harleyville, Pa., 1965-66; part-time chap., Palmetto State Hosp., Columbia, S. C., 1959-61; Dir., Norristown Sch. Dist. 1965; Norristown Sch. Adv. Bd., 1968-71; v. p., Norristown Coun. of Ch.; Central Union Assn. of Amer. Bapt. Conv., 1966-present; sec., Visiting Nurses Assn. of Norristown; Norristown Parking Authority, 1967-pres.; mem., Human Relations Coun. of Norristown, 1967; Bd. Phila. United Negro Coll. Fund, 1968; Youth Referral Com., 1965-66; Bd. Geo. Wash. Carver Com., 1964-67; mem., Alpha Kappa Mu Hon. Soc.; Alpha Phi Alpha; Mason; Home: 240 Jacoby St., Norristown, Pa., 19401; Office: 204 E. Oak St., Norristown, Pa.

FAULKNER, Robert Huntt, b. Garrard Co., Ky., Mar. 22, 1899; s. A. W. and Ellen (Rayston) F.; A. B., B. D., D. D. (hon.), Simmons Univ., 1926, 27, 45; m. Genevieve W. Warren (deceased), Nellie B. Hughes; Children--Genevieve (Mrs. Pritchett), Robert Huntt, Jr., Lauretta (Mrs. Burleson), Barbara (Mrs. Lee Roach), Lois P. (Mrs. Craig), Arthur, Patricia Ann (Mrs. Virgil Tharp); pastor, Little Benson Bapt. Ch., Franklin Co., Ky., 1922; Second Bapt. Ch., Bloomfield, Ky., 1926; First Bapt. Ch., Nicholasville, Ky., 1929; First Bapt. Ch., Stanford, Ky., 1933; Alpha Bapt. Ch., Franklin, Ky., 1939; dir., Chrstn. Edu., Ky., 1944-49; pastor, Second Bapt. Ch., Bloomfield, Ky., 1949-51; dean, Central Bapt. Theol. Sem., Indianapolis, Ind., 1951; St. Paul Bapt. Ch., Marion, Ind., 1952--; State dir., Chstn. Edu., Gen. Bapt. State Conv. of Ind. (currently serving); current dean, State Bapt. Sunday Sch. and Bapt. Trng. Union Congress; pres., Bapt. Fellowship, Marion and Anderson, Ind.; pres., Marion Congress of Social Action; mem., Exec. Bd., Urban League; Exec. Bd., Congress for Rel. and Race; Commission of Chaplaincy Service; Marion Area Min. Assn.; state chrmn., Ten Million Dollar Edu. Found. of the Natl. Bapt. Conv., USA, Inc.; Office: St. Paul Bapt. Ch., 1615 W. 7th St., Marion, Ind.

FAULKNER, William John, dean of chapel, b. Society Hill, S. C., Nov. 16, 1891; s. Lawrence and Hanna J. (Dobey) F.; Normal Dept., Mayesville Coll., S. C.; Bachelor of Humanics, YMCA Coll., Springfield, Mass.; A. M., Univ. of Chicago (Practical Tehol.); grad. courses, Univ. of Pa.; D. D. (hon.), Chgo. Theol. Sem., 1946; m. Elizabeth Abele Cook; Children--William John, Jr. (deceased), Mrs. Chas. H. Webster, Mrs. John O. Brown; sec., YMCA, Phila., Pa. and Atlanta, Ga.; personnel placement sec., YMCA War Coun. (WW I); pastor, First Congre. Ch., Atlanta, Ga.; dean of men and min., Fisk Univ., 1934-42; dean of the chapel, 1942-53; pastor, Congre. Ch. of Park Manor, Chicago, Ill., 1953-62; dean of the Chapel, Dillard Univ., New Orleans, La., 1963-64; promoted "Build Better Homes" movement for Negroes; Atlanta, Ga.; estab. first summer camps for Negro Boys, Phila. & Atlanta; former moderator, Tenn. State Conf. of Congre. Chs.; twice v. moderator, Gen. Coun., Congre. Chrstn. Chs.; mem., Congre. Chrstn. Chs.; Soc. Action Committees; Ch. Exten. Div.; Race Relations Dept.; former pres., Nashville Interdenom. Min. Alliance; former pres., NAACP; Univ. Chaplains Assn.; Edw. W. Hazen Foundation; Bd. of Dirs., Disciplined Order of Christ; Fellowship of Southern Churchmen; Southeastern Regional Coun.; former pres., NAACP Nashville, 7 yrs.; the suit to equalize teachers salaries, Nashville, Tenn., won in 1942 under presidency; mem., Bd. of Dirs., Welfare Coun. of Metro. Chgo.; Adv. Bd., Chgo. Theol. Sem.; v. chairman, Adv. Bd., Chgo. Assn. of Congre. Chrstn. Chs.; Bd. of So. Chgo. Community Center; Administrative Comm., Chicago Ch. Federation; Grand Crossing Min. Alliance; Evangelism and Devotional Life Comm., Ill. State Conf.; mem., Apostles Club; Foreign Missions Conf. of No. Amer.; contributes articles edu. and rel. magazines; has recorded several folk stories for sale by Bd. of Edu., Meth. Ch.; Home: 128 W. Roberts Ave., Wildwood, N. J.

FAUNTROY, Walter E., b. Wash., D. C., Feb. 6, 1933; s. Wm. T. and Ethel V. F.; A. B., Va. Union Univ., Richmond, Va., 1951-55; B. D., Yale Univ. Div. Sch., 1955-58; grad. sch., Catholic Univ., 1958-59; 1959-60; pastor, New Bethel Bapt. Ch., Wash., D. C., 1959--; dir., Wash. Bureau, SCLC, 1964; regional repr. Southern Chrstn. Leadership Conf., 1961--; D. C. coordinator, for the Aug. 28, 1963 March on Wash. for Job and Freedom; Exec. Bd. Wash. Urban League Project; Citizens

Committee on Homes and Highways; Coun. of Chs. of Greater Wash.; Howard Univ. Community Service Project; Interreligious Com. on Race Relations; Jr. Citizens Corps; NAACP, D.C. br.; "Stay-in-School" Comm.; Wash. Action for Youth; Wash. Home Rule Comm.; Wash. Planning & Housing Assn.; Bapt. Min. Conf., Wash., D.C.; Central Northwest Civic Assn.; Kappa Alpha Psi; Leadership Conf. on Civil Rights; Wash. Min. Assn; YMCA; Citizen of the Year, 1963; Home: 4105 17th St. NW, Wash., D.C.; Office: 812 S. St. NW, Wash., D.C.

FEAST, James Floyd, b. Beaumont, Tex., Aug. 22, 1930; s. Allen and Virginia (Feast) F.; A.B., Wiley Coll., Marshall, Tex., 1946-47, 1947-48; A.B.; Gammon Theol. Sem., Atlanta, Ga., 1951; 1952-55, B.D.; m. Cecelia Fagans; Children--Reginald Eugene, Angelia Elaine, Edwin Jeffrey; pastor, The Trinity Circuit, Huntsville, Tex., 1955-56; Bethlehem Meth. Ch., Hempstead, Tex., 1956-57; St. Paul Meth. Ch., Galveston, Tex., 1957-60; Grace Meth. Ch., Houston, Tex., 1960-63; current, Union Meml. Meth. Ch., Houston, Tex., 1963--; sub. tchr., Galveston Independent Sch. Dist., 1958-60; Dist. dir. of Temperance, 1958-60; Bd. mem., Financial Sec., Gibson Br. YMCA Galveston United Fund, Amer. Chrstn. Social Concerns; sec., Bd. of Pensions; Jurisdictional Repr. of So. Central Jurisdiction, Bd. of Christian Concerns; mem., Local Min. Alliances, Houston; Mason; Home: 4307 Wipprecht St., Houston, Tex. 77026; Office: 4712 Calvacade St., Houston, Tex. 77026

FEATHERSTONE, Rudolph Richard, b. Wash., D.C., Dec. 26, 1934; s. James Samuel and Annie Rebecca (Brown) F.; B.A., Gettysburg Coll., 1952-56; B.D., Gettysburg Sem., 1956-60; m. Carmella Delores Walker; bd. missionary, St. Johns Luth. Ch., Bronx; pastor, The Luth. Ch. of the Incarnation, Jamaica, N.Y., 1961--; Home: 119-41 Sutphin Blvd., Jamaica, N.Y.; Church: 150-14 Foch Blvd., Jamaica, N.Y.

FEDLER, Clifford Samuel, coll. prof., b. Douglas, Ga., Aug. 9, 1909; s. Isaac and Lillie (Buckin) F.; B.S., Fla. Meml. Coll., St. Augustine, Fla.; B.D., Detroit Div. Inst., 1935; m. Vera Mitchell; Children-- Cullen C., Clifford F., Leo W.; pastor, St. Marys Bapt. Ch. Ga.; Bapt. Ch., Tetusville, Fla.; current pastor, Bapt. Ch. Petersburgh, Fla., 1941--; instr., Dept. of Rel.,

Fla. Meml. Coll., St. Augustine, Fla.; dean, asst. to the pres., Fla. Meml. Coll.; head teacher and supervisor, Adult Edu. Euclid Center, Deland, Fla.; pres., Fla. State Sun. Sch. and B. T. U. Congress; Bd. mem. of the Natl. Congress, USA, Inc.; mem., Mason; NAACP; Pub. Relation Office; Citizen's Taxpayer Assn., Daytona Beach; Inter-Racial Alliance, Deland, Fla.; Min. Alliance, Daytona Bch., Fla.; author: Syllabus for Workers of Rel. Edu.; Home: 635 Bellevue Ave., Daytona Bch., Fla.

FERGUSON, Clarence F., church official, b. Easley, S. C., Dec. 1, 1900; s. William and Amanda F.; A. B., Clark Coll., 1921; B. D., Gammon Theol. Seminary, 1925; D. D. (hon.), Gammon Theol. Sem.; m. Etta J. Brwer; Children--William, Clifford, Mildred (Mrs. Greer); present pastor, Mt. Mark Meth. Ch., S. C.; mem., The So. Carolina Conf. of the Meth. Ch.; (former) two Gen. Conf. of the Meth. Ch.; mem. of five the Central Jurisdictional Conf. of the Meth. Ch.; Gen. Bd. of the Meth. Ch., 12 yrs.; Dist. supt., S. C. Conf. of the Meth. Ch.; mem., Bd. of Trustees, Claflin Coll.; Mason; NAACP; Home: 101 Hardale Lane, Greenville, S. C.; Office: same.

FERGUSON, John Columbus, b. Cleveland, O., s. John and Daisy; A. B. Baldwin Wallace Coll., Berea, O., 1954; B. D., Oberlin Grad. Sch. of Theol., 1958; m. Edith Hughes; Children--John, Beverley; pastor, St. Paul Meth. Ch., Cleveland, O., 1948-54; 2nd Meth. Ch., Anderson, Ind., 1954; Rust Meth. Ch., Oberlin, O., 1954-58; Werner Meth. Ch., Cleveland, O., 1958-61; Adm. asst., Bishop Clair, St. Louis, Mo., 1961-64; pastor, Normal Pk. Meth. Ch., Chgo., Ill., 1964-66; Stockton Meth. Ch., Stocton, Ill, 1966-present; Bd. of Dir., Trumbull Pk. Comm. Center, Chgo., Ill., 1964-66; US Army Air Corps, 1942-45; awards, Owen-Ruggles, Oberlin Grad. Sch. of Theol., Oberlin, O., 1958; mem. Lions Internatl.; Home: 302 E. Front St., Stockton, Ill. 61085; Office: Hudson & Benton St., Stockton, Ill. 61085

FERGUSON, William Melanthcon, b. Greenwood, S. C., Mar. 14, 1927; s. C. F. and Addie (F.); A. B., Claflin Coll., Orangeburg, S. C., 1947; B. D., Gammon Theol. Sem., Atlanta, Ga., 1950; S. T. M., Boston Univ., Sch. of Theol., 1951; m. Myrtis Williams; Children--Leonardo M., Enrocardo L.; pastored United Meth. Chs., Minus

Chapel, Wesley Chapel, 1947-50; St. Paul & Macedonia Chs., Camden, S. C., 1951-53; Field Repr. Bd. of Temperance, The Meth. Ch., Wash., D. C., 1953-56; pastor, Mt. Pleasant United Meth. Ch., Gainesville, Fla., 1956-67; Dist. Supt., The No. Florida Dist. of the United Meth. Ch., currently; former prof. Mather Acad., Camden, C. C., 1951-53; tchr. in the Summer pastor sch., Atlanta Coast Area U. Meth. Ch., Gammon Theol. Sem., Atlanta, Ga., 1958-68; former pres. NAACP, Gainesville, Fla.; mem., Mason; Omega Psi Phi; Home: 1135 S. E. 13th St., Gainesville, Fla. 32601

FERRELL, Clarence J., tchr., b. Early Branch, S. C., Oct. 18, 1927; s. Clarence and Bessie (Williams) F.; A. B., Benedict Coll., Columbia, S. C., 1957; m. Minnie Albany; Children--Delores, Clarence; pastored in Chrstn. Meth. Episc. Chs. in St. Peters, Walterboro, S. C., 1960-63, and Canaan Fair, Williston, S. C., 1963-present; tchr. of English and Speech, Estill Trng. School, Estill, S. C., 1957-present; US Army, 1952-55; Good Conduct medal; mem., Progressive Educational Assn. and the Palmetto Edu. Assn.; Home: P. O. Box 197, Estill, S. C.; Office: Canaan Fair, Post Office, Willston, S. C.

FERRELL, Horace Albion, b. Phila., Pa., April 11, 1913; s. Isaiah P. and Lillian (Johnson) F.; B. S., N. J. State Coll., 1932; Th. B., Phila. Div. Sch., 1947; Th. M., 1954; m. Sylena Anderson; vicar, Ch. of St. Mary the Virgin, Pleasantville, N. J., 1947-50; Ch. of the Ascension, West Chester, Pa., 1950-56; chaplain, Douglas Hosp., Phila., Pa., 1947-52; Cheyney State Coll., Cheyney, Pa., 1950-56; Episc. chaplain, Howard Univ., faculty, Howard Univ. Sch. of Rel., 1956--; consultant, Juvenile Court of Atlantic County, N. J., 1948-50; Bd. of Dirs., Family Service Agency of Chester Co., Pa., 1953-56; Bd. of Dirs., Health and Welfare Coun., Chester Co., Pa., 1954-56; mem., Dist. of Columbia Parole Bd., Five member bd., 1963; Omega Psi Phi Fraternity, Beta Chapter; Distinguished Service Award, 1949; mem., Amer. Acad. of Polit. and Soc. Sci.; Negro Community Coun. of the Natl. Capitol Area; Intl. Chaplain Frontiers Internatl. Inc.; Wash. Urban League; NAACP; Assn. of Professors of Practical Theology; Pigskin Club of Wash.; Omega Psi Phi; Acad. of Religion and Mental Health; Oxen Blades Golf Club; Home: 2333 First St. NW, Wash., D. C.

FINISTER, Abbot, b. Jena, La., Aug. 6, 1926; s. Mady and Rosie (Jenkins); attended rel. sch., 1946-48; Progressive Northwestern Bapt. Sem., 1961-64; D. D. (hon.) 1964; m. Dorothy Green; Children--Abbott, Jr., Danny, Wanda Jean Loretta, Kenneth; asst. pastor, Goodwill Bapt. Ch., Seattle, Wash., 9 mos.; St. John Bapt. Ch., Seattle, Wash., Mission Seattle, Wash., Kings Crest Bapt. Ch., Vancouver, Can., six mos.; Greater Faith Missionary Bapt. Ch.; in 1967 he reactivated a small and abandoned ch. (18 mi. from town) that was greatly needed... and named it Mars Hill Bapt. Ch.; Home: 3318 S. 24th Ave., Seattle, Wash.; Office: 1607 S. Forest St., Seattle, Wash., 98144

FISHER, Carl Anthony, Navy chap., b. Pascagoula, Miss., Nov. 24, 1945; s. Peter Wm. and Evelyn Gertrude (Grant); Epiphany Apostolic Coll.; Mary Immaculate Novitiate, Walden, N. Y.; B. S., St. Joseph Sem. Coll., Wash., D. C., 1968; grad. student present; mem., Josephites, a Cath. order working for the incorporation of the Negro into the church and society; tutor, Uplift House, Wash., D. C.; counselor, tchr., Kennedy Inst. for the Retarded, Wash., D. C.; advisor, Neighborhood Improvement Com. for everyone (NICE), Wash., D. C.; currently, asst. to the Bur. of Naval Personnel's spec. asst. for the science of human relations, Wash., D. C.; chaplain, Wash., D. C., Jr. Chamber of Commerce, Knights of St. Peter Claver; Freedom Democratic Party of Miss.; Urban League; awards: Diploma, Catechist Elem. Sch. of Rel. for Mentally Retarded Children (May 1968); author, Urban Affairs Seminar, The Negro in the Inner City Communicates to the Church, The Josephite Harvest, May-June 1967; Home: 615 N. Market St., Pascagoula, Miss., 39567; Office: 1200 Varnum St. N. E., St. Joseph's Seminary, Wash., D. C. 20017

FITZGERALD, Charles Harris, ch. official, b. Mandeville, La.; A. B., B. D., Morehouse Coll.; M. A., Hartford Sch. of Rel.; courses: Gammon Theol. Sem.; Atlanta Univ. Summer Sch.; m. Mary Elizabeth Shute; Children --Vivian Lisette, Karen Lavette; prof., registrar, dean, Amer. Bapt. Theol. Sem., Nashville, Tenn., 1956-64; pastor, Roger Heights Bapt. Ch.; current dir., Promotion, Tenn. Bapt. M. & E. Conv., Nashville, Tenn.; former moderator, Stone River Dist. Assn., Nashville; dean, Tenn. Bapt. Leadership Congress; dir., The Administration Workshop of the Natl. Sun. Sch. and Bapt.

Bapt. Trng. Union Cong. of the Natl. Bapt. Conv., USA, Inc.; chrmn. Program Comm. of the Bd. of Dirs., Bethlehem Center, Nashville, Tenn.; mem., Exec. Comm. of the Joint Comm. of the Natl. Bapt. Student Union, Nashville, Tenn.; Office: Tenn. Bapt. M & E Conv., PO Box 5645 North Station, Nashville, Tenn. 37208

FLACK, French Ziezler, b. Alexander, N. C., Apr. 6, 1896; s. Berry Raleigh and Mary Maggie F.; A. B., Knoxville Coll., Knoxville, Tenn., B. D. Livingstone Sem. & Coll., 1923; D. D. (hon.), Miller Univ., 1958; m. Mabel C. Freeman; ordained elder, 1920; retired pastor, A. M. E. Z. Ch. after 43 yrs.; mem., Com.-at-large, N. Y. Coun. of Chs.; Trustee Bd., Pa. Coun. of Chs.; mem., Human Rel. Com. of York, Pa.; mem., Trustee Bd., Crispus Attucks Assn., York, Pa.; Home: 254 So. Pershing Ave., York, Pa. 17403

FLANAGAN, William Carl, b. Moundville, Ala., Nov. 6, 1909; s. Abe and Ethel F.; Miles Meml. Coll.; private tutorship in Theology; m. Ora Mae Moore; Children--William C., Samuel Lee, Ronald; ordained minister of the Chrstn. Meth. Ch.; pastored in Ala., Ky., Ohio, Indiana, Va., Md.; present: pastor, Central Metro. C. M. E. Ch. and presiding elder, Jacksonville Dist. Fla. C. M. E. Annual Conf.; arrested twice in struggle for Civil Rights in the City of Jacksonville, Fla.; Home: 526 West 21st St., Jacksonville, Fla.; Office: 1079 Davis St., Jacksonville, Fla.

FLEMING, John Wilson, sem. prof., b. Morganton, N. C., July 7, 1916; s. Wm. T. and Rebecca (Avery) F.; A. B., Shaw Univ., Raleigh, N. C., 1935-38, 1946-47; B. D., Grad. Sch. of Theol., Oberlin, O., 1947-50; S. T. M., 1950-51; m. Hortense Gilmore; Children--Sundar Wilson; Dir. of Chrstn. Edu., Gen. Bapt. State Conv., 1951-53; instr., Shaw Univ., 1953-54; Gen. Bapt. State Conv., 1955-63; pastor, Brookston Bapt. Ch., Henderson, 1961 --; assoc. prof., Humanities, two summers; columnist, Norfolk Journal & Guide, 1959-60; reporter, Associated Negro Press, 1963; founder and first pres., Raleigh Theater; mem., NAACP; No. Carolina Council of Chs.; Conf. on Race and Religion; Mayor's Adv. Comm.; Phi Beta Sigma; Young Democratic Club; editor, Bapt. Informer, official organ of Gen. Bapt. Conv. of N. C., 1959-60; Home: 1816 Charles St., Raleigh, N. C.;

Office: Shaw Univ., Raleigh, N. C.

FLEMING, Maryland Taft, b. Henrico Co., Va., Nov. 12, 1908; s. Claude Julian and Sarah Miles F.; A. B., Va. Union Univ., 1948; B. D., Va. Union Univ. Sch. of Rel., 1950; D. D. (hon.), Va. Theol. Sem. & Coll., 1962; m. Hattie L. Chamberlayne; children--Ruth, Lloyd, M. T., Jr., Geneva Dallas, John H., Dorothy B. Bradley; pastor, St. James Bapt. Ch., Jetersville, Va., 1936-42; Shady Grove Bapt. Ch., Louisiana, Va., 1936-42; St. Peter Bapt. Ch., Glen Allen, Va., 1939-55; Jerusalem Bapt. Ch., Doswell, Va., 1943-55; Bethany Bapt. Ch., Montpelier, Va., 1952--; St. John Bapt. Ch., 1942-55; Zion Bapt. Ch., Richmond, Va., 1955--; pres., Bapt. Min. Conf. of Richmond & Vicinity, 1954-55; moderator, Tuckahoe Bapt. Assn., Va., 1948--; Hampton Min. Conf. Exec. Bd., 1961--; mem., Trustee Bd. of Va. Bapt. Negro Childrens Home, 1959--; Bd. of Broad St. Civic Club, Richmond, Va.; Bapt. Min. Assn.; Bapt. Min. Alliance, Richmond, Va.; Mason; Home: 7302 W. Broad St., Richmond, Va.; Office: 2006 Decatur, Richmond, Va.

FLORENCE, Franklin D. R., Sr., b. Miami, Fla., Aug. 9, 1933; s. Henderson and Bertha (Bensley) F.; Nashville Chrstn. Inst.; George Pepperdine Coll.; m. Mary Edna; Children--Franklin Jr., Clifford, Joshwyn M.; pastor, Reynold St. Ch. of Christ, Rochester, N. Y.; Non Violent Integrated Comm.; Exec. Bd. NAACP; Police Adv. Bd. for the City of Rochester; v. p., Love and Goodwill Corp., Home: 37 Reynolds St., Rochester, N. Y.

FLOYD, Harris Limual, chaplain, b. Wilmington, N. C., May 15, 1929; s. Clarence Limual Thomas and Callie (Floyd) T.; A. B., Shaw Univ., 1952; B. D., Berkeley Bapt. Div. Sch., 1959; m. Ethel Lee Rogers; US Army Chaplain, 1958-60; pastor, Mt. Zion Missionary Bapt. Ch., 1961--; auditor, No. Pacific Bapt. Conv., Washington and Idaho; vice moderator, Olympic Assn., Bremerton, Port Angles, Port Townsend; Good Conduct Medal; Defense Medal for Service in the US Army; mem., Bremerton Min. Assn.; Phi Beta Sigma; Home: 420 Union Ave., Bremerton, Wash.; Office: 4650 Werner Rd., Bremerton, Wash.

FLOYD, Massey, Jr., b. Rock Hill, S. C., July 25, 1915; s. Floyd and Alice (M.); A. B., Johnson C. Smith Univ.,

1936; B.D., Colgate Rochester Div. Sch., 1949; D.D. (hon.), Johnson C. Smith Univ., 1955; m. Ethel E. Hurley; Children--Floyd, III, Donald Bruce, Thomas Rickie; pastor, Pilgrim Bapt. Ch., St. Paul, Minn., 1944-65; Macedonia Bapt. Ch., L.A., Calif., 1965-pres.; mem., Mason; Omega Psi Hi; Democrat; former v.p., Minn. Conv. Amer. Bapt. Ch. (Twin City Bapt. Union), Bd. of Dir., Amer. Bapt. Foreign Mission Soc.; Conf. preacher, Amer. Bapt. Assembly, Green Lake, Wis., v. chrmn., Minn. Gov.'s Commn. on Human Rights; sec., Planning Bd. (St. Paul), Bd. of NAACP; Urban League; Hallie Q. Brown Comm. House; awards: Ramsey Co. T.B. Assn.; Sterling Blub Man of the Year, 1953; radio sta. WCCO Good Neighbor, 1964; Indian God of Peace trophy; pres., Minn. State Pastors Conf.; v.p., Minn. Coun. of Chs.; present, Bd. of Dir., L.A. Coun. of Chs.; So. Calif. Bapt. Conv.; L.A. Bapt. Assn.; L.A. Bapt. City Mission Soc.; S. Central YMCA; Home: 1415 W. 124th St., L.A., Calif. 90047; Office: 1751 E. 114th St., L.A., Calif. 90056

FOGGIE, Charles H., tchr., b. Sumpter, S.C., Aug. 4, 1912; s. James Legree and Marie Louise F.; A.M., Livingstone Coll., 1936; S.T.B., S.T.M., Boston Univ., 1939; D.D. (hon.), Livingstone Coll., 1949; m. Madeline Sharpe; asst. pastor, Afr. Meth. Episc. Zion Ch., Boston, 1931-32; pastor, Providence A.M.E.Z. Ch., R.I., Cambridge, Mass., 1936-39; current, Wesley Center, A.M.E.Z. Ch., Pittsburgh, 1944--; mem., Bd., Univ. Pittsburgh Rel. Fellowship; Pittsburgh Courier Award in Religion; pres., NAACP (Pittsburgh); Alpha Phi Alpha; frequent speaker on TV and radio and colleges; Home: 3131 Evart Drive, Pittsburgh, Pa.; Office: 2701 Center Ave., Pittsburgh, Pa.

FORBES, James Alexander, Jr., b. Burgaw, N.C., Sept. 6; s. James A. and Mable F.; B.S., Howard Univ., 1957; B.D., Union Theol. Sem., N.Y., 1962; m. Bettye Jeanne Franks; asst. pastor Binkley Meml. Bapt. Ch., current pastor, Holy Trinity Bapt. Ch., Wilmington, N.C. and St. Paul Holy Bapt. Ch., Roxboro, N.C.; instr., Bible Trng. Inst., Goldsboro, N.C.; mem., Fellowship of Southern Churchmen; Home: 516 N. 4th St., Wilmington, N.C.; Office: Holy Trinity Church, Corner of 4th and Campbell Sts., Wilmington, N.C.

FORDHAM, Walter Wraggs, church official, b. Charleston,

S. C., Oct. 20, 1912; s. Henry Joseph and Katherine (Wraggs) F.; Oakwood Coll., 1927-34; A & I State Univ., 1931-32; Univ. of Pittsburgh, 1940-41; A & I State Univ., 1958-59; m. Maybelle Lois Winston; Children--Frankie (Mrs. Charles R. Clay), Audrey Elaine (Mrs. Robt. L. Booker), Walter Wraggs; began ministry in N. J.; pastore Camden, Asbury Park, Burlington, Bridgeton, N. J., 1934-39; Pittsburgh, Pa., 1939-42; State of Fla., Sec. of Dept. of Evangelism, 1942-46; Southwest Region area conf. pres., 1946-54; present: conf. pres. of So. Central Conf., Kansas City, Mo., 1959--; Riverside Hosp. Bd., Nashville Tenn.; Porter Hosp. and Boulder Hosp. Bds., Denver and Boulder, Colo.; Oakwood Coll. Bd., Huntsville, Ala.; Union Coll. Bd., Lincoln, Nebr.; Pacific Press Pub. Bd., Mountain View, Calif.; Loma Linda Med. B., Los Angeles, Calif; Human Relations Comm., Gen. Conf. of S. D. A., Wash., D. C.; Chrmn. of Membership Dr., Centre Ave. br. of YMCA, 1940, rec'd the Loving Cup Award; mem., NAACP; editorial bd. of The Message Magazine pub. in Nashville, Tenn.; Home: 3501 Bellefontaine St., Kansas City, Mo. 64128; Office: 2528 Benton Blvd., Kansas City, Mo. 64127

*FORKKIO, John A., b. Kumasi Ghana, Sept. 27, 1924; s. Philip and Mary (Akomah) F.; A. B., Evangel. Coll., Springfield, Mo., 1961; M. Div., Howard Univ. Sch. of Rel., 1968; m. Esther Owush; Children--Elizabeth, James, Samuel, John, Jr.; student pastor, Chrstn. Meth. Episc. Chs., Kumasi, Ghana, 1953-55; pastor, Chase Circuit United Meth. Ch. Chase, Whitemarsh & Joppa, Md., 1968--present; tchr. & principal, elem. sch. Accra, Ghana, 1952-55; Home: P. O. Box 3288, Kumasi Ghana, W. Africa; Office: P. O. Box 112, White Marsh, Md. 21162

FORTUNE, Allen Ethan, b. Mayesville, S. C., Sept. 9, 1899; s. Thomas J. and Rebecca; A. B., Johnson C. Smith Univ., 1926; B. D., 1929; Harvard Univ., Cambridge, Mass. chaplains sch., 1942; Columbia Theological Sem., Decatur, Ga., 1951; m. Annie M.; Children--Carolyn, Alleyne; v. p., Albian Acad., Franklinton, N. C., 1929-30; tchr. of sociology & psychology, Haynes Jr. Coll., Augusta, Ga., 1930-32; pastor, Grace Presby. Ch., Winston-Salem, N. C., 1932-37; pastor, United Presby. Ch., Norfolk, Va., 1937-42; Army chap., 1942-46; v. p., Chaplain Assn., Atlanta, Ga., 1954-58; chrmn. Church Extension Comm., Ga. Presby., 1950-58; chrmn.

"Minister and His Work," 1958--; pres., Christian Inter-racial Group, Winston-Salem, N. C., 1947-48; US Army chaplain, 1945-46; awards: three battle stars, Cert. of award for meritorious service; mem., Omega Psi; Home: 309 N. Sanborn St., Florence, S. C.

FOSTER, Richard A. G., b. Lawrenceville, Va., Dec. 19, 1900; s. Walter Scott and Mary M. (Vaughans) F.; A. B., Livingstone Coll., 1925; Hood Theol. Sem., 1927; Syracuse Univ., 1930; Yale Div. Sch., 1950-51; Indian Central Coll.; Calif. State Coll.; m. Thelma Louise Brooks; Children--Ethel Jane (Mrs. Hillard), Mary Anne (Mrs. Cobb), Richarda Louise, Lillian Brooks, Ellen Eugenia; pastor, People's A. M. E. Z. Ch., Syracuse, N. Y.; St. John A. M. E. Z. Ch., Wilson, N. C.; Varick A. M. E. Z. Ch., New Haven, Conn.; current pastor, Cooper Afr. Meth. Episc. Zion Ch., Oakland, Calif.; elected alderman of 19th Ward, New Haven, Conn.; chrmn., Railroads and bridges of Aldermatic Bd.; mem., Mayor's Comm. on Edu. and Sch. Survey; New Haven Coun. of Chs.; Rent Control Bd. of State of Conn. & Oakland, Calif.; v. chrmn., Republican Coun. Central Committee, 10 yrs.; Bd. of Dirs. and V. Pres., of Oakland Coun. of Chs.; Trustee, Peralta Jr. Coll. Dist. of 6 cities including Oakland; Trustee and Bd. Mem., Booth Hosp., Oakland, Calif.; mem., Nat. Coun. of Chs., Bd. of Dirs., March of Dimes; Birth Defects Comm.; Mason; Elks; Alpha Phi Alpha; Republican; active in civil rights; mem., NAACP; Founding mem., Men of Tomorrow (civic organization); Home: 1927 Filbert St., Oakland, Calif.; Office: Greater Cooper A. M. E. Z. Ch., Oakland, Calif.

FOSTER, Wendell, b. Ala.; attended Columbia Univ., Union Theol. Sem., m. Helen Somersall; Children--Rebekah; pastor, A. M. E. Chs., Woodbury, N. J., Springfield, Mass., Hamilton, Bermuda, N. Y. C., Niagara Falls, N. Y.; chrmn., exec. bd. mem., Youth Coun., Jersey City, N. J.; pres., NAACP, Springfield, Mass.; mem., CORE; appt. assoc. dir., Amer. Com. on Africa, 1965-; US Navy; award, Servant of the Public, TV, WWLP, Springfield, Mass.; prod., dir. of plays, telecast, "A Man Called Allen"; Home: 1225 Woodycrest Ave., Bronx, N. Y.

FOUNTAIN, Major Lee, b. Angus, Tex. (Navarro Co.), Sept. 29, 1934; s. Jaycee and Pearline (Quarles) F.;

B. A., Jarvis Chrstn. Coll., Tex., 1957; current, Brite Div. Sch., Tex., 1963--; m. Perlean Simpson F.; Children--Bennie Lee, Laneda Jo, Donald Ray, Linda Gale, Lydia Denise; pastor, 13th Ave. Chrstn. Ch., Corsidana, Tex., 1955-57; Puget St. Chrstn. Ch., Dallas, Tex., 1958-60; Cedar Grove Chrstn. Ch., Rockwall, Tex., 1960-62; current, E. Annie Chrstn Ch., Ft. Worth, Tex. 1963--; annual counselor & instr., Youth Groups at summer fellowships; Home: 1312 E. Leuda St., Ft. Worth, Tex.; Office: 1234 E. Annie St., Ft. Worth, Tex.

FOUSHEE, Warren Raymond, presiding elder, b. Bynum, N. C., Mar. 31, 1907; s. John B. and Lula (Snipes) F.; Berry O'kelly Training Sch., 1938-41; Shaw Univ., 1941; Paine Coll. Summer Schs.; Student Bible Inst., m. Sylvia B. Roberson; Children-- Warren Raymond, Jr.; pastor, Young Chapel Chrstn. Meth. Episc. Ch., Raleigh N. C., 1938-41; Mt. Pleasant & Pine Ridge Ch., Union Mills, N. C., 1941-43; Sweet Spring Ch., Holly Springs, N. C., 1943-45; St. Matthew Ch., High Point, N. C., 1945-47; Durham Dist. N. C. Conf., presiding elder, 1947-48; pastor, Brown Temple C. M. E. Ch., Asheville, N. C., 1948-54; Beebe Meml. Ch., Washington, N. C., 1954-55; St. Joseph C. M. E. Ch., Chapel Hill, N. C., 1955--; pres., Inter-racial Min. Assn., 1956-57; Sec., Chapel Hill Min. Alliance, 1958-59; mem., Chapel Hill City Planning Bd., 1960-61; The Fellowship for Better Schs., 1956-61; chrmn., Citizen's Comm. for Schs., 1960-63; Mayor's Human Relation Comm., 1963--; v. p., Chapel Hill Chapter, NAACP; The Ex. Comm. for Open Movies, 1960; The Exec. Comm. for Open Business, 1961-63; The Exec. Comm. for Integration, 1963--; chrmn., The Finance Comm. for building $50,000 swimming pool (The Chapel Hill-Carrboro Swimming Pool Inc.), 1961--; Bd. of Dirs. of Community Action, Chapel Hill, N. C., 1963--; Mason; Royal Arch; Elks; Voter's Registration Comm.; Home: 520 W. Rosemary St., Chapel Hill, N. C.

*FOWLER, Andrew, sem. prof., b. Inman, S. C., Feb. 23, 1910; s. John C. and Ina (Newbitt) F.; A. B., Tuskegee Inst., 1937; B. D., M. A., Howard Univ., 1940, 1943; D. D. (hon.), Lynchburg Sem. and Coll., 1960; m. Henrietta Roberta Hatter; Children--Andretta I., Andrew H., Henrietta E., John I.; current pastor, Capitol View Bapt. Ch., 1941--; current prof. of Biblical Interpretation and English, Wash., D. C. Bapt. Sem., 1949--; visiting lecturer, Howard Univ. Sch. of Rel., 1962--; dir., Wash. Bureau, Natl. Fed. Coun. of Chs., 1951--; D.C., Chrmn. Foreign Missions Com. of Natl. Bapt. Conv. Mission Bd.; mem., Bd. of Dirs., Lott Carey Bapt. Foreign Mission Conv.; Bd. of Dirs. D.C. TB Assn.; Gen. Assembly, Health Welfare Conv., D.C.; Bd. of Dirs., Stoddard Bapt. Home; mem., Soc. of Biblical Lit. and Exegesis; Bd. of Dirs., New England Bapt. Missionary Conv.; Bapt. Conv., D.C. and Va.; former pres., Bapt. Conv., D.C. & vicinity; cited by Natl. Fraternity Coun. of Chs., 1962, Wash., D.C.; Home: 249 10th St. NE, Wash., D.C.; Office: Division Ave. and Ames St. NE, Wash., D.C.

FOWLIS, Ronald Preston, b. Springfield, Ohio, June 6, 1934; s. Charles O. and Edna (January) F.; Butler Univ., Indianapolis, Ind.; m. Coralee Harper F.; Children-- Joy, Rondalee, Connie; 1957--to date, pastor, Third Chrstn. Ch., Warren, O.; activities: counselor for YMCA Outpost; Club advisor, Warren Urban League; mem., Mayor's Housing Comm.; Warren Urban League Bd.; NAACP; Frontiers of Amer.; Warren Min. Assn.; Trumbull Co. Min. Alliance; Home: 849 Tod Ave., Warren, O.; Office: 241 1st St. SW, Warren, O.

FOX, William K., b. Sept. 25, 1917, Beloit, Wis.; s. George and Nettie Artist (F.); B.S., Tenn. A & I Coll., Nashville, Tenn., 1940; B.D., Univ. of Chgo. Div. Sch., 1943; M.S., Butler Univ. and Chrstn. Theol. Sem., 1963; courses Drew Univ.; Wash., Univ.; m. Reubena Mae Stultz; Children-- Wm. K., Jr., Katherine; field worker, comm. on War Services (Disciples of Christ), 1943; asst. pastor, Southside Chrstn. Ch., Chicago, 1940-43; dir. Rel. Ext., Southern Chrstn. Inst., 1943-47; Dean of Men, Coll. chap., assoc. prof., Tenn. A & I Univ., 1947-50; pastor, Gay-Lea Chrstn. Ch., Nashville, 1947-50; Centennial Chrstn. Ch., St. Louis, Mo., 1950-60; Dir. Spec. Studies and Lilly Endowment Planning Fellow, Ch. Fed., Greater Indianapolis, 1961-65; Asst. Gen. Sec., N.J. Coun. of Chs., 1965--present; former pres., v. pres., sec., Min. Alliance, St. Louis; v.p., Bd. of Mgrs. United Chrstn. Missionary Soc. (Chrstn. Ch.); pres., Natl. Chrstn. Missionary Conv.; pres., Ministers Fellowship (Natl.); Bd. mem., NAACP area; pres., Community Improvement Assn., St. Louis; present, pres., Tri-City Citizens Union for Progress and Tri-City Citizens Economic Union, Inc.; v.p., N.Y. Metro.

Dist. of Chs.; Chrmn. Com. of Program and Structure, Natl. Chrstn. Missionary Conv.; Bd. mem. Bd. of Ch. Ext. for Chrstn. Chs.; Finan. sec., N.W. Atlantic Churchmen's Conf.; mem., Dept. for Coun. of Chs.; Natl. Coun. of Chs.; mem., Assn. for Clin. Pastoral Ed., Inc.; N.J. Social Welfare Coun.; Bd. of Dir., Natl. Assn. of Coun. Secs.; Natl. Com. of Negro Churchmen; Ed. Conv. Journal of Chrstn. Chs., 3 yrs.; ed., Chrstn. Ch. Weekly newspaper, 4-1/2 yrs.; Home: 6 Union St., Montclair, N.J. 07042; Office: 116 N. Oraton Parkway, E. Orange, N.J. 07017

FOY, James Douglas, b. San Antonio, Tex., Sept. 10, 1907; s. Thomas H. and Ida L. F.; A.B., Samuel Huston Coll.; B.D., Gammon Theol. Sem.; S.T.M. Boston Univ. Sch. of Theol.; resident wk. for doctorate, Amer. Univ.; m. Venera R.; pastor, Aliquippa, Pa., 1938; Lewisburgh, W.Va., 1939-41; Pittsburgh, Pa., 1941-48; Georgetown, D.C., 1948-54; Dist. Supt. of the Wash. Dist. of the Meth. Ch., 1954-55; pastor, Asbury Meth. Ch., 1955-68; Dist. Supt., United Meth. Ch., 1969-pres.; mem., Phi Beta Sigma; Mason; Wash. Annual Conf. Meth. Ch.; frequent contributor to ch. publications; Home: 3801 S. Dakota Ave. NE, Wash., D.C. 20018.

FRANCIS, David Curtis, Sr., b. New York City, Jan. 1, 1926; s. Wallace A. and Jodena (Thomas) F.; B.S., S.C. State Coll., 1951; B.D., J.J. Starks Sch. of Theol., Benedict Coll., 1960; working for S.T.M., Interdenom. Theol. Center, Atlanta, Ga.; m. Francis B. Grant; Children--David, Jr., Thomas L., Willie B.; pastor, St. John Bapt. Ch., Bamberg, S.C., 1954-59; Beauty Hill Bapt. Ch., Orangeburg, S.C., 1952-59; Bethlehm Bapt. Ch., Newberry, S.C., 1959-63; Springfield Bapt. Ch., Greenville, S.C., 1963--; mem., Bd. of Trustees, Morris Coll., Sumpter, S.C., 1960--; pres., Greenville br. NAACP, 1964--; historian, Bapt. Miss. & Ed. Conv., S.C., 1965--; sec., S.C. Conf. of brs., NAACP, 1966-; v.p., Greenville Chrstn. Min. Assn., 1965-66; mem., Foreign Miss. Bd., Natl. Bapt. Conv. of Amer.; volun. Chap. Greenville Gen. Hosp.; exec. comm.-man, Ward 5, Box 4, Greenville Co. Democrat; US Navy, 1944-46; mem., Alpha Phi Alpha; PTA; Amer. Legion; Home: 604 E. McBee Ave., Greenville, S.C., 29601; Office: 602 E. McBee Ave., Greenville, S.C. 29601

FRANCIS, John, b. New Orleans, La., Nov. 13, 1907; s. John and Alice (Johnson) F.; Union Bapt. Theol. Sem.; D.D. (hon.); Children--John, Jr., Arnada, Mildred Jean; pastor, Evening Star Bapt. Ch., and Pilgrim Progress Bapt. Ch., 1937, 1941-present; moderator, La. Freedmen Bapt. Gen. Assn., 1957--; chrmn. Finance Com., 1963-present; treas., Natl. Bapt. Conv. of Amer., 1966; mem., Bd. Trustees, Leland Coll. and Union Bapt. Sem.; mem., YMCA; Orleans Progressive Voters League; Democrat; Home: 3710 Dryades St., New Orleans, La.; Office: 3600 Loyola Ave., New Orleans, La.

FRANCIS, Joseph Abel, b. Lafayette, La.; s. Joseph Abel and Mabel (Coco) F.; St. Augustine's Sem., Bay St. Louis, Miss. 1936-41; St. Mary's Coll., Techny, Ill., B.A., 1942-47; St. Augustine's Major Sem., Bay St. Louis, Miss., 1947-51; M.A. Cath. Univ. of America, 1959; Mt. St. Mary's Coll., Los Angeles, 1962; Loyola Univ., Los Angeles, 1963; Xavier Univ., New Orleans; Asst. Dir. Holy Rosary Inst., Lafayette, La.; pastor, Holy Cross Cath. Ch., Austin, Tex.; instr., Pius X High Sch., Downey, Calif.; princ. Verbum Dei High Sch., L.A., Calif.; Home: 3 St. James Park, Los Angeles, Calif.; Office: 11100 S. Central Ave., Los Angeles, Calif.

FREEMAN, Edward Anderson, church official, b. Atlanta, Ga., June 11, 1914; s. James Henry Watts and Ollie Watts F.; A.B., Clark Coll., Atlanta, 1939; B.D., Central Bapt. Sem., Kansas City, Kan., 1949; Th.M., 1950; Th.D., 1953, Central Bapt. Sem.; m. Ruth Anthony; Children--Edward Anderson, Constance Marie, William Norman; ordained to ministry Bapt. Ch., 1935; prin., Austell, Ga., pub. sch., 1939-42; pastor, First Bapt. Ch., Kansas City, Kan., 1946--; pres., Missionary Bapt. State Conv. of Kan., 1957--; mem., State v.p., Natl. Bapt. Conv., USA, Inc.; dir., Kan. City, Kan. City Planning Commissions; Kansas City, Kansas Human Relations Commission; Trustee, Amer. Bapt. Theol. Sem., Nashville, Tenn.; Western Bapt. Bible Coll., Kansas City, Mo.; Douglas Hosp., Kansas City, Kan.; The Greater Kansas City Bapt. and Community Hospital Assn., Kansas City, Mo.; Kansas City, Kan. Bapts. Min. Alliance; KCK Min. Inter-racial & Interdenom. Alliance; US Chaplain Corps, 1942-46, 1st. Lt. to Major; Man of the Year, Wyandotte Coun. of Chs., 1949; Man of the Year, Natl. Bapt. of So. India, 1958; candidate,

Kansas City Bd. Ed., 1950, 1954; candidate for rep. State Legislature, 1952; author: The Epoch of Negro Baptists and the Foreign Mission Board, 1953; paper: The Role of Integrated Seminaries in Meeting Educational Needs of Negro Students; Home: 3620 Oak Ave., Kansas City, Kans.; Office: Fifth & Nebraska, Kansas City, Kan.

FREEMAN, James Jasper, b. Bertie Co., N. C., Sept. 8, 1907; s. Maggie P. Freeman; A. B., Shaw Univ., 1937; B. D., Shaw Univ., 1938; D. D. (hon.), Va. Sem., 1944; M. A., New York Univ., 1962; L. H. D. (hon.), Shaw Univ., 1966; m. Mary C. Taylor; Children--James, Jr., Clarence Eugene, Gloria B., Carolyn E., Maggie R.; pastor, Brown's Missionary Bapt. Ch., Clinton, N. C., 1934-39; New Mt. Zion, Roxboro, N. C., 1935-39; Lawson Chapel Bapt. Ch., Person Co., N. C., 1937-39; First Bapt. Ch., Norfolk, Va., 1939-49; Queen St., Bapt. Ch., Norfolk, 1949-present; tchr., evening coll., Norfolk Div., Va. State; Roanoke Inst., Shaw Univ., Elizabeth City, N. C.; trustee, Va. Sem. & Coll., 1944-present; trustee, Shaw Univ., 1960-present; Norfolk Community Hosp., 1947-62; Hunton YMCA, 1948-65; sec., Lott Carey Bapt. Conv., 1954-present; sec., Hampton Inst. Min. Conf., 1966-present; coun., Child-Family Service, 1945-58; Home: 730 E. 28th St., Norfolk, Va. 23504; Office: 413 E. Brambleton Ave., Norfolk, Va. 23510

FREEMAN, Thomas F., prof., b. Richmond, Va., June 27, 1920; s. Louis H. and Louise E. F.; A. B., Va. Union Univ., Richmond, Va.; B. D., Andover Newton Theol. Sch., Newton Center, Mass.; Ph. D., The Univ. of Chgo, Chgo., Ill.; further study: Boston Univ.; Harvard Univ., Cambridge, Mass.; m. Clarice Estelle; Children --Thomas F., Jr., Carter Evan, Carlotta Vanessa; assoc. minister, Concord Bapt. Ch., Boston, Mass., 1940; pastor, Pleasant St. Bapt. Ch., Westerly, R. I., 1941-42; assoc. pastor, Monumental Bapt. Ch., Chgo., Ill., 1942-44; pastor, Mt. Carmel Bapt. Ch., Richmond, Va., 1944-50; prof., Va. Union Univ., 1944-48; guest lecturer, Bishop Coll., Marshall (current prof.) Tex. Southern Univ., 1949--; coach of the T. S. U. Debate Team, 1949--; advisor, Alpha Beta Chapter Alpha Kappa Mu, 1950--; Alpha Mu Omega Philosophical Fellowship, 1949--; Sigma Pi Alpha Symposium, 1949--; chrmn., Com. on University Ushers, 1949--; chrmn., Comm. on

Rel. Activities, 1949-54; and pastor, The Mt. Horem Bapt. Ch., Houston, Tex., 1951--; frequently engaged as speaker for Releigious Emphasis Week Programs; Ministers Institutes, Honors Convocation; High Sch. and Coll. Baccalaureate Services; High Sch. and Coll. Commencement exercises; awards: The Kappa Gamma Chi Debate Key for 4 yrs - Collegiate debating; The Chick Scholarship for maintaining the highest scholastic standing for three consecutive years at Andover Newton; Turner Fellowship for Grad. Study from Andover Newton; Divinity Fellowship for Grad. Study at the Univ. of Chgo.; Faculty mem. of the Year, 1951, 1952; pres., Southern Intercollegiate Forensic Conf., 1951-55; Exec. sec., 1955--; sec., Southwest Debate League, 1952-54; regional director, Region VII Alpha Kappa Mu Natl. Honor Soc., 1954-62; Natl. pres., Alpha Kappa Mu, 1962; mem., Amer. Philosophical Assn.; Amer. Forensic Assn.; Southwest Philosophical Assn.; Southern Speech Assn.; Natl. Edu. Assn.; Assn. of Higher Edu.; Natl. Assn. of Univ. Chaplains; Amer. Acad. of Science; YMCA; Natl. Bapt. Conv.; Home: 2522 Calumet St., Houston, Tex.; Office: 1915 Lockwood Drive, Houston, Tex.

FREEMAN, William Lee, presiding elder, b. Charleston, S.C., Nov. 11, 1906; s. Kitt and Elizabeth (K.) F.; The Natl. Bible Inst., New York City, 1942 (now Shelton Coll.); D.D. (hon.), Payne College, Birmingham, Ala.; D.D. (hon.), Monrovia Coll., Monrovia, Liberia; D.D., Allen Univ.; D.D., Edward Waters Coll., Jacksonville, Fla.; mem., Mason; Elk; Oddfellow; Knights of Pythians; mem., Genl. Conf. of the Afr. Meth. Episc. Ch. for the past 25 yrs.; Home: 1928 Prospect Ave., Bronx, N.Y. 10457; Office: same.

FULFORD, Fergus Maurice, b. Norfolk, Va., Mar. 21, 1917; s. James Edward and Annie (Brehon) F.; B.S., St. Augustine's Coll., Raleigh, N.C.; B.D., Bishop Payne Div. Sch., Petersburgh, Va.; Grad. Sch. of Applied Rel., Cincinnati, O.; ordained deacon, St. Paul's Chapel, Lawrenceville, Va., 1941; served Mission Chs. in Diocese of So. Va.; ordained priest, Novice-Order of St. Francis, Mt. Sinai, N.Y., 1942-43; curate, Ch. of the Crucifixion, NYC, 1944-46; present pastor, St. Barnabas' Ch., Bklyn, 1946--; Father Benedict, Oblate Tertiary of the Order of St. Francis, A Monastic Order of Men in the Episc. Ch.; Bd. mem., Youth Consultant on Service of the Diocese of Long Island; mem., Diocesan Youth

Commission as Clerical Advisor; mem., Exec. Com. of Archdeaconry of Bklyn, Diocese of L.I.; Chap. (Maj.) in US Army Reserves; mem., Amer. Ch. Union; NY Cath. Club; L.I. Clerical League; NYC Commission on Human Rights; Home: 417 Elton St., Brooklyn, N.Y.; Office: St. Barnabas' Ch., 727 Belmont Ave., Brooklyn, N.Y.

FULLILOVE, Paul Allen, b. St. Louis, Mo., Oct. 17, 1917; s. Oliver V. and Elnora (Johnson) F.; Amer. Bapt. Theol. Sem., Nashville, Tenn., 1941-42; B.Th., Gordon Coll. of Theol., Boston, Mass., 1944-48; Hartford Sem., Hartford, Conn., 1951-52; m. Josephine Daniels; Children--Paul, Jr., Jo-Ethel; asst. pastor, Peoples Bapt. Ch., Boston, Mass.; pastor, Union Bapt. Ch., New Bedford, Mass., 1946-59; current, Third Bapt. Ch., Springfield Mass., 1950--; mem., Bd. of Dirs., Dunbar Community Center, Springfield, Mass.; Bd. mem. at large, Child and Family Service, Springfield, Mass.; NAACP; treas., United Bapt. Convention of Mass. and R.I.; Bd. of Dirs., Natl. Bapt. Conv., Inc., USA; treas., New England Bapt. Missionary Conv.; treas., Pastor's Council of Greater Springfield, Mass.; Afr. Comm., Natl. Coun. of Chs.; Pres. Johnson's Bapt. Joint Comm. on Public Affairs; Syracuse Lodge, Knights of Pythias; Home: 150 Buckingham St., Springfield, Mass. 01109; Office: 151 Walnut St., Springfield, Mass. 01109

FURBRLUR, Harold Alonzo, b. Boston, Mass., June 13, 1936; s. Harry A. and Beatrice (Johnson) F.; Cardinal O'Connell Minor Sem., Jamaica Plain, Mass., 1954-56; St. John's Major Sem., Brighton, Mass., 1956-62; curate, St. John-St. Hugh's Parish (Roxbury-Dorchester Sec.) Boston, Mass., 1962--; Boy Scouts of America (volunteer), 1949--; Home: 62 Lincoln St., W. Medford, Mass.; Office: 26 Lawrence Ave., Dorchester, Mass.

GADSDEN, James Solomon, b. Berkeley Co., S.C., June 12, 1930; s. Wm. & Rosalee (Snipe) G.; A.B., Claflin Coll., Orangeburg, S.C., 1954; B.D., Gammon Theol. Sem., Atlanta, Ga., 1957; m. Ruth Lee Adams; Children--James Solomon II, Cynthia Ann; pastored United Meth. Chs., So. Carolina, Isaiah-Dorman Chapel, Walterboro, 1952; Summerville-Lincolnville, Summerville, 1953; W. Anderson, Anderson, 1954-56; Lamar, 1957-58; St. Mark, Sumter, 1959; Camden, 1960-66; Staff, Bd. of Ed.

United Meth. Ch., 1967-present; tchr., Boylan-Haven-Mather Acad., Camden, S. C., 1959-63; Home: 909 E. Clayton Ave., Nashville, Tenn. 37204; Office: 201 Eighth Ave., So. Nashville, Tenn. 37203

GAINES, Renford George, b. Halifax, Apr. 21, 1930; s. Wm. & Blanche, (R.); A. B., Western Reserve Univ., 1964; D. MN., Univ. of Chgo, Meadville Theol. Sch.; m. Harriet June Latimore; Children--Henry, Irene; pastor, Unitarian-Universalist Ch., Urbana, Ill., 1968--; Dir., Channing-Murray Found., Univ. of Ill., Aug. 1968; spec. staff chaplain, Univ. of Chgo. Hosp., 1967-68; former tchr., English; Lithographer, Manager (Cleveland, O.) 1957-61; counselor, terminally ill patients; Home: 401 W. Wash., Urbana, Ill. 61801; Office: 309 W. Green St. (P. O. Box 326), Urbana, Ill., 61801

GALAMISON, Milton Arthur, b. Phila., Pa., Jan. 25, 1923; s. Gladstone and Dorothy (Wood); A. B., Lincoln Univ., 1945; B. D., Lincoln Univ., 1947; Th. M., Princeton Theol. Sem., 1949; D. D. (hon.), Lincoln Univ., 1963; m. Gladys Hunt; Children--Milton Arthur; pastor, Witherspoon Presby. Ch., Princeton, N. J.; Siloam Presby. Ch., Brooklyn, N. Y., 1949-present; mem., Presby. Ch., USA, NYC, Commn. Rel. and Race; Presby., NYC Com. on Administration; Natl. Com. of Negro Churchmen; Bd. of Dir., Interfaith Community Services, Bklyn; chrmn., Bd. of Dir., OIC, NY; Bedford-Troop Neighborhood Assn.; mem., NYC Coun. Against Poverty; exec. dir., Sch. and Community Org. for Partnership in Ed.; chrmn., NYC Peoples Bd. of Ed.; cons., Central Brooklyn Coordinating Coun.; Bd. of Dir., Willia Hardgrow Mental Hygiene Clinic; v. moderator (former) Presby. of Brooklyn-Nassau; advisor, Geneva Fellowship, Presby. of Brooklyn-Massau; mem., Gen. Assembly Spec. Com. on Segregated Synods and Presby., Presbyterian Ch.; former pres., NAACP, Brooklyn br.; Parents Workshop for Equality, NYC; Bd. of Trustee, Woodward Sch.; Bd. of Dir., Big Bros. Inc.; Bd. of Dir., Bedford-Stuyvesant Youth in Action; chrmn., Stuyvesant Community Center Bd. of Dir.; Bklyn TB and Health Assn.; Good-will Emissary to the Young People of Presby. Ch. to Europe and Fr. Cameroun, W. Africa, 1955; represented Westminster Fellowship of Presby. Ch.; Spec. Mission for Dept. of Evangelism to Cuba, 1959; conducted sem. at various Synod Sch. for Min. in USA; prof. Ed. and Urban Studies, Harvard Grad. Sch.

of Ed., Cambridge, Mass., 1969-present; Home: 1494 President St., Brooklyn, N.Y., 11212; Office: Harvard Univ. Grad. Sch. of Education, Cambridge, Mass.

GALLOWAY, Horace Ely, b. Chicago, Ill., Apr. 5, 1913; s. Milton I. and Marie (Ely) G.; B.D., McCormick Theo Sem., 1957; LL.B., Chgo-Kent Coll. of Law; courses, Univ. of Ill.; m. Martha Johnson; children--Horace Mark; employed Cook Co. Probation Dept.; private law practice; pastor, St. James A.M.E. Ch., Chgo., Ill.; St. John, E. Chgo., Ind.; Bethel A.M.E. Ch., Robbins, Ill.; pres., A.M.E. Min. Alliance of Chgo.; mem., NAACP; Urban League; Cook Co. Bar Assn.; Home: 9248 S. Wabash Ave., Chicago, Ill. 60619

*GANDY, Samuel Lucius, sem. dean, chaplain, b. Anderson, S.C., Nov. 28, 1916; s. Charles F. and Belle Victoria (Brock) G.; B.A., S.C. State Coll., 1935; B.D., Howard Univ. Sch. of Rel., 1938; Ph.D., Univ. of Chgo. 1952; post-doctoral, Danforth Fellow, 1958; m. Frances Elizabeth Williams; asst. dean of men and asst. minister Fisk Univ., 1938-41; acting pastor, Ch. of the Good Shepherd, Chgo., 1941-44; dir. of rel. activities and pro of rel., Va. State Coll., Petersburg, 1944-55; dean of the chapel, Dillard Univ., New Orleans, La., 1955-61; pastor, Kenwood United Ch. of Christ, 1961-64; current, dean of Sch. of Rel., Howard Univ., Sept. 1964--; consultant, Southern Regional Coun. Mid-West Round Table, Natl. Conf. of Chrstns. & Jews; dir., European Seminar for Students Studying the Heritage of the Ch., 1960; Bd. mem., No. Kenwood Oakland Community Conf.; Neighborhood consultant to military establishments, especially Ft. Lee, Va.; mem., Com. on Urban Renewal; Dialogue Group of Ministers, Rabbis and Priests, Chicago Chapter Natl. Conf. Chrstns & Jews; Bd. mem., Mich. Ave. Hosp.; Peoples Co-op Credit Union; Nursing Sch., Provident Hosp.; Advisory Com., Bd. of Health, Elem. Sch. Girl Pregnancies; Urban Missions Com.; Rel. Ed. Assn. Natl. Assn. of Coll. and Univ. Chaplains; mem., Urban League; NAACP; author: Chapel, publication of NACUC; booklet on Prayers in the Chapel; Research in urban ch. activities; Office: Sch. of Rel., Howard Univ., Wash., D.C.

GARDNER, LeRoy, b. Wichita, Kan., Nov. 25, 1924; s. Littleton and Lena (Washington); A.A., Bethel Coll., St. Paul, Minn., 1946; m. Katherine A. Darling; Children--

LeRoy, Jr., Sharon, Gordon; pastor, No. Central Bapt. Ch., St. Paul, Minn., 1956-present; Ober Boy's Club, St. Paul, Minn., 1942-46; author: The Truth About Interracial Marriage; Black Muslim Truth or Heresy; Home: 728 Iglehart Ave., St. Paul, Minn; Office: No. Central Bapt. Ch., 400-408 W. Central Ave., St. Paul, Minn., 55103

GARNER, Frank Travis, Jr., b. Cincinnati, O., Jan. 30, 1924; s. Frank T. and Lillian (Wright); 1963, Bishop Coll., Dallas, Tex.; m. Mayme Carrol Watson; Children--two sons, two daus.; asst. pastor, 1953-55, Wehrman Ave. Chrstn. Ch., Cincinnati, O.; pastor, Elm St. Chrstn. Ch., Oxford, O.; 1961-63 E. Vine Ave. Chrstn. Ch., Knoxville, Tenn.; currently: Denley Drive Chrstn. Ch., Dallas, Tex.; US Army 1943-45; mem. Mason; Amer. Legion 636; Home: 1407 Glen Ave., Dallas, Tex.; Church: 1702 Denley Dr., Dallas, Tex.

GARTRELL, C. L., b. Washington, Ga., June 11, 1927; s. George G. and Rosa (Wellmaker) G.; A. B., Johnson C. Smith Univ., 1948; B. D., 1951; further study: Ft. Valley State; m. Gladys Maloy; pastor, Chrstn. Meth. Episc. Chs., Union Mill, N. C., 1948-50; Forest Chapel C. M. E. Ch., Fair Forest, S. C., 1950-52; Bethel C. M. E. Ch., Macon, Ga., 1952-55; Trinity C. M. E. Ch., Milledgeville, Ga., 1955-57; chaplain, State Mental Inst., Milledgeville, Ga.; current pastor, Jeffersonville C. M. E. Ch., 1957--; chrmn., Examining Bd., Central Ga. Conf. C. M. E. Ch.; tchr., Bettis Acad. and Jr. Coll., 1951-52; elem. sch., 1952-54; Ballard-Hudson Sr. High Sch., 1954--; mem., Masons; Phi Beta Sigma; Alpha Phi Omega; Natl. Serv. Fraternity; Boy Scouts of Amer.; NEA; ATA; PTA; Home: 409 Lilly Ave., Macon, Ga.

GASKINS, Walter Wesley, b. Middleburg, Va., Feb. 10, 1934; s. Dadley Scott and Martha (Lloyd) G.; Paine Coll., Augusta, Ga., 1 sem.; m. Marion Fox Brown; Children--Walter Wesley, II; pastor, Monroe Chapel Chrstn. Meth. Episc. Ch., Ashburn, Va., 1 yr.; Lawrenceville circuit, 2 yrs.; St. Stephen C. M. E. Ch., Winchita, 2 yrs.; Williams Chapel & St. Paul C. M. E. Ch., Va.; active in the civic affairs of Front Royal and Warren Co.; mem., Human Relations Coun.; Home: 15 E. Prospect St., Front Royal, Va.

GASTON, Joseph Alexander, church administrator, b. Winnsboro, S. C., Jan. 3, 1928; s. John N. and Lilla (Russe A. B. & B. D., Johnson C. Smith Univ.; M. A., Univ. of Denver; pastor, Edward Webb Ch., Mt. Airy, N. C.; First Presby. Ch., Boonsville, N. C., 1952; Sun. Sch. Missionary, United Presby. Ch., 1952-56; Johnson C. Smith Univ., 1956--; consultant Counseling and Guidanc for Vocation and Ch. Occupations, Catawba Synod; mem Amer. Personnel and Guidance Assn., Natl. Assn. of Personnel Worker, Mental Health Assn., Omega Psi Ph Fraternity; Home: 301 Campus St., Charlotte, N. C.; Office: Johnson C. Smith Univ., Charlotte, N. C.

GATEWOOD, Clifton Emory A.; b. Dorsey, Md., July 4, 1925; s. Alphonso E. and Elestine (G.); attended Bates Coll., 1939-43; A. B., Morgan State Coll., 1951; studen Howard Univ., 1952; B. D., Drew Univ., 1956; student, Union Theol. Sem., 1956; m. June Howston; Children-- Chanelle Elestine; assoc. pastor, Salem Meth. Ch., 1956-63; pastor, Epworth Meth. Ch., NYC, 1963-preser Exec. Bd., Bronx NAACP; mem., Child Study Assn. of Amer.; Prot. Fed. of Welfare Agencies; Air Force, 1943-46; Good Conduct Award; Home: 226 W. 150th St. New York, N. Y. 10039; Office: 834-36 Concourse Village E., Bronx, N. Y., 10451

GATHINGS, Samuel Alonzo, b. Gibson, Miss., April 5, 1923; s. Alonzo and Jazzie; B. A., Rust Coll., Holly Springs, Miss., 1949; M. S., Univ. of Indiana, 1954; M. A., Univ. of Chgo., 1965; m. Callie Jordan; pastor, Sherman Methodist Ch., Evanston, Ill., 1959-64; New Hope C. M. E. Ch., Evanston, Ill., 1964-present; tchr., Miss., 1949-57; Chgo. pub. sch., 1959-present; pres., Evanston Min. Conf., 1964-68; v. p., NAACP, 1959-66; Democrat Club; US Army, 1942-45; awards: Good Conduct; 2 Battle stars; mem., Elks; Mason; NEA; Home: 1924 Brown Ave., Evanston, Ill. 60201; Office: 1840 Grey Ave., Evanston, Ill. 60201

GAYLOR, Stewart Richard, b. Buffalo, N. Y., Jan. 19, 19 s. Thomas and Madeline (Johnson) S.; B. S., Livingstone Coll., Salisbury, N. C., 1962; B. D., Hood Theol. Sem., Salisbury, N. C., 1965; certificate, Inst. of Pastoral Care, Buffalo, N. Y., 1961; pres., Ch. Youth Coun., Buffalo, N. Y., 1955-58; treas., Youth Div., Coun. of Chs., Buffalo, N. Y., 1956; asst. camp mgr., Camp Dorothy Walls, Black Mountain, N. C., 1960, 1961; asst. pastor, Soldier's Meml. Ch., Salisbury, N. C., 1958-60;

pastor, Zion Chapel A. M. E. Z. Ch., Hiddenite, N. C., 1961-65; pastor, Mt. Vernon A. M. E. Z. Ch., Statesville, N. C., 1961-65; pastor, St. Mary A. M. E. Z. Ch., Laurel Hill, N. C., 1965-present; sub. tchr., Laurel Hill, N. C., 1965-present; founder-first pres., NAACP, Livingstone Coll., Salisbury, N. C., 1959-62; mem., NAACP, Buffalo, 1956-58; a leader in the Freedom Struggle in the Salisbury, N. C. area, 1958-65; Outstanding Youth of Year, Westminster House, Buffalo, N. Y., 1954; Lula Montgomery Award (student award) for outstanding contribution of year (given for civil rights work), 1962; NAACP Plaque for service to humanity, Salisbury, N. C., 1965; mem., Scotland Co. Ministerial Fellowship, 1965-present; mem., Phylanx Club (Prof. & Bus.) Laurinburg, N. C.; Omega Psi Phi; Home: Rt. 2, Box 167, Laurel Hill, N. C. 28351; Office: 422 Cameron St., Laurel Hill, N. C. 28331

GEORGE, Arthur Henry, dean, Camden, S. C., 1894; s. Henry and Elvira (Beckham); A. B., Johnson C. Smith Univ., 1917; S. T. B., J. C. Smith Sem., 1920; S. T. M., Western Theol. Sem., 1921; Auburn Sem., Union Sem.; m. Minnie B. Jones; Children--Arthur Allen, Henry Hamilton, Bryant; pastor, Calvary Presby. Ch., Wilson, N. C., 1921-29; Stated clerk of Cape Fear Presby.; Shiloh Presby. Ch., Knoxville, Tenn., 1930-34; prof. Homiletics, Johnson C. Smith Univ., 1934; dean, J. C. Smith Sem., 1946-60; dean, Emeritus prof. of homiletics, 1960; Home: Johnson C. Smith Univ., Charlotte, N. C.

GEORGE, Bryant, administrator, b. Wilson, N. C., Nov. 19, 1927; s. Arthur Henry and Minnie (Jones); B. A., Johnson C. Smith Univ., Charlotte, N. C., 1950; B. D., 1953; m. Marion Frances Gater; Children--Arthur Henry II; Fraternal Worker, UPUSA Ch. to Pakistan 1953-57; assoc. Genl. Sec. Pakistan Student Chrstn Movement; Dir. of Youth Work Lahore Ch. Coun.; Ch. Extension Bd. Presby. of Ch.; asst. to exec. dir. and sec. South Central Planning Coun., 1957-61; UPUSA Bd. of Natl. Missions; asst. dir. Dept. of Urban Ch., 1961-63; assoc. chrmn. Div. of Ch. Strategy and Development, UPUSA, 1963--; lecturer in Mission World Mission Inst., Evanston, Ill., 1960; lecturer Home Missions Chrstn. Theol. Sem., 1959; Spiritual Emphasis Week Macalester Coll., 1964; mem. Bd. of Dirs. Englewood Urban League (N. J.), Bd. of Managers Commission on Missionary Educa. (Friendship Press), Bd. of Mgrs., Urban Dept. Natl.

Coun. of Chs.; mem., Masons; Omega Psi Phi; Elks; Home: 52 Beveridge St., Teaneck, N. J.; Office: 1151, 475 Riverside Dr., New York, N. Y.

GEORGE, Carrie Leigh, sem. prof., b. Winder, Ga., Sept. 28; dau. Elijah J. and Olian (Owens) L.; A. B., Clark Coll., 1932-36; M. A., Atlanta Univ., 1936-37; B. D., Gammon Theol. Sem., 1948-54; P. C. R. E., New York Univ., 1961; Ed. R. D. (Hon.), Burton Coll. and Sem., 1963; Ohio State Univ., 1942; Hartford Sem. Found., 1958, 59; Garrett Theol. Sem., Sum. 1960; Atlanta Univ., 1963-64; m. Domotory T.; Children--Faith Olian, Donald T.; assoc. prof., Gammon Theol. Sem., Atlanta, 1954-57; Interdenom. Theol. Center, Atlanta, 1957--; minister of Rel. Ed., Antioch Bapt. Ch., Atlanta, 1955-62; dir., "People's Sch. of Christian Education" at the Interdenom. Theol. Center, 1964--; instr., Turner Theol. Sem. (Morris Brown Coll.), Atlanta, 1957-58; Head of Mathematics Dept., Samuel Howard Archer High Sch., Atlanta, 1957-58; instr., Spelman Coll., 1959-60; dean, Mission Study Inst., Mt. Hermon Assn., 1954-64; mem., Com. on Chrstn. Edu. of Children, Natl Coun. of Chs., 1962--; recipient, Woman of the Year Award in Religion, Iota Phi Lambda, 1956; Most outstanding minister's wife of the year award, Nat. Assn. of Ministers' Wives, 1954; del., World Bapt. Alliance in London, England and given a tour of eight other countries including the Holy Land, 1955; author: What Matters Most, 1948, Logan Press, Atlanta, Ga.; mem., Amer. Assn. of Women Ministers; Amer. Assn. of Univ. Profs. Amer. Personnel and Guidance Assn.; Rel. Education Assn. of Greater Atlanta; Amer. Assn. of Rel. Educators; Mid-Eastern Assn. of Religious Educators; Bapt. Minissters' Wives Coterie; YMCA; ITC Women's Fellowship; Alpha Kappa Alpha Sorority; Home: 1652 Detroit Ave. NW, Atlanta, Ga. 30314; Office: 671 Beckwith St., Atlanta, Ga.

GERALD, William church official, editor, radio announcer, b. Fitzgerald, Ga., Dec. 15, 1918; s. Percy and Bitha Wilcox (Collins) G.; Cortez Peters Business Coll., 1951; Howard Univ., 195 ; Bible Way Training School, 1950-62; m. Fannie Mae Braxton; Children--Edmond, Clarence, Frank, Raymond; mem., Bible Way Ch. Our Lord Jesus Christ World-wide, Inc., 1947--; Sec. pastor Bishop S. E. Williams; Exec. sec. Bd. of Bishops of Bible Way Ch. World-wide, Inc.; editor, official paper of organization, The Bible Way News Voice; chrmn., Ministers and Elders' Club; Gen. mgr., Sacred Composers' United Coun.; Gospel and semi-classic song composer; music arranger; pianist; organist; accordionist; interior decorator; pastor of the Lighthouse Ch., Annapolis, Md.; artist; sign painter; photographer; visiting minister to area penal institutions in nearby Va., 1951-58; author: musical compositions "My Hope is Fixed in Christ," "You Can Make It," "Have You Ever Been Touched by the Master," "When I Get Through," (Gospel songs); "My Ship Will Come In," "Tell Me Now," (Semi-classic); religious drama: "Three Deaths," Laughing At Wisdom;" weekly broadcast (Annapolis, Md.); Home: 4708 Sheriff Rd., NE, Wash., D. C.; Office: Bible Way Ch., 1130 N. J. Ave., NW, Washington, D. C.

GIBBS, Carey Abraham, bishop, b. Madison, Fla., Mar. 20, 1892; s. Jack and Lila G.; A. B., Edward Waters Coll., 1917; B. D., Payne Sem., 1923; D. D. (hon.); LL. D. (hon.), Edward Waters Coll.; pastor, Afr. Meth. Episc. Chs., Ohio, Fla., Missouri; presiding elder, 13 yrs.; pres., Edward Waters Coll., 1929; elected bishop, 1948; current, presiding bishop, 7th Dist., A. M. E. Ch.; mem., Gen. Bd., Natl. Coun. of Chs.; chrmn, Trustee, Edward Waters Coll., 1932; 1936--; US Forces, WW I; served as A. M. E. bishop in Africa and West Indies; mem., Mason; Pythian; Amer. Woodman; Republican; Elk; Gen. Bd., Coun. of Chs.; Home: 1011 W. 8th St., Jacksonville, Fla.

GIBBS, Ernest, b. Cropley, Md., Oct. 8, 1891; s. Wm. H. and Rose; Theol. ed., Frelinghuysen Univ., Wash., D. C., 1949; m. Apr. 6, 1914; asst. pastor, Rock Creek Bapt. Ch., Wash., D. C., 1920-28; organizer, St. Paul Bapt. Ch., 1926; pastor, Mt. Glory Bapt. Ch., Chropley, Md. 1945-48; pastor, Rock Creek Bapt. Ch., Wash., D. C., currently; vet. WWI; mem., Urban League; NAACP; Police & Boys Club; Bapt. Ministers Conf., Wash., D. C.; Lott Carey Missionary Assn.; The Oldest Inhabitants of D. C.; Stoddard Bapt. Home for Older People; Progressive Bapt. Assn.; Home: 4423 9th St., Wash., D. C.

*GILL, W. O.; B. D., Howard Univ. Sch. of Rel., 1941; three children; pastor, United Christian Ch., Jackson, Miss., 1956-62; dean of instruction & prof. of rel., Jarvis Christian Coll., 1942-55; dean of students, Jackson

State Coll.; Home: 1009 Eastview St., Jackson, Miss.

GILLESPIE, Sylvester Thaddeus, b. Starkville, Miss., May 23, 1938; s. Charles Franklin Golden and Ida (Smith) G.; B.A., Rust Coll., Holly Springs, Miss., 1962; B.D., Gammon Theol. Sem., Atlanta, Ga., 1965; m. Ora J. Andrews; Children--Dekovan Thaddeus; summer worker, Bd. of Natl. Missions of the Meth. Ch., Chattanooga, Tenn.; pastor, Clearwater, Fla.; pub. relations Min. Alliance, Clearwater, Fla., 1965; pastor, Stewart Meml. Meth. Ch., 1966-present; Home: 763 Lotus Lane, Daytona Beach, Fla.

GILLESPIE, William George, b. Knoxville, Tenn., May 12, 1931; s. Matt Wm. and Virginia (McBrayer); B.S., Knoxville Coll., 1948-52; B.D., Johnson C. Smith Theol. Sem., 1952-55; Concordia Sem., 1958-59; Wash. Univ., 1962-63; m. Martha Bele Cox; Children--Vendetta Elizsebeth, Wm. Edward, Harry Edmund; pastor, Davie St. Presby. Ch., Raleigh, N.C., 1955-56; Cote Brilliante Presby. Ch., St. Louis, Mo., 1956-; pres. Carver House of Directors, 1961--; mem., Alpha Phi Alpha Fraternity, Frontiers Intl., Presby. Interracial Coun., Democrat; Home: 4665 Labadie, St. Louis, Mo.; Church: 4673 Labadie, St. Louis, Mo.

GIPSON, Waymon Jefferson, b. Red Bay, Fla., Oct. 10, 1898; s. Finley Jefferson and Christiane Nellie (McClendon) G.; Stillman Inst., 1924-36; Dillard Univ., 1937-38; A.B., Southern Univ., 1945-46; B.D., Gammon Theol. Sem., 1956-57; m. Laura Ernestine Powell; Children--Hilda Marie; pastor, Berean Presby. Ch., New Orleans, La., 1934-47; pastor, Faith Presby. Ch., Jackson, Miss., 1947--; served on Comm. on Negro Work Gen. Assembly, Presby. Ch., U.S., 1942-50; chrmn., Synod's Comm. on Chrstn. Education, 1946-50; Stated clerk, Central Louisiana Presby., 1936-50; chrmn., Chrstn. Edu., 1950--; Trustee of Stillman Coll., 1952-63; mem. of Bd. of Farish St., YMCA Bd. Management, 1950-58; Home: 2407 Morton Jackson, Miss.; Office: 2219 Morton, Jackson, Miss.

GIVENS, Howard Washington, b. Waynesboro, Aug. 4, 1904 s. Howard W. and Ada (Handkerson) G.; A.B., Johnson C. Smith Univ., Charlotte, N.C., 1932; B.D., Johnson C. Smith Univ., 1935; A.M., Columbia Univ., N.Y., 1949; D.D. (hon.), Johnson C. Smith, 1960; pastor, Ben

Salem and Lloyd Churches, 1935-40 (Presby. of Catawba); Biddleville-Emmanuel Presby. Ch., Charlotte, N. C., 1940--; del. to Gen. Assembly of United Presby. Ch. USA (three times); Stated clerk of the Synod of Catawba, Presby. Ch., USA, 1957--; mem., Adv. Comm. (Boggs Acad., Keysville, Ga. 1959--.); exec. comm. Human Relations Coun.; exec. comm. Charlotte br. NAACP; pres., Mecklenburg Min. Assn., 1961; official repr. the Synod of Catawba to N. C. Coun. of Chs., mem. the Comm. on Desegregation Comm. of Friends, 1960--; certificate of recognition from NAACP (Charlotte br.), 1960; mem., Phi Beta Sigma; Home: 401 Campus St., Charlotte, N. C.; Church: 403 Mattoon St., Charlotte, N. C.

GLADNEY, Harvey Levi, tchr., b. Moundville, Ala., Apr. 14, 1914; s. Lee Andrew and Nettie (Bishop) G.; Stillman Coll., 1937-39; B. S., Rust Coll., 1945-47; B. D., Johnson C. Smith, 1955; m. Gladys Miller; Children--Jean, Clevie, Edith and Beverly; pastor, Greenfield and McKinney Presby. Ch., 1940-48; pastor, Bethel and New Liberty Presby. Chs., Dillon, S. C., 1948-57; pastor, Second Presby. Ch., Thomasville, Ga., 1957-59; current pastor, Carver Heights Presby. Ch., Columbus, Ga., 1959--; pub. sch. tchr. and prin., 2 yrs. in Miss., 2 yrs. in Dillon, S. C.; Home: 3313 Decatur St., Columbus, Ga.; Office: Carver Heights Presby. Ch., 8th St. & Illges Rd., Columbus, Ga.

GLENN, Lawrence Talmadge, administrator, b. Winnsboro, S. C., July 20, 1963; s. James W. and Mattie A. G.; B. A., Johnson C. Smith Univ.; B. D., Theol. Sem., Johnson C. Smith Univ., 1947-54; S. T. M., Temple Univ., 1954-56; Dir. St. John's Presby. Neighborhood House, Detroit, Mich., 1956-58; asst. on staff of the Inst. on the Church in Corporate Soc., 1959-61; pastor the Broadstreet United Presby. Ch., Detroit, Mich., 1961--; mem., Bd. of the Greater Detroit Comm. for Fair Housing Practices; Home: 4082 Cortland, Detroit, Mich.; Church: 12065 Broadstreet, Detroit, Mich.

GLOVER, Benjamin James, b. Greenwood, S. C., Oct. 26, 1915; s. Charles George and Esther (Massey) G.; A. B., Wilberforce Univ.; B. D., Payne Theol. Sem.; D. D. (hon.), Allen Univ.; LL. D. (hon.), Kittrell Coll.; courses, Union Theol. Sem., N. Y.; m. Madrian Lynette; Children--Madrian Lynette, Lydia Oveta, Benjamin Bruce,

Shawn DeWayne, Gail Audelia; pastor, Mt. Lebanon Ch., Due West, S. C.; Quinn Chapel Ch., Wilmington, Ohio; Chappelle Sta. and builder of Chappelle Meml., Columbia, S. C.; Morris Brown Ch., Charleston; presiding elder, Edisto Dist.; currently, Emanuel Ch., Charleston, S. C.; tchr. pub. schs., Due West, S. C.; prof., Allen Univ.; head of dept. of Systematic Theol., Dickerson Sem.; dean, Charleston Extension, Allen Univ.; dir., Public rel., Allen Univ.; ed., The Epsic. Messenger; chrmn., "The Friends of Allen" Drive; mem. in past, Gen. Bd. of Ed., A. M. E. Ch.; pres., Citizens Org. of Charleston; Phi Beta Sigma; sec., Bd. of Dirs.; Reid House of Chrstn. Service; chrmn., Bd. of Dirs. Mc Clennan-Banks Hosp.; mem. at present, Gen. Bd. of A. M. E. Ch.; pres., Interdenom. Min. Alliance; Bd. of Dirs., Reid House; S. C. Coun. on Race Relations; Exec. Bd. of Citizens Com.; pres., Allen Univ., Columbia, S. C.; del. Ecumenical Intersem. Conf., Zeist, Holland; four consecutive Gen. Conf.; WCC, Amsterdam, Holland; NCC, San Francisco; Coun. on Race and Rel., Chicago; Home: 2322 Taylor St., Columbia, S. C., Office: Allen Univ., Columbia, S. C.

GOLDEN, Charles Franklin, bishop; b. Holly Springs, Miss. Aug. 24, 1912; s. L. W. and Mary P. (Tyson) G.; A. B., Clark Coll., Atlanta, 1936; B. D., Gammon Theol. Sem., 1937; D. D. (hon.), 1958; S. T. M., Boston Univ., 1938; grad. study, 1946-47; m. Ida Elizabeth Smith; ordained to deacon, Meth. Ch., 1936; elder, 1938; pastor, Birmingham, Ala.; Atlanta, Cooksville, Tenn.; Clarksdale, Miss., 1935-38; Wesley Ch., Little Rock, 1938-42; prof., Dept. of Rel. and Philosophy, Philander Smith Coll., 1938-41; dir., field service, Dept. of Negro Work, Meth. Bd. Missions, 1947-52; assoc. sec., Div. of Natl. Missions, 1952-56; dir., Div. of Natl. Missions, 1956-60: bishop, Nashville-Birmingham area, Meth. Ch., 1960-68; Bishop, U. Meth. Ch., Calif., 1968-pres.; repr., Div. of World Missions to India Centennial, Lucknow, India, 1956; chrmn., Bd. of Trustees, Gulfside Assembly, Rust Coll.; Capt., Chaplains Corps, US Army, 1942-46; mem., Interdenom. Min. Alliance; Natl. Coun. Ch. of Christ in America; Meth. Rural Fellowship (sec. 1952-56); contributor of articles to religious publications; Office: Box 467 San Francisco, Calif. 94101

GOLDSBERRY, Harry Willis, bishop, b. Helena, Ark., Jan.

11, 1895; s. William and Elizabeth; D. D. (hon.), Trinity Hall Coll. and Sem., 1965; Oral Roberts Univ., 1968; sch. and coll., Dallas, Tex., Portland, Ore.; m. Theace Helen Mitchell; founder, pastor, Faith Temple Mission, Chgo., Ill., 1928-present; appt. Bishop, Ch. of God in Christ, 6th Diocese of Ill., 1966; radio min., daily, March of Faith, stations WOPA, WVON; chrmn., Bd. of Dir., Internatl. Youth Congress, 1968; trustee, Ellen Dosie Golden Age Found.; Bd. of dir., US Bd. of Health; USO Mental Health Counsellor, 1966-67; US Army WW I; donor, Goldsberry Scholarship Award Fund; awards, Achievement, Rel. Workers Guild, Ch. of God in Christ; del., Internatl. Pentecostal Conf., Helsinki, Finland; Democrat; Home: 855 W. 73rd St., Chgo., Ill. 60621; Office: 7158 S. Peoria St., Chgo., Ill. 60621

GOMEZ, Joseph, bishop, b. Trinidad, West Indies, Nov. 29, 1889; A. B., Wilberforce Univ., 1914; M. A., Eden Grad. Sch. of Rel.; m. Hazel Thompson; Children--Eula Viviana, Annetta Louise; pastor, Afr. Meth. Episc. Chs.; Mission field of Bermuda and Canada; elected bishop, 1948; current, presiding bishop 4th Dist.; prof., Payne Theol. Sem.; chrmn., Ration Bd., 11-18, Auyahoga Co.; pres., Interdenom. Min. Alliance; mem., Exec. Comm., Fed. Coun. of Chs.; Bd. of Dirs., Cleveland Ch. Fed.; Trustee, Wilberforce Univ.; chrmn., Payne Theol. Sem.; Bd. of Dirs., Cedar Br. YMCA, Cleveland; Financial Bd. A. M. E. Ch.; Corporation of Schauffer Coll. of Rel. & Social Work; mem., Kappa Alpha Psi; dir., St. James Literary Forum; del., World Conf. of Methodism, 1956, 1961; World Coun. of Chs., New Delhi, India; chrmn, Connectional Com. on Missions, 1959-60; sec., Coun. of Bishops; pres., Coun. of Bishops, 1960-61; Home: 11009 Wade Park Ave., Cleveland, Ohio.

GOODEN, DeFarris, b. Madisonville, Tex., Sept. 28, 1937; s. Burnice Rogers and Alice Lee (Tarrow); A. B., Wiley Coll., Marshall, Tex., 1958; B. D., Gammon Theol. Sem., Atlanta, Ga., 1961; pastor, Mt. Vernon United Meth. Ch., Richmond, Tex., 1961-62; Commissioned chap., 1962; served US ATC, Ft. Sill, Okla., 1962-63; Gun Batt., Bamberg, Germany, 1963-64; HQ. 317th Engineer Batt., 1964-66; Hq. 5th Signal Batt., Ft. Hood, Tex., 1966-present; mem., Inner-City Ministry Trinity United Meth. Ch., Bronx, N. Y., summer 1959; Natl. Bd. of Mission United Meth. Ch., Bluefield, W. Va., sum.

1958; Ex. com. Douglass USO, Lawton, Okla., 1962-63; Bd. of trustees, The Madison Co. Health & Recreational Center, 1967-; Military Chaplains Assn., Natl. Coun. on Fam. Relations; Knights of Pythias; Home: 1316 Massey St., Killeen, Tex.; Office: Hq. 57th Signal Bn., Ft. Hood, Tex., 76544

GOODEN, Samuel Ellsworth, b. Jamaica, W. Indies, Aug. 25, 1916; s. Thomas and Ethel (Perrin) G.; A.B., Union Coll., Lincoln, Nebr., 1949; M.A., Columbia Univ., N.Y., 1958; m. Elita (Powell) G.; Children--Sharon, Rose Marie; Missionary, Nigeria, Seventh-Day Adventist Ch., 1963-67; Youth Dir., & Supt., SDA Ch., 1967-present; former tchr. SDA Schs., 1953-63; pres., Fed. Credit Union, NYC; Alpha Phi Alpha; Phi Delta Kappa; Home: 3068 Lynn Dr., S.W., Atlanta, Ga. 30311; Office: 235 Chicamauga Ave. S.W., Atlanta, Ga. 30314

GOODWIN, Kelly Oliver Perry, b. Washington, D.C., Dec. 24, 1911; s. Oliver Perry and Martha (Duncan) G.; A.B., Howard U., Wash., D.C., 1935; B.D., United Theol. Sem., Dayton, O., 1941; Grad. study, Temple Univ., Phila., Pa., 1941-42; Counselling cert., N.C. Bapt. Sch. of Pastoral Care, Bowman Gray Sch. of Med., Winston-Salem, N.C., 1948; D.D. (hon.), Shaw Univ., Raleigh, N.C., 1960; ordained Bapt. Minister, 1936; pastored, Friendship Bapt. (student asst.), Wash., D.C., 1935-36; Supply pastor, Zion Bapt. Ch., Reading, Pa., 1936; pastor, Zion Bapt., 1937-47; pastor, Mt. Zion Bapt., Winston-Salem, N.C., 1947--; consultant & mem., Exec. Comm., Town and Rural Inst. Ministers, N.C.A. & T. Coll., Greensboro, N.C.; mem., The Amer. Acad. of Pol. & Soc. Science; mem., Natl. Assn. of Housing and Redevelop. Officials; vice chrmn., Commissioner, Winston-Salem Housing Authority, 1958--; mem., Chaplain, Comm. of Management YMCA, 1960--; v.p., Emancipation Assn., Winston-Salem and Forsyth Co., 1961--; Coll. chap., Winston-Salem State Coll., 1958-59; mem., Omega Psi Phi; Masons; IBPOE of W; travelled, N. Amer., Caribbean Is., Europe, W. Africa; mem., Natl. Bapt. Conv. USA, Inc., 1945--; mem., Exec. Bd. Phyllis Wheatley Home, Winston-Salem, N.C. Home: 501 26th St. NW, Winston-Salem, N.C. 27105; Office: 1304 N. Highland Ave., Winston-Salem, N.C. 27101

GOPAUL, Paul Albert, educator, b. San Francisco, Calif., June 11, 1926; s. Paul Mortimer and Ivy Grace (Gibbs) G.; B.A., St. Michael's, 1952; M.A., St. Michael's 1954; Ph.D., Univ. of Ottawa, 1958; Ph.D. cand., Univ. of N. Mex., 1958--; ordained priest Roman Cath. Ch., 1952; tchr., Eng., Hist., Humanities, Rel., Phil., St. Michael's; Med. Ethics, Marr., Jeanne Mance Sch. of Nursing, Burlington, Vt.; Ch. Hist., Patrology, Pius XII Maj. Sem., Albuquerque, N. Mex.; Psych., Regina Sch. of Nursing, Albuquerque, N. Mex.; founder, co-curricular program in Communication Arts, St. Michael's 1957-58; Prof. hist., Univ. of New Mex. Newman Extension, 1962-63; Pius X High Sch., Alb., N. Mex., 1962-63; U.S. Hist., Academic Counsellor, St. Charles Borromeo Sem., El Paso, Tex., 1964; priesthood: Week-end ministries, 40 hrs., Sodality, Days of Recollection, Sisters' Renovation, Children's Retreats, Vermont Cath. Hr., Columnist, Vermont Catholic Tribune; Editor, Sponsor Magazine, Newman Apostolate, Vermont and New Mexico, Hosp. chap.; prof. Soc.; Amer. Cath. Hist. Assn., Amer. Hist. Assn.; life mem., Calif. Scholarship Fed., J.H. Card. Newman Hon. Soc.; asst. pastor, Blessed Sacrament Ch., El Paso, Tex., 1963--; assoc. editor, Southwest Cath. Register, El Paso, Tex., 1964; Home: 90-25 Diana Dr., El Paso, Tex.; Office: same.

GORDON, Frank R., tchr., b. Hague, Va., Jan. 23, 1918; s. John and Marie; A.B., Lincoln Univ., 1939; S.T.B., 1942; m. Evelyn Crabb; Children--Sandra Dale, Lee David; pastor, Penna., Ga., Mo.; current: Shiloh Presby. Ch., Knoxville, Tenn.; Missouri; Bible tchr. Knoxville Coll.; mem. Natl. Comm. on Rel. and Race, U.P. Ch., USA; served as moderator of the Presbytery and Synods; mem., Gov. Comm. on Human Relations, Tenn.; Bd. of Managers YMCA. Juvenile Court, 1954-57; pres., Knoxville NAACP; pres. Tenn. State Conf., NAACP branches; chrmn., Ch. Work Comm. of Min. SE Region, NAACP; leader sch. integration, City of Knoxville; mem., Elk, Mason, Kappa Alpha Psi; Church: 1015 E. Church St., Knoxville, Tenn.

GORDON, Maxie Sylvester, educator, author, b. Greenville, S.C., Dec. 10, 1910; s. John Oscar and Hattie (Byrd) G.; A.B., Benedict Coll., Columbia, S.C.; B.D., Oberlin Grad. Sch. of Theol., 1937; M.A., 1938; S.T.M., 1939; Additional study, Univ. of Chgo., Sorbonne Univ., Paris, France; D.D. (hon.), Benedict Coll., 1956; m.

Ethel Mae McAdams; 2 sons, Maxie S. Jr. (2nd Ltd.), Thomas Asbury; pastor, Royal Bapt. Ch., Anderson, S. C., 1940-45; New 1st Calvary Bapt., Columbia, S. C., 1945--; instr. Mod. Lang. & Rel., Friendship Jr. Coll., 1939-42; asst. then assoc. prof., Fr. and Bib. Lit., Benedict Coll., 1942-60; acting dean, Starks Center of Training, Benedict Coll., 1960--; Research scholar and author, Flashlights, Sun. Sch. Pub. Bd., Natl. Bapt. Conv. USA.; S. C. Repr., Foreign Mission Bd., Nat. Bapt. Conv.; chrmn. Standing Comm. on Intercultural Relationship; appeared in Who's Who in Amer. Education, Vol. 20, 1961-62; Who's Who in Colored America, 1950; mem., (sub. life) NAACP; Coll. Lang. Assn.; Natl. Assn. Bible Instrs.; Coun. on Higher Edu.; Palmetto Edu. Assn.; Omega Psi Phi; Home: 2221 Marguerette St., Columbia, S. C.; Church: 1401 Pine St., Columbia, S. C. School: Benedict College, 1618 Oak St., Columbia, S. C.

GORDON, Robert Charles, b. Akron, Ohio, Feb. 20, 1931; s. Buford Franklin and Thelma (Pierce) G.; A. B., Fisk Univ., Nashville, Tenn., 1952; Oberlin Coll., Ohio, 1950-51; Johnson C. Smith Univ. Sem., 1952-53; Reformed Presby. Theol. Sem., Pittsburgh, Pa., 1956-57; Pioneer Theol. Sem., 1956-58; B. D., Th. M., D. D. (hon.), Pittsburgh-Xenia Theol. Sem., Pa. 1957-58; M. A., Fairfield Univ., Fairfield, Conn., 1965-66; (cand. Ph. D.), Hartford Sem. Found.; m. Lois Catherine Jackson; Children--Joan, Catherine; pastor, Cedar Creek A. M. E. Z. Ch., Heath Springs, S. C., 1952-54; St. Matthews A. M. E. Z. Ch., Sewickley, Pa.; A. M. E. Z. Ch., Indiana, Pa., 1960-62; First A. M. E. Z. Ch., So. Bend, Ind., 1962-65; Walters Meml. A. M. E. Z. Ch., Bridgeport, Conn., 1965-present; dir. of Rel. radio and TV operations, Dept. of Chrstn. Edu. of the A. M. E. Z. Denomination., 1956-present; served as news and pub. service direc. of radio stations in Ohio, Tenn., N. C., Pa., 1951-62; part-time rel. programming on radio and TV, So. Bend, Ind.; mem., Bd. of dirs., Ind. Coun. of Chs., 1962-65; mem., Div. of Audio-Visual and Broadcast Educ., Natl. Coun. of Chs.; faculty mem., Quadrennial Chrstn. Edu. Conv., A. M. E. Z. Ch., 1958-66; faculty mem., Grad. Sch. of Edu., Fairfield Univ., Conn.; mem., Bd. of Dir. of Bridgeport YMCA; Bridgeport Mental Health Assn. NAACP; co-chrmn., United Negro Coun. of So. Bend, Ind., 1964-65; mayor's bi-racial commn., 1964-65; cand. for City Council, So. Bend, 1963; cand., State Senator, 1964;

del., Dem. State Conv., 1964; exec. dir., Peace Corps; sec., Pastor's Assn., Bridgeport, Conn.; pub. service award, assisting in recruiting for US Army, Air Force, Navy, 1959-62; Tri-State Citizens Award for state of Ind.; mem., Omega Psi Phi, Chi Alpha Omega; exec. comm., Young Democrats; presently preparing for publication, revisions of two books by the late Bishop Buford Gordon (father)--Pastor and People, and Teaching for an Abundant Living; composed words and music to "On My Knees"; Home: 10 Wendy Rd., Trumbull, Conn. 06611

GOW, Francis Herman, bishop, b. Cape Town, S. Africa, Sept. 29, 1896; s. Francis McDonald and Sarah Elizabeth G.; A. B., Wilberforce Univ.; Tuskegee Inst., Miami Univ., Ohio; Lane Theol. Sem.; D. D. (hon.), Morris Brown Coll.; Wilberforce Univ.; LL. D., Allen Univ.; m. Louise Ballon; Children-- Teepho; pastor, Cincinnati Afr. Meth. Ch., Charleston, W. Va.; Cape Town, S. Africa; presiding elder, Cape Town Dist.; supt., Cape Natl. Conf.; elected bishop, 1952, 15th Epsic. Dist., S. Africa; mem., Comm. on Revision of the Discipline, Edu. and Missions, A. M. E. Ch.; Omega Psi Phi; Mason; Coun. of Chrstn. Chs., S. Africa; pres., African Peoples' Organization; chrmn., Colored Adv. Council; commandant, Civilian Protective Services, S. Africa; pres., Afr. Students Union; Home: 40 Prince George Dr., Wynbert, Capetown, S. Africa.

GRADY, James Crawford, b. New Hanover Co., N. C., Sept. 19, 1900; s. Luke and Rebecca (Aycock) G.; A. B., B. D., Kittrell Coll.; further study: Harvard Univ.; Shaw Univ., Cortez W. Peters Sch. of Business; m. widower; Children--Marion (Rev. Reuben Dicks), Charles; pastor, Chs., No. Carolina, Western N. C., Va., Md.; prin., Ross Hill, N. C. elem. sch., 1929; present pastor, St. John Afr. Meth. Episc. Ch., Wilmington, N. C.; mem. Exec. Bd., Wilmington, N. C., chap. NAACP; 1st Lt. Chap., US Army, 1944-46; Commendation award; Good Conduct Award; mem., Voters Registration; Mason, Civic League; mem., Writers Staff Second Episc. Dist. of the A. M. E. Ch.; Home: 216 So. 7th St., Wilmington, N. C.; Office: St. John A. M. E. Ch., Wilmington, N. C.

GRADY, Zedekiah LaZett, b. Laughman, Fla., Mar. 28, 1931; s. Walter and Sylvira (Bynum) G.; B. Th., Edward Waters Coll.; B. A., Allen Univ., 1957; B. D., Dickerson Theol. Sem., D. D. (hon.), Kittrell Coll.; m. Carrie Etta

Robertson; Children--Zedekiah LaZett, Jr., Judith Felita; pastor, Bethel A. M. E. Ch., Laurens, S. C., 1954-58; Bethel A. M. E. Ch., Anderson, S. C., 1958-59; St. Stephen A. M. E. Ch., Georgetown, S. C., 1959-62; Morris Brown A. M. E. Ch., Charleston, S. C., 1962-present; tchr., Dickerson Theol. Sem. Extension Sch.; mem., NAACP; Citizens Com.; Interdenom. Min. Alliance; Bd. of Trustee, Bd. of Control of Allen Univ.; Ad. Bd. of OEO, Charleston Co., 1965; award: Service Award from Morris Brown A. M. E. Ch., 1966; mem., Phi Beta Sigma; Mason; World Meth. Conf.; Home: 194 St. Philip St., Charleston S. C. 29403

GRAHAM, John Harry, b. Corinth, Miss., Apr. 6, 1915; s. Joseph Nathan and Bessie (Chambers) G.; A. B., Clark Coll., Atlanta, Ga., 1939; B. D., Gammon Theol. Sem., Atlanta, Ga., 1940; M. A. Drew Univ., Madison, N. J., 1941; D. D. (hon.), Rust Coll., Holly Springs, Miss., 1950; Grad. course Boston Univ., Boston, Mass., 1957-59; m. India Mae Gordon; Children--James Arthur, Patricia Viberneice; Dir., Bd. of Missions of the United Meth. Ch., 1960--to present; pastor, Corinth Circuit, Upper Miss., 1941-44; Dist. Supt., Starkville Dist., 1944-46; Holly Springs, Miss., 1951-53; Prof., Socio., Gammon Sem., Atlanta, Ga., 1953-60; Bible and Socio., Rust Coll., Holly Springs, Miss. 5 yrs.; Dean of New Orleans Area, Pastor's Sch., 4 yrs.; Dir. Dept. of Town and Country Work, Natl. Dir. Bd. of Missions of the Meth. Ch.; Trustee of Rust Coll., Holly Springs, Miss. and Gulfside Assembly, Waveland, Miss.; Dir. of recruiting and field supervisor, Gammon Sem., 1953-60; del. to Gen. Conf., 1948, 1952, 1960, and 1964; Jurisdictional conf., 1948, 52, 56, 60, 64; Seventh Meth. Ecuminical Conf., mem., Springfield, Mass., 1947; World Meth. Conf., London, 1966; chrmn., Central Jurisdictional Adv. Coun.; mem., Phi Beta Sigma; Mason; Republican; Meth. Rural Fellowship; author, Mississippi Circuit Riders, Parthenon Press, 1967; Office: 475 Riverside Dr., New York, N. Y. 10027

GRAHAM, Tecumseh Xavier, b. Wash., D. C., Mar. 14, 1925; s. James W. and Marjorie G.; B. A., Livingstone Coll., 1955; B. D., Hood Theol. Sem., 1958; m. Loreda Branch; Children--Tecumseh Jr., Majorie Ella; asst. pastor, First Afr. Meth. Episc. Ch., Brooklyn, N. Y., 1948-50; pastor, St. David A. M. E. Z. Ch., Sag Harbor, N. Y., Hood Meml. Ch., Belmont, N. C.; Waddell Chapel,

1956-60; A. M. E. Z. Ch., Portland, Ore., 1960-64; St. Mark Ch., Cincinnati, 1964-present; tchr., Cleveland Co., N. C.; instr., Portland Continuation Center, Portland St. Coll.; former pres., NAACP, Shelby, N. C.; pres. Shelby Voter's Registration League; pres., Greater Shelby Min. Assn.; served on Shelby Public Commn.; v. p., NAACP Portland chapter; pres., Albina Min. Assn.; co-chrmn., Albina Neighborhood Improvement Com.; Adv. Com., Portland Coun. of Chs.; Bd. of Dir., Ore. TB & Health Assn.; Bd. of Mgrs., No. Branch YMCA; presently, pres., A. M. E. Z. Minister's Fellowship; pres., Inter-denom. Min. Alliance, Cincinnati; v. p., NAACP, Cincinnati; Sigmo Rho Sigma; Omega Psi Phi; treas., Opportunities Indus. Centre; mem., Mayor's Adv. Com. Apprenticeship Inform. Center, Cincinnati; Home: 2181 Crane Ave., Cincinnati, Ohio 45207; Office: St. Mark A. M. E. Z. Ch., 3006 Eden Ave., Cincinnati, O.

GRANBERRY, James Madison, Jr., ch. official, b. Coweta, Okla., Apr. 29, 1914; s. James Madison Sr. and Naomi Eva G.; A. A., Western Univ., 1934; A. B., Lane Coll., 1936; D. D. (hon.), Campbell Coll., Jackson, Miss., 1952; LL. D. (hon.), Monrovia Coll., Liberia, W. Africa, 1955; m. Ethel Lee Hymes; pastor, Brown Chapel Afr. Meth. Episc. Ch., Bristow, Okla.; Bethel A. M. E. Ch., Claremore, Okla.; St. Peter A. M. E. Ch., Clarksville, Tenn.; St. John A. M. E. Ch., Nashville, Tenn.; St. Paul A. M. E. Ch., Columbia, Tenn.; served as pastor churches in Okla., and Tenn. from 1939 to May 1964; current, sec.-treas., Pension Dept., A. M. E. Ch.; chrmn., State Ch. work, NAACP, Tenn., 1962; one of the organizers of the Brotherhood of the A. M. E. Ch.; mem., Exec. Bd., T. V. A.; Citizen of the Year, Radio station WVOL; outstanding minister's award from Payne Theol. Sem., Wilberforce, O.; Citation from Davidson Co. by Mayor Briley, Honorary Citizen of Tenn.; Home: 1131 E. Delmas Ave., Nashville, Tenn.; Office: 414 Eighth Ave. S., Nashville, Tenn. 37203

GRANT, David Cooper, b. Attapulgus, Ga., Apr. 16, 1912; so. Henry W. and Lula G.; B. S., Ga. State Coll., Savannah, Ga., 1931-35; M. Ed., Fla. A & M Univ., 1953; courses, Gammon Turner Theol. Centers; m. Ella Mae Hardwich; Children--Adrain Deloris; Margaret Cecile; David, Jr.; pastor, A. M. E. Chs. in Louisville, Stillmore, Pelham, Watley, Valdosta, Columbus, Bainbridge, Waycross, pastor, Steward Chapel, 1963-present; Macon, Ga.;

tchr., Voc. Agric. and Music; prin., Jr. High Sch. & High Sch., Ga.; instr., Rel. Edu., Morris Brown Coll., Ga.; chaplain, Griffin Hosp., Bainbridge, Ga., 1956-60; Civic leader, 1958-present; mem., NAACP; del., Gen. Conf., 1956-present; mem., Trustee Bd., Morris Brown Coll.; sec., Annual Conf., 1950-present; pres., A. M. E. Min. Alliance; 1966-present; mem., Connectional Coun., A. M. E. Ch.; mem., Race Rel. Com.; Democrat; Mason; wrote articles for Christian Recorder Magazine; Home: 657 Spring St., Macon, Ga. 31201; Office: 887 Spring St., Macon, Ga. 31201

GRANT, Edward James, b. Wash., Ga., Aug. 21, 1899; s. Edgar Poe and Clara Julia; A. B., Morehouse Coll., Atlanta, Ga. 1925; M. A., Atlanta Univ., 1959; B. D., D. D. (hon.), Union Bapt. Sem. 1956; Grad. courses, Hampton Inst. Va., Gammon Theol. Sem. Univ. of Chgo.; m. Rubye Brown; Children--Barbara (Mrs. Tyler Hall); Carolynne J.; Sheryl R.; pastor, New Salem Bapt. Ch., Jacksonville, Ala., 1941-42; First Bapt. Ch., Montgomery, Ala., 1943; Mt. Zion Bapt. Ch., Albany, Ga., 1944-present; former asst. mgr. and auditor, Atlanta Life Ins. Co., Montgomery Ala., Natl. Benefit Ins. Co., agent, Pilgrim Health & Life Ins. Co.; mem., Voters League, Montgomery, Ala.; Urban League; NAACP; Operation Breadbasket, Regional call man; SCLC, chrmn. Pub. Relations, com., Albany br.; mem., Hosp. Biracial com., Albany, Ga.; US Marine Corps; Community Relations Com.; Mason; Elk; Omega Psi Phi; pres., Interracial Interdenom. Min. Assn.; former prin., E. Baker Elementary & High Schs., Newton, Ga.; dir., Daugherty Co. Resources and Dev.; pres., Albany Bapt. Min. Conf.; sec., pres., Interdenom. Min. Allince, v. p., Gen. Missionary Bapt. Conv., Ga.; Bd. of dirs., Natl. Bapt. Conv., USA, Inc.; pres. & chrmn. of Bd. of dirs., Harlem Cut Rate Drug Store; awards, "Man of the Year" 1962, Omega Psi Phi; "Citizenship Award" Albany State Coll.; 1965, included in "Personalities of the South," 1970; Home: 618 Whitney Ave., Albany, Ga. 31701; Office: 326 Whitney Ave., Albany, Ga. 31702

GRAY, Arthur Douglas, b. Sheffield, Ala., Jan. 17, 1907; s. William L. and Hattie (Shine) G.; A. B., Talladega Coll., 1929; B. D., Chicago Theol. Sem., 1934; D. D. (hon.) Chgo. Theol. Sem., 1948; m. Edna Brown; 1 dau. Clarice; pastored, Plymouth Cong. Ch., Wash., D. C., 1934-44; Ch. of the Good Shepherd Cong. Ch., Chgo.,

Ill., 1944-52; Park Manor Cong. Ch., Chicago, Ill., 1962--; assto to pres., Talladega Coll., Ala., 1930-32; pres., Talladega Coll., 1952-62; mem. Alpha Phi Alpha; Sigma Pi Phi; Home: 1450 E. 55th Pl., Chicago, Ill. Office: 7000 S. Park Ave., Chgo, Ill.

GRAY, L. Charles, b. Camden, N.J., May 3, 1915; s. Jules and Georgia Ann G.; A.B., Lincoln Univ., 1935; S.T.B., M.A., New York Univ., 1938; courses toward Ph.D.; m. Maude E. Johnson; Children--Charles Jr., Denis Jules; pastor, Faith Presby. Ch., Phila., Pa., 1938-40; tchr. and pastor, Swift Meml. Jr. Coll., Rogersville, Tenn., 1940-42; pastor, Gibson Chapel, Springfield, Mo., 1942-43; St. Paul Presby. Ch., Kansas City Lafayette Presby. Ch., Jersey City, 1951-62; current pastor, Presby. Ch. of St. Albans, 1962--; visiting lecturer, Lincoln Univ. Seminary, 1957-59; tchr., pub. schs. Springfield, Mo., 1941-42; English and Public Speaking, Synder High Sch., Jersey City, N.J., 1960-62; chaplain, Hosp. for Mental Diseases, Secaucus, N.J., 1957-60; pioneer in summer camping program for Jr. and Sr. High Schs. in Synod of Missouri for 11 yrs.; former moderator, Presby. of Palisades; former pres., Jersey City Coun. of Chs.; organized Operation Clean Up (St. Albans) by recognition to serious housing problems; honored by Long Island Chapter of Omega Fraternity, 1964; mem., CORE - arrested many times on picket line; mem., Alpha Phi Alpha; Author, plays: "Broken Threads" three acts; "A Rose by Any Other Name," "Magnets and Magic;" Home: 119-11 190 St., St. Albans, N.Y.; Office: Presbyterian Ch. of St. Albans, 190 St. and 119th Ave., St. Albans

GREENE, Horace Henry, Sr., b. Louisville, Ky., Apr. 12, 1907; s. George Isaac and Eva (Bloomer) G.; B.Th., Gammon Theol. Sem.; m. Daisy Mae English; children--Horace Jr., Elwood La Monte; pastor, Irvington, Ky., 1929-31; New Zion, Ky., 1931-39; Gunn Meth. Ch., Lexington, Ky., 1939-48; Dist. Supt., Louisville, Dist., Lexington Conf., 1948-52; Calvary Ch., Cincinnati, O., 1952; Jones Temple Meth. Ch., Louisville, Ky., 1953--; Louisville Min. Assn., 1961-62; chrmn. Bd. of Dirs., Wesley Club, Ky. State Coll., 1960--; Exec. Bd., Boy Scouts, 1956-62; former pres., Interdenom. Min. Assn.; chrmn., Bd. of Evangelism, Lexington Conf.; chrmn., Common Conf. Relations; Central Jurisdiction Conf. Meth. Ch., 1964; Home: 1816 W. Jefferson, Louisville, Ky.;

Office: 1921 W. Jefferson, Louisville, Ky.

GREGG, Howard Decker, b. Sumer, S. C.; s. William J. and Cornelia; A. B., Lincoln Univ.; B. D., Yale Univ.; A. M. Columbia Univ.; Ph. D., Univ. of Pa., 1936; LL. D. (hon.) Lincoln Univ.; m. Mabel C. Hart; Children-- 3 sons and 1 dau.; tchr., Howard Univ., Wash., D. C.; dean, Wilberforce and Fisk Univ.; pres., Del. State Coll.; present pres. Daniel Payne Coll.; pastor, Morris Brown A. M. E. Ch., Charleston, S. C.; St. Paul A. M. E. Ch., Newport News, Va.; Bethel A. M. E. Ch., Richmond, Va.; mem., Exec. Com. on Institutions, A. M. E. Ch.; NEA; State Tchrs. Assn.; Omega Psi Phi; Home: 6415 Washington Blvd., Birmingham, Ala. 35212; Office: Daniel Payne Coll., Birmingham, Ala. 35212

GREGORY, Henry C., III, b. New York City, July 31, 1935; s. Henry C. and Louise A. G.; Howard Univ. Sch. of Rel., 1951; A. B., Howard Univ., 1952-56; B. D., Drew Univ., 1957-59; asst. pastor, Shiloh Bapt. Ch., Wash., D. C. (currently); mem., Eta Sigma Phi (Natl. Hon. Classical Fraternity); Alpha Phi Alpha; Home: 3915 13th NW, Wash., D. C. 20011; Office: 1500 9th NW, Wash., D. C.

*GRIFFIN, James C., b. Norfolk, Va., June 21, 1908; s. James and Chestina (Lark) G.; A. B., Johnson C. Smith Univ., 1932; B. D., Howard Univ., Sch. of Rel., 1935; M. S. T., Boston Univ.; military chp. courses, Ft. Oglethorpe, Ga. and Howard Univ.; D. D. (hon.), Johnson C. Smith Univ., 1959; m. Delya Stitt; entered service, 1941; during WW II, served at Army posts in Kan., Tex. and So. Pacific area from Guadalcanal to the Philippines; transferred to US Air Force, Okinawa during Korean War; stateside assignments include service as wing and base staff chap. with the Tactical Air Command, Lockbourne AFB, Ohio; Air Training Command, Lackland AFB, Tex. and Chanute AFB, Ill., Strategic Air Command, Fairchild AFB, Wash.; present installation chap., McClellan AFB, Calif.; awards, Bronze Star Medal, Korean & UN Service; Armed Forces Longevity Service Award; mem., Inst. of Pastoral Care; Amer. Hosp. Assn. of Chaplains; Military Chaplains Assn., Wash., D. C.; life mem., NAACP; Assn. for the study of Negro Life & History; Mason; Omega Psi Phi; Home: 980 Anna St., Norfolk, Va. 23502; Office: 603rd Air Base Wg., APO New York 09130

GRIFFIN, Marvin Collins, church official, b. Wichita, Kans., Feb. 20, 1923; s. Jessie and Beulah (Howell) G.; B. A., Bishop Coll., 1943; B. D., Oberlin Coll, 1947; M. R. E., Southwestern Theol. Sem., 1955; m. Lois Jesse King; Children--Marva Lois, Gaynelle, Ria Joy; ordained to ministry Bapt. Ch., 1942; prof., Okla. Bapt. Sch. of Rel., 1944-48; supt., City Missions, Dallas, 1948-50; pastor, New Hope Bapt. Ch., 1951--; sec., Ministers' Conf. of Missionary Bapt. Gen. Conv. of Tex.; mem., Doris Miller br. YMCA, 1952--; pres., Democratic Progressive Voters' League of Waco and McLennan Co., Tex., 1956--; Grass Roots Comm. of Waco, Tex., 1957--; Bd. of Dirs., Tex. Southern Univ.; author column, Historian, Natl. Bapt. Conv. of America, 1958--; Home: 1324 N. 6th Waco, Tex.; Office: 915 N. 6th Waco, Tex.

GRIFFIN, Theolia John, b. Fort Smith, Ark, Apr. 29, 1907; s. Butler John and Eliza (Simpson) G.; Philander Smith Coll., 1927-31; A. B., Atlanta Univ., 1934; B. D., Gammon Theol. Sem., 1931-34; D. D., Shorter Coll., 1941; LL. D., Natchez Coll., 1951; pastor, Tenn., Okla. West Va. Ark. Ill. Ark. and again Tenn., at which time edited newspapers and worked in the NAACP; tchr., St. Louis area Meth. Sum. Sch., 7 summers; Chaplain, Talf, Okla. Mental Hosp.; mem., Phi Beta Sigma; author: Book of Sermons; Home: 268 Edsel Ave., Memphis, Tenn.; Office: 1606 Kansas St., Memphis, Tenn.

GRIFFIN, Thomas J., ch. official, b. Carroll Co., Miss., July 4, 1917; A. B., Jarvis Chrstn Coll., 1947; B. D., Garrett Theol. Sem., 1947; courses, Columbia Univ. Sch. of Social work, 1959; seminars: Economics, Politics, Education, Religion and United Nations; m. Geneva Brown; Children--Robert Eugene; Thomas J. II; Reginald De Koven, Rayford Galen; student pastor, Ft. Worth Chrstn. Ch., Tex.; Muskogee Chrstn. Ch., Okla.; Jacksonville Chrstn. Ch., Tex.; asst. pastor, Indiana Ave. Chrstn. Ch., Chgo, Ill.; pastor, E. Sixth Chrstian Ch., Okla. City, 1950-56; Natl. Field Sec., Chrstn. Ch., Dept. of Christian Action and Community Service, 1956-60; current pastor, Univ. Chrstn Ch., Houston, Tex., 1960--; former sec., Intl. Christian Youth Fellowship, Christian Ch.; former pres., Interdenom. Min. Alliance; Chrstn. Exec. Bd. NAACP, Okla. City; organizer, Houston Conf. on Rel. and Race; mem., editorial staff, Social Action News Letter, Chrstn. Ch. Publication; mem., NAACP; Bd. of Houston Coun. of Human Relations; co-chrmn. Houston

Conf. on Rel. and Race; mem., Dept. of Cultural and Community Relations, Texas Coun. of Chs., Office: 3610 Southmore St., Houston, Tex. 77004

GRIGGS, Andrew L., b. Forrest City, Ark., Apr. 15, 1931; s. Americus and Virginia (Castel) G.; A.B., Ark. A. M. & N. Coll., 1959; courses, Interdenom. Theol. Center, Atlanta, Ga.; Univ. of Buffalo, 1964-65; m. Ruby J. Griggs; Children--Andrew Jr., Carolyn Marion, Michael, William, Brenda; soc. coun., Oneida Co. Welfare Dept., 1960-64; pastor, St. Paul Bapt. Ch., Utica, N.Y., 1965-66; dir., Cora Hill Opportunity Center, Utica, N.Y., 1966-present; chap., Oneida Co. Migrant Comm., 1960; mem., Oneida Co. Migrant Comm., 1961-64; armed services, 1951-55; natl. defense service medal; Home: 704 Faye St., Utica, N.Y.; Office: 1117 Nealson St., Utica, N.Y.

GRISHAM, Dubro Merriweather, ch. official, b. Murfreesboro, Tenn., Dec. 12, 1911; s. Henry and Alice Mariah (Smith) G.; B.S., Tenn. A & I State Coll., 1938; B.D., Gammon Theol. Sem., 1941; m. Frazelia Belle Walker; Children--Frazelia Metia, Daniel Wesley; pastor, Brooks Chapel Meth. Ch., Brentwood, Tenn., 1933-38; Clark Meml. Meth. Ch., Nashville, Tenn., 1941-53; Centenary Meth. Ch., Memphis, Tenn., 1953-62; Nashville Dist. Supt., Tenn. Conf., 1962--; pres., Trustee Bd. Gorine Coll., Memphis, Tenn.; Trustee Morristown Coll., Morristown, Tenn.; mem., James A. Myers Lodge; J.A. Henry Consistory; Home: 2207 Elliott Ave., Nashville, Tenn. 37204.

GUIDRY, Raymond James, b. July 30, 1928, Abbeville, La., s. Erastus and Anita; Schs. Our Lady of Lourdes, Abbeville, La., St. Augustine Sem., Bay St. Louis, Miss., 1942-47; St. Mary Sem., Techny, Ill., 1947-49; Cath. Univ. of Amer., Wash., D.C. 1966-68; St. Paul Sem., Epworth, Ia., 1947-51; St. Augustine Sem., 1951-57; ordained May 1957; Missionary Diocese of Accra, Ghana, W. Africa, 1957-66; entered US Chaplaincy 1968-present; Office: Hq. Fourth Cambat Support Training Brigade, Office of the Brig. Chaplain, Ft. Ord, Calif. 93941

*GUILES, Samuel Everette, b. Pamplico, S.C., Oct. 17, 1921; s. William Samuel and Areta (Green) G.; A.B., Allen Univ., 1944; B.D., Howard Univ. Sch. of Rel., 1947; Howard Univ. Law School, 1948; D.D. (hon.), Kittrell Coll., 1950; m. Anne Gertrude Rowe; pastor, Dent Chapel Afr. Meth. Episc. Ch., Bladensburg, Md., 1947; Campbell A. M. E. Ch., Wash., D. C., 1949-56; current, Turner Meml. A. M. E. Ch., Wash., D. C., 1956--; pastoral clinical training: chaplain intern, Natl. Trng. Sch. for Boys, D. C.; D. C. Gen. Hosp.; St. Elizabeth's Hosp., Wash., D. C.; mem., Coordinating Comm. of Anacostia, D. C. and Vicinity, 1950-55; Consolidated Parent Group, 1953-54; Bd. of the Wash. Fed. of Chs., 1953-56; Bd. of Dirs., Iona Whipper Home for Unwed Mothers, 1959-63; D. C. Commissioner's Youth Coun., 1959-63; Exec. Bd. of the D. C. br. of the NAACP; Institutional chaplaincy Comm. of the Coun. of Chs., Natl. Capital Area; Bd. of Dirs., The Wash. Urban League; Volunteer worker, United Givers Fund; Citation, Coordinating Comm. of Anacostia and Vicinity, for progressive community work, especially among the youth, 1954; Citation of Appreciation as Volunteer Worker for the United Givers Fund, 1957; Citation, Wash. Urban League, for outstanding community work, 1959; Trophy Award from the Intl. Dance Studios for exemplary achievements in the field of culture, especially among the youth, 1964; Cited in Washington Post, Jan. 11, 1964, "Washington Church," for outstanding pastoral work with the youth; mem., Republican State Comm., D. C.; President's Comm. on Government Contracts (Under Eisenhower admin.;) Phi Beta Sigma; Home: 1605 Crittenden St. NW, Wash., D. C. 20011; Office: 600 I St., NW, Wash., D. C., 20001

GUY, John Francis, b. Cleveland, O.; s. Frank L. and Bertha L. G.; B. A., Andrew Univ., 1958; M. A., Andrews Univ., 1960; m. Evelyn Alicia Phipps; son: John Kendall; asst. pastor, Shiloh Seventh-Day Adventist Ch., 1960-61; present: pastor, Ecorse and Bellivelle S. D. A. Chs., Ecorse, Mich.; mem., Local Min. Assn.; Most Sportsmanship Award in basketball; Home: 3788 19th St. Ecorse, Mich.; Office: 3834 10th St., Ecorse, Mich.

HADDEN, Thomas Paul, educator, b. Raleigh, N. C., May 31, 1929; s. Thomas Gary and Clarice (Mallette) H.; B. A., St. Meinrad College, 1950-55; S. T. B., The Pontifical Gregorian Univ. (Rome), 1955-59; Pastorates: Newton Grove Cath. Ch., Newton Grove, N. C., 1959-60; Consolation Cath. Ch., Charlotte, N. C., 1960-61; St. Theresa's Cath. Ch., Durham, N. C., 1961-62; St. Joseph's Cath. Ch., New Bern, N. C., 1962--; tchr., Charlotte Cath. High Sch., 1960; Wm. Gaston Cath. High Sch., New Bern, N. C., 1962--; Bd. of Dirs., West St. Pub. Library, New Bern, 1962--; NAACP Youth Coun. Advisor, New Bern, 1963; N. C. Conf. on Race and Rel.; N. C. Cath. Clergy Cred. Union; Home: 306 Bern St., New Bern, N. C.

HAIG, Albert Randolph, publishing sec., b. Jamaica, West Indies, Oct. 9, 1903; s. Reginald and Hannah (Fuertado) H.; "Jamaica Gov't Edu. Certificate," Jamaica, W. I., Govt. Elem. Prep., 1910-18; "Coll. Edu. Cert." W. Indian Training College (S. D. A. Denominational), 1923-27 Atlantic Union Coll., Mass., extra-mural dept. (NY Center) - Sem. course; m. Marian Louise Parchment; Children--Iralyn Patrice (Mrs. Gladwin Trott), Myrnelle Faunglow, Anne Alberga (Mrs. Albert Jahn); Jamaica Conf. of Seventh-Day Adventists, Jamaica, W. I., publishing sec., 1928-29; Bahamas Mission of S. D. A., Bahamas, pub. sec., 1929-30; Jamaica Conf. of S. D. A., Jamaica, W. I., literature-evangelist, 1930-32; Jamaica Conf. of S. D. A., pastor-evangelist, 1932-40; Jamaica Conf. of S. D. A., pub. sec., 1940-43; British, French and Dutch Islands and Colonies of W. Indies, pub. dept. sec., 1943-46; Brit. W. I. Union of Seventh-Day Adventist, Jamaica, W. I., publishing, educational, youth-leade temperance, home-missionary and sabbath-sch., sec., 1946-56; pub. sec., Northeastern Conf. of S. D. A., N. Y. current pastor, Evangelist and Supt. of "Hanson Place S. D. A. Ch." "Park Place S. D. A. Ch." 1959--; Youth movement organizer; mem. of the following boards: Andrew's Meml. Hosp., W. Indies Coll., and Kingsway High Sch., all of Jamaica, W. I. Annual Scholarship to W. Indies Training Coll., Mandeville, Jamaica, W. I., awarded for exceptional accomplishments in rel. literatu salesmanship, 1921-26; Educational scholarship to W. I. Coll. awarded for faithfulness and other accomplishments in pastoral-evangelism, 1936-37; American Temp. Soc., Amer. Red Cross; Home: 560 W. 150th St., New York, N. Y.; Office: 88 Hanson Pl., Brooklyn, N. Y.

HAIRSTON, Andrew Jasper, b. Clemons, N. C., July 9, 1932; s. James and Laura (W.) H.; B. A., Southwestern Christian Coll., 1955; B. A., B. S., Paul Quinn, 1956, 57; B. D., Johnson C. Smith Univ.; Texas Chrstn. Univ. 1960; Residence work completed for Th. M.; m. Jeanne Turner; Children--Kenneth Andrew, Norma Jeannean, Ke

Lynn; current pastor, The Church of Christ, Atlanta, Ga., 1962--; mem., Greater Atlanta Coun. on Human Relations; NAACP; Home: 245 Simon Terr., E. Atlanta, Ga.; Office: 810 Simpson St., N.W., Atlanta, Ga.

HAIRSTON, John Carl, Sr., Lexington, N.C., Aug. 17, 1894; s. Jim and Minnie B. (Crowell) H.; course in Chrstn. Edu. Southern Bapt. Conv., 1936; Moody Bible Inst., 1938; D.D., (hon.), Va. Theol. Sem. and Coll., Lynchburg, Va., 1956; m. Bessie Roberta Rock; Children--James Roland, John Carl; Aliese Frances (Mrs. Robinson); ordained July 20, 1920, Columbus, Ohio; pastor, Second Bapt. Ch., Milford Center, Ohio; First Bapt., Woodstock, O.; Mt. Zion, St. John, Pilgrim St. John, Columbus, Ohio; Sixth Mt. Zion Bapt. Ch., Pittsburgh, Pa., 1928-present; treas., Pa. Bapt. State Conv.; pres., Lott Carey Bapt. Foreign Miss. Conv., USA, Inc., 1964, 1965; WW II vet.; mason; instr. in pub. schs.; Home: 7303 Hermitage St., Pittsburgh, Pa. 15208; Office: 6556 Shetland Ave., Pittsburgh, Pa. 15206

HAIRSTON, Samuel Henry, b. Henry Co., Va., Nov. 24, 1891; s. Jack and Thenie H.; diploma ed. courses: Hampton Inst., St. Paul, Va. State Coll.; m. Mamie Lee Foster; Children--Mrs. Christiana Napper, (Mrs. Wilson Napper,) Mrs. Irene Ramey, Mrs. Estes Barnes (Mrs. James C. Barnes); present pastor, Mt. Olive Chrstn., Antioch Chrstn. Ch., Meadow Chrstin Ch., New Bethel Chrstn. Ch., 1916-to date; tchr., pub. schs., Henry Co., Va. (50 yrs.); mem. trustee bd., Community Hosp., Martinsville, Va. honored; Samuel H. Hairston Consolidated Elem. Sch., Rt. 3, Martinsville, Va.; former editor, Natl. Chrstn. Messenger; Home: RFD 3, Box 156, Martinsville, Va.

HALE, Samuel Wesley, b. Chicago, Ill., Nov. 17, 1942; s. Samuel W. and Toledo E.; A.B., Amer. Bapt. Theol. Sem., Nashville, Tenn., 1966; M. Div., Southern Bapt. Theol. Sem., Louisville, Ky., 1969; m. Gloria Marie Harris; child--Samuel Wesley III; youth coordinator, Mt. Calvary Bapt. Ch., Chgo., Ill., 1963; summer youth dir., Shiloh Bapt., Chgo., Ill., 1966; dir. of Mission 7-0, Mt. Lebanon Bapt. Ch., Louisville, Ky., 1966-69; pastor-director, Johenning Bapt. Ch.-Center, Wash., D.C., 1969-present; former dir., Longview Area Recreation Center, Decatur, Ill., summer, 1962; coun., Pre-college program, Fisk Univ., Nashville, Tenn., 1965;

tchr., Project Push-Up, Chicago, Ill., summer, 1966; instr., Simmons Univ., Louisville, Ky., 1969; Southern Bapt. Sem., Louisville, Ky., 1968-69; sec., Bd. of Dirs OIC, Louisville, Ky., 1967-69; treas., Neighborhood Planning Coun., Area 20, Wash., D. C., 1969-70; Home: 833 Bellevue St., SE, Apt 101, Wash., D. C. 20032; Office: 4025 Ninth St., SE, Wash., D. C. 20032

HALE, William Henry, b. Pine Bluff, Ark., May 12, 1918; s. William N. and Edna Mae H.; Western Bible Coll., Kan. City, Mo., 3 yrs.; Hannibal LaGrange Coll., Hannibal, Mo., presently; m. Alice Hutchinson; Children--William H., Jr.; Jerome; pastor, Md. St. Bapt. Ch., Louisiana, Mo., 1960-64; Eighth & Centers Sts. Bapt. Ch., Hannibal, Mo., 1965-present; proprietor, Carver Co. (a pest control operation); mem., Mason; Home: 204 No. Eighth St., Hannibal, Mo. 63401; Office: 722 Center St., Hannibal, Mo.

HALL, James Harold, b. Brunswick, Ga., June 20, 1928; B. A., Talladega Coll., 1944-47; St. Augustine's Coll., 1948-50; B. D., Nashotah House Sem., 1950-53; M. A. course, Mont. State Univ. (current); pastor, St. Matthew' Delray Beach, Fla., 1953; pastor, St. Christopher's Ft. Lauderdale, Fla., 1955; Timothy's Daytona Beach Episc. Chap. to Bethune-Cookman Coll.; mem., NAACP, Fla. Coun. on Human Rel., Mental Health Assn. of Volusia Co., Omega Psi Phi; Home: 200 Agnes Ave., Missoula, Mont.

HALL, Laurence Edward, YMCA official, b. Baltimore, Md., Mar. 11, 1920; s. Wallace James and Lula Mae (Hall) L.; Jarvis Chrstn. Coll., Hawkins, Tex., B. A., 1950; M. A., Southern Meth. Univ., Dallas, Tex., 1952; grad. study, Coll. of the Bible, Philip's Univ., Enid, Okla., 1953; Major, Rel. Edu., Amer. Ch. History; m. Irene Deniese Watson; Children--Thaddeus Waldof; pastor Romine Ave. Chrstn. Ch., Dallas, Tex., 1947-52; vicar, St. Philip's Episc. Ch., Muskogee, Okla., 1952-56; rector, St. Luke's Episc. Ch., New Orleans, La., 1957-62; Exec.-sec., James Rhodes YMCA, Ft. Pierce, Fla., 1963; adult edu. tchr., New Orleans Pub. Sch. Sys., 1958-62; mem., The Commission of Social Action, Diocese of La., 1960; the Northeastern Okla. Mental Health Assn., 1954; the Psychiatric Achievement Awards Comm. 1952-56; founder of the Interfaith A. A. Group, New Orleans, La., 1958, part-time chap., Taft State Mental

Hosp., Taft, Okla., 1953-56; US Army during WW II; 1st Lt. during Korean conflict; awards: Good Conduct Medal, US Army WW II; Citizenship Awards from Md. and La.; mem., Mason, NAACP, CORE; radio speaker WARN; Home: 1214 Ave. L., Ft. Pierce, Fla.; Office: 3100 Ave. G., Ft. Pierce, Fla.

*HALL, Lloyd Dalton, coll. prof., b. Dallas, Tex., Sept. 11, 1935; s. Lloyd Dalton, Sr. and Elizabeth (Hayden) H.; B. A., Bishop Coll., 1959; B. D., Howard Univ. Sch. of Rel., 1962; m. Virginia Ambler; Children--Clyde Allen, Lloyd Burnett; student pastor, Shiloh Bapt. Ch., Wash., D. C., Honeywell Heiland Div., Denver, Colo.; assoc. prof., Rel., Bishop Coll., Dallas, Tex.; Rockefeller Theol. Award, 1961-62; mem., Alpha Phi Alpha; Home: 3837 Simpson-Stuart Rd., Dallas, Tex.; Office: Bishop Coll., Dallas, Tex.

HALL, Marzella Warren, b. Birmingham, Ala., Mar. 18, 1898; dau. John and Gertrude (Merriweather) Hutchens; widow; children--Frances M. Hutton; organizer, pastor, Holiness Community Temple Gospel Center, Chgo., 1937-present; organized first community center, Holiness Ch., Chgo., 1941; organized the Universal Fellowship Coun. of All Nations, 1942; mem., Grace Lee Stevens Federated Club; Oscar DePriest Federated Civic & Charity Club; Professional & Business Women's Federated Club; Hyde Park-Kenwood Community Conf.; founder, The Intl. United Conv., 1960; founded, The Universal Forum Coun., 1965; Office: Holiness Community Temple Gospel Center, 5536 So. Indiana Ave., Chgo., Ill.

HALL, Richard Wesley, b. Md., Jan. 11, 1913; s. Richard Wesley and Mary (Haley) H.; courses, Howard Univ., 1939; m. Eleanor Lewis; Children--Richard Wesley, Eleanor M., Charles W., Mary M., Richard David; pastor, Bowie Lanham Ch., Prince George Co., Md., 10 yrs.; Simms Mem'l. Meth. Ch., Wash., D. C.; construction contractor, Real Estate Dealer; mem., Mason; Democrat; Home: 7301 16th St., NW, Wash., D. C.

HALL: Shelvin Jerome, b. Yoakum, Tex., May 3, 1916; s. Will and Mayme H. (S.); B. A., Bishop Coll.; grad. work, Prairie View Coll.; m. Lucy Mae Lewis; Children --Luberdie Priscilla; Shelvin Louise; Lewis Jerome; prin., Mt. Eden Elem. Sch., Texas; Ralph Bunche High Sch.; pres., Mid-West Commun. Coun., 1958-60; pastor,

St. John's Bapt. Ch., Corpus Christi, Tex., 1954; Friendship Bapt. Ch., Chgo., Ill., 1955-present; pres., West Side Bapt. Min. Conf., Ch. Fed. of Chgo.; dean, Bapt. Gen. State Congress of Chrstn. Edu.; 1st v. moderator, Salem Bapt. Dist. Assn.; instr., Natl. Bapt. Sun. Sch. and B. T. U. Congress; Urban League, NAACP; Chicago City miss. Soc.; Chgo Comm. on Rel. and Race; Home: 424 S. 17th Ave., Maywood, Ill.; Office: 3411 W. Douglas Blvd., Chicago, Ill.

HALLER, Herman, b. Angleton, Tex., Feb. 10, 1936; s. Jackson and Emma H.; B. A., Bishop Coll., Dallas, Tex. 1959; B. D., Perkins Sch. of Theol., Dallas, Tex., 1966; m. Oletha Epps; asst. pastor, Bethel Bapt. Ch., Houston Tex., 1958-60; Bethlehem Center Boys Worker, Dallas, Tex., 1965-66; co-pastor, Fellowship Community Ch., United Ch. of Christ, 1966-present; mem., Youth Com., United Ch. of Christ; Dir., Wisc. Coun. of Chs.; mem., Urban Seminar, Milwaukee Assn. in Urban Ministries; chrmn., Northtown Assn. Project; Army, 1959-61; Good Conduct Medal in military service; mem., Econ. Opportunity Bd.; Opportunities Industrialization Bd.; Northtown Planning Bd., Alpha Phi Alpha; Home: 2208 W. Locust, Milwaukee, Wis. 53206

HAMILTON, Charles Spencer, educator, b. Cedartown, Ga., May 12, 1927; s. Lindley D. and Clifford (Mozelle) W.; A. B., Morehouse Coll., 1950; B. D., Morehouse Coll. Sch. of Rel., 1953; courses: Fla. A & M Univ., 1954; M. S. T., Interdenom. Theol. Center, 1964; m. Sallye Butler; children--Ronald Spencer, Charletta Gale; student pastor, First Bapt. Ch.; pastor, The Arbor Grove Bapt. Ch., LaGrange, Ga.; The Woodward Bapt. Ch., Atlanta, Ga.; The First Bapt. Ch., Thomasville, Ga., 1953-56; Tabernacle Bapt. Ch., Augusta, Ga., 1956--; tchr., The Boston High Sch., Boston, Ga.; coach, girls and boys basketball; employee, The Atlanta Life Ins. Co.; mem., Bd. of Dirs., Augusta Richmond Co. Voters League, 1962-64; Richmond Co. Exec. Democratic Comm., 1962; State Adv. Comm. of Commission on Civil Rights, 1962; US Merchant Marines, 1945-46; US Army, 1946-47; awards: Man of the Year, 1963; Omega Phi Fraternity; YMCA award for service, 1963; Augusta Richmond Co. Voters League Freedom award, 1963; mem., Bd. of Dirs Shiloh Orphanage; YMCA; Bethlehem Center; Human Relation Coun.; Omega Phi Fraternity; v. p., State Conf. NAACP; pres., Augusta Chapter, NAACP; treas., New

Era Bapt. Conv., Ga.; pres., The Gwinnett St. Investment Co.; Home: 1224 Gwinnett St., Augusta, Ga. 30901; Office: 1223 Gwinnett St., Augusta, Ga. 30901

*HAMILTON, McKinley, John, b. Lake Charles, La., Nov. 24, 1921; s. Lincoln and Jennie (Keys) H.; A. A., Butler Jr. Coll., Tyler, Tex., 1941-43; A. B., Bishop Coll., Marshall, Tex., 1943-45; Crozer Theol. Sem., 1947; B. D., Howard Univ. Sch. of Rel., 1955-58; m. Mary Stone; pastor, New Hope Bapt., Alto, Tex., 1942-43; St. James Bapt. Ch., 1942-43; The Good Samaritan Bapt. Ch., Wash., D. C., 1947-58; First Bapt. Ch., Rocky Mt., Va., 1958--; chap., Migrants, Lake Shore area of Westfield, N. Y., 1957; v. p., Sun. Sch. Conv., Franklin Co., Va., 1962--; moderator, The Pigg River Assn.; Franklin Co., Va., 1963--; pres., Lee M. Waid PTA, 1962-63; vice dist. chrmn., Algonquin Dist. of Boy Scouts, 1960--; instr., Week-Day Rel. Edu., Lee M. Waid Sch., 1964--; mem., Franklin Co. Minister's Assn.; Va. Coun. of Human Relations, Roanoke, Va.; Home: 137 Patterson Ave. SE, Rocky Mount, Va. 24151; Office: 137 Patterson Ave. SE, Rocky Mount, Va. 24151.

HANDY, James Albert, b. Tyaskin, Md., June 1, 1881; s. John and Julia (Hester) H.; St. Paul Episc. Sch. (Va.); Delaware State Coll.; Morgan Coll. (Baltimore); Honorary degree, Phila. Sch. of the Bible; widower; present: presiding elder, Norfolk Dist., Chrstn. Meth. Episc. Ch.; Ch. extension sec., 1957-63; one of the organizers of Community Hosp., Norfolk, Va.; mem., Intl. Union of Gospel Missions; founder and sec., Seaview Hotel and Beach Corp.; former probation officer, Norfolk, Va.; Home: 2527 Virginia Beach Blvd., Norfolk, Va.; Office: 408 Main St., Norfolk, Va.

HANDY, John Wm., Jr., b. Oct. 10, 1918, Harrisburg, Pa.; s. John Wm. Sr. and Cora Shirley (H.); B. S., Shaw Univ., Raleigh, N. C., 1941; Shaw Univ. Sch. of Rel., 1941-42; Diploma, US Army Chaplain's Sch., Harvard Univ.; advanced courses: Ft. Oglethorpe, Ga., 1946; M. Ed., Univ. of Colo., 1959; M. A., NYU, 1961; career course, Ft. Slocum, N. Y., 1959; Ed. D. (candidate) Univ. of Colo., 1961-63; diploma US Army Management Sch., Ft. Belvoir, Va., 1963; Certificate Sr. Army Exec. Automatic Data Processing Course, Ft. Shafter, 1968; US Army Personnel Management Sch., Ft. Benjamin Harrison, Ind., 1968; US Army Command and Gen.

Staff Coll., Ft. Leavenworth, Kan., 1964; m. Lois E. Reed; children--Wm. M., Chie A.; chaplain, 1943, England, France, Germany, Philippines, Staten Island, N.Y., Ft. Dix, N.J., Camp Kilmer, N.J., Japan, Korea, Ft. Eustis, Va., Ft. Carson, Colo., Ft. Monroe, Va., 1968-present; pastor, concurrent with military service St. Luke United Meth. Ch., New Rochelle, N.Y., 1959-61; instr., Chaminade Coll., Honolulu, 1967-68; Dela. Conf., Bronx, N.Y., 1941-59; Prof. Dept. US Army Chaplain's Sch.; Ft. Slocum, N.Y., 1959-61; consult. Dept. of Ed., Univ. of Hawaii, 1966-68; workshop leader for guidance and guidance tchrs., Hawaii, 1966; mem., Mayor's comm. on children and youth, Hawaii, 1966-68; Bd. of dirs., Armed Forces YMCA, Honolulu, 1966-68; Bd. of trustees, Del. Annual Conf. United Meth. Ch., 1957-64; Rotary Intl.; awards, Legion of Merit 1968; Bronze Star, 1951; Army Commendation Medal, First Oak Leaf Cluster, 1963; Amer. Theater Ribbon, 1943; European Theater Ribbon w/4 Battle Stars; Asiatic-Pacific Theater Ribbon w/1 Bronze Star, 1945; Philippine Liberation Medal, 1946; Occupation medal, Japan and Europe, 1949, 1954; Nat. Defense Medal; Certificate of Achievement, State of Md., 1946; Certificate of Appreciation, United Meth. Ch., 1947; V. Corps, US Army 1956; Rotary Fellowship Foundation, 1968; Certificate of Appreciation, Mayor City and Co. of Honolulu, 1968; mem., Acad. of Rel.; Phi Delta Kappa; Amer. Personnel and Guidance Assn.; Natl. Voc. Guidance Assn.; Amer. Rehab. Coun. Assn.; Military Chaplain's Assn.; 1966-67; sec., Natl. Military Chaplain's Assn., US, 1968-present; Honolulu Min. Assn.; pres., Hawaii Chapter Military Chaplain's Assn.; Home: 124 Diggs Dr., Hampton, Va. 23366

HANDY, William Talbot, Jr., b. New Orleans, La., Mar. 26, 1924; s. Wm. Talbert, Sr.; Tuskegee Inst., 1940-42; A.B., Dillard Univ., 1948; B.D., Gammon Theol. Sem., 1951; S.T.M., Boston Univ., Sch. of Theol., 1952; m. Ruth Odessa Robinson; Children--Wm. Talbot, III (deceased), Dorothy Denise, Stephen Emanuel; pastor, Newman United Meth. Ch., Alexandria, La., 1952-59; St. Mark U. Meth. Ch., Baton Rouge, La., 1959-68; publishing repr., Meth. Publishing House, Nashville, Tenn; Staff mem. Central Jurisdiction Meth. Ch., Gammon Course of Study Sch., 1956-present; mem., following U. Meth. Ch., Uniting Conf., 1968; Chrmn. New Orleans delegation, gen. & central conf., 1964; Co-chrmn., South western area, delegation, Uniting Conf. 1968; Chrmn. Bd. of Ministerial Training & qualifications, La. Conf. 1958; mem., Gen. Advance Com., United Meth., 1964--; Ex. Bd. Gen. Comn. on Promotion & cultivation; Organizational Com. La. Coun. of Chs., Bd. of Dirs. La. State Coun. of Chs.; past chrmn. Bd. of Evangelism; past trustee, La. Annual Conf., New Orleans area; mem., La. commission on civil rights; Bd. of Dirs., Community Advancement, Inc. (anti-poverty), Baton Rouge, La.; Manpower Develop. Inc., Adv. Com. Amer. Friends Ser. Com., Baton Rouge Area Ministers Assn.; Ex. Com., Baton Rouge Coun. on Human Relations; NAACP; Prot. Com. on Scouting, Baton Rouge; Bd. of Mgrs., YMCA, Baton Rouge; Mason; Frontiersman of the Year, 1963; US Army, 1943-46; European and Pacific Theater; Office: Publishing Representative, Meth. Publishing House, 201 Eighth Ave. So., Nashville, Tenn. 37202

HANEY, William Riley, b. Cataula, Ga., July 26; S. John Henry and Celia H.; A.B., Central Univ., Ind., 1947; B.Th., 1941, B.D., 1942 and D.D. (hon.), 1953, Birmingham Bapt. Coll.; grad. study: Wayne State Univ., 1949-54; Univ. of Mich., 1954, 55; m. Anne Clara Andrew; former pres., Woverine State Missionary Bapt. Conv.; mem., editorial staff, Sun. Sch. Pub. Bd. of the Natl. Bapt. Conv., USA, Inc.; Exec. bd., Woverine State Missionary Bapt. Conv.; Bd. of Dirs., Detroit Coun. of Chs.; Bd. of Dirs., Gleiss Meml. Center; pres., Bd. of Trustees, Bapt. Training Sch., Detroit; instr., Natl. Sun. Sch. and Bapt. Training Union Congress in the Ministers' Div.; corresponding sec., Metro. Dist. Assn.; pastor (current), Dexter Ave. Bapt. Ch., 1946--; mem., Mason; Home: 4048 Fullerton Ave., Detroit, Mich.; Office: 13500 Dexter Ave., Detroit, Mich.

HARGRAVES, James Archie, ch. official, b. Greensboro, N.C., Aug. 2, 1916; s. Archie and Geneva (McCollum) H.; B.S., N.C. Agricultural and Tech. Coll., 1940; B.D., Union Theol. Sem., 1948; Columbia Univ., 1948-51; m. Inez Boger; 1 dau. Janet Delmanda; pastored: E. Harlem Prot. Parish, NYC, 1948-51; Lawndale Community Presby. Ch., Chgo., 1954-56; Nazarene Congre. Ch., Bklyn, 1956-61; instr., Soc. Sciences and Dir., Pub. Relations, N.C. Agr. & Tech. Coll., Greensboro, N.C., 1940-41; prof., Soc. Problems, Biblical Sem., NYC, 1958-60; lecturer, Inst. for Religious and Social

Studies, Jewish Theol. Sem., NYC, 1961-64; Dir., Westside Chrstn. Parish, Chgo., 1951-56; Sec. Urban Ch., United Ch. Bd. for Homeland Ministries, NYC, 1961-64; Dir., Metro. Ministries, The Urban Training Center for Chrstn. Mission, Chgo., 1964--; Info. Specialist, Office of Public Admin., Wash., D. C., 1941-42; Sgt. 92nd Inf. Div., 1943-44; 2nd Lt., AOS (Calcutta, India), 1945-46; recipient, Gen. Alumni Award, N. C. Agr. & Tech. Coll. 1962, Social Action Award, Phi Beta Sigma, 1960, YMCA Service Award, 1955; mem., Religious Research Assn., Long Range Planning Comm., U. Ch. of Christ, No. Amer. Study Comm., World Coun. of Chs.; Del. Third Gen. Assembly, World Coun. of Chs., New Delhi, India, 1961; author: Stop Pussyfooting Through a Revolution, 1963; Office: 40 N. Ashland Ave., Chicago, Ill.

HARGROVE, Beverly Milton, II, chaplain, b. Birmingham, Ala., Oct. 20, 1920; s. Beverly Milton and Ruth (Shortridge) H.; A. B., Miles Meml. Coll., Birmingham, Ala., 1942; B. D., Gammon Theol. Sem., Atlanta, Ga., 1948; m. Blanche Day; Children--Beverly III, William, John, Gayle, Ruth; pastor, Ebenezer Meth., Sparrows Point, Md., 1948-49; Eastern Meth. Ch., Balto., Md., 1949-52 Asbury Meth. Ch., Hagerstown, Md., 1952-56; Buena Vista Meth. Ch., 1956-59; Simpson Meml. Meth. Ch., Charleston, W. Va., 1959--; former tchr., Jr. High Sch. Birmingham, Ala.; current, dir. of the Wesley Foundation on the campus of West Va. State Coll., 1961--; Merit award, NAACP; mem., Bd. of Min. Training of the Wash. Annual Conf. Meth. Ch.; Bd. of Ed., Ministerial Training of the Wash. Annual Conf. Meth. Ch.; Bd. of Christian Social Concerns, Ministerial Training of the Wash. Annual Conf. Meth. Ch.; articles in the Central Chrstn. Advocate and local newspapers; Home: 212 Brooks St., Charleston, W. Va.; Office: 607 Shrewsburg St., Charleston, W. Va.

HARLEY, Philip A., b. Philadelphia, Pa., May 26, 1921; s. Fred and Elizabeth (Jackson) M.; A. B., Morgan State Coll., Balto., Md., 1945; B. D., Garrett Theol. Sem., Evanston, Ill., 1956; m. Ireleen Jones; Children--Antoinette, Anthony, Michael, Richard, Bruce; pastor, St. James Meth. Ch., Milwaukee, Wis., 1951-52; assoc., Corey Meth. Ch., Cleveland, O., 1952-53; pastor, Wheatland Ave., Meth. Ch., Columbus, O., 1953-55; Wesley Meth. Ch., Harvey, Ill., 1955-56; Neighborhood Meth. Ch. Center, Ft. Wayne, Ind., 1956-63; First Meth

Ch., Mitchell, So. Dakota, 1963-65; St. James Meth. Ch., Chgo., Ill., 1966-present; min. of ed., Christ Meth. Ch., Ft. Wayne, Ind., 1956-62; First Meth. Ch., Mitchell, So. Dakota, 1962-65; chrmn., Ind. Regional Consultative Com. on Race; mem., Mayor's Comm. on Human Relations, Ft. Wayne, Ind., 1958-62; candidate, City Councilman, Ft. Wayne, Ind., 1959; Dist. dir. of Surveys and Research Meth. Ch., N. C. Conf., 1958-60; v. p., Frontiers Club of Amer., Ft. Wayne Chapter, 1959; Bd. Ministerial Training, N. C. Conf.; Bd. Christn. Soc. Concerns, N. C. Conf.; Bd. Ed. N. Ind. Conf.; tchr., meth. Hosp. Sch. of Nursing, 1963-65; instr., Adult Ed., Ind.; mem., Bd. Ed., So. Dakota Conf.; Bd. Wesley Found., Univ. of Chicago; Exec. Com. Hyde Park Coun. of Chs. and Synagogues, Chgo., Ill.; Adv. Bd. So. Park Urban Progress Center, Chgo., Ill.; Adv. Bd. Ada Mc Kinley Community Center for Mentally Retarded, Chgo., Ill.; Com. Promotion and Cultivation, Rock River Conf.; Com. Rel. and Race, Rock River Conf.; US Navy, 1944-46; mem., Phi Beta Sigma; Mason; Home: 1313 E. 55th St., Chgo., Ill. 60615

HARPER, Theophilus E., b. Newberry, S. C., Oct. 23, 1906; s. J. S. W. and Josephine (Sims) H.; A. B., Allen Univ., Columbia, S. C.; D. D. (hon.), Wilberforce Univ., Daniel Payne Coll., Monrovia Coll., W. Africa; m. Callie O. Bryant; Children--Theophilus E., Jr., Brenda Joyce, Linda Kay; pastor, Cherry St. Afr. Meth. Episc. Ch., Dothan, Ala., 1941-42; St. Paul A. M. E. Ch., Birmingham, Ala., 1942-44; pres., Daniel Payne Coll., Birmingham, Ala., 1944-48; St. James A. M. E. Ch., Atlantic City, N. J., 1948-55; St. Matthew A. M. E. Ch., Phila., Pa., 1955--; prin., Shiloh Jr. High Sch., Prosperity, S. C., 1933-36; asst. prin., Dothan Col. High Sch., 1941-42; pres., Atlantic City br. NAACP, 1951-52; chrmn., Equal Housing Com., Phila., Fellowship Commission; mem., Urban League; Educational Bd., A. M. E. Ch.; Home: 6212 Wash. Ave., Phila., Pa.; Office: 59th and Summer Sts., Phila., Pa.

*HARRIS, Charles Poindexter, b. Franklinton, N. C., June 2, 1897; s. Caswell Powell and Elizabeth (Tharrington) H.; Franklinton Chrstn. Coll., N. C., 1914-18; B. D., Howard Univ., Sch. of Rel., 1927; courses: Columbia Univ.; Roanoke Coll.; D. D., Shaw Univ., 1946; m. Mattie Louise Sears; Children--Charles Warren; tchr., Roanoake Inst., Elizabeth City, N. C., 1921-22; pastor,

First Bapt. Ch., Warrenton, Va.; tchr., Wash. Bapt. Sem., Wash., D. C., 1927-31; pastor, Mt. Ararat Bapt. Ch., Rutherford, N. J., 1931-38; current, Calvary Bapt. Ch., Plainfield, N. J., 1938--; pres., Genl. Bapt. Conv. of N. J., 1953-57; exec. sec., The Home Mission Bd., The Natl. Bapt. Conv., USA, Inc., 1958--; v. p., The New England Bapt. Missionary Conv., 1959--; dean, Natl. Bapt. Sun. Sch. and Training Union Congress, 1947-52; dir., Rel. Education, 1943-50; pres., Plainfield, N. J. br. NAACP, 1950-52; Mayor's Commission on Civil Rights, 1952-59; chrmn., Local Co-ordinating Comm. for Fair Housing, 1950-51; v. p., New England Bapt. Missionary Conv., USA, 1928; editor, The Home Mission Journal; Home: 1283 E. Second St., Plainfield, N. J.; Office: Calvary Bapt. Ch., 1000 W. 4th St., Plainfield, N. J.

HARRIS, Elbert Ferdinand, tchr., b. Harriston, Miss., Sept. 26, 1933; s. Alvin E. and Alice (Porte) H.; Epiphany Coll., Newburgh, N. Y., 1949-53; St. Joseph's Sem. Wash., D. C., 1954-60; St. Michael's Coll., Winooski, Vt., 1956-59, B. A., 1961; Cath. Univ. of Amer., Wash. D. C., 1960; Assumption Coll., Worcester, Mass., 1961; Sorbonne, Paris, France, 1962; ordained priest, Rom. Cath. Ch., 1960; tchr., Latin, French, Epiphany Apostolic Coll., mem., Nat. Fed. of Modern Language Tchrs. Office: Epiphany Apostolic Coll., Newburgh, N. Y.

*HARRIS, Henry Benton, b. Bloomfield, N. J., Oct. 17, 1898; s. Pleasant and Lucy (Roberts) H.; B. Th., Shaw Univ., 1916; A. B., Talladega Coll., 1922; Drew Univ., 1926; B. D., Howard Univ., Sch. of Rel.; B. D., Andover New Sch. of Rel., 1931; M. S. T., Boston Univ., 1938; grad. studies: Harvard Univ. Div. Sch.; m. Icilmah Athrin Thompson; pastor, Shiloh Bapt. Ch., Hartford, Conn., 1928-30; Peoples' Bapt. Ch., Portsmouth, N. H., 1930-38; Union Bapt. Ch., New Bedford, 1939-45; Bethlehem Community Ch., Holyoke, Mass. and Second Bapt. Ch., Greenfield, Mass., 1945-49; John St. Bapt. Ch., Worcester, Mass., 1945-49; Western Ave. Bapt. Ch., Cambridge, 1949-55; US Army, 92nd Div., 350 Field Artillery Overseas (France), 1918-19; moderator, Franklin-Millers River (Mass.) Bapt. Assn.; v. p., Holyoke (Mass.) Ministers Assn.; pres., Worcester (Mass.) Ministers Assn.; moderator, Worcester Bapt. Assn.; mem., The Adv. Comm. (38 persons) of the City of Worcester, Mass. Planning Bd. (appt. by mayor); Clerk of the Worcester Bapt. City Mission Bd.; Clerk of the Permanent Council of the Worcester Bapt. Assn.; Corresponding sec. United Bapt. Conv. of Mass. and R.I., 1942-52; pres., U. Bapt. Conv. of Mass. and R.I., 1952-54; counselor and tchr., Royal Ambassador Boys' Camp, Ocean Pk., Maine, 1944-54; mem. of the Finance Comm. and also mem. of the Bd. of the New England Bapt. Missionary Conv., 1950; mem. of the Bd., Person-Simpson Rest Home, Worcester, Mass., 1955; del. to Fed. Coun. of Chs., Cleveland, O., from the Greater Worcester Area Coun. of Chs.; student on two occasions to the Town and Country Sch., Green Lake Wis.; mem. of the Bd., Greater Worcester Area Coun. of Chs., 1955-56; mem. of the Bd., Hampton Ministers Conf., Hampton Inst., 1954-56; mem. of the Inst. of Rel., Sch. of Rel., Howard Univ., Wash., D.C.; del., Churchmen's Seminar, Wash., D.C. (Social Action Comm. of the Amer. Bapt. Assn.), 1955; Home: 168 Western Ave., Cambridge, Mass.; Office: Western Ave. Bapt. Ch., 299 Western Ave., Cambridge, Mass.

HARRIS, Marquis Lafayette, bishop, b. Macon Co., Ala., Mar. 8, 1907; s. William Eugene and Estelle Marie (Glen); B.S., Clark Coll., Atlanta, Ga., 1928; B.D., Gammon Theol. Sem., 1929; S.T.M., Boston Univ., 1930; Spec. Studies, Phil. of Rel., Howard Univ., Psychology of Econ., Western Res. Univ., Ohio; Ph.D., Ohio State Univ., 1933; Fellow Natl. Coll. of Canada, 1940; D.D. (hon.), Gammon Theol. Sem., 1941; LL.D. (hon.), Southwestern Coll., 1960; m. Geneva Magnolia Nelson; Children--Ison, Marquis Lafayette, Jr.; Elder, Meth. Ch., 1932; pastor, Columbia and Martins Ferry, O.; elected bishop of The Meth. Ch. Atlantic Coast Area, 1960; 7 yrs. Ex. sec. Chrstn. Ed., Lexington Conf.; tchr, Clark College, 1927-29; Chaflin Coll., 1930-31; Coll. dean and prof., Samuel Huston Coll., 1933; pres. and prof., Philander Smith Coll., 1936-60; mem., Gen. Bd. of Ed., Meth. Ch., Gen. Conf. Comm. on Ch. Union; mem., the Meth. Ecumenical Conf., Oxford, England, 1951; mem., the World Meth. Conf., Oslo, Norway, 1961; Accredited del. The World Coun. on Ch. Union, Chicago, 1954; mem., The Gen. Conf. Comm. on Rules, 1952; v. chrmn., 1952 Gen. Conf. Comm. on Education; chrmn., The Comm. on Educa. of the Jurisdictional Confs. of 1952 and 1956; mem., The Bd. of Trustees of the Meth. Ch.; Exec. Comm. of the Gen. Conf. Comm. on Advance Projects, 1952-56; mem., The Gen. and

Jurisdictional Conf. of the Meth. Ch., 1940, '44, '48, '52, '56, '60; mem., Bd. of Dirs. of the Southwest Reg. of the YMCA, 1939-52; The Mid-Century Conf. on Children and Youth, 1950; mem., the Ark. State Conf. on Child Welfare and Youth, 1950-54; mem., The Mayor's Comm.; mem., The State Adv. Bd. of UN, Little Rock, Ark., 1951-54; Ex. Comm. of the Pulaski Co., Ark. Health Assn.; Governing Bd. of the Coun. of Social Agencies and Comm. Chest, 1955-58; Sponsoring Comm. of the 1955 South Wide Conf. on Integration in the pub. schs elected Man of the Year in Race Relations by the Urban League of Greater Little Rock, and presented a certificate of merit, 1955; Adv. Bd. on Tchr. Edu. for the state of Ark., the Little Rock Meth. Coun., v.p., of the Ark. Coun. of Chs. and founder and pres., of the Gulf Coast Inter-collegiate Athletic Conf. 1955; Amer. Philosophical Assn.; Southern Soc. of Philosophy and Psychology; Southwestern Philosophical Soc.; Amer. Mathematics Soc.; Amer. Acad. of Soc. and Political Sci.; Alpha Delta Alpha, Alpha Phi Alpha, Beta Kappa Chi, Alpha Kappa Mu, Sigma Pi Phi, Mason, Elk; mem. The Bd. of Trustees of Atlanta Univ. and the Interdenom. Theol. Sem.; chrmn. of the Bds. of Trustees, Bethune-Cookman Coll. (Fla.), Claflin Coll. (S. C.), Clark Coll., Gammon Theol.. Sem. (Ga.); mem., Fed. Coun. of Chs., 1944-51 official voting mem., Natl. Coun. of Chs., successor to the Fed. Coun. of Chs., 1951; mem. (current), The Gen Bd. of Dirs. of the Natl. Coun. of Chs.; author: "Some Conception of God," "Values in One World," "Voice in the Wilderness," "Life Can Be Meaningful." Contributor to magazines: Together; Central Christian Advocate; Adult Teacher; The Methodist Story; Adult Student; Home: 250 Auburn Ave., NE, Atlanta, Ga.

HARRIS, Odell Greenleaf, ch. official, b. Warren Co., N. C., Sept. 3, 1903; s. Robert L. and Susanna (Russell H.; A. B., St. Augustine's Coll.; B. D., Payne Div. Sch. Columbia Univ. & Union Theol. Sem., A. M.; m. Lizzie Elnora Henderson; children--Odell Greenleaf, Marion Elizabeth (Mrs. Mervin E. Perry); rector, All Saint's Ch., Warrenton, N. C., 1933-37; warden & prof., Bishop Payne Div. Sch., Petersburg, Va., 1937-48; Archdeacon of diocese, S. Virginia, 1946-51; director-chaplain, Ft. Valley Coll. Center, Ft. Valley, Va., 1951-61; Archdeacon of Negro Work-Diocese of Atlanta, 1956-61; rector, St. Peter's P. E. Ch., Richmond, Va., 1961--; mem., Diocese of Southern Va., 3 yrs.; Ex. Comm. of

Diocese of S. Va.; Dept. of Chrstn. Educa. in Third Province; Alternate to Genl. Conv.; pres., Petersburg Rec. Assn., Petersburg, Va., 1959-61; dean, St. Augustine's Conf. on Chrstn. Educa., 1950-56; examining chap., Diocese of Atlanta, 1952-56; dir. of camp for boys and girls, Diocese of Atlanta, 1952-61; Exec. Comm. in Diocese of Atlanta, 1958-61; Dept. of Missions, Diocese of Atlanta, 1957-61; Deputy to Genl. Conv., Diocese of Atlanta, 1958; alternate to Genl. Conv., Diocese of Atlanta, 1961; Testimonial of Merit Certificate, Delta Omega Chapter, Omegi Psi Phi, for outstanding community service, 1961; mem., Alpha Phi Alpha; Mason; editor, Handbook of Objectives, Methods, and Plans for our Work, 1947-56, Prot. Episc. Ch.; Home: 1907 N. 23rd St., Richmond, Va.; Office: 1719 N. 22nd and X Sts., Richmond, Va.

HARRIS, Otha Carruthers, b. Norfolk, Va., Dec. 19, 1916; s. John Alexander and Julia (West) H.; A. B., Johnson C. Smith, 1939; B. B., 1942; M. A., McCormick Sem., 1946; M. A., Columbia Univ.; m. Wyndell Griffin; pastor, Trinity United Presby. Ch., Smithfield, N. C., 1942-45; Mizpah Presby. Ch., So. Boston, Va., 1947-50; John Calvin U. Presby. Ch., Petersburg, Va., 1953--; Assoc. in Rel. Activities, Va. State College, Petersburg, Va., 1954--; Rel. and Cultural Seminar to Latin America; mem., Va. Coun. on Human Relations, PTA, NAACP; Va. Soc. Sci. Assn.; Southern Sociological Soc.; Alpha Kappa Delta, Natl. Sociology Honor Soc.; author: History of Johnson C. Smith Sem.; Home: 231 New, Petersburg, Va.; Church: Westminster U. Presbyn. Ch., Petersburg, Va.

HARRIS, Robert Lee, b. Asheville, N. C.; s. John and Lessie (Norris) H.; Southeastern Commercial Coll., Asheville, N. C., 1950; B. D., New Era Theol. Inst., Phila., Pa. 1953; Temple Univ., 1963; m. Clara Lee Lindsay; Children--Robert, Ophelia, Henrietta, Paul, Gladys, James, Charles Calvin, Minerva; assoc. pastor, Temple Meth. Ch., Asheville, N. C.; student supply pastor, Janes Meml. Meth. Ch., Phila., Pa.; current pastor, St. Thomas Meth. Ch., Phila., Pa.; US Navy Reserve, 1942-45; Home: 5539 Morton St., Phila., Pa.; Office: 4701 Tackawanna St., Phila., Pa.

HARRIS, Simon E., b. New Orleans, La., Dec. 21, 1930; B. S., Southern Univ., Baton Rouge, La., 1962; B. D.,

Gammon Theol. Sem., Atlanta, Ga. 1966; m. Carolyn Hines; Children--Valerie Lucille, Albert Sylvester; pastored U. Meth. Chs., Denham Springs, La., 1959-62; Whitesville, Ga., 1963-64; Dublin, Ga., 1965-66; Mansfield, La., 1966-68; Newman U. Meth. Ch., Alexandria, La., current; US Army, 1950-52; Mason; Home: 1616 Eighth St., Alexandria, La. 71301

HARRIS, William Henry, b. Selma, Ala., June 3, 1922; s. William and Frances H.; Knox Acad., 1939; Selma Univ. High Sch., 1941; Daniel Payne Coll., A. B., 1945; B. D., Ruffin Nicholas Theol. Sem., 1950; D. D., Daniel Payne Coll., 1954, D. D., Monrovia Coll.; m. Bertha King; Children--William Henry, Jr.; pastor, St. Mary Afr. Meth. Episc. Ch., Piper, Ala., 1942-45; Sadlers Chapel A. M. E. Ch., Bessemer, Ala., 1945-50; Nicholas Temple A. M. E. Ch., Birmingham, Ala., 1950-59; current pastor St. John A. M. E. Ch., Montgomery, Ala., 1959--; ordained itinerant deacon, 1942; itinerant elder, 1944; mem. A. M. E. Min. Alliance; Gen. Bd. of the A. M. E. Ch.; Interdenom. Min. Alliance; Legal Bd. of Trustees, Daniel Payne Coll.; Pastoral Coun. by appointment; faculty mem., Daniel Payne Coll. High Sch., 1949-51; award of merit for outstanding work in religion - Pi Lambda Sigma 1963; mem., Democrat; Home: 1928 Pearson Ave., SW, Birmingham, Ala.; Office: 809 Madison Ave., Montgomery, Ala.

HARRISON, Earl Leonard, b. Alto, Tex., Jan. 23, 1891; B. Th., Bishop Coll. Theol. Sch., 1919; Post-grad. studies, Union Theol. Sem., NYC; D. D. (hon.), Bishop Coll. 1936; m. Eula Mae Anderson (dec.); Ella B. Snell, 1948; 1 son, Earl; 2 daus., Earline Zane Sampson (Mrs.), Eulene Kay James (Mrs.); pastored rural chs. Antioch Bapt. Ch., Houston, Tex.; Shiloh Bapt. Ch., Wash., D. C., 1930--; chrmn. Bd. Trustees, Wash. Bapt. Sem., D. C., 1958--; pres., Bapt. Conv. D. C. and Vicinity; trustee, Butler Coll., Tyler, Tex.; trustee, Bishop Coll. Dallas, Tex.; pres., Bishop Coll., 1951-52; Republican; Mason; In Who's Who in Religious Leaders of Amer., 1941-42; Home: 1743 Webster St., N. W., Wash., D. C.; Church: 1500 9th St., N. W., Wash., D. C.

*HARVEY, Raymond Francis, b. Hempstead, L. I., N. Y., June 20, 1918; s. Martin Luther, Sr. and Rosa (Monroe) H.; A. B., Va. State Coll., Petersburg, Va., 1940; B. D. Howard Univ. Sch. of Rel., Wash., D. C., 1943; courses

Sch. of Theol., Oberlin Coll., Oberlin, O., 1943-44; D.D. (hon.), Birmingham Bapt. Coll., 1964; m. Lillian Holland; Children--Lind Kathleen, Paul Timothy, Peter Charles; acting chap., Tuskegee Inst., Ala., 1944-46, 1949-50; rel. dir., Interracial group of Southern Coll. students to Danzig, Poland, 1946; pastor, Bethesda Bapt. Ch., Opelika, Ala., 1950-54; Greenwood Missionary Bapt. Ch., Tuskegee Inst., 1954--; rel. emphasis week speaker: Fla. A & M, Tuskegee Inst., Ala. A & M; Morehouse Coll., Prairie View A & M; Ark. A & M; Va. State Coll.; Miss. Vocational Coll.; visiting preacher: Appalachian Preaching Mission, Howard Univ., Southern Univ., N. C. Coll.; Bapt. State Conv. of N. C.; Home: 909 Washington Ave., Tuskegee Inst., Ala.; Office: same.

HARVEY, Wardelle Green, b. Boonville, Ind., June 12, s. Elner and Inez Mae (Green) H.; B.Th., Tri-State Bapt. Coll., 1955; D.D. (hon.), Bapt. Theol. Center, Houston, Tex., 1962; m. Josephine Boling; Children--Marion Jeanette, Wardelle Green, Jr.; pastor, First Ebenezer Bapt. Ch., Evansville, 1956-62; current pastor, Harrison St. Bapt. Ch., Paducah, Ky., 1962--; pres., Non-partisan League; mem., Local Human Rights Commn.; chap., Paducah Area Min. Fellowship; pres., Bapt. Min. Fellowship; 2nd v. moderator, The First Dist. Bapt. Conv. of Ky. Bapt.; Mason; mem., publisher, Harrison St. Messenger (newspaper), official organ of Harrison St. Bapt. Ch. and Community; Mayor's Adv. Bd., Paducah, Ky.; Home: 1126 Harrison, Paducah, Ky; Office: 1124 Harrison, Paducah, Ky.

*HASKINS, Joseph Franklin, b. Durham, N.C., Jan. 8, 1913; s. Arthur and Martha (H); Johnson C. Smith Univ.; A.B., Howard Univ., 1952; B.D., Howard Univ. Sch. of Rel., 1955; grad. courses, Boston Univ., 1956; m. Florence Greene; Children--Joseph Jr., Denise Annette; present pastor, Galloway U. Meth. Ch., Falls Church, Va.; mem., Health & Welfare Coun., Natl. Cap. Area; Northern Va. Min. Assn.; Falls Church Community Action Program; NAACP; Fairfax Co. Fair Housing Commn.; Omega Psi Phi; organizer & v. chrmn., Saunders B. Moon Community Action Program, (UPO); mem., Conf. Bd. of Bd. of Missions, U. Meth. Ch. (Va. Conf.); tchr., N. Va., 1964-66; chrmn., Fairfax Co. Voter Reg. Drive, 1963-64; mem., Rolating Hosp. Chaplaincy, N. Va., 1965-present; US Army, 1943-46, (ETO); Mason; Research, Meth. Ch. Commission; Va. Methodist Look Ahead, E.

Pluribus Unum, pamphlet on proposed Union of the Meth. Ch. and the abolition of the Central Jurisdiction; Overlook Press, 1966; Let My People Go, A controversy on radicalism, 1967; Home: 2752 Annandale Rd., Falls Church, Fa. 22042; Office: 306 Annandale Rd., Falls Church, Fa. 20042

HATCHER, Eugene Clifford, bishop, b. Eufaula, Ala., Sept. 12, 1902; s. Clarence George and Julia Ann (Watts) H.; A. & T. Coll., Greensboro, N.C.; A.B., Daniel Payne Coll.; D.D. (hon.), Payne Univ., 1930; D.D. (hon.), LL.D. (hon.), Wilberforce Univ.; LL.D., Shorter Coll.; Flipper Curry Coll., 1944; Morris Brown Coll.; J.U.D. (hon.), Nasson Coll., Springfield, 1960; m. Oretha Mae Tillman; children--Rubye (Mrs. Crawford), Eugene Clifford, Jr.; pastor, Wayman Chapel, Afr. Meth. Episc. Ch., S. Jackson, Jacksonville; South St. Afr. Meth. Episc. Ch., Dothan, Ala.; presiding elder, 1930, Fla. & Ozark Dists., elected bishop, 1952; now presiding bishop 3rd dist., prof., Payne Univ. and Bethel Coll.; trustee, Daniel Payne Coll.; chrmn., Wilberforce Univ. Trustee Bd.; mem., Wilberforce Foundation; Natl. Coun. of Chs.; Phi Beta Sigma; NAACP; pres., Gen. Bd. of Ed. (A.M.E.), World Meth. Coun.; one of the chief celebrant community services, Oslo, Norway, 1961 World Meth. Conf.; mem., Elks; Mason; editor, Southern Chrstn. Recorder, 1940-48; author: What We Saw, Heard and Accomplished in West Africa; Home: 110009 Wade Park, Cleveland, O.

HAWKINS, Alexander Amos, social worker, b. Gainesville, Fla., Sept. 3, 1923; s. George Washington and Pearl Williams; Cookman Coll., Bethune, 1942-44; Assoc. of Arts, Morehouse Coll., 1944-46; B.A., Univ. of Pittsburgh Law Sch., 1946-47; Master of Social Work, 1949; post-grad. courses: Sch. of Soc. Work, 1953--; m. Mable Teola Emanuel; children--Alexander A., Jr., Clinton M.; pub. asst. case worker, 1949-50; Amer. Red Cross case worker, 1951-53; Va. Hosp., Pittsburgh Psychiatric Soc. Worker, 1954-60; Supervisor Correctional Services-Salvation Army, Pittsburgh, 1960-62; Dir., Soc. Service Dept. of Justice, Bur. of Correction-Central Office, 1962--; asst. pastor, Brown Chapel Afr. Meth. Episc. Ch., Pittsburgh, 1955-56; asst. pastor, Calvary A.M.E. Ch., Braddock, Pa., 1956; Interim pastor, Bethel A.M.E. Ch., Greensburg, Pa., 1956-57; pastor, Quinn Chapel A.M.E. Ch., Elizabeth, Pa., 1957-60;

asst. pastor, Bethel A. M. E. Ch., Pittsburgh; pastor, Bethel A. M. E. Ch., Monroeville, Pa., 1960--; field instr., Univ. of Pittsburgh Soc. Work, 1960--; Adult Ed. Dept. of Pub. Instr.-Evening Correctional In-service training Program, 1960--; mem., United Negro Coll. Fund; sec.-treas., Pittsburgh Univ. Soc. Wk. Alumni Assn.; past. sec., Psychiatric Soc. Wk. Assn, Pittsburgh; US Army, 1942-43; mem., NAACP; Natl. Assn. of Soc. Workers; Acad. of Certified Soc. Workers; Natl. Conf. of Crime & Delinquency; Middle Atlantic States Conf. on Correction; Pa. Assn. on Probation, Parole and Correction; author of article: "Casework in Corrections" The Quarterly; presently writing book, Principles & Practice of Social Work in the Bureau of Correction; Home: 253 Travella Blvd., Pittsburgh, Pa. 15235; Office: Bethel A. M. E. Church, Box 365, Wilmerding, Pa.

HAWKINS, Elder Garnett, b. New York City, June 13, 1908; s. Albert and Annie (Lee) H.; B. A., Bloomfield Coll., 1935; D. D. (hon.), 1938; B. D., Union Theol. Sem., NYC, 1960; m. Thelma Burnett; Children--Renee, Ellen; ordained to ministry, Presby. Ch., 1938; founder and present pastor, St. Augustine Presbyn. Ch., N. Y.; moderator, Presbytery, N. Y., 1958-60; v. moderator, Gen. Assembly United Presby. Ch., USA, 1960-61; moderator, 1964; mem., Bd. of Chrstn. Edu., 1959--; Bd. of Dirs., Natl. Big Bros. America, Bronx Mental Hygiene Assn.; pres., Bd. of Forest House, Bronx; Adv. Com., Bronx Community Coll.; awards: Amer. War Mothers; Natl. Council Negro Women Natl. Urban League; Bronx Borough President's Office; Home: 834 E. 16th St., New York, N. Y.; Office: St. Augustine Presby. Ch., Prospect Ave., 165th St., Bronx, N. Y.

HAWKINS, Reginald Armistice, dentist, b. Beaufort, N. C., Nov. 11, 1923, s. Charles C. and Lorena (Smith); B. S., Johnson C. Smith Univ., 1941-44; D. D. S., Howard Univ., 1944-48; B. D., Johnson C. Smith Univ., 1953-56; LL. D., Johnson C. Smith Univ., 1962; m. Catherine Elizabeth Richardson; children--Paulette Charlene, Reginald Armistice, Jr., Wayne Beauregard, Lorena Bernice; practicing dentist, 1948--; Capt. in US Army Dental Corps, 1951-53; pastor, United Presby. Ch. USA, (Minister-at-large of Catawba Presby), 1956--; mem. Bd. of Mecklenburg Co. TB and Health Assn.; Bd. of Charlotte-Mecklenburg Youth Council; Bd. of Mecklenburg Mens Democratic Club;

chrmn. Democratic Precinct 25; Exec. Comm. of Bd. of Trustees of N. C. Coll. at Durham; Good Neighbor Comm. of N. C.; Capt. US Army Dental Corps, Korean conflict, 1951-53; decorations: 1961 Dentist-of-the-Year of Old North State Dental Soc. (N. C.); 1962 Dentist-of-the-Year of Natl. Dental Soc.; rec'd honorary Doctor of Laws Degree from Johnson C. Smith Univ. in 1962; mem., Old North State Dental Soc., Natl. Dental Soc., Exec. Comm. of local Democratic Men's Organization; chrmn. of Mecklenburg Organization on Political Affiars; United Presby. Ch., USA; NAACP; Kappa Alpha Psi; author: "Status of Negro Doctors in Municipal Hospitals," feature article in Charlotte Observer, May 4, 1962; feature article of Washington Post, Nov. 1962; featured in Howard Univ. Journal, Apr. 1963; interview on natl. CBS and ABC network feature on civil rights; interview on Radio Free Europe feature on civil rights; Home: 1703 Madison Ave., Charlotte, N. C.; Office: 1218 Beatties Ford Rd., Charlotte, N. C. 28208

HAWKINS, Zachariah, tchr., b. Salisbury, N. C., Aug. 10, 1923; s. Wm. A. and Lou W. (Pogue) H.; B. S., Johnson C. Smith Univ., 1946; B. D., 1949; M. A., N. C. Coll. at Durham, 1955; post-grad. work at NYU and Rutgers Univ. pastor, Mebane Second Presby. Ch., Mebane, N. C., 1949-55; Scott Elliott Meml. Presby. Ch., Graham, N. C. tchr., Pub. schs., New Jersey, 1955-59; pub. schs., N. Y., 1959--; mem., NAACP; Civic Assn. of Wyandanch, L. I., N. Y.; mem., Omega Psi Phi; NY State Tchrs. Assn.; Home: 804 Mount Ave., Wyandanch, L. I., N. Y.

HAYES, Joshua William, b. Alabama, Aug. 2, 1905; s. Joshu and Florence E.; A. B., Livingstone Coll., 1944; m. Josephine Moore; 1 dau., Josephine Moore; pastor, Trinity Afr. Methodist Episc. Zion Ch., Birmingham, Ala.; one of the organizers of the Montgomery Improvement Assn.; pres., Ensley Voter League; mem., Chrstn Movement for Human Rights; Democratic Preachers Party, Birmingham, Ala.; active in 1963 Birmingham demonstrations; Home: 1810 19th St., Birmingham, Ala.; Office: 1800 19th St., Birmingham, Ala.

HAYGOOD, Lawrence Franklin, college prof., b. Coffee Springs, Ala., Mar. 29, 1933; s. Roy W. and Venetta (Tyrus) H.; Stillman College, Tuscaloosa, Ala., 1951-55, B. A.; B. D., Union Theol. Sem., Richmond, Va.; m.

Bennie S. Taylor; children--Lawrence F., Jr., Rouetta, Jocasta, Chiquita Anastasia; pastor, Covenant Presby. Ch., Norfolk, Va., 1959-62; present pastor, Parkway Gardens Presby. Ch., Memphis, Tenn., 1962--; instr., Dept. of English at Norfolk Div. of Va. State Coll., Norfolk, Va., 1961-62; mem., Health & Welfare Planning Commn. for Memphis & Shelby Co.; mem., Memphis Comm. on Community Relations; ch. work chrmn. of Memphis br. NAACP; Stillman Coll. Alumni Assn.; Home: 1253 Worthington, Memphis, Tenn.; Office: 1683 S. Parkway, E., Memphis, Tenn.

*HAYLING, Mapson Forkau, b. Grenada, W. Indies, June 12, 1877; s. George and Rosetta H.; B.D., Howard Univ. Sch. of Rel., 1912; Children--Mapson, Jr.; pastor, The Meth. Ch., 1911-50; retired 1950; current, v.p., Ministorium, Verona, Pa.; mem., Mason; Home: 505 Church St., Verona, Pa.

HAYNES, Roosevelt, b. Summer Co., Tennessee, Feb. 17, 1933; s. Henry Grant and Maude (Macmurry) H.; A.B., Stillman Coll., 1959; B.D., Louisville Presby. Theol. Sem., 1962; m. La Pearl Hamilton; Children--Terrence De Wayne; student pastor, Good Hope Presby. Ch., 1957-59; Cecelia Presby. Ch., 1959-61; student pastor at Bowling Green, Ky.; asst. pastor, Grace Presby. Ch., Louisville, Ky., 1961-62; pastor, Washington St., Presby. Ch. of Dublin, Ga., 1962--; US Army, 1953-55; Natl. Defense Service Medal, United Nations Service Medal, Korean Service Medal, Good Conduct Medal; mem., Democratic Party; Home: 112 Carter St., Dublin, Ga.; Office: 975 S. Washington, Dublin, Ga.

HAYWOOD, John Wilfred, b. Maury Co., Tenn., July 3, 1880; s. Charles and Jennie (Kennedy) H.; A.B., Lincoln Univ., Chester, Pa., 1903; S.T.D., Union Theol. Sem., 1912; grad. courses, Univ. of Pa., 1924, '25, '28; D.D. (hon.), Gammon Theol. Sem., 1925; LL.D. (Hon.), Lincoln Univ., 1928; LL.D. (hon.), L.H.D. (hon.), Morgan State Coll., 1963; m. Lottie Juanita Burnett; Children--John Wilfred Jr., Rondall Burnett, Violet Geraldine; pastor, Ebenezer Meth. Ch., Marshall, Tex., 1913-17; dean, Wiley Coll., Marshall, Tex., 1917-19; assoc. exec. sec., N.O. Area Meth. Centennial, 1919-20; prof., Morgan State Coll., 1920; prin. Morgan Acad., 1921-23; dean, Morgan State Coll., 1924-36; pres., Morrison Jr. Coll., Morristown, 1936-44; pres., Gammon Theol. Sem.,

1944-48; field sec. Meth. Bd. of World Peace, 1948-53; retired 1953; mem., A. D. A.; asst. sec., Meth. Gen. Conf., 1940-44, 1948, 1952; frequent contributor, rel. publications; Home: 1439 Irving St. NE, Washington, D. C. 20017

HAZZARD, Walter R., b. Golts, Md.; s. John E. and Minnie B. (H.); Morgan Coll.; A. B., Lane Coll., 1939; M. A. Howard Univ., 1941; B. D. Crozer Theol. Sem., 1945; D. S. T. Temple Univ., 1953; m. Alexina A.; Children--Walter R. Jr., Alexina E., Lois A.; pastor, Oddessa Port Penn Charge Meth. Ch., Delaware Conf., 1942-45; Hamilton Meml. Meth. Ch., Atlantic City, N. J., 1945-54; Supt., Phila. Conf. Meth. Ch., 1954-57; pastor, Tindley Meth. Ch., Phila., 1960-65; Supt., South Dist., Phila. Conf.; Meth. Ch. Tchr. Crozer Theol. Sem.; Dean of Wilmington Dist. Youth Inst., 1945-54; faculty mem. Conf. Youth Assembly; tchr. in Balto. Area Pastor's Sch. of Bennett Coll., leader of seminars at Gammon Theol. Sem. and Drew Coll.; pres. of Interracial Ministerium of Absecon Island, N. J.; chrmn. Bd. of Dirs. Reg. Pastor's Sch.; dean of Reg. Pastor's Sch.; mem. Comm. to study the Metro. area of greater NYC; v. chrmn. of the Jt. Comm. to study problems of ministering to people in the city of Phila.; v. chrmn. of Billy Graham Greater Phila. crusade; mem., YMCA; NAACP; Convocation Comm. on Urban Life of 1966; Gen. Bd. of Chrstn. Social Concerns of the Meth. Ch.; sec., Meth. Comm. for Overseas Relief; chrmn. of the 25th anniversary Comm. of MCOR; treas., Meth. Student Movement of the Chesapeake Area; mem., Mayor Tate's Adv. Comm. on Human Relations; Bd. of Managers of Corp. of Ch. World Service; founder and pres., Chrstn. Benevolent Assn.; Supt. So. Dist. of Phila. Conf.; dir., So. Dist. Missionary Project in Chester, Pa.; pres., Comm. Action Coun., Chester, Pa.--present; mem., Bd of Gov. of Wesley Theol. Sem.; Bd. of Mgrs. of Morgan Chrstn. Center, Balto., Md.; trustee, Comm. Coll. Del. Co., Pa.; chrmn. Bishop's comm. on City Work; mem., Comm. for Overseas Relief; Quadrennial Program Comm. of Meth. Ch.; v. chrmn., Legislative Comm. on Chrstn. Social Concerns at the Uniting Conf.; v. p., Pa. Coun. of Chs.; Home: 940 Clover Hill Rd., Wynnewood, Pa. 19096

HEACOCK, Roland Tilman, b. New Milford, Conn., Dec. 30, 1893; s. Stephen and Mary (Gregory) H.; B. A., Howard Univ., 1921; B.D., Yale Univ. Div. Sch., 1924; S.T.M., Boston Univ., 1925; D.D. (hon.), Amer. Intl. Coll., Springfield, Mass., 1951; m. Lucile LaCour; Children--Don R., Mrs. Marshal Layton, Mrs. Jean Musson; ordained Congre. min., 1924; pastor, Lincoln Congre. Ch., Springfield, Mass., 1926-39; pastor, St. John's Congre. Ch., Springfield, Mass., 1926-29; pastor, Community Congre. Ch., Phila., Pa., 1929-31; St. John's Congre. Ch., Springfield, Mass., 1931-45; pastor ad interium, Stafford Springs Congre. Ch., Stafford Springs, Conn., 1948-49; pastor, Staffordville, Conn., 1950-59; retired, 1959; Natl. Conf. of Chrstns. and Jews in Tulsa, Okla.; US Army, WW I, 1917-18; chaplain, Amer. Leg. Post, Stafford Springs, Conn., 1947-49; chap. (Capt.), WW II, 1942-45; citation by the Chicago Defender for advance race relations in the past year; author of articles in the rel. press on race relations; chrmn., Social Action Comm.; Comm. on the Ministry; pres., Springfield Congre. Union, Springfield, Mass.; dir., Bd. of the Springfield Goodwill Industries; arbitrator on a labor-management dispute; mem., Jewish Lecture Bureau on Race Relations; mem., Alpha Chapter, Omega Psi Phi; Howard Univ., 1920; Home: Hydeville Rd., Stafford, Conn.

HEDGLEY, David Rice, b. Mobile, Ala., Apr. 22, 1907; s. Noah M. and Pauline (Rice) H.; A.B., Va. Union Univ., 1931; A.M., Univ. of Chicago, 1935; B.D., Northern Bapt. Theol. Sem., 1945; D.D. (hon.), Shaw Univ., 1953, Va. Union Univ., 1955; m. Christine Kelly; Children--David, Jr., Christine Lunah; chap., Fla. A & M Coll., 1936-44; pastor, First Bapt. Ch., Winston-Salem, 1944--; moderator, Rowan Bapt. Assn., 1958-62; pres., Missionary & Educational Union; pres., Ministers Assn.; mem., Urban League Exec. Comm., 1957--; Mayor's Goodwill Comm., 1964; Mason; Phi Beta Sigma; Democrat; Home: 901 13th NE, Winston-Salem, N.C.; Office: 912 7th NE, Winston-Salem, N.C.

HEGMON, Oliver Louis, b. Boling, Tex., Feb. 8, 1908; s. John Charles and Martha (Robins); B.Th., Conroe Normal Indus. Coll., Conroe, Tex., 1937; D.D., LL.D. (hon.), Union Bapt. Sem., Houston, Tex., 1950, 1958; m. Emma Louise Jones; pastor, True Light Bapt. Ch., Houston, Tex.; Mt. Rose Bapt. Ch., Liberty, Texas; Mt. Olive Bapt. Ch., Dayton, Tex.; Mt. Calvary Bapt. Ch., Galveston, Texas; Chapel Bapt. Ch., Waco, Tex.;

Calvary, Los Angeles; Antioch Missionary Bapt. Ch., Ft. Worth, Tex. present; tchr., Conroe N & I Coll. (4 yrs); founder, The Truth Seekers Bible Sch.; v.p., Progressive Voters League, 1947-49; mem., Mayor's Com. on Human Relations, Waco, Tex., 1949-51; v.p., Negro Cham. of Commerce, Waco, 1949-51; pres., McLennan Co. br. NAACP, 1948-58; Chrmn., Ch. Work State Com. NAACP, 1958-present; Chrmn. & Trustee Rel. Dir. Ft. Worth & Tarrant Co. United Fund, 1967-68; Exec. sec., Missionary Bapt. Gen. Conv. of Tex.; pres., Bapt. Min. Union of Ft. Worth & Tarrant Co.; chrmn., Civic Com. of Interdenom. Min. Alliance, Ft. Worth; radio broadcaster, 1935-present; editor, The Truth Seeker (newspaper); Home: 800 E. Baltimore Ave., Ft. Worth, Tex. 76104; Office: 1063 E. Rosedale St., Ft. Worth, Tex., 76104

HEMPHILL, James Thomas, b. Jan. 13, 1931, Buffalo, N.Y.; s. John Elliott and Viola (Barber) (H.); A.B., Livingstone Coll., Salisbury, N.C.; B.D., Hood Theol. Sem., Salisbury, N.C.; Children--Jacquelyn, Viola, James, Jr.; pastor, Pleasant Hill A.M.E.Z. Ch., Heath Springs, S.C., 1953-54; St. John A.M.E.Z. Ch., Thomasville, N.C., 1954-58; Walls Meml. A.M.E.Z. Ch., Buffalo, N.Y., 1958-present; tchr., East High Sch., Buffalo, N.Y.; tchr., Emotionally Disturbed Children, Child Care Center, Buffalo, N.Y.; mem. Bd. Black Men's Business, Inc., Buffalo, N.Y., 1968; Black Men's Development, Inc., 1968; Community Action Organization, Erie Co., 1965-68; pres., Thomasville, N.C. NAACP, 1954-58; pres., Buffalo NAACP, 1958-60; Dist. Com. Democratic Party, Erie Co., 1960-present; chrmn., Walls Meml. Cultural Center, Inc., Buffalo, 1968; mem., Masons; Alpha Phi Alpha; Home: 115 Utica St., Buffalo, N.Y., 14208; Office: 455 Glenwood Ave., Buffalo, N.Y. 14208

HENDERSON, Elo Leon, b. Shelton, S.C., Mar. 29, 1909; s. Elijah and Essie; B.S., Johnson C. Smith Univ., Charlotte, N.C., 1939; B.D., Johnson C. Smith Sem., Charlotte, N.C., 1942; m. Doris Stephens; Children--Sula Eileen; pastor, St. Lloyd, Ben Salem United Presby. Chs. 1942-43; Grier Heights United Presby. Ch., 1943-45; Field rep., Synod of Catawba, 1955-56; Synod exec., Catawba Synod, 1966-68; rep., Synod at formation of Natl. Coun. of Presby. Men, 1948; chrmn., S.E. Evaluation Conf., United Presby. Ch.; del., United Presby. Ch.,

N. A. Area Coun.; cons., Gen. Assembly's Commn. on Theol. Ed. in S. E.; chrmn., Personnel Practice Com., Bd. of Natl. Missions; mem., exec. com., N. C. Coun. of Chs.; pres., Bd. of Dir., Charlotte OIC, Inc.; org., Charlotte Frontier Assoc., 1961; chrmn., Black Solidarity Com.; Democrat; Omega Psi Phi; Home: 1716 Washington Ave., Charlotte, N. C., 28208; Office: Johnson C. Smith Univ., Charlotte, N. C. 28208

HENDERSON, James Franklin, Sr., b. Blackstock, S. C., Dec. 31, 1912; s. John Loyd and Carrie (Carylon) H.; A. B., Allen Univ., 1933; B. D., Johnson C. Smith Univ., 1936; D. D. (hon.), Johnson C. Smith Univ., 1958; post-grad. work, Auburn Sem., in assoc. with Union Sem. (Columbia Univ., N. Y.); m. Frank Mildred Simmons; Children--James Franklin, Jr.; pastor, Zion Presby. Ch., Charleston, S. C.; Allison U. Presby. Ch., Little Rock, Ark.; pres., Min. Union, Charleston, S. C. and Greater Little Rock Min. Alliance, Little Rock, Ark.; v. moderator The Oklahoma-Ark. U. Presby. Synod; served on jury First Div. of Circuit Court of Pulaski Co.; assoc. prof. of Rel. and Sociology at Philander Smith Coll. and Ark. Bapt. Coll.; (current) pastor, Allison Meml. Presby. Ch., Little Rock, Ark.; mem., Mayor of Little Rock's Interracial Comm. Ark. Valley Presby.; chrmn., Interracial Min. Alliance Comm. on Community and World Affairs; Adv. Bd. Natl. Urban League; Florence Crittendon Home; dir., Canadian Summer Conf. for Westminster Fellowship; v. p., Quapaw Area, Boy Scouts of Amer.; Ad. Comm. Presby. Men's Forum of Canadian Synod; moderator, Canadian Synod and White River Presbytery; Community War Chest Campaign of Little Rock Merit Award, 1944; author: "The Way to Walk and The Light to Follow," "A Report on Racial and Cultural Relations," "A History of the Negro in Zion Presbyterian Church." Home: 1620 W. 21st St., Little Rock, Ark.; Church: 901 Gaines St., Little Rock, Ark.

HENDERSON, Jefferson Winston, b. Kansas City, Kan., Sept. 29, 1915; s. Roscoe C. and Ethel H.; B. A., Indiana Central Coll.; B. D., Payne Theol. Sem.; m. Frances Marie Harris; Children--Gloria (Mrs. Robert Alford), Sylvia, Jefferson, Jr.; pastor, Afr. Meth. Episc. Chs., Nashville, Tenn., 1942; Urbana, O., 1944; Pittsburgh, Pa., 1947; current, Cincinnati, O. (Brown Chapel A. M. E. Ch.); draftsman, Gen. Elec., Evandale, 1951-52; Psychiatric Social Worker (Univ. Pittsburgh); former pres., NAACP, Urbana, Ohio; cad. for City Council, Cincinnati, O., 1961; Democrat; RCIN - radio-outstanding Cincinnati citizen; mem., Mason; pres., A. M. E. Min. Alliance; Home: 1711 Crane, Cincinnati, Ohio; Office: 2804 Alms Peace, Cincinnati, Ohio.

HENDERSON, Lewis Duke, principal, b. Dallas, Tex., June 2, 1924; s. Eddie and Francis (Hubbard) H.; B. A., Oakwood Coll., 1950; M. A., Texas Southern, 1953; D. D. (hon.), Union Bapt. Theol. Sem., Houston, Tex., 1955; m. Earnest M. Boss; Children--Lewis, Jr., Carolyn Elaine, Ann Laverne, Lynda K.; began ministry in Ft. Worth, Tex., 1950-51; tchr. and pastor, Houston, Tex., 1951-55; pastored: Lake Charles, La., 1955-62; present: pastor, Seventh Day Adventist Ch. and prin. of sch., Shreveport, La.; US Army Med. Corps, 1942-44; Home: 1960 Anna St., Shreveport, La.; Office: 1143 Madison St., Shreveport, La.

HENNING, Cornal Garnett, b. Memphis, Tenn., Oct. 12, 1935; s. Herman William and Mattie Elizabeth (Miller) H.; Lemoyne Coll., Memphis, Tenn., 1952-53; Wilberforce Univ., Ohio, 1953-57; Payne Theol. Sem., Ohio, 1957-60; Kansas Sch. of Rel., 1964; m. Ernestine Donesta Lee; Children--Helaine Aleece; assoc. pastor, Greater Allen A. M. E. Ch., Dayton, Ohio, 1956-60; pastor, Salem A. M. E. Ch., Nashville, Tenn., 1960; St. Luke A. M. E. Ch., Nashville, Tenn., 1960-64; St. Luke A. M. E. Ch., Lawrence, Kan., 1964-65; assoc. pastor, First A. M. E. Ch., Los Angeles, Calif., 1965-present; asst. to the exec. sec. of the div. of Chrstn. Edu., A. M. E. Ch., Nashville, Tenn., 1960-64; mem., Planning Com. for the Connectional Youth Congress, 1962; Exec. Com. of Nashville Chrstn. Leadership Coun.; NAACP; CORE; Alpha Phi Alpha; Bd. mem., Univ. of Kansas Rel. Assn.; Home: 2670 Ellendale Pl., Los Angeles, Calif.; Office 801 Towne Ave., Los Angeles, Calif.

HENRY, Vincent DePaul, tchr., b. Charleston, S. C., Sept. 2, 1931; s. Freeman and Estelle (DeVeaux) H.; St. Francis Sem., 1949-51; Assumption Sem., 1952-54; St. Anthony-on-Hudson Sem., 1954-57; S. T. L., Cath. Univ. of Amer., 1957-58; B. Mus., B. Sac. Mus., Manhattanville Coll. - Pius X Sch. of Liturgical Music; Res. Chap., Manhattanville Coll., 1958-59; student, Manhattanville,

1958-60; St. John's Grad. Sch. of Library Sci., 1960-62; tchr., librarian, organist, St. Francis Sem., Staten Is., N.Y., 1960--; dir., St. Louis Fraternity, 3rd Order of St. Francis, Staten Is., N.Y.; mem., Natl. Cath. Music Educators Assn.; Cath. Library Assn.; Home and Office: St. Francis Sem., Todt Hill Rd., Staten Island, N.Y.

HERRON, Vernon Mack, b. Charlotte, N.C., Oct. 7, 1928; s. Samuel and Mamie (McPherson) H.; A.B., Shaw Univ.; B.D., Johnson C. Smith Univ.; further study: Pittsburgh-Xenia Grad. Sch.; m. Louise Christine Oliphant; Children--Vernease Marcelinia; Leila McPherson; Frenshetta Louise; pastor, First Bapt. Ch., Dallas, N.C., 1952-55; Friendship Bapt. Ch., Pittsburgh, Pa., 1957-62; prison chap., State Pen., 1961--, Joliet, Ill.; trustee, Woodville State Mental Hosp., 1961; mem., Alpha Phi Alpha; Home: 156 S. Joliet St., Joliet, Ill.

HERZFELD, Will Lawrence, b. Mobile, Ala., June 9, 1937; s. Julius and Clarice; A.A., Immanuel Luth. Coll., Greensboro, N.C.; Immanuel Luth. Sem., 1961; grad. courses, Concordia Sem., St. Louis, Mo.; m. Thressa Alston; Children--Martin Everett, Katherine Elizabeth, Stephen Lawrence; pastor, Christ Luth. Ch., Tuscaloosa, Ala., (5-1/2 yrs.); Urban minister, Calif. & Nevada Dist., Luth. Ch. Mo. Synod, present; former organizing mem. S.C.L.C. Conf.; pres., Ala. S.C.L.C. Conf.; mem. Dist. Stewardship Com. Luth. Ch.; Dist. Parish Ed. Com.; chrmn., Family Life Com.; present, v.p., Luth. Human Relations Assn. of Amer.; bd. of dirs., Wheat Ridge Foundation; first v.p., Bay Area Black Clergymen's Assn.; bd. of dirs., East Bay Conf. on Rel. and Race and Social Justice; Home: 2470 Mavis St., Oakland, Calif. 94601; Office: 506 - 41st Street, Oakland, Calif. 94609

HEWLETT, Everett Augustus, Sr., b. Virginia; s. Augustus and Adelaid (Sykes); A.B., Lincoln Univ., Chester Co., Pa., 1953-59; S.T.B., Lincoln Sem., 1939-41; m. Mary Still; Children--Everett A., Jr., Deborah A., Michelle K.; pastor, First Presby. Ch., Richmond, 1941-43; US Army chap., 1943-46; So. Pacific Bd. of Natl. Missions, Presby. Ch., 1947; N.Y.C. Sargent Meml. United Presby. Ch., USA, 1948--; June 1965 - elected mem., Dist. of Columbia, Bd. of Ed.; 3rd v.p., D.C. Citizens Coun.; v. chrmn., Washington, D.C. Presby.

Com. on Race; Interracial mem., Natl. Capitol Area Presby. Coun.; Home: 4300 Ord St. NE, Wash., D.C.; Church: Grant St. at 51st NE, Wash., D.C.

HICKMAN, Ernest Lawrence, bishop, b. Fayetteville, Tenn., June 8, 1903; s. Edgar and Lilla Ann (Brown) H.; B.D., Turner Coll., 1928; D.D. (hon.), Payne Theol. Sem.; Shorter Coll., both in 1953; LL.D., Wilberforce Univ., 1956; m. Cleopatra Watkins; Children--Bertha, Othella (Mrs. Leroy Green); pastor, Afr. Meth. Episc. Chs., Cleveland, Chattanooga, Memphis, Knoxville, Fayetteville, Tenn.; presiding elder, elected bishop, 1956; now presiding 13th Dist., A.M.E. Ch.; mem., Civilian Defense Coun., Chattanooga; Chattanooga Interracial Com.; Natl. Fraternal Coun. of Negro Chs.; Southern Recorder Bd., A.M.E. Ch.; v.p., Pension Bd., A.M.E. Ch.; v.p., Bd. of Payne Theol. Sem.; mem., Mason; NAACP; Urban League; Coun. of Chs.; YMCA; Mayor's Com., Louisville; Office: 451 Halden Dr., S.W., Atlanta, Ga.

HICKS, E.B., b. Kansas; B.A., Washburn Municipal Univ., Topeka, Kan.; B.D., Central Bapt. Theol. Sem., Kan. City, Kan.; D.D. (hon.), Monrovia Coll. & Indus. Inst. of Monrovia, Liberia, W. Africa, 1961 m. Effie Mae (deceased); m. Roena S. Starks; Children--four; pastor, Calvary Bapt. Ch., Duluth, Minn., 1938-42; Army chap., 1942-45; dir., Bapt. Ed. Center of Topeka, 1946-56; exec. sec., Mission Bapt. Conv. of Kan., 1946-56; Natl. dir., Ed. Centers for the Amer. Bapt. Home Missions Soc., 1956-present mem., Natl. Staff, Div. of Ch. Missn., Amer. Bapt. Home Missn. Soc., Topeka, Kan.; acts as liaison betweeen the Amer. Bapt. Conv. and the Natl. Bapt. Conv.; mem., Second Bapt. Ch., Topeka, Kan.; served as pres., local Sun. Sch. & B.Y.P.U. Congress; v.p., Topeka Interdenom. Interracial Alliance; pres., Bapt. Min. Union; served as auditor, KAW Valley Dist. Bapt. Assn., Kan.; moderator, Lake Superior Bapt. Assn., ABC of Minn.; served 11 yrs. as exec. sec. and missionary, Missionary Bapt. State Conv., Kan.; field repr., Amer. Bapt. Home Missn. Soc.; camp advisor; supt. of missns.; registrar-sec., Extension Sch. Central Bapt. Sem.; sec., Natl. Bapt. Conv. Flood Relief Com., 2 yrs.; mem., Bd. of Dirs., Civil Rights Legislation Com., Natl. Bapt. Conv., USA; V. pres., Kan. Coun. of Chs., 2 yrs.; instr., Topeka Coun. of Ch. Women's Sch. of Missions; editor, Kansas Missionary; Home: 1228 Buchanon St., Topeka, Kan.

HICKS, H. Beecher, b. Uniontown, Ala.; s. Wm.; A. B., Leland Coll., Baton Rouge, La.; B. D., Oberlin Grad. Sch. of Theol., Ohio; courses: Univ. of Pa.; D. D. (hon.), Leland Coll., Baton Rouge, La.; m. Eleanor V. Frazier; Children--Sandra, H. Beecher Jr., William; student pastor, Second Bapt. Ch., Medina, Ohio; pastor, Union Bapt. Ch., Brusly, La.; Mt. Olivet Bapt. Ch., Columbus, Ohio, 1946-present; former tchr., prof., prin., Plaquemine, La.; dean of Chapel, Leland Coll., Baton Rouge, La., 1944-46; mem. Ed. com. Columbia Area Cham. of Commerce; Natl. Negro Churman; mem., Gen. Bd. Natl. Coun. of Chs., USA; past pres., Columbus Chapter Frontiers Intl., Inc.; former mem., Franklin Co. Rent Control Bd.; mem., Pastor's section Div. of Ed., Natl. Coun. of Chs., USA; mem., Columbus Planned Parenthood Clinic; Omega Psi Phi; Mason; chrmn., Ohio Pastor's Convocation, 1957; awards: Omega Man of the Year, Columbus Chapter, 1957; Office: 428 Main St., Columbus, Ohio.

*HICKS, Jessie Mae, evangelist, b. Grapeland, Tex., Sept. 28, 1915; dau. James B. and Jeola H.; Mary Allen Jr. Coll., Crockett, Tex.; B. S., Tillotson Coll., Austin, Tex.; B. D., Howard Univ. Sch. of Rel.; currently evangelist, Natl. Bapt. Conv. of America; tchr., Sun. Sch., Zion Star Bapt. Ch., San Antonio, Tex.; mem., NAACP; Bd. of Dirs., Ella Orphanage Home; organizer and pres., San Antonio Bapt. Missionary Coun.; pres., Texas Beauty Culturist League; v. p., Natl. Beauty Culturist League; organizer and pres., San Antonio Beauticians; founder and instr., The Hicks Beauty School; statistician, The Senior Auxiliary of the Natl. Bapt. Conv. of Amer.; travels extensively, made two trips to Liberia, Africa to secure deeds to 1000 acres of land for the Natl. Bapt. Conv. of America to do mission and educational work; 1964 guest speaker, Jamaica (Natl. Bapt. Conv.); toured the Holy Lands, 1956; awards: Woman of the Year, Zeta Phi Beta Sorority; citation by Tillotson Coll; awarded an honorary degree, the Union Bapt. Sem., Houston, Tex.; citation by the Business Dept. of Tex. Teacher Assn.; a community award by San Antonio Cham. of Commerce for outstanding work; a trophy by San Antonio Cham. of Commerce for outstanding business and religious personality; Home: 802 Dekota, San Antonio, Tex.; Office: New Branufels Ave., San Antonio, Tex.

HICKS, Jimmie Charles, b. Crystal Springs, Miss., Dec.

3, 1935; s. Clifton L. and Artimessia H.; m. Eunice Catchings; pastor, St. James A. M. E. Z. Ch., Tallulah, La., 1963-present; ordained elder, A. M. E. Z. Ch., 1965; owner, H. & T. Grocery, Crystal Springs, Miss.; pres. local br. NAACP; asst. dir., Copiah Co. Voter's Edu. Project; Mason; Bd. of Dir., Little League Baseball Team Bd. of Dir., Crystal Improvement Club; Home: 329-1/2 Bell St., Crystal Springs, Miss. 39059

HICKS, John Josephus, b. Bronwood, Ga., Feb. 13, 1915; s. Noble and Julia Mae Dasher; A. B., Paine Coll., Augusta, Ga., 1938; B. D., Gammon Theol. Sem., Atlanta, Ga., 1941; Th. M., Univ. of So. Calif., 1944; D. D. (hon.), Gammon Theol. Sem., 1956; m. Pollie Bledsoe; Children--John, Jr., Eldon, Raiford, Paula, Emma; pastor, Barnesville Meth. Ch., Ga., 1940-41; St. Johns Meth. Ch., Los Angeles, Calif., 1941-55; Union Meml. Meth. Ch., 1955--; prof., Reid Coll. of Rel., 1952-54; pres., St. Louis Bd. of Ed.; mem., Bd. of Dirs., Page Park; YMCA; awards: Natl. Assn. of Coll. Women, 1962; Man of the Year 1959; Assn. of Colored Womens Clubs, 1964; Public Service Award, St. Louis Argus; mem., Phi Beta Sigma; Frontiers of America Intl.; Chi Alpha Fraternity; Home: 4160 Enright, St. Louis, Mo.; Office: St. Mark's Meth. Ch., 49 Edgecomb Ave., New York, N. Y.

HICKS, Luther Clemon, b. Norfolk, Va., Apr. 27, 1922; s. Elijah and Hattie; B. A., Va. Union Univ., 1956; D. of Optometry, Monroe Coll. of Optometry, 1950; B. D., Va. Union Univ. Sch. of Rel., 1959; courses: Jane Adams Sch. of Soc. Work, Chgo., Ill.; m. Doris Wood; Children--Luther, Lawrence; pastor, 1st Bapt. Ch., Portsmouth, Va., 1955-59; asst. to chap., Va. State Penitentiary, Richmond, Va., 1958-59; Cook Co. Hosp., Chgo, Ill., 1959-60; pastor, St. Paul Meth. Ch., Robbins, Ill., 1960-62; case worker, Cook Co. Dept. of Public Aid, Chgo., Ill, 1962-63; chap., Ill. State Pen., Pontiac, Ill., 1963-66; pastor, Riverside Park Meth. Ch., Indianapolis, 1966-present; instr., Chrstn. Theol., Chgo., Bapt. Inst.; commn., Min. in Inst., Ch. Fed. of Indianapolis dist. repr., Com. on Soc. Concerns, NW Indiana Conf., Meth. Ch.; Com. Housing, Ch. Fed., Indianapolis, Ind.; pres., NAACP, Indianapolis, Ind.; repr. NAACP, Pontiac, Ill.; mem., Citizens Adv. Com., Indianapolis; Adv. Com. CAAP; pres., Riverside Civic League, Indianapolis; Adv. Com., NW Action Coun.,

Indianapolis; US Coast Guard, 1942-46; awards, merit, NAACP; mem., Mason; Home: 1517 W. 25th St., Indianapolis, Ind. 46208; Office: 2440 Harding St., Indianapolis, Ind.

HICKS, Richard Louis, Jr., b. Alexandria, La.; son Richard Louis, Sr. and Agnes (Moses) H.; B.A., Fla. A & M Univ., Tallahassee, Fla., 1949; M.A., Western Res. Univ., Cleveland, O., 1952; B.D., The Div. Sch. of Kenyon Coll. (Bexley Hall), 1956; m. Pearly Mae Wilson; Children--Cyntia Delores, Patricia Agnes, William Joseph, Richard Lami; instr. of dramatics, Fla. A & M Univ., 1949-53; curate, St. Andrew's Episc. Ch., 1956; chap., Cuttington Coll. & Div. Sch., 1957-60; rector, Trinity Pro-Cathedral, 1957-60; chap. A & T and Bennett and priest-in-charge, Ch. of the Redeemer, Greensboro, N.C., 1960--; chrmn., Greensboro Ministers Forum, 1962--; recording sec., Greater Greensboro Ministers Fellowship; mem., Mayor's Special Bi-Racial Comm., 1962; chrmn., Greensboro Citizens Coordinating Comm., 1962--; US Army, 1942-48; awards: Knight Commander; Order of Afr. Redemption (Liberian govt.); mem., Inst. of Pastoral Care, Acad. of Rel. and Health, Episc. overseas Missionary Soc., Episc. Soc. for College Wk., NAACP, Omega Psi Phi; article--Liberia: Land of Change; Home: 1605 Lansdown Ave., Greensboro, N.C.; Office: 901 E. Market St., Greensboro, N.C.

HICKS, Richard Ross, b. Milford, Del., Oct. 20, 1931; s. Wellington Oswald and Georgia (H.); B.S., Hampton Inst., Hampton, Va., 1958; B.D., Crozer Theol. Sem., Chester, Pa., 1964; courses, Md. State Coll., Princess Anne, Md., 1967-68; m. Thelma Miller; Children--Terri Lynn, Stephanie Wynne, Georgia Sue; pastored United Meth. Chs., Townsend, Del., 1961-63; Chestertown, Md., 1963-67; Princess Anne, Md., May 1967-present; mem., Bd. of Ed., Peninsula Conf. of U. Meth. Ch.; dist. dir., Adult Ed., Salisburg, Dist., Peninsula Conf., Bd. of ministerial training & qualifications, Peninsula Conf.; dist. dir., counseling Elder Program, Salisburg Dist. U. Meth. Ch.; dir., Wesley Found., Md. State Coll.; former dist. youth coun., Chestertown Dist. U. Meth. Ch. (Peninsula Conf.); ex. com., Somerset Co. br. NAACP; mem., Somerset Co. Men for Progress; former counselor, youth services commn. state of Del.; tchr., Bridge House, Del.; tchr., Charlotte, N.C., 1959-60; Williamsburg, Va., 1958-59; US Army, 1952-55; Home:

33 E. Broad St., Princess Anne, Md. 21853; Office: 35 E. Broad St., Princess Anne, Md. 21853.

HIGGINS, Samuel L., b. Ft. Worth, Tex., May 11, 1923; s. L. J. and Elnora (Evans) H.; B. S., Univ. of Denver, 1954; Th. B., Western Theol. Sem., 1963; m. Virginia Ricks; Children--Donald, Benita; realtor, accountant; pastor, Chrstn. Meth. Episc. Chs.; St. Mark, Oakland, Calif.; Amos Meml., Ogden, Utah; current, Coleman C. M. E. Chapel, Memphis, Tenn.; reg. treas., Omega Psi Phi; sec., Bd. dirs., Men of Tomorrow, Inc.; mem., Western Urban League, San Francisco; awards: Purple Heart; Amer. Defense and Weapons Medals; mem., Mason; Elks; NAACP, Rocky Mtn.; Cham. of Commerce Bd.; Home: 988 Springdale St., Memphis, Tenn. 38108; Office: 1154 Argyle St., Memphis, Tenn. 38107

HIGGS, Raymond Clarence, b. Poplar Bluff, Mo., Aug. 30, 1925; s. Rufus and Arcadia (Mitchell); B. A., Bishop Coll., Marshall, Tex., 1949; B. Th., Western Bapt. Bible Coll., Kan. City, Mo., 1967; m. Catherine Montgomery; children--Brenda Gale; pastor, Mt. Zion Bapt. Ch., Abilene, Kan., 1950-51; Mt. Olive Bapt. Ch., S. Pk., Kan., 1951-55; Mt. Carmel Bapt. Ch., Topeka, Kan., 1955-58; Bethel Bapt. Ch., Kan. City, Kan., 1959-present counselor, Kaw Valley Dist. Camp; tchr., Booker T. Wash. Sch.; volunteer chap., Doug. Hosp., Benthany Hosp., Primrose Villa Sr. Citizens Home; US Army, 1944-46; award: Good Conduct Medal; mem., Civic Club; Bapt. Min. Union, Kan. City, Kan.; Home: 4135 Bellefontaine, Kan City, Mo. 64130; Office: 2415 N. Sherman, Kan. City, Kan. 66101

HILDEBRAND, Richard Allen, b. Winsboro, S. C., Feb. 1, 1916; A. B., Allen Univ., 1938; B. D., Wilberforce Univ., 1941; S. T. M., Boston Univ., 1948; D. D. (hon.), Wilberforce Univ., 1951; m. Anna B. Lewis; children--Camille; pastor, in S. C., Jonestown and Akron, O., Providence, R. I., New York, Wilmington, Del.; current pastor, Bethel Afr. Meth. Episc. Ch., 1954--; 1st Negro pres., Manhattan Div. of Prot. Coun. of New York; pres., NAACP (NYC); mem., Alpha Phi Alpha; Mason; Home: 52 W. 132nd St., New York, N. Y. 10037; Office: 54-60 W. 132nd St., New York, N. Y. 10037

HILL, Abraham Alton, b. Lockhart, Tex., May 6, 1908; s. Isaac and Mary Elizabeth H.; Tillotson Coll., Austin,

Tex., 1921-22; Guadalupe Coll., Seguin, Tex., 1925-31; m. Jewell V. Lockhart; Children--Walter LaDell, A. Alton, Jr., Herman M. Davis; pastor, Mt. Moriah Bapt. Ch., Hillsboro, Tex.; Plastine Bapt. Ch., San Antonio, Tex.; Mt. Moriah Bapt. Ch., Elgin, Tex.; First Bapt. Ch., Memphis, Tenn.; Mt. Zion Bapt. Ch., Evanston, Ill., 1953--; pres., Evanston Coun. of Chs.; trustee bd., F.O.R.; mem., N. Suburban Bd.; NAACP bd.; Evanston's Urban Renewal Bd.; chrmn. Bd. of Bapt. State M. & E. Conv. of Ill.; Bapt. World Alliance, London, 1955, Brazil, 1961; mem., Gen. Natl. Bapt. Conv.; Home: 1109 Clark St., Evanston, Ill. 60201

HILL, Charles Andrew, b. Detroit, Mich., April 28, 1893; s. Edward and Mary (Lantz) H.; B.Th., Lincoln Univ., Chester, Pa., 1918; D.D. (hon.), Rust Coll., Miss.; m. Georgia R.; Children--4 sons, 3 daus.; assoc. pastor, Second Bapt. Ch., Detroit (3 yrs.); pastor, Hartford Ave. Bapt. Ch., 1920-present; past pres., Detroit NAACP; chrmn., Sojourner Truth Housing Com.; Com. to secure jobs for women during WW II; Com. opposed to police brutality; Progressive Bapt. Conv., Natl. Publishing Com.; candidate City Council (5 times); mem., Interracial Com. (1943); Home: 1660 W. Grand Blvd., Detroit, Mich. 48208; Office: 6300 Hartford Ave., Detroit, Mich. 48210

HILL, Daniel Graxton, sem. dean, prof., b. Annapolis, Md., May 26, 1896; s. Daniel G., Sr. and Margaret (Peck) H.; B.A., Lincoln Univ., Pa., 1917; B.D., Iliff Sch. of Theol., Denver, Colo., 1928; soc. work, Univ. of Oregon, 1930; M.A., 1932; S.T.M., Pacific Sch. of Rel., 1935; Th.D., Iliff Sch. of Theol., 1946; D.D. (hon.), Lincoln Univ., 1963; m. May Louise Edwards; children--Jeane M. (Mrs. Sidney Flateau), Margaret T. (Mrs. Harry I. Martin), Daniel E., III, Doris M. (Mrs. Salter Cochran); pastor, Afr. Meth. Chs., Mo., Colo., Oregon, Calif., 1921-45; mem. faculty, Sch. of Rel., Howard Univ.; dean, Chapel, Howard Univ., 1945-57; dean, Sch. of Rel., Howard Univ., 1958-64; pastor, Wash. Conf. Meth. Ch., 1950--; tchr., Berean Sch., Phila., Pa., 1919-20; tchr., History and Ethics, Western Univ., Kan. City, Kan., 1923-24; probation officer, Court of Domestic Relation, Portland, Ore., 1930-33; case aide and supervisor, State Relief Adm., Oakland, Calif., 1936-40; US Army, 1917-19, 2nd Lt.; mem., Acad., Political and Soc. Science; Natl. Assn. of Coll.

and Univ. Chaplains; Alpha Phi Alpha; editor, Well Springs of Life, book of chapel sermons; contributor: Best Sermons, 1947; article on Afr. Meth. Episc. Ch. in the Encyclopedia Americana, 1951; Home: 2946 Chain Bridge Rd. NW, Wash, D. C. Office: Howard Univ. Sch. of Religion, Wash., D. C.

HILL, Robert Arlander, church official, b. Sturgis, Ky., Aug. 16, 1913; s. Henry H. and Rebecca (Fortson) H.; Evansville Coll., 1952; Tri-State Bapt. Bible Coll., Evansville, Ind., 1955; m. Minnie Mary Dunlap; Children--Herman, George Sherman; pres., Central Dist. Assn., Ind., 1957-64 pres., Mt. Olive State Sun. Sch. & B. T. U. Cong. of Ind., 1956-64; financial sec., Natl. Bapt. Song Leaders Convention, 1960--; pastor, Second Bapt. Ch., Vincennes, Ind., 1954-64; current pastor, Seventh St. Bapt. Ch., 1964; mem., Citizens Participation Comm. & Spec. Comm., Minority Group Housing, Vincennes, Ind., 1963--; Bd. of Chaplains, Knox Co. Min. Alliance; Good Samaritan Hosp., Vincennes, Ind., 1962-63; Home: 903 Clark St., Paducah, Ky.; Office: 504 So. 7th St., Paducah, Ky.

HILL, Wright Albert, b. Pollocksville, N. C., Nov. 4, 1890; s. Senus and Mary H.; Eastern Acad., 1912 m. Emma Murphy; children--Ernest Franklin, Mrs. Ella Payton, Mrs. Nancy J. Peyton, Mrs. Emma Davis, Wright A., Jr., Mrs. Georgie Mae Lorick, Robert Louis; tchr., pub. schs. in Jones, Onslow, Pamlico Counties, N. C., 30 yrs.; pastor, N. C. Conf., A. M. E. Z. Chs., 52 yrs.; retired, 1966; v. p., Community Assn., Pollocksville, N. C.; Knight of Pythias, Mason, Oddfellow; Home: Pollocksville, N. C. 28573

HINES, Lincoln Fisher, b. Birmingham, Ala., Mar. 31, 1940; s. Janie Emma H.; A. B., Daniel Payne Coll., Birmingham, Ala.; Pacific Sch. of Rel., Los Angeles, Calif.; m. Bessie Marie Belden; children--Artrina Marie assoc. pastor, Grant Chapel A. M. E. Ch., Long Beach, Calif., 1960-64; pastor, Union Bethel A. M. E. Ch., Great Falls, Mont., 1964-66; pastor, Quinn Chapel A. M. E. Ch., Jefferson City, Mo., 1966-present; mem., Bd. of local NAACP; mem., Adv. Bd. of Jefferson City, Commn. on Rel. and Race; rec'd Citizenship Award for outstanding public service, Birmingham, Ala., 1958; Mason; Home: 1107 E. Dunklin St., Jefferson City, Mo. 65101; Office: 529 Lafayette St., Jefferson City, Mo.

HINES, Thomas E., Jr. Capt. (Chaplain), b. Grantville, Ga., July 10, 1939; s. Thomas E. and Louise (H.); B. A., Clark Coll., Atlanta, Ga., 1961; B. D. Interdenom. Theol. Center, Atlanta, Ga., 1964; m. Peggy C. Slade; Children--Trina L., Thomas E. III; pastor, Fullers Chapel United Meth. Ch., Zebulon, Ga., 1961-64; M. L. Harris Meth. Ch., 1964-67; chap., Ft. Knox, Ky., 1967-68; 9th Inf. Div., So. Vietnam, 1968-present; tchr., Columbus, Ga., 1966-67; Home: 437 Pryor St., Atlanta, Ga. 30303; Office: HHC 2/60 Infantry, 9th Infantry Div., APO San Francisco 96371

HODGES, Sloan Stanley, b. Hodges, S. C., May 15, 1913; s. George and Malissa (Vaughns) H.; B. Th., Amer. Bapt. Theol. Sem., Nashville, Tenn., 1948; m. Martha Ruth Treece; licensed to preach in St. John Bapt. Ch., Miami, Fla., 1939; ordained at Sylvan St. Bapt. Ch., Nashville, Tenn., 1942; asst. pastor, Hartford Ave. Bapt. Ch., Detroit, Mich., 1940-44; First Bapt. Ch., Toronto, Canada, 1944-46; pastor, Thankful Bapt. Ch., Johnson City, Tenn., 1946-50; current, Pilgrim Bapt. Ch., Hamilton, Ohio, 1950--; relocation supervisor, Hamilton Urban Renewal Agency, 1958-61; trustee of Ft. Hamilton Hosp., Hamilton, Ohio, 1953--; pres., Second Ward Community Center Bd., 1960 and presently a mem. of the Bd.; mem., Goodwill Industry Adv. Bd. of Hamilton, Ohio; The Mayor's Friendly Relations Comm.; Home: 1028 S. Second St., Hamilton, Ohio 45011; Office: 337 Chestnut St., Hamilton, Ohio 45011

HOGGARD, Dennie W., b. Bertie Co., N. C., June 5, 1897; s. Morgan and Alice (Rainer) H.; Roanoke Collegiate Inst., Elizabeth City, N. C.; Moody Bible Sch.; D. D. (hon.), Va. Sem., Lynchburg, Va.; m. Isabel E. Ricks; Children--Dennie W., Jr., Olga Elizabeth, Phyllis Yolards, Watson; pastor, Calvary Bapt. Ch., Plainfield, N. J., 10-1/2 yrs.; current pastor, Mt. Carmel Bapt. Ch., Phila., Pa., 30 yrs.; former mem., State legislature for 4 terms, 8 yrs.; chrmn., Foreign Mission Bd., Natl. Bapt. Convention, USA, Inc.; mem., NAACP; Home: 558 No. 58th St., Philadelphia, Pa.; Office: 5732-34 Pace St., Phila., Pa.

HOGGARD, J. Clinton, b. Jersey City, N. J., Aug. 9, 1916; s. Jeremiah Matthew and Symera (Cherry) H.; A. B., Rutgers Univ., 1939; B. D., Union Theol. Sem., N. Y. City, 1942; D. D. (hon.) Livingstone Coll., Salisbury,

N. C., 1956; m. Eva Stanton; Children--J. Clinton Jr., Paul S.; pastor, St. Francis Afr. Meth. Episc. Zion Ch., Mt. Kisco, N. Y., 1940-42; Inst. A. M. E. Z. Ch., Yonkers, N. Y, 1942-51; Little Rock A. M. E. Z. Ch., Charlotte, N. C., 1951-52; sec., treas., Bd. of Foreign Missions, A. M. E. Z. Ch., NYC, 1952-present; lecturer, Consult. Div. of Chrstn. Life and Work, Gen. Assembly, and Bd., Natl. Coun. Chs. USA; v. chrmn., Municipal Housing Authority, Yonkers, N. Y., 1945-51; mem., World Coun. Chs., Div. World Missions and Evangelism World Meth. Conf.; Urban League; NAACP; Alpha Phi Alpha; Republican; editor, Official Missions pub., The Missionary Seer; Home: 715 S. 6th Ave., Mt. Vernon, N. Y. 10550; Office: 475 Riverside Dr., Room 1910, New York, N. Y. 10027

HOLLOMAN, John Lawrence Sullivan, educator, b. Powellsville, N. C., Apr. 24, 1885; s. Turner and Amy (Freeman) H.; A. B., Union Univ., Richmond, Va.; M. A., Frelinghuysen Univ., Wash., D. C.; pastorates, Hertford, Bertie, and Northampton Cos., N. C.; Second Bapt. Ch., Wash., D. C., 1917-present; m. Rosa Victoria Jones; 4 daus., Carolyn H. Troupe, Jessie H. Jackson, Dr. Marjorie H. Parker, Miss Grace F., 1 son, Dr. J. L. S. Holloman, Jr.; mem., four Bapt. World Alliance congresses, Toronto 1928, Atlanta 1939, Cleveland 1950, London, Eng., 1955; instr. Waters Normal Inst., 1910-1917; dean, Wash. Bapt. Sem., Wash., D. C.; Home: 403 P St., NW, Wash., D. C.; Office: 816 3rd St., NW, Wash., D. C.

HOLLOWAY, Frederick Douglas, Sr., b. Mexia, Tex.; s. Samuel and Ammy H.; Paul Quinn Coll., 1916-17, 1925-26; Houston Coll., Rel., Austin, Tex. 2 summers; Prairie View, Tex., 3 sessions; m. Oleta Carruthers; Children--Minne Lee (Mrs. Williams), Freddie Marie (Mrs. Brown), Ruby Faye (Mrs. Hendrix), Ethelyn (Mrs. Harbert), F. D. Jr., Ada Mae (Mrs. Lewis), Samuel; pastor and pres. elder, Afr. Meth. Episc. Ch., Corpus Christi, Temple, and Corsicana Dists.; Anderson Chapel, Wichita Falls; Bethel, Cameron; Grant Chapel, Palestine Payne Chapel, Houston; Jones Chapel, Houston; Bethel, Belton; St. James, Terrell; Bradford Chapel, Bonham; Wesley Chapel, Georgetown; Dallas Howard, Waco and a number of others; tchr., pub. sch., 7 yrs.; mem., Connectional Bd. of Evangelism; Republican; chrmn., Precinct 10A, Waco, Tex.; del., McLennan Co. to State

Republican Conv., Houston, Tex.; mem., Waco Min. Assn.; Interdenom. Min. Alliance; 10 musical compositions; several poems, ed., The Minister's Digest No. 1-3; Home: 506 Rose St., Waco, Tex., 76704

HOLLOWAY, James Romeo, b. S.C., June 20, 1912; s. Tucker and Rosa Holloway; (H.); A.B., Morehouse Coll., 1943; B.D., Colgate-Rochester, 1945; S.T.M., Boston Univ., Sch. of Theol., 1964; m. Christine Heard; Children--Edwin McNeill; James R. Jr.; pastor, First Bapt. Ch., La Grange, Ga., 1945-47; dir., Mecklenburgh Bapt. Inter-racial Commn., 1947-51; pastor, Mt. Pleasant Bapt. Ch., Cambridge, Mass., 1952-54; Western Ave. Bapt. Ch., Cambridge, Mass., 1954-59; Zion Bapt. Ch., Mpls., Minn., 1959-present; Home: 6829 Medicine Lake Rd., Mpls., Minn.; Office: 1023 Lyndale Ave., No. Mpls., Minn.

HOLMAN, Alonzo William, b. Lincolnville, S.C., Oct. 9, 1934; s. Alonzo Franklin and Lillie Bell (Ross) H.; A.B., Allen Univ., 1955; B.D., Dickerson Theol. Sem., 1958; m. Gerald Eloise Smith; pastor, Waterloo Circuit, Laurens Co., S.C., 1954; Mt. Zion A.M.E. Ch., Graniteville, S.C., 1956-59; Cumberland A.M.E. Ch., Aiken, S.C., 1959-present; mem., Aiken Coun. Min. Alliance; Chrstn. Action Coun.; Trustee bd., Allen Univ.; pres., Aiken br. NAACP; first v.p., S.C. Conf. of branches of NAACP; chrmn., Aiken Coun. Voter Educ. Project; mem., Aiken Coun., Bd. of Dir., Amer. Cancer Cos.; mem., S.C. Coun. on Human Relations; first Negro mem., Greater Aiken Cham. of Commerce; mem., Manpower Devel. Trng. Commn. for Aiken Co.; mem., Campaign Comm., Democrat; del., Co. and State Conventions (Democrat) 1966; Mason; Home: 111 Kershaw St., SE, Aiken, S.C. 29801

HOLMES, J. Arthur, b. Georgetown, S.C., Oct. 26, 1920; s. Saul and Mary H.; A.B., Allen Univ., Columbia, S.C.; D.D. (hon.), Monrovia Coll., Liberia, Africa; B.D., Payne Theol. Sem., Wilberforce Univ., Wilberforce, O.; courses: Syracuse Univ., N.Y.; m. Edith Reynolds; Children--Arthuretta, J. Arthur, Jr.; instr., pub. schs., S.C.; prof., Ethics, Biblical Lit. and Psych. of Rel., Allen Univ.; pastor, Greater Trinity A.M.E. Ch., Spartanburg, S.C.; pastor, Little White Hall Mission, Spartanburg; presiding eleder, Columbia Dist., A.M.E. Ch., Columbia Conf.; pastor, Bethel A.M.E. Ch., Columbia,

S. C., 1949-present; pres., A. M. E. Alliance of Columbia; pres., Interdenom. Min. Alliance, Columbia; v. p., Columbia Min.; mem., City Hall Bi-racial Comm. on Better Human Relations; Adv. Comm., S. C. State Hosp.; Operation Com., USO; former mem., Commn. on Ed., A. M. E. Ch.; Alpha Phi Alpha; Mason; v. chrmn., Richland Co. Anti-Poverty Program; trustee, Allen Univ.; Home: 2507 Waites Rd., Columbia, S. C.; Office: 1528 Sumter St., Columbia, S. C.

HOLMES, John William, b. Hawkinsville, Ga., Dec. 24, 1913; s. Thomas and Louise (Harrell) H.; A. B., Livingstone Coll., Salisbury, N. C., 1934-38; B. D., Yale Univ. Div. Sch., New Haven, Conn., 1938-43; pastor, St. Stephen A. M. E. Z. Ch., Branford, Conn., 1938-41; McKinley A. M. E. Z. Ch., Norwich Conn., 1942-46; Mt. Pleasant A. M. E. Z. Ch., Danbury, Conn., 1946-49; Douglass Meml. Ch., New Bedford, Mass., 1949-51; Watertown, N. Y., 1951-54; Rush Meml. A. M. E. Z. Ch., Cambridge Mass., 1954-55; St. Paul A. M. E. Z. Ch., Amsterdam, N. Y., 1955-61; Myers Tabernacle Ch., Charlotte, N. C., 1961-present; hosp. chap., Amsterdam, N. Y., 1955-61; mem., Mason; Elk, Omega Psi Phi, Republican; Pub. Relations Dir., First Episc. Dist. of A. M. E. Z. Ch.; Home: 509 Cherry St., Charlotte, N. C. 28204; Office: 511 Cherry St., Charlotte, N. C. 28204

HOLMES, Wesley Clyde, b. Vaiden, Miss., Apr. 25, 1917; s. Wess and Mary Jane (Brooks); B. S., Rust Coll., Howe Sch. of Rel., Memphis, Tenn., 1939-40; M. Div. Memphis Theol. Sem., Memphis, Tenn., 1969; m. Earline Towns; children--Lynn Renee, Jan Michels; pastor, Elcanaan Bapt. Ch., Whiteville, Tenn., 1939-45; Everdale Bapt. Ch., Water Valley, Miss., 1943-48; St. John Bapt. Ch., Memphis, Tenn., 1943-48; Mt. Vernon Bapt. Ch., Memphis, Tenn., 1948-55; Beulah Bapt. Ch., Memphis, Tenn., 1955-present; pres., Sardis Coll., Sardis, Miss., 1945-48; chrmn. Non-partisan Voters Regis. Org. 1960; Dev. Com. of Orange Mound Nursery Bd.; Exec. Com. of Trustee Bd. of Owen Coll., 1968; mem., NAAC moderator, Tenn. Bapt. Missionary & Ed. Assn.; chrmn. of Mission Div. of Tenn. Coun. of Chs.; Home: 2399 Douglass, Memphis, Tenn. 38114; Office: 2407 Douglass Memphis, Tenn.

HOLMES, Willie Lawnsie, coll. pres.; b. Ealnor, Ala., Apr. 13, 1913; s. Joe and Elizabeth (Lewis); A. B., Univ.

of Louisville, 1950; B.D., Th.M., Southern Bapt. Sem., 1954, 1957; D.D. (hon.), Simmons Univ., 1959; Cincinnati Theol. Sem., 1962; m. Annie Beatrice Woods; pastor, First Baptist Eminence Ch., Eminence, Ky., 1951-56; pres., Simmons Univ., Louisville, Ky., 1956--; instr., Simmons Univ., 1954--; Rel. Adv. Bd., Jefferson Co. Jail, Louisville, 1958--; chrmn., Bd. of Dirs., Louisville Area Health Center; Counseling Staff mem., Jefferson Co. Jail, 1956--; mem., Planned Parenthood Adv. Bd., 1961--; US Forces, 1943-45; Home: 900 So. 42nd, Louisville, Ky.; Office: 1811 Dumesnil St., Louisville, Ky. 40210

HOLMES, Zan Wesley, Jr., b. San Angelo, Tex., Feb. 2, 1935; s. Zan Wesley and Blakely Naomi H.; A.B., Huston-Tillotson Coll., Austin, Tex., 1956; B.D., Perkins Sch. of Theol., Southern Meth. Univ., Dallas, Tex.; S.T.M.; m. Dorothy Burse; pastor, Hamilton Park Meth. Ch., Dallas, Tex., 1958--; treas., Dallas Pastors Assn.; chrmn., Conf. Comm. on Min. Recruitment; chrmn., Conf. "Our Mission Study"; mem., Bd. of Carnation Charity Home; Dallas Traffic Commission; Dallas Chapt. of Amer. Red Cross; Alpha Phi Alpha; Democrat; Dallas Pastors Assn.; Meth. Ministers Fellowship; Interdenom. Min. Alliance, Dallas; Home: 8418 Bunche, Dallas, Tex.; Office: 11881 Schroeder, Dallas, Tex.

HONORÉ, Thomas Francis, b. Baton Rouge, La., Sept. 7, 1936; s. Marshall and Evelyn (Darensbourg) H.; A.B., St. Joseph's Sem. & Coll., 1965; tchr., Epiphany Apostolic Coll., 1965-May 1968; Newburgh, N.Y., mem., Bd. of Dir. Lander St. Community Center; Ex. comm. NAACP Newburgh, N.Y.; currently pursuing degree, Urban studies, Chgo.; Home: 758 S. Springfield Ave., Chgo., Ill. 60624

HOOD, Robert E., author, b. Louisville, Ky., Feb. 29, 1936; s. G.R. and B. (Tubbs) H.; A.B., Ohio Wesleyan Univ., 1957; Union Theol. Sem., 1957-59; S.T.B., Gen. Theol. Sem., 1960; Oxford Univ., England, 1962-63; asst. pastor, St. Philip's Ch., New York City, 1960-62; asst. pastor, Chapel of the Intercession, Trinity Parish, New York City, 1962--; mem., Soc. for Biblical Exegesis; Episc. Soc. for Cultural and Racial Unity; Beta Sigma Tau; Omicron Delta Kappa; Phi Beta Kappa; Theta Alpha Phi (Dramatics honorary); Delta Sigma Rho (Debate honorary); author: The Absurdity of Corporate Worship;

Home: 550 W. 155th St., New York, N.Y.

*HOPKINS, Thomas Ewell, social worker, b. Sontag, Va., Aug. 30, 1908; s. Daniel Thomas and Cora Ann H.; A.B., W. Va. State Coll., 1933; B.D., Howard Univ., Sch. of Rel., 1938; Grad. Sch. of Howard Univ., M.A., 1939; m. Esther Harrison; Children--Susan, Thomas, Jr.; dir., Rel. Edu., Vermont Ave. Bapt. Ch., Wash., D.C.; pastor, First Bapt. Ch., W. Washington, D.C.; pastor, The Union Bapt. Ch., Stamford, Conn.; Rockview-Brookside Community Ch., New Haven; tchr., pub. sch. system, Va. and The Wash. Bapt. Sem.; social investigator, Dept. of Welfare, City of New Haven; exec. sec., Dixwell Min. Alliance; chap., Masons; Home: 77 Beers, New Haven, Conn.; Office: City Welfare Dept., 196 Bassett, New Haven, Conn.

HORSLEY, Leroy, b. Kinston, N.C., Dec. 22, 1930; s. William and Beaddie (Rouse) H.; B.S., Fayetteville Tchrs Coll., Fayetteville, N.C., 1959; B.D., Johnson C. Smith Univ., Charlotte, N.C., 1963; m. Geneva Louise Knight; Children--Cynthia, Edwin; current, pastor, Mt. Pelier Presby. Ch., U.S., Rowland, N.C., 1962-63; pastor, Anys Chapel Presby. Ch., U.S., Maxton, N.C., 1963; pastor, Covenant Presby. Ch., U.S., Kannapolis, N.C., 1962-63; Bellefonte President, UP USA Harrisburg, N.C. 1962-63; Area Voluntary Worker for state vocational rehabilitation; Adv. to Community Improvement Assn.; US Army, 1951-52; Good conduct medal; mem., NAACP Elks, American Legion, Republican; Home: Box 581, Rowland, N.C.

HORTON, Frank Lewis, Granttown, W. Va., July 18, 1937; s. Timothy and Mattie; A.B., Salem Coll., Salem, W. Va., 1965; Rel. D., Claremont, Sch. of Theol. (Calif.), 1968; D.D. (hon.), Reed Coll. of Rel., Los Angeles, 1968; m. Carolyn Yvonne Blackmon; Children--Monica, Cynthia Reneé, Frances Louise; pastored, United Meth. Chs., McKendree, Cumberland, Md., 1963-64; Trinity, Clarksburg, W. Va., 1964-65; Bethel, Los Angeles, 1965-68; pastor to the House of the Carpenter, Wheeling, W. Va., 1968-present; prof., Wheeling Coll., present; US Navy, 1955-58; US Air Force, 1958-62; mem., Alpha Phi Omega; Bd. Dir., Black Meth. for Church Renewal; Home: Box 49A Rd 3 Stone Church Rd., Wheeling, W. Va 26003; Office: 96 Zane St., Wheeling, W. Va. 26003

HORTON, James Aguinaldo, b. Chicago, Ill., Feb. 13, 1925; s. Andrew and Marie; B. Th., Chgo. Bapt. Inst., 1954; m. Janie King; Children--James, JoAnne, David, Stephanie; pastor, Central Pk. Bapt. Ch., 1963; Grt. Union Bapt. Ch., 1967; sec., ILA Local 19 Longshoremen, 1964-67; tchr., Chgo. Bapt. Inst.; sec., Northwood River Dist. Assn.; 2nd v. p., Bapt. Min. Alliance of Chgo.; mem., Rosicrucian Order; Home: 4320 Wilcox St., Chgo., Ill., 60624; Office: Grt. Union Bapt. Ch., 1956 W. Warren Blvd., Chgo., Ill.

HOUSTON, Charles Edward, b. Benham, Ky., Jan. 4, 1914; s. John and Agnes (Bradley) H.; A. B., Morehouse Coll., Atlanta, Ga., 1939; B. D., Union Theol. Sem., NYC, 1942; Adv. Study, N. T. Greek, Union, 1949-50; m. Mary Ann Patterson; Children--Charles, Jr., Cornelia, Mary, Jeanne; ordained Bapt. min., 1942; pastoral asst., Providence Bapt. Ch., Atlanta, Ga., 1935-39; field work stu., Ch. of the Master, NYC, 1939-41; Salem Meth. Ch., 1941-42; pastor, Shiloh Bapt. Ch., Tuckahoe, N. Y., 1946--; mem., faculty and Bd. Dir., Bapt. Edu. Center, N. Y., N. Y.; chrmn., Chrstn. Edu. Comm., Empire Missionary Bapt. Conv.; faculty and Bd. Dir., Empire Miss. Sun. Sch. & B. T. U. Congress; Commissioner, Tuckahoe Housing Authority, 1957-- (chrmn., 1962); treas., Central Hudson Bapt. Assn. (7 yrs.); dean, Sun. Sch. & B. T. U. Aux. (7 yrs.); pres., Sun. Sch. & B. T. U. Aux. (8 yrs.); Home: 61 Washington St., Tuckahoe, N. Y.; Church: 15 Marbledale Rd., Ruckahoe, N. Y.

HOUSTON, William Eugene, Jr., ch. administrator, b. Hot Springs, Ark., July 1, 1920; s. Wm. Eugene and Abbie (Austin) H.; A. B., Johnson C. Smith Univ., 1941; B. D., Johnson C. Smith, 1944; D. D., 1961, Johnson C. Smith Univ., Charlotte, N. C.; m. Lilla M. Johnson; children--Bjorn Lorenz, Cheryl Jeanne; pastor, Rendall Meml. Presby. Ch., 1944--; chap. NYC Hosp., Welfare Is., 1950-57; chap., Elmhurst Gen. Hosp., Queens, N. Y., 1957-60; chap. Dept. of Sanitation, NYC, 1960--; also v. moderator Presby. of NY, 1960-62; moderator Synod of NY U. P. Ch., 1962-63; exec. dir., Commission on Rel. and Race, Presby. of NYC, 1963; Bd. of Dirs., N. Y. J. B. Assn., 1957--; Bd. of Pensions United Presby. Ch., USA, 1960-66, chrmn., Central Harlem Coun. for Community Planning, 1957-59; chrmn. Public Relations Comm. and Ch. College Comm. Synod of N. Y., 1963--; chrmn. Commission on Rel. and Race, Presby. of NYC, 1964;

polemarch NY Alumni Chapter of Kappa Alpha Psi Fraternity, 1958-60; chrmn. Grand Chapter of Kappa Alpha Psi Nominating Committee, 1958-62; chrmn. Northern Manhattan Volunteers for Stevenson, 1952-56; Bd. of Dirs., Henry Hudson Historical Society Assn.; pres., Presby. Min. of NY & N.J., 1946-60; pres., Presby. Coun. of The North and West, 1956-58; v.p., Interdenor Min. Meetings of NY & Vicinity, 1947--; pres., Johnson C. Smith Univ. Club of N.Y., 1945-48, 1956-58; treas., N.Y. Tennis Association, 1960--; Umpire in Chief, NY State Championships A.T.A., 1959--; alternate referee, Natl. Championships Amer. Tennis Assn., 1962--; mem. Alpha Kappa Mu, Kappa Alpha Psi, Chi Alpha, Natl. Presby. Health and Welfare Assn., Acad. of Rel and Mental Health, Assn. of Amer. Prot. Hosp. Chaplains, County Comm., Democratic Party, N.Y. County, chaplain to NY State Legislature, NY City Council and twice to Democratic State Comm.; written for The Presbyterian, Presby. Tribune, Social Progress, Monday Morning, Football News, Social Compositions: Agnus Dei, Ordination Prayer, and musical setting for the Eucharist; Home: 2255 Fith Ave, New York, N.Y.; Church: 59-61 W. 137th St., New York, N.Y.

HOWARD, Arthur R., Jr., b. Allendale, S.C., Sept. 3, 1908; s. Arthur R., Sr. and Adelaide (Moses) H.; A.B., Claflin Coll., Orangeburg, S.C., 1932; S.T.B., S.T.M., Boston Univ., 1935, 1936; m. Emma Wathers; pastored, St. Andrews United Meth. Ch., Worcester, Mass., 1933-36; Second Meth. Ch., Anderson, Ind., 1938-39; Border Meth., Minneapolis, Minn., 1939-42; Asbury, Lexington, Ky., 1946-49; Mary Palmer Meth. Ch., Detroit, Mich., 1949-56; Hartzell Meml. U. Meth. Ch., Chgo., 1956-present; tchr., Rust Coll., Holly Springs, Miss.; Alcorn A & M Coll., Alcorn, Miss., Dir. chrmn Ky. United Charity Fund; chrmn., Cancer Drive, Chgo. (2 yrs.); T.B. Unit, Chgo.; chap., US Army (4 yrs.); awards, 2 service stars; mem., Kappa Alpha Psi; Mason editor & sec., Lexington Annual Conf. (8 yrs.) Home: 6129 So. Langley Ave., Chgo., Ill.; Office: 3330 Martin Luther King, Jr. Dr., Chgo., Ill.

HOWARD, Lawrence Wester, Sr., tchr., b. Blount Co., Tenn., Sept. 23, 1920; s. George and Bertha Elizabeth H.; Swift Meml. Jr. Coll., Rogersville, Tenn., 1935-37 A.B., Knoxville Coll., Knoxville, Tenn., 1943; courses: Howard Univ. Sch. of Rel.; Lincoln Univ.; m. Alice

McIver Turner; Children--Bertha Alice, Lawrence W., Jr.; pastor, Sanders Afr. Meth. Episc. Zion Ch., E. Tenn.; Jones Meml. A. M. E. Z. Ch., Greenville, Tenn.; St. Paul A. M. E. Z. Ch., Maryville, Tenn.; Allenyen A. M. E. Z. Ch., Phila., Pa.; A. M. E. Z. Chs., Harrisburg, Gettysburg, Allentown, Pa.; current pastor, St. Paul A. M. E. Z. Ch., Salisbury, Md.; county sch. tchr.; pres., PTA, Salisbury, Md.; former pres., Min. Alliance; current sec., Salisbury Min. Alliance; mem., Mason; Elk; Democrat; Scout Master; Home: 408 Delaware Ave., Salisbury, Md.

HOWELL, Cajus B., b. Nov. 7, 1911, Cabarrus, N. C.; s. James Edward and Dollie (Forest); A. B., Livingstone Coll., Salisbury, N. C., 1939; S. T. B., Eden Theol. Sem. and Boston Univ. Sch. of Theol., 1950; grad. studies, Iliff Sch. of Theol., Denver, Colo., 1957-58; m. Celeste Nadine Fearrington; Children--Oznathylee A. (Mrs. Richard Hopkins); pastor, Parker Chapel Circuit, A. M. E. Z. Ch., 1933-40; State St. Ch., Mobile, Ala.; chaplain, US Army, 1943-67; presiding elder, Dec. 1954, Canton-Jackson A. M. E. Z. So. Mississippi Conf. (2 yrs.); estab. first A. M. E. Z. Ch., Denver, Colo., 1956-64; pastor, Zion Hill A. M. E. Z. Ch., Concord, N. C., 1964-present; tchr., US Army Reserve Sch., Charlotte, N. C., 1965--; former Bd. of Dirs., Denver Coun. of Chs.; Denver Min. Alliance, 1957-58; Bd. mem. Denver Anti-Discrimination Comm., Chrmn., Social Action Comm., Cabarrus Co., Ministerial Assn., 1966-67; mem., YMCA; Alpha Phi Alpha; awards: Seven Bronze Stars; WW II Victory Medal; UN Ribbon; AM Theatre Ribbon; 4 O/S bars; Natl. Defense Medal; Occ. Medal Korean President Citation; K. S. Medal; Home: 215 Cabarrus Ave. West, Concord, N. C., 28025

HUCLES, Henry Boyd, III, hosp. chap., b. New York, N. Y., Sept. 21, 1923; s. Henry Boyd and Alma (Lewis) H.; B. S., Va. Union Univ., 1943; B. D., Bishop Payne Div. Sch., 1946; m. Manie Dalceda Adams; Children--Henry B. IV, Michael Edward; priest-in-charge, Grace Prot. Episc. Ch., Millers Tavern, Va.; St. Andrews Ch., Upright, Va., 1946-49; rector, St. George's Ch., Brooklyn, N. Y., 1949--; senior protestant chap., Bklyn House of Detention for Men; mem., Bd. of Mgrs., St. John's Episc. Hosp.; Bklyn Prot. Coun.; Alpha Phi Alpha; Home: 255 Monroe St., Bklyn, N. Y.; Office: 800 Marly Ave., Bklyn, N. Y.

HUDSON, Arthur Eaton, b. Halifax Co., N.C., Feb. 22, 1882; s. Eaton and Julia (H.); grad. Plymouth State & Industrial Sch., Plymouth, N.C., 1901; m. Rosa A. Jenneth (deceased), Esther Richardson; Children--Julia C. (Mrs. John Sweetner) deceased; pastored, Afr. Meth. Epis. Zion Chs., 1913-28; presiding elder, 1928-present; former tchr. Edgecombe Co., N.C.; Railway mail clerk, 1905-13; mem., Mason; Republican; Home: 1005 N. John St., Goldsboro, N.C. 27530

HUDSON, James, coll. prof., b. Birmingham, Ala., Oct. 1, 1903; s. Berry Henry and Alta (Hawkins) H.; A.B., Morehouse Coll., 1926; Oberlin Coll., 1928-29; B.D., Colgate-Rochester Div. Sch., 1929-31; A.M., Ph.D., Boston Univ., 1935, 1946; m. Augustine Josephine Lagarde; Children--James Lagarde; pub. sch. tchr., Lincoln Jr. High Sch., 1927-28; tchr. and coll. pastor, Leland Coll., Baker, La., 1931-42; pastor, Bradley Meml. Baptist Ch., Oak Bluffs, Mass., 1943-46; tchr. and chap., Fla. A & M Univ., 1946--; 3d v.p., Fla. A & M Univ. Clinical Assn., 1963-64; mem., Exec. Bd. of Inter-Civic Coun. (Tallahassee, Fla., 1956--); pres., Tallahassee Non-Partisan Voters Crusade, 1960--; mem., Exec. Comm. of Tallahassee Community Awakening Crusade, 1962--; mem., Alpha Phi Alpha Scholarship award; Phi Beta Sigma Social Action Award from Chapter at Fla. A & M Univ., 1956; former pres., Fla. Philosophical Assn.; Amer. Tchrs. Assn.; Natl. Assn. of Coll. and Univ.; Home: 712 Gamble St., Tallahassee, Fla.; Office: Box 251 Fla. A &M Univ., Tallahassee, Fla.

HUDSON, James Hammie, tchr., b. St. Harles, Lee Co., S.C., June 13, 1917; s. James and Jannie H.; Mayesville, Inst., 1926-34; Coulter Meml. Acad., Cheraw, S.C., 1936-37; Coulter Jr. College, Cheraw, S.C., 1936-39; A.B., Johnson C. Smith Univ., Charlotte, N.C. 1939-41; B.D., Seminary, 1946; '49; m. Mozelle Delois Peay; Children--James Hammie, Jr.; pastor, Pleasant Ridge Univ. Presby. Ch., Lancaster, S.C. and Pageland 2nd U. Presby. Ch., Pageland, S.C., 1948-51; Mt. Vernon U. Presby. Ch., Palatka, Fla. and Mather-Perit U. Presby. Ch., St. Augustine, Fla., 1952; Westminster U. Presby. Ch., Spartanburg, S.C., 1953-57; Calvary U. Presby. Ch. and Shiloh 1st U. Presby. Ch., Winnsboro, S.C., 1957--; dir. and tchr. of Rel. Ed., Harbison Jr. Coll., S.C., 1957-58; pres. Spartanburg Co. NAACP br. 1955-57; moderator, Atlantic Synod U. Presby. Ch.,

1962-63; moderator Fairfield, McClelland and the merged Fairfield-McClelland Presbyteries several terms; US Army 1941-46 (9 mos. overseas duty in the Southwest Pacific Theater-Okinawa); awards: Good conduct medal, Amer. Defense Service Medal, Amer. Campaign Medal, Asiatic-Pacific Campaign Medal with Bronze Star, WW II Victory Medal and Army of Occupation Medal with Japan Clasp.; mem., Atlantic Synod, United Presby. Ch. in USA; Fairfield-McClelland Presby, U. Presby. Ch. in USA; Jenkinsville, S. C. br. NAACP; Fairfield High Sch. PTA; Sanctorium Lodge 25, Cheraw, S. C. and Cairo Temple 125, Columbia, S. C.; Home: 501 W. Moultrie, Winnsboro, S. C.

HUDSON, R. T., ch. official, b. Jackson, Miss., Dec. 4, 1912; s. Joseph Bell and Anna Lee (Cotton) H.; Oakwood Coll., 1930-34; Queens Coll., 1960-61; Andrews Univ., 1961-62; m. Dorothy Mae Warren; Children--Romona Mouzon, Sharon Rose, Robbin Denise, Ricardo Tilden; pastor, Phila. Seventh-Day Adventist Ch., DesMoines, Iowa, 1935-41; sec., Region Work, Tex. Conf. of S. D. A., 1941-45; minister, Allegheney Conf. of S. D. A., 1945-55, pastoring in Pittsburgh, Pa., Wash., D. C., and Cleveland, O.; pastor, Ephesus S. D. A. Ch., 1955-62; former tchr., Elem. Sch., Huntsville, Ala., 1933-34; present: pres., Northeastern Conf. of S. D. A. Ch., 1962--; mem., Oakwood Coll. Bd., Atlantic Union College Bd.; Atlantic Union Conf. Exec. Comm.; mem., New England Sanitarium Bd.; chrmn., Northeastern Conf. Exec. Comm.; chrmn., Northeastern Acad. Bd.; co-author, State paper presented to the NY Legislature assembly on "The Fair Sabbath Law," Jan. 29, 1962; Home: 457 Lafayette Ave., Rockville Center, N. Y.; Office: 560 W. 150th St., New York, N. Y.

HUDSON, Theodore; s. Howard Wilson and Pearlene Early; H.; A. B., Wilberforce Univ., 1949; B. D., Payne Sem., 1944; m. Joyce Marie Brooks; Children--Bryan; Charles; Lori; served on Jayne Boyd Commun. House Bd., Cedar Rapids, Iowa; pres., NAACP; chrmn., FEPC Comm.; mem., Coun. of Soc. Planning; pres., PTA; pres., Mich. City Interdenom. Min. Alliance; mem., Mayor's Comm. on Human Relations and pastor, Bethel A. M. E. Ch.; first Negro nominated for city coun.; Home: 2317 Warsaw St., Ft. Wayne, Ind.; Office: 836 E. Jefferson St., Ft. Wayne, Ind.

HUGHES, Carl Donald, educator, b. Indianapolis, Ind., June 10, 1918; s. Twidell and Lillian (Haslewood) H. Ford; A. B., Ind. Univ., Bloomington, Ind., 1939; B. S., Bus. Adm., W. Va. State Coll., Inst., W. Va., 1942; M. A., Finance, Wharton Sch. of Finance, Univ. of Pa., 1943; B. D., Grad. Sch. Rel., Butler Univ., Indianapolis, 1957; M. A., Grad. Sch. of Rel., Butler Univ., 1958 Sch. of Law, Ind. Univ. (2 yrs.); grad. work in Education, Wayne State Univ. and Univ. of Detroit (Mich.); m. Louise Cox; 1 son, Carl D., Jr.; 2 daus., Karen Louise, Beverly Jean; tchr., Business Ed., Det. Pub. Schs.; instr., Calvary Dist. Assoc., Detroit, Mich.; Wolverine State Conv. Sun. Sch. & B. T. U. Cong., Mich.; Natl. Bapt. Sun. Sch. & B. T. U. Cong.; Prog. chrmn., Interdenom. Min. Conf., Detroit, Mich.; recipient, 1st John L. Webb Award, Natl. Bapt. Conv. USA, Inc., (contr. field of rel. ed.), Houston, Tex., 1948; Who's Who in Amer. Coll. and Univ., 1943; Who's Who in Colored Amer., 1950; membership comm., YMCA and NAACP; mem., Kappa Alpha Psi; Mason, Budg. Comm., Nat. Negro Bus. League; ordained Bapt. minister, 1952; Second Bapt. Ch., Lafayette, Ind., 1952-56; Greater St. John Missionary Bapt. Ch., Det., Mich., 1956-60; dir., G. Ed., Metropolitan Bapt. Ch., Det., 1960; pastor, Bethel Bapt. Ch., East Det., 1961--; Home: 258 Trowbridge Ave., Detroit, Mich. 48202 Church: 5715 Holcomb, Detroit, Mich. 48213

HUGHES, Henderson Randolph, b. Hemingway, S. C., Dec. 23, 1908; s. Silas M. and Hattie (M.) H.; A. B., Allen Univ., Columbia, S. C.; B. D., Oberlin Grad. Sch. of Theol.; D. D. (hon.), Allen Univ.; Daniel Payne Coll.; m. Ruth Henderson; Children--Henderson R.; pastor, Shiloh Afr. Meth. Ch., Charleston, 4 yrs.; St. John A. M. E. Ch., Birmingham, Ala., 8 yrs.; Emanuel A. M. E. Ch., 17 yrs.; pres., Daniel Payne Coll., Birmingham, 4 yrs.; tchr., Allen Univ., Columbia; Berkley Co. Training Sch.; mem., YMCA; NAACP (local br.); Urban League; Mason; Elk; Home: 400 Convent Ave., New York, N. Y.; Office: 37 W. 119th St., New York, N. Y.

HUGHLEY, Judge Neal, coll. prof., b. Columbus, Ga., Dec. 10, 1907; s. William Wilkins and Ozella (Jones) H.; A. B., Morehouse Coll., 1929; M. A., Columbia Univ. B. D., Union Theol. Sem., 1932; Ph. D., Columbia Univ. 1947; m. Sadie Sawyer; Children--Mario Neal; prof., Bishop Coll., 1932-37; pastor, First Bapt. Ch., Okmulg

Okla., 1938-39; Mt. Calvary Bapt. Ch., Coffeyville, Kans., 1939-41; current prof., N. C. Coll., Durham, N. C., 194-; current pastor, Mt. Calvary Bapt. Ch., Durham, N. C., 1959--; chrmn., Fellowship of Southern Churchmen, 1947-49; Danforth Assoc., 1955-65; mem., Selection Comm. for Danforth Grad. Fellowships; Howard Univ. Inst. of Rel., 1942-65; Exec. Bd. N. C. Coun. on Human Relations; Exec. Bd. N. C. Coun. of Chs.; author: Rethinking Our Christianity, Dorrance Press, 1942; Trends in Protestant Social Idealisms, Columbia Univ. Press, 1948; Home: 203 Pekoe St., Durham, N. C. 27707; Office: North Carolina Coll., 312 Administrator Bld., Durham, N. C. 27707

HUNT, Blair Theodore, tchr., b. Memphis Tenn., Oct. 1, 1888; s. Blair Theodore and Emma (House) H.; B. A., Morehouse Coll.; T. H. B. and M. S., Tenn. State Univ.; m. Ernestine Jacobs H.; Children--Blair, Wilson, Ernest; present pastor Miss. Blvd. Chrstn. Ch.; tchr., 46 yrs., Memphis sch. system, the last 27 yrs. princ. of B. T. Washington High Sch.; retired in 1959; mem., former pres., of the Natl. Conv. of Chrstn. Chs.; Co. Bd. of Ed., Shejby Co., Tenn.; Bd. of Trustee, Owen Coll., Memphis, Tenn. and Tougaloo Coll., Tougaloo, Miss.; World War I, 1st Lt.; mem., Alpha Phi Alpha; Elks; Urban League; NAACP; 1952, weekly sermon for "The Memphis World" (newspaper); Home: 931 Hastings St., Memphis, Tenn.; Church: 978 Mississippi Blvd., Memphis, Tenn.

HUNT, James Louis, Asheville, N. C., Apr. 18, 1926; s. Edward H. and Sarah F. (H.); A. B., Livingstone Coll.; m. Kathleen Moore; Children--James Edward Louis, William Henry; pastor, A. M. E. Z. Ch., Connly Chapel, Plum Tree, N. C.; Carsons Chapel, Rutherford Co., N. C.; Matthews Chapel, W. Asheville, N. C.; New Moss Temple, Black Mt., N. C.; Weaverville Ch., Weaverville, N. C.; Mt. Zion, Marion, N. C.; Slades Chapel, Morganton, N. C.; prsent pastor, Goler Meml., Winston-Salem, N. C.; pres., Morganton Burke Co. NAACP, 3 yrs.; special deputy, Burke Co. Sheriff Dept.; treas., Burke Co. Min. Alliance; mem., Mayor's Bi-racial Comm., 1962-65; Mason; Democrat; Home: 2300 Glenn Ave., Winston-Salem, N. C. 27105

HUNT, Lawrence Everett, b. Baltimore, Md., July 12, 1938; s. Edward and Roselle; A. B., Capital Univ., 1958;

B.D., Evangelical Luth. Theol. Sem., 1962; m. Carolyn Keeley; Children--Jacqueline; asst. pastor, Advent Luth. Ch., Milw., Wis., 1962-63; pastor, Ch. of the Abiding Savior, Durham, N.C., 1964-68; mem., Worship and Ch. Music Com., E. Dist., The Am. Luth Ch.; chap., Durham Jr. Cham. of Commerce, 1965; bd. of dir., Durham Jr. Cham. of Commerce, 1966-67; mem., Coordinating Comm., Black Luth. Clergymen; Comm., Inner-City Min.; ALC; Home: 2503 Janet St., Durham, N.C., 27707; Office: 1625 So. Alston Ave., Durham, N.C. 27707

*HUNTER, Charles Alvin, tchr., b. Longview, Tex., May 7, 1926; s. Wallace Alvin and Ivernia (Fleming) H.; B.A Bishop Coll., 1947; B.D., Howard Univ., 1950; M.Th., 1954; Th.D., Div. Sch., Phila., Pa., 1958; m. Annie Mary Alexander; Children--Alpha Angela, Rhonda Fleming, Rhashell Debra, Byron Charles; minister, Trinity Congre. Ch., Athens, Ala., 1950-52; tchr. of Soc. Studies, Trinity High Sch., 1951-2; tchr. of Soc. Studies and Common Learning, Phila. pub. schs., Pa., 1954-57 Dir. of United Campus Chrstn. Fellowship, Fla. A & M Univ., 1959-61; minister, Trinity U. Presby. Ch., Tallahassee, Fla., 1959-61; assoc. prof. of Sociology, Bishop Coll., Dallas, Tex., 1961-present; minister, Hope Presby. Ch., 1962-present; associate, Amer. Sociological Soc., SW Regional Sociological Assn., Southwest Philosophical Soc.; Home: 4425 Meadow St., Dallas, Tex.; Church: 4411 Meadow St., Dallas, Tex.

HUNTLEY, Thomas Elliott, b. Wadesboro, N.C., June 28, 1903; s. John P. and Lula (Brewer) H.; grad. Va. Theol. Sem. and Coll., Lynchburg, Va., 1928; A.B., Morehouse Coll., Atlanta, 1934; Atlanta Univ., 1937; Union Theol. Sem., N.Y.; D.D. (hon.), Friendship Coll., Rock Hill, S.C., 1943; Selma Univ., 1954; m. Kiffie Elizabeth Esther Maddox; ordained to ministry of Bapt. Ch., 1928; pastor, St. Louis Bapt. Ch., 1942--; founder Ch. on Wheels, 1947; leader, Natl. Ministers' Prayer March on Wash., 1948; mem., Soc. Service Com., Natl. Bapt. Conv. Inc., 1948-52; Hist. Com., 1956-58; former mem., Pastor's Adv. Com., Natl. Coun. Rel. Edu.; founder, Natl. Bapt. Publication House of So. India, 1956 chrmn., ed. staff foreign publications of Bharath Social and Cultural Trust, Publishers of So. India, 1957; mem. NAACP; Protestants and Other Americans United for Separation of Church and State (v.p.); Phi Beta Sigma; Mason author: As I Saw It, 1954; Devil on the Moon; When People Behave Like Sputniks; Sense and Common Sense in a World of Non-Sense; A Baptist Manifesto in Three Epistles; 1940, while in pastorate at Pensacola, Fla., influenced (without organizational help) editor of the white daily Pensacola New Journal, to change his policy of spelling the word "Negro" with a small "n"; 1946, to curtail juvenile delinquency in St. Louis, founded The Church on Wheels (a sch. bus, used as a ch. house in the blighted areas, with staff of Sun. Sch. tchrs., evangelistic and soc. workers); 1948, led Ministers' Prayer March on Wash. in an effort to influence and World Peace; 1955, His book As I Saw It (not commUnism but CommOnism) was sold, for the first time in a foreign land, by the Carey Kingsgate Press, London, England; 1956, As I Saw It was trans. and pub. in three languages of India, with a preface in the Telugu lang. by Dr. B. Pattabhi Sitaramayya, (Gov. Madhya Pradesh) referred to the book as "a great contr. to the advancement of the moral and spiritual development of India;" 1956, cited by the Hindustan Times of India as "a priest of the highest type of liberalism and toleration instead of the maxim, "My country right or wrong;" 1963, author: Huntley's Manual for Every Baptist (Some Things Every Member Should Know); founded, The Family Fireside Inst. (designed to teach children, at an early age, in the home, the fundamentals of good citizenship as well as Baptist doctrine; 1963, through the Oct. 25, 1963 ed. of The St. Louis Argus, made an appeal to Negro citizens of St. Louis to withdraw their deposits from most of the banks and establish a bank of their own, upon an integrated basis, due to an accute "sit in" controversy that was taking place at the Jefferson Bank over the hiring of Negroes--a bank where most Negroes deposited their money; 1964, his appeal materialized into the organization of the Gateway Natl. Bank with 15 Negro workers and one white cashier, two white bd. members; his book, Huntley's Manual for Every Bapt., was adopted by the Natl. Bapt. Conv., USA, Inc. (in its 1964 sess. at Det., Mich.) as a standard guide in Bapt. ch. administration--the first such doctrinal guide from a lone au. ever to be adopted by this rel. body; cited and recommended for membership in the Intl. Platform Assn. by the Comm. on Associates: Lowell Thomas, Drew Pearson, Edgar Bergen and Hal Holbrook (The Intl. Platform idea dates back to the days of Aristotle and repr. the highest type of literary and artistic chracters); he holds membership certificate from this org.; Home: 4959 Cote Brilliante Ave., St. Louis, Mo.; Office: Central Bapt. Ch., 2842

Washington Ave., St. Louis, Mo.

HURDLE, Isaiah Q., tchr., b. Greenville, Tex., Aug. 12, 1886; s. Andrew J. and Viney J. (Sanders) H.; B.S., Prairie View State Coll., 1927; grad. study, Univ. of Colo., 1929; grad. study, Univ. of Denver, 1937; later, at Prairie View and also Tex. Southern Theol., Brite Coll., Ft. Worth, Tex., 1960; m. Erma Bowser; Children--Irving Q, Zenobia L., James R.; ordained, 1912; pres., Northeast Tex. Chrstn. Theol. and Indus. Coll., Palestine, Tex., 1912-58; served as sch. prin. during the years of ministerial wk. for 26 yrs.; interim preaching since 1958, when retired from Willow Pk. Chrstn. Ch., San Antonio, Tex.; pastor, Holland Chapel, Holland, Tex.; organized Crest View Chrstn. Ch., Temple, 1942, also New Hope in Marlin, Friendship Chrstn. Ch., Taylor, Tex. and Friendship Chrstn. Ch., Davilla, Tex.; served as parliamentarian for Natl. Chrstn. Missionary Conv., Disciples of Christ; served as instr. summer camps; Austin, Tex. 1934-36, Hiram Coll., Ohio, 1950, San Antonio, Tex., 1956-58; ch. schs. and evangelistic campaigns, pres. of Tex. Chrstn. Missionary Conv., 1939-45; Boy Scout Commissioner, 1934-37; Samuel Huston Coll. (summer sch. dir., 1922); visiting prof., in Tillotson Coll., 1936; Jarvic Coll., 1945-46 (summer activities); pres., Tex. Tchrs. State Assn., 1936-37; mem., Bd. of Trustees, Jarvis Chrstn. Coll., 1945-57; current-interim pastor, Friendship Chrstn. Ch., Davilla, Tex.; Forty Year serv. pen from Natl. Chrstn. Missionary Conv., 1954; 50 yr. service medal from the Intl. Conv. of Disciples of Christ; del. from the US, the World Conv. on Chrstn. Edu., Toronto, Can., 1950; current, recording sec., the Most Worshipful St. Joseph Grand Lodge, Tex. Jurisdiction, Scottish Rite Ancient Free and Accepted Masons; ed., The Tex. Chrstn. Evangelist, 1912-16; ed., Tex. Standard, 1937-38; Home: 1416 E. 12 St., Austin, Tex.

HUTCHINS, Joshua, Jr., ch. official, b. Huntingtown, Md., Apr. 6, 1937; s. Joshua and Lillian Brown H.; B.S., St. Paul's Coll., 1960; B.D., Interdenom. Theol. Center, Gammon Theol. Sem., 1962; m. Gloria M. Walker; licensed to preach, 1954; chrmn., Bd. of Ed.; Wash. Conf. Meth. Ch.; Alpha Phi Alpha, Student Chrstn. Movement, Crusade Scholar, 1961-63; Home Missions, 1962-63; pastor, Trinity Meth. Ch., 1962-64; Conf. Youth Dir. Ch. Bd. of Ed., Meth. Ch., Wash. Conf., 1964--;

pres., NAACP, Clarksburg, W. Va.; mem., Alpha Phi Alpha; Republican; Office: Bd. of Ed., Wash. Conf., The Meth. Ch., 1206 Etting St., Baltimore, Md.

HUTCHINSON, Charles Lesley, b. Talladega, Ala., Oct. 5, 1933; s. Alphus and Emily B.; B. S., A & T Coll. of N. C., 1958; B. D., Gammon Theol. Sem., Atlanta, Ga., 1962; m. Eunice L. Underwood; 1 child; pastor, Village View Meth. Ch., Athens, Ala., 1959-62; St. Paul Meth. Ch., Tuscaloosa, Ala., 1962-65; Dist. Supt. of Birmingham Dist. Meth. Ch., 1965-present; tchr., Tuscaloosa, Ala., 1963; award, Rust Coll., Holly Springs, Miss.; mem., Tuscaloosa Citizens for Action Comm.; NAACP; Interdenom. Min. Alliance, Greater Birmingham Min. Assn.; Min. Leadership Training Program; SCLC; Home: 625 10th Ave. W., Birmingham, Ala. 35204.

HUTCHINSON, Harry T., Jr., b. Pittsburgh, Pa., May 4, 1924; A. B., Bethany Coll., Bethany, W. Va., 1946; S. T. B., Western Theol. Sem., 1948; course requirement M. A. English; Library Service M. L. S., 1969, Univ. of Pittsburgh & Grad. Sch. Library & Info. Serv.; pastor, Presbyn. Chs., Ohio, 1948-50; Southside Presby. Ch., Pittsburgh, 1950-56; Avalon Presbyn. Ch., Avalon, Pa., 1956-59; asst. pastor, Presbyn. Ch. of Sewickley, Pa., 1959-present; Home: 521 Nevin Ave., Sewickley, Pa. 15143

HYLTON, Samuel Wilbur, Jr., tchr., b. Roanoke, Va., Feb. 14, 1927; s. Samuel W. and Idenia (White) H.; 1946-49, B. A., Morehouse Coll.; 1951-54, B. D., Boston Univ.; Butler Univ. (Chrstn. Theol. Sem.); m. Mildred McLeod H.; children--Samuel Wilbur III, Karen Elizabeth; pastor, Second Chrstn Ch., Indianapolis, Ind., 1951-54; Cleveland Ave. Chrstn. Ch., Winston-Salem, N. C., 1954-61; Centennial Chrstn Ch., St. Louis, Mo., 1961-present; mem., Faculty, Winston-Salem, Tchrs. Coll., Winston-Salem, N. C.; Bd. of Mgrs., Patterson Ave. YMCA, Winston-Salem; Omega Psi Phi; Beta Chi Honorary Soc.; Home: 771 N. Euclid Ave., St. Louis, Mo. 63108; Church: 4950 Fountain Ave., St. Louis, Mo. 63113

IMES, William Lloyd, b. Memphis, Tenn., Dec. 29, 1889; s. Benjamin Albert and Elizabeth (Wallace) I.; Knoxville Coll., 1905-08; B. A., M. A., Fisk Univ., 1910, 1912;

B.D., Union Theol. Sem., NYC, 1915; M.A., Columbia Univ., 1915; D.D. (hon.), Lincoln Univ., 1929; m. Grace Virginia Frank; pastor, Plainfield, N.J., 1915-19; Phila., Pa., 1919-25; NYC, 1925-43; pres., Knoxville Coll., 1943-47; staff, NY State Coun. of Chs., 1947-55; lecturer, Howard Univ., Sch. of Rel., 1940-43; visiting dean of chapel, Fisk Univ., 1957-58; Dillard Univ., 1958-59; instr., Dillard Univ., 1958-59; retired 1955; chap., YMCA, N.J., 1918; hon. mem., Dundee Rotary Club, 1947-present; mem. bd. dir., v.p., NAACP; anniv. award, Trinity Meth. Ch., New Orleans, La.; alumni award, Fisk Univ., 1960; pub. chapters in Best Sermons, Book Four (Sermon of "Faith"); We Believe in Immortality; The Music of the Gospel (Hunter), 1932; The Christian Way in Race Relation (Nelson), 1948; author, Integrity: Studies in the Book of Job, Presby. Bd. of Chrstn. Edu., May 1939; The Way of Worship in Everyday Life, Light and Life Press, 1947; The Black Pastures, A Pilgrimage in Two Centuries, The Hemphill Press, 1957; Home: 16 Bigelow Ave., Dundee, N.Y. 14837

ISOM, Dotcy Ivertus, Jr., b. Feb. 18, 1931, Detroit, Mich.; s. Dotchy Ivertus and Laura; B.S., Wayne State Univ., Detroit, 1956; M.A., M. Div., Chrstn. Educa., Eden Theol., 1966, 1967; m. Esther Ladon Jones; Children--Dotcy III, Jon Mark, David Carl; pastor, Allen Temple C.M.E. Ch., Paris, Tenn., 1957-58; St. Luke C.M.E. Ch., Saginaw, Mich., 1958-61; Carter Chapel C.M.E. Ch., Gary, Ind., 1961-62; Pilgrim Temple C.M.E. Ch., E. St. Louis, Ill., 1962-present; tchr., mentally retarded; mem., Human Relations Comm., City Planning (PACE); chrmn., Comm. of "30"; Bd. of Dirs. St. Clair Co. E.O.C.; Bd. Mayor's Spec. Task Force; US Army 1948-52; awards: 5 bronze stars, Korean Service Medal, Combat duty in Korea; mem., Alpha Phi Alpha, Frontiers, NAACP, CORE, Intl. Coun. Exceptional Children, Youth Div. Natl. Coun. of Chs.; tchr., C.M.E. Leadership Training Sch.; Home: 700 N. 39th St., E. St. Louis, Ill. 62205; Office: 1800 Trendley Ave., E. St. Louis, Ill.

JACKSON, A. Patterson, b. Batesville, Miss., Nov. 22, 1918; s. Durmon Z. and Mary; A.B., Morehouse Coll., 1941, B.D., Garrett Biblical Inst.; m. Elizabeth Williams; Children--Duane Myron, Darrell Lamar; pastor,

Cuberty Bapt. Ch., 1952-present; bd. mem., Urban League, 1961-65; v.p. Chgo. NAACP; bd. mem., Ch. Fed. Soc. Ser. Dept., Chgo.; tchr. Chgo. Bapt. Inst.; Sun. Sch. and B. T. U. Congress; Phi Beta Sigma; Mason; author: pamphlet The Sacred Truth, A Primer for Baptists; Home: 1223 Hyde Park, Chgo, Ill. 60615; Office: 4851 So. Pkway, Chgo, Ill.

JACKSON, D. Manning, b. Monroe, La., July 5, 1906; s. Gabriel and Mattie; A. B., Southern Univ., 1928; Bishop Coll., 1934; D. D. (hon.), Monroe Coll., 1944; m. Minnie Ruth Hawkins; pastor, Golden Gate Bapt. Ch., 1930-36; First Bapt. Ch., San Antonio, Tex., 1936-49; First Afr. Bapt. Ch., Phila., Pa., 1949-52; Fellowship Bapt. Ch., Phila., Pa., 1952-54; Live Oak Bapt. Ch., Beaumont, Tex., 1954-59; El Bethel Bapt. Ch., San Francisco, Calif., 1959--; dean of rel., Guadalupe Coll., 1941-45; dir. of ed., Phila. Pastors Conf.; sec., Bills and Accts., Natl. Bapt. Conv. of America, since 1958; author: Pulpit Meditations; Home: 127 Thrift St., San Francisco, Calif.

JACKSON, Edward Franklin, b. Pensacola, Fla., July 19, 1911; Fla. A & M Coll., Edward Waters, Jacksonville, Fla.; further study, Tuskegee Inst. and Univ. of Buffalo, D. D., Livingstone Coll., 1948; m. Mildred Dodson; Children--Edward, Jr., Cameron W., Darryl J., Gloria J.; pastor, Ala., Tenn., Buffalo, N. Y.; current pastor, John Wesley A. M. E. Z. Ch., Wash., D. C., 1952--; 1955 led ch. comm. for NAACP campaign; 1957 led ministers in successful effort to place Negroes in sales positions in downtown dept. stores; 1959, elected pres. D. C. br. NAACP; 1960 led campaign for Frank D. Reeves as Natl. Democratic Committeeman; elected to Central Democratic Comm. and elected del. to Democratic Natl. Conv.; v. p., Central Democratic Comm.; led and assisted in successful efforts to reorganize US Employment Serv.-D. C. and to place Negro divers on trucks of major oil companies; v. chrmn., Citizens Adv. Comm. to Presidents Civil Rights Commn.; natl. pres., of Min. and Laymen's Assn. of the A. M. E. Z. Ch. since 1953; mem., Bd. of Dirs., Coun. of Chs.; Adv. Comm. Northwest Settlement House; Comm. of Management YMCA; Bd. of Dirs. United Givers Fund; Steering Comm. Inter-religious Comm. on Race; chrmn. Person-to-Person Communication Sub-Comm.; Natl. Speakers Bur. Democratic Party; Mason, Omega Psi Phi; Elk; awards: Afro Man of the

Year, D. C., 1957; recalled to Buffalo to rec. citation for outstanding service 1958; chosen for 12th St. YMCA's "1963 Oustanding Citizen's Award"; Office: 1615 14th St., NW, Wash., D. C.

JACKSON, Henry Brown, music tchr., b. Alden Bridge, La. Feb. 11, 1889; s. Silas and Sallie (Brown) J.; A. B., Philander Smith Coll., 1919; studied medicine, Howard Univ.; studied law at Howard Univ.; studied theol. at Shaw Univ.; music, Detroit Conservatory of Music; m. Elizabeth Reid; Children--Henry Brown, Jr., Charles Lee; minister, Chrstn. Meth. Episc. Ch.; mem. of three Gen. Conferences; piano tchr. for fifty-one yrs.; recording artist, OK Recording Co., N. Y.; present: minister, C. M. E. Ch., Spartanburg, S. C., pres., Inter-denom. Min. Assn., Spartanburg, S. C.; Home: 176 Amos St., Spartanburg, S. C.

JACKSON, Henry Ralph, b. Birmingham, Ala., Aug. 22, 1915; s. William Morgan and Delia (Bennings) J.; A. B., Shorter and Daniel Payne Colls.; B. D., Jackson Theol. Sem.; grad. studies, Fisk Univ.; D. L. (hon.), Wilberforce Univ., Monrovia Coll., Daniel Payne Coll.; D. D. (hon.), Campbell Coll.; D. H. (hon.), Allen Univ.; m. Hattie Elie; children--Zita Ralphayne, Cheri Estelle; pastor, St. Andrew A. M. E. Ch., Memphis, Tenn., 1941-present; dir., Mimimum Salary Dept., A. M. E. Ch., 1966-present; former pres., Brotherhood A. M. E. Ch. and A. M. E. Pastor's Coun. Memphis; mem., Gen. Conf. A. M. E. Ch., 1944, 48, 52, 56; Gen. Commn. and Sub Commn.; Gen. bd., A. M. E. Ch., Exec. Bd. and Budget Comm.; Natl. Coun. Chs.; Fraternal Coun. Chs., Exec. Bd.; Mason; Urban League; NAACP; cited by A. M. E. Ch. for meritorious service to A. M. E. Ch.; Mayor of Memphis for outstanding leadership in civic and political service; Home: 167 Honduras, Memphis, Tenn.

*JACKSON, James Castina, b. Okla. City, Okla., Mar. 24, 1922; s. Wade D. and Rosie (Owens) J.; A. B., Morehouse Coll., 1944; B. D., Howard Univ. Sch. of Rel., 1947; Okla. Sch. of Rel., D. D. (hon.), 1964; m. Barbara Mae Sparks; Children--Janice C., Merdith Patrice; dir., No. Tulsa Bapt. Center, Tulsa, Okla., 1947-56; pastor, Paradise Bapt. Ch., Tulsa, 1956--; prof. of preaching, Okla. Sch. of Rel., Langston, Okla., 1950-54; sec., Tulsa br. NAACP, 1954-60; Bd. of Dirs., Tulsa Co. Assn. for Mental Health; Bd. of Dirs., No.

Tulsa Coordinating Comm.; Bd. of Dirs., Okla. Sch. of Rel.; pres., Okla. State Bapt. Pastors' Conf; dean, Creek Dist. Congress of Chrstn. Ed.; Bd. of Dirs., Hutcherson br. YMCA; Bd. of Dirs., Okla. Bapt. State Conv.; contributor: "Oklahoma Eagle;" former editorial staff of the Natl. Bapt. Sun. Sch. Pub. Bd.; Home: 503 E. Young St., Tulsa, Okla; Office: 507 E. King St., Tulsa, Okla.

JACKSON, James Conroy, chap., b. Scranton, Pa., May 9, 1913; s. James Conroy and Ella Glascoe (Smith) J.; B.S., Cheyney State Tchrs. Coll., Cheyney, Pa., 1938; B.Th., Phila. Div. Sch., 1949; m. Daisy Louise Ledgister; Children--Patricia Ann; ordained deacon in the Episc. Ch., 1949; priest, 1949; vicar, St. Philip's P.E. Ch., Dallas, Tex., 1949-56; priest-in-charge, St. Augustine's Mission, Dallas, 1950-52; priest-in-charge, St. Simon's Ch., Ft. Worth, Tex., 1949-56; vicar, St. Philip's, P.E. Ch., Little Rock, Ark., 1956-62; St. Mary's P.E. Ch., Hot Springs, 1956-62; St. Andrew's P.E. Ch., Pine Bluff, 1956-61; St. Augustine's P.E. Ch., Ft. Smith, 1961-62; current, chap., Voorhees Coll.; priest-in-charge of Philip's Chapel, Voorhees Coll., Denmark, S.C.; pres., Greater Little Rock Urban League, Little Rock, Ark., 1960-62; served overseas in Solomon Is. and the Philippines during WW II, 1942-45; mem., Kappa Alpha Psi; Amer. Ch. Union-Episc. Soc.; award: Good Conduct Medal; Home: Voorhees Coll., Denmark, S.C.

JACKSON, Jesse Louis, Civil Rights Leader, b. Oct. 8, 1941, Greenville, S.C.; s. Charles H.; B.S., A & T Coll., Greensboro, N.C.; Chgo. Theol. Sem. (2 yrs.); m. Jacquelin Lavinia Brown; Children--Santita, Jesse Louis, Jr., Jonathan Luther; assoc. pastor, Fellowship Bapt. Ch., Chgo., present; Natl. Dir. Operation Breadbasket, SCLC Conf., Chgo., present; former, dir. of Field Activities for the Coordinating Coun. of Community Organizations (CCCO); dir., spec. projects and economic develop. (SCLC); organizer, Young Democrat Clubs, Negro Colleges, 1964; del., US Youth Coun., 1963-64; World Assembly of Youth, 1963; Natl. 2nd v.-grand basiteus, Omega Psi Phi, 1962-64; N.C. State student legislature, A & T Coll.; former field repr., CORE Southeastern reg.; pres., N.C. Intercollegiate Coun. on Human Rights; Liaison officer to Gov. Sanford's office; directed state-wide TV tutorial; leader, Greenville, S.C.

Civil Rights Movement, June, 1960; A & T Coll. Civil Rights Movement, 1963; honors, Greensboro Citizen of the Year (1964) Windsor Com. Recreation Center; Omega "Man of the Year," 6th dist.; Gate City chap., Alumni award (A & T Coll.); "Man of the Year (Chgo.) Frontiers Intl., 1968; Home: 6725 S. Ridgeland, Chgo., Ill. 60649; Office: SCLC's Operation Breadbasket, 366 E. 47th St., Chgo., Ill. 60653

JACKSON, John Henry, Jr., b. Oakwood, Tex., Sept. 24, 1919; s. John Henry, Sr. and Aggie (Williams) J.; A.B., Samuel Huston Coll., Austin, Tex.; M.A., Atlanta Univ., Atlanta, Ga.; B.D., Gammon Theol. Sem.; D.D. (hon.), Turner Sem., Kan. City, Kan.; m. Verna Maude Worthy; Children--Linda Joyce, La Verne, Janis Harlene; pastor, and prin. of High Sch., Kynette Forsyth, Ga. for 16 yrs. Exec. sec., Bd. of Ed., Central West Conf. Meth. Ch.; pastor (current), Scott Meth. Ch., 1959--; summer workshop leader, Oregon, Colo.; former pres., E. Denver Min. Alliance; pres., Rocky Mountain Min. Alliance; chap., House of Repr., Denver, Colo.; Devotional speaker for Sun. morning radio program, KIMN sta.; certificate from Gov. Talmadge; mem., Mason, Sigma Phi Beta; pub. two books of prayer given in House of Repr.; Home: 2830 Eudera St., Denver, Colo., 80207; Office: 2201 Ogden St., Denver, Colo. 80205

JACKSON, Joseph Harrison, ch. administrator, b. Jonestown, Miss., Sept. 11, 1900; s. Henry and Emily (Johnson) J.; A.B., Jackson Coll., 1926; B.D., Colgate Rochester Div. Sch., 1932; M.A. Creighton Univ., 1933; D.D. (hon.), Central State Coll., Wilberforce, O., 1954; LL.D., Bishop Coll., Marshall, Tex., 1956; m. Maude Thelma Alexander, 1926; children--Kenny; ordained Bapt. ministry, 1922; pastor, 1st Ch., Macomb, Miss., 1925-27; Bethel Bapt. Ch., Omaha, Nebr., 1927-34; Monumental Bapt. Ch., Phila., Pa., 1934-41; Olivet Bapt. Ch., Chgo., Ill., 1941--; pres., Natl. Bapt. Conv. Inc., 1953--; sec., Foreign Mission Bd., Natl. Bapt. Conv., 1934-41; mem., Bapt. World Alliance (Exec. Comm.); mem., Natl. Coun. Chs. (Gen. Bd.); Phi Beta Sigma; Mason; author: A Voyage to W. Africa and Some Reflections on Modern Missions, 1936; Stars in the Night, 1950; Home: 4937 Kimbark Ave., Chgo, Ill.; Office: 3101 S. Parkway, Chgo., Ill.

JACKSON, Lester Kendel, b. Ft. Gaines, Ga., May 18,

1895; s. Edwin and Maria (Booyer) J.; Chatahoochie Inst., Ga. State Univ., Va. Theol. Sem. & Coll.; m. Emma Lee Hawkes; Children--Lester K., Jr., Mrs. Veora Maxine Proctor, Mrs. Joyce Estelle Swain, Mrs. Sarah Yvonne McCall; prof. rel. ed., Va. Theol. Sem. & Coll., 1924-27; bus. mgr., 1929-31; pastor, Rivermount Bapt. Ch., Lynchburg, Va., 1925-34; Ebenezer Bapt. Ch., Passaic, N.J., 1934-36; Second Bapt. Ch., Long Branch, N.J., 1936-42; St. Paul Bapt. Ch., Gary, Ind., 1943--; pres., Interdenom. Min. Alliance, Gary, Ind.; pres., Gary Fellowship of Ministers (interracial, interfaith); sec., Ind. Bapt. State Conv.; mem., Gary Cham. of Commerce; life mem., NAACP; life mem., Natl. Frat. Coun. of Chs.; mem. , CORE; SCLC (Southern leadership Conf.); Republican; recipient, Citation, Interdenom. Min. Alliance and Luther Morris Award, NAACP, outstanding service in Civil Rights, 1962; Home: 2541 Madison St., Gary, Ind.; Church: 1938 Adams St., Gary, Ind.

JACKSON, Mance C., Jr., b. Ft. Worth, Tex., Oct. 13, 1930; s. Mance and Mildred; B.A., Calif. State Coll., L.A., Calif, 1960; B.D., Interdenom. Theol. Center, 1966; m. Joy A. Rogers; Children--Diantha, Claudius, Darlene, Deborah, Doreen, Myron, Donna; mem., Calif. Conf., C.M.E. Ch.; pastor, Fontana Mission, Fontana, Calif., 1958-60; Phillips Chapel, Santa Barbara, Calif., 1960-61; Bethel C.M.E. Ch., Seattle, Wash., 1961-63; Rome Circuit, Rome, Ga., 1963-66; Phillips Temple, Berkeley, Calif., 1966-68; Community Organization Spec., E.O.A., Atlanta, Ga.; dir., Neighborhood Service Center, Atlanta, Ga.; cons., E. Bay Conf. on Rel., Race and Social Justice, Oakland, Calif.; cons., Berkeley Center for Human Interaction; asst. prof., Interdenom. Theol. Center, Atlanta, Ga., 1968-present; mem., Manpower Commn. City of Berkeley, 1968; bd. of dir., NCNC; Western regional v.p., NCNC, 1967-68; bd. of dir., NAACP, Seattle, Wash., 1962-63; NAACP, Rome, Ga., 1964-66; CORE, Seattle, Wash., 1962-63; Berkeley Area Coun. of Chs., 1966-68; N. Calif. Coun. of Chs., San Francisco, Calif., 1967-68; org. Com., OIC, Berkeley, Calif.; King Co. Metro. Planning Commn.; US Army, 1950-52; mem., Ephebian Soc.; Prot. Fellow, Rockefeller Found.; Theta Phi Honor Soc.; Home: 1424 Channing Way, Berkeley, Calif., 94702; Office: 3334 Adeline St., Berkeley, Calif.

*JACKSON, Theodore Clifton, Jr., tchr., b. Baltimore, Md., Aug. 4, 1933; s. Theodore Clifton and Lucy (Milbourne) J.; Howard Univ., Coll. of Liberal Arts, 1952-54; Va. Theol. Sem., Lynchburg, Va., 1955-57, A. B.; Howard Univ., Sch. of Rel., 1957-59; Morgan State Coll., 1962-63; m. Marlene Young; Children--Patricia Ann, Carla Rae; chap., Anna Mae Hunter Home for the Blind, Baltimore, Md., 1958; pastor, St. Matthews Chrstn. Meth. Episc. Ch., Wash., D. C., 1949-62; present pastor, Herberts Chapel C. M. E. Ch., Balto., Md., 1962--; tchr., Balto. City pub. sch. system, 1960-64; US Army, 86th Airborne; mem., Mason, Mt. Zion Lodge 10; Kappa Alpha Psi; NAACP; Interdenom. Min. Alliance; Meth. Youth Fellowship; C. M. E. Min. Alliance; Urban League; Home: 4019 Grantley Rd., Balto., Md. Office: 3300 Fairfield Rd., Baltimore, Md.

*JACKSON, Moses Lester, b. Florence, S. C., Aug. 16, 1921; s. Moses L., Sr. and Alma (Williams) J.; electro-tech. certificate, Milwaukee, Wis. Sch. of Engineering, 1949-50; B. A., Va. Union Univ., 1958; B. D., Howard Univ. Sch. of Rel., 1961; m. Cora Lee Moore; Children--Velvenia Lestine, Timothy Demetrius; ordained Mt. Airy Bapt. Ch.; asst. pastor, Jr. Ch., 1950-58, Mt. Airy Bapt. Ch., Wash., D. C.; pastor, Beulah Bapt. Ch., 1961--; mem., NAACP; Bapt. Min. Conf.; Far North East Min. Assn.; Dir. of Teen-age Problems for the Far North East Civic Assn.; US Coast Guard, sea duty in S. Pacific, 1943-46; Gen. Services Administration Suggestion Award, 1964; Home: 802 49th St., NE. Washington, D. C.; Office: 5901 Dix St. NE, Wash., D. C.

JACKSON, Walter Kinsley, b. Boley, Okla., Mar. 28, 1914; s. Eddie and Adlade J.; A. B., Bishop Coll., 1937; B. Th Okla. Sch. of Rel., Langston, Okla., 1947; D. D. (hon.), Morris-Booker Coll., Dermont, Ark., 1955 and Okla. Sch. of Rel., 1964; advance study, Union Theol. Sem., NYC, 1963-64; m. Eula Lee Wilhite; 1 dau., Waltine Lynette; pastor, Corinth Bapt. Ch., Ardmore, Okla., 1937-45; St. John Bapt. Ch., 1945--; pres., Bapt. Min. Assn., 1947-64; pres., Citizen's Action Comm., 1950-58 seminar leader, Ch. Admin., Bishop Coll., 1952, 53, 54; Bd. of Regents, Okla. Sch. of Rel., 1960-64; serve, Gov.'s Human Relation Comm., 1962-64; Urban League, NAACP, YMCA; mem., Boy Scouts of Amer., Amer. Legion, Omega Psi Phi, Democratic Party; moderator, E. Zion Dist. Assn.; contr. editor, Natl. Bapt. Voice,

Nat. Bapt. Conv., USA, Inc., 1959--; Home: 1200 NE Euclid, Okla. City, Okla. 73117; Church: 805 NE Second St., Okla. City, Okla. 73104

JACOBS, Donald Gustavus, b. Chelsea, Mass., Aug. 24, 1916; s. Burchell and Melissa (Van De Zee) Gustavus; A.B., Wilberforce Univ., 1939; B.D., Payne Theol. Sem., 1943; Duquesne Univ., Pittsburgh, Pa., 1946-47; Oberlin Sch. of Theol., 1954-56; D.D. (hon.), Wilberforce Univ., 1956; LL.D. (hon.), Edward Waters Coll., 1965; pastor, Circuit of Hillsboro and Bainbridge, O., 1940-43; Circuit of Milton, Danville and Bloomsburg, Pa., 1943-45; Payne Chapel A.M.E., Pa., 1945-46; Quinn Meml., Stephenville, O., 1946-51; St. Paul, Canton, O., 1951-55; St. James A.M.E. Ch., Cleveland, O., 1955-present; pres., Greater Cleveland Min. Assn., 1961-62; sec., Wilberforce Univ. Bd. of Trustees, 1960-present; pres., Cleveland br. NAACP, 1964-present; mem., Kappa Alpha Psi, Mason, A.M.E. Connectional Coun., Meth. Min. Alliance, Cleveland; Home: 10925 Pasadena, Cleveland, O. 44108

JACOBS, Solomon Napoleon, b. Panama, Nov. 21, 1920; s. Hiram A. and Lucia M. Wilson (J.); A.B., Va. State Coll., Petersburg, Va., Theol. ed., Bishop Payne Div. Sch.; m. Lynette G. Henry; Children--Gregory A., David G., Lisalyn; ordained deacon, Prot. Episc. Ch., June 1948; priest, Cathedral of St. Luke's, Ancon, Canal Zone, 1949; priest-in-charge, St. Mary's Rainbow City and St. George's, Gatun, Canal Zone, Panama; rector, St. Philips, Omaha, Nebr., 1952-58; St. Andrew's, Cleveland, O., 1958-70; Church of the Atonement, Mar. 1970-present; mem., NAACP, Urban League, Friendly Inn Settlement, Cleveland, O., Family Service Assn.; Home: 78 - 53rd Place S.E., Wash., D.C. 20019; Office: 5073 E. Capitol St., Wash., D.C. 20019

JAMES, Alexander Lincoln, b. Houston, Tex., Oct. 18, 1920; s. Samuel H. Sr. and Tannie Etta; B.A., Va. Union Univ., 1945; B.D., 1947; D.D., 1952, Va. Theol. Sem. and Coll., Lynchburg, Va.; m. Clara Thompson; Children--Alexander, Jr., Linda, Clara, Ronald, Andrea; pastor, First Afr. Bapt. Ch., Richmond, Va., 1942-47; First Bapt. Ch., Suffolk, Va., 1948-54; Greater Bethesda Bapt. Ch., Chgo., Ill, 1954-66; faculty, Va. Theol. Sem. and Coll., 1952-54; mem., Adv. Commn. to the Youth Commn. of Suffolk, Va., 1950-54; mem., Ill. Civil

Rights Commn., 1957-60; Youth Commn., City of Chgo., 1961-63; Home: 355 E. 90th Pl., Chicago, Ill.

JAMES, Allix B., v.p., b. Marshall, Tex., Dec. 17, 1922; s. Samuel Horace, Jr. and Tannie (E.) J.; A.B., Va. Union Univ., Richmond, Va., 1944; B.D., Va. Union Univ. Sch. of Rel., 1946; Th.M., Th.D., Union Theol. Sem., 1949, 1957; course, Boston and Penn St. Univs.; m. Sue B. Nickens; Children--Alvan Bosworth, Portia Veann; dean, Sch. of Rel., Va. Union Univ., 1956-60; v.p., Va. Union Univ., 1960-present; pastor, Third Union Bapt. Ch., King Williams, Va.; present mem., Alpha Phi Alpha; exec. bd., Bapt. Gen. Assn., Va.; Commn. on Chrstn. Ed., Va. Coun. of Chs.; Adminstrn. Commn. Dept. Ministry, Natl. Coun. Chs.; Mayor's Commn., Human Relation (Richmond, Va.); pres., Clergy Assn. (Richmond, Va.); pres., Norrell Sch. PTA, Richmond, Va.; v.p., Coun. on Theol. Ed., Amer. Bapt. Conv.; Home: 608 Overbrook Rd., Richmond, Va. 23220; Office: 1500 N. Lombardy St., Richmond, Va. 23222

*JAMES, Bose Moses, b. Memphis, Tenn., Feb. 12, 1922; s. Bose Moses and Beulah (Moss) J.; A.B., B.D., Howard Univ., 1953, 1959; m. Dorothy Elizabeth Cox; Children--Lois Michelle; pastor to migrants, N.Y. State Coun. of Chs., 1956-57; asst. pastor, Canaan Bapt. Ch., Wash., D.C., 1957-61; pastor, No. Community Ref. Ch., Kalamazoo, Mich., 1961--; chrmn., Kalamazoo Community Rel. Bd., Bd. of Ed., Ref. Ch. in America; present, mem., Kalamazoo Co. Bd. of Supervisors; Former Kalamazoo Coun. on Human Relations; Mayor's Law Enforcement Adv. Com., organizer Martin Luther King, Jr., meml. fund; Bd. Chrstn. Action Commn., Reformed Ch. in Amer.; chrmn., Nat. Black Coun., Reformed Ch. in Amer.; Kiwanis Club; NAACP; Dir., Day Care Center, (No. Community Ref. Ch.); US Army, 1942-43; Home: 325 Norway Ave., Kalamazoo, Mich.; Office: 324 W. Frank St., Kalamazoo, Mich.

*JAMES, Daniel Finney, b. Richmond, Va., June 23, 1911; s. Nathaniel Loved and Missouri (Finney) J.; B.S., Va. Union Univ., Richmond, Va., 1939; B.D., Howard Univ. Sch. of Rel., Wash., D.C., 1955; courses toward M.T.H., 1966--; m. Doris Courtney; Children--Joletta A., Wanda M., Daniel F., Jr.; staff mem., Shiloh Bapt. Ch., Wash., D.C., 1950-55; White Rock Bapt. Ch., Wash., D.C., 1956-60; asst. pastor, Good Will Bapt.

Ch., Wash., D. C., 1960-68; pastor, Ebenezer Bapt. Ch., Luray, Va.; US Navy, 1943-45; Area Campaign Medal; WW II Victory Medal; mem., Phi Beta Sigma, Democrat; Home: 804 Crittenden St., NE, Wash., D. C. Office: 1862 Kalorama Rd., NW, Wash., D. C.

JAMES, Eugene Marshall, b. Princess Anne, Md., Apr. 26, 1938; s. William Henry, Sr. and Pauline Ballard (Fields) J.; Somerset Jr.-Sr. High Sch., 1956; A. B., Md. State Coll., 1956-60; B. D., Theol. Sem., Johnson C. Smith Univ., 1960-62; Post Sem. Intern (for the Bd. of Natl. Missions) at St. Augustine Presby. Ch., 1963-64; mem., NAACP; Home: E. 172nd St. Bronx, N. Y., Church: 838 E. 16th St., Bronx, N. Y.

JAMES, Eugene Willis, b. Chiborne Co., Miss., Apr. 12, 1917; s. Cary and Janie James; A. A., Southern Chrstn. Inst., 1942; A. B., Jarvis Chrstn. Coll., 1944; m. Johnie Elizabeth; Children--Eugene, Jr.; Roserine; Daniel; Peter; Titus; Timothy; John; pastor, Crocket St. Chrstn. Ch., San Antonio, Tex.; Pine St. Chrstn. Ch., Tulsa, Okla.; Loudon Ave. Chrstn. Ch., Roanoke, Va.; Third Chrstn. Ch., Warren, O. (present); pres., Natl. Chrstn. Missionary Conv.; mem., Interdenom. Min. Alliance; Roanoke Min. Conf.; Roanoke Area Coun. (Disciples of Christ); Clergy Club; worked with the first Bi-Racial Comm.; program chrmn., Interdenom. Min. Conf.; v. p., pres., Piedmont-Tri State Conv., (Disciples of Christ); Home: 325 Spring St., Warren, O. 44485; Office: 241 First St., Warren, O. 44485

*JAMES, Frederick C., b. Prosperity, S. C., Apr. 7, 1922; s. Edward and Rosa (Lee) J.; A. B., Allen Univ., 1943; B. D., Howard Univ., Sch. of Rel., 1947; further study, Union Theol. Sem.; Columbia Univ.; D. D. (hon.), Allen Univ.; Monrovia Coll., W. Africa; m. Theresa G.; instr., Allen Univ.; dean, Dickerson Theol. Sem., Allen Univ., 6 yrs.; pastor, Friendship Afr. Meth. Episc. Ch., Irmo, S. C.; Bishop's Meml. A. M. E. Ch., Columbia, S. C.; Wayman A. M. E. Ch., Winnsboro, S. C., 3 yrs.; Chappelle Meml. A. M. E. Ch., Columbia, S. C., 3 yrs.; current, Mt. Pisgah A. M. E. Ch., Sumter, S. C., 10 yrs.; author of the 1960 Social Action Bill which created the A. M. E. Commn. on Social Action; elected the 1st consultant-director, Social Action Commn., A. M. E. Ch.; mem., The Gen. Bd. of the A. M. E. Ch.; sec., Commn. on Finance and Statistics of the A. M. E. Ch.;

supt., A. M. E. Sun. Schs. of S. C.; Denominational Staff Council, Natl. Coun. of Chs.; President's 30 member Commn. on Rel. and Race; Natl. Coun. of Chs., 1963; Home: 215 W. Bartlett St., Sumter, S. C.

JAMES, Goree Leon, b. Daingerfield, Tex., Sept. 5, 1930; s. Aaron and Loan Mae (J.); Prairie View A & M Coll., 1949; A. B., Okla. City Univ., 1960; m. Kate Lee Mc Cann; Children--Goree II, Kerwin Lemarr; ordained as an elder in the Chrstn. Meth. Episc. Ch., 1958; present pastor, St. Mary's C. M. E. Ch., 1961--; private sec. to Bishop B. Julian Smith and Bishop. W. H. Amos; chrmn., Conf. Bd. of Chrstn. Ed., C. M. E. Ch., 1961--; v. p., Okla. Coun. of Chs.; present, Dean of the Okla. City Dist. Leadership Training Sch., 1963--; mem., Okla. Coun. on Rel. and Race; Speaker's Bur. for the Natl. Coun. of Chrstns. & Jews; chrmn., comm. on housing, Okla. City NAACP; rel. consultant, Okla. City Urban League; mem., Adv. Comm. for the Okla. City Urban Renewal Authority, 1963-64; US Army, 1950-53; served in Korea 18 mos.; Korean Service medal; v. p., Interdenom. Min. Alliance, Okla. City; Democrat; Home: 3332 NE 16th St., Oklahoma City, Okla.; Office: 1700 NE 4th St., Okla. City, Okla.

JAMES, H. Rhett, b. Baltimore, Md., Dec. 1, 1928; s. Samuel H. and Tannie E.; A. B., Va. Union Univ., 1950; M. Ed., Our Lady of the Lake, 1952; B. D., Va. Union Univ., 1957; M. Th., Tex. Chrstn. Univ., 1960; m. Leora Thompson; children--Gregory Michael, Cedric Dwight, Pamela Denese, Stephen Anthony; instr., pub. schs., San Antonio, Tex., 1950-55; prof. educ., Va. Union Univ., 1955-58; assoc. pastor, Moore St. Bapt. Ch., Richmond, Va., 1957-58; pastor, New Hope Bapt. Ch., Dallas, Tex., 1958-present; teacher, Bishop Coll. Dallas, Tex., 1962-present; del. to four White House Conf.; pres., Comm. on Equal Employment; del., White House Civil Rights Conf., 1966; Bd. mem., Tex. Coun. of Chs., Amer. Civil Liberties Union; pres., John F. Kennedy Chapter of NAACP; Bd. of Solicitation, Dallas, Tex.; pres., Dallas Chapter of Frontiers Intl., Inc., pres., Youth Opportunities, Inc.; mem., Natl. Employment Assn., Spec. Deputy Constable of Dallas Co.; mem., Amer. Assn. of Univ. Professors; pres., Careers Diversified Inc.; mem., Comm. on Programming, Amer. Bapt. Conv.; Bd. mem., Family Serv. Inc.; chrmn., Metropolitan Coun. of NAACP; invited by Pres. John F.

Kennedy to the One Hundred Years Celebration of the Emancipation Proclamation held at the White House; Home: 5042 Lark Lane, Dallas, Tex.

JAMES, Isaac, b. Grifton, N. C.; s. Edward and Daisy; A. B., B. D., Va. Union Univ.; courses, Univ. of Md., Wash. Sch. of Psych., Wash. D. C.; Richmond Prof. Inst., Richmond, Va.; St. Elizabeth's Hosp., Wash., D. C.; m. Pearl Woodly; asst. min., Mt. Zion Ch., Richmond, Va.; pastor, Fountain Bapt. Ch., Richmond, Va.; present--chap., Central State Hosp., Petersburg, Va.; mem., exec. bd., Lott Carey Foreign Mission Conv.; Bd. Dir., Bapt. Allied Bodies of State of Va.; Min. Relief Bd., Natl. Bapt. Conv.; exec. bd., Goodwill Bapt. Conv.; Bapt. Min. Conf., Richmond, Va.; Crusade for Voters League; NAACP; Sigma Phi Beta; author: The Sun Do Move, Cong. Rec., 89th Congress, 1st session, No. 56, V. 3, Wash. D. C.; Home: 2615 Edgewood Ave., Richmond, Va. 23222; Office: Central State Hosp., Petersburg, Va. 23803

JAMES, Leroy, chaplain, b. Oakfield, Ga., Dec. 24, 1928; s. Perry and Fannie (J).; A. B., Morehouse Coll., Atlanta, Ga., 1955; B. D., Andover Newton Theol. Sch., Mass., 1960; m. Clara Alice Price; Children--Carlton Leroy; pastor, Lincoln Congre. Ch., Brockton, Mass., 1956-57; asst. pastor, Union Bapt. Ch., Hartford, Conn., 1951-56; Lay preacher and student asst., Providence Bapt. Ch., Atlanta, Ga.; Lay preacher, First Bapt. Ch., W. Tampa, Fla., 1950-51; chap. major, US Army, 1961-present, Ft. Hamilton, N. Y.; Ft. Devens, Mass., 1961; Korea; Pittsburgh Air Defense Command; Vietnam; Ft. Knox, Ky.; recipient, Army Commendation Medal, 1968; politics, Independent; mem., Phi Beta Sigma; Military Chaplains Assn., United Ch. of Christ; Home: Qtrs. Bldg. 136-A, Apt. 6-E, Hamilton Manor, Ft. Hamilton, N. Y.; Office: Student Detachment, Chaplains Officers Advanced course, Ft. Hamilton, N. Y., 11252

JAMES, Samuel H., b. a native Texan; Tenn. State Coll.; B. D. and S. T. M., Andover Newton Theol. Sem.; Grad. Work, Boston U. and Harvard U.; D. D. (hon.), Selma Univ.; LL. D., Bishop Coll.; m. Catherine J. Lomans; 2 sons, Samuel H., III; Carl Austin; 1 dau., Angela Inez; former dean of men, instr., Dept. of Rel., Bishop Coll.; pastor, Second Bapt. Ch., San Antonio, Tex.; moderator, La Grange Bapt. Dist. Assn., Texas; v. p.,

State Bapt. Missionary and Ed. Conv., Texas and State Sun. Sch. & B.T.U. Cong., B.M. & E. Conv.; mem., Bd. Dirs., Coun. of Chs., Metro. San Antonio; mem., Bd. Dirs., Community Welfare Coun., San Antonio; mem., Bd. Dirs., Central br. San Antonio YMCA; travelled, England, Europe, Holy Land, Africa, Scandinavian countries, Switzerland and Russia; mem. Planning and Zoning Commn., City of San Antonio. Home: 430 No. Pine St., San Antonio, Tex.; Church: Chestnut & Center Sts., San Antonio, Tex.

JAMES, William M., b. Meadville, Miss., June 4, 1915; s. Warren and Rosa; A.A., Southern Univ., Scotlandville, La.; A.B., Mt. Beulah Coll., Miss.; Butler Univ., Indianapolis, Ind., B.L.S.; B.D., Drew Univ., Madison, N.J.; courses: Jewish Theol. Sem., NYC; Chgo. Univ.; m. Juanita Taylor; Children--Edward; asst. pastor, Sampson United Meth. Ch., Indianapolis, Ind., 1936-39; pastor, E. Calvary Ch., NYC, 1941-44; Trinity Ch., Bronx, N.Y., 1944-52; Metro. Community U. Meth. Ch., NYC, 1952-present; former, Coun. Bronx Home Term Court; lectr. Min. Sch. for City Work; mem., Independt (politically); Fellowship Cambridge Univ., England, 1939; Fellowships, Harvard, Yale & Hartford Sem.; Curricula Bldg. & Philosophy; chrmn. Min. Interfaith Assn.; chrmn., Bd. Dirs. E. Calvary Nursery; mem., Natl. Bd. of Ed. Meth. Ch.; del., Gen. Conf. Meth. Ch., 1964-68; mem., Bd. Dirs. HARYOU Act; mem., Mon. Club; mem., Bd. Chaplains Prot. Coun.; mem., Bed. Ed. Prot. Coun.; mem., Bd. Dirs. HARCAP; mem., City-wide Coordinating Comm., N.Y.; mem., Meth. Camp Adv. Bd.; mem., Bd. MUST; ex. comm. OIC (N.Y.); mem., Harlem Coun. Service; Steering Comm. ACM; Home: 1981 Madison Ave., New York, N.Y.; Office: 1975 Madison Ave., New York, N.Y. 10035

JAY, Grover Cleveland, b. Ocilla, Ga., Aug. 14, 1914; s. John B. and Lizzie (Wells) J.; A.B., Paine Coll., Augusta, Ga., 1941; B.D., Gammon Theol. Sem., 1948; m. Jonnie Mae Mitchell; Children--Grover Anthony; ordained, 1942; pastor, Church Hill Circuit, Webster Co., Ga.; pastor, Scotts Mater Chrstn. Meth. Episc. Ch., Americus, Ga.; Holsey Temple C.M.E. Ch., Atlanta, Ga.; Flat Rock Circuit, Elbertony Dist.; current pastor, presiding elder, Trinity C.M.E. Ch., Augusta, Ga.; tchr., Eatonton, Ga. pub. sch.; Holsey Cobb Inst.,

Cordale, Ga.; dir., Student recruitment, Paine Coll., 1932-64; mem., Bd. of Trustees, Philip Sch. of Theol., Atlanta; Bd. of Trustees, Paine Coll.; v.p., Bd. of Chrstn. Educ., Chrstn. Meth. Episc. Ch.; Augusta Richmond Co. Voters League; Ga. Coun. on Human Relations; NAACP; Div. of Chrstn. Ed., Natl. Coun. of Chs.; Home: 731 Taylor, Augusta, Ga., 30901; Office: 818 Eighth St., Augusta, Ga.

JEFFERSON, Cattrall T., b. Kingston, Jamaica, Oct. 8, 1932; s. Scott S. and Helen Louise (Johnson) J.; A.B., B.S., Pacific Union Theol. Coll., Angwin, Calif., 1968; A.A., Diablo Valley Coll., Concord, Calif., 1965; m. Robbie M. Sibley; Children--Katherine V.; pastor, Liberty Park Seventh Day Adventist Ch., Salt Lake City, Utah, 1953-present; mem., Utah State Apprentice Commn.; Salt Lake City Jr. Acad. Sch. Bd.; Salt Lake City NAACP; T/Sgt. US Air Force, 1950-54; awards: Good conduct, Korea, Purple Heart, United Nations; Home: 1881 W. 100 South, Salt Lake City, Utah; Office: 820 S. Third St. E. Salt Lake City, Utah 84119

JEFFERSON, Frederick Douglas, b. Ardmore, Pa., Sept. 22, 1928; s. Frederick Douglas, Sr. and Ruth E. (J.); B.S., Wilberforce Univ., Ohio, 1950; B.D., Yale Univ., 1956; Th.M., Harvard Univ., 1958; M.A., Univ. of Chgo., 1968; m. Ruby M. McIntosh; Children--Janie Lue, Frederick Douglas, III, Norman; pastor, Bethel Afr. Meth. Ch., Lynn, Mass., 1957-59; instr., Payne Theol. Sem., Wilberforce, O., 1959-63; pastor, Holy Trinity A.M.E. Ch., Wilberforce, O., 1960-63; asst. prof. & dir. of rel. activities, Wilberforce Univ., 1964-66; dir., field ed., and lectr. homiletics, McCormick Theol. Sem. Chgo., Sept., 1968-present; acting personnel off. Great Lakes Reg. Office, O.E.O., Chgo.; Equal employment opportunity reviewer, consumer & marketing service, US Dept. of Agriculture; pres., Lynn, Mass. NAACP, 1958-59; mem., Alpha Phi Alpha; joined United Presby. Ch., Nov. 1968; US Army 1950-52; mem., Zeta Sigma Pi (Natl. Soc. Sci. Fraternity); Sen Mer Rekh Honor Soc., Wilberforce Univ.; Alpha Kappa Mu Natl. Honor Soc.; Home: 1025 E. 48th St., Chgo, Ill. 60615; Office: McCormick Theol. Sem., 800 W. Belden Ave., Chgo., Ill. 60615

*JEFFERSON, June Lee, Jr., b. June 25, 1924, Edgefield Co., S.C.; m. Rosa Lewis; Children--Justin Lee, Jay

Michael; B.S., Howard Univ., 1954; B.D., Howard Univ. Sch. of Rel., 1959; certificate, "Clinically Trained Clergyman," Laurel, Md., Lorton Reformatory, Va., 1966; asst. pastor, Zion Bapt. Ch., Alexandria, Va., 1957-present; chap., Graterford Correctional Inst., Graterford, Pa., 1964-65; chap., Dist. of Columbia, Dept. of Corrections, D.C. Jail, 1965-present; ordained Bapt. min., Apr. 23, 1960; charter mem., Steering Comm., SW br. YMCA; mem., SW Neighborhood Planning Council; Wash. Min. Conf.; Correctional Chaplain's Assn. of Amer.; bd. mem., Luther Rice Coll.; pres., Amidon Parents Recreational Coun.; sec., Health and Welfare, Crime and Delinquency Control Group; Bd. mem., Black Economic Union Adv. Coun.; mem., OIC, UPO; Wash. Concentrated Employment Program; awards: Outstanding award for volunteer work to the youth of Wash., D.C; US Navy, 1943-46; Home: 622 H St. SW, Wash., D.C. 20024; Office: Chaplain's Office, Dist. of Columbia Jail, Wash., D.C.

JENKINS, Bradley Palmer, b. Wilcox Co., Ala., July 17, 1916; s. Silas and Bessie J.; Snow Hill Inst., Snow Hill, Ala., 1938; Immanuel Luth. Coll. and Sem., 1954; summer courses: Concordia Sem., St. Louis, Mo., 1955 and 1960; m. Leila Scott; pastor, Faith Luth. Ch., Mobile, Ala., 1954-61; pastor, St. Philip Luth. Ch., 1962-; prin., Chrstn Day Sch., Faith Luth. Ch., Mobile, Ala.; v.p., Ala. Luth. Conf., 5 yrs.; Home: 803 Eddings St., Chattanooga, Tenn.; Church: 51 W. 25th St., Chattanooga, Tenn.

JENKINS, Charles Edward, Sr., b. Paris, Tenn., Aug. 24, 1928; s. Charles Atkins and Louise (George) J.; Lemoyne Coll.; Ala. A & M Coll.; Union Bible Sem.; D.D. (hon.), Monrovia Coll., Monrovia, Liberia, W. Africa; m. Lula Mae Reynolds; Children--Charliese, Lunelle, Mary Louise, Charles Edward, Jr.; pastor, St. Mary's Afr. Meth. Episc. Ch., Sahillo, Tenn., 1949; St. Mary and Lewis Chapel A.M.E. Chs., Lexington and Parson, Tenn., 1949-50; pastor, Ebenezer A.M.E. Ch., Clarksville, Tenn., 1951-55; St. Paul A.M.E. Ch., Fayetteville, Tenn., 1955-60; St. Paul A.M.E. Ch., Chattanooga, Tenn., 1960--; St. Mark A.M.E. Ch., Rossview, Tenn., 1951-52; Kelso Ciacoit, Kelso, Tenn., 1959-60; radio speaker and programs on stations, WTPR, Paris, Tenn., WDXI, WJZM, Clarksville, Tenn., WEKR, Fayetteville, Tenn.; former pres., A.M.E. Alliance of Chattanooga;

former v.p., Interdenom. Alliance, Chattanooga; sec., Central Tenn. Conf., 1950-55; del. to Gen. Conf. of A.M.E. Ch., 1960-64; contr. ed. of A.M.E. Christian Recorder; Home: 2524 Williams, Chattanooga, Tenn.; Office: 2514 Williams, Chattanooga, Tenn.

JENKINS, John Dallas, Sr., tchr., b. Luray, Page Co., Va., Oct. 12, 1919; s. Isaac Isaiah and Minnie (Jeffries) J.; studies: Storer Coll., Harpers Ferry, W. Va.; Capital, University, Columbus, Ohio; Conf. of Va. Negro Coll. on Rural Life, Va. State Coll., Ettricks, Va., 1947; Amer. Bible Coll., B.Th., 1960; Amer. Div. Sch.; D.D. (hon.), 1962; m. Marian Elizabeth Dennis; Children--Mrs. Grover Cleveland Banks, Mrs. Lewis E. Dodley, Mrs. Richard Vern Smith, John Dallas, Jr., Carver Robeson, Dennis Lee; ordained at Shepherdstown, W. Va., 1938; pastor, Bapt. Chs. in Shenandoah Valley of Va., 1938-48; reordained Deacon and Elder in A.M.E.Z. Ch., 1949; pastor, Poplar St. A.M.E.Z. Ch., Phila., Pa., 1949-52; pastor, A.M.E.Z. Ch., Lisbon, O., 1951-52; pastor, Avery Meml. A.M.E.Z. Ch., Pittsburgh, Pa., 1952-54; pastor, Caldwell Temple, A.M.E.Z. Ch., Columbus, Ohio, 1954--; instr., Central Sch. of Rel., Columbus, O.; instr., 4th Dist. Inst.; resource person, Gen. Conv. on Chrstn. Ed.; chrmn., Ch. comm., Columbus NAACP, 1959-60; sec., Columbus Area Coun. of Chs., 1958-59; mem., Admin. Bd., Ohio Coun. of Chs., 1955-63; chrmn., Commn. to Study Evangelism in A.M.E.Z. Ch., 1964; pres., A.M.E.Z. Min. Conf. of Columbus, 1955--; v.p., Interdenom. Min. Alliance of Columbus, 1960-63; mem., Pastor's section NCCC USA, 1962; mem., Ex. bd., Women's Charity Coun.; mem., Ex. bd., Poindexter Center, 1962-63; chrmn., Budget Comm. Ohio A.M.E.Z. Ch.; mem., Steering Comm. Organic Union of A.M.E.Z. and C.M.E. Chs.; chrmn., Columbus Chapter, Amer. Negro Emancipation Centennial Authority; Extraordinary Serv. Award in Chrstn. Ed., presented by the Chrstn. Ed. Dept. of the A.M.E.Z. Ch., 1959; mem., NAACP, Mason, Elks, YMCA, Urban League; author: Toward Order (handbook for Zion Meth. on the sacraments and ordinances). contr., A.M.E.Z. Quarterly Review (a homiletic journal); Home: 1750 E. Long, Columbus, O.; Office: 925 Bryden Rd., Columbus, O.

JENKINS, Thomas J., b. Nov. 18, 1900, Waldo, Fla.; s. Thomas B. and Emma (J.); Fla. Bapt. Acad., Jacksonville, Fla., 1913-16; Drew Theol. Sem., 1931-32; Israelite Heritage Inst., NYC, 1964; m. Margaret Jenkins; Children--three boys, 1 girl; pastor, Angelic Bapt. Ch., Bayonne, N.J., 1922-27; Ebenezer Bapt. Ch., Poughkeepsie, 1934-45; Sec. Bapt. Ch., 1946; moderator, Mt. Zion Assn., 21 yrs.; mem., Mayor's Adv. Com.; sec., Poughkeepsie Hous. Authority; 1st chrmn. of Evangelism Progressive Bapt. Assn. Inc.; mem., Mason; Home: Glenwood Ave., Poughkeepsie, N.Y. 12303

JENKINS, Warren Marion, ch. official, b. Cowpens, S.C., Mar. 15, 1915; s. James E.C. and Maggie E.J.; A.B., Claflin Coll., 1933-37; B.D., Gammon Theol. Sem., 1944; M.A., Drew Univ., 1946; m. Alma Louise Williams; Children--Patricia Elaine; chap. and tchr., Claflin Coll., Orangeburg, S.C., 1946-49; chap., S.C. State Coll., Orangeburg, S.C., 1949-53; pastor, Trinity Meth. Ch., Camden, S.C., 1953-57; Cumberland Meth. Ch., Florence, S.C., 1957-61; Exec. sec., S.C. Conf., Bd. of Ed., 1961--; mem., Phi Beta Sigma, Mason; Bd. of Ed. The Meth. Ch., 1956--; mem., The Assn. of Historical Soc. of the Meth. Ch.; Home: Muller St., Orangeburg, S.C.; Office: Claflin Coll., Orangeburg, S.C.

JESSIE, William R. Sr., b. Greensboro, N.C., July 1, 1926; s. James and Mary J.; B.D., Phila. Bible Inst., 1947; m. Ethel Studivant; Children--Mrs. Campbell Roland, Mrs. Vernon Shaw, Mrs. Willie Johnson; minister, Rel. Ed., Full Gospel Pentecostal Ch., Bridgeport, Conn., 1953-56; pastor, Pentecostal Temple, Ch. of God in Christ, Conn.; state chrmn. of finance, Chs. of God in Christ, 1965-present; State Evangelist Bd., sec., Ordination Bd., Conn., 1966-present; co-minister, Pastoral Psych., Bd. of Dir., Ch. of God in Christ; tchr., in other courses; N AACP organist, Conn., 1965-66; S/Sgt. US Signal Corps., 1947-53; mem., Mason; Home: 245 Larkin Ct., Stratford, Conn. 06497; Office: 434 Stratford Ave., Bridgeport, Conn. 06608

JOHNS, Vernon, administrator, b. Darlington Heights, Va.; s. William and Sally Branch (Price) J.; Va. Theol. Sem. and Coll., Lynchburg, Va., 1915; Oberlin Coll. Grad. Sch. of Theol., Oberlin, O., 1918; m. Altona Trent; 3 sons, Vernon, William, John; 3 daus., Adelaide, Enid, Jean; ordained Bapt. min., 1918; pastored, Court St. Bapt. Ch., Lynchburg, Va., 1920-26, 1941-48; Holy

Trinity Ch., Phila., 1933; First Ch., Charleston, W. Va., 1937-41; Dexter Ave. Bapt. Ch., Montgomery, Ala., 1948-53; Dir., Bapt. Educational Center, NYC, 1926-29; pres., Va. Theol. Sem. and Coll., 1929-33; mem., Alpha Phi Alpha; author: "Human Possibilities," Best Sermons, 1926; editor, Second Century Magazine, 1961 Deceased 1968.

JOHNS, Paul, b. Bristol, Pa., Feb. 7, 1887; s. Reading Beatty and Maria Caroline (Barney) J.; B.A., Howard Univ., 1913; B.D., Yale Univ., 1918; m. Grace Alma Wellmon; pastor, Congre. Chs., Knoxville, Tenn., 1918-24; Newport, R.I., 1924-27; Phila., Pa., 1927-28; New Haven, Conn., 1928-30; Savannah, Ga., 1930-34; retired, 1947; tchr., Brewer Normal Sch., Greenwood, S.C., 1913-14; Gregory Inst., Wilmington, N.C., 1914-15; Home: 173-54 103rd Rd., Jamaica, N.Y. 11433

JOHNSON, Albert Norman, b. Ivondale, Va., Apr. 27, 1898; s. Julius Caesar and Eudora; Va. Union Univ., 1921-24; B.Th., Va. Union Univ., 1934; pastor, Queen Ester Bapt. Ch., Mollusk, Va., 1931-42; Willie Chapel Bapt. Ch. and Second Mt. Zion Bapt. Ch., 1942-62; Mt. Vernon Bapt. Ch., Whitestone, Va., 1962-present; tchr., Westmoreland Co., 1935-50; Richmond, Va., 1950-58; certified Red Cross Tchr., Northern Neck Dist., Va.; moderator, Northern Neck Bapt. Assn. (4 yrs.); Home: 2814 Fendall Ave., Richmond, Va. 23222

JOHNSON, Andrew Lincoln, chap., b. Memphis, Tenn., Sept. 14, 1911; s. Aron and Sarah J.; B.A., Johnson C. Smith Univ.; B.D., Oberlin Grad. Sch. of Theol.; M.A., Oberlin Coll.; D.D., Payne Theol. Sem.; m. Dora K. Kennedy; Children--Dennis Harowe; Elder, Afr. Meth. Episc. Ch., No. Ohio Conf.; entered Reserve Chaplaincy of US Army, 1938; active duty Chap., 1941--; Lt. Col., 1954; Deputy Post Chap. Ft. Carson, Colo., 1961-65; assoc. chap., Tuskegee Inst., 1965-present; 1st chap., in 93rd Div. to earn bronze star, 1944; Army Commendation Ribbon; mem., Alpha Phi Alpha, Mason; Office: Tuskegee Inst., Tuskegee, Ala.

JOHNSON, Arthur L., b. Orangeburg, S.C., July 21, 1928; s. Henry and Eloise (Dash) J.; A.B., S.C. State Coll., 1953; B.D., Eastern Bapt. Theol. Sem., Phila., 1956; further study, Drexel Inst. and Temple Univ.; m. Frances Harris; Children--April Laurance, Ava Louise; asst.

pastor and pastor, St. Paul Bapt. Ch., Phila., Pa., 1965-present; mem., Good Shepherd Min. Com., Phila., Bapt. Assn.; Omega Psi Phi; awards: Korean Service Ribbon; Purple Heart Medal, two campaign ribbons; mem., Mercy-Douglass Hosp., Stephen Smith Home for the Aged, Friends Neighborhood Guild, Fellowship Commn., Downington Indus. Sch., Columbia br. YMCA, Crime Prevention Assn., Amer. Acad. of Pol. and Soc. Sci. and of Kappa Alpha Psi; active in movement for adoption of Phila. Home Rule Charter; Phila. Civil Service Commn.; 2nd Assembly of WCC, 1954; Commn. on Theol. Ed., Natl. Bapt. Conv.; speaker to numerous student groups; Home: 534 Orchard Ave., Yeadon, Pa. 19050; Office: 10th & Wallace Sts., Phila., Pa. 19123

JOHNSON, Charles Edward, b. Glen Alpine, N. C., Dec. 14, 1912; s. Edward Washington and Lessie Jane J.; B. A., Kittrell Coll., N. C., 1941; D. D. (hon.), Kittrell Coll., 1962; m. Irene Vivian Fitzgerald; pastor, Union Bethel A. M. E. Ch., Carey, N. C., 1938-40; Emmanuel A. M. E. Ch., Durham, N. C., 1940-43; Carroll Circuit A. M. E. Chs., Baltimore, Md., 1943-51; St. Stephen A. M. E. Ch., Essex, Md., 1951-54; Rocks Circuit A. M. E. Chs., Rocks, Md., 1956-62; Grace A. M. E. Ch., Catonsville, Md., 1962-present; mem., Baltimore Co. League for Human Rights; mem., W. Baltimore Inter-Faith, Inter-Racial Coun.; former mem., Hartford Co. Min. Alliance; mem., Baltimore Preacher's Meeting; mem., Catonsville Ministerium & Interdenom. Min. Alliance, Baltimore, Md.; Mason; Home: 67-1/2 Winter Ave., Catonsville, Md. 21228

JOHNSON, Coolidge Milford, b. Honea Path, S. C., Dec. 30, 1923; s. Milford E. and Bertha (Mattison) J.; B. A., Benedict Coll., 1946; B. D., J. J. Starks School of Rel., 1949; D. D. (hon.), Friendship Coll., 1952; m. Freeda Mae Moore; Children--Freeda Lynne; current pastor, Majority Bapt. Ch., 1955--; pres., State Bapt. Cooperative Conv., 1957--; sec., State Sun. Sch. and B. T. U. Cong., 1954--; prin., Geer High Sch., Belton, S. C., 1950-57; tchr., Benedict Sch. of Rel. Extension Class; pres., Palmetto Voters League; Bd. of Trustees, Morris Coll. and Friend Coll.; pres., Spartanburg br. of CORE, 1957-60; mem., NAACP, 1944--; State Youth Br. (coll.); active in Boy Scouts of Amer. since 1948; chrmn., Piedmont Div. of Boy Scouts of Amer.; Bd. of Natl. Sun. Sch. and B. T. U. Congress, USA, Inc.; Bd. of the Home

Home Mission, Natl. Bapt. Conv., USA, Inc.; Silver Beaver Award, 1963; mem., Mason, Omega Psi Phi; Home: 199 W. Park Ave., Spartanburg, S. C.; Office: 199 W. Park Ave., Spartanburg, S. C.

JOHNSON, Harvey Eligah, chap., b. Atlanta, Ga., Apr. 19, 1898; s. Harvey, Sr. and Indiana M (Oneal) J.; B. D., Taladega Coll., Ala., 1923; B. S. L., Chrstn. Bible Coll., 1924; M. A., Atlanta Univ., Ga., 1939; D. C., (Hon.), Natl. Spiritual Sch., 1960; m. Fannie Ramsey; Children --Marcine A. (Mrs. Sylvester Hall); pastor, First Congre. Ch., Chattanooga, 1923-29; Rush Meml. Congre. Ch., 1929-31; Beecher Congre. Ch., New Orleans, 1931-33; Talladega and Kymulga Congre. Chs., 1933-36; The First Congre. Chs., Montgomery and Selma, Ala., 1936-41; US Army Chap., Lt. Col., 1941-54; instr., High Sch., Lawrenceville, Ga.; Notary Public; mem., Mason; Home: 568 Auburn Ave., Atlanta, Ga.; Office: 18 So. Jackson, Atlanta, Ga.

JOHNSON, Julius Caesar, b. Baltimore, Md., Sept. 1894; s. Julius Caesar and Lillie Virginia (Matthew) J.; Temple Univ., 1911; Gammon Theol. Sem., 1916; grad. work: Boston Univ., 1921; D. D. (hon.), Wiley Coll., Marshall, Tex.; m. Emma Pepper; son--John Henri Watkins; pastor, Wash. Conf. Meth. Ch., 1916; dir., Sharp St. Meml. Ch. Educational Center, 1920-21; dir., Community Center and Playgrounds, Lexington, Ky. and part-time pastor: Denver, Colo., 1923-30; Hot Springs, Ark., 1930-32; Nashville, Tenn., 1932-34; Min. and Dir. of Chrstn. Ed., Tenn., Ark., Okla., 1930--; summer sch. instr., Meth. Ministers through Ministerial Training Meth. Ch., Philander Smith Coll., 16 yrs.; mem., Chrstn. Bd. Dirs., So. St. Community Center; Chaplains Training Sch., WW I; citation, plaque for serv. in pub. sch. by Cameron High Sch.; mem., Mason, Omega Psi Phi; Home: 1109 First Ave., So. Nashville, Tenn.; Office: 1116 First Ave., So. Nashville, Tenn.

JOHNSON, Lawrence Washington, tchr., b. Clifton, Tenn., Feb. 24, 1901; s. Frank and Ida (Briggs) J.; B. S., Tenn. State Coll., 1937; M. A., Fisk Univ., 1946; m. Lucille Jackson; children--Sharon, Ralph, Deborah, Roy; pastor, Shorter Chapel Afr. Meth. Episc. Ch., Franklin, Tenn., 1951-52; Cedar Grove Circuit, Rutherford Co., Tenn., 1956-57; Lewisburg Circuit, Lewisburg, Tenn., 1958, 1962-63; Woodford Chapel A. M. E. Ch., Shelbyville,

Tenn., 1959; St. Luke A. M. E. Ch., Gallatin, Tenn., 1963--; prin., High Sch., Winchester, Tenn. , Princeton, Ky., Trenton, Tenn., Midville, Ga., Rochell, Ga.; mem., Amer. Legion and Brotherhood Club; chap. asst., US Army, 1943; mem., Ministerial Interracial Group; Home: 355 Blythe Ave., Gallatin, Tenn.; Office: 357 Blythe Ave., Gallatin, Tenn.

JOHNSON, Leroy, chaplain (Major); b. Independence, La., Oct. 13, 1928; s. Archie and Armer (Lee) J.; A. A., City Coll., San Francisco, Calif., 1949-51; A. B., San Francisco State Coll., 1952-56; B. Th., Western Theol. Sem., El Cerrito, Calif., 1960-61; B. D., Golden Gate Theol. Sem., Mill Valley, Calif., 1961-63; m. Simmie Mae DeLoney; Children--Leana Marie, Darlene Arneil, Leroy Jr.; pastor, St. James Chrstn. Meth. Episc. Ch., Salinas, Calif., 1954-58; Laymen Chapel C. M. E. Ch., Oakland, Calif., 1958; David Chapel C. M. E. Ch., Richmond, Calif., 1958-63; US Army chaplain, 1963-present; mem., G. O. P. Central Comm. (county) Contra Costa, Richmond, Calif., 1961-63; 1st v. p., NAACP, Richmond Calif., 1961-63; Western Chrstn. Leadership Conf., Min. Alliance of Richmond, Calif.; rec'd Bronze Star; Army Commendation; Naval Unit Commendation; Vietnam Serv. Award; Amer. Defense Award; Home: 1611 Virginia Ave., Richmond, Calif.; Office: Hg. Rheinland-PEALZ, Supdist, APO New York, 09227

JOHNSON, Louis, b. Earl, Ark., Apr. 6, 1930; s. Omie and Zenobia; B. S., Wayne State Univ., Detroit, Mich., 1954; Northern Bapt. Theol. Sem., Chgo., Ill., 1956; Oberlin Grad. Sch. of Theol.; D. D. (hon.), Ark. Bapt. Coll., May 19, 1965; m. Beulah Stokes; children--Kevin, Quintin, Eric, Roderic; tchr., spec. ed., Chgo., Ill., 1955; pastor, Greater Zion Temple Bapt. Ch., Chgo., Ill., 1956-58; Friendship Bapt. Ch., Detroit, Mich., 1958-present; mem., Div. of Strategy and Planning, Detroit Coun. of Chs., 1959-65; Bd. of Dir., Open Door Rescue Mission, 1960-67; Bd. of Dir., Detroit Assn. of Amer. Bapt. Chs., 1964-67; Bd. of Mgrs., Mich. Bapt. Conv., 1964-67; chrmn., Min. Coun., Home Fed. Savings & Loan Assn., 1962-67; Detroit Fellowship of Urban Renewal Chs., 1960-67; Urban Renewal Com., 1964-67; Coun. of Bapt. Pastors, 1964-67; v. p., Wolverine Bapt. State Conv., 1963-66; v. moderator, Calvary Bapt. Dist. Assn., 1963-67; pres., Detroit Bapt. Pastors Union, 1966-67; mem., Detroit Urban League Housing Com.,

1963-67; Higher Ed. Opportunities Com., 1965-67; Mayor's Com. for Human Resources Dev., 1965-67; Fair Campaign Practices Commn., State of Mich., 1962-67; Detroit-Wayne Mental Health Services Bd., 1966-67; Home: 17417 San Juan Dr., Detroit, Mich. 48221; Office: 3900 Beaubien Ave., Detroit, Mich. 48201

JOHNSON, Meredith Elbert, b. Port Gibson, Miss., May 17, 1910; s. Henry E. and Phanada J.; A.B., Alcorn A. & M. Coll., 1935; D.D. (hon.) Campbell Coll., 1943; LL.D. (hon.), Monrovia Coll., Monrovia, Liberia, W. Africa; m. Kitty Ann Bourgeois; Children--Mrs. Alton Washington, Jr.; Gwendolyn Geneva; Meridith Warren; pastor, A.M.E. Ch., Mound Bayou, Miss., 5 yrs.; New Orleans, La., 13 yrs.; present pastor, Bethel A.M.E. Ch., Baton Rouge, La.; princ., pub. sch. sys., Miss.; Dean, Campbell Coll., Jackson, Miss.; trustee, Campbell Coll., 1941-43; mem., Connectional Coun., A.M.E. Ch., 1965; La. Coun. of Chs., 1965; defense worker, WW II; mem., NAACP, Urban League, Mason, Elk; Home: 1356 So. Blvd., Baton Rouge, La. 70802

JOHNSON, Ned Howard, b. Wheeling, W. Va., Nov. 8, 1934; s. Arthur F. and Elizabeth (Jackson) J.; A.B., Clark Coll., Atlanta, Ga., 1957; B.D., Gammon Theol. Sem., 1960; D.D. (hon.), The Coll. of Philosophy, Kans. City, Miss., 1963; m. Sarah Hughes; Children--Ned Jr., Geneva, Yvonne, Karen; pastor, First Congre. Ch., Marietta, Ga., 1956; First Congre. Ch., Macon, Ga., 1958-59; St. Paul Meth. Ch., Montgomery, Ala., 1959-60; Trinity Meth. Ch., Clarksburg, W. Va., 1961-62; Ronceverte-White Sulphur Charge, Ronceverte, W. Va., 1962--; mem., Alpha Phi Alpha, Masons, Alpha Kappa Delta Sociological Honor Soc.; Democrat; Home: 231 Main St., Ronceverte, W. Va., 24970

JOHNSON, Paul Edwin, chaplain, b. Buffalo, N.Y., Dec. 27, 1933; Sidney O.B. (grandfather), Maggie J. (J.); A.B., Talladega Coll., Talladega, Ala., 1955; B.D., Hartford Theol. Sem., Hartford, Conn., 1958; M.A. Harvard Univ., Cambridge, Mass., 1957; m. Shirley Ann Williams; Children--Paula Rene, Darryl Edwin; licensed and ordained, NYC Metro. Assn., United Ch. of Christ; assoc. minister, Congre. Ch. of No. N.Y. (Bronx, NY); chap., US Army 1962-present; Ft. Monmouth, N.J., 1962-64; 7th Inf. Div., Korea 1966; Teaching Fellow, Univ. of Michigan--summer, 1958; Consult., Rel. Ed.

for Bronx Co., NY City Prot. Coun. of Chs., 1959-61; guest lectr., Union Theol. Sem., NYC, 1960-61; instr., Univ. of No. Carolina at Ft. Bragg, N.C., 1967-68; mem., Dist. 15 & 16 Bd. of Ed., Bronx Co., 1961-62; Bd. of Dir., Big Brothers, Bronx, 1959-62; Bd. of Dir. So. Bronx Community Coun., 1960-62; pres., Bronx Co. Boy Scouts of Amer., 1961-62; Ex. Com. Liberal Pary, Bronx, 1959-61; pres., Min. Alliance, Long Branch & Red Bank, N.J., 1964-65; awards: Bronze Star; Army Commendation Medal; Air Medal; Master Parachute Badge Armed Forces Expeditionary Medal; Natl. Defense Medal; Citizenship Award; mem., Alpha Phi Alpha, Delta Phi Kappa Honor Soc., NAACP, SCLC, Democrat, Met. Assn. UCC; author: The Amistad Incident, Conn. Hist. Soc.; Home: 118 Elm Drive, Waugh, Ala.; Office: HQS 5th Spe. For., (Air), 1st Spe. For., APO San Francisco, 96240

*JOHNSON, Richard Hanson, b. Balto., Md., Sept. 8, 1904; s. Charles A. and Anna Elizabeth H.; A.B., B.Th., Howard Univ. Sch. of Rel., 1934; A.M., Howard Univ., 1952; courses: Gammon Theol, Sem., 1959; m. Julia Louise Taylor; Children--Richard Hanson, Jr., Charles Albert II, Beverly (Mrs. Kelly), Florence (Mrs. Richard I. Ray), Joan M., Alexander P., Edgar A.; current Dist. supt., No. Balto. Dist., Meth. Ch.; mem., Bd. of Pensions; Chaplains Com.; Comm. on Ministry to Neglected Areas; treas., Wesley Foundation, Howard Univ.; mem., Omega Psi Phi; author: Faith Through Victory, Wash., D.C., Campbell Press; Home: 3208 Carlyle Ave., Balto, Md.; Office: 828 N. Carollton Ave., Balto., Md.

JOHNSON, Robert Josiah, b. Hartford, Conn., Oct. 12, 1884; s. Robert and Elnora (Hurb) J.; St. Augustine's Collegiate Inst., Raleigh, N.C., 1906; Bishop Payne Div. Sch., 1909; attended Coll. of Preachers, Wash., D.C., 1945-52; D.D. (hon.), Shaffer Theol. Sem., Kans. City, Kans., 1930; m. Anna Turner Burgess; Children--Elnora, Robert, James, Ann, Theodore, Francis; vicar, St. Titus, Durham, N.C., 1909-13; St. Auden's, Paterson, N.J., 1919-23; Good Shepherd, Lynchburg, Va., 1913-19; St. Augustine's, Wichita, Kans., 1923-25; Church of the Ascension, Kans. City, Kans., 1925-30; St. Mary's, Hot Springs, Ark., 1930-40; All Saint's, Warrenton, N.C., St. Mark's, Wilson, 1943-57; retired 1957; dir. of Young Peoples Groups of Conf., Diocese of N.C.,

1945-56; sec., Bd. of Trustees of St. Augustine's Coll., 1957--; mem., The Exec. Coun. of the Diocese of N. C., 1943-47, 1951-54; Home: 1304 Fidewood, N. Wilson, N. C.; Office: Vicar Emeritus of St. Mark's Church, Wilson, N. C.

JOHNSON, Robert Pierre, b. Jersey City, N. J., 1914; A. B., Bloomfield Coll., 1937; B. D., Union Seminary, NYC, 1940; Ed. M., Univ. of Pittsburgh, Pa. 1947; D. D., Bloomfield Coll., 1964; m. Florence V. Bond, 1941 (deceased 1962); children--Lydia; Elayne; Alex; Deborah; ministry: ordained by Presbytery of Jersey City, 1940; Bethesda Presby. Ch., 1940-50; asst. sec., Dept. of City and Indus. Work, Bd. of Natl. Missions (Presby.) 1950-54; pastor, 15th St. Presby. Ch., 1954; Inst. of Racial and Industrial Relations; co-founder, Pittsburgh, 1946, Comm. of Reorganization of Presbytery, 1949-50; Westminster Found., 1954-60, 1961-64; chrmn., Pensions Comm., Wash. Presbytery, 1956-62; Gen. Counc. 1959-62, 1963; moderator, 1964--; 102nd Synod Preacher, 1957; tchr., Wilson Leadership Sch., 1959-62; chrmn., Natl. Missions, 1963; Permanent Commn. on Inter-Ch. Relations, 1955-58; del., World Alliance of Ref. Chs. holding the Presby. Order, 1958-64; Trustee, Natl. Presby. Ch. and Center, 1962-64; Commissioner, 1953, 1963; mem., Bd. of Dirs. of Children and Fam. Serv., Pittsburgh, Pa., 1948-50; sec., Bd. of Dirs., Coun. of Chs., Nat. Cap. Area, 1958-60; chrmn., Dept. of Soc. Welfare, Coun. of Chs. of Nat. Capitol Area, 1960-62; pres., Macfarland PTA, 1958-59; Housing Comm., Wash.; Urban League, 1960; Home: 4503 17th St., NW, Wash., D. C.; Office: 15th and R Sts., NW, Wash., D. C.

JOHNSON, Robert Ross, b. Spokane, Wash., June 26, 1920; s. John J. and Meha (Nickleberry) J.; B. A., Whitworth Coll., 1939-43; B. D., Colgate Rochester Coll., 1943-46; m. Ernestine N.; Children--Michele, Stephen Ross, John Ernest; instr., Fla. Normal Ind. Coll., 1946-47; pastor, 2nd Bapt. Ch., LeRoy, N. Y., 1947-48; co-minister, So. Congre. Ch., Chgo., Ill., 1947-52; pastor, Nazarene Congre. Ch., Brklyn, N. Y., 1952-56; St. Albans Congre. Ch., 1956--; mem., NYC Dept. of Correction; former mem., Oakwood-Kenwood Community Council; Hyde-Park Community Conf.; Bd. mem., Chicago Coun. Against Racial and Rel. Discrimination; v. p., Ch. Federation of Chicago; pres., Chicago Congre. Minister's Union; pres., Ill. State Conf. of NAACP; Bd. mem., Chicago NAACP;

chrmn., Chrstn. Ed. Dept., Bklyn, Prot. Counc. 2 yrs.; Bd. mem., NYC Congre. Ch. Assn.; Urban League of Jamaica, N.Y.; pres., Brooklyn-Long Is. Min. Alliance; Alpha Phi Alpha; chrmn., Com. on Church Extension and Home Missions of the NYC Congre. Ch. Assn.; local sch. bd. Dist 50, Queens; Bd. of Jamaica br. NAACP; Natl. Conf. of Chrstns. & Jews; Queens Mental Health Soc.; Queens Fed. of Chs.; Queens Center; Queens TB and Guidance Health Assn.; Home: 175-46 Murdock Ave., St. Albans, N.Y.; Office: 172-17 Linden Blvd., St. Albans, N.Y.

JOHNSON, Samuel T., b. New York, N.Y., Oct. 20, 1925; s. John L. and Carolyn (Russell) J.; N.Y.U., 1941-43; B.A., Roosevelt Coll., Chgo., Ill., 1948; Th.B., Chgo. Bapt. Inst., 1951; B.D., N. Bapt. Theol. Sem., 1955; m. Korin Clark; 1 son, Samuel T., Jr.; 2 daus., Saundra Anita, Cheryl Dennese; ordained Bapt. Minister, 1954; assoc. minister, Union Evangelistic Bapt. Ch., Chgo. Heights, Ill., 1951-54; asst. minister, Union E. Bapt. Ch., Chgo. Heights, 1954-58; pastor, New Mt. Zion Bapt. Ch., Daytona Beach, Fla., 1958--; faculty staff, Natl. Sun. Sch. & B.T.U. Congress, 1959--; pres., Interracial Coun. on Human Relations; v.p., Min. Alliance, (integrated), Halifax Area, Fla.; officer local NAACP (5 yrs.); coordinator, Assoc. Br. SCLC (So. Chrstn. Leadership Conf.); pres. (protem), Coun. on Human Relations for full compliance to Civil Rights Law, 1964; US Army, overseas (China, India, Burma theater), 1943-46; recipient, Good Conduct Service Medal and Bronze Star; mem., Social Engineers; (Pres.) business and prof. club for better community improvement; Home: 251 Weaver, Daytona Beach, Fla.; Church: PO Box 863 Daytona Beach, Fla.

JOHNSON, Ulysses Samuel, b. Fairfield Co., S.C., Oct. 13, 1909; s. Robert and Ida (Sanders) J.; A.B., Livingstone Coll., 1938; B.D., Johnson C. Smith Univ., Theol. Sem., 1942; D.D. (hon.), Livingstone Coll., 1952; m. Marie Jennings; Children--Norris Jennings; pastor, St. Paul A.M.E.Z. Ch., Hendersonville, N.C.; Hunters Chapel A.M.E.Z. Ch., Tuscaloosa, Ala.; St. Luke, A.M.E.Z. Ch., Wilmington, N.C.; current pastor, St. John's A.M.E.Z. Ch., Wilson, N.C.; sub. teaching-instr., Ministers & Laymen's Inst., South Port, N.C.; trustee, Clinton, N.C., Rock Hill, S.C.; mem., Men's Civic Club, Wilson, N.C.; NAACP; Home: 119 Pender

St., Wilson, N. C.; Office: St. John A. M. E. Z. Ch., Wilson, N. C.

JOHNSON, Wilbur R., b. Chicago, Ill., Sept. 28, 1920; s. L. C. and Corinne A.; B. S., Wilberforce Univ., 1945; S. T. B., Boston Univ. Sch. of Theol., 1949; m. Ernestine Range; Children--Gayle, Karen; pastor, Easter Hill Meth. Ch., Richmond, Calif., 1951-59; Normandie Ave. Meth. Ch., Los Angeles, Calif., 1959-61; Enterprise Meth. Ch., Compton, Calif., 1961-63; current, Pueblo Gardens Meth. Ch., Tucson, Ariz., 1963--; rec'd world-wide news coverage over appt. as first Negro to be assigned as minister-in-charge of all-white ch. (July '63); first Negro in Richmond, Calif. Rotary Club; mem., Mason, Alpha Phi Alpha, NAACP, Democrat; Christmas sermon in Pulpit Digest, Dec., 1963; Home: 2303 So. Norris Ave., Tucson, Ariz. 85713; Office: 2520 So. Plumber Ave., Tucson, Ariz. 85713

JOHNSON, William, b. Florence, S. C., Jan. 9, 1927; s. James and Alean (Johnson) J.; B. C., Lane Coll., Jackson, Tenn., 1960; B. D., Vanderbilt Univ., Nashville, Tenn., 1963; m. Clara V. Conley; Children--Frederick Devon; pastor, St. James C. M. E. Ch., Parksville, Mo., 1952-56; Wash. Chapel C. M. E., Jackson, Tenn., 1956-59; Denmark-Mercer C. M. E. Ch., Jackson, Tenn., 1956-59; Salem C. M. E. Ch., Jackson, Tenn., 1959-63; Miles Chapel C. M. E. Ch., Little Rock, Ark., 1963-present; mem., Greater Little Rock Min. Assn.; Little Rock Conf. of Rel. and Race Steering Comm.; Mason; Comm. on Community Affairs; Urban League of Greater Little Rock; Ark. Coun. on Human Relations; Ark. Voters Assn.; NAACP; No. Ark. Conf. C. M. E. Ch., 1965-66; Dist. chrmn., Boy Scouts of Amer.; awards for community service, Urban League, 1965; N. Ark. Conf. C. M. E. Ch., 1965, 1966; Office: 1804 E. Capitol Ave., Little Rock, Ark. 72202

JONES, Arthur Samuel, b. Mebane, N. C., Aug. 8, 1923; s. Pinkney Otto and Gertrude (Moore) R.; N. C. Coll., 1939-40; Kittrell Coll., 1943; Wilberforce Univ., 1944-46; D. D. (hon.), Kittrell Coll., 1962; m. Erma Vashti Knight; Children--Arthur Lewis, Joseph; pastor, Union Chapel A. M. E. Ch., Narragansett, R. I., 1954-55; Bethel A. M. E. Ch., Lynn, Mass., 1955-56; Allen Temple A. M. E. Ch., Somerset, Bermuda, 1957-61; Metropolitan A. M. E. Ch., Phila., Pa., 1961-present; instr., Prospect

Sch. for Boys, Pembroke, Bermuda; mem., Bd. of Dir., Phila. Coun. of Chs.; US Army WW II; Kappa Alpha Psi; Home: 723 S. 20th St., Phila., Pa.

JONES, Aubry, b. Texarkana, Ark., Feb. 22, 1933; B.S., Ark. A.M. & N. Coll., Pine Bluff, Ark.; 1954; M.Ed., Univ. of Ark., Fayetteville, Ark., 1961; Wesley Sch. of Theol., 1962; m. Joyce Young; Children--Aubry Jones, jr.; pastor, Smith Chapel Meth. Ch., Sikeston, Md., 1960--; tchr., pub. sch., 1956--; chrmn., The Recreational Comm., Sunset Cham. of Commerce; US Army, 1954-56; mem., Kappa Alpa Psi; NEA; Mo. Education Assn.; Ind. Arts & Vocational Education Assn.; Home: 4680 Essex Pl., St. Louis, Mo.; Office: 200 Young St., Sikeston, Mo.

JONES, Bennie J., b. Danville, La., Nov. 12, 1909; s. Billie and Edna Essie; Grambling Coll., La.; Bishop Coll.; Langston Univ., B.S.; m. Ada B. Hewitt; Children--Geneva, Marjorie, Bennie, Jr.; tchr., 15 yrs; chap., WW II; pastor, First Bapt. Ch.; moderator, S.E. Dist. Bapt. Assn.; dean, Okla. Bapt. Congress of Chrstn. Ed.; two battle stars; mem., Mason; Home: 4 NW Enid St., Idabel, Okla.

JONES, E. Theodore, b. Savannah, Ga., B.A., Va. Union Univ., Richmond, Va.; B.D., Crozer Theol. Sem., Chester, Pa.; M.A. Univ. Pa., Phila., Pa.; Ed.D., Tchrs. Coll., Columbia Univ., N.Y.; D.D. (hon.), Shaw Univ., Raleigh, N.C.; m. Dorothy L. Rice; Children--Cheryl Laconia, Theodore B., Eric Todd; pastor, Riverview Bapt. Ch., Richmond, Va., 1950-62; Dean of Chapel, Dir., Student Chrstn. Ctr., Va. Union Univ., 1947-60; prof., Socio. and anthro., Va. Union Univ., 1947-62; asst. dir., Dept. Schs. and Coll., Amer. Bapt. Conv., Valley Forge, Pa., 1962-67; Dir. Dept. Collegiate Educ., Amer. Bapt. Conv., 1967-68; present- Dir. Martin Luther King Sch. of Social Change, Crozer Theol. Sem., Chester, Pa.; mem., Salem Bapt. Ch., Jenkintown, Pa.; sch. bd. of Ellwood sch., W. Oak Lane, Phila.; Phi Delta Kappa--Honorary Men's Ed. Research Frat.; Kappa Alpha Psi; Natl. Ed. Assn.; NAACP; Natl. Assn. Coll. and Univ. Chap.; Rel. Ed. Assn.; Student Guidance and Personnel Assn.; Amer. and Coll. and Personnel Assn., United Bd. for Coll. Development; Natl. Coun. of Chs. of Christ in Amer.; United Negro Coll. Fund; Y's Men of Chrstn. St. YMCA; Scout Comm.

Troop 12, BSA.; Bd. of Dir. of Amer. Univ. Sch. of Intl. Service; Bd. of Mgrs. of Amer. Bapt. Hist. Soc.; Bd. of Dir. of Cooperative Coll. - Registry; Bd. of Trustees: Shaw Univ., Benedict Coll., Fla. Meml. Coll., Ellen Cushing Jr. Coll., Alderson-Proaddus Coll.; Office: Martin Luther King School of Social Change, Crozer Theol. Sem., Chester, Pa.

JONES, Enoch, b. Biloxi, Miss., Aug. 19, 1922; s. Lee and Martha; B. Th., Amer. Bapt. Theol. Sem., 1964; B. A., M. A., Fisk Univ., 1961, 1968; courses, Scarrit Coll., Nashville, Tenn.; m. Annabelle James; Children--Enoch Lee, Stephen, Janet; pastor, Friendship Bapt. Ch., Nashville, Tenn. (8 yrs.); 15th Ave. Bapt. Ch., 1961-present; founder, sponsor, Low Rent Housing Proj., Nashville, Tenn.; trustee, Amer. Bapt. Sem.; treas., Stones River Dist. Assn.; officer, Min. Conf., Nashville, Tenn.; v. p., Nashville Chrstn. Leadership Coun.; mem., Tenn. Bapt. Missn. and Ed. Conv.; Natl. Bapt. Conv., Inc.; former prof., Amer. Bapt. Sem.; WW II, three battle stars, Purple Heart; Home: 655 Moorman's Arm Rd., Nashville, Tenn. 37207; Office: 1203 Ninth Ave., North, Nashville, Tenn.

JONES, James E., b. Prince George Co., Va., Apr. 16, 1916; s. Mike and Minnie (Williams) J.; A. B., Va. Union Univ., 1947; B. D., Va. Union Univ., 1950; D. D., Birmingham Univ., 1961; m. Martha Carter; Children--Jameson C., Maudine W.; pastor, Va., 1953-56; Army chap., 1956; Spec. Sec. of the Amer. Bible Soc.; mem., Gethsemane Bapt. Ch., Wash., D. C.; Dir., Chrstn. Ed. Gethsemane Bapt. Ch.; rec'd achievement award while serving as Army Chaplain; Home: 614 Oneida St. NE, Wash., D. C.; Office: Amer. Bapt. Soc., 1435 G St., NW, Wash., D. C.

JONES, James Miller, b. New York, N. Y., Aug. 2, 1921; s. (adopted) Mary Nelson Jones; B. S. Ed., W. Va. State Coll., 1949; S. T. B., Boston Univ. Sch. of Theol., 1953; m. Margaret Ruth Howard; 2 daus., Nathlie Eloise, Valerie Teresa; Mig. ministry, Home Miss. Div., Natl. Coun. of Chs. of Christ, USA, 1951, 52, 1953-57; Assoc. Chap., Hampton Inst., Hampton, Va., 1957-61; pastor, Lemuel Haynes Congre. Ch., Jamaica, N. Y., 1961--; part-time chap., Vet. Adm. Hosp., NYC; mem., NAACP, Bd. of Dirs., Soc. Action Comm., U. Ch. of Christ; US Army, 33 mos. overseas duty, 1942-45; Home: 160-35

119th Drive, Jamaica, N.Y. Office: 146-09 116th Ave., Jamaica, N.Y.

*JONES, James Ricardo, Jr., b. Baltimore, Md., Feb. 21, 1934; s. James and Annie (J.); A.B., Morgan State Coll., Balto., Md., 1958; M. Div. Howard Univ. Sch. of Rel., 1968; m. Janice Matthews; Children--Rodney, Ricardo Leonard; asst. pastor, Christ-Edmondson United Meth. Ch., Balto., Md., 1967-68; pastor, Prince Frederick Circuit, Prince Frederick, Md., 1968-present; mem., Bd. of Recreation and Parks, Calvert Co., Md., 1968-70; Sponsor--to build Carroll-Western United Meth. Recreation Area; mem., Elks, Mason; Beta Sigma Tau, Democrat; Address: Route 1, Box 21, Prince Frederick Md. 20678

JONES, John Garth, b. Huntsville, Ala., Nov. 14, 1909; s. Mathew and Martha J.; attended Bishop William Sch. of Rel., 1942-44; A.B., B.D., Wilberforce Univ., 1947-52; pastor, Handy Chapel, Joplin, Mo., 1952; Ward Chapel A.M.E., Festus, Mo., 1954; A.M.E. Ch., Farmington, Mo.; Bethel A.M.E. Ch., Churchwelston, Mo.; St. Mark A.M.E. Ch., St. Louis, Mo.; mem., NAACP; Community Club; Mason; Home: 4516 Newberry Terrace, St. Louis, Mo. 63113

JONES, John Luke, b. White Plains, Va., Aug. 28, 1886; s. Wilkins E. and Elizabeth (Tanner) J.; Downingtown Indus. Sch., 1913; Lincoln Univ. Theol. Dept., Pa., 1917; Carswell Inst. of Speech; m. Estella Rose Morgan; former missionary of the Bethany Bapt. Assn., N.J., 1918; instr., The Liberty Bapt. Inst., Camden, N.J.; pastor, Union Bapt. Ch., Pawtucket, R.I., 1922-24; Grace Temple Bapt. Ch., Lawnside, N.J., 1927-29; Current pastor, Miller Meml. Bapt. Ch., 1936--; pres. (former), UNIA, R.I.; gospel singer, 1910-18; studied as crayon artist, house and sign painting, mail order business, compositor-printer and journalism; editor and founder, Northwest Truth magazine; Bd. of Penna Bapt. State Conv.; Grand Order Moses; NAACP; Fellowship Commn; Crime Prevention Assn.; The Wharton Center Assn.; Home Mission Dept. of the Natl. Coun. of Christ in America; Home: 2225 No. College Ave., Phila., Pa.; Office: 22nd St. and Jefferson, Phila., Pa.

JONES, Lawrence Neale, educator, b. Moundsville, W. Va., Apr. 24, 1921; s. Eugene Wayman and Rosa (Bruce) J.;

B. S., Ed., W. Va. State Coll., 1942; M. A., Univ. of Chgo., 1948; B. D., Oberlin Sch. of Theol., 1955; Ph. D., Yale Univ., 1961; m. Mary Ellen Cooley; dau., Mary Lynn, son, Rodney Bruce; West Salem Charge Evan. and Ref. Ch., 1953-55; Student Chrstn. Movement, Middle Atlantic Region, 1957-60; Dean, Fisk Univ. Chapel, Nashville, Tenn., 1961--; US Army 1943-46; 1947-53; ROTC Asst. Prof. of Military Sci., Va. State Coll.; Capt., US Army, Europe, 1951-53; mem., Bd. Dirs., Nashville NAACP, 18th Ave. Comm. Ctr., Nashville Assn. for United Nations; v. p., Nashville Human Rel. Coun.; mem., Soc. Action Comm., Tenn. Coun. of Chs.; pres., U. Ch. Fellowship of Campus Ministry; mem., Commn. on Higher Education, Natl. Coun. of Chs.; recipient, Rosenwald Scholarship, Lucy Monroe Scholarship, Rockefeller Doctoral Fellowship; Present Dean of Students Assn., Union Theol. Sem., NYC; Office: Union Theol. Sem., New York, N. Y.

JONES, Leon Cooper, social worker; b. Laurel, Miss., Apr. 16, 1919; s. Robert Franklin and Addie (Mobley) J.; certificate, Cornish Musical Conservatory, Seattle, Wash., 1952; B. A., Seattle Pacific Coll., 1962; m. Rubye Brown; Children--Kathryn Louise; asst. pastor, Mt. Olive Bapt. Ch., Seattle, Wash., 1957-60; pastor, Second Bapt. Ch., Everett, Wash., 1960--; case worker, Wash. State Dept. of Pub. Assistance; mem., Mason; v. moderator, Cascade Assn., Amer. Bapt. Chs. of Pacific Northwest, 1963; US Navy, 1938-46; Defense Medal; Good Conduct Medal; Asiatic Pacific Ribbon; Philippines Campaign; WW II Victory Medal; The Amer. Theater Medal; Home: 1424 31st Ave., Seattle, Wash.; Office: Second Bapt. Ch., 2807 Virginia, Everett, Wash.

JONES, Leonard McKinley, b. Painter, Va., Feb. 8, 1927; s. William and Viola; B. S., Va. Union Univ., Richmond, Va., 1950; S. T. M., Temple Univ., 1954; S. T. M., Temple Univ., Phila., Pa., 1955; M. P. H., Columbia Univ., NYC, 1965; m. Hattie; Children--Leonard, Wyndel, Timothy; pastor, Zion Bapt. Ch., Ardmore, Pa., 1953-present; regional supervisor, Pa. Dept. of Health; mem., Bd. of Trustees, Mont. Co. Com. Coll., Norristown, Pa.; chrmn., Loner Merion Township, Housing Authority, Ardmore, Pa.; US Army; award: Commonwealth of Pa. Civil Service League; US Army Commendation; pres., Environmental Health Sec.; mem., Pa. Public Health Assn.; Nat. Assn. of Sanitarians; Amer.

Bapt. Conv.; Home: 221 W. Spring Ave., Ardmore, Pa.; Office: 1400 W. Spring Garden St., Phila., Pa.

JONES, Major J., coll. prof., ch. official; b. Rome, Ga.; A. B., Clark Coll., Atlanta, Ga.; B. D., Gammon Theol. Sem.; S. T. M., Oberlin Coll., Ohio; Th. D., Boston Univ. Mass.; m. Mattie P.; children--Chandra J.; pastor, coll. prof., conf. dir. of Chrstn. Edu. in the Meth. Ch.; current supt., The Knoxville Dist. of the E. Tenn. Conf. of the Meth. Ch.; mem., 1964 Gen. Conf. the Meth. Ch.; 1964 Central Jurisdictional Conf. of the Meth. Ch.; Gen. Bd. of Ed. of the Meth. Ch.; The Commn. on Stds. for Wesley Foundations of the Meth. Ch.; The Chattanooga Mayor's Bi-Racial Comm.; Chattanooga Cham. of Commerce; Bd. of Dirs., Tenn. Coun. on Human Relations; The Bd. of the Comm. of Southern Churchmen; The Bd. of the Southern Chrstn. Leadership Conf.; The Comm. of Management of the YMCA; The Bd. of the Chattanooga Area Literacy Movement; The Bd. of the Natl. (Chattanooga) Conf. of Chrstns. and Jews; Office: 3709 Rogers Rd., Chattanooga, Tenn.

JONES, Matthew Aurelius, Sr., tchr., b. Bethel, N. C., Au 17, 1913; s. Henry Fred and Isabella (Payton) J.; 1937, A. B., St. Augustine's Coll.; 1947, B. D. Bishop Payne Div. Sch.; m. Oliva Beatrice Browning; Children: Matthew, Jr., Marshall R., Rose J. Hicks, Brenda J. Frazier; headmaster, John Moncure High Sch., 1937-38 (Millers Tavern, Va.); principal-tchr., Marie McIver High Sch., 1939-43, Littleton, N. C.; chap., Voorhees Sch. & Jr. Coll., 1947-51, Denmark, S. C.; priest-in-charge, St Cyprian's Episc. Ch., Pensacola, Fla., 1951-58; priest-in-charge, St. Luke's Episc. Ch., Knoxville, Tenn., 1958; tchr., WPA Adult Ed., 1936-38, Raleigh, N. C.; mem. chrmn., Fricker Rec. Center Bd., Pensacola, Fla. 1952-53; pres., Knoxville Br. NAACP, 1961; sec. Comm Associated Coun. for Full Citizenship, Knoxville, Tenn., 1960-61; Adv. Bd., Homemakers Service, State Dept. Pub. Welfare, Tenn.; Urban League Award; Home: 2201 McCalla Ave., Knoxville, Tenn.; Office: 600 Chestnut St., Knoxville, Tenn.

JONES, Ozro Thurston, Jr., b. Phila., Pa., s. Ozro Thurston and Neaza; B. S., B. S. T., D. S. T., Temple Univ., 1945, 1946, 1949, 1953, 1962; pastor, Young People's Ch. of Holy Temple Ch. of God in Christ, 1941-49; missionary and liaison minister of Ch. of God in

Christ, Liberia, W. Africa; Holy Temple Ch. of God in Christ, Phila., Pa., 1953-63; assoc. min., Meml. Ch. of God, Haverford, Pa.; organized Young People's Tue. Night Service, Phila, Pa., Sons of Gideon and Daughters of Ruth; Young People's Chorus of Holy Temple; Upper Room Fellowship; assoc. ed., Young People's Willing Workers Quarterly; co.-ed., The Christian View of Life; What Are Young People In Your Church Doing? Who Is This Man Called Jesus? Doctoral dissertation, The Meaning of the 'Moment' in Existential Encounter According to Kierkegaard; co-organizer, Pentecostal Student Youth Conf.; organizaer, Big Brothers and Big Sisters Fellowship, Ch. of God in Christ; ad. asst., chrmn., Program and Steering Comm., Int. Youth Congress, Ch. of God in Christ; pres., Intl. Youth Dept., Ch. of God in Christ, 1964; Office: Holy Temple Ch. of God in Christ, 60th & Callowhite Sts., Phila., Pa.

JONES, Quintus Leon, b. Nov. 21, 1917, Canton, Miss.; s. W. L. and Mary Ann (J.); A. B., Jackson State Coll., Jackson, Miss.; Th. B., A. B., Am. Bapt. Theol. Sem., Nashville, Tenn.; D. D. (hon.), Simmons Univ., Louisville, Ky.; m. Gertrude Chess; Children--Marian (Mrs. Cole); pastor, Hill's First Bapt. Ch., Athens, Ga., 1943-47; Fourth St. Bapt. Ch., Queensboro, Ky., 1947-60; So. Liberty Bapt. Ch., Canton, Miss., 1960-present; moderator, pres., Ky. Bapt. State Congress, 1948-60; past. chrmn., Soc. and mem. Bd. of Dirs., Service Comm. Natl. Bapt. Conv.; former tchr., Miss. Bapt. Sem., Jackson, Miss.; mem., Progressive Bapt. Conv.; S. C. L. C.; NAACP; Home: 1413 Brinkley Dr., Jackson, Miss. 39213; Office: 531 So. Liberty St., Canton, Miss. 39045

JONES, Robert L., b. Elizabeth, N. J., July 29, 1936; s. Samuel O. and Eva (Taylor) J.; B. A., Atlantic Union Coll., 1959; M. A., Andrews Univ., 1961; m. Dawn Lee Reynolds; conducted evangelistic crusade, 1963; Lake Region Conf. of Seventh-Day Adventists, 1961; asst. pastor, Benton Harbor, Mich.; present: pastor, Seventh-Day Adventist Ch., Kalamazoo, Pontiac and Millan, Mich.; Phi Delta Chi Soc.; Urban League; Home: 3263 Avon Manor, Rochester, Mich.; Office: London S. D. A. Ch., London, Mich.

JONES, Sercy Leonard, b. Conroe, Tex., Nov. 7, 1917; s. John and Ella Foster; Samuel Huston Coll., 1940; A. B.,

Gammon Theol. Sem., B.D.; Drew Univ., grad. study, 1943; S.T.M., Temple Univ., 1943; m. Mary Elizabeth Randolph; Children--Randolph L., Carroll W., Iris Faye, Francis Robert, Marcus Edwin; pastor, Woodbury Meth. Ch., 1944-45; Delair, N.J., 1945-47; Fordville, N.J., 1947-49; Chester, Siloam, 1949-55; Cambridge, Md., 1955-61; Haven Meth. Ch., Phila., Pa., 1961--; mem., Bd. of Mgrs. of YMCA, Chester & Phila., Pa.; Bd. of Mgrs., Columbia br. YMCA; Bd. of Dirs., The Inter-ch. Child Care Soc.; Citizens' Adv. Comm. of the Dept. of Pub. Assistance of the City of Phila.; mem., Omega Psi Phi; Home: 6700 Cresheim Rd., Phila., Pa. 19119; Office: 23rd and Oxford St., Phila., Pa. 19121.

JONES, Sidney St. Clair, b. Rep. of Panama, Dec. 22, 1919; s. Charles and Louise (Skeete) J.; B.S., Univ. of Panama, Rep. of Panama 1946-49; M.A., Univ. of Notre Dame, So. Bend, Ind.; Gen. Elec. Fellowship, Rennselaer Polytech. Inst.; m. Marjorie Harris; Children--Lois, Hubert, Albert; ordained Oct. 29, 1963; asst. pastor, First Bapt. Ch., Bay Shore, N.Y., 1962-65; pastor, First Bapt. Ch. 1965-present; prof. of Math., Colegio Abel Brave, Rep. of Panama; tchr., Brentwood High Sch., Brentwood, N.Y.; mem., Bd. of Dir., NAACP, Bay Shore, N.Y., 1967-68; Bd. of Dir., Bay Shore Community Coun., 1966-68; NEA; Mason; L.I. Progressive Missionary Bapt. Ch. Assn.; Islip Min. Coun., Islip, N.Y.; Home: 31 Anna, Bay Shore, N.Y.; Office: 175 Second Ave., Bay Shore, N.Y. 11706

JONES, Vernon Algernon, Jr., chaplain, b. Brunswick Co., Va., Sept. 19, 1924; s. Vernon A. and Harriet (Rhodes) J.; A.B., Va. Union Univ., Richmond, Va., 1941-45; B.D., Bishop Payne Div. Sch. (Va. Theol. Sch., Alexandria), 1945-48; m. Lillian Liressarine Clark; Children--Frances Cecilia, Harriet Ethelyn, Lillian Vernelle; pastor St. Andrew's, Danville, Christ, Halifax, St. Luke's Chatham (Va.), 1948-49; pastor, St. James, Emporia, Va. and St. Thomas', Freeman, Va., 1949-53; pastor, St. Stephen's, Petersburg, Va., 1953-57; rector, St. Andrew's Ch., Tuskegee Inst., Ala., 1957--; Episc. chap. to students, Tuskegee Inst., with counseling and hosp. ministry assignments; mem., Tuskegee Civic Assn., Omega Psi Phi; Mason; Home: 301 Neal St., Tuskegee Inst., Ala.; Office: 429 Montgomery Rd., Tuskegee Inst Ala.

JONES, William Augustus, Jr., b. Louisville, Ky., Feb. 24, 1934; s. William A., Sr. and Mary E. J.; A.B., Univ. of Kentucky, 1958; B.D., Crozer Theol. Sem., 1961; m. Natalie Barkley Brown; Children--William III, Elsa, Lesley; pastor, First Bapt. Ch., Phila., Pa., 1959-62; Bethany Bapt. Ch., Bklyn, N.Y., 1962-present; former, Chrmn. Bd. of Dirs., Bedford-Stuyvesant Youth in Action, Brklyn Anti-poverty program; bd. mem., Urban League, Bklyn.; United Epilepsy Assn.; mem., Borough President's Comm. on Equal Opportunity; Bd. mem. Dept. of Social Justice; Natl. Coun. Chs., chrmn., Greater NY Operation Breadbasket; pres., Eastern Reg. Conv.; Progressive Natl. Bapt.; awards: "Man in the News," NY Times; cited, NY Post for efforts to secure equal job opportunities for minorities; "Man of the Year," Bklyn Jr. Cham. of Commerce; former ed., "Mission Outlook," official pub. Bapt. Foreign Mission Bur., USA; US Army 1954-56; Home: 1377 President St., Bklyn, N.Y. 11213; Office: 460 Sumner Ave., Bklyn, N.Y., 11216

JONES, William Clarke, ch. official, b. Detroit, Mich., Sept. 18, 1927; s. Gilbert Emmanuel and Lue Alma (Clarke) J.; Oakwood Acad., 1944-45; B.A., Oakwood Coll., 1949; m. Doris Willia Mae Kimble; Children--William, jr., Cynthia R. Mera; SW Reg. Conf. of Seventh-Day Adventist, 1949--; pastored, Lubbock, Tex., 1950-53; Ft. Worth, Tex., 1953-57; Tyler, Tex., 1957-62; San Antonio, 1962-63; present: sec., Sabbath Sch. and Home Missionary of S.A.D. Ch., Dallas, Tex. Office: 1900 South Blvd., Dallas, Tex.

JONES, William Ronald, b. Louisville, Ky., July 17, 1933; s. Henry Wise, Jr. and Lannie Belle (Brogsdale) J.; 1955, A.B., Howard Univ.; 1958, B.D. Harvard Univ. 1960, Candidate for Ph.D., Brown Univ.; m. Lauretta Adalyne Hicks J.; Child: Jeffrey; current: asst. min., First Unitarian Ch., Providence, R.I.; tchr. asst. Brown Univ. (present); Phi Beta Kappa; Natl. Defense Ed. Act Fellowship; Rockefeller Bros. Theol. Fellowship; Rockefeller Doctoral Fellowship in Rel.; Home: 2715 Magazine St., Louisville, Ky.; Office: Dept. of Religious Studies, Brown Univ., Providence, R.I.

JORDAN, Frederick Douglass, bishop, b. Atlanta, Ga., Aug. 8, 1901; s. D. J. and Carrie (Thomas) J.; A.B., Northwestern Univ.; B.D., Garrett Theol. Sem.; grad.

work, Chgo. Theol. Sem., Univ. of Chgo.; D.D. (hon.), LL.D. (hon.), Wilberforce Univ., Payne Sem., Campbell Coll., Morris Brown Coll., Kittrell Coll., Allen Univ., Monrovia Coll., Liberia; m. Artishia Wilkerson; dean of Sch. of Rel., dean of Coll., organizer and pres., Bishop Wms. Sch. of Rel., Western Univ., Quindaro, Kans.; dean, Intl. Coun. of Rel. Ed.; pastor, St. Paul Afr. Meth. Episc. Ch., So. Chgo.; St. Paul, A.M.E. Ch., Moline, Ill.; Carey Temple and St. Mary A.M.E. Ch., Chgo., Ill.; First A.M.E. Ch., Gary, Ind.; Bethel A.M.E. Ch., Leavenworth, Kans.; Bethel A.M.E. Ch., Kans. City, Mo.; 1st A.M.E. & Ward A.M.E. Ch., Los Angeles, Calif.; Episc. supervision: Union of S. Africa, Central Afr. Fed., Ghana, Liberia, Sierra Leone and Nigeria, on the W. Coast of Africa; Fifth Episc. Dist.: Missori, west to Calif.; Eighth Dist.: La. and Miss.--forced to leave the latter because of integration activities, voter registration and etc.; mem., Ex. bd. of NAACP Comm. of Management, YMCA, Los Angeles; Natl. Ed. Comm. of CORE; Urban League; So. Chrstn. Ed. Comm.; Amer. Civil Liberties Union; Amer. Chrstn. Palestine Comm.; Ex. Comm. and chrmn., Race Relations Commn. of Los Angeles Ch. Federation; Mason; Alpha Phi Alpha; Sigma Pi Phi; NAACP; Home: 5151 Franklin Ave., Hollywood, Calif.

JORDAN, Isaac Matthew, b. Perquimans Co., July 28, 1906; s. Wilson and Mary J.; State Tchrs. Coll., Elizabeth City, N.C., 1931; B.S., NY Univ., 1956; M.A., New York Univ.; m. Clara Alexander; asst. pastor, First Bapt. Ch., New Bern, N.C., 1949; pastor, Bethel Meml. Bapt. Ch., New Bern, N.C., 1951; Rountree Meml. Bapt. Ch., Wilson, N.C., 1954; Banks Chapel Meml. Bapt. Ch., Rt. Kinston, N.C., 1956; tchr., public sch., Snow Hill, N.C. since 1934; Mason; Home: PO Box 273, Snow Hill, N.C. 28580

JORDAN, Robert Lee, b. Knoxville, Tenn., May 20, 1906; s. Henry and Emma (Matteney) J.; Va. Union Univ., 1928-30; A.B., Chapman Coll., 1936; Univ. of So. Calif. 1932; M.A., Univ. of Mich.; m. Maisie Norman; Children--Robert Lee, Emma Goldie, Kenneth Samuel; asst. supt., West Side Community Center, Los Angeles, Calif. 1933-35; chrmn., Comm. on Friendly Relations, Chrstn. Chs., 1934-36; asst. pastor, Hooper Ave. Chrstn. Ch.; current pastor, United Chrstn. Ch., Detroit, Mich., 1937--; pres., Natl. Chrstn. Missionary Cov., 1958-60;

chrmn., Social Action Comm., Chrstn. Ch., 1954-58; bd. mem., Delta Home for Girls, 1956-58; program chrmn., Denominational Min. Alliance, 1963--; mem., Selective Ratings Group of Negro Preachers of Detroit, Mich.; award: 25 yr. citation for serving one ch., Detroit Min. Conf.; pres., West Side Pastors Union, Detroit; Interdenom. Min. Alliance; Kappa Alpha Psi; author: Two Races in Fellowship; Negro Disciples in Michigan; former mgr., Western Challenger (newspaper, Los Angeles); Home: 2421 W. Forest, Detroit, Mich.; Office: 2415 W. Forest, Detroit, Mich.

JOSEPH, Charles David, b. Centerville, Ala., July 30, 1936; s. Walsh and Avie (Smelley) J.; B.S., Oakwood Coll., 1957; B.A., Oakwood Coll., 1961; M.A., Andrews Univ., 1962; m. Vivian Holland; Seventh-Day Adventist Ch., intern work in Gary, Ind., 1961-62; intern work in Chgo., Ill., 1962; intern work in Minneapolis, Minn., 1962; present: pastor, Greenwood S.D.A. Ch., 1962--; tchr. of academy sci. and coll. biology, 1960-61; Home: 1016 Eastlawn Dr., Greenwood, Miss.

JOSEPH, Ray Kennington, b. St. Thomas, Virgin Is., Jan. 27, 1932; s. Arthur W. and Dassilda L.; B.A., Moravian Coll., Bethlehem, Pa., 1963; Moravian Theol. Sem., 1963-66; M. Div. Chrstn. Theol. Sem., Indianapolis, Inc., 1967; m. Shirley June Elizabeth James; youth worker, Salem United Ch. of Christ, Allentown, Pa., student asst. min., Schoeneck Moravian Ch., Nazareth, Pa.; pastor, Fourth Moravian Ch., N.Y., 1 yr.; chap., migrant workers; B.S.A. Coun., Bethlehem, Pa.; US Navy, 1968; present: Chaplin III Marine Amph. Force, Vietnam military; Natl. Def. Award (twice); Good Conduct Medal, 1957; San Diego, Mar. and Aug., 1968; tchr., 1967; mem., Central Chrstn. Ch., San Diego; N.J., Pa. Regional Coun. of the United Campus Chrstn. Fellowship; Intl. Club, Moravian Coll., Disciples of Christ Ministers Fellowship; Disciples of Christ Military Chaplains Group; Democrat; Home: 5487 Rosewell St., San Diego, Calif. 92114; Office: Lt. Ray K. Joseph, CHR, USNR, c/o Force Chaplain's Office, Hqs., III Marine Amphibious Force, FPO San Francisco, Calif. 96602

JUSTISS, Jacob, Jr., ch. official, coll. prof., b. Mt. Pleasant, Tex., May 2, 1919; s. Jacob and Beatrice (Price) J.; Univ. of Toledo, 1937-39, Jr. Coll.; B.A.,

Emmanuel Missionary Coll., 1939-42; Wayne Univ., Detroit, 1943; S. D. A. Theol. Sem., 1944-45; S. D. A. Theol. Sem., 1945-46, advanced wk. toward B. D.; Harvard Univ., summer 1950, pastoral training; Ohio State Univ., 1951-52, grad. doctoral work toward Ph. D. in history; m. Mae Elizabeth Smith; Children--Joan Andree and Jacob III; Mich. Conf. of S. D. A., pastor-evangelist, 1942-44; S. D. A. Theol. Sem., 1944-45; head of History Dept., Pine Forge Inst., Pine Forge, Pa., 1946-48; assoc. in History Dept., Oakwood Coll., 1948-50; prin., Wash. Union Acad., Wash., D. C., 1950-51; pastor, Columbus, Ohio, 1951-53; pastor, Cincinnati, O., 1958-62; present: chrmn. of Youth Activities, Allegheny Conf. of S. D. A., chap., Natl. Service Organization and Temperance Coordinator, Pine Forge, Pa., 1962--; marriage counselor; chrmn. of the Bd. of Dirs., Chrstn. Benefit Assn., mem., Ex. comm. of Allegheny Conf., 1960-62; Ex. Bd. of Pine Forge Inst., 1958-62; chap., Hadley Meml. Hosp., Wash., D. C., 1956-58; chap., Adv. Comm., Metropolitan Boys Club, 1956-58; author: _History of Health Work of S. D. A. among Negroes_; _History of Riverside Sanitarium and Hospital to 1945_. Home: PO Box 21, Pine Forge, Pa.; Office: Allegheny Conf., Pine Forge, Pa.

KEARNS, Curtis Andre, b. Charlotte, N. C., Aug. 29, 1916; s. Andrew B. and Belle Harrell; A. B., Johnson C. Smith, Charlotte, N. C., 1935-39; B. D., Theol. Sem., 1939-42; grad. work, Union Sem., Richmond, Va., 1949; m. Laura Lee Henderson; Children--Ida Isabella, Curtis A., Jr., Ronald; coll. pastor and rel. ed. tchr. Mary Allen Jr. College, Crockett, Tex., 1942-43; pastor, Pine St. Presby. Ch., Durham, N. C., 1943-44; Davie St. Presby. Ch., Raleigh, N. C., 1944-54; Fifth Ave. Presby. Ch., Roanoke, Va., 1955--; pianist Roanoke Min. Conf.; pres., Clergy Club (Inter-Faith - Inter-racial); state clerk Presby of Southern Va.; mem.: YMCA; NAACP; Home: 311 Patton Ave., N. W., Roanoke, Va.

KELLER, Cyrus Samuel, Sr., b. Lake Charles, La., Jan. 9, 1920; s. Cyrus S., II, and Bertha (Scott) K.; B. A., Univ. of Calif., Los Angeles, 1940; Chrstn. Ed., Bible Inst. of L. A., 1943; Theology, Noah Williams Sch. of Rel., 1946; m. Hazel Maurie Tackett; Children--Edward (deceased), Juliebeth Maurie, Cyrus Samuel, Jr., Marjo Renee, Michelle Evon; pastor, Bethel A. M. E. Ch., Elwood, Kans., 1943-45; pastor, Allen Chapel, Salina, Kans., 1946-48; Quinn Chapel, Independence, Kans., 1948-51; Ward Chapel, Kans. City, Mo., 1952-56; St. John A. M. E. Ch., Topeka, Kans., 1956-58; Cain Meml. A. M. E. Ch., Bakersfield, Calif., 1956-58; St. Andrews A. M. E. Ch., Sacramento, Calif., 1958---; examining chap. for the Annual Conf. A. M. E. Ch. since 1952; pres., Sacramento Min. Alliance, 1961; advisor, Youth Coun., Coun. of Chs., Kans. City, Mo., Bakersfield, Cal., Sacramento, Calif.; trustee mem., Payne Theol. Sem., 1951-56; mem., Comm. of Administration Douglas Hosp., 1953-56; trustee bd. Douglas Hosp., 1943-56; Western Univ. Holding Corp., 1958-64; mem., NAACP since 1951; currently pres., Sacramento br. NAACP; mem., Human Relations Comm., Sacramento; chrmn., Conf. Rel. & Race; mem., Div. of Chrstn. Ed.; mem., Natl. Coun. of Chs.,; Democrat; Southern Chrstn. Leadership Conf. (western sec.); prepared and presented radio and TV programs for the Coun. of Chs. and the min. alliances; Home: 3825 44th St., Sacramento, Calif. 95820; Office: 2131 8th St., Sacramento, Calif. 95818

KELLER, Richard Carol, b. La., Nov. 7, 1910; s. George G. and Phoebe (McDowell) K.; B. A., B. Th., Va. Union Univ., 1928-34; Chaplain's Sch., USA, 1950-63; m. June R. Elder; Children--Richard C. Jr., Edward George; asst. pastor, Pilgrim Bapt. Ch., Chgo., Ill., 1933-39; pastor, Beth Eden Bapt. Ch., Chgo., Ill., 1939-present; Rel. ed., The Chicago Defender, Chgo., Ill., 1934-63; chap., 178 RCT Ill. Army Natl. Guard, 1947-64; Chgo. Metro. Ins. Co., 1937-65; Metro. Funeral Parlors, 1946-present; mem., Bd. Dirs., Morgan Park and Loan Assn., Chgo., Ill., 1960-present; instr., Chgo. Bapt. Inst., 1937-43; founder, Morgan Park Beverly Hills Coun. of Human Relations; Chap. Corp., US Army, 1947-65 (Lt. Col.); mem., Kappa Alpha Psi; Inter Ch. Coun.; Home: 1352 W. 112 Pl., Chgo., Ill. 60643

KELLOGG, Reginald John, tchr., b. Ann Arbor, Mich., July 2, 1933; s. Francis Bernard and Anna Theresa (Roney) K.; Assumption Sem., 1955-61; Our Lady of Carey Sem., 1953-55; Laval Universite, 1961-63; ordained priest, Roman Cath. Ch., 1961; tchr., Religion, French, Central Cath. High Sch., Toledo, Ohio; study and teach, Universite Laval, Quebec, Canada, 1961-63; French tchr., Our Lady of Carey Sem. & Coll., Carey, O., 1963-64; Home: 2425 Cherry, Toledo, Ohio, 43608;

Office: Our Lady of Carey Sem., Mt. St. Francis, Ind.

KELLY, James C., b. Bethlehem, Pa., Sept. 29, 1928; s. Samuel H. and Mabel O. (K.); B.A., Va. Union Univ., Richmond, Va., 1964; cand. B.D., Va. Union Univ., Richmond, Va., June, 1967; m. Loretta M. Barnes; Children--Susan, James Jr., Lynne; pastor, Gravel Hill Bapt. Ch., Richmond, 1963-65; Fifth Bapt. Ch., Richmond, 1965-present; served in Armed Forces; recd. Combat Infantry Badge; Mason; Home: 3218 Griffin Ave., Richmond, Va. 23222; Office: 1400 W. Cary St., Richmond, Va.

KELSEY, George Dennis Sale, b. Columbus, Ga., July 24, 1910; s. Andrew Z. and Marie H. K.; A.B., Morehouse Coll., 1934; B.D., Andover Newton Theol. Sch., 1937; Ph.D., Yale Univ., 1945; m. Leola B. Hanks; Children --George D.S., Everett Newton; prof., Morehouse Coll., 1938-45; dir., Morehouse Coll. Sch. of Rel., 1945-48; assoc. dir., Field Dept., Natl. Coun. of Chs., 1948-52; guest lecturer, Drew Univ., 1950-51; prf., Drew Univ., 1952--; mem., Assn. of Prof. of Chrstn. Ethics; Bd. of the Morris County (N.J.) Urban League; Fellowship of Southern Churchmen; Soc. of Rel. in Higher Ed.; author: Racism and the Christian Understanding of Man, 1965; sabbatical 1965-66, research study and teaching at the London Sch. of Economics; mem., Kiwanis Club; Mason; Sigma Pi Phi; Office: Madison, N.J.

KENDRICK, Arthur Lee, Sr., b. Atlanta, Ark., Dec. 19, 1901; s. Alfred Daniel and Lula; courses two years, Philander Smith Coll.; m. Elizabeth Williams; Children--Arthur Lee, Jr., Ernestine (Mrs. Norman Cleaver), Franklin, Joe Louis, Alfred Daniel; licensed to preach, Chrstn. Meth. Episc. Ch., 1930; ordained deacon, 1936; ordained elder, 1942; present pastor, Ashdown Chrstn. Meth. Episc. Ch., Ashdown, Ark.; tchr. in Ark., 15 yrs.; treas., So. West and So. Ark. Conf., C.M.E. Ch., 1961-date; Home: 1320 Ray St., Texarkana, Ark., 75501

KENNARD, Messie Lewis, Jr., b. Chicago, Ill., Oct. 23, 1918; s. Massie L. Kennard and Helen Q. K.; Univ. of Ill., 1935-36; 1941-42 Roosevelt Univ., 1946-47 B.A.; Garrett Biblical Inst., 1947-50; B.D., Chgo. Lutheran Theol. Sem., 1956-57; pastor, Concordia Luth. Ch., Buffalo, N.Y., 1959-68; present, sec., Urban Personnel,

Luth. Ch. of Amer.; mem., Alpha Phi Alpha; Office: 227 LaSalle St., Chicago, Ill.

KENNEDY, William Thomas, b. Washington, D.C., Mar. 18, 1928; s. William and Hattie (Turner); B.S., Miner Tchrs. Coll., Wash., D.C., 1953; S.T.B., Wesley Theol. Sem., 1964; S.T.M., Wesley Theol. Sem., 1967; m. Blanche Bryant; Children--Stephanie Sorena; asst. pastor, John Wesley A.M.E.Z. Ch., Wash. D.C., 1947-52; pastor, St. Luke A.M.E.Z. Ch., Westfield, N.J., 1952-56; Martin Temple, Chgo., Ill., 1956-58; Clinton Chapel, Detroit, Mich., 1958-60; Holiday Meml., Braddock, Pa., 1960-64; Mt. Olive, Waterbury, Conn., 1964-present; tchr., Hertzl Elem. Sch., Chgo., 1956-58; inst., Waterbury Hosp. Nursing Sch., 1967; pres., NAACP; v.p., Waterbury CAP Agency; Waterbury Legal Aid Soc.; chrmn., Waterbury Development Corp.; US Army, 1947-48; Home: 82 Pearl St., Waterbury, Conn. 06704

KENT, Reginald H., b. Virginia; s. Basil and Bettie (Coleman) K.; St. Paul's Coll., 1933-36; A.B., St. Augustine's Coll., 1941-43; B.D., Va. Sem., 1943-46; courses: Union Sem., Columbia Univ.; grad. study: Univ. of Pa.; m. Mrs. Reginald H.; children--four boys; pastor, St. Matthew's, Detroit; St. Cyprice, Detroit; St. James, Philip; St. Luke, Va.; St. Marks, St. Mary's, St. Matthrew's and St. John's, St. Matthew's Prot. Episc. Ch., So. Hill, Va.; current rector, St. Mary's Prot. Episc. Ch., Chester, Pa.; hosp. chap., mem., NAACP; Home: 1905 W. 4th St., Chester, Pa.; Office: 7th and Edwards Sts., Chester, Pa.

KEYES, Wilbert David, b. Jamesville, N.C., May 17, 1913; s. Ivory V. and Nancy Daisy (Barber) K.; 1962-63, Shaw Univ. (Roanoke Inst.); 1963-64, Goldsboro Chrstn. Inst., Goldsboro, N.C.; m. Tyress Maryland Wilkins; pastor, 1951-57, Promised Land Chrstn. Ch., Jamesville, N.C.; White Oak Chapel Ch., Bath, N.C.; 1958-64, Antioch Chrstn. Ch., Hookerton, N.C.; Speller's Chapel Ch., Windsor, N.C.; Union Chapel Chrstn. Ch., Roper, N.C.; Zion Grove Chrstn. Ch., Columbia, N.C.; Minister's Inst., Roper, N.C.; statistician, Wash.-Norfolk Dist. Assembly; pres., Jt. Union, Wash.-Norfolk Dist.; gen. sec., Gen. Assembly (Eastern seaboard); consultant, Interracial Consultation, Coll. of the Bible, Lexington, Ky.; consultant on Negro Evangelism at United Chrstn. Missionary Soc., Indianapolis, Ind.; Democrat; Mason;

Home: PO Box 72, Roper, N. C.

KIBBLE, Harvey Ward, ch. official, b. Huntsville, Ala., Jan. 28, 1908; s. Edward and Mittie (Livingston) K.; Oakwood Coll., 1928; Andrews Univ. (Extension Div.), 1962; m. Thelma Lois Winston; Children--Harvey, Jr., Herman Loris, William Harold, Marie Lois (Mrs. Edward Robinson), Ann La Verne, Alvin Maurice; pastor, S. D. A. Chs. in Houston, Tyler, and San Antonio, Tex., 1929-35; Newark, Jersey City, Montclair and Englewood, N. J., 1935-42; Chicago, Ill., 1942-48; Bklyn, N. Y., 1948-51; radio broadcast (weekly) WAIT, Chgo., Ill., 1943-45; pres., Lake Region Conf. S. D. A., Chgo., Ill., 1951-62; present: chrmn., Lake Reg. Conf. Ex. Comm. Chicago, Ill.; radio and TV devotional messages (The Dept. of Radio and TV of the Ch. Fed. of Greater Chgo. over NBC Channel 5 and WGN radio)--"Time to Reflect" and WGN TV Channel 9, "Five Minutes to Live By," 1960-61; mem., Oakwood Coll. Bd., 1951-62; Riverside Sanitarium and Hosp. Bd., Nashville, Tenn., 1951-62; Hinsdale Sanitarium and Hosp. Bd., 1951-62; Emmanuel Missionary Coll. Bd., 1951-62; Andrews Univ. Bd., 1960-62; Urban League Bd., Newark, N. J., 1938-42; Boy Scouts Coun. Comm., Newark, N. J., 1941; S. D. A. Min. Fellowship Coun. mem., Chicago, Ill.; Republican; contributing ed. to The Message magazine, Nashville, Tenn., 1951-62; Home: 782 Janos Lane, W. Hempstead, N. Y.; Office: Northeastern Conf. Seventh-Day Adventist, 560 W. 150th St., New York, N. Y.

KILGORE, Claude Columbus, tchr., b. Macon, Ga., Dec. 1, 1921; s. Jackson and Alice (Smith) K.; B. S., Hampton Inst., 1942-47; B. C., Lincoln Univ., 1948-51; post-grad. work in Rel. Ed., Evangelical & Reformed Sem., Lancaster, Pa., 1952-53; adjunct fellow, Dept. of Urban Studies, Rutgers Univ., 1963-64; m. Mildred Elizabeth Holmes; children--Darryl, Lynda, Robert, David; mem., personnel staffs, Hampton Inst., 1946-48, Lincoln Univ., 1948-49; pastor, Faith Presby. Ch., York, Pa., 1951-56; fabricating inspector, York-Hoover Body Corp., York, Pa., 1951-57; minister-to-migrants, Pa. Coun. of Chs., 1954-55-summer; Thirteenth Ave. Presby. Ch., Newark, N. J. 1956-63; Westminster-Bethany United Presby Ch., Bklyn, N. Y., 1963--; tchr., summer camps and conf., Synod of N. J.; v. moderator, Presbytery of Newark, N. J. rep. of radio-TV, Synod of N. J. and the N. J. Coun. of Chs.; chrmn., Gen. Missions Interpretation Comm.,

Presbytery of NYC; mem. of NYC Presbytery's Comm. on Candidates and Ch. Vocations; mem., Urban League of Essex Co., Newark, N. J.; Comm. of Management of Jones St. YMCA, Newark, N. J.; Bd. of Dirs., Planned Parenthood Assn., Clergy Adv. Comm. to the Mayor's Commn. of Human Rights, Newark, N. J.; sec., The Red Shield Boy's Club, Bklyn, N. Y., 1964--; local sch. bd. districts 32, 33, 34, Bklyn, N. Y. (appointment from June 31-1964 to July 1, 1969); mem., Omega Psi Phi, Elks, Masons; originated the community radio show "Perspective" - a program dealing with the lives of the minorities in urban N. J.; guest soloist with the Religious TV Show "The Evangel Hour, Sta. WPIX, NY; guest preacher for the Prot. Coun. of NYC on the program "Morning Meditations," WPIX; scholarship recipient to act and study drama in the ch., Wagner Coll., S. I., N. Y., 1964, as a result of amateur and prof. acting experience; Home: 555 Bainbridge St., Bklyn, N. Y.; Office: Howard Ave. & McDonough St., Bklyn, N. Y.

*KILGORE, Thomas, Jr., b. Woodruff, S. C., Feb. 20, 1913; s. Thomas and Eugenia (Langston) K.; A. B., Morehouse Coll., 1935; Howard Univ. Sch. of Rel., 1944; D. D. (hon.), Shaw Univ., 1956; B. D., Union Theol. Sem., 1957; D. D., Morehouse Coll., 1963; m. Jeannetta Scott; Children--Lynn Elda, Jini Medina; pastor, New Bethel Bapt. Ch., Asheville, N. C., 1936-38; Friendship Bapt. Ch., Winston-Salem, N. C., 1938-47; exec. sec., N. C. Gen. Bapt. Convention, 1945-47; pastor, Friendship Bapt. Ch., NYC, 1947-63; Second Bapt. Ch., Los Angeles, Calif., 1963--; chap., Winston-Salem Tchrs. Coll., 1942-44; mem., Bd. of Trustee, Natl. Trade and Professional Sch., Wash., D. C.; YMCA Service Award, Harlem br., NY, 1963; mem., Chi Alpha; Omega Psi Phi; Home: 1238 Westchester Pl., Los Angeles, Calif. 90019; Office: 2412 Griffith Ave., Los Angeles, Calif. 90011

KIMBROUGH, Walter Lee; b. Atlanta, Ga., July 30, 1940; s. J. B. and Myrtice; A. B., Morris Brown Coll., Atlanta, Ga., 1964; B. D., Interdenom. Theol. Center, Atlanta, Ga., 1966; m. Marjorie Ann Lindsay; Children--Walter Mark; pastored, Calvary United Meth. Ch., Chgo., 1966-68; Auburn Park United Meth. Ch., Chgo., 1968-present; mem. pres., Auburn Park neighborhood Civic Assn., 1967-68; Alpha Phi Alpha; Home: 49 E. 75th St., Chicago, Ill., 60619; Office: 335 W. 7th St., Chgo. Ill. 60620

KINARD, David Lee, b. So. Carolina, June 5, 1915; s. Wymon C. and Julia (Glover) K.; m. Ruth Taylor; children--Ruthalie, (Mrs. James Wooten, Jr.), Helen (Mrs. Joseph S. Solomon), Magdalen (Mrs. Rodgers L. Shelton), Patricia, Sandra, David Lee, Jr.; pastor, 1942-50, Calvary Chrstn. Ch., Bklyn, N.Y.; current: 1953, St. Philips Chrstn. Ch., Bklyn, N.Y.; activities: pres., Eastern Seaboard Chrstn. Convention, 1949-56; Home: 304 Kosciusko St., Bklyn, N.Y. 11221; Church: 345 Throop Ave., Bklyn, N.Y. 11221

*KING, Dearine Edwin, b. LaGrange, Tenn., Feb. 9, 1910; s. Martin A. and Effie K.; A.B., LeMoyne Coll., Memphis, Tenn.; B.D., M.A., Howard Univ. Sch. of Rel.; m. Mae Evelyn Rudder; children--Dearine Ed., Michael Earl, Maderia Evonne; coll. minister and instr., Ala. State A & M Coll., 1942-43; pastor, Wash. St. Bapt. Ch., Paducah Ky., 1942-46; Zion Bapt. Ch., Louisville, Ky., 1946-63; Friendship Bapt. Ch., NYC, 1963-67; pastor, Monumental Bapt. Ch., Chgo., 1967--; former sec., Natl. Bapt. Conv., USA; Exec. Bd., Louisville Area Coun. of Chs.; chrmn., Advisory Bapt. Fellowship Center; mem., Bd. of Trustees, Natl. Trade & Professional Sch., Wash., D.C.; Bd. of Dir., Natl. Coun. of Chs., 1953-58; Institution rep., Boy Scouts Bd. of Dirs., Red Cross Hosp.; trustee, Simmons Univ.; mem., NAACP; Omega Psi Phi; Mason; published sermon: "The Shepher Heart;" Office: 729 Oakwood Blvd., Chgo., Ill.

KING, John Lucas, Jr., b. Greenville, Miss., Apr. 14, 1920; s. John Lucas K., Sr. and Lena (Coleman) K.; A.B., Rust Coll., 1938-42; B.D., Gammon Theol. Sem., 1943-45; m. Madice Nickson; children--Matie Channice, Claude Raymond, Madice Eileen, Mable Maxine, Claudette Denise; pastor, Columbus Ct., Columbus, Miss., 1946-49; St. Paul Meth. Ch., Moss Pt., Miss., 1949; St. Stephenes Meth. Ch., Yazoo City, Miss., 1949-53; St. Paul Meth. Ch., Biloxi, Miss., 1953-55; Lynch Chapel Meth. Ch., Forest, Miss., 1955-58; St. Mark Meth. Ch., Dekalb, Miss., 1958-59; Franklin, La., 1959-62; St. James Meth. Ch., Shreveport, La., 1962--; tchr., related subjects, Columbus Vet. Sch., Columbus, Miss., 1946-49; Bd. of Ed., La. Annual Conf., 1959--; Bd. of Min. Training, La. Annual Conf., 1959--; mem., NAACP, Shreveport, La. Chapter; parliamentarian, Intl. Min. Alliance; Home: 945 Lewis Pl., Shreveport, La. 71103; Office: 850 Hope St., Shreveport, La. 71101

KING, Robert Henry, b. Sunny South, Ala., April 1, 1922; B.D., Immanuel Luth. Sem., 1949; M.Ed., Univ. of Pittsburgh, 1956; m. Edna Jean McCord; Children--Jocelyn, Jann, Roger; pastor, Victory Luth. Ch., Youngstown, O., 1949-57; pastor, St. Philip's Luth. Ch., Chgo. Ill., 1957--; pastoral advisor, Walther League of Northern Ill., Dist. of Luth. Ch-Missouri Synod, 1961-63; Home: 6731 Eberhart, Chicago, Ill.; Church: 6732 Eberhart, Chicago, Ill.

*KING, William Joseph, chaplain, b. Selma, Ala., July 21, 1921; s. Joseph and Lillian (Davis) K.; A.B., Talladega Coll., 1943; B.D., Howard Univ., Sch. of Rel., 1946; m. Clarice Robinson; Children--Eris Evermont; Home Missions Councils of No. American Chaplain to migrant workers, 1946-48; pastor, Third Bapt. Ch., Suffield, Conn., 1948-51; current chap., US Air Force, 1951--; mem., Alpha Phi Alpha; Mason; Home: 5312 Arnold Ave., Otis AFB, Mass.

KING, William P., b. Columbia, Ga., Jan. 26, 1922; s. E.R. and Mary King (Batin) K.; Morris Brown Coll.; Turner Theol. Sem.; Interdenom. Theol. Center; m. Yvonne Arnold; Children--Carl, Wm. III, Janette, Carole; asst. pastor, Shiloh Bapt. Ch., Atlanta, Ga.; pastor, Hills First Bapt. Ch., Athens, Ga., 1959-present; Army Air Force, 1943-46; mem., Morris Brown Coll. Alumni Club; Voter Registration Award; Urban League; Home: 704 Aline Dr., N.W., Atlanta, Ga. 30318

KING, Willis Jefferson, b. Rose Hill, Tex., Oct. 1, 1886; s. Anderson William and Emma (Blackshear) K.; A.B. Wiley Coll., Marshall, Tex., 1910; S.T.B., Boston Univ. Sch. of Theol., 1913, Ph.D., 1921; D.D. (hon.), Boston Univ., 1933; student Harvard Div. Sch.; m. Permella J. Kelly, (deceased); Children--Velma Norine, Eloise Aurora, Grace Evangeline; married 2nd, Emma Clarissa Arnold, June 28, 1944; entered ministry Meth. Episc. Ch., 1908; pastor, Greenville, Tex., 1908-10; assoc. pastor, St. Mark's Ch., NYC, 1911; pastor, Fourth Ch., Boston, St. Paul Ch., Galveston, Tex., Trinity Ch., Houston, until 1918; prof. O.T. and Chrstn. sociology, Gammon Theol. Sem., Atlanta, 1918-30, pres., 1932-48, lectr., 1952; elected bishop, 1944; assigned to Liberia, W. Africa; reassigned, 1948; assigned to La., Miss. and Upper Miss. Confs., 1953; resident bishop New Orleans area, central jurisdiction The Meth. Ch., 1956--; pres.,

Samuel Huston Coll., 1930-32; Fellow Julius Rosenwald Fund, for research, Oxford Univ. and Palestine, under auspices Am. Sch. of Oriental Research (on leave of absence from Gammon Theol. Sem.), 1929-30; represented Negro students at World's Student and Chrstn Fed., Peking, China, 1922; recipient of the Great Band of the Humane Order of African Redemption, Liberia, 1956; Knight Commander of the Order of African Redemption, Knight Commander Order of African Pioneers, Mem., Gen. Conf. M. E. Ch., 1924, 28, 32; del. to Conf. on Life and Work, Oxford, England, 1937; del. to World Coun. Meth. Ch., Oxford, 1951; rep., Bishop's Coun. to Africa Central Conf., Belgian Congo, 1952; mem., Natl. Preaching Mission Staff, 1936-37; Commn. of Unification of Meth. Chs. in America; Atlanta Sch. of Social Work; Commn. on Interracial Cooperation since 1940; Amer. Oriental Soc., Southern Sociol. Soc., Am. Acad. Polit. and Social Sci., Omega Psi Phi, Republican; author: The Negro in American Life, 1926; collaborator: Personalism in Theology and Christian Bases of World Order, 1943; Address: 631 Baronne St., New Orleans, La.

KIRKENDOLL, Chester Arthur, coll. pres., b. Searcy, Ark., June 3, 1914; s. Chester Arthur and Mattie (Wyatt) K.; A. B., Lane Coll., 1938; M. A., Northwestern Univ., 1941; Litt. D., Tex. Coll., 1957; D. D., St. Andrew's Sem., 1962; m. Alice Elizabeth Singleton; children--Chester Arthur III, Loretta Jean, Leland Kapel; Dir. of Leadership Ed., Gen. Bd. of Rel. Ed., Chrstn. Meth. Episc. Ch., 1940-50; pastor, St. Paul C. M. E. Ch., Bolivar, Tenn.; Lane Chapel C. M. E. Ch., Whiteville, Tenn.; Walls Chapel C. M. E. Ch., Chgo., Ill.; pres., Lane Coll., 1950--; Bd. of Dirs., United Negro Coll. Fund, Inc., 1950--; Tenn. Coun. on Human Relations, 1957--; Omega Psi Phi Achievement Award, 1952; Alpha Phi Alpha; Mason; author: Improving the Educational Program of the Local Ch.; Home: 566 Lane Ave., Jackson, Tenn.; Office: Lane Coll., Jackson, Tenn.

KIRTON, Edwin Eggliston, b. Trinidad, B. W. I., Dec. 13, 1907; s. Christopher and Lucretia (Hope) K.; B. S., Coll. of the City of NY, 1932; NY Law Sch., 1938; Gen. Theol. Sem., 1948-49; m. Eunice Brothwaite; children--Eunice, Edwin E., Jr., Elsie Elise; vicar, St. Michael Prot. Episc. Ch., Medford, N. Y., 1949-51; rector, St. Mark's Prot. Episc. Ch., Wilmington, 1951--; mem., Deputy to Gen. Convention Prot. Episc. Ch., 1961; Ex.

Coun.-Diocese of E. Carolina, 1963-65; chrmn., Dept. of Missions-Diocese of E. Carolina, 1963-65; staff mem., St. Augustine's Summer Sch., 5 yrs. of Rel. Ed.; Wilmington-New Hanover Bi-Racial Comm., 1963--; Mental Health Adv. Coun., 1963--; Bd. of Dirs., New Hanover Co. Mental Health Assn., 1958-63; Comm. Coun., City of Wilmington, 1961--; Gov.'s Comm. on Juvenile Delinquency and Youth Humane Service by Omega Psi Phi; mem., Polemarch-Wilmington Alumni Chapter, Kappa Alpha Psi; alumnus, Coll. of Preachers, Wash., D.C.; del. to the Provincial Synod-4th Province, 1954, 55, 63; Dir., Oceanside Episc. Youth Camp, 1953--; mem., Dept. of Chrstn. Ed.; mem., Comm. on Camps and Confs.; Home: 601 Grace St., Wilmington, N.C.; Office: 6th and Grace Sts., Wilmington, N.C.

KNOTT, Moses Alexander, Jr., b. Feb. 22, 1932, Meridian, Miss.; s. Moses A., Sr. and Jeanetta E. (K.); A.B., Va. Union Univ., Richmond, Va., 1957; B.D., Va. Union Sch. Rel., 1960; m. Neaera LaVerne Taylor; Children--Moses A. III, LaWana R.; pastor, Union Grove Bapt. Ch., Petersburg, Va., 1958-60; asst. chap., Central St. Hosp., Petersburg, Va., 1960-61; Ex. sec., Bible Soc. of Liberia, 1961-64; Ch. Relations Sec., Amer. Bible Soc., 1964-66; Natl. Distribution Sec., 1966-present; US Army, 1952-54; award: Bergen Co. Chapter Natl. Assn. of Chrstn. & Jews, 1968; mem., NAACP; Omega Psi Phi; Democrat; Home: 27 Elm St., Rutherford, N.J. 07070; Office: 1865 Broadway, New York, N.Y. 10023

KNOX, Wilbur Benjamin, author, b. Smith, S.C., Nov. 25, 1912; s. Milas J. and Carrie (Minor) K.; A.B., B.D., Johnson C. Smith Univ., 1950; m. Susie Boulware; Children--Kathleen, Wilbur, Jr., Paul; pastor, First Wash. Bapt. Ch., Lancaster, S.C., currently, writing plays and speeches, addresses for special days and all special ch. occasions; tchr., pub. sch., 1941-43; pres., NAACP, Rock Hill, S.C.; mem., Phi Beta Sigma; contributor: The 1949 Anthology of Poetry and The 1950 Gold Medal Series of Contemporary Poets; Home: 307 W. Moore, Rock Hill, S.C.; Office: 123 Pleasant Hill, Lancaster, S.C.

KYLE, Curtis, b. Rusk, Tex., Nov. 16, 1912; s. Henry Leonard and Victoria Brown (K.); Howard Univ., 1948-49; Univ. of Md., 1951-53; Howard Univ., Sch. of Rel.,

1963; Wash. Bible Sem. (4 yrs.); m. Eula Powell; Children--Cynthia, Elaine; ordained to deaconate, Shiloh Bapt. Ch., 1960-64; pastor, Sixteenth Bapt. Ch., Wash., D.C., 1964-present; Defense Doc. Center, US Fed. Govt. Tech. Information Documentation Specialist, 1945-present; ex-officio Chap. Defense Doc. Center; holds noon services in Chapel of D.D. center daily; ed. vi.-pres.; pres., Intl. Toastmasters Club, 1969; Mason; Home: 1419 Longfellow St., N.W., Wash., D.C. 20011; Office: 16th St. Bapt. Ch., 5333 16th St., N.W. Wash., D.C. 20011

KYLES, Samuel Billy, b. Sept. 26, 1934, Shelby, Miss.; s. Joseph Henry and Ludie (K.); Northern Bapt. Inst., Chgo.; Chgo. Bapt. Inst., Chgo., Ill.; m. Gwendolyn Louise Hart; Children--Dwain J.; Dwania P.; Dursheena T., Devin C.; asst. pastor, Mt. Pleasant Bapt. Ch., Chgo., 1954-56; Tabernacle Bapt. Ch., 1956-59; pastor, Monumental Bapt. Ch., Memphis, Tenn., 1959-present; Adv. Youth OEO, Memphis; tchr., Natl. Bapt. Congress; US Comm. on Civil Rights (Tenn.); mem., Memphis Manpower Comm.; Trustee, Co. Hospital., Memphis; mem., exec. bd., NAACP; repres., SCLC (Memphis); Home: 2215 S. Parkway East, Memphis, Tenn. 38114; Office: 704 S. Parkway East, Memphis, Tenn. 38106

LAKEY, Othal Hawthorne, b. Shreveport, La., Apr. 6, 1936; s. Clarence J. and Zandree (Ashley) L.; B.A., Whitman Coll., 1954-57; B.D., Drew Univ., 1957-60; m. Narsis Beard; Children--James Othal; pastor, St. James Chrstn. Meth. Episc. Ch., Pasco, Wash., 1954-57; asst. pastor, Salem Meth. Ch., N.Y., 1958-60; pastor, Allen Temple Chrstn. Meth. Episc. Ch., Portland, Ore., 1960-63; Williams Meml. C.M.E. Ch., Shreveport, La., 1963--; chief sec., La. Annual Conf., C.M.E. Ch.; chrmn., Educational Comm., Portland Urban League, 1960-63; Pi Kappa Delta Natl. Forensic Honorary; Natl. Thespian Soc.; pres., Albina Community Coun., Portland, 1962-63; v.p., Greater Portland Coun. of Chs.; Bd. of Dirs. of the Oregon Coun. on Alcoholic Problems, 1961-63; Standards Comm. for Child-Caring Institutions of the Oregon State Pub. Welfare Commn., 1963; Bd. of trustees, Miss. Indus. Coll., Holly Spring, Miss.; Home: 1853 Logan St., Shreveport, La.; Office: 1501 Peabody St., Shreveport, La.

LAMBERT, Rollins Edward, b. Chicago, Ill., Mar. 3, 1922 s. Monroe E. and Martha (Rollins) L.; A.B., U. of Chgo

1942; M.A. and S.T.L., St. Mary of the Lake Sem., 1942-49; asst. pastor, St. Malachy Ch., Chgo., 1949-57; asst. pastor, St. Dorothy Ch., Chicago, 1957-61; asst. Cath. Chaplain, Univ. of Chgo., Ill. Inst. of Tech., 1961-68; dir., Black Catholic Clergy Caucus, 1968--; mem., Bd. Adult Ed. Center, Archdiocese of Chgo.; Chgo. Conf. on Rel. and Race; Home: 5735 University Ave., Chgo., Ill. 60637; Office: 2942 S. Wabash Ave., Chgo., Ill. 60653

LATTA, William Clarence, tchr., b. Oxford, N.C., Feb. 20, 1932; s. Wilber E. and Lulamiller (Allen) L.; Cortex W. Peters Business Sch., 1952-53; Wash. Bible Coll., 1956-60, B.A.; m. Lelia Mae Turner; Children--William Clarence, Jr.; pastor, The Bible Way Ch., Columbus, O., 1960-63 (Bible Way Chs. of our Lord Jesus Christ World-Wide, Inc.); tchr., The Aenon Bible Sch., Columbus, O., 1960-63; US Forces, 1954-56; Natl. Defense Service Medal; Army of Occupation Medal (Germany); Good Conduct Medal; mem., Local Minister's Fellowship, Columbus, O.; Home: 685 So. Highland Ave., Columbus, O. 43223; Office: 453 So. Wheatland Ave., Columbus, O.

*LAVALL, John W., b. Charleston, S.C., Jan. 17, 1893; s. Jacob and Melissa (Ross) L.; Th.B., Howard Univ., Sch. of Rel., 1928; m. Blanche Etta Stuart; current pastor, Shiloh Bapt. Ch., Middleburg, Va., 1964--; tchr., church history, Frelinghuysen Univ., Wash., D.C., 1931-42; Home: 1227 Walter, Wash., D.C. 20003; Office: Shiloh Bapt. Ch., Middleburg, Va.

LAVALAIS, Joseph George, tchr., b. Mansura, La., Sept. 13, 1913; s. George J. and Mary (Lucendia); St. Paul's Luth. Elem. Sch., Mansura, La., 1919-27; Luther Coll., New Orleans, La., 1927-31; Luth. Univ., Baton Rouge, La., 1931-34; Immanuel Luth. Coll. & Sem., Greensboro, N.C., 1934-37; m. Elizabeth L. Smith; children--George, Juanita, Gwendolyn; tchr., Ala. 4 yrs.; services in parishes: Kingslanding Luth. Ch., Maplesville, Ala., 1937-38; Montrose, Ala., 1938-39; Kinbrough, Ala., Lamison, Ala., 1939-41; Pine Hill Luth. Ch., Arlington, Ala., Abshi, Ala., Vineland, Ala., 1941-43; St. Philip's Luth. Ch., Pa., 1943--; mem., serving as Circuit Counselor, Phila. Circuit, Eastern Dist., Luth. Ch.-Missouri Synod; Missionary Bd. of the Luth. Synodical Conf. Youth Conservation Assn.; Commn. on Human Relation, Lutheran

Church-Missouri Synod (Eastern Dist.); Home: 533 N. 56th St., Phila., Pa.; Church: 53rd & Wyalusing Ave., Phila., Pa.

LAWING, Raymond Quinton, b. Chesterfield Co., Va., Mar. 3, 1910; s. Willie and Mary Lou; B.S., Va. State Coll., Petersburg, Va., 1932; studies, Va. State, Moody Bible Inst., Chgo., Ill., 1936-66; m. Florence Jones; Children--Leon, Jacqueline (Mrs. Poteat), Mary (Mrs. Fleshman), Raymond, Timotheous, Florence; pastor, Galilee Bapt. Ch., Mt. Shiloh, Promised Land Bapt. Chs., Appomattox, Va., 1946-present; moderator, Hasadiah Bapt., Va., 1964; financial clerk, Cornerstone Bapt. Assn., Va. 1940; tchr., Carver Price High Sch., Appomattox, 1932-present; org. Appomattox Improvement Assn., 1939; pres., E., W. Bound Sunday Sch. Union; chap., NAACP 1966-68; mem., Appomattox Voters League; Appomattox Cancer Soc., 1960; pres., Appomattox Health Project; mem., Va. Tchrs. Assn.; Old Dominion Vocational Assn. NEA; Masons; awards: Cert. of Merit, 1952; Service award, 1967; Cert. for being teacher of teachers, 1968; mem., G. U. O. of Moses; Phi Beta Sigma; ed., weekly column, "Times Virginian;" Home: 97 Evergreen Ave., Appomattox, Va. 24522; Office: Carver Price High Sch. Appomattox, Va.

LAWRENCE, Cephas Worrick, b. Sampson Co., N. C., May 18, 1894; s. P. W. and Margaret; B. S., A. & T. Coll., Greensboro, N. C., 1910; Theol. Sem., Lincoln Univ., Pa., 1913; m. Estley T., deceased; m. Irene Mendenhall; Children--Annie (Mrs. Neyson Taylor); Viola (Mrs. Timothy Crain), Nadline (Mrs. W. Henley), Cephas W.; pastored, A. M. E. Z. Chs., Shippingburg, Pa., 1913; Graham, N. C.; Greensboro, N. C.; High Pt., N. C., 1940-46; dist. presiding elder, W. Central N. C. Conf., 1931-40; Natl. Exec. Sec., Ch. Ext. Dept., 1946-48; sr. presiding elder, W. Central N. C. Conf., A. M. E. Z. Ch., 1948-present; del. to Gen. Conf.; sec., 33 degree Mason mem., Oddfellows; Knights of Pythias; Order Eastern Star; mem., Gen. Bd. of Chrstn. Ed., Chgo., Ill.; Home: 1211 Willow Rd., Box 20152, Greensboro, N. C.

LAWSON, James Morris, Jr., ch. official, b. Uniontown, Pa., Sept. 22, 1928; s. James Morris and Philane May (Cover) L.; A. B., Baldwin-Wallace Coll., Berea, O., 1947-52; Oberlin Coll., Grad. Sch. of Theol., 1956-58; S. T. B., Div. Sch., Vanderbilt Univ., 1958-60; Boston

Univ.; m. Dorothy Dolores Wood; Children--John Clifford L., III; v.p., Natl. Conf. of Meth. Youth, 1949-53; chrmn., Natl. Meth. Youth Fellowship Commn., 1948-49; field worker, Intl. Chrstn. Univ. of Japan, 1950-51; pastor, Turner Chapel Meth. Ch., 1950-51; Meth. Missionary in India, 1953-56, Hislop Coll., Nagpur, India; pastor, Scott Meth. Ch., 1960-62; Centenary Meth. Ch., Memphis, Tenn., 1962--; spec. consultant, Southern Chrstn. Leadership Conf., 1960--; southern sec., Fellowship of Reconciliation, 1958-60; editorial contributor, Fellowship Magazine; Office: Centenary Meth. Ch., 653 Alston Ave., Memphis, Tenn.

LAWSON, William Alexander, Jr., b. June 28, 1928; s. William A. Sr. and Clarisse L.; A.B., Tenn. A & I State Univ., 1950; B.D., M.Th., Central Bapt. Theol. Sem., 1953, 55; candidate Ph.D., Univ. of Chicago, 1961; m. Audrey Ann Hoffman; Children--3 daus. and 1 son; pastor, Mt. Hebron Bapt. Ch., 1952-55; dir., Bapt. Students and Prof. of Bible, Tex. Southern Univ.; current pastor, Wheeler Ave. Bapt. Ch., Houston, Tex., 1962--; organizer, United Ministers, Tex. Southern Univ.; chrmn. of Chaplains, 1963--; mem., Alpha Phi Alpha; Danforth Foundation; Missions and Evangelism Assignments, Southeast Asia, Middle East; speaker, Bapt. World Alliance Youth Conf., Beirut, Lebanon, 1963; frequent speaker, Coll. and Univ.; Office: 3124 Wheeler Ave., Houston, Tex. 77004

LEDBETTER, Theodore S., b. Goliad, Tex., Jan. 15, 1910; s. Caesar S. and Maggie (Clemons) L.; A.B., Atlanta Univ., 1932; B.D., Oberlin Grad. Sch. of Theol., 1935; m. Orelia Washington; children--Theodore S., Jr., Leslie M., Charles A.; Plymouth Congre. Ch., Louisville, Ky., 1937-47; Dixwell Ave. Congre. Ch., New Haven, Conn., 1947-58; Plymouth Congre. United Ch. of Christ, Wash., D.C. 1958--; Dir., Plymouth Social Settlement, Louisville, Ky., 1937-47; Dean of Men, Tillotson Coll., Austin, Tex., 1935-37; del. Natl. Dem. Conv., 1960; mem. Dem. Central Comm., D.C., 1960-64; trustee, United Planning Organization; mem., Public Welfare Adv. Bd.; Assoc. Moderator, Middle Atlantic Conf., UCC; Assoc. Mod., Wash. Assn., UCC; v. chrmn., Comm. on Amendment to Constitution, UCC; mem., Kappa Alpha Psi; Home: 1737 Webster, N.W., Wash., D.C.; Church: 5313 N. Capital, Wash., D.C.

LEDOUX, Jerome Gaston, educator, b. Lake Charles, La., Feb. 26, 1930; s. Peter Louis and Gastonia (Petrie) L.; St. Paul's Coll., Epworth, Iowa, 1949-51; St. Augustine's Major Sem., 1951-57; J. C. D. and S. T. L., Gregorian Univ. (Rome); ordained priest, Roman Cath. Ch., 1957; author: doctoral thesis, Coarctatio jurisdictionis sacramentalis, 1962, (a study of sacramental jurisdiction as restricted by the Code of Canon Law); "Defender of the Bond" for the marriage tribunal of the diocese, Natchez-Jackson, Miss.; Home and Office: Divine Word Missionaries, Bay St. Louis, Mississippi, 39520

LEE, Alfred Leonard, b. Castleberry, Ala., Dec. 2, 1935; s. Morgan P. and Mable W. (L.); Fla. Meml. Coll., 1962; The Interdenom. Theol. Center; Morehouse Sch. of Rel., 1967; US Army Chaplain Sch., 1967; m. Retha Pew; Children--Sylvia Elizabeth, Brenda Leontyne; former assoc. pastor, First Bapt. Ch., St. Augustine, Fla.; dir., Wesley House Center, Atlanta, Ga.; Program Developer Chattahoochee Flint Area Planning & Development Commn., Lagrange, Ga.; pastor, Arbor Grove Bapt. Ch., Lagrange, Ga.; present, US Army Chaplain; sch. tchr., cert. Fla. & Ga.; Dir. Voters Registration; cons., Legrange Voters League; US Marine Corp, Korean War; mem., Mason; NAACP; Phi Beta Sigma; Military Chaplains Assn.; SCLC; Democrat; Natl. Bapt. Conv. of Amer.; honors, Natl. Defense; Oak leaf Cluster; Good Conduct; Home: 208 S. Hubbard St., Bonifay, Fla.; Office: US Army Garrison, Ft. Devens, Mass. 01433

LEE, Carleton Lafayette, coll. prof., b. Clayton, N. C., Mar. 30, 1913; s. Frank Joshua and Aurelia Gertrude (Hill) L.; A. B., Talladega Coll.; M. A., Univ. of Chgo.; B. D., Chgo. Theol. Sem., 1937; Ph. D., Univ. of Chgo., 1951; m. Maggie Ada Latta; Children--Carleton Henry; pastor and tchr., Midway Congre. Ch. and Dorchester Acad., McIntosh, Ga., 1935-57; Lincoln Congre. Ch., Kings Mountain, N. C., 1937-38; Case-Aide, Chgo. Relief Administration, 1938-39; assoc. sec., Southern Area Coun., YMCA, Atlanta, Ga., 1939-44; acting dean, Turner Theol. Sem., 1944-45; Research and Survey Natl. Coun., YMCA, 1946-47; chap., Tuskegee Inst., 1947-53; Fraternal Worker, World Coun. of Chs., Mainz Kastel an Rhein, 1953-55; Prof. of Philosophy, Tougaloo Coll., Miss., 1955-57; dor., Rel. Life & Prof., Phil., Central State Coll., Wilberforce, O., 1957-67; prof., Cheyne State Coll., 1967-69; head, Black Americana Program,

Univ. of Western Mich., 1969-present; mem., Adv. Comm. NCCF, 1951-53; mem., Kent Fellow, 1949--; former pres., Exec. Comm., Natl. Assn. of Coll. and Univ. Chaplains; Coll. Language Assn. (mem.); mem., Assn. of Soc. Sci. Tchrs.; Assn. for the Study of Negro Life and History; NAACP; Mason; Alpha Phi Alpha; Alpha Phi Gamma; Phi Alpha Theta; AAUP; contributor: Assuring Freedom for the Free, ed. by Arnold Rose, 1963; Office: Black Americana Program, Univ. of Michigan, Kalamazoo, Mich.

*LEE, Gabriel S., Jr., b. Junction City, Ark., July 6, 1922; s. Gabriel S. and Mollie Elder L.; B.A., Bishop Coll., Marshall, Tex., 1949; B.D., Howard Univ., Sch. of Rel., 1954; m. Leona Jean Williams; pastor, Fellowship and New Land Bapt. Chs., Lillie, La., Bernice, La., 1949-51; Hollywood Hgts. Presby. Ch., Shreveport, La., 1956-60; co-pastor, Beacon & Glenham Reformed Chs., Beacon, N.Y., 1960-62; current pastor, Nazareth Bapt. Ch., Wash., Pa., 1965--; dir., Men's and Boy's Work, Westminster House, Buffalo, N.Y., 1954-55; caseworker, Erie Co. Dept. of Soc. Welfare, Buffalo, N.Y., 1962-65; mem., NAACP; Ad. Bd., Child Welfare, Wash. Co., Dept. of Welfare, Wash., Pa.; US Army, 1942-46; awards: Good Conduct Medal; Asiatic-Pacific Campaign Medal; WW II Victory Medal; mem., Phi Beta Sigma; Wash., Pa. Lions Club; dir., former, Buffalo Host Club Intl.; Home: 143 Chestnut Street, Washington, Pa. 15301; Office: 123 N. Lincoln St., Washington, Pa. 15301

LEE, Marshall Williams, b. Fagner Co., Va., Apr. 1, 1886; s. Abram M. and Agnes B.; courses, Temple Univ.; Crozier Sem.; m. Hannah May King; Children--Sarah (Mrs. E. Herbert), Agnes (Mrs. Theo. White), Mary (Mrs. Raymond Thompson), Olive (Mrs. E. Banks); pastor and org., St. Paul's Bapt. Ch., 1925-to date; v. chrmn., Mont. Co. Housing Authority; chrmn., Rent Control, 1940-present; pres., Visiting Nurses Assn., 1966-67; moderator, Central Union Bapt. Ch. Assn.; treas., Bapt. Min. Conf. (Phila.); mem., Health and Welfare Soc. of Mont. Co., 1959-66; TB Assn., Mont. Co., 1959-66; Cham. of Commerce (Conshohocken, Pa.); pres., Conshohocken Min. Assn., rec'd Daniel Whiteman Mem. Award, 1966; org. Human Rel. Soc., 1955; Dir., Union Mutual Insurance Co., 1923-64; treas. and trustee, Mental Hygene Soc., Mont. Co., Pa., 1955-60; mus. dir.,

Silvam Bapt. Ch. Choir, 1912-25; Home: 316 Hollowell St., Conshohocken, Pa. 19428

LEE, Morris William, b. Isle of Wright Co., Va., Oct. 19, 1935; s. Peter Haywood and Mannie (Crocker) L.; A. B., B. D., Va. Union Univ., 1958, 1960; pres., Student Participation Assn. of Va.; at coll., chief justice of Student Court; pres., Lyceum, Bartone Soloists, narrator of choir, Basileus of Zeta Chapter, Omega Psi Phi; licensed to ministry, May 30, 1953; called to pastorate of Jerusalem Bapt. Ch., Doswell, Va., 1957; current pastor, Third Bapt. Ch., Youngstown, O., 1960--; mem., Mahoning Co. Welfare Bd.; Ex. comm., Citizens Assn., Youngstown; pres., Youngstown Min. Assn.; mem., Ex. comm. of Youngstown Coun. of Chs.; Home: 1175 Park Hill Drive, Youngstown, O.; Office: 1177 Park Hill Dr., Youngstown, O.

LEE, Robert Edgar, b. Kane, Pa., Aug. 14, 1920; s. Thomas and Anna (Culver); A. B., Livingstone Coll., 1949; courses, Western Theol. Sem., Pittsburgh, Pa., 1953; m. Ruby Nell Slaton; Children--Anita, Vanessa, Robert, William; pastor, Wright Meml. A. M. E. Z. Ch., Wash., Pa., 1949-54; Zion Temple A. M. E. Z. Ch., Madisonville, Ky., 1954-59; Jacob St. Tabernacle A. M. E. Z. Ch., Louisville, Ky., 1959-61; First Congre. Meth. Ch., Louisville, Ky., 1961-present; sec., Rel. Groups Com. of Louisville, Ky., 1962-64; chrmn., Human Rel. Com.; Pub. Rel. Com. of Interdenom. Min. Alliance of Louisville, Ky.; Voters Ed. Com.; Bd. mem., Allied Organ. for Civil Rights; awards: Public ser., Livingstone Coll. Choral Union Ensemble, 1949; Work with Youths, Ky. Col Cert., 1966; Home: 3428 So. Ave., Louisville, Ky. 40211; Office: 3810 Garland St., Louisville, Ky. 40211

LEE, Shelton C., b. Aiken, S. C., Benedict Coll., N. Western Coll., (D. C.); founder and organizer, Metrotone Bapt. Ch., Wash., D. C., 1939-present; mem., officer, Mt. Bethel Assn.; The Bapt. Conv. of Wash., D. C.; Natl. Bapt. Conv., USA, Inc.; Office: 5211 B St., SE, Wash., D. C.

LEE, Willie Samuel, ch. official, b. Dothan, Ala., May 29, 1915; Oakwood Coll., 1936; m. Ruth Althea Reid; Children--Althea Grace (Mrs. Arthur Kennedy), Willie Samuel, Jr., Brenda Ruth; pastored: five S. D. A. Chs., Okla. City District, 1936-40; Tampa, Fla., 1940-43,

Jacksonville, Fla., 1946-50, New Orleans, 1950-55, Ephesus - New York, 1955; Reg. sec., Pacific Union Conf., S. D. A. Ch.; Home: 2283 El Sereno Ave., Altadena, Calif.; Office: PO Box 146, Glendale, Calif.

LEHMAN, Harvey John, tchr., b. Mansura, La., Oct. 10, 1905; s. Paul Marius and Harriett (Thompson) L.; Luth. Parochial Sch., 1911-20; Luth. Coll., New Orleans, La., 1920-24; Immanuel Coll. and Sem., Greensboro, N. C., 1925-30; children--Harvey J. Jr., Lillian E., Philip M.; ordained into the ministry, July 5, 1930; pastor, Trinity Luth. Ch., Selma, Ala.; pastor, St. Paul and Christ congregation, Oak Hill and Rosebud, Ala., 12 yrs.; pres., Ala. Conf.; pastor, Matthews, Baltimore; current pastor, The Luth. Ch. of Our Savior, Buffalo, N. Y.; tchr., Luth. Parochial Sch., Ala.; service on the Mission Bd. of the Southeastern Dist.; service on the Profession Youth Bd., Buffalo, N. Y., 1960--; part-time chp., the Erie Co. Home, Alden, N. Y.; Home: 30 Brunswick Blvd., Buffalo, N. Y.; Office: 26 Brunswick Blvd., Buffalo, N. Y.

LESSER, Leo, Jr., b. Indianapolis, Ind., Apr. 28, 1928; s. Leo, Sr and Katie (Jones) L.; B. S., Indiana Univ., 1950; B. Th., Burton Coll., 1958; B. D., Burton Coll., 1960; D. D. Monrovia Coll., 1959; D. D., Chgo. Div. Coll., 1962; pastor, Parks Chapel A. M. E. Ch., Chattanooga, Tenn., 1957-61; pastor, St. John A. M. E. Ch., 1961-62; pastor, Greater St. James A. M. E. Ch., Louisville, Ky., 1962; prof., Business Dept., Zion Coll., Chattanooga, Tenn.; administrative asst. to pres., Zion Coll., Chattanooga, Tenn.; chap., Geriatric Unit Central Hosp., Anchorange, Ky.; apptd. by gov. as mem. of Ky. Commn. on Aging; Dir. of Research and Training for St. James Literacy Center, Louisville; served in ETO 1945, served in Korea 1961; outstanding contributions in the field of illiteracy, establishing centers in Louisville and throughout the state of Ky.; mem., Ex. bd. NAACP; Inst. of Pastoral Care, Acad. of Rel. and Mental Health; Mason; Natl. Coun. of Senior Citizens, Urban League; YMCA; Boy Scouts of Amer.; paper, Ministry for Mental Health; Publication - A Program for the Ch. and It's Senior Citizens, paper read at Gov.'s Conf. on Aging--The Ch. and the Ministry to The Old Member; column, "In Times Like These," Home: 2104 W. Oak St., Louisville, Ky.; Office: 2100 W. Oak St., Louisville, Ky.

LESTER, Woodie Daniel (W. D.), b. Sardis, Miss., Nov. 5, 1902; A. B., Philander Smith Coll., Little Rock, Ark., 1924; B. D., Gammon Theol. Sem., Atlanta, Ga., 1927; courses: Univ. of Chgo.; D. D. (hon.); LL. D. (hon.), Philander Smith Coll., 1952; 1959; m. Julia Beatrice; Children--Woodie Daniel, Julius Bernard; ordained deacon, 1922; United Meth. Ch. elder, 1927; pastored Pine Bluff, Arlk, 1920-24; Wiley Meml. Meth. Ch., Atlanta, Ga., 1924-26; McGehee, Ark., 1927-29; Conway, Ark., 1929-30; Muskogee, Okla., 1931-35; Samaritan Temple Meth. Ch., St. Louis, Mo., 1937-41; Mason Meml. Meth. Ch., Kans. City, Kans., 1941-48; supt., Little Rock Dist., 1935-37; Ex. sec. of Chrstn. Ed., Central West Conf., 1948-52; staff mem. and dir. of the Dept. for Spec. Activities, the Bd. of Evangelism, the United Meth. Ch., 1952-present; dean, Fargo A & M Coll., Fargo, Ark., 1921-22; instr., Math and History, Conway High Sch., Conway, Ark., 1929-30; Chap., Okla. State Hosp., Taft, Okla., 1931-35; princ., St. Louis Week Day Sch. of Chrstn. Ed., 1937-41; del. and mem., Com. on Procedure, Rules of Order and Organization, Meth. Gen. Conf., 1948, 56, 60, 64; del., Central Jurisdictional Conf., 1944, 48, 56, 60, 64; chrmn., Episc. Com., 1964; trustee, Philander Smith Coll., 1931-present; Douglas Hosp., Kans. City, Kans., 1943-present; dir., Douglas State Bank, 1946-present; trustee, Wesley Found., Tenn. Agr. & Indus. Coll., 1962-present; mem., Phi Beta Sigma; One Hundred Thousand Mile Club; Ambassadors Club; Jupiter Rex; Mason; Office: Bd. of Evangelism, United Meth. Ch., 1908 Grand Ave., Nashville, Tenn. 37203

LEWIS, Alexander Leonard, chap., b. St. Pauls, N. C., Dec. 10, 1910; s. Wade and Emma J. (Davis) L.; Redstone Acad., 1931; A. B., Johnson C. Smith Univ., 1935; B. D., Theol. Sem., 1941; Boy Scout Natl. Sch., Mendham, N. J., 1944; m. Addie J. Jones; Children--Alexander L., Jr., Gertrude L.; pastor, Salem Presby. Ch., Anderson, S. C., 1941; Wash. Ave. Presby. Ch., 1942-44; Boy Scout Field Exec., Macon, Ga.; mem., YMCA Coun.; chrmn., Youth Community Center and other community organizations; princ., Panthersford Sch., Buies, N. C., 1935-36; princ., Fremont Negro High Sch., 1936-39; chrmn., Robeson Co. Sch. Master Organization, 1935-36; mem., Boy Scouts of Amer., Honolulu, Hawaii, 1962; counselor USA Stockade Scho. Bks, Hawaii, 1963; chap., US Army, 1st Lt., 1944; Capt., 1946; Major, 1952; served as chap. in both theaters of war; first chap.

to enter Korea during occupation 1946; POW Camp in Kojedo, Korea, 1950-52; stockade chap., Port chap., Bn. chap., Regimental chap., sub area chap., post chap., Ft. Hampton, N.Y., 1957-59; asst. Div. chap., Schofield Barracks, Hawaii, 1952-60; hosp. chap. in Germany; sch. counselor and sch. officer for Kassel sub area, Kassel, Germany; Youth Counselor to the Youth Center, AYA officer and advisor; athletics dir. for both youth and soldiers; Boy Scout Master, chrmn. of Boy Scout Committeeman, Cub Scout Den Dad, Cub Scout Committeeman in Kassel, Germany; chrmn., Social and Civic Comm. of the five nations located in that area: Americans, French, German, English and Belgium forces; mem., Phi Beta Sigma, Alpha Epsilon Chapter, Cosmopolitan Consistory 291, Honolulu, Hawaii, Cosmopolitan Lodge 82, Honolulu, Hawaii, local YMCA, The Lions Club; pres., the Leilehua High Sch. PTA, Eastern Star, the Mental Health Soc. of Honolulu, Hawaii; NAACP; State of Hawaii PTA; Home: 110 So. Cane St., Wahiawa, Hawaii

LEWIS, Benjamin E., b. Alcoa, Tex., Sept. 13, 1930; s. John and Beatrice; A.B., Knoxville Coll., 1962; B.D., I.T.C., Atlanta, Ga., 1966; grad. courses, Univ. of Alaska; m. Dorothy M.; Children--Benjamin E., Jr., Bridgett, John, Warren; pastor, First United Ch. of Christ, Sweetwater, Tenn., 1960-present; minister, Community Relations and Human Resources; (part-time) Alcoa, Tenn., tchr.; pres., Monroe Co. Welfare Adv. Com.; dir., Anti-poverty program (five counties); organizer, Sweetwater, Tenn. NAACP; mem., Racial Justice Now Com. (UC of Christ); mem., Planned Parenthood Assn.; sec., Tenn.-Ky. Min. Assn.; organizer Young Democrats; mem., Masons; Home: PO Box 405, Sweetwater, Tenn. 37874; Office: 85 Kentucky Ave., Oak Ridge, Tenn. 37830

LEWIS, Henry T., b. Cotton Valley, La., Aug. 28, 1926; s. Raford and Effie (M.); B.A., Western Bapt. Coll., Kan. City, Mo., 1966; courses, Kan. Univ. Ext. Sch., 1968; m. Louise Milligan; Children--Cynthia, Sandra, Michael, Curtis; assoc. pastor, Mt. Pleasant Bapt. Ch., Kan City, Mo.; pastor, 2nd Bapt. Ch., Platte City, Mo.; 2nd Bapt. Ch., Independence, Mo.; Sec. United Prayer Movement; US Army, 1945-46; Home: 2522 Jackson St., Kansas City, Mo. 64127

LEWIS, Mahlon Montgomery, contractor, b. Bedford, Va.,

July 29, 1890; s. Chas. Shepherd and Mary (Ellen) L.; C. N. & I. Dept. Wilberforce, Univ., Payne Theol. Sem., Wilberforce, O., B. D., 1916; D. D. (hon.), Payne Theol. Sem., 1936; m. Cornelia B. Reed; 55 yrs. an ordained itinerant elder; 40 yrs. in the A. M. E. Ch.; resigned from A. M. E. Ch., 1949; organized Greater St. Matthew Independent Ch., Phila., Pa.; builder of St. Matthew A. M. E. Ch.; Mahlon M. Lewis Boys Club; builder of Bethel A. M. E. Ch., Walnut Ave.; builder of Bethel A. M. E. Ch., Ardmore, Pa.; mem., Mason, Crime Prevention Comm., Phila., Pa.; Office: Greater St. Matthew Independent Ch., Race and Vadges Sts., Phila., Pa.

LEWIS, Samuel Archibald, b. San Juan, Puerto Rico, Mar. 25, 1908; s. Charles A. and Basilisa A.; A. B. Wagner Coll., Staten Is., N. Y. 1939; B. D., Luth. Theol. Sem., Phila., Pa., 1942; M. A., Columbia Univ., 1949; courses toward Ed. D.; pastor, St. Phillip's Luth. Ch., Balto., Md., 1943-44; asst. pastor, Transfiguration Luth Ch., NYC, June 1942-Dec. 1942; entered US Army 1944; Chap., (Capt.) China-Burma-Indian Theater of War and Alaska, 1944-48; Lt. Col., USA, France, Germany, Trieste, 1950-56; pastor, Holy Trin. Luth. Ch., Jamaica, NY, 1964-present; tchr., NY 1949; Missionary, St. Croix, Virgin Is., 1962-63; mem., Military Chap. Assn., Manhattan Chapter; Mayor's Staff, NY Emergency Control Bd. of Civil Defense, 1968-present; Luth. Coop. Parishes (Queens, N. Y.); St. Croix Friends of Denmark Soc., Inc.; Queens Fed. of Chs., Inc., Richmond Hill, N. Y.; Home: 217 W. 115 St., New York, N. Y. 10026; Office: Holy Trinity Luth. Ch., 161-28 Mathias, Jamaica, N. Y. 11433

LEWIS, Willie, b. Gainesville, Fla., July 29, 1939; s. Willie and Bessie (Jones) L.; B. A., Oakwood Coll., 1960; M. A., Andrews Univ., 1961; m. Barbara Ann Stokes; 1 son: William Stokes; present: South Atlantic Conf. of S. D. A., Atlanta, Ga., 1961--; Home: 1302 Heidt St., Columbia, S. C.; Office: 1750 McFadden St., Columbia, S. C.

LEWIS, Willie B., b. Nash Co., N. C., Sept. 17, 1925; s. Willie and Hazel L.; A. B., B. D., Shaw Univ., 1945-53; m. Lillie Hilliard; Children--Lileta Ynettee, Wilhelmia; pastor, Wake Chapel Bapt. Ch.; Bethlehem Bapt. Ch.; current pastor, Fayetteville St. Bapt. Ch., Raleigh, N. C.; tchr., Natl. Bapt. Sun. Sch. and Training Union Cong.; organizer, Voters League, Fayetteville Bapt. Ch.;

Home: 1013 S. Person St., Raleigh, N. C.; Office: 751 Fayetteville St., Raleigh, N. C.

LIGGIN, Carl Crutcher, b. Louisville, Ky., Feb. 20, 1929; s. Clyde A. and Jennie (B.); L.; Tuskegee Inst., 1946-47; Ky. State Coll., 1947-49; Wilberforce Univ. & Payne Theol. Sem., 1952-53; m. Lois Jean Gray; Children--Karen Renee, Katrina Rochelle, Karl Clyde; entered ministry of Afr. Meth. Episc. Ch., Quinn Chapel, Louisville, Ky., 1950; dir., Youth Work, A. M. E. Ch., appointed to Clayborn Chapel Mission, Lexington, Ky., 1951; ordained deacon; pastor, St. John A. M. E. Ch., Louisville, 1956; current pastor, Ebenezer, Clarksville; one of organizers, Sch. of Practical Nursing & Business, 1958; dir., Ebenezer Kindergarten-Nursery & Business Enterprises, 1961 --; dean, Louisville Sch. of Rel. Ed., Louisville Coun. of Chs., 1960--; dir., Citizen's Comm. of Local Affairs; v. p., Clarksville Chrstn. Leadership Corps, NAACP, Kappa Alpha Psi, Democratic Party, League of Montgomery Co., Interdenom. Min. Alliance; currently conducting rel. census and voter's registration survey, Clarksville, Tenn.; Home: 131 Edmondson Ferry Rd., Clarksville, Tenn.; Office: 129 Edmondson Ferry Rd., Clarksville, Tenn.

LIGGINS, Lyman William, tchr., b. Gallipolis, O., Jan. 12, 1921; s. Elmer Lewis and Irene (Smith) L.; Univ. of Toledo, Toledo, O., 1940; Howard Univ., 1941-43; Ohio State Univ., A. B., 1946; M. A., Ohio State Univ., 1951; Ohio State Univ. work towards Ph. D.; m. Grace Elizabeth Busby; Children--Denis, Cheryl; asst. pastor, Minister Allen Temple A. M. E. Ch., Cincinnati, O., 1956; pastor, Quinn Chapel A. M. E. Ch., Wilmington, O., 1957-63; current pastor, Holy Trinity, Wilberforce Univ., Wilberforce, 1963--; visiting lecturer, Philosophy of Law, Wilberforce Univ., 1951, Philosophy of Rel., Payne Sem., Wilberforce, 1960-61, Pastoral Psychology, Payne Sem., Wilberforce, 1960-62; staff position, Juvenile Diagnostic Center, Columbus, O., 1952-55; full-time consultant, Legislative Service Commn., State of Ohio, 1955; conducted statewide study of juvenile delinquency; research consultant, Ohio Dept. of Mental Hygiene & Correction, 1956; directed statewide evaluation of the effectiveness of tranquilizing medications; research statistician, Ohio Bur. of Unemployment Compensation, 1957; Employment trends for U. S. Dept. of Labor; Asst. research sec., Gov.'s Adv. Commn. on Civil Rights, 1958; statewide statistical study of employment patterns; mem., Alpha Phi Alpha; Home: 742-B N. Nelson Rd., Columbus, O.; Office: Wilberforce Univ., Wilberforce, O.

LIGGINS, Thomas Elmer, b. Wolfdale, Pa., Nov. 10, 1935; s. Edward S. and Eura Maxine (Patterson) L.; Ohio State Univ., Columbus, Ohio; Payne Theol. Sem., Wilberforce, O.; m. Mary Frances Slade; Children--Thomas E., Threase E., Terri E., Toni E., Timothy E.; pastor, Bethel Afr. Meth. Episc. Ch., Westerville, O., 1955-56; St. John A. M. E. Ch., Worthington, O., 1956-57; current pastor, Zion A. M. E. Ch., Marysville, O, 1957--; Allen Chapel A. M. E. Ch., Marysville, O., 1957--; visiting minister, Ohio Reformatory for Women, Marysville, O.; mem., Liberty Community Center Bd., Delaware, O., 1960--; Red Cross Bd., Delaware Co., 1961-63; chrmn., Del. Civil Rights Com., 1963--; mem., Mental Health Bd., Del. Co., 1964--; Outstanding Citizen Award by the Human Relation Coun. of Delaware, O.; mem., Mason; Ohio Republican Coun.; Kiwanis Intl.; NAACP; Home: 81 Park Ave., Delaware, O.; Office: 140 S. Washington St., Delaware, O.

LIGGINS, Wendell, b. Xenia, Ohio, Oct. 21, 1914; s. Frank and Aroma H. L.; A. B., Denver Univ.; B. D., Payne Theol. Sem., Wilberforce Univ.; course on Th. D., Iliff Sch. of Theol.; D. D. (hon.), Ark. Bapt. Coll., Little Rock Ark.; m. Louise Helen; Children--Wanda Faye; current pastor, Zion Bapt. Ch., Denver, 1940--; mem., Library Commn., Denver, Colo.; former pres., Western Bapt. Conv.; General Bd., Natl. Coun. of Chs.; editorial writer, Natl. Bapt. Sun. Sch. Publishing Bd.; instr., Nat Sun. Sch. and Bapt. Training Leadership Union Congress; Exec. mem., Bd. of Natl. Trade & Professional Sch., Wash., D. C.; former mem., Speakers Bur., Republican State Committee of Colo.; mem., Phi Beta Sigma; writer of devotional literature, Natl. Bapt. Sun. Sch. Pub. Bd.; former rel. column writer, The Denver Call; Home: 3200 Monaro, Denver, Colo.; Office: 933 E. 24th, Denver, Colo.

LIGHTSEY, Joseph Hancock, b. Irwin Co., Ga., Mar. 1, 1909; s. John W. and Cora Bell (Mclain) L.; Holsey Cobb Inst., Cordele, Ga., 1922-30; inservice training - Bennett Coll., 1948; A & T Coll., 1954; Univ. of N. C., 1962-63; m. Ruth Mozella Martin; Children--Malvea Joan, Joseph Martin, Phoebe Mozella; pastor, Mt. Calvary Chrstn.

Meth. Episc. Ch., Bridgeport, Conn., 1933-36; pastor, N. C. Annual Conf. C. M. E. Ch., 1940-64; conf. dir., Chrstn. Ed., 1949-58; present: presiding elder, Durham Dist., N. C. Conf., 1961--; N. C. Coun. of Chs., Durham Minister Assn.; Mason; NAACP; Home: 510 S. Alston St., Durham, N. C.; Office: 510 S. Alston St., Durham, N. C.

*LILE, Alfred T., b. Bonora, Pa., Oct. 27, 1928; s. Horace and Hattie; diploma, Chgo. City Coll., 1954; M. R. E., Bethany Theol. Sem., 1963; B. Ed., Chgo. Tchrs. Coll., 1958; B. D., Howard Univ., Sch. of Rel., 1964; pastor, Apostolic Faith Ch., Chgo., Ill., 1958-62; Trinity United Congre. Ch., Chgo., Ill., 1962-63; asst. to min., United Chrstn. Coll., Durham, N. C.; tchr., Chgo., Ill.; repre., law students civil rights research coun., N. C. Coll., Durham, N. C.; US Army, 1954-56; Home: 8536 S. Ingleside, Chgo., Ill.

LINCOLN, C. Eric, author, coll. prof.; b. Athens, Ala., June 23, 1924; A. B., Lemoyne Coll., 1947; A. M., Fisk Univ., 1954; B. D, Univ. of Chgo., 1956; Ph. D., Boston Univ., 1960; M. Ed., 1960; m. Lucy Cook; Children--Cecil Eric, Joyce Elaine, Hilary; pastor, John Calvin Presby. Ch., Nashville, 1953-54; Dir. of Public Relation, Lemoyne Coll., 1950-51; asst. personnel dean, asst. prof., rel. & philosophy, Fisk Univ., 1954-57; resident chap., Boston Univ. Sch. of Theol., 1958-59; dir. of panel of Amer., Human Relations Center, 1958-60; assoc. prof. and asst. to pres., Clark Coll., 1961-63; prof. and dir., Inst. for Social Relations, 1963-68; present: asst. prof. Sociology and Rel., Union Theol. Sem., NYC; awards: John Hay Whitney Fellow; Crusade Fellow; mem., Soc. Psychological Study of Soc. Issues; Natl. Assn. of Univ. Prof.; Natl. Assn. of Intergroup Relations Officials; Amer. Acad. of Political and Social Science; Kappa Alpha Psi; Frontiers; guest appearances on local TV and radio shows in Boston, St. Louis, Memphis, Atlanta, Chattanooga, Cleveland; lecturer, univ. and learned societies; author: The Black Muslims in America, 1961; My Face Is Black, 1964; "The Nation of Islam" and "The Black Muslims in America" in The Encyclopaedia Britannica, 1963; contributed to many books and periodicals, such as The Reporter, The New Englander, New South, The Negro Digest, The Journal of Soc. Issues, Phylon, Christian Century and many others; Home: 2937 Collier Dr., NW, Atlanta, Ga.; Office: McGiffert Hall, Union Theol. Sem., New York, N. Y.

LINDSEY, Merrill Winston, tchr., b. Holly Springs, Miss., Feb. 21, 1911; s. Albert and Molly (Burns) L.; A. B., Rust Coll., 1948; M. A., Denver Univ., 1953; D. D., (hon.), Rust Coll., 1956; m. Alberta Lee Michael; Children--Merill W., William Bernard, Delores Elnora (Mrs. Roland McJunkins); Masheetta Uylanda, Michael Forsythe; pastor, Algoma, Miss., 1933-36; Ripley, Miss., 1936-41;Griffin Ch., Starkville, Miss., 1941-46; Haven Ch., Clarksdale, Miss., 1946-50; Wesley Ch., Greenwood, Miss., 1950-60; Asbury Ch., Holly Springs, Miss., 1960-62; current, Dist. supt., Aberdeen Dist. Upper Miss. Conf., Meth. Ch.; tchr., city and co. schs. of Tippah Co., Miss., 1941-46; prof., Coahoma Jr. Coll., Clarksdale, Miss., 1948-50; prof., Sociology, Miss. Vocational Coll., Itta Bena, Miss.; guest lecturer, Grad. Sch., Jackson State Coll., Jackson, Miss.; Rust Coll., 1960-62; candidate for Congress, First Congressional Dist., Miss., 1962; mem., Adv. staff, Democratic Party; Home: 425-5 St., West Point, Miss.,

LINK, John Lewis, b. Milton, N. C., Sept. 4, 1884; s. Stephen and Susan L.; B. A., Lincoln Univ., 1909; S. T. B. Lincoln Univ. Theol. Sem., 1912; Derrick Business Sch., 1921; journalism, Univ. of Pa., 1936; Crozer Sem., 1938; m. Nora Helen Cameron Watson; pastor, Afr. Meth. Episc. Ch., Shippensburg, Pa., 1912-13, Downingtown, Pa., 1914-17, Columbia, Pa., 1917-20, Media, Pa., 1920-25; Murphy Ch., Chester, Pa., 1925-33; presiding elder, Delaware Conf., 1933--; mem., Chester City Sch. Bd., 1947-63; pres., Inter-Racial; treas., br. YMCA, Chester, Pa.; mem., Lincoln Univ. Alumni Assn.; Mason; Home: 524 Flower St., Chester, Pa., 19013; Office: 524 Flower St. Chester, Pa.

*LINSEY, Nathaniel, b. Atlanta, Ga., July 24, 1926; s. Sam and L. E. (Forney) L.; A. B., Paine Coll., 1948; B. D., Howard Univ., 1951; m. Mae Cannon Mills; Children--Nathaniel L., Ricardo Mills, Julius Wayne; pastor, Halifax Circuit, 1949-51; Natl. Youth Dir., Chrstn. Meth. Episc. Ch., 1951-52; pastor, Walterboro Circuit, Walterboro, S. C., 1952-53; presiding elder, Greenville Dist., S. C., 1953-54; pastor, Vanderhorst Meml. C. M. E. Ch., Charleston, S. C., 1954-55; pastor, Mattie E. Coleman Ch., Knoxville, Tenn., 1955-62; pastor, Thirgood C. M. E. Ch., Birmingham, Ala., 1962--; Birmingham Diist., Dir. of Evangelism, C. M. E. Ch.; pres., NAACP, Knoxville, Tenn., 1960; chrmn., Bd. of Man-

agement, YMCA, Knoxville, 1961-62; mem., Mayor's Bi-racial Comm., Knoxville, Tenn., 1960-62; Community Service Award 1964 Zeta Phi Beta Sorority, Birmingham Ala.; rec'd Citation in Rel. from Pi Lambda Sigma Honor Soc., Birmingham, Ala., 1963; Ala. Chrstn. Movement for Human Rights; Strategy Comm. YMCA; Adv. Comm. of Planned Parenthood; mem., Ministers and Layman's Coun., C. M. E. Ch.; Home: 932 Center Pl., S. W., Birmingham, Ala.; Office: 1029 7th Ave., N. Birmingham, Ala.

LITTLE, Harlee Hoover, b. Richmond Co., N. C., Nov. 15, 1917; s. Harlee and Owen; B. A., Livingstone Coll., 1939; B. D., Hood Theol. Sem., 1947; M. A., Drew Univ., 1952; graduate diploma, Teachers Coll., Columbia Univ., 1958; studies, Union Theol. Sem., NYC, m. Meriam Sanders; Children--Harlee, LaVerne, Maurice, Annie, Helen, Bernice; pastor, A. M. E. Z. Ch., Parish, 1938-43; US Army chap., 1943-46; parish minister, 1946-48; prof., Livingstone Coll., 1949-59; Pub. relations dir., 1959-66; Dir. of Development, Livingstone Coll., Salisbury, N. C., 1967--; cons., rural ch. work, Chrstn. Ed.; pres., Rowan Co. NAACP; adv. commn., sch. integration; Bd. of dir., Rowan Co. United Fund; awards: Five battle stars, WW II; Livingstone Coll. Alumni Meritorious Service; mem., Rural Sociology; Town and Country Commn.; Com., Chrstns. Approach to Jews, Natl. Coun. of Chs.; NCCJ; Sec., Inter-racial Coun.; chap., Natl. Coun., UNCF; Democrat; Omega Psi Phi; Alumni ed., Livingstone Coll.; extensive research, rural life in South; Home: 502 Milford Hills Rd., Salisbury, N. C. 28144; Office: Livingstone Coll., Salisbury, N. C.

LITTLE, John Franklin, b. Rock Run, Ala., Mar. 5, 1908; s. Hampton Wiley and Lula (Thomason) L.; B. S., Bluefield State Teacher's Coll., W. Va., 1940; B. D., Payne Theol. Sem., Wilberforce, O., 1935; further study: Denver Univ., 1960 and Pittsburgh Univ.; m. Mabel Sterns; Children--Marjorie Loretta (Mrs. Howard Cockrell); Laura Jane (Mrs. John Okumu), Jo-Anne Murray; pastor, A. M. E. Chs., Ohio, W. Va., Pa., Liberia, 1931-62; prof., Univ. of Liberia, 1953-56; pres., Monrovia Coll. & Indus. Training Sch., 1953-60; tchr., Cape Palmas High Sch. and A. M. E. Day Sch., Harper City, Liberia, 1961; current pastor, Trinity A. M. E. Ch., Pittsburgh, Pa.; pres., United Nations Organization, Harper City, Liberia; preached in John Wesley Chapel, London, Eng.,

July 31, 1951; preached and lectured in Germany, 1951; Home: 560 Clow Ave., Newcomerstown, O.; Office: 2702 Wylie Ave., Pittsburgh, Pa. 15219

LLOYD, Gil Burton, b. Nashville, Tenn., Nov. 9, 1916; s. Grant, Sr. and Johnella (Stewart) L.; A.B., Fisk Univ., 1939; B.D., Chicago Sem., 1941; m. Doris Watts; Children--Doris Diane; asst. pastor, Sylvan St. Bapt. Ch., Nashville, Tenn., 1935-37; pastor, St. Mary Congre. Ch., Abbeville, La., 1938; chap., US Army, 1942-46; pastor, Mt. Zion Bapt. Ch., Seattle, Wash., 1955-57; exec. dir., Englewood Chrstn. Center, 1957-59; pastor, Herry Hill Bapt. Ch., Seattle, Wash., 1959--; assoc. dir., Parkway Community House, Chgo., Ill., 1946-47; community worker, Southside Community Comm., Chgo., Ill., 1948-52; chap., 1st Lt., Chap. Corps, 1942-46; Bronze Star Medal; mem., Amer. Public Welfare Assn.; 1st v.p., No. Pacific Bapt. Conv.; Bd. of Home Missions Natl. Bapt. Conv. USA, Inc.; former editor, The FACTS, Northwest weekly, Seattle, Wash.; Home: 325 19th Ave. E. Seattle, Wash. 98102; Office: 700 22nd Ave., Seattle, Wash. 98122

*LOCKMAN, Irvin Charles, b. Baltimore, Md., June 22, 1929; s. William and Elizabeth (Griffin) L.; A.B., Morgan State Coll., 1952; B.D., Howard Univ. Sch. of Rel., 1955; m. Joan Carroll; ordained Meth. Ch., 1952; pastor, John Mann Meth. Ch., Winchester, Va., 1952-56; St. Matthew's Meth. Ch., Baltimore, Md., 1956-58; Epworth Meth. Ch., Bronx, N.Y., 1958-63; current pastor, Mt. Clavary Meth. Ch., New York City, 1963--; mem., Bd. of dirs., Bethel Meth. Home, Ossining, N.Y.; Ch. campaign comm., YMCA, Harlem br.; Prot. Fed. of Welfare Agencies; sec., Metro. Sub-district Meth. Minister's Fellowship; treas., Meth. for Ch. Renewal, N.Y.; sec., Interdenom. Chap., NY Chapter; Howard Univ. Alumni; Home: 227 W. 149th St., New York, N.Y. 10039; Office: 116 Edgecombe Ave., New York, N.Y. 10030

LOGAN, John Richard, Jr., chap., b. Phila., Pa., May 12, 1910; s. John R., Sr. and Mary L. (Harbison) L.; Lincoln Univ., 1930-34; Phila. Div., 1934-37; m. Sarah U. Johnson; Children--John R. III; present rector, St. Simon Cyrenian Prot. Episc. Ch.; mem., The Exec. Coun.; mem., Bd. of Missions; Bd. of Triers of the Diocese of Pa.; Episc. chap., the Mercy-Douglas Hosp.; Bd. of Dirs., of the Chrstian St. br. of the YMCA; St.

John's Settlement House; The Amer. Red Cross; adv., Reed St. Community Coun.; awards recd. from American Red Cross, Christian St. YMCA, Pt. Breeze Community Coun., Boy Scouts of Amer.; mem., Sigma Pi Phi; Alpha Boule; Alpha Phi Alpha; Mason; Elks; Home: 1230 So. 21st, Phila., Pa.; Office: 2122 Reed, Phila., Pa.

LOGAN, Thomas W. S., b. Philadelphia, Pa., Mar. 19, 1912; s. John Richard and Mary (Harbison) L.; A. B., Lincoln Univ., 1935; Gen. Theol. Sem., 1938; S. T. B., Phila. Div. Sch., 1941; m. Hermione Hill; 1 son--Thomas W. S., Jr.; deacon, Phila., Pa., 1938; priest, Phila., Pa., 1939; vicar-in-charge, St. Augustine's Prot. Episc. Ch., Yonkers, N. Y., 1938-39; curate, St. Philip's Parish, N. Y. C., 1938-39; vicar, St. Michael's Chapel, Phila., Pa., 1940-45; current rector, Calvary Prot. Episc. Ch., Pa., 1945--; dean, Sch. of Rel., Meth. Ch., Wilmington, Del., 1951--; dean, Summer Sch. of Rel., St. Paul's Coll., 1944-46; chap., Summer Sch., St. Augustine's Coll., 1947-49; former pres., Natl. Ch. Workers Conf. of Episc. Ch., 1952-61, and the Hampton Interdenom. Conf., 1961-62; Distinguished Serv. Cert., Amer. Legion of Pa., 1960; Distinguished Serv. Award, Prince Hall Masons, Pa., 1961; Distinguished Serv. Award by Afro-Amer., 1945; mem., Alpha Phi Alpha; Elks; Mason; Democrat; former pres., local and present chap., of Frontiers of America; Home: 46 Lincoln Ave., Yeadon, Pa.; Office: Calvary Episc. Ch., 814 N. 41st St., Phila., Pa.

LOMAX, Rhea Swann, b. Mountain City, Tenn., June 28, 1911 s. George W. and Elizabeth; A. B., B. D., Lincoln Theol. Sem., 1944; 1948; grad. courses: Temple Univ., of Pa.; m. Mary Louise Smith; Children--Rhea Jr.; Curtis Blaine; Millicent Anne; Beverly Jill; Deborah Jean; pastor, Mt. Tabor A. M. E. Z. Ch., Avondale, Pa., 1945-48; John Wesley A. M. E. Z. Ch., Chambersburg, Pa., 1948-52; West St. A. M. E. Z. Ch., Carlisle, Pa., 1952-56; Alleyne Meml. A. M. E. Z. Ch., Phila., Pa., 1956-present; former pres., Franklin Co. NAACP, Chambersburg, Pa.; Exec. dir., Carlisle Community League; pres., Ministerial Assn. of Carlisle; mem., Chambersburg Min. Assn.; mem., Franklin Co. Bd. of Examiners of BSA; mem., Bd. of Dirs., Cumberland Co. Amer. Red Cross; Carlisle Intercultural Coun.; mem., Carlisle Athletic Assn.; mem., W. Phila. Min. Assn.; past pres., A. M. E. Z. Minister's Assn.; Probation Dept., Phila. Co.

Court; New Jersey Natl. Guard, 1940-42; Mason; Phi Beta Sigma; Republican; Home: 1236 No. 53rd St., Phila., Pa. 19131

LONG, Harold David, b. Stamford, Conn., Jan. 8, 1929; s. Carson and Fannie; A. B., Lincoln Univ., 1950; B. D., Yale Div. Sch., 1953; pastor, 1st Congre. Chrstn. Ch., B'ham, Ala., 1954-67; Ch. of the Open Door (UCC), Miami, Fla., 1967-present; mem., Jefferson Bd. of Mental Health, 1956-68; treas., B'ham Coun. on Human Rel., 1960-65; Bd. dir., YMCA, 1956-62; award: Man of the Year, Frontiers Club, 1963; Home: 6001 NW 8th Ave., Miami, Fla. 33127

LOUD, Irwin C., chap., Major, b. Anderson, Tex., Nov. 15, 1925; s. Irwin C. Sr. and Jessie Lee (L.); A. B., Samuel Huston Coll., Austin, Tex., 1950; B. D., Gammon Theol. Sem., Atlanta, Ga. 1953; further study, New Mexico State Univ., 1961, Univ. Park, N. M.; m. Emma Lucy Johnson; Children--Yvonne Lynette, Irwin C. III; ordained deacon, United Meth. Ch., 1947; elder, 1951; pastor, St. Luke United Meth. Ch., Dallas, Tex., 1953-54; Mt. Vernon U. Meth. Ch., Lubbock, Tex., 1954-58; Myrtle Ave. United Meth. Ch., El Paso, Tex., 1958-62; commissioned a Chap., 1st Lt., US Army 1962; chap., 36th Art. Group, Germany, 1964-67; student, US Med. Center for Fed. Prisoners, 1967-present; Home: 1228 Gholston Rd., Waco, Tex.; Office: 606 N. Benton Ave., Springfield, Mo. 65806

LOVE, Edgar Amos, bishop, b. Harrisburg, Va., Sept. 10, 1891; s. Julius C. and Susie (Carr) L.; Morgan Acad., 1905-09; A. B., Howard Univ., 1913; B. D., 1916; S. T. B. Boston Univ., 1918; D. D. (hon.), Morgan Coll., 1935; Gammon Theol. Sem., 1946; Boston Univ., 1956; m. Virginia Louise Ross; Children--Jon Edgar; ordained to ministry, Meth. Ch., 1915; princ., acad., Morgan Coll., Balt., 1920-21; coll. prof., 1919-21; pastor, Wash., Pa., 1921-26, Annapolis, Md., 1926-29, Wheeling, W. Va., 1929-31, 1931-33; dist. supt., Wash. Dist., Wash. Conf. Meth. Ch., 1933-40; supt. dept. Negro Work Bd. Missions, Meth. Ch., 1940-52; bishop since 1952, assigned Balt. area; sometime lecturer, numerous colls. and univs.; trustee, Morgan Coll.; mem., Bd. of Governors, Gammon Theol. Sem., Atlanta, Morristown Jr. Coll.; Bd. Missions; v. p., Bd. Evangelism, Coordinating Coun. of Meth. Ch.; Meth. Com. on Chaplains; Gen. Com on

Chaplains; Natl. Coun. Chs. of Christ in USA; mem., Omega Psi Phi; Elk; Mason; Frontiers of Amer. (Balto.); retired 1964; Home: 2416 Montebello Terr., Baltimore, Md.

LOWE, Richard A., chap., editor, b. Cleveland, O., June 12, 1898; s. Robert B. and Martha (Lane) L.; B.Th., Wilberforce Univ., 1917; B.S., Univ. of Chgo., 1926; Lewis Inst., Chgo.; Harvard Univ., 1940; D.D. (hon.), Texas Bapt. Coll; m. Ruth Wheeler (1st), Catherine Redman (present); Children--Anna Belle, Richard, David; field missionary, Western Bapt. Conv., 1919-21; ordained A.M.E. elder, 1922; pastor, Afr. Meth. Episc. Chs., 1922-30; assoc. pastor, Shiloh Bapt. Ch., Cleveland, O., 1930-35; Providence Bapt. Ch., 1935-37; Greater El Bethel Bapt. Ch., Dallas, Tex., 1937-41; current, Mt. Zion Bapt. Ch., Newark, N.J.; public relations practitioner, 1926-40; pub. relations consultant, 1940--; editor, Missionary Bapt. Digest, official organ New England Bapt. Conv. and Amer. Negro Missionary Bapt., 1956--; Pub. Relations Counsel: Natl. Negro Independent Civic & Political Assn., Inc., 1952--; US Vet. WW I, 1918-19; Chap., US Army, 1941-43, 1st Lt.; mem., Mason; Commissioner of Pub. Relations, Gen. Bapt. Conv.; ed., These Changing & Clashing Worlds 1948; Home: 214 W. Market St. (Apt. 5), Newark, N.J.; Office: Third Floor East, 160 Broadway, New York, N.Y.

LUCAS, Lawrence Edward, b. New York, N.Y., July 8, 1933; s. George Alvin and Miriam (Grant) L.; Cathedral College, N.Y., 1947-53; St. Joseph's Sem., Yonkers Coll., 1953-59; ordained Roman Cath. priest; St. Joseph's Ch., Croton Falls, N.Y., 1959; St. Peter's Ch., Barclay St., N.Y., 1959-61; Resurrection Ch., NYC, 1961--; Bd. of Dir., Harlem Neighborhood Assn.; Mayors Comm. of Rel. Leaders; Home and Office: 276 W. 151st St., New York, N.Y.

LYLES, James J., coll. chap., b. Texarkana, Tex., July 4, 1928; s. F. O. and Laura (Stucky) L.; B.A., Philander Smith Coll., 1952; B.D., Perkins Sch. of Theol., Southern Meth. Univ., 1955; further study: Hogg Found. on Mental Health; Univ. of Tex., 1960; m. Shirley Robinson; Children--Marquis Denzell; youth dir., St. Paul Meth. Ch., Dallas, Tex., 1952-53; Bd. of Evangelism of the Meth. Ch., 1953-54; organized Golden Meth. Ch.,

Memphis, 1954-56; US Air Force chap., 1956-61; chap., pastor, tchr. and counselor of Bethel Ch., Morristown Coll., 1961--; registrar, E. Tenn. Annual Conf., 1963--; mem., Bd. of Mgrs., Gulfside Meth. Assembly Sch.; Cultural and Civic Comm. of the Morristown Coll.; Cham. of Commerce; Democrat; Amer. Philosophical Soc.; 42nd Bomb Wing Unit Citation; 5th Motor Transport Unit Citation; B'nai B'rith Award of Outstanding Achievements in the field of Soc. Ethics; mem., Alpha Phi Alpha; NAACP; Urban League; Natl. Coun. of Chrstns. & Jews; mem., Ed. bd. of The Red Knight Journal; Home: 307 E. 6th St., N. Morristown, Tenn.; Office: Morristown Coll., Morristown, Tenn.

LYNCH, Lorenzo Augustus, b. Oak City, N.C., Apr. 21, 1932; s. Augustus and Carrie (Burnett) L.; A.B., Shaw Univ., Raleigh, N.C.; B.D., Shaw Univ., Sch. of Rel.; grad. courses: Southeastern Bapt. Theol. Sem., Univ. of N.C.; candidate, Ph.D., Boston Univ.; m. Lorine Harris; Children--Lorenzo Jr.; Leonao; Loretto; pastored at Bapt. Chs., N.C.; Providence Bapt. Ch., Durham, N.C., 1958-66; pastor, White Rock Bapt. Ch., 1966-present; tchr., Boston Coun. Week-Day Rel. Ed.; present adv., Bapt. Student Union, A & T Coll., Greensboro, N.C.; mem., Greensboro Citizens Assn.; exec. bd. Rowan Bapt. Assn.; Bd. of Missions, Gen. Bapt. State Conv.; Bd. of Dir., United Southern Chrstn. Fellowship Found., A & T Coll.; Bd. of Dir., Cumberland Courts, Inc.; mem., Guildford Co. Young Democratic Club; candidate, Guilford Co., Bd. of Commissions, Democratic Primary; chrmn., Com. on Ed., Greensboro Human Rel. Commn.; Natl. Coun., Family Rel.; assoc. mem., The Natl. Assn. of Coll. & Univ. Chaplains, USA; Home: 1219 Fayetteville St., Durham, N.C. 27707

McCALL, Aidan Maurice, coll. prof., b. Washington, D.C., July 25, 1926; s. Henry A. and Eva (Thompkins) M.; B.A., St. John's Univ., 1950; A.M., Univ. of Mich., 1959; ordained priest, Roman Cath. Ch., 1954; instr., Latin, St. John's Prep Sch., 1950-54; Latin and Scripture, St. Augustine's Coll., Nassau, Bahamas, 1954-57; Latin and Greek, St. John's Univ., 1957--; asst. prof., St. John's Univ., 1962--; mem., Linguistic Soc. of Amer., Classical Assn. of Midwest & South, Minnesota Classical Conf.; Home and Office: St. John's Univ., Collegeville, Minn.

McCALL, Emmanuel Lemuel, b. Sharon, Pa., Feb. 4, 1936; Simmons Univ., Louisville, Ky., (1 yr.); A.B., Univ. of Louisville, 1958; B.D., M.R.E., So. Bapt. Theol. Sem., 1962-63; 1968, M. Div.; D.D., Simmons Univ., 1966; m. Emma Marie Johnson; Children--Emmanuel, Evalya Lynnette; assoc. pastor, Joshua Tabernacle Bapt. Ch., Louisville, Ky., 1954-60; pastor, 28th St. Bapt. Ch., Louisville, Ky., 1960-68; assoc. sec., Dept. of Work with Natl. Baptist, So. Bapt. Home Mission Bd., Atlanta, Ga., May 1968-present; prof., Simmons Univ., 1958-68; pres., Louisville Bapt. Min. Conf., 1956-67; Brotherhood sec., Central Dist. Assn., Ky., 1958-60; Natl. Youth Leader, Natl. Progressive Bapt. Congress of Ed., 1963-68; pres., Ky. State Bapt. Congress of Chrstn. Ed., 1965-68; awards: Outstanding Young Man of 1965 (YMCA); Ambassador of Good Will, Louisville, Ky., 1967; Ky. Col. award, 1968 (State of Ky.); editor, Simmons Univ.: Past & Present; This Is My Story, This is My Song; author: The Centennial Story. Gen. Assn. of Ky. Bapts.; Office: Home Mission Bd., Southern Bapt. Conv., 1350 Spring St., N.W., Atlanta, Ga. 30309

McCALL, H. Carl, b. Boston, Mass., Oct. 17, 1935; s. Herman and Carol (Ray) M.; A.B., Dartmouth Coll., 1954; M.A., Univ. of Edinburgh, Scotland, 1960; B.D., Andover-Newton Theol. Sem., 1962; m. Cecelia Hodges; Children--Marcella Jennifer; dir., Blue Hill Chrstn. Center, Boston, Mass., 1961-63; NYC Mission Soc., N.Y., 1963-64; sec., Urban Ch., United Ch. of Christ, N.Y., 1964-65; project dir., Taconic Found., N.Y., 1965--; consultant to action, Boston Community Development, 1963; mem., Task Force for Human Resources Development Project, N.Y., 1966; program dir., Emergency Summer Youth Program, summers of 1964-65; mem., Bd. of Bedford-Stuyvesant Youth-in-Action; mem., Adv. Comm., Urban Ch. Dept. of U. Ch. of Christ; Publications Comm., Coun. for Soc. Action, U. Ch. of Christ; Home: 2 Washington Sq. Village, 3-0, New York, N.Y. 10012; Office: Taconic Found., Inc., 666 Fifth Ave., New York, N.Y. 10019

McCALLUM, James Hector, tchr., b. Robeson Co., N.C., Sept. 23, 1918; s. P. Jefferson and Jackie Anne (Anderson) M.; B.S., Fayetteville State Coll., Fayetteville, N.C., 1942; M.S., A & T Coll., Greensboro, N.C., 1953; Th.M., Amer. Div. Sch., Chgo., Ill., 1963; m.

Wilhelmenia Powell; Children--Rachelle; pastor, Meth. Ch., N.C. Conf., 21 yrs.; 10 yrs. in Maxton and surrounding areas; 8 yrs. in Laurinburg and surrounding areas; 3 yrs., Fayetteville, N.C.; tchr., pub. schs. 20 yrs.; pres., Local Tchrs. Assn.; mem., State Nominating Comm.; mem., NAACP; NCTA; NEA; Home: 806 Frolic St., Fayetteville, N.C.; Office: 616 Cumberland St., Fayetteville, N.C.

McCLAIN, Herbert Linton, chap., b. Decatur, Ga., Apr. 14, 1920; s. Herbert and Frances (Beasley); B.A., Johnson C. Smith Univ., 1946-49; B.D., 1949-51; US Army Chaplaincy, Ft. Slocum, N.Y. 1949; m. Rebecca Washington; Children--Sharon, Carolyn, Leroy; US Army chap. serving both Far East and Europe, 1952-58; Dir. of Camp and Rel. Ed., Westminster House, Buffalo, N.Y., 1958-61; Dir. of Community Center, Bethel United Presby. Ch., Phila., Pa., 1963--; sec., for 22nd Dist. of Youth Conservation Service sponsored by the Dept.; served as Private and Chap. Asst. with grade of Tech. 5th Grade, 1941-45; Bronze Star Medal for Meritorious Serv. during the Korean War, 1953; Cert. of Meritorious Serv. from Phila. Dept. of Police (Juvenile Aid Div.), June 1963; mem., Alpha Phi Omega Scout Fraternity, Phi Beta Sigma, The Fraternity of the Humanities at Johnson C. Smith Univ., Alpha Kappa Mu Natl. Honor Soc., US Chaplain Military Assn., Wash., D.C.; Home: 5933 N. 21st St. Philadelphia, Pa.; Church: Bethel Center, 19th & York Sts., Phila., Pa.

McCLAIN, Wm. Bobby, b. May 19, 1938, Gadsden, Ala.; s. Frank Bural and Malinda Williams (Mc); A.B., Clark Coll., Atlanta, Ga., 1960; St. B., Boston Univ., Sch. of Theol., completed courses Ph.D., Boston Univ.; m. Pamela Jane Wilson; son--Wm. B. Jr.; pastor, Haven Meth. Ch., 1962-64; dir., Dept. Guidance and Counseling, Gadsden St. Coll., 1962-64; pastor, Messiah Bapt. Ch. and Stu., Boston Univ., 1964-66; dir., Youth Mental Health Prog., Boston, 1964-66; pastor, Union United Meth. Ch., Boston, Mass., 1968-present; dir., Urban Training Center, 1967-present; Consult. Mass. Coun. for Pub. Schs.; mem., Mass. Migrant Health and Ed. Prog., Boston, Univ.; Boston Univ. Law-Medicine Inst.; Boston Police-Comm. Relations Prog.; Urban League, Affiliate Boston Univ. Human Relations Center; prof., Northeastern Univ. Sch. of Ed.; ad hoc pres., Ala. br. SCLC, 1962-63; mem., Mayor's Coun. on Human Relations, Anniston,

Ala., 1962-63; chrmn., Confrontation Comm. Brookline Civil Rights Comm.; Bd. of Dirs., Black Meth. for Ch. Renewal; awards: Alpha Phi Omega; Grad. scholarship Rockefeller Found. Fellowship; Boston Univ. Walker Fellowship; Crusade Scholarship of the Meth. Ch.; mem., Alpha Phi Omega; CORE; NAACP; Bd. of Dirs., Uni-Loyal, Inc., SCLC; Home: 78 Crowninshield Rd., Brookline, Mass.; Office: 485 Columbus Ave., Boston, Mass.

*McCLELLAN, James F., Jr., coll. prof., dean, b. Nashville, Tenn., Sept. 24, 1925; s. James F. and Robbie (Bell) M.; B.S., Tenn. A & I State Coll., 1944; Howard Univ., Sch. of Rel., B.D., 1947; Amer. Univ., summer session, 1946; Teachers Coll., Columbia Univ., M.A., 1951; Ed.D., 1956; m. Lois Jean Dedeaux; Children--Jean Elizabeth; pastor, Faith Presby. Ch., Pine Bluff, Ark., 1961-62; Wash. Heights Ch. of Christ, NYC, 1949-51; Release-time Tchr., City Mission Soc., NYC, 1948-49; pastor, Migrant Laborers, NJ Coun. of Chs., Princeton, N.J., 1948; pastor, Harlem Ch. of Christ, NYC, 1948; asst. dean and prof. of Education, Psychology, Ky. State Coll., Frankfort, Ky., 1963--; prof. of ed., Ark. A M & N. Coll., Pine Bluff, Ark., 1954-63; dir. of student personnel, Ark. A M & N. Coll., Pine Bluff Ark., 1959-60; assoc. in student personnel, Ark., A M & N Coll, 1956-59; counselor, Liberal Arts Counseling Serv., Howard Univ., Wash., D.C., 1953-54; educational dir., Geo. W. Cook Hall, Howard Univ., Wash., D.C., 1951-53; Bd. mem., Pine Bluff NAACP (incl. chrmn., Ed. Comm.; chrmn., Legal Redress Comm.); sec., State Conf. (Ark.) NAACP; Bd. mem., Ark. Coun. on Human Relations; chrmn., Citizenship Comm.; Delta Sigma Lambda Chapter; Alpha Phi Alpha; Townsend Park Sch. award for Outstanding Community Serv. (Pine Bluff, Ark., 1961); Tenn. A & I State Univ. Golden Anniversary Alumni Award, Nashville, Tenn., 1962; Pine Bluff br. NAACP Citizenship Citation, 1963; Delta Sigma Lambda Chapter, Alpha Phi Alpha Frat. Serv. Award, 1963; mem., Alpha Kappa Mu Natl. Honor Soc.; Kappa Delta Pi Honor Soc. in Ed.; Phi Delta Kappa Honor Frat. in Ed.; Amer. Assn. of Univ. Prof.; Amer. Tchrs. Assn.; Assn. of Higher Ed.; Natl. Ed. Assn.; Coll. and Univ. Personnel Assn.; Natl. Assn. of Personnel Workers; Southern Coll. Personnel Assn.; Alpha Phi Alpha; unpub. doctoral project: Seminary Training in Pastoral Counseling; Home: Ky. State Coll., Frankfort, Ky.; Office:

Kentucky State Coll., Frankfort, Ky.

McCLENDON, John Ruben, b. Chgo., Ill., June 24, 1905; s. Anderson and Mary (Williams); B.A., Northwestern Univ., 1922; B.D., Payne Theol. Sem., 1926; student, Cincinnati Ohio Law Sch., 1941; m. Margaret Vance Jones; Children--Charles R.; John H., Ronald S.; ordained elder, A.M.E. Ch., 1925; pastor, Moundsville, W. Va., 1924-26; Elkins, W. Va., 1926-27; W. Va. State Coll., Clarksburg, W. Va.; Uniontown, Pa., 1930-33; Oil City, Pa., 1933-35; Wilkes Barre, Pa., 1935-36; Youngstown, O., 1936-39; Allen Temple, Cincinnati, O., 1939-43; Homestead, Pa., New Castle, Pa., St. Paul, McKeesport, Pa., 1950-57; presiding elder, Scranton Dist., Pittsburgh, Pa., 1957-present; Omega Psi Phi; Home: 126 Freeland St., Pittsburgh, Pa. 15210

McCLONEY, Leon H., coll. pres., b. Beaumont, Tex., Aug. 27, 1924; s. Robert, Sr. and Minnie M.; A.B., The Coll. of Emporia, Emporia, Kans.; B.D., Western Univ. Sem.; D.D. (hon.), Paul Quinn Coll.; Wilberforce Univ.; m. Juanita; Children--Bruce Alan, Brena Ann; pastor, Wayman Temple Afr. Meth. Episc. Ch., Troy, Kans., 1943-44; Bethel A.M.E. Ch., Elwood, Kans., 1945; Quinn Chapel A.M.E. Ch., St. Louis, Mo., 1945-47; Mt. Olive A.M.E. Ch., Emporia, Kans., 1947-52; Brooks Chapel A.M.E. Ch., Corpus Christi, Tex., 1952-58; St. Luke A.M.E. Ch., Waco, Tex., 1958-62; current, pres., Paul Quinn Coll., Waco, Tex.; mem., City of Waco Adv. Comm.; The Budget Comm. of the Waco U. Fund; The Bd. of Dirs. of the Doris Miller YMCA; Waco Urban Renewal Commn.; Waco Progressive Coun.; Ed. Comm. of the Waco Cham. of Commerce; Office: Office of President, Paul Quinn Coll., Waco, Tex.

McCLOUD, J. Oscar, b. Waynesboro, Ga., April 10, 1936; s. George and Sophronia (Foley); 1954-56 Warren Wilson Jr. Coll; 1956-58 B.A., Berea Coll; 1958-61, B.D., Union Theol. Sem. (NYC); m. Robbie Juanita Foster; dau., Ann Michelle; asst. pastor, 1951-61 Willis Ave. Meth. Ch., Bronx, N.Y.; 1961, The United Ch., Raleigh, N.C. (White); 1961-present, Davie St. United Presby. Ch., Raleigh, N.C.; mem. 1962, Bi-racial Comm., Raleigh, N.C.; 1963, v.p., Raleigh br. NAACP; pres., Min. Alliance; Psi Chi Honor Soc. (Psychology); N.C. Young Democrats Club; Home: 913 S. East St., Raleight, N.C., 27601; Church: Cor. Davis and Person

Sts, Raleigh, N. C. 27601

McCORMICK, Bennie Lionel, Pineland, Tex., May 13, 1915; s. Benjamin and Ilee (Scott); B. A., Huston-Tillotson Coll., 1958; courses, Univ. of Tex., 1959; Austin Presby. Sem., 1959; D. D. (hon.), Paul Quinn Coll., Waco, Tex., 1963; m. Lillie Mae Brown; Children--Leroy Henry; pastored, New Willard Mission, 1937-38; Kountze Circuit, 1938-39; Dayton Circuit, 1939-43; Sealy Circuit, 1943-47; St. John, Brenham, 1947-54; Grant Chapel, Austin, 1954-61; St. Paul A. M. E. Ch., Dallas, 1961--; sec., Austin Coun. of Chs., 1957-61; pres., Citywide Ch. Union, Brenham, 1950-54; pres., Travis Co. Voters League, 1959-61; Bd. of Dirs., Paul Quinn Coll., Waco, Tex., 1948-60; v. p., Tex. Coun. of Chs., 1963-64; sec., Interdenom. Min. Alliance of Dallas, 1963--; pres., S. Dallas, NAACP, 1964--; Mason; Home: 2410 Metropolitan Ave., Dallas, Tex. 75215; Office: 2410 Metropolitan Ave., Dallas, Tex.

McCOWN, Lowell Malcolm, b. So. Boston, Va., Oct. 24, 1937; s. Clarence P. and Sally C. (Coleman); A. B., Va. Sem., & Coll., Lynchburg, Va., 1961; B. D., Va. Union Univ., Richmond, Va., 1965; m. Buelah Boulden; Children--Lowell Malcolm, Kevin L'Mann; pastor, Beautiful Plain Bapt. Ch., Charlotte Court House, Va.; Five Forks Bapt. Ch., Saxes, Va.; New Hope Bapt. Ch., Ashland, Ky., 1966-present; tchr., Charlotte Ct. House, Va.; coordinator, New Careers Program, Huntington, W. Va., 1967-68; dir., New Careers Prog., Huntington, W. Va., Oct. 1968-prs.; pres., NAACP (Ashland, Ky.); Bd. mem., Citizens Adv. Com., Ky.; sec., Human Rights Commn., Ky.; Bd. mem., Amer. Red Cross, Ashland, Ky.; mem., Masons; Elks; Democrat; Home: 2720 Carter Ave., Ashland, Ky. 41101; Office: 2717 Carter Ave., Ashland, Ky. 41101

*McCOY, Cleo Milam, coll. chap., b. Winnfield, La., Sept. 29, 1912; s. Matt Milam and Hattie (Lee); A. B., Paine Coll., Augusta, Ga., 1939; B. D., Howard, Univ., Sch. of Rel., 1942; courses: A & T Coll., N. C.; m. Mabel Amelia Madden; Children--Ellen O'Hear, David Madden; US Civil Serv., Wash., D. C., 1942-46; chap. & tchr. of Philosophy, rel., history and soc. sci., A & T Coll. of N. C., Greensboro, N. C., 1946--; organized Dir., Town & Rural Min. Inst.; Dir. of Chrstn. Ed., N. C. Annual Conf. Chrstn. Meth. Episc. Ch., mem., Div. of

Chrstn. Ed.; Natl. Coun. of Chs.; contribution in the area of community leadership during the civil rights demonstrations crisis of 1963 resulted in the creation of The Greensboro Community Fellowship, a nonsectarian, non-political, interracial fellowship; mem., Assn. for the Co-ordination of Univ. Rel. Affairs; Natl. Assn. of Chaplains and Dirs. of Rel. Life; The N. C. Assn. of Tchrs. of Rel.; N. C. Chrstn. Student Workers Assn.; The Inst. of Rel., Howard Univ., Wash., D. C.; The Greensboro Min. Fellowship; The Pulpit Forum of Greensboro and Vicinity; The Assn. of Soc. Sci. Tchrs.; The Greensboro Citizens Assn.; The Greensboro Community Fellowship, v. p.; The Greensboro Community Coun.; Rural Ch. Comm., N. C. Coun. of Chs.; Comm. on Continuing Ed. for Town and Country Pastors, Landgrant Univ.; Home: 1009 Martin St., Greensboro, N. C. 27406; Office: Box H-23, A & T Coll., 312 N. Dudley St., Greensboro, N. C. 27411

*McCRAY, Maceo Edward, librarian, b. Bucksport, S. C., Feb. 10, 1935; s. Vetus C. and Grace (Wallace) M.; B. S., S. C. State Coll., 1956; B. D., Howard Univ., Sch. of Rel., 1962; Drexel Inst. of Tech., Sch. of Library Scie., summers of 1963-64; ordination, 1961; served with several chs. in the Wash. area, S. C. and Springfield, Mass; asst. pastor, Mt. Sinai Bapt. Ch., 1959-63; chap. to migrants in western NY, summers of 1960-61; asst. circulation librarian, Howard Univ., 1962--; mem., Wash. Urban League; Visiting Nurses Assn.; Howard Univ. Library Assn.; D. C. Library Assn.; Omega Psi Phi; Home: Rte 1, Box 14, Bucksport, S. C.; Office: Medical Lib., Howard Univ., Wash., D. C. 20001

McCRAY, Thomas L.; A. B., Wilberforce Univ.; Bucknell Univ.; B. D., Payne Theol. Sem., Wilberforce, O.; m. Elizabeth J.; Children--Lois, Thomas, Tereas; circuit pastor, A. M. E. Z. Ch., Pa., 3 yrs.; assoc. pastor & minister of Chrstn. Ed., St. James A. M. E. Ch., Cleveland, O.; pastor, Mt. Moriah A. M. E. Ch., Maple Hghts, O., 1958-present; mem., Div. of Home Missns., Natl. Coun. of Chs. of Christ; former v. chrmn., Dept. Chrstn. Ed., Third Episc. Dist.; mem., Cedar br., YMCA; Youth Com., NAACP; mem., Dept. Youth Ministry, Exec. Com., Natl. Coun. of Chs.; Gov.'s Com., Migrant Labor; v. p., Admin. Com., Cleveland Coun. of Chs. Child Devel. Program; pres., A. M. E. Minister's Fellowship, Cleveland; Home: 4253 East 163rd St. Cleveland, Ohio 44128

McDANIEL, Abraham H., b. March, 1905, Lee Co., S.C.; s. James and Julia (Mc); B.D., Hood Theol. Sem., Livingstone Coll., Salisbury, N.C., 1947; M.Th., Pioneer Theol. Sem., 1953; D.D. (hon.), Morris Coll., 1967; m. Ioye Nelle Gaither; Children--Albert Ernest, Cecilia Lynette, Russell Keith, Branelsia Kaye; pastor, Union Bapt. Ch., Winston Salem, N.C., 1953-present; moderator, Rowan Bapt. Assn., 1962-66; mem., Lott Carey Bapt. Foreign Mission Conv., 1942-present; Natl. Bapt. Conv., Inc., 1939-present; mem., Kate Bidding Reynolds Hosp.; Urban Correlation (Winston-Salem); Bapt. Min. Conf.; Forsyth Co. Min. Assn.; pres., Paisley Sch. PTA; City-Co. Sch. Com.; Bd. mem., NAACP, Winston-Salem; Mason; Democrat; Home: 3779 Carver Rd., Winston-Salem, N.C. 27105; Office: 406 N.W. Blvd., Winston-Salem, N.C. 27105

McFARLANE, Percival Alan Rex, b. Montreal, Canada, Jan. 25, 1928; s. Clarence Percival and Irene Louise (Arnold); McGill Sch. Cert., 1947; Episc. Sem., Haiti; St. Peters Coll., Jamaica, B.W.I.; McGill Univ. (Certificate in Theol), 1951; Columbia Univ., B.S. and M.A., 1962; curate, St. Boniface Ch., Assiniboia, Canada, 1951-52; Curate, St. Paul's Cathedral, Regina, Canada, 1952-55; vicar, St. Thomas Ch., Red Bank, N.J., 1955-58; curate, All Soul's Ch., NYC, 1958-60; curate, St. Philip's Ch., Bklyn, N.Y., 1961--; chap., Anglican Young People's Assn. for Alberta, Manitoba, Saskatchewan, Canada, 1953-55; current, study dir., Campus Ministry Study, Inst. of Urban Studies, Tchrs. Coll., Columbia Univ.; sec., Columbia Univ. Student Coun., Head of Columbia Univ. Delegation to 1963 US Natl. Student Assn. Congress; Office: Institute of Urban Studies, Teachers College, Columbia Univ., New York, N.Y.

McGEE, C.L., b. Phila., Pa.; A.B., B.D., Bloomfield Coll. & Sem., N.J., 1937, 1939; M.A., New York Univ.; S.T.D., Miller Univ., Princeton Theol. Inst., 1961; D.D. (hon.), Bloomfield Coll. & Sem., 1963; m. Mabelle Pierce; pastor, Trinity United Presbyn. Ch., Montclair, N.J., 1935-present; pastor, Trinity United Presbyn. Ch., Bloomfield, N.J., 1938-63; mem., Bd. of Dir., Bloomfield Coll., Bloomfield, N.J., 1962-65; mem., Citizen Adv. Com. of the Montclair Urban Renewal Agency, 1962-63; mem., Bd. of Dir., Community Welfare Coun., Montclair, 1962-65; moderator, Newark Presbytery, 1958-59; mem., Montclair br. NAACP, 1950-63; candidate, Republican for Freeholder in Essex Co., N.J., 1961; served on Presbytery comms.; mem., Sod. Ed. and Action Comm.; pension, Evangelism, Ministerial Rel. Nominating, Natl. Missn., permanent clerk; mem., Synod of N.J.; committees served: Coun., 1960-62; Nominating, 1959-61; Natl. Missn., 1961-66; Coun. of Chs., 1961-63; Bd. of Trustees, Synod Homes, 1961-66; mem., Bd. of Trustees, Edith-George Brown Meml. Home for Aged, Montclair, 1949-63; mem., Montclair Min. Assn., 1950-63, pres., 1954-55; mem., Bloomfield Coun. on Race Rel., 1940-63; mem., Presbyn. Min. Assn., N.Y., N.J., 1940-62; mem., Urban League, Essex Co., 1960-63; pres., Montclair Community Assn., 1955-62; mem., Acad. of Rel. & Mental Health, N.Y., 1960-63; mem., N.J. Welfare Coun., 1960-63; mem., Montclair Human Rel., 1961-62; mem., Intercultural Assn., Montclair, 1961-62; supervisor, Essex. Co. Coun. of Rel. Ed., 1934-39, Spec. Project, Newark, N.J., 1937-39; sec., 2nd Ward Republican Club, Orange, N.J.; pres., Chrstn. Endeavor Soc., 1925-33; pres., Fed. of Adult Men's Bible Classes, Phila., Pa.; Mason; chap., US Army, WW II; awarded the Bronze Star Medal; author, God In Action, N.Y. Carlton Press, 1964; Office: Trinity Presbyn. Ch., Orange Rd. & High Sts., Montclair, N.J.

McGEE, Lewis Allen, chap., b. Scranton, Pa., Nov. 11, 1893; s. Charles A. and Gay Ruth M.; Univ. of Pittsburgh, 1912-13; B.D., Payne Theol. Sem., Wilberforce, O., 1916; Loyola Univ., Chgo., 1933-35; B.A., Carthage Coll., Ill., 1936; Meadville Theol. Sch., Chgo., 1946-47; m. Mary Marcella Walker; Children--Lewis A., Jr. (deceased), Charles E., Mrs. Jacob Downs; pastor, A.M.E. Ch., Parkersburg, W. Va., 1916-17; instr., Kittrell Coll., N.C., 1917-18; US Army chap., 1918-19; A.M.E. minister, Cleveland, O., Morgantown and Charleston, W. Va., 1919-25; instr., Edward Waters Coll., Fla., 1925-27; social worker with Illinois Childrens Home and Aid Soc., 1927-31; Chgo. Municipal Court, 1931-37; A.M.E. minister, Chicago, Ill. and Gary, Ind., 1937-43; US Chap., 1943-45; minister, All Souls Unitarian Ch., Chgo., 1947-53; admin. asst., Amer. Humanist Assn., Yellow Springs, Ohio, 1953-57; assoc. minister, First Unitarian Ch., L.A., 1958-61; minister, Unitarian Fellowship, Chico, Calif., 1961-62; interim minister, Orange Co. Unitarian Ch., Anaheim, Calif., 1962-63; Minister of Ed., Throop

Meml. Unitarian-Universalist Ch., Pasadena, 1936-present; pres., Amer. Civil Liberties Union, Yellow Springs, O., 1956-57; Alpha Phi Alpha; Mason; Amer. Legion and Amer. Vets. Comm.; Amer. Assn. of Soc. Workers; Democrat; Home: 4384 Risinghill Rd., Altadena, Calif; Office: 300 S. Los Robles Ave., Pasadena, Calif.

*McINTYRE, DeWitt T., b. July 12, 1932, Newport News, Va.; s. Willie A. and Kizzie H. (Mc); B.S., Hampton Inst., 1958; grad. courses, Hampton Inst., 1961-62; Norfolk State Coll., 1952-54; Wesley Theol. Sem., 1965-66; M.Div., Howard Univ., Sch. of Rel., 1968; L.H.D. (hon.), Balto. Coll. of the Bible and Sem. (Md.), 1967; m. Correan D. Woodson; Children--Disraeli, Descartes, DeWitt T. II; co-pastor, Friendship Bapt. Ch., Newport News, Va., 1960-61; asst. pastor, St. John's Bapt. Ch., Balto., Md., 1962-64; pastor, Reisterstown, Md. Circuit United Meth. Ch., 1964-66; Chase Charge, Chase, Md., 1966-68; Asbury United Meth. Ch., Mt. Vernon, N.Y., 1968-present; former tchr., Balto. Pub. Schs.; social worker, Carroll Co., Md.; Employment sec., claims adjuster, N.Y. state; Insurance agent, tax adjuster, N.Y. and Va.; dean and prof., Balto. Coll. of the Bible and Sem.; NAACP; Urban League Reisterstown Dem. Improvement Club, 1964-66; Balto. Police Community Rel. Coun., 1966-68; awards, D.B. Barton award, (Pastoral Theol.) Howard Univ., 1968; Balto. Annual Conf. United Meth. Ch.; S.E. Dist. Ch. of the Year Award; sec., Peninsular Bapt. Min. Conf., 1957-58 (Newport News, Va.); NEA 1962-65; mem., Balto. Co. Ministerium, 1966-68; Coun. of Chs., 1964-present; Home: 58 W. Seventh St., Mt. Vernon, N.Y. 10550

McINTYRE, John Henry, b. Sylacauga, Ala., June 1, 1925; s. Willie M. and Georgia Ann; A.B., Emmanual Bible Coll., 1964; Carver Bible Inst., 1956; Friendship Bapt. Ch., 1956-64; Shiloh Bapt. Ch., 1960-present; Tallageda Springs, Ala.; Army service, 1943-46; mem., Mason; former pres., NAACP, Sylacauga Min. Assn.; Home: Rte 3, Box 690-A, Sylacauga, Ala. 35150; Office: Shiloh Bapt. Ch., Sylacauga, Ala.

MACK, Charles Henry, b. Mobile, Ala., Jan. 19, 1918; s. John and Eliza M.; A.B., B.D., Lincoln Univ., Pa., 1950, 1953; grad. courses, Temple Univ., Pa.; m. Gladys Roberts; Children--Charlotte; Carlton; Deshera;

asst. pastor, Pa. Ave. A.M.E.Z. Ch., Balt., Md., 1946; pastor, Trinity A.M.E.Z. Ch., Delta, Pa., 1947-48; St. James A.M.E.Z. Ch., Salisbury, Md., 1948-present; migratory worker's minister, 1946-present; chap. Poplar Hill Correctional Camp, Md. Penitentiary Sys., 1959-present; sub.-tchr., Md., 1954; US Army, 1943-45; author, Through An Open Door, 1965; Independent; supervisor, Wicomico Co. Recreation Commn.; Bi-racial Commn.; Fed. Housing Commn., Salisbury; v. chrmn., Wicomico Md. Housing Authority; Home: Jersey Rd., Salisbury, Md. 21802; Office: St. James A.M.E.Z. Ch., School St., Salisbury, Md. 21802

MACKEY, Andrew, Jr., b. Lancaster, S.C., Dec. 10, 1939; s. Andrew Sr. and Mattie Jane Mackey; A.B., Livingstone Coll., Salisbury, N.C., 1961; B.D., Hood Theol. Sem., Salisbury, N.C., 1964; m. Cora Lee Smith; Children--Sandra Lorraine, Andrea Benita; student minister, Cedar Grove Circuit A.M.E.Z. Ch., New London, N.C., 1959-61; pastor, New Zion Circuit A.M.E.Z. Ch., Robbins, N.C., 1961-63; Wesley A.M.E.Z. Ch., Bklyn, N.Y., 1964-65; St. Mark A.M.E.Z. Ch., Dallas, Tex., 1965-present; dir., St. Simon Child Care Center, Dallas, Tex., 1965-; NAACP; Dallas Pastor's Assn.; Dallas Interdenom. Min. Alliance; Greater Dallas Coun. of Soc. Agencies, 1965--; Home: 2312 E. Kiest Blvd., Dallas, Tex.; Office: E. Illinois Ave. & Kiest Blvd., Dallas, Tex.

McKENNEY, Martin Luther, Jr., b. Charles Co., Md., May 12, 1933; s. Martin Luther and Ahean (Frazier) M.; A.B., Morgan State Coll., 1959; S.T.B., Wesley Theol. Sem., 1962; m. Dorothy Ross; served, Westminster, Md., 1961-63; asst. pastor, Metropolitan Meth., Balto., Md., 1963-64; US Air Force, 1951-55; Good Conduct Medal; mem., Mason; Home: 3009 Lyttleton Rd., Baltimore, Md.; Office: Metropolitan Meth. Ch., Baltimore, Md.

McKINNEY, Carnes, b. Lancaster, S.C., Nov. 17, 1898; s. Daniel and Sallie Mae (Wilson) M.; Lancaster Normal and Indus. Inst.; courses, Shelton Coll.; D.D. (hon.), Livingstone Coll., 1961; m. Marvelen Johnson; Children--Marcellus, Sidney; pastored, St. Thomas A.M.E.Z. Ch., Haverstraw, N.Y., 1933; St. Francis A.M.E.Z. Ch. Mt. Kisco, N.Y., 1937; St. Phillip A.M.E.Z. Ch., Nyack, N.Y., 1941; current pastor, Caldwell A.M.E.Z. Ch., Bronx, N.Y., 1943--; tchr., Lancaster Sch., S.C.;

v. p., Bronx Div. Prot. Coun.; New York A. M. E. Z. Min. Alliance; organizer, the Bronx br. NAACP, 1952; chrmn., Bd. of Dirs., The Carnes McKinney Apartments; award: Bethune Award; Achievement Award from the NY A. M. E. Z. Conf.; mem., Forest Neighborhood House Assn.; NAACP; Urban League; Hunts Pt. Coordinating Coun; Mason; Democrat; Home: 1281 Chisholm, Bronx, N. Y. 10459; Office: 1288 Stebbins Ave., Bronx, N. Y. 10459

McKINNEY, Richard Ishmael, educator, b. Live Oak, Fla., Aug. 20, 1906; s. George P. and Sallie R. (Ellis) M.; A. B., Morehouse Coll., 1931; B. D., Andover Newton Theol. Sch., 1934; S. T. M., Andover Newton, 1937; Ph. D., Yale Univ. 1942; added study, Pendle Hill, Univ. of Chgo., Univ. of Paris, Columbia Univ.; m. Phyllis Vivian Kimbrough, 1933; 1 son, George K., 1 dau., Mrs. Osban W. Bynum, Jr. (Phyllis); pastor, Pond St. Bapt. Ch., 1934-35; dir., Rel. Activities and asst. prof., phil. and rel., Va. Union Univ., Richmond, Va., 1935-42; dean, Sch. of Rel., Va. Union Univ., 1942-44; pres., Storer Coll., Harpers Ferry, W. Va., 1944-50; acting dir., Rel. Activities, Va. State Coll., Petersburg, Va., 1950-51; head, Dept. Phil., Morgan State Coll., Balto., Md., 1951--; mem., Summer Sch. Grad. faculties, Tex. Southern Univ., Fla. A & M Univ., Southern Univ.; visiting lecturer, Amer. Friends Serv. Comm.; mem., Bd. Dirs., Balto. Urban League, 1956-59; mem. bd. Trustees, Union Bapt. Ch., 1962--; mem., Phi Sigma Tau Natl. Honor Soc. (past pres.); Amer. Phil. Assn., Natl. Soc. for Rel. in Higher Education; Alpha Kappa Mu Honor Soc.; Amer. Assn. Univ. Profs.; Soc. for Existential Phil., and Phenomenology; Inst. of Rel.; Mason; Omega Psi Phi; Sigma Pi Phi; author: Religion in Higher Education Among Negroes, 1945; contributor, The Christian Way in Race Relations, 1948; Home: 2408 Overland Ave., Baltimore, Md. 21214; Office: Morgan State College, Baltimore, Md. 21212

McKINNEY, Samuel Berry, b. Flint, Mich., Dec. 28, 1926; s. Wade Hampton and Ruth (Berry) M.; A. B., Morehouse Coll., Atlanta, Ga., 1952; B. D., Colgate-Rochester Div. Sch.; m. Louise Jones; Children--Lora Ellen, Rhoda Eileen; Inner-Mission of Rochester, N. Y. and student asst. minister, The Aenon Bapt. Ch., Providence, R. I., 1954-58; current pastor, Mt. Zion Bapt. Ch., Seattle, Wash., 1958--; pres., No. Pacific Bapt. Conv., 1960-63;

v.p., Washington-Northern Idaho Coun. of Chs., 1964-65; mem., Mayor's Human Rights Commn.; pres., Amer. Bapt. Black Churchmen; US Forces, WW II; mem., Alpha Phi Alpha; Home: 828 33rd Ave., Seattle, Wash.; Office, 1634 19th Ave., Seattle, Wash.

McKINNON, Snowden Isaiah, b. Streetman, Navarro Co., Texas, Nov. 17, 1913; s. John Marshall Ewatt and Ardella Edna (Orange) M.; A.B., Fisk Univ., 1950; B.D., Louisville Presby. Theol. Sem., 1953; m. Linda Rhoda Samuels; Children--Snowden Isaiah, Jr.; pastor, St. James Bapt. Ch., Chattanooga, Tenn., 1954-58; pastor, Hope Presby. Ch., Dallas, Tex., 1958-61; current pastor, Highland Hills Presby. Ch., USA, Dallas, Tex.; sec., Local Bapt. Min. Union; YMCA Youth Comm., Dallas, Tex.; Boy Scouts of America; "certificated" tchr., Bapt. Bible Center, Chattanooga, and Tenn. State Bapt. Educational Training, Memphis; Owen Jr. Coll.; Bd. of Dirs., Moorland br., YMCA, Dallas; USAAF, 1942-46; awards: Good Conduct Medal; United Negro College Fund, Colll. Div. Award; mem., Alpha Phi Alpha; Home: 7334 Vecino Dr., Dallas, Tex. 75241; Office: Highland Hills Presby. Ch., 6352 Bonnie View Rd., Dallas, Tex. 75241

McKINNON, Udalga Zorosha, prof., b. Corsicana, Tex., Oct. 9, 1903; s. John M.E. and Ardella Edna (Orange) M.; A.B., Tex. Coll., 1927; A.B., Clark Coll., 1944; B.D., Gammon Theol. Sem., 1945; A.M., Drew Univ., 1950; D.D. (hon.), Miss. Ind. Coll., 1949; grad. studies in Perkins Sch. of Theol., S.M.U., summer 1952; spec. study in Human Relations, Boston Univ., summer 1962; m. Beatrice Winifred Smark; tchr., pub. schs. of Ellis Co., Texas, 1929-31; pastor, Chrstn. Meth. Episc. Chs., Texas, Ga. and Tenn.; presiding elder, 1957-58; prof., rural work, Phillips Sch. of Theol., Jackson, Tenn., 1946-51; ex. dean, 1954-59; Dir. of Extension, Interdenom. Theol. Center, 1959--; mem., Local sec. & pres., NAACP since 1946; v. p., Tenn. State Coun. of Branches, NAACP, 1948-49; candidate for state constitutional Conv. in 1952; the first Negro to seek office in Jackson, Tenn. since reconstruction; mem., Mason; Alpha Phi Alpha; Democrat; Adult Ed. Assn. of Amer.; master's thesis on Study of Financial Methods of Negro Chs. for Drew Univ. Edited booklet on Stewardship in the Church; wrote and pub. booklet on Achieving a Minimum Salary for Full-time Pastors in Our Church (1949);

and Handbook for Recruiting for the Christian Ministry (1960); Home: 641 Beckwith St., SW, Atlanta, Ga. 30314; Office: 671 Beckwith St., SW, Atlanta,. Ga., 30314

McKISSICK, John H., b. Dec. 11, 1913, Pickens, S.C.; s. John H. and Mary J. (Mc); A.B., Benedict Coll., Columbia, S.C.; B.D., Benedict Coll. of Theol.; D.D. (hon.), Allen Univ., Columbia, S.C., 1938; m. Willie Pearl Hazzard; pastor, Second Bapt. Ch., Aiken, S.C., 1943-57; First Bapt. Ch., St. Augustine, Fla., 1957-64; Galilee Bapt. Ch., Phila., Pa., 1964-present; former tchr., S.C.; trustee, Morris Coll., Sumter, S.C., 1946-57; v.p., NAACP, Aiken chapter, 1956; pres., St. Augustine NAACP, St. Augustine, Fla., 1962; Democrate; mem., Phila. Minister's Conf., Progressive Natl. Bapt. Conv.; Home: 457 Roxborough Ave., Philadelphia, Pa. 19128; Office: 459 Roxborough Ave., Philadelphia, Pa. 19128

McKISSICK, William J., b. Philadelphia, Pa., Apr. 30, 1925; s. Wm. and Pauline; Phila. Coll. of Bible, 1954-59; Conwell Sch. of Theol., 1959-60; B.D., Boston Univ., 1964; m. Phyllis L. Harris; Children--Deborah (Mrs. R.K. Edwards), Wm., Jerry Steven; pastor, New Tabernacle Bapt. Ch., Phila., Pa., 1958-61; founder and pastor, Christ Tabernacle, Phila., 1961-62; pastor, Union Bapt. Ch., Cambridge, Mass., 1962-67; First Bapt. Ch., Greenwich, Conn., 1967-present; former tchr., Mass., 1964-67; Bd. mem. Natl. Urban League; NAACP; Bd. mem., NAACP, Cambridge, Mass., 1967-present; mem., Cambridge Corp., Mayorls comm. Pastoral award, New England Bapt. Conv.; Certificate of Merit, Progressive Natl. Bapt. Conv.; mem., Fairfield Co. Ed. Assn.; Elks; Progressive Bapt. New England Conv.; Epsilon Delta; Home: 4 Northfield St., Greenwich, Conn. 06830; Office: 10 Northfield St., Greenwich, Conn. 06830

McLEAN, Edward Clifton, b. Harnett Co., N.C., May 30, 1928; s. Alexander and Gertrude S. M.; B.A., Livingstone Coll., Salisbury, N.C.; B.D., Hood Theol. Sem., Salisbury, N.C.; m. Mildred Ennis Raye; Children--Edward C., Jr., Michael Eldred; pastor, Afr. Meth. Episc. Z. Ch., 1928--; mem., Minister's & Laymen Assn., A.M.E.Z. Ch., 1954--; present pastor, Old Ship A.M.E.Z. Ch., 1964--; Interdenom. Min. Alliance,

1963--; Durham Min. Assn, 1963--; Rel. Affiliate, Redevelopment Commn., 1963--; NAACP; NCTA; 1958-60; NEA, 1958-60; Comm. on Negro Affairs, 1963--; United Campus Ministry, 1963--; N. C. Coll., 1963--; US Forces, 1949-53; mem., Sigma Rho Sigma; Omega Psi Phi; Democrat; Home: 120 Mildred St., Montgomery, Ala.; Office: 483 Holcombe St., Montgomery, Ala.

*McLELLAN, Daniel Christopher, b. Pittsburgh, Pa., Feb. 9, 1937; s. Daniel and Olivia Pygate (Mc); A. B., Wilberforce Univ., Wilberforce, O., 1963; M. Div., Howard Univ., Wash., D. C., 1968; m. Jacquelyn R. Lowery; Children--Daniel Thomas III, Lenard Wm.; licensed to preach, Wesley Center, Afr. Meth. Z. Ch., Oct. 1961, Pittsburgh, Pa., pastor, Chase charge, Balto., Md., 1963-66; ordained deacon, Meth. Ch., Wash. Conf. June 1964; Martinsburg Circuit, 1966-69; ordained elder, United Meth. Ch., 1968; pastor, Garrison Blvd. United Meth. Ch., Balto., Md. 1969-1970; candidate, Council-at-large, Martinsburg, W. Va., 1968; mem., Min. Assn., Interdenom. Min. Alliance, Balto., Md.; Home: 2510 Elsinore Ave., Balto., Md. 21216; Office: Wesley Foundation, Howard Univ., Washington, D. C.

McLEOD, Norman Stinson, b. Englewood, N. J., June 17, 1912; s. James R. S. and Lelia (Dunn); B. A., Pacific Union Coll., Angwin, Calif., 1934; Certificate, McAllister Sch. of Embalming, NYC, 1949; m. Grace Dobson; Children--Norma (Mrs. Kelso Barrett), James P., Howard S.; asst. pastor, S. D. A. Ch., San Diego, Calif. 1934; pastor, S. D. A. Chs., San Francisco, Buffalo, Rochester, New Rochelle, Mt. Vernon, White Plains, Springfield, Mass., Hartford, Conn., Murfreesboro, Tenn.; pastor, Westside S. D. A. Ch., 1967-present; former asst. Prot. Chap., San Francisco, Calif.; Home 205 Doolittle Ave., Las Vegas, Nev.; Office: PO Box 447, Las Vegas, Nev. 89101

*McNEIL, James Henry, tchr., b. Ennis, Tex., Sept. 21, 1915; s. Jake N. and Haydie (Johnson) M.; B. S., Prairie View A & M Coll., 1947; Howard Univ., Sch. of Rel., B. D., 1950; summer of grad. study in Education, No. Texas State Univ., Denton, Tex.; m. Bessie Velton Mellon; Children--James M., Mimi Vern, Lini Fern; student council advisor & tchr. of soc. studies, Turner High Sch., Waxahachie, Tex., 1950--; pastor, 4th Ward Bapt. Ch., Ennis, Tex., 1956--; dir., Youth Dept.,

No. Texas Dist. Missionary Bapt. Assn., 1963--; dean, of chapel, Religious Counselor & spec. lecturer, Prairie View A & M Coll., Tex., summer 1952; US Navy, company officer & yoeman, 1943-45; mem., State Tchrs. Assn., Tex.; No. Tex. Tchrs. Assn.; Natl. Ed. Assn.; Waxahachie Classroom Tchrs. Assn.; Ministers Conf. of No. Texas Missionary Bapt. Dist. Assn.; Interracial Min. Alliance, Ennis, Tex.; Home: 1006 N. Kaufman St., Ennis, Tex. 75119; Office: 1301 N. Shawnee St., Ennis, Tex.

McPHATTER, Thomas Hayswood, tchr., b. Lumberton, N.C., Oct. 8, 1923; s. Thomas Matthew and Elizabeth Morrisey; 1948, A.B., Johnson C. Smith Univ.; 1951, B.D.; m. Genevieve Redona Bryant; dau. Mary Elizabeth, Doretha, sons, Thomas Jr., George Howard, Joseph D.; 1951-58, pastor, St. Paul's Presby. Ch., Kans. City, Mo.; 1958-63, US Navy chap.; certified tchr., grad., Presby. Inst. of Indus. Relations; mem., Hearing Bds, Naval Repair Facility, San Diego, Calif.; advisor, Equal Opportunities Comm. (same installation); Penal counseling, US Navy Brig, San Diego, 1962-63; Urban League; Wheatly Hospital; Paseo br. YMCA; Linwood YMCA; NAACP; Wayne Minor Post Amer. Legion 149, and 5th Dist. Chap.; 1958, v.p., Coun. Chs. of Greater Kans. City; v.p., Mo. State Conf. NAACP; moderator, Presbytery of Kans. City; 1955-57, Human Relations Comm., Coun. Chs.; 1956 Commissioner to Gen. Assembly of the Presby. Ch. in USA; 1958, Pres. Eisenhower's Minority Leaders Conf.; military record--1944-46, Sgt., US Marine Corps; 1945, WW II at Iwo Jima and in the occupation of Japan; 1958-63, US Navy Chap., Lt.; awards: Presidential Unit Citation; expert rifleman; Navy Unit Citation; WW II Medal; Occupation Medal--letter of appreciation for outstanding service, US Navy Brig, San Diego, Calif.; letter of commendation for serving as Hearing Bd. Mem. (Industrial Relations); citations, Boy Scouts of America; Misato Ch. of Christ (Okinawa-Civic); mem., Omega Psi Phi; Sigma Rho Sigma; Democrat; 1957-58, articles pub. in Kans. City in Civil Rights struggle--"A Passport to Eat;" "Abuse of Authority." Home: 902 Ballensacher St., San Diego, Calif.; Office: US Naval Station, San Diego, Calif. (Box 139) 92136

McQUEEN, Charles Waldo, b. Montgomery, Ala., Apr. 25, 1916; s. J.W. and Maggie (Broodenax); A.B., Miles Coll., Birmingham, Ala.; B.S., Ala. State Coll., Montgomery,

1941; Seabury-Western Theol. Sem., Evanston, Ill., 1948; Univ. of Cincinnati, 1949-50; Univ. of Southern Calif., 1953-54; m. Ruby Phifer; Children--Gwendolyn Yvonne, Charles W., Jr., Barbara Ann, Henry, William Earl; headmaster-priest-in-charge, St. Christopher Episc. Ch., Columbus, Ga., 1950-53; curate, St. Philips, L.A., Calif., 1953-54; chaplain-priest-in-charge, Bethune Cookman Coll., 1954-56; current priest-in-charge, St. Mathews, Delray, St. Mary, Deerfield Beach; St. Cuthberts, St. John, St. Cuthbert's, Boynton Beach, Fla., 1956--; instr. High Sch., Delray Beach, Fla.; US Forces, 1941-48; Home: PO Box 1412 Delray Beach, Fla.; Office: same.

McWILLIAMS, Alfred Edward, b. Guthrie, Okla., July 5, 1911; s. Max and Sarah (Offutt) M.; A.B., Lane Coll., Jackson, Tenn., 1933; student, Gammon Theol. Sem., Atlanta, Ga., 1933-34; B.D., Yale Div. Sch., New Haven, Conn., 1936; D.D., Lane Coll., Jackson, Tenn., 1958; candidate, M.A., Univ. of Miss., 1967; m. Elvira Minerva Bowles; Children--Alfred Edward, Jr., Stanley W., Patricia E.; ordained, 1937; pastor, Kans. & Okla., 1936-40; prof. of Rel., Tex. Coll, Tyler, Tex., 1940-43; Army chap., Southwest Pacific, May 1943; retired Lt. Col., Aug. 1964; present pastor, Anderson Chapel C.M.E. Ch., Holly Springs, Miss.; mem., Dir. Placement, Miss. Indus. Coll., Holly Springs, Miss.; Dir. of Evangelism, Miss. 4th Episc. Dist. C.M.E. Ch.; sec., Marshall Co. Citizen's for Progress; sec., Rust Coll. Head Start Adv. Comm., v.p., Marshall & Benton Co. NAACP, Holly Springs, Miss.; mem., Holly Springs Human Rel. Commn.; Army, 1943-64; rec'd Bronze Star Commendation Ribbon; Mason; Alpha Phi Alpha; Lion's Club; Democrat; Home: 214 No. Memphis St., Holly Springs, Miss. 38635

MALLOY, Culberth Jerome, b. Charlotte, N.C., Dec. 30, 1936; s. Culberth Jerome, Sr. and Annie (Enloe) M.; A.B., Va. State Coll., 1963; Va. Union Univ., 1965; m. Phyllis J. Goodson; student pastor, Lake Harriet Meth. Ch., Minneapolis, Minn.; pastor, West End Collegiate Ch., NYC, 1966-present; exec. sec., West Minister's Assn., N.Y., 1966; chrmn., Boy Scouts Activities, Manhattan Div., 1966-present; US Air Force, 1955-59; Good Conduct Medal; Outstanding Airman Award; "Good Citizenship Award," Mayor of Petersburg, Va. for efforts and success in promoting the desegregation of the Petersburg Pub. Library, 1959; Home: 792 Columbus

Ave., Apt. 17M, New York, N.Y., 10025; Office: West End Collegiate Ch., 77th St., one block west of Broadway, New York, N.Y.

MALOY, Rufus Charles, b. Nashville, Tenn., Nov. 24, 1895; s. Henry and Hattie (Winston) M.; 1916, Sch. for Blind, Nashville, Tenn.; 1921-22, post-grad. course at Knoxville, Tenn.; m. Robbie Erzell; pastor, 1921-22, Chrstn. Ch., Straberry Plains, Tenn.; 1923-40, Gay St. Chrstn. Ch., Nashville, Tenn.; current, Alameda St. Chrstn. Ch., 1940--; Disciples of Christ; awards: Disciples of Christ Service Pin (40 yrs. ministerial serv.) 1957 and 1962; Oldfellows; Home: 333 21st Ave. No. Nashville, Tenn. 37203; Office: 2422 Alameda St., Nashville, Tenn. 37208

*MANGRAM, John Dee, coll. prof., b. Pittsburg, Tex., June 18, 1924; s. Ruther and Viola Ruth (Reed) M.; A.B., Jarvis Chrstn. Coll., 1945; Howard Univ., Sch. of Rel., 1948, B.D.; S.T.M., Yale Univ., 1958; presently studying toward Th.D., at Pacific Sch. of Rel., Berkeley, Calif.; m. Bobbye Ella Durham; asst. dir., Social Studies, Pendle Hill, Wallingford, Pa., 1948-49; univ. minister, Lincoln Univ., 1949-50; coll. chap., Tougaloo Coll., Tougaloo, Miss.; asst. prof. of rel., Tougaloo Coll., 1950-61; pastor, First Congre. Ch., Meridian, Miss.; moderator, Ala.-Miss. Conf. of Congre. Chrstn. Chs., 1959-61; Trustee Conv. of the South, Greensboro, N.C., 1959-61; interim pastor, The Church for the Fellowship of All Peoples, San Francisco, Calif., 1963-67; present, prof. Bishop Coll., Dallas, Tex.; v.p., Jackson, Miss. NAACP, 1954-61; chrmn., Bd. of Dirs., Jackson, Miss., NAACP; v. chrmn., Southeastern Region NAACP, 1955-57; Bd. Dirs., Miss. Council on Human Relations, 1953-60; Bd. of Dirs., Progressive Voters' League of Miss.; advisor, Youth Chapters of NAACP, State and Jackson, Miss. br., 1953-61; awards: Citizenship Award from Alpha Phi Alpha, Tougaloo, Miss., 1956; Danforth Campus Chrstn. Worker Fellowship to Yale Univ., 1957; Danforth Study Grant for work toward Doctorate, 1961; mem., Natl. Assn. of Coll. Univ. Profs.; Natl. Assn. of Coll. and Univ. Chaplains; Danforth Associates; Home: 1716 Routh St., Dallas, Tex.; Office: Bishop Coll., 3837 Simpson Stuart Rd., Dallas, Tex.

MANIGO, George Franklin, Jr., b. Bamberg, S.C., Nov.

10, 1934; s. George Franklin and Etta Mae (Ramsey) M.; Voorhees Jr. Coll., 1952-53; B. S., Claflin Coll., 1959; B. D., Gammon Theol. Sem., 1962; m. Rosa Lee Lewis; Children--Marcia Benita; student work, Central Meth. Ch., Atlanta, Ga., 1959; pastor, Horst Meml. Meth. Ch., 1960-62; current pastor, St. Paul Meth. Chs., Johnson City & Elizabethton, Tenn., 1962; Clinical training at High Spaulding Hosp., Atlanta, Ga., 1960-62; mem., Young Democrats of Johnson City; Exec. Comm. of local NAACP chapter; US Forces, 1953-56; Natl. Defense Service Medal; Army Occupation Medal; Good Conduct Medal; mem., Phi Beta Sigma; Johnson City Progressive League; Community Relation Comm.; Democrat; Home: 402 Chilhowie Ave., Johnson City, Tenn.

MARCUS, Chester Lee, ch. official; b. Swiftown, Miss., Feb. 14, 1917; s. Frank and Eliza M.; B. S., Alcorn A & M, 1940; B. D., Lincoln Univ., Pa., 1943; Albright Coll., Pa.; m. Warnetta Patton (dec.); 1 son, Chester Lee, Jr.; ordained, Phila. Presbytery, 1943; pastored, Wash. St. Presby. Ch., Reading, Pa., 1943-54; sec., Racial and Cultural Relations of E & R Ch., Cleveland, O., 1954-62; tchr. and Goodwill Ambassador, Ghana, 1960; present, Africa Secretary, United Ch. of Christ, 1962; named outstanding alumnus, Alcorn A & M, 1962; recipient, Africa Gold Star for contribution to labor understanding, Ghana, 1960; Reading Fellowship Medal for contribution to Racial Understanding, 1954; Dir., Natl. Coun. of Chs. Inst. on Racial and Cultural Relations, 1957-58; mem., World Coun. Comm. on Christian Ed.; mem., Phi Beta Sigma; author, The Bible and Race, 1959; Home: 201 Irvington Rd., Teaneck, N. J.; Office: 475 Riverside Dr., N. Y. C.

MARINO, Eugene Antonio, coll. prof., b. Biloxi, Miss., May 29, 1934; s. Jesus Maria and Irene (Bradford) M.; Epiphany Apostolic Coll., Newburgh, N. Y., 1952-55; St. Joseph's Sem., Wash., D. C., 1956-62; St. Michael's Coll., Winooski, Vt., 1957-60; Loyola Univ., New Orleans, La., 1961-63; ordained priest, Roman Cath. Ch., Wash., D. C. (Natl. Shrine of the Immaculate Conception) 1962; mem., St. Joseph of the Sacred Heart; instr., physical sci., biology, Cath. doctrine, Epiphany Apostolic Coll., Newburgh, N. Y.; mem., Amer. Assn. for the Advancement of Sci.; Home and Office: St. Joseph's Sem., 12th & Varnum Sts., Wash. D. C. 20017

MARSH, Clinton McClurkin, ch. administrator, b. Annemanie, Ala., Oct. 28, 1916; s. Thomas P. and Sadie; A.B., Knoxville Coll., 1939; B.D., Pittsburgh-Xenia Theol. Sem., 1944; D.D. (hon.), Knoxville Coll., 1955; grad. courses, Univ. of Pittsburgh; m. Dorothy Cosby; Children--Walter Francis; pastor, United Presby. Ch., Chase City, Va., 1944-45; Witherspoon U. Presby. Ch., Indianapolis, Ind., 1946-63; Dir. of Evangelism, N. Central Area, United Presby. Ch.; pres., Indianapolis Ch. Fed. Bd. of Dir., Indianapolis Coun. of Chs. Gen. and v.p., Bd. Natl. Coun. of Chs.; Bd. of Dir., Eastside Ch. Center of Indianapolis; Bd. of Dir., Indianapolis Center Sr. Citizens; Bd. of Dir., Ind. Health & Welfare Council; Bd. of Natl. Missions, United Presby. Ch., USA; mem., Counseling Comm. on Ch. and Society, U. P. USA; Adv. Bd., Marion Co. TB Assn.; Gov't Youth Coun.; Comm. on Segregated Presbyteries and Synod; moderator, Indianapolis Presbytery; pres., Ind. Min. Assn.; moderator, Second Synod, U.P.C.; chrmn., Chrstn. Ed., Ind. Presbytery; pres., Lord's Day Alliance of Ind.; Bd. Weekday Rel. Ed. of Marion Co., Ind.; Home: 436 W. 25th St., Indianapolis, Ind.

MARSH, Henry Levander, b. Wadesboro, N.C., Dec. 14, 1904; s. Henry and Annie; A.B., B.D., Va. Union Univ., Richmond, Va., 1944, 1955; grad. work, Union Theol. Sem., Richmond, Va.; m. Vanbureau Hall; Children--Marian (Mrs. Jones), Henry, Frederick, Harold; pastor, A.M.E.Z. Chs., St. Philips Cir., 1948-50; Taylor's Chapel, 1950-52; Piney Grove, Waverly, Va., 1952-54; Oberry, Franklin, Va., 1954-59; Mt. Zion, Alberta, Va., 1959-62; St. Paul Tabernacle, Hendersonville, N.C., 1962--; rep., Va. Coun. of Chs., 1956-62; N.C. Coun. of Chs., 1963--; Sch. Bd., Hendersonville, N.C., 1965-present; mem., Mayor's Comm. on Race Rel.; v.p., Henderson Co. Min. Assn.; bd. of dir., Henderson Co. United Fund; mem., Omega; Home: 813 6th Ave. W., Hendersonville, N.C.

MARSHALL, Arthur Jr., b. High Pt., N.C., Mar. 2, 1914; s. Arthur M., Sr. and Nellie (Kindle) M.; B.A., Livingstone Coll., 1937; S.T.B., Boston Univ., 1941; M.A., Boston Univ.; D.D. (hon.), Livingstone Coll., 1962; m. Mary Ann Stotts; Children--Arthur Clifton; pastor, St. Phillip Circuit, Greensboro, N.C., 1933 Dean, Walter's Southland Inst., Lexa, Ark., 1938; presiding elder, Pine Bluff Dist., Ark. Conv.; pastor, Wadsworth St. A. M. E. Z., Providence, R. I., First A. M. E. Z. Ch., Syracuse, N. Y., 1944; John Wesley A. M. E. Z. Ch., Pittsburgh, Pa., 1947; Metropolitan A. M. E. Z. Ch., Kansas City, Mo., 1955; Metropolitan Ch., St. Louis, Mo., 1961; mem., Natl. Bd. of Publications, A. M. E. Z. Ch., 1949; exec. bd., Health and Welfare Assn., Pittsburgh, Pa., 1950; Bd. of Dir., Commun. Comm. for Soc. Action, Kans. City, Mo., 1955; Bd. of dir., Natl. Bd. Chrstn. Ed., A. M. E. Z. Ch., 1955; ex. bd., Pasea br. YMCA, Kans. City, Mo., 1955; initiated and led civil rights movement in Kans. City to desegregate public facilities, 1957; pres., Interdenom. Min. Alliance, Kans. City, Mo., 1958; candidate, Mo. State Legis., 1960; ex. bd., St. Louis br. NAACP, 1961; trustee bd., Livingstone Coll., 1963; mem., Public Housing Bd., A. M. E. Z. Ch., 1963; mem., Ex. Comm. on Rel. and Race, 1964-65; Bd. of Dir., Mo. Coun. of Chs.; mem., Gen. Bd. and Commn. of Urban Chs. of the Natl. Coun. of Chs.; recd. award from Paseo br. YMCA for membership drive to highest in history of the inst., 1957-58; recd. meritorious award from the Kans. City Call for outstanding achievement in the field of rel. and meritorious serv. to the community; mem., Zeta Sigma Pi; Alpha Phi Alpha; Mason; Home and Office: 3008 Lucas St., St. Louis, Mo. 63103

MARSHALL, Calvin B., III, b. Brooklyn, N. Y., June 13, 1932; s. Evans Bromlee and Edythe (Best) M.; B. A. Anderson Theol. Sem., 1958; m. Delma Louise Mann; Children--Edythe Louise; youth minister, the Lafayette Ave. Ch. of God,, Brooklyn, N. Y., 1958-59; staff, St. Augustine's Chapel, Trinity Episc. Ch., NYC, curate, Christ's Episc. Ch., Newark, N. J., 1960; pastored, A. M. E. Z. Ch., 1960; Park St. A. M. E. Z. Ch., Peekskill, N. Y.; mem., NY Annual Conf., A. M. E. Z. Ch., 1961; pres., Peekskill Area Pastor's Assn.; co-chrmn., Upper Westchester Fair Housing Council; chrmn., the Exec. bd. of the Peekskill Anti-Poverty Coun.; mem., NAACP local bd.; Westchester Public Health Assn.; Kiwanis Club; staff, the Conf. Bd. of Admissions, the NY Conf. Inst. and N. Y. Conf. Advisory Comm.; Omega Psi Phi; leader, Episc. Protocol of NY Annual Conf.; v. p., Hudson River Valley of A. M. E. Z. Ch. Min. Assn.; Home: 1207 Lincoln Terrace, Peekskill, N. Y., 10566

MARSHBURN, J. Dett, b. Maple Hill, N. C.; B. D., D. D., (hon.), Va. Univ., Richmond, Va.; Union Theol. Sem.,

N. Y. C. ; pastor, Wine St. Bapt. Ch., 1932-36; Zion Bapt. Ch., Phoebus, Va., 1936--; Bd. of Dirs., Bapt. Children's Home, Petersburg, Va.; chrmn., Prov. of Ch. supported schs. & coll., Natl. Bapt.; dean, Lebanon Va. Bapt. Assn.; current pastor, Antioch Bapt. Ch. and Zion Bapt. Ch., Phoebus, Buckroe, Va., 1937--; organizer, Phoebus Comm. Center, 1942, Louise Davis Playground, Phoebus, Va.; mem., Coord. Comm., Lower Peninsula Voters League; Ex. bd. mem., King St. Communication Center; candidate City Coun., 1955 and 1961; del., Bapt. World Alliance, 1948, Copenhagen, Denmark; mem., Mental Health Bd., Lower Peninsula Assn. for Mental Health; mem., Omega Phi Psi; mem., Peninsula Min. Alliance; Office: 11 No. Hope St., Phoebus, Va.

MARTIN, Richard Beamon, tchr., b. Peak, S. C., Feb. 23, 1913; s. Benjamin Butler and Violet (Glasgow) M.; A. B., Allen Univ., 1933-37; B. D., Bishop Payne Div. Sch., 1939-42; Grad. Sch. of Theol., Univ. of the South, 1962; Union Theol. Sem., 1958; m. Annella Hoover; Children --Richard Beamon Jr., Garnett Hoover; priest-in-charge, St. Augustine's, Sumter Co. and Ch. of the Good Shepherd, Sumter, S. C., 1942-44; rector, Grace Ch., Norfolk, Va., 1944-63; archdeacon, Dioces of Southern Va., rector, St. Philip's Ch., Bklyn, N. Y., 1963--; pub. sch. tchr., Howard High Sch., 1937-39; tchr., Morris Coll., Sumter, S. C., 1943-44; former mem. of Bd. of Dirs., Norfolk Journal & Guide; Amer. Ch. Inst.; St. Paul's Coll., Lawrenceville, Va.; Youth Consultation Service, Diocese of Long Is.; Bklyn TB & Health; Presiding Bishop's Comm. on Racial Minorities; mem., Alpha Phi Alpha; former weekly column in Norfolk Journal and Guide, Norfolk, Va.; Home: 195 Willoughby Ave., Bklyn, N. Y.; Office: 265 Decatur St., Bklyn, N. Y.

MARTIN, Samuel Joseph, b. Huntsville, Ala., June 5, 1905; s. John Thomas and Hubbard (Dorrence); B. S., Boston Univ.; Tufts Coll., Chicago Univ.; B. D., Inst. of Tech., 1933; Episc. Sem., 1930; S. T. M., Seabury Theol. Sem., 1935; D. D., Seabury Western Sem., Evanston, 1954; m. Clarice White; Children--Annette, John Craighead, Samuel Martin, Jr.; pres., Standing Comm., Diocese of Chicago; mem., Diocesan Coun., Diocese of Chgo.; current, Dean of the Chicago Deanery, Diocese of Chgo.; dir., NAACP, Chicago br.; founder, St. Edmunds Parochial Sch.; Distinguished Serv. Cross for outstanding service to diocese presented by Bishop Steward, 1936--; Bishop Payne Episc. Sem.; numerous articles in "The Living Church" Episc. weekly; Home: 8515 Indiana Ave., Chicago, Ill.; Office: 6105 Michigan Ave., Chicago, Ill.

MASHAW, Samuel Jones, b. Pickneyville, Ala., Nov. 25, 1891; s. Benjamin Frank and Luella (Wilson) M.; A.B., Miles Coll., Birmingham, Ala., 1937; B.D., Miles Coll., 1938; Study in Rel. Ed., Tuskegee Inst., 1942; study in rel. ed., Fisk Univ., 1944; m. Addie Ernestine Reynolds; children--Mattie (Mrs. Theo. Douglas Gill); pastor, 7 yrs. in Ohio; 19 yrs. in Ala.; current pastor, St. Peter Chrstn. Meth. Ch., Kans. City, Kans., 12 yrs.; elected to Judiciary Court of C.M.E. Ch., 1950; elected Chief Justice of the court, 1962; del., C.M.E. Gen. Conf., 1930, 34, 38, 42, 46, 50; mem., Commn. from C.M.E. Ch. of the state of Kans. to Coun. of Chs. on Political Action at Univ. of Nebraska, 1963; mem. Bd. of Dir., Douglas Hosp., Kans. City, Kans.; Bd. of Trustee, Miles Coll.; Trustee of Phillips Sch. of Theol., Atlanta, Ga.; Republican; Exec. bd. of NAACP, Kans. City, Kans.; Home: 743 Oakland Ave., Kansas City, Kans. 66101; Church: St. Peter C.M.E. Ch., 8th & Okland Sts., Kansas City, Kans. 66101

MASON, Cleveland L., b. Daingerfield, Tex., Jan. 23, 1908; s. Thomas and Bessie (Whitmore) M.; A.B., 1949; Extension Sch., Prairie View Coll., Prairie View, Tex.; m. Evelyn D. Burgess; Children--Cleveland L. Jr., Oland D., Oreantha D.; pastor, Mt. Zion Chrstn. Meth. Episc. Ch., Daingerfield, Tex., 1915-30; pastor, Miles Chapel C.M.E. Ch., Norfolk, Va., 1930-59; present: pastor, St. John C.M.E. Ch., Petersburg, Va., 1959--; former tchr., Veteran's Sch., and insurance agent, 1933-40; US Army, Ft. Sill, Okla., 1941-44; Europe, 1944-45; 5 battle stars, 1 bronze star medal, unit citation; mem., NAACP, YMCA, Mason, Democrat; Office: St. John C.M.E. Ch., 428 St. Mark St., Petersburg, Va.

MASSEY, Floyd Jr., b. Rock Hill, S.C., July 24, 1915; s. Floyd Sr. and Alice (Massie) M.; A.B., Johnson C. Smith Univ., Charlotte, N.C., 1936; B.D., Colgate Rochester Div. Sch., 1944; D.D. (hon.), Johnson C. Smith Univ., 1955; m. Ethel Hurley; Children--Floyd III; Ronald Bruce, Thomas Rickie; pastor, Pilgrim Bapt. Ch., St. Paul, Minn., 1965; Macedonia Bapt. Ch., Los Angeles, Calif., 1965-present; instr., Booker T. Washington High

Sch., Columbia, S. C., 1936-41; sec., Planning Bd., City of St. Paul, Minn., 1955-65; v. chrmn., Minn. Gov.'s Commn. on Human Rights, 1958-65; chrmn., Minn. State Pastor Conf., Jan. 1958; v. p., Minn. Coun. of Chs., 1964-65; pres., Minn. Bapt. Conv. of Natl. Bapt. Chs., 1952-62; pres., Amer. Bapt. Foreign Miss. Soc., 1962; mem., Foreign Miss. Bd., Amer. Bapt. Conv., 1956-66; mem., St. Paul Urban League Bd.; NAACP; St. Paul "Man of the Year," 1953; Good Neighbor Citation, radio sta., WCCO; Mason; Omega Psi Phi; edited, Pictorial History, Pilgrim Bapt. Ch. during Centennial Yr., 1963; contributing ed. to The Mission, study book for Natl. Bapt. Women; Home: 861 E. 116th Pl., Los Angeles, Calif.; Office: 1755 E. 114th St., Los Angeles, Calif.

MATTHEWS, Verner Randolph, b. New York, N. Y., Apr. 27, 1923; s. Charles and Rebecca (Campbell); B. A., Shelton Coll., N. J., 1955; S. T. B., Biblical Sem., New York, 1961; courses, E. Bapt. Sem., Phila., Pa.; m. Emily Louise Cadwell; Children--Darryl, Jonathan; asst. pastor 1st Bapt. Ch., Madison, N. J., 1955-57; Antioch Bapt. Ch., Bedford Hills, N. Y., 1957-60; Ebenezer Bapt. Ch., Poughkeepsie, N. Y., 1960-present; tchr., Empire State Bapt. Sunday Sch., Bapt. Training Union Congress; military duty, 1942-46; awards, Good Conduct Medal, Pacific Theater Medal; mem., Poughkeepsie Rotary Club; Family Couns. Serv.; OEO; Home: 11 Winnker Ave., Poughkeepsie, N. Y. 12601

MAYES, Allen Mercer, ch. official, b. Jefferson, Tex., Sept. 20, 1920; s. F. D. and N. Allen; B. S., Wiley Coll., 1941; B. D., Gammon Theol. Sem., 1944; S. T. M., Boston Univ. Sch. of Theol., 1946; additional study: Harvard Univ., 1945-46; m. LaVerne Hadnott; Children--Janis Alene; supervisor, Migrant Ministry in NY State, Natl. Coun. of Chs., 1944-45; pastor, Asbury Meth. Ch., Houston, Tex., 1946-50; St. James Meth. Ch., Beaumont, Tex., 1950-63; current, asst. sec., Gen. Bd. of Pensions of Meth. Ch., Evanston, Ill., 1963--; dean, New Orleans Area Pastors' Sch., 1960--; sec., Central Jurisdictional Conf., 1964--; mem., Bd. of Mgrs., Gen. Bd. of Missions of Meth. Ch., 1960-64; sec., Section of Ch. Extension, Gen. Bd. of Missions, 1960-64; Jt. Comm. of Missionary Personnel, Bd. of Missions, 1960-64; Bd. of Dirs., Wesley Found., Tex. Southern Univ.; del., Meth. World Conf., 1956; Reserve del. to Gen.

Conf., Meth. Ch., 1956-, 60; Conf. Bd. of Ministerial Training, 1946--; chrmn., Tex. Conf. Bd. of Ed., 1948--; Tex. Conf. Missionary Sec., 1948-64; Home: 2416 Crain St., Evanston, Ill. 60202; Office: General Bd. of Pensions of Meth. Ch., 1200 Davis St., Evanston, Ill.

MAYS, Benjamin Elijah, coll. pres., sem. dean, author, b. Epworth, S.C., Aug. 1, 1895; s. S. Hezekiah and Louvania (Carter) M.; A.B., Bates Coll., 1920; M.A., Univ. of Chicago, 1925; Ph.D., 1935; D.D. (hon.), Howard Univ., Wash., D.C.; Bates Coll., Lewiston, Me., 1947; Bucknell Univ., Lewisburg, Pa., 1954; Berea Coll., Berea, Ky., 1955; Kalamazoo Coll., Kalamazoo, Mich., 1959; LL.D. (hon.), Denison Univ., Granville, O., 1945; Va. Union Univ., Richmond, Va., 1945; Univ. of Liberia, Monrovia, Liberia, 1960; St. Augustine's Coll., Raleigh, N.C., 1963; LH.D. (hon.), S.C. State Coll., Orangeburg, S.C., 1946; HH.D. (hon.), Boston Univ., 1950; DH.L, Keuka Coll., Keuka Park, N.Y., 1962; Ed.D. (hon.), St. Vincent Coll., Latrobe, Pa., 1964; m. Sadie Gray; prof. Morehouse Coll. and pastor, Shiloh Bapt. Ch., Atlanta, Ga., 1921-24; instr., S.C. State Coll., 1925-26; ex. sec., Tampa Urban League, Fla., 1926-28; Natl. Student Sec., YMCA, 1928-30; dir., a study of Negro chs. in the US under the auspices of the Inst. of Soc. & Rel. Research, NYC, 1930-32; dean, Howard Univ., Sch. of Rel., 1934-40; pres. Morehouse Coll., 1940-68; author: The Negro's God; Seeking to be Christian in Race Relations; A Gospel for the Social Awakening; Disturbed About Man; contributed articles in sixty-nine magazines such as Christian Century, Crises, Journ. of Negro Education in Life, etc.; Kent Fellow of Natl. Coun. on Rel. in Higher Ed.; repr. the YMCA of America at the Plenary session of the World Com., Stockholm, Sweden, 1938; repr., the US at the Oxford Conf. on the Ch., Community and State, Oxford Univ., England, 1937; leader, Youth Conf. at Amsterdam, Holland, 1939; mem., Delta Sigma Rho, Delta Theta Chi, Omega Psi Phi, Phi Beta Kappa, Southern Ed. Found.; contributing editor, Journal of Negro Ed.; mem., Theol. Discussion Group; Bd. of Natl. YMCA; v.p., The World Student Serv. Fund; del., World Coun. of Chs., Amsterdam, Holland, 1948; mem., Central Comm., World Coun. of Chs., 1949-53; Central Com. Meeting of the World Coun. of Chs., Chichester, England 1949; attended the meeting of the Central Com. of World Coun. of Chs., Rolle, Switzerland, 1951; del. and leader,

Bapt. World Alliance Assembly, Cleveland, O., 1950; attended the meeting of the Central Comm. of World Coun. of Chs., Lucknow, India, 1952, 1953; attended meeting of the Commn. on the Church Amidst Racial and Ethnic Tensions, Geneva, Switzerland, 1953; Bd. mem., Inst. of Intl. Ed.; Bd. mem., Booker Wash. Agri. & Indus. Inst. of Liberia; trustee, Natl. Fund for Medical Ed.; trustee, Danforth Found.; Bd. mem., Southern Assn. of Coll. and Schs.; v.p., The Fed. Coun of Chs. of Christ, USA, 1944-46; named on the Schomberg Honor Roll of Race Relations, 1944; recipient of Letter Award from Letter Magazine, Ada P. McCormick, ed.; named "The Alumnus of the Year" by the Div. Sch. of the Univ. of Chgo.; recipient of the 2nd Annual State Fair Negro Achievement Award of Tex., 1950; The Distinguished Service Award for effectiveness in public speech given by Delta Sigma Rho at its 50th Golden Jubilee; pres., The United Negro Coll. Fund, Inc., 1958-61; Adv. Coun. of the US Com. for the UN, 1959; mem., Natl. Adv. Coun. to the Peace Corps, 1961; mem., US Natl. Commn. for UNESCO; repr. the US at the state funeral of Pope John XXIII, 1963; Home: 820 Fair St. NW, Atlanta, Ga. 30314; Office: 223 Chestnut St., Atlanta, Ga.

MAYS, Willie, b. New Orleans, La., May 14, 1927; s. George and Ruby M.; B.S., Grambling Coll., 1959; B.D., Interdenom. Theol. Center, 1962; m. Queen Elizabeth Coleman; Children--Wayne Wendell; ordnance worker, Port Chicago, Calif., 1950-51; current pastor, Chrstn. Meth. Ch., 1954--; pres., Bd. of Dirs. of the Calcasieu Co-ordinating Coun., 1963--; chrmn., The World Service Comm., YMCA, 1963--; Mem., Mason; Home: 308 S. Lyons St., Lake Charles, La.; Office: 1439 Winterhalter St., Lake Charles, La.

MAYSON, Henry Irving, b. Cleveland, O., Feb. 1, 1925; s. Edwin Lawson and Josephine Bell (Hill) M.; 1948, B.A., St. Augustine's Coll.; 1951, B.D., Bexley Hall, Div. Sch., Kenyon Coll.; m. Alma Marie Harris; Child, Heather Kim; founder and rector, St. Philip's Episc. Ch., Akron, O., 1951--; Akron Chapter of CORE (ex. bd.); Omega Psi Phi; Urban League (ex. bd.) 1957-61; NAACP (ex. b.) 1960; YMCA; Glendale Bd., 1951; Metropolitan Bd.; Ohio, W. Va. Area Coun.; Natl. Coun.; Frontiers of America, 1951; Coun. of the Diocese of Ohio, 1960; Home: 885 Storer Ave., Akron, O. 44320; Church: St. Philip's, 1130 Mercer Ave., Akron, O. 44320

MEACHEM, Robert Allen, tchr., b. Warren, Ark., Nov. 21, 1926; s. Allen Scott and Wheatley Joina (Todd) M.; B. A., Johnson C. Smith Univ., 1949; B. D., 1958; grad. work, Univ. of Mich.; m. Jean Frances Jackson; Children--Sherry Lynn, Robert Lynette; pastor, Freedom East U. P. Ch., Mt. Olive and Mars Hill U. Presby. Ch., 1956-57; Caldwell & Miranda U. Presby. Chs., 1958; Catawba U. Presby. Ch., 1959--; tchr., Mary Homes Jr. Coll., West Point, Miss., 1954; typing instr., '52 Hugo, Okla.; dir. of Recreaction Center, Charlotte, N. C., 1957-63; service in USAF Control Tower operator; mem., certified Recreator State of N. C., Amer. Rec. Soc.; Kappa Alpha Psi; Polemarch '57 Johnson C. Smith Univ., Min. Relations Comm.; Catawba Presby. of the U. Presby. Ch., USA; Home: 3033 Bellaire Drive, Charlotte, N. C.; Church: Rte 2, Box 105 Huntersville, N. C.

MEDFORD, Hampton Thomas, bishop (retired), b. Marion, N. C., Jan. 29, 1887; s. Charles M. Greenlee and Cecelia Godfrey Greenlee; Livingstone Coll., 1909-20; D. D. (hon.), 1920; m. Elizabeth Kemp; Children--Booker T., Alma, Cordella, Thomas A.; pastor, A. M. E. Z. Ch., Cherryville, N. C.; Morris Chapel, Salisbury, N. C.; Jacob St. Ch., Louisville, Ky.; Logan Temple, Knoxville, Tenn.; John Wesley A. M. E. Z. Ch., Wash., D. C.; Gen. Sec. of Foreign Missions, A. M. E. Z. Ch., 1930-50; Bishop to Africa, 1950-54; retired as bishop, 1960; mem. Bd. of Trustee, Livingstone Coll.; editor of "From the Depths," "From Rags to Riches;" Home: 4615 16th St. NW, Wash., D. C.; Office: 1421 U St. NW, Wash., D. C.

MERCER, William Summer, b. Providence, R. I., Oct. 1, 1917; s. Miah William and Abolle (Seter); B. A., Lincoln Univ., 1941; S. T. B., Lincoln Sem., 1944; M. A., McCormick Theol. Sem., Chgo., 1948; D. D., Knoxville Coll., 1964; m. Cecilia McCoy; Sun. Sch. Missionary, Southern, Va., 1944-45; pastor and larger parish dir., Burke Co. Ga., 1945-46; social group worker, Neighborhood House, Buffalo, N. Y., 1946-47; Dir. of Goodwill Larger Parish-Sumter, Lee and Clarendon Counties, So. Carolina, 1948-53; pastor, Redcliffe U. Presby. Ch., Atlanta, Ga., 1953--; moderator, Knox-Hodge Presby.; moderator, Atlantic Synod; chrmn., Christn. Ed. Knox-Hodge; Evangelism chrmn., Knox-Hodge Presbytery; chrmn., The Adv. Comm. of Boggs Acad., Keysville, Ga.

Bd. mem., Gate City Nursery Assn., Atlanta; mem., Alpha Phi Alpha; ex. comm., Southern Chrstn. Leadership Conf.; ex. comm. NAACP; Home: 284 Hightower Rd., NW, Atlanta, Ga. 30318; Church: 290 Hightower Rd. NW, Atlanta, Ga. 30318

MYERS, Samuel David, b. New York, N.Y., Nov. 26, 1925; s. Theodore Troup and Louvenia (Meyers); B.S., Emmanuel Missionary Coll., 1947; m. Gloria Lee Vaughn; Children--Anthony Lloyd, Pamela Marie, Charles Weldon, Donna Louise, Sibyl Diane; Southwest Region Conf. of S.D.A., Hdq. in Dallas, Tex.; pastored 1947-52, in New Orleans and Baton Rouge, La., Dallas and Ft. Worth, Tex.; Central States Conf. of S.D.A., Hdq. in Kans. City, Mo., pastored 1952-60, in Kans. City, Kans. and Omaha, Nebr.; Lake Reg. Conf. of S.D.A., Hdq. in Chicago, Ill., presently pastor, S.D.A. Ch., Chgo., Ill. Home: 7020 S. Michigan Ave., Chicago, Ill.; Office: 7008 So. Michigan Ave., Chgo., Ill.

MICHAEL, Euilious Raphael, b. Rutherfordton, N.C., b. Mar. 6, 1907; s. John Wiley and Margaret A.; A.B., Livingstone Coll., 1927-31; D.D., Hood Sem., Livingstone Coll., 1960; spec. studies: Harvard Univ. Div. Sch., 1961-63; m. Elizabeth Lee Arnold; Children--Margaret Anna, Veronica Louise; pastor, A.M.E.Z. Ch., Indianapolis, Inc., 1933-1936; Kentucky, 6 yrs.; N.C., 5 yrs.; New York, 6 yrs.; Massachusetts, 5 yrs.; New Jersey, 2 yrs.; Pennsylvania, 3 yrs.; "A Historic Pulpit Swap with Reverend Wilson Bridge of The United Church Lachute, Quebec, Canada"; present pastor, Big Wesley Afr. M.E.Z. Ch., Phila., Pa.; pres., PTA Northwest Jr. High, 2 yrs.; mem., Elk, Mason; Home: 4918 Walnut St., Phila., Pa. 19139; Office: 1500 Lombard St., Phila., Pa. 19146

MICHAUX, Solomon Lightfoot, b. Buckroe Beach, Va.; m. Mary E.; entered ministry, 1917, Hopewell, Va.; here began to broadcast services over local radio sta.; established the Ch. of God (Gospel spreading assn.); had large coast-to-coast audience CBS radio network. Deceased 1968.

MICKLE, John Charles, b. Birmingham, Ala., Dec. 3, 1914; s. John Charles and Ethelyn (Simmons) M.; Ala. A & M Coll., 1931-32; A.B., Talladega Coll., Ala., 1936; Howard Univ., Sch. of Rel., 1936-37; B.D., Chgo.

Theol. Sem., 1939; Univ. of Chgo. Div. Sch., 1939-40; m. Sadie Blanche Thomas; Children--Elva Louise, Blanche Naomi, Gregory Thomas; Dir. of Rel. Ed., Ch. of the Good Shepherd, Chgo., 1940-41; pastor, Mt. Zion Congre. Ch., Cleveland, O., 1941-47; (co-), S. Berkeley Community Congre. Ch., Calif., 1947-53; Second Congre. Ch., Memphis, Tenn., 1954--; personnel counselor, LeMoyne Coll., Memphis, 1954--; mem., Ex. Comm., Memphis Comm. on Community Relations, Ex. Comm., Budget Comm., United Ch. of Christ; Publications Comm., United Ch. Herald; Southern Personnel and Guidance Assn.; pres., Memphis Interdenom. Min. Alliance; Home: 762 Walker Ave., Memphis, Tenn; Office: 764 Walker Ave., Memphis, Tenn.

MIDDLETON, James Peter, Jr., b. So. Carolina, Apr. 12, 1928; s. James Peter and Joetta (Chaplin) M.; B.A., Oakwood Coll., 1951; m. Marilyn Lindsay; Children--Yvonne, Elizabeth, James, Eric; Ariz. Conf. of S.D.A. 1951; built and pastored the Sharon S.D.A. Ch. in Tucson, Ariz., 1954-61; present: pastor, Beacon Light S.D.A. Ch., 1961--; tchr., Ariz. Conf. of S.D.A., 1951-53; mem., NAACP Bd., 1958-61; Tempe Hosp. Bd., 1962; Indian Sch. Bd., 1959-62; Urban League, 1963-; mem., ex. comm. of Ariz. Conf. of S.D.A. since 1958; Men of Tomorrow Group, 1963--; Ch. Interracial Comm. for States of Ariz., Nev., Utah, Calif., Hawaii; Home: 1424 E. Granada Rd., Phoenix, Ariz.; Office: 963 E. Monroe St., Phoenix, Ariz.

*MIDDLETON, John Albert, coll. pres., b. Foreston, S.C., Jan. 2, 1914; s. Brewington and Lula M.; A.B., Allen Univ., Columbia, S.C., 1939; B.D., Howard Univ., Sch. of Rel., 1942; Th.M., Iliff Sch. of Theol., Denver, Colo., 1956; m. Merlissie Ross Tyson; Children--Ann, Johnsy and Philip; pastor and tchr. in Smithfield; pastor, Allen Temple A.M.E. Ch.; tchr., Morris Brown Coll., Atlanta, Ga., 14 yrs.; pres., Morris Brown Coll., Atlanta, Ga., 1965--; present, tchr., Gammon Theol. Sem., Atlanta, Ga.; pres., Atlanta Chapter SCLC; pres., Turner High Sch. PTA; co-chrmn., Operation Breadbasket; mem., NAACP, Alpha Phi Alpha, Soc. of Biblical Instructors; writes weekly column, Atlanta Inquirer; Home: 601 Univ. Place, NW, Atlanta, Ga. 30314; Office: 643 Hunter St. NW, Atlanta, Ga. 30314

*MILES, Henry, b. Heflin, La., July 4, 1919; s. Mack C.

and Viola (Bailey) M.; A.B., Morehouse Coll.; B.D., Howard Univ., Sch. of Rel.; Amer. Univ., Wash., D.C.; m. Mary Goggins; chap. and counselor, migrant workers, NY state; assoc. pastor, 19th St. Bapt. Ch., Wash., D.C., 1954-58; asst. pastor, Third Bapt. Ch., Wash., D.C., 1959; acting pastor, Third Bapt. Ch., 1960; current pastor, Third Bapt. Ch., 1960--; mem., Bd. of Dirs., Stoddard Bapt. Home, 1959--; Brighwood Civic Assn., 1962; Neighbors, Inc.; NAACP; YMCA; US Army, 1941-45, 1st Sgt.; mem., Ex. Bd., Lott Carey Bapt. Foreign Mission Conv.; Ex. Comm., Bapt. Min. Conf. of Wash., D.C. and Vicinity; Civil and Social Comm. of the Conf., Wash., D.C.; Morehouse Alumni Club; Phi Beta Sigma; Home: 1355 Tewkesbury Pl., NW, Wash., D.C.; Office: 5th and Que Sts. N.W., Wash., D.C.

MILES, Joel Leonard, Sr., chap., b. Boswell, Okla., Jan. 1, 1936; s. Isaiah Garrett & Lillian (Thomas) M.; A.B., Langston Univ., Langston, Okla., 1958; B.D., Interdenom. Theol. Center, Atlanta, Ga., 1964; diploma, US Army Chap. Sch., Apr. 1967-June 1967; widower; Children--Joel L., Kevin; pastor, James Metropolitan Chrstn. Meth. Episc. Ch., Idabel, Okla., 1964; Fla. Chrstn. Migrant Ministry, Belle Glade, Fla., 1964-67; US Army Chap., 1967-present; Regional Bd. Dir., Palm Beach Co. Community Action Coun., 1966-67; v.p., and pres., Parents Without Partners, Inc., 1967, 1968; awards, Good Conduct Medal; Expert Rifleman Badge; Marksman badge; mem., Phi Beta Sigma; First Armored Div. Assn. (Old Ironsides); Home: 5904-2 Fisher Ave., Ft. Hood, Tex. 76545; Office: 685-5011 52nd St., Chapel, Ft. Hood, Tex. 76545

MILES, Joseph A., Sr., b. Mar. 23, 1907, Garysburg, N.C.; Wash. Bapt. Sem.; courses: Howard Univ.; m. Ollie Marshall; Children--Joseph A., Patricia; asst. pastor, Shiloh Bapt. Ch., Wash., D.C.; organizer and pastor Shiloh Bapt. Ch. Mission, Brookland Union Bapt. Ch., 1945-present; Home: 3101 14th St. NE, Wash., D.C. 20001; Office: Brookland Union Bapt. Ch., 14th and Irving St. N.E., Wash., D.C. 20017

MILLER, Clyde Horace, Jr., b. Middleboro, Ky., Dec. 9, 1927; s. C.H., Sr. and Daisy (Anderson) M.; Ky. State Coll., 1945-47; A.B., Talladega Coll., 1954; B.D., Chgo. Theol. Sem., 1958; m. Eva Whitlock; Children--Claire, Joy; pastor, Ch. of the Good Shepherd Congre.,

1958-64; consultant, Chrstn. Ed., Ch. Fed. of Greater Chgo., 1964-67; pastor, Kenwood United Ch. of Christ, 1967-68; consultant in Christian ed. to local chs. and denominations in the metro. area; also served in several capacities to Natl. Coun. of Chs.; Natl. Dir., Project Equality (Natl. Coun. Chs.), Chgo., Ill., 1968-present; Armed Forces, 1950-52; Home: 1348 E. 48th St., Chgo., Ill. 60615

MILLER, Oliver Howard, b. Longview, Tex., May 2, 1914; s. Jap and Roxie; B.S., Ohio State Univ., Franklin Univ., 1948; B.D., Capital Univ., Oberlin Theol. Sem., 1966; m. Jescenia; Children--Elaine, Janet, William H.; Christine; asst. pastor, Trinity Bapt. Ch., pastor, Second Bapt. Ch., Circleville, O., Pleasant Green Bapt. Ch., Portsmouth, O.; present, tchr., Fourth Bapt. Gen. Assn.; mem., Mason, Republican; Home: 1216 Union St. Portsmouth, O.; Office: Wallter and 15th Sts., Portsmouth, O.

MILLER, Roy L., b. Newberry, S.C., May 22, 1915; s. Oscar; A.B., Allen Univ., Columbia, S.C., 1940; B.Th., Payne Theol. Sem., O., 1945; further study, Duquesne Univ., Pittsburgh, Pa., 1946; Univ. of Pittsburgh, 1947; D.D. (hon.), Allen Univ., 1960; D.E.L. (hon.), Shorter Coll., Little Rock, Ark., 1962; pastor, Meth. Chs., S.C., Mich., Ohio, Pa., Islands of Bermuda, Ind.; Greater Inst. A.M.E. Ch., Chgo., Ill., 1954--; mem., Chatham-Avalon Coun.; YMCA; NAACP; Dept. of Home and Foreign Missn.; Bd. of A.M.E. Ch.; appeared bef. Subcom. on Afr. Com. in Foreign Affairs, House of Rep., Wash., D.C., Mar. 1966; pres., Chgo. Conf. on expanded housing for low and middle incomes and the elderly; operates in ch., Head Start Prog.; Employment Serv.; sch. for mentally retarded; day nursery; boy and girl Scouts; Credit Union; Office: 7800 S. Ind. Ave., Chgo., Ill. 60619

MILLER, Wilbert Daniel, Sr., b. April 12, 1921, Miami, Fla.; s. Prince A. and Ida; A.B., Morehouse Coll., Atlanta, Ga., 1950; B.D., Gammon Theol. Sem., Atlanta, Ga., 1963; m. Pearl Harrison; Children--Austin, Wilbert Jr., Brenda and Dorcas; Mobile ministry, U. Presby. Ch. Migrant Workers; organized Sun. Schs., Vacation Ch. schs., 1955-57; pastor, Laura St. Presby. Ch., Jacksonville, Fla., 1957-60; asst. pastor, St. Augustine Presby. Ch., 1960-61; pastor, St. Luke's Ch., Brooklyn,

N. Y., 1962-present; past chap. Vets. Hosp., NYC; tchr., Rel. Dept., Fla. Normal Coll., 1957, St. Augustine, Fla.; social worker, NYC, 1961; Bd. of Dirs., Bklyn TB Soc.; Bd. of Dirs., Brownsville Comm. Coun.; US Army 1943-45; Army awards: European Theater of Operation; Community Leaders Award; Mason; Natl. Black Churchmen; Home: 313 Grafton St., Bklyn, N. Y. 11212; Office: 142 Watkins St., Bklyn, N. Y. 11212

MILLS, Cedric Earl, bishop, b. Hartford, Conn., Dec. 17, 1903; s. Patrick Henry and Sophannia (Blount) M.; A. B., Lincoln Univ., 1926; S. T. B., Phila. Div. Sch., 1929; M. A., Univ. of Pa., 1929; D. D. (hon.), Lincoln Univ., 1946; D. D. (hon.), Phila. Div. Sch., 1960; LL. D. (hon.), St. Augustine's Coll., 1963; m. Rebecca Esther Taylor; Children--Damon Foster; vicar, Chapel of Ascension, West Chester, Pa.; vicar-in-charge, St. Cyril's Mission, Coativille, Pa., St. Mary's Ch., Chester, Pa.; chap., Episc. students, Lincoln Univ., Cheyney State Tchrs. Coll. and Downingtown Indus. Sch., 1929-37; comdt. of boys and tchr. of math and sci., Downingtown Sch.; rector, St. Mark's Ch., Plainfield, N. J., 1937-40; rector, St. James' Ch., Baltimore, Md., 1940-63; bishop, The Missionary Dist. of the Virgin Is., 1963--; mem., Ex. Coun. of the Diocese of Md., 1944-50, 1954-57; sec., The Army and Navy Commn. of the Diocese of Md. during WW II; pres., Md. Clericus, 1950; chrmn., Adult Ed. in the Diocese of Md.; deputy, Gen. Conv., 1961; Standing Comm. of the Diocese of Md., 1958-63; chrmn., The Associate Study Comm. of the Diocese of Md.; charter mem., Balt. Chap. of the Frontiers of Am., Inc.; Bd. of Dirs., NAACP; The Gov.'s Commn. on Problems Affecting the Colored Population; Bd. of Dirs., Balt. Coun. of Social Agency's, 1951; chrmn., Survey Comm., PTA Fred. Doug. H. S., 1952; chrmn., Parent's Citizens Com. on Ed.; Bd. of Mgrs., The Geo. F. Bragg Fund; Bd. of Dirs. of Mental Hygiene Soc. of Greater Balt.; Adv. Comm. Henryton Practical Sch. of Nursing; v. p., Bd. of the Citizens Planning and Housing Assn.; v. p., Bd. of Dirs., Balt. Urban League; trustee, Provident Hosp.; mem., Harlem Park Neighborhood Coun.; counselor student nurses, Provident Hosp. and chrmn., Bd. of Dirs., The Lafayette Sq. Community Center; Home: PO Box 1589 Charlotte Amalie, St. Thomas, US Virgin Island

MILLS, Luther Hunter, b. Danville, Va., Nov. 29, 1895;

s. William and Emma; Wash. Natl. Bapt. Sem.; Laurena Polnele Sem.; courses, Howard Univ., 1937-38; m. Carolyn Spencer; pastor, Mt. Grove, Danville, Va.; Oakland Bapt. Ch., Alexandria, Va., 26 yrs.; former pres., Min. Alliance, Alexandria; treas., Wash. Min. Dist. Conf.; mem., NAACP, Mason; served in WW I; mem., One Hundred Min.; Fraternal Coun. of Chs., N. Va. Bapt. Assn.; author, A Model Investment; Youth Ought to Know; Seven Cardinal Diseases of Man; Office: 3408 King St., Alexandria, Va.

MILLS, William G., fieldwork tchr., b. Newport, R.I., Aug. 30, 1906; s. Laurence and Essie (Gray) M.; Hampton Inst., 1926; NYC Coll., 1928; Oakwood Coll, 1933; Andrews Univ., 1963; m. Cora Reid Davis; Children--Wm. Laurence, Eleanor (Mrs. Aaron R. Wright), Aaron N., Phyllis A., Earl N.; pastored: 1933-43 S.D.A. Chs. Ala., Miss.; 1944-55, Fla., Ariz.; 1956, Ind., Mich.; present: pastor, S.D.A. Ch., Calvin Center Rd. and Cossopolis, Mich.; mem., 1948-52, Ariz. Acad. Sch. Bd.; field work tchr. for sem. students (Andrews Univ.); Amer. Red Cross, First Aid instr., 1953-63; NAACP; Community Chest leader; Home: 1708 S. 3rd St., Niles, Mich.; Office: 215 Johnson St., So. Bend, Ind.

MITCHELL, Henry Bryant, hosp. chap., b. Ahoskie, N.C., Nov. 12, 1918; s. Bryant M. and Mary (Lewter) M.; B.S., Hampton Inst., 1939; Va. Theol. Sem. (Episc.), Alexandria, Va.; Yale Univ., Sch. of Alcohol Studies, 1960; m. Gertrude Marion Phillips; Children--Carolyn P., Henry Bryant; tchr., School for Blind and Deaf, Raleigh, N.C., 1939-41; employee, Norfolk Navy Yard, 1941-42; postal employee, Newport News P.O., 1942-54; vicar, Danville Cure, 1957-58; rector, Trinity Episc. Ch., Charlottesville, Va., 1958-present; real estate broker, 1950-54; pastoral clinical training (advanced), Univ. of Va. Hosp., 1963; pres., Charlottesville Min. Assn., 1962-63; ex. bd. of Charlottesville br. NAACP, 1963-present; v. chrmn., Charlottesville Bi-racial Comm. 1963-present; pres., Coun. of Human Relations, 1962-63; mem., bd. of Charlottesville Mental Health Assn. and bd. of Va. Skyline Coun. of Girl Scouts, 1963; mem. Omega Psi Phi; Home: 415 10th St., NW, Charlottesville, Va.; Office: Trinity Episc. Ch., 10th St. at Grady Ave., Charlottesville, Va.

MITCHELL, Henry Heywood, b. Columbus, O., Sept. 10,

1919; s. Orlando and Bertha (Estis); A. B., Lincoln Univ., Pa., 1941; B. D., Union Theol. Sem., 1944; M. A., Fresno State Coll., 1966; m. Ella Pearson; Children--Henry, Muriel, Kim, Elizabeth; asst. pastor, Concord Bapt. Ch., Bklyn, N. Y., 1943-44; acting dean of Chapel, Inst., N. C. Coll. at Durham, 1944-45; exec. staff, N. Calif. Bapt. Conv., 1945-59; pastor, 2nd Bapt. Ch., Fresno, 1959-66; Calvary Bapt. Ch., Santa Monica, Calif., 1967-present; pres., Fresno Co. Ec. Opportunities Commn., 1966; Ext. tchr., Fresno State Coll., 1966; pres., N. Calif. Bapt. Conv., 1961-62; chrmn., Bd. of trustees, Berkeley Bapt. Div. Sch., Berkeley, Calif., 1960--; chrmn., Housing Comm.; exec. comm., Mayor's Bi-racial Comm., Fresno, Calif., 1963-66; 1st v. p., Western Chrstn. Leadership Conf., SCLC, 1964; pres., W. Fresno Interdenom. Min. Alliance, 1961-63; chrmn., Evangelism Commn., 1956; Comity Commn., 1957; Strategy and Planning Commn., 1958-60; Ch. architecture, 1959-60; exec. bd., N. Calif. Nev. Coun. of Chs., 1951-60; mem., Mayor's Comm. on Capital Improvements, Berkeley, Calif., 1958-59; mem., Phi Kappa Epsilon, Phi Kappa Phi; author, various articles; Home: 1420 S. Victoria Ave., L. A., Calif.; Office: Calvary Bapt. Ch., 1502 20th St., Santa Monica, Calif. 90404

MITCHELL, James Carl, b. Greenville, Ga., Oct. 20, 1900; s. Richard Calvin and Laura (Bowles) M.; A. B., Morehouse Coll., 1925; B. D., Va. Union Univ., 1935; M. A., Marshall Univ., 1953; LL. D. (hon.), Monrovia Coll., Liberia, W. Africa; m. Ora Esttels Fain; pastor, Flaggs Chapel Bapt. Ch., 1929-31, Milledgeville, Ga.; Va. Union Univ., 1931-33; current pastor, Sixteenth St. Bapt. Ch. and Community Center, Huntington, W. Va., 1933--; pres., Bapt. State Minister Union, 1934-35; pres., W. Va. Bapt. State Conv., 1935-40; pres., Bapt. Min. (Inter-racial); pres., Tri-State Bapt. Brotherhood, 13 yrs.; pres., Huntington br., NAACP, 14 yrs.; sec., State Conf., NAACP; organizer, Guardian Nursing Home, Inc.; pres., Negro Co-operative Plan, Inc.; Guardian Securities Co.; exec. bd., Mental Health Assn.; del., Natl. Republican Conv., 1948; v. chrmn., Co. Republican Ex. Comm.; mem., City Council, Huntington; former basileus, Omega Psi Phi; mem., Mason; Elk; Psi Chi Natl. Honorary Soc. (Psychology); Home: 1653 9th Ave., Huntington, W. Va.; Office: 1647 9th Ave., Huntington, W. Va.

MITCHELL, James William, b. Boston, Mass., July 3,

1898; s. James Dennis and Julia (Linehan) M.; Bates Coll.; Boston Univ., Bishop Payne Div. Sch.; m. Martha Jefferson (2nd); Eleanor M. Brown; Children--Mary, Elyne, Michael, Sherri, Jacqueline, Peter, James, David, William; pastor, St. John's P. E. Ch., Wash., D. C., 1928-30; pastor, St. Mary's, Wash., D. C.; pastor, St. Bartholomew, Cambridge, Mass.; retired as rector, 1963; Grace Ch., Millers Tavern, Va.; Home: 216 Blue Hill Ave., Dorchester, Mass.

MITCHELL, Kelly Karnale, Sr., b. Atlanta, Ga., May 18, 1928; s. Jerry C. and Marie T. M.; B. A., Fisk Univ., 1952; Ala. State Coll., 1961-62; m. Andrea Marie Martin; Children--Kelyne Andrienne, Kelly Karnale, Jr.; pastor, Green St. Ch. of Christ, Nashville, Tenn., 1951-54; current pastor, Holt St. Ch. of Christ, Montgomery, Ala., 1955--; former asst. mgr., Martin's Funeral Home, Nashville, Tenn.; staff writer, Chrstn. Echo; mem., Adv. Bd. for the Found. for Chrstn. Education; Natl. and Intl. Evangelist; Phi Beta Sigma; Ala. State Tchrs. Assn.; Natl. Tchrs. Assn.; Dansford Found. Honor Roll for Leadership; Min. Alliance, Montgomery, Ala.; Home: 3404 Santee Drive, Montgomery, Ala. 36108; Office: 726 Columbia, Montgomery, Ala. 36108

MITCHELL, Raymond S., b. Morton, Pa., Nov. 6, 1918; s. Howard and Edna B. (Scott) M.; B. S. Ed., Cheyney Coll.; S. T. B., Phila. Div. Sch. (Episc.); m. Mildred S. Johnson; Children--Monica, Ingrid; pastor, St. Cypriani, Phila., 1947-54; St. Philip's, Syracuse, N. Y., 1954-57; St. Augustine, Norristown, Pa., 1957-61; present, St. Philip's Prot. Episc. Ch., Richmond, Va., 1961--; former tchr. (language--French, German), organist, pianist, clinical training (mentally ill); chap., Crouse Irving Hosp., 1954-57; pres., Eastside Comm. Council, Syracuse, N. Y.; mem., Bd. of YMCA; Escru; NAACP; Child Therapy Center, Richmond, Va.; Honorable discharge, WW II; Clericus of Richmond-Race Relations consultant; Richmond Va. Bd. Dir. (US); first Negro pres., Clericus (Episc. clergymen's assn.); Home: 614 Overbrock Rd., Richmond, Va.; Church: 2900 Hanes Ave., Richmond, Va.

MITCHELL, Roscoe Marron, b. Greenville, S. C., Oct. 5, 1908; s. William E. and Mary E. (McWilliams) M.; Shelton Coll., New York; Burton Coll.; B. Th., Th. M., D. D. (hon.); m. Bessie Louise Gillard; Children--Mary

Alice (Mrs. Benjamin Warren), Roscoe M., William Allen; pastor, Shiloh Bapt. Ch., Southhold, N.Y., 1929; Mt. Pleasant Bapt. Ch., NYC, 1930-34; Ebenezer Bapt. Ch., Newbough Bapt. Ch., NY, 1934-41; New Hope Bapt. Ch., Tarrytown, N.Y., 1941-55; current pastor, Faith Bapt. Ch., Buffalo, NY, 1955--; instr., Natl. Sun. Sch. & B.T.U. Congress; pres., Faculty Club; Republican; mem., YMCA Bd.; Welfare Bd., Buffalo and Erie Co.; Exec. bd., local NAACP; moderator, Great Lakes Bapt. Assn. of Western New York; Mason; author, Principles of Stewardship; Stewardship for Today; Home: 630 Humboldt St., Buffalo, N.Y. 14211; Office: 626 Humboldt St., Buffalo, NY 14211

MITCHELL, Wallace Jefferson, b. No. Birmingham, Ala., Apr. 27, 1916; s. Doss and Georgia (Dix) M.; B.A., Oakwood Coll., 1948; m. Charlotte Rebecca Boysaw; pastor, S.D.A. Chs. in Tenn., Ala., Miss., and Ky.; present: pastor, Univ. Ave. S.D.A. Ch., Knoxville, Tenn. and S.D.A. Chs. in Morristown, Harriman and Greenville, Tenn., 1948--; mem. of Min. Coun., Seminar and Supervisor of youth activities; field repr. of Bible Sch., Voice of Prophecy, Southern Union Sch. of Bible Prophecy and Faith for Today Telecast; voluntary worker for Heart Fund, March of Dimes, Civic Moral Booster for God; US Army, 1943-45; ETO; honorable discharge in 1945; Good Conduct Ribbons in US Army; beyond the call of duty min. activities; Ambassador for good will and peace, for the cause of God; independent political affiliations; Biblical research on Truth not Theory; Home: Racuule Village, Rt. 5, Milroy Lane, Knoxville, Tenn.; Office: University Ave. S.D.A. Ch., 1300 University Ave., Knoxville, Tenn.

MONK, J. Paul, Jr., b. Phila., Pa., Jan. 24, 1940; s. J. Paul and Burdon; A.B., Oakwood Coll., Huntsville, Ala., 1961; M.A., B.D., Andrews Univ., Berrien Springs, Mich., 1962, 1964; m. Carolyn Woodard; Children--Carmela Arlene, Kimberly Rene; mem., So. Atlantic Conf. S.D.A. Ch., 1964; district pastor, Macon, Ga.; Ft. Lauderdale, Fla., currently; mem., Ft. Lauderdale Housing Develop. Bd.; Home: 3841 N.W. 6th St., Ft. Lauderdale, Fla. 33311; Office: 649 NW 15th Way, Ft. Lauderdale, Fla.

MONTGOMERY, Leroy Jeremiah, author; b. Crockett, Tex., Sept. 12, 1902; s. Walter and Fanny (M.); A.B., Morris-

Brown Coll., 1925; S. T. B., Boston Univ., Sch. of Theol., 1928; S. T. M., Union Theol. Sem., 1930; m. Beatrice Duren; pastored, Meth. Chs. in Danbury, Conn., 1954-56, Buffalo, N. Y., 1956-60; Wm. Temple C. M. E. Ch., Phila., Pa., 1960-62; Russell Temple C. M. E. Ch., Alexandria, Va., 1962-64; Author: "The Race Problem," "Two Distinct Religions," and "My Trip Abroad." Home: 1930 Mississippi Ave. S. E., Wash., D. C.; Office: 507 No. Alfred St., Alexandria, Va.

MONTGOMERY, Simon Peter, ch. official, b. Pineville, S. C., Feb. 12, 1922; s. Lee and Lizzie (Jenkins) M.; B. D., Cummings Theol. Sem., 1946; Benedict Coll., 1946-47; Claflin Coll., 1958-59; A. B., Garrett Biblical Inst., 1952-53; M. A., Boston Univ., 1955; m. Bessie Mathilda Allen; Children--Simon Peter, Jr., Vernita Renee, Keith Allen; pastor, Rock Hill Meth. Ch., 1947-49; Gaffney Meth. Ch., 1949-50; dir., Chrstn. Ed., Mobile Unit South Fla. Conf. Meth. Ch., 1950-52; Old Mystic Meth. Ch., 1955-57; Rockville Meth. Ch., 1957-59; current, ex. dir. and pastor-at-large, Inner City Parish, Stamford-Darien Coun. of Chs., 1959--; principal, Chesney Sch., Chesney, S. C., 1949; instr., Norwich Tech., 1955-56; dir., Intercultural and Interfaith project at Emmanuel Luth. Ch., Boston; first Negro chap. of the Conn. Gen. Assembly, 1957-58; pres., Stamford Alumni Chapter Claflin Univ., 1959--; chrmn., Social and Economic Comm. of NE Southern Conf., Meth. Ch., 1956-59; mem., Commn. of Social Concern, NE Southern Conf., 1959-64; consultant, Young Adult Fellowship Weekend Retreat, summers of 1956-59; staff mem., Northern NE Sch. of Rel. Ed., 1956-61; spec. consultant, The Congre. Family Conf. of Conn. Conf., 1964; current, Exec. bd. of the W. Main St. Community Center; TB & Health Assn., Southern Fairfield Co.; Psychiatric Clinic for Children, Stamford-Darien-New Canaan Heart Assn.; Conn. Heart Assn.; Stamford-Darien Coun. of Chs.; NAACP Stamford chapter; Comm. on Rel. and Race, Conn. Coun. of Chs.; Bd. of dirs., Conn. Coun. of Chs., 1955-58; v. p., Stamford-Darien Min. Assn., 1963; mem., Exec. Bd. Senior Citizens Assn., Stamford; award from Conn. State for outstanding service as Chaplain in the House of Rep.; certificates of appreciation for faithful service from the Norwich Lions Club, Rockville Rotary Club; Research developer of the Inner City Parish of the Stanford-Darien Coun. of Chs.; Home: 36 Bonner St., Stamford, Conn.

MOODY, James Luther, chap., b. McLain, Miss., Mar. 17, 1937; s. Frank and Fannie R.; A.B., Rust. Coll., Holly Springs, Miss.; B.D., Interdenom. Theol. Center, Atlanta, Ga., 1964; m. Barbara A. James; Children--Jamie B., James Leonias; pastor, Centre-Woodben Circuit, United Meth. Ch., Centre, Ala., 1963-64; Walthall Parrish, Tylertown, Miss., 1964-65; Metropolitan Meth. Ch., Montgomery, Cala., 1965-66; chap., US Army, Chu Lai, Vietnam, Jan. 1967-present; Medals, Bronze Star, Army Nat. Defense, Vietnam Campaign, Presidential Unit Citation; mem., Mason, Montgomery Improvement Assn.; NAACP; Home: PO Box 484, Bayspring Rd., Centre, Ala. 93560; Office: HHQ, 3/21, 196th Inf. Brigade, APO San Francisco, Calif. 96256

MOORE, Arthur Chester, b. Philadelphia, Pa., Jan. 4, 1894; s. James Henry and Anna (Brice) M.; S.T.B., Temple Univ., Philadelphia, Div. Sch. of Episc. Ch., 1924; Th.M., Temple Univ., 1940; m. Marguerite Carmen Young; pastored: St. Cyprian's Ch., Phila.; St. Mary's Ch., Chester; St. Monica's Ch., Phila., St. Luke's Ch., NYC, 1945-51; present: St. Simon's Prot. Episc. Ch., New Rochelle, N.Y., 1951--; chrmn., Ch. Sch. Tchrs. Training Sch. under the New Rochelle Coun. of Chs., 1961; mem., New Rochelle Chap. of NAACP; New Rochelle Hosp. Assn.; Coun. of Unity, New Rochelle; Urban League of Westchester; award for Phila. Afro-American for Better Housing; Gov. Award for Civilian Defense in State of New York; pres., Prot. Min. Assn. of New Rochelle, N.Y., 1962 and Interdenom. Min. Alliance, 1963-present; mem. and chap., Alpha Phi Alpha, Westchester chap.; mem. and former sec., Westchester Clericus of Episc. Clergy; mem., Dept. of Chrstn. Ed. Diocese of Pa. and Dept. of Chrstn. Social Relations; sec., Convocation of W. Phila. Home: 135 Remington Pl., New Rochelle, N.Y. Office: 133 Remington Pl., New Rochelle, N.Y.

*MOORE, Douglas, b. July 3, 1928, Hickory, N.C.; s. Jack and Forney (Steavson); A.B., N. Carolina Coll., 1949; Howard Univ., Sch. of Rel., 1949-50; S.T.B., Boston Univ., Sch. of Theol. 1953, S.T.M., 1958; grad. courses N.C. Coll., and Univ. of N.C.; Boston Univ. African Studies Program, 1960; Univ. of Grenoble, Grenoble, France, 1960-61; m. Dasie Haynes; Children--four; pastor, United Meth. Chs., in Ramseur, Leaksville, and Durham, N.C., 1953-60; tchr., Livingstone Coll., Salisbury, N. C., 1955-56; asst. dir., Amer. Friends Serv. Comm. Merit Employment Program, Greensboro, N. C., 1954-55; ex. sec., bd. of ed. of the N. C. Conf. of the Meth. Ch., 1956-60; current pastor, Calloway United Meth. Ch., Arlington, Va.; current, asst. dir., D. C. Redevelopment Land Agency Assn.; pres., Leaksville, N. C. NAACP; organized sit-in·in Durham, N. C. in 1957; one of the founders of So. Christ. Lead. Conf., N. C. bd. mem., 1957-61; organized statewide conf. on voter regis., Durham, N. C., 1957; organized the first meeting of student-sit-in leaders in N. C. and the Raleigh Easter Conf. for students who had participated in the sit-in protest movement, 1960; v. p., D. C. Citizens for Better Govt., 1968; candidate, D. C. Bd. of Ed. mem. at large, 1968; tchr., chap., coun., Elizabethville, Katanga Province, Congo, Leopoldville, 1962-65; Home: 2628 Monroe St., NE, Wash., D. C.

MOORE, Earl B., b. Little Rock, Ark., Feb. 2, 1931; s. Luther H. and Esma M.; Ark. Bapt. Coll., 1950-53; Va. Union Univ. Sch. of Rel., 1953-56; m. Cora L. Thornton; Children--Melvin; mem., N. Y. Bapt. City Miss. Soc., 1956-60; pastor, Shiloh Bapt. Ch., Tarrytown, N. Y., 1960-63; St. Paul Bapt. Ch., N. Y., 1960-present; mem., Civic Com., Westchester Co., 1960-63; Amer. Bapt. Conv.; Bapt. Ministers Conf.; Bapt. Ed. Center; N. Y. Bapt. City Miss. Soc.; Empire State Bapt. Conv.; Prot. Coun., United Miss Bapt. Assn., N. Y.; Central Hudson Assn., 1960-63; N. Y. City Chap. (prisons), 1964-present; Home: 216 Station Pl., Mt. Vernon, N. Y.

MOORE, Emerson John, b. May 16, 1938, New York, N. Y., s. Emerson and Dorothy Williams (E.); Cathedral Coll. Prep. Sem., NYC, 1956-58; B. A., St. Josephs Sem. & Coll., Yonkers, N. Y.; Parish work, Holy Family Ch., NYC, 1964-68; Kennedy Community Center, NYC, 1968-present; mem., Central Harlem Head Start Program; Cath. Interrracial Coun.; E. Harlem Triangle Assn.; Home: 47 E. 129th St., New York, N. Y. 10035; Office: 34 W. 134th St., New York, N. Y. 10037

MOORE, Ezra Julius, businessman, b. Maysville, N. C., Apr. 30, 1922; s. Geo. Israel and Everlenner (Ashwood); B. S., A & T Coll., 1953; B. D., Johnson C. Smith Univ., 1960; m. Lula Mae Stanton; Children--Michael Julius, Ezra Maceo, Beverly Joanne; cashier and bookstore mgr., Claflin Coll., 1953-57; pastor, Macedonia First Presby.

Ch., 1957; Sadalia Congre., Haw River, N. C. and Sadalia Congre. Ch., Sadalia, N. C., 1958-60; current pastor Bklyn United Presby. Ch., 1960--; mem., Bd. of Dirs., Charlotte Coun. on Alcoholism, bd. of dirs., Mecklenburg Organization on Political Affairs; active service in the US Navy, 1940-46; mem., Kappa Alpha Psi, Second Ward High Sch. PTA, YMCA, YWCA, Northwest Jr. High PTA, Univ. Park PTA, NAACP, Democratic Party, Boy Scouts; Home: 2027 Syracuse Dr., Charlotte, N. C.; Church: 418 So. McDowell St., Charlotte, N. C.

MOORE, James Robert, B. Petersburg, Va.; s. Robert and Sarah M.; A. B., City Coll., N. Y.; Va. Theol. Sem.; courses, Columbia Univ., Union Theol. Sem., N. Y.; D. D. (hon.), Va. Theol. Sem.; m. Gladys Pritchett; asst. pastor, Union Bapt. Ch., N. Y.; pastor, Amity Bapt. Ch., Jamaica, N. Y., 1928-present; sec., Manhattan, Bronx, Westchester and Staten Is. Assn.; mem., Nat. Bapt. Conv., Inc.; bd. of trustees, NY Bapt. Home for the Aged; Bd. of Trustees, Va. Theol. Sem. & Coll.; pres., Sun. Sch. & B. T. U. of the Eastern Bapt. Assn.; moderator, Eastern Bapt. Assn.; Home: 18717 Rome Dr., Jamaica, N. Y. 11412; Office: 164-18 108th Ave., Jamaica, N. Y.

*MOORE, Jerry A., coll. chaplain; b. Minders, La., June 12, 1918; s. Jerry A., Sr. and Mae Dee (Abner) M.; B. A., Morehouse Coll., 1940; B. D., Howard Univ., Sch. of Rel., 1943; M. A., 1957; post grad., Univ. of S. C. and American Univ.; m. Ettyie H. Hill; Children--Jerry A., III, Juran D.; pastor, 19th St. Bapt. Ch., 1946--; Councilman, Dist. of Columbia, 1969-; Bapt. Univ. Chap., Howard Univ., 1956--; mem., Republican State Comm., D. C.; exec. comm. Bapt. World Alliance; Natl. Comm. for Support of Pub. Schs.; Phi Beta Sigma; Bapt. Minister's Conf., D. C. & vicinity; Home: 1612 Buchanan St. NW, Wash. D. C. Office: 19th St. Bapt. Ch., 19th & Eye Sts., NW, Wash., D. C. 20009

MOORE, Jesse Lee, b. York County, Rock Hill, S. C., Sept. 1, 1929; s. Albert and Sadie (Ervin) M.; A. B., Johnson C. Smith Univ., 1957; B. D., Johnson C. Smith Univ., Charlotte, N. C., 1960; pastor, The Grandview United Presby. Ch., Chesterfield, S. C.; The Pageland Second United Presby. Ch., Pageland, S. C.; chrmn., The Upper Fairfield-McClelland Larger Parish; chrmn.,

The Chesterfield Community Civic Club; mem. Alpha Phi Alpha; NAACP; Home: PO Box 72, 203 Mill St., Chesterfield, S. C.; Church: PO Box 72, 203 Mill St., Chesterfield, S. C.

MOORE, John Dewey, b. Macon, Ga., Feb. 18, 1904; s. John and Annie M.; Hampton Inst., 1919-26; B. D., Gammon Theol. Sem., 1930-33; B. S., Clark Univ., 1927-30; B. D., Oberlin Div. Sch., 1933-34; m. Frankie Reid Neal; Children--Evelyn Dametta Evans, Cecil Evans, Karna Lotthene; pastor, Evergreen Congre. Ch., Beachton, Ga., 1932; First Congre. Ch., Florence, Ala., 1934-35; Joe Wheeler Dam Office Interviewer, 1935-36; current pastor, Pilgrim Congre. Ch., 1936--; Omega Man of Year; Boy Scout "Silver Beaver," and Girl Scout "Thank You Badge;" mem., Omega Psi Phi, YMCA, NAACP, Independent (politics); pres., PTA Coun. Harris Co.; v. p., State PTA; v. p., W. L. Davis Boy Scouts; treas., Houston Assn., United Ch. of Christ; pres., Turner PTA; mem., Bd. Huston-Tillotson Coll.; Eden Home for Aged; San Jacinto Girl Scouts of America; Houston Assn. of Chs.; T. S. U. Conf. Ministers of United Ch. of Christ; Human Relations; Planned Parenthood; Home: 3547 Rosedale Ave., Houston, Tex.; Office: 3519 Live Oak St., Houston, Tex.

MOORE, Noah Watson, Jr., bishop; b. Newark, N. J., Mar. 28, 1902; s. Noah W. Moore, Sr. and Eliza A. M.; A. B., Morgan Coll., Baltimore, Md., 1926; B. D., Drew Univ., Dept. of Theol., 1931; grad. study, Crozier Theol. Sem., 1945-46; D. D., Gammon Theol. Sem., 1951; LL. D., Morgan State Coll., 1961; m. Carolyn W. Lee; children--Carolyn O.; ministry: New Rochelle, N. Y., 1930-31; Upper Hill, Md., 1931-35; Fairmount Circuit and Upper Hill, Md., 1935-37; Camphor Meml., Phila., Pa., 1937-41; St. Daniels, Chester, Pa., 1941-43; Supt. of the Eastern Dist., 1943-47; Tindley Temple, Phila., pa., 1949-60; activity: Trustee and v. p., Morgan Coll. Corp., 1950-60; trustee, Morristown Coll., Morristown, Tenn., 1956-60; mem., Meth. Coun. on World Serv. & Finance, 1960; mem., The World Meth. Coun. and Exec. Comm.; chrmn., Commn. on Higher Ed., Del. Conf., Balto. Area, 1949-60; mem., The Masonic Order; Omega Psi Phi; bd. mem. and sec. -treas., Phila. Housing Authority; mem., Bd. of Mgrs., Chrstn. St. YMCA, Phila., Pa.; mem., Frontiers of America; trustee, United Fund, Phila., and vicinity; three-time mem. Gen. and Jurisdictional Conf., The Meth. Ch., Southern Area; Phila. Health and Welfare; elected Bishop, The Meth. Ch.; Cleveland Ohio, July 14, 1960; consecrated July 17, 1960; assigned to New Orleans area (Louisiana, Texas and W. Tex. Conf.); publications and lectures: selected articles in Central Chrstn. Advocate and The Church Sch. Jour.; including book reviews, articles and Lenten messages in the weeklies and the Phila. daily papers; tchr. and lecturer at pastor's schs., including Bennett Coll., Emory and Henry Coll.; Lenten series speaker for eight consecutive yrs. for Wilmington Coun. of Chs. and Coun. of Chs. of Pulaske, N. Y. and Ogdensburg, N. Y.; study tour of W. Germany and Berlin, as guest of the govt. of the Fed. Republic of Germany - one of nine clergymen (Prot., Cath., and Jewish) from the US, 1959; elec. pres. of Coll. of Bishops, 1962; Home: 631 Baronne St., New Orleans, La.

MOORE, Prentis Monroe Dumas, b. Garrison, Tex., Jan. 13, 1936; s. Wm. M. & Addie (Bell) M.; A. B., Tex. Southern Univ., Houston, 1958; LL. D. (hon.), Andover Newton Theol. Sem., Newton, Mass., 1962; D. D. (hon.), Union Bapt. Theol. Sch., Houston, 1962; courses, Portia Law Sch., Boston, 1968; m. Mary Johnson; Children--Carol Edith, Tracey Marie; jr. pastor, Mt. Horem Bapt. Ch., Houston, 1955-58; staff minister, Andover Newton Inner City Project, 1958-59; asst. pastor, Eliot Ch., Roxbury, Mass., 1959-61; pastor, Graham Congre. Ch., Beaumont, Tex., 1961-62; Eliot Ch., Roxbury, Mass., 1962-present; instr., Union Bapt. Theol. Sem., Houston, 1961-62; ex. dir., Progressive Youth Assn., Houston, 1961-62; dean, South-end Roxbury Christ Inst.; business mgr., King Bee Enterprises, Houston, 1956-58; lectr., Race Relations; consult. Urban Affairs; sec., Greater Boston Min. Alliance, 1967-present; pres., Inter-faith Urban Finance & Develop. Corp.; Bd. of Dirs., City Miss. Soc. of Boston; trustee, Fellows Athaneaum Lib. of Boston; treas., Checkerboard Housing Corp.; mem., NAACP; Democrat; Home: 1018 Boylston St., Newton Highlands, Mass. 02161; Office: 120 Walnut Ave., Roxbury, Mass. 02119

MORGAN, Eugene Edward, Jr., b. Mobile, Ala., Nov. 24, 1918; s. Eugene Edward Sr. and Sallie (Croshon) M.; A. B., Dillard Univ., 1941; B. D., Hood Theol. Sem., 1947; B. D., Oberlin Grad. Sch. Theol.; m. Guernia Dae Morgan; children--Eugene Edward, III, Winifred Lynne;

instr., Wayne Co. Pub. Sch., N.C., 1942-44; pastor, Avery Meml. A.M.E.Z. Ch., Pittsburgh, 1949-51; St. Matthews A.M.E.Z. Ch., Sewickley, Pa., 1951-53; Wesley Temple A.M.E.Z. Ch., Akron, O., 1953-present; dean, Fourth Dist. Inst., A.M.E.Z. Ch., Counseling serv. under Ohio Dept. of Mental Health; bd. mem., Akron Urban League, 1963; United Community Coun. of Akron, 1963; Mayor's Commn. on Employment, 1956-60; bd. mem., Hood Theol. Sem., 1956-60; mem., Connectional Budget Bd., A.M.E.Z. Ch., 1964; A.M.E.Z. Commn. on Organic Union, 1964; Home: 799 Diagonal Rd., Akron, Ohio 44320; Office: 104 N. Prospect St., Akron, O.

MORGAN, Frank Douglas, b. Durham, N.C., Sept. 26, 1917; s. Walker Hargrove and Maggie Daisy; A.B., Johnson C. Smith Univ., 1949; B.D., 1950; grad. study, Yale Univ.; m. Ida Lee Coleman; pastor, First Congre. Ch., 1953-63; current pastor, Goodwill Presby. Ch., 1963--; moderator of Conf., 1953-59; chrmn., March of Dimes, 1957-60; mem., The ex. br. of the Fla. Coun. on Human Rights; pres. of the Interdenom. Min. Alliance, 1958-58; certificate of award from the Natl. Found. of Infantile Paralysis; mem., Democrat, Omega Psi Phi, Master Mason; Home: 516 No. 8th St., Ft. Pierce, Fla.

MORGAN, Philip Henry, b. Birmingham, Ala., July 28, 1914; s. Philip M. and Belle (Palmore) M.; Oakwood Coll., Huntsville, Ala.; Andrews Univ., Mich.; m. Rosalia Clark; children--Philip H., Jr., Willie Charles, Rosalyn L., Maurice C.; pastor, S.D.A. Chs., 1938-60 in Columbus, Ga., Knoxville, Tenn., Albany, Ga., Raleigh, N.C., Durham, N.C., Columbia, S.C., Tulsa, Okla., and Los Angeles, Calif.; present: pastor, S.D.A. Ch., Palmdale, Calif., 1960--; tchr., Columbus, Ga., 1938-40; sec., Negro Cham. of Commerce, Knoxville, Tenn., 1941-43; pres., Interdenom. Min. Alliance, Albany, Ga.; sec., NAACP, Albany, Ga., 1947-48; former mem., Ga. State Negro Democratic Comm.; Home: 234 W. 124th St., L.A., Calif.; Office: 1007 Aves St., Little Rock, Calif.

MORRIS, Donald Eugene, Sr., b. Watseka, Ill., July 3, 1907; s. James Curtis and Eva Alice (Brady) M.; St. Louis Area Pastor's Sch.; Great Lakes Coll., Detroit, Mich.; m. Phyloese Robinson, Viola Eldridge, Louella Robinson; Children--Donald Eugene, Jr., Carol Evonne (Mrs. Hemphill); asst. pastor, Indiana Ave. United Meth.

Ch., Chgo., Ill., 1947-48; pastor, Calvary Meth. Ch., Milford, O., 1948-50; Taylor Chapel Meth. Ch., Batavia O., 1949-50; Saulters Chapel Meth. Ch., Terre Haute, Ind., 1950-51; Wiley Meth. Ch., New Castle, Ind., 1951-53; St. John Meth. Ch., Pontiac, Mich., 1953-57; Mitchell Meml. Meth. Ch., Detroit, Mich., 1957-59; Bethel United Meth. Ch., Flint, Mich., 1959-present; pres., Greater Flint Min. Assn., 1965-66; Home: 1909 Whittlesey St., Flint, Mich. 48503; Office: 421 E. 12th St., Flint, Mich. 48503

MORRIS, John Batiste, b. Gretna, La., April 3, 1920; s. Amos F. and Agnes (Shorter) M.; A.B., Leland Coll., 1943; B.D., Oberlin Grad. Sch. of Theol.; m. Gloria Butler; Children--Deborah Gail; pastor, First Free Mission Bapt. Ch., New Orleans, La., 1945; instr., the Layman's Dept. of the Natl. Bapt. Conv., 1946; instr., Natl. Bapt. Sun. Sch. and B.T.U. Congress, USA, Inc.; tchr., Dept. of Chrstn. Ed., State Convention; mem., Interracial and Interfaith Clergy Fellowship; chrmn., Religious Life Comm. of Interdenom. Min. Alliance; Devotion Leader for the Youth Encampment; pastoral advisor, Dillard Univ. Student Union; current pastor, First Free Mission Bapt. Ch., New Orleans, La.; mem., Bd. First Dist. Missionary Bapt. Assn.; Bd. of Management, Dryades St. YMCA; The Urban Leage of Greater New Orleans; v. chrmn., The Citizen's Comm; Desire St. Project Spec. Comm.; del., Bapt. Alliance, London, England, 1955; mem., Frontiers of America; NAACP; Mason; Home: 7612 Zimple St., New Orleans, La. 70118; Office: 919 Adams St., New Orleans, La. 70118

MORRIS, John Charles, b. Bristol, Va., May 16, 1924; s. Fred H. and Estalla Ruth M.; Va. State Coll., 2 yrs.; Buffalo Bible Inst.; children--Veronica E.; Mosetta Charline; organized Faith Temple Ch. for All People, 1962; Union coun., Steelworker's Local 2601, 1964-67; spec. minister, Western NY for Steel Workers Hosp. & Welfare Assn.; pres., Joint Ed. Dept. of Elk for Frontiers and Elite of Buffalo, N.Y., 1958-60; mem., Boy Scouts of Amer.; Home: 317 Madison St, Buffalo, N.Y. 14212

MORRIS, Lloyd Belton, b. Charlotte, N.C., Nov. 21, 1938; s. John Henry and Grace (Henderson); B.A., Johnson C. Smith Univ., 1955-59; B.D., 1959-62; summer service projects: Matton United Presby. Ch., Wash., D.C.; ordained by the Fairfield McClelland Presby.; pastor,

Hermon United Presby. Ch., Rock Hill, S.C. in 1962; v.p., Rock Hill NAACP, youth adv. NAACP Youth br., dir., Negro voter registration campaign in York Co., S.C.; mem., Phi Kappa Alpha, Humanities Honor Soc., Omega Psi Phi; Home: 442 So. Trade St., Rock Hill, S.C.; Church: 446 So. Trade St., Rock Hill, S.C.

*MORRIS, Ronald Elliot, b. Malden, Mass., Nov. 20, 1931; s. Stanley C. and Dorothy Mae M.; A.B., Boston Univ., 1952; B.S., Boston Univ., 1954; B.D. Howard Univ., Sch. of Rel., 1962; chap., New York State Coun. of Chs., Migratory Ministry, 1960-62; Dir. of Religious Ed., Mt. Zion Congre. Ch., Cleveland, O., 1963; pastor, Antioch United Ch. of Christ, Suffolk, Va., 1964; chrmn., Suffolk-Nansemond Coordinating Comm.; v.p., Suffolk Min. Alliance; US Air Force, 1954-58; Good Conduct Medal; mem., Omega Psi Phi; Home: 24 Deckard, Boston, Mass.; Office: 424 Smith, Suffolk, Va.

MORRIS, Samuel Solomon, b. Norfolk, Va., Nov. 1, 1916; s. Samuel Solomon, Sr. and Mayme (Lawson) M.; B.S., Wilberforce, Univ., 1937; B.D., Yale Univ., 1940; courses, Ohio State Univ.; Univ. of Chgo.; D.D. (hon.), Payne Sem.; Shorter Coll.; LL.D. (hon.), Kittrell Coll.; Monrovia Coll.; m. Ermine Smith; Children--Joyce, Ermine, Samuel III; pastor, St. Luke A.M.E. Ch., Gallatin, Tenn.; St. John A.M.E. Ch., Springfield, Tenn., 1940-41; St. Paul A.M.E. Ch., Nashville, Tenn., 1943-46; assoc. pastor, Bethel A.M.E. Ch., Detroit, Mich., 1948-49; pastor, First A.M.E. Ch., Gary, Ind., 1949-56; prof., Payne Sem., Wilberforce Univ., 1941-43; pres., Shorter Coll., No. Little Rock, Ark., 1946-48; present pastor, Coppin A.M.E. Ch., Chgo., Ill.; Mayor's Comm. on New Residents; pres., Chgo. br. NAACP, 1960-62; Chgo. Conf. on Rel. and Race; Ch. Fed. of Greater Chgo.; Chgo. Urban League; Ex. Comm. on Educ. Inst., A.M.E. Ch.; organizer and chrmn., Clergy for Quality and Equality in Educ., Chgo.; Alpha Phi Alpha; Masons; Frontiers Internatl.; author, An African Methodist Primer; attended World Coun. of Chs., New Delhi, 1961, including World Tour of fourteen countries in Europe, Africa, the Holy Land, Near and Far East; toured Jamaica, W.I., 1965; Home: 5621 S. Mich. St., Chgo., Ill.; Office: 5627 S. Mich. St., Chgo., Ill.

MORRIS, Wm. Wesley, b. Aug. 7, 1937, Baltimore, Md.; s. Wm. Wesley and Daisy Franklin (M.); A.B., Ohio

Wesleyan Univ., 1957; B.D., Garrett Theol. Sem., 1960; m. Eva Muldrow; children--Loretta Jeanette, Ava Janine; staff mem., Jewish Comm. Center, Chgo., 1959; student pastor, Bethany United Meth. Ch., 1959; Pastor Union Ave. Comm. Center Ch., Chgo., 1959-60; Christ Meth. Ch., 1960-62; Stanley United Meth. Ch., 1962, Chattanooga, Tenn.; dir., Youth Work, United Meth. Ch., Chattanooga, Tenn. 1961; chrmn., Minimum Salaries Comm., Tenn.-Ky., Conf.; chrmn., Hamilton Co. TB Assn.; bd. of mgrs., YMCA; mem., Bd. Bethlehem Com. Center; Amer. Cancer Soc. Achievement Award, 1962; mem., Greater Chattanooga Min. Assn.; Inter-Alliance; Home: 1001 Acklen Ave., Nashville, Tenn. 37203; Office: 901 Benton Ave., Nashville, Tenn. 37203

MORSE, Savarhett, b. Jacksonville, Fla., July 30, 1910; s. Richard and Mamie (Sims) M.; B.Th., Wilberforce Univ., 1945; A.B., Howard Univ., Wash., D.C., 1950; m. Elaine Weyms; Children--Sharon Elett, Savarhett, Jr., Raymond Ellis; pastor, St. Paul A.M.E. Ch., Danville, Va., 1951-55; Trinity A.M.E. Ch., Norfolk, Va., 1956-58; Ebenezer A.M.E. Ch., Hagerstown, Md., 1959-62; current, Pilgrim Afr. Meth. Episc. Ch., Wash., D.C., 1963--; mem., Phi Beta Sigma; Republican; Home: 718 19th St. NE, Wash., D.C.; Office: 700 17th St. NE, Wash., D.C.

MORTON, Charles Evans, coll. prof., b. Bessemer, Ala., Jan. 31, 1926; s. Hodge M. and Mary M.; B.A., Morehouse Coll., 1943-46; B.D., Union Theol. Sem., N.Y., 1949; Heidelberg Univ., Germany, 1955; Garrett Biblical Inst. of Northwestern Univ., 1956; Ph.D., Columbia Univ., 1958; m. Jean Estelle Braboy; Children--Joan Maria, Carla Estelle; youth dir., Greater New York Inter-racial Fellowship, 1947-48; student minister, St. James Presby. Ch., 1946-47; instr., Morehouse Coll., Atlanta, Ga., 1949-51; pastor, Ebenezer Bapt. Ch., Poughkeepsie, N.Y., 1951-53; assoc. prof., Knoxville Coll., Knoxville, Tenn., 1953-57; chrmn., Div. of Hamnities and prof. of Rel. & Philosophy, Dillard Univ., New Orleans, La., 1957-62; academic dean, Fayetteville State Coll., Fayetteville, N.C., 1962-63; current pastor, Metropolitan Bapt. Ch., Detroit, Mich.; assoc. prof., Albion Coll., Albion, Mich., 1964--; mem., Mayor's Exec. Comm. on Voters Registration; Wayne Co. Commn. on Juvenile Delinquency; Bd. of Dirs., Detroit br. NAACP; The Founders Soc., Detroit Inst. of Arts; chrmn., Detroit br. NAACP membership campaign, 1964; The Ministerial Adv. Comm., Detroit Planned Parenthood Assn.; Detroit Prot. Coun. of Chs.; Comm. on Radio and TV Communication and co-chrmn. of the Min. Comm. of the African Art Gallery Fund; Phi Beta Sigma Award for Serv. to Education, New Orleans, 1962; NAACP Membership Campaign Award, Detroit, 1962; Pittsburgh Couriers Min. Award, 1964; mem., Phi Beta Sigma; Urban League; NAACP; Natl. Coun. of Chs. & World Coun. of Chs.; article, "The South Today;" author: The Teaching of Religion in Church Related College, Bd. of Higher Ed., The Meth. Ch., Nashville, Tenn., 1962; Home: 17510 Ohio Ave., Detroit, Mich.; Office: 13110 14th St., Buena Vista, Detroit, Mich.

MOSELEY, Alexander Dumas, b. Lewiston, N.C., Jan. 20, 1915; s. Samuel Henderson and Burnettie (Wiggins) M.; A.B., Shaw Univ., 1948; M.A., Univ. of Denver, 1953; N.C. Coll., Durham, N.C., 1950; Union Theol. Sem., N.Y.C., 1959; D.D. (hon.), Kittrell Coll., 1960; Neotarian Coll. of Philosophy, 1961; m. Earle Cleves; children--Alexis Earle; tchr., pub. sch., N.C., 1935-41; pastor, New Sawyer Creek Bapt. Ch., Bell Cross, N.C., 1947-51; Union Bapt. Ch., Tarboro, N.C.; St. John Bapt. Ch., New Bern, N.C., 1951-56; First Bapt. Ch., Weldon, N.C., 1956-61; Mt. Gilead Bapt. Ch., Durham, N.C., 1961--; dir., Chrstn. Education, Old Eastern Assn., Greenville, N.C., 1950-57; exec. sec., Eastern Bapt. Dist. Conv. an aux. to The Gen. Bapt. State Conv. of N.C., Inc., 1950-61; dir., Veterans Training Program, P.S. Jones High Sch., Wash., N.C., 1952-55; Commissioner of Civil Liberties, N.C., 1950-60; pres., Walker-Lassiter Defense Fund, Weldon, N.C., 1957-61; chrmn., Fuller Sch. Precinct, Durham, N.C., 1962--; pres., Durham Min. Assn., 1964; v.p., Durham Comm. on Negro Affairs, 1962--; ex. bd., John Avery's Boys Club, Durham, N.C., 1962--; NAACP; CORE; SCLC; US Air Forces, 477th Bomb Group, 1945; cited for Meritorious Service; mem., Neotarian Fellowship; Alpha Phi Alpha; Mason; Elk; Pythian; Eastern Star; Democrat; Office: 401 Dowd St., Durham, N.C.

MOSELEY, Calvin Edwin, Jr., b. Demopolis, Ala., Jan. 7, 1906; s. Calvin Edwin Sr. and Lily Belle (Dixon) M.; Oakwood Jr. Coll., 1926; B.A., Emmanuel Miss. Coll., Berrien Springs, Mich., 1929; M.A., S.D.A. Theol. Sem., Wash., D.C., 1946; courses, Northwestern and

Chicago Univs.; m. Harriet Frances Slater; children--Mrs. Donáld L. Keith; Mrs. Mervyn A. Warren; pastor, S. D. A. Chs., Evanston, Ill., 1929-31; Springfield, Ill., 1931; Kansas City and St. Louis, Mo., 1932-34; head, Bible Dept., pastor, Oakwood Coll., 1934-51; assoc. sec., North Amer. Regional Dept. of the General Conf. of S. D. A., 1951-58; Gen. field sec. for conf., 1958-present; mem., Gen. Conf. exec. com.; Bd. of dir., Oakwood Coll., Huntsville, Ala.; Regional Adv. Comm.; Denominational books to public libraries comm.; S. D. A. Welfare Comm.; received plaque for dedicated service to Religious Ed., Oakwood Coll. Alumni Chapter, 1960; columnist and ed. consultant for The Message Magazine, editorial consultant, Youth's Instructor; Home: 49 Jefferson Ave., Takoma Pk, Md. 20012

MOSES, Jesse Daniel, tchr., b. San Antonio, Tex., Dec. 18, 1914; s. Jesse Daniel and Veinita (Bryan) M.; B. A., Univ. of Redlands, 1937; M. A., B. D., Berkeley Bapt. Div. Sch., 1937-40; Univ. of So. Calif., Th. D., 1945-55; m. Regenia Audrey Payne; Children--Jesse Daniel, Jeffrey Dennis; sec., Gleiss Center, Detroit, Mich., 1941-42; US Army chap., 1942-45; pastor, St. Barnabas Ch., Pasadena, 1950-51; asst. pastor, St. Paul's Cathedral, L. A.; tchr., Pasadena City Schs., 1950--; tchr. and v. prin., Jr. High Sch., Pasadena, Calif., 1949--; pres., Pasadena Ed. Assn., 2 terms; pres., Calif. Tchrs. Assn., Southern Sec.; mem., Urban League, Red Cross, 1942-45; mem., Alpha Phi Alpha, Phi Delta Kappa; Home: 1148 Wotkyns Dr., Pasadena, Calif.; Office: 325 So. Oak Knoll, Pasadena, Calif.

MOSS, Otis, Jr., b. La Grange, Ga., Feb. 26, 1935; s. Otis, Sr. and Magnolia (R.) M.; B. A., Morehouse Coll., 1956; B. D., Morehouse Sch. of Rel., 1959; m. Sharon Joann Howell; Children--Daphne Rachelle; pastor, Old Mt. Olive Bapt. Ch., La Grange, Ga.; Providence Bapt. Ch., Atlanta, Ga., 1956-61; current, Mt. Zion Bapt. Ch., Ohio, 1961--; former v. p., Atlanta br. NAACP; former sec., Atlanta Coun. on Human Relations; area repr., So. Chrstn. Leadership Conf., Cincinnati, Ohio; mem., Alpha Phi Alpha; Home: 69 Chestnut, Cincinnati, O.; Office: 325 N. Wayne Ave., Cincinnati, O.

MOUCHETTE, Edward Donley, clergyman, b. Bermuda B. W. I., May 27, 1930; s. Brownlow and Blanche (C.) M.; A. B., Wilberforce Univ., 1955; B. D., Payne Theol.

Sem., 1953-56; m. Anna Mary Shipes; Children--Franscine, Edward Donley III, Sherri Lynn; pastor, Bethel Afr. Meth. Episc. Ch., Shelley Bay, Bermuda, 1956-58; First United A. M. E. Ch., Lockport, N. Y., 1958-59; Bethel A. M. E. Ch., Bay Shore, N. Y., 1959-61; Allen Meml. A. M. E. Ch., Bklyn, N. Y., 1961-62; US Army chap. since 1962; pres., NAACP, Bay Shore, N. Y. br., 1961-62; Found. for Mentally Retarded Children, Suffolk Co., N. Y., 1960-62; German Occupation Ribbon and Medal; mem., Alpha Phi Alpha; Zeta Sigma Phi; Natl. Soc. Sci. Honor Soc.; Assn. of Military Chaplains; contributor: The A. M. E. Chrstn. Recorder; Home: 319-1 Pollan, Ft. Riley, Kans. 66442; Office: 2nd Bde, St. Inf. Div., Ft. Riley, Kans.

MURCHISON, Elisha P., bishop, prof., b. Ft. Worth, June 18, 1907; s. Elisha P., Sr. and Gertrude (Moore) M.; A. B., Clark Coll., 1929; B. D., Gammon Theol. Sem., 1930; A. M., Boston Univ., 1932; Univ. of Chgo., 1932-34; 1939-40; D. D. (hon.), Paine Coll., 1958; m. Imogene Ford; Children--Ellen (Mrs. Joseph Pierce); licensed preacher, Chrstn. Meth. Episc. Ch., 1921; pastor, chs. in Texas, Ga., Mass. and Ill.; dir., Leadership Ed., C. M. E. Ch., 1935-38; dist. supt., Chicago Dist., 5 yrs.; editor, The Christian Index, 1946-54; elected bishop of the C. M. E. Ch., Fifth Episc. Dist. (Ala., Fla., Ghana, Nigeria), 1958--; prof.; Tex. Coll., 1932-35; Missionary to Africa; chrmn., Bd. of Trustees, Miles Coll.; Bd. of Trustees, Phillip's Sch. of Tehol.; v. p., Natl. Fraternal Coun. of Chs.; mem., 1st World Coun. of Chs. Assembly; Natl. Coun. of Chs.; exec. mem., Natl. Conf. on Race and Rel.; Omega Psi Phi; established Historical Lib. of the C. M. E. Ch.; research in field of psychology of religion; chrmn., Public Resolutions C. M. E. Ch.; Home: 308 Tenth Ave., W. Birmingham, Ala.

MURPHY, Maximilian Edward, b. Dallas, Tex., Dec. 4, 1902; s. Robert Louis and Viola (Wiley) M.; St. Augustine Sem., Bay St. Louis, Miss.; St. Patrick's Sem., Menlo Park, Calif.; Charles Univ., Prague Czechoslovakia, 1930-34; ordained priest, Roman Cath. Ch., 1930; dean, Trinidad, B. W. I., 1935--; Canon, Metropolitan Cathedral, Port of Spain, Trinidad, 1961--; chrmn., Aquinas Sponsoring Scholarship Comm.; regular contributor to German language papers; Home and Office: The Presbytery, Chaguanas, Trinidad, British West Indies.

MURPHY, Thurman H., b. Cumberland Co., Jan. 10, 1927; s. Clyde E. and Annie (McDonald) M.; B.S., Fayetteville St. Tchr. Coll., Fayetteville, N.C., 1956; B.D., Hood Theol. Sem., Livingstone Coll., Salisbury, N.C.; m. Ophelia Richardson; Children--Linda Rise, Thurmetta Arlene; pastor, St. Matthews A.M.E.Z. Ch.; Kesler Temple A.M.E.Z. Ch.; currently Franklin Chapel, A.M.E.Z. Ch., Laurinburg, N.C.; mem., State Burial Assn.; Mason; Carpenters Consistory; US Army, 1950-52; mem., Interracial Com., Henderson, N.C.; sec., Interracial Min. Fellowship; chrmn., N.C. Volun. Serv. Program; dir., Vista Training Groups; Home: 359 Grant St., Laurinburg, N.C.; Office: 1103 S. Caledonia Rd., Laurinburg, N.C.

MURRAY, Allen Levi, b. Jenerette, La., Apr. 1, 1903; A.B., B.D., Wilberforce Univ., Payne Theol. Sem., 1926; S.T.M., Western Theol. Sem., Pittsburgh, Pa., 1940; Ph.D., Univ. of Pittsburgh, 1944; m. Ida Page; Children--Mrs. Glenn Abbott; pastor, Afr. Meth. Episc. Chs.; presiding elder, Eastern Dist. of Balto. Annual Conf.; Professional marriage counselor; prof., Religious Ed., Howard Univ., 1946-48; former dean and v.p., Wiley Coll., Marshall, Tex.; former, dean, dir., tchr. ed., Philander Smith Coll.; mem., Ford Found. Fund; present, trustee, Kittrell Coll., Kittrell, N.C.; served as Army chap., and psychologist, 1944-46; Alpha Kappa Mu; Alpha Phi Alpha; author, <u>School Plants and Facilities in Texas Negro Public Schools</u>; <u>Freedom of Wills and Fundamentals of Education</u>; Home: 3706 Garrison Blvd., Balto., Md. 21215

MURRAY, Lindsay Clifton, b. Leesburg, Va., Oct. 24, 1889; s. Bushrod W. & Martha F. (M.); Frelinghuysen Univ., Wash., D.C. (religious training); m. Marguerite J. Carroll; Children--Meredith, Louise, Howard, James, Lindsay, Marguerite, Robert, Eugene; pastor, First Bapt. Ch., Loudoun Co., Va., 1929-61; Morning Star Bapt. Ch., 1936-present; mem., Va. State Bapt. Ed. Congress, 1950-64; North Va. Bapt. Assn., 1929-present; Mt. Bethel Bapt. Assn., 1936; Lott Carey Bapt. Foreign Mission Conv., 1936-present; Bapt. Min. Conf. of D.C.; clerk, US Govt. Printing Office, 1925-46; chap. com. on Community Improvement; mem., Public Interest Civic Assn.; mem., N.E. Fed. Com. on Sanitation; Home: 616 G St., NE Wash., D.C. 20002; Office: 531 T St., NW, Wash., D.C. 20001

MYERS, French Whycliff, Jr., b. Wash., D.C., Oct. 10, 1933; s. French W. and Eleanor B.; courses, Howard Univ., Wash., D.C., 1964; Voice of Prophecy Bible Sch., Los Angeles, Calif., 1966; pastor, St. John Afr. Meth. Episc. Z. Ch., Odenton, Md., 1966-present; Home: 1526 - 10th St., N.W., Wash., D.C. 20001

MURRAY, Chasteen Theophilus, b. Va., Sept. 16, 1887; s. Fountain and Casanda (Mont) M.; A.B., B.D., D.D. (hon.), Va. Sem. and Coll., 1911-18; THM, Zenia Sem., Pittsburgh, 1927-28; m. Sadie Jeneva Reynolds; Children--Chasteen T., Jr., Gregory Carlyle, Rosalyn Jeneva, Windell Contee; James Hamilton, Sadie Evelyn (Mrs. Harold Minor); pastor, Dearington Hill Baptist Church, 1914-1919; Loyal Baptist Church, Danville, Va., 1920-24; Carron Baptist Church, Pittsburgh, Pa., 1925-29; Vermont Ave. Baptist Church, Wash., D.C., 1929-64; mem., Gen. Bd. Natl. Coun. of Chs., Bd. of Dirs., Lott Carey Foreign Mission Conv.; Bd. of Dirs., Coun. of Chs. Natl. Capitol Area; Crime Council-Precinct No. 2, Wash., D.C.; Republican State Committeeman; Mason; former pres., Bapt. Conv., Wash., D.C. and vicinity; Natl. Frat. Coun. of Chs.; Home: 1001 3rd St. SW, Wash., D.C.; Office: 1630 Vermont Ave., NW, Wash., D.C.

MURRAY, Earl, ch. official, b. Lapine, Ala., June 2, 1922; s. William and Maggie (Trotter) M.; B.D., Daniel Payne Sem.; children--Earl, Willie L., Thomas L., Samuel J., Gloria E.; pastor, Eleventh St. Chrstn. Ch.; Pres., Christian Missionary Conv., Jefferson Co., Ala., 1953-63; v.pr., Ala. Chrstn. Missionary Conv., 1957-63 and current pres., 1962--; mem., Bd. of trustees, YWCA, Birmingham, Ala.; chrmn., Auxiliary Bd. Amer. Cast Iron Pipe Co., 1961--; mem., Recommendation Comm., Intl. Conv. of Chrstn. Chs.; US Forces, 1944-46; Home: 10 So. 20th Court St., Birmingtham, Ala.

NABRIT, H. Clarke, sem. prof., b. Augusta, Ga.; s. James M. and Gertrude (West) N.; A.B., Morehouse Coll., 1937; B.D., Crozer Theol. Sem., 1942; D.D. (hon.), Simmons Univ., 1957; m. Vernice Smith; Children--H. Clark, Jr., Barbara Anne, Charles M.; prof., Hurch History, Amer. Bapt. Theol. Sem., 1942; pastor, Ebenezer Bapt. Ch., 1942-45; editor, Young Adult and Senior Quarterlies, 1950-58; current pastor,

First Bapt. Ch., Memphis, Tenn., 1947--; instr., Owen Coll., Memphis, Tenn., 1960-61; dir., Negro Work in Education, Northern Bapt., W. Va., 1946-47; mem., Bd. of Dirs., Natl. Training Sch., Nashville, 1948-60; pres., Memphis Chapter Frontiers of America, 1960-63; chrmn., Legal Redress Comm.; mem., NAACP; chrmn., Freedom Comm., NAACP, Memphis br., 1960--; mem., Omega Psi Phi; Home: 682 So. Lauderdale, Memphis, Tenn. 31805; Office: 807 E. McLemore, Memphis, Tenn. 38106

NEAL, Warren Joseph, b. Columbus, Ohio, Feb. 10, 1921; s. Porter A. and Charlotte (Rivers) N.; B. A., Oakwood Coll., 1949; post-grad. work at La Sierra Coll., 1961, and Andrews Univ., 1962-63; m. Roberta Mae (N.); Children--Brian L. and Warren A.; pastor, Blythe, Calif., 1952-54; present: pastor, Emmanuel S. D. A. Ch., Riverside, Calif., 1954--; youth counselor in jr. camps; Army Air Force, hosp. orderly, 1942-46; Good Conduct Medal, WW II; Home: 7446 Lincoln Ave., Riverside, Calif.; Office: Emmanuel S. D. A. Ch., 2719 - 11th St., Riverside, Calif.

NEALY, Fred Rogers, b. Winter Garden, Fla., Aug. 8, s. Paul and Katie; B. A., Oakwood Coll., Huntsville, Ala., 1952-57; Andrews Univ., Berrien Springs, Mich. (1 yr.); m. Lucia J. Anderson; Children--Judy Faye, Joy Angelia; pastor, Chicamauga Ave. S. D. A. Ch., Atlanta, Ga., 1958-present; sub. tchr., 1961-63; mem., So. Atlanta Conf. S. D. A. Ch., Home: 75 Race St., Charleston, S. C. 29403

NEBBLETT, Milton Elmer, b. Honduras, Central Amer., Jan. 21, 1924; s. Edwin and Lea (Douglin) N.; A. B., Oakwood Coll., Huntsville, Ala., 1950; M. A., Andrews Univ., Berrien Springs, Mich., 1952; m. Ivy S. Tynes; Children--Edwin, Marina, Judith, Milton Jr., pastor, Woodbrook Ch., Trinidad, W. Indies, 1954; youth dir., Guyana Mission S. D. A. Ch., So. Amer., 1956; pastor, Leeward Is. Mission 1957-59, Barbados; youth dir., Caribbean Union of S. D. A. Ch., E. Caribbean, 1960-62; pres., Guyana Mission, S. D. A. Ch., S. Amer., 1963-66; pastor, Juniper Ave. S. D. A. Ch., Fontana, Calif., May 1968-present; Rehabilitation Counselor, L. A. Co., 1966-68; Home: 5383 Rose Ave., Riverside, Calif.; Office: 7347 Juniper Ave., Fontana, Calif. 92335

NELSON, Clarence Theodore Roosevelt, b. Little Rock, Ark., July 5, 1903; s. Duncan William and Lydia (Durant) N.; A. B., Philander Smith Coll., Little Rock, Ark., 1920; B. D., Garrett Theol. Sem., Evanston, Ill., 1932; M. A., Northwestern Univ., Evanston, Ill.; D. D. (hon.), Philander Smith Coll.; 1959; m. Juanita Jackson; Children--Lydia Juanita, Sandra Diane; pastor, Taylor Meth. Ch., Batavia, O., 1932-34; Broaddus Meth. Ch., Springfield, O., 1934-35; Penn. Ave. and Lincoln Heights Meth. Chs., Columbus, O., 1935; Braden Meth. Ch., Toledo, O., 1935-38; Camphor Meml. Meth. Ch., St. Paul, Minn., 1938-47; exec. sec., Lexington Conf. (Meth. Ch.) Bd. of Ed., 1947-52; McKinley Meth. Ch., Dayton, O., 1952-55; supt., The Columbus Dist. of the Lexington Conf., 1955-61; Scott Meml. Meth. Ch., Detroit, Mich., 1961--; dir., Public Relations and correspondent for Meth. Information of the St. Louis Area of the Meth. Ch., 1951-64; Natl. chrmn of Operation Freedom (a Civil rights organization); v. p., Meth. Fed. for Social Action of the Meth. Ch.; co-chrmn., The Religious Freedom Com., Inc.; life mem., The Ohio Pastor's Conv.; former sec., Ohio Coun. of Chs., 1959-61; mem., Phi Beta Sigma; author: The Romance of the Negro and the Meth. Ch. (to be published); Home: 262 E. Boston Blvd., Detroit, Mich., 48202; Office: 609 E. Kirby St., Detroit, Mich. 48202

NELSON, James Herbert, I. b. Ridgeway, S. C., July 7, 1919; s. Warren Julius and Maggie Sarah (Grant) N.; A. B., Johnson C. Smith, 1940; B. D., Johnson C. Smith Univ., 1949; m. Johnalee Barnes; Children--Louise Ja Malla and James Herbert, II; pastor, Congruity Westminster P. Chs.; current pastor, St. Luke U. P. Ch., Orangeburg, S. C.; dir., Westminster Found., S. C. State Coll.; tchr., Sumter Co. pub. schs., S. C.; Morris Coll., Sumter, S. C.; Atlantic Presbytery co-dir., Goodwill Larger Parish, United Presby. Ch., S. C.; mem., S. C. Coun. on Human Relations, Southern Regional Coun. ex. comm. Orangeburg NAACP; S. C. Counc. of br. NAACP; state v. p., NAACP; US Army, WW II, Pacific Theatre, 372nd Inf. Div.; award: Omega Man 9th yr.; mem., Mason, Omega Psi Phi; Home: Box 1574 State Coll., Orangeburg, S. C.; Church: Loman at Amelia, Orangeburg, S. C

NELSON, R. Wendell, b. Charlotte, N. C., Apr. 18, 1916; s. Arthur and Anna May (Stephens) N.; B. A., Pacific

Union Coll., 1941; courses: Univ. of So. Calif., Pacific Sch. of Rel., Loma Linda Univ. and Andrews Univ.; m. Margaret Ellen Perry; Children--Marilynn Elaine, R. Wendell, Jr., Walter Ronald; Regional evangelist, Texico Conf. of the S. D. A. Ch., 1941-45; dist. pastor-evangelist, Lake Region Conf. of S. D. A., 1945-46; pastor-evangelist, North Calif. Conf. of S. D. A., 1946-57; Market St. S. D. A. Ch., Oakland, Calif; present: pastor, Evangelist, So. Calif. Conf. of S. D. A., Sunset Ave. S. D. A. Ch., Pasadena, Calif., 1957--; mem., Conf. Ex. Comms. of Texico Conf., 1945, No. Calif. Conf., 1948-54, So. Calif. Conf., 1959-63; pres., Min. Fellowship, No. Calif. Conf., in Oakland, Calif.; chrmn., Yosemite Nature Camp, 1952-61; mem., So. Calif. Conf. Min. Chorus (2nd Bass Sect.), 1958-present; mem., Southern Harmonious Quartet, 1939-present; Home: 1530 Poppy Peak Dr., Pasadena, Calif.; Office: 1281 Sunset Ave., Pasadena, Calif.

NELSON, William Stuart, univ. v. p., b. Paris, Ky., Oct. 15, 1895; s. William Henry and Emma (Kersands) N.; A. B., Howard Univ., 1920; LL. D. (hon.), 1936; Union Theol. Sem., New York, 1920-21; B. D., Yale Univ., 1924; grad. student, Sorbonne and Prot. Theol. Sem., Paris, 1921-22; Univ. of Marburg and Univ. of Berlin, 1922-23, 25, 26; LL. D. (hon.), Shaw Univ., 1936; LL. D., Daniel Payne Coll., 1962; m. Blanche Louise Wright; instr., Howard Univ., 1924-26; asst. prof., 1926-29; assoc. prof. and asst. to pres., 1929-31; pres., Shaw Univ., Raleigh, N. C., 1931-36; pres., Dillard Univ., New Orleans, La., 1936-40; dean, Sch. of Rel., Howard Univ., 1940-49; dean, 1948-61; v. p., Howard Univ., 1961; US Army, 1st Lt.; Fullbright Research Fellow to India, 1958-59; mem., Conf. on Science, Philosophy and Religion; Fellow Natl. Coun. of Rel. in Higher Ed.; Religious Educational Assn.; Acad. Polit. Science; Omega Psi Phi; Bapt. ed., _The Christian Way in Race Relation_, 1948; ed., _Jour. of Rel. Thought_; lecture at Univs. in India, 1947-48; author: _Bases of World Understanding_, 1949; _La Race Noir Dans La Democratic Americaine_, 1921; contributor: articles to journals; Home: 1722 Varnum St., NW, Wash., D. C. 20011

NESBY, Robert Nathaniel, b. Green Co., Ala., May 3, 1931; s. Robert Nathaniel & Susie Will (N.); A. B., Univ. of Colo., Boulder, Colo.; B. D., Colgate Rochester Div.

Sch., N.Y., 1964; m. Carolyn Brantly Pulliam; Children--Nathaniel Tyrone, Robert Cornell; pastored Bapt. chs., Alliance & Scottsbluff, Nebr., 1953-54; Second Bapt. Ch., Boulder, Colo., 1959-61; pastor, First Inst. Bapt. Ch., Phoenix, Ariz., 1965-present; dean, Western Bapt. Bible Coll., Denver Extension, 1964-65; tchr., Phoenix Valley Coun. of Chs., Leadership Sch.; commercial artist; staff, Biological Sciences Curriculum Study; Boulder, Colo.; illustrator, Wards Sci. Supply House, Rochester, N.Y.; pres., Min. Fellowship, Phoenix Coun. of Chs.; mem. LEAP Commn. (Leadership & Education for the Advancement of Phoenix); mem., Human Relations Commn., (Phoenix); US Air Force, 1951-55; mem., NAACP; Home: 1139 E. Jefferson, Phoenix, Ariz. 85034; Office: 1141 E. Jefferson St., Phoenix, Ariz. 85034

NEWBERRY, Earl Edward, b. Wilcox Co., Ala., June 2, 1918; s. Frank and Mollie Josephine (N.); A.B., Morris Brown Coll., 1951; B.D., Gammon Theol. Sem., 1954; m. Inez Platt; Children--Edward Bernard, Brenda Y., Beucenia D.; organizer, pastor, Trinity Presby. Ch., Decatur, Ga., 1943-56; current pastor, S. Tryon Presby. Ch., Charlotte, N.C., 1958--; princ., pub. sch.; dir., City recreation; leader, Boys Club; pres., Decatur Civic Club, 1953-55; counselor, Housing Projects; mem., Phi Beta Sigma; Home: 2201 English Dr., Charlotte, N.C.; Office: 2616 S. Tryon St., Charlotte, N.C.

NEWBOLD, Robert Thomas, Jr. coll. tchr., b. Miami, Fla., Feb. 26, 1920; s. Robert Thomas, Sr. and Irene (Johnson); A.B., Fla. A & M Univ. 1942; B.D., Theol. Sem., Lincoln Univ., Pa., 1945; M.A., McCormick Theol. Sem., Chgo., 1946; m. Ann Worrell; pastor, Second Presby. Ch., Brunswick, Ga., 1944-46; pastor, Radcliffe Meml. Presbyn. Ch., Atlanta, Ga., 1946-53; pastor, Grace United Presby. Ch., Balto., Md., 1953--; lecturer, Homiletics, Gammon Theol. Sem., Atlanta, Ga., 1948-53; lecturer, Public Relations, Cortez Peters Bus. Sch., Balto., Md., 1955-58; instr., Philosophy, Morgan United Presby. Ch., Balto., Md., 1953--; mem., Bd. of Strategy, Balto. Presby. 1962--; mem. Comm. on Nominations, Balto. Presby. 1962--; Comm. on Race and Rel., Gen. Assembly; mem., Bd. of Dirs., Wilson Leadership Sch., mem. Bd. of Dirs., Balto. Urban League; mem. Bd. of Dirs., Patuxent Institution; mem., Mayor's repr. Steering Comm. Human Renewal Commn.; mem.,

YMCA, NAACP, Urban League, Frontiers of Amer., Citizens Planning and Housing Assn., the Gov.'s Comm. on Juvenile Delinquency, Interdenom. Min. Alliance, Theo. R. McKeldin Republican Club, Northwestern United Protective Assn., Pi Omega Chapter, Omega Psi Phi; Clergy Visiting Staff-Balto. City Hosps., mem. of the Balto. Grand Jury, the Fed. Grand Jury, The Balto. Petty Jury, Natl. Rehabilitation Assn., Adult Ed. Assn.; columnist-Afro-Amer. newspapers, bd. of dirs., Md.-Del. Coun. of Chs., Clergy Coun. of the Urban League, Bd. of Dirs., Balto. Urban League, Bd. of Dirs., Patuxent Inst., the Mayor's repr. Steering Comm. Human Renewal Commn; Home: 3610 Grantley Rd., Balto., Md. Church: Dolphin and Etting Sts., Baltimore, Md.

*NEWBORN, Ernest J., tchr., b. Whiteville, Tenn., Mar. 19, 1927; s. James H. and Josephine (McKinney) N.; A.B., Tenn. State Univ., 1951; B.D., Howard Univ., Sch. of Rel., 1954; Kent State (Ohio) Univ., 1962--; m. Janice Robinson; Children--Ernest J. Jr., Mary-Jo; pastor, Gay-Lee Chrstn. Ch., Nashville, Tenn., 1950-51; chap., Migrant Farm Workers, Pa., N.C., Ohio, 1954-55; pastor, Cherry Chrstn. Ch., Canton, O., 1954-69; asst. pastor, First Congre. Ch., Wash., D.C., 1969--; tchr., Social sci., Canton, O., 1956-69; dean, Chrstn. Sch. of Rel. for Community Leadership Sch., Canton, O.; Bd. mem., YMCA; Ohio Soc. of Chrstn chs.; treas., Canton Leadership Coun.; Adv. bd., Canton Urban League; Stark Co. Min. Assn.; Canton Professional Educators Assn.; Natl. Ed. Assn.; Office: First Congre. Ch., 945 C St., NW, Wash., D.C. 20001

NEWMAN, Omega Franklin, b. Nov. 8, 1930, Latta, S.C., s. Mellon C. and Serena Hamilton (N.); B.S., Claflin Coll., Orangeburg, S.C.; B.D., Gammon Theol. Sem., Atlanta, Ga., 1966; courses, S.C. State Coll., Orangeburg, S.C.; m. Louise Vernell Williams; Children--Cheryl, Gayle Michelle, Karen; pastor, John Wesley U. Meth. Ch., Gresham, S.C., 1956-57; Springfield, 1957-60; Greer, 1960-64; York, 1964; Dir., Bd. of Ed., S.C. Conf., U. Meth. Ch., 1968-present; chap., Migrant Ministry; Parents Coordinator and Consult., York Co., S.C.; Notary Pub., N.C.; mem., Natl. Conf. of Black Meth.; Leader, First Protest, Orangeburg, S.C., May 1954; pres., York br. NAACP, 1965-68; area v.p., State Conf. NAACP, 1967; State Adv. Youth and Coll. Chapters, NAACP, 1967; Ch. Work Comm. Chrmn., 1968;

SCLC State chrmn., 1960, 61, 68; US Army 1950-53; awards, Pacific Theatre Medal; Korean Service Award; United Nations Medal; Rifleman Medal; mem., Mason; Elk; Alpha Phi Alpha; Democrat; pres., York Min. Assn.; v.p., Western York Min. Assn., organizer, Greater Greet Community Civic Club; Natl. Bd. of Ed. U. Meth. Ch.; Natl. Fellowship; Home: 561 King Rd., Orangeburg, S.C.; Office: P.O. Box 2096 State Coll., Orangeburg, S.C.

NICHOLS, Henry H., b. Phila., Pa., June 6, 1916; B.S., S.T.B., Temple Univ., Tchrs. Coll. and Sch. of Theol., 1940, 1941; m. Thelma T. Shaw; pastor, St. Thomas U. Meth. Ch., Frankford, Ky., 1940-47; St. Johns Ch., Spring Lake, N.J. and Bethsaida Meth. Ch., Phila., 1937-40; Janes Meml. U. Meth. Ch., Phila., Pa., 1947-present; mem., Phila. Annual Conf. U. Meth. Ch., 1965-present; Conf. Bd. of Hospitals and Homes; v.p., Bd. of Ed., 1965-present; Co. chrmn., Mayor's Adv. Comm. on Civil Rights; vol. chap., Children's Reception Ctr. (Germantown, Pa.); sponsor, paroles; v.p., Ex. Comm. & Trustee United Fund; Bd. of Dir., United World Federalist Natl. Conf. Chrstns. & Jews; Settlement Music Sch.; Temple Area Community Pool; United Health Ser.; Citizens Bank; Greater Phila. Enterprise Develop't Corp.; Bd. of Commissioners Phila. Fellowship Commn.; Crime Commn. of Phila., Inc.; Natl. Com. of Phila., Inc.; Natl. Com. for the Support of Pub. Schs.; Bd. of Dirs., of Phila. Housing Develop't Corp.; Adv. Comm., The Working Blind Steering Com., Phila., Urban Coalition; honors, "Man of the Year" (Germantown, Dept. of Welfare); Morristown Coll., Distinguished Service; Outstanding service to the people and community, Janes Meml. Meth. Ch.; Achievement Award for civic and religious services; Brotherhood Award, Phila. Club Frontiers Internatl.; Del. Annual Conf. Award for outstanding Chrstn leadership; KYW TV Civic and Religious Leader Annual Interfaith Award of the Men and Women's B'nai Brith Coun. of Greater Phila.; Gen. Alumni Award, Temple Univ.; Community Leadership Award, 59th St. Bapt. Ch.; Distinguished Service in Rel. Ed., Pub. Ed. and Social Action by Va. Union Univ., Alumni Assn.; Bd. of Mgrs. Award, No. Branch YMCA; "Man of the Year" Award, Chrstn St. br. YMCA; Distinguished Serv. Award, Alumni of Fla. A & M Coll.; Cardozo Lodge 400 Brith Sholom Community Service Award; Omnia-Bona, Inc. Citizenship Award; tribute from

Phila. Youth Serv. Award Volunteer Serv., City of Phila.; Del. Conf. Meth. Youth Fellowship, Award for service as Conf. Dir. of Youth Work; Home: 328 W. Earlham Terrace, Phila., Pa. 19144; Office: Janes United Meth. Meml. Ch., Germantown, Pa.

NICHOLS, Roy C., bishop, b. Hurlock, Md., Mar. 19, 1918; s. Roy C. Sr. and Mamie (Waters) N.; A. B., Lincoln Univ., Chester, Pa., 1941; B. D., D. D. (hon.), Pacific Sch. of Rel., Berkeley, Calif., 1947, 1964; D. D. (hon.), Univ. of the Pacific, 1961; m. Ruth Richardson; children--Melisance, Allegra, Nathan; pastor, So. Berkeley Com. Ch., Calif., 1943-46; Downs Meml. Meth. Ch., Oakland, 1949-64; Salem Meth. Ch., NYC, 1964-68; elected president bishop of Pittsburgh area United Meth. Ch., July, 1968; mem., World Coun. Chs. Central Com., 1968; former del., Meth. Gen. Conf., 1960, 1964; Berkeley Bd. of Ed., 1963-64; mem., Alpha Phi Alpha; author, Motivation for a New Age, 1964; Office: 408 Seventh Ave., Pittsburgh, Pa.

*NOISETTE, Ruffin Nichols, b. Summerville, S. C., Mar. 20, 1923; s. Joseph Edward and Louise (Nichols) N.; A. B., Howard Univ., 1946; B. D., 1949; D. D. (hon.), Wilberforce Univ.; m. Thelma Irene Anderson; children--Shelley, Karin, Robin, Louis; asst. dean of chapel, Fisk Univ., 1949-50; pastor, Ebenezer Afr. Meth. Episc. Ch., Rahway, N. J., 1950-51; Bethel A. M. E. Ch., Wilmington, Del., 1951--; volunteer rel. instr., Ferris Sch. for delinquent boys, Wilm., 1958-61; Woodshaven Kruse Sch. for Delinquent Girls, 1961-62; pres., Wilmington Ministerium, 1955-57; pres., Wilmington Coun. of Chs., 1959-61; mem., Bd. of Dirs., Walnut St. br. YMCA, Wilmington, 1962--; Outstanding Citizen Award, 1959; Red Cross Outstanding Service Certificate, 1957; mem., NAACP; YMCA; Alpha Phi Alpha; Boy Scouts of Amer.; Mayor's Comm. on Housing; Bi-Racial Comm.; Home: 905 N. Rodney St., Wilmington, Del. 19806; Office: Walnut St., Wilmington, Del. 19801

NOLEN, Benjamin Julius, b. Camden, Ariz., Sept. 25, 1910; s. Ben and Arrilla Lilly N.; A. B., Wilberforce Coll.; B. D., Daniel Payne Theol. Sem.; D. D. (hon.), Wilberforce Univ., Allen Univ., Kittrell Coll., Shorter Coll., Daniel Payne Coll.; LL. D. (hon.), Campbell Coll., Daniel Payne Coll.; D. LLt. (hon.). Campbell Coll.: m. Cleo Mildred Childers; Children--Esther (Mrs. Samuel A.

Baldwin, Benjamin J. Jr., Barbara (Mrs. James Buchanan); pastored, Afr. Meth. Episc. Ch. in Ohio, Ark., W. Va., Penna., Miss., Ala., Ga., 1956-64; editor, A. M. E. Chrstn. Recorder; current pastor, A. M. E. Ch., Topeka, Kans.; dean, Shorter Coll., N. Little Rock, Ark.; Campbell Coll., Jackson, Miss.; pres., Leavenworth br., NAACP; mem., Masons, Elks, Odd Fellows, Kappa Alpha Psi; author, The Place of Preaching in the Christian Ministry; Office: 511 7th St., Topeka, Kans.

*NORMAN, Clarence, b. Goldsboro, N. C., Apr. 30, 1930; s. Doniver and Viola Archer; B. A., Bloomfield Coll., N. J., 1959; B. D., Howard Univ., Sch. of Rel., Wash., D. C., 1964; grad. courses, Long Island Univ., Bklyn, N. Y., 1960; m. Ellen Harrell; Children--Clarence, Jr., Edward James; pastor, First Bapt. Ch., Williamsburg, Inc., Brooklyn, N. Y., 1953-present; tchr., NYC pub. sch.; tchr., Whitelaw Reid Jr. High Sch., Bklyn, N. Y.; chrmn., Liberty Civic Assn.; mem., Exec. Com., Queens Co. Liberal Party; the independent candidate for State Senator in 1964; mem., Bd. of Dir., Youth in Action, the Anti-Poverty Agency, Bedford-Stuyvesant; chrmn., Adv. Com., NY Bapt. Assn., mem., Progressive Natl. Bapt. Conv.; Home: 214-11 110th Ave., Queens Village, N. Y. 11429

NORRIS, Hills Edward, b. Columbia, S. C., Mar. 15, 1927; s. Hills and Lottie B.; A. B., Benedict Coll., 1960; B. D., Starks Sch. of Theol., 1962; S. T. M. Interdenom. Theol. Center, Atlanta, Ga., 1966; m. Helen Johnson; Children--Kenneth Earl, Karl Edward; pastored Bapt. Chs., So. Carolina, Florida, 1949-64; chap., Dept. Corrections; Veterans Admin., Otun, N. C., 1964-present; former advisor, NAACP Youth 1950 and 60, Columbia, S. C.; mem., Natl. Acad. of Rel. & Mental Health Assn.; chrmn., Interfaith Comm. on Housing & Com. on Ed. Affairs of Ashville, Human Rel. Coun.; mem., Nat. Com. of Negro Churchmen; Progressive Bapt. Conv.; US Army 1946-48; Public Service certificate, March of Dimes, Columbia, S. C.; Home: Apt. 6-D, Veterans Drive, Otun, N. C.; Office: 124 Veterans Admin. Hosp., Otun, N. C.

NORTHCUTT, Robert Robinson; Prairie View Univ.; Perkins Sch. of Theol.; Chrstn. Meth. Episc. Chs., 32 yrs.; current pastor, Be Bee Tabernacle C. M. E. Ch., 1950--; mem., Interdenom. Min. Alliance; Houston Min.

Alliance; Houston Min. Assn. of Greater Houston; treas., The Tex. Annual Conf.; The Judiciary Court of the C. M. E. Ch.; Alumni Assn. of Texas Coll., Tyler, Tex.; Trustee and Exec. mem., Tex. Coll.; instr., Pastor's Sch. 10 yrs.; mem., Long Range Planning Com., C. M. E. Ch.; mem., United Fund and the Red Cross Comm., YMCA; Office: BeBee Tabernacle C. M. E. Ch., 822 W. Dallas Ave., Houston, Tex.

NORWOOD, John Fredrick, ch. official, b. Darlington, S. C., Nov. 28, 1927; s. John Ruben and Benzena (Mc Curry) N.; B. A., Claflin Coll., Orangeburg, S. C., 1951; B. D., Gammon Theol. Sem., Atlanta, Ga., 1957; m. Zanthia L. Bush; Children--John Fredrick Jr., Iris Regina; served four charges in S. C. and one charge in the Central Ala. Conf. of The Meth. Ch., 1951-56; Dist. supt., The Huntsville Dist., The Meth. Ch., Huntsville, Ala.; mem., Exec. Com., General Bd. of Lay Activities of The Meth. Ch.; del., Jurisdictional Conf. of the Central Jurisdiction, Meth. Ch.; mem., Gen. Bd. of Missions of The Meth. Ch.; prin., Hickman Elem. Sch., Kershaw Co., Camden, S. C.; volunteer chap., Macon Co. Jail, 1957-62; mem., NAACP; Tuskegee Civic Assn.; Ala. Provisional Coun. of Chs., Exec. Com., Citizen Service Com., Huntsville, Ala.; The Voters League; award: "Ruptured Duck." mem., Mason; Madison Co. Mental Assn.; Min. Alliance; Home: 1605 Armstrong St. NW, Huntsville, Ala.; Office: PO Box 1454, Huntsville, Ala.

NUTTER, Homer Eckler, b. Harrison Co., Ky., Mar. 9, 1895; s. Harrison and Amelia; A. B., B. D., Simmons Univ., Louisville, Ky., 1922, 1926; D. D. (hon.), Simmons Univ.; m. Ida Coleman; pastor, First Bapt. Ch., Lexington, Ky., 1926-present; officer, Gen. Assn. of Negro Bapt. Ky. (26 yrs.); moderator (9 yrs.); present, treas., Lexington & Fayette Counseling Bd. mem.; Lexington Red Cross; Adv. Bd. Fayette Co. Children's Assn.; chrmn of bd. of trustees, Lexington Colored Orphans Home; v. chrmn. Bd. of Regents, Ky. State Coll.; v. chrmn., bd. of trustees Simmons Univ.; rec. sec., Consolidated Dist. Assn.; mem., Lexington Cham. of Commerce; Lexington Com. on Rel. & Human Rights; former pres., Lexington Min. Alliance; Bd. United Community Fund; Home: 407 No. Upper St., Lexington, Ky. 40508; Office: 266 E. Short Street, Lexington, Ky. 40507

OATES, Bernard Dennis, b. Neptune, N. J., July 2, 1941; s. Caleb Eugene and Arthella R.; (O.); B. A., Lincoln Univ., Pa. 1963; Crozer Theol. Sem., Chester, Pa., 1963-65; m. Doris Frederick; Children--Anita Charlotte; asst. pastor, Bethany Bapt. Ch., Famingdale, N. J.; probation officer, Freehold, N. J.; mem., Neighborhood Coun., Anti-Poverty Program, Omega Psi Phi; Home: Rte 1, Box 115, West Farms Rd., Farmingdale, N. J. 07727

OATES, Caleb E., b. Shelby N. C., Apr. 6, 1917; s. David Pilgrim and Emma Ethel; courses, Union Theol. Sem., 1946-7; NY Sch. of Business, 1937-39; m. Authelia R. Walker; Children--Bernard D., David C.; pastor, Bethany Bapt. Ch., Farmingdale, N. J., 1947-present; purchaser, US Govt., 1941-57; mem., adv. bd. of Planned Parenthood, 1957-67; Ex. bd. mem., Monmouth Community Action Program, 1964-67; v. moderator, Seacoast Missionary Assn., 1966-67; chrmn., Neighborhood Coun., 1964-67; US Army, 1943-46, Asst. chap. Bronze Star Medal, 5 Battle Stars; Afro-Amer. Award, 1954; Publication Certificate of Merit, Jewish War Veterans, US Amer., 1961; author, The Deacon and His Work; Home: RFD 1, Box 116A, Farmingdale, N. J. 07727; Office: Bethany Bapt. Ch., Farmingdale, N. J.

OBEY, Edward Rudolph, b. Olivia, N. C., Dec. 2, 1927; s. James Edward and Viola (Johnson) O.; 1944-48, B. A., Johnson C. Smith Univ., Charlotte, N. C.; 1948-51, B. D. (Theol.); m. Elizabeth Ann Frazier; Children--Vickie Lynn, Valerie DeAnna, Veronica Elizabeth; 1951-53, pastor, Lenoir N. C. and Morganton, Lenoir and Morganton Presby. Chs.; 1953-Aug. 1955, Lincolnton and Shelby No. Carolina (Presby. Chs.); dir., Friendship House, Lackawanna, N. Y.; 1959-Oct. 1960, assoc. pastor, Bethel Presby. Ch., Lackawanna, N. Y.; pastor, 1960--; Cherry Hill Community Presby., Balto., Md.; mem., Balto., Md. Coordinating Coun. of Cherry Hill; Big Bros. of Balto., Synod Westminster Found. Comm., Min. Alliance of Baltimore, Inner City Coun.; Omega Psi Phi; Home: 2516 Terra Firma Rd., Balto., Md. Church: 819 Cherry Hill Rd., Balto., Md.

ODEN, Hobart Edward, b. Birmingham, Ala., June 7, 1918; s. Hobart and Emma Jane O.; A. B., Miles Coll., 1940; M. S., Ala. A & M Coll., 1964; Children--Hobart Edward, III; dean, Greenville Indus. Coll., Greenville

Miss., 1940-41; prin., New Convert Jr. High Sch., Maplesville, Ala., 1941-42; asst. pastor, Sixteenth St. Bapt. Ch., Birmingham, Ala., 1954-66; presént pastor, Forty Fifth St. Bapt. Ch., Birmingham, Ala; present Boy's Advisor, Carver High Sch., Birmingham, Ala.; mem., Birmingham Min. Conf.; Ala. Bapt. State Conv.; Natl. Bapt. Conv., USA, Inc.; mem., Birmingham Progressive Ed. Assn.; Ala. State Tchrs. Assn.; Natl. Ed. Assn.; Armed Forces, 1942-45; Mason; Home: 1132 North 24th Ave., Birmingham, Ala.

OFFUTT, Garland Kimble, b. Louisville, Ky., May 9, 1908; s. Elmore Theval and Joeanna (Kimble) O.; student, Morehouse Coll., 1930; B. A., Ky. State Coll., 1936; student, Simmons Univ., 1931-32; B. Th., Southern Bapt. Sem., 1945; M. Th., 1948; D. Th.; D. D. (hon.), Simmons Univ., 1954; m. Katherine Wilson; Children--Garland Kimble Jr., Annett; pastor, Bracktown Bapt. Ch., Bracktown, Ky., 1932-37; New Hope Bapt. Ch., Ashland, Ky., 1938-43; moderator, Consolidate Assn., 1938-43; dean, Amer. Bapt. Theol. Sem., Nashville, Tenn., 1944-45; pastor, W. Chestnut St. Bapt. Ch., Louisville, Ky., 1948-present; prof., Biblical Theol., Simmons Univ., 1946-present; regional repr., Fund for Theol. Ed. Inc., pres., Ky. Bapt. State Cong., 1960-65; chrmn., Ky. Amer. Bapt. Rel. Pub. House, 1960-present; pres., Natl. Bapt. Progressive Cong. of Chrstn. Ed., 1960-present; mem., Foreign Missn. Bureau, Progressive Natl. Bapt. Conv., 1961-present; mem., Family Welfare Bd., 1956-57; NAACP, 1957-61; v. p., Central Area Community Action, 1962-present; Bd. mem., Ky. SCLC; mem., Planning Com., Louisville Conf. on Rel. & Race, 1962-63; Phi Beta Sigma; Mason; Home: 1131 Cecil Ave., Louisville, Ky.

*OGLESBY, Jacob C., b. May 13, 1918; s. John and Ida Mae; A. B., Lane Coll., 1940; M. A., B. D., Howard Univ., Sch. of Rel., 1942, 44; D. D. (hon.), Birmingham Bapt. Coll., 1963; m. Anne H.; courses for Th. D., Sch. of Rel., Boston Univ., 1963; m. Anne H. Harris; Children--2 sons; chap., Fla. Normal and Indus. Coll., 1944; tchr., Lane Coll., 1945-47; pastor, Bapt. Ch., Tenn., 2 yrs.; Fla. 3 yrs.; current pastor, Christ Bapt. Ch., Detroit, Mich., 1956--; Bd. mem., Detroit Coun. of Chs.; Great City Projects for New Schools; awards: NAACP award; "Minister of the Week" (Mich. Chronicle), 1963; presented plaque for Community Service by Eta Phi

Beta Sorority, 1964; dean, Bapt. Training Sch.; past pres., Bapt. Min. Conf. of Detroit and Vicinity; mem., Commn. for Establishment of a Seminary for Detroit (Detroit Coun. of Chs.); Alpha Phi Alpha; Home: 4428 Burns St., Detroit, Mich.; Office: 3544 Iroquois Ave., Detroit, Mich.

OLIVER, Archie S., Jr.; b. Oct. 5, 1917, DeSota, Mo.; s. Archie S. Sr. and Daisy (McSpadd); B.S. Univ. of Wis., 1947; M.A., N.W. Univ., 1953; courses: Univ. of Wis., 1938-41; Chgo. Tchrs. Coll.; Howard Univ. Sch. of Rel., 1968--; m. Gladys A. Byrd; Frances M. Fulton; Children--Archie Lee, Darlene, Frances F., Ashby; asst. pastor, Mt. Zion Bapt. Ch., Madison, Wis., 1939; Calvary Bapt. Ch., Milwaukee, 1944-50; Mt. Zion Missionary Bapt. Ch., Evanston, Ill., 1951-52, 1954-68; pastor, "Happy Club" (Sunday ch. for the trainable mentally retarded) 1950-68; pastor, Johnson Chapel, Jr. Rehab. Nursing Home, Chgo., Ill., 1966-68; assoc. pastor, Ingram Congre. United Ch. of Christ, Wash., D.C., Oct. 1968-June 1969; tchr., mentally handicapped, 1947-63; asst. dir., N. Shore Summer Play Sch. (mentally handicapped), 1952-57; hd. tchr., Research Pilot Project on the Trainable Mentally Handicapped Child, Champaign-Urbana, Univ. of Ill., 1953-54; tchr. Americanization Program, Chgo. Bd. of Ed. to Spanish-speaking Adults, 1961-67; instr., part-time, YMCA Comm. Coll., Chgo., Ill., 1965-68; Coun., Chgo. Bd. of Ed., 1962-64; tchr. illiterates, Welfare Program, Chgo. Bd. of Ed., 1962-64; Coun. and tchr., Fed. Defenders Program, Chgo., 1967-68; Program Cons., Aurora, Ill., United Cerebral Assn. of Greater Chgo.; Area Coordinator, Chg. Bd. of Ed., Neighborhood Youth Corps; Sept. 1965-Apr. 1966; Sch. Comm. Coordinator, Chgo. Bd. of Ed., Manierre Elem. Sch. Dist. 7; sup., Mentally Retarded Programs, Glenview, Ill. Bd. of Ed., 1964-65; Parent Comm. Coordinator, Motley Girls Social Adjustment Sch., Chgo., Ill.; Instr., Howard Univ., Wash., D.C.; field work sem. for Observation and Participating Student Tchrs. Feb. 1969-June 1969; mem., Mayor's Commn on Human Rights, Milw., Wis., 1948-50; sec.-treas., v.p., pres., YMCA Men's Club, Chgo., Ill; Neighborhood Commissioner Boy Scouts Coun.; chrmn., Community Fund Dr., Evanston, Ill., 1950-51; co-chrmn. CARE Drive; mem., Glencoe, Ill. Bd. of Human Relations, Glencoe, Ill., 1961-62; Glencoe Rec. Adv. Bd., Glencoe, Ill., 1963-65; Bd. of Dirs., "The Lambs" (semi sheltered Workshop for Mentally Retarded Young Adults) Chgo., 1962-65; Adv. Bd. Evanston Towship High Sch. Dad's Club, 1958-60; awards: Human Relation Award, Evanston Coun. on Human Relations, 1954; Outstanding tchr. of Mentall Retarded for the city of Chgo., Chgo. Coun. for Exceptional Children; Home: 3060 16th St., NW, Wash., D. C. 20009; Office: Howard Univ., Sch. of Rel., Wash., D. C. 20001

OLIVER, Jesse M., b. Pulaski Co., Mar. 10, 1900; s. Henry and Mary (Taylor) O.; Ark. Bapt. Coll., Little Rock, Ark., 1930-42; Bishop Coll. Inst.; D. D. (hon.), 1937; m. (deceased); Children--Jesse, Jr.; pastor, First Bapt. Ch., Sweet Home, Ark., 1938-59; Maccedonia Bapt. Ch., England, Ark., 1937-42; Centennial Bapt. Ch., Hensley, Ark., 1932-59; St. John Bapt. Ch., Little Rock, 1942-59; St. James Bapt. Ch., Ft. Smith, Ark., 1959--; Boy Scouts of Amer., 1950--; mem., Mason; Home: 3324 Broadway, Little Rock, Ark. 72206; Office: 701 So. 6th St., Ft. Smith, Ark.

OLIVER, Leonard James, administrator, b. Lake Charles, La., Oct. 12, 1923; s. James Lawrence and Mathielde (Rochon) O.; St. Augustine's Sem., 1939-41; St. Mary's Sem., Techny, Ill., 1942-46; St. Augustine's Sem., Phil. and Theol., 1946-52; M. A., Cath. Univ. of Amer., 1961; asst. dean of students, St. Augustine's Sem., Bay St. Louis, Miss., 1952-56; Head dean, St. Augustine's, 1956--; mem., Natl. Bd. of Ed., Society of the Divine Word (S. V. D.); Natl. Cath. Educational Assn.; Miss. Ed. Assn.; Nat's Assn. of Secondary Sch. Principals; M. A. Thesis: "History of the Origin and Development of Saint Augustine's Seminary;" Home and Office: Ullman Ave., Bay St. Louis, Miss. 39520

OLIVER, William Raoul, tchr., educator, b. New Orleans, La., Aug. 27, 1928; s. Henry J. and Iola V. (Duvernay) O.; M. A., Soc. Sci., Cath. Univ. of Amer.; Xavier Univ.; instr., Seminary Divine Word Fathers, Riverside, Calif., 1959-60; asst. dir., Holy Rosary Inst., 1960-62; dir., Holy Rosary Inst., 1962--; Home and Office: Holy Rosary Inst., PO Box 2219, Lafayette, La.

OSLEY, William Edgar, b. Dallas, Tex., Aug. 27, 1932; s. Edgar Sr. and Luella (Wilkerson) O.; Prairie View A & M Coll., Prairie View, Tex.; m. Gloria Mitchell; pastor, St. Michael Ch. of Christ, 1965-present; M/Sgt.

US Army, 1947-60; Good Conduct Medal; Mason; Home: 258 S. 7th St., Newark, N.J. 07103; Office: St. Michael Ch. of Christ, Newark, N.J.

OWEN, Samuel Augustus, b. Stanton, Tenn., July 21, 1886; s. Henry Clay and Fannie (Ware) O.; Roger Williams Univ., Nashville, Tenn.; Walden Univ., Nashville, Tenn.; A.B., Atlanta Bapt. Coll., 1911; M.A., Morehouse Coll., Atlanta, Ga., 1922; D.D. (hon.), Roger Williams Univ., 1922; grad. work, Divinity Sch., Univ. of Chgo, 1920-35; m. Mary Jane Wood; Children--Samuel Augustus, Jr.; tchr., Fla. Inst., Live Oak, Fla., 1912-17; pres., Fla. Meml. Coll., Live Oak, Fla.; pastor, Jethro Bapt. Ch., 1913-16; pastor, Mt. Bethel Bapt. Ch., Daytona Beach, Fla. 1917-20; pres., Roger Williams Coll., Nashville, Tenn., 1920-23; pastor, Metropolitan Bapt. Ch., Memphis, Tenn., 1923-63; moderator, W. Tenn. B.M. & E. Assn., 1928-61; pres., Tenn. Bapt. M. & E. Conv., Inc., 1936-63; chrmn., Bd. of Dirs., Griggs Business Coll.; chrmn., Bd. of Dirs., Owen Jr. Coll.; v. chrmn., Bd. of Trustees, LeMoyne Coll., Memphis; v.p.-at-large, Natl. Bapt. Conv., Inc., 1953-57; designated Minister of the Year in Memphis, 1953; US Army chap., WW II, 1942-44, Capt.; mem., Mason; Odd Fellows; Knights of Pythians; Republican; Phi Beta Sigma; Home: 761 Walker Ave., Memphis, Tenn.; Office: 767 Walker Ave., Memphis, Tenn.

*OWENS. Chester Howard, b. Huntington, Tenn., July 27, 1902; s. Alonzo and Corrine; S.C. State Coll., 1933; B.D., Howard Univ., Sch. of Rel., 1936; B.D., Va. Sem. and Coll., 1946; m. Edlyn Elaine Bentley; pastor, Mt. Zion Bapt. Ch., Fredericksburg, Va., 1933-39; High St. Bapt. Ch., Danville, Va., 1939-49; Zion Bapt. Ch., Reading, Pa., 1949--; chap., Wernersville State Hosp., Wernersville, Pa., 1963--; dean, Dept. of Rel., Wernersville State Hosp.; deceased 8/13/68.

PAIGE, Charles Thomas, professor, b. Phoebus, Va., Sept. 25, 1911; s. Charles Henry and Ethel (Webb) P.; A.B., Hampton Inst.; B.D., Va. Union Univ.; current student for S.T.D., Temple Univ.; m. Mary Elizabeth Manning; Children--Milton Thaddeus, Helen Elizabeth, Jeanette Claire, Sarah Ethel, Inena Mae, Carlena Faye, Vivian Jo-Ann, Robert Charles; instr., Rel. & Acting, chrmn., of Religion Dept., Bishop Coll., Marshall, Tex.

coll. minister and chrmn. of rel., Owen Coll., Memphis, Tenn.; pastor, Riverview Chrstn. Ch.; chap., Western State Hosp.; tchr., Shelby Co., Tenn.; Gloucester and Warwick Counties, Va.; chrmn., Bd. of Helping Hand Assn., 1958-60; bus. mgr., Zuber Bymun Coun., 1960-62; mem., Kappa Alpha Psi; Chap. Western State Hosp.; Home: 1120 So. Lauderdale St., Memphis, Tenn.; Office: 1982 Riverside Blvd., Memphis, Tenn.

PAIGE, Walter Ellis, b. Green Bay, Va., Feb. 8, 1914; s. Edward and Minnie; A.B., Morgan State Coll., D.D. (hon.), Lynchburg, Sem.; m. Irene Woods; pastor, Faith Bapt. Ch., Balto., Md., 1955-present; mem., NAACP; YMCA; Mason, Bd. mem., Advanced Saving & Loan Assn.; Lynchburg Sem. and Coll.; Bapt. Aged Home of Md.; Home: 3110 Liberty Heights Ave., Balto., Md. 21215; Office: 833 N. Bond St., Balto., Md. 21205

*PAIR, James David, b. Wake County, N.C., Aug. 31, 1873; s. Harmon and Alie (Lassates) P.; A.B., Shaw Univ., 1898; B.D., Howard Univ. Sch. of Rel., 1911; m. Lula N. Thornton; Children--Clarence A., James M., Hubert B., Lois, Harmon E.; ordained Bapt. min., 1912; pastor, chs., Va. and Md., 1912-58; retired, 1958; mem., Federation Civic Assn., 1924--; sec., N.C. Bapt. Sun. Sch. Conv., 1897-1904; v.p., D.C. Bapt. Sun. Sch. Conv., 1906-10; pres., Wash., D.C. Congress of Parents and Tchrs., 1932-34; mem., chrmn., D.C. Selective Serv. Draft Bd., 1940-45; mem. and sec., D.C. Selective Draft Bd., 1948-64; financial dir., D.C. Natl. Congress of Colored Parents and Tchrs (Atlanta, Ga.); spec. awards from Presidents, Truman, Eisenhower, Kennedy for service to the nation in selective service sys., 1940-63; mem., Mason; former v.p., Interdenom. Min. Alliance, Wash., D.C.; pastor-emeritus, First Bapt. Ch., No. Brentwood, Md.; Home: 745 Girard St., Wash., D.C. 20001

PARHAM, Thomas David, b. Mar. 21, 1920, Newport News, Va.; s. Thomas David and Edith S. (P.); A.B., N.C. Coll., Durham, N.C.; S.T.B., S.T.M., Western Theol. Sem., Pittsburgh, Pa.; grad. courses, N.C. Coll. Grad. Sch., Univ. of Pittsburgh, Univ. of Chgo., Univ. of Calif.; Univ. of R.I.; certificate, marriage counseling, Menninger Found., Topeka, Kan.; m. Marion Cordice; Children--Edith Evangeline, Mae Marion, Thomas David

III; pastor, Butler Meml. Presby. Ch., Younstown, O., 1944-50; Navy chap., 1944-46; 1951-present; asst. to Chief of Naval Personnel for Human Relations and asst. to Chief of Chaplains for Plans, present; mem., Mahoning Presby. Com. on Chrstn. Ed.; examiner in Hebrew; Mayor's Com. on Indus. Relations; faculty Synod of Ohio (Presby.) summer conf. and camps, Bethany Coll.; Coll. of Wooster; Camp Zion; Office: Dept. of the Navy, Bureau of Naval Personnel, Wash., D.C. 20370

PARIS, William A., b. Monessen, Pa., May 18, 1923; s. John Wesley Banks (stepfather) and Mildred Agnes (P.); N.Y. Sch. of Theol., 1955; Boston Theol. Sem., 1959; Hartford Sem. Found., 1962; Purdue Univ., 1965; m. Rosemarie Tyler; Children--Stephen Michael, Patricia Maria; pastor, Goodwill Afr. Meth. Episc. Z. Ch., Riverhead, N.Y., 1957-58, 1960-61; Rush A.M.E.Z. Ch., Cambridge, Mass., 1958-60; Redeemer A.M.E.Z. Ch., Gary, Ind., 1964-present; Regional Bd. of dirs., NAACP, 1966-67; Hosp. and Police Chap., (Gary), 1957-present; US Army, 1943-46; awards, European Theater (2 bronze stars); Croix de Guerre; European Theater (Arrow Head); mem., Mason; Human Relations Commn.; Adv. Coun. to Mayor Hatcher (Gary); Home: 1306 Jackson St.; Office: 1300 Jackson St., Gary, Ind. 46407

PARKER, Arthur John, b. Daytona Beach, Fla., Dec. 23, 1926; s. Arthur L. and Ella M. (P.); B. Mus. Modern Sch. of Music; B.D. Hood Sem., Livingstone Coll.; m. Evelena Lee; Children--Michelle, D.; 1950-61, US Patent Office, Wash., D.C.; 1953-61, concert soloist; asst. pastor Trinity A.M.E.Z. Ch.; student pastor, Hood Meml. A.M.E.Z. Ch., Belmont, N.C.; present, presiding elder, St. Croix, Virgin Is.; missionary pastor, US Virgin Is. for A.M.E.Z. Ch.; 1945-46, US Army; mem., NAACP; Ministerial Assn.; Home: No. 3, Richmond, PO Box 1137 C'sted, St. Croix, Virgin Is.

*PARKER, Charles Edward, b. Annapolis, Md., Oct. 18, 1923; s. John Wesly and Carrie (Parker) P.; B.S. Ed., Wilberforce Univ., O., 1953; M.S. Ed., Loyola Coll., Balto., Md., 1957; B.D., Howard Univ., Sch. of Rel., 1960; m. Joan Isaacs; Children--Tanya, Toxcy, JoAnn; tchr., Kittrell Coll., Pastor, Galatia Afr. Meth. Episc. Ch., Nashville, N.C., 1953-55; ex. officer, Service Co., US Army and betweeen 1955 and 1957 did grad. study at Loyola Coll, Balto., Md. and worked at N.C.

Mutual Ins. Co.; pastor, Ebenezer A. M. E. Ch., Wash., D. C., 1957-60; Eastminster-Woodville Interracial Parish, Richmond, Va., 1961-63; current, Bethel Presby. Ch., Alexandria, Va.; trustee, Wilberforce Univ. Found.; mem., Church and Civil Rights Comm., Presbytery of the Potomac; Adv. Bd., YMCA, Alexandria, Va.; Chrstn. Ed. Com., Hanover Presbytery, Richmond, Va.; US Army, 2nd Lt., Inf. and Engineer Corps, 1953-55; Republican; mem., Omega Psi Phi; Zeta Sigma Phi; Sen Mer Rhek; pres., Zeta Sigma Phi; mem., NAACP; Home: 605 So. Fayette St., Alexandria, Va.; Office: 634 No. Patrick St., Alexandria, Va.

PARKER, Fred William, b. Tampa, Fla., Dec. 18, 1924; s. William and Amanda (P.); A. B., Oakwood Coll., 1949; m. Mildred P.; Children--Fred W., Willie Samuel, Walter Wayne, Yvonne; pastor, S. D. A. Ch., Fayetteville, N. C.; sub. tchr., elem. sch.; US Navy, 1944-46; Home: 1874 Gola Dr., Fayetteville, N. C.; Office: 330 Old Wilmington Rd., Fayetteville, N. C.

PARKER, Lynnwood, ch. official, b. Arrow Rock, Mo., June 19, 1920; s. Henry and Sophia P.; B. S., Univ. of Nebr., 1948; M. S., Univ. of Omaha, 1951; B. D., Gammon Theol. Sem., 1958; Univ. of Nebr., 1959-60; m. Gertrude Elizabeth Jones; Children--Lynnette; exec. sec., Central West Conf. Bd. of Ed., St. Louis, Mo., 1958--; pastor, Clark Meth. Ch., McMinnville, Tenn., 1955-58; tchr., English & Social Studies, Chrispus Attucks High Sch. in Adult Ed. Dept., Indianapolis, Ind., 1954-55; dir. of guidance, Wash. Tech. High Sch. and sub. tchr. in English and Social Studies, Adult Ed. Dept., St. Louis, Mo., 1952-53; ex. sec., Urban League, Lincoln, Nebr.; ed., The Omaha Star (weekly newspaper), Omaha, Nebr., 1950-51; Boys counselor, Boys Town, Nebr.; Battalion Adj., The Infantry Sch., Ft. Benning, Ga., 1944; Chrstn. Ed. in all Central Jurisdiction Chs. in the states of Mo., Kan., Colo., Nebr., Ill., Iowa; Bd. of Mgrs. and Dean of St. Louis Area Leadership Sch.; mem., Gen. Comm. on Family Life of the Meth. Ch.; Interconference Commn. on Student Work of Mo.; Greater Kans. City Metro. Area Planning Com.; Mo. Coun. of Chs.; set up workshops and clinics and provide camping and conference opportunities for youth and young adults; former mem., Nebr. Comm., White House Conference on Children & Youth; Lincoln, Nebr.: Mayor's Comm. on Human Relations; Nebr. Social Action Coun.; Nebr. State Parole Bd.;

Natl. Meth. Scholarship Award; mem., Alpha Phi Alpha; Mason; Home: 4324 Marcus St., St. Louis, Mo.; Office: 4903 Delmar Blvd., Suite 201, St. Louis, Mo.

*PARKER, Sidney Bayne, tchr., b. Jamaica, West Indies, July 13, 1922; s. Luther Augustus and Rachel (Salmon) P.; Mico T. Coll., 1941-43; B.D., Howard Univ. 1945-52; B.S., 1949; M.A. 1953; Louisiana State M.S., 1954; Nashotah House, Wis., 1960; Gen. Theol. Sem., NYC, S.T.B. 1961; m. Bernice Eleanor Martin; Children--Philip Sidney, Cynthia Victoria Elaine; high sch. tchr., Jamaica 1944-45; mem., Amer. Univ. faculty in social sci., 1952-53; vicar, St. Michael's Episc. Ch., Baton Rouge, La., 1953-57; Montclair, N.J., 1957-61; rector, Trinity Episc. Ch., Montclair, 1961--; sub. tchr., high schs., E. Orange, N.J.; mem., Bd. of Trustees, Visiting Nurse Assn. of Montclair; mem., Mayor's Comm., United Nations; pres. of Student Behaviour Comm., Montclair; instr., Leland Coll., Baker, La., 1954-57; mem., The Fellowship of the Inst. for Rel. & Social Studies; Home: 43 Gates Ave., Montclair, N.J.; Office: 19 No. Willow St., Montclair, N.J.

PARKER, Walter Procter Hall, b. Philadelphia, Pa., Sept. 23, 1919; s. William Edward and Blanche Hall; B.S., Temple Univ. 1938-41; S.T.B., Temple Univ., 1943-45; m. Christine Rider; Children--Carolyn, Janet, William, Gloria; vicar, Chapel of the Ascension, West Chester, Pa. and St. Cyrill's Chapel, Coatesville, Pa., 1946-50; priest-in-charge, St. Philip's Ch., Syracuse, N.Y., 1950-54; rector, The Ch. of The Holy Cross, Pittsburgh, Pa., 1954; youth advisor, Diocese of Central N.Y., Syracuse, N.Y., 1952-54; ex. coun., Diocese of Pittsburgh, Pa., 1957-60; mem., Pittsburgh Bd. of Dirs., Lemington Ave. for the Aged, Pittsburgh, Pa.; Homewood-Brushton Community Improvement Assn.; Homewood-Brushton Renewal Coun.; Religious Adv. Comm.; Planned Parenthood Assn.; Negro Foster Home Adoption Comm.; Family and Children's Service; 1962 Simon Gratz Distinguished Service Award; mem., Omega Psi Phi; NAACP; Frontiers of Amer.; Mason; Home: 7507 Kelly St., Pittsburgh, Pa.

PARKS, Lyman S., b. Mar. 12, 1917, Princeton, Ind.; s. Madison and Minnie E. (P.); A.B., Wilberforce Univ., Wilberforce, O., 1944; Payne Theol. Sem., Wilberforce, O., 1944; D.D. (hon.), 1951; m. Cleo Imogene Sweat;

Children--Linda S. (Mrs. Henry Waddington), Larry S., Leo S., Lana S., Londa S., Lyman S., Jr., Lawana S.; pastor, Wayman A.M.E. Ch., Kokomo, Ind., 1943-44; Bethel A.M.E. Ch., Richmond, Ind., 1944-47; pastored A.M.E. Chs., Ann Arbor, Mich., River Rouge, Mich., 1952-66; First Community A.M.E. Ch., Grand Rapids, Mich., 1966-present; former mem., City Planning Commn., Richmond, Ind., 1951-52; v.p., Ann Arbor Min. Assn.; Human Relations Comm.; Bd. of Religious Affairs Com., Univ. of Mich.; Citizens Adv. Commn. OEO, River Rouge, Mich.; present Citizens Adv. Comm.; sec., Grand Rapids Area Coun. of Chs.; Relocation Comm. for Urban Renewal; Citizens Comm. to study City Charter; NAACP; Mason; Downtown Kiwanis Club; treas., Henry Sch. PTA; Alpha Phi Alpha; Bd. Chrstn. Youth Home; Div. chrmn., Boys and Girls Comm. of Kiwanis; elected to City Comm., Grand Rapids, Mich., 1968-72; Home: 530 Madison Ave. S.E., Grand Rapids, Mich., 49503; Office: 500 James Ave. S.E., Grand Rapids, Mich. 49503

PARRIS, Henry Phares, b. Holly Grove, Ark., Nov. 17, 1906; s. John and Ivory Dove P.; Minister's Institues, Langston Univ. and Bishop Coll.; m. Mary Alice Lemmons; pastor, Okla. in the following chs.: Mt. Olive Bapt. Ch., Chickasha, 1931-34; New Bethel Bapt. Ch., Blanchard, 1935-38; Mt. Olive Bapt. Ch., Chickasha, 1939-40; First Bapt. Ch., Purcell, 1940-43; First Bapt. Ch., Kingfisher, 1943-47; Union Bapt. Ch., Shawnee, 1947-49; current pastor, Union Bapt. Ch., Lawton, Okla. 1949--; dir. of ed., New Hope Bapt. Ch., Chickasha, Okla.; dean, Chickasha Dist. Congress; dean, Western Dist. Congress, 4 yrs.; pres., three Min. Alliances; current pres., Lawtonview Improvement Assn.; moderator, Western Dist. Bapt. Assn.; 1st v.p., Okla. Bapt. State Congress on Chrstn. ed.; state v.p., Natl. Bapt. Congress; mem., Chickashaw Dist. Bapt. Assn.; Home: 1606 Garfield, Lawton, Okla.; Office: Union Bapt. Ch., 16th at Garfield, Lawton, Okla.

PATTERSON, Bernardin Joseph, tchr., b. Clarksdale, Ark., Dec. 24, 1924; s. Alonzo and Johnnie (Wilson) P.; B.A., Philosophy, B.A., Classics, St. John's Univ., Collegeville, Minn., 1949; J.C.B., Catholic Univ., 1958; J.C.L., Cath. Univ., 1959; ordained priest, Roman Cath. Ch., 1954; instr., Classics, St. John's Univ., 1949-53; Classics and linguistics, St. John's Univ., 1953-

55; Greek and Latin, St. Maur's Sem., So. Union, Ky., 1955-57; Cannon Law, Moral Theol., St. Maur's Sem., 1959-63; asst. Superior, St. Maur's Interrracial Sem., So. Union, Ky., 1960-63; first Negro Superior of Cath. Inst. in US, So. Union, Ky., Dec. 1963; founder, Natl. Inst. for Race and Rel., So. Union, Ky., 1963; pres., St. Maur's Interracial Sem., 1963--; pres., Mid-West Clergy Conf. on Negro Welfare, 1963; Home and Office: St. Maur Interracial Sem., So. Union, Ky. 42283

PATTERSON, Clinton David, b. Marengo Co., Nov. 11, 1936; s. David and Mattie (Mason) P.; B. Th., Birmingham Bapt. Coll., 1963; m. Lillie Young; Children--Florencia L.; Clintonia M.; Donneta A.; pastor, New Morning Star, Demopolis, Ala. 1965-present; asst. mgr., Booker T. Wash. Ins. Co., Ensley Dist., 1963-present; tchr., Macedonia Bible Class, 3 yrs.; tchr., Missionary Soc., Peace Bapt. Ch.; pres., No. Ensley Civic League, 1959-60; sec., No. Ensley Civic League, 1965-present; mem., Bd. of Dir., BBM Fed. Credit Union; mem., Adv. Com., Demopolis Civic Club; recd. C. J. McNear English Award, 1962; Mason; YMCA; Chrstn. Aid Soc. Progressive Democratic Club; Home: 811 Ave. H., Birmingham, Ala.; Office: 119 So. Ash St., Demopolis, Ala. 36732

*PATTERSON, Rossie L., b. Abbeville, Ala., Nov. 26, 1918; s. Hezikiah and Lucy (Panty) P.; B. S., Ala. State Tchrs. Coll., 1947; B. D., Howard Univ. Sch. of Rel., 1951; m. Mattie Martha Pringle; Children--Marilynn, Carolynn, Leonard; dir. of Chrstn. Ed., Mt. Carmel Bapt. Ch., Wash., D. C., 1951-55; pastor, First Institutional Bapt. Ch., Winston-Salem, N. C., 1955-59; current pastor, Mt. Carmel Bapt. Ch., Wash., D. C., 1959--; pres., Bapt. Ed. Congress of D. C. and vicinity; sec., Bd. of Trustees, Wash. Bapt. Sem., Wash., D. C.; auditor, Progressive Natl. Bapt. Convention; mem., Comm. of 100 Clergymen; US forces, 1942-45; mem., Mason, Democrat, NAACP, Southern Chrstn. Leadership Conf.; Home: 1728 Webster St., Wash. D. C. 20011; Office: 3rd and Eye Sts., Wash., D. C. 20011

PAYTON, Benjamin Franklin, coll. pres., Orangeburg, S. C., Dec. 27, 1932; s. Leroy R. and Sara Mack P.; S. C. State Coll., 1955; B. D., Harvard Univ., 1958; M. A., Columbia Univ., NYC, 1960; Ph. D., Yale Univ., New Haven, Conn., 1963; m. Thelma Plane; pastor,

Friendship Bapt. Ch., Orangeburg, S. C., 1951-55; Savannah Créek Bapt. Ch., Ehrhardt, S. C., 1952-55; asst. pastor, Ebenezer Bapt. Ch., Boston, Mass., 1955-58; asst. pastor, The Riverside Ch., NYC, 1958-60; head, Dept. of Sociology of Rel. and Social Ethics in the Howard Univ. Sch. of Rel.; dir., Howard Univ. Community Service Project; ex. dir., Natl. Coun. Chs., USA, Comm. on Rel. & Race, 1967-68; present, pres., Benedict Coll., Columbia, S. C.; mem., Amer. Soc. of Scholars; Soc. for Rel. in Higher Ed.; Alpha Phi Alpha; Amer. Sociological Assn.; NAACP; The Wilkinson High Sch. Natl. Honor Soc.; Alpha Kappa Mu Honor Soc.; Danforth Grad. Fellowship to study for doctorate, Harvard Univ. Billings Prize, 1st place, 1957; Nathan W. Scott Award for Meritorious Serv. from Fla. Meml. Coll., St. Augustine, Fla.; Office: Benedict Coll., Columbia, S. C.

PAYNE, Arthur Jerome, b. Balto., Md., Nov. 1894; s. James Henry and Maggie (Bonaparte) P.; Wayland Acad. of Va., Union Univ., 1918; A. B., Morgan Coll., 1928; A. M., Columbia Univ., 1939; D. D. (hon.), Va. Union Univ., 1936; m. Elizabeth Welch; (2nd) Odell Watkins; Children--Arthur Jerome, Jr.; ordained Bapt. ministry, 1915; pastor, Union Bapt. Ch., Ekridge, Md., 1913-14; Good Hope Bapt. Ch., Balto., Md., 1914-15; asst. pastor, Abyssinian Bapt. Ch., NYC, 1920-23; current pastor, Enon Bapt. Ch., Balto., Md., 1923--; former pres., Coun. of Chs. and Chrstn. Ed. of Md. and Del.; dir., Dept. Store, Balto., Md.; pres., United Bapt. Conv., Md., 1929; v. p., Natl. Bapt. Conv., Inc., 1929; trustee, Northern Univ., Long Branch, N. J.; mem., Bd. of Dirs., Mt. Bethel Assn.; Bd. of Dir., Urban League; NAACP; YMCA; recd. Boy Scouts Silver Beaver Minister of the Year-New England Bapt. Conv., 1960; Cert. of Merit from the city of Balto. for service in the Civilian Mobilization during 1945; Welfare Assn.; Alpha Phi Alpha; Vocational Guidance Group; Bapt. Worlds Alliance; Republican; Bd. of Morgan Coll. Chrstn. Center; Bd. of Provident Hosp., Balto., Md.; author: Bible Meditations, Church Programs and Parent Education, Distinctive Characteristics of American Public Ed.; dean, Preachers of Balto., Md.; Home: 5901 Old Frederick Rd., Balto., Md. 21228; Office: Edmondson Ave. & Shroeder Sts., Baltimore, Md. 21223

*PEARSON, Augustus Japheth, b. Pine Bluff, Ark., Oct.

29, 1916; s. Carl W. and Bessie (O.) P.; A. B., Ark. A. M. & N. Coll., 1939; B. D., Howard Univ., Sch. of Rel., 1940; M. Ed., M. A., Fisk Univ., 1947; Univ. of Ark., 1954; m. Jane Lee Nichols; Children--Roslyn, Jessie Y., Augustus J., Marguerite D., Nichola; pastor, Shiloh Bapt. Ch., Camden, Ark., 1942-47; Ninth St. Bapt. Ch., Ft. Smith, Ark., 1947-60; Shiloh Bapt. Ch., Topeka, Kans., 1960--; tchr., Lincoln High Sch., Camden, Ark., 1942-47; counselor, Ark. Bapt. Coll., 1956-57; second Negro elected to Central Democratic Comm. Ark., 1956-58; chrmn., Housing Comm., NAACP, Topeka, Kans.; mem., Mason; author: Literature for the Senior High Bapt. Sun. Sch.; Home: 1211 W. 12th, Topeka, Kans.; Office: 1202 Buchanan St., Topeka, Kansas

PEARSON, George Isaac, tchr., b. Steelton, Pa., Feb. 3, 1930; s. William H. W. and Lassie (Adams) P.; St. Phillips Coll., 1956; B. A., Oakwood Coll., 1959; M. A., Andrews Univ., 1960; m. Lou Ethel Duckworth; tchr., Dupont Park High Sch., Wash., D. C., 1960-62; pastor, Greenville Dist., Miss. So. Central Conf. of S. D. A., 1962-present; US Air Force, 1952-56; Natl. Defence Serv. Medal, Good Conduct Medal; mem., Greenville Min. Assn.; Home: 328 So. Ninth St., Greenville, Miss.; Office: Cateley at Belle Aire, Greenville, Miss.

PEAY, Ralph Preston, b. Greensboro, N. C., Jan. 31, 1931; s. John Henry and Mary (Irby) P.; A. B., Oakwood Coll., Huntsville, Ala., A. M., Andrews Univ., 1954; m. Erma Juanita Jackson; 1 dau.--Ralita Alene; S. D. A. pastoral evangelist since 1954; pastored in Ala., Miss. (Delta area), Ky., Chattanooga; present: pastor, S. D. A. Ch., Memphis, Tenn.; pres., Interdenom. Min. Alliance in Chattanooga, Tenn.; mem., Mayor's Comm. for Desegregation of pub. schs., Chattanooga, Tenn.; frequent contributor to Message Magazine; Home: 4922 Ortie Dr., Memphis, Tenn.; Office: 1051 Mississippi Blvd., Memphis, Tenn.

*PENN, Leon Sinkler, Sr., b. Wash., D. C., Aug. 21, 1905; s. Robert Sinkler and Nannie B. (Austin) P.; Th. B., Howard Univ., Sch. of Rel., Wash., D. C., 1927; D. D. (hon.), Kittrell Coll., Kittrell, N. C., 1959; m. Myra Virginia Gibson; Children--Leon S., Jr., Edward N., Nanita (Mrs. Donald G. Riddick), Joseph A., Ruth C.; pastor, Seaton Afr. Meth. Episc. Ch., Lincoln, Md.,

1931-33; Petersville Circuit, A. M. E. Ch., Petersville, Md., 1933-36; Mt. Pleasant Circuit, A. M. E. Ch., Frederick Co., Md., 1936-39; Bethel A. M. E. Ch., Chestertown, Md., 1939-44; Wright's A. M. E. Ch., Elkton, Md., 1944-45; Robinson A. M. E. Ch., Grasonville, Md., 1945-48; Bethel A. M. E. Ch., Easton, Md., 1948-49; presiding elder, Easton Dist., Balto. Conf., A. M. E. Ch., 1949-52; Quinn A. M. E. Ch., Frederick, Md., 1952-53; St. Paul A. M. E. Ch., Raleigh, N. C., 1953--; v. p., Min. Alliance, Easton, Md.; v. p., Raleigh Min. Alliance; mem., Troop Com. Boy Scouts, Easton, Md.; treas., Crosby-Garfield Sch. PTA, Raleigh, N. C.; Mason; former associated ed., The Allen Chrstn. Endeavor Quarterly (A. M. E. Ch.); v. p., Raleigh Coun. of Chs.; mem., Chrstn. Soc. Action Comm., N. C. Coun. of Chs.; Home: 217 E. Lenoir St., Raleigh, N. C. 27601; Office: 407 W. Edenton St., Raleigh, N. C.

PENN, Robert Earl, b. Keystone, W. Va., Mar. 7, 1916; s. George and Phoebe; A. B., Clark Univ., Atlanta, Ga., 1938; B. D., Gammon Theol. Sem., Atlanta, Ga., 1941; Th. M., Th. D., Central Bapt. Theol. Sem., 1948, 1952; Lois Neale; Children--Barbara (Mrs. Stembridge), James; pastor, New Hope Bapt. Ch., Covington, Ga., 1941-42; 1st Bapt. Ch., Macon, Ga., 1942-43; US Army chap., 1942-46; pastor, Pleasant Green Bapt. Ch., Kan. City, Kan., 1946-52; 1st Bapt. Ch., Gary, Ind., 1952-present; tchr., pub. sch., Newton Co., Ga., 1938-41; Ext. Dept., Clark Coll., Atlanta, Ga., 1940; bd. of trustees, Gary pub. sch., 1956-60; bd. of dir., Campbell Friendship House; Gary Neighborhood House; Gary Urban League; Gary United Fund; trustee, Amer. Bapt. Theol. Sem., 1954-60; award, CBI Theatre Ribbon; mem., Alpha Phi Alpha; Gary Fellowship of Ministers; Bapt. Min. Conf., Am. Bapt. Conv.; Home: 537 W. 19th Pl., Gary, Ind., 46407; Office: 626 W. 21st Ave., Gary, Ind. 46407

PEOPLES, Robert Hayes, b. Hollywood, Miss., Jan. 25, 1903; A. B., Eureka Coll.; Univ. of Chgo., 1 yr.; Chrstn. Theol. Sem., Indianapolis, Ind., 2 yrs.; m. Zellie M. Simpson; Children--Perle (Mrs. Fowler); United Chrstn. Missionary Soc., 16 yrs; tchr. of Rel., Jarvis Chrstn. Coll., Hawkins, Tex., 8 yrs; field sec. for Negro Chs. of Chrstn. Ch., 8 yrs; current pastor, Second Chrstn. Ch., Indianapolis, Ind., 1923--; sec., Ch. Federation of Greater Indianapolis; v. p., Ch. Federation; Home: 2700 No. Capitol, Indianaspolis, Ind., 46208; Office: 2901 No. Kenwood Ave., Indianapolis, Ind. 46208

PERRY, Harold Robert, bishop, b. Lake Charles, La., Oct. 9, 1916; s. Frank J. and Josephine (M.) P.; Divine Word Sem., Bay St. Louis, Miss.; St. Mary's Sem., Techny, Ill.; Holy Ghost Sem., E. Troy, Wis.; ordained priest, Roman Cath. Ch.; pastoral work: Lafayette, La., St. Martinville, La., Mound Bayou, Miss., Broussard, La., Pine Bluff, Ark., 1944-58; rector, Sem. at Bay St. Louis, Miss., 1958-63; Provincial Superior and rector 1964, 1965; Natl. chap., Knights of St. Peter Claver; mem., ex. bd., Cath. Interracial Coun.; apptd. Auxiliary Bishop of the New Orleans archdiocese, 1965-pres.; Home and Office: St. Augustine Sem., Bay St. Louis, Miss.

PERRY, Michael, ch. official, b. West Point, Miss., Feb. 27, 1909; s. Will and Lucy (Collins) P.; Rust Coll.; Jackson State Coll.; m. Lula Tuy; Children--Lucile Walker, Meredith P. Blanks; Albernia Holliman, Michael, Jr.; pastor, Strong Hill Bapt. Ch.; pres., NE Miss. State Sun. Sch. and B. T. U. Congress; Mt. Olivet Dist. Sun. Sch. & B. T. U. Congress; principal, Southside Elem. Sch.; instr., Dept. of Rel. Ed., Min. Institute & Coll.; trustee, M.I. & I. Coll. and West Point Municipal Schs.; mem., Modern Math Club; Mason; Home: 319 Moore, West Point, Miss.; Office: Box 515, West Point, Miss.

*PERRY, Nathaniel Patrick, ch. official, b. New Orleans, La., Mar. 17, 1912; s. Willie and Esther Redd (Bums); B.A., Dillard Univ., 1935; B.D., Howard Univ., 1937-40; Master Soc. Work, Howard Univ., 1951-52; and 1955-56; m. Clytie Fears; pastor, John Wesley Meth. Ch., Wash., Pa., 1940-42; pastor, Mt. Zion Meth. Ch., Silver Spring, Md., 1942-46; ex. sec., La. Conf. Meth. Ch., 1946-52; Dist. supt., La. Conf. Meth. Ch., 1952-54; pastor, Trinity Meth. Ch., New Orleans, La., 1954-55; pastor, Cherry Hill Meth. Ch., Balto., Md., 1956-64; social worker State of Md., including 3-1/2 yrs. of supervisory status, 1964--; tchr. and princ., W. Baton Rouge Parish, La., 1 yr.; tchr. in Adult Ed. in E. Baton Rouge Parish, La., 1 yr.; supervisor of students in field work at Maryland Training Sch. for Boys from Howard Univ., Sch. of Social Work and Univ. of Pa. Sch.

of Social Work; dir. of leadership training for Wash. Conf. of Meth. Ch.; participated in survey on social and rel. status of rural Negro in Md. by Univ. of Md.; v.p., Cherry Hill Coordinating Coun., 1959-64; mem., Meth. Conf. on Chrstn. Ed.; Acad. of Certified Social Workers; Natl. Assn. of Soc. Workers; NAACP; YMCA; Mason; Omega Psi Phi; several articles on Christian ed. in Meth. periodicals; Home: 946 No. 23rd, Baton Rouge, La.; Office: 544 Government St., Baton Rouge, La. 70802

PERRYMAN, Samuel Chester, b. Coy, Ala., July 25, 1921; s. Henry Lee and Irene P.; Daniel Payne Coll., 1948; B.Th., Birmingham Bapt. Coll., 1951; D.D. (hon.), Birmingham Bapt. Coll., 1965; m. Georgia Lillie McPherson; Children--Celestine, Chesterlene, Samuel, Granville, Leola, Madie Chester, George, Gladys, LaVera, Alonzo; pastored chs. in Ala., New Caanon Bapt., Graysville, 1951-52; First Bapt., Booker Hghts., 1952; New Bethel Bapt., Avondale, 1952-62; Mt. Zion, Key Hghts., 1962-64; Great Bethel Bapt., Alex City, 1964-present; auto mechanic; operated garage and serv. sta., Birmingham; chrmn., Minority Com., Alex City, 1966-67; chrmn., Ala. Pub. Bd., Birmingham; owner, Perryman & Son Funeral Home, Alex City; US Army, 1942-45; Mason; Home: 523 Christian St., Alexander City, Ala. 35010; Office: 520 Christian St., Alex City, Ala.

PETERS, James D., Wash. Bapt. Sem.; D.C. Tchrs. Coll.; courses, Howard Univ. Sch. of Rel.; m. Diane Eaton; pastor, Little Zion Bapt. Ch., Burke, Va. (2 yrs.); Third Bapt. Ch., Alexandria, Va. (3 yrs.); East End Tabernacle Bapt. Ch., Bridgeport, Conn., 1960-present; instr., Natl. Bapt. Sun. Sch. & B.T.U. Congress; state pres., N.B.S. Sch. & B.T.U.; sec., Conn. Bapt. Missionary Conv.; Regional repr. S.C.L.C.; Bridgeport chrmn. March on Wash.; pres., Conn. state NAACP; ex. dir., Youth Services, (CAP Agency); co-chrmn., CDAP Advisory Com.; radio speaker WICC (Negro history); Office: East End Bapt. Ch., 548 Central Ave., Bridgeport, Conn. 06607

PETERSEN, Claude Tedford, chap., b. St. Croix, Virgin Islands, July 21, 1927; s. Hugh Valdemar and Petrina (Edney) P.; B.A., Inter-Amer. Univ., Puerto Rico; B.D., Luth. Theol. Sem., Phila., Pa.; m. Anna Marynda Dorsey; Children--Diane Elizabeth, Trina Marie;

assoc. pastor, Bethany Luth. Ch., Bronx, N.Y., 1958-61; pastor, Christ Luth. Ch., Phila., Pa., 1961--; protestant chap., Phila. Gen. Hosp., 1962--; pres., Bd. of Dirs. Christ-Bethlehem Community Center, 1962-63; Central Dist. Stewardship Representative Eastern Pa. Synod, 1962-64; service during Korean conflict as supply specialist, 1952-54; Home: 3008 W. Diamond, Phila., Pa.; Church: 3006 W. Diamond, Phila., Pa.

PETETT, Weldon Durell, b. Thomson, Ga., Apr. 2, 1908; s. Edmond and Georgia (Martin) P.; Walker Bapt. Inst. Grade & High Sch., 1919-28; D.D. (hon.), Inter-Bapt. Theol. Center, 1964; m. Lillie Robinson; Children--Bessie (Mrs. Paul Dykes), Erma (Mrs. Lee Bert Williams), Johnie Mae (Mrs. Earl Sandidge), Ann Elizabeth, Audrey Lee, David Edmond, Jacqueline Lee; pastor, Morningside Bapt. Ch., 1936-41; treas., Bapt. Min. Conf. 1956-60; v. moderator, Allegheny Union Bapt. Assn., 1957-60; chap., C. Howard Brushton Coun. of Chs., 1956-58; moderator, Allegheny Union Bapt. Assn., 1961-65; mem., NAACP; United Protest Com.; Homewood Brushton Improvement League; Home: 7420 Hermitage St., Pittsburgh, Pa. 15208; Office: 7053 Hamilton Ave., Pittsburgh, Pa. 15208

*PHIFER, Solomon Crooms, b. New Bern, N.C., July 12, 1931; s. Willie and Mary (Bryce); Md. State Coll., Princess Anne, Md., 1954-56; B.A., B.D., Howard Univ., Wash., D.C., 1958-1961; certificate, Coun. for Clinical Training, 1961; m. Elizabeth Louise Tracy; Children--Solomon C., Jr.; asst. pastor, Antioch Bapt. Ch., Cleveland, O., 1962; pastor, Wash. Park Bapt. Ch., Seattle, Wash., 1963--; dean, Seattle Bapt. Ministers Inst., Volunteer chap. for Seattle Coun. of Chs.; mem., NAACP; US Marine Corps, 1951-53; Korean Presidential Unit Citation; United Nations Campaign Medals; Three Battle Stars; mem., Phi Beta Kappa; Kappa Delta Phi; Phi Alpha Theta; Seattle Bapt. Min. Coun.; contributor to; Missions Magazine; Home: 3115 E. Madison St., Seattle, Wash. 98102; Office: 624 Lake Washington Blvd., Seattle, Wash. 98102

*PHILLIP, Lee C., coll. chap., b. Harrison Co., Texas, Sept. 15, 1902; s. Alex Phillip and Julian (Bradley) P.; B.S., Prairie View A & M Coll., 1924-28; B.D., Howard Univ., 1928-31; M.A., Rel. Ed., Howard Univ., 1939; m. Jimmie Ruth McDonald; Children--Jimmie Lee

(Mrs. Poindexter), Cecelia (Mrs. Boldon); prof., philosophy and ed., Prairie A & M Coll., 1932--; mem., Ex. Comm. Natl. Assn. of Univ. and Coll. Chaplains (4 yrs.); mem., Natl. Ed. Assn.; State Tchrs. Assn.; Area Coun. of the Southwest YMCA; cited by Prairie View A & M Coll. for outstanding work in public relations and human relations; Home: Box 2002 Prairie View A & M Coll., Prairie View, Tex.

PHILLIPS, Channing Emery, b. Brooklyn, N.Y., Mar. 23, 1928; s. Porter W. and Dorothy (Fletcher) P.; Carnegie Inst. of Tech. (Art scholarship); Univ. of Utah, 1945-46; A.B., Va. Union Univ., 1947-50; B.D., Colgate Rochester Div. Sch., 1950-53; grad. studies, Drew Univ.; teaching ministry: instr., N.T., Howard Univ., Sch. of Rel., Wash., D.C., 1956-58; visiting lectr., Greek, Prot. Episc. Sem., Alex., Va., 1958; visiting lectr., N.T., Amer. Univ., Wash., D.C., 1957-58; pastorates, Educ., Ch. of the Open Door, Bklyn, N.Y., 1956; Interim, Plymouth Congre. Ch., Wash., D.C., 1958; assoc., Grace Congre. Ch., NYC, 1958-59; Lemuel Haynes Congre. Ch., Jamaica, N.Y., 1959-61; former pastor, Lincoln Meml. Congre. Temple, Wash., D.C., 1961-1970; pres., OEA Housing Development; m. Jane Celeste Nabors, 1956; Children--Sheilah Nahketah, Tracy Jane, Channing Durward; mem., Natl. Assn. Biblical Instr. Soc. of Biblical Lit. and Exegesis, Inst. of Rel., Alpha Phi Alpha, Alpha Kappa Mu Honor Soc., NAACP; nominated Primary D.C. Nat. Committeeman Democratic Party, May 1968; nominated for Presidency of US at Natl. Dem. Conv., Aug. 1968; Home: 1373 Locust Rd., N.W., Wash., D.C.

PHILLIPS, Ernest Blake, b. Banks, Ark., Mar. 9, 1906; s. Joe and Mattie (Green) P.; Ideal Bible Coll. Corresponding, 1937; D.D. (hon.), Natchez Coll., Natchez, Miss., 1950; courses: John W. Wilkerson Bapt. Inst., St. Louis, Mo., 1930-34; m. Cortie Golden Timms; Children--Lorenza, Steve; pastor, Pleasant Land Bapt. Ch., 1934-41, St. Louis, Mo.; St. Paul Bapt. Ch., Terre Haute, Ind., 1941-53; current pastor, The Greater Galilee Bapt. Ch., Milwaukee, Wis., 1953--; v.p., Gen. Bapt. State Conv., Wis.; pres., Bapt. Min. Conf.; chrmn., Public Relations Comm., Interdenom. Min. Conf.; chrmn., Greater Milwaukee, Coun. of Chs. Evangelistic Com.; mem., NAACP; Urban League; North

Town, Community Organization; Near Northside Non-Partisan Conf. "Young Men's" Chrstn. Assn.; Home: 628 W. Wright St., Milwaukee, Wis. 53212; Office: 2432 N. Teutonis, Milwaukee, Wis. 53212

PHILLIPS, Oscar George D., b. Moneague, St. Ann, Jamaica, May 28, 1914; s. Joshua B. and Ida (Jackson) P.; A.B., Bishop Coll., Marshall, Tex., 1947; M.Ed., 1949; B.D., Andover Newton Sem., Newton Centre, Mass., 1953; S.T.M., Boston Univ. Grad. Sch. of Theol. 1955; m. Miriam Faulcon; Children--Peter Joshua, Miriam Elaine; pastor, Macedonia Bapt. Ch., Marshall, Tex., 1946-49; Dean of men, Bishop Coll., Marshall, Tex., 1947-49; pastor, Shiloh Bapt. Ch., Medford, Mass., 1950--; chap., Tewksbury Hosp., Tewksbury, Mass., 1958--; visiting lectr., Andover Newton Theol. Sem., 1961--; clerk, Boston East Bapt. Assn., 1957-60; Bd. of Dirs., Mass. Bapt. Conv., 1959-61; Bd. of Dirs., W. Medford Community Center, 1959--; mem., Conf. on Rel. and Race, 1965--; Bd. of Governors for Inst. of Pastoral Care, 1965--; pres., Mystic Valley Credit Union, 1960-63; Bd. of Dirs., Mystic Valley Credit Union, 1960--; Accreditation as Chaplain Supervisor in Inst. of Pastoral Care, 1961--; ecclesiastical endorsement of Amer. Bapt. Conv. as professional counselor, Amer. Assn. of Pastoral Counselors; Home: 94 Monument St., Medford, Mass. 02155; Office: 33 Lincoln St., Medford, Mass. 02155

PHILLIPS, Porter William, Jr., b. Wash., D.C., May 24, 1925; s. Porter W. Sr. and Dorothy (Fletcher) P.; A.B., Soc., Va. Union Univ., 1949; B.D., Union Theol. Sem., N.Y., 1952; m. Dorothy Bobo; 4 daus.--Stephanie Laverne, Adrienne Lorraine, Claudia Leslie, Dorothy LaNell; pastor, Humboldt Parkway Bapt. Ch., Buffalo, NY, 1953--; pres., Bapt. Min. Conf., Buffalo and vicinity; pres., Coun. of Chs. of Buffalo and Erie Co.; mem., Citizens Coun. of Human Relations, Psychiatric Clinic of Buffalo, Hickory St. Chrstn. Center, Buffalo Bapt. Assn.; Office: 794 Humboldt Pkway, Buffalo, N.Y.

PHILLIPS, Porter William, Sr., b. Little Richmond, N.C., Oct. 7, 1897; s. John Emery and Mollie Belle (Davis) P.; Slater State Normal; A.B., Va. Union Univ.; M.A. Columbia Univ.; B.D., Union Theol. Sem.; D.D. (hon.), Va. Union Univ.; m. Dorothy Anne Fletcher, 1924; 1 dau. Marie Belle Cary; 5 sons, Treadwell Oliver, Wendell Har rison, Fletcher Allison, Porter William, Jr., Channing Emery; pastorates, Trinity Bapt. Ch., Newport News, Va., Brown Meml. Ch., Bklyn, N.Y., Carrone Bapt. Ch., Pittsburgh, Pa., 1938--; dean, Ft. Greene Tchrs. Training Sch., Bklyn; chrmn., Comm. of Labor and Management, Natl. Bapt. Conv. of America, Inc.; mem., ex. bd., YMCA and NAACP; pres., Homewood Brushton Coun. of Chs.; mem. ex. bd., Allegheny Union Assn. and Pa. Bapt. State Conv.; "Father of the Year"Award, 1958, Pittsburgh Courier; Home: 312 Lowell St., Pittsburgh, Pa.; Office: 7119 Frankstoun Ave., Pittsburgh, Pa.

PHILLIPS, Walter McLoyd, b. Wilson, N.C., Aug. 25, 1903; s. Walter and Mary (Davis) P.; student, Wash. Business Inst.; Smith Sch. of Instrumental Music, NYC; courses, Temple Univ., 1958-59; diploma, New Era Theol. Inst., Phila., Pa., 1960; student, Shaw Univ., Raleigh, N.C.; m. Beulah Turner; present pastor, Mt. Moriah A.M.E.Z. Ch., Henderson, N.C.; organized classes in rural N.C. in voter registration, reading, writing; Organized Boy, and Girl Scout troops; mem., NAACP, Southern Chrstn. Leadership Conf.; Home: Rt. 1, Box 314A, Apex, N.C.; Office: P.O. Box 177 Holly Springs, N.C. 27540

PHILLIPS, Wendell Harrison, b. Brooklyn, N.Y., Nov. 19, 1934; s. Porter Wm. Sr., and Dorothy (Fletcher) P.; Pa. State Univ.; B.S., Va. Union Univ., 1956; B.D., Colgate Rochester Div. Sch., 1961; m. Dorothy Harris; Children--Wendell Fitzgerald; Hubert Hau Community Center, Rochester, N.Y., 1959-60; pastor, Second Bapt. Ch., Mumford, N.Y., 1961-64; Heritage United Ch. of Christ, Balto., Md., 1964-present; chrmn. N.W. Police Community Relations Coun., 1966-67; mem., bd. dir., Central Atlantic Conf. U. Ch. of Christ; Adv. Coun. Ch. Extension Dept. U.C.C.; pres., Bd. dir. Fellowship House, Inc.; Monumental Foods, Inc.; pres., Ministerium, U.C.C. (Balto., Md.); mem., Alpha Phi Alpha; Home: 3604 Edgewood Rd., Balto., Md. 21215; Office: 3106 Liberty Heights Ave., Balto., Md.

PICKNEY, Aurelius D., b. June 28, 1898, Dublin, Ga., A.B., Brown Univ., Providence, R.I.; Morehouse Coll., Atlanta, Ga.; courses: Harvard Univ., Chgo. Univ.; pastor, Yoked Parish, Liberty, Ga.; Second Congre. Ch., Memphis, Tenn.; Plymouth Congre. Ch. and Settlement

House, Louisville, Ky.; past moderator, Ky.-Tenn. Conf. UCC; mem., Bd. of trustees, UCC Conf. So. Carolina; moderator, Ind.-Ky. Conf.; mem., Com. of structure, Racine, Wis.; mem., nominating com., UCC; organizer Ch. of Chrstn. Fellowship, San Diego, Calif., 1967; present organizer UCC, Tampa, Fla., 1968--; Home: 334 E. 108th St., Apt. 11A, New York, N.Y. 10029

PIERCE, Isaiah Benjamin, presiding elder, b. Winfall, N.C., Sept. 28, 1907; s. William Dallas and Annabelle (White) P.; B.A., Knoxville Coll., 1932; S.T.B., Pittsburgh Theol. Sem., 1935, M.Th., 1947-49; M.Ed., Univ. of Pittsburgh; advance work toward Ph.D., 1950; D.D., Livingstone Coll., 1957; m. Carrie Bedgette; Children--Isaiah B., Jr., Jane Carolyn Cook, William D. II; presiding elder, A.M.E.Z. Ch., mem., Mason, Borough Pk. Comm., Sewickley, Pa.; chap., U.S.A.R., 1951--; served WW II in Europe and Africa, rec'd Bronze Star Medal, w/4 battle stars; Lt. Col., U.S.A.R. Chap. Corps; author: "My Church Believes," booklet, 1956; "Worship in the A.M.E.Z. Ch., 1946, revised 1954; life's work with A.M.E.Z. Ch.; presiding elder, 10 yrs.; pastor, Knoxville, Tenn.; Pittsburgh, Pa.; Uniontown, Pa.; Sunbury, N.C.; Newport News, Va.; Youngstown, O.; Sewickley, Pa.; at present, pastor of Jones Tabernacle A.M.E.Z. Ch., Indianapolis, Ind., 1960--; host to the 37th Quadrennial Gen. Conf. A.M.E.Z. Ch., 1964; mem., Gen. Bd. Natl. Coun. of Chs., also Rel. & Race; author: "Ushers In Our Church," 1960; "Why We Worship as We Do," 1962; pres., Interdenom. Min. Alliance of Greater Indianapolis and Vicinity, 1964-65; Home: 135 W. 43rd St., Indianapolis, Ind.; Office: 440 N. Blackford, Indianapolis, Ind.

PIERRE, Maurice C., b. Barbadoes, B.W.I., Nov. 12, 1917; s. Clifford and Ida; A.B., Combermere Coll. (MWI), 1935; D.D. (hon.), Union Bapt. Theol. Sem., Birmingham, Ala.; m. Sarah Smith; pastor, First A.M.E.Z. Ch., Amityville, L.I., N.Y., 1956-58; Asbury A.M.E.Z. Ch., Pascogoula, Miss., 1958-60; Jacob Tabernacle, Louisville, Ky., 1960-63; Cornish Chapel, A.M.E.Z. Ch., Key West, Fla., present; Mayor's Human Rel. Com., Louisville, Ky.; pres., Monroe Co. Assn. for Retarded Children, Key West, Fla.; Bd. mem., Key West Chapt. Red Cross; Bd. Salvation Army; ex. comm. NAACP Key West Chapt.; Canadian Army, 1939-46; Min. Assn., Key West, Fla.; Home: 702 Whitehad St., Key West, Fla. 33040

PINDER, Nelson Wardell, b. Miami, Fla., July 27, 1932; s. Geo. L. and Colleen (Saunders) P.; Bethune-Cookman Coll., Daytona Beach, Fla., 1956; Nashotah House Sem., Nashotah, Wis.; m. Marian E. Grant; Children--Gail Yvonne; current pastor, The Episc. Ch. of St. John the Bapt., Orland, Fla., 1959--; state officer, Fla. Congress of Parents and Teachers Assn., 1961-62; US Army, 1953-55; Home: 438 Cottage Hill Rd., Orlando, Fla.; Church: 1000 Bethune Dr., Orlando, Fla.

PINN, Walter S., b. Feb. 5, 1907, Astoria, N.Y.; s. Howard and Elizabeth (P.); Columbia Univ., 1924-27; Nat. Bible Inst. (Shelton Coll.), 1934-37; D.D. (hon.), Va. Sem.; Va. Union Univ.; Miller Univ. (Phila.); m. Peggy Delores Aldridge; Children--Walter Royal (deceased), Louise; asst. pastor, Metro. Bapt. Ch., NYC, 1935-37; 1938-46; Jr. Pastor; pastor, Calvary Bapt. Ch., Jamaica, N.Y., 1946-present; sec. and v.p., Bapt. Min. Conf., Greater NY; pres., Gen. Bapt. Assn. Youth Dept. (2 yrs.); Bd. chrmn., and founder Allied Fed. Savings & Loan, Jamaica, NY; mem., Bd. of Dirs. Commercial Progressive Assn., NYC; mem., NAACP; Bd. mem., Progressive Bapt. Conv.; Eastern Bapt. Assn.; Jamaica, NY Cham. of Commerce; awards: United Negro Coll. Fund; Allied Fed. Savings; Jamaica br. NAACP; Ebony Oil Corp. Comm. Award; founder, United Democrats, Queens - Jamaica; mem., Amer. Bapt. Conv.; Natl. Negro Churchman; Interfaith Clergy; frequent sermons, CBS "Church of the Air." Home: 175-05 139th Rd., Springfield Gardens, N.Y. 11434; Office: 111-10 New York Blvd., Jamaica, N.Y. 11433

*PITTS, W. Lyndsai, b. Essex Co., Va., Oct. 18, 1912; s. William Albert and Lettie (Washington) P.; B.S., Howard Univ., 1945; B.D., 1951; M.A., 1957; Coll. of Divine Metaphysics, 1959; Dr. of Psychology, Yale Univ., 1959; Northwestern Coll., 1959; D.D. (hon.); m. Annie B. Cain; Children--Brenda L.; W. Lyndsai Pitts, Jr.; asst. pastor, Mt. Lebanon Bapt. Ch., 1940-46; asst. pastor, Metro. Bapt. Ch., 1946-47; Minister-in-charge, First Mt. Calvary Bapt. Ch., 1947-48; pastor, First Mt. Calvary Bapt. Ch., Balto., Md., 1948--; tchr., Md. Bapt. Center, 1953-56; prof., Mt. Royal Coll., Balto, Md.; lectr., Coppin State Coll.; mem., Phi Beta Sigma; Big Brothers of Baltimore; Interdenom. Min. Alliance; Bapt. Ministers Conf.; YMCA; Balto. Area Coun. of Alcoholism; Howard and Yale Univs. Alumni Assn.;

Home: 2916 Archeutonly Terr., W. Balto., Md. 21217; Office: 1142 N. Fullton Ave., Balto., Md. 21217

POGUE, King David Solomon, chap., b. Sumter, S. C., Aug. 21, 1912; s. Solomon and Mary Elizabeth Pearson P.; 1930-34 A. B. and 1934-37, B. D. Johnson C. Smith Univ.; 1959, D. D. Burton Theol. Sem.; m. Ruby Louise Mitchell; 1 son--David Eugene; pastor, 1937-41, Salem United Presby. Ch., Anderson, S. C.; 1946-48, Sargeant Meml. Presby. Ch., Wash., D. C.; chap. (Lt. Col.) US Army, 1941-45; 1958-63, Vets. Admin. Hosp., Tuskegee, Ala.; mem., Adv. Bd. of YMCA-YWCA, 1958-63, Tuskegee Inst., Ala.; 1958 served as consultant for establishing Denominational Chaplaincy at the John A. Andrew Hosp. of Tuskegee Inst.; military rec.: 1941-43 Regimental Chap., 99th CA(AA) US and Overseas; 1944-45 Regimental Chap., 27th Troop, 2D Calvary Div.; 1944-45, Regimental Chap., 371st Infantry, 92D Inf. Div. US and Overseas; awards: Mediterranean Battle Stars and Commendation for Italian Campaign; mem., The Acad. of Rel. and Mental Health; Omega Psi Phi; Tuskegee Civic Assn.; Home: 121 Colvert St., Tuskegee Institute, Ala.; Office: Veterans Administration Hosp., Tuskegee, Ala.

POINTER, Louis Waylon, b. Feb. 18, 1933, Granville Co.; s. Willie A. and Rosetta D.; A. B., Johnson C. Smith Univ., Charlotte, N. C.; B. D., Shaw Univ. Sch. of Div., Raleigh, N. C.; m. Catherine Carter; Children--Kathryn; pastor, Round Branch Bapt. Ch., Bladenboro, N. C., 1957-65; First Bapt. Ch., Clarkton, N. C., 1958-65; First Bapt. Ch., Jacksonville, N. C., 1965-67; chap., US Army, 1968-present; mem., Chaplain Bd. of Onslow Meml. Hosp., Jacksonville, N. C., 1966-67; Adv. Bd. Onslow Co., Bd. of Ed., Jacksonville, N. C.; v. p., Min. Assn., Lumberton, N. C., 1965; mem., Bladen Co. Health Club, 1959-65; Lumberton Citizens Civic Club, 1962-65; v. p., Fellowship Civic League, Jacksonville, N. C., 1965-67; v. p., Onslow Co. Fund, Inc., 1966-67; Public Housing Comm., 1966-67; mem., Trustee Bd. Gen. Bapt. State Conv. (N. C.), 1966-67; USO Coun., Jacksonville, N. C., 1965-67; Alpha Phi Omega; Mason; Home: 1707 Nevada Ave., Lumberton, N. C. 28358; Office: 131 Gregg St., Ft. Jackson, S. C., 29207

POLK, Robert Lawrence, b. Chgo., Ill., May 1928; s. Tillman and Lilly (Bell) P.; Wilson Jr. Coll., Chgo., Ill.; B. A., Doane Coll., Crete, Neb.; B. D., Hartford

Theol. Sem.; pastor, Berthold Congre. Ch., Berthold, N. D., 1955-57; Youth Work Sec., YMCA, Minot, N. D., 1957-60; Minister to Youth, The Riverside Ch., NYC, 1960-68; chap., Dillard Univ., 1968--; Office: Dillard Univ., New Orleans, La. 70122

POLLAR, Alfred, b. New Orleans, La., Oct. 1, 1927; s. Henry and Isabell (Russell) P.; A. B., Clark Coll., 1949; B. D., Gammon Theol. Sem., 1955; m. Barbara Lee Walker; Children--Alfred, Jr.; Columbus Charge, 1958-59; Commerce-Lawrenceville Charge, 1959-63; pastor, Palen Meth. Ch., Savannah, Ga., 1963--; mem., Bd. of Frank Callen Boy's Club; US Army, 1952; mem., Alpha Phi Alpha; Home: 1907 Burroughs St., Savannah, Ga. 31401; Office: Palen Meth. Ch., 601 W. 35th St., Savannah, Ga. 31401

POOLE, John Douglas, b. Greensville, S. C., May 25, 1927; s. Theodore T. Morehead and Emily E.; Luth. Jr. Coll., 1946-48; Immanuel Luth. Sem., 1948-52; m. Myrtice Hicks; pastor, St. James Luth. Ch., Southern Pines, N. C., 1951-52; pastor, Mt. Calvary Luth. Ch., Kannapolis, N. C., 1952-53; pastor, St. Marks Luth. Ch., Atlanta, Ga., 1953-59; pastor, St. John's Luth. Ch., Salisbury, N. C., 1959--; chrmn., Program Comm. of N. C. Sun. Sch. Conv., N. C.; contact pastor, The Stewardship Dept. for Chs. in this circuit; mem., the Luth. Human Relation of America; mem., Rowan Co. Civic League; Home: 623 W. Horah St., Salisbury, N. C.; Church: Cor. S. West & Innes, Salisbury, N. C.

POPLEON, K. Edward, b. Plaquemine, La., May 10, 1918; s. Alexis and Italy M. (Collins); B. S., Denver Univ., 1941; M. S., Wash. Univ., 1949; S. T. M., Pac. Sch. of Rel., 1961; m. Maggie Louise O'Neal; Children--Gene, Wayne, Connie, Kenneth; ordained 1954; pastor, Union Bapt. Ch., Yuma, Ariz., 1954-57; Sec. Bapt. Ch., Vallejo, Calif., 1957-67; ex. dir., Manpower Training Div., La. State, 1967-pres.; former tchr., Vallejo Jr. Coll.; mem., Amer. Bapt. Conv. Finance Comm.; Maj., US Army, 1938-64; Home: Rte. 1, Box 214, Plaquemine, La. 70764; Office: 3615 Gov. St., Baton Rouge, La. 70806

PORTER, Florezel Louis, Sr., b. Hattiesburg, Miss., Feb. 17, 1896; s. Granville and Josephine; B. Th., Bishop Coll., Marshall, Tex., 1930; courses, Univ. of Chgo.;

Inter-Bapt. Theol. Center, Houston, Tex., 1964, D.D. (hon.); m. Emry Spencer; Children--Florezel Louis, Jr., Josephine (Mrs. Aldrich), Granville, Anna Bell (Mrs. Adkins), Florine (Mrs. Fesby), Willa Bee (Mrs. Denman), Henrietta (Mrs. Tolbert); pastor, 11th St. Bapt. Ch., Texarkana, Tex., 1926-30; St. Paul Bapt. Ch. (5 yrs.); St. Stephen Bapt. Ch., Chgo., 1939-present; instr., Prot. Natl. Sun. Sch. & B. T. U. Congress, State Sun. Sch. & B. T. U. Congress; former pres., Bapt. Pastors' Conf. (Chgo.); pres., Moderators Coun., Prog. Natl. Bapt. Conv., Moderator, New Fellowship Assn.; candidate, Pres. Bapt. Ministers Conf. (Chgo.); Home: 652 E. 92nd St., Chgo., Ill. 60619; Office: 658 E. 92nd St., Chgo., Ill. 60619

PORTER, Herman Anthon, b. Chicago, Ill., Feb. 8, 1917; s. Shirley and Ellen (Moreland) P.; Loyola Univ., 1941; B.A., Sacred Heart Monastery, 1947; M.A., Univ. of Notre Dame, 1952; Dean of Studies, Divine Heart Sem., Donaldson, Ind., 1952-60; asst. pastor, Sacred Heart Ch., Sterling, Ill., 1960-63; dir., Cath. Info. and Counseling Ctr., Chap., Cath. Interracial Coun., Rockford, Ill., 1963--; author, 25 article series on the Cath. Ch. and the Negro, The Steubenville Register, Steubenville, O., 1964; Home and Office: Catholic Information and Counseling Center, 1722 Chestnut St., Rockford, Ill.

PORTER, John Richard, b. Mineral Springs, Ark., Apr. 2, 1932; s. Steve and Retha Porter; B.A., Iowa Wesleyan Coll., 1959; B.D., Garrett Theol. Sem., 1962; m. June Carol McIntosh; Children--John Thomas, Joseph Dubois, Julia Magdalene; US Army, 1954-57; asst. pastor, Normal Park Meth. Ch., Chgo., 1960-62; pastor, Christ Meth. Ch., June 1962-present; pres., Englewood So. Chrstn. Leadership Conf., pres., Southtown Clergy Assn. mem., Urban League; NAACP; CORE; Amer. Civil Liberties Union; YMCA; lectr., on civil rights; has written several articles for local papers; Home: 6409 S. Sangamon St., Chicago, Ill.; Office: 6401 S. Sangamon St., Chicago, Ill., 60621

PORTER, John Thomas, b. Birmingham, Ala., Apr. 4, 1931; s. Robert Sr. and Emma (Daniel) P.; B.S., Ala. State Coll., Montgomery, Ala., 1955; B.D., Morehouse Coll. Sch. of Rel., Atlanta, Ga., 1958; m. Dorothy Rogers; Children--Jon Roderick, Mark Kelvin; Mia Lachone; asst. pastor, Dexter Ave. Bapt. Ch., Montgomery,

Ala., 1954-55; Ebenezer Bapt. Ch., Atlanta, Ga., 1955-58; pastor, First Bapt. Inst. Ch., Detroit, Mich., 1958-62; Sixth Ave. Bapt. Ch., Birmingham, Ala., 1962-present; lectr., Birmingham Bapt. Coll.; mem., Minister's Assn., Birmingham, Ala., 1966; Bd. of Management, YMCA; Alpha Phi Alpha; Home: 620 Center Way, S.W., Birmingham, Ala. 35211; Office: 1531 Sixth Ave., S., Birmingham, Ala. 35333

PORTER, Richard Sylvester, tchr., b. Gloster, Miss., June 9, 1923; s. Ishop and Bertha (Lusk) P.; Amite Co. Training Sch.; A.B., Leland Bapt. Coll., Baker, La., 1949-53; m. Annie Mae Matthews; Children--Louise, Dorothy, James, Shirley, Richard, Linda, Patricia, Eric, Laura, Lawrence; pastor, First Bapt. Ch., Gloster, Miss., 1949-53; Owens Chapel Bapt. Ch., Columbia, Miss., 1953-59; First Union Bapt. Ch., Meridian, Miss., 1959--; tchr., pub. sch. sys. of Miss., 1953-57; dean, Harper Bapt. Sem., Magnolia, Miss., 1957-59; assoc. bd. mem., Leland Bapt. Coll., 1953-55; bd. of trustees, Meridian Bapt. Sem.; 1st v.p., E. Miss. Bapt. State Conv.; organizer and pres., Meridian and Lauderdale Co. Human Rights Assn.; Coun. of Federated Organization; Vet. of WW II, European Theatre of Operation; Bronze Stars; mem., Natl. Bapt. Conv., USA, Inc.; 2nd New Hope Consolidated Bapt. Assn.; Leland Coll. Alumni Assn.; NAACP; Mason; Home: 602 39th Ave., Meridian, Miss.; Office: 610 38th Ave., Meridian, Miss.

POTTER, William Abraham, tchr., b. Demopolis, Ala., Apr. 18, 1916; s. William A., Sr. and Mary G. P.; B.S., Ala. State Coll., 1938--; B.D., Gammon Theol. Sem., 1948; courses: Oberlin Coll., Oberlin, O.; m. Sadye Mae Watson; Children--Savannah, Sadye; prin., Jr. High Sch., Tuscaloosa, Ala., 1932-40; Field Scout Ex.-Boy Scout of Ala., 1940-42; minister, No. Ala. Conf.; tchr., Caner Vocational Sch, 1946-63; pastor, Shaw Tenyle A.M.E.Z. Ch., Atlanta, Ga. 1951--; asst. chap., Grady Hosp., Atlanta, Ga., 1958-64; pres., Atlanta Min. Alliance; mem., ex. bd. Ga. Coun. of Chs.; mem., Operation Breadbasket, Atlanta, Ga.; mem., Civic Liberties Assn.; chaplain's asst. in US Forces; mem., Elks, Mason, Phi Beta Sigma, YMCA; mem., Gen. Conf. A. M.E.Z. Ch.; Home: 38 Hightown Rd. NW, Atlanta, Ga.

POULARD, Grady Emory, b. Crowley, La., Aug. 15, 1936; s. Grady E., Sr. and Leola (Green) P.; Temple Univ.,

Phila., Pa., 1953-54; A. B., Southern Univ., Baton Rouge, La., 1957; B. D., Yale Univ., 1960; courses on Ph. D., Columbia Univ., New York; m. Marguerite Marie Brown; Children--Michael; pastor, Second Bapt. Ch., Greenfield, Mass.; interim minister, Dixwell Ave. Congre. Ch., New Haven, Conn.; Migrant chap., Pa. Coun. of Chs.; camp counselor, Camp Cononicus, Worwick, R. I.; assoc. min., Concord Bapt. Ch., Bklyn, NY; field repr., Natl. Student Chrstn. Fed., Commission on World Mission; visiting traveling field sec., World Student Chrstn. Federation, Europe and the Middle East; chap., Chrstn. Med. Coll., Vellore, So. India; field sec., Natl. Coun. of Chs., Commission on Rel. and Race; current pastor, People's Congre. Ch., Wash., D. C.; awards from: Who's Who Among Students in American Coll. and Univ.; "Debater of the Year," Southwest Forensic Conf.; award of merit for role as student body pres., Southern Univ.; mem., Alpha Phi Alpha; Home: 2000 N St., N. W. Washington, D. C.; Office: 4704 13th St., NW, Wash., D. C.

POWELL, Adam Clayton, Jr., congressman, author, b. New Haven, Conn., Nov. 29, 1908; s. Adam Clayton and Mattie Fletcher (Schafer) P.; A. B., Colgate Univ., 1930; M. A., Columbia Univ., 1932; D. D., Shaw Univ., 1935; LL. D., Va. Union Univ., 1947; m. Isabel Geraldine Washington, Mar. 8, 1933 (sep. Nov. 1944); married 2d, Hazel Scott Aug. 1945 (divorced); one son, Adam Clayton III; married 3d, Yvette Diago; minister, Abyssinian Bapt. Ch., 1937-60; elected to City Coun. of NY, 1941; founder People's Voice, editor-in-chief, co-publisher, 1942; elected to Congress Nov. 1945; mem. 79th-87th Congress from NY 16th Dist., chrmn., com. on ed. and labor; del. Parliamentary World Govt. Conf., London, 1951-52; ILO Conf. Geneva, Switzerland, 1961; decorated Knight of the Golden Cross, Ethiopia, 1954; mem., World Assn. Parliamentarians on World Govt. (v. p.); author: Is This a White Man's War? 1942; Stage Door Canteen, 1944; Marching Blacks, 1945, Adam Clayton Powell, 1960; Home: 120 W. 138th St., New York, N. Y.; Office: U. S. House of Representatives, Wash., D. C.

POWELL, Grady Wilson, b. Brunswick Co., Va., Aug. 6, 1932; s. Herbert Vermont and Lille (Taylor) P.; B. S., St. Pauls Coll., Lawrenceville, Va., 1954; B. D., Va. Union Univ., Richmond, Va., 1959; m. Bertie Jeffress; Children--Sandra Z., Dorthula H., Grady, Jr., Herbert

C.; pastor, Beautiful Plain Ch., 1959-60; Gillfield Bapt. Ch., Petersburg, Va., 1961-present; Quioccasin Bapt. Ch., 1959-60; tchr., Emporia, Va., 1954-56; Richmond, Va., 1961; mem., Biracial Com. of Petersburg; v.p., United Givers Fund, Petersburg; mem., Welfare Adv. Bd., Petersburg, Va.; past pres., Clergy Assn. of Petersburg; mem., Bd. of Ed. & Publication Com. (Amer. Bapt. Conv.); Home: 312 S. Dunlop St., Petersburg, Va.; Office: 209 Perry St., Petersburg, Va.

POWELL, John Lewis, b. McKeesport, Pa., Nov. 2, 1902; s. John and Rachel (Deering) P.; A.B., Johnson C. Smith Univ., 1931; B.D., 1934; M.Ed., Univ. of Pittsburgh, 1947; D.D. (hon.), Johnson C. Smith Univ., 1956; m. Ruth Marie Davidson; pastor, Friendship Bapt. Ch., Charlotte, N.C., 1932-47; tchr., Social Sciences, Unity High Sch., Statesville, N.C., 1944-47; prof., Chrstn. Ed., Ch. History, Dean of Students, Amer. Theol. Sem., Nashville, Tenn., 1947--; pastor, Progressive Bapt. Ch., Nashville, Tenn., 1950--; dir., Extension Classes of Amer. Bapt. Theol. Sem., Nashville, Tenn.; Bd. of Dirs., So. St. Community Center, 1950-58; Bd. of Dir., Bethlehem Community Center, 1958--; pres., Nashville Min. Conf.; mem., NAACP; NCLC; Democratic League of Voters; Natl. Assn. of Coll. Deans & Registrars; Alpha Phi Alpha; Mason; Home: 611 Young's Lane, Nashville, Tenn.; Church: 1419 12th Ave., So., Nashville, Tenn.

POWELL, Joseph Tiffany, chap., Lt. Col., b. Balto., Md., Nov. 11, 1923; s. Clarence F. and Alethia B.; A.B., Oakwood Coll., Huntsville, Ala., 1946; M.A., Andrews Univ., Berrien Springs, Mich., 1951; courses: N.C. Coll., Durham, N.C.; m. Alice Pettiford; Children--Cynthia R. and JoAnne M.; dean of men and pastor, Pine Forge Acad., Pine Forge, Pa., 1947-52; Army chap., 1952-60; pastor, Immanuel Temple S.D.A. Ch., Durham, N.C., 1960; Lt. Col., US Army chap., Ft. Bragg, N.C., 1962-65; Dominican Republic, 1965-66; Ft. Ord., Calif., 1966-present; sec., Interdenom. Fellowship of Min., Durham, 1968-69; mem., Durham Com. on Negro Affairs, 1960-61; head, Sp. Education sub. comm. for student re-assignment and integration, Durham, Aug. 1969; Army Commendation Ribbon, 1966; Home: 236 Ardennes Circle, Ft. Ord, Calif. 93941; Office: Hq. 1st BCT. Bde., Ft. Ord., Calif. 93941

POWELL, Robert Bernard, sem. prof., b. Petersburg, Va., Nov. 2, 1894; s. Henry William and Hattie Rebecca (Valentine) P.; A. B., Va. Union Univ., 1923; B. D., Oberlin Grad. Sch. of Theol., 1926; D. D. (hon.), Simmons Univ., 1948; m. Maggie Webster Winstead; Children--Clara Margaret (Mrs. Willie B. Satterfield), Elfrida Roberta (Mrs. John Henry Scott, Jr.), Gloria Violet (Mrs. Norman M. Winsmore, Jr.), Chrystal Garrell (Mrs. Chrystal Powell Tibbs); pastor, Mt. Zion Bapt. Ch., Oberlin, O., 1924-26; Shiloh Bapt. Ch., Southold, L. I., N. Y., 1927-28; Ebeneza Bapt. Ch., Williamsport, Pa., 1928-38; Macedonia Bapt. Ch., Wheeling, W. Va., 1938-42; chap., US Army, 1942-46; prof., Bible and English, Lynchburg Sem. and Coll., Va., 1947-48; dir., Negro and Interracial Work, W. Va. Bapt. Conv., 1948-61; serve as interim pastor where needed; dir., Chrstn. Ed. for W. Va. Bapt. State Conv. and the Mt. Zion Dist. Bapt. Conv., 1948--; mem., Bd. of Dirs. Planned Parenthood Assn.; Brotherhood Activities Comm.; Gov.'s Human Rights Commn., 1963; Alpha Phi Alpha; Masons; Amer. Legion; Home: 1325 Oak St., Parkersburg, W. Va

POWELL, Robert Meaker, b. Cumberland, Md., Apr. 23, 1930; s. William Edward and Edna (Williams) P.; A. B., Morgan State Coll., Balto., Md., 1954; B. D., Va. Prot. Episc. Theol. Sem., Alexandria, Va., 1957; vicar-in-charge, Holy Trinity Episc. Ch., Balto., 1957-58; Gen. Diocesan Missionary, Diocese of Maryland, 1958-63; ex. dir., Lafayette Square Community Center, Balto., 1958-63; asst. priest, St. James' Episc. Ch., Balto.; assoc. priest, St. James' Episc. Ch., Balto., Md., 1958--; mem., Md. Commn. on Interracial Problems and Relations; Chrstn. Social Relations Commn. of the Diocese of Md.; Citizen's Planning and Housing Assn.; Harlem Park Urban Renewal Exec. Coun.; Volunteer Consulting Staff at Rosewood State Training Sch.; Md. Coun. of Chs.; Bd. of Dir., Lafayette Sq. Community Center; citation by the Balto. Jr. Assn. of Commerce for its Distinguished Service Award, 1961; citation by the Balto. Afro-Amer. News; Home: 827 N. Arlington Ave., Balto., Md.; Office: St. James' Episc. Ch., 827 No. Arlington Ave., Baltimore, Md.

POWELL, W. J., b. Montgomery Co., Ala., Nov. 2, 1908; s. Joseph and Bertha (Lee) P.; A. B., Livingstone Coll., Salisbury, N. C., 1947; B. D., Hood Sem., 1950, Salisbury, N. C.; m. Bessie Ford; worked as common laborer during high sch. days with the Amer. Cast Iron Pipe Shop of Birmingham, Ala., 1925-27; served as YMCA sec. in Birmingham after grad. from Indus. High Sch., 1927-42; began preaching, 1942; pastor, Birmingham, Ala., Cherryville, N. C., Charlotte, N. C., Salisbury, N. C., Montgomery, Ala.; current pastor, Afr. Meth. Episc. Ch., Montgomery, Ala.; one of the organizers of Montgomery Improvement Assn.; served as sec., 1st v. p., chrmn. of program comm., etc.; served as pres., Montgomery Emancipation Comm.; bd. mem. br. YMCA; mem., local bi-racial comm.; sec., bd. of trustees, Lomax-Hannon Coll., Greenville, Ala.; Home: 120 Mildred St., Montgomery, Ala., 36104; Office: Holcombe St., Montgomery, Ala. 36104

PRESSLEY, Calvin Oliver, b. New York, Nov. 10, 1937; s. George W. and Pansy C. P.; B. A., Drake Univ., 1959; B. D., Drew Univ., 1962; m. Iona Adams; pastor, Metro. Community, The Meth. Ch., 1961-62; Ch. of the Open Door, 1963--; NYC Bd. of Ed., local sch. bd., 1925-27; Lay Adv. Bd. Cumberland Hosp., Bklyn; Community Sch. zoning comm., Faregist-Hghts.; mem., Chi Jota Phi; Home: 175 Willowby St., Bklyn, N. Y.; Office: 201 Gold St., Bklyn, N. Y.

PRICE, Alonzo, b. Pittsburgh, Pa., May 1, 1933; s. Alonzo and Bessie (Shannon); B. A., San Francisco State Coll., 1954-58; B. D., Ch. Div. Sch. of the Pacific, 1958-61; Youth dir., St. Johns Episc. Ch., San Francisco, 1961; Missionary, Diocese of Alaska, 1962; asst. rector, St. James Episc., San Francisco, 1962; present, deputy organist and asst. minister, Grace Cathedral, San Francisco, 1963--; US Air Force, 1949-53; mem., Phi Mu Alpha-musical fraternity; Home: 625 Scott, Apt. 301, San Francisco, Calif.; Office: 1051 Taylor, San Francisco, Calif.

PRIMES, Joseph Ronald, b. Akron, O., Sept. 11, 1926; s. George Walter, Sr. and Annabelle (Holsey) P.; Kent State Univ., 1948; A. B., Claflin Univ., 1955; B. D., Gammon Theol. Sem., 1958; m. Minerva Hollaway; Children--Joseph Ronald, Jr.; pastor, Haven Meth. Ch., Dadeville, Ala., 1956; Richards Chapel Meth. Ch., Troy, O., 1958; Cory Meth. Ch., Cleveland, O., 1960; pastor, St. Paul Meth. Ch., Cleveland, O., 1961--; mem., Phi Beta Sigma; Home: 16408 Telfair Ave., Cleveland, O.; Office: 4720 Lee Rd., Cleveland, O.

PRIMM, Howard Thomas, bishop, b. Brentwood, Tenn., June 23, 1903; s. Zack and Addie (Curtis) P.; A.B., Wilberforce Univ. (Ohio), 1924; B.D., Payne Theol. Sem., 1927; D.D. (hon.), Wilberforce Univ., 1940; LL.D. (hon.), Edward Waters Coll, 1944; m. Edythe Mary Hailey; Children--Rita Mae; pastor, Trinity Afr. Meth. Episc. Ch., 1926-28; Gilchrist A.M.E. Ch., Memphis, 1928-29; Allen A.M.E. Ch., Memphis, 1929-31; Bethel A.M.E. Ch., Alexandria, La., 1931-32; St. Peter A.M.E. Ch., Port Gibson, Miss., 1932-33; Union A.M.E. Ch., Ark., 1933-35; Visitors' Chapel A.M.E. Ch., Ark., 1935-41; Union Bethel A.M.E. Ch., New Orleans, 1941--; elected bishop, 1952; currently serving the 5th Episc. Dist.; organized the Sarah Allen Child Welfare Sta., New Orleans, 1942; Sun. Sch. Bd., 1930; Book Concern, 1940; trustee of Shorter Coll., 1936-39; Campbell Coll., 1939--; pres., Gen. Bd. of the A.M.E. Ch., 1962-64; sec., Coun. of Bishops, 1963; pres., Coun. of Bishops, 1964; builder of denomination's first home for senior citizens Kans. City, Kans., 1964; chrmn., Minimum Salary Commn. A.M.E. Ch.; Mason; NAACP, Urban League; del., World Conf. of Chrstn. Youth, Amsterdam, Holland, 1939; mem., Omega Psi Phi; Home: 1724 Villa Place, Nashville, Tenn.

PRIMO, Quintin Ebenezer, Jr., b. Liberty Co., Ga., July 1, 1913; s. Quintin and Alvira; A.B., Lincoln Univ., Pa., 1934; S.T.B., Lincoln Univ. Sem., 1937; B.D., Bishop Payne Div., Petersburg, Va., 1941; cert., Yale Univ. Sch. of Alcohol Studies, 1956; Leadership Training, Div. Inst., Roslyn, Va., 1964-65; m. Winifred Thompson; Children--Cynthia, Quintin, Susan; curate, St. Agnes' Ch., Miami, Fla., 1941-42; vicar, St. Gabriel's, Rutherfordton, N.C., 1942-44; St. Stephen's, Winston-Salem, N.C., 1944-45; St. Timothy's Ch., Bklyn, N.Y., 1945-47; rector, St. Simon's, Rochester, N.Y., 1947-63; St. Matthew's, Wilmington, Del., 1963-present; asst. prin., St. Alban's Vocational Sch., Coconut Grove, Fla., 1937-38; founded St. Simon's Community Center; St. Mathew's Tutorial and Job Traning Program; co-founder, Community Training Found.; appt. by Gov., 29-man comm. to investigate causes of civil unrest, Del.; chrmn. Block Blight, Code Enforcement Comm.; mem., Gen. Conv., Diocese of Rochester, N.Y.; mem., bd. Planned Parenthood; UNCF; NAACP; pres., Community Training Found.; NCCJ; pres., Union of Black Clergy and Laity of the Episc. Ch.; Natl. Comm. of Negro Churchmen; chrmn

Diocesan Comm. to study confirmation practices; pastoral services comm., Coun. of Chs.; chrmn., Chrstn. Social Relations Spl. Comm. to study discrimination in cemetery burial plots; chrmn., treas., Natl. Clergy Comm. to remove discrimination in hiring and personnel practices; Clergy Dialogue Group; Clergy Adv. and Mobile Operations; Episc. Action Group on Poverty, Nat. Ch.; mem., Del. Fair Housing Coun.; Mental Health Assn.; Commn., Deployment of Clergy, Exec. Coun., Episc. Ch.; appt. Episc. rep., Project Equality Bd., Del.; chrmn., transportation, Wilmington's Poor People's Campaign; awards, Citation of Merit, St. Augustine's Coll., Raleigh, N. C.; mem., Phi Beta Sigma; Home: 3901 Monroe St., Wilmington, Del. 19802; Office: 700 Walnut St., Wilmington, Del. 19801

PRITCHETT, Clayton Robinson, b. Felton, Del., Apr. 20, 1927; s. Alvin and Annie (Harris) P.; B. A., Oakwood Coll., 1949; m. Jessie Vivinee Raymond; Children--Jerald David, Cherrie Elaine, Steven Lloyd; teacher-pastor, Southwest Reg. Conf. of S. D. A. serving in priv. schs. in Houston and Dallas, Tex., 1949-52; tchr., denominational schs. in Pasadena and Los Angeles, 1952-54; present: pastor, Santa Monica and Monrovia, 1954--; mem., Prohibitionist Political Party; Home: 144 E. Evergreen St., Monrovia, Calif.; Office: 1003 So. Ivy Ave., Monrovia, Calif.

PROCTOR, James Melvin, b. Monticello, Fla., Sept. 13, 1929; s. James Alfred and Queen Ester P.; B. S., Fla. Agric. & Mech., 1956; B. D., Interdenom. Theol. Cent., 1965; m. Rosa L. Gallen; Children--Reginald Melvin; tchr., Voc. Agric., Delray Beach, Fla., 1956-62; student asst. pastor, Flipper Temple A. M. E. Ch., Atlanta, Ga., 1962-64; asst. dir., Rel. Activities, Morris Brown Coll., Atlanta, Ga., 1964-65; pastor, Good Hope A. M. E. Ch., Pensacola, Fla., 1965-66; chap.-dir., Genesee-Orleans Ministry of Concern, N. Y. Coun. of Chs., 1966-present; program chrmn., Orleans Co. br. NAACP; v. p., Albion Parent Tchrs. Assn.; US Army Signal Corps, 1952-54; recd. Natl. Defense Service Medal; Democrat; mem., Bd. of Dir., Orleans Legal Aid Bureau, Inc.; mem., Orleans Community Action Comm., Inc.; Home: 114 Platt St., Albion, N. Y. 14411

PROCTOR, Samuel Dewitt, coll. pres., gov. official, b. Norfolk, Va., July 13, 1921; s. Herbert Q. and Velma

G. P. ; Va. State Coll., Petersburg, Va., 1937-39; US Naval Apprentice Sch., 1939-40; A. B., Va. Union Univ., 1940-42; B. D., Crozer Theol. Sem., 1945; Univ. of Pa. Grad., 1944-45; Grad. Sch., Yale Univ., 1945-46; Th. D. Boston Univ., 1950; pastor, Pond St. Bapt. Ch., Providence, R. I., 1945-49; prof., Va. Union Univ., 1949-50; dean, Sch. of Rel., Va. Union Univ. 1950-55; v. p., Va. Union Univ., 1953-55; pres., Va. Union Univ., 1955-60; pres., A. T. Coll. of N. C., 1960-61; Peace Corps repr. to Nigeria, 1962; assoc. dir., Peace Corps, 1963-1964; Assoc. Gen. Sec. for communication, Nat. Coun. of Chs. 1964--; 1965 elected v. p., Amer. Bapt. Conv.; mem., Exec. Bd., So. Reg. Coun.; Gen. Bd. of Natl. Coun. of Chs.; Natl. Comm. 1960 White House Conf. of Children and Youth; Commn. on Liberal Ed. of the Assn. of Amer. Coll.; Sigma Pi Phi; Kappa Alpha Psi; Outstanding Alumnus Award, Sch. of Theol., Boston Univ.; mem., Bd. of Trustees, Crozer Theol. Sem.; Bd. of Mgrs., Amer. Bapt. Bd. of Ed. and Publication; Office: 457 Riverside Dr., New York, N. Y.

PRYOR, Thomas, b. Seabrook, S. C., Jan. 5, 1932; s. Philip and Clara P.; m. Ethel Preston; Children--Janice, Marilyn, Cheryl, Tharon; pastor, La Pageville Bapt. Ch., Savannah, Ga.; mem., NAACP; YMCA; acting sec., Union Missn. Bapt. Assn.; Mason; Home: 816 Carroll St., Savannah, Ga. 31401

PUGH, Alfred Lane, b. Pleasantville, N. J., May 31, 1927; s. Wilfred B. and Mamie P.; A. B., Lincoln Univ., 1944-48; B. D., Theol. Sem., Lincoln Univ., Pa., 1948-51; Rutgers Univ., New Brunswick, N. J.; m. Cleora; Children--Kevin, Karen; pastor, Mt. Ararat Bapt. Ch., Rutherford, N. J., 1951-56; Second Bapt. Ch., Asbury Pk, N. J., 1956--; pres., Asbury Park, Shore area br. NAACP, 1957-60; Home: 158 Fisher Ave., Neptune, N. J.; Office: 120 Atkins Ave., Asbury Park, N. J.

*PUGH, Robert Milton, b. Donalsonville, Ga., Mar. 8, 1915 s. Cary and Elizabeth; B. S., Savannah State Coll., Savannah, Ga.; B. D., Howard Univ., Sch. of Rel., Wash., D. C.; courses: Howard Grad. Sch., Drew Univ., D. C. Tchrs. Coll., Amer. Univ.; m. Lillian Robinson; dir., Neighborhood House, Gary, Ind., 1945-46; rel. activities Fla. Normal Coll., St. Augustine, Fla., 1946-50; acting pres., Fla. Normal Coll., 1949-50; pastor, Shiloh Bapt. Ch., 1949-50; Dean of Men, Storer Coll., Harpers Ferr

W. Va., 1950-52; pastor, Wainwright Bapt. Ch., Charles Town, W. Va.; sec., YMCA, 1953-58; chap. interviewer, Lorton Reformatory, Va., 1959-60; couns., Childrens' Center, Laurel, Md., 1960-61; pastor, 1st Bapt. Ch., Warrenton, Va., 1955-61; assoc. min., Albright EUB Ch., 1961-64; chap., inst. min., Coun. of Chs., Wash., D. C., 1964-present; tchr., Wash. Bapt. Sem., 1955-61; dir., Adult Ed., YMCA; mem., Cham. of Commerce, 1954-58; D. C. Adult Ed. Assn., 1954-58; D. C. Ed. TV, 1955-58; Neighbors Inc., Civic Assn., 1958--; NAACP, Urban League, Coun. for Clinical Tng.; awards: Cit. of Merit, UGF; YMCA; Natl. Cap. Housing Authority; Boy Scouts of Amer.; commendation, Public Welfare; author: article; Home: 323 Quakenbos St., N. W., Wash., D. C. 20011; Office: 1751 N St., N. W., Wash., D. C. 20036

PUGH, Thomas Jefferson, sem. prof., b. Lewiston, N. C., Oct. 25, 1917; s. John David and Otebia (Parker) P.; A. B., Clark Coll., 1940; B. D., Gammon Theol. Sem., 1942; M. A., Atlanta Univ., Ga., 1947; Drew Univ., 1948; Ph. D., Boston Univ., 1955; m. Lillian Ruth Raper; Children--Jon Raper; dir., Rel. Ed. to migrants, Jas. Andrew Farm, Hurlook, Md., 1942; prin., Dickens Co. Jr. Sch., Tate, Ga., 1942-44; pastor, Bethesda Bapt. Ch., Americos, Ga., 1943-45; tchr., Bryant Theol. Sem., 1944-47; chap., Albany State Coll., Ga.; 1948-58; current assoc. prof., and pastor, Interdenom. Theol. Cent., Atlanta, Ga., 1958--; consultant, Human Relations, Miles Coll., 1960; worship leader to worship in secondary education for the Philip State Fund, 1960; consultant, pastoral counseling to in-service ministers, Chrstn. Meth. Episc. Ch., 1961; counselor, Alcoholics Helping Hand Soc., Atlanta, Ga.; mem., Alpha Phi Alpha; Intl. Theol. Scholastic Soc.; The Acad. of Rel. & Mental Health; The Natl. Soc. for the Sci. Study of Rel.; The American Psychological Assn.; Amer. Assn. of Univ. Profs.; Home: 2806 Engle Rd. NW, Atlanta, Ga. 30318; Office: 671 Beckwith St., Atlanta, Ga. 30314

PUTNEY, Ellis, Jr., b. Pine Bluff, Ark., Sept. 13, 1926; s. Ellis Sr. and Emma (Harris) P.; Metro. Sch. of Music, 1950; m. Lucille Murphy; Children--Manuela, Denise, Donellis; pastor, Rayfield Miss. Bapt. Ch.; mem., Brotherhood Dist. Assn.; Central Conv. of Ill.; Natl. Bapt. Conv. of USA; US Army, 1945-57; mem., Mason; Democrat; Home: 1221 W. 72nd St., Chicago, Ill.;

Office: 1217-19 W. 72nd St., Chicago, Ill.

QUICK, Jerry Alphonzo, b. Raeford, N.C., July 8, 1935; s. James and Myrtle (McL.); A.A., Clinton Jr. Coll., 1964; B.A., Barber Scotia Coll., 1966; M. Div, Hood Theol. Sem., 1969; m. Ruth Melvin; Children--Mavis Jerruth; farmer 1953-59; instr., pub. sch.; Concord and Landis, N.C., pastor, Hunter Chapel and Zion Hill Ch., Maxton, N.C., 1959-62;. Weeping Willow Ch., Charlotte, N.C., 1962-64; O'Connors Grove Ch., Belmont, N.C., 1964-67; Sandy Ridge A.M.E.Z. Ch., Landis, N.C., 1967-present; mem., Afr. Meth. Episc. Zion Ch., Negro Civic League, NAACP, Democrat, Alpha Phi Alpha, So. Rowan Min. Assn.; Mason; Inst., Rep. Boy Scouts of Amer.; Home: PO Box 518, Raeford, N.C., 28376 Office: PO Box 101, Landis, N.C. 28088

RAND, David George, b. Indianapolis, Ind., Jan. 26, 1930; s. Frank and Helen (Ubanks) R.; A.B., Emmanuel Missionary Coll., 1957; M.A., Andrews Univ., 1959; m. Martha Nola Wideman; princ., Ch. Sch. and asst. pastor, S.D.A. Ch., Gary, Ind., 1959-61; present: pastor, Battle Creek, Jackson and Kalamazoo, Mich. S.D.A. Chs., 1961--; US Army, 1951-53; Home: 320 N. Wash. Ave., Battle Creek, Mich. 49017; Office: 420 W. Van Buren, Battle Creek, Mich.

RANDALL, Eugene, b. New Orelans, La., Nov. 19, 1927; s. Wilson and Calvie (Haughton) R.; 1949, B.S., Tuskegee Inst., (Ala.)1963, B.D. Johnson C. Smith Univ., Charlotte, N.C.; m. Helen Juanita Rudisell; supply min., 1963, Ebenezer Presby. Ch., Morven, N.C., Greenstreet Presby. Ch., Morganton, N.C., 1963--; Relocation dir., Charlotte Redevelopment Commn; sec., Ex. bd., Charlotte NAACP; organized the Brooklyn Day Care Center in Charlotte for deprived children; military rec.: 1955-56, Corp., US Army, 2nd Armored Div., 48th Med. Battalion (Germany); Home: 1900 Aileen Dr., Charlotte, N.C.

RANGE, King Solomon, business man, b. Lexington, Miss., Apr. 3, 1893; s. Ambrose M. and Dycie (Archer) R.; Henderson Bus. Coll., Memphis, Tenn., 1915-17; Moody's Bible Inst., Chgo., Ill., 1923-25; m. Marguerite Washington; Children--Marguerite Range Champman,

Warren C. Chapman, Dycolene Range Bland, Oscar Bland, Thelma Range Smith, Chester Smith; asst. pastor, Olivet Bapt. Ch., Chgo., Ill., 1936-49; organizer and founder, Range Meml. Bapt. Ch., 1949, Chgo., Ill.; founder, King S. Range Real Estate Co., 1929; founder, Ill. Fed. Savings Loan Co., Chgo., Ill.; mem., Bapt. Ministers Conf.; pastors Conf. of Chicago & Vicinity; chap., Frederick Douglas Repub. League; 2nd & 6th Ward Republican Organization; US Army, 1918-19; mem., Elk, Mason; publisher, first Negro greeting cards; Home: 1318 72nd St., Chicago, Ill.; Office: 3808 Indiana, Chicago, Ill.

RANSOME, William Lee, sem. prof., b. Nottoway Co., Va., Mar. 7, 1879; s. Geo. W. and Lucy (Fowelks) R.; A.B., Va. Union Univ.; M.A., Va. Union Univ.; B.D., LLB, D.D. (hon.), Va. Union Univ.; Th.M., Union Theol. Sem., Richmond, Va.; m. Mary E. Wingfield, Mary M. Cobb; Children--Esther (Mrs. Miller), Clarence, George W., Mary E., J. Rodman; pastor, Shiloh Bapt. Ch., Fredericksburg, Va.; tchr., Fredericksburg High Sch., 1906-20; pastor, First Bapt. Ch., So. Richmond, Va., 1920--; tchr. in Va. Univ., 22 yrs.; pastor, White Rock Bapt. Ch., Durham, N.C. (1 yr.); pres., NAACP, Richmond; founder, Richmond Civic Coun.; candidate for Richmond City Council; Va. State Legislature; (former) Grand master Prince Hall Grand Lodge of Masons; present, ed. and founder of Masonic Organ the "Bee Hive;" pres., Bapt. Gen. Assn., 7 yrs; chrmn., Lott Carey Bapt. Foreign Mission Soc.; Ed. Bd., Natl. Bapt. Conv.; co-organizer and sec., Goodwill Bapt. Conv., Va.; mem., Phi Beta Sigma; author: Stewardship and Negro Baptists; "Old Story for This New Day," Central Pub. Co., 1954; Home: 1507 Decatur St., Richmond, Va. 23224; Office: 1501 Decatur St., So. Richmond, Va.

*RASBERRY, Hosea, b. Idabel, Okla., Apr. 17, 1914; s. Richard and Currie (Moore) R.; A.B., Clark Coll., Atlanta, Ga., 1942; B.D., Howard Univ., Sch. of Rel., 1945; m. Ozella Smith; Children--Richard; pastor, Milton Congre. Chrstn. Ch., Milton, Del., 1942-44; pastor, Graham Congre. Chrstn. Ch., Beaumont, Tex., 1945-47; Pioneer Presby. Ch., Beaumont, Tex., 1947--; organized in 1950 as the second Negro Presby. Ch., US of the state of Tex. 1956, del. Gen. Assembly of the Presby. Ch., U.S., repr. the Synod of Tex., served on various comm. on the Presbytery and Synod level; (Comm. of Chrstn. Ed. and printed minutes); tchr. 1947-49; 1950-63 served as counselor or director of summer camp, Camp Cho Yeh, Livingston, Tex.; volunteer worker for the United Appeals, 1960-63; institutional repr. for the Boy Scouts - Trinity Neches Coun. of the Boy Scouts of Amer., 1959; chrmn. of Bd. of the Beaumont Coun. of Campfire Girls of Beaumont, Tex., mem. of the Beaumont Min. Assn.; mem. of the Minister's Discussion Group (this group contributed much in the smooth integration of many of the public facilities of the city--parks, swimming pools, theatres, dept. store clerks, etc.); mem., Alpha Phi Alpha; YMCA; Ministers Assn. of Beaumont; Home: 2480 Houston, Beaumont, Tex.; Office: 3520 Pine St., Beaumont, Tex.

READYE, David E., b. N. Little Rock, Ark., June 30, 1916; s. David E., Sr. and Carrie (Everett) R.; A. A., Shorter Coll., 1939; B. A., Wilberforce Univ., 1942; D. D., Monrovia Coll., 1955; D. D., Jackson Theol. Sem. of Shorter Coll., 1963; m. Alberta Covington; Children--David E. III; Mary Gaynell; pastor, St. Peters A. M. E. Ch., 1952-60; Antioch Miss. Bapt. Ch.; pastor, Greater St. John A. M. E. Ch., 1960--present; pres., Decatur chap. NAACP for 5 yrs.; first Negro elected to Bd. of Ed., Decatur, Ill.; pres., Englewood Commun. Organ of Chgo. for 5 yrs.; mem., Bd. of Southtown Planning Assn., Chgo.; elected del. to Gen. Conf. of the A. M. E. Ch.; mem., Ch. Advancement Comm. of the Assn. of Commerce, Decatur, Ill.; Interdenom. Pastor's Alliance; chap. of the Decatur City Coun; recd. testimonial and award from the Bd. of Ed. in Decatur, Ill.; award from W-BEE Radio for outstanding work in the commun.; salute from W-VON local radio sta.; award for outstanding work in the community from the Bulletin Newspaper; Home: 6200 S. Elizabeth St., Chicago, Ill. 60636

REAVIS, Ralph, b. Lawrenceville, Va., July 3, 1940; s. Hallie and Fannie; B. A., Va. Sem. and Coll., 1962; B. D., Va. Union Univ., 1966; m. Marion E. Langhorne; Children--Ralph; pastor, Promise Land Bapt. Ch., Bedford Co., Va., 1959-61; Mt. Zion Bapt. Ch., Clarksville, Va., 1960-62; Mt. Nebo Bapt. Ch., Surry, Va., 1961-66; Mt. Sinai, Holland, Va., 1963-66; Gethsemane Bapt. Ch., Suffolk, Va.; Grove Bapt. Ch., Churchland, Chesapeake, Va., 1966-present; appt. Com., Churchland Adv. Citizens Com.; cons., Newtown poverty area; official repr. to high schs., Va., Va. Sem. and Coll.; cons., Pres. of Va. Sem. and Coll.; awards, Citizenship from Va. Sem., 1961; mem., Amer. Bapt. Conv.; Portsmouth Urban Coalition; Portsmouth Min. Assn.; Home: 6005 Campbell, Portsmouth, Va., 23703; Office: Grove Bapt. Ch., Churchland, Portsmouth, Va.

*REDD, Albert Carter, b. Mar. 13, 1917, Columbia, S.C.; s. Artis and Polly; A.B., Benedict Coll., Columbia, S.C., Howard Univ. Sch. of Rel., 1951; YMCA Cert., Howard Univ. Sch. of Rel.; courses, Union Theol. Sem., NYC; m. Georgia; Children--Althea, Brenda, Albert Jr.; pastor, Chrstn. Meth. Ch.; Grace C.M.E. Ch., Md.; S. Carolina; Fla.; Mich.; pastor, Cleaves Meml. C.M. E. Ch., Denver, Colo., present; dir., Chrstn. Ed., Detroit C.M.E. Ch., 5 yrs Dean of Leadership Training, C.M.E. Detroit; ex. sec., S.C. Conf. NAACP; chrmn., Bd. of Dir. S.C. Human Relations; Adv. Bd., Inter-Civic Coun., Tallahassee, Fla.; ch. work sec. Conf., state NAACP; spec. resource com. on Civil Rights (voting) Gadsen Co., Fla.; mem., Citizens Adv. Bd., Urban Renewal, Mt. Clemens, Mich., chrmn., Fair Practices Com., Macomb Co., Inter-racial Assn.; pres., Mt. Clemens Min. Assn.; part-time chap., V.A. Hosp., Allen Park, Mich.; mem., Prosecuting Attorney Juvenile Com.; Bd. of Prot. Community Chs.; chrmn., comm. on Audio visual services; Bd. of Dir. Guild of Ch. Musicians; mem., Metropolitan Detroit Coun. of Chs.; Planning comm. of the Interfaith Coun.; mem., Alpha Phi Alpha; Home: 2210 Marion St., Denver, Colo., 80205; Office, Cleaves Meml. Ch., 2222 Marion St., Denver, Colo. 80205

REDDICK, Albert Joseph, b. Madison, Fla., Aug. 2, 1921; s. Albert and Josie (Dixon) R.; A.B., Edward Waters Jr. Coll., 1941; A.B., Morris Brown Coll., 1944; B.D., Hamma Div. Sch., 1947; D.D., Monrovia Coll., 1956; LL.D., Campbell Coll.; m. Clara Louise Roberts; Children--Cleo Alberta, Patricia Louise, Marian Joanne; pastor, St. Paul A.M.E. Ch., Dallas, Ga., 1942-43; Allen A.M.E. Ch., Milford, O., 1944-45; Allen Chapel A. M.E. Ch., Williston, Fla., 1947-49; Hurst Chapel A.M. E. Ch., Orlando, Fla., 1949-52; St. James A.M.E. Ch., Miami, Fla., 1952-58; Bethel A.M.E. Ch., Tallahassee, Fla., 1958-61; Bethel A.M.E. Ch., St. Petersburg, Fla., 1961--; tchr., pub. schs. Levy Co., Fla., 1947-49; Seminole Co., Fla., 1949-52; former state pres., NAACP;

del. and sec., to 1956, 1960, 1964 Gen. Conf. of the A. M. E. Ch.; mem., Adv. Bd. of FAMU Univ., 1959-61; mem., Bd. of Management and Trustee Bd. of Edward Waters Coll.; mem., Knights of Pythian, Elks, Alpha Phi Alpha; editorial staff, A. M. E. Chrstn. Recorder; author: "The History of the Negro Branches of Methodism;" Home: 912 3rd Ave. No., St. Petersburg, Fla. 33705; Office: 3rd Ave. & 10th St., No., St. Petersburg, Fla.

REDDING, James, b. Chattanooga, Tenn., May 1, 1910; s. Daniel and Mary; courses, Bapt. Bible Inst., Cleveland, O.; m. Margaret Johnson; pastor, 2nd Mt. Sinai Bapt. Ch., Cleveland, O.; Pleasant Valley Bapt. Ch., Cleveland, O.; Master Bapt. Ch., Cleveland, O.; present, asst. chap., Cleveland Workhouse, Chief steward, Universal Wire Spring; financial sec., treas., local 12; hon. attorney gen., state of Ohio; chrmn., Hough Cultural Center Scout Troop 468; Dep. auditor, Cuyahoga Co. Aud. Office; ex. dir., Hough Cultural Center; award, James Dodman Nobel Humanitarian; mem., Bapt. Min. Conf.; Adv. Bd., Mary B. Martin Sch.; Adv. Bd., Drug Addiction and Alcohol, Case Western Res. Univ.; Home: 16102 Biltmore Ave., Cleveland, O. 44128; Office: 1874 E. 82nd St., Cleveland, O. 44103

REDDS, Harry Lee, b. Greenwood, Miss., Feb. 12, 1938; s. Monroe and Lessie B. (Terry); pastor, Payne Chapel Chrstn. Meth. Episc. Ch., 1961-65; Dir. Ed., Grace Hill Settlement House, St. Louis, Mo., 1965-67; pastor, Wesley Chrstn. Meth. Episc. Ch., Beloit, Wis., 1967-present; consult., Inter-Religious Found. for Community Organization (IFCO); candidate, City Coun., Beloit, Wis.; mem., Beloit Public Housing Authority (4 yrs.); Community Action Program Bd. of Dirs.; (3 yrs.) Bd. of Dirs., Rock Co. Day Care Service (3 yrs.); mem., Nat. Comm. of Negro Clergymen; Mason; US Air Force (4 yrs.); Home: 1762 Poole Ct., Beloit, Wis. 53511; Office: 1760 Shore Drive, Beloit, Wis. 53511

REECE, John Henry, Jr., b. New York, N. Y., Jan. 16, 1919; s. John H. and Lenora (Smith); Govt. schs., Nassau, Bahamas, 1925-36; Bishop Payne Div. Sch., Petersburg, Va., 1945-48; asst. tchr., Nassau, Bahamas, 1937-39; headmaster, Bahamian Schs., 1939-45; ordained deacon, Jan. 19, 1949; priest, Jan. 21, 1950; deacon and priest-in-charge, All Saints', Clarksburg, W. Va.,

1949-50; present, vicar, St. Peter's, Key West, Fla., 1950--; mem., Republican Party, Mason, NAACP, ACV; Home: 800 Center St., Key West, Fla.

REED, Carother N., b. Haynesville, La., May 5, 1911; s. Judge T. and Suddie (White); A.B., Tex. Coll., Tyler, Tex., 1950; S.M.U., Perkin Sch. Theol.; D.D., Union Bapt. Sem., 1955; LL.D., Tex. Coll., 1957 (hon. deg.); widower; son--Winston D.; Dean and minister, Texas Coll.; mem., Bd. of Trustees and Ex. Comm. of Bd., Tex. Coll.; mem., Commn. on Organic Union of Chs. C.M.E.; treas., NY-Wash. Conf. C.M.E.; present, pastor, Holsey Temple Chrstn. Meth. Episc. Ch., Phila., Pa.; consult., Natl. Coun. of Chs.; certified instr., Bd. of Chrstn. Ed.; Man of the Year, Citizens' League, Houston, Tex., 1950; Natl. Negro Business League Award for work done at S.M.U., Dallas, Tex., 1951; mem., Mason, Natl. Negro History Soc.; Home: 1631 W. Grange St., Phila., Pa.; Office: 1641 W. Hunting Park Ave., Phila., Pa.

*REED, Daniel Lee, b. Clarksville, Tex., Feb. 8, 1877; s. Houston and Louise Beatty; 2 yrs., Bishop Coll; Sequin Coll., Sequin, Tex. Normal Sch. Certificate; B.D., Howard Univ., Sch. of Rel., 1910; m. Mollie Coleman; pastor, Mt. Zion Bapt. Ch., Fredericksburg, Va., 1911-18; chap., WW I, 1918; lectr., Negro in WW I, 2 yrs.; worker, Natl. Bapt. Conv.; Evangelist pastor, 2nd Bapt. Ch., Matawan, N.J., 3 yrs.; Mt. Olive Bapt. Ch., 3 yrs.; founder, Ebenezer Bapt. Ch., NYC, 8 yrs.; evangelist, Wash., D.C., 25 yrs., govt. worker, present; mem., Natl. Bapt. Conv.; Min. Conv. of N.J.; N.J. Bapt. Assn.; NAACP; pres., Bapt. Min. Fellowship Coun., Newark; Assoc. ed., Natl. Bapt. Voice, 35 yrs.; Home: 157 Ward St., Orange, N.J.

REED, Nathaniel, b. July 28, 1914, Atlanta, Ga.; s. Humphrey and Ellen; course, Clark Univ., Atlanta, Ga., 1932-33; diploma, B.Th., Cincinnati Bible Coll. and Sem., 1966; 1969; m. Annie Velma Brown; Children--Sylvia (Mrs. Paul Marshall, Jr.); assoc. pastor, Union Bapt. Ch., Cincinnati, O.; Macedonia Bapt. Ch., Covington, Ky., 1966; pastor, Sec. Trinity Bapt. Ch., Cincinnati, O., 1966-present; mem., Prog. Bapt. Conv. Inc.; Cincinnati Bapt. Min. Conf.; Interdenom. Min. Alliance; Bd. of Dirs. NAACP; Meritorious Service Award NAACP; Mason; Home: 860 Blair Ave., Cincinnati, O. 45229;

Office: 1813 Hewitt Ave., Cincinnati, O. 45229

REID, Arlond N., b. Indiana, May 8, 1913; s. Grant and Minnie; B.S., Univ. Chgo., 1936; D.D., Phillip Sem., 1942; Grad. deg. theol., Amer. Bible Coll., 1962; m. Cosetta Marie Martin; Children--Siritha (Mrs. John Mc Callister), Arlond N., Jr., Debra, Daniel; pastor, Quinn Chapel, Cassopolis, Mich., 1954-58; Conner Chapel, Dowagiac, Mich., 1949-51; assoc. pastor, Allen Temple, Dayton, O., 1952; pastor, Marcellus Meth. Ch., Marcellus, Mich., 1953-60; assoc. pastor, Allen Chapel, Kalamazoo, Mich., 1946-49; pastor, Lewis Chapel, Albion, Mich., 1960-63; Newman A.M.E. Ch., Pontiac, Mich., 1963-present; chrmn., Labor & Industry; chap., Pontiac Gen. Hosp., 1966; pres., Pontiac Pastor's Assn., 1966; mem., NAACP; Strategy and Planning Commn., Mich. Coun. of Chs.; Oakland Poverty Commn.; Human Relations Bd.; US Navy, 1942-46; recd. award for outstanding service to the community, 1960, Gary, Ind.; award for service rendered to the Chrstn. Ed. Dept., Coun. of Chs., Pontiac, Mich.; award for service rendered to the Chaplain Commn., Pontiac Gen. Hosp., 1965; chrmn., membership and evangelism for Mich. Annual Conf., A.M.E. Ch.; dir., Rel. Ed., So. Detroit; elected del. for Community Chest, Albion, Mich., 1962; Home: 155 Judson St., Pontiac, Mich.

*REID, Edgar Leroy, b. Brownsville, Tenn., July 7, 1925; s. Robert L. and Annie (Morgan) R.; A.B., Lane Coll., 1950; B.D., Howard Univ., Sch. of Rel., 1955; m. Christene Crues; Children--Rita A.; asst. pastor, Walker Meml. Bapt. Ch., Wash., D.C.; pastor, Oakrum Bapt. Ch., Thoroughfare, Va., 1957-58; pastor, Second Bapt. Ch., Jefferson City, Mo., 1958-65; pastor adv., Bapt. Student Union, Lincoln Univ.; pastor, Walbrook Bapt. Ch., Balto., Md., 1965-; trustee, Western Bapt. Bible Coll., Kans. City, Mo., 1962; pres., Jefferson City br. NAACP, 1963-64; pres., Jefferson City Min. Alliance, 1963-64; US Navy, 1944-46; Office: Walbrook Baptist Ch., Rosedale and Walbrook Ave., Baltimore, Md. 21216

REID, George Ransom, b. Louisville, Ky., Oct. 30, 1932; s. Frank Madison and Beatrice Victoria (Andrews) R.; A.B., Allen Univ., Columbia, S.C., 1953; S.T.B., Boston Univ.; Union Theol. Sem.; m. Mary Ann Brown; Children--Gina Ann, George R.; pastor, Calvary Afr.

Meth. Episc. Ch., Louisville, S.C.; Campbell A.M.E. Ch., Wash., D.C.; current, St. Paul A.M.E. Ch., Wash., D.C., 1956--; dean of rel., Kittrell Coll., Kittrell, N.C., 1957-64; counseling staff, Boston Mass. Gen. Hosp.; mem., Alpha Phi Alpha, Mason; Home: 5302 Kansas Ave. NW, Washington, D.C. 20011; Office: 4901 14th St., NW, Wash., D.C. 20011

REID, Robert Edward, presiding elder, b. Como, Miss., Sept. 13, 1903; s. John Jackson and Laura Ann (Danner); A.B., Lane Coll.; B.D., Gammon Theol. Sem.; m. Alyce W. Monroe; Children-- Orien E.; pastor, Chrstn. Meth. Episc. Chs., Ga., Tenn.; presiding elder, Topeka, Kan.; dean, Leadership Sch., C.M.E. Ch., 4 yrs.; v.p., City Alliance, Topeka, Kan.; sec., repr. Coun. of Chs., Coun. of Rel. and Race; attended Seminary, Hebrew Sem., Jerusalem, Israel, 1964; mem., NAACP; Home: 3344 So. Benton St., Kansas City, Mo.

REID, Wilfred, b. Detroit, Mich., Oct. 9, 1923; s. William N. and Marguerite (Newman) R.; B.A., Univ. of Ill., 1952; D.D. (hon.), Monrovia Coll., 1964; m. Loretta Adams; Children--Paul Wilfred, Lorna Joyce; pastor, Bethel A.M.E. Ch., Muscatine, Iowa, 1956; Allen Chapel, A.M.E. Ch., Galesburg, Ill., 1957; Bethel A.M.E. Ch., Evanston, Ill., 1960; St. Stephen A.M.E. Ch., Chgo., Ill., 1964-present; v. chrmn., Leadership Development, Chgo. Urban League, 1965; chrmn., the Evangelistic Crusade for the Fourth Dist. of the A.M.E. Ch.; asst. sec., Chgo. Annual Conf. of the A.M.E. Ch., NAACP; chrmn., N. Shore Coordinating Coun., 1963; pres., Pastors Conf., Evanston, Ill., 1963; chrmn., Investigative Com. of the Human Relations Coun., Galesburg, Ill., 1958; chrmn., Social Action Com., Coun. of Chs., Galesburg, Ill., 1959; bd. mem., Evanston Coun. of Chs., 1962; US Forces, 1943-46; mem., Pi Kappa Delta; Home: 6800 S. Constance Ave., Chgo., Ill. 60649

REUBEN, Odell Richardson, coll. pres., b. Silverstreet, S.C., June 21, 1918; s. James and Matilda Stewart) R.; A.B., Benedict Coll., 1942; B.D., Benedict Coll., 1954; S.T.M., Oberlin Coll., 1947; LL.D., Allen Univ. (hon.), 1955; Pd.D. (hon.), Benedict Coll., 1959; m. Anna Daniels; Children--Wilhelmina, Lucy, Anna Maria, Odell, Jayne, Janice Reuben; pastor, Happy Home Bapt. Ch., Allendale, S.C.; Dunn Creek Bapt. Ch., Ware Shoals, S.C.; instr., Theology, Morris Coll., 1947-48; pres.,

Morris Coll., 1948--; sec., S.C. Chrstn. Action Coun. Bd.; mem., Community Hosp., Sumter, S.C.; Penn Community Service, St. Helena Is., S.C.; Coun. on Human Relations; mem., NAACP, Odd Fellows; Masons; Amer. Acad. of Political Sciences, etc.; Office: Morris Coll., Sumter, S.C.

REYNOLDS, Abraham Lincoln, b. Warrenburg, Miss., May 2, 1907; s. Abraham and Minnie (Tolbert) R.; B.A., Rust Coll., Holly Springs, Miss., 1931; B.D., Th.D., Burton Sem., Manitou, Col., 1950, 1953; m. Louise Robinson; Children--Abraham Lincoln III, Theon Leroy; pastor, Meth. Ch., Ft. Scott, Kan., 1947; St. John Meth. Ch., Independence, Kan., 1948-51; Peoples Meth. Ch., Colorado Springs, Colo., 1951-54; Mt. Olive Meth. Ch., Topeka, Kans., 1954-55; currently, Sixth United Presby. Ch., Chgo., Ill., 1956--; mem., Chgo. Presbytery; pres., Min. Woodlawn Alliance; Intl. Min. Alliance; mem., Bd. of Dirs., Chgo. Woodlawn Boys Club, Wash. Park YMCA; Presby. Interracial Coun.; South Central Planning Coun.; Assn. Clubs of Woodlawn; Chadburn Mission, Colorado Springs; Lions Club, Lamar, Colo.; awards: plaque, Interdenom. Min. Alliance; plaque, Boy Scouts of Amer.; Certificate of Merit, Mayor's office; Brotherhood Award; Natl. Conf. of Chrstns. and Jews; the Wash. Park YMCA; Woodlawn Service Com.; mem., Bd. of Dirs., Porter Found. of the United Presby. Ch. on campus of Univ. of Chgo.; Home: 1210 E. 62nd St., Chgo., Ill. 60637

RICE, Deual Convers, b. Kings Mt., N.C., Feb. 11, 1911; s. Converse and Dathula (Roberts); B.A., Rutgers Univ., 1934; B.D., Va. Union Univ., 1940; M.Th., Bloomfield Coll. and Sem., 1950; M.A., Columbia Univ., 1953; m. Edith Latimore; Children--Donna Karl and Jane Denise; pastor, Bank St. Bapt. Ch., Norfolk, Va., 1938-41; chap., US Army, 1941-45; Union Bapt. Ch., Montclair, N.J., 1945-66; tchr., hist. and soc., Hackensack, N.J., 1955-68; mem., Equal Employ. Oppt. Commn., Wash., D.C.; Home Improvement Adv. Bd., N.J.; Kappa Alpha Psi; Masons; Home: Lackawanna Ave., W. Paterson, N.J.; Office: Hackensack Middle Sch., 360 Union St., Hackensack, N.J.

*RICE, James Donald, sem. prof., b. Union, S.C., Oct. 6, 1926; s. J.D. and Mildred (Rosborough) R.; A.B., S.C. State Coll., 1950; B.D., Howard Univ., Sch. of Rel.,

1953; m. Ellen Vincienne Smithwick; Children--Donnelida L., James Donald, Jr.; chap., Natl. Coun. of Chs.; NY City Mission Soc.; chap. & tchr., Leland Coll., Baton Rouge, La.; coll. minister & tchr., Morris Coll., Sumter, S. C.; pastor, Enon Bapt. Ch., Sumter, S. C.; pres., Western Bapt. Sem. (Bible Coll.), Kansas City, Mo.; current pastor, Roanoke Bapt. Ch., Hot Springs Natl. Park, Ark., 1962--; occasional tchr., religious institutes; guest lectr. and rel. emphasis Week Leader on various coll. campuses; mem., Bd. of Community Coun. for Social Action of Greater Kansas City, 1960-62; First v.p., Kansas City, Mo. br. NAACP; currently, pres., Hot Springs Natl. Park Br. NAACP, and chrmn. Legal Redress Comm., Ark. Conf., NAACP; S.W. Reg. Ch. Sec. of NAACP; mem., Kansas City Coun. Ex. Bd., Coun. of Chs., 1958-62; WW II Vet, served overseas; 1961 Phi Beta Sigma Award, Kansas City, Mo.; Man of Year for work in desegregation; mem., Phi Beta Sigma; Home: 737 Pleasant,Hot Springs National Park, Ark.; Office: Roanoke Bapt. Ch., PO Box 1201, Hot Springs, Ark.

RICE, Warner Myron, ch. official, b. Minneapolis, Minn., Oct. 29, 1932; s. Warner E. and Myra (Riley) R.; Oakwood Coll., 1954-57; Wash. Missionary Coll., 1957-58; Union Coll., 1958-59 - B. A.; Drake Univ., post-grad. courses, 1963--; m. Shirley I. Smith; 1 son--Lowel V.; asst. pastor, S. D. A. Ch., Wichita, Kan., 1959-60; pastor, Compress Rd. S. D. A. Ch., Sikeston, Mo., 1960-62 and Philadelphia S. D. A. Ch., Des Moines, Iowa, 1962-63; present: pastor, Central States Conf. of S. D. A., Kansas City, Mo.; part-time tchr., 1960-61; v.p., NAACP, 1961, Sikeston, Mo.; sec., Interdenom. Min. Alliance, Sikeston, Mo.; v.p., Interdenom. Min. Alliance, Des Moines, Iowa, 1963-present; cub-scout master, Sikeston, Mo., 1961; Home: 1433 Fremont St., Des Moines, Iowa; Office: 1150 13th St., Des Moines, Iowa.

RICH, Archie L., b. Apr. 7, 1934; married; 4 children; A. B., Southwestern Coll., Winfield, Kans., 1957; B. D., Garrett Sem., 1961; pastor, John Wesley Meth. Ch., River Rouge, Mich., 1961-66; Berea United Meth. Ch., 1966-present; mem., Conf. Bd. of Chrstn. Concerns, U. Meth. Conf.; chrmn., Com. on Race and Cultural Relations, Bd. of Chrstn. Concerns; registrar and asst. dir., 1965 U. N., Wash. Peace Seminar, (Detroit); former pres., River Rouge - Encorse br. NAACP, 1964-66;

v. chrmn., Com. on Peace & Cultural Relations, Detroit Coun. of Chs., 1965-66; chrmn., Com. on Ecumenical Affairs, (Detroit) 1968-69; Natl. Bd. Dirs., Blatch Meth. for Church Renewal; pres., "Mission Now," (ecumenical summer prog.); organizer and dir., Berea Com. Development Organization, (Urban renewal prog.), Highland Pk, Mich. (Model cities prog.); established "John Stewart Hut," storefront ministry, (tutoring, arts, drama, black history, reading courses to pre-sch. and un-churched children); organizer, Berea Neighborhood Senior Citizens Group; participated in developing, 12 week course for use in local ch. "The History and Culture of Black People;" frequent contributor to newspapers, periodicals and journals; Home: 3274 Lawrence, Detroit, Mich. 48206; Office: 400 LaBelle Ave., Highland Park, Mich.

RICHARDSON, Ben; A.B., Fla. A & M, 1936; S.T.B., Harvard Univ., 1939; Certificate in Ed., Newark State Tchrs. Coll, 1948; pastor, Presby. Chs., 1940-54; dir., Erie Neighborhood House, Chgo., Ill.; Office: 1347 W. Erie St., Chicago, Ill.

RICHARDSON, Harry Van, sem. dean, b. Jacksonville, Fla., June 27, 1901; s. Martin V. and Bertha I. (Witsell) R.; A.B., Western Reserve Univ., 1925; S.T.B., Harvard Univ. Div. Sch., 1932; Ph.D., Drew Univ., 1945; D.D. (hon.), Wilberforce Univ., 1941; m. Selma T. White; chap., Tuskegee Inst., Ala., 1934-48; pres., Gammon Theol. Sem., 1948, 1950; pres., Interdenom. Theol Cent., 1959-69; retired. mem., Bd. of Dir., So. Reg. Council, Inc.; mem., Natl. Coun. of Chs. of Christ in the US; Southern Advisory Com., Gen. Bd.; mem.-at-large, Greater Atlanta Coun. of Chs.; mem., Bd. of Dirs., Atlanta Urban League; mem., Citizens Adv. Com. for Urban Renewal of Atlanta; Bd. of Dirs., Atlanta TB Assn.; Assn. of Meth. Theol. Schs., pres. of the Assn. 1955; Ex. com. of the Amer. Assn. of Theol. Schs.; mem., Bd. of Dirs. of the Community Chest; Bd. of Dirs., Ga. Assn. for Pastoral Care; Mayor's Com. of the Atlanta Coordinating Coun.; Bd. of Dir. of Family Service Soc., Public Relations Com.; Coun. of Evangelism of the Meth. Ch.; Bd. of Mgrs., Gulfside Pastors Sch., Meth. Ch.; chrmn., Negro Div. of Community Services Campaign; field dir. of program for training of the Negro rural ministry under the auspices of Home Missions Coun. of No. Amer. and the Phelps-Stokes Fund; author: Dark Glory: A Study of the Rural Church; contributor to: Best Sermons,

The Christian Way in Race Relations, Journal of Religious Thought, Opportunity, New York Times Magazine, The Negro Educational Review, The Central Christian Advocate, The Upper Room, Ebony, and others; Office: 671 Beckwith St., SW, Atlanta, Ga.

RICHARDSON, Louis Melvin, b. Johnstown, Pa., Nov. 7, 1927; s. Louis M., Sr. and Elizabeth (Hemphill) R.; student, Johnstown Div., Univ. of Pittsburgh; B.S., Livingstone Coll., 1955; B.D., Hood Theol. Sem., 1958; student, St. Francis Coll.; m. Allie Dimery; Children--April V., Louis II, Emmett, Alan, Hope C., Peter C.; pastor, Pilgrim Congre. Chrstn. Ch., High Point, N.C., 1955-56; Rickert Chapel A.M.E.Z. Ch., Wilkesboro, N.C., 1956-58; Zion Wesley Sta., Troutmans, N.C., 1958-60; Goler Meml. A.M.E.Z., Winston-Salem, N.C., 1960-65; First A.M.E.Z. Ch., Paterson, N.J., 1965-present; tchr., consultant, Domestic Rel. Court; pub. relations, Paterson Task Force; Bd. of Dir., Visiting Homemakers; exec. com., Paterson Coun. of Chs., mem., NAACP, Rotary Intl., Alpha Phi Alpha; Home: 326 Ellison St., Paterson, N.J. 07501

RILEY, Negail Rudolph, sem. prof., b. Oklahoma City, Okla., Sept. 15, 1930; s. Tilton and Estella Lucille (Sneed) R. Caruthers; B.A., Howard Univ., 1952; B.D., Perkins Sch. of Theol., So. Meth. Univ., 1955; Boston Univ., 1955-candidate for Th.D.; m. Gwendolyn Maurine Allen; Children--Beryl Elise; asst. pastor, St. Paul Meth. Ch., Dallas, Tex., 1952-55; interim dir., Brooks Meml. Community Center, Jamaica, L.I., N.Y., 1955; dir., Chrstn. Ed., Ch. of All Nations, Boston, Mass., 1955-57; dir., Morgan Meml. Youth and Children's Settlement House, Boston, Mass., 1958-62; interim pastor, Union Bapt. Ch., Cambridge, Mass., 1962; pastor, Wesley Chapel Meth. Ch., Little Rock, Ark., 1962-68; ex. sec., City Work Dept. Bd. of Missions, The United Meth. Ch., 1968-present; asst. prof., Rel. and Sociology, Philander Smith Coll., Little Rock, Ark., 1962 ret.; mem. bd. of dir., Carver br. YMCA, Little Rock, Ark.; bd. of dirs., Urban League of Greater Little Rock; Bd. of dir., Ark. Coun. on Human Relations; bd. of dir., Aldersgate Meth. Camp, Little Rock, Ark.; first v.p., Ark. Cun. of Chs.; v.p., Little Rock Coun. on Community Affairs; treas., Little Rock Interracial and Interdenom. Min. Alliance; exec. comm., Prof. of Rel. Section, Meth. Conf. on Chrstn. Ed.; Alpha Phi Alpha; articles: The Chrstn.

Advocate; Power Magazine; The Annals of Political and Social Sciences; Together Magazine; Home: 112-54 175th Pl., St. Albans, N.Y. 11433; Office: 475 Riverside Dr., New York, N.Y. 10027

RILEY, Sumpter Marion, Jr., ch. official, b. Greenwood, S.C., June 10, 1903; s. Sumpter Marion and Amy Jane (Fisher) R.; A.B., DePauw Univ., 1926; B.D., Garrett Biblical Inst., 1930; S.T.M., Boston Univ., 1938; completed the residence for Ph.D., 1941; D.D. (hon.), Philander Smith Coll., 1952; m. Varina Wilhelmenia Lone; Children--Phyllis (Mrs. Richard Williams); pastor, Browns Meth. Ch., Ill; Patoka Meth. Ch., Ind., 1926; 2nd Meth. Ch., Princeton, Ind., 1927; asst. pastor, So. Park Meth. Ch., Chgo., Ill., 1928-30; asst. dir., Negro Work of Bd. of Home Missions and Ch. Extension, 1930-31, Phila., Pa.; pastor, Centenary Meth. Ch., Akron, O., 1931-32; Scott Meth. Ch., Denver, Colo., 1932-34; Burns Meth. Ch., Des Moines, Iowa, 1934-36; LaSalle Meth. Ch., St. Louis, Mo., 1936-37; 4th Meth. Ch., Boston, Mass., 1937-42; Asbury Meth. Ch., Columbus, O., 1942-44; Berea Meth. Ch., Detroit, Mich., 1944-45; Gorham Meth. Ch., Chgo., Ill., 1945-51; Dist. supt. of Chgo. Dist., 1951-57; pastor, Cory Meth. Ch., Cleveland, O., 1957--; mem., Mason; Alpha Phi Alpha; Democrat; Home: 10515 Grantwood Ave., Cleveland, O.; Office: 1117 E. 105th St., Cleveland, O.

ROBERTS, Frederick Raymond, b. Phila., Pa., Nov. 27, 1921; s. Pleas and Emma; A.B., Va. Theol. Sem. and Coll., Lynchburg, Va., 1942; studies, E. Bapt. Theol. Sem., Phila., Pa., 1947-49; m. Ernestine Skelton; Children--Rochelle (Mrs. R. Stanley), Frederick; pastor, Main St. Bapt. Ch., Clifton Forge, Va., 1940; chap., Yokohama, 1945; asst. pastor, Mt. Zion Bapt. Ch., Germantown, Pa., 1947-49; Monumental Bapt. Ch., Elmira, N.Y., 1949-51; asst. pastor, Siloam Bapt. Ch., Norristown, Pa., 1952-54; Mt. Olive Bapt. Ch., Coatesville, Pa., 1954-58; Calvary Bapt. Ch., Merchantville, N.J., 1965-present; instr., New Era Theol. Inst., Phila., Pa., 1949 and 1959; instr., Bethany Bapt. Assn., Jericho, N.J., 1968; v.p., Darby area br. NAACP; 1968; chrmn., Community Rel. Org., Darby, Pa., 1964-present; military duty, 1944-46; awards, Asiatic-Pac. Theater Award; 2 Bronze Stars; Good Conduct Medal; Sharpshooters Award; Home: 22 Spruce St., Merchantville, N.J. 08109

ROBERTS, Harry Walter, b. Phila., Pa., Oct. 5, 1902; s. Wallace and Frances (Jackson); A. B., Wilberforce Univ., Wilberforce, O., 1929; B. D., Yale Div. Sch., New Haven, Conn., 1932; M. A., London Univ., London, England, 1934; Cert. Oxford Univ., Oxford, Eng., 1933; Ph. D., Yale Univ., New Haven, Conn., 1943; courses, Univ. of Chgo., Chgo., Ill., 1935; Va. Polyt. Inst., 1951-52; m. Leo Butler; A. M. E. Ch. Hd., Dept. of Soc., Va. State Coll., Petersburg, Va., 1935-present; Dir., summer sch. for min., Va. State Coll., 1943-50; spec. res. asst., Va. Polyt. Inst., 1937-40; mem., Amer. Sociological Soc.; So. Sociological Soc.; Rural Sociological Soc.; Va. Soc. Sci. Assn.; Va. Soc. for Res.; Natl. Coun. Fam. Rel.; Soc. Study of Soc. Prob.; Assn. for Study of Negro Life; Va. Coun. on Fam. Relations; SE Coun. on Fam. Rel.; Amer. Acad. Pol. and Soc. Sci.; author, contrib. to many prof. periodicals; awards, cert. of appreciation and esteem for 25 yrs. serv. in soc. sci., Asson. of Soc. Sci. Tchrs., 1960; pres., Ser. Cert. of Va. Soc. Ser. Assn., 1964; cert. of award for meritorious serv. to So. Organ. for Visually Handicapped, Petersburg, Va.; mem., Mason, Alpha Phi Alpha, Sigma Pi Phi; Home: 401 4th Ave., Ettrick, Va., 23803; Office: Va. State Coll., Dept. of Soc., Petersburg, Va.

ROBERTS, James Deotis, Sr., sem. prof.; b. Spindale, N. C., July 12, 1927; s. J. C. and Edith (Godde) R.; A. B., Johnson C. Smith, 1947; B. D., Shaw Univ., 1950; B. D., Hartford Theol. Sem., 1951; S. T. M., Hartford Theol. Sem., 1952; Ph. D., Edinburgh Univ., Scotland, 1957; m. Elizabeth Caldwell; Children--James Deotis, Jr.; edin Charmaine, Carlita Rose; pastor, Union Bapt. Ch., Tarboro, N. C., 1947-50; asst. pastor, Union Bapt. Ch., Hartford, Conn., 1950-52; dean, Religion, Ga. Bapt. Coll., Macon, Ga., 1952-53; assoc. prof. and chaplain, Shaw Univ., 1953-55; 57, 58; current prof., Theology, Howard Univ. Sch. of Rel.; visiting prof., Swarthmore Coll., Phila., Pa., 1969; mem., Institutional Ministry Comm., Coun. of Chs. Natl. Capitol Area; Kappa Alpha Psi; Alpha Kappa Nu Natl. Honorary Soc.; Amer. Assn. of Univ. Profs.; author: Faith and Reason; Comparative Study of Pascal Bergson and James; From Puritanism to Platonism in Seventeenth Century England; Home: 1428 Whittier Pl. N. W., Wash., D. C.; Office: Sch. of Rel., Howard Univ., Wash. D. C.

ROBERTS, Joseph Lawrence, Jr., b. Chgo., Ill., Feb. 17, 1935; s. Joseph L.; B.A., Knoxville Coll., 1956; B.D., Union Theol. Sem., 1959; m. Esther Jean; Children--Cheryl, Cynthia; field worker, Ch. of the Master, NYC, 1956-58; First Ch., Hoboken, N.J.; pastor, Weequahic Ch., Newark, N.J., 1959-62; Elmwood United Presby. Ch., E. Orange, N.J., 1962--; mem., Presby. Comm. on Ecumenical Mission & Relations; v. chrmn., Synod's Com. on Rel. and Race; v.p., Min. Assn. of Orange & Maplewood, N.J.; Office: Elmwood United Presby. Ch., Elmwood Ave. & Eppert Sts., E. Orange, N.J.

ROBERTSON, Benjamin William, Sr., b. Roanoke, Apr. 6, 1931; s. Clarence and Anna Mary (Holland) R.; A.B., Va. Union Univ., 1954; B.D., Va. Sem. & Coll., 1957; D.D. (hon.), Va. Sem., 1959; LL.D. (hon.), Union Bapt. Sem., 1965; m. Dolores Wallace; Children--Benjamin, Jr.; pastor, First Union Bapt. Ch., Chesterfield, 1950-52; Piney Grove Bapt. Ch., Va. Beach, 1952-55; Cedar St. Mem. Bapt. Ch., 1955--; nat. sec., Prog. Nat. Sun. Sch. & B.T.U. Congress; founder, Robertson's Kiddie Kollege; tchr., Natl. Sun. Sch. & B.T.U. Leadership Course; campaign dir., Richmond br. NAACP, 1960-61; ex. sec., Va. Sem. Managerial Bd., 1962--; mem., Trustee Bd., Bapt. Ch. Children's Home, 1961-63; ex. bd., Va. Coun. of Chs., 1963--; award: Citizenship Award, Alpha Phi Alpha, 1960; Outstanding Citizenship Award, East End Civic Assn., 1961-62; Minister of the Month, 1961; sec., East End Lodge, Mason; St. Luke; Moses, Inc.; Knights of Damons; NAACP; Ex. bd., Union Savings & Loan Assn.; Adv. Bd., The Citizen (newspaper); Home: Rte 5, Box 312y, Richmond, Va.; Office: Cedar St. Meml. Bapt. Ch., 24 & N Sts., Richmond, Va.

ROBERTSON, Burnell Jacob, b. Patterson, La., June 13, 1924; s. Jacob and Alma Bridget R.; Southern Univ.; Campbell Coll., Miss.; Lampton Sem.; R.R. Wright Sch. of Rel.; m. Gaynell Blake; Children--Joycelyn Ann, Lorraine Theresa, Emily Marie; ordained 1957; pastor, St. Paul (Congre.) United Ch. of Christ, New Iberia, 1956; current pastor, Teche United Ch. of Christ, New Iberia, La.; chap., New Orleans Coun. Parent Teacher Assn., 1942-45, 1950-52; awards; Good Conduct, Three Battle Campaign Stars; Boy Scout Eagle Badge; mem., La. Pub. Health Assn., Boy Scout Troop Scoutmaster; Home: 1920 N. Mao New Orleans, La. 70119; Office Teche United

Ch. of Christ, New Iberia, La.

ROBINSON, Arthur Alexander, Jr., b. Napoleonville, La., Feb. 20, 1928; s. Arthur Alexander and Odessa (Noel); A. B., Dillard Univ.; B. D., Gammon Theol. Sem., 1954; US Army Chap. Sch.; m. Jeanette Wyne; Children--Adrienne A., Arthur A., III, Anthony A., Angelique A.; pastor, Camphor Meml. Meth. Ch., Baton Rouge, La., 1954-56; Phillips Memorial Meth. Ch., New Orleans, La., 1956-60; Baynton Meth. Ch., Gretna, La., 1948-51; Kynett Meth. Ch., Forsyth, Ga., 1952-54; current pastor, St. James Meth. Ch., 1962--; sub. tchr., Pine Bluff, Ark., pub. sch. sys.; adult organizer and adviser, Pine Bluff Student Movement, 1963; mem., New Orleans Interdenom. Min. Alliance, 1956-60; Scotlandville br. NAACP; Baton Rouge Interdenom. Min. Alliance; US Navy Unit Commendation Award, 1944; Stars for four battles, WW II; Democrat; chrmn., Bd. of Pension of the La. Conf. of the Meth. Ch. and Bd. of Min. Training of the same Conf.; called a boycott of the merchants of downtown Pine Bluff and the shopping center area which led to interracial negotiation, Mar. 1963; led and called the first march over 500 people in the downtown area of Pine Bluff seeking equality for all the races; St. James Meth. Ch. where he was the pastor was bombed because of its integration activities; Home: 314 So. Poplar, Pine Bluff, Ark.; Office: 316 So. Poplar, Pine Bluff, Ark.

ROBINSON, Dillard, b. San Antonio, Tex., June 8, 1934; s. Dillard and Naomi; B. A., Drew Univ., Madison, N. J., 1955; S. T. B., Berkeley Div. Sch., New Haven, Conn., 1958; vicar, St. Philip's Episc. Ch., San Antonio, Tex., 1958-66; canon of Trinity Cathedral, Newark, N. J., 1967-present; clinical training; Amer. Inst. of Rel. and Psychology; Watson Fellow of Bexley Hall, Gambier, O., 1965; Home: 381 Broad St., Newark, N. J., 07104; Office: 24 Rector St., Newark, N. J. 07102

*ROBINSON, G. Dewey, bishop, b. Sumter Co., S. C., Feb. 22, 1910; s. Powell and Carrie (James) R.; A. B., Allen Univ.; B. D., Howard Univ. Sch. of Rel., Wash., D. C.; further study: Harvard Univ., Cambridge, Mass.; m. Darrie Mae Chandler; pastor, Young Chapel, S. C.; Little Mountain Circuit, S. C.; Burlington Ct., N. C.; Allen Afr. Meth. Episc. Ch., Baltimore, Md.; Ward Meml. A. M. E. Ch., Wash., D. C.; Campbell A. M. E. Ch., Wash., D. C.; Waters, A. M. E. Ch., Balto., Md.;

pastor, Metro. A. M. E. Ch., Wash., D. C.; elected bishop 15th Episc. Dist. A. M. E. Ch., 1968--; US Army chap., 1941-44; mem., Rel. Comm., YMCA, Balto.; Chrstn. Ed. Comm. Urban League, Balto., Md.; trustee, Kittrell Coll.; treas., Kittrell Coll.; trustee & treas., Balto. Conf.; mem., Bd. of dirs., Coun. of Chs.; Natl. Coun. of Chs.; World Coun. of Methodism; treas., Wash. Conf. A. M. E. Ch.; mem., Mason; Phi Beta Sigma; author: What We Believe and Why We Believe It (Afr. Methodism); Home: 1715 Webster St., N. W. Wash., D. C.

ROBINSON, Hubert Nelson, bishop, b. Urbana, O., Apr. 28, 1912; s. John H. and Rovilla Ontario (Hill) R.; A. B., Ohio State Univ., 1935; B. D., Hamma Div. Sch., 1934; Univ. of Pittsburgh, 1945; Wilberforce Univ., D. D. (hon.), 1943; D. D., Allen Univ., 1952; m. Mary Isley; children --Cassandra Lee; entered Afr. Meth. Episc. Ch. ministry, 1930; elder's ordination, 1934; pastor, Smithfield A. M. E. Ch., Ohio, 1935; Jones Tabernacle A. M. E. Ch., Cincinnati, O., 1935; Steubenville A. M. E. Ch., Ohio, 1938; St. Paul A. M. E. Ch., Columbus, O., 1940; St. James A. M. E. Ch., Pittsburgh, Pa., 1944; St. James A. M. E. Ch., Cleveland, O., 1948; Ebenezer A. M. E. Ch. Detroit, Mich., 1955-64; elected bishop, A. M. E. Ch., Cincinnati, O., Mav 1964; tchr., Payne Sem., Wilberforce Univ., 1943; lectr., Minister's seminars at Paul Quinn Coll., Tex., 1950-53; Edward Waters Coll., Jacksonville, Fla., 1960-63; Bd. of Ed., A. M. E. Ch., 1944-60; Trustee bd., Wilberforce Univ. and Payne Sem.; v. p., Detroit Coun. of Chs.; pres., Detroit Metro. Pastor's Union; Gov's. Commn. on Morals & Ethics, Mich., 1962-64; Gov's. Commn. on Traffic Safety, Mich., 1964; mem., Kappa Alpha Psi, Mason, Elks, NAACP, Urban League, Frontier Club of America; Bd. of Dir., Children's Adoptive Agencies, Cleveland, O., Detroit, Mich.; Home: 131 Arden Park, Detroit, Mich.; Office: 5151 W. Chicago Blvd., Detroit, Mich.

ROBINSON, J. E., coll. prof., b. Drawdy, S. C.; A. B., Paine Coll.; B. D., Howard Univ., Sch. of Rel.; residential work for M. A., Howard Univ.; M. A., Drew Univ.; two children; asst. pastor, Wash., D. C., Tenn.; pastor, Chrstn. Meth. Episc. Chs., S. C., Del., Va., Tenn.; presiding elder, Jackson-Memphis Annual Conf. (C. M. E. Ch.); current pastor, Miles C. M. E. Ch.; head of dept. of rel., Miles Coll., Birmingham, Ala.; administrative asst.

to Bishop E. P. Murchison (C. M. E. Ch.); dean and registrar, Phillips Sch. of Theol. Sem.; 6 yrs.; dean, Leadership Training Sch., Tenn., 4 yrs.; mem., C. M. E. Ministers' Alliance; Birmingham Brotherhood of Clergymen; Ala. Coun. on Human Relations; lesson writer, Gen. Bd., Chrstn. Ed. (C. M. E. Ch.); pres., Birmingham Brotherhood of Clergyman; mem., YMCA, Mason, Alpha Phi Alpha; Office: Miles Coll., Birmingham, Ala.

ROBINSON, James Herman, consultant, State Dept., b. Knoxville, Tenn., Jan. 24, 1907; s. Henry John and Willie (Banks) R.; A. B., Lincoln Univ., 1935; B. D., Union Sem., 1938; D. D. (hon.), Wesleyan Univ., 1957; Dartmouth Coll., 1963; LL. D., Lincoln Univ., 1949; LH. D., New Sch. for Social Research, 1958; D. D., Occidental Coll., 1964; m. Gertrude Cotter; Youth dir., NAACP, 1938-40; pastor, Ch. of the Master, NYC, 1936-61; Dir., Morningside Comm. Center, Inc., 1936-61; Emeritus Ch. of the Master, 1957-present; consultant on Africa for United Presby. Ch.; consultant on Afr. Desk, Dept. of State; v. chrmn., Natl. Adv. Comm. to Peace Corps; mem., Bd. of Syndenham Hosp.; Boys' Club of New York; Greater New York; Safety Coun.; former mem., Bd. of NAACP; Natl. Urban League; author: Road Without Turning; Tomorrow is Today; Adventurous Preaching; Love of This Land; Africa at the Crossroads; Home: 549 W. 123rd St., New York, N. Y.

ROBINSON, Milton Benerdine, b. Harris, N. C., June 29, 1913; s. Plato and Connie R.; cert., N. C. State Coll., 1957; A. B., Johnson C. Smith Univ., Charlotte, N. C., 1963; cand., M. S., A & T Coll., Greensboro, N. C., 1968; m. Lois Mosley; Children--Mrs. Theodore Mercer; Mrs. Willie L. McDaniel; Connie M.; Milton, Jr., Mrs. Levi Evans, Mrs. Bobby McKesson, Arthur, Charles, Priscilla, Phyllias, Kenneth; pastor, St. John A. M. E. Z. Ch., Rutherford, N. C.; presiding elder and pastor, Western N. C. Conf.; del., Gen. Conf., 1960, 1964; Zion repr. on Dept. of Ch. bldg. and architecture, Natl. Coun. of Chs.; mem., Bd. of Statistics & Recors A. M. E. Z. Ch.; instr., Dept. of Trade-Indus. Ed., Carver H. S., Spindale, N. C.; mem., Rutherford Co. Human Rel. Coun.; statistical sec., Blue Ridge Annual Conf.; mem., Planning Com., Community Action Program, Rutherford; NAACP, Rutherford Co.; mem., Rutherford Co. Min. Assn.; mem., Rutherford Co., N. C. Tchrs. Assn.; mem.,

N. C. Natl. Vocational Assn.; sec., Mason; Home: Rt. 1 Box 398A, Forest City, N. C. 28043

ROBINSON, Paul Mitchell, b. High Point, N. C., June 23, 1928; s. Carrows William and Senas (Barnes) R.; A. B., B. D., Johnson C. Smith Univ., 1952; m. Maggie Lee Brown; Children--Carolyn, Beatrice, Paul Jr., Kevin, Twila; pastor The Bethel and Shinnecock Presby. Ch., Southampton, L. I., N. Y., 1952--; also moderator L. I. Presbytery, 1959; chrmn., So. Fork Migrant Comm., Eastern L. I., 1956-60; chrmn. L. I. Presbytery's Comm. on Bill & Overtures, 1955-61; pres., Community Improvement Assn., Southampton, N. Y., 1960; selected "Man of the Year" 1959, Southampton, N. Y.; chap., Tyre Lodge 91, Riverhead, N. Y.; mem., Mason, 1956-61; Office: Shinnecock Indian Reservation, Southampton, L. I., N. Y.

RODNEY, John Joseph, b. Chicago, Ill., June 4, 1931; s. Onazie Jos. and Blanche (Young) R.; St. Paul's Coll., Epworth, Iowa, 1952-54; St. Mary's Sem., Techny, Ill., 1954-60, B. A., 1956; 10 summers, Loyola Univ., Chgo., M. A. 1964; ordained priest, Roman Cath. Ch., 1960; asst. pastor, St. Anselm's Ch., Chicago, 1960-61, Our Lady of the Gardens Ch., Chgo., 1961-63; St. Nicholas Ch., St. Louis, Mo., 1963--; Chgo. Urban League, Coun. of Rel. Leaders, 1961-62; March on Wash. for Jobs and Freedom, Aug. 1963; Home: 18th and Lucas St., St. Louis, Mo.

RODNEY, Joseph Conway, b. Darrow, La., Feb. 7, 1938; s. Joseph Conway and Rosalie Gaudin (R.); Epiphany Apostolic Coll., Newburgh, N. Y., 1958-61; St. Joseph's Sem., 1964, B. A.; St. Joseph Sem., Wash., D. C., 1962-68; tchr. confraternity of Chrstn. Doctrine, Holy Comforter Ch., Wash., D. C., 1963-present; mem., Police Community Relation Bd. 14th precinct; Far North East Community Coun.; Coun. of Concern; Min. Alliance; vol. worker "Head Start" (U. P. O.); Step up Program, (U. P. O.); Voter registration, Baton Rouge, La., summer 1967; Home: 4925 E. Capitol St., Wash., D. C. 20019

ROGERS, Cornish Romeo, b. N. Y. City, Dec. 3, 1929; s. Neal and Mollie (Morris) R.; A. B., Drew Univ., Madison, N. J., 1947-51; S. T. B., Boston Univ., Sch. of Theol., NYC, 1952-55; grad. courses: Union Theol. Sem., NYC, 1955-57; m. Elsie Virginia Daniels; Children--

David Bruce; assoc. pastor, Ch. of All Nations, Boston, Mass., 1953-55; Metro. Community Ch., NYC, 1955-57; pastor, Willis Ave. Meth. Ch., Bronx, N.Y., 1957-58; Calvary Meth. Ch., Los Angeles, Calif., 1958-66; Wesley United Meth. Ch., Los Angeles, 1967-present; Credentialled instr. in Negro History, L.A. pub. adult sch. prog.; consult., Human Relations, L.A. sch. sys.; guest lectr. Univ. of Calif., L.A., Extension; pres., L.A. County Fed. of Community Councils, 1966; Bd. mem., EYOA (Poverty progr.), L.A., 1966; Bd. dir., Welfare Planning Conf. (L.A.) 1964-66; mem., Calif. State Adv. Com. on Children & Youth, 1966-present; honorary life mem., PTA; Fed. of Community Coordinating Councils; Home: 4847 Presidio Dr., Los Angeles, Calif. 90043; Office: 112 W. 52nd St., Los Angeles, Calif. 90037

ROGERS, Jefferson Paramore, b. Quincy, Fla., Jan. 27, 1918; s. Jefferson and Dovie R.; A.B., Fla. A & M Coll., 1940; M.A., Howard Univ. Rel. Ed., 1949; B.D., Yale Univ., 1947; m. Mary Grace Harris; Children--Anita Darrielle, Alain Burghardt, Weldon Douglass; Dir., Chrstn. Ed., Jones Tabernacle, A.M.E. Ch., Phila., Pa., 1944; pastor, St. Johns A.M.E. Ch., Phila., Pa., 1945; pastor, Bethel A.M.E. Ch., New Haven, Conn., 1945-46; race relations sec., Evangelical and Reformed Ch., Cleveland, O., 1947-54; pastor, Plymouth Congre. Ch., Wash., D.C., 1954-57; founder and pastor, Ch. of Redeemer Presby. Ch., Wash., D.C., 1957--; pres., D.C. Chapter So. Christn. Leadership Conf., 1964; organizing mem., Fellowship of Concern, Presby. Ch., USA, 1963--; rel. ed., Phila. Tribune, 1945; columnist of Religion in Modern Times, Phila. Tribune, 1945-47; staff mem., editorial bd. of Social Action, monthly organ of Congre. Chs.; organizer, New Haven Social Action Com., 1945; mem., NAACP; race relations div., Fed. Coun. of Chs.; Comm. on Chrstn. Social Action of the Evangelical and Reformed Ch.; bd. of Natl. Missions of Evangelical and Reformed Ch.; Inst. of Rel., Howard Univ.; Home: 4340 Argyle Terr., NW, Wash., D.C., 20011; Office: 15th at Girard St., NE, Wash., D.C.

ROGERS, Leslie Thomas, tchr., b. San Jose, Calif., Dec. 31, 1929; s. Covel and Alice (Berry) R.; B.A., Maryknoll Coll., Glen Ellyn, Ill., 1954; M.R.E., Maryknoll Sem., Maryknoll, N.Y., 1959; ordained Roman Cath. Ch. priesthood, June 13, 1959; tchr., Minor Sem., Musoma, Tanzania, E. Africa, 1959-61; asst. pastor, Komuge Cath.

Ch., Musoma. Home: U. S. Maryknoll P. O., New York; Office: Komuge Cath. Ch., PO Box 109, Musoma, Tanzania, E. Africa

ROGERS, T. Y. Jr., b. Oct. 8, 1935, Sumter Co., Ala.; s. T. Y. Sr. and Mrs. T. Y. Rogers; B. S., Ala. State Coll., 1955; B. D., Crozer Theol. Sem., 1960; m. La Pelzia Rankins; Children--Gina LaTruette; asst. pastor, Dexter Ave. Bapt. Ch., Mont., Ala., 1956-57; Youth dir., Camden Chrstn. Center, N. J., 1957-58; pastor, Galilee Bapt. Ch., Phila., Pa., 1960-64; ex. sec., Phila. Fellowship of Reconciliation, 1960-64; present pastor, First Afr. Bapt. Ch., Tuscaloosa, Ala., 1964-present; Dir. of Affiliates, S. C. L. C., Atlanta, Ga., 1967-present; visiting prof., Black Ch. Affairs, Interdenom. Theol. Center, Atlanta, Ga., 1968-present; pres., Tuscaloosa Citizens for Action Acomm., 1965-present; Comm. of Management, Barnes br. YMCA, 1965-67; pres., Confed. of Ala. Political Organizations, 1966-67; mem., Bd. of Dirs. S. C. L. C., 1964-67; mem., Bd. of Dirs. S. C. E. F., 1967-present; contributing ed., Bapt. Foreign Mission Outlook; mem., Alpha Phi Alpha, Intl. Platform Assn.; awards, Lily Found. Fellowship, 1959; Alumni of the Year, Va. Union Univ., Phila. chapter, 1963; Citizenship Award, Omega Psi Phi, 1965; Youth Service Award, Barnes br. YMCA, Tuscaloosa, Ala., 1967; Outstanding Young Man of Amer., 1967; 1968 ed. Who's Who in the South and Southwest; Home: 3267 Magnum Lane S. W., Atlanta, Ga. 30311; Office: 334 Auburn Ave. N. E., Atlanta, Ga. 30303

ROLAND, Garther William, b. New London, N. C., Feb. 12, 1911 s. Arthur and Mary (Smith) Owens (adopted parents); Slater Normal Sch. (now Winston-Salem State Coll.), 1927; B. S., Piedmont Bible Inst., 1953; m. Daisy Lee Chavis; Children--Mary Deloise (deceased), James Peters, Alphonzo Crosby (foster children); pastor, Middle Fork Chrstn. Ch., Winston, N. C., 1934-48; Little Salem Chrstn. Ch., Reidsville, N. C.; current, 1st Chrstn.Ch. Concord, N. C.; tchr., Rel. and Bible Ed., Winston-Salem and Reidsville, N. C., 2 yrs.; pres., Piedmont Tri-State Dist. Conv., 2 yrs.; chrmn., Bd. and sec.-treas., Dixie Shores Realty Co., Inc.; consultant, Interracial Consultation; minister of the south, Lexington, Ky. (Coll. of the Bible); Home: 2309 E. 1st St., Winston-Salem, N. C.; Office: Mahan & Rone Sts., Concord, N. C.

*ROLAND, Harold, b. Elko, S. C., Nov. 24, 1908; s. W. B. and Eliza; A. B., S. C. State Coll., 1934; B. D., Howard Univ., Sch. of Rel., 1937; courses: Univ. of Pa., Union Sem., Yale Univ., and Univ. of Ga.; m. Juanita (Reddish); Children--Harriet Anita; pastor, Beth. Bapt. Ch., Barnwell, S. C.; Central Bapt. Ch., Charleston, S. C.; Mt. Gilead Bapt. Ch., Durham, N. C.; New Mt. Zion Bapt. Ch., Orangeburg, S. C., present; chrmn., Corps of Chaplains, S. C. State Coll., 1967; princ., Macedonia High Sch., Blackville, S. C., 1937-42; cons., AA, Durham, N. C., 1951-52; del., Democratic State Conv., N. and S. C., 1957, 1966; mem., Omega Psi Phi; pres., New Hope Union, 1957-60; chrmn., Soc. Action Com., Bapt. State Conv., S. C.; 1964-68; author: Sermonettes, Carolina Times, Durham, N. C., 17 yrs.; various articles; author: booklet, Gems from Genesis; Home: Rte. 1, Box 875, Orangeburg, S. C.; Office: New Mt. Zion Bapt. Ch., Orangeburg, S. C.

ROLLINS, Joseph Metz, b. Newport News, Va., Sept. 8, 1926; s. Joseph and Alice; A. B., Johnson C. Smith Univ., Charlotte, N. C., 1947; B. D., Theol. Sem., Johnson C. Smith Univ., 1950; m. Julia (Boone); Children--Cecilia, Joseph; instr., Johnson C. Smith Univ., 1950-53; pastor, Trinity Presby. Ch., Tallahassee, Tenn., 1953-58; v. p., Nashville Chrstn. Leadership Conf. (SCLC), 1958-63; office, Bd. of Chrstn. Ed., United Presby. Ch., 1958-63; assoc. dir., Presby. Commn. on Rel. and Race, NYC, 1963-68; ex. dir., Nat. Com. of Negro Churchmen, NYC, 1968--; mem., Kappa Alpha Psi; FOR, Nyack, N. Y.; award, Citizen of Year, Omega Psi Phi; Home: 42 McKinley Ave., White Plains, N. Y.; Office: 354 Covent Ave., New York, N. Y. 10031

ROLLINS, Richard Albert, educator, b. Phila., Pa., Nov. 30, 1927; s. Nathaniel and Alyce R.; A. B., Lincoln Univ., Pa., 1952; B. D., Union Theol. Sem., N. Y., 1955; S. T. M., Boston Univ. Sch. of Theol., 1960; m. Audrey Joan King; assoc. minister, Enon Tabernacle Bapt. Ch., Phila., 1949-52; asst. minister, Cornerstone Bapt. Ch., Bklyn, 1954-55; Youth Dir., Manhattanville Neighborhood Center, NYC, 1952-53; Interim pastor, Park Manor Presby. Ch., N. Y., 1953-54; Bishop Coll., Dean of Men, 1955-58; instr., Div. Rel. and Phil., 1955-57; asst. instr., Div. Rel., 1957-59; Dean of the Chapel, 1959-64; asst. dir., Rel. Ed., Jerusalem Bapt. Ch., Marshall, Tex., 1959-61; assoc. prof. and chrmn., Div. of Rel.

and Phil., Bishop Coll., 1959; author: "Principles and Procedures in Improving Prayer in Public Worship," 1955; mem., Nat. Assn. of College and Univ. Chaplains; Amer. Soc. Society; Amer. Assn. of Univ. Profs.; Tex. State Tchrs. Assn.; Nat. Assn. of Biblical Instrs.; Amer. Psychological Soc.; Amer. Bapt. Ed. Assn.; Kappa Alpha Psi, Natl. Urban League, NAACP, YMCA; Dir. Natl. Bapt. Survey (Tex.), 1964; coll. adv., United Nations Week, 1960; Danforth tchr., 1964; Home: 2371 E. Ledbetter Dr., Dallas, Tex.; Office: 3837 Simpson Stuart Rd., Dallas, Tex.

*ROLLINS, Robert Lee, b. Louisa Co., Va., Nov. 17, 1903; s. William and Sallie; A.B., Storer Coll., Harpers Ferry, W.Va., B.D., Howard Univ. Sch. of Rel., 1941; D.D. (hon.), Va. Theol. Sem., 1948; m. Geneva C. Gillis; children--Elois Viola (Gibson); pastor, Fla. Ave. Bapt. Ch., Wash., D.C., 1938--; tchr., Bible Course in the Natl. Bapt. Congress; statistician, New England Bapt. Missionary Conv., 1950-63; mem., Ledroit Civic Assn; Mason; former pres., D.C. Bapt. Educational Congress; outstanding alumnus award from Storer Coll., 1950; mem., Natl. Sun. Sch. Pub. Bd.; Home 720 Quebec Pl., Wash., D.C.; Office: 623 Fla. Ave. NW, Wash., D.C.

*ROMAN, Gus, chap., b. New Orleans, La., Dec. 20, 1932; s. Gus and Mary Ballard) S.; Dillard Univ., 1952-54; A.B., B.D., Howard Univ., Wash., D.C., 1956, 1959; m. Eunice Helena Matthews; Children--Marcus, Tonai, Derrick; assoc. pastor, Sixth Mt. Zion Bapt. Ch., Richmond, Va., 1954-56; assoc. pastor, Mt. Pleasant Bapt. Ch., Wash., D.C., 1956-59; pastor, First Bapt. Ch., Balto., Md.; Prog. dir., O.T.C., Phila., Pa.; US Army chap., 1959-62; commendation medal; Home: 108 W. Coulter St., Philadelphia, Pa.

ROOKS, C. Shelby, administrator, b. Beaufort, N.C., Oct. 19, 1924; s. Shelby A. and Maggie (Hawkins) R.; B.A., Va. State Coll., 1949; B.D., Union Theol. Sem., N.Y., 1953; m. Adrienne Martinez; 1 son, Laurence Gaylord, 1 dau., Carol Ann; minister, Shanks Village Prot. Ch., Orangeburg, N.Y., 1951-53; Lincoln Meml. Congre. Temple, Wash., D.C., 1953-60; assoc. dir., The Fund for Theol. Ed., Inc., Princeton, N.J., 1960--; US Army, 1943-46, Overseas (Guadalcanal & Philippines), S/Sgt.;

Natl. Coun. of Chs., Dept. of the Ministry, Commn. on Higher Ed.; Bd. of dirs., U. Southern Chrstn. Fellowship; Theol. Commn., U. Ch. of Christ; del., World Congre. Coun., Rotterdam, Holland, 1962; moderator, Middle Atlantic Conf., UCC; Bd. of Dirs., Middle Atlantic Conf., UCC (pres., 1960-62) Adv. and Study Comm. on Realignment of Middle Atlantic Area, UCC; Steering Comm. of Consultation on Theol. Sch. and Student Financial Aid; Adv. Bd., Christianity and Crisis Magazine; author, "The Image of the Ministry in the Prot. Fellowship Program," "A Cross to Bear," The Journal of Religious Thought; "We Can't Ignore the Negro Campus," Presbyterian Survey; The Shortage of Negro B.D. Students," Union Seminary Tower; surveys, Rockefeller Doctoral Fellows, Negro Ph.D.'s and Th.D.'s 1953-63, and Negro B.D. students enrolled in Amer. Assn. of Theol. Schs. Home: 152 Guyot Ave., Princeton, N.J.; Office: 163 Nassau St., Princeton, N.J.

ROSS, Solomon David, b. Sumpter Co., Ga., Aug. 29, 1886; s. Esquire and Haggar; A.B., Morehouse Coll., Atlanta, Ga.; Univ. of Chicago; m. Lucinda Moore (deceased), Mary Olivia Brookins; Children--Abigail, Judson, William, Angelene, Darene McKinney; principal, high sch., Griffin, Ga., 3 yrs.; High sch., Sardis, Miss., 5 yrs.; pastor, Bapt. Ch., Pelham, Ga., 3 yrs., Second Bapt. Ch., Savannah, Ga., 6 yrs.; current pastor, Shiloh Bapt. Ch., Detroit, Mich., 1929--; moderator, Metro. Assn. (Detroit), 8 yrs.; chrmn., Race Relations Com., Nat. Bapt. Conv.; officer, Bapt. World Alliance; mem., Natl. Coun. of Chs.; Nat. Sun. Sch. & Bapt. Training Union Congress; Detroit Coun. of Chs.; testimonial resolutions, Detroit City Coun., 1959; mem., Omega Psi Phi; Home: 584 Arden Pk., Detroit, Mich.; Office: 557 Benton, Detroit, Mich.

ROSTON, David Williamson, b. Milledgeville, Ga., Sept. 8, 1904; s. John Maxwell and Anna (Williamson) R.; Tuskegee Normal and Industrial Inst., 1921; Natl. Bible Inst., N.Y., 1935; m. Hattie Foster (divorced); Children--Philip, Robert; pastored, Chrstn. Meth. Episc. Chs. in New Haven, Syracuse, N.Y., Bridgeport, Conn., Boston, Mass., 1936-40; pastored C.M.E. Chs. in Apex-Fuquay-Varina, Greensboro, Chapel Hill, Wash. and Gastonia, N.C., 1941-54; present: pastor, C.M.E. Chs. in Allendale, Lexington, Spartanburg, Saluda and Estill, S.C., 1955--; sec. to Bishop H.P. Porter, 1937-38; sec., Wash.

-Va. Conf. C. M. E. Chs., 1938-40; sec. to Bishop C. H. Russell, 1943-48; sec., N. C. Conf., 1942-54; sec., S. C. Conf., 1955-present; sub. tchr., Estill Training Sch., S. C.; mem., Knights of Pythians, Masons, NAACP, 1930-64; Democratic Ex. Comm., Greensboro, N. C., 1944-47; Demo. Ex. Comm., Columbia, S. C., 1956-58; v. p., Ward 9, Co. Democrats, 1956-58; del., Richland City Conf., Spartanburg, S. C., 1960; Home: PO Box 703, Estill, S. C.; Office: Wilmot St., Estill, S. C.

ROUSSEVE, Maurice Louis, educator, b. New Orleans, La., Sept. 22, 1906; s. Bartholomew Abel and Valentine Marie (Mansion) R.; Xavier Prep., 1918-20; St. Augustine's Sem. 1920-34; ordained priest, Roman Cath. Ch., May 23, 1934, first class of Negro S. V. D.; pastoral work 1934-50; 1952-64; tchr., asst. provincial and master of clerical novices, 1950-52; mem., Knights of Peter Claver, 4th degree; Home and Office: St. Joseph Ch., Box 278, Julien Rd., Broussard, La.

ROUTTE, Jesse Wayman, b. Macon City, Mo., June 13, 1906; s. Louis William and Lu Lu Belle (Smith) R.; B. A., M. A., Augustana Coll., 1929; B. D., Augustana Sem., 1932; m. Enid Gomez; Children--Luther, Jess (deceased), Enid, Carmen; ordained NY Synod, 1932; pastor, Holy Trinity Ch., Jamaica, Queens, 1934--; pres., Queens Luth. Pastors Assn.; mem., Adv. Comm. on Juvenile Delinquency, Jamaica, NY; Home: 111-46 167th St., Jamaica, N. Y.; Church: Holy Trinity Luth. Ch., 162-28 Mathies Ave., Jamaica, N. Y.

ROWE, Franklin R.; b. York, Ala., Oct. 1, 1910; s. Brag and Sarah; B. D., Gammon Theol. Sem., Atlanta, Ga., 1947; m. Rosa Lee Duncin R.; Children--Roosevelt, P. J.; pastored Chrstn. Meth. Episc. Chs., 25 yrs.; retired; present, pres. Ed. Inst. for the Advancement of Minority Groups; pres., Ben-Hill Co. br. NAACP (10 yrs.); chrmn., Legal Redress Com. NAACP, Fitzgerald, Ga.; chrmn., Ga. Chapter Human Relation Coun.; del., White House Conf. "To Fullfil These Rights," 1966; Democratic Party Conv., Chgo., 1968; candidate, Justice of Peace, 1964, Fitzgerald, Ga.; mem. bd. of ed., 1965; Home: 703 N. Meade St., Fitzgerald, Ga.; Office: 408 S. Hooker St., Fitzgerald, Ga. 31758

RUDOLPH, George A., b. Hanesville, Ala., Oct. 18, 1916;

s. John and Sillia R.; Birmingham Bapt. Coll., 1964; m. Elizabeth Lewis; Children--George C.; present pastor, Sixth Ave. Bapt. Ch., Birmingham, Ala.; mem., Clark Robinson Post 311, Birmingham, Ala.; Jefferson Co. Progressive Democratic Club; YMCA; Rose Mark Civic League; Armed services, 1942-43; Mason; Home: 34 16th Ave. West, Birmingham, Ala. 35204

RUFFIN, Andrew Jackson, b. Lisman, Ala., Nov. 11, 1893; s. Spencer P. and Gora Ann R.; A.B., State Tchrs. Coll., 1918; B.S., Morehouse Coll., 1929; B.Th., Western Bapt. Coll., 1937; m. Jennie Roberts; minister, Religious Ed. Dept., Pilgrim Bapt. Ch., Chgo., Ill., 1930-42; supply pastor, Bethel Bapt. Ch., Dayton, O., 1943-45; pastor, Jerusalem 2nd Bapt. Ch., Urbana, O., 1946--; tchr., Natl. Sun. Sch. & B.T.U. Congress, 1943; Ohio State Sun. Sch. & B.T.U. Congress, 12 yrs.; trustee, Champaign Co. Home Hosp., 1960--; mem., Urban Bi-Racial Comm.; pres., NAACP; Home: 127 Hill St., Urbana, O. 43078

*RUFFIN, James Shepard, b. Clayton, N.C., Mar. 6, 1928; s. Shepard and Gladys (Goodson) R.; A.B., Shaw Univ., Raleigh, N.C., 1954; B.D., Howard Univ., Sch. of Rel., 1959; grad. courses, Wesley Theol. Sem., Wash., D.C.; chrmn., Ex. Com., Youth Coun., 1955-56; Youth Dir., 1956-58; Jr. Ch. pastor, 1959-62; dir., Chrstn. Ed., 1963-65; First asst. pastor, 1965-66; coun., Cedar Knoll Sch., Wash., D.C., 1957-63; Receiving Home for Children, 1963-65; asst. Natl. Capitol Housing Project, 1965-67; Wash., D.C., Pupil Personnel Services, Team Leader, 1967-present; mem., Natl. Bapt. Conv.; Progressive Bapt. Conv.; pres., United Neighbors, Parkwood Pl., 1957-67; US Army, 1950-52; awards, Combat Badge, Korean Serv. Medal (3 Bronze Ser. Stars); United Nations Ser. Medal; Army Occupation Medal (Japan); mem., Bapt. Ed. Congress (D.C.); Bapt. Min. Conf.; Jr. Police Boys Club; Southwest Assembly; meritorious ser. award Mt. Methel Bapt. Ch., 1958; Home: 1422 Parkwood Pl., N.W., Wash., D.C. 20010; Office: 3242-A Penn., SE, Wash., D.C.

*RYCE, Amos, b. Ft. Valley, Ga., Apr. 7, 1912; s. Amos and Janie; A.B., Paine Coll., Augusta, Ga., 1937; B.D., Howard Univ., Sch. of Rel., Wash., D.C., 1940; D.D. (hon.), Eden Theol. Sem., Webster Groves, Mo., 1964; m. Emma Burton; Children--Sylvia, Amos, Julia (Mrs.

Ronald Marshall); George; pastor, Lane Tabernacle, St. Louis, Mo., 1954-66; Holsey Temple, Atlanta, Ga., 1941-44; Bethel C.M.E. Ch., Cordele, Ga., 1944-46; Trinity C.M.E. Ch., Augusta, Ga., 1946-49; Israel Metro. Ch., Gary, Ind., 1949-50; Indus. sec., Atlanta Urban League, Atlanta, Ga., 1942; prin., Austell pub. sch., Austell, Ga., 1943; pres., Holsey Inst., Cordele, Ga., 1944-46; v.p., Metro Ch. Fed. of Greater St. Louis, 1964; adm. asst. to pres., Miles Coll., Birmingham, Ala., 1966-present; mem., Clergy Adv. Com. of Planned Parenthood St. Louis, Mo.; Legal Aid Soc., St. Louis, Mo.; Bd., Family and Children's Serv., St. Louis, Mo.; Dialogue Group of Cath., Prot., Jews; Exec. bd., Conf. on Rel. and Race; Mayor's Comm. on Equal Employment Opportunity; Bd. of dir., United Fund, St. Louis, Mo.; Bd. of Dir., United Negro Coll. Fund; Bd. of dir., Metro. YMCA, St. Louis, Mo.; Girl Scout Coun. of St. Louis; Bd. of Ed., St. Louis, Mo., 1965; award, Frontier's of Amer. Choice for Man of Yr., St. Louis, 1961; Fellowship, Amer. Peace Mission, Rel. and Internatl. Diplomacy, NYC, 1958; study, Mid-East; W. Africa; Home: 723 3rd Ave., NW, Moultrie, Ga.

SABOURIN, Clemonce, b. New Orleans, La., Oct. 6, 1910; B.D., Immanuel Luth. Coll., Greensboro, N.C., 1935; A.B., Johnson C. Smith Univ., 1939; LL.D., Valparaiso Univ., Ind., 1963; m. Glenice James; one son--Clemonce James; asst. pastor, Grace Luth. Ch., Concord, N.C.; pastor, St. Paul's Luth. Ch., Charlotte, N.C., 1936-39; pastor, Grace-Luth. Meml. Luth. Ch. in Greensboro, N.C., 1939-44; pastor, Mt. Zion Luth. Ch., NYC, 1947--; dir., Mt. Zion Parochial Sch., sec., Gen. Conf. (a natl. organization of Synodical Conf. Negro Luth. Congregation); pres., Gen. Conf. of Synodical Conf. Negro Luth. Congregation; mem., The Synodical Conf. Survey Comm.; mem., first bd. of dirs., of Luth. Interracial Service, now a dept. of Luth. Soc. Serv. in NYC; mem., the Bd. of Dirs. of Luth. Child Welfare Assn. in NYC; mem., Bd. of Dirs. of Adopt-A-Child; sec., Lutheran Welfare Coun.; pres., Luth. Human Relations Assn.; pres., the Bronx-Manhattan-Westchester Pastoral Conf.; author: Let the Righteous Speak; Home: 421 W. 145th St., New York, N.Y.

SALMON, Harold Anthony, tchr., New York, N.Y., Nov. 27 1929; s. Harold and Dorothy (Henderson) S.; St. Joseph's

Sem. & Coll., 1950-56; asst. dir., Mission of Immaculate Virgin, S.I., N.Y., 1956-59; tchr., English and Rel., Cardinal Hayes High Sch., Bronx, N.Y., chrmn., Family Life Coun., Harlem-Wash. Heights Area; mem., Comm. of Religious Leaders of NYC, NAACP, Cath. Interracial Coun., Natl. Coun. of English Tchrs.; Home: 650 Grand Concourse, Bronx, N.Y. 10451

SALMON, John Luther Jr., b. Manhattan, N.Y., Oct. 9, 1932; B.S., B.D., Bloomfield Coll., N.J., 1955, 1958; m. Jeanne Mitchell; Children: Rebecca, Anne; David Benjamin, Jeanne Ellen; pastor, Trinity Presby. Ch., Rochester, N.Y., 1958-68; Tabor United Presby. Ch., Nov. 17, 1968-present; youth adv., St. Paul Presby. Ch., Newark, N.Y., 1953; Totowa Presby. Ch., Paterson, N.J., 1954-56; Central Presby. Ch., Paterson, N.J., 1956-58; clergy v.p., Flight Group, Rochester, N.Y., 1966; Coun., Industry State Sch. Industry, N.Y.; Camp Sharparoon (NY Mission Soc.); pres. mem. Bd. of Dir. Presby. Home, Wash., D.C.; Presby. Com. Metro. Missions; Presby. Com. Ch. and Soc.; certified hosp. chap., citation, Empire State Fed. Women's Clubs, Inc., 1965; Home: 910 Lawrence St. NE, Wash., D.C. 20017; Office: 150 S St. NW, Wash., D.C. 20017

*SAMPSON, Frederick George, b. Port Arthur, Tex., Aug. 9, 1925; s. Frederick and Florence S.; A.B., B.Th., Bishop Coll., 1946, 1947; B.D., Howard Univ. Sch. of Rel., 1950; D.D. (hon.), Va. Theol. Sem. & Coll.; Bishop Coll.; m. Earlene Zone Harrison; Children--Frederick G., III, Freda Gelene; dir., Religious Life and tchr., Bishop Coll., 1947; acting pastor, Coll. Hill Bapt. Ch., Ark., 1946-47; asst. pastor, Shiloh Bapt. Ch., 1948-52; pastor, High St. Bapt. Ch., Roanoke, Va., 1952-60; current pastor, Mt. Lebanon Bapt. Ch., Faculty mem., Ky State Sun. Sch. & B.T.U. Congress, Natl. Sun. Sch. & B.T.U. Congress; lectr., Natl. Bapt. Conv. USA, Inc., Women's Auxiliary; mem., Alpha Phi Alpha; consultant to Gov. of Ky. on Human Relations; Worship Leader, Women's Missionary State Convention; mem., YMCA; YWCA; Home: 950 SW Parkway, Louisville, Ky. 40211; Office: 2224 Chestnut St., Louisville, Ky.

SAMS, Roosevelt, Coll. prof., b. Lee Co., Texas, Feb. 15, 1923; s. Teb and Joe (Anna) S.; B.S., Paul Quinn Coll., 1949; M. Ed., Tex. So. Univ., 1953; Tex. Coll.-Spec. Study, 1964; m. Izetta Christman; Children--

Donna Jeanine, Cynthia Gale; interim minister, Ch. of Christ, Waco, Tex., 1951-52; conducted Gospel meeting in many cities in Tex. & Oregon; lectr., The Annual Lectureship in many states--Tex., Ill., Tenn., Calif.; US Army, 1943-55; current pastor, Coll. Ch. of Christ, Terrel, Tex.; dean, Southwestern Chrstn. Coll., Terrell, Tex.; tchr. 6 yrs., Paul Quinn Coll.; broadcast 1 yr, radio sta. KTER, Terrell, Tex.; awards: three battle stars (Europe), Marksman and Good Conduct Medal; mem., Tex. State Tchrs. Assn.; Tex. Assn. of Coll. and Univ. Registrars; Home: 605 W. End, Terrel, Tex.; Office: 205 W. End, Terrell, Tex.

SARGENT, Charles Jackson, Jr., b. Hampton, Va., Oct. 23, 1927; s. Charles J., Sr. and Ruth (Jackson) S.; B. A., Va. Union Univ., 1944-49; B. D., Drew Theol. Sem., 1949-52; Biblical Sem. of New York; m. Virginia Adele Evans; Children--Hope Irene; pastor, Migrant laborers, Va. Coun. of Chs., 1950-51; First Bapt. Ch., Madison, N. J., 1952-55; Ebenezer, Bapt. Ch., Poughkeepsie, N. Y., 1955-59; current, Union Bapt. Ch., Stamford, Conn., 1959--; v. p., The Lott Carey Bapt. Foreign Mission Conv., Conn.; moderator (former): The Dutchess Bapt. Assn. of the Amer. Bapt. Conv.; 1965 Nominating Comm. of the Amer. Bapt. Conv.; mem., Omega Psi Phi; Home: 15 Fifth St., Stamford, Conn.; Office: 28 Adams Ave., Stamford, Conn.

SATTERWHITE, John H., sem. dean, prof., b. Newberry, S. C., Jan. 1, 1913; s. Modock and Lucretia S.; A. B., Benedict Coll., 1934; B. D., S. T. M., Oberlin Grad. Sch. of Theol., 1937, 38; Th. D., Boston Univ. Sch. of Theol., 1947; D. D. (hon.), Johnson C. Smith and Benedict Coll., 1950, 64; m. Lucille C. Mills; Children--Joan C. (Mrs. Cartwright), John M.; instr., Livingstone Coll., Salisbury, N. C., 1938-40; dean, Hood Theol. Sem., and prof. of theol., 1940-57; prof., Systematic Theol. and Ecumenics, Wesley Theol. Sem., Wash., D. C., 1958--; pastor, Afr. Meth. Episc. Zion Ch.; mem., Philadelphia-Balto., Conf.; dir., The Amer. Soc. of Chrstn. Social Ethics; Coun. of Chs. of Greater Wash.; Exec. comm., Dept. of Racial and Cultural Relations, Natl. Coun. of Chs.; Howard Univ. Inst. of Rel.; NAACP; Fellowship of Profs. of Ecumenics and Missions; Interreligious Comm. on Rel. and Race; Inter Ch. Club of Wash., D. C.; Min. Assn. of Greater Wash.; chrmn., Comm. on Ecumenical Ed., Coun. of Chs. of Greater Wash.; author: "Christian Action in Racial and Ethnic Relations: Its Biblical and Theological Basis." Dept. of Racial and Cultural Relations, Natl. Coun. of Chs., NYC, 1963; Home: 3208 19th St. NW, Wash., D.C. 20010

SAUNDERS, Lenwood Daniel, b. Richlands, Mar. 21, 1927; s. Louis Johnson and Hanah (Cox) S.; B.Th., Kittrell Coll., Kittrell, N.C., 1956; m. Lena Malie Davis; Children--Alinda, Gwendolyn, Louis, Frank, Wayman; pastor, Dak Chapel A.M.E. Ch., Warrenton, N.C.; pastor, Shocco A.M.E. Ch., Bethel A.M.E. Ch., both at Spring Hope, N.C.; Enfield, N.C.; current pastor, Mt. Olive Afr. Meth. Episc. Ch., Wilmington, N.C.; mem., Exec. Bd. of Gegony Elem. Sch.; treas., Interdenom. Alliance; mem., Ministerial Assn.; mem., Fannis Nawood Home Bd. Dirs.; mem., Exec. Bd., NAACP; mem., Civic League, v. chrmn., 5th Ward, 2nd Precinct (Wil., N.C.); Good Conduct Medal, US Army; mem., Mason; Home: 712 Wright St., Wilmington, N.C.; Office: 1001 Seventh St., Wilmington, N.C.

*SAUNDERS, Monroe Randolph, bishop, b. Florence, S.C., Apr. 13, 1919; s. Lawrence and Millie (Fleming) S.; Va. State Coll., 1937; A.B., B.D., Howard Univ., 1953, 1957; m. Alberta Brockington; Children--Monroe Randolph Jr., Jackqueline Faye, Esther Karen, Adrian Jason; pastor, Rehoboth Ch. of God (Apostolic), Wash., D.C., 1953--; Gen. sec., Ch. of God in Christ Jesus (Apostolic), 1954--; presiding bishop, The Central Dist. of the Ch. of God in Christ Jesus (Apostolic), 1957--; Ex. dir., Rehoboth Ed. and Welfare Center, Sykesville, Md.; dir., Rehoboth Bible Inst., Balto., Md.; spec. consultant, presiding bishop of the Ch. of God in Christ Jesus (Apostolic) on Ministerial Training and Youth Affairs; editor, "The Rehoboth Beacon," official publication of the denomination; pres., Clergymen's Assn. for Soc. Service in the Second Precinct, D.C.; mem., Policy Comm. of the Community Service Project, Howard Univ., 1962-63; chrmn., Housing Comm., Clergymen's Assn., 1964; chap., Apostolic students, Morgan Coll.; mem., Chrstn. Coun. of Morgan Coll., 1962--; US Army, 1942-45; Good Conduct Medal; mem., Alpha Kappa Delta, Honorary Sociological Fraternity; NAACP; Home: 3002 N. Hilton St., Baltimore, Md.; Office: 700 Poplar Grove St., Baltimore, Md.

SAUNDERS, Robert Lee Sr., b. Louisville, Ky., Oct. 21,

1932; s. Wellington S. and Norveline Swanagan (Wade) S.; courses, Butler Univ.; Ind. Central Coll.; Central Bapt. Theol. Sem., Ind.; Simmons Univ., Louisville; D.D. (hon.), Inter Bapt. Theol. Center, Houston, Tex.; married; Children--Karen Denise, Angela Faye, Pamela Jean, Robert Lee, Jr.; acting pastor, New Bethel Bapt. Ch., Indianapolis, Ind., 1953-55; pastor, Second Bapt. Ch., Shelbyville, Ind., 1955-59; Second Bapt. Ch., Anderson, Ind., 1959--; mem., Bd. of Dirs., Madison Co. Family Service; pres., Ind. Bapt. State Sun. Sch. & B. T. U. Congress; chrmn., Mayor's Commn. on Human Relations, Anderson, Ind.; Exec. Bd. mem., Ind. State Conf. of brs. of NAACP; v.p., State Conf., NAACP; mem., State Ed. Bd., Ind. Miss. State Conv.; mem., Community Services Coun., Anderson, Ind.; Home Miss. Bd., Natl. Bapt. Conv. of Amer.; mem., Bapt. Min. Alliance of Indianapolis and vicinity; v. chrmn., Bd. of Dirs., Westside Community Center; mem., Bd. of Madison Co. Soc. Actions Coun. (War on Poverty Program); Home: 1207 W. 10th St., Anderson, Ind.; Office: 1101 Sherman St., Anderson, Ind. 46011

SAVAGE, Horace C., author, coll. pres., b. Portsmouth, Va.; M.A., New York Univ., 1948; LL.D., Lane Coll., 1959; pastor, Chrstn. Meth. Episc. Ch., Goolettsville, Tenn.; Mission Ch., Haiti; Foreign Missionary, Haiti and Cuba; prof., Lane Coll., 1952-54; Tenn. State Univ., 1954-64; pres., Texas Coll., Tyler, Tex., 1964--; mem., Assn. for Study of Negro life and history; Miss. Valley His. Soc.; Tenn. Educational Congress; Southern Historical Soc.; Assn. of Univ. Profs.; Mason; Democrat; author: Life and Times of Bishop Isaac Lane; co-publisher and founder, Capitol City Defender (newspaper), Nashville, Tenn.; Office: Texas Coll., Tyler, Tex.

SAVOY, Clarence Monroe, ch. official, b. Croom, Md., July 1, 1924; s. Walter and Mary (Pinkney) S.; A.B., Lane Coll., Jackson, Tenn., 1954; B.D., Gammon Theol. Sem., 1957; m. Florence Louise Penn; pastored, Bowden Hills Chapel Chrstn. Meth. Episc. Ch., 1953-54; Rock of Ages C.M.E. Ch., Augusta, Ga., 1957-59; Hamlet Chapel, Stanton Meml. C.M.E. Chs., Pittsboro, N.C., 1959-63; Calvary C.M.E. Ch., Jersey City, N.J., 1963-64; chap., migrants summers of 1956-57; present: Episc. dir., Chrstn. Ed. for the Seventh Episc. Dist. of the C.M.E. Ch., 1959--; US Marine Corps, 1943-46; Omega Psi Phi; Home: 25 Oak St., Jersey City, N.J.

Office: 27-29 Oak St., Jersey City, N.J.

SCALES, William Clinton, Jr., b. Charleston, W. Va., Mar. 18, 1935; s. Wm. Clinton and Myra (Davis) S.; B.A., Oakwood Coll., 1956; M.A., Andrews Univ., 1958; m. Lois Nila Ruth Yates; Sedalia, Mo. S.D.A. Ch., Sedalia, Mo., 1958-60; Prospect Ave. S.D.A. Ch., Springfield, Mo., 1960-61; Phila. S.D.A. Ch., Des Moines, Iowa, 1961-62; present: pastor, Bethel S.D.A. Ch., Kansas City, Kan., 1962--; teaching of various Bible classes regularly and counseling from time to time; ministerial alliance. Home: 645 Oakland Ave., Kansas City, Kans. 66101; Office: 713 Freeman Ave., Kansas City, Kans. 66101

SCOTT, Claude Caesar, tchr., b. Lenoir, N.C., Dec. 25, 1894; s. William Barham and Tempie (E.) S.; A.B., Kittrell Coll., Shaw Univ., 1925; D.D. (hon.), 1933; m. Margaret Helen Deloatch; Children--Claude Jr. and Zenobia Mae; ordained elder 1922 in A.M.E. Ch. at Morganton, N.C.; pastor, St. James A.M.E. Ch., 1925; pastor, St. Paul A.M.E. Ch., 5 yrs.; St. James A.M. E. Ch., Winston-Salem, 7-1/2 yrs.; St. Paul A.M.E. Ch., Raleigh, 7 yrs.; Bethel A.M.E. Ch., Greensboro, 3 yrs; present, St. James A.M.E. Ch., Asheville, 15 yrs.; prin., The Orange Co. Trg. Sch., Chapel Hill, N.C., 3 yrs.; mem., The Trustee Bd. and Bd. of Control, Kittrell Coll.; current, Dir. of Rel. Ed., 2nd Episc. Dist. A.M.E. Ch., etc.; pres., Interdenom. Alliance of Winston-Salem, Raleigh and Asheville, N.C.; sec., Asheville and Buncombe Citizens Organization; pres., Citizens Civic Organization, Winston-Salem, N.C., 1933-34; Home: 2001 McConnell Rd., Greensboro, N.C. Office: 134 Broad St., Asheville, N.C.

SCOTT, Edgar Lloyd, b. Shreveport, La., Mar. 31, 1936; s. Jack and Bessie (Sanders) S.; Compton Jr. Coll., 1955-56; George Pepperdine Coll., 1958-59; Antelope Valley Coll., 1957-58; m. Minnie Pear Washington; Children--Edgar Jr., Freddie, Gregory; pastor, Missionary Bapt. Ch.; Ch. of God in Christ, San Francisco; founder and pastor, Good News Ch. of God in Christ, Chambersburg, Pa.; mem., Housing Comm., NAACP; spec. minister to migrants (summer, 1964); Dist. supt., Sun. Sch., Harrisburg, Pa.; Home: 546 Black Ave., Chambersburg, Pa. 17201; Office: 544 Black Ave., Chambersburg, Pa.

SCOTT, James Arthur, b. Phila., Mar. 10, 1931; s. James S. and Mable (Bridgeford) S.; B.A., Lincoln Univ., Pa., 1952; B.D., Yale Div. Sch., 1956; Inst. for Advanced Pastoral Trng.; m. Beverly Norine Dunston; Children--Linda Louise; pastor, Pleasant St. Bapt. Ch., Westerly, R.I., 1953-56; field repr., Amer. Bapt. Home Missn. Soc., 1956-62; Dir., Urban Ch. Program, Amer. Bapt. Home Missn. Soc., 1962-63; pastor, Bethany Bapt. Ch., Newark, N.J., 1963-present; research asst., Natl. Coun. of Chs., Dean, Community Sch. of Chrstn. Leadership; v.p., Youth Devel. Clinic; Bd. of Dir., Essex Co. Urban League; Dir., Robert Bruce House; Dir., Edith George Brown Home for Aged; Dir., United Community Fund; Exec. Bd., Greater Newark Coun. of Chs.; mem., Family Life Coun.; former adv., Youth Chapter, NAACP; Alpha Phi Alpha; Home: 57 Clifton Ave., Newark, N.J.

SCOTT, Julius Samuel, Jr., coll. chap., ch. official, b. Houston, Tex., Feb. 26, 1925; s. J.S. Sr. and Bertha (Bell) S. (deceased); A.B., Wiley Coll., 1945; B.D., Garrett Biblical Inst., 1949; M.A., Brown Univ., 1964; Ph.D. candidate, Boston Univ., 1956-60; m. Ianthia Lucille Harrell; Children--Julius S. III, David Kumar; Missionary to India, 1949-52; dir., Public relations, Wiley Coll., 1952-55; Meth. chap., Brown Univ., 1958-60; Meth. chap., MIT, 1961; dir., Wesley Found., Tex. Southern Univ., 1961-63; Exec. sec., Brown Univ. Chrstn. Assn., 1963--; lecturer, World Religions, Boston Univ., 1958-60; lectr., World Religions, Boston Adult Ed. Center, 1958-60; mem., Omega Psi Phi; Democrat; FOR; CORE; NAACP; Home: 95 Brown St., Providence, R.I. 02906; Office: Brown Univ., Providence, R.I. 02912

SCOTT, Nathan A., Jr., coll. prof., author, b. Cleveland, O., Apr. 24, 1925; s. Nathan A. and Maggie (Martin) S.; A.B., Univ. of Mich., 1944; B.D., Union Theol. Sem., 1946; Ph.D., Columbia Univ., 1949; m. Charlotte Hanley; Children--Nathan A. III, Leslie Kristin; ordained Prot. Episc. priest; mem. of faculty, Howard Univ., Div. of Gen. Ed. Prog. in the Humanities, 1948-55; present, prof., Theol. and Lit., Div. Sch., Univ. of Chicago, 1955--; Major publication: <u>Rehearsals of Discomposure: Alienation and Reconciliation in Modern Literature</u> (King's Crown Press, 1952); <u>The Tragic Vision and the Christian Faith</u> (Associated Press, 1957); <u>Modern Literature and the Religious Frontier</u> (Harper & Bros., 1958); <u>Albert Camus</u> (Hillary House, 1962); <u>Reinhold Niebuhr</u> (Univ. of

Minn. Press, 1963); The New Orpheus: Essays Toward a Christian Poetic (Sheed & Ward, 1964); The Climate of Faith in Modern Literature (Seabury press, 1964); Samuel Beckett (Bowes & Bowes Ltd., 1964); Forms of Extremity in the Modern Novel, Man in the Modern Theatre, and Four Ways of Modern Poetry; (pub. by John Knox Press, 1965); contributor, Religious Symbolisum (Harper & Bros., 1955); Literature and Belief (Columbia Univ. Press, 1958); Symbolism in Religion and Literature (Geo. Braziller, Inc., 1960); Christian Faith and the Contemporary Arts (Abingdon Press, 1962); Society and Self (Free Press); Graham Greene: Some Critical Considerations (Univ. of Ky. Press, 1963); Nature and Grace (Harper & Row, Inc., 1964); The Search for Identity: Essays on the American Character (Harper & Row, Inc., 1964); Religion in American Literature (Univ. of Wash. Press, 1965); The Christian Doctrine of Man (Seabury Press, 1965); has contributed articles to numerous scholarly periodicals; Home: 5242 S. Greenwood Ave., Chgo., Ill.; Office: The Divinity Sch., Univ. of Chgo., Ill.

SCOTT, Simon H., Jr., b. Aug. 3, 1926; A. B., Johnson C. Smith, 1948; B. D., McCormick Theol. Sem., 1950; m. Gloria Jean Reynolds; commissioned Air Force Res., June 1951; served foll. interior bases: Westover, AFB, Mass., 1951-52; Hamilton AFB, Calif., 1961-63; McGuire AFB, N. J., 1954-58; Scott AFB, Ill., 1967-present; served foll. overseas areas: Okinawa, 1953-54; France, 1958-61; Greenland, 1963-64; present Chief Professional Airlift Command Chaplains Office, Scott AFB, Ill.; awards: four 1st pl. awards Annual Toastmaster Intl. Speech Contests, Voconaires T. M. Club, McGuire AFB; Area 17, Wash. Crossing, Pa.; E. Section 38th Dist., Camden, N. J., Cherry Hill, N. J., Bethlehem, Pa., 1966-1967; Office: Professional Div. Comm. Chaplains Office, Hq. Military Airlift Command, Scott AFB, Ill.

SCOTT, Spencer Lendrus, b. Norfolk, Va., June 22, 1919; s. Spencer and Cora; A. B., B. S., B. D., Ch. C., D. D. (2) B. T. H., State Tchrs. Coll., Elizabeth City, N. C.; Va. State Tchrs. Coll., Norfolk, Va.; Va. Union Univ., Richmond, Va.; Harvard Univ. Chaplain Sch., Cambridge, Mass.; hon., Va. Sem. and Coll., Lynchburg, Va.; Wash. Natl. Univ., Chgo., Ill.; m. Beulah Rodgers; Children--Rhonda Jane; pastor, 4th Bapt. Ch., Portsmouth, Va.; Union Bapt. Ch., Va. Beach, Va.; chap., WW II; pres., Bapt. Min. Conf., Norfolk, Portsmouth vicinity; v.p., Hampton Inst. Min. Conf.; mem., Exec. Bd., Bapt. Gen. Assn.; Home Mission Bd. of Natl. Bapt. Conv.; Bd., Norfolk Co. Cancer Soc.; Adv. Bd., City of Chesapeake, Va.; mem., Elks, Masons, St. Luke, Omega Psi Phi; Home: 1408 Spring Rd., Chesapeake, Va.; Office: 730 S St., Portsmouth, Va.

SETTLE, William Henry, b. Norristown, Pa., Oct. 25, 1924; s. Oliver and Ida; A.B., Howard Univ., Wash., D.C., 1943; M.A., Howard Univ., 1945; B.D., Temple Univ. Sch. of Theol., 1945; m. Mary Green; Children--William, Iris, Stuart; asst. pastor, Metro. A.M.E. Ch., Wash., D.C., 1942-45; Campbell A.M.E. Ch., Wash., D.C., 1944-45; pastor, Great Pleasant A.M.E. Ch., Andrews, S.C., 1949-53; Felderville A.M.E. Ch., Kinstree, S.C., 1958-63; St. Luke A.M.E. Ch., Charleston, S.C., 1963-present; instr., Jackson High Sch., Charlestown, W.Va., 1945-47; Storer Coll., Harpers Ferry, W.Va., 1945-47; instr., Rosemary High Sch., Andrews, S.C., 1945-53; prin., St. James Elem. Sch., Eutawville, S.C., 1953-present; pres., Georgetown Co. Tchr. Assn., 1947-50; Holly Hill Sch. Dist. Tchr. Assn., 1954-57; mem., Mason; NAACP; min., Palmetto S.C. Annual Conf., A.M.E. Ch.; Home: 11 S. Beach Ave., Andrews, S.C.; Office: 245 S. Philip St., Charleston, S.C.

*SETTLES, Paul, b. Phila., Pa., Apr. 2, 1929; s. Thomas and Pearl; B.A., Wilberforce Univ., 1956; B.D., Howard Univ., Sch. of Rel., 1964; m. Alberta Wall; Children--Lawrence, LaVerne; pastor, St. Paul's A.M.E. Ch., Waynesboro, Pa., 1956-63; Bethel A.M.E. Ch., Smyrna, Del., 1963-67; asst. Dean of Men, Del. State Coll., Dover, Del., 1967-68; Exec. Dir., Kento Co. Community Action Agency, 1967-68; present, pastor, Macedonia A.M.E. Ch., Seaford, Del., 1968--; Home: 416 N. St., Seaford, Del.; Office: Box 913 Court House, Dover, Del.

SEWELL, George Alexander, coll. prof., b. Newnan, Ga., Oct. 12, 1910; s. J. Otis and Pearl (Clark) S.; A.B., Morris Brown Coll., 1934; S.T.B., Boston Univ., 1944; S.T.M., Boston Univ., 1946; Ph.D., Boston Univ., 1957; LL.D., Monrovia Coll., 1956; m. Lillie Mae White; Children--Annita Pearl (Mrs. Marvin Oliver); pastor, Decatur Mission A. M. E. Ch., Decatur, Ga., 1933-34; Post Oak Mission, Sneads, Fla., 1934-36; Greenwood-Neal's Landing Circuit, Jackson Co., Fla., 1936-42; St. Andrews Meth. Ch., Worcester, Mass., 1942-44; Trinity A. M. E. Ch., Atlanta, Ga.; Gaines Chapel A. M. E. Ch., Waycross, Ga., 1951-52; Steward Ch., Louisville, Ga., 1960-62; coll. min., LeMoyne Coll., Memphis Tenn., 1944-45; coll. min., instr., Bible & Rel., Morris Brown Coll.; coll. min. and Dean of Men, Ark. A. M. & N. Coll., Pine Bluff, Ark.; Dean: Turner Theol. Sem., Atlanta, Ga., 1957-62 (Dir., ITC); Prof. Sociology, Alcorn A & M Coll., Lorman, Miss., 1962--; Distinguished Community Serv. Award (plaque) Interracial group, Macon, Ga., 1956; mem., A. M. E. Gen. Conf., 1954--; mem., Soc. Biblical Lit.; sec., Gen. Bd. of Ed. A. M. E. Ch., 1962--; del. (Youth sec.) 2nd Assembly Natl. Coun. of Chs., Evanston, Ill., 1957; mem., Mason; author: A Motif for Living, and other sermons, Vantage Press, NYC, 1963; Home: 74 Ashby St., Atlanta, Ga.; Office: 409 Church St., Port Gibson, Miss.

SHANNON, David Thomas, sem. prof., b. Richmond, Va., Sept. 26, 1933; s. Charlie Lee and Phyliss (Gary) S.; A. B., Va. Union Univ., 1954; B. D., Va. Union Univ. Sch. of Rel., 1957; S. T. M., Oberlin Grad. Sch. of Theol., 1959; Union Theol. Sem., 1960--; m. Averett Powell; Children--Vernitia Averett, Davine Berlinda; licensed, Bapt. Ch., 1950; ordained, 1954; pastor, Fair Oaks Bapt. Ch., Fair Oaks, Va., 1954-57; student asst. pastor, Antioch Bapt. Ch., 1957-59; Ebenezer Bapt. Ch., 1960--; prof., Va. Union Univ., 1959--; Women's Leadership Training Sch., Bapt. Ch., 1960-63; ch. chrmn., NAACP, 1960; mem., Exec. Com. Richmond Chaplaincy; v. p., Area of Allied Bodies of Va., 1962--; Exec. Com., Lott Carey Foreign Mission Conv., 1961--; Com. on Theol. Ed., 1962--; Amer. Bapt. Conv., 1962--; 2d v. p., Bapt. Min. Conf. of Va., 1963--; Phi Beta Sigma; Y's Men Intl.; author: The Life and Teachings of Paul, Townsend Press, Nashville, Tenn.; Meditations - Upper Room Disciplines; contributor to: The New Testament Image of the Redeemed Community, ed. by Jessie Jei McNeil, 1962; Home: 2712 Seminary Ave., Richmond, Va.; Office: Ebenezer Bapt. Ch., 216 W. Leight St., Richmond, Va.

SHANNON, Sylvester Lorenzo, chap. (Capt.), b. Pelham, Ga., May 25, 1933; s. J. Powell and Maude L. (Kelley)

S.; A.B., Fla. A & M Univ., Tallahassee, Fla., 1955; B.D., Duke Univ., 1966; further studies: Univ. of Colo.; m. Doris Brooks; Children--Glenn LeRoy, Keith Lester, Theresa LaVonne; pastor, United Presby. Chs., Mebane and Graham, N.C., 1964-66; commissioned 2d Lt., Infantry, 1955; served US Army, Ft. Benning, Ga.; Ft. Jackson, S.C.; So. Vietnam, 2nd Brigade Chaplain, 25th Inf. Div., Ft. Carson; 1967-present; sr. Boy Scout Committeeman; mem., Bd. of Dir., Ft. Jackson Fed. Credit Union, 1966-67; Sch. Bd. Ft. Jackson, 1966-67; mem., Alpha Phi Alpha; NAACP; Military Chaplain's Assn.; feature writer, Post Military Publications; Home: 1303 Shenandoah Dr., Colorado Spring, Colo., 80910; Office: Hdq., 2nd Brigade 5th Inf. Div., Ft. Carson, Colo. 80913

SHAW, C. Alexander, b. Cleveland, O., Apr. 4, 1927; s. Edward E. and Curlie A. (Brocks) S.; A.B., Wilberforce Univ., 1953; B.D., Payne Theol. Sem., 1956; m. Marjorie B. (S.); 1 dau., Bonita Elaine; pastored: Miles Chapel Chrstn. Meth. Episc. Ch., Fairmont, W.Va.; Peoples Community C.M.E. Ch., Dayton, O.; Phillips Chapel C.M.E. Ch., Springfield, O.; St. Phillips C.M.E. Ch., Hamilton, Ohio; mem., Phi Beta Sigma; Home: 64 Hanover St., Charleston, S.C.; Office: 66 Hanover St., Charleston, S.C.

SHAW, Harry Wilbert, ch. admin., b. Mayesville, Sumter Co., Sept. 3, 1907; s. Benjamin and Alice (Monroe) S.; 1942, A.B. and 1949, B.D., Theol. Sem., Johnson C. Smith Univ.; m. Rosetta L. White; Children--Harry Eugene, Michael Monroe, Jacquelyn Yvone, and James Wilbert; pastor, 1947-50, Salem U. Presby. Ch., Anderson, S.C.; 1950-56, Goodwill U. Presby. Ch., Ft. Pierce, Fla.; 1956-62, Trinity U. Presby. Ch., Key West, Fla.; Sun. Schs. Missions and Mobile Ministries, with Bd. of Natl. Missions; Sun. Schs. Missions: Dyersbury, Tenn., Miller, Miss., Selma, Ala., Camden, S.C.; current: 1962, dir., Community Center for Youth and Adults, James Is., Charleston, S.C.; beginning Oct. 1963 called to pastorate of St. James U. Presby. Ch.; dir. of youth work; mem., Omega Psi Phi, Ministerial Alliance, Mason, NAACP, Democrat; Home: 1008 Park Ave., Charleston, S.C.; Office: Route 5, Box 286, Charleston, S.C.

SHAW, Herbert Bell, bishop, b. Wilmington, N.C., Feb.

9, 1908; Fisk Univ. ; Howard Univ. Sch. of Rel. ; D. D. (hon.), Livingstone Coll. , Salisbury, N. C. ; ordained elder, A. M. E. Z. Ch. , 1928; pastored 1929-37; presiding elder, Wilmington, N. C. Dist. , A. M. E. Z. Ch. , 1937-43; sec. -treas. , Dept. of Home Missions Pensions and Min. Relief, 1943-52; presiding bishop, Third Episc. Dist. , A. M. E. Z. Ch. , 1952-present; mem. , Gen. Commn. of Army and Navy Chaplains; Natl. Coun. Chs. of Christ, USA; v. p. , World Meth. Conv. ; N. C. Coun. Chs. , Bd. of Dir. , 4-H Club Foun. of N. C. ; Boys Club of Amer. , Wilmington, N. C. ; chrmn. , Curriculum Com. , Dept. Christn. Ed. , A. M. E. Z. Ch. ; v. chrmn. , Bd. of Trustees, Livingstone Coll. , Salisbury, N. C. ; v. chrmn. , Bd. of Trustees, Clinton Coll. , Rock Hill, S. C. ; Bd. of Trustees, Lomax Hannon Coll. , Greenville, Ala. ; mem. , Johnson Meml. Inst. , Batesville, Miss. ; Mason; Omega Psi Phi; del. , 8th, 9th, 10th World Meth. Conf. , 1950, 56, 61, 66; Office: 520 Red Cross St. , Wilmington, N. C.

SHAW, Talbert Oscall, b. Jamaica, W. I. , Feb. 28, 1928; s. Albert and Albertha S. ; B. A. , Emmanuel Missionary Coll. , 1960; M. A. , B. D. , Andrews Univ. , 1963; m. Lillieth Hamilton Brown; pastored: E. Jamaica Conf. of S. D. A. , Kingston, Jamaica, 1952-55; Bahamas Mission of S. D. A. , Nassau, Bahamas, 1956-58; present: Lake Region Conf. of S. D. A. Ch. while pursuing studies at the Univ. of Chgo. on doctoral program; former chrmn. , Sch. Bd. , Nassau, Bahamas; social worker with Cook Co. Public Assistance, Chgo. , Ill. Home: 5427 University Ave. , Chgo. , Ill. ; Office: 8517 So. State St. , Chgo. , Ill.

SHEARES, Reuben A. , II, Charleston, S. C. , Sept. 3, 1933; s. Reuben A. and Lucille S. ; B. A. , Talladega Coll. , Talladega, Ala. , 1955; B. D. , Colgate-Rochester Div. Sch. , Rochester, N. Y. , 1959; m. Ora Myles; Children-- Reuben, III, Bradley T. , Craig A. ; pastor, Second Bapt. Ch. , Leroy, N. Y. , 1955-59; Blackwell Chapel, Jamestown, N. Y. , 1959-61; Howard U. Ch. , Nashville, Tenn. , 1961-63; minister, Metro. Missns. , Staff of Southern Calif. & Southwest Conf. , Los Angeles, Calif. , 1963-65; sec. , Urban Dept. , United Ch. Bd. for Homeland Ministries, N. Y. , 1956-present; Home: 97-11 Horace Harding Expressway, Corona, N. Y. 11368; Office: 287 Park Ave. So. , New York, N. Y.

SHEPARD, Norman Clayton, b. Chilton Co., Ala., 1894; s. Richard and Lucy; Selma Univ. (3 yrs.) D. D. (hon.), Selma Univ.; married; Children--Mrs. Roland Smith; pastor, Hopewell Bapt. Ch., Clanton, Ala., (14 yrs.); Rising Star Bapt. Ch., Sylacauga, Ala. (41 yrs.); former pres., City Civic Club, 1948-54; Sylacauga Adv. Com.; Natl. Bapt. Conv., Inc.; trustee and statistician, Ala. State Bapt. Conv.; Mason; Home: 325 W. Park St., Sylacauga, Ala. 35150

SHEPPARD, Garrett Augustus Hobart, b. Greenville, Tex., Feb. 9, 1897; s. A. D. and Susie (Greesy) S.; B. Th., Bishop Coll., 1930; B. R. E., Hartford Sem., 1931; B. D., Yale Univ., 1934; Th. D., 1936; D. D., Ark. Bapt. Coll., 1940; LL. D., Bishop Coll., 1961; m. Bertha Mae Watson; pastor, Antioch Bapt. Ch., Mexia, Tex., 1934-38; Sunset Bapt. Ch., Texarkana, Tex., 1938-41; sec., Amer. Bible Soc., Dallas Div., 1941-45; pastor, Greater Bethlehem Bapt. Ch., Dallas, Tex., 1946--; current pres., B. M. & E. State Congress of Tex., since 1936; pres., St. Paul Jr. Coll., Mexia, Tex., 1936-38; trustee, Bishop Coll., Dallas, Tex., 1961--; mem., Bd. of Dirs., Dallas Negro Cham. of Commerce, 1963--; Committeeman, Boy Scouts of Amer., Circle Ten Coun.; life mem., NAACP; mem., Mason, Kappa Alpha Psi, Epsilon Delta Chi Religious Soc., The Amer. Acad. of Political and Soc. Sci., Editorial Bd., Western Star; author: several booklets, many news articles; Home: 2808 Sutton St., Dallas, Tex.; Office: 4401 Spring Ave., Dallas, Tex.

SHEPPARD, Marshall Lorenzo, b. Oxford, N. C., July 10, 1899; s. Robert and Pattie (Gilliam); Va. Union Univ., Richmond, Va.; Pendle Hill Quaker Grad. Center, Wallingford, Pa.; m. Willie L. Owens; Children--Marshall, Jr.; asst. pastor, Abyssinian Bapt. Ch., 1923-26; pastor, Mt. Olive Tabernacle Bapt. Ch., Phila., Pa., 1926--; rel. work sec., 135th St. br. YMCA, NYC, 1922-23; Bd. of Dirs., Chrstn. St. YMCA, Phila., Pa.; mem., Comm., Div. of Chrstn. Life & Work, Natl. Coun. of Chs.; Pa. State Legislature, 1934-36-40; recorder of deeds, Wash., D. C., 1944; recorder of deeds, Phila., Pa., 1951; councilman-at-large, Phila., Pa., 1955-59-64; del. and speaker, World Bapt. Alliance, Copenhagen, Denmark, 1947; mem., Alpha Phi Alpha; Mason; Elks; Home: 1331 N. 57th St., Phila., Pa.

SHERARD, Robert Douglas, educator, b. Memphis, Tenn., June 10, 1922; s. Major James and Elizabeth (Perkins) S.; A. B., Morehouse Coll., Atlanta, Ga., 1949; B. D., Gammon Theol. Sem., Atlanta, Ga., 1952; m. Lois Johnson; 1 son, Robert Douglas, Jr., 2 daus., Lynn Chase, Dawna Jean; tchr., Carver Vocational High Sch., 1949-52; minister, Beecher Meml. United Ch. of Christ, New Orleans, La., 1953-58; Corona Congre. Ch. (UCC), Corona, N. Y., 1958--; mem., Mayor's Task Force for Youth, NYC, Mayor's Comm. on Explotation, NYC, State Soc. Action Comm., NY State Conf., United Ch. of Christ; co-chrmn., Civil Rights Comm. for Reference on Rel. & Race for NYC; sponsor, Northeast Queens Fair Housing Comm., NYC; Bd. of Dirs., NY Assn. of Congre. Chs.; pres., Corona-E. Elmhurst br. NAACP, 1959--; chrmn., Bd., Independent Citizens for Good Govt., Corona, NY.; Bd. Mem., Community Coun. of Corona, NY; First Class Petty Officer, US Navy, 1942-45; recipient, 4 Battle Stars for European Theatre of Operation; Human Relations Award, North Shore Bus. & Prof. Women's Club, NY, 1962; Community Interest Award, Elmview Women's Club, NY, 1963; mem., Omega Psi Phi; Home: 27-21 99th St., E. Elmhurst, N. Y., 11369; Office: 102-18 34th Ave., Corona, N. Y. 11368

SHERMAN, Odie Lee, bishop, b. Jacksonville, Tex., 1897; Tex. Coll.; A. B., Shorter Coll., 1927; D. D. (hon.), Shorter Coll.; Wilberforce Univ.; m. Ruth Andy Jones, Edna Othenia Daniels; Children--John Oliver Davis, Mary Etta; pastor, Afr. Meth. Episc. Chs., Arkansas; presiding elder, Augusta, Arkansas, Camden, Central Ark. Conf., Hot Springs; elected bishop, 1956; now presiding bishop 10th Dist., A. M. E. Ch.; award for outstanding services during the integration crisis, Little Rock, Ark.; mem., NAACP; mgr., State campaign for ex-Gov. McMath; State Bd. of Dirs., Girls Indus. Sch., Fargo, Ark.; chrmn., Civil League, Little Rock; pres., Publication Bd., A. M. E. Ch.; Home: 128 Garrison St., Waco, Tex.

*SHIELDS, Landrum Eugene, coll. prof., b. Winston-Salem, N. C., Mar. 17, 1927; s. Joanna (Berry) S.; A. B., Lincoln Univ., Pa., 1949; Oberlin Grad. Sch. of Theol., 1950-51; B. D., Howard Univ., Sch. of Rel., 1958; M. R. E., Chrstn. Theol. Sem., 1960; candidate for Ph. D., Indiana Univ.; m. Marjorie Earley McDaniel; Children--

Landrum Eugene Jr., Sharyn Camille, Laurita Eileen; pastor, First Congre. Ch., Greensboro, N.C., 1952-55; YMCA sec., Adult Prog., Indianapolis YMCA, 1955-57; asst. pastor, Witherspoon Presby. Ch., Indianaplis, Ind., 1959-61; current, Adult Ed. Specialist, Bd. for Fundamental Ed., Indianapolis, Ind., 1963--; Prof., Indiana Central Coll., 1963--; Democrat; Alpha Phi Alpha; mem., Adult Ed. Assn., USA; Amer. Soc. of Training Dirs.; Mason; Indianapolis Presbytery; Home: 1055 Pomander Pl., Indianapolis, Ind. 46208

SHIPLEY, Anthony Jerome, b. May 19, 1939, New York, N.Y.; s. Oscar and Lillian (S.); A.B., Drew Univ., Madison, N.J., 1961; Garrett Theol. Sem., 1961-64; m. Barbara Jean McCullough; pastored, United Meth. Chs., Metropolitan Community Meth. Ch., NYC, 1958-61; St. Matthew Ch., Chgo., Ill., 1961-64; Metro.-Duane Ch., Greenwich Village, NYC, 1964-66; Union Meth. Ch., Bklyn, NY, 1966-68; Assn. Prog. Dir., Coun. on Prog. and Adm., NY Conf. United Meth. Ch., 1968-present; research asst., Gabrini House, Chgo., 1961-62; asst. chap., Cook Co. Hosp., Chicago, 1963; consult., Metropolitan Urban Serv. Trng. Service, 1967-68; Ed. and Vocational Testing Fr. Green Community Prog. Center, 1968; consult. N.J. Community Action Trng. Inst.; Dir., Head Star Prog., 1967-68; consult., Clergy Service; Abortion Crown Hghts. Anti-Povety Bd.; mem., Personal Comm. N.E. Missionary Soc.; mem., Welfare Improvement League; mem., NAACP; Meth. Action Coun.; Chelsa Area Meeting for Planning Lower West Side, Anti-Proverty Bd.; Natl. Negro Clergy; Black Meth. for Ch. Renewal; Home: 773 Concourse Village, E. Bronx, N.Y., 10451; Office: 210 Boston Post Rd., Rye, N.Y. 10580

SHOCKLEY, Grant S., b. Phila., Pa., Sept. 3, 1919; A.B., Lincoln Univ., Pa., 1942; B.D., Drew Univ., N.J., 1945; M.A., Ed.D., Union Theol. Sem. & Tchrs. Coll., Columbia Univ., NY, 1946, 1953; m. Doris Taylor; Children--Muriel Elizabeth; ordained elder, 1944; assoc. pastor and dir., Rel. Ed., St. Mark's Meth. Ch., NY, 1942-46; pastor, Whatcoat Meml. Meth. Ch., Dover, Del., 1951-53; Janes Meml. Meth. Ch., Bklyn, N.Y., 1953-59; asst. prof., Rel. & Phil., Clark Coll., Atlanta, Ga., 1946-49; prof., Rel. Ed. & Psych., Gammon Theol. Sem., Atlanta, Ga., 1949-51; instr., Rel. Ed., Sch. of Ed., NY Univ., 1957-59; lectr., Rel., Northwestern

Univ., 1960-62; visiting prof., Rel. Ed., Interdenom. Theol. Center, 1964; acting head, Div. of Practical Studies, Garrett Theol. Sem., Northwestern Univ., Evanston, Ill., 1959-66; visiting prof., Educacion Christiana, Cnetro Evangelico Unido, Mexico, 1966; presently serves as Functional Exec. Sec. for Chrstn. Ed., World Div., Bd. of Missn., The Meth. Ch.; mem., Gen. Bd. of Ed., The Meth. Ch.; Curriculum Com., Meth. Ch.; Lay Career Workers Study Com., Meth. Ch.; World Meth. Family Life Com.; Coordinating Com., Parish Ed. Staffs, Consultation in Ch. Union; Program Bd., Div. of Chrstn. Ed., Natl. Coun. of Chs.; No. Amer. Regional Com., World Coun. on Chrstn. Ed.; editor-at-large, The Christian Century; contributor, Westminister Dictionary of Christian Education (K. B. Culley, ed.); A History of American Methodism (E. S. Bucke, ed.) Abingdon Press, 1964; An Introduction to Christian Education (J. J. Taylor, ed.) Abingdon Press, 1966; Bicentennial of American Methodism (A. Godbald, ed.) Assn. of Methodist His. Societies, 1967; Encyclopedia of World Methodism (N. B. Harmon, ed.) Abingdon Press, 1968; recd. Merit Award for Disting. Serv. in Promoting Better Intergroup Relations, Northshore, Ill. Human Rel. Coun., 1961; World Coun. of Chrstn. Ed. Sabbatical Services Travel & Research Fellowship in Mexico, 1966; was elected mem., Bd. of Ed., Evanston, Ill., 1963-66, 1966-67; Office: Rm. 1544, 475 Riverside Dr., New York, NY 10027

SHOCKLEY, John Richard, b. Fruitland, Md., Jan. 18, 1914; s. John Wilmore and Effie (Allen) S.; Clark Coll., Atlanta, Ga., and Gammon Theol. Sem., Atlanta, Ga. Diploma, 1933-36; m. Edith Matthews; Children--Richard, Carol, Zarina, Audrey; ministry: Wachapreague, Va., 1936-39; St. Andrews Meth. Ch., Upper Hill, Md., 1939-42; Shiloh, Crisfield, Md., 1942-49; Waugh, Cambridge, Md., 1949-55; Ezion, Wilmington, Del., 1955-61; Dist. Supt., Wilmington Dist., Del. Conf. of the Meth. Ch., 1961-present; mem., Phi Beta Sigma; Home: 412 N. Clayton St., Wilmington, Del. 19805

SHORTS, Robert Buell, presiding elder, b. Gloster, Miss., Dec. 10, 1905; s. Nathan and Eliza S.; A. B., Miss. Indus. Coll., 1930; B. D., Gammon Theol. Sem., 1934; m. Helen Jenetta Clift; thcr., pub. sch., Miss., 5 yrs.; pastor and presiding elder, Chrstn. Meth. Episc. Ch.; present pastor, Linden St. C. M. E. Ch., Atlanta, Ga.; mem., Fulton Co. Democratic Club; Leadership Summit

Conf., Atlanta, Ga.; Adv. Comm., Natl. Conf.; Ga. Coun. of Chs.; Voter's League; NAACP; Mason; Democrat; Home: 601 Hightown Rd. NW, Atlanta, Ga.; Office: Linden St. Institutional C.M.E. Ch., 286 Linden Ave., NE, Atlanta, Ga.

SHUTTLESWORTH, Fred Lee, civil rights leader, b. Muggler, Ala., Mar. 18, 1922; s. Will and Alberta (Roberson) S.; Cedar Grove Inst., Mobile, Ala.; A.B., Selma Univ.; B.S., Ala. State Tchrs. Coll.; m. Ruby Keeler; Children--Patrica (Mrs. Eugene Barnes), Ruby, Fredricka, Carolyn Fred, Jr.; Pastor, First Bapt. Ch., 1952-55; Bethel Bapt. Ch., Birmingham, Ala., 1957-60; current, Revelation Bapt. Ch., Cincinnati, O., 1960--; organizer and pres., Ala. Chrstn. Movement for Human Rights, Birmingham; pres., So. Conf. Educational Fund; sec., Southern Chrstn Leadership Conf.; mem., Natl. Adv. Bd. of CORE; nationwide speaker for civil rights movement; awards: Natl. Newspaper Publishers Assn. for Russwurm Award, 1958; display of self sacrifice, gallantry and bravery, Cincinnati Business League, 1963; tribute to brave leadership, Back Our Bros. Inc., 1963; humanitarian award, Md. St. Conf. NAACP br., 1962; Capitol Press Club Award for Human Relations, 1962; distinguished citizen award, Birmingham Frontiers Club, 1962; for self sacrifice in field of human rights, Honors & Awards Commn.: ACMHR, 1962; admiration, Cincinnati Newswomen, 1963; personal contribution and leadership in fight for human dignity, Cincinnati br. NAACP, 1964; Home: 965 Dana St., Cincinnati, O.; Office: 1556 John St., Cincinnati, O.

SHY, P., Randolph, bishop, b. Kelly, Jasper Co., Ga., May 5, 1898; A.B., Paine Coll.; M.A., Fisk Univ.; M.A., Columbia Univ.; Coll. prof., Miles Coll., Birmingham, Ala., 10 yrs.; pastor, Chrstn. Meth. Episc. Chs., Decatur, Athens and Birmingham, Ala.; pastor, Capers Meml. C.M.E. Ch., Nashville, Tenn., 1940-48; academic dean, Lane Coll.; pastor, St. Paul C.M.E. Ch., Jackson, Tenn.; elected 30th bishop C.M.E. Ch., May, 1958--; repr. C.M.E. Ch. Conv. on Chrstn. Ed., Mexico City; mem., Alpha Phi Alpha; Home: 2780 Collier Dr., NW, Atlanta, Ga.

*SIDEBOARD, Henry Yergan, ch. official, b. Centerville, Miss., Oct. 9, 1909; s. Richard and Mary L. (Montgomery) S.; A.B., Paine Coll., 1935; B.D., Howard

Univ., Sch. of Rel., 1938; m. Christina White; Children--Jean Carolyn, Rosemary, Cheryl Ann; pastor, Chrstn. Meth. Episc. Ch., Georgia, Va., N. J., S. C.; ordained elder, 1938; pastor, Sidney Parker C. M. E. Ch., Columbia, S. C.; current pastor, Bethel C. M. E. Ch., Seattle, Wash.; dir., Chrstn. Ed., C. M. E. Ch.; prin., Holsey-Cobb Acad., Cordele, Ga., 1940-42; dean, Leadership Training Sch., N. C., S. C.; US Army chap.; Bronze Star Medal, Korea; mem., Omega Psi Phi; Office: 172 23rd St., Seattle, Wash.

SIMMONS, Dimpson Waycross, b. Atlanta, Ga., Apr. 21, 1917; s. Dean E. and Minnie B. S.; B. A., Lane Coll., 1955-59; B. D., Interdenom. Theol. Center, 1960-63; m. Lillie V. Wallace; Children--Mrs. Benton Strode, Mrs. Paul Boyd, Mrs. Geraldyne Johnson; pastor, St. Paul Meth. Ch., Paris, Tenn.; Burdettes Chapel Meth. Ch., Capleville, Tenn., 1951-55; St. Paul Meth. Ch., Dover, Tenn., 1949; Clark Meth. Ch., McMinnville, Tenn., 1959; present pastor, Pickett Chapel Meth. Ch., McMinnville, Tenn., 1960--; Home: 207 E. Market St., Lebanon, Tenn.

SIMMONS, Julius Caesar, b. New Rochelle, N. Y., Nov. 24, 1925; s. Charles and Priscilla (Dilligard) S.; A. B., Va. Union Univ., 1952; B. D., Va. Union Univ. Sch. of Rel., 1955; further study: Ft. Valley State Coll., m. Alma Alexander; Children--Patricia Diane, Julius C., Jr.; chrstn. soc. worker, Dayton Chrst. Center, Dayton, O., 1955-57; dir., Rel. Activities, Ft. Valley State Coll., 1957--; pastor, Trinity Bapt. Ch., Ft. Valley, Ga., 1957--; v. p., So. Regional Va. Union Univ. Alumni Assn., 1959--; pres., Ft. Valley Min. Alliance, 1959--; mem., Frontiers Intl.; Natl. and Regional officer, Phi Beta Sigma (former); US Navy, Pac. Theatre of War, 1944-46; WW II Medal; Pac. Battle Ribbon; Honor Man during Boot training; mem., Natl. Assn. of Univ. and Coll. Chaplains; Prog. Natl. Bapt. Conv.; Assn. of Coll. Personnel Workers, Bapt. Student Union; advisor, YMCA; Home: Ft. Valley State Coll., Ft. Valley, Ga.

SIMMS, David McDaniel, research asst., b. Richmond, Va., Aug. 28, 1933; s. Obadiah B. and Rebecca (McDaniel) S.; A. B., Va. Union Univ., 1950-54; B. D., Prot. Episc. Theol. Sem., Va., 1955-58; NYU, 1960--, (Ph. D. candidate); chap., Dept. of Corr., NYC, 1960--; Chapel of Intercession (curate), Trinity Parish, NYC, 1961-62;

research asst., Bur. of Research and Survey, Natl. Coun of Chs., USA, 1962-63; mem., Soc. for Scientific Study of Rel.; assoc., Amer. Soc. Assn.; mem., Acad. of Rel. and Mental Health; author: "Understanding the Adolescent Offender," Journal of Pastoral Care, Summer, 1961; "Communicating With the Adolescent Delinquent," Journal of Educational Sociology, Summer, 1962; "The Liturgical Movement in the Roman Catholic Church: Path to Dialogue?" Journal of Religious Thought, No. 2, 1962-63; Home: 45 Tiemann Pl., Apt. 4A, New York, N. Y.

*SIMMS, Virgil Andrew, social worker, b. Ronceverte, Va., Aug. 5, 1931; s. Edward F. and Evelyn (Peck) S.; A. B., West Va. State Coll., 1954; B. D., Howard Univ., Sch. of Rel., 1958; present--Sch. of Social Work, Howard Univ., 1962--; m. La Verne Wilmer; Children--Dwayne Kerin, Deborah Leyna; tchr., The Lewisburg, W. Va., 1954-1954; counselor, to delinquent boys, 1955-58; pastor, First Bapt. Ch., Lex., Va., 1955-62; tchr., Rockbridge, W. Va., 1960; counselor to delinquent children, Wash., D. C., 1962-64; psychiatric soc. worker, St. Elizabeth Hosp., 1962-63; assoc. pastor, Second Bapt. Ch., 1951-53; US Forces, 1952; Home: 5017 The Alemeda, Balto., Md.

SIMON, Joseph Donald, tchr., b. Natchitoches, La., June 30, 1932; s. Charlie and Ida (LaCour) S.; St. Mary's Sem., Techny, Ill., 1951-53; St. Paul's Sem., Epworth, Iowa, 1953-55; L. C. H., Gregorian Univ., Rome, 1961-63; ordained priest, Roman Cath. Ch., 1961; tchr., Church History, Amer. and World History, St. Augustine's Sem., Bay St. Louis, Miss., 1963--; Home: St. Augustine Sem., Bay St. Louis, Miss.

SIMPSON, William Bratton, b. St. Louis, Missouri, Aug. 26, 1933; s. Wm. Emanuel and Lillian Mae (Bratton) S.; Wayne Univ., Detroit, Mich., 1952-55; B. A., Wilberforce Univ., Wilberforce, O., 1962-64; m. Anna Christie Brown; asst. pastor, Ward A. M. E. Ch., Los Angeles, Calif., 1959-61; pastor, Primm Tabernacle A. M. E. Ch., Pomona, Calif., 1961-62; pastor, Shorter A. M. E. Ch., So. Charleston, O., 1962-63; asst. pastor, St. John A. M. E. Ch., Xenia, O., 1963--; US Navy, 1955-57; mem., Alpha Phi Alpha; Home: Emery Hall, Wilberforce Univ., Wilberforce, O.

SIMS, David Henry, bishop, b. Ala., July 18, 1886; s. F. R. and Evelyn S.; A. B., Ga. State Coll., 1905; A. B., Oberlin Coll., 1909; B. D., Oberlin Theol. Sem., 1912; A. M., Univ. of Chgo., D. D. (hon.), Allen Univ.; Morris Brown Coll.; Wilberforce Univ.; Livingstone Coll.; m. Mayme; Children--Careve S. Dudley, Mayme Anna; pastor, Afr. Meth. Episc. Chs., Painesville, O., Rhode Island; pastor, Morris Brown Coll., Greenwood, S. C.; elected bishop, 1932; has served as bishop, So. Africa, Ala., 1936-40; retired, 1940; prof., Morris Brown Coll.; dean, Allen Univ.; dir., Citizens & Southern Bank & Trust Co., Phila., Pa.; dir., Phila. Tribune (weekly newspaper); dir., Union Mutual Life Ins. Co.; mem., Elk; Mason; Alpha Phi Alpha; Knight of Pythias; author: History of the A. M. E. Ch. in the 14th District; The Function of the Presiding Elder; The Office of Presiding Elder; Rel. Ed. in Negro Colleges; The Function of Worship; Home: 211 N. 53rd St., Phila., Pa.

SIMS, Frank Kentworth, b. Union, S. C., July 20, 1911; s. Ernest and Bessie (Jeter) S.; A. B., Benedict Coll., 1940; courses, Biblical Sem., 1941-42; Union Theol. Sem., N. Y., 1943-45; M. S., Tenn. A & I Univ., 1959; currently studying at Chgo. Theol. Sem.; m. Eunice Robinson; Children--Frankie Lamar, Sylvia Antenet; pastor, New Mt. Zion Bapt. Ch., Orangeburg, S. C., 1942-47; Bethesda Bapt. Ch., Georgetown, S. C., 1947-55; Mt. Olive Bapt. Ch., 1955-59; Ebenezer Bapt. Ch., 1959--; tchr., Cameron Elem. Sch., S. C., 1944-47; mem., Trustee Bd., Benedict Coll., 1961--; Bd. of Selective Serv. Bd. Area XII, Chgo.; Natl. Bapt. Conv. of Amer.; Bapt. World's Alliance; Gen. Bd., Natl. Chrstn Ed., NCC; Ch. Fed. of Greater Chgo.; Home: 8201 So. Champlain Ave., Chgo., Ill. 60619; Office: 4501 So. Vincennes Ave., Chgo., Ill. 60653

SIMS, George Turner, b. Thebes, Ga., July 23, 1897; s. Felix R. and Emma (E.) S.; A. B., Morris Brown Coll., 1915-19; B. S. T., Lincoln Univ., 1920-23; D. D. (hon.), Wilberforce Univ., 1960; m. Beatrice Childs (1924), Victoria Hargon (1960); Children--George Turner, Jr.; ordained A. M. E. Ch., 1920, to the deaconate; ordained A. M. E. Ch. to the eldership, 1923; pastor, Afr. Meth. Episc. Ch., Muskogee, Okla., 1925-27; Pine Bluff, Ark., 1928-31; Hot Springs, Ark., 1931-35; presiding elder, Cleveland, O., 1935-39; pastor, St. John A. M. E. Ch., Cleveland, 1950-55; current coll. prof., Campbell

Coll., and presiding elder, A. M. E. Ch., 1963--; sec., Bd. of Wilberforce Univ., 1955-61; tchr., Campbell Coll., 1963; Office: Campbell Coll., Jackson, Miss.

SINGLETON, Harold Douglas, b. Valdosta, Ga., Dec. 10, 1908; s. Joseph Pinkney and Annie (King) S.; student, Oakwood Coll.; Union Coll.; Andres Univ.; m. Mary Louise Miller; Children--Mrs. Maurice Mitchell, Harold Jr., Alvin, Kenneth, Marilyn, Dwight; pastor, Chattanooga, Tenn., 1929-31; Ocala and Gainesville, Fla., 1932-34; Belle Glade, Fla., 1934-35; Daytona Beach and New Smyrna, Fla., 1935-37; Miami, Fla., 1937-39; Raleigh, N. C., 1939-42; sec., Negro Dept., S. D. A. Ch., 1942-45; pres., So. Atlantic Conf., S. D. A. Ch., 1946-53; pres., Northeastern Conf., S. D. A. Ch., 1954-62; sec., No. Amer. Regional Dept., Gen. Conf., S. D. A. Chs., Wash., D. C., 1962; assoc. sec., Gen. Conf., S. D. A., Ch., 1966-present; mem., Denom. Inst. Bds., Oakwood Coll., 1942; Riverside Hosp., 1942; Atlantic Union Coll., 1954-62; New England Sanitarium, 1954-62; Home: 700 Oglethorpe St., Wash., D. C. 20011

*SINGLETON, William Matthew, b. Conway, S. C., Oct. 11, 1920; s. George W. and Elizabeth S.; A. B., Va. Union Univ., 1943; Howard Univ., Sch. of Rel., B. D., 1946; D. D. (hon.), Western Bapt. Bible Coll., 1964; m. Florence Revels; Children--Margout Ann, Elizabeth Ann, William M., Jr.; pastor, Bethlehem Bapt. Ch., Tyler, Tex., 1947-49; First Bapt. Ch., Madison, N. J., 1951-52; Second Bapt. Ch., Minova, Mo., 1957-62; dir., Rel. Activities, Butler Coll., Tyler, Tex., 1946-50; tchr., Bible, Butler Coll., Tyler, Tex.; dean, Western Bapt. Bible Coll., 1958-61; pres., Western Bapt. Bible Coll., 1962--; mem., Independent Voters League, Kans. City, Mo., 1951; Lincoln Community Coun., 1963--; Trustee Bd. Western Bapt. Bible Coll., Kans. City, Mo., 1961--; Spec. spuv., Surgeon Gen. Office, Wash., D. C., 1945-46; Kans. City Theol. Soc.; YMCA; Urban League; NAACP; Min. Alliance, Kans. City, Mo.; Religion and Labor Found.; Omega Psi Phi; author: History of Missouri Bapt. State Conv., 1964; Home: 2119 Tracy, Kans. City, Mo. 64108

SKEETE, F. Herbert, b. New York, N. Y., Mar. 22, 1930; s. Ernest A. and Elma I. S.; A. B., Brooklyn Coll., 1959; B. D., Drew Univ. Theol. Sem., 1962; grad. work towards M. A., New Sch. for Social Research; m. Shirley

Clarissa Hunte; Children--Michael Herbert, Mark Curtis; student asst., Metro. Community Meth. Ch., NYC; student pastor, Union Meth. Ch., New York; ordained elder, NY Conf., 1962; pastor, Union Meth. Ch., So. Ozone Pk., New York; social investigator, NYC Dept. of Welfare, 1959; mem., Exec. Bd., Ed. Chrmn., United Neighbors Civic Assn., 1961-64; mem., Exec. Com., Second Van Wyck Civic Assn.; co-chrmn., Queens Assn. for Integrated and Quality Ed.; membership chrmn., Exec. Com., So. Ozone Pk. Coordinating Counc., 1962--; mem., NY Conf. Bd. of Social Concerns of the Meth. Ch., 1962-64; mem., Committee on Health Care Agencies, NY Conf. of the Meth. Ch., 1964; v. chrmn., NY Chapters of Meth. for Ch. Renewal, 1963; chrmn., Ed. Com., Queens Interfaith Clergy Coun., 1964; Chapel Com. at Kennedy Airport, 1964; Evangelism Com., Queens Fed. of Chs., 1962; US Air Forces, Aptitude Testing Unit; dir., Emergency Youth Work Project in Bedford-Stuyvesant, Bklyn, N.Y., 1964; Home: 130-32 149th St., So. Ozone Park, New York, N.Y.; Office: Union Meth. Ch., 150 St. Rockaway Blvd., So. Ozone Pk., New York, N.Y.

SKINNER, John Thomas, chap., b. Jackson, Ala., July 15, 1915; s. Hayes W. and Bettie (Dickinson) S.; B.D., Luth. Coll., 1934-40; m. Lai Levonne Ramsey; pastor, Calvary, Holy Cross, St. Mark's, Gethsemane, Christ, St. Paul's Luth. Ch., Ala., 1940-48; Mt. Calvary, Kannapolis, N.C., 1948-55; Calvary, Memphis, Tenn., 1955-59; Trinity Luth. Ch., Montgomery, Ala., 1959-62; Bethlehem. Luth. Ch., New Orleans, La., 1962-63; Institutional chap., New Orleans, 1963--; Dept. of English, Ala. Luth. Acad., 1946-48; sec. of Bd. of Control, Immanuel Luth. Coll., Greensboro, N.C., 1953-58; Institutional chap., Charity Hosp., New Orleans; mem., NAACP, Democrat; Home: 4402 Anthony Ave., New Orleans, La.; Office: Charity Hospital, New Orleans, La.

SMALLS, Leonard L., b. White Plains, N.Y., Jan. 20, 1930; A.B., Va. Union Univ., 1952; S.T.B., Temple Univ. Sch. of Theol., 1955; Cert., Clinical Pastoral Trng.; m. Edna Beatrice Lee; Children-- Leonard, Linda; radio announcer, WANT, Richmond, Va., 1951; pastor, 1st Bapt. Ch., Morton, Pa., 1956; Beth. Bapt. Ch., Penllyn, Md., 1958; Sr. Prot. Chap., Graterford State Penitentiary, 1961; pastor, 59th St. Bapt. Ch., Phila., Pa., 1963-present; cons., Phila. Bd. of Ed., consumer ed., Fidelity Bank, Phila., Pa.; candidate, State Senate, 8th Dist., 1966; Mayoralty candidate, 1967; US Army, 2 yrs.; awards, Joshua Simpson Alumni for Outstanding Service, Va. Union Univ., 1968; mem., Omega Psi Phi; Pride of Ethiopia Lodge, Phila., Pa.; Cham. of Commerce; Bd. of Dir., Little Neighborhood Schs.; Amer. for Democratic Action; Phila. Coun. for Comm. Adv.; Chrmn., Bd. and organizer, United Purchaser Services, Inc.; Home: 4632 Larchwood Ave., Phila., Pa. 19143; Office: 59th St. Bapt. Ch., 59th and Pine St., Phila., Pa. 19143

SMITH, Allen Hart, b. Chgo., Ill., Oct. 20, 1935; s. Dewight and Josephine; B.A., Elmhurst Coll., Elmhurst, Ill., 1958; B.D., Yale Univ. Div. Sch., New Haven, Conn., 1961; assoc. min., St. Albans Congre. Ch., St. Albans, L.I., N.Y., 1961-62; pastor, Chrstn. Tabernacle Bapt. Ch., Hamden, Conn., 1962-present; asst. dean of students, financial aid officer, Yale Univ. Div. Sch., New Haven, Conn., 1965-present; tchr., Hillhouse High Sch., New Haven, Conn., 1962-65; Bd., New Haven br. NAACP; OIC; Home: 475 Mansfield St., New Haven, Conn. 06511; Office: 409 Prospect St., New Haven, Conn. 06511

SMITH, Benjamin Julian, bishop, b. Barnesville, Ga., Dec. 27, 1899; s. Rev. John Benjamin and Matha Angeline (Thomas) S.; A.B., Howard Univ., 1924; B.D., Garrett Theol. Sem., 1927; student Northwestern Univ.; D.D., Lane Coll., 1944; m. Hermion V. Jackson; Children--Roy Morgan, Carol Susan (Mrs. Earle Anthony), Benjamin Julian; ordained to ministry Chrstn. Meth. Episc. Ch.; asst. pastor, Israel Meth. Ch., Washington, 1922-24; pastor, New Hope Ch., Evanston, Ill., 1924-28; dir., redl. ed., 8th Episc. Dist.; acting pastor, Williams Institutional Ch., NYC, 1928-29; pastor, Jubilee Temple, Chgo., 1929-30, Jamison Temple, Kansas City, Mo., 1930-35; gen. sec., bd. rel. ed., C.M.E. Ch., 1935-54, bishop, 1954--; also pres., Bd. Chrstn. Ed., v.p. Interdenom. Theol. Center, Atlanta; mem., Natl. Coun. Boy Scouts; pres., Bd. of Trustees Lane Coll., Jackson, Tenn.; trustee, Miss. Indus. Coll.; dir., Rockefeller Bros. Fund for Theol. Ed., mem., Natl. Coun. Chs. Christ US (v.p.), World Coun. Chrstn. Ed. and Sun. Sch. Assn. (v.p.), World Coun. Chs. (exec. com. US conf.), So. Conf. Human Welfare, NAACP, Phi Beta Sigma; Home: 8128 S. Calumet Ave., Chgo., Ill.

SMITH, Bennett W., b. April 7, 1933, Florence, Ala., s. Q. T. Miles and Pearlene Smith; B. S., Tenn. A & I State Univ.; Moody Bible Inst., Chgo.; D. D. (hon.), Cincinnati Bapt. Theol. Sem.; m. Trixie Clement; Children--2 sons, 2 daus.; pastor, First Bapt. Ch., Mt. Auburn, Cincinnati, O.; Lincoln Hgts. Bapt. Ch., Cincinnati, present; mem., Bd. Dirs. Coun. of Chs., Cin-Cinnati, O.; com. Race and Rel.; com. on Scouting; Cincinnati Chrstn. Leadership Conf. Chrmn.; Bd. of Dirs. OIC; sec., Bd. of Trustees, Cincinnati Bapt. Coll. and Sem.; sec., Western Union Dist. Assn.; statistical sec., Ohio Bapt. Gen. Assn.; v. p., Valley Chrstn. Improvement Assn; mem., Faculty Natl. Bapt. Congre. of Chrstn. Ed.; Home: 1102 Byrd Ave., Cincinnati, O.

SMITH, Charles Mifflin, b. Wilmington, Del., Jan. 10, 1921; s. W. Hibberd and Louise Coursey S.; A. B., Livingstone Coll., 1962; m. Theodora Shippy; Children--Charles Mifflin, Jr., Edgar Hibberd; pastor, Ernest Robinson Meml. Afr. Meth. Episc. Z. Ch., Chester, Pa., 1950-52; Alloyne Meml. A. M. E. Z. Ch., Phila., Pa., 1952-55; Union Chapel A. M. E. Z. Ch., Albermarle, N. C., 1955-57; Russell Chapel A. M. E. Z. Ch., Rogersville, Tenn., 1957-59; Mt. Zion A. M. E. Z. Ch., Lancaster, S. C., 1959--; tchr., pub. sch., Albermarle, N. C., 1 yr.; Lancaster, S. C., 1 yr.; trustee, Clinton Coll.; mem., Connectional Dept. Budget Bd. A. M. E. Z. Ch.; mem., A & A; NAACP; author: Our Heritage, 1867-1958; Home: 401 Clinton Ave., Lancaster, S. C.

SMITH, Charlie Jasper, b. Angelus, S. C., Nov. 12, 1929; s. Charlie and Eula (McQueen) S.; A. B., Claflin Coll., Orangeburg, S. C., 1959; B. D., Gammon Theol. Sem., Atlanta, Ga.; m. Doris Frances Webb; pastor, Landrum and Inman Meth. Ch., 1951-53; McBee Meth. Ch., S. C., 1953-54; York Meth. Ch., 1954-60; Spartanburg Meth. Ch., 1960-62; Dist. Supt. of the Sumter Dist., The Meth. Ch., 1962--; chrmn., The Com. on Urban Work; v. chrmn., Bd. of Min. Trng. and Qualification; mem., The Commn. on World Serv. and Finance in the S. C. Conf.; v. chrmn., The Sumter Movement; Democrat; mem., Alpha Phi Alpha; Odd Fellows; Masons; Home: 514 S. Main St., Sumter, S. C., 29151

SMITH, Earnest Andrew, b. Macon, Ga., Aug. 25, 1913; s. Thomas and Pauline (Washington); A. B., Rust Coll., Holly Springs, Miss., 1937; M. A., Oberlin Coll., Oberlin, O., 1938; doctoral studies, Hartford Sem. Found., 1948-50; m. Milverta Alice (Gooden); pastor, United Meth. Ch., Alexander City, Ala., Marion, Ala., 1939-43; St. Paul Meth. Ch., San Antonio, Tex., 1951-57; dir., Lincoln Sch., Marion, Ala.; ex. sec., Bd. of Ed., Meth. Ch., Holly Springs, Miss.; pres., Rust Coll., Holly Springs, Miss.; dir., Dept. Rel. & Race, Bd. of Social Concerns, United Meth. Ch., Wash., D.C., 1966-present; mem., Bd. of Dirs., YMCA, San Antonio, Tex., 1953-57; NAACP San Antonio, Tex., 1952-55; NAACP, Holly Springs, Miss., 1958-66; Phi Beta Sigma; author: Civil Disobedience, A Stance for Christians, 1969; Home: 5110 Que St., SE, Wash., D.C. 20027; Office: 100 Maryland Ave., NE, Wash., D.C. 20002

SMITH, Ernest Clarence, sem. prof., b. Cumberland, Va., Jan. 16, 1897; s. Booker and Alice (Epps) S.; A.B., Va. Union Sem. & Coll., 1923; A.B., B.D., Va. Union Univ., 1926, 1929; Union Theol. Sem., NY, 1936; D.D. (hon.), and LL.D. (hon.), Va. Sem., 1953; D.D. (hon.), Va. Union Univ., 1940; m. Dorothy B. Butler; Children--Oswald C., Ernest C., Jr.; pastor, Mt. Carmel Bapt. Ch., Lynchburg, Va., 1919-24; Second Bapt. Ch., S. Richmond, Va., 1924-28; pastor, Metropolitan Bapt. Ch., Wash., D.C., 1928--; instr., Howard Univ., Sch. of Rel., 1935-58; lectr., Bapt. Sun. Sch. Congress; Home: 1551 Hemlock NW, Wash., D.C.

SMITH, George Walker, b. Montgomery, Apr. 28, 1928; s. Will and Amanda (Tyler) S.; B.S., Knoxville Coll., Tenn.; B.D., Pittsburgh Theol. Sem., 1956; m. Elizabeth Hightower; children--Anthony Tyrone, Carolyn Yvonne, Joyce Lorraine; youth dir., Third U. Presby. Ch., Pittsburgh, Pa., 3 yrs.; current pastor, Golden Hill U. Presby. Ch., 1956--; v.p., Bd. of Ed.; mem., Adv. Bd. of the Salvation Army; Bd. of Dirs., San Diego Co. Coun. of the Boy Scouts of Amer.; Resolutions Comm. of the Calif. Sch. Bd. Assn., 1964--; Bd. of Dirs., The Big Bros. of San Diego, Inc.; Bd. of Dirs., USO Coun. of San Diego; Civil Service Oral Review Bd.; chrmn., Support of Chs. Commn. for Southeastern Kiwanis Club; Bd. of Trustee, Univ. Rel. Found., Univ. of Calif., San Diego; chrmn., Bd. of Mgrs., Southeast YMCA; mem., Metro. Bd., San Diego City-County YMCA; San Diego Mental Health Com.; supt., Schs. Commn. dealing with culturally handicapped; San Diego Unified Sch. Dist. Bd. of Ed.; Outstanding Young Clergyman of the Yr., by the

Jr. Cham. of Commerce, San Diego; Outstanding Young Men of America, by the Natl. Bd. of Dirs. of the Jr. Chamber of Commerce; Home: 5514 Mira Flores Dr., San Diego, Calif.; Office: 2130 Market St., San Diego, Calif.

SMITH, Herald Leonydus, ch. official, b. Smithfield, O., Apr. 20, 1907; s. Ira Rufus and Mary (West) S.; B. D., Payne Theol. Sem., 1945; m. Dorothy Irene McClinton; Children--Herald Smith, Jr., Verl, Rosalie Foster, David; assigned to St. Andrew Coshocton, 1939; St. Paul, London, 1941; Quinn Chapel, Ironton, 1945; St. Paul, Cincinnati, 1953; asst. pastor, St. John, Cleveland, 1957; Quinn Chapel, Cleveland, 1962; chief sec. of So. Ohio, Ohio Conf. from 1943-57; sec., Tawawa Sch. of Rel., Dist. Conf., v.p., of Tawawa Sch. of Rel., Editor of Tawawa and a Trustee of No. Ohio Conf., instr., Seminary sponsored by ministers in Cleveland; sec., Meth. Min. Alliance, A. M. E. Fellowship; treas., Meth. Alliance; 2nd v.p. of NAACP of Cincinnati, O., active in community work in Cincinnati Masonic Lodge, Boy Scout Institutional and Regional repr., Dir. of Rel. Ed., Soc. Relation of Coun. of Chs. in the City of Cleveland; mem., Bd. of Kinsman Area chs. in the City of Cleveland; mem., Bd. of Kinsman Area Recreational Bldg; award given in 1950 for best letter on theme "My City" in Ironton, Ohio; many other citations; Royal Crescent Club of Wilberforce, Sphinx Club and Republican, Literary Societies; columnist in the Call & Post, Negro weekly of Cincinnati, "Extending the Pulpit Beyond the Sanctuary," Cincinnati Enquire, Cleveland Press, Metro, Forum and others; Home: 3359 142nd, Cleveland, O.; Office: 3241 130th, Cleveland, O.

SMITH, James Alfred, b. Kansas City, Mo., May 19, 1931; s. Clyde and Amy Elnoro; B. S., Western Bapt. Sem. Coll., 1952; B. D., Mo. Sch. of Rel., Columbia, Mo., 1959; Th. M., Mo. Sch. of Rel., 1966; courses, Pacific Sch. of Rel., Berkeley, Calif.; m. Joanna Goodwin; Children--Amy, James, Shari, Ronald, Craig, Anthony; pastor, 2nd Bapt. Ch., Columbia, Mo.; prin., Lincoln Sch., Keytesville, Mo.; asst. to pres., Bishop Coll., Dallas, Tex; present, Min. of Comm. Witness, Amer. Bapt. Conv., Oakland, Calif.; cons., Human Rel. Dept., Berkeley, Calif.; police dept., Oakland, Calif.; mem., Citizens Adv. Com., E. Bay Skills Center, Oakland, Calif.; Internatl. Min. Alliance; Bd. of Dir. OIC, Oakland, Calif.; award, United Negro Coll. Fund, Bishop Coll., Dallas, Tex.; guest, Bapt. Union for Sweden, 1968; repr., Amer. Bapt. Home Mission Soc., Sweden and Norway, 1968; author of various articles; Home: 5401 Gately, Richmond, Calif.; Office: 268 Grand Ave., Oakland, Calif. 94623

SMITH, James Wynetotte, b. Cherokee Co., S.C., Mar. 15, 1893; s. Cooper Samuel and Nancy (Meachem) S.; A.B., Johnson C. Smith Univ., 1920; B.D., J.C. Smith Univ., 1923; D.D., Johnson C. Smith Univ., 1945; m. Margaret Arthur; Children--James Wynetotte, Jr., Wm. Arthur, Estelle Ida Mae (Mrs. Wm. Gayman), Gloria Margaret (Mrs. James Thomas Burch); pastor, E. Vine Ave. Presby. Ch., Knoxville, Tenn.; Davie St. Presby. Ch., Raleigh, N.C.; (current), Seventh St. Presby. Ch., Charlotte, N.C.; sec., Trustee Bd., Johnson C. Smith Univ., Charlotte, N.C.; mem., Trustee Bd., Barber Scotia Coll., Concord, N.C.; chrmn., Natl. Missions Comm., Catawba Synod; 1st class pvt., WW I, 1918-19; 1961 "Father of the Year" by W.P.O. of Seventh St. Presby. Ch.; mem., Mason, Finance Comm. order Eastern Star, Ex. Bd., Coun. of Chrstns. & Jews, Commn. on Church Relations, Presby. Ch.; Home: 1901 Patton Ave., Charlotte, N.C.; Church: 406 N. College St., Charlotte, N.C.

SMITH, John Conway, ch. official, b. Little Rock, Ark., Jan. 4, 1927; s. John C. Smith; B.A., Oakwood Coll., 1950; m. Helen L. George; Children--Laura Janet, Jonathan C.; publishing sec., Southwest Reg. Conf. of S.D.A., 1952; Home Missionary - Sun. Sch. Sec., SW Reg. Conf., Dallas, Tex., 1962; pastor, Phil. S.D.A. Ch., Shreveport, La., Ephesus S.D.A. Ch., San Antonio, Tex; present: pastor, Bethel S.D.A. Ch., Toledo, Ohio, 1963--; US Army, WW II. Home: 1703 Parkdale St., Toledo, O.; Office: 660 Vance St., Toledo, O.

*SMITH, Kelly Miller, b. Oct. 28, 1920, Mound Bayou, Miss.; s. Perry M. and Priscilla (Anderson); A.B., Morehouse Coll., 1942; B.D., Howard Univ. Sch. of Rel., 1945; grad. study, Vanderbilt Univ., 1955; former pastor, Mt. Heroden Bapt. Ch., Vicksburg, Miss., 1946-51; Hd. Dept. of Rel., Natchez Coll., 1946-48; ex. tchr., Alcorn Coll., Alcorn, Miss., 1949-50; instr., Am. Bapt. Theol. Sem., 1959-61; pastor, First Bapt. Ch., Capitol Hill, Nashville, Tenn., 1951-present; instr.,

Vanderbilt Univ. Div. Sch.; pres., Nashville NAACP, 1956-59; moderator, Stone's River Dist. Assn., 1954-61; pres., Nashville Chrstn. Leadership Coun., 1958-63; present, pres., Bapt. Leadership Ed. Congress; Bd. Pres. OIC; Exec. Bd. mem., Tenn. Coun. on Human Relations; SCLC; Bd. of Managers Amer. Bapt. Foreign Mission Soc.; Bd. mem., Nashville Urban League; Southern Reg. Coun.; Family and Children's Services; Exec. Bd. mem., Nashville Chrstn. Leadership Coun.; Senior Citizens, Inc., mem., War on Poverty Prog.; chrmn., Comm. on Southern Churchman; awards, listed "One of America's Ten Most Outstanding Preachers" by Ebony Magazine, 1954; listed among "Outstanding Civic Leaders of America;" citations from - Fellowship House (Cincinnati, O.); Natl. Coun. Negro Women (Nashville, Tenn.); Agora Assembly (Nashville, Tenn.); Freedom Jubilee (Pittsburgh, Pa.); Nashville NAACP; Tenn. St. Alumni Assn.; Fed. of Colored Women's Clubs (Nashville, Tenn.); "Citizen of Nashville" Tenn. Bapt. Youth Encampment; Khayyams Klub (Cleveland, O.); ed., Katallagete Mag., pub. by Comm. of Southern Churchmen; former ed., Young Adult Quarterly, 1958-59; Home: 1229 Caldwell Ave., Nashville, Tenn. 37212; Office: 319 Eighth Ave. N., Nashville, Tenn. 37203

SMITH, Kenneth Wayne, b. Covington, Ky., Oct. 28, 1932; s. James and Olivia; B.A., Oakwood Coll., Huntsville, Ala., 1958; M.A., Potomac Univ., Wash., D.C., 1961; m. Shirley Yvon (Dixon) S.; Children--Yvon, Joslyen, Diedre, Wayne; pastor, assoc., Phila. S.D.A. Ch., 1963-64; assoc. E. Palo Ch., Calif., 1964-65; pastor, Seaside S.D.A. Ch., Seaside, Calif., 1966-present; Chr. Dupont Park Acad., Wash., D.C., 1961; San Francisco Jr. Acad., 1962-63; consult., Welcome Wagon, Monterey Peninsula; coun., Seaside Elem. Sch., Calif.; asst. sec., Min. Assn. Monterey Peninsula; mem., Amer. Med. Technologist M.T.; Democrat; founder, radio program, "The New Dimension," Seaside, Calif.; Home: 1920 Paralta St., Seaside, Calif. 93955; Office: PO Box 38, Seaside, Calif. 93955

*SMITH, Lawrence Benjamin, b. Washington, D.C., Nov. 2, 1925; s. Alice Smith; A.B., Dickinson Coll., Carlisle, Pa.; B.D., Howard Univ., Sch. of Rel.; m. Estelle Augusta Holsey; Children--Jonathan Darryl, Lawrence Benjamin, Jr., Kevin Augustus (Jameson), Timothy Bruce; pastor, Mt. Zion Meth. Ch., Silver Spring, Md., 1951-

52; Nottingham-Croom Charge, The Meth. Ch., Nottingham and Croom, Md., 1955-56; chap. to students, Wesley Found., Howard Univ., Wash., D. C., 1953-54; Metro. Community Meth. Ch., NYC, 1957-59; pastor, Trinity Meth. Ch. of Morriania, Bronx, NY, 1959--; chrmn., Children's Work Comm., The Prot. Coun. of the City of NY, 1958-59; chrmn., Chrstn. Ed. Comm., The Prot. Coun of the Bronx, 1961-63; chap., Ten Mile River Scout Camps, Narrowsburg, NY, 1960-63; mem., Bd. of Dirs., Claremont Neighbor Community Centers, Inc.; Clergy Adv., Parents for Leadership and Action Now (pub. sch. action group organized May 1964); US Army, Overseas duty in Italy, Germany and France, 1944-46; Ehrenfeld Service Award; affiliated in active capacity and role with Bronx Coun. of Greater NY Couns., Boy Scouts of America; Home: 1074 Washington Ave., Bronx, NY 10456; Office: 1076 Washington Ave., Bronx, NY 10456

*SMITH, Oswald Garrett, b. Richmond, Va., Apr. 17, 1925; s. Ernest Clarence and Odile (Davis) S.; B. A., B. D., Howard Univ., Wash., D. C., 1947, 1950; M. A., Columbia Univ., NY, 1951; D. D. (hon.), Va. Theol. Sem., & Coll., 1954; m. Berta Elizabeth Mills; Children--Oswald, Jr., Alicin Odile; current, Dir. Activities & asst. pastor, Metro. Bapt. Ch., Wash., D. C., 1947--; pastor, Mt. Zion Bapt. Ch., Arlington, Va., 1952--; lectr., Lott Carey Summer Conf., 1954; instr., Natl. Bapt. Sun. Sch. & B. T. U. Congress; instr., Dist. Bapt. Ed. Congress; pres., Capitol Funeral Service Inc., 1959-62; v. p., Reynolds Smith Investment Co.; mem., Bd. of Civic Welfare; Bapt. Min. Conf.; US Army, 1944-46; Good Conduct Medal; Expert Rifleman Award; Bd. of Dirs., Vets. Meml. YMCA; Bd. of Dirs. Lott Carey Foreign Mission Conv.; Bd. of Dirs., Northern Va. Bapt. Assn.; Arlington Min. Assn.; Family Services of Northern Va.; So. Chrstian Leadership Congress; Home: 1938 Bunker Hill Rd., NE, Wash., D. C.; Office: 19th So. Glebe Rd., Arlington, Va.

SMITH, Otis Artis, chap., b. Helena, Ark., Mar. 22, 1934; s. Willie and Mary Lee; A. B., Lemoyne Coll., Memphis, Tenn., 1962; B. D., Interdenom. Theol. Center, Atlanta, Ga., 1965; m. Nettie Mae McQuerter; Children--Adrienne LaJuanna, Mia Chandra; asst. pastor, Radcliffe United Presbyn. Ch., Atlanta, Ga., 1963-65; pastor, Christ United Presby. Ch., Augusta, Ga., 1965-66;

chap., US Army, 1966-present; mem., NAACP; pres., Augusta chapter SCLC, 1965-66; Com. Chrmn., Coun. on Human Relations, Augusta, 1966; chrmn., Operation Breadbasket, 1966; EM (Air Force) 54-60/off-Chaplain, Capt.; US Army Soldier's award; Alpha Phi Alpha Award; Bronze Star; Army Commendation Medal; Purple Heart; Vietnam Campaign Ribbon (Clusters); mem., Omega Psi Phi; Theta Phi (Scholarship); Democrat; Home: 3103 Bellemeade Dr., Augusta, Ga. 30906; Office: Office of the Hosp. Chaplain, Ft. Gordon, Ga. 30905

*SMITH, Perry Anderson III, b. Mt. Bayou, Miss., May 16, 1934; s. Perry Anderson and Elease (Williams) Wilson S., A.B., B.D., Howard Univ., Wash., D.C., 1955; 1958; pastor, First Bapt. Ch., No. Brentwood, Md., 1958-present; Ex. dir., Poverty Program, Prince Georges Md., NAACP; Tech. adv., Model Cities Prog., Natl. Civil Service League, 1969; Home: 7836 Lake Crest Dr., Greenbelt, Md.; Office: 1028 Connecticut Ave., Wash., D.C.

SMITH, Robert Johnson, b. Chgo., Ill., Sept. 26, 1920; s. James H. L. and Anne (Eugenia) S.; A.B., Morehouse Coll., 1937; B.D., Andover Newton Theol. Sem., 1940, S.T.M., 1946; M.S.W., Bryn Mawr Coll., Sch. of Soc. Work; D.D. (hon.), Morehouse Coll., 1956; m. Jennie M.; Children--Everett, Robert II; chap., Va. Hosp., Roanoke, Va., 1946-53; pastor, High St. Bapt. Ch., Roanoke, Va., 1947-52; Hill St. Ch., 1953-55; Salem Bapt. Ch., Jenkintown, Pa., 1956-present; counselor, Phila. Sch. Dist., 1960-present; mem., Penna. State Human Relations Commn.; trustee, Va. Sem. and Coll.; Berean Inst., Phila., Pa.; United Fund, Phila., Pa.; dir., Health and Welfare Coun., Phila., Pa.; US Army, 93rd Inf. Div. (Major), 1941-45; awards: Five Battle Stars, Bronze Star; mem., Rotary, Omega Psi Phi, Fellow of Acad. of Certified Social Workers, Democrat, NEA; Research: John Wycliffe, Precursor of the Modern Age; Religious Beliefs of Servicemen Before and After World War II; Factors Influencing Referrals of Ministers; Home: 191 Serrill Rd., Elkins Park, Pa. 19117; Office: 610 Summit Ave., Jenkintown, Pa.

SMITH, Roland, b. Decatur, Ga., Feb. 26, 1902; s. Anderson and Mattie S.; A.B., Morehouse Coll., 1929; A.M., Atlanta Univ., 1961; D.D. (hon.), Selma Univ., Selma, Ala.; Allen Univ., Columbia, S.C.; Morris Brown Coll.,

Atlanta, Ga.; LL. D. (hon.), Ark. Bapt. Coll., Little Rock, Ark.; Monrovia Coll., Liberia, W. Africa; m. Mary S.; pastor, Metropolitan Bapt. Ch., Columbia, Ga., 1929-31; First Afr. Bapt. Ch., Tuscaloosa, Ala., 1931-36; First Bapt. Ch., Macon, Ga., 1936-37; First Bapt. Ch., Little Rock, Ark., 1947--; statistician, Natl. Bapt. Conv., USA, Inc. 1932-54; sec., Negro Work, Home Mission Bd., Southern Bapt. Conv., 1938-49; sec., Natl. Bapt. Trng. Union Bd., Natl. Bapt. Conv., USA, Inc., 1954-57; editor, The Georgia Bapt. Paper, 1941-49; mem., Natl. Coun. of Chs. of Chrst in Amer.; former mem., Joint Commn. of Pub. Affairs, Natl. Bapt, Southern Bapt., and Amer. Bapt. Conventions; former sec., Joint Commn. on Min. Ed. and Race Relations, Amer., Southern, and Natl. Bapt. Conventions; mem., World Bapt. Alliance Executive Comm., Copenhagen, Denmark, 1947; World Bapt. Alliance Relief Commn., 1947-50; dir., Citizens Trust Co., Atlanta, Ga.; dir., South Eastern Fidelity Fire Ins. Co., Atlanta, Ga.; mem., Kappa Alpha Psi; Delta Sigma Rho Honorary Soc.; Mason; former chrmn., Bd. of Trustees, Ark. Bapt. Coll., Little Rock, Ark.; pres., Ark. Chrstn. Movement (led in the declaring of all four segregated laws nullification by the Supreme Court of State of Ark. as proposed by Gov. Oval Faubus); Home: 613 W. 7th St., Little Rock, Ark.; Office: 7th S. Gaines St., Little Rock, Ark.

SMITH, Thomas, Sr., b. Ansonville, N. C., July 15, 1922; s. Thomas, Jr. and Callie (Windfield) S.; B. S., St. Paul's Coll., 1946-50; S. T. B., Phila. Div. Sch.; Temple Univ. Sch. of Theol., 1950, 1953; Coll of Preachers, 1960, 60; m. Mary Jackson; Children--Carolyn, Clarise, Cynthia, Thomas, III; priest-in-charge, St. James Prot. Episc. Ch., Emporia, Va., St. Thomas Prot. Episc. Ch., Freeman, Va., 1953-57; current vicar, St. Stephens Ch., Winston-Salem, 1957--; chap., Episc. Faculty and Students, Winston-Salem State Coll. and the Sch. of Nursing and the Kate Bitting Reynold's Hosp.; mem., Ex. Coun. of the Diocese of N. C. Dept. of Missions, Chrstn. Social Relations, Dept. of College Work; chrmn., YMCA Fund raising campaign, Winston-Salem, 1962-63; Group chrmn., United Fund, Business Section, 1963; co-chrmn, The Congress of Racial Equality, Winston-Salem, 1963; Exec. Bd. of the NAACP, 1961-62; US Army, 1941-45; Good Conduct Medal; Campaign Medals for the Pacific operation with five battle stars; mem., Financial

Com., Democratic Party, Winston-Salem, N. C.; Home: 810 No. Cameron Ave., Winston-Salem, N. C.; Office: 1104 No. Highland Ave., Winston-Salem, N. C.

SMITH, Walter Louis, b. McKinney, Tex., Jan. 1, 1919; s. Walter Louis and Hattie Luper; A. B., Tex. Coll., Tyler, Tex., 1943; widower; Children--Mary (Mrs. Percy Knox), Bettye Lou (Mrs. Thermon Holiday), W. Louis, III, James Richard, Edward Louis, William Lee, Howard Daniel; pastor, Pilot Pt., Sherman, Tex., 1941-43; Independent Springs Sta., Rural Parish, Tex., 1943-45; NW Tex. Conf. St. Mark C. M. E., Pampa, Tex., 1945-49; Bethel C. M. E., Seattle, Wash., 1950; Allen Temple C. M. E., Portland, Ore., 1953-60; mem., C. M. E., Tacoma, Wash., 1960-66; Miss. Temple C. M. E., San Francisco, Calif., 1966-68; Bd. of Trustees, Tex. Coll.; Ed. Western Index, Citizens Adv. Com. to Alamo Sq., San Franc.; sec., Presiding Bishop, Calif. Conf., tchr., Pilot Grove, Tex., 1940-41; Booker T. Wash. High, Bonham, Tex., 1941-2; awards, Amer. Cancer Soc. Cert. of Merit; Kiwanis Club Outstanding Citizen, Tacoma, Wash.; First Negro Abbot of Trey Frairs of Portland, Ore.; Cert. of Merit, Episc. 3d Dist., C. M. E. Ch.; mem., Masons; Home: 1455-75 Golden Gate Ave., San Francisco, Calif.

SMITH, William T., chap., b. Memphis, Tenn., Nov. 25, 1931; A. B., Lane Coll., Jackson, Tenn., 1959; B. D., Philips Sch. of Theol., Atlanta, Ga., 1962; m. Lois Willingham; Children--Ronald, Charlet, Wm., Jr.; pastored, St. Paul Chrstn. Meth. Episc. Ch., Bolivar, Tenn.; Allen Temple, Marietta, Ga., 1959-61; Trinity, Toccoa, Ga., 1961-62; Williams Meml. C. M. E. Ch., Augusta, Ga., 1962-64; enlisted US Army 1952-54; chap., 1964-present; former v. p., Min. Assn., Augusta, Ga., 1963-64; asst. sec., Ga. Annual Conf., 1960-64; awards, Natl. Ser. Defense Medal; Good Conduct Ribbon; Korean Service Ribbon; United Ser. Ribbon; Army Commendation Medal; Home: 1521 Estill St., Memphis, Tenn. 38109; Office: Office of the Chaplain, NATO/ Shape Support Group, APO, N. Y. 09055

SNELL, Simon, b. Rosenberg, Ft. Bend Co., Tex., Feb. 8, 1912; s. Isome and Marcella (Stewart) S.; Wiley Coll., Marshall, Tex., A. B., Clark Coll., Atlanta, Ga., 1949; B. D., Gammon Theol. Sem., Atlanta, Ga.; further study: Atlanta Univ.; m. Mary Lee Tinner; Children--

Dr. Edna Faye Snell Houston (Dr. Sam Houston); ministry: Warren Meth. Ch., Macon, Ga., 1949; Porch Chapel Meth. Ch., Calhoun, Ga., 1950, First Pastor of Bowen Meth. Ch., Atlanta, Ga., 1951-52, Lawrenceville Circuit, Lawrenceville, Ga. 1953-59; St. Paul Meth. Ch., Texarkana, Tex., present: pastor, Meth. Ch., Marshall, Tex.; mem., Conf. Bd. of Ed.; asst. sec., Bd. of Dirs. of the Wesley Found.; chrmn., Conf. Commn. on Evangelism; tchr. in the Dist. Inst., Marshall, Tex.; sub. tchr., Texarkana pub. sch. sys.; mem., YMCA, Red Cross; Citizens Comm.; chrmn., Min. Comm.; mem. of Political Action Comm. of NAACP; Civil Defense, US Army, 1941-44, served in No. Africa, Italy, France; recd. the EAME Campaign Medal with four bronze stars, Good Conduct Medal, Victory Ribbon, one service stripe, four overseas bars; mem., Phi Beta Sigma, American Woodmen; Home: 908 Whetstone St., Marshall, Tex.

SOMERSILLE: James Humphries, b. Albay, Legaspi, Philippine Is., June 27, 1915; s. Albert E. and Maude (Humphries) S.; A. B., Capital Univ., 1937-40; B. D., Capital Univ. Theol. Sem., 1940-43; Major in Psychology and Soc. Work in Howard Univ.; m. Elizabeth Beatrice Adams; pastor, Evangelical Luth. Ch. of Our Redeemer (LCA), 1943--; Home: 3644 13th St. NW, Wash., D. C.; Office: 2 Rhode Island Ave., NE, Wash., D. C.

SOMERVILLE, Wendell Clay, sem. prof.; b. Reidsville, N. C., Mar. 10, 1900; s. Addie Louise Brown; A. B., 1929, B. D., 1931, Shaw Univ.; A. M., Grad. Sch. of Theol., Oberlin Coll., 1939; D. D. (hon.), Shaw Univ., 1943; LL. D. (hon.), Howard Univ., 1960; m. Alice E. Cooper; Exec. sec., Gen. Bapt. State Conv., N. C.; Exec. sec., Lott Carey Bapt. Foreign Mission Conv., 1940--; visiting prof., Sch. of Rel., Howard Univ.; US Navy, WW I; Cert. of Achievement, Wash. Afro-Amer., 1941; mem., Omega Psi Phi; author: Around the World for Others, 1960; Home: 4408 16th St., Wash., D. C.; Office: 1501 11th St., Wash., D. C.

SPARROW, Eugene, educator, b. Clinton, Mass., Oct. 6, 1921; s. William N. and Mae (Chant) S.; A. B., Mich. Univ., Ann Arbor, Mich., 1946; S. T. B., Tufts Coll., Crane Theol. Sch., 1949; Harvard Div. Sch., Cambridge, Mass., 1946-47; m., divorced; Children--Debra, Rebecca; Dean of Men, Tex. Coll., Tyler, Tex.; acting head, Soc. Studies Dept., Jarvis Chrstn. Coll., Hawkins,

Tex.; tchr., Elem. Sch., Plainville, Conn., 1953-56; acting dir., Urban League, Springfield, Mass., 1956-58; dir., Field Service, Unitarian Universalist Conf.; present asst. dir., Mayor's Friendly Relations Comm., Cincinnati, O.; consultant, The Midwest Unitarian Fellowship Comm.; camp dir., 1957-58; mem., Mayor's Comm. Springfield, Mass., 1957-58; US Air Force; mem., Natl. Educational Assn.; Unitarian Universalist Min. Assn.; Natl. Assn. of Intergroup Officials; weekly column, daily newspaper, Cincinnati, O.; Home: 1491 Baymiller Walk, Cincinnati, O.; Office: 909 Plum St., Cincinnati, O.

SPEAKS, Ruben Lee, sem. prof., b. Lake Providence, La., Jan. 8, 1920; s. Benjamin and Jessie B. S.; A. B., Drake Univ., Des Moines, Iowa, 1946; B. D., Drew Univ., Madison, N. J., 1949; S. T. M., Temple Univ., Phila., Pa., 1952; Duke Univ., Durham, 1960-61; m. Janie Angeline Griffin; Children--Robert, Joan Cordelia, Faith Elizabeth; pastor, St. Thomas Afr. Meth. Episc. Zion Ch., Somerville, N. J., 1946; Wallace Chapel A. M. E. Z. Ch., Phila., Pa., 1950; St. Mark A. M. E. Z. Ch., Durham, 1956; First Ch., Bklyn, N. Y., 1964; prof., Hood Theol. Sem.; Livingstone Coll., Salisbury, N. C., 1959-64; mem., Commn. on the Ed. of Exceptional Persons; Natl. Coun. of Chs. USA; Episc. Comm., A. M. E. Z. Ch.; Durham Comm. on Negro Affairs, N. C.; trustee, Lincoln Hosp., Durham, N. C.; NAACP; Citation and plaque, Outstanding community service to city of Durham; Democrat; mem., Mason; editorial staff, devotional book, Strength of My Life; Home: 1455 Carroll, Brooklyn, N. Y.; Office: 480 Tompkins Ave., Brooklyn, N. Y.

SPIVEY, Bennett, b. Newmarket, Tenn., Aug. 30, 1932; St. Joseph's Jr. Coll., 1953-55; A. B., Philosophy, Our Lady of Angels Sem., 1956-58; St. Josephs Maj. Sem., 1959--; 1963, victim of multiple sclerosis.

SPIVEY, Charles Samuel, sem. dean, b. Washington, O., Feb. 28, 1921; s. Charles Samuel Sr. and Ruth Elizabeth (S.); B. S., Wilberforce Univ.; B. D., Payne Sem.; B. D., Yale Div. Sch.; courses, Oberlin Grad. Sch. of Theol.; m. Ruth Elizabeth Everette; Children--Charles; Ruth Elizabeth; Elaine; Dean, Sch. of Rel., Allen Univ., Columbia, S. C.; pastor, Allen A. M. E. Chapel; Brown A. M. E. Chapel; Bethel A. M. E. Ch., Pittsburgh, Pa.; present Dean, Payne Theol. Sem., Wilberforce, O.;

mem., State FEP Commn., Pa., 1957; mem., Meth. Theol. Study Conf., Oxford Univ., 1965; mem., Faith & Order Commn., Natl. Coun. of Chs., World Wide Coun. of Chs.; mem., Exec. Com., Devel. Conf.; Dept. of Ministry; Com. on long-range planning, Natl. Coun. of Chs.; Alpha Phi Alpha; Home: Box 474 Wilberforce, O. 45384

SPOTTSWOOD, Stephen Gill, bishop, b. July 18, 1897; s. Abraham Lincoln and Mary Elizabeth (Gray) S.; Allbright Coll.; Gordon Div. Sch.; Yale Univ.; D. D. (hon.), Livingstone Coll., 1939; m. Viola Estelle Booker (deceased); 5 children; pastor, 34 yrs. Wash., D. C., Buffalo, Indianapolis, Winston-Salem, New Haven, Portland, Me., W. Newton and Lowell, Mass.; elected 58th Bishop of the Afr. Meth. Episc. Zion Ch., 1952--; (Dist., Alleghany, Ohio, Mich. and Indiana Conf.); pres., NAACP, Wash., D. C. br., 1947-52; mem., Natl. Bd. of Dirs., NAACP, 1954-61; pres., Bd. NAACP, 1961--; chrmn., Bd. A. M. E. Z. Ch., Bd. of Finance; Transportation and Statistics; Commn. on Chaplains; Gen. Conf. and Contennial of Freedom Campaign; mem., World Meth. Coun.; Natl. Coun. of Chs.; Bd. of Trustees, Livingstone Coll., N. C.; Home: 1931 16th St., NW, Wash., D. C.

STALNAKER, Calvin Kersey, b. Edgefield, S. C., Dec. 12, 1891; s. Calvin and Amelia; Hodges Acad., Wash., Ga.; Benedict Coll., Columbia, S. C.; A. B., Paine Coll., Augusta, Ga.; grad. studies, Chgo. Univ. Div. Sch.; Garrett Div. Sch., Evanston, Ill.; Univ. of Toledo, O.; D. D. (hon.), Benedict Coll., S. C.; m. Celeste Kibler (dec.); Children--Spencer (dec.); Dorothy (dec.); Gloria (Mrs. Raleigh E. Taylor); Fern (Mrs. Veryl A. Switzer); LeRoy, Frank; served as Army-Navy sec., Camp Hancock, Ga., 1918-19; pastor, Union Bapt. Ch., Augusta, Ga., 1919-24; exec. dir., Booker T. Washington Community Serv., Hamilton, O., 1924-26; organizer and exec. sec., Sylvania Williams Community Service, New Orleans, La., 1926-29; exec. sec., Douglas Community Center, Toledo, O., 1929-32; pastor, Third Bapt. Ch., Toledo, O., 1932-42; nat. instr., Walker Bapt. Inst., Augusta, Ga., 1942-46; lectr., coll. and univ.; served in both wars with Army-Navy; mem., YMCA; recd. Distinguished Serv. Citation; mem., Com. on Min. Credentials and Ordination, Toledo Bapt. Assn. of Amer. Bapt. Conv.; mem., Exec. Bd., Toledo Coun. of Chs.; pres., Toledo Min. Alliance of the Coun. of Chs.; mem., Planning Com. for City Manager form of govt.; Mayor's Com. on Human Rights, 1932-43; pastor, First Bapt. Ch., No. Tulsa, Okla., 1946-61; sec., Okla. Bapt. State Conv.; Amer. Com. of the World Coun. of Chs.; pres., Interdenom. Min. Alliance, 1952; mem., Ed. Bd., Natl. Bapt. Conv., Inc.; mem., Amer. Assn. of Soc. Workers; NAACP; Mason; Alpha Phi Alpha; ed., Advance Studies for Older Young People, Sun. Sch. Pub. Bd.; contrib. to religious mag.; author: "The Parish Visitor;" "Week Day Religious Education," handbook, Church Membership And You; Home: 1225 Pierce St., Sandusky, O. 44870; Office: 908 So. Depot St., Sandusky, O.

STANLEY, Alfred Knighton, b. Greensboro, N. C., July 15, 1937; s. Rev. and Mrs. J. Taylor S.; A. B., Talladega Coll., 1959; B. D., Yale Univ. Div. Sch., 1962; ordained min., Congre. Ch., 1962; m. Beatrice Alice Perry; dir., Youth Act. and asst. min., Bunker Hill Congre. Ch., Waterbury, Conn., 1959-60; consult. for Youth Work, Wider City Parish, 1960-61; grad. asst., assoc. chap., Yale Univ., 1961-62; summer asst., Central Congre. Ch., New Orleans, La., 1959-62; minister-dir., United So. Chrstn. Fellowship Found., N. C. A & T Coll., 1962-64; mem., State Adv. Comm. of all Civil Rights organizations; appointed to Greensboro Human Relations Commn., 1962 (chrmn. Comm. on Progress & Info.); mem., Reg. Bd. of Selections, N. C. Volunteers (state Peace Corp type organ.); assoc. min., Plymouth Congre. Ch., Detroit, Mich., sum. 1964; asst. prof., Phil. and Rel., Bennett Coll., Greensboro, N. C., 1964-present; mem., Alpha Phi Alpha; recipient, Sumner and DeForest Scholarships, Buel Gallagher Award, Avery Speech Award, Woodrow Wilson Fellowship, Rockefeller Theol. Fellowship; author: "Freedom and Responsibility in Religious Perspectives," "The Current Crisis in the Negro State supported University" and several other articles; listed among 100 Negro leaders in The Negro Revolution in America (Newsweek publication); Address: Bennett Coll., Greensboro, N. C.

STANLEY, Othello Doremus, b. Beaufort, N. C., July 4, 1904; s. John B. and Annie (Gibble) S.; St. Augustine's Coll., 1925-27; B. A., Lincoln Univ., 1930; Univ. of Penna., 1932-33; Th. B., Phila. Div. Sch., 1933; pastored: St. Titus' Episc. Ch., Durham, N. C., 1933-45; St. Cyprian's Ch., Oxford, N. C., 1943-52; vicar, St. Matthew's Ch., Balto., Md., 1953-55; present, pastor,

St. Cyprian's Ch., N. C., 1956--; Home: 404 Granville St., Oxford, N. C.; Office: 408 Granville St., Oxford, N. C.

STANLEY, Walter Payne, b. Balto., Md., Feb. 18, 1890; s. Wm. and Grace (Carroll) S.; B. D., Lincoln Univ. (Pa.), Pittsburgh Sem.; m. Edythe Hume; Children--Edythe Powell, Patricia, Walter; pastor, Prot. Episc. Chs. in New York, Kentucky, Toledo, Louisville; retired in 1954 as rector of St. Augustine's Prot. Episc. Ch., Youngstown, O.; mem., Sch. Bd., Toledo; former pres., Douglas Community Center, Toledo, O.; Welfare Bd.; YMCA sec. (14 mos.); pres., Min. Assn.; Youngstown; Mason; Elks; Democrat; organist; Home: 703 Parmalee St., Youngstown, O.

STANTON, Robert Louis, b. Bessemer, Ala., Apr. 24, 1932; s. Wright and Laura (Newell) S.; Armed Forces Inst., 1950-51; Lasalle Ext. Univ., 1954-56; m. Frances O. Clark; children--Robert Louis, Jr., Edgar Lowell, Paul Clark, Fredrick Douglas, Naomi Louise; ordained Elder, Afr. Meth. Episc. Ch., 1961; pastor chs., Smith Co., 1957-58; Buckatunna, 1958-59; Meridian, 1959-61; pastor, Bethel A. M. E. Ch., Brookhaven, Miss., 1961-present; Scoutmaster, 1953-57; 1959-61; pres., Youth Coun., NAACP, Meridian, Miss., 1953-56; pres., Meridian br., NAACP; helped organize Meridian Crusade for voters, 1958; mem., Meridian Negro Bus. League, 1958-60; mem., Lauderdale Co. Improvement Assn.; organizer, pres., Brookhaven NAACP; US Air Force, 1949-52; Home: 212 Gulledge St., Brookhaven, Miss., 39601

STELL, Louis Scott, b. Fayetteville, Ga., Aug. 13, 1911; s. Louis Scott, and Ida (Harp); m.; Children--Louis Scott III, Larry James, Ralph Lamar, and Carey Benton (dec.); pastor, Friendship Bapt. Ch., Adairsville, Ga., Dec. 1942 to Sept. 1948; Zion Hill Bapt. Ch., 1944-47 Douglasville, Ga. Bethesda Bapt. Ch., 1945-48; Austell, Ga., Sardis Bapt. Ch., 1947-52; Dawson, Ga., Big Bethel Bapt. Ch., 1948-52; Bethlehem Bapt. Ch., 1952-present; Ex. sec., Savannah Emancipation Assn., 1959-present; mem., Bd. of Dir. and chrmn., Ed. Com., Savannah br. NAACP, 1960-present; Bd. of Dir., W. Broad St. YMCA 1955-58, 1968-present; sec. of Savannah Transit Authority, 1967-present; Chatham Co. Commissioner, 1969-73; Savannah Housing Authority Adv. Bd.,

1964-present; Boy Scouts of Amer.; Mason; Home: 1616 Eleanor St., Savannah Ga., 31401; Office: 702 W. Park Ave., Savannah, Ga. 31401

STEVENS, Junius Ray, b. Hugo, Okla., July 4, 1914; s. Joe and Lula B.; Howard Univ., 1948-51; grad. courses: US Dept. of Agriculture, Wash., D. C., 1952-54; m. Esther Bowers; Children--Justice Bowers; assoc. pastor, Ch. of Christ, 13th & Irving Sts., Wash., D. C., 1952-55; pastor, Davisville Ch. of Christ. Hopewell, Va., 1955-62; current pastor, Northeast Church of Christ, Wash., D. C., 1962--; tchr., Camp Mawava, Front Royal, Va.; Home: 100 Madison NW, Washington, D. C. 20011; Office: 5026 E. Capitol, Wash., D. C. 20019

STEVENS, Robert Matthew, coll. pres., b. Quincy, Fla.; s. W. S. and Annie (Kent) S.; A. B., Fisk Univ.; B. D., Payne Theol. Sem.; D. D. (hon.), Wilberforce Univ., 1954; LL. D., Monrovia Coll., 1955; m. Dorothy Chappell; one son; mem., Gen. Bd., Afr. Meth. Episc. Ch.; former pastor, Afr. Meth. Episc. Ch., presiding elder, A. M. E. Ch.; dean, Theol. Sem.; current pres., Campbell Coll.; mem., Mason; Kappa Alpha Psi; NAACP; Home: 1352 Alamo, Jackson, Miss.; Office: 1500 W. Lynch, Jackson, Miss. 39203

STEWART, James Edward Woodson, b. Moston, Mass., July 24, 1911; s. Edward Tyler and Pearl Langhorne (Woodson) S.; B. A., Livingstone Coll., 1939; B. Th., Clark & Gammon Theol. Sem., 1936; courses, Chaplain's Sch., Harvard Univ., 1943; courses, Union Theol. Sem., 1949-50; Natl. Trng. Sch. for Scout Exec., 1946; m. L. Juanita Hampton; Children--Lt. James Meredith; Helen Langhorne; ordained Afr. Meth. Episc. Z. Ch., 1936; chap., 1943-present; served annual Conf., Western, N. C., 1936-39; New England, 1940-42; Va., 1947-48; N. Y., 1948-50; New England, 1950-present; presently, Chap. (Maj.) 2d BCT Bde, Ft. Dix, N. J.; Boy's worker, Carrie Steele Orphanage, Va., 1933-36; Field Scout Exec., Boy Scouts of Amer., Lynchburg, Va., 1942-43; Richmond, Va., 1946-48; Chap., Armed Forces, 1943-present; recd. Amer. Defense Medal, Afr. Middle Eastern Campaign Medal; WW II Victory Medal; Asiatic-Pacific Campaign Medal; Korean Service Medal; United Nations Serv. Medal; Natl. Defense Serv. Medal; Rep. of Korea Pres. Unit Citation; Commendation Ribbon with Medal Pendant, 1953; Armed Forces Reserve Medal; Army

Commendation, Ft. Chaffee, Ark., 1962; Reserve Officers Assn. of US.; mem., New England Annual Conf., A. M. E. Z. Ch.; mem., Military Chap. Assn.; Min. and Layman's Assn. of A. M. E. Ch.; Mason; NAACP; Home: 1656-A Cedar St., Ft. Dix, N. J.; Office: HQ, 2d BCT Brigade, Ft. Dix, N. J. 08640

STINES, Henri Alexandre, b. Port-au-Prince, Haiti, Oct. 29, 1923; s. George A. and Denise B. (Francisco) S.; B. A., Univ. of Haiti; B. D., St. Louis De Consague Theol. Sem., 1946; student, Law Sch., Port-au-Prince, Haiti, 2 yrs.; S. T. B., Gen. Theol. Sem., NYC, 1948; m. Gladys A. Robinson; Children--Denise, Gabriell, Suzette; ordained to Deaconate, 1945; canon, Port-au-Prince Cathedral, 1948-50; vicar, St. James Ch., Charleston, W. Va., 1950; Episc. chap., W. Va. State Coll., 1950-53; rector, Grace Episc. Ch., Detroit, Mich., 1953-64; dir., Southern Field Service, Atlanta, Ga., 1964-66; rector, Episc. Ch. of the Atonement, Wash., D. C., 1966-present; instr., Theol. Sem., Port-au-Prince, Haiti; Dean, Central Convocation, Detroit; mem., Exec. Coun. of the Diocese, Mich.; mem., Cathedral Chap., Dept. of Missions; com. mem., Dept. of Chrstn. Soc. Rel., Dept. of Urban Work; mem., Mayor's Com., Rehabilitation of Narcotics; Home: 78 53rd St., SE, Wash., D. C. 20019; Office: 5073 E. Capitol St., Wash. D. C. 20019

STINSON, Olden Hixon, b. Woodbury, Ga., Oct. 25, 1905; s. Edd L. and Carrie (Hixon) S.; A. B., B. D., Morehouse Coll. and Morehouse Sch. of Rel., 1927, 1949; post. grad. study, Univ. of Chgo., 1951; m. Eddie Bay Curgil; Children--Jeanne M., Olden Edward; pastor, Mt. Zion First Bapt. Ch., Griffin, Ga., 1943--; pres., New Era Missionary Bapt. Conv., Ga., 1961--; instr., New Testament, Exten. Dept. of the Interdenom. Theol. Cent., Atlanta, Ga., 1962--; pres., Citizens Improvement League of Griffin and Spalding Co.; clerk, Cane Creek and Cabin Creek Bapt. Assn.; mem., Griffin Staff on Alcoholic Rehabilitation Service, Counseling; former sec., Republican Party, Spalding Co.; author: Handbook, A Glimpse of Negro Baptists in Georgia; Home: 123 S. 4th St., Griffin, Ga.; Office: Mt. Zion Bapt. Ch., Cor. of E. Taylor and 4th St., Griffin, Ga.

STITT, Robert Elemaker, b. Charlotte Courthouse, Va., June 8, 1909; s. William Banks and Alice (Morris) S.

1940, B.S., Lane Coll., Jackson, Tenn.; 1947, B.D., Lincoln Univ.; m. Wilhemenia Gertrude Christmas; Children--Robert, Jr.; pastor, United Presby. Ch., USA, 1940--; mem., Moderator of Cape Fear Presbytery (1 yr.); chrmn., Ecumenical Mission and Relations Comm. (10 yrs.); chrmn., Ministerial Relations Comm. (presently); mem., Phi Beta Sigma, Ancient Egyptian Order, Nobles of the Mystic Shrine of No. and So. Amer.; Home: PO Box 524, Lillington, N.C.

STOKES, Frank Augustus, b. Griffin, Ga., Nov. 13, 1916; s. Frank and Pauline S.; B.A., Oakwood Coll., 1951; M.A., Oakwood Coll., 1952; m. Ruth Bracy; Children--Barbara, Lewis, Edward, Frank III, Paul; pastored: Atlantic City, N.J., Rome, Ga., Greenville, S.C., W. Palm Beach, Fla.; present: Mt. Sinai S.D.A. Ch., Orlando, Fla.; served on Mayor's Comm., Urban Renewal Comm. and Voters' League; Ex. v.p., NAACP; former mem., Civil Service Bd. of Palm Beach Co.; active duty in WW II, Okinawa and Philippines; Home: 2316 W. South St., Orlando, Fla.; Office: 514 So. Parramore St., Orlando, Fla.

STOKES, Rembert Edwards, coll. pres., b. Dayton, O., June 16, 1917; s. Wm. Otis and Hoyel Marie S.; B.S., Wilberforce Univ., 1940; S.T.B., Boston Univ.; Th.D., Boston Univ.; studies in Harvard Univ.; m. Nancy Philips; Children--Linda, Deborah, Celesto; pastor, A.M.E. Ch., Jamestown, Rhode Island, Cambridge, Mass., Canton, O.; Dean, Payne Theol. Sem., 1951-56; pres., Wilberforce Univ., Wilberforce, O., 1956--; mem., Admin. Coun., Ohio Coun. of Chs., Faith and Order Conf., World Coun. of Chs., Bd. of Trustees, Natl. Conf. of Chrstns. & Jews; mem., Gov.'s Commn. on Ageing; Ohio Commn. on Ageing; Greene-Montgomery Co. Red Cross Board; mem., Alpha Phi Alpha; Frontier Intl., Dayton, O.; Home: PO Box 453, Wilberforce, O. 45384; Office: Office of the President, Wilberforce Univ., Wilberforce, O. 45384

STONE, Lee Owen, b. Lexington, Ky., Apr. 27, 1903; s. Walter And Lillace (Peasons) S.; 1936, B.D., Bishop Payne Div.; 1944, B.S., Lewis and Clark Coll.; m. Eva Lena Wilson; 1926-28, tchr., Ky. House of Reform; 1936, vicar, St. Philips Episc. Ch., Portland, Ore.; Bd. of Portland Urban League, 1946-50; Bd., Portland Coun. of Soc. Agencies, 1950-56; Bd., Portland USO,

1946-58; Deputy to Gen. Conv. of Episc. Ch., 1952-61; Home: 6920 27th Ave. NE, Portland, Ore.; Office: 120 Knott St., NE, Portland, Ore.

STRASSNER, William Russell, coll. admin., b. Morrilton, Ark.; A. B., Ark. Bapt. Coll.; B. D., Va. Union Univ.; M. S. T., Andover Newton Theol. Sem.; further study: Union Theol. Sem. and Tchrs. Coll., N. Y.; D. D. (hon.), Shaw Univ.; LL. D. (hon.), Va. Union Theol. Sem., 1962; student pastor, Zion and Galilee Ch., W. Va.; Zion Bapt. Ch., Boston; pastor, Mt. Zion Bapt. Ch., Charlottesville, Va., 7 yrs.; current co-ordinator, Coll. Community Relations, Hampton Inst., 1962--; Dean of Rel., Bishop Coll.; Dean of Sch. of Rel., Shaw Univ., Raleigh, N. C.; pres., Shaw Univ., 1951-62; mem., Fellowship of Southern Churchmen, Southern Reg. Educational Bd.; Va. Tchrs. Assn.; Natl. Ed. Assn.; Jt. Comm. on the Negro Baptist; YMCA; Alpha Phi Alpha; Odd Fellows; organizer, Civil League, Inter-Fraternal Coun., Recreational Center, Charlottesville, Va.; Office: Hampton Inst., Hampton, Va.

STRAYHAND, Thomas Lewis, chap., b. Newman, Ga.; s. John L. and Mattie L.; A. B., Paine Coll., Augusta, Ga., 1949; B. D., Gammon Theol. Sem., Atlanta, Ga., 1952; US Chap. Sch., 1953, 1957; m. Deborah E., Mary L. Children-- pastor, Holsey Meml. Chrstn. Meth. Episc. Ch., Sparta, Ga., 1948-52; Vanderhorst C. M. E. Ch., McRae, Ga., 1952-53; US Army Chap., 1953-present; former US Air Force, 1942-45; awards, Bronze Star; Good Conduct Medal; Army Commendation Medal; European Theater Ribbon (3 o/s bars); Amer. Defense Ribbon; WW II Victory Medal; United Nations Ribbon; Reserve Forces Medal; Korean Serv. Medal; Vietnam Campaign and Serv. Medal; mem., Military Chap. Assn.; Mason; Home: Qtrs. 680-S Oakland Army Base, Okland, Calif.; Office: US Army Personnel, Oakland, Calif. 94626

STREET, John Franklin, b. Millsboro, Del., Jan. 8, 1906; s. Gardner Ross and Della (Norwood) S.; Oakwood Jr. Coll., Huntsville, Ala., 1936; m. Ruth Evelyn Burton; 1 dau., Della Ruth Evelyn; pastor, S. D. A. Chs., Ala., Miss., Ariz. and So. Atlantic Conferences, 1939-59; present: pastor, Allegheny Conf., 1959--; farm supt., Oakwood Coll., 1936-39; Home: 532 E. Commerce St., Bridgeton, N. J.

STRICKLAND, Frederick William, b. Van Buren, Ark., Nov. 25, 1915; s. William Stafford and Annie Elizabeth (s.); B. A., Ottawa Univ., Ottawa, Kan.; B. T. H., D. D. (hon.), Ark. Bapt. Coll., Little Rock, Ark.; cand., M. S., Univ. of Tulsa, Grad. Sch.; m. Ardene; Children--Fred W. Jr., Rickie, Vickie; pastor, First Bapt. Ch., Hoisington, Kan.; Second Bapt., Winfield, Kan.; Independent Bapt., Leavenworth, Kan.; present pastor, Calvary Bapt. Ch., Coffeyville, Kan., 1951; moderator, Southeastern Dist. Assn., Kan.; auditor-statistician, Missn. Bapt. State Conv., Kan.; seminar speaker, Minister's Coun., Kan.; instr., Rel. for the Minister's & Chrstn. Workers Retreat, Kan.; mem., Finance Com., Natl. Bapt. Conv.; chrmn., Commn. on Civil Rights, Coffeyville, Kan.; former pres., local br. NAACP; Democrat; cand., City Commissioner, Coffeyville, Kan.; author, book of poems, Logic and Laughter in Verse; author of rel. songs: "I Know Someone Who Cares," "I Have Tasted Heaven's Manna," "Joy Bells in My Soul," "There's A Better Day Ahead;" author of rel. plays: The Retrial of Jesus, The Coroner's Inquest; The Jericho Road; Home: 404 E. 6th St., Coffeyville, Kan. 67337

STRICKLAND, Marshall Haywood, b. Chattanooga, Tenn., Oct. 8, 1933; s. Allen Albert and Elzia (Greer) S.; B. A., Livingstone Coll., Hood Theol. Sem., Salisbury, N. C.; Howard Univ., Wash., D. C.; courses toward Ph. D. Vanderbilt Univ., Sch. of Rel., 1964; m. Ruby Gaston; Children--Marshall Haywood II; pastor, Big Zion A. M. E. Z. Ch., Mobile, Ala.; at the nation-wide meml. serv. held in memory of the late Pres. John F. Kennedy, message was selected to be pub. in the book entitled, "That Day With God;" selected fraternal del., Gen. Conf. of the A. M. E. Ch., 1964; mem., Exec. Budget Bd.; mem., Connectional Budget Bd., A. M. E. Z. Ch., Omega Psi Phi; Home: 110 So. Bayou, Mobile, Ala. 36602

STRINGER, Emmett James, chap., b. Yazoo Co., Miss., Sept. 16, 1919; s. Young Marion and Jane (Hargrove) S.; B. S., Alcorn Coll., Alcorn, Miss., 1937-41; D. D. S., Meharry Med. Coll., Nashville, Tenn., 1946-50; m. Flora Charlene Ghist; US Army, 1941-46; steongrapher, The Vets Admin., 1946; engaging in practice of general dentistry in Columbia, Miss., since 1950; current pastor, Mt. Olive Missionary Bapt. Ch., Boligee, Ala., 1959--; v. moderator, Mt. Olive-Green Co., Ala., Bapt. Dist.

Assn.; faculty mem., Natl. Bapt. Sun. Sch. and B.T.U. Congress, USA, Inc., 1961--; chap., Natl. Dental Assn., 1962--; Adv. Comm. of Mary Holmes Jr. Coll., 1962--; pres., NAACP, Columbus, Miss., 1953-58; pres., Miss. State Conf. of NAACP brs., 1953-54; the first Negro since reconstruction days to register to vote in Lowndes Co., Columbus, Miss., 1952; chap., treas., Columbia Negro Assn. for Retarded Children; pres., Dental Sec., John A. Andrew Clinical Soc., Tuskegee, Ala.; Man of the Year, 1960, by Miss. Reg. Coun. of Negro Leadership; Dentist of the Decade Award from the Dental Class of 1950 of Meharry Med. Coll.; pres., Miss. Dental Soc., 1961-62; pres., No. Miss. Med., Dental, Pharmaceutical & Nurses Soc., 1960; mem., Mason; Elk; Phi Beta Sigma; Home: PO Box 146, Columbus, Miss.; Office: 114-1/2 So. 4th St., Columbus, Miss.

STROUD, Norman L., b. Harnett Co., N.C., July 18, 1929; s. James F. and Pearl S.; B.A., Livingstone Coll., 1952; M.S., A & T Coll., 1965; chrmn., Language Dept., Speight High Sch., Wilson, N.C., 1952-59; chrmn., Language Dept., Shawtown High Sch., Lillington, N.C., 1959-67; pastor, O Bryant A.M.E.Z. Ch., Chapel Hill, N.C.; St. John, Mt. Hebrew Chs., Fayetteville, N.C.; athletic dir.; mem., NTA; NEA; NCTE; FLTA; Phi Beta Sigma; v.p., Fayetteville Expansion Assn.; pres., Professional Improvement Club, Sanford, N.C., 1964; Home: Rt 6, Box 844, Sanford, N.C. 27330

SULLIVAN, Leon Howard, b. Charleston, W. Va., Oct. 16, 1922; W. Va. State Coll. Union Theol. Sem., NYC; Columbia Univ.; m. Grace Banks; Children--Howard, Julie, Hope; asst. pastor, Abyssinia Bapt. Ch., NYC, pastor, First Bapt. Ch., So. Orange, N.J., 1945; pres., So. Orange Coun. of Chs. (first Negro) 1945; pastor, Zion Bapt. Ch., Phila., Pa. 1950-present; founder and chrmn., Opportunities Industrialization Center; helped in organizing the Phila. Citizens Comm. Against Juvenile Delinquencies and Their Causes, later devel. Natl. Citizens Comm., 1965; founded the Zion home for the retired, Pa., 1960; awards: one of the Ten Outstanding Young Men in Amer., Outstanding Young Man of Phila., 1955; City of Phila., Good Citizen Award; Afro-Amer. Achievement Award, 1956; Boy Scouts of Amer., Silver Beaver Award, 1957; Outstanding Alumnus Award, 1960; Russworm Award (awarded annually to ten oustanding Negroes),

1962; Phila. or BOK Award for outstanding public serv., 1966; Home: 6825 Milton St., Phila., Pa.

SUMMERS, Vance, Jr., b. Orangeburg, S.C., Aug. 20, 1948; A.B., Chaflin Coll., Orangeburg, S.C., 1964; B.D., I.T.C., Atlanta, Ga., 1967; student pastor, Warren Meml. United Meth. Ch., Atlanta, Ga., 1964-65; summer asst. pastor, Trinity Meth. Ch., Orangeburg, S.C., 1965; administr. asst. Bishop Golden, Nashville, Tenn., 1966-68; area dir., Promotion & Public Relations, Nashville-Carolina, United Meth. Ch., 1966-68; editor, The Voice, Nashville-Carolina, U. Meth. Ch., Nashville, 1966-68; field dir., The Dorchester Com. of New York, Inc.; The Dorchester Project, St. George, S.C., 1968-present; public relations dir., Central Jurisdictional Conf., The Meth. Ch., Nashville, 1967; circulation mgr., Daily Chrstn., Advocate Magazine, 1967; mem., Omega Psi Phi; S. Carolina Conf.; mem., Dorchester Ministers Alliance; NAACP; Home: 204 Whitridge Lane, St. George, S.C. 29477; Office: PO Box 487, St. George, S.C. 29477

SUMPTER, Augustus Cicero, tchr., b. Sumter Co., S.C., 1895; s. Marcus J. and Ella (Dorothy) S.; Allen Univ., Columbia S.C.; Wilberforce Univ., Wilberforce, O.; Howard Univ., Wash., D.C.; Tuskegee Inst.; D.D., Payne Theol. Sem.; m. Mary Maude Brown; principal, Bishopville High Sch., S.C.; pastor, Bethel Afr. Meth. Episc. Ch., Conway, S.C.; Bethel A.M.E. Ch., Dillon, S.C., 3 yrs.; Allen Temple, Greenville, S.C., 5 yrs.; Allen Temple, Cin., O., 7 yrs.; Mt. Vernon A.M.E. Ch., Columbus, O., 4 yrs.; Exec. Comm., Natl. Coun. Chs., 1950-57; current pastor, St. James A.M.E. Ch., Pittsburgh, Pa.; mem., Bd. of Dirs., Coun. of Chs., Pittsburgh area; US Forces, WW I, 8 mos.; Home: 7334 Monticello, Pittsburgh, Pa.; Office: 208 No. Euclid Ave., Pittsburgh, Pa.

SUMPTER, Benjamin Franklin, presiding elder, b. Sumter, S.C., Mar. 11, 1916; s. M. J. and Cleopatra S.; Allen Univ.; Dickerson Theol. Sem.; D.D. (hon.), Allen Univ., 1954; D.D., Monrovia Coll., W. Africa, 1954; m. Thelma O. Brown; Children--two sons and five daus.; pastor, St. Peters Afr. Meth. Episc. Ch., Cameron, S.C., 1938-40; pastor, Miller Chapel A.M.E. Ch., Newberry, S.C., 1940-46; pastor, Mt. Zion A.M.E. Ch., Charleston, S.C., 1946-59; current, presiding elder, The Manning and Wateree Dists., 1959--; principal, Jr. High Sch., Newberry, S. C., 1942-46; first Negro Commissioner of the city of Charleston; chrmn., Bd. of Reid House of Chrstn. Serv.; pres., NAACP (Charleston, S. C.); mem., Alpha Phi Alpha; Mason; Elk; Home: 193 Smith St., Charleston, S. C.

SWANN, Melvin Chester, b. Balto., Md., Nov. 6, 1914; s. Isaiah and Grace Viola (Chester) S.; A. B., Clark Univ., Atlanta, Ga.; D. D., Allen Univ.; Kittrell Jr. Coll.; m. Dorothy Elizabeth Whitaker; Children--Melvin Chester, Jr.; pastor, Hosana A. M. E. Ch., Berkeley, Md.; Hemingway Temple, A. M. E. Ch., Balto., Md.; Bethel A. M. E. Ch., Greensboro, N. C.; pastor, St. Joseph's A. M. E. Ch., Durham, N. C., 1957-66; pastor, Waters A. M. E. Ch., 1966-present; trustee, Kittrell Jr. Coll., Kittrell, N. C.; US Army, Capt., 3 yrs. (chap.); chrmn., v. p., Durham Min. Assn.; mem., Exec. Comm., Durham Comm. on Negro Affairs; co-dir., Audio-Visual and Radio Ed., A. M. E. Ch.; Audio and Radio Ed. Comm. of the Natl. Coun. of Chs.; Gen. Bd. of the A. M. E. Ch., Office: Waters A. M. E. Ch., Balto., Md.

SWEET, Henry Beauregard, b. Augusta, Ga., July 8, 1902; s. Henry B. and Grace (Brown); Lincoln Univ., Pa., 1924, A. B., B. D., McCormick Sem., 1953; grad. study, Univ. of Chgo.; m. Sarah Evelyn Christian; Children--Fred S. Cummings, Renee, Alan Lloyd; pastor, Second Presby. Ch., Oxford, Pa., 1951-53; pastor, Ch. of the Master, NYC, 1953-54; current pastor, Westhills Presby. Ch., USA, Atlanta, Ga., 1954--; Boys Worker, Jones Meml. Community Center, 1946-48, Chgo. Heights, Ill.; sec., Atlanta Chapter, Lincoln Univ. Pa. Alumni; chap., Eta Landa Chapter, Alpha Phi Alpha, 1959; state clerk, Ga.-Carolina Presbytery, 1957-62; Home: 3518 Fairburn Pl., Atlanta, Ga.; Office: 1745 Springview Rd., Atlanta, Ga.

SYDNER, Calvin Herbert, b. Bryn Mawr, Pa., June 12, 1940; s. Calvin and Crystal; B. S., Cheyney State Coll., 1965; M. Div., Lexington Theol. Sem., 1968; m. Charlotte; Children--Gloria, Calvin; pastor, Shorter Chapel A. M. E. Ch., Paris, Ky., 1966-present; dir., Ruckerville Improvement Assn., Paris, Ky., 1967-present; cons., Mayor and City Commissioners, Paris, Ky., 1968; chrmn., Chapel and Convocation Comm., Lexington Theol. Sem., 1967-68; award, Time Magazine Current Affairs;

mem., Lampodoes Club, Omega Phi Psi; Inquisitors Soc. Club, Paris, Ky.; author articles; mem., Bd. of Examiners, Ky. Annual Conf., A.M.E. Ch., Bd. of Rel. Ed.; chrmn., State of the Country Com., 1968; sec., Ky. Annual Conf., A.M.E. Ch.; Lex. Dist., Ky. Annual Conf.; del., Natl. Coun. of Chs. of Christ, Louisville, Ky., 1968; del., Exec. Prog. Coun. of Intl. Soc. of Chrstn. Endeavor, Columbus, O., 1967; Home: 116 Chaplin St., Paris, Ky. 40361

SYLVESTER, Joseph, b. Opelanna, La., 1915; studied, Moody Bible Inst.; Chgo. Bible Inst.; Children--Jean (Mrs. Lynwood Harris); pastor, Landmark Missionary Bapt. Ch., 1953-present; US Army, 6 yrs.; award, 1966 "Minister of the Year;" Office: 2700 Wilcox Ave., Chicago, Ill.

TALBERT, Melvin George, b. June 14, 1934, Clinton, La.; s. Nettles and Florence (T.); A.B., Southern Univ., Baton Rouge, La., 1959; B.D., Gammon Theol. Sem., Atlanta, Ga., 1962; m. Ethelou Douglas; student pastor, Boyd Chapel and Rising Sun Meth. Chs., Jefferson City and Sunrise, Tenn., 1960-61; St. John's United Meth. Ch., Los Angeles, 1961; Wesley United Meth. Ch., Los Angeles, 1962-64; assoc. pastor, Hamilton Meth. Ch., Los Angeles, 1964-67; pastor, Assn. Gen. Sec., Coordinating Coun. of Southern Calif.-Ariz. Conf., United Meth. Ch.; Exec. Sec., Bd. of Evangelism, Bd. of Chrstn. Soc. Concerns; Bd. of Lay Activities, 1967-68; Dist. Supt., Long Beach Dist., United Meth. Ch., 1968-present; former Dist. Adv. Sen. Youth, Los Angeles Dist., 1962-64; Dist. Sec. and Evangelism, 1964-65; Bd. of Dirs., All Nations Found., 1965-67; Bd. of Missions, Urban Dept. Chrmn., 1966-67; Conf. Nominating Com., 1966-67; Conf. Study Com., 1966--; Bd. of Dirs., Los Angeles City Soc., 1965; present mem., United Meth. Chs. Coordinating Coun.; Strategy Com., Gen. Bd. Coun. of Chs. (So. Calif.); Gen. Conf. Del., 1968; Jurisdictional Conf. del., 1968; mem., Interdenom. Min. Alliance (Los Angeles); NAACP; Bd. United Crusade (Central Los Angeles); Crisis Coalition, Los Angeles; Home: 26801 Rolling Vista Dr., Lomita, Calif., 90717

TALBOT, David Arlington, coll. admin., b. British Guiana, Jan. 25, 1916; s. David Patterson and Maude (Roberts) T.; cert., Queen's Coll. of British Guiana-Oxford and

Cambridge Sch.; B. A., Morris Brown Coll., 1935-39; Turner Theol. Sem., 1938-40; Columbia Univ., 1940-42; M. A., 1951; m. Phyllis Snow Willis; Children--David Arlington, Jr., James Patterson, Eric Maurice; instr., Morris Brown Coll., 1939-40; circulation mgr., and assoc. ed., Tan Town Stories, 1945-46; soc. worker, Dept. of Welfare, NYC, 1947-51; coll. min. and chrmn., Div. of Languages, Literature and Art, Shorter Coll., 1952-57; pastor, Bethel Afr. Meth. Episc. Ch., Blytheville, Ark., 1954-57; chap., A. M. & N Coll., 1957--; Psychometrist, A. M. & N. Coll., 1957-60; current dean, of students, A. M. & N. Coll., 1960--; mem., Bd. of Dirs., Tiny Tim Sch., Pine Bluff, Ark.; US Army, 1942-45, Sgt. Major; Bronze Star Medal, 1945; mem., Amer. Coll. Personnel Assn.; Natl. Assn. of Personnel Workers; Southwestern Reg. Assn. of Guidance Workers; author: Comparative Study of Freshmen Entering A. M. & N. Coll. from 1957-62; Home: Box 154, A. M. & N. Coll., Pine Bluff, Ark.; Office: 1300 Magnolia St., Pine Bluff, Ark.

*TANKERSON, Richard Earl, b. New Orleans, La., Mar. 17, 1940; s. James R. and Winnie Franklin (T.); B. A., Dillard Univ., New Orleans, La., 1961; Howard Univ., Sch. of Rel., 1967; m. Louise Jennings; Children--Roderick Earl, Karen Louise, Linda Marie; ordained 1959, asst. pastor, St. James Afr. Meth. Episc. Ch., New Orleans, 1959-61; Turner Meml. A. M. E. Ch., 1961-63; pastor, Robinson A. M. E. Ch., Grasonville, Md., 1963-68; Ward Meml. A. M. E. Ch., Wash., D. C., 1968-present; asst. bookkeeper, Financial Dept. A. M. E. Ch., Wash., D. C., 1963-68; Demographic Survey Coordinator, Shaw Urban Renewal Project, Wash., D. C., 1967; coordinator, New Careers Prog., D. C. Redevelopment Land Agency, 1968; Employee Relations Specialist, D. C. Redevelopment Land Agency, 1968-present; mem., Capitol Hill Jay Cees of Amer.; NAACP; D. C. Prayer Breakfast Fellowship; Natl. Coun. of Chs., Natl. Coun. of Black Churchemn; Home: 3675 Highwood Dr., SE, Wash., D. C. 20020; Office: 241 42nd St., NE, Wash., D. C. 20019

TAYLOR, David Lawson, b. Camden, N. J., June 28, 1933; s. David and Eula; A. B., Oakwood Coll., Huntsville, Ala., 1957; Pepperdine Coll., Calif., 1958-59; M. A., Andrews Theol. Univ., Berrien Springs, Mich., 1961; m. Maxine Janet Clark; Children--Daryle Alan, Cheryle

Ann; pastored, S. D. A. Ch., San Diego, 1961-64; S. D. A. Ch., Santa Ana, 1964-66; S. D. A. Ch., Fontana, 1966-68; Berea S. D. A. Ch., Valleyo, Calif., 1968-present; tchr., Teen Post, Fontana, Calif.; counselor, Santa Ana and Valleyo, Calif.; organizer, Bykota Youth Club (Be Kind One to Another); Strona Dynamic Youth Club, Valleyo, Calif.; mem., Min. Assn., San Diego and Fontana; Bd. mem., Napa Jr. Acad.; Sch. Bd. mem., Orangewood, Fairview and Paradise Valley, Calif.; Home: 193 Marquette Ave., Valleyo, Calif. 94590; Office: 833 Louisiana St., Valleyo, Calif. 94590

TAYLOR, G. Herfin, b. Shreveport, La., Apr. 7, 1911; s. Hezekiah and Lillie (Morris) T.; A. B., Dillard Univ., New Orleans, La., 1935; m. Evelyn Smiler; Children--G. Herfin, Jr., Raymond A., Barbara A., Brenda A.; Colo. Conf. of S. D. A., Denver, Colo., 1946-48; Central States Conf. of S. D. A., 1948-63; pastored: Denver Beth Haven, Denver, Colo., 1946-51; New Hope S. D. A. Ch., Pueblo, Colo., and Sharon S. D. A. Ch., Omaha, 1951-59; New Hope S. D. A. Ch., Sioux, Iowa; Allon Chapel, Lincoln, Nebr., 1959-60; present: Beacon Light S. D. A. Ch., and Berean S. D. A. Ch., St. Louis, Mo., 1960--; YMCA Service Award, 1957, Omaha, Nebr. Home: 5440 Clemens Ave., St. Louis, Mo.; Office: 1244 No. Union Blvd., St. Louis, Mo.

TAYLOR, Gardner Calvin, b. Baton Rouge, June 18, 1918; s. W. M. and Selma G. (Taylor) T.; A. B., Leland Coll., 1937; D. D. (hon.), 1944; B. D., Oberlin Grad. Sch. Theol., 1940; m. Laura Scott; Children--Martha Lyn; ordained to ministry Bapt. Ch., 1939; pastor, Elyria, O., 1938-40; New Orleans, 1941-43; Baton Rouge, 1943-47; Brooklyn, NY, 1948--; prof., Colgate-Rochester Div. Sch., Rochester, N. Y.; former pres., Prot. Coun., NYC; v. p., Bd. of Dirs., Urban League Greater New York; v. p., Progressive Natl. Bapt. Conv., Inc.; mem., Bd. of Ed., NYC; Kappa Alpha Psi; Mason; Home: 833 Marey Ave., Bklyn, N. Y.

*TAYLOR, George Shedrick, b. Sumter, S. C., Jan. 3, 1927; s. William M. and Ada N.; B. A., A & T Coll., Greensboro, N. C., 1951; Amer. Univ., Wash., D. C., 1954-55; B. D., Howard Univ., Sch. of Rel., Wash., D. C., 1958; M. Soc. Work, Univ. of Okla., Norman, Okla., 1967; m. Rebecca Ham; Children--Jana Cordele, Lynne Shedrica; assoc. pastor, Mt. Zion Bapt. Ch., Arlington, Va.,

1954-58; Chap., US Army, 1958-62; supervisor, Field Youth Counselors, Okla. City, Okla., 1962-present; pastor, First Bapt. Ch., Luther, Okla., 1962-present; mem., Okla. Past. Inst.; Kimbro Parents Music Assn., Inc.; Prog. Bapt. Conv., Bd. of Dir. CAP, Luther, Okla.; NE Commn. for Comm. Improvement, 1966-pres.; pres., E. Zion Dist. Assn. Bapt. Chs., Okla.; mem., Alpha Phi Alpha; Intern. Frat.; YMCA; Natl. Assn. Soc. Workers; Mason; Health, Welf. Com., Urban League, Okla. City, Okla.; author, Res. Proj. An Analysis of Public Assistance Rate in Okfuskee Co., Okla. in assn. with Certain Ec. Factors Relating to Gen. Pop.; Home: 1417 NE 33, Okla. City, Okla. 73111; Office: Sequoyah Bld., Room 200, Okla. City, Okla.

*TAYLOR, Julian Augustus, ch. official, b. Hertford, N. C., May 14, 1903; s. William A. and Roberta (Fortune) T.; B. A., B. D., Howard Univ., Univ. of Chgo, Columbia Univ.; D. D. (hon.), Norther Sch. of Rel.; m. Margaret Pauline Morris; Children--Mauryne Brant, Doris Kaith, Jewells Gibbs, Julian, Jr., Shirlee Haizlip, Patricia Williams; pastor, Ebenezer Bapt. Ch., Martinsburg, W. Va., 1927-30; First Bapt. Ch., Stratford, Conn., 1933-38; Macedonia Bapt. Ch., Ansonia, 1938--; pres., New England Bapt. Trng. Union, 1950--; pres., Conn. Bapt. Missionary Conv., 1956--; pres., Tri-County Interdenom. Min. Alliance; mem., Bd. Conn. Coun. of Chs.; Adv. Bd. Salvation Army; 'Bd. of Dirs., Natl. Bapt. Conv., USA, Inc.; Bd. of Amer. Bapt. Theol. Sem., Nashville; hearing examiner, Civil Rights Commn., Conn., 1955--; chrmn., Ansonia Municipal Planning Comm., 1955--; organizer, pres., Ansonia br. NAACP, 1944--; mem., Mason; Kiwanis Intl. Admin. Consultant Sen. Abraham Ribicoff; spec. commn. from Natl. Bapt. to Liberian Govt., 1961-62; del.-at-large, 1960 Natl. Democratic Conv.; del.-at-large, 1964 Natl. Democratic Conv.; Home: 133 W. Park Ave., New Haven, Conn.; Office: 24 Clifton Ave., Ansonia, Conn.

TAYLOR, Noel Calvin, b. Bedford, Va., July 15, 1924; s. Noel A. and Hettie L. Taylor; B. S., Bluefield State Coll., 1949; Va., 1955, M. A., New York Univ., 1964; D. D. (hon.) Va. Union Sem. & Coll., 1959; courses, Ph. D., New York Univ.; m. Barbara Jean Smith; Children--Sabrina Leochia, Deseree Charlalla; pastor, First Bapt. Ch., Clifton Forge, Va., 1955-58; First Bapt. Ch., Norfolk, Va., 1958-61; High St. Bapt. Ch., Roanoke, Va.,

1961-present; principal, Western Light Elem. Sch., Bedford, Va., 1949-50; Longwood Elem. Sch., 1950-52; auditor, Va. Bapt., State Conv.; trustee, Va. Sem. & Coll.; Bd. of Mgrs., Hunton YMCA; Bd. of Dirs., Amer. Red Cross; Roanoke, v. moderator, Valley Bapt. Assn.; mem., Roanoke City Library Bd.; Health Planning Coun.; adv. bd., Public Welfare, Roanoke; former pres., Roanoke Min. Conf.; pres., O.I.C. Roanoke Valley; Alpha Phi Alpha; Mason; awarded "Man of the Year," Roanoke chapter, Omega Psi Phi Fraternity; Office: High St. Bapt. Ch., 21 Center Ave., NW, Roanoke, Va. 24016

TAYLOR, Paul Jones, b. Lake Providence, La.; s. Cornelius and Dilay (T.); courses, Ark. Bapt. Coll., Little Rock, Ark.; Leland Coll. Ext. Sch., Baker, La.; m. Jerusha Morehouse; Children--Timothy, David, Leo, Eddie, Jean, Pauline, Ruthie Mae, Ernest, Dennis, Doris; pastor, Progressive Chapel Missionary Bapt. Ch., Lake Providence, La.; North State Missionary Bapt. Ch., Lake Providence, La.; Ephesus Missionary Bapt. Ch., St. Louis, Mo., 1951-present; mem., Voter Registration Comm., Mississippi; Mason; v.p., NAACP, Lake Providence, La., 1945; Home: 4205 St. Louis Ave., St. Louis, Mo. 63115; Office: 3520 N. Newstead Ave., St. Louis, Mo. 63115

TAYLOR, Paul Lawrence, college prof., b. Darien, Ga., Oct. 26, 1913; s. Joseph David and Martha (Covington) T.; A.B., J.C. Smith Univ.; M.A., Hartford Sem. Sch. of Rel.; B.D., McCormick Theol. Sem.; M.Th., Western Theol. Sem.; Ed.D., Indiana Univ., 1933, 1936, 1938, 1949 and 1958 respectively; m. Bessie Carpenter pastor, Laura St. Presby. Ch., USA, Jacksonville, Fla., Trinity Presby. Ch., Smithfield, N.C., 1937-39, 1939-41; US Army chap., 1941-46; pastor, Faith Presby. Ch., Pine Bluff, Ark., 1952-57; Dean of instr., Barber-Scotia Coll., Dir. of Testing & Guidance, Savannah State Coll.; Dir., Student Personnel, Ala. A & M Coll.; chrmn., Dept. of Ed., Miss. Vocational Coll., Itta Bena, Miss.; decorations: Five Battle Stars, was chosen along with five other chaplains to study the crimes of the Army personnel and make recommendation; mem., APGA-Phi Delta; Masons; Omega Psi Phi; abstract of doctoral dissertation was published--"An Analysis of Religious Counseling Practices of Nine Selected Negro Colleges;" master thesis "The Social Teaching of St. Paul;" Home: PO Box 446, Itta Bena, Miss.

TAYLOR, Prince Albert, Jr., bishop, b. Hennessey, Okla., Jan. 27, 1907; A. B , Samuel Huston Coll., Austin, Tex. 1931; B. D., Gammon Theol. Sem., Atlanta, Ga., 1931; M. A., Columbia Univ., New York, 1940; Ed. D., New York Univ., NYC, 1948; D. D., (Hon.), Rust Coll., Holly Springs, Miss., 1949; Gammon Theol. Sem., 1950; LL. D., Philander Smith Coll., Little Rock, Ark.; ordained, 1931, elder, N. C. Conf.; pastor, Kernersville, N. C., 1931; N. W. Greensboro, N. C., 1931-34; St. John Meth. Ch., Thomasville, N. C., 1934-37; E. Calvary, NYC, 1937-40; St. Mark's Meth. Ch., NYC, 1940-42; 1945-48; elected a bishop of the Meth. Ch. at the Central Jurisdictional Conf., New Orleans, La., 1956; assigned to Monrovia, Liberia area; New Jersey area; instr. and asst. to the pres., Bennett Coll., Greensboro, N. C., 1940-43; Hd. of Dept., Chrstn. Ed. and Psychol., Gammon Theol. Sem., 1943-48; Exchange tchr., Clark Coll., Atlanta, Ga., 1943-48; adult counselor, Central Jurisdiction Natl. Meth. Student Com., 1944-48; dir., Correspondence Sch. for Commn. on Min. Trng., Central Jurisdiction, 1945-48; ed., Central Christian Advocate, New Orleans, 1948-56; pres.-designate Coun. of Bishops; mem., Com. on the Structure of Meth. Overseas; Gen. Bd. of Missions; Com. for Ecumenical Affairs; trustee of several educational institutions; Phi Beta Sigma; awards: Gov. of Liberia for dist. service (twice); The Venerable Knighthood of the Pioneers; Highest Decoration given by the govt., second private citizen to rec. it; recipient, St. George's Award given by Old St. George's Ch., Phila., Pa.; mem., State Youth Com., N. J.; Citizen's Coun. for Economic Opportunity, N. J.; Home: 70 Nassau St., Princeton, N. J.

*TAYLOR, Rafe Monroe, b. May 10, 1931, Clearview, Okla.; s. Cary and Mary (Mayo); B. A., Bishop Coll., Marshall, Tex., 1958; B. D., Howard Univ., Sch. of Rel., 1962; Clinical Trng. St. Elizabeth's Hosp., Wash., D. C.; m. Bennie Jewel Shaw; Children--Rafe, Ralph, Natalie; pastor, Mt. Olive Bapt. Ch., Marshall, Tex., 1957-58; asst. pastor, Shiloh Bapt. Ch., Wash., D. C., 1958-59; pastor, Antioch Bapt. Ch., King George, Va., 1959-62; pastor, Faith Tabernacle Bapt. Ch., Stamford, Conn., 1962-June, 1968; present, Ebenezer Bapt. Ch., Boston, Mass.; mem., Mayor's Human Relations Comm.; 8th Charter Revision Comm. of Stamford, Conn.; Bd. of Dirs., Fam. and Children's Services; Friendship Housing; Bd. of Management, Prog. Natl. Bapt. Conv.; Bd.

Foreign Mission Bureau of Natl. Bapt. Conv.; Stamford-Darien Clergy Assn.; Fairfield Co. Bapt. Ed. Fellowship; sec., Kiwanis Club, Stamford, Conn.; Exec. Dir., New Hope Corp.; Bd. of NAACP; Omega Psi Phi; awards: Okla. State Medal of Honor; 4 Battle Stars; Good Conduct; Office: 157 W. Springfield St., Boston, Mass.

TAYLOR, Theodore Roosevelt, b. Ark., 1905; s. Albert and Lula T.; attended Little Rock, Ark. Coll., 2 yrs.; m. Juldine Boyd; Children--Jerome; pastor, Chrstn. Meth. Episc. Ch., St. Louis, Mo.; Dist. Sup. of A. M. E. Ch., 22 yrs.; repr., Sch. Bd., St. Louis, Mo.; Home: 5176 Cates St., St. Louis, Mo.; Office: 1915 Wagner St., St. Louis, Mo.

TAYLOR, Virgil Thomas, b. Harrods Creek, Ky., May 1889; s. Wm. and Maggie; m. Mable Harris (T.); pastored, Bapt. chs., Harrods Creek, Ky. (4 yrs.); Paramount Bapt. Ch., Wash., D. C. (4 yrs.); Parker Meml. Bapt. Ch., Takoma Pk., Md. (29 yrs.); retired; honors, Plaque, Mayor Takoma Pk, Md.; Plaque, City Council; pastor emeritus, Parker Meml. Ch.; Vet. WW I, 92nd Div., France; postal clerk, Wash., D. C. (25 yrs.); Home: 2109 Osage St., Louisville, Ky. 40210

TEAMER, James William Robert, educator, b. Greenville, S. C., Jan. 3, 1908; s. Jesse and Minnie (Evans) T.; A. B., Johnson C. Smith Univ., 1943; B. D., 1945; courses: Moody Bible Inst., Gammon Theol. Sem., Turner Theol. Sem.; Morris Brown Coll.; D. D. (hon.), James W. Teamer Sch. of Rel., 1958; pastor in North Carolina, South Carolina and Georgia; current pastor, Cosmopolitan Community Ch. (non-denominational), Charlotte, N. C.; founder, James W. Teamer Sch. of Rel., Teamer Sch. of Ed., Teamer Sch. of Commercial Ed.; Boy Scout Commissioner, 3 yrs.; chrmn., Bd. of Management, Henry Lawrence McGorey, YMCA; mem., Democrat; Mason; NAACP; Phi Beta Sigma; Home: 2524 Newland Rd., Charlotte, N. C.; Office: 2600 Newland Rd., Charlotte, N. C.

*TERRELL, Leonard Earl, coll. dean, b. Montgomery Co., Miss., Jan. 27, 1908; s. William H. and Addie V. T.; A. B., B. D., Howard Univ., Wash., D. C., 1935; Drew Univ., Madison, N. J.; M. A., New York Univ., 1959; Ph. D. candidate, Drew Univ.; m. Louise F. Moorhead; Children--Leonard Howard; acting dean, Chapel of Howard

Univ., 1938-39; pastor, New Hope Bapt. Ch., Hackensack, N.J., 1939-46; pastor, Bethel Bapt. Inst. Ch., Jacksonville, Fla., 1946-52; pres., Storer Coll., Harpers Ferry, W.Va., 1952-55; dir., Rel. Activities, Va. State Coll., Petersburg, Va., 1955-63; current, Union Bapt. Ch., New York, 1963--; prof., Sch. of Rel., Howard Univ., 1937-38; Va. State Coll., 1952-53; organizer and treas., Civic League, Jacksonville, Fla., 1949; trustee, Bd. of Fla. Normal & Indus. Coll., St. Augustine, Fla., 1946-52; citation from Fla. Normal & Indus. Coll., 1951; mem., Phi Beta Sigma; NAACP; Southern Chrstn. Leadership Conf.; Rel. Ed. Assn.; Bd. of Sloane House, YMCA; Supervisory Com. over Chaplaincy, New York City; Home: 408 Tecumseh Ave., Mt. Vernon, N.Y.; Office: 240 W. 145th St., New York, N.Y. 10039

THIGPEN, Lee Allen, Jr., b. Houston, Tex., Jan. 8, 1920; s. Lee Allen, Sr. and Lena (Mills) T.; B.A., Wiley Coll., Marshall, Tex., 1941; B.D., Gammon Theol. Sem. 1944; S.T.M., Boston Univ., 1947; m. Arvon Rainey; Children--Regina Allene; Lee Allen, III; Wilford D'Artagnan; pastor, St. Paul Meth. Ch., Clarksville, Tex., 1944-45; chap., US Army, Okinawa and Japan, 1945-46; chap., VA Hosp., Tuskegee, Ala., 1947-52; chap., 82nd Airborne Div. 505th Airborne Inf. Regiment, Ft. Bragg, N.C., 1952-54; chap., VA Med. Teaching Gp. Hosp., Memphis, Tenn., 1954-61; chap., VA Hosp., Lyons, N.J., 1961-present; Regimental chap. (Major), 78th Regiment, Camp Kilmer, N.J., 1961-65; Lt. Col., USAR, 1965-present; Omega Psi Phi; Mason; collaborated with the writers of the book entitled, <u>From Custodial to Therapeutic Patient Care in Mental Hospitals</u>; Home: Veterans Administrn. Hosp., Lyons, N.J. 07939

THOMAS, Clarence Harris, coll. tchr., b. Mooresville, N.C., June 29, 1924; s. Theodore Roosevelt and Lovell; A.B., Johnson C. Smith Univ., 1944-50; B.D., 1950; Th.M., Union Theol. Sem., 1957-58; m. Adelaide Maxwell; Children--Deborah Carol; pastor, Chase City United Presby. Ch., Chase City, Va., 1950-56; Haymount Presby. Ch., Fayetteville, N.C., 1956--; tchr., Fayetteville State Coll., 1960--; founder of and adv. to Chase City Service Club; moderator, Tenn. Presbytery, 1953; treas., Mecklenburg Co., Va. br. NAACP, 1954-56; mem., No. Carolina Tchrs. Assn., NEA, ATA, Alpha Phi Alpha; Home: 420 Chatham St., Fayetteville, N.C.; Church:

611 Hay St., Fayetteville, N. C.

THOMAS, Cornelious Egbert, coll. prof., b. Marion, Ala., May 4, 1923; s. James A. and Serna (A.) T.; A. B., Daniel Payne Coll., 1946; B. D., Gammon Theol. Sem., 1949; D. D. (hon.), Payne Coll., 1954; m. Susie Mae Jamar; Children--Cornelia S., James E.; pastor, St. Mark A. M. E. Ch., Dora, Ala., 1943-49; pastor, Bethel A. M. E. Ch., Ensley, Ala., 1949-52; pastor, St. John A. M. E. Ch., B'ham, Ala., 1952--; part-time instr., Daniel Paine Coll., Birmingham, Ala.; trustee, Daniel Payne Coll., mem., Gen. Citizens Federation; mem., Bd. of A. M. E. Ch.; mem., Adv. Bd., Savings & Loans; mem., Progressive Democratic Party; mem., Mason, Knight of Pythians; author: "As He Spoke To Me;" Home: 431 12th Terr., B'ham, Ala.; Office: 708 15th, No. B'ham, Ala.

THOMAS, George, b. Pittsburgh, Pa., Jan. 8, 1931; s. David Prince and Georgia (Bailey) Ware; B. A., Univ. of Toledo, 1954; Western Res. Univ., Cleveland, O., B. D., Oberlin Coll., 1958; m. Delores Mabel Shoecraft; 1 dau., Sheila Delores, 2 sons, George David, Anthony Adrian; Dir., Chagrin Falls Pk. Community Center, 1957-60; pastor, Coronado Congre. Chrstn. Ch., Norfolk, Va., 1960-61; pastor, St. Mark Congre. Ch., Boston, Mass., 1961--; sec.-treas., Boston Conf. on Rel. and Race, 1964-65; Bd. Mem., Roxbury Comm. Coun.; mem., United Comm. Services-Spec. Service Comm.; life mem., NAACP; Home: 34 Elm Hill Ave., Boston, Mass. 02121; Church: 210 Townsend St., Boston, Mass.

THOMAS, George Benjamin, b. McKees Rocks, Pa., July 11, 1924; s. George M. and Naomi (Sykes); A. B., Lincoln Univ., 1950; B. D. and S. T. M., Hood Theol. Sem. and Boston Univ., 1950-54; courses, Scarritt and American Univ.; m. Farrel Harmon; Children--George Chana, Rosana Lorraine, Eric Allen; pastor, Community Ch., Courtland, Va., 1947-49; A. M. E. Z. Ch., Cambridge, Mass., 1953-58; tchr., Livingstone Coll., 1954; Hood Theol. Sem., 1955-58; missionary, Div. of World Missions of the Meth. Ch. in Belgium, 1-1/2 yrs.; Congo, 3 yrs.; currently, staff, Hood Theol. Sem., A. M. E. Z. Ch., 1964--; counseling minister for Palmer Meml. Inst., Sedalia, N. C.; consultant lectr. on Missions, Africa; organizer, Movement for Social Betterment, McKees Rocks, Pa., 1947; chrmn., Prayer and Action Cell Movement,

Lincoln Univ., 1948-49; worked with NAACP, Salisbury, Rowan Co., 1955-58; probation officer in Juvenile Court, Pittsboro, Alleghany Co., 1963; mem., Bd. of Dirs., Natl. Coun. of Chrstns. & Jews; sec., Initial Integrated Salisbury, Rowan Min. Fellowship; US Army, T5 HQ Detachment, 1945-46; award: A star from the New Guinea Campaign; Philippine Invasion Campaign; organizer, Afro-Am. Literary Soc., Livingstone Coll., Salisbury, N.C.; mem., N.C. Tchrs. Assn.; N.C. Tchrs. of Rel.; Natl. Ed. Assn.; author: devotional series, Strength of My Life, Profile of Congo, Stereotypes-Stigmas of Shame; Home: 904 W. Monroe St., Salisbury, N.C.; Home: 904 W. Monroe St., Salisbury, N.C.; Office: Hood Theol. Sem., Livingstone Coll., Salisbury, N.C.

THOMAS, James J., ch. official; b. Charleston, S.C., s. Joseph J.; St. Colmes Theol. Sem., 1943; B.D., Lincoln Univ., Pa., 1946; M.A., Drew Univ., 1950; M.A., Union Theol. Sem., 1954; D.Ed., Tchrs. Coll., Columbia Univ., 1957; m. Winell Mae Thorpe; Children--Ralph, Joy, Howard; Presbyn. minister (United), 1945; pastor, Mott Haven Ref. Ch. in America, 1953-61; area sec., Japan and Southeast Asia areas (Ref. Ch. in Amer.) mem., Com. on Ministry Personnel in Far East; China Com., Com. on Overseas Union Chs.; The East Asian Chrstn. Conf. Com.; The Japan Com., S.E. Asia Com., Natl. Coun. of Chs.; Com. on Chrstn. Higher Ed., Southeast Asia; pres., Synod Ref. Ch. in America, NY area; mem., Bd. of Trustees, Western and New Brunswick Theol. Sem.; mem., Bd. of World Missions; Home: 3216 Paulding Ave., Bronx, N.Y. 10469; Office: 475 Riverside Dr., New York, N.Y.

THOMAS, James Samuel, bishop, b. Orangeburg, S.C., April 8, 1919; s. James Samuel Sr. and Dessie (Merks) T.; A.B., Claflin Coll., 1939; B.D., Gammon Theol. Sem., 1943; M.A., Drew Univ., 1943; Ph.D., Cornell Univ., 1953; D.D. (hon.), Claflin Coll., 1953; LL.D. (hon.), Bethune Cookman Coll., 1963; m. Ruth Naomi Wilson; Children--Claudia, Gloria, Margaret, Patricia; principal, Hickson Grove Sch., Florence Co., S.C.; pastor, Orangeburg Co., S.C.; chaplain, S.C. State Coll.; pastor, York, S.C.; prof., Gammon Theol. Sem.; assoc. dir., Div. of Higher Ed., Meth. Bd. of Ed.; prof., Friendship Union Coll., 1947; visiting prof., Southern Meth. Univ., 1958; mem., Bd. of Trustees,

Bennett Bethune Cookman Coll., Claflin Coll., Clark Coll., Huston Tillotson Coll., Philander Smith Coll., Philander Smith Coll., Rust Coll., Wiley Coll., Paine Coll.; Kappa Delta Pi; Phi Kappa Phi; Phi Delta Kappa; consultant, Danforth Found.; Home: 3500 Kingman Blvd., Des Moines, Iowa 50309; Office: 508 Tenth, Des Moines, Iowa

THOMAS, Nathaniel Charles, ch. official, b. Jonesboro, Ark., June 24, 1929; s. Willie James and Linnie (T.); Miss. Indus. Coll., 1951; A.B., Lincoln Univ., 1954; B.A., Lancaster Theol. Sem., 1953; m. Juanita Fannie Jefferson; 1 dau., Gina Charlies; migrant ministry (student) in Oxford, Pa., 1953-54; dir., Chrstn. First Episc. Dist. C.M.E. Ch. (comprising Ark. and Okla.), 1955; pastor, Cottrell C.M.E. Ch., Hot Springs, Ark., 1957-60; v.p., youth sec. of the Div. of Chrstn. Ed., Natl. Coun. of Chs., 1959; pastor, Bullock Temple C.M.E. Ch., Little Rock, Ark., 1960-62; sec., Interracial Min. Alliance, Little Rock, Ark., 1961; present: Dir. of Chrstn. Ed., and Admin. Asst. to presiding Bishop, C.M.E. Chs. (Ark. and Tenn.), 1962--; mem., Interracial Coun., Lancaster, Pa., 1953-53; Steering Comm. Natl. Conf. of Rel. and Race, 1961--; Steering Comm., Little Rock Conf. on Rel. and Human Relations, 1963--; dir. of Leadership Trng. for C.M.E. Chs. in Okla., Ark. and Tenn., 1954-58; Distinguished Serv. Award by YMCA, Little Rock, Ark., 1961; mem., C.M.E. Min. Alliance of Greater Memphis area; Interdenom. Min. Alliance, Memphis, Tenn.; Gen. Bd. of Chrstn. Ed., C. M.E. Ch.; chrmn., Comm. on location of the C.M.E. Gen. Conf.; published Chrstn. Youth Fellowship Guide (1st in C.M.E. Ch.), 1956; ed. and compiled three publications for Bd. of Chrstn., 1957, 1959, 1960; author: "Living Up to My Obligations of Church Membership," 1963; Home: 664 Vance Ave., Memphis, Tenn. 38126

THOMAS, Robert Colby, b. Abbeville, La., July 2, 1922; s. Robert and Orear (F.) Th.; A.B., Leland Coll., 1943; courses, Denver Univ., San Francisco State Coll., Pacific Sch. of Rel.; M.R.E., Golden Gate Sem.; m. Juanita Foote; Children--Ronita Barbara, Robert Jerome, Kelesha Lei; principal, Elem. Sch., Madisonville, La., 1946-48; tchr., San Francisco Unified Sch. Dist., 1948-52; pastor, Mt. Zion C.M.E. Temple, Minden, 1952-56; Williams Meml. C.M.E. Temple, Shreveport, La., 1956-63; Bebee Meml. C.M.E. Temple, 1963-65; current pastor, All Faiths Community Ch., Oakland, Calif., 1965--; visiting tchr., Pastor's Sch., Texas Coll.; dean, Leadership Trng. Sch., Grambling Coll. Chrstn. Meth. Episc. Ch.; mem., City Recreation Bd., Minden, La.; Bd. of Management, YMCA, Shreveport, La.; United Chrstn. Movement; chrmn., Human Relations Com. Bd. of Dirs.; NW br. YMCA; Metro. Bd. of Dirs., Oakland, Calif.; Caddo parish chrmn. of voting drive in Shreveport, 1958; public relations officer in Europe, WW II; mem., Mason, NAACP, Democrat, Alpha Phi Alpha, Oakland Coun. of Chs.; Home: 1858 Melvin Rd., Oakland, Calif. 94602; Office: 2267 Telegraph Ave., Oakland, Calif.

*THOMAS, William Neamon, b. Malvern, Ark., Aug. 18, 1927; s. Felix Neamon and Arvilla T.; A.B., Storer Coll., Harpers Ferry, S. Va., 1953; B.D., Howard Univ. Sch. of Rel., 1959; m. Elsie Virginia Tucker; Children--Deborah, William; current pastor, Zion Bapt. Ch., 1954--; mem., Com. on Racial Unity, 1963; Democratic Committeeman, 1962; chrmn., CORE, 1963; mem., Bd. of Dirs., NAACP, Alexandria, Va.; US Forces, 1946-49; Outstanding Citizens Award, 1963, Alexandria, Va.; Democrat; mem., Mason; Home: 916 Queen St., Alexandria, Va.; Office: 114 S. Lee St., Alexandria, Va.

THOMPSON, Albert A., educator, b. So. Carolina, May 14, 1909; s. T.A. and Mary (Gill) T.; A.B., B.D., J.C. Smith Univ., 1936; Ph.D., Harvard Univ., 1952; m. Willie Mae Callaham; 1 dau., Gloria, 1 son, Albert; pastor, Laura St. Presby. Ch., Jacksonville, Fla., 1940-41; Faith Congre. Ch., Hartford, Conn., 1960--; Head, Sci. Dept., Tenn. State Univ., 1953-60; Adjunct prof. of Hist., Univ. of Hartford; mem., Citizens Charter Comm., Family Serv., Hosp. Chaplains Assn.; Home: 87 Rosemont, Hartford, Conn.; Church: 2030 Main, Hartford, Conn.

THOMPSON, Charlie Roosevelt, b. Warren, Ark., May 22, 1933; s. Charlie and Minnie, A.B., Livingstone Coll., Salisbury, N.C., 1955; B.D., Hood Theol. Sem., Salisbury, N.C., 1958; m. Dorothy L. Little; Children--Christopher, Roosevelt, Lee, Carrie; pastor, Smithville A.M.E.Z. Ch., Cheraw, S.C., 1955-59; Payne Chapel, Little Rock, Ark., 1959-65; Metropolitan A.M.E.Z. Ch., Monticello, Ark., 1963--; dir., Youth Min., 1965-66; chrmn., Commn. on Youth Min., 1967--; presiding elder, Hot Springs Dist., N. Ark. Conf., 1967--; instr. Annual

Conf. Inst., 1963-65; dean, Mobile Unit of Walters Inst.; chrmn., Finance Com., pres., Little Rock PTA Coun., 1964-65; mem., Greater Little Rock Min. Assn., 1960-65; Little Rock Conf. on Rel. and Race; Home: 4157 W. Jackson St., Chgo., Ill. 60624; Office: 128 E. 58th St., Chgo., Ill. 60637

THOMPSON, Floyd Wm., b. Columbia, S. C., May 19, 1900; s. Thomas Wm. and Mary (Rowls); B. D., Allen Univ., 1923; D. D. (hon.), Campbell Coll., 1951; m. Juanita Lancaster; Children--Floyd W. Jr., Mary E., Leon W., Vivian; pastor, Jones Tabernacle Aft. Meth. Episc., 1945-50; Grace A. M. E. Ch., Warren, O., 1951-57; Brown Chapel A. M. E. Ch., Pittsburgh, 1958-59; St. Paul A. M. E. Ch., Wash., 1959-63; current pastor, St. Paul A. M. E. Ch., Lima, O., 1963--; mem., NAACP Family Serv. Bd., Wash., Pa.; Hosp. chap.; mem., Elks, Masons; Home: 1328 W. Elm, Lima, O.; Office: 1103 Spring St., Lima, O.

*THOMPSON, John Andrew, b. McCool, Miss., Dec. 24, 19--; s. Isaac J. L. and Susie T.; A. B., Jackson Coll., Jackson, Miss., 1933-40; Univ. of Atlanta, Atlanta, Ga., 1942; Univ. of Chicago, 1945, 46; B. D., Howard Univ., Sch. of Rel., 1950; m. Maudie Louise Lee; Children--John Andrew, Karl Anthony; principal, Weir Jr. High Sch., 1941-44; principal, Oakland Jr. High Sch., 1946-47; College Hill High Sch., Pontotoc; Homes Co. Trng. Sch., Durant, Lawrence Co. Trng. Sch.; pastor, First Bapt. Ch., Ronceverte, W. Va., 1947-50; Tabernacle Bapt. Ch., W. Palm Beach, Fla., 1951; Bethel Bapt. Ch., Omaha, Nebr., 1952-54; current, Corinth Meml. Bapt. Ch., 1955--; Bd. mem., NAACP; Exec. sec., New Era Bapt. State Conv. of Nebr.; founder and pres., Intl. League for Brotherhood and Peace, 1962--; Bd. mem., Omaha Coun. of Chs., 1953-63; dir., Western Bapt. Bible Coll. (Omaha Center), 1964--; Home: 2709 Spaulding St., Omaha, Nebr. 68111

THOMPSON, Paul Frederick, b. Kinston, N. C., Apr. 2, 1933; s. John and Hortense; A. B., Morehouse Coll., Atlanta, Ga., 1956; B. D., Colgate Rochester Div. Sch., 1959; m. Sybrnee (Jones); Children--Alicia; dir., Chas. D. Hubert Chrstn. Center, N. Y.; asst. pastor, Antioch Bapt. Ch., Cleveland, O., 1959-61; pastor, Emmanuel Bapt. Ch., Niagara Falls, NY, 1961-64; v. p., Niagara Coun. of Chs.; sec., Min. Coun. of Niagara Falls; Niagara Co. Migrant Chaplain; pres., Niagara Falls br. NAACP; chrmn., Human Rel. Commn., Niagara Falls; mem., Central Budget Com., UGF; mem., Bd. of Dir., Community Center; Fam. and Children Service; Jr. Achievement; Parks and Recreation Adv. Bd., Niagara Falls; pastor, Olney St. Bapt. Ch., Providence, R.I., 1964-present; sec., Min. Alliance of Providence; chrmn., Lippitt Hill Neighborhood Adv. Com.; mem., Bd. of Dir., E. Side YMCA; exec. com., E. Side Neighborhood Coun.; pres., Bapt. Ed. Soc., R.I. Bapt. State Conv.; Human Rel. Commn. of Providence; awards, Public Serv. Appreciation, City of Niagara, 1964; "Niagara Personality of the Week," Niagara Falls Gazette, 1964; 2nd v.p., R.I. Bapt. State Conv., 1968; pres., Mt. Hope Day Care Com., 1965-68; Home: 51 Mt. Hope Ave., Providence, R.I.; Office: 100 Olney St., Providence, R.I. 02906

THOMPSON, Randolph, b. Pt. Howe, Cat Is., Bahamas, B.W.I., Oct. 28, 1927; B.A., Shaw Univ., Raleigh, N.C., 1954; B.D., Colgate Rochester Div. Sch., Rochester, NY, 1957; m. Bernice Coleman; Children--Evania, Denita, Randolph, Stephen; pastor, Jackson Chapel, 1st Bapt. Ch., Wilson, N.C., 1964-67; Brownsville Bapt. Ch., Miami, Fla., 1960-64; exec. dir., Bapt. Ed. Center, NYC, 1966-present; dir., Rel. Ed., Mt. Zion Bapt. Ch., Miami, Fla., 1958-59; Supt. of Mission, Fla. E. Coast Bapt. Assn., 1959-62; spec. admin. asst., 2nd Canaan Bapt. Ch., NYC, 1957-58; Dean, Fla. E. Coast J.T. Brown Sch. for Min., 1959-64; natl. accredited instr., Sun. Sch. and B.T.U. Congress, Fla. E. Coast Assn., 1958-64; bible expositor, Greater Miami Bapt. Coun., 1959-64; pres., NAACP, Wilson, N.C., 1964-67; pres., organizer, Wilson Co. Citizens' League, 1964-67; sec., Pastors' Fund Raising Drive; chrmn., Fund Raising Sec., State of N.C., for liquidation of indebt., Shaw Univ., Raleigh, N.C.; mem., Wilson Co. Min. Assn.; volunteer chap., Wilson Co. Meml. Hosp., 1964-66; co-chrmn., registration com., Local Steering Com., World's Bapt. Alliance, Miami, Fla., 1965; v.p., Greater Miami Coun. of Chs., 1963-64; coordinator, Parliamentarian Greater Miami Min. Alliance, 1959-64; mem., YMCA; Commn. missionary, Home Mission Soc., Amer. Bapt. Conv., 1966; mem., Task Force Com., Black Caucus of Amer. Bapt. Conv., 1968; mem., Roger Williams Fellowship of Amer. Bapt. Conv.; mem., NCNC; Office: 2190 Valentine Ave., Bronx, N.Y. 10457

THOMPSON, Roy Lee, b. Pineville, Ky., July 9, 1922; s. Quiller and Bertha; B.S., W. Va. State Coll., Inst., W. Va., 1949; B.D., Colgate Rochester Div. Sch., Rochester, N.Y., 1958; studies, Western Res. Univ., Cleveland, O., Univ. of Rochester, Rochester, N.Y.; m. Lois Reese; Children--Kemberly Ann; US Army, 1942-46; staff mgr., Supreme Liberty Life Ins. Co., 1953-55; asst. min., Meml. A.M.E.Z. Ch., Rochester, N.Y., 1955-57; supply pastor, Ogden Bapt. Ch., Ogden, N.Y., 1957-58; assoc. pastor, 2nd Bapt. Ch., L.A., Calif., 1958-61; pastor, Manchester Bapt. Ch., L.A., Calif., 1961-66; dir., World Mission Support, N.Y. Bapt. City Soc., N.Y., 1966-present; mem., NAACP, CORE; pres., Welfare Planning Coun., L.A., Calif., 1964-66; awards, 2 Bronze Stars, Philippine Liberation Medal, Meritorious Achievement; Community Award, Radio KDAY, L.A., Calif.; Merit Award, Welfare Planning Coun., L.A.; mem., Alpha Phi Alpha; Home: 115-15 220th St., Cambria Heights, N.Y. 11411; Office: 297 Park Ave. S., New York, N.Y. 10010

THURMAN, Howard, sem. dean, author, b. Daytona Bch., Fla., Nov. 18, 1900; s. Saul Solomon and Alice (Ambrose) T.; A.B., Morehouse Coll., 1923; D.D. (hon.), 1935; B.D., Rochester Theol. Sem., 1923; D.D., Wesleyan Coll., Conn., 1946; D.D. (hon.), Lincoln Univ.; Howard Univ., 1955; LL.D. (hon.), Ohio Wesleyan Univ., 1954; LL.D., Wash. Univ., 1955; Allen Univ., 1954; Litt.D. (hon.), Tuskegee Inst., 1956; D.D., Oberlin Coll., 1958; LL.D., Va. State Univ., 1959; m. Sue E. Bailey; Children--Anne, Olive; ordained to ministry, Bapt. Ch., 1925; pastor, Mt. Zion Bapt. Ch., Oberlin, Ohio, 1926-28; prof., Morehouse Coll., 1928-31; prof. and dean of chapel, Howard Univ., Wash., D.C., 1932-44; pastor, Ch. for Fellowship of All Peoples, San Francisco, 1944-53; dean, Marsh Chapel; prof., spiritual disciplines and resources, Boston Univ., 1953-67; lectr., on immortality of man, Harvard Univ., 1947; Merrick lectr., Ohio Wesleyan Univ., 1953; mem., Bd. of Dirs., Urban League Greater Boston, Inc.; dir., Travelers Aid Soc.; Mass. Commn. Against Discrimination; Bd. of Natl. Mental Health Assn.; Natl. Coun., Rel. in Higher Ed.; Amer. Acad. of Arts and Sciences; Alumni Assn., Colgate Rochester Div. Sch.; Fellowship of Reconsiliation Clubs; Book of Calif., Mass. Schoolmasters Commonwealth; author: The Greatest of These, 1945; Deep River, 1946, 1955; Meditations for Apostles of Sensitiveness, 1947; The Negro Spiritual Speaks of Life and Death, 1947; Jesus and the Disinherited, 1948; Deep is the Hunger, 1951; Meditations of the Heart, 1953; The Creative Encounter, 1954; Apostles of Sensitivenss, 1956; The Growing Edge, 1956; Footprints of a Dream, 1959; contributor to: Interpreter's Bible, Vol. 7; Inward Journey, 1961; Mysticism and the Experience of Love, 1961; Disciplines of the Spirit, 1963; The Luminous Darkness, 1965; Home: 2018 Stockton St., San Francisco, Calif.

TIEUEL, Robert C. D., Jr., b. Boley, June 26, 1914; s. Robert C. D. and Nodie E. (T.); Lane Coll., 1930-32; Tenn. State Coll., 1932-33; LeMoyne Coll., 1933-34; spec. study at Harvard Div. Sch., 1934-36; A.B., Tex. Coll., 1950; m. Mary Porter; present, pastor, Brown Chapel Chrstn. Meth. Episc. Ch., San Angelo, Tex., 1946--; dir., Public Relations of Eighth Episc. Dist. C.M.E. Ch., including states of Tex. and Ky.; mem., Hobbs Cham. of Commerce and Bd. of Chrstn. Ed. of the Northwest Texas-New Mexico Conf. C.M.E. Ch.; chrmn., Ex. Comm. of the Progressive Citizens League, Inc. of New Mexico; candidate, State repr. in 1958 Democratic primary race (Lea Co., N.M.); cited by Pres. Eisenhower--efforts in bldg. Chrstn. inter-racial goodwill and relations as editor of the magazine Christian Call; ex. mem., NAACP, San Angelo br., Tex.; editor, Who's Who in the C.M.E. Ch., 1962; publisher, Christian Call, publication of C.M.E. Ch.; Home: 914 S. Dal Paso St., Hobbs, N.M.; Office: 200 W. 14th St., San Angelo, Tex.

*TILLMAN, Eugene C., b. W. Palm Beach, Fla., Apr. 10, 1926; s. William and Laura T.; A.B., Howard Univ., 1948; B.D., Howard Univ. Sch. of Rel., 1951; m. Vivian; Children--Eugene C., Jr., Thurmond Neil; minister to the Migratory Farm Workers, Pompano Beach, Fla. and Bridgeton, N.J., 1948-54; pastor, Mt. Bethel Bapt. Ch., Daytona Beach, Fla., 1954-63; pres., The Sun. Sch. and B.T.U. Congress, Fla. E. Coast Assn., 1962--; instr., Sun. Sch. and B.T.U. Congress, State Conv., Fla., 1951--; instr., Natl. Sun. Sch. and B.T.U. Congress, 1952--; present pastor, Shiloh Bapt. Ch., Brunswick, Ga.; one of two Negroes apptd. to the State Bi-Racial Comm. of Gov. Leroy Collins; mem., The Fla. Adv. Comm. to the Fed. Civil Rights Commn., apptd. by the late John F. Kennedy; The Urban Renewal Bd.,

Daytona Beach, Fla.; state-wide coordinator for Negro and minority vote to elect Mayor Robt. King High of Miami for Governor, Fla.; US Naval Res., 1944-46; many citations from human relations groups, NAACP Groups, colleges, fraternities; mem., Phi Beta Sigma; Exec. Bd., Fla. Coun. on Human Relations; Bd. of the NAACP, State of Fla.; Home: 1221 Egmont St., Brunswick, Ga.

TIMPSON, George William, tchr., b. Frederick, Md., Aug. 16, 1927; s. James Thomas and Cora Bell (Leeks) T.; B.S., 1952, Oakwood Coll., Huntsville, Ala.; m. Cynthia Eleanor Knight; 1 son, Dane Anthony; pastored: 1st S.D.A. Ch., Ellenville, N.Y., 1959-60; Bethesday S.D.A. Ch. of Amityville, N.Y., 1960-61; Mt. Zion S. D.A. Ch. of New Haven, Conn., 1961--; principal, Ephesus Jr. Acad., Birmingham, Ala., 1952-53; tchr., Bethel Elem. Sch., Bklyn, N.Y., 1953-61; US Navy combat - Okinawa, 1944-46; awarded a life-time teaching cert. from the Gen. Conf. Educational Dept. of S.D.A., Wash., D.C.; mem., Min. Alliance of New Haven, Conn.; Home: 79 Thompson St., New Haven, Conn.; Office: 64 Marlboro St., Hamden, Conn.

TINSLEY, Raymond Earl, chap., b. Flack-Lick, Ky., Oct. 15, 1921; s. Ernest and Eula Dean; B.S., Livingstone Coll., Salisbury, N.C., 1949; B.D., Hood Theol. Sem., Salisbury, N.C.; M.A., New Mexico State Coll., 1960; Sacramento State Coll., 1966; m. Aurelia Pearson; Children--Ernestine (Mrs. Wayland Mitchell), Roberta Jannett, Margaret Ann (Mrs. Leonard Bloom); Air Force chap., Amarillo AFB, Tex., 1952-54; Itazuke AFB, Japan, 1954-57; Whiteman AFB, Mo., 1957-58; Biggs AFB, Tex., 1958-60; Thula AFB, Greenland, 1960-62; Mather AFB, Calif., 1962-66; Spangdahlam AFB, Germany, 1966-168; Offuth AFB, Nebr., 1968-present; Office: Base Chapel, 3902 AB Wg., Offuth, AFB, Nebr. 68113

TIPTON, B. Cortez, b. May 31, 1913; s. Garfield F. and Mary M. (T.); A.B., Knoxville Coll.; M.S.W., Howard Univ., Sch. of Soc. Work; courses, Cath. Univ. of Amer.; Cambridge Univ. (St. John's Coll.), England; Hartford Sem., (Conn.); m. Elizabeth H. Howase; Children--Cassandra, Bensonetta, Eunice, Libbee; licensed and ordained minister, United Ch. of Christ, served as minister 20 yrs.; tchr.-principal, Bonny Oaks Indus. Sch.; Wash. High Sch., E. Chattanooga, Tenn.; Extension tchr., Tenn. A & I State Univ.; Chief of Casework, Bur. of

Rehabilitation, Wash., D.C.; and Sup. of Occ. Therpay, D.C. Health Dept. (10 yrs.); field work instr., Howard Univ. Sch. of Soc. Work, (4 yrs.); Sch. of Soc. Sciences, Cath. Univ. of Amer. (3 yrs.); part-time staff, Fed. Bur. of Prisons, Dept. of Justice; asst. dir., Soc. Service Dept., Denver, Colo., Coun. of Chs.; dir., Soc. Service Dept., Hartford Coun of Chs.; founder and coordinator, Volunteer Sponsor Prog., Conn. Prison Assn.; asst. dir., Conn. Public Schs. Bussing Prog., W. Hartford; ex. dir., Coun. of Chs. of Greater Bridgeport (present); Sensitivity Trng. Coach, Bridgeport Bd. of Ed. (part-time, 1967-69); mem., Mayor's Housing Com. (Chattanooga, Tenn.); Mayor's Intercultural Com. (Tenn.); chrmn., Commissioner's Sub-Com. Study of Probation & Parole Systems; Bd. of Dirs., Wash. Fed. of Chs. (7 yrs.); chrmn., Mayor's Com. on Alcoholism, Denver, Colo.; Bd. of Dirs., Conn. Half-Way House, Inc.; mem., Adv. Bds., Community Action Develop. Proj.; Office of Humane Affairs; Bridgeport Mental Health Assn.; awards: Humanitarian award, Conn. Guardians, Hartford; Religious award, Natl. Coun. of Negro Women, Bridgeport; Oustanding service, Anglo-American Discussion Groups, Ollerton-Knotts, England; pres. elect, Natl. Assn. of Coun. Secretaries; mem., Natl. Coun. on Family Relations; Natl. Assn. Social Workers; Natl. Conf. of Soc. Welfare; Natl. Coun. on Crime; Home: 30 Elmwood Pl., Bridgeport, Conn. 06604; Office: 3030 Park Ave., Bridgeport, Conn. 06604

TIVY, Cleveland Burie, coll. prof., b. Kingston, Jamaica, W.I., June 19, 1916; s. Charles Caleb and Doris (Roslyn) T.; Oakwood Coll., Huntsville, Ala., A.B., 1950; m. Gloria Olena Bonterre; Children--Julie Lillian, Janice Oleana, Joy Linda; pastored S.D.A. Chs. in: Richmond, Petersburg, Crewe, Va., 1950; Dayton, Germantown, Springfield, O., 1955; Jerse City, Englewood, Montclair, N.J., 1958; present: Pine Forge, Pa., 1959--; tchr. of Bible courses, Pine Forge Inst., Pine Forge, Pa., 1959--; US Army, 1942-45; Home: Box 34, Pine Forge, Pa.

TOATLEY, Robert George, missionary, b. Irmo, S.C., May 6, 1922; s. Robert Nelson and Lottie (Watts) T.; A.B., B.D., Johnson C. Smith Univ., 1943, 1946; m. Juanita Bernice (Williams) T.; Children--Johnie Mae, Robert George Jr., Juanita Laverne; supply minister, Pleasant Ridge Presby. Ch., Lancaster, S.C., 1944-45;

Lincoln Acad. (Congregational), King Mountain, N. C., 1945-46; Calvary and Shiloh Presby. Chs., Winsboro, S. C., 1946-47; missionary, Fairfield-McClelland Presby., Atlantic Synod, 1957; instr., Veteran Farm Trng. Prog., New Home Sch., 1948-52; co-dir., Audio-Visual Workshop, Atlantic and Catawba Leadership Trng. Sch., Johnson C. Smith Univ., Charlotte, N. C., 1957--; mem., Presbytery chrmn. of Com. on Social Ed. and Action, 1957-60; sec., Local Com. for Promotion of Human Rights, 1960; mem., Phi Beta Sigma; Home: 927 Crawford St., Rock Hill, S. C.

TONEY, Patrick W., educator, b. Mayesville, S. C., Nov. 1, 1897; s. Gaston and Virginia (Ceasar) T.; A. B., B. D., Johnson C. Smith Univ.; m. Albertha Plowden; Children--Lydie (Mrs. Kearns), Patrick W. Jr., Boyd G., Lloyd; pastor, Trinity Presby. Ch., Marion, N. C., 1920-22; Green St. Presby. Ch., Morganton, N. C., 1902-22; Faith Presby. Ch., Aberdeen, N. C., 1923-30; Good Will Presby. Ch., Ft. Pierce, Fla., 1930-33; current pastor, Mt. Sinaie and Mt. Lisborn Presby. Chs., 1933--; principal, Kisler Acad., Morganton, N. C., 3 yrs.; principal, Sarah Lincoln Acad., Aberdeen, N. C.; principal, Curry High Sch., St. Charles, S. C., 15 yrs.; mem., Masons; Sons and Daughters of Job, St. Charles, S. C.; Office: Mt. Sinai and Mt. Lisbon United Presby. Ch., St. Charles, S. C.

TOPPIN, Edwin Noel, b. Barbados, W. I., Jan. 10, 1933; s. Edwin A. J. and May B. (T.); A. B., Harrison Coll., Barbados, W. I., 1953; B. D., Union Theol. Sem., 1958; Jewish Inst. of Rel. and Soc. Science; m. Sally Ann Murray; Children--Sandra, Michele, Jonathan; Youth leader, Ebenezer United Meth. Ch., Barbados, 1946-51; Boy Scouts Commissioner, Grenada, St. Vincent, Barbados, 1958-64; pastor, Mardela Springs United Meth. Ch., Md., 1964-65; pastor, New Rochelle United Meth. Ch., 1965-68; pastor, Bklyn United Meth. Ch., 1968-present; couns., Grahamn Sch. for Children; Pleasant Ville Jewish Sch.; Dir. of Component & Couns., Community Action Program; cert. of appreciation, Women's League, New Rochelle, N. Y.; mem., Jewish Inst. of Rel.; Masons; United Meth. Ch. Bd. of Evangelism & Chrstn. Concern (N. Y. Conf.); Home: 1204 St. Jons Pl., Bklyn, N. Y. 11213

TOTTRESS, Richard E., b. Newby, Okla., Nov. 25, 1917;

s. M. M. and Louise (Headspeth) T.; B.A., Pacific Union Coll., Angwin, Calif.; Oakwood Acad. & Coll., Oakwood, Calif.; m. Margareau F. Norton; pastor, Oakwood Coll. Ch. of S.D.A., Huntsville, Ala.; mem., Oakwood Coll. Acad. Admissions Com. governing Com. Administr. Coun.; author: Heaven's Entrance Requirements for the Races; Pastor Tot's Poems and Points; broadcast, WEUP, "Your Bible Speaks;" Huntsville, Ala.; Home: Oakwood Coll. 135, Huntsville, Ala.; Office: Moran Hall, Oakwood Coll., Huntsville, Ala. 35806

TRAYLOR, Horace Jerome, coll. pres., b. La Grange, Ga., Mar. 15, 1931; A.B., Zion Coll., Chattanooga, Tenn., 1953; B.D., Gammon Theol. Sem., 1958; grad. study: Atlanta Univ., 1956; Univ. of Chattanooga; m. Thelma Dennis; Children--Sheryl Lynn; Linda Gail, Yohanna Fayl, Chequeta Renee, Tonya Yvonne; prof., Zion Coll., 1951--; admin. asst., Zion Coll., 1951-54; dean, 1954-59; current pres., Zion Coll., 1959--; current pastor, First Congre. Ch., 1958--; chrmn., Commn. on Resolutions, Tenn. Ky. Conf., Congre. Chrstn. Chs., 1959-61; pres., Coun. for Cooperative Action; mem., Auditorium and Tivoli Bd.; The Adult Educational Coun.; Bd. of Chattanooga Area Literacy Movement; Bd. of Family Service Agency; Mayor's Bi-Racial Comm.; Chattanooga Cham. of Commerce; selected as one of seven outstanding men from Chattanooga area by Jr. Chamber of Commerce, Chattanooga, Tenn., May 1964; Office: Zion Coll., Chattanooga, Tenn.

TROTTER, Walter Constello, b. Miss., June 16, 1898; s. William A. and Cannie (Brown) T.; B.Th., Okla. Bapt. Coll.; D.D. (hon.), Ideal Bible Coll.; D.D. (hon.), Inter-Bapt. Theol. Center, Houston, Tex.; m. Lurline Walls; Children--Walter, James; present pastor, World Bapt. Ch., Chicago; exec. sec., Dept. of Evangelism, Natl. Bapt. Conv., USA, Inc., 13 yrs.; pres., Bapt. Pastor's Conf.; Home: 6029 Michigan St., Chicago, Ill.

TROUT, Nelson Wesley, b. Columbus, O., Sept. 29, 1920; s. William N. and Bertha (Alston), T.; Wilberforce Univ., 1929-40; A.B., Capitol Univ., 1948; Ohio State Univ., 1949-50; B.D., Evangelical Theol. Sem., 1952; post grad. study, Univ. of So. Calif., 1962; m. Jennie V. Foster; Children--Cassandra, Paula, Philip; pastor, Trinity Luth. Ch., Montgomery, Ala., 1952-55; pastor,

Community Luth. Ch., Los Angeles, Calif., 1955-62; dir., Youth Evangelism, The Amer. Luth. Ch., Minneapolis, Minn., 1962-66; assoc. pastor, Grace Lutheran Ch., Eau Claire, Wis., 1966-present; consultant, rel., civic, and educational groups in human relations; mem., Bd. of Dir., Minneapolis Urban League, 1964-66; US Army, 1941-46; 1st Lt., Chaplain's Corps, 1958; promoted to Capt., Chaplain's Corps, 1960; prepared study documents for Youth Dept., Amer. Luth. Ch.: The Word for the World, Vol. I & II; The Youth Service Corps: The Journey to the City; Home: 520 Third Ave., Eau Claire, Wis. 54701

TRUEHEART, Gregory, b. King Wm. Co., Va., June 13, 1919; s. Gregory and Addie (Temple) T.; Wash. Bapt. Sem., 1943-47; m. Ada Baylor; current pastor, Mt. Horeb Bapt. Ch., Wash., D. C., 1952--; Home: 2000 Lawrence St. NE, Wash., D. C.; Office: 1507 No. Carolina Ave. NE, Wash., D. C.

TUCKER, Charles Eubank, bishop, b. Baltimore, Md., Jan. 12, 1896; s. William A. and Elivia (Clark) T.; m. Amelia Moore; 1 dau., Bernice; ed. Beckford and Smith's Coll., Jamaica, B.W.I., 1913; Lincolun Univ., Pa., 1917; Temple Univ., 1919; read law under Hon. Chas. Gogg, Pt. Pleasant, Va.; pastor, A. M. E. Zion Ch., Middletown, Pa., 1916; Delta, Pa., 1917; Salem Ch., Williamsport, Pa., 1919; Hilliard's Chapel, Montgomery, Ala., 1920-22; A. M. E. Z. Ch., Sharon, Miss., 1922-23; Mt. Zion Ch., Augusta, Ga., 1923-27; Cornish Temple Ch., Key West, Fla., 1927-29; Stoner Meml. Ch., Key West, Fla., 1927-29; Stoner Meml. Ch., Louisville, Ky., 1929-30; Jones' Temple Ch., New Albany, Ind., 1930-31; Elder, Phila. and Balto. Conf., A. M. E. Z. Ch., 1918-19; presiding elder, So. Ga. Conf., 1923-27; became presiding elder, Madisonville Dist., Ky., 1931; began criminal law practice, Louisville, Ky., 1929; candidate, assembly, Louisville, Ky., 1933; mem., Lincoln Bar Assn., NAACP; Independent in politics; present, Bishop, A. M. E. Z. Ch., 7th Episc. Dist.; Home: 1625 W. Kentucky St., Louisville, Ky.

*TUCKER, Frank D., b. Mar. 17, 1939, Blackstone, Va.; A. B., B. D., Howard Univ., Wash., D. C., 1961, 1964; m. Brenda Barbour; Children--Lisa Elizabeth; Dir. of Chrstn. Ed. and Minister of the Youth Ch., First Bapt. Ch., Wash., D. C., 1960-64; asst. pastor and minister of Chrstn. Ed., Shiloh Bapt. Ch., 1965--; research asst., Howard Univ. Community Serv. Proj., 1964-65, supervisor, Neighborhood Workers (Anti-Poverty) Prog., 1964-65; coll. minister and asst. prof. of Theol., Fla. Meml. Coll., 1965-66; pastor, Jones Meml. Bapt. Ch., Phila., Pa., 1966--; chrmn., Social Concern Com., Phila., Bapt. Assn.; mem., Foreign Mission Bd. Natl. Bapt. Conv., USA, Inc.; President's Adv. Coun. Disadvantaged, Eastern Bapt. Coll. and Sem.; auditor, Bapt. Min. Conf.; chrmn., Denominational Outlook Com.; Bd. of Dirs., Phila. Bapt. Assn.; NAACP; Office: Jones Meml. Bapt. Ch., 20th and Dauphin Sts., Phila., Pa. 19132

*TURNER, David, Jr., chap., b. Anderson, Tex., May 12, 1930; s. A. B. and Bertha W. (Lewis) T.; B.S., Prairie View A & M Coll., Tex., 1953; B.D., Howard Univ., Sch. of Rel., 1959; m. Sylvia Larkins; Children--David Fernando, Frank Lenous; pastor, First Bapt. Ch., Anderson, Tex., 1955; Tabor Presby. Ch., Wash., D.C., 1955-56; asst. pastor, First Bapt. Ch., Wash., D.C., 1956-61; counselor, Dept. of Pub. Welfare, Wash., D.C., 1956-61; assoc. Prot. chap., Dept. of Correction, 1961--; US Army chap., 1959--; certified as a Clinically Trained Clergyman, Bd. of Dirs., Natl. Coun. for Clinical Trng. USA, 1962; Natl. Defense and Good Conduct Medal; mem., US Army Reserve Officers Assn.; Home: 3208 Park Pl., NW, Wash., D.C.; Office: Box 25, Dept. of Corrections, Lorton, Va.

TURNER, Eugene Burns, b. Goldston, N.C., Sept. 16, 1924; s. Samuel David and Ollie (Emerson) T.; A.B., Shaw Univ., 1947; B.D., Shaw Div. Sch., 1950; M.Th., Midwestern Grad. Bible Sch., 1954; D.D. (hon.), Friendship Coll., 1963; m. Georgia Ann McNeil; Children--Andrea Lisa, Roslyn Arlene; pastor, First Bapt. Ch., 1948--; moderator, Robeson Bapt. Union, 1959-63; pres., Lumberton Civic Comm., 1958-63; chrmn., Central Divisional Comm. Boy Scouts of Amer., 1963; mem., Exec. Comm. Lott Carey Foreign Mission Conv., USA; Sun. Sch. Bd. Natl. Bapt. Conv., 1961; Exec. Comm. Gen. Bapt. State Conv. of N.C.; recording sec., Gen. Bd., Gen. Bapt. State Conv.; Bd. of Dirs., Robeson Co. TB Assn.; Chaplain's Adv. Comm., Southeastern Gen. Hosp.; N.C. Coun. of Chs.; N.C. Comm. on Rel. and Race; Lumberton City Coun., 1961; register, Voting Precinct No. 6; mem., Precinct Comm. No. 4; del., State Democratic Conv., 1964; Community Service Award, 1962;

mem., Mason; N.C. Municipal Assn.; N.C. Assn. of Licensed Day Care Facilities; Child Welfare League of Amer.; author: "A Biography of Wm. Henry Knuckles," 1962; "The Pastor's Helper," 1961; Home: 139 Spruce St., Lumberton, N.C.; Office: 504 W. 2nd St., Lumberton, N.C.

TURNER, Franklin Delton, b. Norwood, N.C., July 19, 1933; s. James and Dora S.; A.B., Livingstone Coll., Salisbury, N.C., 1956; S.T.B., Berkeley Div. Sch., New Haven, Conn., 1965; social work courses, W. Va. Univ., Morgantown, W. Va., 1961-62; m. Barbara Dickerson; Children--Jennifer Lynn; Kimberly Jill; vicar, Ch. of the Epiphany and chap., Bishop Coll., Dallas, Tex., 1965-66; rector, St. George's Prot. Episc. Ch., Wash., D.C., 1966-present; pres., Com. of Community Improvement, Inc., 1968-present; mem., Wash. Episc. Clergy Assn., pres., Wash. Clericus, Diocese of Wash., 1968-69; Home: 1340 Jackson St., NE, Wash. D.C., 20017; Office: 2nd and You Sts. NW, Wash., D.C. 20001

TURNER, Howard Ellis, b. Wash., D.C., May 10, 1919; s. Howard W. and Ida E.; B.Th., Frelinghuysen Sch. of Rel.; D.D. (hon.), Northwestern Coll.; m. Virginia M. Nickens; pastor, 1952-54, Mt. Calvary Bapt. Ch., Orange, Va.; Carron Bapt. Ch., Wash., D.C., 1954-present; mem., Com. of 100 Ministers; v.p., Natl. Capitol Bapt. Conv., 1944-46; Med. Corp. Army Med. Tech., Military awards, Asiatic Pacific Theater, Philippine Liberation and Army Occupation of Japan; Home: 525 Van Buren St. NW, Wash., D.C. 20012; Office: 3104 Ga. Ave. NW, Wash., D.C. 20010

TURNER, Jury Ethward, b. New Albany, Miss., Aug. 15, 1915; s. Rogers G. and Rena (Jackson) T.; Fisk Univ., 1934-36, B.S., A & T. Coll., Greensboro, N.C.; B.D., Gammon Theol. Sem., Atlanta, Ga., 1947; grad. study, Univ. of So. Calif., Los Angeles, Calif., 1942-43; Cornell Univ., Ithaca, N.Y., 1961; m. Ophelia Turner; Children--Joyce Rena, Floy Christina, Jaunell Denitra, Lyris Agvett; ministry: Clark Chapel Meth. Ch., 1943-46, McMimmville, Tenn., Stone River Circuit, Murfreesboro, Tenn., 1946-47; Patterson Meml. Meth. Ch., Nashville, Tenn., 1947-present; principal, Bernard High Sch., McMimmville, Tenn., mathematics tchr., Cameron H.S., Nashville, Tenn., (18 yrs.) ; mem., Nashville Chrstn.

Leadership Coun.; Tenn. Educational Congress; Middle Tenn. Tchrs. Assn.; Tenn. Mathematics Assn.; NEA Mathematics Assn.; Kappa Alpha Psi; Home: 1111 32nd Ave. N. Nashville, Tenn.; Office: 316 Whitsitt St., Nashville, Tenn. 37211

TURNER, Maynard Philip, Jr., sem. pres., b. St. Louis, Mo., s. Maynard Philip and Alma Elizabeth; A. B., Fisk Univ., 1934; B. D., Eden Theol. Sem., Webster Grove, Mo.; Th. D., Central Bapt. Theol. Sem., Kansas City, Kans.; m. Edna Earl Hall; sci. instr., Western Coll., Kansas City, Mo.; dean, Western Bapt. Sem., Kansas City, Mo., 1944-49; dean, Sch. of Rel., Bishop Coll., 1949-50; pres., Western Bapt. Sem., 1950-55; pastor, Mozart Bapt. Ch., Chgo., Ill., 1957; Mt. Zion Bapt. Ch., Nashville, Tenn., 1960--; v. p., Interdenom. Min. Fellowship; v. p., Middle Region, Tenn. Bapt. Miss. & Ed. Conv.; former mem., Comm. on Theol. Ed., Natl. Coun. of Chs.; Mayor's Comm. on the Aging; Comm. on Chs., Nashville br. NAACP; mem., Bd. of Nashville Chrstn. Leadership Coun.; chrmn., UNCF Drive, Nashville, 1964; mem., Alpha Phi Alpha; Frontiers Intl.; Soc. of Biblical Lit. & Exegesis; Sigma Rho Sigma; Kappa Delta Pi; articles and address, Bulletin of Negro History; Congressional Record; Laymen Sun. Sch. in former; Home: 1910 15th Ave., So. Nashville, Tenn.; Office: 1112 Jefferson St., Nashville, Tenn.

*TURNER, Samuel, Jr., coll. prof., b. Memphis, Tenn., Aug. 21, 1935; s. Samuel and Lelia (Bland) T.; B. S., LeMoyne Coll., 1958; B. D., Howard Univ., Sch. of Rel., 1961; m. Naomi Turner; Children--Samuel III, Ruth E.; pastor, Hollywood Heights Presbyn. Ch., Shreveport, La., 1961-62; dean of instruction, Butler Coll., Tyler, Tex., 1962--; Mt. Olive Bapt. Ch., Winona, Tex., 1964--; mem., NAACP; Democrat; Home: Butler Coll., Tyler, Tex.

TURNER, William Davis, b. Charleston, S. C., Jan. 4, 1911; s. Richard M. and Lillie (Davis) T.; A. B., St. Augustine Coll., 1934; Bishop Payne Div. Sch., Petersburg, Va.; S. T. B., Temple Univ., Div. Sch., 1948; m. Dorothy Virginia Norris; Children--Anne Yvonne (Mrs. Anthony Avelino), Alice Patricia, William Davis, Jr.; vicar, Ch. of the Good Shepherd, Sumter, S. C.; St. Augustine's Ch., Sumter Co., 1938-40; St. Stephen's Ch., Savannah, Ga., 1940-42; rector, St. Stephen's Prot.

Episc. Ch., Petersburg, Va., 1942-43; St. Augustine's P. E. Ch., Phila., Pa., 1943-present; mem., Bd. of Dirs., Volunteers in Sickle Cell Anemia, Phila., Pa.; Humanitarian Award, Volunteers in Sickle Cell Anemia, 1960; Home: 3825 Pulaski Ave., Phila., Pa.; Office: 27th St. and Girard Ave., Phila., Pa.

*TYMS, James Daniel, sem. prof., b. Aberdeen, Miss., Jan. 2, 1905; s. Lawrence and Nancy T.; A. B., Lincoln Univ., Jefferson City, Mo., 1934; B. D., Howard Univ., Sch. of Rel., 1937; M. A., Grad. Sch., Howard Univ., 1938; Ph. D., Boston Univ., 1942; D. D., Western Bapt. Sem., Kansas City, Mo., 1958; m. Brittie Ann Martin; pastor, New Hope Bapt. Ch., Winchester, Mass., 1940-42; tchr., Morehouse Coll., 1942-47; Sch. of Rel., Howard Univ., 1947--; Fellow, Gen. Ed. Bd., 1944-45; mem., Religious Ed. Assn.; Assn. Sem. Profs. in Practical Field; Inst. of Religion; Fullbright Research Scholar, Gold Coast, W. Africa; lectr., State Dept. (U. S.) Inst. Foreign Affairs on Chrstn. Ed. in Ghanain Culture; book review ed., Journal of Religious Thought; author, The Rise of Religious Education Among Negro Baptists. Contrib. Roucek, J. S. ed. The Negro Impact on Western Civilization. Home: 1729 Varnum St. NW, Wash., D. C. 20011; Office: School of Rel., Howard Univ., Wash. D. C.

TYNES, Morris Harrison, b. Lynchburg, Va., May 12, 1923; s. Joseph W. and Lucy (Rich) T.; B. S., N. C. Agri. & Tech. Coll., 1944; B. D., Yale Div. Sch., 1947; studied, Univ. of Mich.; LL. D. (hon.), Va. Theol. Sem. & Coll., 1957; D. D. (hon.), Western Theol. Sem., 1958; m. Lillian Marguerite Payne; Children--Lillian Marguerite, Sharon Rose, Morrisine Marie; Dean of Theol., Va. Sem., Lynchburg, Va., 1947-49; pastor, 8th St. Bapt. Ch., 1947-49; Mt. Zion Bapt. Ch., Staunton, Va., 1949-53; Monumental Bapt. Ch., Chgo., Ill., 1953-present; mem., NAACP; mem., Adv. Bd. of Chgo. Ch. Federations Social Service Dept.; Bd. mem., Chgo. Urban League; former chrmn., Chrstn. Action Comm., Univ. of Chgo.; pres., United Chrstn. Fellowship of Chgo.; v. p., Chgo. League of Voters; chrmn., Adv. Bd., Gen. Bapt. State Conv.; Bd. mem., Minister's Civic League; Bd. mem., Dept. of Chrstn. Life & Work, Natl. Coun. Chs. of Chrst; participant in United Chrstn. Preaching Mission in Knoxville, Tenn.; Bd. mem., Chgo. Conf. for Brotherhood and chrmn. of Exec. Comm.; Alpha Phi Alpha; Mason; Home: 6757 St. Lawrence Ave., Chgo., Ill.;

Office: 729 E. Oakwood Blvd., Chgo., Ill.

TYSON, Charles Edward, b. Asheboro, N. C., July 25, 1925; s. Levy and Martha T.; B. S., A & T Coll., N. C., 1960; B. D., Southeastern Bapt. Theol. Sem., 1964; Internship, Pastoral Clinic Trng., Duke Univ. Med. Center, 1966; m. Maude Brady; Children--Angeline A.; pastor, St. Homes Meth. Ch., Wilkesboro, N. C. and The Phila. Meth. Ch., Durham, N. C., 1962-66; Asbury Temple Meth. Ch., Durham, N. C.; chap., S. C. Dept. of Corrections, 1966-present; mem., Bd. of Dir., Campus Ministry, Duke Univ., 1962-65; mem., Bd. of Dir., The United Campus Ministry, N. C. Coll., 1962-67; ran for membership in the Asheboro City Sch. Bd., 1957; ran for City Coun., 1959; US Navy, 1943-46; 1950-51; mem., Columbia Coun. on Human Rel.; Columbia Ministerial Assn.; Republican; mem., S. C. Law Enforcement Officer's Assn.; mem., Amer. Correctional Chaplains Assn.; The Amer. Prot. Correction Chaplains Assn.; Home: 4211 Grant St., Columbia, S. C. 29203; Office: 1515 Gist St., Columbia, S. C. 29202

UPSHAW, Robert Lee, presiding elder, b. Union Springs, Ala., Sept. 28, 1900; s. William and Lucretia U.; A. B., B. D., Payne Sem., 1939; D. D. (hon.), Monrovia Univ., W. Africa; m. Sylvia A. Matthews; Children--Robert C., Connie M.; tchr., Pike Co., Houston Co., Bullock Co., Ala.; dean, Central Coll., Birmingham, Ala.; v. p., Ministers Conf., Hampton, Va., 2 yrs.; presiding elder, The Allegheny Dist., Afr. Meth. Episc. Ch.; Home: 1322 Sylvan Ave., Homestead, Pa.

UPTON, Milton Leon, educator, b. Sweetwater, Tenn., Nov. 23, 1925; s. Elihu Howard and Hattie (Cleveland) U.; A. B., Knoxville Coll., 1950; B. D., Gammon Theol. Sem., 1956; grad. studies, Gammon Theol. Sem. and Atlanta Univ. toward S. T. M., Soc. of Rel.; m. Marcella Ellis; Children--Linda Carol, Mildred Elaine, Leander Howard; pastor, Freedmen Cumberland Presby. Ch., Athens, Tenn., 1947-50; St. James C. P. Ch., Cleveland, Tenn., 1948; Pulpit Assn., 1st Congre. Ch., Atlanta, Ga., 1954-56; minister, 1st Congre., Marietta, Ga., 1955-56; Rush Meml. Congre., Atlanta, 1956-58; present, Beecher Meml. Congre. Ch., New Orleans, La., 1958--; Dean of Men & Instr., Alcorn A & M Coll. (Miss.), 1950-53; research asst., Ford Found., Dillard Univ.; mem., Bd.

Dirs., Met. Assn. for Blind, Carrie-Steele-Pitts Children's Home (Atlanta), 1957-58; Campfire Girls, Atlanta, 1956-58; Bd. mem., NAACP, New Orleans, 1959-63; Community Relations Coun. of N. O., 1964; N. O. Urban League, 1960--; dir., Voter Reg., Coord. Coun. of N. O., 1961; v. p., Interdenom. Min. Alliance, N. O.; chrmn., Soc. Action Comm., So. Central Conf., UCC, 1963--; US Navy, Seaman 1st Class, 1944-46; recipient, Victory Medal, Battle of Philippines, et al, Baden Powell Statuette; Outstanding Citizen Award, Radio Sta. WYLD; Outstanding Civic Leader Award, N. O. A. M. E. Ch.; Citizenship Award, Omega Psi Phi; mem., Omega Psi Phi; Prince Hall Mason, Frontiers Intl., YMCA, Toastmasters Club, Y's Men's Club, Consumers League of N. O., Greater New Orleans Assn. of Day Care Centers; sec., Chrstn. Communications Fellowship of New Orelans; partial research for The Negro Leadership Class, Thompson, D. C.; contributor to church journals; Home: 1912 N. Miro St., New Orleans, La. 70119; Church: 1914 N. Miro St., New Orleans, La.

*VAN BUREN, William George, b. Monticello, Ga., 1929; B. A., Dillard Univ., New Orleans, La., 1957; M. Div., Howard Univ., Sch. of Rel., 1968; m. Barbara Wells; Children--George and Emily; Counselor, D. C. Welfare Dept.; dir., Com. Service, Joint Community Prog. Bd., St. Louis, Mo.; Hotel and Restaurant Loc. 781, Wash., D. C., 1958-63; D. C. Public Welfare Dept., coun., 1963-68; Dir. of Community Services of Pilgrim Congre. Ch., Union Ave. Chrstn. Ch., and Westminster Presby. Ch., St. Louis, Mo., 1968--; Office: 5300 Delmar Blvd., St. Louis, Mo. 63112

VAN CROFT, William Arthur, Jr., s. William Arthur and Gertrude Dillon V.; A. B., St. Augustine's Coll., Raleigh, N. C., 1946-49; S. T. B., The General Theol. Sem., 1949-52; Shaw Univ., summer 1948; m. Ruby May Rainey; Children--William Arthur III; ordained in Diocese of Newark, 1952; curate, St. Luke's Episc. Ch., Wash., D. C., 1952-62; current rector, St. Luke's Episc. Ch., 1962--; chap., D. C. Natl. Guard, 1955--; chap., Boys Village of Md., 1953--; mem., Bd. of Dirs., Northwest Settlement House, 1962--; Diocesan Com., State of the Ch.; Com. on the Deacons Trng. Program; Com. on the Diocese of Wash. Summer Urban Program; staff mem. on Summer Conf. for Diocesan Youth Conf.; Dept. of Chrstn. Ed. (Diocese of Wash.); US Army,

N. Africa, Italy, France, Germany, 1943-45; awards: Four bronze stars; Good Conduct Medal; Meritorious Service Award; mem., Omega Psi Phi; Home: 2705 13th St. NE, Wash., D.C. 20019; Office: 1514 15th St. NW, Wash., D.C. 20005

VARNER, Samuel Lee, b. Opelika, Ala., Oct. 19, 1937; s. Will and Sarah; B.A., Livingstone Coll., Salisbury, N.C., 1962; B.D., Interdenom. Theol. Sem., 1966; m. Ruth Suggs; student pastor, Inner-city Prot. Parish, Cleveland, O.; E. Harlem Prot. Parish, NYC; Iona Community, Ch. of Scotland, Greenock, Scotland; Work-study travel seminar, Kenya, E. Africa; pastor, 1st Ref. Ch. UCC, Cincinnati, O.; former grad. asst., Scarritt Coll., Nashville, Tenn.; mem., SNCC; CORE; Fellowship of Reconciliation, Iona Community; Omega Psi Phi; Home: 1512 F. Dudley St., Cincinnati, O. 45214; Office: 1809 Freeman Ave., Cincinnati, O. 45214

*VAUGHAN, Alfred Austin, b. Beckley, W.Va., June 6, 1922; s. Charles and Lillian (Poney) V.; B.A., Morehouse Coll., 1946; B.D., Howard Univ., Sch. of Rel., 1952; courses M.A.; m. Martha Butterworth; Children--Michael Phillip, Charles, Mechele; pastor, Cherry Hill Meth. Ch., Balto., Md., 1954-56; Prince Frederick Meth. Charge, 1956-60; Union St. Meth. Ch., Westminster, Md.; current, Union Meth. Ch., Aberdeen, Md., 1961--; tchr., Jr. High Sch., Elbert Co., Ga., 1946-47; dean of chapel, tchr., Fla. Indus. Sch., St. Augustine, Fla., 1949-50; mem., NAACP; Hartford County Human Relations Coun.; Meth. Min. Assn.; Home: Old Post Rd., Box 9, Aberdeen, Md.

VERRETT, Joseph C., educator, b. New Orelans, La., Jan. 17, 1930; s. Joseph C. and Mary Stella (Smith) V.; Epiphany Apostolic Coll., Newburgh, N.Y.; St. Joseph's Sem., Wash., D.C.; B.S. Ed., Loyola Univ., New Orleans, La., 1958; S.T.L., Angelicum Univ., Rome, 1962; J.C.B., Cath. Univ., Wash., D.C., 1963; M.A. Ed., Xavier Univ., 1964; ordained priest, Roman Cath. Ch., 1955; instr., Engl., Lat., dramatics, St. Augustine H.S., New Orleans, 1959-60; asst. prin., 1960-61; instr., Latin and English, couns.-teach., moderator of dramatics, asst. prin., St. Augustine H.S., New Orleans, La., 1963--; mem., Natl. Cath. Theatre Conf., Natl. Coun. Tchrs. of Eng.; mem., of the Josephite Fathers; Home: St. Augustine H.S., 2600 London Ave., New Orleans,

La., 70119

WACTOR, James Wesley, b. Hoke Co., N. C., Sept. 13, 1908; s. Henry Lee and Annie Bell (Campbell) W.; A. B., Livingstone Coll., Salisbury, N. C., 1935; D. D. (hon.), Livingstone Coll., 1955; courses, Union Theol. Sem., N. Y. C.; Harvard Univ. Sch. for Chaplains; m. Hildred Anita Henry; pastor, Mainville Circuit, Salisbury Dist., Granite Quarry and New Hope Salisbury Dist., Western N. C. Conf.; Young's Chapel, Morristown, Tenn., Asheville Dist.; Keslser Temple, N. C.; Mattocks Meml., Fayetteville, N. C.; Red Springs, N. C.; Barry Ave. A. M. E. Z. Ch., Long Is., N. Y.; Hood Meml. A. M. E. Z. Ch., N. Y. C.; Big Zion, Mobile, Ala., 1960-64; Metro. A. M. E. Z. Ch., Birmingham, Ala., 1964-present; mem., Evangl. Com., Prot. Coun. of Chs., 1954-56; Inter-racial Com., Billy Graham Crusade for N. Y. C.; Bd. of Dirs., Citizens Fed. Savings & Loan Assn., Ala.; dean, A. M. E. Z. Minister's & Laymen's Inst., Birmingham; tchr., "Spiritual Life of the Meth. Ch., A. M. E. Z. Conf.; mem., Ch. Extension Bd., A. M. E. Z. Ch., Bd. of Trustees, Lomax-Hannon Jr. Coll., Greenville, Ala.; Bd. of Trustees, A. M. E. Z. Ch. for the North Ala. Conf.; Bd. of Dir., A. G. Gaston Boys Club, Ala.; US Army Chap., 1943-48; cited for erecting first Amer. Chapel on German soil, 1946; dir., German Youth Activities Prog. for Kaiser Wilhelm Kaserne; Bd. of Dir., German Youth Activities, Manheimn, Germany; Home: 1524 4th Ave., No. Birmingham, Ala. 35203

WADSWORTH, James Edward, Jr., b. Indianapolis, Ind., May 17, 1923; s. James Edward and Catherine (Carpenter) W.; Va. State Coll., 1942-47; B. S., Butler Univ., Indianapolis, Ind., 1948-49; B. D., Pittsburgh Theol. Sem., 1949-52; pastor, First United Presbyterian Ch., Tenn., 1952-53; St. Mark's Community Ch., Detroit, Mich. 1953--; corrections commissioner, Mich. Dept. of Corrections; pres., Detroit br. NAACP; commissioner, Fair Election Practices Commn., 1964; an active participant in the selective buying prog. sponsored by the Negro Ministers of Detroit; mem., Detroit Pastor's Union; Detroit Interdenom. Min. Alliance; Kappa Alpha Psi; Democrat; Guardian Club; NAACP; Pioneer Club; Thursday Luncheon Club; Home: 2212 Atkinson, Detroit, Mich.; Office: 9321 Twelfth St., Detroit, Mich.

WALDEN, Charles Eugene, Jr., b. Washington, D.C., Feb. 2, 1922; s. Charles Eugene and Lillian (Coleman) W.; Wilberforce Univ., 1937-38; A.B., Magna Cum Laude, How. Univ., 1941; B.D., Grad. Sch. of Theol., Oberlin Coll., 1943; grad. work, Drew Univ.; m. Wilhelmina Brower; Children--Charles Clayton, Karen Laverne, Deborah Hean, Frances Marlene, Stephanie Charlene; prof., Rural Sociology and Ch. Administration, Turner Theol. Sem., Morris Brown Coll., Atlanta, Ga., 1945-46; pastor, Trinity A.M.E. Ch., Ridgely, Md., 1947-50; asst. to vicar, Atonement Episc. Chapel, 1950-52; present: vicar, St. Philip's Episc. Ch., 1952--; visiting lectr., Rural Ch. Extension Program, Phelps-Stokes Fund (N.C. - Shaw Univ. & Livingstone Coll.; Ala., Miss., Tenn., (Fisk Univ.) Kentucky, Fla., Va., Ga. (Ga. State Coll.); visiting preacher, D.C. Village; counselor, Diocese of Wash. Youth Conf., 1953; mem., Dept. of Promotion, 1956-58; mem., Ch. School Div., Dept. of Chrstn. Ed., 1960-62; Chaplain and Bd. mem., Whipper Home for Unwed Mothers, 1958-60; chrmn., Area Commissioners' Youth Coun., 1956-58; bd. mem., Planned Parenthood Assn. of D.C., 1959-61; mem., Clergy Adv. Comm., Planned Parenthood; mem., Parents' Adv. Comm. Ripon Coll., Wis., 1962-64; chap. (Capt.), Natl. Capitol Wing, Civil Air Patrol; pres., Davis Sch. PTA, 1961-62; mem., Adv. Comm., Spec. Services, D.C. Tuberculosis Assn.; prog. chrmn., Potomac Area Coun., Campfire Girls, 1961; merit badge counselor, Natl. Capitol Coun., Boy Scouts of America; citation: J. Finley Wilson Meml. Lodge No. 1371, IBPOE of W., "for effective performance measuring to the high standards in community service... sharing skills and knowledge ..." 1958; Omega Psi Phi; Home: 1200 45th Place, SE, Wash., D.C.; Office: 2431 Shannon Pl., SE, Wash., D.C.

*WALKER, Arnold George, b. Talladega, Nov. 9, 1935; s. Arnold George and Doris (Vick) W.; B.S., B.D., Howard Univ., Wash., D.C., 1956, 1959; chaplain-trainee, D.C. Gen. Hosp., 1959; chap. intern, Med. Coll., Va. Hosp. Div., 1960; pastor, Bethany Presby. Ch., Lumberton, N.C., 1962--; pres., Lumberton Citizens Civic Comm.; Good Neighbors Coun., 1964; sec., Lumberton Min. Assn., 1963--; mem., Omega Psi Phi; Lumberton Interracial Organization; Home: 523 Ninth, Lumberton, N.C.; Office: Elizabethtown Rd., Lumberton, N.C.

WALKER, Henry W.B., b. Charlotte Co., Va., Sept. 27,

1903; s. Charlie and Lucy Walker (Slaughter); A. B., Va. Seminary; B. D., Temple Univ.; S. T. M., Union Sem., N. Y.; completed work for Th. D. from Temple Univ.; m. Anita Freeman Barettee; Children--Mrs. Helen Hunt (adopted); pastor, Mt. Zion Bapt. Chs., Appomattox, Va.; Brooksville Bapt. Ch., Lynchburg, Va.; Bapt. Chs., Piedmount, Yanceys, Mills, Va.; mem., Mason; Elk; Phi Beta Sigma; tchr. and dean of the Theol. Dept. of Va. Sem. and Coll., 9 yrs.; current pastor, Second Calvary Bapt. Ch., Norfolk, Va.; pres., The Bapt. Min. Conf. of Norfolk, Portsmouth and vicinity; v. p., Inter-Racial Min. Assn.; pres., Civic League, 2 yrs.; mem., Hampton Min. Conf. Bd.; v. p., Va. Bapt. Conv.; Natl. Bapt. Conv. of Amer.; v. p., Trustee Bd., Va. Sem., Lynchburg, Va.; US chap., 1941-44; Capt.; Home: 6740 Newtown Rd., Va. Beach, Va.; Office: Croprew and Godfrey Ave., Norfolk, Va.

WALKER, John Thomas, b. Barnesville, Ga., July 2, 1925; s. Joseph and Mattie (Wyche) W.; B. A., Wayne State Univ., Detroit, Mich., 1951; B. D., Episc. Theol. Sem., Alexandria, Va., 1954; m. Rose Maria Flores; Children --Thomas Peyton; pastor, St. Mary's Prot. Episc. Ch., Detroit, Mich.; tchr., St. Paul's Sch., Concord, N. H., 1957-64; mem., New Hampshire Adv. Com. of the US Civil Rights Commn.; Office: St. Paul's Sch., Concord, N. H.

WALKER, Lucius, Jr., b. Roselle, N. J., Aug. 3, 1930; s. Lucius and Bertha (W.); B. A., Shaw Univ., Raleigh, N. C., 1954; B. D., Andover Newton Theol. Sem., Newton Centre, Mass., 1958; M. S., Soc. Work, Univ. of Wis., Milwaukee, Wis., 1963; Clinical Trng. Lab., Wash., D. C., 1959; Inst. on Administration, Hull House, Natl. Fed. of Settlements and Neighborhood Centers, Jan. 1962; mem., research team, "The People of the Inner Core - North;" research, No. Neighborhood House; pastor of youth, Beth-Eden Bapt. Ch., Waltham, Mass., 1954-57; dir., Boys Activities, Milwaukee Chrstn. Center, 1957-61; lectr., Theory and Practice of Group Leadership, Sch. of Soc. Welfare; Univ. of Wis., Milwaukee, 1964-67; Ex. Dir., Northcott Neighborhood House; Ex. Dir., Inter-Religious Found. for Community Organization, N. Y., 1967-present; Home: 615 Piermont Rd., Demarest, N. J. 07627; Office: Inter-Religious Found. for Community Organization, 815 Second Ave., Room 1603, New York, N. Y. 10017

WALKER, William James, b. Detroit, Mich., May 29, 1937; s. James and Mattie; B.A., Lane Coll., Jackson, Tenn., 1958; M.A., McCormick Theol. Sem., Chgo., Ill., 1961; Grad. Cert., Gen. Theol. Sem., N.Y., 1962; Cert., Clinical Pastoral Trng., Augustana Hosp., Chgo., Ill., 1962; m. Guelda Joyce White; curate, Grace Episc. Ch., Detroit, Mich. 1962-64; rector, St. Philip's Episc. Ch., Jacksonville, Fla., 1964-65; staff, All Saints' Episc. Ch., Indianapolis, Ind., 1965-67; rector, St. Augustine's Episc. Ch., Gary, Ind., 1968-present; instr., Flanner House, Indianapolis, Ind., 1966-67; mem., NCNC; Assn. for Clinical Pastoral Ed.; chrmn., Citizens Com. for Adoptive Parenthood; Bd., Lake Co. Inner-city Task Force; mem., Alpha Phi Alpha; Home: 2406 Madison St., Gary, Ind. 46407; Office: 2425 W. 19th Ave., Gary, Ind. 46404

WALKER, William Raphael, b. Clarksville, Tex., May 26, 1918; s. George Henry, Sr. and Nettie (Burks) W.; B.S., Wilberforce Univ., O., 1950; B.D., Payne Theol. Sem., Wilberforce, O., 1951; m. Vera Marie Fossett; Children--Vickie Sue, William Jr., John Edward, George Henry, Vera Marie, Vivian Kaye; pastor, Quinn Afr. Meth. Episc. Ch., Wilmington, O., 1947-51; St. Paul A.M.E. Ch., Bellaire, O. and Wayman A.M.E. Ch., Martins Ferry, O., 1951-61; current pastor, Trinity A. M.E. Ch., Springfield, O., 1961--; chrmn., Inter-racial Comm., Clark Co., O.; sec., Bd. of Dirs., Grace Tatum Nursery Sch.; Bd. of Dirs., Union Settlement House; mem., Budget Comm. of the United Appeals Fund of Clark Co.; mem., Trustee Bd. of Trustee Bd. of the United Appeals Fund of Clark Co., O.; US Air Forces, staff sgt., 3 yrs.; Cert. of Merit, Third Episc. Dist., Afr. Meth. Ch. for Distinguished and Unselfish Service, for Faithful Devotion to Duty, for Loyalty to the cause of Chrstn. Ed., 1954; Mason; pres., Inter-denom. Alliance of Springfield, O.; chief sec., Ohio Annual Conf., Trustee of the Ohio A.M.E. Ch. Annual Conf.; Trustee, Payne Theol. Sem.; Home: 506 W. Southern Ave., Springfield, O.; Office: Trinity A.M.E. Ch., 554 Selma Rd., Springfield, O.

WALKER, Wyatt Tee, civil rights leader, b. Brockton, Mass., Aug. 15, 1929; s. John Wise and Maude (Pinn) W.; B.S., Va. Union Univ.; B.D., Sch. of Rel., Va. Union Univ.; m. Theresa Edwards; Children--Anne Patrice, Wyatt Jr., Robert, Earl; pastor, Gillfied Bapt.

Ch., Petersburg, Va. (8 yrs.); ex. asst., Southern Chrstn. Leadership Conf.; v.p. in charge of marketing and service, Amer. Ed. Heritage, Inc. (For 2 yrs. on loan from So. Chrstn. Leadership Conf. to help in developing and distributing Negro History Library; to help diminish the "cultural block out" that has been imposed on the Negro community in Amer.); pres., NAACP, Va., 5 yrs.; state dir., CORE; Natl. Bd. Mem., So. Chrstn. Leadership Conf.; Trustee, Va. Theol. Sem. & Coll.; pres., PTA; Visitors League; pres. and Bd. mem., Va. Coun. on Human Relations; Elks Awards; Natl. Civil Rights Award; mem., Alpha Phi Alpha; Office: American Educational Heritage, Inc., 733 Yonkers Ave., Yonkers, N.Y.

WALLACE, Eustace Fieldings, b. Bearden, Ark., Nov. 23, 1896; s. Christopher C. and Mary (Walker) W.; attended Philander Smith Coll. 1937, and 1951-54; m. Mamie Swinger; Children--Mrs. Elren Hutchinson, Mrs. Edith Harris, Mrs. Agnes Myers, Marion; ministry: pastor in Ark., 1927-48; Dist. supt., 1948-54; pastored in Okla., 1954-61; pastored in Ark. 1961-62; present, Dist. Supt. of the Little Rock Dist., Ark., of the Meth. Ch., 1962; taught pub. sch., 1916-18; 32nd degree Mason since 1940; mem., Republican Pary; Home: 3215 Arch St., Little Rock, Ark.

WALLACE, Robert Clayton, b. Galveston, Tex., Nov. 20, 1905; s. William and Margaret (Roper) W.; B.A., Knoxville Coll., 1937; (cand. M.A.), Howard Univ. Sch. of Rel., 1939; m. Arnetta McKamey - Gravely; ordained 1943, Mt. Zion Bapt.; asstd. in founding Prairie Ave. Bapt. Ch., Chgo., Ill., 1930; asst. pastor, Prairie Ave. Bapt. Ch., 1930-33; mail clerk, Tenn. Valley Authority, Knoxville, Tenn.; USO dir., United Service Organ., Clarksville, Tenn.; Pensacola, Fla., 1943-46; dir., Chrstn. Ed. and asst. pastor, Mt. Zion Bapt. Ch., Knoxville, Tenn., 1946-48; edited ch. paper; mem., Natl. Bapt. Conv., 1948-50; pastor, Prairie Ave. Bapt. Ch., Chgo., 1954-58; Exec. Dean, Chgo. Bapt. Inst., 1954-present; consultant on Chrstn. Ed., First Bapt. Ch., Nashville, Tenn.; educ. consultant, Tenn. Bapt. Leadership Ed. Congress; educ. consultant of 4-yr. prog. commn., Natl. Sun. Sch. & B.T.U. Congress, Natl. Bapt. Conv.; mem., Natl. Coun. of Chs., Div. of Chrstn. Ed.; Ex. Comm., 23rd Intl. Sun. Sch. Conv., Cleveland, O., 1955; Bd. of Mgrs., Chicago Bible Soc.; Theol. and Biblical commentator, Chrstn. Ed. Conf., Bapt. Assembly; del., Observer Natl. Conf. on Rel. and Race, Chgo., 1963; del., Natl. Conf. on Civil Rights Legis., Univ. of Nev., 1963; del., Race Relations Inst., Fisk Univ., 1964-65; Adv. Comm., Soc. Welfare Dept., Ch. Federation, Chgo., 1965; Operation Breadbasket; SCLC, Chgo., 1966; contributing editor, The Independent Call, (ch. paper); co-author, Leadership in the Sunday School and Youth Program Vol. II; meditation speaker, TV and radio series; TV panelist, "New Trends in Theol. Ed.;" Cert. of Merit, Tenn. Bapt. Leadership Congress, 1951; Cert. of Achievement, Sun. Sch. Pub. Bd., 1958; Oscar award Women's Auxiliary, New Era Dist. Assn., 1956; Cert. of Merit, Bapt. State Conv., Ill., 1961; Award of Merit, Mt. Zion Bapt. Ch., Chgo., 1961; Citizens Award, radio sta., WBEE, Chgo, 1965; Home: 5120 S. Parkway, Chicago, Ill. 60615

WALLER, Alfred M., Sr., b. Va., Dec. 8, 1920; s. Alexander C. and Elizabeth W.; A. B., Va. Union Univ., 1946; B. D., Union Univ., Sch. of Rel., 1948; grad. courses, Univ. of Pittsburgh; m. Belva Williams; Children--Alfred, Alexander, Wendy, Alyn; pastor, Westwood Bapt. Ch., Richmond, Va., 1945-48; New Hope Bapt. Ch., Braddock, Pa., 1948-63; Shiloh Bapt. Ch., Cleveland, O., 1963-present; moderator, Allegheny Union Bapt. Assn., (Western Pa.), 4 yrs.; pres., Bapt. Min. Conf., Pittsburgh, 2 yrs.; co-chrmn., Com. on Human Rights; NAACP (E. Burroughs br.); repr., Natl. B. T. U. Bd. (Natl. Bapt. Conv.), 1 yr.; asst. to chaplain, State Penitentiary, Richmond, Va.; Republican; Omega Psi Phi; Mason; Office: 5500 Scoville Ave., Cleveland, O. 44104

WALLS, William Jacob, bishop, b. Chimney Rock, N. C., May 8, 1885; s. Edward and Harriet (Edgerton) W.; A. B., Livingstone Coll., Salisbury, N. C., 1908; B. D., Hood Theol. Sem., 1913; D. D., (Hon.), Livingstone Coll., 1918; LL. D. (hon.), 1943; A. M., Univ. of Chgo., 1941; m. Dorothy Louise Jordan; pastor, Eleveland, N. C., 1905-07; Lincolnton, N. C., 1908-10; Salisbury, N. C., 1910-13; Louisville, Ky., 1913-20; editor, Star of Zion, Charlotte, N. C., 1920-24; bishop, Afr. Meth. Episc. Zion Ch., 1924; chrmn., Bd. of Publ., 1930; chrmn., Bd. of Home Missions, Resident in Chgo., 1930; chap., WW I; chrmn., Bd. of Trustees, Livingstone Coll.; trustee, Gammon Theol. Sem.; chrmn., Afr. Meth. Episc. Zion Sesquicentennial, 1946; del., Gen.

Con. M. E. Ch., South, 1918; M. E. Ch., 1928; del., Ecumenical Meth. Conf., London, England, 1921; Atlanta, Ga., 1931; Springfield, Mass., 1947; Oxford, England, 1951; v. p., World Meth. Conf. 1951; mem., Pres.'s and War Sec.'s Amer. Clergymen's Comm. to occupied countries in Europe, 1947; mem., Exec. Bd., Natl. Coun. of Chs. of Christ in USA; mem., Commn. Cultural and Human Relations, 1954; del., World Coun. of Chs., Amsterdam, Holland, 1948; mem., Message and Central Committees since 1948; Exec. Comm., World Meth. Coun., 1956; del., World Chrstn. Ed. and Sun. Sch. Conv., Tokyo, 1958; v. p., Divinity Sch.; trustee, United Intl. Chrstn. Endeavor Soc.; mem., Religious Educational Assn.; Intl. Coun. Religious Ed.; World's Sun. Sch. Assn.; Natl. Coun. of Chs. of Christ America (Gen. bd.); treas., Fraternal Coun., Chs. of America; mem., NAACP; Amer. Acd. Political Science; chap., Natl. Negro Business League; mem., Phi Beta Sigma; Republican; Mason; Odd Fellow; K. P.; Elk; author: J. C. Price Educator and Race Leader; Pastorates and Reminiscences; What Youth Wants; The Dream of Youth; The Romance of A College; Home: 4736 So. Parkway, Chgo., Ill.; Retired.

WALLS, William Roscoe, b. Winston-Salem, N. C., Nov. 3, 1926, s. Porvioys and Nannie (Barber); A. B., Johnson C. Smith Univ., B. D., J. C. Smith Univ., 1949 and 1952 respectively; m. Gertrude Hinos; pastor, Phila. Meth. Ch., Rockingham, N. C., 1952-53; Laughton Meth. Ch., Greensboro, N. C., 1953-55; Broad Presby. Ch., Statesville, N. C.; 1955-61; Timothy Darling Presby. Ch., 1961--; Oxford, N. C.; mem., The Mayor's Bi-Racial Comm.; Home: 121 Halifax St., Oxford, N. C.

WALTON, Joseph Louis, Sr., b. New Orleans, La., June 24, 1936; s. Samuel D. Sr. and Isabell (Atherly) W.; A. B., Livingstone Coll., Salisbury, N. C., 1959; B. D., Hood Theol. Sem., Salisbury, N. C., 1962; m. Joel Conway; Children--Joseph L., Jr. and Dennis Earl; pastor, Zion Believers A. M. E. Zion Ch., Independent, La., 1955-57; Ard's Chapel A. M. E. Zion Ch., Lexington, N. C., 1958-60, Show Hill A. M. E. Zion Ch., Maiden, N. C., 1960-62; Pilgrim Rest A. M. E. Zion Ch., 1962-present; financ. sec., Hogan Lib. Bd., Prichard, Ala.; mem., Bd. of Dir., NAACP, Lexington, N. C.; Mason; Dep. Grand Chancellor, Knights of Phythians, N. C.;

CORE; SCLC; Home: 125 N. Ozark Ave., Whistler, Ala.

WAMBLE, Amos Sylvester, Sr., b. Warren, Ark., Aug. 16; s. James Oscar and Lula (Dorn) W.; B. Th., Western Coll., Kansas City, Mo., 1951; attended Rockhurst Coll., Kansas City, Mo., 1951-52; m. Earlene Collins; Children--Edwin, Brenda, John, Amos, Jr., Marcus, Minnie, Carl, Theresa, Phillip, Angelia, Eunice; ministry: Young's Chapel, Blackburn, Mo., Crutchfield Chapel, Malta Bend, Mo., White Oak, Independence, Mo., Grace Meth., Kansas City, Mo., St. James Meth., (formerly Kelly Chapel) Kansas City, Mo., St. James Meth., Coffeyville, Kan., Second Meth., Independence, Kan.; present: Quayle Meth., Okla. City, Okla; Govt. employee, 1946-55, inc. Post Office, Vets. Admin., Govt. Ser. Assn., CCC, Quartermaster, all in Kan. City, Mo.; mem., Census Bd., Independence, Mo., Planning Bd. Comm., Coffeyville, Kansas, 1960; US Army, July 3, 1940-Sept. 11, 1945; Good Conduct Medal, 4 Campaign Ribbons; Sec. of Southwest Conf. of the Meth. Ch.; mem., Okla. Coun. of Chs., Sec. of Interdenom. Interracial Alliance; mem., NAACP; Urban League; YMCA and YWCA; chrmn., Conf. Bd. of Promotion and Cultivation; chrmn. of Conf. Bd. of Publications; edit and pub. Annual Conf. Minutes and Journal; Home: 2801 N. Missouri St., Oklahoma City, Okla. 73111

*WARD, Charles W., b. Georgia, Nov. 1915; s. Willie and Cerrender (R.) W.; A. B., Morehouse Coll., 1942; B. D., Howard Univ., Sch. of Rel., 1946; cert., Psychosomatic medicine, Bowman Gray Sch. of Med.; m. Roberta Ernestine Gore; Children--Charles Winfred, Jr.; pastor, West End Bapt. Ch., Winston-Salem, N. C., 1944-49; Rising Star Bapt. Ch., Walnut Grove, N. C., 1946-52; Ex. sec., Ga. Missionary and Educational Conv.; current, First Bapt. Ch., Raleigh, N. C., 1959--; mem., YMCA Boards; United Fund Drives; Min. Assn.; Human Relation Comm.; State-wide chrmn. of Voter Registration for N. C.; NAACP, 1964; Young Democratic Club of N. C.; del. to State Democratic Conv., 1964; Home: 501 S. Bloodworth St., Raleigh, N. C.; Office: 101 So. Wilmington St., Raleigh, N. C.

WARD, Edgar William, b. Newport News, Va., Sept. 26, 1925; s. Charles A. and Mattie Lee (Snowden) W.; A. B., Johnson C. Smith Univ., 1947; B. D., Sch. of Theol.,

Johnson C. Smith Univ., 1950; m. Marjorie A. Johnson; Children--Lucia A.; pastor, Allen Temple; Cameron Presby. Ch.; Pleasant Grove Presby. Ch., N. C., 1950-52; Cherry Hill Community Ch., Balto., Md., 1952-60; Grace Presby. Ch., Chgo., Ill, 1960-present; acting sec., So. Central Planning Coun. of Presbytery of Chgo. v. moderator of Presbytery of Balto., 1959; pres., Cherry Hill Coordinating Coun. of Balto., 1957-59; So. Balto. Polit. Action Comm., 1958; Douglas Coordinating Coun., Chgo., Ill.; mem., Planned Parenthood Bd. of Chgo.; recd. Afro-Amer. Man of Year Award, Afro Newspapers, Balto., Md.; Alpha Phi Alpha; Acad. of Rel. and Mental Health; Democrat; mem., Bd. of Dir., Forman Neigh.; Home: 3001 So. Parkway, Apt. 1217, Chgo., Ill. 60616

WARD, Eric Calvin, coll. prof., b. Los Angeles, Calif., Nov. 11, 1924; s. Galbourne A. and Estelle (W.) W.; Los Angeles Union Acad., 1936-40; Lynwood Acad., 1940-42; Th. B., Pac. Union Coll., 1946; m. Gwendolyn M.; Children--Carolyn, Prince, Golbourne, Beverly, Linda, Della; pastor, So. Atlantic Conf. of S. D. A., Atlanta, Ga., 1954-63; present: pastor, 31st St. S. D. A. Ch., San Diego, Calif., 1963--; instr., Field Sch. of Evangelism and Pastoral Care, Andrews Univ., June-Sept. 1963; visiting lectr., on Pastoral and Evangelistic methods for Oakwood Coll., 1953-62; spec. articles for The Message magazine and The Ministry magazine of Wash., D. C. Home: 422 Los Angeles Pl., San Diego, Calif.; Office: 414 So. 31st St., San Diego, Calif.

WARD, Martin DePorres, tchr., b. Boston, Mass., Mar. 20, 1918; s. William Henry and Clara (Irby) W.; ordained Franciscan Friar, 1955; prof., English, prof. of Com. English, prof. of Sacred Music; Franciscan missionary in Brazil; has formed choirs for execution of Gregorian chant; Home: Ginasio Santo Antonio, Sao Luiz Gonzaga, Rio Grande DoSul, Brazil, S. America

WARREN, Charles Lacy, ch. official, b. Victoria, Tex., Aug. 1, 1911; s. John W. and Helen (Coffey) W.; A. B., Huston-Tillotson Coll., 1933; B. D., Gammon Theol. Sem., 1936; S. T. M., Boston Univ. Sch. of Theol., 1937; D. D. (hon.), Huston-Tillotson Coll., 1948; D. D., Gammon Theol. Sem., 1950; m. Alice H. Jones; Children--Charles Lacy, Oscar Wesley, Madelynn Louise; pastor, Taylor Meml. Meth. Ch., 1940-58; St. Mark's Meth.

Ch., N.Y.C.; current Dist. Supt., Metro. Dist., N.Y. Conf., The Meth. Ch.; former v.p., Oakland Coun. of Ch., Dept. of Human Relations; mem., Bd. of Dirs., Welfare Bureau; del., Western Jurisdictional Conf., Meth. Ch., 1948, 52, 56; del., Gen. Conf., Meth., 1952; del., NE Jurisdictional Conf., 1964; mem., Ex. Com., Dept. of Racial and Cultural Relations, Natl. Coun. of Chs.; Com. of Religious Leaders, N.Y.C.; Harlem Adv. Bd.; Adv. Bd., Sydenham Soc.; Adv. bd., Harlem br. YMCA; Clergy Com., Sch. Dist. 12, 13, 14; Bd. of Dirs., Meth. Deaconess Home; Bd. of Dirs., N.Y.C. Soc.; N.Y. Region Personnel Com., Bd. of World Missions; In the N.Y. Annual Conf., the chrmn of the Interboard Coun.; mem., Urban Life Com.; v.p., Bd. of Missions; mem., British-American Preachers Exchange, Preaching Scotland and England, 1961; Chi Alpha; Alpha Phi Alpha; Mason; Home: 72 Holls Terr. N. Yonkers, N.Y.; Office: 475 Riverside Dr., New York, N.Y. 10027

WARREN, Glendah Hillard, b. Cheyenne, Wyo., Aug. 7, 1914; s. John W. and Ernest (Brady) W.; B.Th., Bishop Williams Sch. of Rel., Western Univ., Kan. City, Kan., 1940; m. Mable Haskin; Children--Frederick; pastor, Brown Chapel A.M.E. Ch., Topeka, Kan., 1963-present; Brown Chapel, Parsons, Kan., 1961-63; St. James, Lawrence, Kan., 1954-61; Bethel, Winfield, Kans., 1952-54; Brown Chapel, Osawatomie, Kan., 1950-52; St. James, Baxter Springs, 1948-50; pres., NAACP, Topeka, 1965-present; pres., Parsons NAACP, 1963-64; clerk-typist, Topeka Air Force Depot, 1951-57; mem., City Commn. on Housing, 1966; Mason; mem., Interdenom. Min. Alliance, Topeka; Home: 1305 Washington St., Topeka, Kan. 66007

WASHINGTON, Curtis Thomas, catholic missionary, b. Coconut Grove, Miami, Fla., Apr. 5, 1917; s. Marion and Rhoda (Smith) W.; St. Emma High Sch. Acad., Rock Castle, Va., 1936; St. Mary's Philosophate, Techny, Ill., 1943; finished coll. course, theol. course, philosophy course at Bay St. Louis, Miss., 1949; ordained 1949; built churches and academic primary, high schs. and colleges and doing social work in credit unions, hospitals and family welfare in Africa; local mgr. of schs. in Ghana, W. Africa in the Diocese of Accra within the Krobo, Adwamu, Shai, Osuduku educational districts; award: expert rifle medal; mem., Intl. Rel. Soc. of the

Divine Word; Home: St. Mary Sem., Techny, Ill.; Office: Catholic Church, Agomanya, Odumase-Krobo, Ghana, W. Africa

WASHINGTON, Dennis Comer, ch. official, b. Hale Co., Ala., Aug. 15, 1905; s. William H. and Mary (Scott) W.; B.S., Ala., State Tchrs. Coll., Montgomery, Ala.; Selma Univ., Selma, Ala.; D.D. (hon.), Selma Univ., 1947; LL.D., Selma Univ., 1954; m. Bessie Randall; Children--William M., Bessie W. Jones, Dennis C., Jr., Harold E.; pastor, Bapt. Ch., Ala., 1924-38; 17th St. Bapt. Ch., Anniston, Ala., 1938-59; asst. sec., Natl. Bapt. Conv., USA, Inc., 1957-59; Ex. Dir., Sun. Sch. Publication Bd., Natl. Bapt. Conv., USA, Inc., 1959--; v. moderator, Snow Creek Bapt. Dist., Assn., Ala.; mem., Exec. Bd., Ala. Bapt. State Conv., 18 yrs.; official del., Anniton Chapter NAACP; White House Conf. on Civil Rights, 1956; tchr., Calhoun Co. Trng. Sch.; trustee, Selma Univ.; trustee, Amer. Bapt. Theol. Sem., Nashville, Tenn.; trustee, Anniston Fed. of Colored Women's Clubs; Democrat; mem., NAACP; Natl. Bapt. Conv., USA, Inc.; Office: 330 Charlotte Ave., Nashville, Tenn.

WASHINGTON, Emanuel Ezra, b. Hoboken, N.J., Dec. 24, 1920; s. George Edward and Mary (Cook) W.; A.B., 1949, B.D., 1951, Johnson C. Smith Univ., Charlotte, N.C.; M.Th., Tex. Chrstn. Univ. (Brite Coll.); m. Mildred Katherine Chisholm; Children--Emanuel, Jr., Ronald Phelton, Granville Calvin; Sabbath Sch. Missionary, Presby. Ch., USA, 1951-54; pastor, St. James Presby. Ch., Kingsport, Tenn., 1954-58; current pastor, St. Peter Presby. Ch., USA, Ft. Worth, Tex., 1958--; US Air Force, 1942-45; mem., Phi Beta Sigma; Mason; Boy Scouts of America; Boys Club; Home: 5549 Patton Dr., Ft. Worth, Tex. 76112; Office: 5801 Truman Dr., Ft. Worth, Tex. 76112

WASHINGTON, James Augustus, b. Marion, S.C., Sept. 9, 1932; s. John and Nancy (Glover) W.; B.A., Oakwood Coll., 1954; M.A., Andrews Univ., 1956; m. Sarah Elizabeth Costen; Children--Costena-Marie, Sarah-Elizabeth, Nancy Ann; pastored S.D.A. Chs. in: Atlantic City, N.J., 1954-55; Akron and Canton, O., 1956-59; Roanoke, Danville, Va., 1959-63; present, pastor, Columbus, O., 1963--; asst. pastor, Dupont Pk. S.D.A. Ch., Wash., D.C., 1955-56; lectur. and pub. evangelist; sec., Roanoke Min. Alliance, 1962-63; former mem., City of Roanoke Bi-Racial Coun.; research on Negro History pre- and post-slavery era; Home: 2110 Maryland Ave., Columbus, O.; Office: 2171 E. Fifth Ave., Columbus, O.

WASHINGTON, Joseph R., Jr., chaplain, author, b. Iowa City, Iowa, Oct. 30, 1930; s. Rev. and Mrs. Joseph W.; B.A., Univ. of Wis., 1952; B.D., Andover Newton Theol. Sch., 1957-58; Th.D., Boston Univ. Sch. of Theol., 1961; m. Sophia May Holland; Children--Bryan Reed; ordained minister, The Central Penn. Conf., The Meth. Ch.; asst. pastor, First Bapt. Ch., Woburn, Mass., 1954-56; pastor, W. Newfield, Maine, Congre. Ch., and Newfield, Maine, Meth. Ch., 1956-57; students pastor, The Bapt. Ch., Brookline, Mass., 1957-58; assoc. Prot. chap., Boston Univ., 1958-61; dean of chapel, Dillard Univ., New Orleans, 1961-63; chap., Dickinson Coll., 1963--; US Army Corps of Military Police, 1952-54; (1st Lt.); Univ. of Wisconsin's Iron Cross, honorary soc. which annually elects twelve men who have contributed significantly to the Univ. during their undergrad. yrs., 1952; author: Black Religion: The Negro and Christianity in the United States; articles: Central Christian Advocate, Mar. 1962; Motive, Jan. 1963; Theology Today, Apr. 1963; Religious Education, June 1963, Sept. 1963, Mar. 1964; Foundations, Jan. 1964; Office: Chaplain to the Coll. and Asst. Prof. of Religion, Dickinson Coll., Carlisle, Pa.

WASHINGTON, L. Barnwell, chaplain, b. Mar. 16, 1910; s. William and Nancy (Fludd) W.; A.B., Johnson C. Smith Univ., 1935; B.D., 1938; M.A., Howard Univ., courses on Ph.D., Union Theol. Sem.; m. Vivian Beatrice Shute; 1939-42, instr., Rel. Ed. and registrar, student pastor, Coulter Jr. Coll. and asst. dir., Cheraw Larger Parish, Cheraw, S.C., pastor, Calvary Presby. Ch., Kannapolis, N.C.; 1942--, chaplains sch., Ft. Benjamin Harrison, Ind., served: 583 FABn, 92 Div.; served Com. and Port Battallions, Indiantown Gap, Pa.; 1943-44, duty S.W. Pacific chap., 97 Ing. Active res. to 1955; part-time instr., Johnson C. Smith Univ., 1946-49; current pastor, New Life United Presby. Ch., Boston, Mass.; 1946-54, pastor Wilson M. P. Ch.; awards: Campaign, Asiatic Pacific Campaign, USA WW II Medal, 1941-45; Cert. of Award for Meritorious Service and Bronze Medal for Devoted Service by the Gen. Assembly of the United Presby. Ch., USA; mem., 1949-58, Acad. Pol. Science; Natl. Travelers Club, N. Y. C.; Phi Beta Sigma; Coordinator and mem. P. L. C. (Presby. Interracial Coun. Clergy Comm.); Wash. Park Redevelopment Assn. Comm.; twice to Church's Highest Court, The Gen. Assembly of the U. Presby. Ch., USA, 1946; repr. Presby. Boston 17th Gen. Assembly, Des Moines, Iowa; Comm. World Responsibility, Mass. Coun. of Chs.; author: "Prayers Before Meals" for Record American; sermonettes for "Boston Herald." Church: 1 Gore St., Boston (Roxbury), Mass.

WASHINGTON, Paul Matthews, b. Charleston, S. C., May 26, 1921; s. Thomas C. and Mayme (Matthews) W.; B. A., Lincoln Univ., 1942; B. D., Phila., Div. Sch., 1946; m. Christine Jackson; Children--Paul Marc; Kemah Carlos; Michael Bravid, Donya Turé; curate, Ch. of the Crucifixion, Phila., 1946-48; tchr., Cuttington Coll. & Div. Sch., Monrovia, Liberia, W. Africa, 1948-54; vicar, St. Cyprians Episc. Ch., Phila., 1954-62; rector, Ch. of the Advocate, Phila., 1962-present; chap., Correctional Inst., 1955-present; Comm. on Human Rel., Phila.; Bd. of Trustees, Commun. Coll., Phila.; mem., Phila. Coun. for Commun. Advancement; Alpha Phi Alpha; co-author, The Death Penalty, 1962; Home: 2120 N. 18th St., Philadelphia, Pa. 19121

WASHINGTON, William Joseph, b. Gonzales, Tex.; B. S., Samuel Huston Coll., Austin, Tex.; B. D., Gammon Theol. Sem., Atlanta, Ga.; S. T. M., Boston Univ.; m. Audrey Vinton Brown; Children--Wm. Joseph, Jr., Aurelia Vedette; ordained deacon, 1951; elder, 1953; pastor, Emanuel United Meth. Ch., Brownwood, Tex., 1953-54; Ex. Sec., Bd. of Ed. United Meth. Ch., 1954-63; dir., Wesley Found., Tex. Southern Univ., 1963-65; staff mem., United Meth. Ch., Gen. Bd. of Ed., Nashville, Tenn., 1965-present; Home: 825 Hillview Heights, Nashville, Tenn.; Office: P. O. Box 871, Nashville, Tenn. 37202

WATKINS, Readus Joseph, b. Pensacola, Fla., July 13, 1931; s. Edward Francis and Berlina (Pickens) W.; B. A., Gordon Coll., 1956; S. T. B., Boston Univ., 1959 Ed. M., Boston Univ., 1960; m. Deborah M. McClure; Children--Bryan Joseph, Dana Linn, Geoffrey Read; assoc. pastor, E. Saugus Meth. Ch., Saugus, Mass., 1956; pastor, Pleasant St. Bapt. Ch., Westerly, R. I.,

1958; Hd. of Counselling & Guidance Dept., Achimota Coll., Ghana, W. Africa, 1959; pastor (current), St. Luke's Meth. Ch., New Rochelle, N.Y., 1962--; mem., Adv. Bd., Planned Parenthood, Southern Westchester Chapt.; Exec. Com., New Rochelle Coun. of Chs.; Bd. of Ed., N.Y. Annual Conf., The Meth. Ch.; Bd. of Dirs., Adoption Service of Westchester Co., New York; v.p., Amer. Red Cross Soc., City of New Rochelle, N.Y.; sec., Prot. Min. Assn., City of New York; Home: 32 Lakeside Dr., New Rochelle, N.Y.; Office: St. Luke's Meth. Ch., 108 Guion Pl., New Rochelle, N.Y.

WATSON, Hughey Willie, b. Mer Rouge, La., Feb. 17, 1907; s. Briscoe and Lorene; Coleman Coll., Shreveport, La.; Leland Coll., Baton Rouge, La.; Bishop Coll., Marshall, Tex., B.Th. (hon.), Coleman Coll., 1943; D.D. (hon.), Conroe Coll., Tex., 1957; m. Rosa M. Price; Children--Hughey W. Jr., Zelma; pastored Bapt. Chs. Monroe, Rustin, Mer Rouge, and Delhi, La., 1932-44; organized and pastored Mt. Calvary Bapt. Ch., Oakland, Calif., 1944-45; pastor, New Hope Bapt. Ch., Oakland, Calif., 1945-60; Bethany Bapt. Ch., Oakland, Feb. 1960-present; mem., Com. on Un-American Activities (Calif.); mem., Bd. of Foreign Missions, Natl. Bapt. Conv.; organizer and moderator, Home & Foreign Mission Assn.; v.p., Calif. State Bapt. Conv.; NAACP; Mason; pres., St. John Bapt. District Assn.; pres., Western Region Progressive Bapt. Conv., Inc.; mem., Progressive Bapt. Assn. Lit. & Foreign Mission Bds.; award, 17th Assembly, Dist. of the State of Calif. & Community, 1967; Home: 6131 Baker St., Oakland, Calif. 94608; Office: Bethany Bapt. Ch., 5400 Adeline St., Oakland, Calif. 94608

WATSON, William Austin, chap., b. Brackettville, Tex., Jan. 15, 1917; s. James D. and Victoria S. (Demery); A.B., Bishop Coll., Dallas, 1943; B.D., Grad. Sch. of Theol., Oberlin, 1945; m. Phyllis Mae Martin; Children--Victoria Jean (Mrs. Geo. H. Russell), Kristine Kay; ordained, United Ch. of Christ, 1945; pastor, U.C.C. Chs., Painesville, O., Memphis, Tenn., 1944-52; entered military service, 1952, Europe, Far East, Ft. Jackson, S.C., Ft. Lee, Va.; Hosp. chap., Brooke Gen. Hosp., Ft. Sam Houston, Tex., Korea; present: staff chaplain, US Signal Center & Sch., Ft. Monmouth, N.J.; awards, Korean Serv. Medal (1 Battle Star), 1953;

Natl. Defense Medal, 1953; United Nations (1962); Commendation Medal First Oakleaf Cluster, 1965; mem., Kappa Alpha Psi; NAACP; Assn. of Military Chaplains; Mason; Home: 35 Megill Rd., Eatontown, N.J. 07724; Office: Office of Post Chaplain, Ft. Monmouth, N.J. 07703

WATTS, Alexander Alfred, b. Portsmouth, Va., May 4, 1897; s. John Henry and Annie May (Elliott) W.; Va. Union Univ., 1920-24; Bloomfield Sem., 1928; B.D., Drew Univ., 1929; M.S., Drew Univ., 1930; Th.D., Drew Univ., 1933; m. Edythe E. Harper; pastor, Second Bapt. Ch., Newport News, Va., 1922-27; Calvary Bapt., Paterson, N.J., 1927-37; Greater Bethesda Bapt. Ch., Chgo., Ill., 1927-52; Emmanuel Park Bapt. Ch., Chgo., 1966-present; Chgo. Bapt. Inst.; Prof., Bishop Coll., Marshall, Tex.; mem., Bd. of Dirs., Chgo. Bapt. Assn., 1938-62; chap. during WW II; Mason; Home: 7722 Morgan St., Chicago, Ill.; Office: 6958 Stewart St., Chicago, Ill.

WATTS, Herman Hayes, b. Portsmouth, Va., Feb. 11, 1922; s. Elmer and Margaret; A.B., B.D., Va. Union Univ., Richmond, Va., 1948, 1952; m. Dorothy Elizabeth; Children--Herman, Jr., Timothy, Colleen, Harding, Steven, Kevin; pastor, Kaighn Ave. Bapt. Ch., Camden, N.J., 1951-68; pastor, Friendship Bapt. Ch., N.Y. City, 1968-present; Chrmn. of Bd., OIC; chrmn., Civil Rights Commn., Camden, N.J., 1961; tchr., Phila., Pa., 1964-66; Employment counselor, state of N.J., 1966-68; Home: 1248 Pelham Parkway (So.), Bronx, N.Y. 10461; Office: Friendship Bapt. Ch., New York, N.Y. 10027

WEATHERS, J. Leroy, b. Georgetown, S.C., May 21, 1936; s. Charles and Rosa Weather; A.B., Allen Univ., Columbia, S.C.; B.D., Allen Univ., Columbia, S.C.; m. Margaret Singleton; pastor, Youngs Chapel A.M.E. Ch., Ermo, S.C., 1960-61; Mt. Olive A.M.E. Ch., Myrtle Beach, S.C., 1961-present; pres. and founder, Myrtle Beach br. NAACP; chrmn., Bi-Racial Comm., Myrtle Beach; v.p., Myrtle Beach Min. Alliance (first and only Negro); vet. of Korean War; merit cert., State Conf. of branches NAACP; Mason; Home: 1311 Hemingway St., P.O. Box 122, Myrtle Beach, S.C.

WEAVER, Seymour Marcus, b. Jan. 6, 1901, Whiteplains,

Ga.; s. Seymour Marcus and Mattie; Th. B., A. B., Morehouse Coll., Atlanta, Ga., 1928, 1929; Th. M., Am. Bapt. Theol. Sem., Nashville, Tenn., 1937; D. D., LL. D. (hon.), Union Bapt. Sem., Houston, Tex., 1949, 1966; m., J. Zenonian; Children--Marliese (Mrs. Johnnie Armstrong), Lavarre (Mrs. A. P. Greene), Seymour Marcuss III; pastored Bapt. Chs. Ga., Tenn., Tex.; pastor, Providence Bapt. Ch., Houston, Tex., 1946-present; prof., Am. Bapt. Theol. Sem., Nashville, Tenn., 1936-40; dean and prof., Union Bapt. Theol. Sem., Houston, Tex., 1946-62; founder and pres., Inter-Bapt. Theol. Center, 1962-present; cor. sec., Home Mission Bd., Southern Bapt. Ch., 1962-66; Home: 5855 Belmark St., Houston, Tex. 77033; Office: 2810 Rosedale St., Houston, Tex. 77004

WEBB, Ercel Franklin, b. Leaksville, N. C., July 24, 1920; s. Charles William and Mamie (Morton) W.; A. B., M. R. E., Eastern Bapt. Sem., 1943-49; B. D., Eastern Bapt. Sem., 1953-54; D. D. (hon.), Eastern Bapt. Coll., 1966; m. Joan Hartzog; Children--Charles, Patricia, Kathleen, Natalie, Michael; asst. pastor, Koign Ave. Bapt. Ch., Camden, N. J., 1943-44; pastor, Monumental Bapt. Ch., Jersey City, N. J., 1944--; tchr., Jersey City High Sch., 1956--; chap. (Major), N. J. Natl. Guard, 1949--; exec. dir., CANDO Anti-poverty prog., 1965-66; mem., NAACP; Bd. of Dirs., Jersey City Red Cross; Bd. of Trustees, Hudson Co. TB and Health League; Mason; Home: 424 Bergen Ave., Jersey City, N. J. 07304; Office: 244 Van Horne St., Jersey City, N. J. 07304

WELLS, Gerald Nathaniel, b. Boca Raton, Fla., Aug. 2, 1934; s. Gerlad Godwin and Tarrah Lee (Jackson) W.; B. A., Oakwood Coll., 1959; M. A., Andrews Univ., 1960; m. Beverly Jean Porter; 1 dau., Desrea Lunn; pastored, Independence Blvd. Ch., Chgo., Ill., 1960-61; Berean S. D. A. Ch., So. Bend, Ind., 1961-62; present: Trendley Ave. S. D. A. Ch., E. St. Louis, Ill., 1962--; Natl. Service Medal and the Good Conduct Medal; Home: 605 Tulane Dr., E. St. Louis, Ill.; Office: 2000 Trendley Ave., E. St. Louis, Ill.

WEST, James Oliver, Jr., b. Richmond, Va., Mar. 2, 1918; s. James O. and Cynthia E. (W.); B. A., Va. Union Univ., 1936; B. D., Va. Episc. Theol. Sem., 1939; S. T. M., Hartford Theol. Sem. and Found., Hart-

Conn., 1940; m. Maxie B. Pearson; Children--Brenda, Paula; served 1 yr. in four mission chapels: Alexandria, Va., Berryville, Va., Milwood, Va., Seminary, Va., 1940; current rector, Calvary Prot. Episc. Ch., Wash., D.C., 1941--; mem., Chrstn. Ed., Social Action and Social Casework Com. of the Episc. Dioces of Wash.; Radio and TV Com. of the Wash. Fed. of Chs.; Bd. of Dirs., D.C. Tuberculosis Assn.; Area P Bd. of D.C. Commissioners Youth Coun.; award: Outstanding Achievement in Rel. Ed. from the Omega Psi Phi, 1953; Outstanding Citizen Award from the Y's Men's Club of Wash., 1962; mem., Omega; D.C. Chapt. of Va. Union Univ. Alumni Assn.; Democrat; Home: 509 Eye St., Wash., D.C. 20002; Office: 820 6th St., Wash., D.C. 20002

WESTON, M. Moran, b. Jarboro, N.C.; s. Milton M. and C. Cornelia (Perry) W.; A.B., Columbia Univ.; B.D., Union Theol. Sem.; Ph.D., Columbia Univ.; D.D. (hon.), Episc. Theol. Sem. (Alexandria, Va.), 1964; New Sch. for social research, 2 yrs.; m. Miriam Yvonne Drake; Children--Karen Yvonne, Philip Gregory Moran; business mgr. and curate, St. Phelp's Episc. Ch., N.Y.C., 1948-51; exec. sec., Div. of Chrstn. Citizenship, Natl. Coun. of Prot. Episc. Ch., 1951-57; current rector, St. Philips Ch., 1957--; social worker; real estate salesman; public relations; founder and mem., Bd. of Dirs., Carver Fed. Savings & Loan Assn.; Bd. of Dirs., Community Coun. of Greater New York; New York City Mission Soc.; Coun. on Rel. in Independent Schs.; Child Adoption Service; State Charities Aid Assn.; Harlem Neighborhood Assn.; Harlem Youth Opportunities Unlimited; Dist. 10 Planning Coun., Manhattan Borough President's Office; Urban League; Elder Craftsman's Shop; New York Clergy Study Com. On Alcholism; Bd. of Dirs., Leake and Watts Children's Home; mem., Administrative Com. Fed. of Prot. Welfare Agencies (NYC); Kappa Alpha Psi; Elks; Pol. Independent; author: Social Policy of the Episc. Ch. in the Twentieth Century, Seabury Press, 1964; Episcopalians at Work in the World, 1952; chapter in: Man at Work in God's World, ed. by Cannon G. E. De Mille; chapter in: Committment and Community in the Schools; frequent speaker at Diocese Conventions and on college campuses; Home: 253 Blvd., New Rochelle, N.Y.; Office: 215 W. 133rd St., New York, N.Y.

WHARTON, Wesley Edward, b. St. Kitts, Brit. W. Indies, Sept. 21, 1918; s. Charles F. and Matilda (Perdrieaux)

W.; A. B., Wilberforce Univ., Ohio, 1952; B. D., Payne Theol. Sem., Wilberforce Univ., 1952; m. Lilla Agnes Harden; pastor, Quinn Chapel A. M. E. Ch., Independence, Kan., 1952; Quinn Chapel A. M. E. Ch., Jefferson City, Mo., 1954-56; Allen Chapel A. M. E. Ch., Danville, Ill., 1956-60; St. Paul A. M. E. Ch., Springfield, Ill., 1960-61; St. Luke A. M. E. Ch., E. St. Louis, Ill., 1962-present; coun., Ill. State Employment Service; pres., NAACP, E. St. Louis, 1963-64; dir., OEO, 1965-pres.; trustee, Freedom of Resident, 1963-present; dir., Community of Progress; mem., Human Relations Commn., E. St. Louis, 1963-66; editorial staff Bermuda Recorder, Hamilton, Bermuda; Home: 412 14th St., E. St. Louis, Ill. 62201; Office: 414 14th St., E. St. Louis, Ill. 62201

WHEELER, Charles Calvin, III, b. Rusk, Tex., Nov. 25, 1913; s. Eli Whitney and Addie M. (White) W.; courses, Western Bapt. Coll., Kan. City, 2 yrs.; A. B., Roosevelt Univ., 1946; B. D., Central Bapt. Theol. Sem., 1951; M. R. E., Drake Univ., 1952; m. Ellen Waller; Children--Mrs. Edward Buckner, Calvin C., Barbara; Mrs. Lester Barlow, Mrs. Jacqueline Condon; asst. pastor, St. John Bapt. Ch., Dallas, Tex., 1941; Morning Star Bapt. Ch., Kansas City, Mo., 1944-51; pastor, Mt. Hebron Bapt. Ch., Pitts., Kan., 1951-52; Westminster Bapt. Ch., Chg., 1953-58; Mid-west Field Div. Minister's Retirement Fund, Natl. Bapt. Conv., USA, Inc.; Dir., Red. Ed., Morning Star Bapt. Ch., 1961-63; organizer, pastor, Westminster Bapt. Ch., Kan. City, Mo., 1963-present; tchr., Bapt. Minister's Conf., Chg.; one of 3 dirs., Ill. Bapt. State Conv., Ed. Dept.; mem., NAACP; chap., US Army, 1942-44; Democrat; Home: 4612 E. 46th St., Kansas City, Mo. 64130; Office: 4733 Elmwood Ave., Kansas City, Mo. 64130

WHITAKER, Arthur L., b. Malden, Mass., July 23, 1921; s. Robert W. and Elizabeth (Hinton) W.; A. B., Gordon Coll., 1949; S. T. B., Harvard Univ. Div. Sch., 1952; S. T. M., Andover Newton Theol. Sch., 1954; doctoral studies, Syracuse, 1964; m. Virginia Carter; Children--Ronald, Paul, Mark, Keith; pastor, Calvary Bapt. Ch., Haverhill, Mass., 1950-55; field repr., Amer. Bapt. Home Miss. Soc., Valley Forge, Pa., 1955-56; Mt. Olive Bapt. Ch., Rochester, N. Y., 1956--; asst. prof., Univ. of Rochester, N. Y., 1958--; cons., Anti-poverty Prog.; Operation Headstart and Trng. Center for Youth Counselors, summer 1965; mem., Bd. of Dirs., Montgomery Neighborhood Center, Rochester, 1956-65; Rochester Rehabilitation Commn., 1959-62; Exec. Com., Rochester br. NAACP, 1956-61; Rochester chapt., Amer. Red Cross, Bd. of Dirs., 1959-65; Exec. Bd., Otetiania Coun., Boy Scouts, 1962--; US Army, WW II; awards: Foggia; Rhineland, Central Europe; Good Conduct Medal; Europe African Middle Eastern Campaign Ribbon; Victory Medal; MacDonald Scholar, Andover Newton Theol. Sem.; citation, Colgate Rochester Div. Sch.; Certified, Prof. Hosp. Chap., Amer. Hosp. Assn.; mem., Soc. for the Scientific Study of Rel.; Acad. of Rel. and Mental Health; Amer. Sociol. Assn.; Rochester Rotary Community and Ch. Studies, Amer. Bapt. Conv.; author: Anatomy of a Riot, 1965; numerous articles on Anti-Poverty Prog. and Negro; cons., John F. Wegman Found., 1964--; Rochester Coun. on Alcoholism, 1964--; Com. on Women Alcoholics, 1965--; Bd. of Dirs., Rochester Hearing and Speech Center, 1966; mem., Harvard Club of Rochester; Rochester Roundtable; City Club of Rochester; Rochester Com., United Negro Coll. Fund, 1957-61; Bd. of Dirs., United Serv. Orga., 1956-61; moderator, Monroe Bapt. Assn., 1958-59; pres., Assn. Officers Coun., N. Y. State Bapt. Conv., 1958-60; pres., Ministers Coun., N. Y. State Bapt. Conv., 1963-65; Bd. of Managers, N. Y. State Bapt. Conv., 1958-65; Bid. of Dirs., Ministers Coun., Amer. Bapt. Conv., 1961-65; Rochester Area Dir., N. Y. -N. J. State Div. of Amer. Negro Emancipation Centennial Authority, Inc., 1963; Home: 141 Trafalgar St., Rochester, N. Y. 14619; Office: 141 Adams St., Rochester, N. Y. 14608

WHITE, Albert McNeil, chap., b. S. C., Dec. 29, 1910; B. S., B. D., Allen and Wilberforce Univ.; grad. study, Boston Univ.; D. D. (hon.), Campbell Coll., 1951; LL. D., (hon.), Kittrell Coll., 1955; m. Aleane Beatrice; Children--Sylvester Jeradin, Ralph McNeil, Frances Renee, Sara Anne; pastor, Afr. Meth. Episc. Chs., Fla., La., Pa., Mass., R. I., Ohio, since 1925; principal, High Sch., S. C.; tchr., Edward Waters Coll., Jacksonville, Fla.; US Army chap., serving in ECOM, FECOM, and PTO during WW II and Korean conflict; 10-1/2 yrs. Amer. Campaign Service Medal; European-African-Middle East Serv. Medal; Asiatic Pacific Serv. Medal; Distinguished Service Ribbons; Five Battle Stars; mem., Phi Beta Sigma; Elks; Mason; Amer. Legion; YMCA; A. M. E. Min. Alliance; A. M. E. Chaplains' Organization; editor,

From a Chaplain's Point of View; Pastoral Counseling; The Pulpit Led Church; Home: 1233 Melon St., Phila., Pa.; Office: Mt. Pisgah A. M. E. Ch., 519 E. Washington, Lake City, Fla.

*WHITE, Andrew, editor, ch. official, b. Moncks Corner, S. C., Mar. 8, 1912; s. Andrew and Annie (Reed) W.; Avery Inst., 1928-32; A. B., Howard Univ., 1936-40; B. D., Howard Univ., Sch. of Rel., 1940-43; M. A., Fisk Univ., 1954-55; D. D. (hon.), Monrovia Coll., 1955; m. Edith Burrel; Children--Andrew N. III, Edith Anne; pastor, Basil Afr. Meth. Episc. Ch., Cockeysville, Md., 1940-43; St. James A. M. E. Ch., Covington, Ky., 1943-48; St. Paul A. M. E. Ch., Nashville, Tenn., 1948-49; Salem A. M. E. Ch., Nashville, Tenn., 1949-56; administrative asst. and editorial associate, Div. of Chrstn. Ed., A. M. E. Ch., Nashville, Tenn., 1948-56; editor-in-chief, Religious Literature, Div. of Chrstn. Ed., A. M. E. Ch., Nashville, Tenn., 1956-60; exec. sec., Div. of Chrstn. Ed., A. M. E. Ch., Nashville, Tenn., 1960--; mem., CIO Political Action Com., Cincinnati br., 1943-48; Com. J. C. Napier Div. Boy Scouts of America, Nashville, Tenn., 1950-56; founding mem. and sec., Nashville, Chrstn. Leadership Coun., 1958-64; pres., Nashville, Chrstn. Leadership Coun., 1964--; mem., Exec. Bd., Southern Chrstn. Leadership Conf., 1963-64, 1964-65; mem., Exec. Bd., Div. of Chrstn. Ed., Natl. Coun. of Chs.; editor, The Journal of Religious Ed., A. M. E. Ch.; publish manuals and work books for use in local churches; Home: 1621 Haynes Mead Circle, Nashville, Tenn. 37207; Office: 414 8th Ave., So. Nashville, Tenn. 37203

WHITE, Edward Augustus, b. Muskogee, Okla., Jan. 25, 1934; s. Joseph and Effie (Huddleston) W.; B. A., Pacific Union Coll., Angwin, Calif., 1958; M. A., S. D. A. Theol. Sem., Wash., D. C., 1959; m. Fleda Toliver; Children--Darrell, Janie, Susan; pastored S. D. A. Ch., Oakland, 1960; present: pastor, Pittsburg S. D. A. Ch., Pittsburg, Calif. and Berea S. D. A. Ch., Valleje, Calif., 1961--; Home: 535 Ridge Ave., Valleje, Calif.; Office: 833 Louisiana St., Valleje, Calif.

*WHITE, Frank Lamar, b. Baltimore, Md., Jan. 5, 1903; s. Harvey and Sarah (Washington); Th. B., M. Div., Howard Univ., Sch. of Rel., 1936, 1938; m. Mary Ellen Woodward; volunteer counsellor, Natl. Trng. Sch., 1941-

43; asst. pastor, Liberty Bapt. Ch., 1936-38; pastor, 1st Bapt. Ch., Manassas, Va., 1938-43; chap., USA, 1943-47; chap., USAF, 1948-63; assoc. pastor, 3rd St. Bapt. Ch., Wash., D. C.; Field repr., instr., Howard Univ. Sch of Rel., 1968-69; Chap., Freedmen's Hosp., 1969-pres.; tchr., Natl. Capitol Sun. Sch. & B. T. U. Congress; pres., Ingrham Block Club; v.p., N. W. Boundary Assoc.; rec'd. Distinguished Unit Citation, Korean Unit Citation; Commendation Ribbon, 1950; mem., Mason; Neighbors, Inc.; Bapt. Min. Conf.; Natl. Bapt. Conv.; Home: 1322 Ingraham St., N. W. Wash., D. C. 20011; Office: Freedman's Hospital, Wash., D. C. 20001

WHITE, John Walter, b. Bertie Co., N. C., May 29, 1908; s. George Washington Lou Willa (Jordan) W.; B. A., Shaw Univ., 1939; B. D., Shaw Univ., 1941; D. D. (hon.), Shaw Univ., 1955; m. Ethel Bunch; Children--John W. Jr., Ralph D., Dianne C.; pastor, Nebo Missionary Bapt. Ch.; St. Francis Bapt. Ch., 1941-48; St. Luke, 1942-48; Indian Wood, 1950-52; dir., Bapt. Trng. Union, Dept. of Gen. Bapt. State Conv., N. C., 1946-49; Mt. Zion Missionary Bapt. Ch., 1948-present; Mt. Hermon Charity League, 1933; St. Luke Credit Union, 1946; founder, Asheville Buncombe Co. Citizens Organ., 1949-62; chrmn., Bd. of Trustees, Shaw Univ., 1959-65; mem., Exec. Comm., Area Coun. on Human Relations, 1959-present; mem., NAACP, 1948-present; pres., Gen. Bapt. State Conv., N. C.; Alpha Phi Alpha; Mason; author - Intermediate Bapt. Trng. Union Quarterly; Home: 211 Asheland Ave., Asheville, N. C. 28801; Office: 47 Eagle St., Asheville, N. C. 28801

WHITE, Joseph Douglas, jr. bishop, b. Macon, Ga., Dec. 25, 1904; s. Isaac and Estella W.; Ch. of Christ Bible Inst., N. Y. C., 4 yrs.; Bible Way Trng. Sch., Wash., D. C., 3 yrs.; m. Geneva Sylvia Strothers; Children--Joseph D. Jr., Shirley M., Isaac M., John H., Reginald J.; licensed for ministry, 1935; ordained 1938; pastored chs. in Atlanta, Ga. (Bible Way Ch. of our Lord Jesus Christ World-Wide, Inc.); Baltimore, Md., Greensboro, N. C.; current pastor, Kernersville, N. C. and Dir. of Rel. Ed. in Western N. C., Ga., Fla.; Jr. bishop over the same area; tchr., Bible Way Trng. Sch., Wash., D. C.; one of organizers and dir. of political action, United Cafeteria Workers Union, Wash., D. C.; US Army, 1923-31; former editor, Bible Way News Voice, Bible Way Church, Wash., D. C.; former v.p., Bible Way Trng.

Sch., Bible Way Church-Wash., D. C.; Home: 181-1/2 Nelson, Kernersville, N. C.; Office: 181 Nelson, Kernersville, N. C.

WHITE, Kenneth, chap., b. Miami, Fla., Jan. 1, 1906; s. Boyer and Millie (J.) W.; Edward Waters Coll., Lee Sem., Jacksonville, Fla., 1940-44; courses: Howard Univ. Sch. of Rel., Wash., D. C.; Graduate Cortez Peters Bus. Sch., Wash., D. C., 1956; m. Lillie H.; Children--Kenneth Jr., Margaret Alston, Henry, Patricia, William Alston; tchr., Taylor Co., Perry, Fla., 1937-39; pastor, Afr. Meth. Episc. Chs., Fla., 1936-44; chap., US Army, 1944-52, Capt.; pastor, A. M. E. Chs., Maryland; current pastor, Reid Temple A. M. E. Ch., Wash., D. C., 1964; chap., Amer. Legion, James Reese Post No. 5, D. C.; Victory Medal, SWP, Japan, Korea; Home: 1519 Queen, Wash., D. C.; Office: 1335 Michigan Ave., Wash., D. C.

*WHITE, Lanneau L., b. Marion Co., S. C., July 13, 1910; s. Claren A. and Lou W.; A. B., Agri. & Tech. Coll., Greensboro, N. C.; B. D., Howard Univ., Sch. of Rel., 1936; M. Re., Union Theol. Sem., N. Y. C.; D. D. (hon.), Reed Coll. of Rel., Oregon; m. Bernice Caldwell; Children--Lanneau, Jr., Franklin Leslie, Robert, Joy Kathleen; pastored Meth. chs., Wash., D. C., Collesville, Md., Roanoke, Va.; current pastor, Holman Meth. Ch., Los Angeles, 1947--; elected del. to the Gen. Conf. of The Meth. Ch.; pres., Los Angeles Coun. of Chs.; chrmn., Architectural Guild of America, 1958; Omega Psi Phi Achievement Award; Masonic Award; Local Coun. of Chs. Award; mem., Omega Psi Phi; 1965 Alumni Achievement Award in Rel., Howard Univ.; Home: 4292 Don Carlos Dr., Los Angeles, Calif.; Office: 3320 W. Adam Blvd., Los Angeles, Calif.

WHITE, Leamon Whitfield, b. Holly Hill, S. C., Sept. 10, 1910; s. Capus C. and Rebecca (Daley) Jaquse W.; Allen Univ., Columbia, S. C., 1929; Wash. Bapt. Sem., 1943; m. Catherine Arnold; Children--Eloyce L., Neil (Mrs. Brooks), Kathy, David, Lydia; pastor, Silver Hill Bapt. Ch., Morrisville, Va., 1945-50; Goldvain, Va., 1948-50; current pastor, Mt. Bethel Bapt. Ch., Wash., D. C., 1950--; sec., Northern Min. Conf., 1948-50; pres., Bapt. Min. Conf., 1962 (Wash., D. C.); v. p., Bapt. Conv. of D. C., 1956--; trustee, Stoddard Bapt. Home, Wash., D. C., 1951, 64; mem., Mason; various

Boards for Assn., 1964; mem., The Bloomingdale Assn.; chap., The Edgewood Civic Assn.; official watcher for Democratic Party Precinct No. 42, 1964; Civilian Award from Dept. of Navy, 1945; Home: 630 Edgewood St., NE, Wash., D. C.; Office: 1915 First St. NW, Wash., D. C.

WHITE, Major Cornelius, b. Muskogee, Okla., May 13, 1926; s. Joseph and Effie (Huddleston) W.; Pacific Union Coll., A. B., 1948; Univ. of the Pacific, 1963, working on M. A.; m. Rue Pearl Haynes; Children--Major Aurelius, Marvin Eugene, Maurice Norvette; pastorates: S. D. A. Chs., Tucson, Ariz., 1948-51, Richmond, Calif., 1951-61; present: Stockton, Calif., 1961--; mem., Bd. of Dirs., Easter Seal Society, Contra Costa Co., Calif.; v. p., Easter Seal Soc., 1957; Home: 1952 So. California St., Stockton, Calif.; Office: 2290 E. Market St., Stockton, Calif.

WHITE, Walter Syrus, chap., b. Sparr, Fla., Sept. 4, 1907; s. Rifus Feldo and Ellen Gloria W.; A. B., B. D., Wilberforce Univ. & Payne Sem.; further study: Bethune-Cookman Coll., Fla. A & M Univ., Northwestern Univ., Chap. Sch.; m. Thelma Lee Skrine; Children--Patricia Ellen, Walter Syrus, Thelma Lee, Gwendolyn Yvonne; pastor, So. Charleston Mission, A. M. E. Ch., Ohio; Bethel A. M. E. Ch., Key West, Fla.; Allen Chapel, Melbourne; Mt. Zion, Ocala; St. Andrews, Palmetto; Allen Chapel, New Smyrna Beach; St. James, Sanford; Mt. Olive, Orlando; Allen Chapel, Pompano Beach; Greater Bethel, Gainesville; presiding elder, A. M. E. Ch., US Army, WW II, 29 mos. overseas; also Chap., Korean War, 36 mos. overseas; total service 8 yrs., rank: Major; current, Inactive Reserve; current pastor, Greater Bethel A. M. E. Ch., Gainesville, Fla.; Four Battle Stars; mem., Omega Psi Phi; Mason; Knights of Pythians; Home: 922 6th St., W. Palm Beach, Fla.; Office: 753 NW 8th St., Gainesville, Fla.

WHITE, William Henry, ch. official, b. Cynthiana, Ky., Aug. 3, 1897; s. William and Fannie (Alexander) W.; A. B., B. D., Wilberforce Univ., and Payne Theol. Sem., 1925-28; B. D., Coll. of the Bible, 1955; D. D. (hon.), Monrovia Coll., W. Africa, 1955; m. Frozene G. Campbell (deceased); Vivian M. Miller; 1 dau., Mrs. George Alston; pastor, Afr. Meth. Episc. Chs., Ky.; current pastor, St. James A. M. E. Ch., Covington, Ky.; thirteen Episc. Dist. A. M. E. Ch. Dir. of Chrstn. Ed.; v. p., Kentucky Coun. of Chs.; mem., Chrstn. Ed. Comm.; Ky. Coun. of Chs. and Northern Ky. Assn. of Prot. Chs.; pres., Interdenom. Min. Alliance; Ex. Comm., NAACP; mem., Northern Ky. Prot. Assn. Commn. on Religion and Race; chrmn., Ed. Comm., NAACP; US Army, WW I; testimonial for 25 yrs. serv. as dir. of Chrstn. Ed. 13th Episc. Dist. A. M. E. Ch.; mem., Mason; A. M. E. Ch.; Home: 118 E. Lynn St., Covington, Ky.; Office: 120 E. Lynn St., Covington, Ky.

WHITE, Woodie W., b. New York, N. Y., A. B., Payne Coll., Augusta, Ga., 1958; S. T. B., Boston Univ., Sch. of Theol., 1961; Dir. of Youth, Trinity Meth. Ch., New Bedford, Mass.; m. Kim White; Children--Kimberly, Hope; pastor, St. Andrews Meth. Ch., Worcester, Mass.; assoc. pastor, E. Grand Blvd. Meth. Ch., Detroit, Mich., 1961; pastor, 1963-67; Urban Missioner for Meth. Ch. (Detroit Metro. Dist.), 1967-68; Dir., Commn. on Rel. and Race, United Meth. Ch., Wash., D. C., 1968-present; mem., NAACP, N. Y. br.; NAACP, past pres., coll. chap.; past pres., Meth. for Ch. Renewal; past pres., East Citizens for Action, Detroit; past pres., Chs. on the East Side for Social Action (CESSA); organizer of Black Meth. for Ch. Renewal; listed in _Who's Who in the Methodist Church_; Bd. mem., Interfaith Action Coun., Inc.; long time participant in organizations for racial justice; (jailed in Jackson, Miss. for attempting to attend church); recently named the recipient of the Urban Award, given by the Office of Economic Opportunity "for outstanding work with the people of the ghetto;" Office: The Commission on Religion and Race, The United Methodist Church, 100 Maryland Ave., NE, Wash., D. C. 20002

*WHITEN, Bennie Edward, Jr., b. Shreveport, La., June 26, 1933; s. Bennie Edward and Leoma (Pryor) W.; A. B., Texas Coll., 1952; B. D., Howard Univ., Sch. of Rel., 1958; m. Gwendolyn Marie Pearson; Children--Leslie Michelle, Bennie Edward III; chap. resident, St. Elizabeths Hosp., Wash., D. C., 1958-60; present: pastor, First Ref. Ch. (United Ch. of Christ), Cincinnati, O.; chrmn., NAACP Housing Comm., 1963-present; Adv. Comm., Better Housing League, 1963-present; trustee, Mayor's Friendly Relations Comm., 1963-present; US Army, Anti-aircraft Artillery Intelligence, 1953-

55; mem., Assn. of Mental Hosp. Chaplains; Kappa Alpha Psi; Home: 1512F Dudley St., Cincinnati, O.; Office: 1809 Freeman Ave., Cincinnati, O.

WHITLOW, Charles Williams, b. Clinton, Okla., Nov. 23, 1925; s. Coleman and Luvina (Johnson) Reece W.; A.B., Langston Univ., 1951; B.Th., Okla. Sch. of Rel., 1957; grad. work: Okla. Univ.; m. Juanita Lewis; Children--Michael, Rubie; pastor, Mt. Olive Bapt. Ch.; St. Paul Bapt. Ch.; Bethlehem Bapt. Ch.; pres., Western Dist. Sun. Sch. & B.T.U. Congress, 1949-61; pres., Chickasaw Dist. Congress, 1963--; principal and tchr., Lakeview, Tex., 1951-53; caseworker, 1953-55; v.p., Min. Alliance, Interracial Comm., 1962-63; Adv. Comm., Mental Health Prog., PTA; NAACP; Democrat; Urban League; US Navy, 1943-45; mem., Alpha Phi Alpha; Home: 311 N. Birch, Pauls Valley, Okla.

WHITTED, Andrew Eugen, b. Delco, N.C., Aug. 29, 1924; s. Manley and Josephine; A.B., Livingstone Coll., Salisbury, N.C., 1956; B.D., Hood Sem., 1959; Cert. Pastoral Couns., Grasslands Hosp., Valhala, N.Y.; m. Annette Estella Williams; pastor, St. Catherine A.M.E. Z. Ch., New Rochelle, N.Y.; A.M.E.Z. Min. Rep., World Coun. of Chs.; chrmn., Finance Com., Brooklyn Dist., A.M.E.Z. Ch.; mem., Budget Com. N.Y. Annual Conf.; pres., A.M.E.Z. Min. Alliance, N.Y.; New Rochelle br. NAACP; Citizens Civic Org.; Prot. Min. Assn.; chrmn., Bd. of Dir., Comm. Org. Prog.; mem., Coun. for Unity; Adv. Bd., Remington br. Boys Club; Mayor's Adv. Com. Bd. of Ed.; Com. Anti-poverty (CAPC); Ex. Bd., Charter League; Citizens Coun.; Home: 21 Lincoln Ave., New Rochelle, N.Y. 10801

WILKES, William Reid, bishop, b. Patnam Co., Ga., Apr. 10, 1902; A.B., Morris Brown Coll., 1928; B.D., 1933; D.D. (hon.), Morris Brown Coll.; LL.D. (hon.), Wilberforce Univ.; m. Nettie Julia Adams; Children--William Reid Jr., Alfred Weyman; coll. pastor, Morris Brown Coll.; pastor, Afr. Meth. Episc. Chs., Atlanta, Ga.; dir., Leadership Education and Min. Inst. (for the Episc. Dist.); elected bishop, 1948; presiding bishop 6th Dist., A.M.E. Ch.; pres., Coun. of Bishops; mem., Bd. of Trustees, Morris Brown Coll.; sec., Interdenom. Theol. Center; Mason; Phi Beta Si; mem., Mayor's Com. on Urban Renewal, Atlanta, Ga.; mem., Citizens Comm.; chrmn., Gen. Conf., Comm. on Finance, A.M.E. Ch.;

1st v.p., Gen. Bd., A.M.E. Ch.; mem., Door of Hope, Atlanta, Ga.; author: Christian Ed. in the Local Ch.; Home: 11009 Wade Park Ave., Cleveland, O. 44106

WILLI, Eddie James, chap., b. St. Petersburg, Fla., Jan. 5, 1925; s. Eddie James Rivers and Rosa Dennis Forman; A.B., Clark Coll., 1949; B.D., Gammon Theol. Sem., 1958; m. Ida Mae Gates Rivers; Children--Jeffrey James, Brenda Rose; asst. pastor, Warren Meml. Meth. Ch., Atlanta, Ga., 1947-48; pastor, Pleasant Hill Meth. Ch., Arcadia, Fla., 1952-55; Steward Meml. Meth. Ch., Daytona Beach, Fla., 1955-61; current, Ebenezer Meth. Ch., Jacksonville, Fla., 1961--; chrmn., Fla. Conf. Bd. of Ed., Meth. Ch.; dir. of music, Fla. Conf., Meth. Ch.; Assoc. Bd. Trustees, Bethune Cookman Coll., 1959; current chap., Bd. of Dirs., Brewster Meth. Hosp.; awards: United Negro Coll. Fund, Religion and Human Relations from Bethune Cookman Coll.; mem., YMCA; Mason; Knight of Pythian; Democrat; Home: 431 W. Ashley St., Jacksonville, Fla.

WILLIAMS, Albert Cecil, b. San Angelo, Tex., Sept. 22, 1929; A.B., Huston-Tillotson Coll., Austin, Tex., 1952; B.D., Perkins Sch. Theol., S.M.U., Dallas, Tex., 1955; M.A., Pacific Sch. of Rel., Berkeley, Calif.; m. Evelyn Robinson; Children--Kimberly, Albert Cecil, Jr.; asst. min., St. Paul Meth. Ch., Dallas, Tex., 1953-55; min., Meth. Ch., Hobbs, N.M.; chap. and instr., Huston-Tillotson Coll., Austin, Tex., 1956-59; min., St. James Meth. Ch., Kansas City, Mo.; dir., Community Involvement Glide Urban Center, 1964; min., Celebration Glide Meml. United Meth. Ch., 1966-present; min., Involvement Glide Urban Center, 1964-present; instr., Episc. Theol. Sem., S.W.; adv. Black Free Store Workers, Bayview Parent Action Group; adv. BUF; co-chrmn., CORE; chrmn., Ed. and Mem. CORE; Coun. Chs., Cir. Comm. Interdenom. Min. Alliance Independent Action Movement; mem., Comm. Martin Luther King, Jr.; Fellow. Prog. (Woodrow Wilson Natl. Fellow. Found.); Citizens Alert, Glide's Task Force; WACO (Western Addition Comm. Org.) worked with Artists' Liberation Front; helped convey the implications of "The Generation Gap;" as manifested by the Love Generation and the Black Power upsurge; Bd. Dir. Coun. Rel. and Homosexual; panelist and speaker, Un. Press Internatl. Conf. and Editors Conf.; speaker, black militants; hippie movement, Haight-Ashbury Dist., initiated thrust of Experimental Worship; recd. Man of Year award, 1967, Sun Reporter Newspaper; Home: 739 32nd Ave., San Francisco, Calif. 94121 Office: Glide Foundation, 330 Ellis St., San Francisco, Calif. 94102

WILLIAMS, Alonzia Kent, b. Scaife, Ark., Aug. 20, 1918; s. Arthur W. and Sophie (Franklin) W.; B.S., Tuskegee Inst., 1941; B.D., Gammon Theol. Sem., Atlanta, Ga.; m. Celia Roberta Foster; Children--Mrs. Harold Early, Arthur Kenneth, Willis Leon; pastor, Bethel Bapt., Tuskegee, Ala., 1941-56; Mt. Pleasant Bapt. Ch., Atlanta, Ga., 1956-57; Providence Bapt. Ch., Atlanta, Ga., 1957-59; The Meth. Ch., 1959-present; chap., V.A. Hosp., Tuskegee, Ala.; instr., Tuskegee Inst., 1945-46; Fla. A & M., Tallahassee, 1946-49; pub. sch., Ala., 1949-56; summer camp, Ridgefield, Conn., 1953-56; Bldg. & Ground Supt., Gammon Theol. Sem., 1956-59; prog. coordinator, Wesley House, Atlanta, Ga., 1959-61; electrician, Engineering Division, Veterans Administration Hosp., Tuskegee, 1962-66; precinct leader, Voters League, Atlanta, Ga.; pres., Mechanicsville, Civic Organ., Atlanta; Com. for Greater Tuskegee, Tuskegee Civic Assn.; Conf. chrmn., Amer. Bible Soc.; Home: 314 N. Jericho St., Tuskegee, Ala. 36083

WILLIAMS, Arthur Benjamin, Jr., b. Providence, R.I., June 25, 1935; s. Arthur and Eleanor; A.B., Brown Univ., Providence, R.I., 1957; S.T.B., Gen. Theol. Sem., N.Y., 1964; asst. rector, St. Mark's Episc. Ch., Riverside, R.I., 1965-67; sub. dean, Cathedral of St. John, Providence, R.I., 1967-68; assoc. rector, Grace Episc. Ch., Detroit, Mich., 1968-present; staff, Leadership Trng. Inst., Province 5, Episc. Ch.; Bd. of Dir., Big. Bro., R.I., 1966-68; State co-chrmn., Easter Seal Campaign, R.I., 1968; Natl. Com. of Inquiry, 1968; US Naval Officer, 1957-61; mem., Episc. Soc. for Cultural and Racial Unity; NCNC; Union of Black Clergy and Laity of Episc. Ch.; R.I. Coun. of Chs., Dept. of Urban Life and Min.; Dept. of Social Action; Home: 16161 Lawton, Detroit, Mich. 48221; Office: 1926 Va. Park, Detroit, Mich., 48206

WILLIAMS, Arthur D., chap., author, b. Abingdon, Va., July 22, 1895; s. Arthur C. and Hattie (Ellison) W.; A.B., Lincoln Univ., 1922; S.T.M., Temple Univ., 1949; Th.D., Harvard Univ., 1955; post grad., Yale Univ., American Bible Sch., Chicago; m. Cleo Dix;

Children--Arthur F., John Mark, Burton D., Dorothea W. (Mrs. Anderson), Sadie (Mrs. Snead), Harriette (Mrs. Batipps); ordained Meth. Ch., 1923; pastor, Second Presby. Ch., West Chester, Pa., 1920-23; Meth. Ch., Pocahontas, Va., 1924-30; Meth. Ch., Hot Springs, Ark., 1930-33; Clark Meml. Ch., Nashville, Tenn., 1933-35; Exec. sec., Nashville YMCA, 1935-38; Faith Presby. Ch., Pa., 1945-50; Second Presby. Ch., W. Chester, Pa., 1953-57; tchr., Phila. pub. schs. of retarded educables; current chap., The Eastern State Penitentiary, Phila., Pa., 1960--; assoc. dir., Skidmore Vocational Sch.; founder, Hattie Pation Williams Clinic; US Military Chap., 1941-47; pres., Natl. John Brown Assn.; mem., West Chester, Cham. of Commerce; Natl. Pastoral Counciling Assn., Phila.; Natl. Writers Assn.; awards: The Geo. Washington Medal of Honor for an outstanding accomplishment in helping to achieve a better understanding of the American way of life by sermon, "All or Nothing," 1964; 1st prize by Sat. Evening Post for the Year, 1962; 1st prize in book writing contest, Random House Publishers for US Fourth Class Citizens, 1963; 1st prize, Natl. Hospitalized Vets. Contest, 1962; 1st prize for NAACP Essay Contest (essay: "The Economic Element in Lynching and Mob Violence"); author: Another Simon of Cyrene; It Will Show in Your Face (poem); Jacob's Ladder; Snow and Ice Service (plays); Home: 2017 W. Girard Ave., Phila., Pa. 19130

WILLIAMS, Curtis, tchr., b. Rhine, Ga., May 13, 1927; s. John Luther and Grace (Harrell) W.; A. B., Western Reserve, 1952; B. D., Payne Theol. Sem., 1957; further study: Union Coll., Alliance, O.; Chgo. Theol. Sem.; m. Etta Belle Harris; Children--Gail, Deborah, Peter, Byron, Faith; pastor, Afr. Meth. Episc. Chs., Ariz., Ohio; current pastor, Bethel A. M. E. Ch., New Castle, Pa.; tchr., Ben Franklin Jr. High Sch., New Castle, Pa.; Dir., Public Relations, NAACP (New Castle, Pa.); US Air Force, 1945-48; Office: Bethel Afr. Meth. Ch., New Castle, Pa.

WILLIAMS, Dogan Wilford, b. Starkville, Miss., Feb. 18, 1920; s. Joseph S. and Penney (Robinson) W.; A. B., Rust Coll., Holly Springs, Miss., 1940-44; B. D., Gammon Theol. Sem., Atlanta, Ga., 1944-47; M. A., Garrett Sem., Northwestern Univ., Evanston, Ill., 1950-52; Children--Donna Wilfretta, Franklin Andrew, Penney Darlene; ministry: Randolph St. Meth. Ch., Lexington, Va., 1947-57; Wiley Meml. Meth. Ch., Chattanooga, Tenn., 1957-61; present: John Wesley Meth. Ch., Bristol, Va.; mem., Democratic Party, NAACP, PTA, Fraternal organization, Ministerial Assn.; Home: 427 Scott St., Bristol, Va.; Office: 311 Lee St., Bristol, Va.

WILLIAMS, Donald James, b. San Bernardino, Calif., Jan. 26, 1928; s. Harry Howard and Violette Lenora (Reynolds) W.; B.A., Oakwood Coll., 1950; M.A., Potomac Univ., Wash., D.C., 1960; m. Pearl Ernestine Harvey; pastor, Smyrna S.D.A. Ch., Lynchburg, Va., 1960-present; US Army, 1953-55; Home: 818 8th St., Lynchburg, Va.; Office: 911 Taylor St., Lynchburg, Va.

*WILLIAMS, Edward Samuel, b. Roanoke, Va., July 1, 1906; s. Edward and Nellie (Finney) W.; A.B., Johnson C. Smith Univ., 1938; B.D., Howard Univ., 1950; m. Annie May Calloway; Children--Camille Adelle, Marguerite May, Edward Samuel, Jr.; Jr. pastor, St. Paul Meth. Ch., Roanoke, Va., 1942; pastor, John Wesley Meth. Ch., Salem, Va., 1942-46; pastor, Mt. Zion Meth. Ch., Silver Springs, Md., 1946-50; pastor, Grace Meth. Ch., Fairmount Hqts., Md., 1950-59; assoc. pastor, Holman Meth. Ch., Los Angeles, Calif., 1959--; chrmn., Commn. on Minimum Salary, Chr. Comm. on State of Country; treasurer's asst., mem. of Comm. on Worship and Fine Arts; Positions held on Wash. District: Dir. of Temperance, mem. of Comm. on Ministerial Qualifications; treas., Local Chapt. NAACP, Salem, Va., 1944; Dir. of Wesley Found., Howard Univ., 1951-53; mem. Bd. of Mgrs. Wesley Found., Howard Univ., Wash., D.C., 1953-59; treasurer, Northeast Min. Alliance, Wash., D.C., 1957-59; mem., Omega Psi Phi; Urban League; NAACP; Home: 4536 W. 17th St., Los Angeles, Calif.; Office: 3320 W. Adams Blvd., Los Angeles, Calif.

WILLIAMS, Ernest Prince, b. Chgo., Ill., Apr. 8, 1910; s. Benjamin and Osceola (Hughes) W.; courses: Northwestern Univ., Campbell Coll., Eden's Sem., Webster Groves, Mo., St. Louis Univ., St. Louis, Mo.; pastored A.M.E. Chs., Frankfort, Ind., New Albany, Ind., Terre Haute, Ind., Peoria, Ill., E. St. Louis, Ill., Des Moines, Iowa; mem., Conf. Trustee for Ch. and Ch. Camp Barber; treas., Wilkie House Community Bd. of Dirs.; award: Merits of Civic Groups for Community Participation; mem., Kappa; Mason; author, Church Guide for Business Records; Home: 695 25th St., Des Moines, Iowa, 50312

WILLIAMS, Floyd Nathaniel, b. Dec. 16, 1928, Houston, Tex.; s. M. C. and Myrtle (W.); A. B. and B. D., Bishop Coll., Marshall, Tex., Tex. So. Univ.; D. D. (hon.), Union Bapt. Sem., Inc., Ala.; Sch. for Chaplains, Pa.; m. Addie Lee Brembry; 1 son, Floyd N. II; pastor, Greater Union Bapt. Ch., Matthews, Tex., 1950-54; Friendship Bapt. Ch.; St. John Missionary Bapt. Ch., Beaumont, Tex.; Antioch Bapt. Ch., Houston, Tex.; present, Bd. of Dirs., Houston Action for Youth; ex. sec., Com. for Excellence in Gov't.; Adv. Bd., Standard Saving and Loan Assn.; v. p., Bapt. Min. Assn.; chrmn., Fact-finding Com. Bapt. Ministers and Wives Coop. Union, Houston; ex. v. moderator, Ind. Dist. Bapt., Tex. auditor, Missionary Bapt. Gen. Coordinator (Tex.); business mgr., Union Bapt. Theol. Sem. (Houston); sec.-treas., Natl. Bapt. Conv. of Amer.; mem., Natl. Com. of Negro Churchmen; Omega Psi Phi; Acres Homes Civic Club, Inc.; awards: Outstanding Citizenship 1960 (Harris Co.); mem., Democrat, NAACP, Democratic Natl. Comm.; write-in candidate for State Repr., Dist. 22; US Army (3 yrs.); Office: 5902 Beall St., Houston, Tex. 77018

*WILLIAMS, Frank Leviticus, city official, b. Barnwell, S. C., Oct. 12, 1917; s. Robert B. and Theodocia E. (Wright) W.; Voorhees Jr. Coll., 1935-37; A. B., Claflin Coll., 1937-39; B. D., Howard Univ., Sch. of Rel., 1939-42; m. Ruth Estella Carr; Children--Frank L. Jr., Beryl C., Cheryl R., Mark Robert; pastor, John Steward Meth. Ch., Wash., D. C., 1942-49; Christ Meth. ch., Balto., Md., 1949-56; pastor, Metro. Meth. Ch., Balto., Md., 1956-67; Asbury U. Meth. Ch., Wash., D. C., 1967--; trustee, Morristown Coll., Morristown, Tenn.; pres., Interdenom. Min. Alliance, Balto., Md., 1960--; Phi Beta Sigma; apptd. to Balto. Community Relations Commn., 1964; Gov.'s Police Adv. Commn., 1964; Home: 3801 So. Dakota Ave., Wash., D. C.; Office: 11th & K Sts., Wash., D. C.

WILLIAMS, Frederick Boyd, curate, b. Chattanooga, Tenn., Apr. 23, 1939; s. Walter Howard and Matlyn (Goodman) W.; B. A., Morehouse Coll., 1959; Howard Univ., 1959-61; S. T. B., Gen. Theol. Sem., 1963; Christopher's

Chapel, N.Y.C., asst. seminarian, 1960; curate, All Saints Aglican Parish, St. Thomas, Virgin Islands, (summer 1962); St. Marks Episc. Ch., Mt. Kisco, N.Y., 1961-63; curate, St. Luke Prot. Episc. Ch., Wash., D.C., 1963--; research assoc. mathematics, Goddard Space Flight Center, NASA, Wash., D.C., 1960; assoc. chap., Boy's Village, Cheltenham, Md., 1963--; mem., Delta Sigma Rho, Pi Mu Epsion, Beta Kappa Chi, Alpha Phi Gamma, ESCRU, Kappa Alpha Psi; Home: 1 Hawaii Ave. NE, Washington, D.C.; Office: 1514 15th St., NW, Wash., D.C.

WILLIAMS, Henry Charlie, b. Burke Co., Ga., Apr. 10, 1886; s. Columbus and Mary; Bogs Acad., Keysville, Ga.; Walker Bapt. Inst. of Augusta; m. Daisy Franklin; Children--Eugene, Henry, Annie Mae (Mrs. Sidney Drayton); Anna Lee (Mrs. Sol Green), Charlie, Lumby, Daisy (Mrs. Fletcher Johnson) Mary (Mrs. Nathan Muller), Robert, Louise (Mrs. Richard Henderson); pastor, Beechwood and Katesville Bapt. Ch., Waynesboro, Ga., Friendly Bapt. Ch., Phila., Pa., 1943-present; pres., Mt. Carmel Min. and Deacons' Union, 1946-62; treas., Bapt. Min. Evening Conf., Phila., 1956-66; Home: 3111 W. Columbia Ave., Phila., Pa. 19121

WILLIAMS, Henry E., b. Charleston Co., S.C.; s. Edward and Hannah (Bryon) W.; A.B., Johnson C. Smith Univ., 1924-28; B.D., Johnson C. Smith Div. Sch., 1928-31; Children--Rose M. Chavis, L.G. Chavis, Henry; pastor, Mizpah Presby. Ch., So. Boston, Va. Ebenezer Presby. Ch., New Bern, N.C., Mt. Pisgor, Presbyn. Ch., Rocky Mt., N.C.; Freedom E. Presbyn. Ch., Raiford, N.C.; Mars' Hill Presbyn. Ch., Hope Mills, N.C.; Ogden Presbyn. Ch., Charlie Hope, Va.; Great Creek Presbyn. Ch., Brasey, Va.; principal and tchr., Mizpah Sch., So. Boston, Va. pub. sch., Charlie Co., Va.; princ. and tchr., pub. sch., Pamplico Co., N.C.; princ. and tchr. pub. sch., Nash Co., N.C.; princ. and tchr., pub. sch., Hoka Co., N.C.; mem., Mason, Phi Beta Sigma; Home: 716 Atlantic Ave., Rocky Mt., N.C.; Church: Ogden Church, Charlie Hoop, Va.

WILLIAMS, James David, b. Lenoir Co., Kinston, N.C., Mar. 30, 1916; s. Walter and Orpha; courses: Va. Union Univ., Richmond, Va.; m. Victoria Blackmon; Children--Lois, Jean, Preston, Vernell, Alma; tchr., 1st Bethel Bapt. Ch.; trustee, Banking Comm.; pastor, Missionary

Star of East; Mt. Herman Bapt. Ch., Richmond, Va.; cons., Mt. Herman Bapt. Ch.; mem., E. End Masonic Lodge, Richmond, Va.; US Air Force, 1944-45; Home: Rte 5, Box 215 G, Richmond, Va., 23231; Office: 2814 Moss Side Ave., Richmond, Va. 23222

WILLIAMS, John F., b. Pittsfield, Mass., B. S., S. T. B., Pa. Bible Inst., Union Univ., Temple Univ., grad. courses, Union Theol. Sem. (NYC) 2 summers; D. D. (hon.), Va. Theol. Sem. & Coll., Lynchburg, Va., 1954; pastor, Bapt. Chs., Phila., Newport News, Va., W. Va., New Orleans; present pastor, Shiloh Bapt. Ch., St. Paul, Minn.; former mem., Newport News Citizens Adv. Bd. and City Planning Commn.; Bd. dirs., Newport News Community Bldg. & Loan Assn. (7 yrs.); pres., State BTU Conv. (Bapt.), (4 yrs.); Dist. Sun. Sch. Conv. (4 yrs.); del., World Coun. of Chs.; World Bapt. Alliance; mem., White House Conf. on Civil Rights; Financial sec., Progressive Bapt. Assn.; present Bd. mem., TCOIC; Bd. mem., TEIP, Racial & Economic Integration Planners; mem., Minority Housing Commn.; pres., St. Paul Interdenom. Min. Alliance, St. Paul; v. p., St. Paul Min. Assn.; Home: 860 Hague Ave., St. Paul, Minn. 55104

*WILLIAMS, John V., army chap., b. Wash., D. C., Aug. 30, 1930; s. Chancellor James and Mattie (McRae) W.; B. A., Howard Univ., 1953; B. D., 1959, M. Div., 1970, Howard Univ., Sch. of Rel., m. Beatrice E. Bryant; Children--John V. Jr., Gregory H., Kenneth T.; asst.pastor, First Bapt. Ch., Deanwood, 1949-52; First Bapt. Ch., SW, 1952-54, 1956-59; US Chap. Corps, 1959-62; serving currently in Mannheim, Germany, 1962--; pres., The Mannheim-Heidelberg Coun. for Retarded Children; award: The Army Commendation Medal for Meritorious Service; mem., Military Chap. Assn.; Home: 5000 Sheriff Rd. NE, Wash., D. C.; Office: HQ 19th Ordnance Bn. APO 166, New York, N. Y.

WILLIAMS, John W.; b. Houston, Tex., Jan. 3, 1908; s. Briscoe and Annie W.; A. B., B. Th., D. D. (hon.), Conroe Normal & Indus. Coll.; B. D., Th. M., Th. D., Central Bapt. Theol. Sem.; D. D. (hon.), Western Bapt. Bible Coll., Kan. City, Mo.; courses, Univ. of Kan.; m. Dorothy Mae McKeever; Children--John Wesley, Jr., Dorothy Mae, Marena Ann; pastor, St. Stephen Bapt. Ch., Kan. City, Mo.; present pres., Gen. Bapt. Conv.

of Amer.; pres., Bd. of Management, Bapt. Home for the Aged, Independence, Mo.; presiding officer, Natl. Bapt. Sunday Sch. & Bapt. Trng. Union Congress; mem., Natl. Bapt. Pub. Bd., Gen. Bd., Natl. Coun. of Chs. of Chrst, USA; Exec. Bd., Bapt. World Alliance; mem., pres.-elect, Commn. on Rel. & Race, Nat. Coun. of Chs., 1965; mem., Exec. Com., Coun. of Chs. of Greater Kan. City; pres., Gen. Min. Alliance, Kan. City; v.p.-at-large, Natl. Coun. of Chs. in Christ, USA; mem., Adv. Com., Independence, Mo. Redevelopment Assn.; mem., Kan. City Chamber of Commerce Redevelopment and Planning Com.; mem., Omega Psi Phi; Mason; recd. Omega Psi Phi achievement award, 1947; Scroll of Honor, 1951; Office: St. Stephen Bapt. Ch., 1414 Truman Rd., Kan. City, Mo.

WILLIAMS, Joseph Henry, b. Kans. City, Kans., Dec. 29, 1928; s. Joseph Henry Sr. and Rhona (Evans) W.; B.A., Tenn. A & I State Univ., 1950; B.D., Central Bapt. Theol. Sem., 1954; m. Constance Loraine Hill; Children--Rhona Loraine, Brent Joseph, Evan Matthew; pastor, St. John Bapt. Ch., Salina, Kan., 1952-55; chap., US Army, 1955-58; cooperative field worker in education and miss., Detroit, Mich., 1958-63; Detroit Assn. of Amer. Bapt. Chs. and Amer. Bapt. Home Miss. Societies and Wolverine State Miss. Bapt. Conv.; pastor, First Bapt. Inst. Ch., Hamtramck, Mich., 1963-present; mem., Coun. of Bapt. Pastors, Detroit and vicinity; supr., Admin. Div., Natl. Sun. Sch. and B.T.U. Congress; auditor, Met. Bapt. Dist. Assn., Detroit; Wolverine State Bapt. Conv.; mem., Detroit and Hamtramck Mich. br. NAACP; recd. letter of commendation from commanding officer, US Army Reception Sta., Ft. Leonard Wood, Mo., 1958; letter of merit, Dir. of Red Cross, Ft. Leonard Wood, Mo., 1958; Alpha Phi Alpha; mem., Detroit Coun. of Chs. Pastors Union; part-time contributr., Natl. Bapt. Sun. Sch. Pub. Bd.; Home: 4130 Kendall St., Detroit, Mich. 48238

WILLIAMS, Julian Leander, b. Albany, Ga., Dec. 20, 1908; s. James A. and Ida (Marshall) W.; B.S., Oakwood Coll., 1951; m. Juanita C. Ward; Children--Irene (Mrs. Leanard Williams), Julian Leander, Jr.; pastored S.D.A. Chs. in: Huntsville, Ala., 1951; Daytona Beach and Ocala, Fla., 1956-60; Fayetteville, N.C., 1960-61; present: pastor, S.D.A. Ch. in Winston-Salem, N.C., 1962-; pub. sec., So. Atlantic Conf., 1951-56; former chap.,

State School, Forest Hills, Fla.; Corp., US Army, 1943-45; Home: PO Box 2755, Winston-Salem, N.C.; Office: 240 N. Dunleith Ave., Winston-Salem, N.C.

WILLIAMS, Lawrence Jesse, b. Atlanta, Ga., Mar. 4, 1917; s. Horace H. and Lizzie W.; Morris Brown Coll., Atlanta, Ga., 1942-44; Wilberforce Univ., Wilberforce, O., 1947-49; m. Libra Holt; Children--Kathaleen; pastor, A.M.E. Chs., Atlanta, Ga., Akron, Bethel, Lebanon, Cleveland, O.; Collins, Lansing, Mich.; present pastor, Community A.M.E. Ch., Jackson, Mich.; volunteer chap., Foote Hosp.; Exec. Bd., O.E.O.; Jackson Co., NAACP Ed. Com.; mem., City Improvement Com.; sub. chap., Mich. State Prison; Democrat; mem., Min. Assn., Jackson, Mich.; Mason; Home: 218 E. Franklin, Jackson, Mich. 49201; Office: 222 E. Franklin St., Jackson, Mich.

WILLIAMS, Linda Colene, b. Laurens, S.C., July 4, 1921; dau., Bravell and Anna Mae (Glenn) Nelson; Moody Bible Inst., Chgo.; Phila. Coll. of Bible; Th.B., Amer. Bible Coll., Chgo., 1957; D.D. (hon.), Miller Univ., Camden, N.J., 1962; m. John E. Selby (dec.); James A. Williams; Children--Garnita M. Selby, Mrs. Cromwell Pope, Reginald Williams; pastor, Holy Temple Ch. of Living God, Penns Grove, N.J., 1953-present; licensed nurse, 1955; natl. pres., Foreign Miss Bd.; brought anti-poverty prog. to Penns Grove, N.J.; wrote creed of Ch. of the Living God, 1953; one of the founders of the Natl. Youth Congress, 1952; sec., Interdenom. Union of Salem Co., 1957; v.p., 1960-present; awarded Phila. Seal by Human Rel. Bd.; Home: 446 S. 49th St., Phila., Pa. 19143

WILLIAMS, Mac James, b. Rutherfordton, N.C., Dec. 11, 1928; s. M. C. and Essie M. Williams; A.A., Gibbs Jr. Coll., St. Petersburg, Fla., 1963; B.S., Fla. Coll., St. Augustine, Fla., 1965; m. Rosa L. Watts; Children --Mac J. Jr., Pamela D., Essie M., Brenda J., Yolanda D.; pastor, Mt. Olive Bapt. Ch., Tampa, Fla., 1955-58; Shiloh Bapt. Ch., Dunedin, Fla., 1958-pres.; Fla. State Chrmn., Collegiate Council for the UN, 1963-64; Intl. Affairs v.p., 1954-65; pres., Dunedin Coun. on Human Relations, 1966; sponsor of Afr. visitors in Fla. under Dept. of State; service repr., Soc. Security Admin., Clearwater, Fla.; asst. Dean of Ed., Progressive Bapt. State Sun. Sch. and BTU Conv. of Fla., 1964-present; mem., Comm. for better housing, apptd. by Mayor of Dunedin, Fla.; first Negro mem., Bd. of Clearwater Mental Health Assn.; cited as Citizen of the Year, Pinellas Co. Commissioners, 1964; Mason; state deputy, Lily Security Assn.; Who's Who In Amer. Coll. and Univ., 1965; UN Assn. of the US, 1965; NAACP; Democrat; Dunedin Min. Assn.; asst. financ. sec., First S. Fla. Bapt. Assn.; mem., State Miss. Bd., Progressive Bapt. State Conv., Fla.; Home: 7902 Fir Dr., Tampa, Fla.; Office: 1106 Douglas Ave., Dunedin, Fla.

WILLIAMS, McKinley, bishop, b. Albany, Ga., Feb. 17, 1901; s. John and Eliza; Albany State Coll.; Amer. Bible Coll., 1950-53, Th. B. M. D.; D. D. (hon.), Amer. Bible Coll.; m. Ethel Mae Thomas; pastor, The Refuge Ch. of Christ, Bible Way World-Wide Inc., Phila., Pa.; current, Bd. of Bishops, The Bible Way Chs. World-wide Inc.; mem., Bd. of Dirs., Carver Loan Investment Co., Columbia Ave., Phila., Pa.; Bd. of 500 Ministers Selective Service; The Downingtown Sch. Bd.; The Geo. T. Mitchell B. & L. Bd. of Dirs.; Home: 523 S. Lansdowne Ave., Yeadon, Pa.; Office: 52nd & Rose Sts., Phila., Pa.

WILLIAMS, Robert, b. White Castle, La., Mar. 12, 1931; s. Sidney Sr. and Effie W.; B. A., Tenn. State Univ., 1957; B. D., Interdenom. Theol. Center, 1966; D. D. (hon.), Interdenom. Theol. Center, 1966; m. Helen Amiker; Children--Rolen DeVelera, Efylma LaMona, Deidre Faye; soc. worker, the La. Dept. of Public Welfare, New Orleans, 1958-63; current pastor, Brooks Meth. Ch., New Orleans, La., 1966--; US forces, 1951-53; mem., Theta Phi Honorary Soc.; Exec. Coun. of the St. Bernard Community Coun.; NAACP; Home: 2611 So. Robertson St., New Orleans, La. 70115

WILLIAMS, Robert Gilmore, b. Fredericksburg, Va., June 19, 1924; s. Charles Beale and Lelia (Wormley) W.; A. B., Va. Union Univ., Richmond, Va., 1945; B. D., 1952; grad. courses: Boston Univ.; m. Doris Inez Brown; Children--Robert Gilmore Jr., Denise Rozelle; pastor, Zion Bapt. Ch., Petersburg, Va., 1947-62; Union Br. Bapt. Ch., Prince Ga., 1956-62; current pastor, Mt. Moriah Bapt. Ch., Wash., D. C., 1962--; career counselor, Va. High Schs.; staff mem., Petersburg Family Counseling Service; mem., Exec. Bd., Southern Chrstn. Leadership Conf.; former mem., Bd. of Management,

USO; Exec. Bd., NAACP; Va. Coun. of Human Rights; Va. Bapt. Children's Home (all Petersburg, Va.); former visiting lectr., Va. Union Univ. and Va. State Coll.; Va. State v.p., Lott Carey and Natl. Bapt. Conv., 1959-62, 1960-62; Trustee Bd., Va. Union Univ., 1960-62; elected pres., Bapt. Gen. Assn., Va., 1960; pres., Petersburg, Improvement Civic Assn., 1961-62; citation from Central N.J. Freedom Assn. (for role in Civil Rights struggle); mem., Mason, Omega Psi Phi, Natl. Frontiers Club of America; leader and coordinator, 1960 Pilgrimage of Prayer for pub. sch. support, Va.; jailed for seeking to use public library, integrate in Petersburg, Va. Trailways Bus Terminals and eating facilities; Home: 7617 12th St. NW, Wash., D.C. 20012; Office: Mt. Moriah Bapt. Ch., 17th & East Capitol St. NE, Wash., D.C.

WILLIAMS, Samuel, b. Brewton, Ala., Mar. 30, 1922; s. James and Gertrude (Mobley) W.; Northwestern Jr. Coll., Orange City, Iowa, 1941-43; A.B., Central Coll., Pella, Iowa, 1946-48; B.D., Western Theol. Sem., Holland, Mich., 1948-51; m. Pauline Hendrieth; Children--Marcia Amelia, Wanda Sylvia, Paula Velucia, Samuel Lloyd; sch. pastor-tchr.-dean of boys, Southern Normal High Sch., Brewton, Ala., 1951-60; current pastor, Pembroke Community Ref. Ch., Saint Anne, Ill., 1960-present; US Army, taught basic reading, writing and arithmetic, Ft. Benning, Ga.; mem., Pembroke Community Consolidated sch., PTA; mem., Saint Anne Min. Prot. Assn.; Kankakee Co. Inter-Faith Comm.; pres., Illiana Classics (Presbytery); mem. of the Bd. of No. American Missions, Ref. Ch. in Amer.; articles for Church Herald, Reformed Ch. in Amer. official magazine; Home: Rte 1, Box 113-A, Saint Anne, Ill.

*WILLIAMS, Samuel, b. Burke Co., Ga., Dec. 7, 1939; s. Linyon and Cora; B.S., Savannah State Coll., Savannah, Ga., 1962; B.D., Howard Univ., Sch. of Rel., 1965; m. Claudia Quarterman; Children--Samuel, Samaithia; asst. min., Cap. View Bapt. Ch., Wash., D.C., 1962-65; dir., Youth Prog., Metro. Mission, Detroit, Mich.; asst. min., St. Mark's UCC, Saginaw, Mich., 1963-64; counselor, Dublin 4-H Club, Dublin, Ga., 1962; chrmn., Fair Repr. Com., Savannah-Chatham Co. Human Rel. Coun., 1967-68; v. chrmn., exec. com., Chatham Coun. on Human Rel., 1964; chrmn., God and Country Award; Chatham Dist. Boy Scouts of Amer., 1966-68; award,

Service, Chatham Dist. Boy Scouts of Amer.; mem., SE Assoc. of Deans of Men; Amer. Coll. Personnel Assn.; Natl. Assn. of Coll.and Univ. Chaplains; NAACP; YMCA; Mason; Ga. Tchrs. Ed. Assn.; Alpha Phi Alpha; Home: 1618 Eleanor St., Savannah, Ga. 31404; Office: Student Personnel, Savannah State Coll., Savannah, Ga. 31404

WILLIAMS, Samuel Jerome, b. Waycross, Ga., Dec. 5, 1907; s. Henry and Jannie; courses, Northan Sch. of Rel., Newark, N.J.; Daniel Paine Coll., Birmingham, Ala.; m. Creola Johnson; pastor, Calvary Bapt. Ch., Norwalk, Conn.; pres., NAACP; Min. Clergy Club; v.p., Coun. of Chs., State of Conn.; mem., Fairfield Co. Assn. of Bapt. Chs.; Conn. Bapt. Missionary Union; Mason; chap., Norwalk Police Dept.; Home: 10 Sable St., Norwalk, Conn., 06854

*WILLIAMS, Samuel Woodrow, coll. prof., b. Sparkman, Ark.; s. Arthur and Annie (Willie) W.; A.B., Morehouse Coll., 1937; B.D., M.A., Howard Univ. Sch. of Rel., 1941, 1942; courses completed Ph.D., Univ. of Chgo.; D.D. (hon.), Ark. Bapt. Coll., 1960; m. Billye Suber; Children--Samuel Golar; chap. and prof., Alcorn Coll., 1942-44; chap. and prof., Ala. A M & N Coll., 1944-46; current prof., Morehouse Coll., 1946--; pastor, Friendship Bapt. Ch., Atlanta, Ga., 1954--; Home: 863-1/2 Fair St. SW, Atlanta, Ga.; Office: 437 Mitchell St. SW, Atlanta, Ga.

WILLIAMS, Smallwood Edmund, bishop, b. Lynchburg, Va., Oct. 17, 1907; s. Edmund and Mary (Broadus) W.; Howard Univ., Sch. of Rel.; B.Th., Amer. Bible Coll., Wash., D.C., 1948; D.D. (hon.), Va. Theol. Sem. & Coll., Lynchburg, Va., 1950; m. Verna L. Rapley; Children--Smallwood Jr., Pearl, Yvonne, Wallace; licensed to preach, 1923, Ch. of Our Lord Jesus Christ of the Apostolic Faith; organized Bible Way Ch. of Our Lord Jesus Christ, Wash., D.C., 1925; current senior bishop and pastor, Bible Way Ch., Wash., D.C.; pres., Commn. on Mental Retardation; del., Democratic Conv., 1964; pres., So. Chrstn. Leadership Conf., Wash., D.C.; estab. recreation center, summer camp, welfare home under sponsorship of Bible Way Ch.; named most popular radio minister, newspaper poll, 1943; mem., Ex. Comm., NAACP, Wash., D.C.; Comm. of Natl. Fraternal Coun. of Chs. in America; dir., The Bible

Way News Voice (bi-monthly); founder and dir., Bible Way Trng. Sch. for Ministers and Christn. workers, 1944; founded sch. and mission in Liberia (1958); mem., Bd. of Dirs., Wash. Home Rule Commn., Inter-religious Commn. on Race Relations, 1963-64, Wash., D. C.; Home: 4720 16th St. NW, Wash., D. C.; Office: 1130 New Jersey Ave., Wash., D. C.

WILLIAMS, Stacy, b. Pontiac, Mich., Mar. 31, 1929; s. Jessie and Martha Ann; A. B., Va. Union Univ., Richmond, Va., 1957; courses, Detroit Bible Coll.; Wayne State Univ., Detroit; m. Elnora Evans; Children--Terry Suzanne, McKinley Anthony, Tracey Evans; pastor, Young Peoples Ch. of the Sacred Cross Bapt. Ch., 1947-52; Lombardy Grove Bapt. Ch., Mecklenburg Co., Va., 1955-56; Swansboro Bapt. Ch., S. Richmond, Va., 1956-63; McKinley Meml. Bapt. Ch., Willow Grove, Pa., 1963-66; Peace Bapt. Ch., Detroit, Mich., 1966-present; tchr., pub. schs., Phila., Pa.; Richmond, Va.; mem., Bapt. Min. Conf., Phila., Pa.; Coun. of Bapt. Pastors, Detroit; former pres., Richmond Tchrs. Assn., Richmond, 1962-64; mem., Hampton Inst. Preaching Conf., 1958-present; organizer, "The Helper's" organ. of pub. sch. tchrs.; Home: 19178 Keystone St., Detroit, Mich. 48234; Office: 13450 Goddard St., Detroit, Mich. 48212

*WILLIAMS, W. Clyde, youth worker, sem. official; b. Cordele, Ga., Aug. 29, 1932; s. M. R. and Annie (Clude) W.; A. B., Paine Coll., 1955; B. D., Howard Univ., Sch. of Rel., 1959; M. R. E., Interdenom. Theol. Center 1961; m. Elaine Wade; Children--Joyce Lorraine, Clyde Randolph; dir. of Boys Work, Bethlehem Community Center, 1953-56; student missionary to Cuba, 1954; State dir. of youth work, Sixth Dist. Chrstn. Meth. Episc. Ch., Ga., 1959-62; dir. of recruiting Interdenom. Theol. Center, 1962-69; Assoc. Gen. Sec. Consultation on Ch. Union (COCU), 1969--; pastor, Trinity C. M. E. Ch., Milledgeville, Ga., 1962-63; chrmn., Com. on Youth Work, Ga. Coun. of Chs.; chrmn., Youth Work, Bd. of Chrstn. Ed. of the C. M. E. Ch., citation for outstanding community service rendered at Bethlehem Community Center, Augusta, Ga., 1955; mem., Masons; YMCA; NAACP; Minister-layman Coun. of the C. M. E. Ch.; MRE Thesis: "The Nature and Development of Youth Work of the C. M. E. Ch.," Ga., 1954-61; Office: Consultation on Church Union, Princeton, N. J.

WILLIAMS, Wilbert Henry, b. Columbus, O., Dec. 13, 1913; s. 'Iradell H. and Nina (Condiff) W.; attended Philander Smith Coll., Little Rock, Ark., Extension studies at Univ. of Pittsburgh; m. Catherine Lois Palmer; Children--Wilbert A. Jr., Clarissa, Jerin, Gabriel Timothy, Stanley Jerome, Linda Joyce, Charles Wesley; ministry: John Stewart Meml. Meth. Ch., Marietta, O., 1943-46; Penna. Ave. Meth. Ch., Columbus, O., 1946-49; Simpson Meth. Ch., Steubenville, O., 1949-52; Wesley Meml. Meth. Ch., Jeffersonville, Ind., 1952-56; St. Johns Meth. Ch., Evansville, Ind., 1956-57; Gunn Tabernacle Meth. Ch., Lexington, Ky., 1957-63; York St. Meth. Ch., Cincinnati, O., 1963-present; agent, superintendent and supervisor for former Domestic Life and Accident Ins. Co. of Louisville, Ky. (12 yrs.); first Negro Jury Commissioner, Steubenville, O., elected as only Negro charter commissioner of Steubenville, O., 1952; youth pres., jr. chapter of NAACP, Steubenville, O.; past pres., of Inter-Group Goodwill Assn. for Civic, Social, Economic, and Cultural Progress, Steubenville, O., 1951; Home: 838 Clark St., Apt. G., Cincinnati, O.; Office: York St. Meth. Ch., Cincinnati, O.

WILLIAMS, Willie George, b. Tupelo, Miss., s. W. M. and Josephine (Glass) W.; Western Bapt. Coll., Kans. City, Kans.; B. Th., Central Bapt. Sem., 1946; B. S., Drake Univ., 1956; M. A., Central Bapt. Sem., 1957; m. Sharlee Annatia West; Children--Jerome Lawrence; supply pastor, First Bapt. Ch., Montserat, Mo.; First Bapt. Ch., Nicodemus, Kans.; Independent Bapt. Ch., Leavenworth, Kans., 1952-64; current pastor, Calvary Bapt. Ch., Wichita, Kans., 1964--; pres., Leavenworth Co. Min. Alliance; mem., Planning Com. for Co. Home; Resolutions Com., Natl. Bapt. Conv., USA; v. p., Natl. Congress; moderator, Northeastern Dist.; former moderator, Smoky Hill River Dist.; instr., Summer Retreat Missionary Bapt. Conv., Kans.; pres., State Bapt. Congress, Kans.; a'golden key from the Mayor, City of Leavenworth; Home: 2344 E. 25th St., Wichita, Kans.; Office: 601 Water St., Wichita, Kans.

WILLIAMS, W. Hazaiah, s. Rev. and Mrs. Wm. H. Willians; A. B., Wayne State Univ., B. S. T., Boston Univ. Sch. of Theol.; grad. courses Univ. of Calif., pastor, Red. Ed. Ch. for the Fellowship of All People, San Francisco, 1955; pastor, So. Berkeley Community Ch., Berkeley, 1956; Ch. for Today, Berkeley Calif., present;

former dir., E. Bay Conf. on Rel., Race and Social Justice; present, prof. and dir., Center for Urban Black Studies, Grad. Theol. Union, Berkeley; former concert mgr. for Robt. Nolan Chorale, Detroit, Mich, 1946; dir., Youth Work Meth. Chs., Sudbury and Maynard, Mass., 1952-55; dir. and organizer Panel of Americans Intergroup Discussion Organization, 1952-55; Boston Univ.; founder-dir., Today's Performing Arts Concerts; founder-dir., Alamo Black Clergy; dir., TV Series Dialogue, Channel 2, Oakland, Calif.; Office: San Fran. Theol. Sem. and Grad. Sch., San Anselmo, Calif.

*WILLIS, Charles Vernon, b. Atlanta, Ga., Sept. 6, 1918; s. Silas and Belle Tigner; B.S., State Teachers Coll., Montgomery, Ala., 1943; B.D., Howard Univ., Sch. of Rel., Wash., D.C., 1947; m. Cecilia; assoc. min., Morning Star Bapt. Ch., Balto., Md., 1953-55; pastor, Tabernacle Bapt. Ch., Coatesville, Pa., 1955; mem., Coatesville Housing Com., 1964-65; Human Rel. Coun., 1966-present; Coatesville Opportunities Coun., 1964--; NAACP Housing Chrmn., 1965--; 1st v. moderator, Salem Bapt. Gen. Assn.; Coatesville Area Ministerium, Greater Phila. Area Bapt. Min. Alliance; mem., Natl. Bapt. Conv.; Home: 417 N. 8th Ave., Coatesville, Pa.19320

WILLIS, Jesse Billinger, b. Calvert, Tex., Nov. 4, 1910; s. Jeff A. and Alice (Tiller) W.; Southern Bible Trng. Sch., Dallas, Tex.; m. Della Hunter; Children--J.B. II, James W., Maggie, Lenora, Victor, Marion; pastor, Marshall Chapel, Marlin, Tex.; Mt. Pleasant, Corsicana, Tex.; True Vine-Ferris, Tex.; Old Mt. Zion, Waxahachie, Tex.; Mt. Rose, Dallas, Tex.; El Bethel, San Fran., Calif.; St. Andrew, San Francisco, Calif.; instr., Bishop Coll. Extension, Dallas, Tex.; mem., Constitutional State Bapt. Conv. of Calif. and Nev.; mem., Progressive Natl. Bapt. Conv., Inc.; Home: 816 Haight St., San Francisco, Calif.; Office: 2565 Post St., San Francisco, Calif.

*WILLIS, Oliver Hunter, b. Harpers Ferry, W. Va., July 12, 1924; s. William and Rose; Storer Coll., Harpers Ferry, W. Va., 1948; Howard Univ., Sch. of Rel., Wash., D.C., 1951; studies, Mich. State Univ., Geo. Peabody Coll., Nashville, Tenn.; m. Viola Nixon; Children--Oliver; instr., S.C. Sch. for the Blind, 1951-present; pastor, New Bethel Ch., Woodruff, S.C.; Home: Evans Acres, Roebuck, S.C. 29376

WILMORE, Gayraud Stephen, Jr., ch. official, b. Phila., Dec. 20, 1921; s. Gayraud S., Sr. and Patricia (Gardner) W.; A.B., Lincoln Univ.; Pa., 1947; B.D., Lincoln Univ. Theol. Sem., 1950; S.T.M., Temple Univ., 1952; D.D. (hon.), Lincoln Coll., 1960; post-grad., Drew Univ., 1961; m. Lee Wilson; Children--Stephen, Jacques, Roberta, David; pastor, Second Presbyn. Ch., West Chester, Pa., 1950-53; regional sec., Student Chrstn. Movement (Mid-Atlantic Region), 1953-56; assoc. sec., Social Ed. & Action, United Presby. Ch., 1956-60; asst. prof., Pittsburgh Theol. Sem., 1960-63; exec. dir., United Presby. Commn. on Rel. and Race, 1963--; consultant, Ch. and Economic Life, United Presby. Bd. of Chrstn. Ed., 1962; candidate for county office - Democratic Party of Del. Co., Pa., 1960; Bd. of Dir., Neighborhood Centers, Inc., Pittsburgh, Pa., 1963; US Army T/4 371st Inf., 92nd Div., Italy, 1944-46; mem., NAACP; Democrat; Presby. Interracial Coun.; Alpha Phi Alpha; editor, "Christian Perspectives on Social Problems" series of Westminster Press; author: The Secular Relevance of the Church, Westminster, 1963; articles in various periodicals; Home: Rd 1, Skillman, N.J.; Office: Rm. 367 Interchurch Center, 475 Riverside Dr., New York, N.Y.

WILSON, Donald Octavio, b. Port Limon, Costa Rica, Central America, Nov. 19, 1915; s. John Christopher and Jeanette Gaynor (Wilson) W.; B.A., Bloomfield Coll. and Seminary, 1942; S.T.B., Gen. Theol. Sem., 1945; Berkely Div. Sch., 1945-46; Union Theol. Sem., 1951-52; Grad. Sch. of Theol., Temple Univ., 1960-62; m. Theda Isabell Morris. Locum Tenens, St. Luke's Episc. Ch., New Haven, Conn., 1945-46; vicar, St. Simon the Cyprenian Ch., Springfield, Mass., 1946-51; and St. Matthew's Ch., Wilmington, Del., 1951-63; present: rector, St. James Ch., Baltimore, Md., 1963--; chrmn., United Negro Coll. Fund Dr., 1952-54; Bd. of Dirs., Child Guidance Center, Bd. of Dirs., St. Matthew's Comm. Center; Mayor's Comm. on Housing; Chap., TB Hosp., 1955-63; Mason; Alpha Phi Alpha; Home: 2701 N. Hilton St., Balto., Md.; Office: 827 N. Arlington Ave., Balto., Md.

WILSON, Edward John, tchr., b. Mobile, Ala., July 31, 1932; s. Edward and Sally (Hobdy) W.; Our Lady of the Lake Sem., 1952-55; Crozier House of Studies, 1956-61; St. Francis Coll., Hastings Coll.; ordained priest, Roman Cath. Ch., 1961; taught St. Cecilia's H. S., Hastings, Nebr.; tchr., Stepinac H. S., White Plains, N. Y.; Home: 30 Gedney Pk. Dr., White Plains, N. Y.; Office: Arch-Bishop Stepinac H. S., White Plains, N. Y.

WILSON, Frank Theodore, educator, b. Maxton, N. C., Jan. 1, 1900; s. James Jacob and Sudie Jane (Harris) W.; A. B., Lincoln Univ., 1921; S. T. B., 1924; D. D. (hon.), 1952; M. A., Columbia Univ., 1932; Ed. D., 1937; D. D. (hon.), Edward Waters Coll., 1953; m. Anna Lucretta Dorsey; Children--Frank Theodore, Anne Elizabeth (Mrs. Edgar M. Cole); nat. student sec., Natl. Coun. YMCA, 1924-36; dean of students, prof., Lincoln Univ., 1936-49; dir., Young People's Summer Confs., Blairstown, N. J., 1945-48; dean, Sch. of Rel., prof. of Religious Ed., Howard Univ., 1949-57; sec. for Educational Commission on Ecumenical Mission and Relations United Presby. Ch. in USA, 1957-67; ex. sec., Temporary Com. on Theol. Ed. in Southeast United Presby. Ch.; guest lectr., Yale Div. Sch., 1950-54; dir., educational survey in Asia, Latin Amer., Middle East; mem., Gen. Comm. of World Student Chrstn. Fed., Mysore, India, 1928-29; mem., Bd. of Chrstn. Ed.; chrmn., Social Ed. and Action Comm., Presby. Ch., USA; Natl. Student Comm., YMCA, 1940--; accredited visitor, World Coun. of Chs., Evanston, Ill., 1954; trustee, Lincoln Univ., 1954--; Fellow Natl. Coun. of Rel. in Higher Ed.; author: Unconditional Spiritual Surrender, 1947; contributor: The Christin Way in Race Relations, 1948; Home: RDI Box 84A, Lincoln Univ., Pa. 19352; Office: 727 Witherspoon Bldg., 130 Juniper St., Phila., Pa. 19107

WILSON, Ivory W., b. Winsboro, La., June 16, 1916; s. Lem and Cura Reed (Carr) W.; Wilberton, Okla. High Sch.; Langston Theol. Sem., Langston, Okla. Univ.; Bishop Coll., Marshall, Tex.; D. D. (hon.), Intl. Bapt. Theol. Center, Houston, Tex.; m. Ollye Lelar Ward; Children--Floyd, Cleaster, Larrayne; pastor, Bethel Bapt. Ch., Las Vegas, Nev.; 1st v. p., Constitutional Bapt. Conv.; 1st v. p., Min. Assn., Clark Co.; mem., Civil Service Bd., 1962-66; NAACP; Coun. for Kit Carson Sch.; 1st v. p., Voter League; mem., Mason; Democrat; Home: 1900 Hassell, Las Vegas, Nevada; Office: 400 Adams & D., Las Vegas, Nevada

WILSON, Robert Henry, b. Columbia, S. C., Aug. 1, 1924; s. Riley M. and Ida (Ellison) W.; A. B., Benedict Coll.,

Columbia, S. C., 1944; B. D., Benedict Sch. of Theol., 1949; D. D. (hon.), Edward Waters Coll., Jacksonville, Fla., Benedict; m. Elise Wider; Children--Roberta Elaine, Robert H., Jr.; asst. pastor, Zion Bapt. Ch., Columbia, S. C., 1940-49; pastor, St. Paul Bapt. Ch., Columbia, S. C., 1950-53; Bethel Bapt. Inst., Ch., Jacksonville, Fla., 1953-66; St. John Bapt. Ch., Dallas, Tex., 1966-present; min., Minister Conf., Coll. Rel. Emphasis Periods and Church Revivals; sec., Bd. of Trustees, Fla. Meml. Coll., St. Augustine, Fla., corres. sec., Natl. Bapt. Conv. of Amer.; Home: 2019 Allen St., Dallas, Tex. 75204

WILSON, S. Russell, b. Norfolk, Va., Aug. 29, 1918; s. Joseph and Maggie (Fuller) W.; A. B., Va. Union Univ., 1937; B. D., Va. Theol. Sem., 1940; M. A., Drew Univ., 1962; courses, St. Margaret's Coll., Amer. Armed Forces Univ. (Italy); m. Carrie Chambers; Children--(adopted), Robt, Christopher; pastor, Prot. Episc. Chs., Millers Tavern (Va.), St. Anna's, Columbia, St. Thomas (S. C.), St. Monica's (S. C.), St. Barnabas (S. C.); present: rector, So. Hill Prot. Episc. Ch., So. Hill, Va.; chap., Elizabeth State Tchrs. Coll. (N. C.); Columbia, S. C. Penitentiary; headmaster, John Moncure Sch., Millers Tavern, Va.; boy's work sec., Leigh St., YMCA, Richmond, Va.; trustee, Voorhees Coll., Denmark, S. C., 1960-61; chap., US Army; Anm. officer - 601 Ord.; 3 combat stars - European-Afr., American; Mason; Kappa Alpha Psi; NAACP; So. Chrstn. Leadership, Fellowship of Reconciliation; Democrat; Home: PO Box 597, So. Hill, Va.; Office: South Hill Cure, So. Hill, Va.

WILSON, William L., b. Greenwood, S. C., Apr. 30, 1908; s. Isam and Susan Devore; A. B., B. D., D. D. (hon.), Benedit Coll.; D. D. (hon.), Morris Coll.; m. Jessie Mae Gibson; Children--one; pres., Bapt. Educational and Missionary Conv. of S. C.; state v. p., Natl. Bapt. Conv., USA, Inc.; moderator, Spartanburg Co. Assn.; pres., Interdenom. Min. Alliance; grand dir., Odd Fellows of America and Jurisdiction; pastor, Macedonia Bapt. Ch., Spartanburg; trustee, Benedict and Morris Coll.; mem., NAACP; Home: 164 Fremont Ave., Spartanburg, S. C.; Office: 301 W. Henry St., Spartanburg, S. C.

WILSON, Wylie Edward, presiding elder, b. Hampton Co., S. C., Aug. 29, 1913; s. William E. and Janie L. W.;

Paine Coll., 1937-38; Allen Univ., 1948-50; Midwestern Grad. Bible Sch., 1955-60; B. D., M. Th., Gammon Sem. Summer Sch., 1957, 1960; m. Hattie Miles; Children--Janie, Willie Marvell, Jerelyn Gayle; pastor, 23 yrs., Chrstn. Meth. Episc. Ch.; presiding elder, 1946-53 and 1955-62; present: pastor, Mt. Carmel Ch., Anderson, S. C.; insurance agent during WW II; mem., Community Fund Drive Comm. (Chapel Hill, N. C.); NAACP, working for better jobs for the Negro of the community; mem., Epsilon Delta Chi; The Min. and Laymen's Council, C. M. E. Ch., Democrat; research: "The Church and its Responsibility in Modern Society." Home: 611 Cleveland Ave., Anderson, S. C.; Office: 609 Cleveland Ave., Anderson, S. C.

WINGATE, Joseph Terry, b. Plymouth, N. C., Mar. 27, 1931; s. Leander and Fannie (Howcott) W.; B. S., Fayetteville Tchrs. Coll.; B. D., Va. Union; courses, Clark Coll., Atlanta, Ga.; N. Y. Univ.; m. Narvella Johnson; Children--Alansieta Josette, Chiquita Valarie, Fravien Colette, Romega Yneather; pastor, Mt. Olive Bapt. Ch., 1957-61; pastor, Willow Grove Bapt. Ch., 1961-present; dir., Willow Grove Child Devel. Center, Chesapeake, Va., 2 yrs.; sec., Bapt. Min. Conf., 1958-61; chrmn., Bd. of Ordination, Sharon Bapt. Assn., 1960-present; dir., Chrstn. Ed., Sharon Assn., 1961-65; mem., NAACP, Fourth Congressional Dist.; Bus. & Prof. Men; Mason; Anti-Poverty Com.; consultant, Child and Family Services, Wash. Co. Schs. 3 yrs.; recd. Man of the Year Award, Southeastern Area, 1965; Outstanding Citizens Award, 1964; papers: "A Guide to Readiness," "The Cause, Cure, and Concepts of the Disadvantaged;" Home: 1025 Main Creek Rd., Chesapeake, Va.

WINKFIELD, Orange Willis, tchr., S. Joseph and Gena (Owens) W.; b. Union Springs, Ala., Sept. 15, 1885; Courses: poetry, literature, psychology; m. Lillian C. Walls; Children--Clyde Julian; ordained in Cataba Presbytery, USA; pastored in Okla., 1914-23; New Vision Bible Ch., Chgo. Hon. Certificate, 1961 from Johnson C. Smith Univ. for 50 yrs. prof. service; Home: 7648 Cottage Ave., Chgo., Ill.

WISNER, Roscoe William, b. Nixa, Mo., Apr. 20, 1894; s. Frank and Julia W.; B. A., Western Univ., Kansas City, Mo., 1926; Chaeffers Theol. Sch., B. D., 1926; teaching certi., Kansas State Tchrs. Coll., 1923; D. D.

(hon.), Allen Univ.; Kittrell Coll.; D. Ed., Monrovia Coll., W. Africa; m. Gladys Vivian; Children--Elbert C., Roscoe W., Richard; pastor, Afr. Meth. Episc. Ch., Ogden, Utah; Salt Lake, Utah; Pueblo, Colo.; Marshall, Mo.; current pastor, Bethel Ch., Hampton, Va.; pres., Kittrell Coll., Kittrell, N.C., 10 yrs.; former tchr., pub. schs.; US Forces, 1918-19; Home: 1422 E. Penbroke Ave., Hampton, Va.; Office: 108 W. Lincoln St., Hampton, Va.

WOMACK, Andrew Australia, b. Prospect, Va., Nov. 11, 1904; s. Lincoln and Virginia (Allen) W.; A.B., B.D., D.D. (hon.), Virginia Sem. and Coll.; m. Helen Lightfoot; Children--Andrew A.; current pastor, Mt. Haven Bapt. Ch., Cleveland, O.; mem., The Min. Conf.; The Cleveland Bapt. Assn.; Natl. Bapt. Conv.; The Amer. Bapt. Conv.; tchr., The State Sun. Sch. Congress; mem., NAACP; Mason; financial sec., State Sun. Sch. Congress; chrmn., The Finance Comm., Northern Ohio Assn.; Bd. of Trustee, Va. Sem. and Coll., Lynchburg, Va.; Home: 15915 Eldamere Ave., Cleveland, O.; Office: Mt. Haven Bapt. Ch., Cedar Ave., Cleveland, O.

WOMACK, P. J., b. Jackson, Tenn., Jan. 28, 1938; s. Byrd and Anna; B.A., Western Bible Coll., 1966; co-pastor, Pleasant Green Bapt. Ch.; Dir., Sun. Sch., 1963-present; v.p., Natl. Alumni Assoc.; pres., Chapt. 3, Western Bible Coll.; mem., St. James Lodge, No. 59; pres., Natl. Bapt. Student Movement, 1964-65; Home: 3419 Euclid, Kansas City, Mo. 64109

WOOD, Marcus Garvey, b. Glucester, Va., June 18, 1920; s. Frank Tucker and Julia (Braxton) W.; A.B., Storer Coll., Harpers Ferry, W.Va., 1948; B.D., Crozer Theol. Sem., Chester, Pa.; m. Bessie Pendleton; Children--Jeanetta W. (Mrs. Eugene Brown), Marcus G.; pastor, Wainwright Bapt. Ch., Charles Town, W.Va., 1945-48; Bethlehem Bapt. Ch., Woodbury, N.J., 1948-52; Providence Bapt. Ch., Balto., Md., 1952--; dir., promotions, Lott Carey Bapt. Foreign Missions Conv., 1963; travels in the area of missions; made a tour of the Island of Haiti and photographed work of mission stations, 1959; spent 2 wks. in Haiti with work team, living on the mission field, 1962; led a survey team to British Guiana in So. America, 1964; Home: 848 Edmondson Ave., Balto., Md. 21201; Office: 850 Edmondson Ave., Balto., Md. 21201

WOODRUFF, James Edward, chap., b. Trinidad, B.W.I., Mar. 2, 1936; s. James Edward and Carmen (Earle) W.; B.S., State Univ. of N.Y., 1953-57; B.D., Seabury Western Sem., 1957-60; Vanderbilt Div., working on S.T.M. in Pastoral Counseling, 1961--; m. Nancy Ann Denson; Children--Mark Francis; dir., YMCA Community Center in Coll., 1955-57; dir., swimmping pool, Buffalo City; Scoutmaster and Cubmaster working with teen-age and early adult; during seminary 1957-60 worked with underprivileged children and gangs in N.Y.C., at St. Christopher's Chapel, 48 Henry St. and at the Ch. of the Epiphany, 111 So. Ashland in Chicago; first pastoral duty was doing the type of work at St. Thomas Ch., 3801 So. Wabash Ave., Chgo; present, Episc. chap., Fisk Univ., Tenn. A & I Univ. and Meharry Med. Coll., 1961--; mem., Omega Psi Phi; Home: 2602 Morena St., Nashville, Tenn.; Office: 2008 Meharry Blvd., Nashville, Tenn.

WOODS, Abraham Lincoln, b. Birmingham, Ala., Oct. 7, 1928; A.B., Miles Coll., 1962; B.Th., Daniel Payne Coll.; Birmingham Bapt. Coll.; current pastor, First Metro. Bapt. Ch., Birmingham, Ala., 1952--; prof., Soc. Science, Miles Coll., 1962--; dir., Miles Coll. Citizenship Work-Study Project, 1963--; instr., Mt. Pilgrim Dist. Congress; sec., Birmingham Bapt. Min. Conf.; mem., Ala. State Teachers Assn.; Amer. Tchrs. Assn.; v.p., Ala. Chrstn. Movement for Human Rights, 1955--; deputy dir. of the south, March on Wash.; mem., Group Relations Sub-Comm. of Birmingham's Interracial Citizens Affairs Comm.; cited by 9th Congressional Dist., Ala. Coordinating Assn. for Voter Registration; cited by WENN radio, Birmingham, for Voter Registration; led march in Ecorse and River Rouge, Mich.; Home: 125 Kappa Ave., So. Birmingham, Ala.

WOODSON, S. Howard, b. Phila., Pa.; B.S., State Coll., Cheyney, Pa.; B.D., Sem. Morehouse Coll., Atlanta, Ga.; post-grad. study, Atlanta Univ., Atlanta, Ga.; m. Audrey J. Manley; Children--Jean, Howard; pres., Coun. of Chs., Trenton, 1953-55; Bd. of Dir., Carver YMCA; Trenton br NAACP; State Conv., NAACP; mem., Bd. of Dir., Central YMCA, Bd. of Dir., Trenton Coun. Human Rel.; Bd. of Dir., Citizens Action Coun., Trenton; Region 2 Steering Com., NAACP; War Meml. Comm., Mercer Co.; pastor, Shiloh Bapt. Ch., Trenton, N.J., 1946-present; co-dir., Worship Natl. Bapt. Conv.; mem.,

Bd. of Dir., N.J. Comm. Against Discrimination in Housing; Bd. of Dir., Amer. Bapt. Sem., Nashville, Tenn.; State Assemblyman, Mercer Co.; Adv. Coun., Trenton Coun. on Human Rel.; chrmn., Co. and Municipal Govt. Comm.; min. leader, House Assembly, N.J.; legislator of the year, Silver Chalice Award, 1968; Outstanding Citizen Award, Natl. Conf. Chrstn. & Jews, 1967; Afro-Amer. Outstanding Citizenship Award, 1956; Kappa Alpha Psi Fraternal Award, 1960; Home: 340 Calhoun St., Trenton, N.J. 08618

*WOOTEN, James Henry, b. Tarboro, N.C., Apr. 30, 1922; s. Curfew and Dollie (Bridges) W.; A.B., Morgan State Coll., Balto., Md., 1954; B.D., Howard Univ., Sch. of Rel., 1957; m. Lois Copeland; Children--Darryl Eugene; pastor, Trinity Meth. Ch., Clarksburg, W. Va., 1957-61; Milton Ave. Meth. Ch., Balto., Md., 1961--; dir., Adult Work, Wash. Annual Conf., Baltimore area; prot. chap., Balto. City Jail; mem., Ex. Bd. NAACP, Balto., Md.; visiting clergy staff, Johns Hopkins Hosp., Balto.; US Forces, 1943-46; Good Conduct Medal; Eliza J. Cummings Award as dept. scholar at Morgan State Coll.; mem., Alpha Phi Alpha; Mason; Democrat seeking nomination as del. to State and National Conventions; Home: 2312 E. Federal St., Balto., Md.; Office: 1500 N. Milton Ave., Balto., Md.

WRIGHT, Byrl Fisher, b. Knoxville, Tenn., Dec. 13, 1913; s. James and Beatrice W.; Stillman Coll. & Sch. of Theology, 1937-40; D.D., Livingstone Coll., 1963; m. Daisy Faucher; Children--Byrl Fisher; pastor, Oakland & Pakgrove A.M.E.Z. Ch., Knoxville, Tenn., 1940-43; Bethel A.M.E.Z. Ch., Knoxville, Tenn., 1943-50; Holiday Meml. A.M.E.Z. Ch., Braddock, Pa., 1950-60; St. Paul A.M.E.Z. Ch., Toledo, O., 1960--; 1st v.p., Toledo br. NAACP; mem., YMCA Bd. of Mgrs.; Courier-Wamo Achievement Award, 1960; Home: 954 Belmont, Toledo, O. 43607; Office: 958 Belmont, Toledo, O. 43607

WRIGHT, Calvin Luther, presiding elder, b. Dolomite, Ala., July 17, 1888; s. Cull Lee and Elvira (Wiley) W.; Payne Univ., 1917-20; post-grad. work: Columbia Univ., 1927-28; D.D. (hon.), Payne Univ., 1928; LL.D., Payne Univ., 1955; Children--Mabel W., Alexander, Calvin Lee, Jr.; first pastorate, 1912; organized nine Afr. Meth. Episc. Chs.; current, presiding elder, W. Birmingham Dist.; former trustee, Payne Univ.; Home: 3517 65th; N. Birmingham, Ala. 35212

WRIGHT, Giles Robert, chap., b. Memphis, Tenn., Mar. 3, 1906; s. Giles and Esther (Wells) W.; B.A., Clark Univ., 1930; B.D., Gammon Theol. Sem., 1933; M.A., Univ. of Kans., 1942; Columbia Univ., residential requirements for Ed.D.; m. Mae Cora Whiten; Children--Grace Eloise, Giles Robert, Jr.; US Army chap., 1942-46 (overseas); Chrstn. Meth. Episc. Ch. minister for 32 yrs.; pub. sch. tchr. for 5 yrs.; present: pastor, Hopps Meml. C.M.E. Ch., Syracuse, N.Y.; dir., Pub. Relations, 7th Episc. Dist., C.M.E. Ch.; mem., Mayor's Commn. on Human Rights, 1963--; dir., Dunbar Center; v.p., dir., Syracuse Coun. of Chs.; mem., Inter-Faith Commn.; European-African Middle Eastern Service Medal; pres., E. Side Cooporate Coun.; Republican; Home: 105 Elk St., Syracuse, N.Y.; Office: 707 So. McBride St., Syracuse, N.Y.

WRIGHT, Jefferson Wendell, b. Bluefield, W.Va., July 24, 1935; s. Thomas and Ethel (Clements); B.A., Marshall Univ., Huntington, W.Va.; S.T.B., Boston Univ., Grad. Sch. of Theol., Boston, Mass.; m. Toni Washington; Children--Jefferson Wendell; pastor, 2nd Bapt. Ch., Harrisburg, Pa., present; mem., Bd. of Dirs., OIC of Dauphin Co.; founder, Harrisburg Community Com.; Bd. of Dir., NAACP; Planned Parenthood; Harrisburg Coun. of Chs.; Wm. Howard Day Cemetery; Temperance League; mem., Urban Strategy Com.; Interdenom. Ministerium; Harrisburg Assn.; Pa. Bapt. Conv.; Amer. Bapt. Conv.; Central Bapt. Assn.; Pa. State Bapt. Assn.; Natl. Bapt. Assn.; chrmn., Political Actions Com. of NAACP; mem., Ways and Means Com., Ed. Com. and Housing Com. of NAACP; Mayor's Adv. Com., Harrisburg; chrmn., subcom. on Housing; pres., Ghetto Enterprises, Inc., Central Pa.; Bd. of Dir., Tri-Co. Family and Children Service; pastor, Sheldon St. Cong. Ch., Providence, R.I. 1961-64; Boys Coun., Hebrew Childrens Home, Bronx, N.Y., 1959; award, commendation, Bd. of Dir., Sta. WITF, Hershey, Pa. for performance as moderator of 4-week forum on educational TV; Home: 1600 Forster St., Harrisburg, Pa. 71703; Office: 2nd Bapt. Ch., 424 Forster St., Harrisburg, Pa.

WRIGHT, Jeremiah Alvesta, b. Caroline Co., Va., June 20, 1909; s. James Allen and Emma (Ellen) W.; B.Th.,

A. B., B. D., D. D. (hon.), Va. Union Univ., 1936, 37, 38, 66; S. T. M., Luth. Theol. Sem., Phila., Pa., 1949; m. Mary Henderson; Children--Mary LaVerne, Jeremiah Alvesta Jr.; pastor, Reedy Bapt. Ch., Caroline Co., Va., 1937-38; Grace Bapt. Ch., Germantown, Phila., Pa., 1938-present; tchr., Phila. pub. sch., 1950-58; award: Recognition for Volunteer Service Child Welfare Center, City of Phila., Dept. of Public Welfare; mem., Mason; Democrat; Acad. of Rel. and Mental Health; Home: 29 W. Johnson St., Phila., Pa. 19144

WRIGHT, Leon E., prof., b. Boston, Mass., Jan. 20, 1912; A. B., Boston Univ., 1934; A. M., Boston Univ., 1937; S. T. B., Harvard Univ., 1943; Ph. D., Harvard Univ., 1945; m. Jesse Mae Wyche; Children--Richard, Wesley; instr., Morgan State Coll., 1937-40; guest lectr., Westminster Choir Coll., Princeton, N. J.; prof., Howard Univ. Sch. of Rel., 1945--; visiting lectur., Va. Prot. Episc. Theol. Sem.; Assoc. ed., Journal of Rel. Thought; US State Dept. & Cultural Attache of Embassy, Rangoon, Burma, 1955-57; Continual assignment as interracial lectr. in chs. and groups in and about Wash., D. C.; mem., Natl. Coun. on Rel. in Higher Ed.; Com. for the Study of Patristic Quotations, Intl. Commn. for New Critical Apparatus to Greek New Testament; Roster of Bd. of Examiners, Middle State Assn. of Secondary Schs. and Coll.; Speakers Bur., Natl. Coun. of Chs.; Soc. of Biblical Literature and Exegesis; Wash. Seminar on Rel. and Psych.; Phi Beta Kappa; awards: Boston Univ. Trustee Scholarship, 1930-34; Grad. Fellowship, 1936-37; Rosenwald Fellow, 1941-43; Fellow, Natl. Coun. on Rel. in Higher Ed., 1942; cited for Hopkins Share, 1942-43, Howard Univ.; Gen. Ed. Bd. Fellow, 1944-45; Guggenheim Fellow, 1951-52; author: Alterations of the Words of Jesus, as quoted in the literature of the second century, Harvard Univ. Press, 1952; Liberty to the Captives: A study in the relationship between Religion and Parapsychology; Bd. for Homeland Ministers, United Ch. of Christ, Comm. Bd. of Rel. and Higher Ed., U. Ch. of Christ; Urban League; NAACP; Assn. of Biblical Instrs.; Natl. Coun. on Rel. in Higher Ed.; first Amer. to be awarded a cert. to teach Buddhist meditation, 1963; Home: 1726 Varnum St. NW, Wash., D. C.; Office: Howard Univ., Sch. of Rel., Wash., D. C.

WRIGHT, Nathan, author, b. Shreveport, La., 1923; B. D., Episc. Theol. Sem., Cambridge, Mass.; S. T. M., Har-

Univ.; Ed. M., State Tchrs. Coll., Boston; Ed. D., Harvard Grad. Sch. of Ed.; m. Barbara Taylor; Children--5; rector, St. Cyprian's Episc. Ch., 14 yrs.; Prot. chap., L. I. Hosp., Boston, 8 yrs; current exec. dir. for Urban Work, Episc. Diocese of Newark; former tchr., Lasell Jr. Coll., Newton, Mass.; consultant, Compensatory education and staff asst., Mass. Ed. Commn.; served on Gov.'s Comm. on Civil Rights; Mayor's Comm. on Housing; former v.p., Mass. Clerical Assn.; v.p., Ch. School Union; mem., Amer. Prot. Hosp. Assn.; former mem., Bd. of Dirs., Boston br. NAACP; Urban League; organizer and first field repr. for New England CORE; author: The Riddle of Life, 1952; The Song of Mary, 1958; One Bread, One Body, 1962; Home: 412 Lawn Ridge Rd., Orange, N. J.

WRIGHT, Richard Robert, Jr., bishop, educator, b. Cuthbert, Ga., Apr. 16, 1878; s. Richard R. and Lydia Elizabeth (Howard) W.; A. B., Ga. State Indus. Coll., 1898; B. D., Univ. of Chgo. Theol. Sem., 1901; A. M., Univ. of Chgo., 1904; studied Univ. of Berlin, 1903, Univ. of Leipzig, 1904; Ph. D., Univ. of Pa., 1911; LL. D., Wilberforce Univ., 1920; m. Charlotte Corgman; Children--Charlotte Ruth (Mrs. Hayre), Richard R. III, Alberta Lavina (Mrs. McClain), Grace Lydia (Mrs. Kyle), Edith (dec.); paymaster's clerk in Spanish-Amer. War, 1898; ordained ministry Afr. Meth. Episc. Ch., 1901; asst. pastor, Institutional Ch., Chgo., 1900-01; instr. in Hebrew, Payne Theol. Sem., Wilberforce, O., 1901-03; pastor, Elgin, Ill., 2 mos., 1904; Trinity Mission, Chgo., 1905; resident, 8th Ward Social Settlement, Phila., 1950-07; research fellow in sociology, Univ. of Pa., 1905-07; field sec., Armstrong Assn., 1908-09; editor, Christian Recorder, Phila., 1909-36; business mgr. Book Concern A. M. E. Ch., 1909-12, 1916-20; founder Citizens and Southern Bldg. and Loan Assn.; pres., Citizens and Southern Bank and Trust Co.; mem., Comm. to draft new charter for City of Phila., 1917-19; Comm. to plan for celebrating 150th anniversary of the Declaration of Independence, 1921; organizer of Soc. Service, City Dept. of Pub. Welfare, Phila., 1921; a founder of the Spring St. Settlement, Richard Allen House; supervisor of social Service for A. M. E. chs. of Phila. and vicinity, 1923; pastor of the Ward A. M. E. Ch., 1928-30, Morris Brown A. M. E. Ch., organizer of Jones Taberncale, A. M. E. Ch., 1930-32; pres., Wilberforce Univ., 1932-36; acting pres., 1941-42; elected bishop Afr. Meth. Episc. Ch., 1936, and assigned to So. Africa, 1936-40; presiding bishop 13th Episc. Dist. (Ky. and Tenn.), 1940-48, and presiding bishop of N.Y., N.J., New England, Bermuda, 1946-48; presiding bishop 6th Episc. Dist., Ga., 1948-51; 12th Episc. Dist., Ark. and Okla., 1951-52; bishop of West Indies and So. America, 1952-56, 8th Episc. Dist. (Miss. and La.), 1956-57, 5th Episc. Dist., 1957-60; historiographer of the A.M.E. Ch., 1960--; founded R.R. Wright Sch. of Rel., Wilberforce Inst., So. Africa, 1938; built 50 new schs. in So. Africa; founder, Sch. of Rel., Memphis, 1944; pres., Missionary Bd. of A.M.E. Ch., 1940-44 (pres., publ. bd., 1946-48, chrmn., bur. history); chrmn., A.M.E. Comm. Army and Navy chaplains since 1940; Exec. sec., Fraternal Cl. Negro Chs. Am. and Africa, 1940-48; mem., Commn. for union of A.M.E. and A.M.E.Z. Chs., 1943--; pres., Bishops' Coun., A.M.E. Ch., 1957-58; mem., Amer. Acad. Political and Social Science, Amer. Sociological Soc., NEA, Amer. Negro Acad., Kappa Alpha Psi; Mason; Elk; author: The Teaching of Jesus, 1903; The Negro in Pennsylvania 1911; Church Financiering, 1919; Social Service, 1922; My Church, Handbook of A.M.E. Ch., 1944; editor: Poems of Phillis Wheatley, 1929; Encyclopedia of African Methodism, 1816 and 1944; The Mission Study Course, 1943; Sermons and addresses, 1943; lecturer on "The Negro in America;" The Bishops of the A.M.E. Ch., 1964; del., Ecumenical Meth. Conf., 1911, 21, 31, 47, 56, 61; Address: 554 N. 58th St., Phila., Pa.

*WRIGHT, Thomas Alexander, b. Mansfield, Ga., Mar. 26, 1920; s. Albert and Roxie (Shy) W.; B.S., Fla. Meml. Coll., 1950; B.D., Howard Univ., Sch. of Rel., Wash., D.C., 1953; m. Affie M. Clatton; Children--Patricia, Thomas, Philorara, Lavon; pastor, St. Mark's Bapt. Ch., St. Augustine, Fla., 1954-62; Mt. Carmel Bapt. Ch., Gainesville, Fla., 1962-present; instr., Fla. Meml. Coll., 1954-62; presently conducts classes for rural ministers in ch.; pres., NAACP, Gainesville, Fla.; cand., City Commn., Mar. 1965; mem., Mental Assn.; Fla.; Home: 503 N.W. 4th St., Gainesville, Fla.

WYATT, James C., b. Dinwiddie, Va., Dec. 25, 1900; s. William and Hattie W.; summer sch., Va. State Coll., 1924-25; Frelinghuysen Sch. of Rel., Wash., D.C., 1936-40; m. Lucy V. Robinson; Children--Mrs. Paul C. Jones, Mrs. Edward Crawford, Mrs. Remon Rhinehart, Angela (Mrs. Jerome Powell), James C. Jr., Justin W.;

dir., Youth Dept., Southern Md. Bapt. Assn., 1940-44; repr., US Bapt. Miss. Conv., 1943-48; pastor, First Bapt. Ch., Highland Pk., Md., 1945-present; sec., Home Miss. Bd., United Miss. Conv.; tchr., Elem. sch. sys., Warren Co., N.C., 1924-27; mem., Prince George Co., Library Bd., 1957-62; mem., Summer Sem. of Ministers, Va. Union Univ., Richmond, Va., 1966; honored by Northwestern Coll., Inc., Wash., D.C. for outstanding rel. and civic work, 1957; mem., Min. Conf., Wash., D.C.; Bapt. Conv., Wash. D.C.; Far Northeast Min. Alliance; Home: 4434 Hunt Pl., NE, Wash., D.C. 20019

WYCHE, Oscar Herbert, b. Henderson, N.C., June 11, 1903; s. Robert Augustus and Lucy Bullock (W.); Shaw Univ., Raleigh, N.C., 1927-31; Va. Union Univ., 1932; m. Cornelia Ann Hill; Children--Carrie Doris (Mrs. Winfield Carlyle Coachman, Sr.); pastor, Community Bapt. Ch., New Canaan, Conn.; mem., Bid. of Dirs., Amer. Red Cross; Comm. of Common Concern; Asst. sec., The Conn. Missionary Bapt. Conv. (New Canaan), Conn.; chap., New Canaan Chapter, NAACP; mem., New Canaan Min. Alliance; Fairfield Co. Bapt. Ed. Fellowship; com. mem., The United Negro College Fund; Democrat; Home: 3 Charles Pl., New Canaan, Conn. 06840; Office: 36 Baldwin Ave., New Canaan, Conn.

*WYNN, Daniel Webster, chap., coll. Prof., b. Wewoka, Okla., Mar. 19, 1919; s. Phay Willie and Mary (Carter) W.; A.B., Langston Univ., 1941; B.D., A.M., Howard Univ., 1944, 1945; Ph.D., Boston Univ., Boston, Mass., 1954; D.D., Eden Theol. Sem., Webster Groves, Mo., profession study, 1941; additional study: Harvard Univ., Cambridge, Mass., professional study, 1950; Hebrew Univ., Jerusalem, Israel, 1963; Colo. Coll., Colo. Springs, Colo., 1959; m. Lillian Robinson; Children--Marian Danita, Patricia Ann; acting chap. and instr. of Sociology and Economics, Ky. State Coll., Frankfort, Ky., 1945-46; acting dean, Sch. of Rel., Bishop Coll., Marshall, Tex., 1946-53; acting chap., Tuskegee Inst., Tuskegee, Ala., 1953-54; dean of students, Langston Univ., Langston, Okla., 1954-55; chap., Tuskegee Inst., Tuskegee, Ala., 1955-68; Assoc. dir., Div. of Higher Ed., United Meth. Ch., Nashville Tenn. 1968-present; mem., Amer. Assn. of Univ. Professors; Natl. Assn. of Biblical Instructors; Natl. Assn. of Coll. and Univ. Chaplains; Religious Ed. Assn.; Inst. of Rel., Howard Univ., Wash., D.C.;

Amer. Philosophical Assn.; Mason; Kappa Alpha Psi; Tuskegee Civic Assn.; NAACP; Ala. Coun. on Human Rights; Distinguished Alumnus Award, awarded by Langston Univ., 1963; author: NAACP Versus Negro Revolutionary Protest, 1955; The Chaplain Speaks, 1956; Moral Behavior and the Christian Ideal, 1962; contributions: Journal of Religious Thought, Howard Univ. Press; Messenger Magazine, Evangelical Ref. Ch.; Royal Service Magazine, Southern Bapt. Conv.; Home Missions Magazine, Southern Bapt. Conv.; National Bapt. Voice, Natl. Bapt. Conv., Inc.; Central Chrstn. Advocate, Meth. Publishing Bd.; Scottish Rite Informer; Upper Room Disciplines, 1963; Motive Magazine, Feb. 1964; Rel. Ed. Magazine, 1964; editor, Developing A Sense of Community, Tuskegee Inst. Press, 1957; Major Issues In Human Relations, Tuskegee Inst. Press, 1961; The Chapel Bulletin, Tuskegee Inst. Press, 1953, 1955--; Newsletter, Natl. Assn. of Coll. and Univ. Chaplains, 1960-63; Home: PO Box 871, Meth. Bd. of Ed., Nashville, Tenn.

WYNN, Master Julius, sem. prof. and official, b. Chattanooga, Tenn., Oct. 17, 1903; s. Clayton and Georgia (Camp) W.; A.B., Clark Univ., 1939; B.D., Gammon Theol. Sem., 1941; M.A., Atlanta Univ., 1957; D.D. (hon.), Clark Coll., 1961; m. Hattie Elizabeth Broughton; Children--George T., Sylvia E.; pastor, The Meth. Ch., Ga. Conf., 1936-49; principal, Chattanooga Co. Trng. Sch., Lyerely, Ga., 1942-47; chap., Bethune-Cookman Coll., 1949-53; prof. and ean of students, Gammon Theol. Sem., 1953-59; current, pres., Gammon Theol. Sem., 1959--; chrmn., Organizational and Extensional Com., Boy Scouts of America; chap., Inter-alumni Coun., United Negro Coll. Fund; mem., YMCA; Omega Psi Phi; editor, "Foundation" magazine published by Gammon Alumni; Office: 653 Beckwill St. SW, Atlanta, Ga.; Home: 9 McDonough Blvd., Atlanta, Ga.

WYNN, Otis James, b. Elizabeth City, N.C., Oct. 7, 1912; s. James Henry and Louise Virginia W.; A.B., Howard Univ., Wash., D.C., 1932-36; Atlanta Univ., Atlanta, Ga., 1939; B.D., Lincoln Univ. Sch. of Theology, 1946-49; m. Pauline D. Childers; tchr., Swift Meml. Jr. Coll., Tenn., 1938-40; current pastor, The First United Presby. Ch., 1949--; current tchr., Crestwood Jr. High Sch., Chesapeake, Va.; princ., Waterford Elem. Sch., Norfolk, Va., 14 yrs.; mem., United Presby. Men; Va.

Tchrs. Assn.; Natl. Tchrs. Assn. and the Amer. Tchrs. Assn.; Democrat; chrmn., Natl. Missions Com. for So. Virginia Ch.; moderator, Presbytery of So. Virginia, 1958-59; chrmn., Comm. on Veterans Affairs, So. Va.; US Army, 1942-46; asst. to the Division Chaplain; Medal for Bravery (So. Pac. theater); Certificate of Award (chaplain); Letter of Appreciation from the Sec. of War, 1946; mem., Natl. Historical Soc., Secondary Tchrs.; Mason; contributor: "Garden of Prayer," Presbyn. Publication; Home: 860 Philpotts Rd., Norfolk, Va. 23513

*YATES, Walter Ladell, Sr., coll. prof., b. Pine Bluff, Ark., Dec. 12, 1912; s. Julias and Ednia (Wilkins) Y.; A. B., Philander Smith Coll., 1942; B. D., Howard Univ., Sch. of Rel., 1945; M. A., Grad. Sch., 1947; S. T. M., Hartford Sem. Found., 1963; Ph. D., Hartford Sem. Theol.; m. Victoria Prince; Children--Walter Ladell, Jr.; assoc. prof. of Church History and Missions, Livingstone Coll. & Hood Theol. Sem., Salisbury, N. C.; prof., Bible, Livingstone Coll., 3 yrs.; counselor, coll. students, 15 yrs.; adv., Overseas Students Club, Livingstone Coll., 1955-60; mem., Omega Psi Phi; Amer. Assn. of Church Histories; Assn. of Professors of Missions, N. C.; unpub. thesis: The History of the A. M. E. Zion Church, West Africa, 1880-1900; Home: 512 Milford Hills Rd., Salisbury, N. C.; Office: Hood Theol. Sem., Salisbury, N. C. 28411

YORPP, Elza Prince; b. Dublin, Ga., Dec. 26, 1906; s. Henry and Lizzie Y.; A. B., Morris Brown Coll., 1945; M. A., New York Univ., 1955; student, Turner Theol. Sem., 1943, 1946, 1956; m. Lucy Mae Thornton; Children--Lee Roy Thornton; tchr. and princ., 1945-58; pastor, Bethel A. M. E. Ch., Albany, Ga., 1963-present; pres., Walton Co. Tchrs. Assn., 1947-51; pres., Atlanta A. M. E. Min. Union, 1958-59; sec., Atlanta Annual Conf., 1946-51, 1958-60; trustee, Morris Brown Coll., Atlanta, 1964-present; mem., Phi Beta Sigma; Democrat; Home: 634 Cherry Ave., Albany, Ga., 31701; Office: 215 S. Washington St., Albany, Ga.

YOUNG, Andrew J., Jr., b. Mar. 12, 1932, New Orleans, La.; s. Andrew J., Sr.; Dillard Univ., 1947-48; Howard Univ., 1948-51; Hartford Theol. Sem., 1952-55; m. Jean Childs; Children--Andrea, Lisa, Paul; pastor, First Congre. Ch., Marion, Ala.; mem., team ministry organizing the Charter Oak Comm. Ch., Hartford, Conn., an inter-racial Chrstn. Fellowship, 1952-53; pastor, Evergreen and Bethany Congre. Chs., Thomasville and Beachton, Ga., 1955-57; field worker, United Chrstn. Youth Movement, 1951; assoc. dir., Dept. of Youth Work, Natl. Coun. of Chs., 1957-61; co-organizer of the Birmingham Civil Rights Movement; St. Augustine, Fla. Movement; Admin. of the Citizenship Ed. Program of SCLC; participant in Ch. of the Brethren Overseas Work Camp Prog., Reid, Austria (summer, 1963); pres., Thomas Co. Bus. and Civic League, 1956-57; head of the US del. to European Ecumenical Youth Assembly, Lausanne, Switzerland (summer 1960); chrmn., Progrm. Comm. Look Up and Live TV program; recd. Citizenship of the Year award, Thomasville, Ga., 1956; articles have appeared in Intl. Jour. of Rel. Ed., The Link, Intercollegian; present, ex. v.pres., SCLC; Home: 177 Chicamauga, Atlanta, Ga.; Office: 334 Auburn Ave., Atlanta, Ga.

YOUNG, Rutus King, prof., b. Dermott, Ark., May 13, 1911; s. Robert and Laura (Scott) Y.; A.B., Shorter Coll., 1937; B.D., Payne Theol. Sem., 1940; D.D. (hon.), Shorter Coll; m. Essie Mae Adams; Children--Essie Mae (Mrs. Richard Norman), Rutus King, Jr., James Robert, Ellen Arneatha, Allena Ann; pastor, Afr. Meth. Episc. Chs., Ark., La., Ala.; current pastor, Bethel A.M.E. Ch., Little Rock, Ark.; dean, Sch. of Rel., Campbell Coll., Jackson, Miss., 1940-44; pres., Daniel Payne Coll., Birmingham, Ala., 1948-50; instr., Shorter Coll., Little Rock, Ark., 1951--; treas., Trustee Bd., Shorter Coll., 1953--; pres., Greater Little Rock Min. Assn., 1961-62; dir., Chrstn. Ed., Miss. & La., 1942-48; Ark. & Okla., 1953--; award: Division Leader in Red Cross Campaign, Hot Spring, 1952; mem., Alpha Phi Alpha, Mason, Non-partisan No. Little Rock Civic League, Little Rock Coun. on Community Affairs; articles on Chrstn. Stewardship in A.M.E. Journal of Chrstn. Ed.; sermons pub. in A.M.E. Review; articles to ch. paper, "Speaking for Myself;" Home: 5000 Glenview Blvd., N. Little Rock, Ark. 72117; Office: 424 W. 9th St., Little Rock, Ark. 72201

ZIMMERMAN, Matthew Agustus, Jr., chap. (Capt.), b. Rock Hill, S.C., Dec. 9, 1941; s. Matthew A. Sr. and Alberta (Brown) Z.; B.S., Benedict Coll., Columbia, S.C., 1962; B.D., Duke Div. Sch., 1965; m. Barbara

Boulware; Children--Tina Yvette, Dana Margaret; Intern Chap., Univ. Prot. Fellowship, Idaho State Univ., 1965-66; coll. min., Morris Coll., Sumter, S.C., 1966-67; chap., US Army, Ft. Gordan, Ga., 1967-68; Vietnam, 1968-present; instr., Rel. Ed., Morris Coll., 1966-67; awards: Natl. Defense Serv. Medal; Vietnam Serv. Medal; Vietnam Campaign Ribbon; mem., Omega Psi Phi; Home: 106 McBeth, Union, S.C. 29379; Office: Advisory Team 51, APO San Francisco, 96402

Sources

For further information on ministers and denominations included in this volume.

AFRICAN METHODIST EPISCOPAL CHURCH

Bishop E. L. Hickman, President
Bishops Council
1212 Fountain Drive
Atlanta, Georgia 30314

AFRICAN METHODIST EPISCOPAL ZION CHURCH

Dr. R. H. Collins Lee
Department of Records and Research
1326 U St., N.W.
Washington, D.C. 20009

BAPTISTS

For a list of Negro ministers related to this convention contact:

AMERICAN BAPTIST CONVENTION
Ministerial Information Bureau
Valley Forge, Pennsylvania 19481

NATIONAL BAPTISTS CONVENTION OF AMERICA

The Rev. G. Goings Daniels
1215 Church St.
Georgetown, South Carolina 29440

NATIONAL BAPTIST CONVENTION, U. S. A., INC.

Record of minutes issued in September at annual meeting includes previous year proceedings, officers and members.

Dr. T. J. Jemison, General Secretary
915 Spain Street
Baton Rouge, Louisiana

PRIMITIVE BAPTISTS

A group of Baptists, mainly through the South who are opposed to all centralization. Fellowship between organizations is maintained by the exchange of minutes and delegates to annual meetings. For further information write:

Primitive Baptist Publishing House
Elon College
Elon, North Carolina

PROGRESSIVE NATIONAL BAPTIST CONVENTION, INC.

Organized as a separate convention in 1962. Geographical lists of ministers may be secured from:

The Rev. L. Venchael Booth,
Executive Secretary
630 Glenwood Ave.
Cincinnati, Ohio 45229

SOUTHERN BAPTIST CONVENTION

For Negro ministers affiliated with this group contact:

Porter Routh, Executive Secretary
460 James Robertson Parkway
Nashville, Tennessee 37219

BAPTIST (Other Sources)

a. Minutes of annual sessions of the National Sunday

Baptist (Other Sources) cont.

School and Baptist Training Union Congress issued yearly and includes committees of ministers and laymen attending conference.

b. Minutes of yearly meetings of the Lott Carey Baptist Foreign Missions. Convention of American Lists Committees, Ministers and Laymen attending annual meeting. For further information contact:

Dr. Wendell C. Somerville
1501 Eleventh Street, N.W.
Washington, D.C.

c. Illinois Historical Records Survey Directory of Negro Baptists Churches in the United States, 2 vols., Chicago, Ill. Issued in 1942 and lists all Negro Baptist Churches geographically by local association.

d. Booth, L. Venchael, ed. Who's Who in Baptist America in the National Sunday School and Baptist Training Union Congress. Ohio, Western Printing Company, 1960.

BIBLE WAY CHURCH OF OUR LORD JESUS CHRIST WORLD WIDE, INC.

Issues yearly minute book. May be secured from:

Bishop Smallwood E. Williams, Presiding Bishop
1130 New Jersey Avenue, N.W.
Washington, D.C.

CATHOLIC, ROMAN

Catholic Directory listing all priests issued yearly. For additional information regarding Negro priests contact:

Registrar
St. Augustine Seminary
Bay St. Louis, Mississippi

CHRISTIAN CHURCHES (Disciples of Christ)

Christian Churches (Disciples of Christ) cont.

A. Dale Fiers, Executive Secretary
221 Ohmer Ave., Box 19136
Indianapolis, Indiana 46219

CHRISTIAN METHODIST EPISCOPAL CHURCH

Meeting of all ministers held every four years. Yearly meetings held for each district. For current information contact:

Bishop Bertram W. Doyle,
Senior Bishop
6322 Elwynne Drive
Cincinnati, Ohio 45236

CHURCH OF GOD IN CHRIST (APOSTOLIC)

For information concerning churches and ministers contact:

Bishop Monroe R. Saunders
Rehoboth Church of God in Christ
1101 8th Street, N. W.
Washington, D. C.

CHURCHES OF CHRIST

For information consult:

Baxter, B. B. & M. Young, eds Preachers of Today, v. 3
The Gospel Advocate, Nashville, Tennessee. 1964.

LUTHERAN CHURCH IN AMERICA

The Board of Publication
2900 Queen Lane
Philadelphia, Pennsylvania 19129

LUTHERAN CHURCH -- MISSOURI SYNOD

Lutheran Church -- Missouri Synod (cont.)

The Lutheran Annual
Concordia Publishing House
St. Louis, Missouri

PRESBYTERIAN CHURCH IN THE UNITED STATES

A branch of the Presbyterian Church established in separate existence in 1861. Sometimes called the "Southern" Presbyterian Church. For directory material write:

Office of the General Assembly.
341-B Ponce De Leon Avenue, N. E.
Atlanta, Georgia 30308

UNITED PRESBYTERIAN CHURCH IN THE UNITED STATES OF AMERICA

Lists of churches, ministers and other directory material may be secured from:

Ministers of the General Assembly of the U. P. O.,
Part III, Statistics
Office of the General Assembly, Witherspoon Building
Philadelphia, Pennsylvania

PROTESTANT EPISCOPAL CHURCH

For lists of Negro clergy, contact:

The Rev. Tollie L. Caution, Associate Secretary
Home Department
National Council of Episcopal Churches
815 Second Avenue
New York, N. Y. 10017

REFORMED CHURCH IN AMERICA

This body was established by the earliest Dutch settlers of New York as the Reformed Protestant Dutch Church in 1628. It embraces many of the historic colonical churches of New York and New Jersey and today has many strong churches in the middle and far West.

Reformed Church in America (cont.).

For yearbook, which lists ministers, contact:

General Synod
475 Riverside Drive
New York, N. Y.

SEVENTH-DAY ADVENTISTS

For information on Negro clergy contact:

Elder H. D. Singleton
General Conference of Seventh-Day Adventists
6840 Eastern Avenue, N. W.
Washington, D. C.

UNITARIAN UNIVERSALIST ASSOCIATION

Yearbook issued. Information secured from:

Dr. Joseph Barth, Director, Department of the Ministry
25 Beacon Street
Boston, Mass. 02108

UNITED CHURCH OF CHRIST

Constitution adopted in 1961 uniting the Evangelical and Reformed Church and the Congregational Christian Churches. Yearbook issued with information for previous year. May be secured from:

The United Church of Christ
297 Park Avenue, South
New York, N. Y. 10010

UNITED METHODIST CHURCH

Formerly The Methodist Church. Merged with the Evangelical United Brethren in General Conference, 1968.

Section of Records
Research and Statistics
1200 Davis Street
Evanston, Illinois

Geographical Index

ALABAMA

ARIZONA

ARKANSAS

CALIFORNIA

Abney, Albert
Adams, John H.
Allison, Jonathan William
Bass, Richard Oliver
Bohler, Lewis Penrose, Jr.
Boswell, Hamilton Theodore
Brookins, H. Hartford
Buie, George Charles, Jr.
Chambers, Timothv Moses
Chambliss, Carroll Randolph
Christian, Gerald Chilton
Coleman, Wm. Hannan, Jr.
Dawkins, Maurice Anderson
Doggette, Jackson Michael
Edwards, Kenneth Pennington
Floyd, Massey, Jr.
Foster, Richard A. B.
Francis, Joseph Abel
Guidry, Raymond James
Harrison. Bob
Henning, Cornal Garnett
Herzfeld, Will Lawrence
Hines, Thomas E., Jr.
Jackson, D. Manning
Jackson, Mance C.
Johnson, Paul Edwin
Jordan, Frederick Douglass
Joseph, Ray Kennington
Keller, Cyrus Samuel, Sr.
Kilgore, Thomas, Jr.
Lee, Willie Samuel
Mangram, John Dee
Massey, Floyd, Jr.
Mitchell, Henry Heywood
Moody, James Luther
Morgan, Philip Henry
Moses, Jesse Daniel
Nebblett, Milton Elmer
Powell, Joseph Tiffany
Price, Alonzo
Pritchett, Clayton Robinson
McGee, Lewis Allen
McNeil, Jesse Jai
McPhatter, Thomas Hayswood
Neal, Warren Joseph
Nelson, R. Wendell
Rogers, Cornish Romeo
Smith, George Walker
Smith, James Alfred
Smith, Kenneth Wayne
Smith, Walter Louis
Strayhand, Thomas Lewis
Talbert, Melvin George
Taylor, David Lawson
Thomas, Robert Colby
Thurman, Howard
Ward, Eric Calvin
Watson, Hughey Willie
White, Edward Augustus
White, Lanneau L.
White, Major Cornelius
Williams, Albert Cecil
Williams, Clarence Joseph
Williams, Edward Samuel
Williams, W. Hazaiah
Willis, Jesse Billinger
Zimmerman, Matthew A., Jr.

COLORADO

Barron, Richard Edward
Coleman, David Cyrus
Jackson, John Henry, Jr.
Liggins, Wendell
Redd, Albert Carter
Shannon, Sylvester Lorenzo

CONNECTICUT

Battles, Richard Arthur, Jr.
Blake, Charles Carols
Clement, Harold
Edmonds, Edwin Richardson
Gordon, Robert Charles
Hopkins, Thomas Ewell
Heacock, Roland Tilman
Jessie, William R.
Kennedy, William Thomas
McKissick, William J.
Montgomery, Simon Peter
Peters, James D.

Sargent, Charles Jackson
Smith, Allen Hart
Taylor, Julian Augustus
Taylor, Rafe Monroe
Thompson, Albert A.
Timpson, George William
Tipton, B. Cortez
Williams, Samuel Jerome
Wyche, Oscar Herbert
Yates, Walter Ladell, Sr.

DELAWARE

Bailey, Howard Andrew
Barnette, James William
Coleman, Rudolph Wesley
Noisette, Ruffin Nichols
Primo, Quintin Ebenezer
Settles, Paul
Shockley, John Richard

DISTRICT OF COLUMBIA

Baber, George W.
Barnes, Frederick Wm.
Bell, Harold Lloyd
Birch, Adolphus Augustus
Blackmon, Thomas O. V.
Bland, Frank Leon
Boyd, Braxton Julian
Brady, Crawford William
Brooks, Charles DeCatur
Broomfield, Oree, Sr.
Browne, Hosea Harold
Bunton, Henry Clay
Burrell, Emma Pinkney
Calhoun, William Edward
Carroll, Edward Gonzalez
Carroll, Richard Allen
Catchings, Lincoln Maynard
Cheek, James Edward
Cleveland, Edward Earl
Clifford, Richard Lorenzo
Coates, James Elliott
Cole, Wilbert C.
Collins, Leon C.
Cousin, Lee Andrew
Craig, Benjamin Howard
Craig, Lawrence Lauman
Crawford, Evans Edgar, Jr.
Crosson, Calvin Ferry
Davis, Arnor S.
Day, Roland Frederick
Dicks, Abel Joseph
Eggleston, George Watkins
Fauntroy, Walter E.
Ferrell, Horace Albion
Fisher, Carl Anthony
Fowler, Andrew
Foy, James Douglas
Gandy, Samuel Lucius
Gerald, William
Gibbs, Ernest
Gregory, Henry C.
Guiles, Samuel Everette
Hale, Samuel Wesley
Hall, Richard Wesley
Harrison, Earl Leonard
Haywood, John Wilfred
Hewlett, Everett Augustus, Sr.
Hill, Daniel Graxton
Holloman, John L. S.
Jackson, Edward Franklin
Jackson, Moses Lester
Jacobs, Solomon Napoleon
James, Daniel Finney
Jefferson, June Lee, Jr.
Johnson, Mordecai Wyatt
Johnson, Robert Pierre
Jones, James E.
Jones, Kelsey A.
Jones, William Ronald
Kyle, Curtis
Ledbetter, Theodore S.
Lee, Shelton C.
McCray, Maceo Edward
Marino, Eugene Antonio
Medford, Hampton Thomas
Miles, Henry
Miles, Joseph A., Sr.
Moore, Douglas
Moore, Jerry A.
Morse, Savarhett

D. C. (cont.)
Murray, Chasteen Theophilus
Murray, Lindsay Clifton
Myers, French Whycliff, Jr.
Nelson, William Stuart
Newborn, Ernest J.
Oliver, Archie
Pair, James David
Parham, Thomas David
Patterson, Rossie L.
Payton, Benjamin Franklin
Phillips, Channing Emery
Poulard, Grady Emory
Pugh, Robert Milton
Reynolds, Louis B.
Roberts, James Deotis, Sr.
Robinson, G. Dewey
Rodney, Joseph Conway
Rogers, Jefferson Paramore
Rollins, Robert Lee
Ruffin, James Shepard
Salmon, John Luther, Jr.
Satterwhite, John H.
Singleton, Harold Douglas
Smith, Ernest Andrew
Smith, Ernest Clarence
Somersille, James Humphries
Somerville, Wendell Clay
Spottswood, Stephen Gill
Stevens, Junius Ray
Stines, Henri Alexandre
Stith, Forrest Christopher
Tankerson, Richard Earl
Trueheart, Gregory
Turner, Franklin Delton
Turner, Howard Ellis
Tyms, James Daniel
Van Croft, William A., Jr.
Veazey, Carlon Wadsworth
Walden, Charles Eugene, Jr.
West, James Oliver, Jr.
White, Frank Lamar
White, Kenneth
White, Leamon Whitfield
White, Woodie W.
Williams, Frank Leviticus
Williams, Frederick Boyd
Williams, Robert Gilmore
Williams, Smallword Edmund
Wright, Leon E.
Wyatt, James C.

FLORIDA

Ball, William Franklin
Brooks, David Henry
Clarke, Elisha Salathiel
Collier, Arthur James, Jr.
Cox, Milton Edward
Davis, Enoch Douglas
Edwards, Isadore
Elligan, Irvin
Felder, Clifford Samuel
Ferguson, Wm. Melanthchon
Flanagan, William Carl
Hall, Laurence Edward
Hudson, James
Gibbs, Carey Abraham
Gillespie, Sylvester Thaddeus
Johnson, Samuel T.
Long, Harold David
McDowell, Henry Curtis
McKissick, John Henry, Jr.
McQueen, Charles Waldo
Monk, J. Paul, Jr.
Morgan, Frank Douglas
Pierre, Maurice C.
Pinder, Nelson Wardell
Reece, John Henry, Jr.
Reddick, Albert Joseph
Stokes, Frank Agustus
White, Albert McNeil
White, Walter Syrus
Willi, Eddie James
Williams, Mac James
Wilson, Robert Henry
Wright, Thomas Alexander

GEORGIA

Alston, Charlie
Anderson, Herbert Forgys
Bearden, Harold Irvin

Borders, William Holmes
Branch, George Murray
Bronson, Oswald Perry
Butler, Grady
Cherry, Maurice Stallworth
Clark, Isaac Rufus
Clarke, Jimmy Ed.
Clayton, Robert Louis
Coan, Josephus Roosevelt
Cook, Payton Brailsford
Creecy, Howard W.
Cunningham, Frank
Darnell, Milner L.
Davis, Edsel M.
Dickerson, Adolphus S.
Eaton, James Alonza
Everett, Ezra
Gartrell, C. L.
George, Carrie Leigh
Gladney, Harvey Levi
Gooden, Samuel Ellsworth
Grant, David Cooper
Grant, Edward James
Hairston, Andrew Jasper
Hamilton, Charles Spencer
Harris, Marquis Lafayette
Haynes, Roosevelt
Hickman, Ernest Lawrence
Jay, Grover Cleveland
Johnson, Harvey Eligah
King, William P.
Lincoln, C. Eric
McCall, Emmanuel Lemuel
McKinnon, Udalga Zorosha
Mays, Benjamin Elijah
Mercer, William Summer
Middleton, John Albert
Pollar, Alfred
Potter, William Abraham
Pryor, Thomas
Pugh, Thomas Jefferson
Richardson, Harry Van
Rogers, T. Y., Jr.
Rowe, Franklin R.
Ryce, Amos II
Shorts, Robert Buell
Shy, P. Randolph
Simmons, Julius Caesar
Smith, Otis Artis
Stell, Louis Scott
Stinson, Olden Hixon
Sweet, Henry Beauregard
Tillman, Eugene C.
Williams, Samuel
Williams, Samuel Woodrow
Wynn, Master Julius
Yorpp, Elza Prince
Young, Andrew J.

HAWAII

Lewis, Alexander Leonard

ILLINOIS

Adamson, Norman R.
Alexander, William Peter
Armstrong, Ernest W.
Austin, Junius Caesar
Bailey, A. Leon
Bailey, Jack Simpson
Blake, David A.
Booker, Merrel Daniel
Bradford, Charles Edward
Brantford, Gerald Henry
Brooks, Jerome Bernard
Brown, Joseph Bernard
Brown, Thomas Emerson
Burrell, Louis Stephen
Campbell, Jesse
Carey, Archibald J., Jr.
Carter, James E.
Christopher, Claude
Clay, W. Benjamin
Clements, George Harold
Clinkscales, John William
Collins, Noel Virginia
Dames, Jonathan Alexander
Daniel, Wilbur Nathan
Davis, Corneal A.
Dickinson, Richard Charles
Dixon, Edward Parker
Dunlap, Theodore Roosevelt

Ill. (cont.)
Eaton, Herbert Hoover
Ellis, Thomas H.
Evans, Clay
Evans, Joseph Henry
Ferguson, John Columbus
Gaines, Renford George
Galloway, Horace Ely
Gathings, Samuel Alonzo
Goldsberry, Harry Willis
Gray, Arthur Douglas
Hall, Marzella Warren
Hall, Shelvin Jerome
Hargraves, James Archie
Harley, Philip A.
Herron, Vernon Mack
Hill, Abraham Alton
Honore, Thomas Francis
Horton, James Aguinaldo
Howard, Arthur R., Jr.
Isom, Dotoy Ivertus, Jr.
Jackson, A. Patterson
Jackson, Jesse Louis
Jackson, John C.
Jackson, Joseph Harrison
James, Alexander Lincoln
Jefferson, Frederick D.
Johnson, William A.
Keller, Richard Carol
Kennard, Massie Lewis
Kimbrough, Walter Lee
King, Dearine Edwin
King, Robert Henry
Lambert, Rollins Edward
Lile, Alfred T.
Martin, Samuel Joseph
Mayes, Allen Mercer
Myers, Samuel David
Miller, Clyde Horace, Jr.
Miller, Roy L.
Morris, Samuel Solomon
Porter, Florezel Louis, Sr.
Porter, Herman Anthon
Porter, John Richard
Putney, Ellis, Jr.
Range, King Solomon
Readye, David E.
Reid, Wilfred
Richardson, Ben
Scott, Nathan A., Jr.
Scott, Simon H., Jr.
Shaw, Talbert Oscall
Sims, Frank Kentworth
Smith, Benjamin Julian
Smith, Kenneth Bryant
Thompson, Charlie Roosevelt
Trotter, Walter Constello
Sylvester, Joseph
Tynes, Morris Harrison
Wallace, Robert Clayton
Ward, Edgar William
Watts, Alexander Alfred
Wells, Gerald Nathaniel
Wharton, Wesley Edward
Williams, Samuel
Winkfield, Orange Willie

INDIANA

Adams, Clyde
Allen, John Claude
Barber, William Joseph
Bedenbaugh, David Roosevelt
Boyd, Cauthion T.
Breeding, M. L.
Burton, H. L.
Butler, Ernest Daniel
Caldwell, John Martin
Carter, John F.
Compton, John Robert
Cummings, James L.
Davis, Cyprian
Dumas, Floyd Earl
Faulkner, Robert Huntt
Hicks, Luther Clemon
Hudson, Theodore
Jackson, Lester Kendel
Kellogg, Reginald John
Marsh, Clinton McClurkin
Mills, William G.
Paris, William A.
Penn, Robert Earl
Peoples, Robert Hayes
Pierce, Isaiah Benjamin

Saunders, Robert L., Sr.
Shields, Landrum Eugene
Smith, Robert
Walker, William James

IOWA

Rice, Warner Myron
Thomas, James Samuel
Williams, Ernest Prince

KANSAS

Bailey, Charles Buford
Brewer, Harold Cole
Darby, Walter A., Jr.
Cunningham, Theodore F.
Easley, Paul Howard, Sr.
Freeman, Edward Anderson
Hicks, E. B.
Higgs, Raymond Clarence
Mashaw, Samuel Jones
Mouchette, Edward Donley
Nolen, Benjamin Julius
Pearson, Augustus Japheth
Scales, William Clinton
Strickland, Frederick W.
Warren, Glendah Hillard
Williams, Willie George

KENTUCKY

Alston, Edward Deedom
Anderson, Felix Sylvester
Berry, Benjamin Donaldson
Dunnaville, Marshall Edward
Greene, Horace Henry, Sr.
Harvey, Wardelle Green
Hill, Robert Arlander
Holmes, Willie Lawnsie
Lee, Robert Edgar
Lesser, Leo, Jr.
McClellan, James F., Jr.
Nutter, Homer Eckler
Offutt, Garland Kimble
Patterson, Bernardin Joseph
Sampson, Frederick George
Sydner, C. H.
Taylor, Virgil Thomas
Tucker, Charles Eubank
White, William Henry

LOUISIANA

Artis, George Henry
Billoups, Edward Doyle
Bowman, John Walter Father
Brown, Ertemus Temple
Carter, George Washington, Jr.
Christopher, Olden Walter
Clark, Moses Julius
Brown, Philip Rayfield
Davis, Abraham Eric
Collins, George Napoleon
Curry, Norris Samuel
Debro, W. L.
Eubanks, John Bunyon
Francis, John
Handy, William Talbot, Jr.
Harris, Simon E.
Henderson, Lewis Duke
Johnson, Meredith Elbert
King, John Lucas, Jr.
King, Willis Jefferson
Lakey, Othal Hawthorne
Mays, Willie
Moore, Noah Watson, Jr.
Morris, John Batiste
Oliver, William Raoul
Perry, Nathaniel Patrick
Polk, Robert Lawrence
Popleon, K. Edward
Ribbons, Jeffery Clarence
Robertson, Burnell Jacob
Rousseve, Maurice Louis
Skinner, John Thomas
Upton, Milton Leon
Verrett, Joseph C.
Williams, Robert

MARYLAND

Barnes, Kenneth Pearle
Bird, Van Samuel
Bourne, Charles Nathaniel
Brooks, Thomas Howard
Brown, Henry
Bryant, Harrison James
Calbert, William Edward
Carter, Harold A.
Coursey, John Henry
Daniels, Reginald James
DeGraffenreidt, Jermit Jesse
Dobson, Vernon Nathaniel
Forkkio, John A.
Garrison, James L.
Hicks, Richard Ross
Howard, Lawrence W., Sr.
Hutchins, Joshua, Jr.
Jackson, Theodore C., Jr.
Johnson, Charles Edward
Johnson, Richard Hanson
Jones, Aubry
Jones, James Ricardo, Jr.
Love, Edgar Amos
McDonald, Harry James
Mack, Charles Henry
McKenney, Martin Luther, Jr.
McKinney, Richard Ishmael
McLellan, Daniel C., Jr.
Moseley, Calvin Edwin
Murray, Allen Levi
Newbold, Robert Thos., Jr.
Obey, Edward Rudolph
Paige, Walter Ellis
Payne, Arthur Jerome
Phillips, Wendell Harrison
Pitts, W. Lyndsai
Powell, Robert Meaker
Roman, Gus
Saunders, Monroe Randolph
Simms, Virgin Andrew
Smith, Perry Anderson, III
Swann, Melvin C.
Wilson, David Octavio
Wood, Marcus Garvey
Wooten, James Henry
Vaughan, Alfred Austin

MASSACHUSETTS

Adjahoe, Alfred Amedjorgbenu
Anderson, Benjamin J.
Bolden, Vernie L.
Breeden, James Pleasant
Brooks, Henry Curtis
Burgess, John Melville
Fullilove, Paul Allen
Furblur, Harold Alonzo
Burton, Horace Edward
Byrd, Cameron Wells
Cobb, Charles E.
Gardner, Elijah Harris
Harris, Henry Benton
King, William Joseph
Lee, Alfred L.
McClain, Wm. Bobby
Mitchell, James William
Moore, Prentis Monroe Dumas
Phillips, Oscar George D.
Taylor, Rafe Monroe
Thomas, George
Washington, L. Barnwell

MICHIGAN

Albert, Xavier Robert
Amos, Walter Hansel
Anderson, Leslie Otto
Bailey, John Seth
Banks, Allen A.
Boone, Theodore Sylvester
Bradley, Fulton Obadiah
Butler, Charles William
Byrd, Cameron Wells
Campbell, Stephen Calhoun
Carpenter, Charles William
Chambers, James Coolidge
Clark, Harold
Cleage, Albert Buford, Jr.
Cone, James Hal
Cooper, Theodore Walter
Crews, Clarence Leo
Dade, Malcolm Gray
Exum, John M.

Glenn, Lawrence Talmadge
Guy, John Francis
Haney, William Riley
Hill, Charles Andrew
Hughes, Carl Donald
James, Bose Moses
Johnson, Louis
Jones, Robert L.
Jordan, Robert Lee
Lee, Carleton Lafayette
Morris, Donald Eugene
Morton, Charles Evans
Nelson, Clarence T. R.
Oglesby, Jacob C.
Parks, Lyman S.
Rand, David George
Redd, Albert Carter
Reid, Arlond N.
Rich, Archie L.
Robinson, Hubert Nelson
Ross, Solomon David
Wadsworth, Jas. Ed., Jr.
Williams, Arthur Benj., Jr.
Williams, Joseph Henry
Williams, Lawrence Jesse
Williams, Stacy

MINNESOTA

Brown, Theophile Waldorf
Gardner, LeRoy
Holloway, James Romeo
McCall, Aidan Maurice
Williams, John F.

MISSISSIPPI

Burns, Charles Dixon
Cameron, Johnnie Earl
Carlen, Gray L.
Chandler, James Cleveland
Cherry, Henry C.
Cox, Sherman Haywood
Fisher, Carl A.
Gill, W. O.
Gipson, Wayman Jefferson
Hicks, Jimmie C.
Jones, Quintus Leon
Joseph Charles David
Ledoux, Jerome Gaston
Lindsey, Merrill Winston
McWilliams, Alfred Edward
Oliver, Leonard James
Pearson, George Isaac
Perry, Harold Robert
Perry, Michael
Porter, Richard Sylvester
Sewell, George Alexander
Simon, Joseph Donald
Sims, George Turner
Stanton, Robert Louis
Stevens, Robert Matthew
Stringer, Emmett James
Taylor, Paul Lawrence

MISSOURI

Anderson, Vinton Randolph
Blair, James Lowell
Blakely, George Wayman
Burgess, Monroe Abel
Chappelle, Ezekiel E., Jr.
Clair, Matthew Walker, Jr.
Clater, Bobbie Daniel
Collins, William
Doggett, John Nelson, Jr.
Edwards, Jos. DuMaine, Sr.
Fordham, Walter Wraggs
Gillespie, William George
Hale, William Henry
Hines, Lincoln Fisher
Huntley, Thomas Elliott
Hylton, Samuel Wilbur, Jr.
Jones, John Garth
Lewis, Henry T.
Loud, Irwin C.
Marshall, Arthur, Jr.
Parker, Lynnword
Reid, Edgar Leroy
Reid, Robert Edward
Rice, George Edward
Rodney, John Joseph
Ryce, Amos, II

Mo. (cont.)
Singleton, William Matthew
Taylor, G. Herfin
Taylor, Paul Jones
Taylor, Theodore Roosevelt
Van Buren, William George
Wheeler, Charles Calvin, III
Williams, John Wesley
Womack, P. J.

MONTANA

Hall, James Harold

NEBRASKA

Brightman, Edward Scipio
Butler, Joseph LeCount
Thompson, John Andrew
Tinsley, Raymond Earl

NEVADA

McLeod, Norman S.
Wilson, Ivory W.

NEW HAMPSHIRE

Walker, John Thomas

NEW JERSEY

Alleyne, Lawrence E. D.
Atchison, Wallace William
Austin, Miles Jonathan
Bagwell, Clarence W.
Blake, Charles Carlos
Bobbitt, Matthew Douglas
Bowie, Harry John
Butts, E. Wellington, II
Christian, Geo. Benjamin
Clarke, Aloysius Roland
Davis, Guilford Kenneth
Davis, Hooker D.
Donaldson, Spurgeon Booker
England, Frank
Faulkner, William John
Fox, William K.
Harris, Chas. Poindexter
Kelsey, George Dennis
McGee, C. Lincoln
Marcus, Chester Lee
Oates, Bernard Dennis
Oates, Caleb E.
Osley, William E.
Parker, Sidney Bayne
Reed, Daniel Lee
Rice, Deual Converse
Richardson, Louis Melvin
Roberts, Frederick Raymond
Roberts, Joseph Lawrence, Jr.
Robinson, Dillard
Rooks, C. Shelby
Savoy, Clarence Monroe
Scott, James Arthur
Stewart, James E. W.
Street, John Franklin
Taylor, Prince Albert, Jr.
Thigpen, Lee Allen, Jr.
Watson, William Austin
Williams, W. Clyde
Woodson, S. Howard
Wright, Nathan

NEW MEXICO

Tieuel, Robert C. D., Jr.

NEW YORK

Anonye, Albert Chinedozi
Anthony, Irving
Asbury, Howard DeGrasse
Austin, Samuel Quincy
Barber, Jesse Belmont
Baron, Herman Alexander
Beasley, Louis James
Bennett, Robert Avon, Jr.
Blackman, Herman E. C.
Bridell, David Wesley
Brooks, Elemit Anthony
Brown, Revl Amos

Brown, Warren M.
Brown, Willard Gardener
Burrus, Lloyd Andros
Calhoun, Raymond L.
Callender, Eugene St. Clair
Carrington, Charles L.
Carrington, John Elmer
Carrington, William Orlando
Carter, Matthew Gamaliel
Cary, William Sterling
Caution, Tollie LeRoy
Churn, Serenus T.
Clark, James I.
Cobb, Charles Earl
Cobham, Dudley DeCosta
Coleridge, Clarence N.
Coles, Joseph Carlyle, Jr.
Cone, James Hal
Cragg, Christopher Morton
Criss, Geo. Washington
Davis, Leon Houston
Daye, Morgan M.
Delaine, Joseph A.
Duckett, Zelma E. (Mrs.)
Dukes, Billie Edward
Epps, Saint Paul Langley
Farmer, James Leonard
Featherstone, Rudolph R.
Florence, Franklin D. R., Sr.
Foster, Wendell
Freeman, William Lee
Fulford, Fergus Maurice
Galamison, Milton Arthur
Gatewood, Clifton Emory A.
George, Bryant
Glanton, Virgil W.
Graham, John Harry
Gray, L. Charles
Griffin, James C.
Griggs, Andrew L.
Haig, Albert Randolph
Harris, Elbert Ferdinand
Hawkins, Elder Garnett
Hawkins, Zachariah
Hayes, William A.
Hemphill, James Thomas
Henry Vincent DePaul
Hicks, John Josephus
Hildebrand, Richard Allen
Hoard, Samuel Lawrence
Hoggard, James Clinton
Hood, Robert E.
Houston, Charles Edward
Houston, Wm. Eugene, Jr.
Hucles, Henry Boyd, III
Hudson, R. T.
Hughes, Henderson Randolph
Imes, William Lloyd
James, Eugen Marshall
James, Leroy
James, William M.
Jenkins, Thomas
Johns, Paul
Johnson, Gray Gould
Johnson, Leroy
Johnson, Robert Ross
Jones, James Miller
Jones, Lawrence
Jones, Sidney St. Clair
Jones, Wm. Augustus, Jr.
Kibble, Harvey Ward
Kilgore, Claude Columbus
Kinard, David Lee
King, Dearine Edwin
Knott, Moses Alexander, Jr.
Lehman, Harvey John
Lewis, Samuel Archibald
Lincoln, C. Eric
Lockman, Irvin Charles
Lowe, Richard A.
Lucas, Lawrence Edward
McCall, H. Carl
McCown, Lowell Malcolm
McFarlane, Percival Alan R.
McIntyre, DeWitt T.
McKinney, Carnes
McLeod, Norman Stinson
Malloy, Culberth Jerome
Marino, Eugene Antonio
Marshall, Calvin B., III
Martin, Richard Beamon
Matthews, Verner Randolph
Miller, Wilbert Daniel, Sr.
Mitchell, Roscoe Marron
Moore, Arthur Chester
Moore, Earl B.
Moore, Emerson John

N. Y. (cont.)
Moore, James Robert
Morris, John Charles
Nichols, Roy
Norman, Clarence
Parker, Walter Procter H.
Phillips, Porter William, Jr.
Phillips, Wendell Harrison
Pickney, Aurelius D.
Pinn, Walter S.
Polk, Robert Lawrence
Pressley, Calvin Oliver
Proctor, James Melvin
Proctor, Samuel Dewitt
Pugh, Alfred Lane
Riley, Negail Rudolph
Robinson, James Herman
Robinson, Paul Mitchell
Rollins, Joseph Metz
Routte, Jesse Wayman
Sabourin, Clemonce
Salmon, Harold Anthony
Sheares, Reuben A.
Sherard, Robert Douglas
Shipley, Anthony Jerome
Shockley, Grant S.
Simms, David McDaniel
Skeete, F. Herbert
Smith, Lawrence Benjamin
Smith, William T.
Speaks, Ruben Lee
Taylor, Gardener Calvin
Terrell, Leonard Earl
Thompson, Randolph
Thompson, Roy Lee
Toppin, Edwin Noel
Turner, Simpson
Walker, Lucius, Jr.
Walker, Wyatt Tee
Walls, William Jacob
Warren, Charles Lacy
Watkins, Readus Joseph
Watts, Herman Hayes
Webb, Ercel Franklin
Weston, M. Moran
Whitaker, Arthur L.
Whitted, Andrew Eugene
Williams, John V.
Wilmore, Gayraud Stephen, Jr.
Wilson, Edward John
Wright, Giles Robert

NORTH CAROLINA

Allen, Frank Murphy
Alston, Justus M.
Anderson, Herman Leroy
Arnold, James Alridge
Barnette, Paul B.
Bell, Asa Lee
Bishop, Cecil
Blakey, Durocher Lon
Blassingame, James Matthew
Boykin, Isaac
Brown, Benjamin Harrison
Brown, Frank Reginald
Brown, William Henry
Bullock, Richard David, Jr.
Burke, DeGrandval
Butler, J. Ray
Cannon, James Alexander, Jr.
Clancy, Bryant Edward
Costen, James Hutten
Costner, Dwight Augustine
Cox, Benjamin Elton
Crawford, William Richard
Davis, Grady Demus
DeVeaux, William Phillips
Drayton, Jerry
Dungee, John Riley, Jr.
Eaton, Herbert Hoover
Eddington, Charles Arthur
Edwards, Chancy Rudolph
Fleming, John Wilson
Forbes, James Alexander
Foushee, Warren Raymond
Gaston, Joseph Alexander
Gaylord, Stewart Richard
George, Arthur Henry
Givens, Howard Washington
Goodwin, Kelly Oliver Perry
Grady, James Crawford
Hadden, Thomas Paul
Hawkins, Reginald Armistice

Hedgley, David Rice
Henderson, Elo Leon
Hicks, Richard Louis, Jr.
Hill, Wright Albert
Holmes, John William
Horsley, Leroy
Howell, Cajus B.
Hudson, Arthur Eaton
Hughley, Judge Neal
Hunt, James Louis
Hunt, Lawrence Everett
Johnson, Robert Josiah
Johnson, Ulysses Samuel
Jordan, Isaac Matthew
Keyes, Wilbert David
Kirton, Edwin Eggliston
Lawrence, Cephas Worrick
Lewis, Willie B.
Lightsey, Joseph Hancock
Little, Harlee Hoover
Lynch, Lorenzo Augustus
McCallum, James Hector
McCloud, J. Oscar
McCoy, Cleo Milam
McDaniel, Abraham H.
Marsh, Henry Levander
Meachem, Robert Allen
Moore, Ezra Julius
Morrison, James W.
Moseley, Alexander Dumas
Murphy, Thurman H.
Newberry, Earl Edward
Norris, Hills Edward
Parker, Fred William
Penn, Leon Sinkler, Sr.
Phillips, Walter M.
Poole, John Douglas
Quick, Jerry Alphonzo
Randall, Eugene
Robinson, Milton Benerdine
Roland, Garther William
Saunders, Lenwood Daniel
Scott, Claude Caesar
Shaw, Herbert Bell
Smith, James Wynetotte
Smith, Thomas, Jr.
Stanley, Alfred Knighton
Stanley, Othello Doremus
Stitt, Robert Elemaker
Stroud, Norman L.
Teamer, James Wm. Robert
Thomas, Clarence Harris
Thomas, George Benjamin
Turner, Eugene Burns
Tyson, Charles Edward
Walker, Arnold George
Walls, William Roscoe
Ward, Charles W.
White, John Walter
White, Joseph Douglas, Jr.
Williams, Julian Leander
Yates, Walter Ladell, Sr.

OHIO

Ackerman, Amos Abraham
Andrews, Richard Taylor, Jr.
Bateman, Melvin
Benton, Elijah
Bodley, Simon, Jr.
Booth, Lavaughn Venchael
Branch, Emanuel S.
Brown, Clifton H.
Caddell, Gerwood Lincoln
Chambers, David Ernest, Jr.
Cleveland, Frank C.
Cochran, Morris Bartlett
Compton, John R.
Deveaux, John Allen, Jr.
Dixon, James Inman
Durden, Lewis Minyon
Evans, Benjamin Bonaparte
Fowlis, Ronald Preston
Gomez, Joseph
Graham, Tecumseh Xavier
Hatcher, Eugene Clifford
Henderson, Jefferson Minston
Hicks, H. Beecher
Hodges, Sloan Stanley
Jacobs, Donald Gustavus
James, Eugene Willis
Jenkins, John Dallas
Latta, William Clarence
Lee, Carleton Lafayette

Ohio (cont.)
Lee, Morris William
Liggins, Lyman William
Liggins, Thomas Elmer
McCray, Thomas L.
Mayson, Henry Irving
Miller, Oliver Howard
Morgan, Eugene Edward, Jr.
Moss, Otis, Jr.
Primes, Joseph Ronald
Redding, James
Reed, Nathaniel
Riley, Sumpter Marion, Jr.
Rivers, Clarence Joseph
Ruffin, Andrew Jackson
Shuttlesworth, Fred Lee
Simpson, Wm. Bratton
Smith, Bennett W.
Smith, Herald Leonydus
Smith, John Conway
Sparrow, Eugene
Spivey, Charles S.
Stalnaker, Calvin Kersey
Stanley, Walter Payne
Stokes, Rembert Edwards
Thompson, Floyd William
Varner, Samuel Lee
Walker, William Raphael
Waller, Alfred M., Sr.
Washington, James Augustus
Whitten, Bennie Edward, Jr.
Wilkes, William Reid
Williams, Wilbert Henry
Womack, Andrew Australia
Wright, Byrl Fisher
Wright, Samuel Ross

OKLAHOMA

Alexander, George W. II
Alexander, Robt. Henry, Sr.
Armstrong, Ernest W.
Chappelle, Thomas Oscar
Curry, Morris Alexander
Jackson, James Castina
Jackson, Walter Kinsley
James, Goree Leon
Jones, Bennie J.
Parris, Henry Phares
Taylor, George S.
Wamble, Amos Sylvester, Sr.
Whitlow, Charles William

OREGON

Stone, Lee Owen

PENNSYLVANIA

Alston, Percel Odel, Sr.
Anderson, Jesse Fosset
Anderson, William H.
Arterberry, Rufus, Sr.
Banks, William Love
Barbour, Josephus Pius
Barrett, William Emanuel, Sr.
Beatty, Joseph Henry
Bottoms, Larence Wendell
Bradley, David H.
Brannon, Thomas Edward
Bright, John Douglas
Burrell, Louis S.
Cannon, James Romeo
Carter, Churchill
Cheatham, William Lee
Cousin, Lee Andrew
Cox, James Alexander
Dunston, Alfred G.
Dyson, William Andrew
Fair, Frank Thomas
Flack, French Ziezler
Foggie, Charles H.
Gray, William Herbert, Jr.
Hairston, John Carl
Hazzard, Walter R.
Harper, Theophilus E.
Harris, Robert Lee
Hawkins, Alexander Amos
Hayling, Mapson Forkau
Hoggard, Dennie W.
Hutchinson, Harry T., Jr.
Johnson, Arthur L.
Jones, Arthur Samuel

Jones, E. Theodore
Jones, John Luke
Jones, Leonard McKinley
Jones, Ozro Thurston
Jones, Ozro Thurston, Jr.
Jones, Sercy Leonard
Justiss, Jacob, Jr.
Kent, Reginald H.
Lavalais, Joseph George
Lee, Carleton Lafayette
Lee, Gabriel S., Jr.
Lee, Marshall Williams
Lewis, Mahlon Montgomery
Link, John Lewis
Little, John Franklin
Logan, John Richard
Logan, Thomas W. S.
Lomax, Rhea Swann
McClain, Herbert Linton
McClendon, John Ruben
McKissick, John H.
Michael, Euilious Raphael
Nichols, Henry H.
Nichols, Roy C. Bishop
Owens, Chester Howard
Peterson, Claude Tedford
Petett, Weldon Durell
Phillips, Porter Wm., Sr.
Reed, Carother N.
Reid, George Ransom
Scott, Edgar L.
Sheppard, Marshall Lorenzo
Sims, David Henry
Singleton, George Arnett
Smalls, Leonard L.
Smith, Robert Johnson
Sullivan, Leon Howard
Sumpter, Augustus Cicero
Tivy, Cleveland Burie
Tucker, Frank D.
Turner, William Davis
Upshaw, Robert Lee
Washington, Joseph R., Jr.
Washington, Paul Matthews
Williams, Arthur D.
Williams, Curtis
Williams, Henry Charlie
Williams, Linda Colene
Williams, McKinley
Willis, Charles Vernon
Wilson, Frank Theodore
Wright, Jefferson
Wright, Jeremiah
Wright, Richard

RHODE ISLAND

Campbell, Amos B.
Campbell, Egbert Alexander
Cook, Wallace Jeffrey
Scott, Julius Samuel, Jr.
Thompson, Paul Frederick

SOUTH CAROLINA

Adair, Joseph H.
Ashford, George
Bailey, John Henry
Barnes, William Heard, Sr.
Bouie, Simon Pinckney
Brockman, Nathaniel J.
Brown, James Walter
Bryant, Lawrence Chesterfield
Calhoun, Clyde Livingston
Cherry, Charles Alexander
Curry, John Wesley
David, Lawrence T.
Dial, James Samuel
Enwright, John Thomas
Ferguson, Clarence F.
Ferrell, Clarence J.
Fortune, Allen Ethan
Francis, David Curtis, Sr.
Glover, Benjamin James
Gordon, Maxie Sylvester
Grady, Zedekiah L.
Holman, Alonzo William
Holmes, J. Arthur
Hudson, James Hammie
Jackson, Henry Brown
Jackson, James Conroy
James, Frederick C.
Jenkins, Warren Marion
Johnson, Coolidge Milford

S. C. (cont.)
Knox, Wilbur Benjamin
Lewis, Willie
Moore, Jesse Lee
Morris, Lloyd Belton
Nealy, Fred Rogers
Nelson, James Herbert
Newman, Omega Franklin
Payton, Benjamin Franklin
Pointer, Louis Waylon
Reuben, Odell Richardson
Roland, Harold
Roston, David Williamson
Settle, William Henry
Shaw, C. Alexander
Shaw, Harry Wilbert
Sideboard, Henry Yergan
Smith, Charles Mifflin
Smith, Charlie Jasper
Summers, V., Jr.
Sumpter, Benjamin Franklin
Toatley, Robert George
Toney, Patrick W.
Tyson, Charles Edward
Weathers, J. Leroy
Willis, Oliver Hunter
Wilson, William L.
Wilson, Wylie Edward

TENNESSEE

Adams, James A.
Alexander, Wm. A., Sr.
Arnold, Lionel A.
Birchette, John Fletcher, Jr.
Britton, John Henry
Brown, Edward Lynn
Bruce, John Carlyle
Burnett, Marshall H.
Byrd, Wm. Theodore, Jr.
Campbell, Abraham A.
Carter, Grover Hester
Coleman, Frederick D., Jr.
Crawford, Peter Griffin
Criglar, Edmond
Donald, Grady H.
Doyle, Bertram Wilbur
Dudley, Charles Edward
Dykes, DeWitt Sanford
Ewing, Isaiah
Fitzgerald, Charles Harris
Gadsen, James Solomon
Golden, Charles Franklin
Gordon, Frank R.
Granberry, James M., Jr.
Griffin, Theolia John
Grisham, Dubro Merriweather
Handy, William Talbot, Jr.
Haygood, Lawrence Franklin
Higgins, Samuel L.
Holmes, Wesley Clyde
Hunt, Blair Theodore
Jackson, Henry Ralph
Jenkins, Bradley Palmer
Jenkins, Charles Edward
Johnson, Julius Caesar
Johnson, Lawrence Washington
Jones, Enoch
Jones, Lawrence Neale
Jones, Matthew Aurelius
Kirkendoll, Chester Arthur
Kyles, Samuel Billy
Lawson, James Morris, Jr.
Lester, Woodie Daniel
Lewis, Benjamin E.
Liggin, Carl Crutcher
Lyles, James
Maloy, Rufus Charles
Manigo, Geo. Franklin, Jr.
Mickle, John Charles
Mitchell, Wallace Jefferson
Morris, William Wesley
Nabrit, H. Clarke
Owen, Samuel Augustus
Paige, Charles Thomas
Peay, Ralph Preston
Powell, John Lewis
Primm, Howard Thomas
Simmons, Dimpson Waycross
Smith, Kelly Miller
Walker, George David
Washington, Dennis Comer
White, Andrew

Woodruff, James Edward
Thomas, Nathaniel Charles
Traylor, Horace Jerome
Turner, Jury Ethward
Turner, Maýnard Philip, Jr.
Varner, Samuel Lee
Washington, Joseph Wm.

TEXAS

Adams, L. Bryant
Ashurst, Harold Teen
Bell, Virgil L., Sr.
Black, Jakie Bernard, Jr.
Bolings, Blaine Arlington
Cooper, Austin Rellins
Cooper, John, Jr.
Cooper, Marcus Lanstern Jr.
Cunningham, Richard T.
Dickson, Melvin Curtis
Feast, James Floyd
Fountain, Major Lee
Freeman, Thomas F.
Garner, Frank Travis
Gooden, DeFarris
Gopaul, Paul Albert
Griffin, Marvin Collins
Griffin, Thomas J.
Hall, Lloyd Dalton
Hegmon, Oliver Louis
Hicks, Jessie May
Holloway, Frederick D., Sr.
Holmes, Zan Wesley, Jr.
Hunter, Charles Alvin
Hurdle, Isaiah Q.
James, H. Rhett
James, Samuel H.
Jones, William Clarke
Lawson, Wm. Alexander, Jr.
Loud, Irwin C.
McCloney, Leon H.
McCormick, Dennie Lionel
Mackey, Andrew
McKinnon, Snowden Isaiah
McNeil, James Henry
Mangram, John Dee
Miles, Joel Leonard, Sr.
Moore, John Dewey
Northcutt, Robt. Robinson
Philip, Lee C.
Rasberry, Hosea
Robinson, Dillard
Rollins, Richard Albert
Sams, Roosevelt
Savage, Horace C.
Sheppard, Garrett A. H.
Sherman, Odie Lee
Snell, Simon
Turner, Samuel, Jr.
Washington, Emanuel Ezra
Weaver, Seymour Marcus
Williams, Floyd Nathaniel
Wilson, Robert Henry

UTAH

Curry, Lacey Kirk
Jefferson, Cattrall

VERMONT

Campbell, Jeffrey

VIRGINIA

Alexander, Lloyd Matthew
Ashby, John Lynwood
Beane, John Solomon
Beasley, Moses W.
Bell, Howard William
Bookee, Austin A.
Bowens, Charles Haywood, Jr.
Chase, Lendall Warren
Clifford, Richard Lorenzo
Coleman, Harry Alexander
Councill, Richard Alvin
Craig, Lawrence Lauman, Sr.
Crews, William Hunter
Daly, Samuel Franklin
Davies, Everett Frederick S.
Davies, Lawrence Anderson

Va. (cont.)
Davis, John Candler
Daye, Linwood Thomas
DeBerry, David
Dennis, Walter Decoster
Elligan, Irvin, Jr.
Evans, Chas. Lawrence
Fleming, Maryland Taft
Freeman, James Jasper
Gaskins, Walter Wesley
Hairston, Samuel Henry
Hamilton, McKinley John
Handy, James Albert
Handy, John William
Harris, Odell Greenleaf
Harris, Otha Carruthers
Haskins, Joseph Franklin
James, Allix Bledsoe
James, Isaac
Johns, Vernon
Johnson, Albert Norman
Kearns, Curtis Andre
Kelley, James C.
Lavall, John W.
Lawing, Raymond Quinton
Marshburn, J. Dett
Mason, Cleveland L.
Michaux, Solomon Lightfoot
Mills, Luther Hunter
Mitchell, Henry Bryant
Mitchell, Raymond S.
Montgomery, Leroy J.
Morris, Ronald Elliot
Murchison, Elisha P.
Parker, Charles Edward
Powell, Grady Wilson
Ransome, William Lee
Reavis, Ralph
Roberts, Harry Walter
Robertson, B. William, Sr.
Scott, Spencer L.
Shannon, David Thomas
Smith, Oswald Garrett
Strassner, Wm. Russell
Taylor, Noel C.
Thomas, William Neamon
Turner, David, Jr.
Walker, Henry W. B.
Williams, Dogan Wilford
Williams, Donald James
Williams, Henry E.
Williams, James David
Williams, John Francis
Wilson, S. Russell
Wingate, Joseph Terry
Wisner, Roscoe William
Wynn, Otis James

WASHINGTON

Adams, John H.
Brazill, Ernest Stonewall
Daw, Matthew Leonard
Evans, John Marvin
Finister, Abbott
Floyd, Harris Limual
Jones, Leon Cooper
Lloyd, Gil Burton
McKinney, Samuel Berry
Phiffer, Solomon Crooms
Sideboard, Henry Yergan

WEST VIRGINIA

Bridges, Ramsey May
Burks, Allen
Dickerson, Noy Jasper
Hargrove, Beverly Milton
Horton, Frank Lewis
Johnson, Ned Howard
Mitchell, James Carl
Powell, Robert Bernard

WISCONSIN

Bowen, Kenneth Athelston
Calvin, Willie James
Haller, Herman
Redds, Harry Lee
Trout, Nelson Wesley

FOREIGN

Bermuda
Byrd, Vernon Randolph

Brazil
Ward, Martin DePorres

Canada
Carter, Lynell Hampton

Ghana
Washington, Curtis Thos.

Italy
Cabey, Edwin Herbert

Liberia
Brown, Dillard Houson

South Africa
Gow, Francis Herman

Tanzania
Rogers, Leslie Thomas

Virgin Islands
Mills, Cedric Earl
Parker, Arthur John

West Indies
Murphy, Maximilian Edw.

Addendum

(Late Biographical Entries)

CREECY, Howard William, b. New Orleans, La., July 6, 1928; s. W. W. and Edna (Fulton) C.; Dillard Univ., 1945-48; Union Theol. Sem., 1944-48; B.S., Ala. State Coll., 1950; B.D., Interdenom. Theol. Center, 1964; m. Marguerite Portis; Children--Doris Glen, Howard W., Gardner, C., Candance M.; pastor, Mt. Pilgrim Bapt. Ch., Morgan City, La., First Miss. Bapt. Ch., Dothan, Ala., 1956-62; Mt. Moriah Bapt. Ch., Atlanta, Ga., 1962-present; Guidance dir., Central High Sch., Mobile, Ala., 1953-54; sec.-treas., Laborer's Local No. 70, Mobile, Ala., 1953-54; dir., Negro Div., So. Bapt. Conv., Morgan City, La., 1954-56; mem., Mayor's Com. on Juvenile Delinquency, Dothan, Ala., 1958-59; candidate for Ga. House of Repre., 1965; v. pres., New Era Bapt. Conv., Ga.; Operation Breadbasket; mem., S.C.L.C.; Advisory Com., Westside Branch, Y.M.C.A., Atlanta, Ga.; mem., Internat. Theol. Hon. Soc., Theta Phi; Democrat; Kappa Alpha Psi; Home: 192 Ashby St., Atlanta, Ga.; Office: 200 Ashby St., Atlanta, Ga.

GARRISON, James Lloyd, b. Jasper, Ala., Mar. 30, 1907; s. John and Mary (Lee) G.; A.B., Clark Coll., 1935; B.D., Gammon Theol. Sem., 1938; m. Elease Witherall; pastor, Asbury Meth. Ch., Savannah, Ga., 1937-39; Centenary Meth. Ch., 1933-37; Rendal Meth. Ch., Wash., D.C., 1941-50; Ames Meth. Ch., Baltimore, Md., 1950-55; Dist. Supt., South Baltimore Dist. Meth. Ch., 1955-59; John Wesley Meth. Ch., 1959-present; mem., CORE; S.C.L.C.; N.A.A.C.P.; Home: 3208 W. North Ave., Baltimore, Md. 21216

GLANTON, Virgil William, b. Abbeville, Ala., Aug. 13, 1897; s. William and Willie (Moore) G.; Selma Univ., Selma, Ala., 1927; grad., 1932; D.D. (hon.) Northern Univ. Sch. of Rel., N.J., 1962; LL.D., Selma Univ., Ala., 1955; m. Vassie L. Brown; Children--Virgil W., Jr., Shirley G. (Mrs. Wilmer A. Petite); pastor, Antioch Bapt. Ch., High Bluff, Ala., 1924-28; First Bapt. Ch., Faunsdale, Ala., 1928-35; First Bapt. Ch., Autaugaville; First Bapt. Ch., Prattville, 1935-45; Stone St. Bapt. Ch., Mobile, Ala., 1945-49; Ebenezer Bapt. Ch., Flushing, N.Y., 1949-61; founder, Holy Unity Bapt. Ch., Corona, N.Y., 1961-present; pres., North Dallas Dist., Sun. Sch. Conv., Ala., 1942-45; v. moderator, Eastern Bapt. Assn., N.Y., 1955-61; promotion sec., Eastern Region, Northern Bapt. Conv., U.S.A.; lectr., Sun. Sch. & B.T.U. Congress, Nat. Bapt. Conv., U.S.A.; instr., Minister's Conf., Greater N.Y. and vicinity; mem., Ch. Union of Brooklyn, N.Y.; mem., N.A.A.C.P.; trustee, Selma Univ.; Mason; Nat. Bapt. Conv.; del., Bapt. World Alliance; Home: 22-46 99th E. Elmhurst, N.Y. 11369; Office: 33-26 107 Corona, N.Y. 11368

HARRISON, Bob, Evangelist and singer; A.B., San Francisco State Coll.; B.D., Bethany Sch. of Theol.; First gained international prominence as a team member with Dr. Billy Graham. Later, was associated with Overseas Crusades, Inc. Palo Alto, Calif.; Dir. & Founder, Bob Harrison Ministries, 1968-present; known as America's "Black Son of Thunder." Travels all over the world preaching and singing, and describes himself as an international evangelist. Recently spent two years in Southeast Asia, Okinawa, Taiwan, Philippines, Indonesia, Malaysia and Ceylon, Congo Africa. Office: Bob Harrison Ministries, 131 Franklin Street, San Francisco, Calif. 94102

JACKSON, John Christopher Jr.; b. Jacksonville, Ill., Nov. 9, 1925; s. John C. Sr. and Myrtle (Farris) J.; A.B., Clark Coll., Atlanta, Ga., 1949; B.D., Gammon Theol. Sem., 1952; Univ. of Kansas, 1957; m. Annie Burt; Children--Celia, John III, Mellessa; pastor, Taylor Meth. Ch., 1949-55; St. James Meth. Ch., Kansas City, Mo., 1955-60; St. Matthew Meth. Ch., Chgo., Ill., 1960-present; v. chrmn., Civic Action Com., Kansas City; chrmn., Com. on Community Organ., 1965; v. pres., Meth. Youth Services of Chgo., 1965-66; v. chrmn., Clergy for Quality Ed., Chgo., Ill.; Community award, 1963; Mayor's citation for service to youth, Chgo., 1964; Omega Psi Phi; Independent Voters, Ill.; U.S. Army, 1944-46; Home: 420 W. Evergreen St., Chgo, Ill. 60610; Office: 348 W. Oak St., Chgo., Ill. 60610

JOHNSON, William A., b. Wash., D.C., Aug. 5, 1900; s.

William Augustus and Missouri (Elliott) J.; Wash. Bapt. Sem., 1929; B.A., Bloomfield Coll., Bloomfield, N.J., 1936; M.A., Univ. of Chgo., 1944; D.D. (hon.) Northern Bapt. Univ., 1951; m. Ophelia Virginia Richmond; pastor, Mt. Pisgah Bapt. Ch., Wash., D.C., 1926-30; Pilgrim Bapt. Ch., Nyack, N.Y., 1930-34; Shiloh Bapt. Ch., Plainfield, N.J., 1934-40; Greater St. John Bapt. Ch., Chgo., Ill., 1940-present; instr., asst. dean, acting, dean, Chicago Bapt. Inst., 1943-64; treas., Interdenom. Ministers Alliance; co-chrmn., Com. on Admissions; mem., Bd. of Dirs., Midwest Bapt. Homes, Chgo., Ill.; pres., Minister's Coun., Chgo. Bapt. Assn.; Amer. Bapt. Conv.; v. pres., The Alumni Assn., Bloomfield Coll.; mem., Bd. of Dirs., Chgo. Bapt. Assn.; Bd. of Trustees, Chgo. Bapt. Inst.; Bd. of Managers, Chgo. Bible Soc.; Dept. of Radio-T.V., Ch. Fed., Greater Chgo.; Exec. Com., Chgo. Coun., Boy Scouts of Amer.; Mayor's Com., New Residents; Chgo. Coun. on Relig. and Race; Adminis. Bd., Half-way House; former pres., Ch. Fed. of Greater Chgo.; chrmn., Dept. of Radio-T.V.; mem., Bd. of Chgo. Urban League; Adminis. Bd., the Beatrice Caffrey Youth Service Organ.; pres., Pastor's Coun., Chgo. Bapt. Inst.; Exec. Bd., Bapt. State Conv. of Ill.; dist. chrmn., Chgo. Coun., Boy Scouts of Amer.; moderator, Middlesex Central Bapt. Assn., N.J.; Union Dist., Bapt. Assn., Ill.; v. pres., Interdenom. Ministers Alliance; rec'd citation, U.S. Board of Trade, 1918; award, the Beatrice Caffrey Youth Service, Inc., Chgo., 1959; award for community service, Bapt. Conv., Ill., 1961; Southside Community Com., Inc., 1961; author, meditation booklets: <u>The Challenge of the Word</u>; <u>The Word in Mine Heart</u>; <u>On Growing As a Christian</u>; Home: 4816 S. Mich. Ave., Chgo., Ill. 60615

JONES, Kelsey A., b. Holly Springs, Mississippi, July 15, 1933; A.B., Miss. Indus. Coll., Holly Springs, Miss., 1955 B.D., Garrett Theol. Sem., Evanston, Ill., 1959 Cert. Clinical Pastoral Care, Univ. of Mich., 1960 Clinical Pastoral Care Wesley Medical Center, Wichita, Kans. 1967 D.D. (Hon.) Miss. Indus. Coll., 1969; m. Virginia Bethel Ford; Children--Kelsey Jr., Cheryl Darlene, Eric Andre, Claude Anthony; pastor, Walls Meml. Chrstn. Meth. Episc. Ch., Chgo., 1956-59; Lane Meml. Ch., Jackson, Mich. 1959-62; Cleaves Temple, Omaha, Nebr., 1962-65; St. Matthews Ch., Wichita, Kans., 1965-70; Israel Metropolitan Ch., Wash., D.C., 1970--; dean, Leadership Ed. Episcopal Districts C.M.E. Ch., former sec. Kansas-Missouri Annual Conf., C.M.E. Ch., former

Chaplin Meth. Population, Cook Co. Joul., Chgo., 1956-58. Counselor, Reception-Diagnostic Center Mich. Correctional Com.; appt. by Governor to State Bd. of Probation & Parole, (4 yrs.); co-organizer, committee for Civil Liberties Omaha 1963; original incorporators of the greater Omaha Action, Inc. (O. E. O.); former v. pres., Wichita Urban League; bd. of dirs. NAACP; past pres., the Greater Wichita Ministerial Alliance; chrmn., North Central Coun., model cities; mem., steering com. "Black United Front." Regular contrib. to magazines and Christians Index (C. M. E. Ch. paper); Office: Israel Metropolitan C. M. E. Ch., 557 Randolph St., N. W., Wash., D. C. 20011

JONES, Ozro Thurston, bishop, b. Fort Smith, Ark.; m. Meaza Jones; Children--six. 1906-1925, organized chs. in Arkansas, Oklahoma and Kansas and appointed Asst. Overseer of Oklahoma Ch. of God in Christ; 1925-pres., pastor, Holy Temple Ch. of God in Christ, Phila., Pa.; 1933 consecrated Bishop; 1962 elected senior bishop; 1925 Overseer of Churches, State of Pa.; 1914 founded Youth Dept. of Ch. and Young People's Willing Workers Quarterly. 1928 organized Nat. Youth Congress.; pres., Nat. Bd. of Ed.; Trustee Corp. of the Ch. of God in Christ; Commissioner, Com. Special Commissioners Ch. of God in Christ; Office: Holy Temple Ch. of Christ, 60th & Callowhite Sts., Philadelphia, Pa.

REYNOLDS, Louis Bernard, b. Verdery, S. C., Feb. 23, 1917; George Albert and Josephine (Washington) R.; certificate, Oakwood Coll., 1936; B. A., Fisk Univ., 1958; m. Bernice Johnson; Children--Dawn (Mrs. Jones), Joan (Mrs. Cruz); pastor, St. Louis S. D. A. Ch., Kansas City, 1936-41; dist. leader, State of Kansas, 1941-44; editor, So. Pub. Assn., 1944-58; curriculum materials, Gen. Conf., S. D. A., 1962-present; lectr., training of adults in rel. ed. program, 45 countries; mem., Bd. Oakwood Coll., Huntsville, Ala.; Riverside Hosp., Nashville, Tenn.; Associated Ch. Press, N. Y.; So. Pub. Assn. Nashville, Tenn.; award: Alumnus of the Year, Oakwood Coll., 1960; author, Dawn of a Brighter Day, 1945; Author Look to the Hill, 1960; Home: 7510 Dundalk Rd., Takoma Pk., Md. 20012; Office: 6840 Eastern Ave., NW, Wash., D. C. 20012

TURNER, Simpson, b. Boston, Mass., Aug. 13, 1923; s. Pelmost A. and L. V. (Simpson) T.; Th. B., Gordon

Coll., Boston, Mass., 1945; M.R.E., N.Y. Theol. Sem., 1958; courses, Boston Univ., Sch. of Theol., 1963; D.D. (hon.), Friendship Coll., Rock Hill, S.C., 1962; m. Laura W. Brown; tchr., priv. coll., 1946-48; Assoc. exec., N.Y. Bible Soc., 1948-51; exec., N.Y. Bible Soc., 1951-64; pastor, Mt. Carmel Bapt. Ch., Brooklyn, N.Y., 1965-present; Bd. mem., Brooklyn YMCA; Afro-Amer. Cooperative Super Market; Vacation for the Aged, Inc.; People's Civic and Welfare Assn.; Waltann Sch. of Creative Arts; mem., Bd. dir., Training Resources for Youth, Inc.; mem., Business and Professional Luncheon Club; Urban League; Mayor's Com. of Rel. Leaders, Brooklyn, N.Y.; pres., Interdenom. Ministers Alliance, Brooklyn and Long Island; couns., Central Brooklyn Coordinating Coun.; Home: 714 Quincy St., Brooklyn, N.Y.; Office: 712 Quincy St., Brooklyn, N.Y. 11221